Paul Ferris's prize-winning biography of Dylan Thomas was published in 1977.
He lives in London but grew up in Swansea.

from ·
Jacqueline

DYLAN THOMAS

The Collected Letters

Edited by Paul Ferris

PALADIN
GRAFTON BOOKS
A Division of the Collins Publishing Group

LONDON GLASGOW
TORONTO SYDNEY AUCKLAND

Paladin
Grafton Books
A Division of the Collins Publishing Group
8 Grafton Street, London W1X 3LA

Published in Paladin 1987

First published in Great Britain by
J. M. Dent & Sons Ltd 1985

Introduction and notes © Paul Ferris 1985
Letters © 1957, 1966, 1985 The Trustees for the
Copyrights of Dylan Thomas
Caitlin Thomas's letter p. 865 © Caitlin Thomas 1985

ISBN 0-586-08578-5

Printed and bound in Great Britain by
Mackays of Chatham Ltd, Kent

Set in Trump Medieval

CONTENTS

FOR CAITLIN

CHRONOLOGY

1914   Born October 27, Swansea.

1925   September, enters Swansea Grammar School.

1927   January 14, newspaper *Western Mail* publishes Thomas's poem 'His Requiem', discovered (forty-four years later) to be plagiarised from a *Boy's Own Paper* of 1923.

1930   April 27, date of the first surviving poem in a poetry notebook, 'Osiris, Come to Isis'.

1931   Summer, leaves school to be a reporter on the local newspaper, *South Wales Daily Post*.

1932   Joins Swansea Little Theatre's company of amateur players.
?December, leaves newspaper.

1933   May 18, *New English Weekly* publishes 'And death shall have no dominion'.
Summer, first visit to London.
September 3, *Sunday Referee* publishes 'That sanity be kept', which leads to correspondence with Pamela Hansford Johnson.

1934   February 23, first meeting with Pamela Hansford Johnson, in London.
November 13, moves into London lodgings.
December 18, *18 Poems*.

1936   August 21, first direct reference to Caitlin Macnamara in a letter.
September 10, *Twenty-five Poems*.

1937   April 21, first radio broadcast, 'Life and the Modern Poet'.
July 11, marries Caitlin Macnamara, Penzance register office.

1938   May, moves to Laugharne; lives there intermittently from now on.
August, applies unsuccessfully for help to Royal Literary Fund.

1939   January 30, Llewelyn Edouard Thomas born, Hampshire.
August 24, *The Map of Love*.
December 20, *The World I Breathe* (USA).

1940   April, *Portrait of the Artist as a Young Dog*.
Summer, with John Davenport at Marshfield, Gloucestershire.

1941   January, applies successfully to Royal Literary Fund.
?Autumn, joins Strand Film Co in London as scriptwriter.

1943   February, *New Poems* (USA).
February 15, 'Reminiscences of Childhood', first of his nostalgic radio talks.
March 3, Aeronwy Bryn Thomas born, London.

1944   September, moves to bungalow at New Quay, Cardiganshire.

1945   Autumn, writes 'Fern Hill' at Blaen Cwm, Carmarthenshire.

1946   February 7, *Deaths and Entrances*.
November 8, *Selected Writings* (USA).

1947   April (until August), in Italy, with family.
June 15, 'Return Journey' (to Swansea), radio feature.
?September, moves to South Leigh, Oxfordshire.

1948   Writing feature films for Gainsborough.
1949   March, commissioned by BBC Television to adapt *Peer Gynt*.
       March, in Prague, guest of Czechoslovak Government.
       April or May, moves to the Boat House, Laugharne.
       May, invited to read at the Poetry Center, New York City.
       July 24, Colm Garan Hart Thomas born, Carmarthen.
1950   February 20, flies to New York: first US trip.
       June 1, sails for England.
1951   January, in Iran, to write film script for Anglo Iranian Oil Co.
       December, living briefly in Camden Town, London.
1952   January 20, arrives in New York, with Caitlin: second US trip.
       February 28, *In Country Sleep* (USA).
       May 16, leaves New York for England.
       November 10, *Collected Poems*.
       December 16, D. J. Thomas, his father, dies.
1953   March 31, *Collected Poems* (USA).
       April 21, arrives New York: third US trip.
       May 14, first performance of *Under Milk Wood* with actors, New York.
       May 14, *The Doctor and the Devils*.
       June 2, returns to London.
       October 19, arrives New York: fourth US trip.
       November 5, collapses at Chelsea Hotel, New York City.
       November 9, dies at St Vincent's Hospital.

INTRODUCTION

Dylan Thomas was born in the Welsh seaport of Swansea in 1914, soon after the First World War began. Both his parents were from working-class families. His father received a good education, and taught English at the local Grammar School; he revered the classic authors, and provided the background of English literature against which the son grew up. A self-centred and precocious child, spoiled by a mother who insisted from an early age that he had 'weak lungs', Dylan Thomas entered adolescence as a serious reader and writer of poetry, whose sense of vocation was usefully complemented by his image of himself as a weakling with a cough.

Thomas made everything subservient to his need to be, and to live as, a Poet with a capital P. He moved to London, saw his talent recognised, married, had children, developed one career writing film scripts and another reading poetry to audiences: all with a disregard for others and a feeling that, somehow, the world owed him a living. He was too intelligent and (when he felt like it) too honest not to see the enormity of this. But dependence was or became a mould that could not be changed. 'Oh, helpless baboon!' he wrote of himself to his American publisher, James Laughlin, in 1949, four years before his death at the age of thirty-nine amid a muddle of drink and debts in New York City. It was a joke; it was a sort of truth.

His letters, of which more than a thousand are collected here, cover just over twenty years, and record a progress out of the darkness of adolescence, and then a return to a worse darkness as middle age approached and his creative powers faltered. But it was progress of an oddly mannered kind.

There is always a hint with Thomas that he planned his life along such lines, that he set up his biographers in advance; and it is this self-conscious approach to the business of being a poet that has done him most harm in recent years. It is not necessarily bad or foolish for a poet to decide that a bohemian life is the thing, complete with poverty, drunkenness and contempt for convention, and to live doggedly within the confines of the cliché, as long as there is an end-product worth having. But Thomas laid it on thick. Many of his poems are statements about the significance of the poet who is writing them, Dylan Marlais Thomas, born into provincialdom, mad with words, beating on the gates of fame, and doing it all *in public*. He has proved too flamboyant or even fraudulent for some of his successors, although a lot of my generation (I was born in 1929) believe he brought it off.

It is possible that Thomas's conscious determination to be taken for a poet was underpinned by a deeper response to demons that pursued him in adolescence and thereafter. There are passages about words and their meaning in his letters to Pamela Hansford Johnson, written when he was nineteen, that sound light-headed with some linguistic obsession. 'Mad with words' could mean just that. The *idea* of madness interested him greatly, although, here again, one is left wondering to what extent he is standing outside himself, treating madness like tuberculosis, a fitting condition for a poet.

But the close-packed letters to Johnson, full of the need to reveal himself to someone, have a genuine air of personal disability. He is undersized, unwell, unemployable. These, in turn, are conditions that suit his vocation. 'A born writer', he tells her (about 21 December 1933), 'is born scrofulous; his career is an accident dictated by physical or circumstantial disabilities.' He revels in the dark side of his nature. 'Everything comes out of yourself,' he advises her (week of 11 November 1933), 'and darkness, despite what you say, has infinitely more possibilities than day.'

The young Thomas was fortunate to have Pamela Hansford Johnson as a correspondent. She was a young woman, employed by a bank, whose life in south London, where she lived with her mother, was as circumscribed as his in suburban Swansea. Like him, she meant to be a writer, and like him, she succeeded. In her case she became a novelist, although when they discovered one another—she wrote to him after reading one of his poems in a newspaper—she was herself trying to be a poet. For more than a year she was in his confidence, and the letters that survive are a remarkable record of his life, both inside and outside himself, while he was writing the poems that made his name.

With two important exceptions, the letters to Pamela are not new, although (as explained later) they have been reorganised. In all, about 300 of Thomas's letters have been published in the past, and so one needs to define the relationship between this volume and its predecessors. There have been two. *Dylan Thomas. Letters to Vernon Watkins* (1957), meticulously edited by the recipient, contained seventy letters, and is an illuminating (if one-sided) record of a relationship between poets. A few passages have been restored in these letters, and two new items added, one of them important; it was found by Mrs Gwen Watkins after her husband's death, and is dated 26 February 1945. *Selected Letters of Dylan Thomas* (1966) was edited by the late Constantine FitzGibbon, who had written the first biography of Thomas, published the previous year. He used about 230 letters, commenting that 'more than half' the available total were omitted. My biography of Thomas was published in 1977; I had access to 5–600 letters in all. This means that several hundred more were identified while the present volume was in preparation.

As the barrel is scraped deeper, of course, the proportion of commonplace letters increases. But it is fair to say that the 'new' letters contain very many that are as striking in their variety and richness as the 'old'.

All now stand together for the first time, a portrait of the artist as a fallen angel.

The most important letters that so far have been unpublished are the group written to Thomas's wife, the former Caitlin Macnamara, an Irish-woman with French blood from Co Clare. Thirty-two of them were in her possession for many years, and there were difficulties in the way of publication, although portions of a few appeared in FitzGibbon's biography and in mine. These thirty-two letters are now privately owned in California, along with another fragment acquired elsewhere. The earliest were written before the Thomases married in 1937, but most of them date from the war years, when they were often apart, and from the early 1950s, when Thomas was visiting America and Iran. The University of Texas has one postcard written in 1936, the earliest item, and a fragment that probably belongs to an incomplete item in the 'thirty-two' group. The Thomas Trustees have two long letters from the 1950s that were found in 1984, as well as two shorter items.

Some are true 'love letters'; others suggest a dependence on her approval—or fear of her disapproval—that is slightly chilling. They are, or they become, the letters of an unhappy man, although sometimes the unhappiness is clearly manufactured for tactical reasons, as when he is anxious to convince her how dreadful a time he is having in the United States. All have echoes of a deep and turbulent relationship. A single letter written by Caitlin Thomas to American friends in February 1953, when her husband's affairs and their life together were at a low ebb, is included in the main text.

Among the other new letters included here are three to his parents, two to his sister Nancy and her husband, and a number to assorted women friends: Veronica Sibthorp, Ruth Wynn Owen, Ellen Kay and Elizabeth Reitell. Thirty-three letters to Desmond Hawkins, written between 1935 and 1940, contain many sidelights on the poet-about-town, as well as detailed discussion of some of his poems. There are nineteen new letters to his American publisher, James Laughlin; seven to T. S. Eliot; eight to his first English publisher, Richard Church; nine to the Royal Literary Fund; more than fifty to the BBC. Among new letters to his friends are about twenty to John Davenport (and three to his wife Clement), ten to Tommy Earp, nine to Margaret Taylor—his most consistent patron over the years—and nine to Princess Caetani, who sent him money and encouragement from Rome. Geoffrey Grigson, Edith Sitwell, Graham Greene, Tambimuttu, Richard Hughes, Glyn Jones, John Lehmann, Stephen Spender, Keidrych Rhys, Henry Treece, Kay Boyle, Ted Roethke, Oscar Williams, Cyril Connolly, Jean Garigue and Oswell Blakeston are among other recipients of hitherto unpublished letters.

Whoever he was writing to, Thomas was a careful, often laborious drafter of letters throughout his life. Original versions were polished up and written out again. In the case of the early, very long letters, this produces copyist's errors, 'poeple' for 'people', 'where' for 'were', 'it's' for 'its'. His begging letters, a major category, were always worked at with elaborate cunning. When he cringed, it was premeditated. He not only wrote direct to patrons, but enlisted supporters to write on his behalf. In 1941, war having finally ruined the precarious Thomas economy, he organised a network of correspondents to help persuade the Royal Literary Fund, which had turned him down three years earlier, to make him a grant. Word reached Thomas that Alec Waugh (who in private supported the application) had remarked, 'advise Dylan to write more stories and fewer letters'; he was furious, but one can see what Waugh was getting at. Drafts of a later letter to Princess Caetani give a gloomy insight into Thomas's painful toying with words and phrases, as though the composition of a begging letter had become a literary end in itself.

The persona that he created for himself was the familiar one of an individual at odds with the world, whose aim in the end was merely to survive in hostile surroundings, a Charlie Chaplin-like figure who seemed without pride. In his letters this made for good comedy as long as his nerve held. Even at first, where he is presenting himself as the introverted poet in poor health, he is high-spirited, clever, scatological, mocking and humorous. He has a casual talent for comic verse. The letter quoted earlier, with the definition of a 'born writer', contained a poem 'to my Aunt, discussing the Correct Approach to Modern Poetry'—

> '. . . Do not forget that "limpet" rhymes
> With "strumpet" in these troubled times,
> And commas are the worst of crimes;
> Few understand the works of Cummings,
> And few James Joyce's mental slummings,
> And few young Auden's coded chatter;
> But then it is the few that matter . . .'

Twelve years later he was writing to a film producer, Donald Taylor, from Wales. The war was just over; America was already the promised land that might make him solvent. The postman knocks, and

> '. . . I reach
> The dog-and-child-chewed mat and find?—yes, yes!—
> A bunch of letters from the far U.S.
> Ah, what epistolary pearls unseen
> Blush in these envelopes! what hippocrene!—
> "Be my pen-pal" from Truman. Or "Dear Friend,
> Shall we arrange a *personal* Lease-Lend?"
> From Betty Hutton . . .
> . . . But, alas, vain hopes!
> There's nothing in those Sam-stamped envelopes
> But a request to write on "Whither Art?"
> For "Cyclorama," "Seed," "Rubato," "Fart,"
> "Prognosis," "Ethic," "Crucible", and "Clef"—
> And other small reviews that pay sweet F.'

But the jokes, the comic element, turned bitter and unfunny as time went on:

'At the bottom of the garden, a man, at 3/- an hour, is digging a new shitpit & will dig on, he says, until he reaches water. By that time I shall owe him this house, which is not mine' (to John Davenport, 26 August 1948).

'On Saturday night I fell down again and cracked some ribs, how many and how badly I won't know till I'm Xrayed tomorrow. . . . The pain is knifing, I cannot sit or lie, and I bellow. I wake the baby with my bullshouts. I cannot sleep. I can hardly write: this is written as I hang off a bed, yelling. Also I have gout in my toe, phlegm on my lungs, misery in my head, debts in the town, no money in my pocket, and a poem simmering on the hob' (to Margaret Taylor, 28 November 1949).

'I grow lazier and fatter and sadder and older and deafer and duller . . . my children grow large and rude; I renounce my Art to make money and then make no money; I fall in love with undesirable, unloving, squat, taloned, moist unlovely women and out again like a trout' (to Ruth Witt-Diamant, 10 October 1951).

Sexual themes and statements abound in his letters. Writing to Pamela Hansford Johnson, it was more a matter of winks and nudges. When they met, she seems to have resisted his advances. No doubt her reluctance to be 'forward'—as it would have seemed to her at that time and place—helped their relationship to disintegrate, once Thomas found freedom and willing partners in London. 'I've always wondered why you won't come to bed with me,' he wrote in October 1934, just before moving to London. The strident sexual imagery of the early poems has always been evident; he liked to dwell on the biological machinery, and his taste spilt over into the letters. 'Man should be two-tooled,' he wrote to a friend, the Swansea journalist Charles Fisher, early in 1935, 'and a poet's middle leg is his pencil. If his phallic pencil turns into an electric drill, breaking up the tar and the concrete of language worn thin by the tricycle tyres of nature poets and the heavy six wheels of the academic sirs, so much the better.'

As Thomas was the first to admit, he had a dirty mind. So have millions; he was just more honest about it. Perhaps he took a long time to develop a mature attitude (whatever that may be) to sex; perhaps he never developed it. During his first years in London he implies in one or two letters that he has caught VD, and clearly regards this as giving some seal of approval to a poet's sex life. His childhood background of cramped morality in West Wales would have helped make the subject more dangerously wicked. As for love letters, the only ones that make erotic declarations, and then briefly, are to Caitlin. If he wrote outspoken letters to other women, they seem not to have survived. A notebook dating from around 1936 that he left with a girl friend, Veronica Sibthorp (it is now at the National Library of Wales), has nonsense rhymes ('If I were Veroniker/I'd give up my moniker'), and scraps of sexual verse, the idle thoughts of a randy young man that turned later on into the controlled bawdiness of *Under Milk Wood*:

> 'I love my love with an A because she Answers
> Both my hands, while both her Breasts are dancers.
> I love my love with a B because she Beats
> All others at Lighthousing up her teats.'

As a commentator on the writing of poetry, Thomas had the reputation of being uninterested, indeed of being ready to flee from anyone who wanted to theorise out loud rather than sit down and write the stuff. This was part of his public act as the man in the loud shirt propping up the bar, but it is not borne out by the letters, which have things to say about his method. In 1933 and 1934 he was giving Pamela Hansford Johnson a running commentary as he wrote the vividly anatomical pieces that went into the book that launched him, *18 Poems* ('Through my small, bonebound island I have learnt all I know, experienced all, and sensed all'). He was also sending lengthy critiques of her own poems, which make a useful complement to what he is saying about his own work.

Henry Treece (who was writing the first book about Thomas) and Charles Fisher were both on the receiving end of interesting technical statements from Thomas in the 1930s. The correspondence with Vernon Watkins was much concerned with the writing of particular poems. There is a letter to Hermann Peschmann (1 February 1938) where Thomas explains, not very succinctly, what a poem, 'I make this in a war-ring absence', is 'about' (the quotation marks are his: he didn't want to be cornered). There is a notable letter (14 August 1939) to Desmond Hawkins, who was poised to review Thomas's book *The Map of Love* for the *Spectator*, and who had written to ask him about five of the more difficult poems. Some of Thomas's exegesis is as confusing as the poems themselves, as Thomas recognised: 'I wrote it down hurriedly for you: not so much to try to elucidate things but to move them about, turn them different ways, stir them up.' But at least it throws light on the process involved, even if it is only light on the muddled frame of mind in which some of these poems of the late Thirties were written.

More nagging by editors might have helped. In an earlier letter (March 1936), Thomas responded to an inquiry from Hawkins, then literary editor of the magazine *Purpose*, who had accepted a poem, 'Find meat on bones', but was puzzled by the phrase, 'a ram rose', in a passage with sexual overtones. 'It's funny about ram,' wrote Thomas. 'Once I looked up an old dictionary and found it meant red, but now I can't find it in any dictionary at all. I wanted ram in the poem to mean red *and* male *and* horny *and* driving *and* all its usual meanings. Blast it, why doesn't it mean red?' Still, 'ram rose' it remained.

Thomas worked long and hard at poems that could achieve the effects he sought. 'You must work at the talent as a sculptor works at stone,' he told Pamela Hansford Johnson (15 April 1934) (employing, incidentally, the kind of phrase that Welsh-language poets use about their strict-metred verse). His poem 'Prologue', written to introduce his *Collected*

Poems (1952), has a first line which rhymes with the last (the 102nd) and so on through second and last-but-one, third and last-but-three, until the rhymes meet in the middle, with lines 51 and 52. It is a scheme that few readers notice unless their attention is drawn to it: 'Why I acrosticked myself like this, don't ask me,' he wrote to his editor at Dent (10 September 1952). To Desmond Hawkins (14 August 1939) he admitted that 'much of the poetry is impossibly difficult; I've asked, or rather told, words to do too much; it isn't theories that choke some of the wilder and worser lines, but sheer greed.' The key phrase is 'sheer greed', the obsession with words for their own sake and for the sake of their intractable nature, at which he must chisel away for ever.

Contemporary poets receive little attention from Thomas, and most of it is dismissive, even contemptuous. Those of whom he said rude things at one time or another include W. H. Auden, Stephen Spender, Ezra Pound, T. S. Eliot, Edith Sitwell, George Barker, C. Day Lewis, Geoffrey Grigson, David Gascoyne and Henry Treece. His judgements in the letters are usually brisk, unkind and unsupported by argument. He also said malicious things about many of his friends and acquaintances, and he never let the facts get in the way of a good story or even a good sentence. He was by nature a teller of tall stories, and the letters only hint at his talent in this department when he had a glass in his hand and a circle of admirers. It would have been excessive to correct each apparent flight of fancy with a footnote. But frequently he needs taking with a pinch of salt, as when he tells his new friend Pamela in distant Battersea that he was born in his Welsh town amid 'the smoke of the tinplate stacks' (the only smoke in his district came from suburban hearths) or declares with mock bravado that he has only four years to live. The complicated begging letters of later years, which lied and manoeuvred as he thought necessary, are another, sadder aspect of the same thing.

But it is not easy to categorise Thomas's letters. For every dissimulation, there is a plain statement of things as they are. For every piece of clowning, a splinter of melancholy. For every gibe at the shortcomings of others, a recognition of his own. Aged nineteen, he wrote to Trevor Hughes of 'my islandic egoism which allows few of the day's waves to touch it'. 'Please help,' he wrote to Margaret Taylor (12 April 1947); 'though I deserve nothing.' He would sacrifice anyone's interests if it helped him stay in business as a poet, but he could also write to a correspondent that 'I don't think it does any harm to the artist to be lonely *as* an artist . . . If he feels personally unimportant, it may be that he is.' His letter to C. Gordon Glover, a passing journalist who had interviewed him for an article (25 May 1948), is a canny assessment of 'this impermanent, oscillating, rag-bag character', a recognition of 'my still only half-squashed and forgotten bourgeois petty values; all my excruciating whimsicality; all my sloth; all my eye!' He caricatured the business of literary reputation even while he was in the process of acquiring one. 'On, on, money to right of them, fame to the left, an income, a new suit, a special party, "Tell me Mr Gluepot how did you start writing? do you believe in the feminine verse-ending? is Europe at the Crossroads?", lobster for tea, champagne every night, a niche in Letters, and an everlasting hole in the earth' (to James Laughlin, 7 May 1938). He knew the reality of things.

*

The present text has been taken from the original manuscripts, except in a few cases where only typescripts are available, and fewer still where the editor has had to rely on the *Selected Letters* version. The text of *Selected Letters* is untrustworthy, as Professor Ralph Maud's 1980 paper, 'Corrections to *Selected Letters of Dylan Thomas*' (*National Library of Wales Journal*, Vol XXI, 435–40), observed. Maud said he had not seen manuscripts of all the letters, so his list was incomplete; he added that his paper ignored 'hundreds of small variations'. The mistakes are scattered throughout the text; many are typists' errors that were left uncorrected. Some letters have few or no errors; others contain dozens of misreadings and omissions. In one case (pages 190–1) two pages of typescript became transposed, and the error was perpetuated. In another (page 69) two pages of manuscript were transposed, with similar effect. It is often not clear whether the dates of letters are Thomas's, or additions by FitzGibbon. And when passages were omitted deliberately, for legal or other reasons, there was sometimes no sign of intervention.

The letters to Pamela Hansford Johnson suffered most of all. The papers of Lady Snow (as she became) went, late in her life, to the State University of New York at Buffalo. Pages of Thomas's letters, kept by her since the 1930s, had become confused. It is not clear whether, in *Selected Letters*, FitzGibbon attempted any rearrangement. He printed everything of substance, twenty-three letters, although he omitted long passages where Thomas was commenting on Johnson's poems and stories, and, more importantly, on methods of writing in general. Apart from these passages (now restored), it turns out that seven of the letters had lost or acquired long sections among one another. With the help of Ralph Maud, who knows more about the Buffalo material than anyone else, I have reassembled and redated these letters (at my responsibility, not his) to make a total of twenty-four, not all of them complete. In addition there are six fragments, a postcard, and two new letters that were found among Lady Snow's papers in London in 1984. A final item, a comic play, 'Spajma and Salnady', sent to her in 1934, is mentioned in Appendix A; but it hardly counts as a letter, and it is not reprinted here.

Concerning the style of presentation, square brackets are used to enclose conjectures of any kind. Where there is an editorial interpolation in addition to the conjectured or uncertain words, the editor's remarks are in italics, the remainder in ordinary type. Where occasional deletions—never of more than a name or a few words—have had to be made, [. . .]

warns the reader. Seventy rather humdrum letters, most of them short, have been banished to Appendix A, near the end of the volume; a one-line entry marks their place in the main text. Sources of biographical information can be found in my life of Thomas. Where there are discrepancies between Life and Letters, for example in dates given to undated items, it means I have decided that I was wrong the first time.

Finally, the matter of Dylan Thomas's spelling. As well as the 'copying' errors already noted, there were many words that gave him trouble, as he remarked in an early letter. Disillusion ('dissilusion'), separate ('seperate'), disappoint ('dissapoint') and propaganda ('propoganda') were among his blind spots. All have been silently corrected, except where it seems they may have been intended to produce some comic or verbal effect. Proper names, often misspelt over years, even in the case of friends, have in general been corrected, sometimes with a footnote reference.

In preparing this collection, I have advertised for Thomas's letters, written to more than a hundred libraries and universities, pestered many individuals and followed up countless clues and hints: all with some success, but with no conviction that I have gathered in copies of every last letter. Appendix B identifies a few known items that I have failed to see. Publication of this volume may stir memories and produce more letters for a future edition. I or the publishers will be glad to hear of any.

ACKNOWLEDGEMENTS

I am grateful to those who have sent me copies of letters and otherwise helped with information. It would have been impossible to write many of the footnotes without the benefit of personal memories.

In particular I would like to thank the following:

Graham Ackroyd, Ben Arbeid, Eric Barton, John Bayliss, Sir Theodore Brinckman (Monk Bretton Books), John Malcolm Brinnin, Victor Bonham-Carter (Society of Authors), Julian Chancellor (Society of Authors), Douglas Cleverdon, John Crichton (The Brick Row Book Shop), Roger Davenport, Michael Davie, H. W. E. Davies, Sean Day-Lewis, Nicolette Devas (sister of Caitlin Thomas), Sheila Dickinson, Laurence Durrell, Valerie Eliot, Charles Elliott, Aeronwy Thomas Ellis (daughter of Dylan Thomas), Charles Fisher, Frances Freeth, Jean Overton Fuller, Roland Gant, David Gascoyne, Clive Graham, Thomas B. Greenslade (Kenyon College archivist), Bernard Gutteridge, Desmond Hawkins, Ian Henderson, Nigel Henderson, Robert Hewison, Jane Aiken Hodge, Barbara Holdridge, G. Thurston Hopkins, Hubert Howard (the Camillo Caetani Foundation), Lord Howard de Walden, Dr Cyril James, Fred Janes, Glyn Jones, Professor Gwyn Jones, Mimi Josephson, P. J. Kavanagh, Ellen de Young Kay, James Laughlin, Laurie Lee, John Lehmann, Michael Levien, Mervyn Levy, Jack Lindsay, Brigit Marnier (sister of Caitlin Thomas), R. B. Marriott, Douglas Matthews, Professor Ralph Maud, Maurice F. Neville (who owns most of Dylan Thomas's letters to his wife), Barbara Noble, John Ormond, Ruth Wynn Owen, Ken Pearson, P.E.N., Hermann Peschmann, Gilbert Phelps, Douglas Phillips, Peter Quennell, Keidrych Rhys, Anthony Rota, Charles W. Sachs (The Scriptorium), D. S. Savage, Rupert Shephard, Philip Skelsey, Elizabeth Reitell Smith, John Sommerfield, Sotheby's (London and New York); Sir Stephen Spender, Professor Jon Stallworthy, Derek Stanford, Meic Stephens (Welsh Arts Council), Lindsay Stewart (daughter of Lady Snow), Harald Sverdrup, Amelia Taylor, Professor Christy M. Taylor, Haydn Taylor (brother-in-law of Dylan Thomas), David Tennant, Georgia Tennant, Clem Thomas, Molly Murray Threipland, Dr Kerith Trick, Meurig Walters, Gwen Watkins, West Glamorgan Public Library, Swansea; E. W. White, John Wilson (bookseller) and Joan Wintercorn.

The author and publisher thank the following corporate holders of Dylan Thomas letters for access to material; all are identified where the letters appear.

We are especially grateful to the Harry Ransom Humanities Research Center of the University of Texas at Austin—which has the largest collection of Thomas letters—and to the State University of New York at Buffalo—whose Poetry and Rare Books Collection at the University Libraries contains the Pamela Hansford Johnson letters and the Thomas Notebooks—for their help with many inquiries.

We also thank the BBC Written Archives Centre; University of Birmingham Library (UK); Bodleian Library; the British Library Board; the Joseph Regenstein Library, University of Chicago; Columbia University Libraries; University of Delaware Library; Houghton Library, Harvard University; Lilly Library, Indiana University; Chalmers Memorial Library, Kenyon College; Pierpont Morgan Library; Mount Holyoke College Library; Henry W. and Albert A. Berg Collection, New York Public Library, Astor, Lenox and Tilden Foundations; Fales Library, New York University; Ohio State University Libraries; Oxford University Press; Royal Literary Fund; Paul Sacher Foundation, Basle; National Library of Scotland; Morris Library, Southern Illinois University at Carbondale; the Department of Special Collections, McFarlin Library, University of Tulsa; National Library of Wales; University of Washington Libraries.

Laurence Pollinger Ltd and the Estate of Mrs Frieda Lawrence Ravagli kindly gave permission to use the three verses from 'Another Ophelia' and the two verses from 'Obsequial Ode', by D. H. Lawrence, which Thomas quoted in a letter dated 30 July 1945. The National Library of Wales and Mrs Gwen Watkins gave permission for the reproduction in facsimile of a letter from Thomas to Vernon Watkins. Mrs Caitlin Thomas gave permission to use her letter on p 865.

I record, sadly, my special gratitude to the late Alan Baker, who proofread this book at all its stages.

ABBREVIATIONS

BBC	BBC Written Archives Centre, Caversham
Berg	Berg Collection, New York Public Library
Buffalo	University Libraries, State University of New York at Buffalo
Carbondale	Morris Library, Southern Illinois University at Carbondale
Delaware	University of Delaware
Harvard	Houghton Library, Harvard University
Indiana	Lilly Library, Indiana University
Ohio	Ohio State University Libraries
Texas	Harry Ransom Humanities Research Center, the University of Texas at Austin

CP	*Collected Poems* of Dylan Thomas
The Poems	*Dylan Thomas: The Poems*, edited by Daniel Jones
'Notebooks'	The four surviving 'Poetry Notebooks' with Thomas's adolescent work, at Buffalo.
SL	*The Selected Letters of Dylan Thomas*, edited by Constantine Fitz-Gibbon
VW	*Dylan Thomas. Letters to Vernon Watkins*, edited by Vernon Watkins.

After a letter, an *SL* or *VW* on the line that notes the location of the manuscript means that the item appeared in the volume indicated. The addition of *(R)* means that text has been restored or rearranged.

The 'incidental' letters, numbered 1 to 70, are identified in the main text by a key-number reference to the Appendix, which in this context always means Appendix A.

Majoda
New Quay
Cards
26 2 45

Dear Vernon,
          I was very very glad to hear and see from
you; it's been a long and complicated time since
we disappointingly met, and I'm happy and
relieved to think that the offence, (for my lost,
preoccupied manner must really have been that)
I gave when we did meet in that gabbling
drunk-grey crush, the worst of the town,
has, I never to be forgotten utterly, lost some
disfavour. (I have just been writing at length
to Llewelyn, on the occassion of a fall from
a tree and a split tongue, and the effort
of not talking to a boy of six has made
me adopt the claptrap periods of a leader-
writer under gas.) I have found, increasingly
as time goes on, or around, or backwards, or
stays quite still as the brain races, the
heart absorbs and expells, and the arteries harden,
that the problems of physical life, of social
contact, of daily posture and armour, of the
choice between dissapations, of the abhorred
needs enforced by a reluctance to "miss
anything", that old fear of death, are as insoluble
to me as those of the spirit. In few and fewer
poems I can despair and, at rare moments
exult with the big last, but the first force
me every moment to make quick decisions
and thus to plunge me into little halls and
rubbishes at which I rebel with a kind
of truculent acceptance. The ordinary moments
of walking up a village streets, opening
doors or letters, speaking good-days to
friends or strangers, looking out of windows,
making telephone calls, are so inexplicably
(to me) dangerous that I am trembling all over
before I get out of bed in the mornings to
meet them. Waking to remember an
appointment at X that coming evening is
to see, before X, galleries of menacing
commonplaces, chambers of errors of the
day's conventions, pits of platitudes and
customary gestures, all beckoning, spurning;
and through, over, & out of these I must

A troubled letter from Thomas to his friend, the poet Vernon Watkins.
It is printed on page 545–6.

2

somehow move before the appointment, the appointment that has now become a shining grail in a dentist's surgery, an almost impossible consummation of illegal pleasure to be acheived in a room like a big gut in a subterranean concentration-camp. And especially, ofcourse, in London. I wish that I could have met Gwen "properly", and glad that she wanted to; I was "myself" in the sense that I was no-one else, but I was broken on a wheel of streets and faces; equally well, I may be just as broken in the peace — what peace? — of the country, hysterical in my composure, hyena-ish in my vegetabledom. I will, if I may, try to come to stay in the pub in Stony Stratford when next I come to London: but oh the bony cupboards and traps and vats before that.

I wish I could see your new poems. The translation in Horizon I did, & remembered much of it, it was beautiful.

I am glad Francis is alive, well, and happy.

I have lost Dan's address again. Will you tell him that we are not going to Ireland for a long time, perhaps not even this year, as another film has risen out of some fool's mind and must be written so that we can eat and tremble at the approach of each quiet, unsensational & monstrous day? The studio is being carefully looked after. I'll write to Dan this week & will send the letter to you.

Love to you and Gwen from us both.

Ever,

Dylan.

I wish I could understand your letter from Heatherslade. It was dated the 24ᵗʰ, which was Saturday, but said that you were afraid we would be unable to meet as you were leaving on Friday. If that was not also, and unfortunately, typical of myself, I should say it was a piece of genuine-accept-no-other Vernon.

Don't mind this silly letter. It was lovely to have yours.

THE LETTERS

Provincial Poet
1931–4

Both Thomas's parents, D. J. (David John) and Florence Thomas, came from rural backgrounds in West Wales, and spoke Welsh. But D. J. Thomas (born in 1876) was of a pre-nationalist generation that accepted English as the dominant culture, and his ambitions looked east to England. D. J.'s youthful writing was unsuccessful, and by 1914, when his son Dylan Marlais was born, he was long established in the post he would occupy until retirement, teaching English to boys from petit-bourgeois families at Swansea Grammar School. A daughter, Nancy, was eight years older than her brother. But it was on his son that D. J. lavished the attention of a disappointed man. Books in general and poetry in particular were part of the daily scene at 5 Cwmdonkin Drive, a semi-detached house on a hill in a suburb of Swansea. Dylan Thomas began to write poetry as a child. Shortly before his eleventh birthday he went to the Grammar School, where his career was undistinguished and a trial to his father, by then the senior English master. But throughout his adolescence, he was filling notebooks with poems.

NANCY THOMAS[1]
[?]   5 Cwmdonkin Drive Uplands on Avon Swansea[2]

Nancy—Sir!
  Before I write I want this to be known:— this is not a news-letter. It is
original, therefore it is a new-letter! BOOKS! Ah! Before I go on we must
stop. Books! What Fasination what charm; what undreamt-of dreams,
what hours of unsuppressed joy lie between the brown-gilt (which has a
guilty look) covers of Messrs (pun!!) Woolworth's classics.
[...]
[an old man in a cemetery is introduced]
                    It was a lonely spot
                    With desolation spread;
                    An eerie, solemn silence reigned,
                    Around the sleeping dead
[...]
[punning verses follow]
       ... a drummer is a man we know who has to do with drums,
       But I've never met a plumber yet who had to do with plums.
       A cheerful man who sells you hats would be a cheerful hatter,
       But is a serious man who sells you mats 'a serious matter'?
[...]
[nursery-type rhymes follow]
                         The Sea
               Behold the wonders of the mighty deep,
               Where crabs & lobsters learn to creep,
               And little fishes learn to swim,
               And clumsy sailors tumble in.
[...]
[a poem about 'wowwies' follows]
('Wowwies' NB – Please drop all the Rs)
               There's a worry in the morning because the coffee's cold,
               There's a worry of the postman & the 'paper' to unfold,
               It's a worry getting on your boots & going to the train,
               And you've got to put your hat on and take it off again

---

[1] This letter, probably written when Thomas was a child, was sold by a godson of his sister
   at Sotheby's, London, in 1981, for £2,200. The pseudonymous buyer, 'Dr Bolus', does not
   reply to letters, and these extracts are taken from the auctioneer's catalogue.
[2] 'On Avon' is a joke. The suburb where the Thomases lived was 'the Uplands'.

[...]

> There are wowwies in the evening, you've got to dress & dine;
> There's the worry of the speeches that accompany the wine;
> There's the wowwy of remembering what card your partner led
> AND THEN THE AWFUL WORRY OF GETTING INTO BED!!!

[...]

> Ah-a-h-a! How tired I am!
> Now comes the awful 'wowwy' of finishing this letter,
> One word before I end Dear—let's hope you're beastly better.

Yours,
Dylan

MS: unknown

TREVOR HUGHES

Dylan Thomas left school in the summer of 1931, aged sixteen, having passed no examinations. Earlier, on June 2, a paragraph in the *South Wales Daily* [presently *Evening*] *Post*, which was soon to employ him for a year or so, announced a 'new literary publication', *Prose & Verse*, edited from his father's address. Trevor Tregaskis Hughes (1904–66), a clerk with literary ambitions, sent him a story. He is the original of 'Raymond Price' in Thomas's later story, 'Who Do You Wish Was With Us?'

10/6/31   5 Cwmdonkin Drive Uplands Swansea

Dear Mr. Hughes,

Thank you very much for your short story, 'Freedom'. It is one of the few contributions I have received so far which does really suit the requirements of the type of periodical I wish to produce. Needless to say, your story is accepted without reservation. But, unless I can foster interest in the notoriously stony bosoms of the local public, neither 'Freedom', nor any of the other material at my disposal, will ever see light in the form of 'Prose & Verse'.

For it is subscribers more than contributors I need now—I am not speaking of your type of contribution which is as gratefully received as it is rarely sent—for out of the 200 subscribers at 2/- [2 shillings] each needed to cover the cost of publication (£20) I have amassed just over twenty. More will be coming this week, but that is all I have been *absolutely guaranteed* so far. Admittedly, I have not written to any of the people who are supposed to [be] interested in literary matters; I put the particulars and my address in the local paper, and trusted to the depth of their interest, which, I am beginning to believe, is almost legendary.

I shall wait a few days before I knock at the houses of the nouveaux riches and the Swansea bohemians, asking, in a hopeless voice, for donations; or at any rate subscriptions.

I wonder whether you could help me in a business way as much as you have helped me in a literary way. If you could gather the names of as many subscribers as possible towards 'Prose & Verse', & then give them into me, you would be doing a great deal towards furthering my project.

Hoping I shall hear from you in the near future,

I am,
Yours faithfully
D. M. Thomas

MS: Buffalo   *SL*

TREVOR HUGHES
[February 1932]   5 Cwmdonkin Drive Uplands Swansea

Dear Trevor,

Your letter was late, but mine is later, and the trouble is I have no real excuse, except the chronic and self-condemnatory one of innate laziness, to offer you. You will, I know, brush aside my faltering cry of 'Work'. You have been one of the World's Workers long enough to realise there is always time enough to complete one's correspondence. So, humbly and with a forced smile upon my lips, I tender—what a curious word that is—apologies as sincere as they are lame. I have such little time. My right hand is injured from a colliery accident. I have no ink.

Now that the bridge of reticence is spanned (God, what style! The man's a Burke!) and the waves of consciousness met (the man's a Lawrence!) writing becomes distinctly easier. A phrase is a phrase again, an image an image now.

The purple of your dreams is untroubled—unstirred as you say. I am glad to hear that. What I shall be gladder to hear is that you are still writing. You may not know it, but you could, with practice & time, become a very considerable prose-writer. You've got something to say & a new way to say it.

My purple is turning, I think, into a dull gray. I am at the most transitional period now. Whatever talents I possess may suddenly diminish or may suddenly increase. I can, with great ease, become an ordinary fool. I may be one now. But it doesn't do to upset one's own vanity, and this letter is gradually becoming a cry from the depths.

I am playing in Noel Coward's 'Hay Fever' at the Little Theatre this season.[1] Much of my time is taken up with rehearsals. Much is taken up with concerts, deaths, meetings & dinners.[2] It's odd, but between all these I manage to become drunk at least four nights of the week. Muse or

---

[1] Amateur players, who performed regularly in the town and district. Thomas was a member from 1932 to 1934. His sister, also a member, was in *Hay Fever*.
[2] Typical events that a junior reporter had to cover.

Mermaid?[1] That's the transition I spoke about. M or M? I'd prefer M any day, so that clears the air a lot.

Job[2] is a very curious man, isn't he? I agree he has no sense of humour and a dislike of alcohol, but I have heard him laugh, and he has told me, quite jocularly, that my voice, inexplicably enough, was always thicker at 3 o'clock than it was at 12.30—you see, I dine in town—(Dine? You compliment yourself, sir.)

When you write next, and I hope you write soon, enclose either a story you have written or the particulars of one you are writing. Otherwise, my insane annoyance will know no bounds.

I can't concentrate. My mind leaps from thought to thought like a wombat. I'll have to stop. Besides, the ink is getting low.

Don't forget to write soon.

Is your Ma any better?

How is London treating you, if at all?[3]

Mermaid?

Are you writing much?

Am I writing much?

Are we writing much?

Can you write, can I write, can we write?

Clear up this lot in your next epistle. Pardon mine, it's a Sunday morning. I've got a head like a wind-mill.

Dylan

MS: Buffalo   *SL*

TREVOR HUGHES
[late 1932/early 1933]   5 Cwmdonkin Drive Uplands Swansea

Dear Trevor,

In my more melancholy moods, when the brightest things can be made to appear the most drab, and when life—you probably detest such a sententious opening to a letter as much as I do—offers little more than the preferably sharp razor and the necessarily painless drug, I turn over, with a certain perverse pleasure, all my ill-fortunate experiences which amount as nearly to heartbreak as one, like myself, who has never felt the desire to fall in love, can realise.

And among those experiences I count that of losing, apparently for ever, my friendship with you. It is easier to write than to talk about it. I have a horrid fear, when talking, of plunging into a hot bath of

---

[1] A pub in the Mumbles, a Swansea suburb.
[2] Chief reporter of the *South Wales Evening Post*, the 'Mr Solomon' of Thomas's story 'Old Garbo'.
[3] Hughes's family had moved to Harrow, London.

sentimentality, but on paper the most girlish thoughts can be expressed without much fear of a sudden immersion into those wicked waters.

I realise I am writing the most utter nonsense. This is what I mean to say: When you left Swansea I thought that the end had come of a friendship, quite short, that I, at any rate, will always think of happily. We wrote letters for a time. Then they stopped for God knows what reason. Laziness on both our parts, probably. I didn't hear from you for six months. My sister stayed the night in Torrington-square & asked where you were. Nobody appeared to know. And then the day before Christmas, a much over-rated holiday, I received a letter. Thanks for it, but don't let it be in the way of a conscience-reliever. Don't lie back, a smug smile on your face, & hands folded over a pious belly, thinking, 'Well, well, everything is alright now. I've let the cat out, done my day's accounts, and written to that little fellow in Swansea—what's his name, now? Thomas I think. No, no, Williams,' and after the strain of such concentration is over, warming your hooves before the fire, letting a contented mind dwell on the beauties of the world-to-come, where suburban gentlemen, small as agates on an alderman's thumb, hymn the Eternal Bowler.

I am writing you a long letter, and I want to hear regularly from you. Let the mind run. If you haven't any facts I won't mind—I rarely have any of my own. Spin a lot of sentences out of your guts. If nothing else, it's practice for that polished prose of yours which one day, and I don't mean maybe, is going to earn you a respectable living and the plaudits of sound literary people. You have a solidity in your writing—for once I use that word in a complimentary, not derogatory, sense—which is bound to get you somewhere one day. It's that solidity & perception of detail, sense of values, if you like, an at-the-root indestructibility of matter, which I haven't got. All I may, eventually, do is to

> Astound the salons & the cliques
> Of half-wits, publicists & freaks.

I was cut out for little else. The majority of literature is the outcome of ill men, and, though you might not know it, I am always very ill. Logically, that means I am producing, or am going to produce, literature. But I have given up believing in logic long ago. Which is a very logical thing to do. Please believe me when I do throw a little bouquet now & then. You'll have enough buckets thrown in your direction because of your literary sincerity. So treasure, like a squirrel, every complimentary bunch of flowers, for though the scent's bound to wither & the stalks drop, &, of course, he who gave the flowers be utterly forgotten, the memory—bring out your tracts! How everyone nowadays is so terribly frightened of becoming maudlin!—will last for a long time. That kind of memory, & the hope that that kind of memory fosters, are among the few things that keep a man alive. Faith, he said, smoothing his tired brow with buffalo's milk, keeps a man breathing.

> When the moon sinks behind the lawn
> With an old smell of camphor & collected roses,
> Will you & I wait for the certain sign,
> And wait for ever, one supposes,
> Watching, our hands cupped holding matches,
> Sun after moon, & then again
> The same celestial repetition.

What you want to keep out is morbidity, even though everything is despondent. Not a forced cheerfulness, nor a preoccupation with the pleasant instead of the dirty side. But there's a fountain of clearness in everyone. Bach found it, Mozart, D. H. Lawrence, W. B. Yeats & probably Jesus Christ. Have a shot at finding it. You may succeed. I never will. And for God's sake don't take to writing poetry in my style. Try Longfellow, not me. This sounds awfully conceited. Try your own style. But then, of course, that's what you really are doing.

To answer a question of yours: I have left the Post. They offered me a five years' contract in Swansea. I refused.[1] The sixteen months or less I was on the staff were already showing signs of a reporter's decadence. Another two years I'd have been done for. Not that I was afraid of the Mermaid's grip. I still sedulously pluck the flowers of alcohol, &, occasionally, but not as often as I wish, am pricked by the drunken thorn (an atrocious image!). No, what I feared was the slow but sure stamping out of individuality, the gradual contentment with life as it was, so much per week, so much for this, for that, so much left over for drink & cigarettes. That be no loife for such as Oi! I am attempting to earn a living now—attempting is the correct word—by free-lance journalism, & contribute, fairly regularly, humorous articles to the Post, less regularly literary articles to the *Herald*,[2] now & then funny verses to the B.O.P.[3] (what a come-down was that, O men of Israel!) seasonable & snappy titbits for the Northcliffe Distributive Press. I had a bad poem in the Everyman,[4] & a story is accepted by Squire in the Mercury,[5]—that's where you want to plant your stuff. When the story 'The Diarists' is published, I'll send you a copy. It isn't particularly good.

I still write poems, of course. It's an incurable disease. I write prose, too, & am thinking of tackling a short novel. Thinking, I said.

The purple of your dreams is, I hope, still purple. I am glad to hear

---

[1] Thomas left the newspaper at the end of 1932. The 'contract' is a fiction. 'His shorthand', the editor remarked later, 'did not become efficient enough to help him at a mothers' meeting.'

[2] *Herald of Wales*, weekly sister-paper of the *Post*.

[3] *Boy's Own Paper*. Thomas's contribution was in February 1927, 'The Second Best'.

[4] In an *Everyman* competition, 1929, two lines of a Thomas poem were commended: 'dim with arrowy air./Asleep and slender with the moon-slow hour.'

[5] The poet and journalist Sir John Squire (1884–1958) founded the monthly magazine *London Mercury* and edited it until 1934. No story signed by Thomas appeared in it.

official responsibilities are not preventing you from writing fiction as they have, in the past, prevented you from writing letters.

Dylan

Remember me, quite sincerely & not as a matter of form, to your sister & mother, & don't, on any account save the imperative dictates of the angels, fail to write soon, again, & again soon.

MS: Buffalo   *SL*

TREVOR HUGHES
[February 1933]   5 Cwmdonkin Drive Uplands Swansea

Dear Trevor,

Thank you for your letter, & excuse mine, written in pencil on the world's worst paper. The only thing I hope is that it is legible.

You certainly did let the mind run, scorning even the mechanical medium of the typewriter, & penning your thoughts—they were, of course, sunk in a deeper melancholy, at least the majority of them, than mine could ever be—in immaculate calligraphy. Your letter was beautifully sincere. In my little ivory temple, immune from the winds and whips of the world, shut, if you like, Proustlike in my conservatory, I find it hard to think, in any but a cynical & theoretical manner, of the blood and withering diseases you have such firsthand knowledge of.[1] Beauty, you say, comes out of suffering. For we are born in others' pain & perish in our own. That, to those who have suffered, & in spite of it are still capable of appreciating and, sometimes, creating beauty, must appear perfectly true. I can't appreciate it, firstly beause I have known little physical suffering & no actual hardships or heartbreaks, and secondly because, at the root of it all, I can't reconcile life & art. Obviously one is born before one can be an artist, but after that it doesn't matter what happens. The artistic consciousness is there or it isn't. Suffering is not going to touch it. Consciousness of beauty—& what that elusive thing is I haven't the remotest idea; woman isn't, because she dies. Nothing that dies is truly beautiful—is born with you or not at all. Suffering is not going to create that consciousness, nor happiness, nor anything else you may experience. True beauty, I shall always believe, lies in that which is undestroyable, &, logically, is therefore very little. But it is there. Not that what you have suffered does not influence you deeply & terribly. It is bound to upset & disillusion, carry you, unless you are careful, to the margins of madness. But it is not going to touch in any way at all that which really makes you an artist—knowledge of the actual world's deplorable sordidness, & of the invisible world's splendour (not heaven with God clothed like a deacon, sitting on a golden cloud, but the unseen places clouding above the brain). Suffer as much as you like, that world remains. It is only the complexion of the outer, & absurd, world that changes.

[1] Hughes had an invalid mother, and his brother had died of tuberculosis.

Words are so misleading. I don't urge a monastic seclusion, &
preoccupation with the invisible places (you see, even my 'facile' flow of
selfconscious images fails, & I am left with the word 'places', which is
quite unsatisfactory). That is Roman Catholicism. (One day I may turn
Catholic, but not yet.) You must *live* in the outer world, suffer in it &
with it, enjoy its changes, despair at them, carry on ordinarily with
moneymaking routines, fall in love, mate, & die. You *have* to do that.
Where the true artist differs from his fellows is that *that* for him is not
the only world. He has the inner splendour (which sounds like a piece of
Lawrence or a fribble of Dean Inge). The outer & inner worlds are not, I
admit, entirely separate. Suffering colours the inner places, & probably
adds beauty to them. So does happiness.

You may think this philosophy—only, in fact, a very slight adaptation
of the Roman Catholic religion—strange for me to believe in. I have
always believed in it. My poems rarely contain any of it. That is why they
are not satisfactory to me. Most of them are the outer poems. Three
quarters of the world's literature deals with the outer world. Most modern fiction does. Some of it, of course, is purely reporting of outer incidents. Not that that need condemn it. Perhaps the greatest works of art
are those that reconcile, perfectly, inner & outer.

There is nothing new in what I have been saying. But it sprang to my
mind when I read your reply to my sincere advice—shun morbidity (as I
haven't).

You say, or at least imply, that you couldn't, because of your terrible
misfortunes. And I say that you can. Morbidity is sickness, un-
healthiness. That need play no *great* part in your stories. They might be
very fine stories anyway. But they will be finer without. This is not a
stirring plea to be British, only to let the inner consciousness, you've got
it because you *are* an artist from the little I have read of yours, develop.
'Raise up thine eyes to the hills.'

And now, when I look back over what I have written, I feel conscious
that there is a terrible lot of priggery in it—intellectual & emotional
priggery. It reads like a chunk of adulterated Chesterton, revised by Sir
Edward Elgar. Looking over it again, I doubt its sincerity, such is the
horribly argumentative, contradictory nature of my mind. Give me a
sheet of paper & I can't help filling it in. The result—more often than
not—is good & bad, serious & comic, sincere & insincere, lucid or
nonsensical by the turns of my whirligig mentality, started from the
wrong end, a mentality that ran before it walked, & perhaps will never
walk, that wanted to fly before it had the right even to think of wings.

Tomorrow, the next moment, I may believe in my beastly inner &
outer. I may be believing it now. It may be facile, immature humbug.
Again, it may be the expression of a real belief. The prince of darkness is a
gentleman. But his satanic convolutions & contradictions abide by no
gentlemanly conditions.

As I am writing, a telegram arrives. Mother's sister, who is in the

Carmarthen Infirmary suffering from cancer of the womb, is dying. There is much lamentation in the family & Mother leaves. The old aunt will be dead by the time she arrives. This is a well-worn incident in fiction, & one that has happened time after time in real life. The odour of death stinks through a thousand books & in a thousand homes. I have rarely encountered it (apart from journalistic enquiries), & find it rather pleasant. It lends a little welcome melodrama to the drawing-room tragi-comedy of my most uneventful life. After Mother's departure I am left alone in the house, feeling slightly theatrical. Telegrams, dying aunts, cancer, especially of such a private part as the womb, distraught mothers & unpremeditated train-journeys, come rarely. They must be savoured properly & relished in the right spirit. Many summer weeks I spent happily with the cancered aunt on her insanitary farm.[1] She loved me quite inordinately, gave me sweets & money, though she could little afford it, petted, patted, & spoiled me. She writes—is it, I wonder, a past tense yet—regularly. Her postscripts are endearing. She still loves—or loved—me, though I don't know why. And now she is dying, or dead, & you will pardon the theatrical writing. Allow me my moments of drama.

But the foul thing is I feel utterly unmoved, apart, as I said, from the pleasant death-reek at my negroid nostrils. I haven't, really, the faintest interest in her or her womb. She is dying. She is dead. She is alive. It is all the same thing. I shall miss her bi-annual postal orders. That's all. And yet I like—liked—her. She loves—loved—me. Am I, he said, with the diarist's unctuous, egotistic preoccupation with his own blasted psychological reactions to his own trivial affairs, callous & nasty? Should I weep? Should I pity the old thing? For a moment, I feel I should. There must be something lacking in me. I don't feel worried, or hardly ever, about other people. It's self, self, all the time. I'm rarely interested in other people's emotions, except those of my pasteboard characters. I prefer (this is one of the thousand contradictory devils speaking) style to life, my own reactions to emotions rather than the emotions themselves. Is this, he pondered, a lack of soul?

There was a certain theatrical quality about your letter, too, a little of the purple dreams of the yellow nineties,[2] the red roses, the wine, & the final falling of the final curtain. And now I wish I hadn't said that. The histrionic quality was sincere. Your answer to my DO NOT BE MORBID statement was enough to shove me under the table. Go on writing future letters just as theatrically. Tons of good stuff comes out of the theatre. This again may sound facetious. I am not deriding what you spoke of. That goes too deep for the playhouse. The selfconscious can escape, momentarily, by dressing their soul-cries in ermine & astrakhan, &

---

[1] Ann Jones, died 7 February 1933. The draft of a poem, later 'After the Funeral', is in a Thomas Notebook, dated 'Feb 10 '33'. The 'insanitary farm' is the Fern Hill of the poem of that title; it is also the 'Gorsehill' of Thomas's story 'The Peaches'.

[2] *The Yellow Book* was an influential magazine of art and literature in the 1890s, a period that Thomas pretended to despise.

letting them stand before the footlights before the footlights fade out.

I am interested in what you say about your story writing—the quick, quiet, dream-come idea, the lifting of the pen, & then the faces of past miseries & horrors obliterating everything. I can realise why your output is so small. In your letter you say it will be something if we can help each other towards, I forget your exact image, the planting of seeds in the forests of literature or something like that. From my seat among the ancients may I, for one moment, shake a few stalactites off my frosty beard, & give you a little advice? I asked you, in a letter, to write from your guts. You did. And, of course, you do in your short stories. But why not, just for a few times, put a sheet of paper in front of you, & without thinking twice, write half or a quarter or all of a short story. Don't begin with a polished idea in which every incident is fixed in your mind. Just shove a girl on the seashore on a summer day & let her make her own story. Write, write, regardless of everything. Your present method of story writing—the draft after draft, the interminable going-over-again, can be compared to the method of the marksman who spends weeks & weeks polishing his rifle, weeks & [weeks] cleaning it, weeks & weeks getting the exact ammunition for it, weeks & weeks deciding on a target, weeks & weeks weighing his rifle in his hand, weeks & weeks weighing it in a different way, &, at the end of the year, having a pop at the bull's eye. Why not, for a change, fire off round after round of ammunition from any old gun you can get hold of. You'll miss hundreds of times, but you're bound to get the bull's eye a lot of times, too. You'll find the hit-or-miss, the writing with no plot, technique will help you considerably in loosening your mind & in getting rid of those old stifling memories which may, unless you are careful, get in the way of your literary progress.

I now rest my beard upon my knees again, & the crows return to their nests.

Swansea still stands where it did. No one has blown up the churches. The Watch Committee still stands on its one leg & hands its glass eye round from member to member. There are the taverns & cafés. There is the hospital & the mortuary. Job—I have seen him several times since I left him—still drones around the edges of the local news like a Cornish bee. My friend Dan[1] still tears his fearsome chords from the entrails of a much-abused piano. I continue writing in the most futile manner, looking at the gas-oven, at periodic intervals, with a wistful glimmer in my eye. My sister is soon to be married.[2] She will live in London. I shall

---

[1] Daniel Jones (b. 1912), Thomas's close friend from childhood; later a professional composer.

[2] Nancy Marles Thomas (1906–53) became engaged to an Englishman, Haydn Taylor, at Christmas 1932. He was then a commercial traveller, and was based in Swansea until September that year. Her letters to him from 5 Cwmdonkin Drive describe an unhappy family ('very quarrelsome') where there were frequent rows about drink and money. According to Nancy, her brother stole from handbags ('a £1 note was missing'), her mother used to steam open Haydn Taylor's letters, and her father frequently raged against life in general.

stay occasionally with her. The London Mercury has not yet printed my story. Neither have I received a cheque for it. I have just evaded a libel action through some pot-boiling article of mine for the Northcliffe Press.[1] A lone tea beckons on the table.

I have been a long time in replying to your last long letter. Please forgive me & let your next be longer.

Dylan

MS: Buffalo   *SL*

TREVOR HUGHES
[May 1933][2]   5 Cwmdonkin Drive Uplands Swansea

Dear Trevor,

Many months passed between the posting of my letter, which, as you say, you found provocative of thought, and the written result. I have a very good mind indeed to send you a shallow letter. You would probably send an answer to it by return post, for the more lengthy and profound (?) my letter, the longer do you seem to take in replying. This little reprimand over, and never, I hope, to be repeated, I can now tackle your correspondence in as serious a manner as I am able.

You ask me for criticism of your story, but I would rather, if it is the same to you, and even if it isn't, criticise the attitude of mind behind its writing & not so much the result of such an attitude.

Again I was struck by the brilliance of your letter, a subterranean brilliance, if you will, and too near the rim to be pleasant. But brilliance, nevertheless, of a high imaginative order as they say in textbooks. But how much do I prefer the passionate wordiness of your letter to the unnecessary wordiness of your story! I am not going to, even if I could, destroy your story in a couple of cheap sentences. It is a bad story, but that doesn't matter. You are, and you know it despite your self-termed apologia, capable of a much better [story] than that. It must be as unsatisfactory to you as it is to me.

This is my main contention: Why, when you can, as you show in your letter, struggle with the fundamentals of belief, & the rock-bottom ideas of artistic bewilderment, morbidity, and disillusionment, when you can write with a pen dipped in fire and vinegar, when you have something to say, however terrible it may be, and the vocabulary to say it with, do you waste time on the machinations of a Stacy Aumonier plot and on the

---

[1] 'Genius and Madness Akin in World of Art', *South Wales Evening Post* (part of the Northcliffe group), 7 January 1933. Nina Hamnett (1890–1956), a painter who thrived on scandal, had published her autobiography, *Laughing Torso*, the previous summer. Thomas referred to it as 'the banned book'. A week later the paper apologised, saying the book had 'a very wide circulation'.

[2] Probably in reply to a letter from Hughes dated May 7 (at Buffalo).

unreal emotions of a pasteboard character whose replica one could find in a hundred novelettes of the nineties? Why go to the cafés, and French cafés at that, for your plots? You are not really interested in people. I doubt whether you are a fiction writer at all. Why go to the cafés for worn plots when the only things you are interested in are the antagonistic interplays of emotions and ideas, the rubbing together of sensibilities, brain chords and nerve chords, convolutions of style, tortuities of new expressions?

My contention boils down to the fact that the short story is not your medium. What your medium is I can do nothing but suggest. It is prose, undoubtedly, but an utterly non-commercial prose, a prose of passionate ideas, a metaphysical prose. I repeat my last letter's advice to you: Write, write, write, out of your guts, out of the sweat on your forehead and the blood in your veins.[1] Do not think about Mr Potter's guide to the salesmanship of short stories produced, apparently, on the lines of the Ford works. Do not bother your head about the length of the stuff you are writing. Don't descend, that is the main point. You descended badly in the story I have at my elbow as I write. You tagged on, under some misapprehension as to the quality of the intellect of your audience, that magazine little bit about the inquest. You see that sort of ending in the Windsor and the Pall Mall periodicals, and even in the London Mercury on an off month. (Please don't think that anything I say in this letter resembles a sneer at your work. I am honestly doing my best to help you.)

You descended from the Stygian heights—a very true paradox—of your real style, which I have only seen in your letters, when you make your pseudo-French characters say, 'It is very difficult—difficile', or words to that effect. Whether the addition of the foreign word is to add atmosphere, or merely to instruct junior readers, I don't know. In either case, it's a ghastly thing to do. What you want to do is to sit down & write, regardless of plot or characters, just as you write a letter to me. You know Middleton Murry's prose and Lawrence's non-fiction prose. Murry is not interested in plots or characters. He is interested in the symbols of the world, in the mystery and meaning of the world, in the fundamentals of the soul. And these things he writes about. These things you are interested in. Write about them. You have a style as individual as Murry's. Murry writes with a sober, contemplative pen, and you with an inebriate pen. But it doesn't matter a bit. Write a story (if you must write stories) about yourself searching for your soul amid the horrors of corruption and disease, about your passionate strivings after something you don't know and can't express. (This is one of the few ways [of] knowing it and expressing it.)

In one letter I remember telling you to steer clear as quickly as you could from morbidity and morbid introspection. Now I am telling you to delve deep, deep into yourself until you find your soul, and until you

---

[1] This advice, however, comes in the last letter but one, according to the order suggested here, which fits the best conjecture.

know yourself. These two bits of advice aren't contradictory. The true search for the soul lies so far within the last circle of introspection that it is out of it. You will, of course, have to revolve on every circle first. But until you reach that little red hot core, you are not alive. The number of dead men who walk, breathe, and talk is amazing.

(I am not taking any trouble over the phrasing of this letter. You, from your peak of sultry glory where the gods of clauses and of commas walk under the exclamatory moon, might be annoyed at my rough way with words and grammar. But the faster I write the more sincere I am in what I write.)

It is not Utopian advice that I am attempting to ladle out to you. It is terribly practical. Forget the 'annihilative reverse' of the rejection slip, and the 'intellectual catarrh'. Plunge, rather, headfirst & boldly into Charon's ferry. And who knows? Charon's ferry may turn at last into the river Jordan & purge you of ills.

You speak of a world in which the effort of thought will be unnecessary. Write of it. You speak of your 'curious surprising of beauty', and its metamorphosis into ugliness, your 'charred crucifix'. Write, write, write.

You are one [of] the dark-eyed company of Poe & Thompson,[1] Nerval[2] & Baudelaire, Rilke and Verlaine. Be a Thompson in prose. You complain that you haven't his genius. Of course you haven't, but you have your own red sparks of genius. And you *must* not allow the old stagnant waters to put them out. You say you have the honey. You say you have nothing but honey and greyness. You have honey and senna. Mix them together, dip your pen into them, and write.

Don't forget: To hell with all the preconceived notions of short story writing, to the world of dyspeptic editors and rejection slips, to the cardboard men & women. Into the sea of yourself like a young dog, and bring out a pearl.

Remember: you are not another Aumonier, another Manhood, another Bullett.[3] You are one of the white-faced company whose tears wash the world.

To hell with everything except the inner necessity for expression, & the medium of expression, [with] everything except the great need of forever striving after this mystery and meaning I moan about.

There is only one object: the removing of veils from your soul & scabs from your body. Reaching a self freedom is the only object. You will get nearer to it by writing as I have suggested—make your own variations — than by all the writing of clever and eminently saleable short stories. And, lastly, it doesn't matter a damn whether your stuff is printed or not. Better a bundle of pages on which you have honestly strived after

---

[1] Francis Thompson (1859–1907), the opium-addicted poet who wrote 'The Hound of Heaven'.
[2] Gérard de Nerval (1808–55), French poet; he was mentally disturbed.
[3] Stacy Aumonier (1887–1928) wrote short stories, as did H. A. Manhood. Gerald Bullett (1893–1958) was a poet and novelist.

something worth striving after, than a story in every magazine & an international reputation.

Come back to Wales in the Neath[1] of adversity. Leave London & come to Neath. That is particularly bad advice, I'm sure, but it is written from purely selfish motives—from a desire to see you and talk to you again, to hear you speak, to read your mad prose, & to read you my mad pomes. 3 months are all too long.

Dylan

MS: Buffalo   SL

TREVOR HUGHES
[summer 1933]   5 Cwmdonkin Drive Uplands Swansea

I looked through a pile of old papers the other day, and found your last letter to me. Reading it again, I realised how very good indeed it was. I know of nothing, in any literature I have read, to compare with it. Among the cribbed and cabinned, the bored and strangled destructivism of so much modern writing, it stands out supremely—a vast wind of pessimism (though that is not the right word) among the despondent farts of the little men. Poe has nothing on you. He had his Ravens, you have a flock of monstrous carrion-pickers. Forget the Hound of Heaven and bay down your own hellhounds. I am looking forward to your sequel to Burton–Hughes's Guts of Melancholia. If I can but make you write always as well as you can write in the letter by my side, then I shall be doing, for once in my life, something worthwhile.

I am writing this near a two-foot statue of Echo, who cocks her marble ear at me, listening to me mouth these words aloud.

Do you want your story back? I have lost it, and one of my own in which there were four characters—a dead man and three hawks. It was very pretty.

I am writing this in an odd mood, smoking, toasting my toes. I have such a bad headache that it is hard to write connected sentences. When a new thought comes I want to put it down, slipshod, in probably a most inapt place. My pen started to write ebony.

Oh, to be a critic! 'Mr X shows promise. This week's masterpiece. Mr Y is bad.' So simple, no bother, no bleeding of writing. I think you bleed more than I do, God help you. Remember the Worm,[2] read a meaning into its symbol—a serpent's head rising out of the clean sea.

Think this selfconscious. A pal o' mine's mad, in Coney Hill, saying all the time, so his aunt says, 'Keep a straight bat, sir'. We have a new asylum.[3] It leers down the valley like a fool, or like a snail with the two

---

[1] A small and unprepossessing town near Swansea.
[2] The Worm's Head, a half-tide island at the end of the Gower Peninsula, near Swansea.
[3] Cefn Coed, on a hill a mile from his home. 'Coney Hill' must be Colney Hatch, once a notorious asylum outside London.

turrets of its water towers two snails' horns.

How good it is to feel that I can write anything to you. Your last letter shows me that you understand, though understand what I shall never know more than I shall know the answer to the looking glass question—'Why is this me?' Remember—'Don't be morbid'. Sometimes I want to go down to the cellar to be nearer the worms. Sometimes only a worm is companion, its grey voice at your ear the only voice.

(This, too, you might laugh off. 'Juvenilia.' A shrug, a slight condescension. Boys will be old men.)

I will be in London for a fortnight, from Bank Holiday on, staying on the Thames with Nancy,[1] my sister, who married some months ago.

Write and tell me when I can come to see you, or where I can meet you sometime. We might go to the ballet together.

Or we might sit and talk. Or sit.

Beachcomber would love this.[2]

Dylan

MS: Buffalo   *SL*

GEOFFREY GRIGSON

Geoffrey Grigson (b. 1905), poet, author and uncompromising critic, was literary editor of the *Morning Post*. In 1933 he found time to start the influential magazine *New Verse*, which appeared every two months, and edited it until it ceased publication in 1939.

[summer 1933]   5 Cwmdonkin Drive Uplands Swansea

Dear Sir,

I am sending you some poems to be considered for publication in 'New Verse', about which I read in 'John O'London's Weekly', a month or two ago. Out of a large number of poems I found it extremely difficult to choose 6 to send you. As a matter of fact, the enclosed poems were picked almost entirely at random.

If you think the poems unsuitable for publication, and if, of course, you are sufficiently interested, I could let you see some more. I probably have far better ones in some of my innumerable exercise books.[3]

A considerable period lies between the writing of some of the enclosed poems, as perhaps you will be able to see. Whether time has shown any improvement I find it hard to say, as I have developed, intellectually at least, in the smug darkness of a provincial town, and have only on rare

---

[1] Nancy Thomas married Haydn Taylor in May 1933. Their first home was a houseboat on the Thames at Chertsey. Thomas's visit, which took place, was almost certainly his first to London.

[2] Pseudonym of J. B. Morton, humorous columnist in the *Daily Express*.

[3] Grigson returned the poems.

occasions shown any of my work to any critics, generally uninterested or
incompetent.

If you could see your way clear to publish any of these poems, or find in
them sufficient merit to warrant the reading of some more, you would be
doing me a very great favour. Grinding out poetry, whether good or bad,
in such an atmosphere as surrounds me, is depressing and disheartening.

Yours sincerely,
Dylan Thomas

MS: Buffalo   *SL*

PAMELA HANSFORD JOHNSON

Soon to find her own feet as a novelist, Pamela Hansford Johnson (1912–81) was
two years older than Dylan Thomas. Their literary friendship, which became a
love affair after they met in February 1934, began with a poem by Thomas, 'That
sanity be kept', published in a newspaper, the *Sunday Referee*, 3 September 1933.
Earlier in the year the newspaper had begun a feature, the 'Poet's Corner', edited
by the eccentric Victor Neuburg (almost invariably spelt 'Neuberg' by Thomas).
Johnson, who worked in a bank and lived with her mother in Battersea, submitted
a poem, which appeared on April 9, and she was drawn into Neuburg's coterie of
young writers. When the *Referee* published Thomas's poem, she wrote to him.

[mid-September 1933][1]   Blaen-Cwm[2] Llangain nr Carmarthen

Beginning this letter in the way I do, removes the necessity of using the
formal, 'madam', the stiff, 'Miss Johnson', (rather ambiguous but entirely
unmeant), and the impudent, 'Pamela', (also ambiguous, also unmeant).
It removes a similar obstacle in your case.

If it is 'gruesome' to reply to letters, then I am as much of a ghoul as you
are. I return frequently, in the characterless scrawl God and a demure
education gave me.

Incidentally, when you reply to this—and let it be long and soon—don't
write to the above address. It is merely a highly poetical cottage where I
sometimes spend week-ends. Reply to my nasty, provincial address.

Thank you for the poems. Mr. Neuburg has paid you a large and almost
merited compliment. 'One of the few exquisite word-artists of our day',
needs little praise or abuse from me. But, still, I must compliment you
upon 'The Nightingale', by far the best of the three poems. Comparing
that with the 'Sea Poem for G', one of the most perfect examples of
bloody verse I have ever seen, and with other Referee poems, is like

---

[1] Johnson's diary, September 9: 'Had nice letter from Referee poet to whom I wrote.'
September 18: 'Charming & very, very modern, not to say rude letter from Dylan
Thomas.' The present letter is the second of these.

[2] A pair of stone cottages, near the Carmarthen–Llanstephan road, occupied by members of
his mother's family. Fernhill (the farm is one word, the poem two) is a mile away.

comparing Milton with Stilton. I like the other two poems you sent me, but not as much, and the first stanza of 'Prothalamium', I don't like at all. Too many adjectives, too much sugar. And the fifth and sixth lines are pure cliché. 'I write from the heart', said a character in some novel I've forgotten. 'You write', was the reply, 'from the bowels as after a strong emetic.' Not that I apply that rude remark to 'Prothalamium'; I'm quoting not because of it but for the sake of it.

Of course you are not an agèd virgin. But many of the contributors to the Poet's Corner are, and woo the moon for want of a better bedfellow. I can't agree with you that the majority of the Referee poems are good. With a few exceptions they are nauseatingly bad. Yours are among the exceptions, of course. Do you remember a poem called '1914' printed a couple of weeks ago? Do you remember the 'Sea Poem'? Do you remember those few diabetic lines about an Abyssinian cat? What did you think of last week's 'Blue Gum Tree'? That is a real test of taste. Like that, you like anything. It would be hard to realise the number of people bluffed into believing 'Blue Gum Tree' to be a good poem. Its sprawling formlessness they would call, 'modern', its diction, 'harsh but effective', and some of its single lines, such as, 'The cloth of silver over a white balustrade', would send them into some sort of colourful rapture. In reality, the formlessness is the outcome of entire prosodical incompetence, the diction is not even tailor-made but ready-to-wear, and the 'colourful' lines are like cheap, vermilion splotches on a tenthrate music- hall backcloth.

In the very interesting copy you sent me of the first Poet's Corner, it is explained that when, during any week, no poetry is received, the best *verse* would be printed. That would be perfectly all right if it did happen. But the pretentious palming off of *doggerel* (not even verse) as 'arty' poetry is too much.

It was on the same grounds that I objected to 'Poet's Corner' as a title. There was a time when only poets were called poets. Now anyone with an insufficient knowledge of the English language, a Marie Corelli sentiment,[1] and a couple of 'bright' images to sprinkle over the lines, is called a poet. He can't even leave his excretion in a private spot. They give him a public 'Corner' to leave it in. (A vulgar metaphor! I hope you don't object.)

This is in no way a biased or personal attack. It's the general principles of the thing I like to use as Aunt Sallies. Pray God I, too, am not 'arty'. A physical pacifist and a mental militarist, I can't resist having a knock—or even a blow at a dead horse—when all I put my faith in is utterly contradicted. I put my faith in poetry, and too many poets deny it.

To return to *your* poetry, (you must excuse my slight soap-box attitude): It shows a tremendous passion for words, and a real knowledge of them. Your grasp of form and your handling of metre is among the best I know to-day. And—the main thing—your thoughts are worth expres-

[1] Marie Corelli (Mary Mackay) (1855–1924), extravagantly romantic novelist.

sing. Have you written a great deal? When do you write? I'm interested to know all sorts of things like that, and to see some more.

What I like about your poems is that they *state*, not contradict, that *they create* not destroy. Poem after poem, recording, in sickening detail, the wrinkles on the author's navel, fill the contemporary journals, poem after poem recording, none too clearly, the chaos of to-day. Out of chaos they make nothing, but, themselves part of the post-war carnage, fade away like dead soldiers. So much new verse (do you know 'New Verse'?) can be summarised into, 'Well, there's been a hell of a war; it's left us in a mess; what the hell are we going to do about it?' The answer is fairly obvious. But is it worth writing about? No, you answer in a loud voice, or at least I hope you do. You are not like that, and your 'not-ness' alone is worth all the superlatives at my command.

So you are the same age as myself.[1] You say one has enough time, when one is 21, to be modest. One has enough time ahead, too, to regret one's immodesty. The more I think of my Referee poem the less I like it. The idea of myself, sitting in the open window, in my shirt, and imagining myself as some Jehovah of the West, is really odd. If I were some Apollo, it would be different. As a matter of fact, I am a little person with much untidy hair.

With this letter you will find two poems of mine. I am sending them to show you, or to hope to show you, that I can do much better than you think from what you have seen of mine. Incidentally, I'd better mention that the poem starting, 'No food suffices', is, though complete in itself, the woman's lament from an unfortunately unfinished play. I think this needs mention; references in the poem would otherwise cast aspersions on the nature of my sex.[2] The second poem you may not like at all; it is distinctly unfashionable.

After my violent outburst against the Referee poets, you'll probably read *my* two poems with a stern & prejudiced eye. I hope you don't, and I hope you like them. Whether you do or not, tell me.

Can I keep your poems for a little longer?

Dylan Thomas

P.S. The Woman poem is to be printed in the Adelphi. I can't resist adding that, because I like the magazine so much. The Jesus poem is probably to be printed in T. S. Eliot's Criterion, though, as a rule, the Criterion doesn't print any metaphysic verse at all. I mention the 'C' for the same reason that I mention the 'A'.[3]

P.P.S. I am staying, as you see, in Carmarthenshire & have forgotten to bring your address with me. I am trusting to luck that 13 is the right

---

[1] She was twenty-one. He was still six weeks short of his nineteenth birthday.
[2] 'The Woman Speaks' was the title of the poem (its first line was 'No food suffices') when it was published the following year.
[3] No 'Jesus poem' appeared in the magazine Criterion.

number. If it is, you will read this explanation. If it isn't, you won't. So there was no point at all in writing it. *D.T.*

MS: Buffalo   *SL*

PAMELA HANSFORD JOHNSON
[1933] [fragment]

Words! Words! I never seem to stop writing. Here is another sentence to add to the already growing confusion.

The two other poems I have included are very recent. For some reason I don't think you will like the needles & the knives.[1] I don't think I do, either, but there we are!

In time you'll have all I've ever written, if I send you such vast quantities at a time.

MS: Buffalo

TREVOR HUGHES
[card, postmarked 11 Oct 1933]   5 Cwmdonkin Drive

Dear Trevor,

First let me apologise for not having written before this, and secondly for writing such a little note now. I have, really, the most concrete excuses, too complicated to put on a post-card. The only thing of importance is this: 'Prose and Verse', that stillborn child, is to be resurrected. Grocer Trick[2] is to do the financial and business part of it, and I, as it was arranged before, am to edit it. The high standards, formerly set, will be strictly adhered to; but there is one important, new condition: 'P & V' will print only the work of Welshmen and women—this includes those of dim Welsh ancestry and those born in Wales—who *write* in English. This condition necessarily restricts, but it is that which will make, I hope and trust, the journal an unique affair. Another highbrow periodical, especially produced from a blowsy town such as this—on the furthest peaks of the literary world—is doomed to hell from the beginning. But a

---

[1] A Notebook poem, 'Take the needles and the knives', is dated September 12. On September 10, Dylan's father, D. J. Thomas, had been admitted to hospital in London, to begin treatment with radium needles for cancer of the mouth, diagnosed two weeks earlier.

[2] Albert Edward ('Bert') Trick (1889–1973), ran his mother's small grocery shop not far from Cwmdonkin Drive. Formerly an income-tax clerk, he was passionately concerned with both literature and left-wing politics. He was married with a small daughter. For a year or so, Thomas's intellectual life revolved around Bert Trick's parlour.

new highclass periodical for Welshmen? Up Cymru! I don't see why it shouldn't be a great success. Already Trick is corresponding with universities, libraries, museums, and other intellectual morgues, with spinsters, knights, and philanthropists. Do you know any Welshmen who might be interested in the project? If so, tell me when you write. And when you can, send me along all your original prose still existing. I'd like to go through it carefully and critically, picking out what is suitable for publication. You've got four or five printed pages at your disposal. I'm not going to write any more now. *Write* and tell me your views.

Dylan

MS: Buffalo   *SL*

PAMELA HANSFORD JOHNSON
[October 15 1933][1]   5 Cwmdonkin Drive Uplands Swansea

Thank you. I should have been very sorry hadn't I posted the card. The mutual outpourings of a crank and a romantic (there is little doubt as to which is which) would have been lost to posterity; creeds and beliefs, that will change as the years change us, but are nevertheless sincere, would have remained unexpressed; insults and compliments, hasty judgments, wisdoms and nonsenses, would have been unsaid; and a considerably nice friendship would have been broken up almost before it began. Even now twelve heartfelt pages are titivating the senses of a Dead Letter superintendent, and three heartfelt poems are lying beneath the pillow of some postmaster's boy in the depths of Llangyfellach or Pwllddu. (I, too, know not a word of Welsh and these names are as fearsome to me as they are to you.)[2]

What have I missed in your letter? Three poems, twelve passionate pages of affirmation and denial, a thought on Shakespeare and a sob for Siegfried! Dear God, and all for three-halfpence.

There is so much to talk about in your last letter, to agree with and to argue with most violently, that I must light my cigarette, and then, with a steady hand and a more-or-less contented mind, tackle the points in order from the very beginning to the last curve on the last letter of the totally unnecessary 'Johnson'.

1) I'm glad you're not as riddled with silliness as I am. I should have carried on for months, never writing your name, consciously avoiding

---

[1] The poems by Pitt and Martineau that Thomas mentions appeared in the *Sunday Referee* on October 8, apparently a week earlier. Johnson's diary, Monday October 16: 'Lovely long & delightful letter from Dylan Thomas.' In those days there was a Sunday post collection, so 'October 15' is a reasonable conjecture.

[2] Llangyfelach (an industrial suburb of Swansea) and Pwlldu (a bay near the town) are both misspelt. Thomas was brought up in an anglicised home. Like most of his friends, he would have been able to pronounce Welsh names, but not necessarily to spell them.

such an ordinary gesture of friendliness as calling you Pamela, or Pam, or whatever I am to call you. My unusual name—for some mad reason it comes from the Mabinogion and means the 'prince of darkness'[1]—rhymes with 'Chillun', as you suggest. I don't know what Pamela rhymes with, unless the *very* cultured way of saying 'family', and therefore cannot reply with a little couplet.

2) The Vicky-Bird,[2] undoubtedly of the parrot variety, doesn't appear to like what we sent him last week. But then I always said his taste was abysmal. I sent him a very short and obscure poem with one indecent line. What did you send him to be so ignominiously placed among the spavined horses? A very short and obscure poem with *two* indecent lines? No, I hardly think so. He doesn't want to give too many prizes to the same people, on principle. He must print the work of others sometimes, and spread the vomit evenly and impartially over his pages. Miss Gertrude Pitt must show her mettle, rusty tin to me; and Mr. Martineau must patch his broken heart with a sentimental song.

3) I am in the path of Blake, but so far behind him that only the wings on his heels are in sight. I have been writing since I was a very little boy, and have always been struggling with the same things, with the idea of poetry as a thing entirely removed from such accomplishments as 'word-painting', and the setting down of delicate but usual emotions in a few, wellchosen words. There must be no compromise; there is always only the one right word: use it, despite its foul or merely ludicrous associations; I used 'double-crossed' because it was what I meant. It is part of a poet's job to take a debauched and prostituted word, like the beautiful word, 'blond', and to smooth away the lines of its dissipation, and to put it on the market again, fresh and virgin. Neuburg blabs of some unsectarian region in the clouds where poetry reaches its highest level. He ruins the truth of that by saying that the artist must, of necessity, preach socialism. There is no necessity for the artist to do anything. There is no necessity. He is a law unto himself, and his greatness or smallness rises or falls by that. He has only one limitation, and that is the widest of all: the limitation of form. Poetry finds its own form; form should never be superimposed; the structure should rise out of the words and the expression of them. I do not want to express only what other people have felt; I want to rip something away and show what they have never seen. Because of the twist in myself I will never be a very good poet: only treading the first waves, putting my hands in deeper and then taking them out again.

---

[1] The word 'Dylan' means nothing more than 'sea', or possibly a sea-god. As a proper name it occurs briefly in the *Mabinogion*—the Welsh medieval prose romances which have echoes of older narratives—where it is bestowed on a child born to Aranrhod: 'a fine boy-child with rich yellow hair'. It was virtually unknown as a name before D. J. Thomas disinterred it for his son.

[2] Victor Neuburg (1883–1940) was not entirely the figure of fun that Thomas portrayed. A bisexual who wrote poetry, he had formerly dabbled in homosexual magic with the necromancer Aleister Crowley.

But even that, to me, is better than the building of perfectly ornate structures in the sand. To change the image, one is a brief adventure in the wilderness, and the other a little gallop on an ordered plot of land.

4) I apologise for No Man Believes, but I really didn't think it was obscure. I understood it so perfectly myself, but I was probably the only one who did. And even that's ungrammatical.

5) But why Wordsworth? Why quote that decay? Shelley I can stand, but old Father William was a human nannygoat with a pantheistic obsession. He hadn't a spark of mysticism in him. How could he be a metaphysicist? Metaphysics is merely the structure of logic, intellect, and supposition on a mystical basis. And mysticism is illogical, unintellectual, and dogmatic. Quote Shelley, yes. But Wordsworth was a tea-time bore, the great Frost of literature, the verbose, the humourless, the platitudinary reporter of Nature in her dullest moods. Open him at any page: and there lies the English language not, as George Moore said of Pater, in a glass coffin, but in a large, sultry, and unhygienic box. Degutted and desouled. Catch him in his coy moods, walking the hills with a daffodil pressed to his lips, and his winter woollies tickling his chest. Catch him in his pompous mood, his Virginity and Victoria mood, his heavy-footed humourlessness pursuing a wanton dogma down a blind alley full of the broken bones of words. I admit the Immortality Ode is better than anything he ever did (with the exception of the pantheistic creed expressed in Tintern Abbey); among the mediocrity and rank badness it stands out like a masterpiece; but judged from a proper perspective, along the lines of Shakespeare, Dante, Goethe, Blake, John Donne, Verlaine & Yeats, it is no more than moderately good. All it says has been said before and better, and all it was incapable of saying. Try to rub away its halo of fame and the mist of veneration that has grown up around it; try to forget the drummed-in fact that he is an English mystic—: and you will see it chockful of clichés, ridiculous inversions of speech and thought, all the tricks-of-trade of the unoriginal verse-writer whose bluff has not yet been called. I put by its side the poems of Matthew Arnold, and think what a delightfully loud splash the two would make if I dropped them into the river.

Perhaps you gather that I don't like Wordsworth. I'm sorry, but he's one of the few 'accepted' whom I refuse in any way to accept at all. *This is my important point about him in summary*: He writes about mysticism but he is not a mystic; he describes what mystics have been known to feel, but he himself doesn't feel anything, not even a pain in the neck. He could well have written his Ode in the form of a treatise: 'Mysticism and its Relations to the Juvenile Mind.' Just as an experiment, read him again with my adverse opinions at the back of your mind. I changed from loving to loathing Swinburne in a day. Enough. You shall have your own back.

6) I, too, should like to meet you. This possibly can be arranged, but not before the beginning of September when I am going to see my sister near Chertsey.[1]

[1] A slip for 'December'. Near the end of the next letter Thomas wrote, 'You are right, of course. December it is.'

Don't expect too much of me (It's conceit to suppose that you would); I'm an odd little person. Don't imagine the great jawed writer brooding over his latest masterpiece in the oak study, but a thin, curly little person, smoking too [many] cigarettes, with a crocked lung, and writing his vague verses in the back room of a provincial villa.

7) David Gascoyne[1] and Reuben Mednikoff! You move in exalted company. I read the Russian Jew's (is he?) effort in the Referee, & thoroughly agree with you—as a poet he's a bloody good painter. But Gascoyne? And seventeen, too? Tut, tut, what are the boys coming to? I read a thing of his—before your letter came—in the new, New Verse,[2] and thought he was raving mad. There are more maggots in his brain than there are in mine. But if he is so young there *is* a hope that the poetry will drop away from him and that the sore it leaves will soon heal. His New Verse poem is called 'And the 7th Dream Is The Dream of Isis'. Without wishing to provide a pornographic interlude over the tea-table, I'll quote some of the actual lines:[3] This is the opening:

> 'White curtains of tortured destinies
> Encourage the waistlines of women to expand
> And the eyes of men to enlarge like pocket cameras
> Teach children to sin at the age of five
> To cut out the eyes of their sisters with nail-scissors.'

And later:

> 'The pavements of cities are covered with needles
> The reservoirs are full of human hair
> Fumes of sulphur envelop the house of ill-fame
> Out of which bloodred lilies appear
> Across the square where crowds are dying in thousands
> A man is walking a tightrope covered with moths.'

And later:

> 'She was standing at the window clothed only in a ribbon
> She was burning the eyes of snails in a candle
> She was eating the excrement of dogs and horses
> She was writing a letter to the president of france.'

And later still:

> 'The edges of leaves must be examined through microscopes
> In order to see the stains made by dying flies
> At the other end of the tube a woman is bathing her husband
> When an angel writes the word Tobacco along the sky
> The sea becomes covered with patches of dandruff
> Little girls stick photographs of genitals in the windows of their homes
> And virgins cover their parents' beds with tealeaves.'

[1] The poet David Gascoyne (b. 1916) published his first book of verse in 1932. During the 1930s he was close to French surrealists, and strongly influenced by them.
[2] The October issue.
[3] There are a number of copying errors, eg 'stairs' for 'stains' six lines from the end, and four lines are omitted.

And so on. All the rest is just as pretty and just as meaningless. Ugliness & eccentricity must have a purpose. So much for Mr Gascoyne. May he teach the bats in his belfry better manners. (By the way, I just thought, I hope he isn't a near & dear friend of yours. If he is, I've been very impolite.)

8) I've heard such a lot about 'Cold Comfort Farm' that I'll have to get hold of it.[1] It sounds incredible. Isn't there a Grandma Doom in it who once saw something frightful in the woodshed?

9) The Steyning incidents[2] are almost too good to be true. Mrs. Runia Tharp![3] I've been muttering the magic names all day. It's enough to Runia, and I hope you'll excuse that. Don't take any notice of what the intellectual bullies told you. Tell 'em you've got more in your little finger than they have in the whole of their fact-crammed brains.

10) But for God's sake don't defend the Sunday Referee literary whippets any more. I'm repeating myself, I know, but I regard the verses printed (with very few exceptions—you, notably) as schoolgirl posies plucked from a virgin garden, and the saccharine wallowings of near-schoolboys in the bowels of a castrated muse. Even the Bentley bodies covering the Ford engines are badly battered. I'd like to carry the image further and say that the chassis is made from a scrapheap of dis-used spare parts. Neuburg indulges in a horrid compromise: between the outlooks of the romanticist and the theorist, the mincing tread of the 'one-line and memorable passage taster and memoriser', and the galumphing of the dogmatic theorist. In fact the compromise [is] between Beer and No Beer. The result is partial inebriation—his muse is never drunk enough to be really emotional and never sober enough to be really intellectual.

11) Please don't type again; the warmest words look cold.

And now I, too, must finish, not because of any business appointment, but because I think I've written plenty. Now it is *your* turn. There are many things I want to write about, but they'll do next time. I'll expect a letter very, very soon—and as long as mine.

Dylan

P.S. Three poems for you. Tell me if you like them or not. And why. I'll do the same if you'll send me some. The 'conversation' poem is very violent, as you will see, the 'Noise' poem very romantic, and the other in my more usual style. Take your choice, mum.

MS: Buffalo   *SL(R)*

---

[1] *Cold Comfort Farm*, Stella Gibbons's parody of the rural novel, was published in 1932.
[2] Neuburg, who lived in London, spent some of his time at Steyning, in Sussex. Johnson had been to literary get-togethers there.
[3] Runia Tharp was the name adopted by Runia Sheila Macleod, a woman of means who was Neuburg's companion.

PAMELA HANSFORD JOHNSON
[late October 1933][1]   Blaen-Cwm Llangain near Carmarthen

One day a very tired and bewildered young man will haunt the steps of the General Post Office, crying aloud, in broken Welsh, this one sad sentence: 'Why, in the name of God and the angelic clerks, cannot my letters be delivered to me?' He will be shooed away, but he will always return, crying his same question to a deaf Post Master and a malicious deity.

The trouble is that, for the last fortnight, I have been leading a very nomad existence, a few days in a rat-infested cottage in the heart of Wales, a few days with an eccentric friend, and a few days at home. Consequently, my letters are delivered to all three addresses, redelivered, and delivered again. Your last letter reached me on Saturday. I am replying with the greatest speed and at the greatest length.

When I came down here there were two letters of yours waiting for me—the proverbial twelve pages, and three typewritten sheets, to say nothing of the three lost poems. Now I reply to your collected correspondence.

I am staying, as you see, in a country cottage, eight miles from a town and a hundred miles from anyone to whom I can speak to on any subjects but the prospect of rain and the quickest way to snare rabbits. It is raining as I write, a thin, purposeless rain hiding the long miles of desolate fields and scattered farmhouses. I can smell the river, and hear the beastly little brook that goes gurgle-gurgle past this room. I am facing an uncomfortable fire, a row of china dogs, and a bureau bearing the photograph of myself aged seven—thick-lipped, Fauntleroy-haired, wide-eyed, and empty as the bureau itself. There are a few books on the floor beside me—an anthology of poetry from Jonson to Dryden, the prose of Donne, a Psychology of Insanity. There are a few books in the case behind me—a Bible, From Jest To Earnest, a History of Welsh Castles. Some hours ago a man came into the kitchen, opened the bag he was carrying, and dropped the riddled bodies of eight rabbits on to the floor. He said it was a good sport, showed me their torn bellies and opened heads, brought out the ferret from his pocket for me to see. The ferret might have been his own child, he fondled it so. His own eyes were as close-set as the eyes of the terrible thing he held in his hand. He called it, 'Billy fach'.

Later, when I have finished this letter, I'll walk down the lane. It will be dark then; lamps will be lit in the farmhouses, and the farmers will be sitting at their fires, looking into the blazing wood and thinking of God knows what littlenesses, or thinking of nothing at all but their own animal warmth.

But even this, grey as it is and full of the noise of sanitating water, and full of the sight of miserably wet fields, is better than the industrial small

---

[1] Dated by Thomas's references to poems which appeared in the *Sunday Referee* on October 22. And a Notebook poem, dated October 25, is marked 'Llangain'.

towns. I passed them in the bus coming down here, each town a festering sore on the body of a dead country, half a mile of main street with its Prudential, its Co-Op, its Star, its cinema and pub. On the pavements I saw nothing but hideously pretty young girls with cheap berets on their heads and paint smudged over their cheeks; thin youths with caps and stained fingers holding their cigarettes; women, all breast and bottom, hugging their purses to them and staring in at the shop windows; little colliers, diseased in mind and body as only the Welsh can be, standing in groups outside the Welfare Hall. I passed the rows of colliers' houses, hundreds of them, each with a pot of ferns in the window, a hundred jerry-built huts built by a charitable corporation for the men of the town to breed and eat in.

All Wales is like this. I have a friend who writes long and entirely unprintable verses beginning, 'What are you, Wales, but a tired old bitch?' and, 'Wales my country, Wales my cow.'

It's impossible for me to tell you how much I want to get out of it all, out of narrowness and dirtiness, out of the eternal ugliness of the Welsh people, and all that belongs to them, out of the pettinesses of a mother I don't care for and the giggling batch of relatives. What are you doing. I'm writing. Writing? You're always writing. What do you know? You're too young to write. (I admit that I very often look even younger than I am.) And I *will* get out. In some months I will be living in London. You shall call every day then and show me the poetry of cooking. I shall have to get out soon or there will be no need. I'm sick, and this bloody country's killing me.

All of which may sound very melodramatic. I don't want to make this letter sound like a third-rate play in which the 'artistic' hero boasts of his superiority over his fellows and moans of his highly poetical disease, or into a mere agony column. I hope you will excuse even the little bit of ranting and self pity I have indulged in.

I *did* like your illustrations, but the drawing of the oysters was far too good for the poem. I've given up tearing my hair at the products of the Neuburg Academy for the Production of Inferior Verse. I read them, put them aside, and try my hardest to forget. 'To The Hen', is the best thing I have seen in the Referee recently, but it is compensated for by the 'Cornflowers' of Miss Arlett. And now, to complete it all, the Sea Poem woman is assistant editor. Ah well. No more will my vague efforts adorn the Neuburg altar. Now even closer will I hug them to me.

But what's this about form? Are you misreading my cryptic comments? Or have I subconsciously (that word has gone sour since Lawrence flung it at his own addled head, and the Vicky Bird roosted on it) written what I did not intend. Rhythm, certainly. It's as essential to poetry as it is to music. Rhyme, certainly, but with qualifications. I've been under the impression that I have defended form in my recent letters and spat me of the sprawling formlessness of Ezra Pound's performing Yanks and others. But, for all I know, I may have reiterated Geoffrey Grigson's vast maxim,

'Modern Art does not need logic or balance', or Herbert Read's[1] statement to the effect that modern art need have no meaning at all.

Now to your twelve pages. Twelve pages, after all, is very little if you have a lot to say. Your flattering description of yourself, aided by the drawing in your last letter, must have given you great amusement. But don't say the drawing's true. And why the desire to look like everbody else? If you were the usual gutless, unimaginative, slang-flinging flapper, your adherence to a conventional style of looks would be excusable. But you aren't. As an individual, you should *look* individual, apart from the mass member of society. For commercial, and sanitary, reasons, it is better to dress cleanly. But I do like colour. *I* don't look a bit like anybody else—I couldn't if I wanted to, and I'm damned if I *do* want to. I *like* conversational (your word) shirts. And I see no reason why I shouldn't. Man's dress is unhygienic and hideous. Silk scarlet shirts would be a vast improvement. This isn't the statement of an artistic poseur; I haven't got the tact to pose as anything. Oh to look, if nothing else, different from the striped trouser lads with their cancer-fostering stiff collars and their tight little bowlers.

I was surprised to hear that you had written only 30 poems; a bus-going life explains it. May the Kiddies' Kompleat Poetry Set be put to severe work in the future, and may I, humbly and yet critically, cast my eyes upon the virgin words.

And now I have eight poems of yours to do what I like with. And I am going to do what I like with them—criticise each in turn, not very minutely, for nothing short of fifty pages would allow it, but at least in some detail. Remember that nothing I say, Pamela, is for the sake of being smart, or to relieve any acid emotions I may have bottled up within me. I mean what I say and I mean it to help. Tell me if it is worth my while and your attention. If it is, then I will willingly, more than willingly, criticise in the same way every and any poem you have written.

Sung In A Garden At Nightfall

Delius should have written this instead of that extremely literary piece of music, Summer Night on the River. His music is a rebound, or, if you like, a second mood. First comes the idea of the creation, then the mental poem, then the composition of the music: a wrong method of approach. The nostalgia that runs through him like a vein drips 'jasmine-sweet' from your song. I'm glad that the colour of your poem book is green, the colour of youth when a minor heartbreak or the twiddly bit on an oboe is more effective than the sight of God or the feel of a surgical needle stuck into the tongue. And this is prejudiced, I know. But I like the Garden Song, and if in places it is more intestinal than emotional, that is all to the good. And I confess to a slight retching at the phrases, 'Woven of saffron with a weft of blue', 'veiled with violet', 'The air is jasmine-sweet'. And I confess that 'The lashes of the rose are sealed with dew' is very pretty. But the whole poem I should like to see upon the cover of a

[1] Sir Herbert Read (1893–1968), author and critic.

chocolate box; its flavours would mix well with the taste of coffee-centres and crême de menthe.

You have such a lot of the abilities that go towards making a *very* good poet that it seems a shame you don't take a firmer grasp on your susceptibilities to the easier emotions and images. The best advice in the world to a poetess is—Be a poet! Think of Mrs Browning and Emily Brontë. One wrote in quite a competent, female manner, the other androgynously. It's Neuburg's Heshe all over again, and Lawrence's Bull-Cow.

Laze, if you will, in a gossamer evening, confiding with your summer lover (impersonal! impersonal!); think your thoughts, and weep over the jail-like attitude of the poplars. But make more out of that experience than a pretty patchwork of derivative images and puce emotions. The garden (God wot!) must fit the mind like a glove. You yourself make it hell or heaven. Nothing is beautiful unless you think it. Make of your Woodforde-Finden garden a valley Wagner might have been proud of, a little place Debussy would have lolled in, a rugby field for an infant Honneger. But don't take it as you find it. The garden was nothing. You descended on it like a bat from Chopin's belfry, and, lo, it was saccharine.

The Béguinage

This is by far the best poem that I've seen of yours. It's hard to imagine that the same mind created this and the previous song. It is beautifully simple; two of the verses are perfect. The idea, the form, & the expression, go hand-in-hand with a most satisfying delicacy. Out of more than fifty lines I can find only two that, in the slightest way, make discord. And those lines, oddly enough, are the two that begin the poem. I read them and expected Sousa orchestrated by Milhaud; I read on and got Mozart—a clumsy way of expressing my delight at fortyeight lines and my dislike of two.

Because I heap calumny on one poem, and immediately cover the next poem in an appreciative pile of roses, don't imagine that I am so easily a victim to my emotions that my opinions are little meditated. I like to spit at what I consider bad or unworthy (and much of what you sent me is unworthy of you), and I like to enthuse over what I consider sincere, real, and valuable. 'Béguinage' is all these three—not a Wordsworth model, or a chic adornment from the 'maison de Christina Rossetti', but an individual and highly successful production from the 'maison de P.H.J.'

Possession

See criticism one, especially the comment upon the poet and the poetess. 'Possession' is essentially a woman's poem. 'Béguinage' belongs to neither sex. It is a poem, and that is all and enough. 'Possession' is, metrically, quite good, but it is aimed at too low a standard.

Promenade Concert

Like the little girl with the curl over her forehead, when you are good you are very, very good, and when you are bad you are horrid. But even in your least inspired moments—and Sir Henry, Wood by name and Wood by nature,[1] seems to have had much effect upon your emotional and little upon your literary centres—good things rise out of the mediocrity as bubbles rise out of a marsh. There is, in the last stanza, an experience nakedly crystallized in a phrase:-

> 'clacking of applause, without even the compliment
> Of an age-old second of silence.'

And that one experience compensates for the hysteria of the preceding lines. Your sincerity is always undeniable, and your hell-paving intentions *do* come out in such phrases as

> 'And the rivers of Eden
> In the cold flute'.

But these are pearls surrounded not only by the pig's ear but by the whole of his bristling body. The 'burning triumph', the 'stinging pain', 'the singing and weeping for glory', are an exhibition (not in the sense of the Steyning highbrow) of emotion rather than a condensing, a torrent rather than a regulated fall, and as such is strictly out of place in a poem. It [is] as though a painter had flung a great mass of colours on to his canvas, and said to his critics, 'This is a landscape, for these are the colours that I see on the hills. The placing, dividing, and forming of those colours I leave to you.'

And while the colours would be bound to have some emotional significance, they no more make a painting than they do a stick of rock.

Tribute

A neat little advertisement, which might prove commercially saleable if 'Poetry' was changed to, say, 'Gibbs' Dentifrice'. One can write of mysticism without being a mystic; Wordsworth proved that. One can write of poetry, too.

Through The Night

Again, many of your merits and nearly all your faults come out in this. There is an obvious desire to say something and quite as obvious a reluctance to know what it is. There are *hints* of loneliness and the *statements* of verbosity. 'Drenched with rose', incidentally, is too reminiscent of de la Mare's 'Nod', in which the words 'dim with rose, and drenched with dew' appear. My dislike of the word 'burgeon' is a purely personal one, as is my dislike of the word, 'primrose'. Unfortunately both appear in this poem (I hope you notice that I have used the 'poem' & 'verse' discriminately in these tiny criticisms) to test my boast of unbias.

'Each window pane shoots fire', is too quick, too impetuous an image to be satisfactory. There, again, you put down the emotional essence of what you wanted to say before you put your literary intelligence to work. I don't know how long you spent over 'Through The Night', but twice the time would have doubled its value, making it a consistently *good* poem, for it is good (careful word) in patches now. The imperative lines are very effective. So is the climax, notwithstanding the 'mother-of-pearl into pallid primrose', the type of line I can only call too easily pretty.

[1] Sir Henry Wood (1869–1944), conductor, closely identified with the Promenade Concerts.

Up Train

Have I ever complimented you upon your command of conventional technique? If not, let me compliment you now, and also upon your ability to command the wider issues of form. 'Up Train' & 'The Symphony' are surprisingly effective in their set-out. Best of all, the form appears inevitable. 'Up Train' could have been written in no other way, the highest thing one can say of a technical experiment. 'Seed Nursery' has the simplicity of a nursery rhyme, set off by a remarkable diction, uninfluenced by any other diction I'm acquainted with.

> 'For the mad sweet-pea he rigs
> Pillories of little twigs'

gives me a most pleasant shock, a *physical* sensation. Few combinations of words have a physical effect upon me.

> 'And he sets between, for brushes,
> Meek and poodle-shaven bushes'.

This, too, and many other lines in this lovely little poem—'little' is the word, the littleness of a certain type of beauty, the littleness of ordered gardens, avenues, and a tidy sky—has the effect upon me of a curious and individual wine out of an old bottle marked with very colourful designs. And if these sentences are, in themselves, too rich and adjectival, blame your odd little muse & not me.

Symphony For Full Orchestra

When I read this first I wasn't sure whether its peculiar form was entirely necessary. But slowly the voices of the orchestra insisted, and the long, drawn-out question of the woodwind became inevitable, until, at the end, I wondered why the whole question, 'O Star In The Dark' was not repeated. Perhaps, if I read it again, I will see a good reason why it should be as it is. The one, sudden entrance of the timpani is remarkably effective. I can hear the harps glissando-ing (can you spell it?) over their strange phrases, the sudden, unharplike sound of the word 'cerements', the sibilant and treble 'Cease!' as they begin. And now any doubts I entertained as to the inevitability of the orchestral form are vanquished. Inevitably the violins say, 'These are his hands on your breast' and as inevitably the brass cry out and say, 'Return, star-crossed, The bloodshed morn is nigh.'

There is, as there was in 'Béguinage', only one phrase I object to.

> '. . . Weave the straining clouds
> Into maddened shrouds',

has too many words—& the wrong words—in it. The rhyme is a jingle. The adjectives add nothing. Polish up or remove that phrase, & I have no quarrel with the poem from beginning to end. In its limits, it is as lovely as anything I know.

And so what a strange, unequal selection of poems and verses you have sent me. You have sent me the sugariest custard, the cheapest port, & the most delicate white wine. I never remember before mixing my drinks so quickly, &, at the same time, so satisfyingly.

Never be pretty for the sake of being pretty. It's always in your power —and yours especially—to lift prettiness into your own sort of beauty. Whether it is the ultimate beauty I don't even care to guess; but much of it is what *I* understand to be beautiful. And that is all I can ever say.

But let me get off the point for a moment, and make what will probably be quite a futile attack upon your creed of simplicity. I admit that everything should be said as simply *as possible*, that meaning should never be smothered by conscious obscurity, that the most prized ornamentations of style and phrase have to go under when the meaning dictates it. But that *all* good poetry is necessarily simple seems to me very absurd. Because I can understand the English of Mrs. Beeton, there is no earthly reason why I should understand the English of Manley Hopkins—or W.H. Davies & W.H. Auden. I see no necessity why the greatest truths of the world, and the greatest variations of these truths, should be so simple that the most naive mind can understand them. There are things, and valuable things, so complicated that even he who writes of them does not comprehend what he is writing.

I admire the simplicity of Shakespeare, the easy language of Twelfth Night and the hard language of Coriolanus. I admire the simplicity of Mozart and the bewildering obscurity of the later Scriabin. Both had a great thing to say, and why the message of Mozart, because of its easiness to understand, is rated above the message of Scriabin, which is a separate message and the devil to follow, I shall never know. It is the simplicity of the human mind that believes the universal mind to be as simple.

Thank you for all you have said about the poems I've sent you. I profit by all criticism; yours is far from puerile, and though I am bound to disagree with much you say I agree heartily with most. With this letter I am enclosing two more poems. They are not typed, I'm afraid, but I hope that won't prevent you from reading and criticising them carefully. There is a sort of finality about the typewritten word which the written word lacks. Spare no compliment—I don't go all girlish; spare no con-demnation—I am used to it and profit by it.

One day I want to send you ten thousand words of prose, 'Uncommon Genesis', a story set in no time or place, with only two characters, a man & a woman.[1] And the woman, of course, is not human. She wouldn't be. If you want it, I'll send it to you. If you don't, I won't.

Whatever you do to letters, story, or poems, don't give them the answer that so shocked the pundits of Steyning. If anyone said 'Sez You' after I had shown him or her a poem I think I should wither up. So, please, be genteel even if you must be condemnatory.

Laleham arrangement, though in the air, is oke by me,[2] and if there is any one expression worse than 'sez you' this is it. You are right, of course. December it is. Yes, I do paint, but very little, and the results are extraordinary.

---

[1] Later published as 'The Mouse and the Woman'.
[2] Nancy and Haydn Taylor lived on the Chertsey houseboat in summer, but in winter moved to a cottage in the nearby village of Laleham.

I should have loved to reply to your hideous drawing with an equally hideous one of myself, but no ordinary pencil can do me justice. If I can find a photograph of myself when in the very far distance I will send it to you.

                                                    Dylan

P.S. Important. I shall be here (Llangain) until Saturday of this week. If you reply before I leave, and I hope you do, send the letter straight here. It can't go wrong.

MS: Buffalo   *SL(R)*

PAMELA HANSFORD JOHNSON
[card, postmarked 30 Oct 1933]   5 Cwmdonkin Drive Uplands Swansea

                Congratulations![1] A *very* long letter

                will arrive in a few days—

                probably by parcel post.

                                        Dylan.

MS: Buffalo

PAMELA HANSFORD JOHNSON
[early November 1933][2]   5 Cwmdonkin Drive Uplands Swansea

Excuses
    I've taken a terribly long time to reply, I know, but, during the last week, I have been so utterly and suicidally morbid that my letter would have read like an excerpt from the Undertakers' Gazette. I hope, in the long week that has passed, you haven't forgotten my existence. And please don't be long in replying because *I* was. I look forward to a letter soon.
    On receiving your photograph I went immediately to have my own likeness taken, there being no existent photograph of myself at this stage

---

[1] The *Sunday Referee* announced on October 29 that it was to sponsor a book of poems by Johnson.

[2] Evidence for the dating is that Thomas was sending her his photograph (paragraph 2), and Johnson's diary for November 6 says, 'Letter from Dylan & photo'. Letters to Johnson were often written over a period of days, using different paper and pen/pencil. As printed in *Selected Letters*, some (including this one) were wrongly assembled. A more likely version begins with the letter in *SL* 46–7; continues with the two headed sections, *SL* 56–57, beginning 'Physiognomical Comment'; and concludes with the letter at *SL* 47–55.

of decline. Either I proved too much for the delicate photographic plates, or else the photographer has gone, moaning, away, for I have had nothing from him. I don't want to hold the correspondence up any longer, so here is a very bad and uncomplimentary passport photograph taken two years ago. It's a poor return, but I shall send you a better and more recent photograph when, or if, it arrives. I do look something like the enclosed snap. Imagine the same face two years older, a bit thinner & more lined. The black shirt (strictly non-political) is the same. I am rarely as tidy or as well-groomed as that, and, pray God, I rarely have that cherub's expression. Still, it has its resemblance. Add a few shadows, draw in a cigarette & ruffle the hair: there I am, in my full glory.

Kind Action

I give you full authorisation to use this new letter form. You'll find it very useful. All you have to do is to write odd notes at different times—on whatever subject, & in whatever mood—and then bung them together under terse little headings. Go ahead, girl!

Congratulatory Hand and Helping Hand

Congratulations. Neuburg, for once, has not gone wrong. It is hardly possible to imagine that he could, for the choice was inevitable. I take as much interest in the publication of your poems as I do in the publication of my own. And if they were my own, I could not be more delighted to hear that your poems are to be published.

You will, I suppose, publish all you have written, but I do advise you to be careful in your editing of the earlier poems. There is no necessity at all why *one* of the printed poems should be bad, providing you use a blue pencil and a scissors with discrimination. If I can help you, in any way, to polish up the final drafts, or to do anything to help your book towards the success it is bound to be, let me know. I'll do my best, too, to advertise the book among those who do not believe Browning to be something to do with gravy. I'll want to buy a copy, too, and to receive a neatly autographed first edition. But don't forget: if there is anything, anything at all, you would like me to do, I should have the greatest possible pleasure in doing it.

Physiognomical Comment

You do look formidable, my Wilhelmina. I did not expect you to be so full and bright and strong, with such a British chin. What a dominant personality! Tut, girl, what a zest for life! And here I am, small, chinless, and like an emasculate Eton boy. Ah, the waves of self pity that engulf me as I gaze first upon your features and then upon mine (even though mine is two and a bit years old, and yours as recent as this morning's dew!) But, to pass from Jest to Earnest, let me thank you for sending your photograph. You are very, very, pleasant to look at. There is meaning and strength in your face. I shall hang you in my room. This is certainly one of the things that could have been expressed better. All I have said is probably in the worst taste [*a line is deleted*: And as I seem to be verging on the edge of vulgarity, I shall] (I don't think I have sent an untidier letter. Excuse it.)

So now, if I look long upon your photograph, and you, looking upon mine, exercise your imagination in the details of age and cleanliness, we shan't be strangers to each other. From your photograph I know the lines of your face, from your poetry the lines of your mind. I'm not a physiognomist—I can't even spell the damned word—but I see how you bristle (images of a herd of porcupine) with individuality. Look like everybody else? No, no. But then I am biased.

Attack On Bats and Defence of Vermin

Believe me or not, the first two lines of 'Béguinage' are as bad as anything you've written. The image is smart and cheap; it falls too easily on the paper. And the attitude behind it is wrong, relying too much on a quick, admittedly vivid, visual impression, instead of upon a mentally digested experience. It is written from the mind's eye, not even from the mind's ear, for the sounds are unintentionally ugly. You have seized on a glimpse of what you wanted to express, and not on the still, slow scrutiny.

Your remark about the end of my Feverish poem is entirely justified. I plead guilty to bathos, but offer in excuse the fact that I copied out the poem as soon as I had written it, wanting to get it off to you and too hurried to worry about its conclusion. In the ordinary way I would never have passed it.

Leave me my 'hatching of the hair'.[1] It's verminous, I know, but isn't it lovely? And what is more refreshing than the smell of vermin? Hardy loved to sit beside a rotten sheep and see the flies make a banquet of it. A dark thought, but good and lively. One of the hardest and most beneficial kicks of life comes from the decaying foot of death. Uncover her face, she died young.

5. Defence of Poesie[2]

What you call ugly in my poetry is, in reality, nothing but the strong stressing of the physical. Nearly all my images, coming, as they do, from my solid and fluid world of flesh and blood, are set out in terms of their progenitors. To contrast a superficial beauty with a superficial ugliness, I do not contrast a tree with a pylon, or a bird with a weasel, but rather the human limbs with the human tripes. Deeply, of course, all these contrasting things are equally beautiful and equally ugly. Only by association

---

[1] The poem, 'From love's first fever', has this phrase in the Notebook version (dated October 14/17). In *Collected Poems* the phrase became 'the breaking of the hair'.

[2] This section of the letter should be numbered '6' if it is to agree with its position after five headed sections. From this point, too, a different writing paper is used. But the internal evidence for making it a single letter is strong.

is the refuse of the body more to be abhorred than the body itself. Standards have been set for us. What is little realised is that it was only chance that dictated these standards. It is polite to be seen at one's dining table, and impolite to be seen in one's lavatory. It might well have been decided, when the tumour of civilisation was first fostered, that celebrations should be held in the w.c., and that the mere mention of 'eating and drinking' would be the height of impropriety. It was decided by Adam and Eve, the first society lawmakers, that certain parts of the body should be hidden and certain be left uncovered. Again, it was chance that decided them to hide their genital organs, and not, say, their armpits or throats. While life is based upon such chance conventions and standards as these, it is little wonder that any poetry dealing impartially with the parts of the anatomy, (not quite impartially, perhaps, for the belly emphasises an abstruse point better than the Atlas-bone), and with the functions of the body, should be considered as something rather hideous, unnecessary, and, to say the least, indelicate. But I fail to see how the emphasising of the body can, in any way, be regarded as hideous. The body, its appearance, death, and diseases, is a fact, sure as the fact of a tree. It has its roots in the same earth as the tree. The greatest description I know of our own 'earthiness' is to be found in John Donne's Devotions, where he describes man as earth of the earth, his body earth, his hair a wild shrub growing out of the land. All thoughts and actions emanate from the body. Therefore the description of a thought or action—however abstruse it may be—can be beaten home by bringing it onto a physical level. Every idea, intuitive or intellectual, can be imaged and translated in terms of the body, its flesh, skin, blood, sinews, veins, glands, organs, cells, or senses.

Through my small, bonebound island I have learnt all I know, experienced all, and sensed all. All I write is inseparable from the island. As much as possible, therefore, I employ the scenery of the island to describe the scenery of my thoughts, the earthquakes of the body to describe the earthquakes of the heart.

Fatal selfconsciousness prevents me from carrying on in the same noble vein. (How about that idiom to help my argument?) It is typical of the physically weak to emphasise the strength of life (Nietzsche); of the apprehensive and complex-ridden to emphasise its naiveté and dark wholesomeness (D. H. Lawrence); of the naked-nerved and blood-timid to emphasise its brutality and horror (Me!)

There has been a great deal of nonsense in this poetical defence. There's some truth, too.

6. Refutation and Explanation

The 'dream' poem that you like is *not* the best I have sent you. Only superficially is it the most visionary. There is more in the poem, 'Before I Knocked',[1] more of what I consider to be of importance in my poetry.

[1] Dated September 6 in the Notebook.

Please, this isn't boasting. I'm incurably pessimistic and eternally dissatisfied.

So the poor old snail has wound his horn before. It is a long time since I read the Ode to Evening, so long that my memory refuses all responsibility.[1]

But surely you haven't missed one of the biggest warps in my poetry. My melting-pot is all sour. In two out of three of all the poems I have sent you, there has been a steady scheme of consonantal rhyming. The 'Eye of Sleep' is rhymed throughout. I never use a full rhyme, but nearly always a half rhyme.

Take the poem published in the Referee last Sunday[2] (did you like it?)

a weather	a earth	a sings	a flower	rocks
b stars	b head	b land	b trees	streams
xa other	a mouth	a gangs	a destroyer	wax
b trees	a death	a wings	b rose	veins
xa feather	b replied	b fade	a fever	sucks
		and so on.		& so on.

I do not always keep to my rhyming schemes with complete faithfulness. As a rule, yes. But perhaps this elaborate explanation has been a waste of time. You may have noticed it all before, for it has a strange effect.

7. Patronising Remark

Certainly let friend Mednikoff read my poems, but don't show him the 'Eye of Sleep' alone. Show him the others, and tell me what he says, won't you, even if, with a sardonic Russian leer, he spits him of all the batch. From your meagre description of him he sounds most interesting, and I'm glad he waxed romantic over your 'Symphony'. But what 'circle' does he move in? The squared circle of the Geometrists? The fleshy circle of the Academicians?

8. Stop Press

The typewriter is still labouring over its 'Uncommon Genesis'. The story was written a year ago, but I have never typed it. The first—and probably the last,—typed copy is for you. It will be ready when I write to you next. I will keep my explanatory comments until then.

---

[1] A poem called 'The eye of sleep' (5 October 1933 in the Notebook) has the line, 'Let fall the snail of time and wound his horn.' Johnson thought that this echoed a line in a William Collins poem, 'Or where the beetle winds his small but sullen horn.'

[2] October 29.

9. FORWARD THE VERSE BRIGADE!

I do not think that I have misunderstood your Creed of Simplicity. Perhaps I attacked it from the wrong angle. You were careful in your wording when you contrasted the beauty of simplicity and the beauty of obscurity, of light and dark, for if I think you a Wilhelmina (and I protest I don't; I think you a Pamela), you think of me as some Stygian cess-hound forever plumbing the intestinal emotions. You may be right, damn you, but all the words you use, 'beauty', 'simplicity', 'obscurity', mean different things to different people, are based upon individual preconceptions. 'Simplicity' to me is the best way of expressing a thing, and the ultimate expression may still be obscure as D. H. Lawrence's Heaven. 'Obscurity' is the worst way. I thought of a definition of beauty, but, like all such definitions, it is too limited. One of the greatest aspects of it is 'acquaintance plus wonder', but the expansion of this would lead me, through many vague pages, to the point where I started. Beauty, too, is the *sense of unity in diversity*. This needs no expansion.

And poetry need not appeal to the intelligent mind more than to the unintelligent. It is appreciated to the greatest extent by the unbiased mind. Each genuine poet has his own standards, his own codes of appreciation, his own aura. Reading a poet for the first time, one cannot be acquainted with him, & therefore, judging him by preconceived standards—however elastic those standards may be—one cannot fully appreciate him. One should take first an empty brain and a full heart to every poem one reads: an impossible task. The only possible way lies in the reading & re-reading, preferably aloud, of any new poem that strikes one as holding some and however little value.

The speaking of poetry should certainly be encouraged. I do hope you read aloud. I myself chant aloud in a sonorous voice every poem I read. The neighbours must know your poems by heart; they certainly know my own, and are bound to be acquainted with many passages of Macbeth, Death's Jester, and the Prophetic Books. I often think that baths were built especially for drowsy poets to lie in and there intone aloud amid the steam and boiling ripples.

10. A Potpourri of Original and Unoriginal Satire

> The Tharp that once through Neuburg's Halls
> The soul of humbug shed,
> Now hangs as mute upon your scrawls
> As if that soul had fled.
> So sleeps the vice of former days,
> So humbug's thrill is o'er,
> And hearts that once gave Tupper praise
> Now praise you all the more.

I don't quite know what this means, but, apart from 'scrawls', which was brought in because it rhymed, it appears to be vaguely complimentary.

God help the Creative Arts Circle. I hope you won't. It would probably be something like this:

> '"I will now call on Alberic Morphine to give a reading."
> The rows of young women look up; their eyes glisten;
>   they shiver
> With the kind of emotion that's very misleading.
> All have fine eyes, yellow faces, vile clothes &
>   a liver.
> They smoke a great deal, bath little, and wear no stays.'

or like this:

> 'You would meet Iris, she who lives serene
> In the intense confusion of the obscene,
> And drags her tea-time sex affair all fresh
> To the dinner table, like a cat with flesh;
> Lesbia, whose outward form proclaims at least
> Some variation on the normal beast;
> Onan, recalling complexes before I speak,
> His childhood roles of cad and sneak,
> Youth's coprolytic loves and grosser fancies
> Derived from reading Ernest Jone's romances.'

You would meet Mrs. Murgatroyd Martin:

> 'She tells you of Pater and Pankhurst, of Tagore and
>   Wilde,
> Of man-made laws and the virtues of proteid peas,
> Of Folk Song and Art and of sterilised milk for
>   the child,
> Of the joys of the Morris Dance and of Poetry Teas.'

You would hear a lot of nice things about Art, and lots of nice people would read your poems and say the nicest things, and you would go home and get sick on the mat.

But, as Ruskin once remarked to Carlyle, Please don't go all stiff-shirted on me. 'Doesn't any man or woman know exactly what sex means before life brings that great experience to them?' Yes, you wrote that, and it will need some explaining away at the gates of heaven where the phallus is taken as a fact and not as a peg upon which to hang one's little platitudes.

11. LOVE and HATE

> Scoff at this enchanted Wood,
> Ye who dare.

I wouldn't jibe at the old war-horse.[1] His hooves have beaten out time

[1] Sir Henry Wood.

to nearly all the great orchestral pieces of the world. He introduced Schönberg to England. He arranged those stirring Sea Tunes that quicken the blood of every true-veined Englishman. What feet have not thumped to his conducting of the marches from Pomp & Circumcision. And I like his beard.

There are only two men in England whom I hate with *all* my heart: Sir Edward Elgar and Mr. Geoffrey Grigson. One has inflicted more pedantic wind & blather upon a supine public than any man who has ever lived. The other edits New Verse. His place is already reserved in the lower regions where, for all eternity, he shall read the cantos of Ezra Pound to a company of red-hot devils.

12. My Life. A Touching Autobiography In One Paragraph

I first saw the light of day in a Glamorgan villa, and, amid the terrors of the Welsh accent and the smoke of the tinplate stacks, grew up to be a sweet baby, a precocious child, a rebellious boy, and a morbid youth. My father was a schoolmaster: a broader-minded man I have never known. My mother came from the agricultural depths of Carmarthenshire: a pettier woman I have never known. My only sister passed through the stages of longlegged schoolgirlishness, shortfrocked flappery and social snobbery into a comfortable married life. I was first introduced to Tobacco (the Boy Scouts' Enemy) when a small boy in a preparatory school, to Alcohol (the Demon King) when a senior member of a secondary school. Poetry (the Spinster's Friend) first unveiled herself to me when I was six or seven years old; she still remains, though sometimes her face is cracked across like an old saucer. For two years I was a newspaper reporter, making my daily call at the mortuaries, the houses of suicides—there's a lot of suicide in Wales—and Calvinistic 'capels'. Two years was enough. Now I do nothing but write, and occasionally make a few guineas out of my dramatic expositions of How Not To Act. A misanthropic doctor, who apparently did not like the way I did my eyebrows, has given me four years to live.[1] May I borrow that foul expression of yours—it isn't yours, really—and whisper Sez You into his ear.

13. A Touching Experience

After my last letter to you, written from the despondency of a Welsh hill cottage, I ran out of cigarettes and walked three miles to the nearest village, Llanstephan, to buy some.

It was a fool of a night. The clouds were asses' ears. The moon was ploughing up the Towy river as if he expected it to yield a crop of stars. And the stars themselves:—hundreds of bright-eyed urchins nudging each other over a celestial joke. It is a long road to Llanstephan, bounded by trees and farmers' boys pressed amorously upon the udders of their dairymaids. But the further I walked the more lonely it became. I found

---

[1] A local doctor is supposed to have told Thomas that he was dying of tuberculosis.

the madness of the night to be a false madness, and the vast horseplay of the sky to be a vaster symbol. It was as if the night were crying, crying out the terrible explanation of itself. On all sides of me, under my feet, above my head, the symbols moved, all waiting in vain to be translated. The trees that night were like prophet's fingers. What had been a fool in the sky was the wisest cloud of all—a huge, musical ghost thumping out one, coded tune. It was a sage of a night, and made me forgive even my own foolishness.

There was, of course, no cigarette machine in Llanstephan.

14. A Rude Poem

Let me explain first that this was written in a violent mood when there seemed little to do but to insult someone. After reading his comments in the last Referee, I picked on Neuburg to be that someone. It's HARDLY CRICKET, I know, & I'm RATHER A CAD considering he is going to publish all your poems & has published a couple of mine, one very recently—but here it is:

> A Sunday paper did its best
> To build a Sunday singing nest
> Where poets from their shells could burst
> With trembling rhymes and do their worst
> To break the laws of man and metre
> By publishing their young excreta.
>
> A highfalutin little bloke
> Conducted (with an artichoke)
> The choir of birds who weekly piped
> From pages very neatly typed.
> Hail to the Referee all plastered
> With products of the pimp and bastard.
>
> With each prophetic phrase or clause
> Dropped from their educated jaws,
> The guts of Logic turn about,
> The swine of Bathos shows his snout.
> With every —— verse they print
> Their Muse develops a worse squint.
>
> Let all rejoice that Victor N
> Is far above the run of men.
> O new Messiah of the Muse
> Would that we could, like those old Jews,
> Place on thy head an ink-filled crown
> And crucify thee upside down.

15. A Piece of Sentiment

How long have I known you? I seem to have been writing these nonsensical letters of mine for ever, and for ever to have been receiving those letters of yours. But it can't have been for more than a few months.

Yet I know you as well as I have ever known anybody in my life. Much of what I write to you is, I know, very silly, and much of it I've regretted as soon as I've posted the letters. But I have written what I wanted to write, I've got all sorts of things off my mind, and I have tried to be honest. I've found a poetess, and one, moreover, who likes *my* poems. I've found a very good friend. No, I refuse to become maudlin, but I'm glad that I've found you or, rather, that you've found me. I write to several people, but to none with the freedom that I adopt in my letters to you. You don't take offence when I become vulgar, as I so often do, or when I say unpleasant things about the poems of yours I don't like; you don't mind if I attack all the windmills in the world with a rusty pen; and, though you say you find much to laugh at in my letters, you don't, I know, laugh at what I am sincere, *really* sincere, in expressing. You like my letters. I hope our meeting, when it does take place, will not disappoint you. I won't run myself down any more; by this time you know as many of my faults and shortcomings as I do myself.

This is the first time, I think, that I've written like this, and it will be the last. I only wanted to tell you how much I appreciate you & your letters. Enough. Enough. Let the correspondence now continue as of yore, and still the postman bear into thy house and mine the brilliant products of the Battersea & Swansea Muse, and the dazzling correspondence of two diverse but well-attuned imaginations.

Dylan

This is not a modernist design but an afterthought on a particular glowing sentence. May it stir your curiosity.
[*Six lines are deleted*][1]

MS: Buffalo   *SL(R)*

PAMELA HANSFORD JOHNSON
[November 5 1933] [fragment][2]

<u>A Story For The Very Young</u>
   Once upon a time there was a little girl. And this little girl, odd to say, was a po-et-ess. She was very ro-man-tic in her out-look, and wrote many

---

[1] Thomas had written:
   I am lying in bed now and
   I have just had a wonderful thought
   A lover [???] tell her how much he loves her.
   He thinks he loves her so much that he [?could change] into a tiny
   insect or fly, & that he could fly [?to where] she slept and go
   to sleep in her hair.
[2] SL 32-3 makes this the end of a letter to which it doesn't belong. The 'glowing article of praise' appeared in the *Sunday Referee* on November 5.

nice ro-man-tic poems, using such words as, 'wings', 'melody', & 'breast', all of which was very nice. But she grew older, and vis-it-ors and rel-at-ives said, Oh, yes, she is a very nice girl, but what is she going to do? It was ob-vi-ous that she would be a po-et-ess always, or even something more im-moral. So she went on being a po-et-ess, and a kind man put her poems in a litt-le book. But one day she became ac-quaint-ed with a little poet, who was the funniest little poet you could imagine. And he wrote vul-gar poems about wombs and things. Well, dears, the po-et-ess and the little poet went on being ac-quaint-ed, and, at last, the po-et-ess took the Wrong Turning. She, too, wrote vul-gar poems, and it was nothing for her to use the horrible word 'Cancer' twice in one stan-za. And the little poet went all flower-faced, and wrote a lot of verses about the sun coming up and the moon going down. But the po-et-ess grew tired of her tu-ber-cular muse, and returned to her babb-ling brooks etc. And the little po-et burnt all his so-nice poems, and returned to his vomit and vul-gar-it-y. And they both lived happy ever after.

Moral   Let Cancer Be.

This seems rather a nasty and un-true story, and I don't know why I wrote it. But, then, this letter is such a terrible hotch-potch, written in odd places and at odd times, that the story fits in with the chaotic atmosphere.

Only half an hour ago I picked up the new Referee, & read Mr. Vicky Bird's glowing article of praise. How it warms the cockles of the heart. Let me very boastfully say this: Take all his praise with a barrel of salt; take mine with none at all. I mean all I have sd about you & your poems; in his pretty little cage, God knows what the editing parrot means or does not mean.

And his infantile remark about 'never faltering in metre' or whatever he sd. It's as if a man sd of Wiley Post, 'What a marvellous flyer; one of the greatest things about his success is the skilful way in which he keeps up in the air!'[1] Oh God, oh Montreal! Oh Neuburg! Oh Jesus!

I agree with a lot he says, and I'll say a lot more in my next letter.

                                                                    Dylan

Pardon all irrelevancies & inconsistencies, the bad grammar & the worse spelling. And take to heart, O Battersea Stick (remark the tonal value of the words) all I have sd from the depths of a tidal, though slightly corrupted, heart.

MS: Buffalo   *SL(R)*

---

[1] Wiley Post, a famous American airman of the time.

PAMELA HANSFORD JOHNSON
[?1933] [fragment]

I have typed & bound on somebody else's official paper sixteen short poems for you. In the past I believe I've only sent you the longer poems. These, as all the others, are chosen haphazardly. Two, to my dim sense of criticism in regard to my own writing, are very bad. Give me a critical study, however short, upon them. And please remember that Quotation No. is not a part of the poem it faces.

MS: Buffalo

PAMELA HANSFORD JOHNSON
[week of November 11 1933][1]

> Excuse the worse than usually terrible writing!

Preface
  In my untidy bedroom, surrounded with books and papers, full of the unhealthy smell of very bad tobacco, I sit and write. There is a beautiful winter sun outside, and by my side the oil-stove shines like a parhelion. On the wall immediately in front of me hangs my pastel drawing of the Two Brothers of Death; one is a syphilitic Christ, and the other a greenbearded Moses. Both have skin the colour of figs, and walk, for want of a better place, on a horizontal ladder of moons. The hot water pipes are swearing at me, and, despite the nearness of the stove, my tiny hands are frozen.
  Last night I slept for the first time this month; today I am writing a poem in praise of sleep and the veronal that stained the ravelled sleeve. These twelve November nights have been twelve long centuries to me. Minute by minute through the eight hours of the dark I lay and looked up into the empty corners of this room. First I would seize upon some tiny thought, hug it close to me, turn it over and over in my brain, hoping, by such concentration, to find my senses dropping away into oblivion. But soon my lips would speak sentences aloud, and I listen to them.
  'The man of substance never walks.' Then my lips say, 'He only wheels a truck', and, a thousand years later, I understand what I have spoken. Then I would repeat all the poetry I knew, but if I forgot a word I could never think of another to put in its place, unless it was a mad word and had no meaning. Then I would hear my heart beat, and count its beats, and hear their regularity.
  And now, thanks to the God who looked with benevolent eye upon the

---

[1] The letter was partly written on Saturday November 11, but not completed for several days. Johnson's diary, November 17: 'Letter from Darling Dylan, which was also morbid.'

antics of Lot's daughters, I have slept. Now I can reply to your letter and do my dance around your poems.

Some of the enclosed notes—I think this newspaper style we have adopted in our last letters suits our particular kinds of mentalities very well indeed—have been written during the last and letterless week. If half your notes are composed during the period between the sending off [of] your letter and the receiving of mine, then much valuable time (the adjective depends on you, of course) would not be lost. This, for me, is a statement of great common-sense, and having delivered myself of such a commonsensible idea, I shall probably be half-witted for the rest of the week.

The moods of the notes I leave to you. One, again, was written in the bath—a striking condemnation of those of my acquaintances who do not believe I ever take one—; one in the bus from Swansea to Trecynon (you have never heard of it, but it boasts a Little Theatre where I occasionally perform); and the rest in the privacy of my pensive and worm-ridden room.

Poisonal Accomplishments and Failings

What a terribly accomplished person you are! I can't sing, can't play any musical instrument, and can't draw. I paint a good deal, but quite untechnically, and the startling effects I sometimes do produce are owing to a diseased mentality and an entire lack of skill. O Wilhelmina Bernhardt! I apologise at once. I'm glad you're an actress, and I'm sure you're a good one. I've been acting on and off—mostly off—both as an amateur and as a vague professional since I was the size of your thumb. But I can't say I'm improved much since that time. My speciality is the playing of madmen, neurotics, nasty 'modern' young men and low comedians—quite straight acting. At the present time I—and the Little Theatre of Wales (it sounds good) are rehearsing 'Strange Orchestra'. Do you know it? I'm playing Val, if you do, and if you don't, I'll explain that Val is a nervous, unhappy writer of unpopular books, in love and yet frightened to be, full of bathetic and half-digested notions on Life with a Capital Letter. What sort of things do you play? Tell me you play hysterical young women with tumours, or erotic young things with Notions, and we'll go round together on the provincial music-halls playing Grand Guignol.

Talking of Grand Guignol, I met Eliot Crawshay Williams last week.[1] He's an old roué with a red face and wrong ideas.

Barter

For one 'jasmine' I will give you one 'belly'.
  "   " 'daffodil' "   "   "   "   " 'senna'.

But I'm damned if I'll swap my wormy wombs for all the fairy bubbles

---

[1] Eliot Crawshay Williams (1879–1962), author, one-time Member of Parliament.

this side of St. Paul's. We're extremists, girl, one upstairs in our lady's chamber and the other downstairs in our lady's chamber-pot. Still, I will do my best to comb out the superfluous horrors in my beard on the one condition that you let Spring pass out next year without bestowing one single lavish spate upon its tomb.

The Publication Of a Book

I said that your book was bound to be successful, successful, that is, compared with any book of poetry recently published, and I repeat it. What harm can it do you? An unbiased reader does not expect a first book to be perfect. All he looks for are parts of promise and fragments of achievement. There have probably been no first poems ever published that have had more to offer than that. And there is certainly promise in all you've written. In two or three instances there has been undeniable and individual achievement. You are young, and can't expect any more than that. Even if you were withered and corseted into shape, there would be no need for you to expect more. Great reputations have been built upon much promise and small achievement.

You are, I know, capable of achieving perfection in a certain type of poetry, a poetry born out of Christina Rossetti and the Georgian and Poetry Bookshop Gang.[1] And you have failed, I know, in attempting a far higher thing—the creation of personal poetry, born out of Battersea, Mrs. Johnson, and wide and haphazard reading. Really, your future as a poetess is capable of developing in one of two ways: along the hedgerows, littered with the PreRaphaelite and Georgian corpses, to a narrow but popular perfection, or in the middle of the road, scorning the hedges and the Referee ruts, towards a wide, unpopular and very splendid failure.

You yourself have to decide which way to go, but the literary people you will associate with will certainly help you to make up your mind. I know which way Neuburg wishes, and I hope to God that my sprawling letters will help you to take the other way. Fear Neuburg and all the Creative Lifers as you would fear the Boojum.

So speaks the Snark.[2]

Pawky (Your Word) Remarks

Why do you call your book Dayspring?[3] It isn't as if the poems in it had sprung out of natural associations. You don't snoop around the country lanes, looking for a ragwort to pour a bellyful of words on, or pimp in the recesses of the gasworks at the amours of stale and repetitive lovers, hoping to hear some words of love that you might jot down upon your pad

---

[1] The Poetry Bookshop, founded 1912, encouraged the 'Georgian poetry' movement that was later frowned upon (not least by Thomas) for writing blandly about a comfortable, countrified England.

[2] 'For the Snark was a Boojum, you see'—a line from Lewis Carroll's nonsense poem, 'The Hunting of the Snark'.

[3] Johnson's original title. It was published as Symphony For Full Orchestra.

of paper. Yours is a selfspring; everything comes out of yourself, and darkness, despite what you say, has infinitely more possibilities than day. There is too much *doing* in life, and not enough *being*. Proof of life lies in the answer to one question, and that question is not troubled with the mechanics of living, with the functions of living, or with the appearances of living—but with the vast verb, To Be. Age is not a matter of years, but of being. Man is pre-occupied with action, never believing Blake's 'Thought Is Action'. Dayspring! I may have missed the point of the title, and, anyway, God knows why I am so suddenly vehement.

Comment upon the Comments upon the Nastiness of the Present Writer
    You ikkle bitch!
    But seriously, it was the attitude behind what you said, rather than *what* you said, that called forth my singular nastiness. To call Sex the Great Experience is to call Birth the Great Adventure, and a prostitute the Lady of Dubious Morals. It is the escape of the coward-worded and the last resort of the prig-moralled journalist (neither of which applies to you). Do you remember Rampion in Point-Counter-Point? He painted a wild picture of a naked man and woman. 'What do you call it?' he was asked. 'Some people call it love', he replied, 'And others call it——.'
    It was not that you made your remarks—with which I thoroughly agree—too 'pretty'; I'm not corrupted enough to ask for the language of the gutter on every possible occasion. But there are only three vocabularies at your disposal when you talk of sex: the vocabulary of the clinic, of the gutter, & of the moralist. Of the three the last is by far the worst; it is compromise and the jargon of the prude. The clinic, at least, talks from knowledge of its subject, and the gutter talks from acquaintance. The moralist, with his half learnt knowledge and his frustrated or perverted acquaintance, cloaks everything in words & symbols. The naked man & woman remain.

Pathos (and forgive the pencil, for I've mislaid the ink)
    Four years, my sweet. 1340 days & nights. And thank you for the optimistic remarks. I don't believe it either, but then it would be very odd if I did. You should hear me cough, though—a most pleasing sound, exactly like a sea-lion peeved.
    No I don't think consumption has very much effect on what I write. (Oh, my bravery with that not-quite-polite word.) I can't help what I write. It is part of me, however unpleasant a part it may be, and however necessary it should be to cauterize and castrate that part. Your belief in my power to write is one of the few things that makes me deny that twice-damned, diabetic doctor. I have another believer—a communist grocer with a passion for obscurity & the Powys family. Both of you shall have a seat in heaven, or in my comfortable, but slightly wormy, hell.
    Just after writing this, I received a rather disquieting note from Richard Rees[1] of the Adelphi, who, last week, asked me to send him some recent

[1] Sir Richard Rees (1900–57) edited the *Adelphi*.

poems. He compliments me upon the high standard & the great originality exhibited, & said my technique was amazing (One Up for Formal Me), but accused me—not in quite so many words—of being in the grip of devils. 'The poems have an insubstantiality, a dreamlike quality', he writes, 'which non-plusses me.' He then goes on to say that the poems, as a whole, reminded him of automatic or trance-writing.

Automatic writing is worthless as literature, however interesting it may be to the psychologist & pathologist. So, perhaps, after all I am nothing but a literary oddity, a little freak of nature whose madness runs into print rather than into ravings and illusions. It may be, too, an illusion that keeps me writing, the illusion of myself as some misunderstood poet of talent. The note has depressed me more than the usual adverse criticism. It shows not dislike, or mere incomprehension, but confession of bewilderment, & almost fear, at the method by which I write my poetry.

But he is wrong, I swear it. My facility, as he calls it, is, in reality, tremendously hard work. I write at the speed of two lines an hour. I have written hundreds of poems, & each one has taken me a great many painful, brain-racking & sweaty hours.

If you like, pay little attention to the following criticisms of your poems, for they are based, as what I write is based, on my own peculiar standards, which may be the standards of a theorising failure & a bilious little crank.

I now stop turning over the dirty pages of my soul, lick my pencil, wipe my cold-filled nose, light a cigarette, & write

Some Frank Criticisms
Twenty To Twelve
Your ability to romanticise an atmosphere & to catch, with some considerable skill, the visual essences of a scene, is well displayed in this. But the whole thing is very slight, and would please the Refereaders more than it does me. It hangs between verse & poetry, and can either be called frail poetry or strong verse. I would prefer to call it the latter; it is a talented piece of versifying, facile, ornamental, & hung about with skilful images. But it lacks subtlety; the images, striking as they are, are too patently obvious for the entire effect to stir much more than one's visual senses. There is no one line I can condemn; the thing is perfect, too perfect. This is more of an achievement than many other poems of yours, but the achievement is very limited. This is to me, the *wrong* direction. It is difficult to explain, in a short note, where the wrongness lies, but I do hope I have made myself clear. It has, apparently, nearly everything a poem needs—an experience, a fairly original diction, & an emotive appeal. Analysed more closely, it has nothing. You haven't given yourself enough to contend with. Knowing your own skill, you pick on something very easy to do, & do it, of course, skilfully & perfectly. Is it worth doing?

February (found the ink again)

The same thing applies. Are you going to be content with a narrow achievement or a wide promise? This, again, is pretty, skilful, and visual. And, I personally, don't care a damn for prettiness or skill, while the putting down of what the eyes have seen (plus a few literary affectations and one or two unusual literary words) has very little to do with poetry. Unless the spirit illuminates what the eyes have mirrored, then all the paraphernalia of the winter scene is as valueless as an Academy picture of Balmoral Castle.

Requiem for Spring

The same criticism applies, with the exception that in this even the skill is a little bowed at the knees.

> 'Of roses she bestows a lavish spate
> The hedgerows and the garden to bedizen'

is as bad as anything the Poet's Corner has ever printed. Indeed, every verse is. I'm glad you didn't send it for my benefit. And God help Neuburg's taste.

What was the matter with you when you wrote this?

Retrospect

All your skill and command of words, added, as you explain, to the cries of a halfmended (or is it fully mended?) heartbreak, make this a moderately good poem, with one or two touches of superlatively good writing. It is narrow, again, but its limits are the essential limits of the subject you impose on yourself.

'Brown into dust upon the morning sun' is an inevitably beautiful line, but the extraction of all the lovely phrases would mean quoting *nearly* every word. The pause in the last line is most effective.

Not perfect but promising. And if you've read all I've written before, (a sudden terrible thought that you show my letters to your mother), you'll know how complimentary this is.

One thing: phrases such as 'the mirage of eternity' are meaningless unless you qualify them.

Black Mess

No, I can't like it. I've tried very hard, but just as I'm beginning to say to myself, 'Oh well, this is quite all right,' along comes a revoltingly saccharine line, or some coy girlish sentiment, or a piece of very ordinary clumsiness.

> The lilies, the innocent lilies, are troubled,
> The trees rub their eyes awake,
> And the mice, the little mice that nibble the grasses,
> Crouch in the stones; their noses shiver with fear.

This is very pleasant; trivial, no doubt, but charmingly done; any moment a selfconscious Pan might come around the corner. Instead, that damned chorus starts again with all their 'silvered intaglio, livid seraglio' business. Occasionally I see something I like—rivers bisecting faces, 'they are surrounding the hills in a ring' (nice & simple), but far more often I see things that sicken me, the jimjackery and jugglebuggery of the *bad* and *pretentious* versifier. If you were bad and pretentious I wouldn't mind, but, as I've repeated so many times, you have nearly everything that contributes towards the make-up of an individual, original, & satisfying poet. If I didn't like you I wouldn't waste ten seconds over the Black Mass. I don't mean to be cruel, but there it is. I see, even in this *very* bad effort, the mentality that produced the Symphonic poem. But in this case you let your taste go down into the sugary vaults. Take a firm grip, for the Lord's sake, on your treacherous aptitudes for prettiness, pretty chaos, & word spinning.

The Morning Sun

By far the most curious poem you have sent me, this moves in a circle of words and feeling, disregarding itself, and falling, inevitably, into its own pattern. Even the touches I do not like do not fail in the general content, but only to the critical eye and ear that, after the first unqualifying response, pursue the ghosts of syllables into the deadends of the purist lanes. Re-reading what I have written I understand very little of it. The fault, dear Pamela, lies in your stars. Your stars are not mine; they twinkle in a different heaven, higher or lower than mine I cannot tell. Perhaps it would be as well if I contented myself with saying of this very individual poem, 'I understand and appreciate,' without bothering to go into the details of appreciation. But I cannot do that; I want you to go on writing like this, never whoring yourself to the fingers of prettiness or the charms of a cheap simile.

All your creeds of simplicity, that surely must comply with the dictates of the ballad form rather than with the long, spongy lines of the sonnet, are obeyed. Indeed, the poem opens on a ballad note, on a naive note thrilling with innumerable and subtle suggestions. The visual element is, again, very strong—I positively can see you, poor stranger in yourself, walking along the crowded pavements and gazing wonderingly down on your 'busy' hips (the perfect adjective)—but, this time, justifiably so. The language is economical and true, with a few exceptions, and the experience *is* a poetical one, and not merely the emotions of a self-confessed romanticist or the romances of a self denied sentimentalist.

Here are the exceptions: 'I think of sunlight & a pile of books.' Many bad poems, imitative of Rupert Brooke's bad poem, 'The Great Lover', include a catalogue of personal likes such as, 'Green apples in the morning sun,' 'The kiss of rain upon the rose,' and, inevitably, the more overpoweringly sentimental like—more overpowering because of its reversed sentimentality—of 'rough blankets on the skin' or 'the smell of tweeds.' The line of yours could easily be included in such a feminine catalogue. It is too sweet & reminds me too much of Percy Lubbock's 'Earlham.'[1] Alter it.

<u>'Of brooks that gargle'</u>
    The associations are absurd, and the sound is ugly. You have said the same of phrases in *my* poems, but this is, strictly, such a beautiful thing that the intrusion of one discordant line must not spoil it.
    'Will be forgotten as a twisted dream.' The adjective is wrong. You want a less sophisticated adjective, such as 'wicked' or even 'ugly', although I am not suggesting these. You will be able to find a better and more harmonious one.
    For the rest I have no complaints.

> 'I feel the stocking pulling at my leg,
> And there is not a stranger in myself'

is severely and *mystically* physical, though many people won't see it. Write like this always, and I shan't grumble.
    'Never strain after prettiness,' my first injunction, is now supplemented by, 'Never use your skill for the sake of skilfulness,' & 'Be yourself in your poetry as you are in your letters.' Morning Sun could have been written by no-one but yourself.
    If you like, I will write more about this poem in my next letter. I have crowds of things to say about it, and some of what I say *may* help you.

<u>Hymn of Despair and Hope</u>
    This is written on Armistice Day, 1933, when the war is no more than a memory of privations and the cutting down of the young. There was panic in the streets, we remember, and the food was bad; there were women who had 'lost' their sons, though where they had lost them and why they could [not] find them, we, who were children born out of blood into blood, could never tell. The state was a murderer, and every country in this rumour-ridden world, peopled by the unsuccessful suicides left over by the four mad years, is branded like Cain across the forehead. What was Christ in us was stuck with a bayonet to the sky, and what was Judas we fed and sheltered, rewarding, at the end, with thirty hanks of flesh. Civilisation is a murderer. We, with the cross of a castrated Saviour cut on our brows, sink deeper and deeper with the days into the pit of the West. The head of Christ is to be inspected in the museum, dry as a mole's hand in its glass case. And all the dominions of heaven have their calculated limits; the stars move to man's arithmetic; and the sun, leering like a fool over the valleys of Europe, sinks as the drops in a test-tube dry and are gone.

---

[1] Percy Lubbock (1879–1965), author and critic. *Earlham* is about his childhood.

This is a lament on the death of the West. Your bones and mine shall manure an empty island set in a waste sea. The stars shall shine over England, but the darkness of England, and the sarcophagus of a spoonfed nation, and the pitch in the slain souls of our children, will never be lit.

'And the earth was without form and void; and darkness was upon the face of the deep.' The old buffers of this world still cling to chaos, believing it to be Order. The day will come when the old Dis-Order changeth, yielding to a new Order. Genius is being strangled every day by the legion of old Buffers, by the last long line of the Edwardians, clinging, for God and capital, to an outgrown and decaying system. Light is being turned to darkness by the capitalists and industrialists. There is only one thing you and I, who are of this generation, must look forward to, must work for and pray for, and, because, as we fondly hope, we are poets and voicers not only of our personal selves but of our social selves, we must pray for it all the more vehemently. It is the Revolution. There is no need for it to be a revolution of blood. We do not ask that. All that we ask for is that the present Dis-Order, this medieval machine which is grinding into powder the bones and guts of the postwar generation, shall be broken in two, and that all that is in us of godliness and strength, of happiness and genius, shall be allowed to exult in the sun. We are said to be faithless, because our God is not a capitalist God, to be unpatriotic because we do not believe in the Tory Government. We are said to be immoral because we know that marriage is a dead institution, that the old rigid monogamous lifelong union of male and female—the exceptions are the exceptions of beauty—is a corrupted thought.

The hope of Revolution, even though all of us will not admit it, is uppermost in all our minds. If there were not that revolutionary spark within us, that faith in a new faith, and that belief in our power to squash the chaos surrounding us like a belt of weeds, we would turn on the tap of war and drown ourselves in its gases.

Everything is wrong that forbids the freedom of the individual. The governments are wrong, because they are the committees of prohibitors; the presses are wrong, because they feed us what they desire to feed us, and not what we desire to eat; the churches are wrong, because they standardize our gods, because they label our morals, because they laud the death of a vanished Christ, and fear the crying of the new Christ in the wilderness; the poets are wrong, because their vision is not a vision but a squint; they look at our world, and yet their eyes are staring back along the roads of the past centuries, never into the huge, electric promise of the future.

There is injustice, muddleheadedness, criminal ignorance, corrupted and inverted virtue, hypocrisy and stone blindness, in every sphere of life. If only for one moment the Western world could drop the veils that, ever since the Reformation, have clung around it like the films of a disease, and look, with lightened eyes, upon the cess it has created, on the greatness it has spilt & strangled, on the starvation it has fostered, on the perversions and ignorances it has taught, then it would die for shame. And we, who have not been long enough alive to be corrupted utterly, could build out of its manuring bones the base of an equal and sensible civilisation.

I will not bore you with any more propaganda, though why it should bore you God knows, for it is near to you as it is to me. Later, in another letter, I will give you a more reasoned outline of Revolution, the hard facts of communism—which is above communism for it holds the individual above everything else—and hope that you, too, may don your scarlet tie, and, striding into the Hampstead dens, scorch the Creative Lifers with an invective their poor bloody brains could never fathom.

But only if it does *not* bore you. The precious seeds of revolution must not be wasted, though I do not think they will be in you.

The Arty Party

The type of party you describe—and you describe it very well indeed—is a menace to art, much as I dislike the phrase. Wyndham (Tar) Lewis has struck them hard in 'Apes of God'; D. B. (Blue Moon) Lewis has poked them gently to see if they bite as well as bark;[1] Roy Campbell,[2] in his 'Georgiad', has trampled them down under the feet of his eighteenth-century charger; but still they flourish. Still do seedy things in their mothers' pyjamas, enthuse over some soon-to-be-forgotten lyricist, or some never-to-be-heard-of painter of nature in the raw and angular. Neuter men and lady tenors rub shoulders with 'the shams and shamans, the amateur hobo and homo of Bloomsbury W.C.1', while their hostess, clad in scarlet corduroy, drinks to their health in methylated spirits.

With a smattering, often incorrectly memorised, of encyclopedia learning, with the names of the transient stars of their decade on the tips of their tongues, with their men's breasts shaped with the aid of wadding, the young women speak on. Sodomhipped young men, with the inevitable sidewhiskers and cigarettes, the faulty livers and the stained teeth, reading Lawrence as an aphrodisiac and Marie Corelli in their infrequent baths, spew onto paper and canvas their ignorance and perversions, wetting the bed of their brains with discharges of fungoid verse. This is the art of to-day: posturing, shamming, cribbing, and all the artifice of a damned generation.

In the corner stands an emaciated female chanting that sentimental ballad, 'Proust A Song At Twilight'. From behind a divan rises a grisly laugh. Someone has made a joke about André Gide.

Seedy Young Thing Do you like Ibsen? *P.H.J.* No, I prefer Glauber.[3]

---

[1] Wyndham Lewis (1882–1957), writer and artist; *Tarr* (1918) was a novel. Dominic Bevan Wyndham Lewis (1894–1969), writer and satirist; *At the Sign of the Blue Moon* was a collection of humorous articles from the *Daily Mail*.
[2] Royston Dunnachie Campbell (1901–57), belligerent poet, later a friend of Thomas.
[3] Glauber salts, an old-fashioned purgative.

Oversight

Thank you for the detailed criticism of the '16 Poems'—a hell of a lot, really, to inflict on you in one dose—but as I haven't kept a copy of the little book I don't [know] which poems you are criticizing. It's terrible: I read 'This is a ghastly line', or 'this is very wormy', and I immediately want to look up the particular poem and agree with you. But I can't. In the next letter send me *all* the first lines with the numbers above them, will you? Don't forget.

On Skeletons

I was neither surprised or revolted at the sight of your little grinning skeleton. When you do sink you sink deep enough into the sugary pits to please all the Women's Friends in England. Don't you dare do it again.

I, too, have a wicked secret. I used to write articles for the Northcliffe Press on 'Do Novelists make Good Husbands?' and 'Are Poets Mad?' etc.—very literary, very James Douglas, very bloody. I don't do that any more now: I ran the Northcliffe Press into a libel suit by calling Miss Nina Hamnett (she wrote the book called 'Laughing Torso', I don't know whether you remember it) insane. Apparently she wasn't, that was the trouble.

Epilogue

I've neglected to touch on several of the points I intended to, and I've left many of your comments unanswered. But five of these huge, tinily written sheets are enough to give you at a time. Write very soon, not in a week but in a few days; I'm giving you a whole week-end to compose your notes. Make them as long as these 'ere. I'm enclosing one poem, just finished. It's quite my usual stuff, I'm afraid, & quite probably you won't like it. But, honestly, the one 'cancer' mentioned *is* necessary. And I will try to be good in future.

Dylan

Looking back over these notes I see many of them to be unusually aggressive & particularly humourless. Sorry!

And another thing before I forget it: If this letter is illegible—you haven't complained of my ugly writing once yet—tell me, & my next letter shall be done on the typewriter.

About the Chertsey trip. I'm terribly dubious at the moment about when I am coming up. I want a really good excuse first. I might be able to arrange a meeting with Middleton Murry[1]—I met him this August in Chelsea. Or even with T. S. Eliot. (God 'elp me.) More about this, & other things, again.

MS: Buffalo   *SL(R)*

---

[1] John Middleton Murry (1889–1957), author and journalist. Thomas had stayed on the houseboat with his sister and brother-in-law.

T. S. ELIOT[1]
[November 1933]   5 Cwmdonkin Drive Uplands Swansea

Dear Sir,

Richard Rees of the Adelphi has already, I believe, given a number of my poems to Mr Herbert Read who wrote to say that he, in his turn, was handing them over to you for your consideration.

Last week Richard Rees asked me to send him some more recent poems. I did so, and received the reply which I am enclosing along with a selection of recently written poems.

I do hope you will be able to find time to read them, if only to corroborate or contradict the suggestion of 'automatic' writing, the slightest idea of which is entirely unfounded. The fluency complained of is the result of extraordinarily hard work, and, in my opinion, the absence of 'knotty or bony passages' is again the result of much energetic labour – however misdirected – and of many painful hours spent over the smoothing and removing of the creakinesses of conflict.

                                   Yours sincerely,
                                   Dylan Thomas

PS: I hope you will not mind my sending the poems or the writing of such a troubled letter.

MS: Valerie Eliot

PAMELA HANSFORD JOHNSON
[?early December 1933][2]

In The Bath
    The water is lapping upon my abdominal shore, and a cigarette-end, slowly disintegrating, is being carried along by the steaming stream that runs, like a stream from the springs of hell, over my feet. No, this is not an abstraction; I am lying in the bath, smoking Woodbines, and staring, through hot mists, on to the paper that lies on my front. I cover the waterfront. The click, click of the geyser sounds like the distant champing of a lady tenor. All is very wet and white, giving rise to thoughts on life and love, on the impermanence of human emotions, the futility of personal effort, the dirty doings of Creative doctors, and the sudden alarming thought of Cinderella. Now it is hot and still. Peace, like an old hat, sits on me.
    This is nonsense, of course, but it is a good opening to a letter; it tears down all formalities; it does away with many of the layers of bluff, double

---

[1] T. S. Eliot (1888–1965) was the director in charge of the poetry list at Faber.
[2] Evidence for the dating is a reference to 'a literary party held in one's own little honour'. Johnson's diary for Saturday November 25 records, 'Party held in my honour by Victor and Runia.' The diary notes letters received from Thomas on December 1 and 11.

bluff, and self-doubt that so often prevent me from saying what I want to say; it is as intimate as the legs of the Pope's pyjamas.

But it is difficult, in this blasted bath, to know what to write about. In the ebullience of my youth and the limitless depths of my greenaged immodesty, I confess to having opinions on everything under the sun. The opinions are often immoderate, generally impetuous, and always verbose. But that matters very little. The great thing is to think, however wrongly.

What shall I regale you with: an attack on George Too Shaw To Be Good? a defence of Lesbia? a belief in vegetarianism? But no—George is clever but visionless; Lesbia is an aestiaboginous (I can't spell it)[1] island; and vegetarianism is inevitable.

Let me, instead, scrub the marks of the roads from my little feet, cough, spit, and whistle, pull up the plug, and retire, like an emaciated Cupid with pen for arrow, to a bleak, unmaidened bed.

In The Bed

Now that the drunkenness of a too-hot bath is wearing off a little, and the water of the bath has got into the ink, I shall write in pencil a few straightforward [*In the margin:* oh yeah?] facts.

THOMAS: HIS IDEAS

I am looking forward to what you've written—or are still writing—of the 'Woman Arisen'; I should love to add my few stanzas, or the ideas for the few stanzas (whichever you like), though my experience of waking with a woman at my side has been necessarily limited.

The medieval laws of this corrupted hemisphere have dictated a more or less compulsory virginity during the period of life when virginity should be regarded as a crime against the dictates of the body. During the period of adolescence, when the blood and seed of the growing flesh need, for the first time and more than ever again, communion and contact with the blood and seed of another flesh, sexual relationships are looked upon as being unnecessary and unclean. The body must be kept intact for marriage, which is rarely possible before the age of twenty; the physical expression of sex must be caged up for six or more years until, for the price of a ring, a licence, and a few hampering words, opportunity is presented with all the ceremony of a phallic religion. But so often the opportunity comes too late; the seed has soured; love has turned to lust, and lust to sadism; the mind has become covered and choked by the weeds of inhibition; and the union of two starved creatures, suddenly allowed the latitude of their sexes, is doomed from the start. The woman carries her marriage licence about with her as a bitch might carry the testimony of its liberated heat.

---

[1] Neuburg popularised and probably coined the word 'ostrobogulous', using it to suggest the bawdy or bizarre (the *OED Supplement*, Vol III, 1982, has an entry). This seems to be what Thomas intended.

Such things may not be pleasant to talk about, but they do exist, and they are evil.

From the first months of puberty, girls & boys should be allowed to know their bodies (I am not trying to twist phrases, nor am I wishing to write down the bare words in all their ugliness). More than that, their sexual expression should be encouraged. It would be very nearly impossible for a young girl to live, permanently, with a young boy, especially if both were in school; they would not live together peaceably; they would have no money, and it would be difficult for them to earn. But the family of the girl should, for a certain time—the time of the mutual devotion of boy and girl—keep the boy in their house. And vice-versa. The lives of the boy and girl would continue individually—there would be school and school associations for both of them—but their domestic closeness and their sleeping together would blend the two individual lives in one, & would keep both brains & bodies perpetually clean. And both would grow up physically and mentally uncontaminated and refreshened.

Don't think I'm regaling you with some crank-ridden, pornographic notion. I really believe in what I say, and no argument has ever shifted my belief. It is not a theory, but an adjustment of the present corrupted facts to uncorrupted ideals. The issues of such an adjustment are, of course, tremendous; they attack the basis of established morals and the foundations of society. But are they wrong?* [*In the margin:* *This is a question to *you*.]

To expand the argument, let me point out that some sort of attraction or devotion would have to be the prelude of the association of the boy and girl. The two sexes, on reaching puberty, would not be lumped inconsiderately together; the honest friendship of boy & girl would be allowed entire freedom and culmination, that is all. There would be no binding agreements between the two families, and boy and girl could have as many lovers as they wished, until, eventually, they find a lover with whom they could [?live] for a longer time, or for ever.

After that—and pray God it didn't sound like Mr. Mybug in an inspired moment—let me return to the beginning. Send me the 'Woman Arises' with your next letter, and, conjuring up the emotions of husbandly love, I shall attempt to send it back—*with* additions—in *my* next.

But real collaboration has to be more than this. The poem *has to be born* in the presence of the two authors. And I hope that it won't be very long before that is possible.

Just a Word

You were very stern about the fragments of poems I sent you. They were written when I was fourteen, remember, and they damned well *had* to be bad.

Uncommon

Tomorrow, when this is posted, I shall send you my 'Uncommon

Genesis', that much-promised story. I'm afraid it's rather long, and will take up a lot of your time. Do read it, though, won't you, and tell me exactly what you think of it. It was written just under a year ago, written straight off and never revised. When I was typing it, I saw all sorts of sentences that, had I been more careful, I should not have hesitated to correct or cut out altogether. Not being careful, I typed out good and bad. And here it is.

The passages in red type should really be in italics. You'll have to excuse the typing all along: in some places it's abominable. But I'm not very nimble-fingered at the best of times, and my machine, as you've noticed from the poems I've sent you, is moody and antique. It possesses all the French accents, but, unfortunately, I write in English.

'Uncommon Genesis' is an uncommon story (I'm sorry to preface it with so many absurd remarks), and you'll either like it, or dislike it very strongly. I'm hoping you'll like it. It has to be read with an unbiased mind, for it is written in a high and wordily romantic style that could, if the attention was shifted only momentarily off its meaning, be turned to bathos. But if you do really read it carefully & without prejudice, I don't think you will laugh. But you tell me all about it, if you will.

It's just struck me: Since we've been writing to one another I've loaded you with an immense quantity of my stuff; crowds of my poems accompany every letter; and now here comes over 20 closely typed sheets to add to the pile. Perhaps it would be better if I gave you a little rest—not from letter-writing, I'll be damned if I'll stop that—but from the inclusion of so much of my stuff. I know you honestly like it—just as I honestly like so much of the little I have seen of yours—but you can have too much of a good thing.

More about Luv

Thank you for telling me about your lost, but not forgotten, lovers, and if the pages did occasionally remind me of Ella M. Ruck, that composite novelist and poet, they were none the less sincere for that.[1]

And that was a horribly patronising remark, the remark of an introvertive crank on the extravertism (what a word!) of a far superior person. I'm very sorry. It probably took a great deal of courage for you to tell me about the frigid reader of newspapers upon whom you wasted such a lot of your affection. And who, by the navel of St. Francis, am *I* to comment on it? You paid me a compliment by telling me about him, & the G.N.L., & the British boy (your taste doesn't seem to lie in the direction of the arty & Poetical young men), & the emotional part of me thanks you very much. Never mind the intellectual part: that is nothing.

But why, if you fall in love again—& you are bound to at some time or another—will you not give again all that you gave before, not necessarily That Which Is Dearer etc., but all the energy of your youngness (youth, here, is the wrong word), your sweetness etc. (I evade saying everything,

---

[1] Perhaps the sentimental poet Ella Wheeler Wilcox and the romantic novelist Berta Ruck.

you know), your brightness & sulkiness and every other bloody mood and feeling you possess. I said your failing was the failing of loving too much. It is, and it always will be. So fasten your affections on some immaculately profiled young man, and love the swine to death. Love among the angels is a perpetual distemper.

(It didn't remind me of Ella M., really. I loved it, only I'm too xxxx selfconscious to say so, damn my rabbit's eyes!)

My Life. The Touching Autobiography Continued From the Last Letter But Three (or Four)

Gower is a very beautiful peninsula, some miles from this blowsy town, and so far the Tea-Shop philistines have not spoilt the more beautiful of its bays. Gower, as a matter of fact, is one of the loveliest sea-coast stretches in the whole of Britain, and some of its tiny villages are as obscure, as little inhabited, and as lovely as they were a hundred years ago.* [In the margin: *this sounds like a passage from a Tourists' Guide.]

I often go down in the mornings to the furthest point of Gower—the village of Rhossilli—and stay there until evening. The bay is the wildest, bleakest, and barrennest I know—four or five miles of yellow coldness going away into the distance of the sea. And the Worm* [In the margin: *Perhaps this accounts for my Complex], a seaworm of rock pointing into the channel, is the very promontory of depression. Nothing live on it but gulls and rats, the millionth generation of the winged and tailed families that screamed in the air and ran through the grass when the first sea thudded on the Rhossilli beach. There is one table of rock on the Worm's back that is covered with long yellow grass, and, walking on it, one [feels] like something out of the Tales of Mystery & Imagination treading, for a terrible eternity, on the long hairs of rats. Going over that grass is one of the strangest experiences; it gives under one's feet; it makes little sucking noises, & smells—and this to me is the most grisly smell in the world—like the fur of rabbits after rain.

When the tide comes in, the reef of needle rocks that leads to the base of the Worm, is covered under the water. I was trapped on the worm once. I had gone on it early in the afternoon with a book & a bag of food, and, going to the very, very end, had slept in the sun, with the gulls crying like mad over me. And when I woke the sun was going down. I ran over the rocks, over the abominable grass, and on to the ridge overlooking the little reef. The tide had come in. I stayed on that Worm from dusk till midnight, sitting on the top grass, frightened to go further in because of the rats and because of the things I am ashamed to be frightened of. Then the tips of the reef began to poke out of the water, &, perilously, I climbed along them on to the shore, with an 18 mile walk in front of me. It was a dark, entirely silent, entirely [?empty] road. I saw everything on that walk—from snails, lizards, glow worms & hares to diaphanous young ladies in white who vanished as I approached them.

One day, when I know you even better than I do now, you must come & stay with me, some time in the summer. Swansea is a dingy hell, and my mother is a vulgar humbug; but I'm not so bad, and Gower is as beautiful as anywhere.

There is one bay almost too lovely to look at. You shall come & see it with me; we shall both utter words of maudlin wonder, and swoon away on the blasted heath.

My father was a master in the Swansea Grammar School, and still would be, for he is not yet old enough to retire. But the last three months he has spent in the London University Hospital, undergoing treatment for cancer of the throat. He is home now, partially cured and exceedingly despondent.[1] His time limit is even shorter than mine (!). Ours is a nice 'ouse.* There is one unintelligent dog, too, with the highly original name of Spot. [*In the margin:* *All this doesn't sound very nice after an invitation, however awkward, does it? I mean it, though.]

I will write more—not, fortunately for you, more of this depressing serial autobiography—tomorrow. Now I am going to wash and shave, preparatory to travelling to Gwaun-cae-Gurwen (I love introducing names like these), where a spirited melodrama will be rendered by a talented cast. Thank you.

Coplans (?) Comment

Why didn't someone kick that perverted doctor in the bottom? Aren't *any* of the Creative Lifers men of action? Here in barbaric Wales, where men are men, he would have been stoned to death by members of Y Gobaith Cymru Wrdd.[2]

There's a charming incident in some novel—I can't remember which —where a very narsty young man lies at the feet of a very nice young girl, &, looking into her eyes, says, 'You remind me of cabbages and big brown messes—I adore you'. It's much the same type of incident, with the exception that I am sure you do not remind anybody of such things. But, really, the astonishing part of that astonishing party—and it must be pleasant to have a literary party held in one's own little honour*—was the way in which the narsty doctor was tolerated for so long. Creative Lifer or not, I should have bitten him severely in the calf. [*In the margin:* *Bah, envy!]

Your aversion to him he most certainly will put down to inhibitions on your part; perverted & unsuccessful lechers of his variety never believe that their love-making (far too good a word) could appeal only to the base of the stomach.

---

[1] No doubt 'throat' sounded more dramatic than 'mouth'. D. J. Thomas was treated in the hospital from September 10 to 20, and from October 10 to 24. The cancer was eradicated by 1934, and he lived another eighteen years.

[2] Urdd Gobaith Cymru, the Welsh League of Youth. Dr Coplans: a friend of Johnson.

Interlude for Refreshments

No, I don't really spit in the piano, so there'll be no need to nail the top down. And I certainly indulge in the singing of lewd roundelays. I shall probably turn shy, & hide myself in the lavatory all day (up the stairs, first to the right).

My only real domestic vice is my indiscriminate sprinkling of cigarette ash over everything and everybody. Apart from this, I am not a particular nuisance, and I smell quite nice. I look about fourteen, and I have a large, round nose; nature gave it to me, but fate, and a weak banister, broke it; in cold weather it is sufficiently glossy to light up any room. When I am about on winter nights there is no need for the gas.

Cough! cough! cough! my death is marching on; the Venus in front of me cocks a marble eye in my direction, & the calendar, with a water-colour view of Lake Como, sways in the incredibly cold wind.

First Epilogue

I was sorry after sending those three sheets of socialism; they were nothing but facts, and facts, unvarnished, are always boring or be-wildering. I am not going to indulge in any more propaganda in this letter; I shall keep two or three red hot notes—along with a note on W. H. Auden, the Poet of Revolution—& send them to you next time.

So the Tharp ranks oratory as one of the Fine Arts? I don't know about that, but the speaking of poetry is certainly one of them. You shall read some 'tweety' poems to me one day, &, rolling my Cymric r's, I shall reply.

Second Epilogue

This letter isn't as long as most of the letters I send you, but the long enclosed story does more than compensate. I'll write a *very* long letter next week; it will probably need a special postman to deliver it all by itself.

And if you don't reply very quickly & at great length, I shall turn myself, with considerable magic, into a winter fly, & come and die in your hair. This is the most terrible threat I know. Let it close the letter, along with an expression of bonhomie, and Old School affection.

Dylan

[*On the back of the sheet—two drawings of himself, cigarette dangling.*]

I'm sorry about this. It was on the back, & I didn't see it. I don't always draw like that, thank God.

MS: Buffalo   *SL*

PAMELA HANSFORD JOHNSON
[about December 21 1933][1]

Unwilling Reply

Nothing I can think of—including the personal delivery of Miss Garbo in a tin box—would please me so much as to spend Christmas with you, and to talk to you (though, really, I don't talk as much as all that) until Boxing Day. The towel and the jar of holly, especially the jar of holly, are terribly big temptations. But I must stand like a little martyr, denying the calls of the flesh (no, I don't mean that at all; it sounds as though you'd invited me to a pyjama party) and obeying, instead, the requests of a benighted family. My sister, brother-in-law and uncle will be down here for the holiday, and great fun will be had by all. Will it, hell! We'll all eat too much, I suppose, read the newspapers, sleep, and crack nuts. There will be no Yuletide festivity about it, and I, in an extra-black shirt, will brood over the fire, contemplating in the coals, the shapes of past Miseries and Follies.

I'm flattered to receive a Christmas invitation from you, from you who have known me for such a little time and in such unusual ways—more flattered (and terribly pleased) than I can tell you.

(By the way, I've discovered a new way of getting ill. You buy an ounce of Sailors' Plug Tobacco, a little machine for making cigarettes, and a packet of cigarette papers. Put a layer of Plug in the machine, put in the paper, turn round, draw out, and smoke the result. It's the worst taste I've ever known. I'm smoking one now.)

Your mother, I suppose, is in the charming invitation, too. Give her my Christmas greetings, and tell her to write separately and give me the low-down on her daughter (how the daughter is a champion ice-skater or steeple-chaser or Derby winner, how she likes Berta Ruck so much more than James Joyce, how she writes novels in her spare time and contributes to the, say to the 'Ladies' Chat' and 'Miriam's Weekly').

By the way, again, have you written any prose? If so, let me see it, won't you? I remember you told me something in a very longago letter about some stories you'd put on the fire. But aren't there *any* stories not used so harshly and, I'm sure, so needlessly? I think you should be able to write very good prose. But then, as I said before somewhere, I'm *very* biased.

I'd love to spend Christmas with you. Circumstances say otherwise, and my father is going up to Hospital in London in the first few days of January to have, as far as I know, several very necessary glands removed.

Three Poems

I don't honestly feel disposed to throw you a bone for your three most recent poems; you certainly deserve a whole puppy biscuit for the sixteen lines of 'Quest', and also, perhaps, a little bit of puppy food for the

[1] Johnson's diary notes receipt of a letter, 'with photo & book of poems from my little Dylan', December 22.

'Motorists'. But you don't get a single mouthful for 'December Trees'.

<u>'Quest'</u> This is a very slight thing but quite successful in its limits, and the last five lines are attractive *because* of their slightness and simplicity. 'Weeps, just because of it', a rather whimsy line, might be improved by the deletion of the comma which makes, to me, a quite unessential pause. I haven't decided yet about the adjective 'unquiet'. As a rule I dislike such negative words, except in very especial instances. If a thing is not quiet there is no real need to say that it is not; it is much better to say what it is. 'Unquiet' doesn't *qualify* the mouse; I've told you of my belief as to the poetical function of the adjective before, haven't I?—'unquiet' doesn't add anything to the mouse. The thing to remember is that everyone has his different associations for every word; one person may, for some Freudian reason, associate 'mouse' with horrors and death's heads, another with a certain soft material and colour. So the poet who is going to put an adjective before 'mouse' must say to himself: I have two alternatives; either I can create such a tremendous and universal adjective that it will *embrace* every association built around the word — that is, it must be an adjective that complies with all the associations from horror to colour—; or I must create an adjective that will *break down* all associations, and make the 'mouse' a new thing with new associations. Does 'unquiet' satisfy either of those tests. I don't know. I rather think, despite my theories, that it is a very effective word. It must be one of those especial instances where such a negation can be used.

<u>The Motorists</u> This is much the sort of thing that another (no, no, please, I don't mean that) of Neuburg's animals produces—one Harry Hodgkinson by name. The last four lines are, unfortunately, for they are good, spoilt for me by the fact that I know a very vulgar schoolboy poem in the same metre. The poem (the 'Motorists', not 'Eskimo Nell') is bright and refreshing, but the sort of cheery poetry that makes me even more depressed than the 'City of Everlasting Night.' That, again, is personal. As a rule I try to criticise your poems from a *pure* poetical standpoint, but various things prevent me from doing it with this. And down comes my omnipotent criticship with a bump. 'And scratch her great, brown face' is clumsy. Why the two bumpy little adjectives? Go on, tell me it's intentional.

<u>December Trees</u> Just what you shouldn't write. Leave these 'Notes from a Rambler's Log Book', to other and far less talented young women. It's the easiest and least valuable form of valueless impressionism.

> 'December trees—
> Brown mists above the fields'

is the sort of opening one comes across on nearly every other page of 'The Best (or Worst) Poems of the Year,' which is a collection of the shattered pieces of sentimental romanticism swept up by that literary charwoman, Mr Thomas Moult.[1]

> 'October fields—
>   A breath of wind about the sedge,
>   A speckled rabbit in a hedge,
>   And cold white snow.'

No, girl, no. This is terribly unworthy of you. Develop—and you *can* develop at a tremendous speed—along the lines of 'Quest' and 'I feel I am a stranger', that lovely poem that does and always will remain in my memory. Write out of yourself, and leave the hedgerows and the *visual* aspects of the countryside. And another thing: don't be afraid, at this stage of your development, to intellectualise more. Intellect alone never makes good poetry. You have the essential attributes of poetry, so can do no harm to yourself by letting your intellect have, now, a certain amount of freedom.

Hints for Recognition

The gradual shrinking you complain of is chiefly mental, for the more despondent I become the littler and weaker I feel.

Height—five foot six (about).

Weight—eight stone ten (about).

Hair—some sort of rat-coloured brown.

Eyes—big, brown and green (this sounds as though one were brown & the other green; the colours are mixed).

Distinguishing Marks—Three moles on right cheek, scar on arm and ankle, though as I generally wear socks you won't see the little mark there.

Sex—male, I think.

Voice—I suppose it would be called baritone, though sometimes it sweeps towards tenor and sometimes droops towards bass. Except in moments of hilarity, I believe I speak without an accent.

Size of Feet—five (this is not number).

Cigarettes—Players, forty a day stuck in centre of mouth.

Food—Hay.

This is neither very funny nor very illuminating, I admit, but I must, by any method possible, steer clear of the soulful outpouring that ended my last letter. I apologise, incidentally, for apologising for the overflow of feeling. I should have known how interesting such overflowing is, because the little, pulsating bits in your letters—when you defend your theism before a pack of negative-brained scoffers, or dwell, unhappily but unbrokenly, upon the passing of juvenile loves—are of immense interest to [me], who am also pleased by the fact that I have your confidence. My little Welsh ear is open for all secrets.

---

[1] Thomas Moult (d. 1974) edited a long-running annual series, *The Best Poems of* . . . , on traditional lines.

But the prospect of being comforted—insubstantially, it is true, but then the substance of life is and always will be to *me* less than the unreality—by a nice and slant-eyed shade, tempts me to indulge in even more abysmal desolations of the spirit.

From a letter to my Aunt, Discussing the Correct Approach to Modern Poetry.[1]

> To you, my aunt, who would explore
> The literary Chankley Bore,
> The paths are hard for you are not
> A literary Hottentot
> But just a kind and cultured dame
> Who knows not Eliot (to her shame).
> Fie on you, aunt, that you should see
> No genius in David G.,
> No elemental form and sound
> In T.S.E. and Ezra Pound.
> Fie on you, aunt! I'll show you how
> To elevate your middle brow,
> And how to scale and see the sights
> From modernist Parnassian heights.
>
> First buy a hat, no Paris model
> But one the Swiss wear when they yodel,
> A bowler thing with one or two
> Feathers to conceal the view.
> And then in sandals walk the street
> (All modern painters use their feet
> For painting, on their canvas strips,
> Their wives or mothers minus hips.)
> Then sport an open skirt and blouse,
> For every arty thing allows
> Her wretchèd bosom to be loosed
> For men to see who talk of Proust.
> Remember this at every table
> Talk as rudely as you're able,
> And never pass the peas with less
> Than *one* remark on sexiness.
>
> Your wardrobe done, (forget the rest,
> The little things like drawers and vest),
> You next must learn the tricks of speech
> (Here nothing rhymes but 'Chelsea Reach').[2]

what a line!

sorry!

---

[1] The poem has had a hard time. *SL* transposed two of the manuscript pages, thus detaching twenty-three lines and placing them above the title. When Daniel Jones included it in *The Poems*, he ignored the misplaced lines altogether.

[2] Johnson's first poem in the *Sunday Referee* (23 April 1933) was 'Chelsea Reach'.

Learn to begin with words like these:
'Chiaroscuro', 'Bright's Disease',
'Timbre', 'soul', 'essential cheese',
'The social art', 'the rhomboid quip',
'The rhythmic works of Stink and Drip',
'The Joyce of Love', 'the D. H. 'Ell',
'The formal spheres of Little Nell'.
With such fine phrases on your tongue,
A knowledge of the old and Jung,
You can converse in any party
And keep the conversation arty.

Perhaps it would be best if you
Created something very new,
A dirty novel done in Erse
Or written backwards in Welsh verse,
Or paintings on the backs of vests,
Or Sanskrit psalms on lepers' chests.
But if this proved imposs-i-bel
Perhaps it would be just as well,
For you could then write what you please,
And modern verse is done with ease.

Do not forget that 'limpet' rhymes
With 'strumpet' in these troubled times,
And commas are the worst of crimes;
Few understand the works of Cummings,
And few James Joyce's mental slummings,
And few young Auden's coded chatter;
But then it is the few that matter.
Never be lucid, never state,
If you would be regarded great,
The simplest thought or sentiment,
(For thought, we know, is decadent);
Never omit such vital words
As belly, genitals, and ——,
For these are things that play a part
(And what a part) in all good art.
Remember this: each rose is wormy,
And every lovely woman's germy;
Remember this: that love depends
On how the Gallic letter bends;
Remember, too, that life is hell
And even heaven has a smell
Of putrefying angels who
Make deadly whoopee in the blue.
These things remembered, what can stop
A poet going to the top?

A final word: before you start
The convolutions of your art,
Remove your brains, take out your heart;
Minus these curses, you can be
A genius like David G.

Take courage, aunt, and send your stuff
To Geoffrey Grigson with my luff,
And may I yet live to admire
How well your poems light the fire.

More Theorising

Only today, after reading for the hundredth time out of the 'Plumed Serpent',[1] have I come to make a valuation of Lawrence. And as nearly everyone today has some sort of set ideas upon that almost legendary figure, it may interest you to know what conclusions I—on the outskirts of the literary world, if any such world exists—have reached. I don't know whether you'll follow all of this note; anyway it isn't worth burrowing into the syntactical tunnels I so often lose myself in.

Lawrence was a moralist, a preacher, but his morals & his sermons were not progressive. He preached a doctrine of paganism and, to the best of his tubercular ability, attempted to lead a pagan life. But the more paganistic, sun-and-sex loving, one becomes, the less one feels the desire to write. A born writer is born scrofulous; his career is an accident dictated by physical or circumstantial disabilities. Lawrence preached paganism, and paganism, as the life by the body in the body for the body, is a doctrine that contents man with his lot. It defies the brain, and it is only through the brain that man can realise the chaos of civilisation and attempt to better it. Aldous Huxley, as his direct protagonist, preaches the sermon of the intellect; his god is cellular, and his heaven a socialist Towards. He would, as someone brighter than myself has said, condense the generative principle into a test-tube; Lawrence, on the other hand, would condense the world into the generative principle, and make his apostles decline not cogitare but copulare.

The young writer, if he would wish to label himself at all, must class himself under one of two headings: under the philosophy (for want of a better word) which declares the body to be all and the intellect nothing, and which would limit the desires of life, the perceptions and the creation of life, within the walls of the flesh; or under the philosophy which, declaring the intellect and the reason and the intelligence to be *all*, denies the warmth of the blood and the body's promise. You have to class yourself under one heading—the labels might overlap a *little*—for the equilibrium between flesh and not-flesh can never be reached by an individual. While the life of the body is, perhaps, more directly pleasant,

[1] D. H. Lawrence's violent novel (1926), set in Mexico.

it *is* terribly limited, and the life of the non-body, while physically unsatisfying, *is* capable of developing, of realising infinity, of getting somewhere, and of creating an artistic progeny.

Lawrence and his disease grew parallel, and one was nothing without the other. If he had had no disease, he would have been a pagan liver, and would never have written at all. As it was, weak and diseased, he wrote of the struggle of the ideas of the pagan strong. And his literature, therefore, however valuable, is a *lie* from start to finish.

Perhaps I haven't developed the argument sufficiently, and perhaps, O uncomplaining receiver of so many half-baked theories, I may be entirely wrong.

You get a rather beastly angle on Lawrence if you read, 'Lorenzo in Taos'.[1] And unless you want to regard the man as a vain, weakchinned, egocentric, domineering little charlatan, *don't* borrow the book.

Us Girls

How is 'Cinderella' going on? This is a really *interested* question, although it leads up to another personal statement. I've just started rehearsals for the 'Way of the World', a play to be carted around the Welsh valleys where they won't understand one bawdy word from the beginning to the end. Do you know the play? (Of course you do.) I'm playing Witwoud, the second consecutive effeminate part. Much more of this type of playing, and I shall be becoming decidedly girlish.

Have you remarked upon the terrible young men of this generation, the willing-buttocked, celluloid-trousered, degenerates who are gradually taking the place of the bright young things of even five years ago? Or is the degeneracy, the almost unbelievable effeminacy, the product of the Welsh slums alone? In an hotel last night a boy, wearing a light green hat, white shirt, red tie, light green trousers and tightly fitting fawn overcoat, went up to the bar and said 'A whate port and a smale Ardathe, girlie'. I heard him. He was the most perfect example I've ever seen, the sort of thing one hears of in coarse stories but rarely encounters in the flesh (God deliver me from the flesh; the outer trappings are enough). I see more and more of them every day. They always existed, but in recent months—it seems months to me—they are coming, unashamedly, out into the open. I saw one with a drunken nigger last night.

It is the only vice, I think, that revolts me and makes me misanthropic. I can—theoretically—tolerate even incest (Tell me, have you read Leonhard Frank's 'Brother & Sister';[2] if not, get hold of it by some method and *do* read it; it's brilliant) and other domestic sins. But the sin of the boy with the nigger goes up like a rocketed scab to Heaven.

I'm trying to borrow that historical novel. Do you still keep up a correspondence with the author, or am I your only deliver[er] of long and literary—not always literary, either—letters?

[1] By Mabel Dodge Luhan (1933).
[2] First published in Germany, 1930; English translation by Cyrus Brooks the same year.

Devils

Today I am starting on a new short story which will in a few weeks, I hope, be finished and good enough to send you. The theme of the story I dreamed in a nightmare. If successful, if the words fit to the thoughts, it will be one of the most ghastly short stories ever written. The action in it will be grisly enough, but—if it will come to pass—the tone of it will be so quiet that the horror should rise up like a clot of blood in the throat. 'I brought the broom for her to brush it into the wall', is the opening sentence which, standing alone, is quite meaningless. But even alone it is horrible to me.

This is no despondency to-day. I feel like a dead man exulting in the company of his beetles, incarnadining the monstrous earth—words, words, words—with the blood of the worms (yes, worms again, my dear) that he breaks—as a housemaid crushes a flea—between the tips of his nails.

Sometimes I am very nice, but to-day I'm awful; I'm caught in my complexes, and they're giving me immense, if unholy, joy.

Do you know the experience of sitting in a corner of a darkened room, a little light coming in through the window, and staring, fixedly and un-movedly, at the face of another in an opposite corner, never taking the eyes off the lines of the other's face? Slowly the face changes, the jaw droops, the brow slips into the cheeks, and the face is one strange white circle, utter darkness around it. Then new features form on the face, a goat's mouth slides across the circle, eyes shine in the pits of the cheeks. Then there is nothing but the circle again, and from the darkness around it rises, perhaps, the antlers of a deer, or a cloven foot, or the fingers of a hand, or a thing no words can ever describe, a shape, not beautiful or horrible, but as deep as hell and as quiet as heaven.

If you don't know the experience, try it. It's all optical illusion, I suppose, but I always call it the invoking of devils. And, mark my grisly words, invoke the devils too much, and by God they will come.

I've got the devils to-day; little blue ones they are, with spats and bowlers and dentists' tweezers. So I'd better not write any more to you until tomorrow. This will delay the letter, I'm afraid, and it's been delayed, for various reasons, long enough already. But I don't want to write you—you of all people—a panegyric on the eyesockets of skeletons.

Words

A new poem accompanies this. I suppose it's my usual stuff again, and even a little more death-struck. But don't be put off by my anatomical imagery, which I explained months ago. Because I so often write in terms of the body, of the death, disease, and breaking of the body, it doesn't necessarily mean that my Muse (not one of my favourite words) is a sadist. For the time at least, I believe in the writing of poetry from the flesh, and, generally, from the dead flesh. So many modern poets take the *living* flesh as their object, and, by their clever dissecting, turn it into a carcase. I prefer to take the *dead* flesh, and, by any positivity of faith and belief that is in me, build up a *living* flesh from it.

Talking of 'Muse', I read in an old John O'London (blast the tit-bitty paper) several individual lists of favourite words, and was surprised to see that the choice depended almost entirely upon the associations of the words. 'Chime', 'melody', 'golden', 'silver', 'alive', etc. appeared in almost every list; 'chime', is, to me, the only word of that lot that can, intrinsically and minus its associations, be called beautiful. The greatest single word I know is 'drome' which, for some reason, nearly opens the doors of heaven for me. Say it yourself, out aloud, and see if you hear the golden gates swing backward as the last, long sound of the 'm' fades away.

'Drome', 'bone', 'dome', 'doom', 'province', 'dwell', 'prove', 'dolomite'—these are only a few of my favourite words, which are insufferably beautiful to me. The first four words are visionary; God moves in a long 'o'. Have you any especial favourites? If so, now's your time, lidy.

Robeyism[1]

Thank you for giving a selection of my poems that might please the mighty Neuburg, but I don't know about the love poem; such a thing is so entirely out of my sphere that I'm frightened to think how bad it might be; I'll send it to the Referee next week, anyway. And thank you for taking all the callous things I said about 'May Day' without being at all annoyed, and for heeding my dogmatic tub-thumpery. Let me see, at the first opportunity, any new poems passed by the acid tests. I love the verses you put in your letters; they have many of the qualities I should like to see exhibited in your more serious work.

You must, you know, be an awfully entertaining little girl. Anyone who can be intelligently artistic, artistically intelligent, and downright vulgar *must* be nice. So your Resolution will be one you can't help fulfilling. It's remarkable how few of the moreorless cultivated young women one meets can be honestly vulgar. They talk, possibly, of matters which, a 100 years ago, were not supposed to exist, but they talk in a sly, subtle, sophisticated way, and their jokes—when they tell any—depend upon innuendoes. Now *you*, to your shame and credit, have a decidedly coarse wit, and your naughty verses about Gascoyne and his morbid preoccupations are little masterpieces in their way. I hope these compliments won't make your Correspondence Muse (a broad creature, not, on any account, to be confused with the slim, doe-eyed apparition of your green book) selfconscious. More power to her, and to you, sweet, Rabelaisian Pamela.

Dylan

Write soon; I *should* like to have a letter for Christmas; and write as long

[1] George Robey was a comedian.

a letter as this. Don't complain of lack of material—these notes should be able to provide enough of that.

MS: Buffalo   *SL(R)*

PAMELA HANSFORD JOHNSON
[December 25 1933]   5 Cwmdonkin Drive Uplands Swansea
*one of the many words I can't spell at all.

<u>Another Aftermath: Christmas Day</u>
Thank you for the cigarettes. The Christmas dinner over, and the memories of it—so far at least—more in the mouth than in the belly, I have been sprawling in an armchair, (yes, we possess one), smoking the first of your so very kind and unexpected present. While the family is collected around the wireless, listening to the voice of His Majesty, let me write a note to you to tell you how glad I was to read your last letter, and how horrified to think that you thought Robert Graves necessarilly* indicated the return of John Player.[1] The reference to my diabolical machine was not a hint to your generosity: I must assure you on that point, even though I have no doubt that the reading of my many letters has established this invisible personality of mine as one too honourable and Balliolic (not to say bucolic) for such an unmannerly action to be possible on my part. Play the game, you cads! And my style this gray December evening (a reference to robins will appear now any moment) is as heavy as the brandied pudding now rising in revolt, deep in the chambers of the intestines, against too much four-and-sixpenny port and vegetables.
Child: Mother, how many pips in a tangerine?
Mother: Shut up, you little bastard.
  My gifts are arrayed in front of me: a startlingly yellow tie and a peculiar pair of string gloves from my sister; a cigarette case from my brother-in-law; ten cigars from my father; 50 cigarettes from an uncle; 50 cigarettes from a young woman in Battersea; a knitted thing from the manageress of the hotel near my Little Theatre; the complete Blake from another uncle; a new edition of the Koran from a friend who writes music (I'll tell you something *very* interesting about him one day); Mrs. Munro's 1923–1933 Anthology (including three poems by the Gascoyne), from a friend who writes communism; two James Joyce pamphlets from myself; while outside hangs a neat, but tight, black hat from my mother, who has despaired for some time of the curves and angles of a decrepit trilby. That is all; and though your gift will vanish far more quickly than some of the others, it will last far longer in my memory than any of them.

[1] He sent her poems by Robert Graves; she sent him Player's cigarettes.

Now could I be more explicit than that.

I have been reading Blake's letters for the first time, and find, among other things, that his headings include: 'Dear leader of my angels', 'Dear sculptor of eternity', 'Dear friend of my angels', 'Dear friend of religion and order'—all of which, in this mellow mood, and with the possible exception of the last, I might apply to you.

Over dinner I told, with no remarkable effect, the following story which I hope may benefit and amuse those of your friends to whom vulgarity, or at least the trimmings of it, is as amusing as it is to you.

A. My sister has just returned from a week's holiday in Paris, and, do you know, she didn't go to the Louvre once.

B. Good lord, change of food, I expect.

I hear the roofs of the ancestral house quake with your laughter. Do I? The story reads badly but speaks well. A story which reads better than it speaks is the story of the two goldfish swimming around in a bowl, one singing to the other that old song,

> 'No roes in all the world
> Until you came.'

I have, as a rule, been averse to including such obvious rudery in my letters to you, but the sight of your crazy supplement (thank you for it), has quelled my aversion. If I could think of another funny story I'd tell you it, but the arms of Morpheus, along with the none-too-nimble fingers of Orpheus (damn that next door Chopin-er), are closing around me. Goodbye until to-morrow, when I hope that the heavy, academic idioms of this note will leave me lucid enough to write more and at more considerable length. The wireless is continually re-iterating the fact that Christmas is here, but Christmas, for me, is nearly over. How many more Christmases will these old eyes be blessed to see approach and vanish? Who knows: one far-off day I may gather my children (though a resolution denies it) around my spavined knee, tickle their chops, and tell them of the miracle of Christ and the devastating effect of too many nuts upon a young stomach.

.X.

A Tragic Conversation

A. Pity the philosophers, the specialists, and the careerists, for, being too acquainted with the fundaments of life or with a very small part of the mechanism of life, they have no time to look upon the vast panorama of social idiocy, of political wise-cracking and literary slapstick. Let us for once be superficial, pull a cracker and blow a whistle before the maggots play noughts and crosses on the delicate structure of our forms.

B. No, let us rather seize upon an aspect of this human tragedy, and pull it to bits, making it even more tragic. Let us walk in the lanes of an English county, remarking upon the futile stirrings of life in the hedges, and, taking out our inevitable notebooks, be vain enough to imagine that the words and rhymes we pen upon the pages are a sufficient excuse for the absurdity of our lives.

C. Pity the cynic and the man of letters, the two creatures in one of all God's creatures furthest removed from God.

Very Serious Question?
  Am I mad?

Librarian's Corner
  An ancient and immovable bias against Mr. Kipling, who stands for everything in this cankered world which I would wish were otherwise; an inexplicable dislike of Washington Irving, fostered by a clergical uncle whose favourite book, as he so often insists, is his Life of Mahomet; a hatred of Latin, fostered by a ridiculously inapt education; an appreciation of what f's can do in the place of s's (look at Graves's poem); a total ignorance of Lady Guff Gordon and Lady Longford; and a theoretical hatred of Byron, Keats, Shelley, and Wordsworth, do not assist me in admiring the Battersea shelves. Stella Gibbons I allow, though Cold Comfort Farm is not half as successful as it should be, owing to some carelessness in the development of the plot and the totally incredible and farcical climax; Gerfalcon I should allow if I knew it; and the Scarlet Letter is splendid. But where are yer moderns? (By the way, I have read, and don't like, most of Dreiser. What he writes of is good and valuable, but he should learn *how* to write. After all, if a writer of English can only express himself awkwardly in that language, he should have a shot at German; as a matter of fact Dreiser's style is thoroughly Teutonic. And, by the way again, I read 'Look Homeward, Angel' a few years ago, and I thought it particularly good.)

  Our books are divided into two sections, Dad's and mine. Dad has a room full of all the accepted stuff, from Chaucer to Henry James; all the encyclopedias and books of reference, all Saintsbury, and innumerable books on the theory of literature. His library contains nearly everything that a respectable highbrow library should contain. My books, on the other hand, are nearly all poetry, and mostly modern at that. I have the collected poems of Manley Hopkins, Stephen Crane, Yeats, de la Mare, Osbert Sitwell, Wilfred Owen, W. H. Auden, & T. S. Eliot; volumes of poetry by Aldous Huxley, Sacheverell & Edith Sitwell, Edna St. Vincent Millay, D. H. Lawrence, Humbert Wolfe, Sassoon, and Harold Monro; most of the ghastly Best Poems of the Year; two of the Georgian Anthologies, one of the Imagist Anthologies, 'Whips & Scorpions' (modern satiric verse), the London Mercury Anthology, the Nineties Anthology (what Dowsonery!);[1] a volume of Cambridge Poetry & Oxford Undergraduate Poetry; most of Lawrence, most of Joyce, with the

---

[1] Another of Thomas's digs at the late Victorians, in the shape of Ernest Dowson (1867–1900), poet.

exception of Ulysses, all Gilbert Murray's Greek translations, some Shaw, a little Virginia Woolf, & some E. M. Forster. This is inadequate, really, but, added to Dad's, it makes a really comprehensive selection of literature. If any of the modern poets I've mentioned are not very well known to you I should truly, truly like to lend you them. All the ones I mentioned are worth knowing well. If you feel like reading, tell me which of the above you'd like to have & I'll lend them to you one by one. Will you?

Legend

What beautiful words are 'legend' & 'island'; they shall certainly go on my list. But Ruth is the loveliest name.

Enclosed is a note to your very kind mother. If you are a good girl you can read it. It doesn't say anything at all. But then what does? And which as well?

Up, Nero!

The last poem I sent you, the one you didn't like, is *not* very good, and I'm glad you attacked it; thank you for the 'White Hope', and thank you, too, for expressing—in your remarks about the hiding of light and the running around in the same weary and minor track—much that I myself have felt and have never been able to express. On one point I disagree: the images are *not* mixed; they are severely physical all through; what gave you the impression of 'mixedness' was the conscious rapidity with which I changed the angles of the images. Yes, the 'iris' is a little bit too facile. But the poem (if you'll still allow me to call it that) is certainly not *mixed* in any way at all; it is on one level and one note, with one idea and one image, changed and transfigured as that image may be. But any bettering in my poetry won't come at one leap; it's going to be, (or it's not going to be, according to the depths of my moods), a very slow and ugly business; the 'hangman' has still a lot of work to do, and the anatomical imagery is not yet exhausted. But one day I hope to write something altogether out of the hangman's sphere, something larger, wider, more comprehensible, and less selfcentred; one day I may even come up to *your* expectations. And if I do, if ever I do, much of the credit will belong to a delightful (I *will* say it) young woman I have never seen.

Your 'Poem' is, at least, serious and simple, with many nice words and rhymes and a lovely little hop-skip-and-jump rhythm. The sentiment is agreeable, a straightforward expression of pantheism; and one or two lines almost transcend pantheistic thought (Jesus!) and hover about on the edges of mysticism. With two such words as 'mysticism' & 'pantheism' on my tongue I could go on for hours; but I'll spare you that.

A thing I have always noticed and always admired in your verses and poems is the directness of the opening lines; there is never any beating about; you say what you have to say as quickly and as simply as possible. And you have never—as you said of me—put anything in to make it more difficult. The 'Poem' is so simple in thought and structure that it loses rather than gains by the repetition of the statement of your alliance with things as diverse as a swallow and a sod. 'Sod' when it rhymes with 'God' is, in itself, a most horrible cliché; whenever I see 'God' in line two of a bad poem I inevitably look down to line four to see how the poor old sod is dragged in there. And although this is not altogether a bad poem the too-close proximity of 'God', 'sod', 'heifer' & 'zephyr' *must* lead one to believe that the thought in which these words appear was dictated by the rhymes, and is therefore false. You started off with a very simple thought (I, for one, will never believe that the most valuable thoughts are, of necessity, simple); you confessed that you were one with the 'sparrow', and then, as a natural conclusion, went on to say that you were one with the 'arrow', too. If it comes to that, you can say you are one with the barrow as well. For you are, my dear, you certainly are. I'm not trying to be flippant; I'm merely trying to show you, by any method, how *essentially* false such writing is.

> I am one with the wind and one with the breezes,
> And one with the torrent that drowns the plain,
> I am one with the streams and one with the seas-es,
> And one with the maggot that snores in the grain.

A rhyming dictionary, a little selection of natural objects, and a halfpenny gift for stringing pretty words together, and one can write like this all day. 'My blood is drawn from the veins of the roses' is on an altogether different plane; here you have *added* to the by-now meaningless repetition of associations, and have contributed something quite lovely both to yourself and to the rose. Is this clear? It's something I'm always hammering at. The man who said, for the first time, '*I see the rose*', said nothing, but the man who said for the first time, '*The rose sees me*' uttered a very wonderful truth. There's little value in going on indefinitely saying,

> 'I am one with the steamship & one with the trolley,
> And one with the airedale & one with the collie';

there's too much 'Uncle Tom Collie & all' about that. Primarily, you see, the reader refuses to believe that *you* believe you are one with all these things; you have to prove it to him, and you most certainly won't by cataloguing a number of other things to which you *say* you are related. By the magic of words and images you must make it clear to him that the relationships are real. And only in, 'My blood is drawn from the veins of the roses', do you provide any proof. You gave the rose a human vein, and you gave your own vein the blood of the rose; now that *is* relationship. 'I am his son' means little compared with 'I am his flesh and blood.'

This is a final compression of what I want to say about the 'Poem', and what I do want you to read. As it is, the 16 lines are all separate, too separate; you could have written one, gone to sleep, woken up, and written the next. Though you talk all through of the relationship of yourself to other things, there is no relationship at all in the poem between the things you example. If you are one with the swallow & one with the rose, then the rose is one with the swallow. Link together these things you talk of; show, in your words & images, how *your* flesh covers the tree & the tree's flesh covers you. I see what you have done, of course—'I am one with the opposites', you say. You are, I know, but you must prove it to me by linking yourself to the opposites and by linking the opposites together. Only in the 'rose' line did you do it.

Is this all clear, or am I talking through my new black hat?

The Green Idyll of the Little Yellow God

Wagner moves me, too, but much in the same way as the final spectacular scene in a pantomime. I won't deny, for a moment, that he's a great composer, but his greatness lies in girth rather than in depth; it lacks humour and subtlety; he creates everything for you in a vast Cecil de Mille way; his orchestration is a perpetual 'close-up'; there is altogether too much showmanship and exhibitionism about him. His Valhalla is a very large and a very splendid place, but built in the style of a German baronial castle: the tapestries are too voluminous & highly coloured, there is too great a display of gold; while the gods that hold dominion over it are florid deities, puffed out with self-importance, wearing gaudy garments and angelic watch-chains.

You know the experience of walking through the palatial chambers at Windsor, admiring the wealth and the magnificence with an open mouth, and longing to sneak away into a small and quiet room where you can eat chips and drink mild beer in comfort. That is the experience which Wagner gives me; he reminds me of a huge and overblown profiteer, wallowing in fineries, over-exhibiting his monstrous paunch and purse, and drowning his ten-ton wife in a great orgy of jewels. Compare him with an aristocrat like Bach!

Still, I admire the way in which you admire him, and realise that it is only natural that Wagner should be one of your high gods. Whatever I can say about him, he is a big man, an overpowering man, a man with a vast personality and an overpowering voice, a dominant, arrogant, gestureful man forever in passion and turmoil over the turbulent, passionate universe. He's all that, I admit; parts of Tristan and Isolde are exquisite; and my sneers are the sneers of a pygmy at a dwarf, not even a David at a Goliath. Yes, he was bound to be the composer you admire, for the qualities (enumerated above) are the qualities that, artistically at any rate, seem to count most with you. You like the raucous, billowy, bawdy historical novel, the 'up-&-at-'em, kick-'em-in-the-belly, God's an Englishman shoutings of Mr. Kipling (though I do not, on any account, call you a hearty), the cloudy brawlings of Shelley, the virility of Washington Irving. If you like all these, how on earth do you like me—if you do? I'm little with no health at all, curled up in an old copy of the 'Funeral Gazette', sneering at the worm.

Neuburg

He didn't appear to like the poem I sent him last week; it was not very inspired, I admit, but it was so wonderfully comprehensible that I felt sure it would appeal to him. However. This week I'll send him that love poem. So your book is to be published in the spring now? Who by? And don't say you're going to call yourself Pamela Hansford Johnson; the three-name method is utterly American. If you do I shall call myself Dylan Marlais Thomas. So there!

Some Resolutions etc:

As this is the season of the year to make resolutions, I shall devote some of my time and, let it be hoped, some of yours, to the propounding of much idealistic nonsense to which it is my intention to adhere. This is such an ugly sentence that the brain naturally turns to the question of ugliness. Now there is nothing on God's earth that is, in itself, an ugly thing; it is the sickness of the mind that turns a thing sick and the dirtiness of the mind that turns a thing dirty. I do not speak of parliaments and committees, eternally ugly things, for they are composed of a collection of ugly minds; I speak of the pig and the popular conception of death. The pig is a particular animal and will eat only what is good for him; because what he eats is not good for us it does not follow that it is a messy food. The pig lies down in dung to sleep, because dung is warm and soft; he would probably think it a very dirty thing indeed to sleep on a sheet. Death is said to be ugly only because we entertain an ugly conception of the body. A live body is a building around the soul, and a dead body a building without it; without the soul a body breaks, but the broken pieces are beautiful and meaningful because the soul has made them so and has left its marks. Just as a live body has its rhythms and its pattern and its promise (promise is perhaps the greatest thing in the world), so has a dead body; and not only an abstract pattern but a physical one. A dead body promises the earth as a live body promises its mate; and the earth is our mate. Looking on one dead, we should say, Here lies beauty, for it has housed beauty, the soul being beautiful; just as, on looking on an empty house, we should say, Here stands strength (or anything else), for it has housed strength, strength being beautiful. What has this to do with a resolution? It leads me to resolve that I shall never take things for granted, but that I shall attempt to take them as they are, that nothing is ugly except what I make ugly, and that the lowest and the highest are level to the eyes of the air.

I resolve not to label the brain into separate compartments; that is, not to differentiate between what is in me that writes poetry and what is in me that says, Here comes one-o'clock; at this time I lunch. That is, again, a resolution not to differentiate between what is called rational and what is called irrational, but to attempt to create, or to let be created, one rationalism. It is said to be mad to write poetry and sane to lunch at one o'clock; but it is the other way about: Art is praise and it is sane to praise, for, praising, we praise the godliness that gives us sanity; the clock is a symbol of the limitation of time, and time is limitless: therefore it is wrong to obey the clock and right to eat not when the hands of the clock, but when the fingers of hunger, dictate. I resolve firstly to *make* poetry and, secondly, to write it; there is poetry in the hands of the clock if only I can realise that the clock is a limitation, and can express, in my poetry, the knowledge of that limitation and the knowledge of illimitability. I can learn, by such resolving, to say that nothing in this world is uninteresting. How can a thing have no interest that *is* in this world, that has the world around it, that has a past, a present & a future, that has all the associations of a million million minds engrained in it. A chunk of stone is as interesting as a cathedral, or even more interesting, for it is the cathedral in essence; it gave substance to the building of the cathedral and meaning to the meaning of the cathedral, for stones are sermons, as are all things. And if I can bring myself to know, not to think, that nothing is uninteresting, I can broaden my own outlook and believe once more, as I so passionately believed and so passionately *want* to believe, in the magic of this burning and bewildering universe, in the meaning and the power of symbols, in the miracle of myself & of all mortals, in the divinity that is so near us and so longing to be nearer, in the staggering, bloody, starry wonder of the sky I can see above and the sky I can think of below. When I learn that the stars I see *there* may be but the backs of the stars I see *there*, I am filled with the terror which is the beginning of love. They tell me space is endless and space curves. And I understand.

And now that I am started I can't stop; I've saddled a bright horse, and his brightness, not his body, keeps me bouncing up and down like a rubber star on his back. I have never raved to you before for as long as this, have I? But it really is a natural raving. Before one gets to a truth in one's own mind one has to cut through so many crusts of self-hypocrisy and doubt, self bluff and hypnotism; the polishing of phrases rubs off the sharp madness of the words and leaves only their blunt sanity. Here I am writing naturally; take it or leave it; this stream is yours if you want it, and can go on for as long as the teeth hold in the gums, for as long as (any image will do) the hairs of your head are as sweet as the ropes that hang down from the hands of the sky, hanging down to be pulled at—if one had the strength.

And to begin, I want to believe in dragons, not the windy, tank-like creature who quarrelled with St. George, but the vast and fiery legend, bearing half a planet on its shoulders, with hell in its nostrils and heaven in its scales, with a comet in the steaming socket of its eye, with a couple of dragon-lets at its side, with a grandmother at home knitting unbelievably large socks and finding counties in her hair.

I want to imagine a new colour, so much whiter than white that white is black.

I want to forget all that I have ever written and start again, informed with a new wonder, empty of all my old dreariness, and rid of the sophistication which is disease. How can I ever lie on my belly on the floor, turning a narrow thought over and over again on the tip of my tongue, crying in my wordy wilderness, mean of spirit, brooding over the death of my finger which lies straight in front of me? How can I, when I have news to scream up to heaven, and when heaven has news to scream down to me? I want to read the headlines in the sky: birth of a star, death of a comet. I want to believe, to believe forever, that heaven is *being*, a state of being, and that the only hell is the hell of myself. I want to burn hell with its own flames.

No, but my wants are not all cloudy as that; I want to live and love & be loved; I want to praise and be praised; I want to sleep and wake, and look upon my sleeping as only another waking; I want to live and die.

We don't worship nature; nature is what we wish it and worships us; we stop the sun, we tell the sun to go on.

'The universe is wild and full of marvels.' In the shape of a boy, and a funny boy at that, I have only a very short time to learn how mad and marvellous it is; I think in cells; one day I may think in rains. All around us, now and forever, a spirit is bearing and killing and resurrecting a body; I care not a damn for Christ, but only for his symbol, the symbol of death. But suicide is wrong; a man who commits suicide is like a man who longs for a gate to be opened and who cuts his throat before he reaches the gate.

There is an imp in your room, looking with my eyes at you.

Finale: the Hat talks

There is a foghorn crying out to the ships in the Bristol Channel as an albatross might have cried to the ancient mariner, over Shakespeare's multitudinous ocean on a deep, dark night. I should like to be somewhere very wet, preferably under the sea, green as a merman, with cyclamen crabs on my shoulders, and the skeleton of a commercial magnate floating, Desdemona-wise, past me; but I should like to be very much alive under the sea, so that the moon, shining through the crusts of the waves, would be a beautiful pea-green.

I am very often—especially in such fantastic frames of mind as have entertained me during the last few days—convinced that the angle of man is necessarily inconducive to the higher thoughts. Walking, as we do, at right angles with the earth, we are prevented from looking, as much as we should, at the legendary sky above us and the only-a-little-bit-more-possible ground under us. We can only (without effort) look in front of us and around us; we can look only at things that are between the earth and sky, and are much in the position of a reader of books who can look only at the middles of pages and never (without effort) at the tops and bottoms. We see what we imagine to be a tree, but we see only a part of the tree; what the insects under the earth see when they look upwards at the tree, & what the stars see when they look downwards at the tree, is left to our imagination. And perhaps the materialist can be called the man who believes only in the part of the tree he sees, & the spiritualist a man who believes in a lot more of the tree than is within his sight. Think how much wiser we would be if it were possible for us to change our angles of perspective as regularly as we change our vests: a certain period would be spent in propelling ourselves along on our backs, in order to see the sky properly and all the time; and another period in drifting belly-downwards through the air, in order to see the earth. As it is, this perpetual right-angle of ours leads to a prejudiced vision. Probably this was the divine plan, anyway; but I certainly intend to spend more time lying on my back, and will even, if circumstances permit, follow Mr. Chesterton's admirable advice, and spend as much time as possible standing on my head.

And so, for the present, I leave you, a short, ambiguous person in a runcible hat, feeling very lost in a big and magic universe, wishing you love and a healthy new year.

Dylan

MS: Buffalo   *SL*

PAMELA HANSFORD JOHNSON
[early January 1934][1] [fragment]

It's a very bad sign when I have to put a little prologue before each letter, and it's some sort of a sign, too, that the letters are becoming heavier. But I don't know whether that's good or bad: it's O.K. by me.

The only reason for this prologue is: I'm sorry, but this isn't a particularly good letter; it's altogether too dogmatic & argumentative; and, reading it through after I'd finished copying the damned thing out, I confess it bored me stiff. Little scraps of it may not be dull as the rest, though: I advise you to find those little scraps, read them, & skip all the rest.

How the last 'Mutter' came to be included in an otherwise sane (too bloody sane & dull, that's the trouble) letter I really don't know; you'll have to pardon that, too.

My next letter, I promise, will be full of beans & epigrams, a highly journalistic affair with a couple of funny stories & a drawing.

Incidentally—a very important incident, too—I don't need to have any maternal low-down on you; I know a young man who has met you & didn't like you. So there, ikkle Pam! Smile that off! I have you now on both hips! Three chairs for the mayor! Here's a toast to the invisible

---

[1] This 'prologue' probably belongs to the next letter. Johnson wrote in her diary on January 10: 'Long fulminating letter from Dylan giving the intriguing information that he'd met someone who knew & disliked me!' The 'someone' was Daniel Jones, who had found his way to Neuburg country, and in summer 1933 visited Steyning. Jones met Johnson there, 'and, I'm afraid', he wrote in 1977, 'was rather rude about her poems.'

Pamela, now done dirt on by a friend of mine! Lift your glasses! Donk your schnozzles, boys, as Florence Nightingale once remarked.

Dylan

!! PROLOGUE !!

MS: Buffalo

PAMELA HANSFORD JOHNSON
[?early January 1934] [incomplete]   Swansea

Night and Day: A Provincial Rhythm

At half past nine there is a slight stirring in the Thomas body, an eyelid quivers, a limb trembles. At a quarter to ten, or thereabouts, breakfast, consisting of an apple, an orange, and a banana, is brought to the side of the bed and left there along with the Daily Telegraph. Some five minutes later the body raises itself, looks blindly around it, and, stretching out a weak arm, lifts the apple to its mouth. Waking is achieved between bites, and, over the now more-or-less clear scrutiny of the fruit, the webs of the last night dreams are remembered and disentangled. Then, still weakly but with increasing certainty of touch, the banana is peeled and the newspaper opened. At the last bite I have taken complete possession of the Thomas body, and read the criminal court cases on page three with great concentration. The orange, incidentally, is never touched until I get downstairs, the process of peeling and pipping being too cold and lengthy for such an hour of the morning. When the reports of rapes, frauds, and murders have been thoroughly digested, I light a cigarette, very slowly lay my head back on the pillow, and then, without any warning, leap suddenly out of bed, tear off my pyjamas, scramble into a vest and trousers, and run, as if the fiends of winter were at my heels, into the bathroom. There, holding the cigarette, I scrape the beard from my face and dab about with a futile sponge. And then downstairs where, after another cigarette, I seat myself in front of the fire and commence to read, to read anything that is near, poetry or prose, translations out of the Greek or the Film Pictorial, a new novel from Smith's, a new book of criticism, or an old favourite like Grimm or George Herbert, anything in the world so long as it is printed. I read on until twelve or thereabouts, when perhaps I have read quarter of a novel, a couple of poems, a short story, an article on the keeping of bees in Upper Silesia, and a review by somebody I have never heard of on a play I never want to see. Then down the hill into the Uplands—a lowland collection of crossroads and shops, for one (or perhaps two) pints of beer in the Uplands Hotel. Then home for lunch. After lunch, I retire again to the fire where perhaps I shall read all the afternoon—and read a great deal of everything, or continue on a poem or a story I have left unfinished, or to start another or to start drafting another, or to add a note to a letter to you, or to type something already completed, or merely to write—to write anything, just to let the words and ideas, the half remembered half forgotten images, tumble on the sheets of paper. Or perhaps I go out, & spend the afternoon in walking alone over the very desolate Gower cliffs, communing with the cold and the quietness. I call this taking my devils for an airing. This takes me to tea-time. After tea I read or write again, as haphazardly as before, until six-o-clock. I then go to Mumbles (remember the women of Mumbles Head),[1] a rather nice village, despite its name, right on the edge of the sea. First I call at the Marine, then the Antelope, and then the Mermaid. If there is a rehearsal I leave these at eight o'clock and find my way to the Little Theatre, conveniently situated between the Mermaid and the Antelope. If there is no rehearsal, I continue to commune with these two legendary creatures, and, more often than not, to conduct metaphysical arguments with a Chestertonian toper, (last night it was 'Existence or Being'), who apparently makes a good living out of designing scanty and dirty costumes for provincial revues. Then a three mile walk home to supper and perhaps more reading, to bed and certainly more writing. Thus drifts an average day. Not a very British day. Too much thinkin', too much talkin', too much alcohol.

We are both slaves to habit. I do not think that either of us are wide, and can never expect to be wide poets, (though, doubtlessly, you are a little wider physically than I am). We both have to concentrate on depth.

Another average day, recorded above, has passed. I am sitting up in bed, none too sober, with a blank sheet of paper on the eiderdown in front of me. But no words will come. The paper is covered with a divinity of thoughts, but it is as naked as the hand that holds it. The smoke of my cigarette reminds me of a lot of things.

I am going to put out the light, and think vain and absurd and never-to-be things until I fall to sleep.

Chestnut Saturday

Very unfortunately your mirth-provoking story of the mental Don Juan was familiar to me (and why my English doesn't permit me to say, 'I know the story about the man in the pub', I can't imagine). My best story is the very long one, spoken in the broadest of Welsh accents, about Marged Ann and the Vicar, but it's very vulgar and I'm afraid it loses nearly all the little point it has if it's written down. I'll keep that as a special treat to tell you, though again I can't imagine why it should be a special treat for you to hear a bawdy story told by a small Welshman in Anglo-Welsh.

Just A Thought

Every thinking man—that is, every man who builds up, on a structure of tradition, the seeds of his own revolution—and every artist—that is,

[1] 'The Women of Mumbles Head' is a lugubrious poem by Clement Scott about an incident of 1883, when the lighthouse-keeper's daughters saved a drowning sailor.

every man who expresses this revolution through an artistic medium —
gradually form a series of laws for living, which he may or may not adhere
to. Those laws are brought about slowly in the individual mind, are
fostered by mental and physical experience. They do not enter the brain
as laws but as the raw matter for thought; it is the brain that explores
them, finds what is worthy in them, and then dogmatises them. And this
is only right. I have theories on the art of poetry, and these theories—as
you know, my poor sufferer of so much of my theoretical nonsense—are
obviously dogmatic. Those theories entered the brain as impressions. On
reading Wordsworth, I was given the impression that, although he talked
of mysticism, he was not a mystic but only a moraliser. Later I stabilised
this impression as a dogma, or rather as two dogmas: Morals are the
imposed trimmings around *inherent* doubt, and: A mystic is a man who
takes things literally. All theories are made in that way. And that, too, is
only right, for by this method alone can the individual have any hand in
the shaping of his own spiritual & mental life. I dislike meat, I dislike
killing, therefore I make my own law: It is wrong to eat meat. Thus all
the laws in the world have been made. The words Jesus said were only his
impressions erected into laws. Rémy de Gourmont has called such an
erection the principle of criticism, and, here again, I am in agreement, for
Jesus was himself a critic more than anything else; he was given God to
read, he read God, understood Him, appreciated Him, and then, stern in
his duty as a critic, decided it was his mission in life to explain the
meaning of God to his fellows.

God is the country of the spirit, and each of us is given a little holding
of ground in that country; it is our duty to explore that holding, to gain
certain impressions by such exploring, to stabilise as laws the most
valuable of these impressions, and, as far as we can, to abide by them. It is
our duty to criticise, for criticism is the personal explanation of
appreciation. Though a man may hate the world he still appreciates it,
and his hate is as valuable as my love; he may hate it for its madness, as I
love it for that; he may hate the whole of humanity as I hate the social
system that is pulling it to buggery; he may hate pain, as I believe in pain.
But we are both critics of life, however misguided. The man who hates &
the man who loves are all right; but there is no room in the country of the
spirit for the man who accepts, or does not accept, without hate or love.

Hate and love, after all, are nearly one; a blow can be a kiss out of
heaven, and a kiss a blow out of hell.

I am writing this at the window. Outside in the cold I see the structure
of the sky. Yes, the structure of the sky, the vast grey erection from the
edge of here to the edge of nowhere. Yes, the erection of the sky, for the
sky is no more than a godly dogma made out of a heavenly impression.

'And if thou wilt, remember,
And if thou wilt, forget.'

Your latest poem has made one thing certain to me: your alliance with the PreRaphaelite school of poets and with Christina Rossetti, the best PreRaphaelite of the whole bunch, in particular. But perhaps you will take the word 'alliance' uncomplimentarily, so let me suggest—and this is most certainly a compliment—that you are the only writer I know to-day who can be said to be in the true PreRaphaelite descent. Again, this is not to say that anything in your work is not your own, for, above all, it is a personal expression; but the merits of that particular, unfashionable, and mis-judged school are shown very clearly in your poems. And, added to those merits, is your own undeniable gusto (a word I hope you won't take exception to), your joy in living and in expressing, and your continual fecundity of natural emotions. Your verse is narrow, but it seems to be a deliberate narrowness, and does not destroy any of its intensity. It is, I am sure, in increased subtlety and elusiveness that you are certain to develop. Christina Rossetti is too little known, [except] by some of her moralistic verses; she had a most delicate command of rhythm, as you have when you take the trouble, a delicate sense of the sounds of words, and a highly competent technical ability which never appeared laboured because of its simplicity; you have all those, too. But it is her perspective of life that interests me most: sweet, small, & narrow, delicate to the point of elusion. Those are four of your qualities, but whereas she was so often caught in semi-theological arguments, was probably too virginal to look at herself in the mirror, and was, on her own admission, disgusted by the sound of laughter, you have a startling sense of humour (I'm not piling on compliments, please, I'm trying to make some sort of a valuation), and a vitality which that other very charming lady never possessed. Walter de la Mare owes much to Christina, and, if there is any labelling to be done, I would put you & de la Mare, that questioning poet, in the same compartment & mark it 'Subtlety and Sensitivity. Perishable. With Care.' You are young, young enough to become subtler and more sensitive, to trust your own sense of harmony much further, and to produce poetry that will stand out far above the singing of even the best lyricists of to-day.

I do not think 'The King Dies' is a good poem, but it is a promising poem; it is not subtle enough, either in rhythm or in the play of vowels; but it is a poem in what I consider to be the right direction for you; it points towards the progress that you are bound to make. I prefer you when you are more personal than this, when you have no guiding thought behind you, but rather when you are in the process of selection—selecting your images to suit your particular moods, selecting your *thoughts* to fit those *images*. The substance of your poetry is always slight, and in 'The King Dies' the slightness is too little redeemed by subtlety of expression. I don't think there is any necessity for me to go into it in detail; all I have to say I've said in this note, and I may appear to have said nothing. That is why I very modestly prefaced the note with a quotation from the Rossetti itself.

Leave the lambkins alone, or never, at least, use them unless you can then take them literally, that is rid of all their associations, or unless you can build new & worth-while associations around 'em. But don't worry about that at the moment; go on writing but more carefully still; submit every syllable to a thorough test; never be afraid of subtlety, even though it may lead you to obscurity (dangerous advice to some, but not to you). And show me all you write.

A Complaint

This method of letter writing, this selection of odd notes, is very satisfying, but it's a swine in some ways. I write the notes for my letters to you at odd times & in pencil on bits of paper. It takes me a hell of a time to copy them all out on these mammoth sheets.

Put this in your Pipe — and if you haven't got one, I'll lend you mine; it reeks.

Ha, child, I was as crafty as you. I confess that my reference to your love of Kipling was no more than a highly titivating bait. Of course you don't like his flagflapping, for you know as well as I do that patriotism is a publicity ramp organised by holders of excess armament shares; you know that the Union Jack is only a national loin-cloth to hide the decaying organs of a diseased social system; you know that the Great War was purposely protracted in order for financiers to make more money; that had it not been for the shares in the armament firms the War would have ended in three weeks; that at one period of the War French and German were shelling each other with ammunition provided by the same firm, a firm in which English clergymen and politicians, French ambassadors and German business men, all had a great deal of money invested; that Kipling, rejected by the army because of weak physique, is nevertheless a 'I gave my son' militarist; that the country which he lauds and eulogises is a country that supports a system by which men are starved, and fish, wheat and coffee are burnt by the hundreds of tons; a system by which men are not allowed to work, to marry, to have children; by which they are driven mad daily; by which children are brought into the world scrofulous; by which the church is allowed to prevent the prevention of sexual diseases; a system so just that a man is arrested on Christmas Day for arrears of rates, when his wife is expecting a baby & his children are dying of typhoid fever caused through the eating of bad fish supplied by a profiteering tradesman. Woah! England, my England. And Kipling still flaps his belly for it, and it is easier to bribe a politician than it is to bribe a costermonger.

And what's all this about the 'delicacy of a silver-point drawing' in the five weak lines you quoted from 'The Way Through the Wood'.[1]

MS: Buffalo   *SL(R)*

---

[1] The surviving MS ends here. *SL* mistakenly adds the section headed 'A Story For the Very Young' which can be dated 5 November 1933.

TREVOR HUGHES
[early January 1934][1]

Ever since I left you alone on the deserted railway platform, waving a last, forlorn handkerchief as the train rushed me onwards to Chelsea and Sir Richard Rees, I have been meaning to write you a long letter. Sometimes the monstrous shape of the Rayner's Lane illuminated sign[2] has risen up in my dreams like the advertisement of my conscience, and I have sworn to jump out of bed the next morning, grab pencil and paper, and write until darkness fell again upon the emptiness of Wales with an accustomed clatter. But the mornings have been cold, the pencil has not been near enough, the paper has been too virgin to deflower, and my own incorrigible laziness has made me postpone, time upon time, the pleasure of continuing our correspondence. Once I can start, then everything's all right; the words, God knows, come easily enough, too easily for some as I will tell you later. But the inspiration to begin has not knocked in the blood nor fingered the fingers. Now—with divine help—this letter can go on for some time. I was with you in September; now Christmas has gone, and the only letters between us during that period have been short and almost business-like in tone. Did I thank you for sending back my story? I know I never sent the new poems as I promised. Let this be my repentance, and may I join you, if only for a little while, in your single wilderness.

You seem no cheerier than when I last saw you, and indeed I would be surprised if you were. Living in Metroland with a crippled mother—and please don't imagine for a moment that these words are flippant in any way—is not conducive to the Higher Optimism, nor, in the midst of such respectability and subservience to the office clock, to the unrespectable creation of literature. I remember advising you to climb out of your morbidity, little realising then, perhaps, that you were not the Jonah swallowed by your own whale, but the whale—I have faith in your ability to write—swallowed by the Jonah of circumstance. And either this is a deeper tortuity than it appears, or it has no meaning at all. Now I understand a little, but only a little, of the circumstance that has played so hard with you, and if it has not swallowed me it is because of my self-centredness, my islandic egoism which allows few of the day's waves to touch it. Soon after I left you, my father went to the University College Hospital to be operated upon for cancer of the throat; today he went back to school, weak and uncured. And only a little while ago I learnt the truth of my own health. But the statement of Dad's disease and the warning of mine have left me horridly unmoved; I become a greater introvert day by day, though, day by day again, I am conscious of more external wonders in the world. It is my aim as an artist—that, too, has been denied, but not by the pontifical Eliot—to bring those wonders into myself, to prove

[1] A letter from Hughes of 13 January 1934, at Buffalo, is probably a reply to this letter.
[2] The sign of the Underground station near Hughes's home.

beyond doubt to myself that the flesh that covers me is the flesh that covers the sun, that the blood in my lungs is the blood that goes up and down in a tree. It is the simplicity of religion. Artists, as far as I can gather, have set out, however unconsciously, to prove one of two things: either that they are mad in a sane world, or that they are sane in a mad world. It has been given to few to make a perfect fusion of madness and sanity, and all is sane except what we make mad, and all is mad except what we make sane.

No, the great Eliot has not damned me, but he has been cautious. Rees, on the other hand, though printing two poems of mine and taking a peculiar interest in all I write, has made one very startling accusation: that much of what I write is not written consciously, that any talent I may have is clairvoyant, and my fecundity is accounted for by 'automatic writing'. Charles Williams of the Oxford University Press, and author, as you know, of several mystic books,[1] has read many of my poems but confesses that he does not understand them; they cannot be 'pooh- poohed' but he could not say that he liked them. And so we go on, meeting nothing but courtesy and interest, and nothing but a rather bewildered refusal to print. I am sending you a few recent poems to criticize, not in the pedantic way of the professors but by your own and far more valuable methods. Be as honest as I am with you. They are, I admit, unpretty things, with their imagery almost totally anatomical. But I defend the diction, the perhaps wearisome succession of blood and bones, the neverending similes of the streams in the veins and the lights in the eyes, by saying that, for the time at least, I realise that it is impossible for me to raise myself to the altitude of the stars, and that I am forced, therefore, to bring down the stars to my own level and to incorporate them in my own physical universe.

Prose and Verse is a sad story, and postponed as often as my letter. Only a little while ago it was budding into light, creeping up even through my lethargy; now it has sunk down again, and is no more than a legend for old men to tell their children: Once upon a time there was a boy who had Literary Pretensions, not only for himself but also for those of his friends who, too, burdened the editors of England with their sad expostulations. And the boy decided to produce a periodical in which he himself and the other unfortunate young men might express the vicissitudes of their spirits in great detail; he advertised it and interested in it many of the leading Intellectuals of his Philistine town. But something happened; one friend went to London, and another to a university, both very big and bewildering places, while the boy was left with a few equally bewildering contributions upon his hands. Time passed, and a new Intellectual arose who, hearing of the boy's frustrated plans, resolved to see that, at long last, those plans should come to fruition. Again something happened, or, to tell the truth, two things happened, and one was the fault of the boy and the other was the fault of the intellectual.

[1] Charles Williams (1886–1945) wrote poetry and criticism as well as supernatural thrillers.

The boy, very suddenly, became disgusted with the mental disease of his country, the warped apathy of his countrymen, and of the essentially freakish nature of himself. And the Intellectual became lazy. So again the periodical was buried under the mists of the mind, and again were the boy's friends done dirt on. But one day 'Prose and Verse' will arise in all its splendour, and be published not out of the bowels of dirty Wales but from the heart of the metropolis. And he and his friends will be older and wiser, and their contributions may even be better than they were before. Yes, 'Prose and Verse' is buried but not forgotten. It shall be published, that I promise. And that some of it, at least, shall be good, you yourself shall see to.

It may be a day or two before this letter is completed for, intent as I am upon writing it, I seem to become busier with every new idle day. In the mornings and afternoons I find I have more and more to write, and the fact that what I write may be valueless does not alter the fact of the time it takes; my evenings are given to rehearsals and performances at the Little Theatre, or to the steady but increasingly copious sinking of drink. Remember, too, that the scrappiness of this letter is owing entirely to the odd minutes I am devoting to it, and not, as it might appear, to such a startlingly untidy brain.

This new year has brought back to my mind the sense of magic that was lost—irretrievably, I thought—so long ago. I am conscious, if not of the probability of the impossible, at least of its possibility, and the paradox has clothed itself like a fairy. It needed courage to say that 'like a fairy', for the young pantomime ladies, gallivanting in gossamer nudity, have robbed the fairy of all but her woman's body. A fairy is not supernatural; she is the most natural thing in the world. How much easier it is to believe in her, in her magnificent transformations, in her wings and wonder, than it is to believe in the invulnerability of the pope, the genius of Bernard Shaw, and the Loch Ness monster. Not that I doubt the existence of the latter, but those who see him look upon him wrongly. A man who perceives a particularly unbelievable sunrise or sunset does not phone the news to the papers; if he sees—as all of us have seen—a firebreathing centaur in the shapes of the clouds he does not take a photograph of it so that his friends might be impressed with its reality. He says, Very wonderful, and he goes on his way. So it should be with the monster in the Loch; the villagers should see it, if it is to be seen, remark upon the legendary curves of its trunk and the horns on its head, then go home quietly to their beds. 'I saw the monster,' they would say to their wives. 'Go on, do you believe that?' 'I don't know about believing it,' would be the reply, 'But I saw it all right, and very unbelievable it was.' There the matter would drop.

Superstition is a moral vice, but a man who believes in the supernatural is a man who takes things literally. It is the aim of the church—that embodiment of a medieval moral—to do away with man's sense of the literal. How much better to say that God is big than that he is 'all-pervading'.

There is no vice (a deliberate contradiction); what we know as vices are social crimes; it is the fault of society that it will not adjust itself so as to make those crimes either uncriminal or unthinkable. But society to adjust itself has to break itself; society should accommodate man, not hinder him; but it has grown up rotten with its capitalist child, and only revolutionary socialism can clean it up. Capitalism is a system made for a time of scarcity, and the truth of today is the truth of fertility. All that renounces fertility is a lie.

The trouble, of course, with preoccupation with the roots and the substance of magic is the frequency with which the devil and his forked apprentices inhabit the mind of the believer; despondency can so easily be put down, not to an organic disturbance or to self-insufficiency or to a misanthropic philosophy, but to the bedevilled paradoxes of the brain; the faults in oneself can be too easily blamed on the things that go squawk in the night; Satanism is too easy a synonym for sadism. The most terrifying figure in history is, to me, the French abbé who became, through some sexual stringency or latitude, a connoisseur of the grave and a worshipper of his sister Worm. He would not lie with a woman unless she dressed herself in a shroud, painted her face as the face of a corpse, and lay as stiff and unbreathing as though she were in the clasp of her last lover. The abbé was probably a gentleman and kind to dogs, but his view on the living was through the lenses of the dead—there is a delightful image somewhere which pictures each blade of grass as the periscope of a dead man—and this, despite my own morbid system of aesthetics, strikes me as an unpardonable fault. The most beautiful thing in the world to Poe was a woman dead; Poe is not to be challenged on the grounds of taste but on those of accuracy, for a woman dead is not a woman at all, the spirit that made her a woman being fled and already metamorphosed. To love a dead woman does not appear to me to be necessarily unhealthy, but it is a love too onesided to be pure. Love is onesided, I admit, for it lies more in what you put into a woman—and for once I am not speaking anatomically—than in what you take out of her. The cynic would say that it is the other way about; but then the cynic is a dead man, and, despite the fact that I consider paganism to be the most evil of doctrines, the body was given to live as much as the stars were given to live up to.

You said once in one of your valuable letters that still, incidentally have a prominent place on my desk, that your troubles at my age encompassed the whole of womanhood, while mine—little toper that I am bound to become—could be circled by the limits of a half pint measure. While disagreeing thoroughly that my adolescent troubles could be confined to a short and bewildered acquaintance with drink, I confess that woman as a generalisation, even as a physical generalisation, has never worried me at all. The actual leaping in my blood has always been caused through the memory of, or the contact with, some particular and actual person. It is also my pleasure or misfortune to confess to a lean and suspicious creator of pathological literature that I am in love. What is more it [is] not an unnaturally onesided love. Laugh as much as you like, though I don't think you will. Will you?

Have you been reading as much as usual, or has that hindered inspiration of yours at last burst out of the womb of the pen? I am looking forward to the reading of your promised story, and am hoping, too, that you are satisfied with it. You know your own faults as well as I know my own, and while I am spending more and more time on the shapes of paragraphs, the slow formation of sentences, and the deletion of commas, it would still be probably advisable for you to spend less and less time on remodelling and more on the redhot creation of your prose. Much is against you, I know, but I find it hard to say whether adverse circumstances are a hindrance or not. The best in a man comes out in suffering; there is a prophet in pain, and an oracle in the agony of the mind. Such things are easy to say; it is easier to recognize the prophet than to heed him; if only I could say with Blake, Death to me is no more than going into another room. How easy, too, it is to say that; there is as much charlatanism in a poet as there is in an astrologer, and it may be that the genuineness and the value of the one is the genuineness and the value of the other; both have a love and an awe of the miraculous world, and both are conscious of horizons.

Does one need 'New styles of architecture, a change of heart'? Does one not need a new consciousness of the old universal architecture and a tearing away from the old heart of the things that have clogged it? Still our minds are hovering too much about our testicles, complaining

> . . . In delicate and exhausted metres
> That the twitching of three abdominal nerves
> Is incapable of producing a lasting Nirvana.

We look upon a thing a thousand times; perhaps we shall have to look upon it a million times before we see it for the first time. Centuries of problematical progress have blinded us to the literal world; each bright and naked object is shrouded around with a thick, peasoup mist of associations; no single word in all our poetical vocabulary is a virgin word, ready for our first love, willing to be what we make it. Each word has been wooed and gotten by a vast procession of dead littérateurs who put their coins in the plate of a procuring Muse, entered at the brothel doors of a divine language, and whored the syllables of Milton and the Bible.

But consciousness of such prostitution need not lead us, as it has led James Joyce, into the inventing of new words; it need not make us, as it has made Gertrude Stein, repeat our simplicities over and over again in intricate and abstract patterns so that the meaning shall be lost and only the bare and beautiful shells of the words remain. All we need do is to rid our minds of the humbug of words, to scorn the prearranged leaping together of words, to make by our own judicious and, let it be prayed for, artistic selection, new associations for each word. Each word should be a basin for us to cough into, to cough our individual diseases, and not a vessel full already of others' and past diseases for us to play about with as a juggler plays with puddings.

> Stands Harrow steeple where it did
> When Horace Vachell[1] was a kid?
> And does the Sign stand like a sinner?
> And is there still too much for dinner?
> Lie my old poems unremoved?
> And is your mother's health improved?
> And other questions I've no time
> Or inclination, too, to rhyme,
> And questions better left unsaid
> Till next I sleep in Trevor's bed.

Now the sooner you write the sooner I shall reply—and I certainly want to—and the more of your work you send me the more shall I be pleased. Write as much as you like, or even more, and I promise that my next letter will be longer than this one and will have much more to say. I hope to be coming up to stay with my sister in the next three or four weeks; no definite date is arranged yet, but I'll let you know as soon as it is; and, if nothing else, we can spend a few hours together in the Fitzroy Tavern.[2] But I hope I'll be able to see you longer than that.

Goodbye and God bless you.

Dylan

MS: Buffalo   *SL*

PAMELA HANSFORD JOHNSON
[January 1934] [A comic one-act play. See Appendix A, letter No. 1.[3]]

PAMELA HANSFORD JOHNSON
[January 1934][4] [fragment]

Epilogue

I shall be coming up to stay with my sister during the next few weeks, but

---

[1] Horace Vachell (1861–1955), novelist.
[2] The Fitzroy Tavern in Charlotte Street, then a landmark for London's bohemians, gave the 'Fitzrovia' district its rather self-conscious name.
[3] Subsequent cross-references to the full version of these 'incidental' letters are all to Appendix A, and give only the identifying number (as, 'Appendix 2', 'Appendix 3' etc).
[4] Probably sent with the 'comic play'. Johnson wrote in her diary on January 17: 'Darling letter—in play form—from Dylan who is coming up soon!' Their first meeting was on Friday 23 February 1934.

the sister is merely an excuse. There are only two reasons for my visit: one is to see you, & the other is to look for a job. I have suddenly decided that I must earn money. If not I shall very soon be on the streets. I am going to look for a job in a publisher's office, though God knows what I have to offer any publisher in return for a living wage.

I hope I won't cut my throat before this reaches you. If I do cut it, I shall start with a meat-saw at the side & cut through & through till my head is hanging down my back.

MS: Buffalo

PAMELA HANSFORD JOHNSON
[?1934] [fragment]

For some forsaken reason someone I have never heard of—Professor Somebody—has written a long article about me. Most of it deals with the fact that I am a better actor than Irving and a greater orator than Disraeli. The excerpts I send you show that I'm a greater poet than Blake.

That article is apt to do an awful lot of harm. I'll be jeered at even more. 'Relating the elemental forces of Earth, Humanity, & the Universe'. 'My philosophy'. Jesus!!

I'm sending it to you to show that someone thinks I *am* good; what if he is nuts? That doesn't matter.

MS: Buffalo

PAMELA HANSFORD JOHNSON
[?1934] [fragment][1]

But enough of this. It sounds, and is not, an alcoholic remorse, the self-pity of gin, the result of constipation. Let me talk to you of rats, or rather of *a* rat with whom I have become acquainted. I was sitting in the porch of the Pwlldu Inn on a cold, sunny afternoon, eating an unnaturally large

---

[1] The MS is not at Buffalo with its companions. Pamela Hansford Johnson must have had it in 1953—which was before she disposed of her Thomas letters—because she wanted to use it in a valedictory article she was writing about Thomas for the magazine *Adam*. She described it when she wrote to the Dylan Thomas Trustees (5 December 1953), saying it was 'an excerpt from a letter'. The Trustees refused permission to publish. In 1965 it was quoted in FitzGibbon's biography of Thomas, and in 1969 appeared in *Dylan Thomas. Twelve More Letters* (Turret Books, copyright of letters retained by the Thomas Trust). Edward Lucie-Smith, who edited *Twelve More Letters*, doesn't know where the Giant Rat letter is now. Nor does anyone else.

sandwich and sipping at a quart mug—both sandwich and mug were almost as large as me. In the midst of my meal I heard a loud stamping (that is the only honest word to describe it), and, looking up, saw a rat standing immediately in front of me, his eyes fixed on mine. A rat? This was a rat with a capital R, a vast iron-gray animal as big as a big cat, with long, drooping white whiskers and a tail like an old frayed whip. Normally I am frightened to death by rats, even by mice, and certainly by moths, but this monstrosity of a creature did not alarm me at all. He couldn't move quickly anyway, he was much too fat. He merely stood there in front of me until I threw him a piece of cheese. He sniffed it, swallowed it, and stamped away. Again 'stamped' is the only word: he went away like a fat old soldier from a canteen. Thinking of him when he had gone, I came to the conclusion that he must be the Father of all Rats, the First Rat, the Rat Progenitive, the Rat Divine.

Only source: Twelve More Letters

GLYN JONES

Glyn Jones (b. 1905), poet and novelist in English, although brought up in a Welsh-speaking household, was a Cardiff schoolmaster when he read Thomas's poem 'The Woman Speaks' in the *Adelphi*, March 1934.

[March 1934]   5 Cwmdonkin Drive Uplands Swansea

Thank you for your appreciation of my *two* poems in the Adelphi. The 'Woman Speaks' but the young man writes, and your doubt as to my sex was quite complimentary, proving (or was it merely my uncommon name?) that I do not employ too masculine a pen.

You ask me to tell you about myself, but my life is so uneventful it is not worth recording. I am a writer of poems and stories (a story of mine is appearing in the Adelphi quite soon)[1] who is trying—quite vainly—to dispute Murry's contention that the object, in which the artist experiences the joy of losing himself, is no longer a recognised exchange for bread-and-butter, shelter, light, and warmth. On the economic level, I have no function.

At the moment I am attempting to form an anthology of English poems and stories written by contemporary Welshmen. So far I have decided nothing definite; but if, sometime in the near future, you wish to contribute to this anthology, I should be delighted to see some of your work. What is this 'Tiger Bay'?[2] Prose or poetry?

If you are ever in Swansea, do call up here. I shall be very pleased to see

[1] 'The Tree', published December 1934.
[2] A poem by Glyn Jones, published in the *Adelphi* under a pseudonym in April 1934. Tiger
. Bay was the cosmopolitan docks district of Cardiff.

you. And if you have half an hour to spare, then I hope you'll send me along a letter.

Dylan Thomas

MS: Carbondale

GLYN JONES
[about March 14 1934]   5 Cwmdonkin Drive Uplands Swansea

If you are not coming to Swansea for some time, why not send me a few of your poems—poems, preferably, that have not been published? If possible, I want only unpublished material for my anthology which, with the grace of God, may be brought out sometime this year. You needn't worry about the poems that I shall accept; W. H. Davies, and all his little nancy parasites, are banned. I don't care so much about the 'hardness' and the 'stiffness' of the poems, so long as they are, in the best sense, modern, and so long as there has been a genuine necessity for writing them. As a matter of fact, I hope that some good 'fluid' verse will find its way to me. There seems to be an aversion today to poems which flow quite evenly along the pages; readers are always looking for knobbly, gristly bits of conflict in modern poems, apparently not realising that a poem can express the most complex of conflicts and yet show none of the actual conflicting gristle. I would really like to see some of the things you write. Are you—I hope you aren't—an admirer of Grigson's 'New Verse', and of the (usually) unutterable bosh that Ross-Williamson prints in his 'Bookman'.[1] You are, I suppose, a good Socialist. As a Socialist myself, though a very unconventional one, I like to read good propaganda, but the most recent poems of Auden and Day-Lewis seem to me to be neither good poetry nor propaganda. A good propagandist needs little intellectual appeal; and the emotional appeal in Auden wouldn't raise a corresponding emotion in a tick. Are you obscure? But, yes, all good modern poetry is bound to be obscure. Remember Eliot: 'The chief use of the "meaning" of a poem, in the ordinary sense, may be to satisfy one habit of the reader, to keep his mind diverted and quiet, while the poem does its work upon him.' And again: 'Some poets, assuming that there are other minds like their own, become impatient of this "meaning" which seems superfluous, and perceive possibilities of intensity through its elimination.' (If you know these quotations, I am sorry.) The fact that a good poem is obscure *does* mean that it is obscure to most people, and its author is therefore—contrary to his own ideas, for every poet thinks that he writes for an universal audience—appealing to a limited public. None of us today want to read poems which we can understand as easily as the

[1] Hugh Ross Williamson (1901–78), author and journalist, was trying to modernise the old-fashioned magazine *Bookman*.

front page of the Express, but we all want to get out of the poems twice as much as we ourselves put into them. It would be possible to catalogue most of the reasons for modern obscurity. Some poets, like Gertrude Stein and the French-American Transitionists of Eugene Jolas,[1] have evolved a mathematically precise method of removing the associations from words, and giving language, or attempting to give language, its *literal* sound, so that the word 'cat' becomes no more than a one-syllabled word with a hard consonantal ending; others, like Joyce, have magnified words, lengthened and animated them with contrary inferences, and built around them a vast structure of unexpected and often inexplicable associations; others, like Auden, have taken their public too much for granted, and have cut out all words that seem to themselves unnecessary, leaving their poems at the end written in an imaginative shorthand; others, again, like Rimbaud, have introduced exclusively personal symbols and associations, so that reading him and his satellites, we feel as though we were intruding into a private party in which nearly every sentence has a family meaning that escapes us; others, like Eliot, have become so aware of the huge mechanism of the past that their poems read like a scholarly conglomeration of a century's wisdom, and are difficult to follow unless we have an intimate knowledge of Dante, the Golden Bough, and the weather-reports in Sanskrit; others, like Graves and Riding,[2] have something intellectually new to inform us, and indulge in a logical game of acrostics. Then there are the Cummings,[3] so very often short, who, obsessed by the idea of form, chop up their poems into little strips and pin them horizontally, diagonally, & upside-down on the pages. My own obscurity is quite an unfashionable one, based, as it is, on a preconceived symbolism derived, (I'm afraid all this sounds very woolly and pretentious), from the cosmic significance of the human anatomy. And I think that is about enough of that.

If this letter sounds too annoyingly dogmatic, send me a picture post-card of the National Museum, will you? (I shall know what to do with it.) No, but I should like to see your work very much, not for the sake of pinning it down and labelling it like a butterfly, as I appear to have done above, but merely to enjoy, or not to enjoy, it.

Now to answer a few questions. I am in the very early twenties. I was self-educated at the local Grammar School where I did no work at all and failed all examinations. I did not go to a university. I am not unemployed for the reason that I have never been employed. I have done nothing but write, though it is only recently that I have tried to have some things published. I have had two poems in the Adelphi, several in the Sunday

---

[1] Gertrude Stein, American avant-garde writer, who lived in Paris. Eugene Jolas, a founder (in 1923) of the periodical *transition*, also in Paris; later, in 1936, it published work by Thomas.

[2] Robert Graves (b. 1895), writer. Laura Riding/Laura (Riding) Jackson (b. 1901), American poet and critic.

[3] E. E. Cummings (1894–1962), American poet, fond of typographical experiment.

Referee (a paper you should take), some stories & poems (there is one story in this week's issue) in the New English Weekly,[1] some poems in the Listener, (I have a very obscure one in this week's, too),[2] many things in an atrocious rag called the 'Herald of Wales', a poem in John O'London's, while the Adelphi, the New English Weekly & other papers including, I hope, the Criterion, are going to print some things in the fairly near future. And that's about all. Not a very formidable list. Oh, I forgot, a poem of mine was read over the wireless from London last year.[3] I believe I am going to live in London soon, but as, so far at least, no-one has offered me suitable employment, living is rather an ambiguous word. I shall probably manage to exist, and possibly to starve. Until quite recently there has been no need for me to do anything but sit, read and write (I have written a great deal, by the way), but now it is essential that I go out into the bleak and inhospitable world with my erotic manuscripts thrown over my shoulder in a sack. If you know any kind people who want a clean young man with a fairly extensive knowledge of morbid literature, a ready pen, and no responsibilities, do let me know. Oh, would the days of literary Patronage were back again!

Write me a letter, and send along some poems. Tell me about yourself. I'm too lazy to ask questions. And if you do really want an obscure poem, invest threepence on a copy of this week's Listener. Even if you don't like my poem there's a good Latin crossword.

Dylan Thomas

MS: Carbondale   *SL(R)*

STEPHEN SPENDER

In 1934 Stephen Spender (b. 1909) was a member of W. H. Auden's 'Gang' of politically minded poets with upper-middle-class backgrounds and left-wing sympathies. His first book of poems appeared that year.

[? March 1934]   5 Cwmdonkin Drive Uplands Swansea

Dear Mr. Spender,

I'm very glad you wrote and very pleased that you like the poems of mine which you have seen. I'm glad in more ways than one that you wrote to me, for I have been trying during the last few weeks to write to *you* and tell you how much I liked your last poem in New Verse. Your poems in New Verse, and the last one especially, seem to me to be by far the most valuable things that have been printed there. I hope you won't think I am saying this merely because you have been so kind about my own poems.

[1] 'After the Fair', issue dated March 15.
[2] 'Light breaks where no sun shines.' It was Thomas's first poem in the *Listener*.
[3] 'The Romantic Isle', submitted for a poetry competition, and read on the BBC's National Programme, 28 June 1933. The poem is lost.

Here, in this worst of provincial towns, I am so utterly removed from any intellectual life at all, that it is a great pleasure for me to receive even the shortest congratulatory letter. The fact that I am unemployed helps, too, to add to my natural hatred of Wales.

Mr. Grigson has asked me, through the Listener, to send him a few poems with a view to having them printed in New Verse. But I don't think he'll like what I sent him. What periodicals are there that publish the sort of verse I am trying to write? I have been printed in the Adelphi, the New English Weekly, the Listener, & the Referee. Do you know of any other papers—or rather, would it be too much trouble for you to write and tell me—which might publish my poems? This is asking rather a lot, I'm afraid. If you're too busy to write, perhaps I could see you in London when I come up next—just after Easter.

Thank you again.

Yours Sincerely,
Dylan Thomas

MS: Harvard   *SL*

T. S. ELIOT
[March 1934]   5 Cwmdonkin Drive Uplands Swansea

Dear Sir,
Some months ago I sent you a few poems for your consideration, but have heard nothing from you since. I am wondering if the poems ever reached you, or whether you have not yet had time to read them.

I enclose a return envelope.

Dylan Thomas

MS: Valerie Eliot

T. S. ELIOT
[March 1934]   5 Cwmdonkin Drive Uplands Swansea

Dear Sir,
Thank you very much for your note. I am more pleased than I can say to think that you found something to like in my poems. Most of the poems you saw were written just about two years ago, when I was eighteen, and I think that my work has improved quite a lot since then.

I will be up in town from Easter Monday, or before, until the end of the week. I wonder whether it would be possible for me to bring you some more recent poems to see?

Thank you again for your kindness.

Yours Sincerely,
Dylan Thomas

MS: Valerie Eliot

PAMELA HANSFORD JOHNSON
Round about March 21 '34

Apology & Regret

I apologise for having delayed this letter so long; usually I write my letters very quickly & then forget to post them, but this time it's quite different. I've been too ill to write, to do anything but sit fatalistically by the fire, sip Turkish tobacco out of a most exotic pipe, and scribble small conceits on the backs of postcards. Which shows you how very ill I must have been. Now I am regaining vitality, and will have to write at a hell of a speed in order that you may receive my honeyed words before the end of the week. I shall also endeavour to keep clear of the emotional element. I still regret that now famous letter with all the conviction of my murky conscience. And I do regret having hurt you, as you said, in my last outpouring. I *do* regret that letter.[1] It gives me a pain where I eat and where I sit down. And the pathos of the second folio is equally regrettable. Of course I know that nothing has, or ever can be, spoilt. Of course … I … know … of course … I … know! The sub-editor can go out of business, and the woolly reporter of the soul regain his position.

Health

The nicest thing that has ever been said to me you put at the foot of the first page of your letter. You won't remember what it was, and I'm not going to tell you. But I shall fight the Spectre of Disease with all my puny powers and grow as pinguid as your melancholy satyr himself, if only to live up to those so many words. And when at last the Great Cricketer disturbs my bails, I shall go serenely back into the Heavenly Pavilion, talking of you & Alma Mater to the enthusiastic crowd, & conscious that my Innings had not let down the prestige you so beneficently granted. This sounds like Mr. Baldwin's humour, but it's deadly true.[2] You alone know how True-Blue I really am, & what a collection of old school ties my vest conceals.

---

[1] No surviving letter fits the description. But Johnson's diary for March 8, three days after Thomas went back to Wales following their first meeting, says: 'Received letter this morning from darling Dylan telling me he loved me. Oh it *is* so difficult to reply!'

[2] Stanley Baldwin (1867–1947), Conservative politician, three times Prime Minister.

Beyond the Agates[1]

I'm so glad your pantomime was a success; it deserved to be; I, from my prophetic couch, willed that it would be so. Mind, I allow *you* a little congratulation for the success; you wrote it and acted it, I admit; but I had an awful lot to do with it, too. But why say it didn't amuse me? It struck me as being very good. It's not the sort of humour that makes me laugh uproariously & bite my neighbour's ears, but that's my fault & not yours. Wit is something entirely out of my comprehension. I can understand slap-stick, rude stories, lunacy & modern verse. And that's about all. Oscar and his little epigrams would have left me as cold as an Eskimo during the breeding season. This is the sort of humour I like & understand (I hope you haven't heard it; you can't stop me, anyway):

A man attended a large Society banquet, & was placed in the next seat to his hostess. When the spinach was brought on to the table, he immediately put his hands into the bowl & rubbed a great deal of spinach into his hair. Sensation. 'Do you *always* rub spinach into your hair at dinner?' enquired his hostess in an icy tone. The man looked flabbergasted. 'What a terrible mistake', he said. 'I thought it was cabbage.'

I find that that story is very rarely successful. But—if it has not already done so—Battersea Rise should roll & retch with its prodigious laughter.

Yes, when we quarrel, your solid Ted shall come & watch us; it should be a very good lesson for him. Do you fling things? When I used to quarrel with friend Jones we used to take it in turns to sit on each other's heads. We might adopt that slightly eccentric method. Had enough? says one. Yes, says the other in an agonised voice. Then the positions are changed. And eventually, tired & hurt, the two arguers sit hiccuping on the floor & wonder what the argument was about.

Your poems are changing, and for the better. The change, not the fulfilment, is quite evident in the poem you sent me. 'Pinguid' *is* a lovely word, but it is also an affected word. It means fat, doesn't it, & is an obvious Latinization. Your first line would be vastly improved if you changed it to its English equivalent. Or even said 'A gray, old satyr, lying in the shade.' Anything like that, the more naive the better. I see that the females who now adorn your poems are a very athletic lot. One woman *would* keep leaping on to vines (probably an alcoholic complex), & now you have a girl who leaps about so indiscriminately that she is called the 'leaping' girl and left at that. I'm not laughing at this sudden introduction of the sporting element. Far from it. I'm just writing a lot of nonsense while I try to define my reactions to the 'Poem' as a whole. The motif — let me have my jargon—is good, and 'curling' into the womb is just the

[1] When he was in London with Pamela Hansford Johnson at the end of February, they went to see Sean O'Casey's play *Within the Gates*. His side-heading in the letter echoes the title and introduces his comments on a pantomime that she had written for a local performance. Then he goes on to criticise her poems, and 'Agates' suggests James Agate, a prolific critic of the day.

sort of juicy anatomical conceit I love. I can't like the second line of the last stanza. I fail to see *why* she should bite her lip, or change colour like a piece of litmus paper. She should have been more subtle in her—what is it?—her loathing, though neither that nor the crossed-off word are the ones I mean. She needn't have gone to the trouble of gnawing her own anatomy. The old boy, pinguid as ever, could merely have looked into her eyes, & seen there, hidden, deeply away, the reason for his letting her go. Which would be much better psychologically, and would probably result in a better poetical line.

The two prose-poems (I'll allow you that) are very uneven. Much of the writing is, for you, almost criminally wrong, being just what you can do so well but shouldn't. You can lavish the best lavishers in the country off their spates when you want to. But don't you dare do it. But what the hell's the good of me talking if you listen with one ear & with the other catch the modulations of the bagpipe and the rippling rill? Piece One is remarkable for the number of entirely meaningless & affected words you have managed to drag in. 'Dulcimer', 'Drumdeep', 'Cohorts', & 'Silken Shadowy Girls'. All the damned abracadabra of the Poet's Corner, and as gutless as a filleted herring. What does it mean, anyway, this coy questioning of the heart (a few centuries ago it would have been the liver, a far better emotional prophet) as to whether you shall, or shall not, do a bit of 'arping? This asking your heart to browse, like a cow, in the lilies? This semi-devotional-mystical voodoo of Saint John and the Seven Candlesticks? What does it mean: I don't want a message; I believe that poetry can have only one message. My latest definition of poetry is 'The expression of the unchanging spirit in the changing flesh' (I may have told it to you before). But I want something more than this insipid un-certainty, this amorous insistence on the 'silk' in girls, this squeaking of 'dulcimers' when the dulcimer is an out-dated and useless thing. In this Piece you adopt the same attitude that makes a person call a poet a 'troubadour'. Why 'cohorts'. Ah. I know the reason. 'Cohorts' is a pretty word, with a lot of nice, dim, tapestry associations. But, my dear, you aren't doing a piece of embroidery. You're writing a poem. And the whole trouble is, of course, that you aren't. This Piece should never have been straggled out as prose. You shd have written them in metre, and they would have been bloody still.

I will knock this romanticist warbling of yours out of your head. I've got a lot to say to you, but I'll wait till I *see* you. Then I can tell you really what I mean. 'The blood-wet rags of the beggar' is good, and so are little patches—I keep coming back, however unconsciously, to embroidery images—in 'Fear', which is, as a whole, almost worse. One of my troubles in slating these is my conscious feeling that the *emotion* in both *is* worth expressing. But, far from there being too little, there is too much 'peace in your pen'. It flows—that's the word—far too quickly & fluidly.

More about these—& a far saner criticism—when I see you. I want you to write *very* well, because I know you can. And, blast my gizzard, I'll do my best to make you drop this willowage and lilery.

I'm sorry Jack Common refused your poems.[1] I advise you to try Squire of the 'Mercury', but I wish you'd let me select them. I know the ones he'll accept.

[*At head of page:* I couldn't—just *couldn't*—finish the poem I told you about. Very caddishly I used the dolphins in another poem which I'm enclosing.]

I've had a few poems in papers lately (New English Weekly, Listener, & John O'London), but I've been frightfully lucky in other ways.[2] After my poem was printed in 'The Listener', Stephen Spender wrote me a letter, saying that he liked it, & offering me some review work on a few good periodicals. I'm going to meet him & have dinner with him when I come up. He might be able to do something for me. Geoffrey Grigson, too, wrote a letter, asking me if I'd like to have some poems printed in New Verse. And, best of all, T. S. Eliot wants me to call & see him. He was, for him, quite complimentary. From a literary point of view this has been a very good week. From every [?other] point it's been terrible. I've been feeling ill, and I've wanted to have you to talk to. Now I'm better, and I'm coming up to town next Thursday. I *will* come to your place on Saturday. Don't say you have visitors or anything like that, will you? (Anyway you asked me, & I know you want me to come).

I'm not going to write any more. This is probably the worst letter I've ever sent you. But I want you to get it before the weekend. Write to me before Thursday, & reassure me.

Love,
Dylan

I'm sending you two poems—one very simple—& a bad short story. The story is included only because it will give you an opportunity to give me the bird as ferociously (what a curious idiom, especially with that adjective) as I gave it to you over the Prose Things. I'm almost frightened that it's whimsy, God deliver me.

Love again
Dylan

MS: Buffalo   *SL(R)*

STEPHEN SPENDER
[late March 1934]   5 Cwmdonkin Drive Uplands Swansea

Dear Mr. Spender,
    Thank you very much for the trouble you have taken in sending me the

---

[1] Jack Common was a left-wing writer associated with the *Adelphi*.
[2] *New English Weekly* printed stories, not poems, in January and March 1934. *John O'London's Weekly* printed a poem, but not until May 5.

names and addresses of those papers. I have already sent half a dozen poems to the Spectator, and have mentioned your name. (Even if I sent poems to every periodical you mention, I would still have enough left over to light all the fires in Wales.) I haven't seen the Spectator recently, but isn't it rather—conservative?

Since your letter I have come across Mrs Munro's 23–33 Anthology for the first time,[1] and again I thought your poems the most valuable there. But who is Gascoyne? I saw a geometrical effort of his in one New Verse, and also a poem in which he boasted of the ocarina in his belly. Is he much subtler or much more absurd than I imagine? It is his sheer incompetence that strikes me more than anything else. (I don't really know why I am writing this, which can be of little interest to you, but his poems seem particularly false by the side of 'Byzantium' and 'After They Have Tired'.)

T. S. Eliot, to whom Richard Rees of the Adelphi showed a few of my poems some months ago, wrote me a very nice note this week, asking me to send him some more recent things. I may still use your name when I write to him, mayn't I?

And yes, I certainly would like to do some reviewing. I need all the money I can possibly get. I shall be very grateful to you if you can get me a little to do. I am coming to town next week for one reason alone: to attempt to make some unsuspecting editor see that, without my assistance, his paper is bound to fail; the point will probably take a lot of seeing.

I shall be in London next Friday, and will stay for a few days. Either the 2nd or the 3rd will suit me perfectly. Would the best thing be for me to give you a ring on one of those days, or could I meet you at some place in town?

Thank you again for your letters and your advice.

Yours Sincerely,
Dylan Thomas

MS: Harvard

GEOFFREY GRIGSON
[late March 1934]   5 Cwmdonkin Drive Uplands Swansea

Dear Mr. Grigson,

Thank you very much. I am glad you are going to print the two poems I sent you. I am enclosing a new poem, just completed, which may be some good to you. I shall send you some more poems later, if I may.

---

[1] Thomas had been given the anthology for Christmas, as he wrote on December 25.

I shall be up in London from Easter Saturday until the end of the following week, and am visiting Hampstead during that time to see some friends. Could I call & see you?

Yours sincerely,
Dylan Thomas

P.S. I have been reading over again my poem starting 'Our eunuch dreams...', and am struck more forcibly than before by what might seem to be the jarring optimism of the first six lines of the fourth part. I suggest that this revised stanza sounds far less false:

> This is the world: the lying likeness of
> Our strips of stuff that tatter as we move
> Loving from rag to bone;
> The dream that kicks the buried from their sack
> And lets their trash be honoured as the quick.
> Suffer this world to spin.[1]

But, of course, it's entirely in your hands. If you think this revised version to be better in any way, I do hope you'll use it.

Dylan Thomas

MS: Buffalo   *SL*

PAMELA HANSFORD JOHNSON
[? late March 1934] [? incomplete][2]

My dear Pamela (I may call you that, mayn't I?)

So glad to have your letter. What a nice hand you have. You must write to me again some time. I do *so* love receiving *intellectual* letters, don't you? It give you a sort of—how shall I put it—a sort of stimulus, don't you find? And when one is plucking one's own little flowers from the Garden of Poesy (such a lovely phrase, don't you think. It was told to me by a Mr. Wheeble), it helps, nay invigorates one to fresh horticultural efforts, to know that far away from one is yet another soul searching for Beauty ('Truth is Beauty', you know, as Keats so aptly put it) in those Evergreen Haunts.

And, my dear, how can I tell you in words—words! ah, frail words! such gossamer cups they be!—the emotions your prosepoems inspired in my bosom. (I have often thought, haven't you, that whereas the Upper Classes have bosoms the Working Classes almost invariably have

---

[1] Thomas was changing two lines: line 3, which previously read 'Loving and being loth', and line 6, previously 'This is the world. Have faith'. The changes were not made, and the unamended version survives in *CP*.

[2] This undated fragment may be the start of the next letter. Paper and pagination match.

breasts.) Those dainty pieces smacked—ah, false pen! See how you play your gay little tricks with me!—of a loveliness which even I, humble in my devotion to the Great God Pan (Elizabeth Browning, you remember) have sought after through many sunny hours. So sweetly indeed did they fall upon my ears (Shakespeare, I think, but if Sir Walter Scott I stand corrected) that I have arranged with Mrs. Grimmfluf that you address our next weekly meeting of the Ladies Culture Guild on 'Inspirations I Have Received'. Is this too personal a title? Perhaps I could arrange for you to speak on 'The Sexual Habits of Moths'. Our Guild is *so* entranced with Natural History. *Do* write to me again. Who knows, maybe I shall let you see my little volume of verse. I call it, 'Thru' Hull with the Muses'.

> Yours,
> Sinfonietta Bradshaw (Miss)

Kind Lady,
  Hearin yew ar a poitess and travel on the tramz I hav beene wonderin if you would care to spare me a 2/6. I have a mutual perculeirity with yew, kind lady; I, too, travel on the tramz, though, being a bachelor of sum 57 years I am no poitess. By perfession I am a Female Impersonator, and I were silk nex to my skin.
  Thankin yew for the 2/6, I hope,

> I am,
> Lesley Pough

Dear Sir,
  We are sorry but we must return your poem. You are, we assume, under a misapprehension. Our offices are the offices of the London Mercury-Manufacturers Association, & not of the Mercury Periodical edited, we believe, by Sir John Sitwell.

> Yours Faithfully,
> Rod, Pole, & Perch Ltd

Dear Madam,
  Will you do us the honour of accepting this small Rhyming Dictionary, a tribute of our sincerest admiration. (Move up the car, please!)
> From,
> The L.C.C. Tramway Workers Union

MS: Buffalo   *SL(R)*

PAMELA HANSFORD JOHNSON
[late March 1934] [incomplete][1]

Thank God, now I can get a word in. You'll be interested to know that the B.B.C. have banned my poetry. After my poem in the Listener ('Light Breaks Where No Sun Shines') the editor received a host of letters, all complaining of the disgusting obscenity in two of the verses. One of the bits they made a fuss about was:

> 'Nor fenced, nor staked, the *gushers* of the sky
> *Spout* to the *rod* divining in a smile
> The *oil* of tears.'[2]

The little smut-hounds thought I was writing a copulatory anthem. In reality, of course, it was a metaphysical image of rain & grief. I shall never darken Sir John Reith's[3] doors again, for all my denials of obscenity were disregarded. Jesus, what are we up against, Pam?

The poem you didn't like, along with 'When the galactic sea was sucked', & a new poem which I'm sending you, is to be printed in the April New Verse.[4] That particular poem isn't as bad as you think. There is no reason at all why I should not write of gunmen, cinemas & pylons if what I have to say necessitates it. Those words & images were essential. Just as some have a complex in regard to lambs & will never mention them even though lambs are necessary for their thought, you, my Christina, refuse to look a pylon in the face. I wasn't conceding anything. I wanted gunmen, and, shatter my hams (your oath, but such a wonderful one that you mustn't be allowed to have it all for yourself) I bloody well had them. Ha!

I'll be up as early as possible on Saturday, but don't hold anything up (I don't mean hold up a flag or an old man's adenoids in a bottle: you know what I mean), because I mayn't be able to leave Swansea until Friday night. More than probably I shall, of course, but I'm telling you this in case.... It's no good me saying I'm looking forward to seeing you again. You know how much I am.

What are we going to do? Smile darkly over the fire?

---

[1] *SL* mistakenly joins this to the letter dated 25 April 1934. Only the first two paragraphs of *SL* 109 belong to the April 25 letter. A third paragraph in the MS of that letter has been omitted by *SL*. The letter from 'Thank God', which begins a fresh MS page, was written earlier, at the end of March, because (1) it is not long after publication of 'Light breaks' on March 14; (2) Thomas writes that he will 'be up as early as possible on Saturday', and Johnson's diary for Saturday March 31 (Easter Eve) says, 'Dylan up at tea-time'.

[2] Thomas is misquoting himself. Line 2 should end with 'rod', line 3 begin with 'Divining'.

[3] John Reith (1889–1971), Baron Reith of Stonehaven, autocratic Director-General of the BBC.

[4] 'When the galactic sea' = 'When once the twilight locks no longer', which, together with 'I see the boys of summer in their ruin', appeared in *New Verse*, June 1934.

I want to see Congreve's 'Love for Love' at Sadler's Wells, if it's still on. Will you come? Or is there something else you'd prefer to see. There's the 'Country Wife'; that should bring out your best bawdy laugh. Find out if 'Juno & the Paycock' is still running. It isn't in the West End, I know, but it may be in some obscure theatre.

What a chatty little letter this. Nothing but facts. It must be—it is—the effect of this pedantic day. The sky looks like the graph of a heavenly calculation.

No, I haven't been doing anything I shouldn't. I have smoked only two cigarettes since I last saw you. You can't—yes, you can—realise how terrible it has been to give them up. I've chain-smoked for nearly five years; which must have done me a lot of good. I am allowed a pipe—mild tobacco, not too much. That keeps me alive, though I hate it like hell. I take walks in the morning and pretend there's a sun in these disappointed skies. I even go without a coat (sometimes) in this cold weather, & tread be-jumpered over the sheepy fields.

I've told you, I think, about the coughing sheep that plague my life. In front of my nice little villa is a field where bankrupt farmers pasture their animals before the time of the slaughter house. It's hard to believe how many of those doomed creatures are consumptive. Good old meat-eaters. In a week that particularly diseased sheep that keeps me awake half the night with its centenarian coughs will be done to death, cut up in various saleable lengths, and hung on hooks in butchers' windows. Some sweet little child will develop a sore throat one of these days, or suddenly his lung will break up like a plate (not a Bell plate). So much for the carnivorous. One day I shall undoubtedly turn into a potato. You won't like me then. And, on that day of Transformation, I certainly shan't like you, salt rasher of bacon!

I like to be tidy-minded, but I so rarely am. Now the threads of halfremembered ideas, the fragments of halfremembered facts, blow about in my head. I can write to-day only awkwardly & uneasily, nib akimbo. And I want to write so differently: in glowing, unaffected prose: with all the heat of my heart, or, if that is cold, with all the clear intellectual heat of the head.

There were no shear-marks visible in my last letter for the reason that I had cut out nothing. I never shall in my letters, though the uncut material may, when I think back on it, hurt me very much. And how horribly easy it is to be hurt. I am being hurt all day, & hurt by the tiniest & most subtle things. So on goes the everyday armour, and the self, even the wounded self, is hidden from so many. If I pull down the metals, don't shoot, dear. Not even with a smile or a pleasant smile or a rehearsed smile. (Like a speech from a Russian drama. Look, little Ivanivitch, there are bodies in the Volga. One is your little aunt Pamela. Go give her a snow-cold kiss. No, O little wretch, that is a dead postman. That is your auntie, the one with the poem in her teeth.)

What a biased child! 'Dolphined' is *your* word. Nothing shall take it away from you. All my words are your words (cue). The only reason I never finished the poem in which *your* word originally appeared was because I failed utterly to make it good enough. You are with me when I write (cue).

And now I shall rise from the lovely fire, jam my hat hard & painfully on my head, & go out into the grey day. I am strong, strong as a circus horse. I am going to walk, alone and stern, over the miles of grey hills at the top of this my hill. I shall call at a public house & drink beer with Welshspeaking labourers. Then I shall walk back over the hills again, alone & stern, covering up a *devastating* melancholy & a tugging, tugging weakness with a look of fierce & even Outpost-of-the-Empire determination & a seven-league stride. Strength! (And I'm damned if I want to go out at all. I want to play discords on the piano, write silly letters or sillier verses, sit down under the piano & cry Jesus to the mice.)

If *I* had money I would go round the world, looking for somewhere where the sun was always shining, beautiful & near to the sea. And there I should build me a house as splendid as Keawe's, so that people should call it the house of light. All day there should be music, and olive-skinned virgins, bearing wine in lotus-coloured bowls, should wait on my littlest want. Women with the voices of harps should read to me all day long. And one day, leaping up from my scented couch, I should cry, 'For Christ's sake give me a tram'.

MS: Buffalo   *SL(R)*

PAMELA HANSFORD JOHNSON
April 15th Sunday [1934][1]

Soliloquy. Morning
    The worms are doing very nicely today. Sunday in Wales. The Sunday-walkers have slunk out of the warrens in which they sleep and breed all the unholy week, have put on their black suits, reddest eyes, & meanest expressions, and are now marching up the hill past my window. Fathers are pointing out the view to their stiff-collared whelps. I'd like a big green stick with a pike on the end. Mothers are resting their bellies on pram-handles; little girls are telling each other their harmless stories of affectionate Sunday School mistresses; boys with pomaded scalps are thinking of picture shows and lingerie; and all the starch, the thin pink blood, the hot salty longings, and the respectable cream on the top of the suburban scum, run down the stones, like a river end up in the Sabbath well where the corpses of strangled preachers, promising all their days a heaven they don't believe in to people who won't go there, float and hide

[1] Thomas had returned to Wales from his Easter visit on April 9.

truth. Life passes the windows, and I hate it more minute by minute. I see the rehearsed gestures, the correct smiles, the grey cells revolving around nothing under the godly bowlers. I see the unborn children struggling up the hill in their mothers, beating on the jailing slab of the womb, little realising what a snugger prison they wish to leap into, how the eyes of men are abused by the town light, how the gasoline has crept under their nostrils like the smell of a new mechanical flower, how the stars have been counted for us, how the smiles of Moon, the seventh planetary god, have been translated to the shapes of hills & shores on which, from the first marking of time, the atomed tides of light break and make no sound, how the God of our image, gloved, hatted, & white, sits no longer playing with his stars but curving his Infinite length to the limits of a Jew's theory, and how, each Easter dawn, the sun moves back a finger's length into the East, rising, to satisfy the Christian convictions of the astrologers, in the sign of Aries, the sign of the Lamb.

I wish I could see these passing men and women as ghosts only, and look on their cheap shapes and substances as the own cheapness of my mind clothing itself, for a minute's maggot, in all these diversities. But I see them solid and brutal; if there are ghosts, *I* am turnip and sawdust, and you are the longest shadow that ever fell under the sun. I wish I could see them as the pagan houses of flesh and blood, as creature-boned and sky-sexed, as the beings that have grown like a bug from a bug out of the garden of Eden, as the fleshes that need no brains but only the conscience of their fleshes and the consciousness of their fleshes and the freedom and the Mexican splendour. If I, incorrigibly romantic, could see them as a Yucatan people, call them to a cat-drinking ceremony, and know their names as childish Nazul, Tilim, & Yum-Chas, my Sunday worm would disappear like a Japanese mouse in a flash of green light—you remember the story—and my letter would be as loving as I wish it. Loving it is now, but recondite and scaly as the zodiacal Scorpion.

I wish I could see these passing men and women in the sun as the motes of virtues, this little fellow as a sunny Fidelity, this corsetted hank as Mother-Love, this abusing lout as the Spirit of Youth, & this eminently beatable child in what was once a party frock as the walking embodiment of Innocence. But I can't. The passers are dreadful. I see all their little horrors.

I wish I could see them as the pitiable products of a capitalist system, wage-slaves, economic eunuchs, mass-systemised, the capitally lettered Workers that Sir Richard Rees, & men who need do no work, are so intent upon making the martyrs of their own intellectual Inquisition. Again I can't. What are these Workers to me? Isn't every thought, every lift of the lids, every smile, every kiss, a Work that no creature but this divine, this rational, meat-eating man can accomplish? Man himself is a work. Today he is a dirty piece of work. But tomorrow he may sprout wings under his serge shoulders, be faced and sided like Aquarius, who is the first sign of the vital year. He may be a bluff, white Tsar, ordering the insects of the earth, the slugs & beetles, the preachers and gangsters, the lovers & lepers, & even the little, loving letter-writers like ourselves, on the maddest missions all over this altering earth. He may be as benevolent as the Alhambra, or gloomy as the Gate.[1] Today he is bloody, and that is a bloody nuff for me.

Comment. Night

I read over what I wrote this morning. All is silly, but why should I cross it out or throw away. It's just a little more me for you to grapple with. Which sounds even more conceited than many of the other things I've put in my letters to you. I've often wondered—I thought of asking you, but am always so vastly happy with you that I don't like introducing morbid & egotistic subjects—whether you think me as conceited a little young man as I often think you must do. I'm not, really; profoundly the other way. But I've noticed that when, for example, you—quite honestly and often misguidedly—run down your poetry, I never retaliate, as every true-blue poet should, by saying how very unsuccessful my own poetry is, too. I never say it, but not because I don't think it. I *know* it. And when you say, of a poem of mine, 'that's bad', & I try to argue & show you how good it really is— that, too, must sound conceit. Darling, it isn't. I'd hate you to think that I was all self-contented, self-centred, self-satisfied in regard to—well, only one little thing, the things I write. Because I'm not. And I'm not half as brave, dogmatic & collected in the company of Literary persons as I might have led you to believe.

Thank God it's dark. Now I can't see the people outside. I might be in a world of my own, owing nothing but the seeds of hate to all the dark passers scuttling to the rub-a-dub-dub in the bebatted belfries of the stinking churches, scuttling homewards again or out on their half-frustrated amatory expeditions after the sin of love has been emphasised by St. Paul & his pimply apostles. I'm going to put on the light; the bad water-colours on the walls will be meaningless, Lake Como a lake of the brain, & even the naked Greek dart-throwers as human as the lumps of stone that clutter up the back garden. I don't want to see my books; a library is a sanatorium of sick minds; I don't want to see my papers all over the floor; why should I take my bed in the sanatorium? There's nothing better now but sitting in a circle of darkness, watching the shape of the body be shapeless, & hearing the intimate rustlings of the room louder & louder. Why aren't you here with me, in my little circle, holding my hand & braving the wicked world with me? Don't tell me—I know. The world is so wickedly wicked it won't let you brave it with me. I have just to go on hoping & waiting. I can make a shape of you to sit with me in this circle; I love the shape, but the shape isn't enough. I try to think of you marooned on your own dark island. Make room, darling. I'm as lean as Ugulino, I don't take much room.[2] There, I'm comfortable now.

---

[1] Alhambra, shorthand for 'music hall'. The Gate, an avant-garde theatre in Covent Garden.
[2] Count Ugolino of Pisa, imprisoned with his sons and starved to death, 1289. In Dante's *Inferno*.

Avaunt, you worm-faced fellows of the night. Pamela & me, on one circled island, sit & poke our fingers at you.

Comment. Tuesday Morning

Monday was a dead day, the hole in space you talk of, such a deep, damp hole as I must have fallen into when I last left you. I can hardly remember a thing about Monday, certainly not the rising & setting of the day. I don't think I read or wrote. I remember lifting up a cushion to see if you were underneath. You weren't. That was early in the morning, & it was after that, I believe, that I fell with a great clatter into space. After all, when you pick up a cushion to find nothing underneath—that's a terrible surprise. Of course it would have been rather a surprise if you had been there. But I haven't got over the idea yet that if I open a cupboard door *very* quickly, I might see you sitting & beaming inside. If you open a furnace door quickly, you'll see the devil, leering on a coal. But you have to shut the door even more quickly. And if, perhaps, you were in the pantry when I opened it one day, the shape of you I saw might—& would be, I think—no more than a very devilish trick. And when I touched you, as I undoubtedly would, I would not be surprised to see you change colour as rapidly as though I were a pinguid satyr, & disappear in an acrid flame through the holes of the cheese.

Monday was dead. I know I wanted to write another section of this letter, & tell you in great detail how much I love you. But I died about ten o'clock, & I think you died with me.

Now Tuesday, today, is quite a different sort of day. It's so abominably warm & bright that I shall have to satisfy my conscience, which, like most other things, is bound up in you, by taking a bus to Gower & walking over the cliffs. I shall hate it because I shall be so lonely. But it shall be done; all your commandments shall be obeyed. I am writing this in a deck-chair under the clothes-line. This should really be a very sexy note (it's not going to be), for above me & around me all the disembodied underclothes of this respectable Drive are doing a very naughty dance. Not so disembodied, though. Those spindle-shanked pants, two lines away, have their own airy limbs; a spring demon has inhabited them: O inhabited pants! And that little vest, (mine, I think) is breathing up & down as though the Carnera[1] wind were developing its chest beneath it.

Lunch. After lunch I go out to do my duty & your commands on the rocky fastnesses of Wales. And, late in the evening, I will finish this letter. Goodbye,——. I left the blank because I can't think of anything lovely enough to call you. Goodbye, darling. And I put such an inflection into the word that it sounds almost as lovely a word as I want to call you.

My latest song: 'Come into the garden, bawd.'

Wednesday Morning

I couldn't write last night, was too tired after my medicinal walk which

---

[1] Primo Carnera was a heavyweight boxer.

led me into the village of Llangennith, miles from anywhere, very near nowhere. Now, quite early on another bright blue day, I am sitting in the untidiest room you ever saw, writing the last few pages. I have just finished an incompetent drawing in pastels of a negro riding on a leopard down the clouds, & although it has made me feel in one of the most airy & unearthly moods, I'll try to answer your question.

I told you the answer over lunch one day, when you were misting the walls near our table with your long breaths of misery. I told you that however much I loved you I would still be able to say 'Lousy' to anything that you wrote, & to tell you to take up raffia work if I thought that your poems had, and could have, no value at all. And I would. I've said 'lousy' to many of your poems, and will undoubtedly do so again, just as you have spat you of my angularities & my blonde bones. But, right deep down in the pit of my belly, I know that you can be good, that you have been good, & that all the little lice in your Muse's ear will one day get up & depart. I can't enthuse over your poetry as yet, & you would know that I was wrong if I did. But I can say, honestly & honestly, that there is a thing in your poetry, in your Lotus Women, Symphonies, Lullabies, & Morning Suns, that is the thing of all true poetry. And if I can't name that thing, it is my fault & not yours. You couldn't give up writing, you know you couldn't. It would be criminal if you did. You have been given certain talents & facilities for the writing of poetry which you must, for the sake of all you believe in, love and live up to. What is wrong is your attitude, or, at least, much of your attitude, towards those talents. Because the talent, which is very easy to see in twenty out of the twenty-four pages of your book, is not enough by itself; the work-woman in your poetess, the intellectual, the thinking craftswoman, has not had half enough to do. You must work at the talent as a sculptor works at stone, chiselling, plotting, rounding, edging & making perfect. You told me, too, over the same lunch, that you hadn't got the time & energy to do all this. My dear, I know; I know you haven't; and I know that it's wrong, as wrong as anything under the sun, that you have to work in a dull, methodical office all the day, all the long, wild & wonderful day that waits for you and can never have you. But instead of going home in the evenings &, after dinner, sitting down to write a poem or two, why not sit down to write perhaps no more than three perfected lines? Instead of three or four mediocre poems, each with a line, a phrase, or a hint of beauty in it, you would, eventually, have *one* poem, or one stanza of a poem, that had all those *collected* lines, phrases & hints in it. You told me that the Lotus Woman was written very quickly, even though I thought it the best thing you had done. I still think so, but I liked it for no more than two lines & two phrases: the rest was ordinary. If, over that same poem, you had spent as many hours as you spent minutes, each line would be one I'd like, & each separate phrase. This advice is easy to give & hard to carry out. But I want you to try to carry it out. You mustn't waste your little bit of genius. You mustn't read bad poetry, must forget your Tennyson & even your

Housman. You must pack your poems tight, work at them every spare moment you have. Whatever you do, I believe in you. I believe in you at your worst & your best. Send periodicals & reviews to hell. Work at your poems. And send me every line you write. As long as I have you at the back of me I'm going to be good. And so are you, with me behind you. And I'm going to be behind you & with you always.

Wednesday afternoon Soliloquy

You are my only friend. I say quite seriously that I have never really spoken to any other human being, & that you are the clear point of faith with which the psalmist lifted his eyes to the hills. When I went away from you, it seemed you had abandoned me to myself. And when I was with you, after all these years of pursuit, we were face to face, alone. And you were a tiny spirit floating around the room, flying faster and faster till you came invisible, & I could hear only your wings. It was a very quiet, monotonous sound, and came from a tail-less, mangy dog which limped across the room. I raised my foot to kick it, but it was the toe of a giant who reached up to take the stars in clusters. Then you were behind me, whispering, 'Juggle with these. Juggle, I say. Go on'.

I wish I knew what that soliloquy meant. It means something very big, but I can't understand it. I know you weren't the mangy dog, dear. But who was? That's the worst of writing without thinking: you write more than you think. I must have been the mangy dog, but I don't feel at all self-pitiful today. Damn the nonsense. Forget it. I seem very, very near to you this afternoon. And being near you is worth all the nonsense in the world.

I'm going to drink some coffee now, & then finish this page. You'll have my letter tomorrow morning. Write over the week-end to me, so that I get your letter by Monday. Coffee. Even coffee has become a symbolical rite. The composition of my own letter and—best of all—the having of yours, has become the greatest event of my week, holier than the ritual of the bath, than the linking of sweet airs & phrases, than the night and its dreams. No more moujik, stomachic depression. No more worm for either of us, or if there must be a worm in our letters let it be the jolly, red-bellied one you told me about & not the grey-whiskered journeyman of the tomb.

> Fathom the wavy caverns of all stars,
> Know every side of every sand in earth,
> And hold in little all the lore of man
> As a dew's drop doth miniature the sun.
> But never hope to learn the alphabet,
> In which the hieroglyphic human soul
> Most changeably is painted, than the rainbow
> Upon the cloudy pages of a shower,
> Whose hinges a wild wind doth turn.
> Know all of each! when each doth shift his thought
> More often in a minute, than the air
> Dust on a summer path.

That's my great Beddoes.[1] I wish to God we were lying by the side of the fire, reading his lovely gloom to one another ere the Spider make a thinne curtaine for our Epitaphes.

> Oh we are not at home in this December world,
> Cold sirs & madams.

Shall we live on an island, somewhere in the Mediterranean, writing & reading, loving & sleeping, singing our sweet, rude rhymes to the seals? I love you, darling. Goodbye.

Dylan
X

MS: Buffalo   *SL*

GLYN JONES
[mid April 1934]   5 Cwmdonkin Drive Uplands Swansea

I must really apologise for not having written before, but I have been spending the last fortnight in town, and have had very little time to do any of the things I had intended. I hope your throat is better, and that you will soon be able to come down and see me. Perhaps, if you are well enough, you might feel like coming down this coming Saturday, or the Saturday after, and spending the week-end here.

I read your 'Tiger Bay' in the Adelphi. I didn't like it very much, but then I am biased against that sort of thing. I liked the 'hooks of her hair', though, and the 'guts' of the thing were undeniable.

If you can in Cardiff, buy a copy of 'New Verse', which will be out in a few days. I have two or three poems in it.[2]

Let me know when you can come down. Any week-end you like, and the sooner the better. Your poetry, &, probably, your theories of poetry, are so opposed to mine that we should have plenty to discuss.

Dylan Thomas

MS: Carbondale

[1] The quotation is from Thomas Lovell Beddoes's play *Death's Jest Book*.
[2] Only 'Our eunuch dreams' appeared. Glyn Jones thinks the issue was published late. Two further poems appeared in June.

(HAMISH) MILES
[? April 1934] [draft][1]

Dear Mr. Miles,

Thank you for your note. I'm sorry to have been so long replying. The poem in your possession is printed in this month's New Verse. I had no idea at all it was going to be, as Geoffrey Grigson told me that he didn't like it very much.

I'm enclosing three poems, all very similar in subject & approach. The one beginning 'I dreamed my genesis' is more or less based on Welsh rhythms, & may seem, rhythmically, a bit [? strange] at first. I do hope you'll like one of them, though I admit their constant anatomical symbols can't be to the taste of many, & are, quite often, not even to the taste of myself.

I am coming up to town sometime next week. May I call & see you then?

> Yours Sincerely,
> Dylan Thomas

MS: Texas

GLYN JONES
[? April 1934]   5 Cwmdonkin Drive Uplands Swansea

I shall expect you on Saturday.

I refuse on paper to quarrel with you about obscurity, fluid verse, T. S. Eliot, Walt Whitman, Worker's Poetry, my own anatomic slap-stick, and other controversial points mentioned in your letter, especially as you're coming down. (I would far rather be Eliot than Whitman, if only because Eliot has a very splendid sense of form.)

And as for the Workers! People have been trying to write to them for years. And they still don't care a damn. The trouble is that in attempting to write for the Workers one generally writes *down*. The thing to do is to

---

[1] Written in a notebook where Thomas and his friend Dan Jones composed alternate-verse poems. Hamish Miles, the likely addressee, was an editor at Cape, the publishers. The 'Welsh rhythms' remark is interesting in the light of Thomas's denials of Welsh-language influence, e.g. in a letter to Spender many years later, 9 December 1952.

bring the Workers *up* to what one is writing. (And, there, I'm starting to argue already.)

MS: *Carbondale*

PAMELA HANSFORD JOHNSON
Wed April 25th '34 [incomplete]

Introduction
　　When I received your mammoth envelope, I had no idea what it contained and began to wonder whether you had sent me your life-story in detail. I was quite expecting to see your letter open with, 'I was born on a cold and lousy May day in a garret in Park Lane', or something of the sort. Instead, of course, you gave me enough literary material to fill a book, and how on earth I'll be able to criticize it all by Thursday I've no idea. You see I'm writing this on Wednesday morning, although I received all those evidences of your teeming brain by the second Post on Monday. I should have started writing before, but I've really been busy—what with my damnable walks (I'm awfully glad you've taken to them, too), rehearsals for a play (I don't know why I keep on doing this), drawing the drawings for the play (it's an arty piece of Coward),[1] typing and revising stuff for

---

[1] A revival of *Hay Fever*.

Vicky, & attempting, quite uselessly, to finish a fairly long short story that I wanted to send you. So now I have only a very few hours in which to tell all the little that's been happening to me, to tell you once more that I love you and think of you all the time, and to do my best with your stories and poems.

Times Literary Blurblement

I agree: it was a gentlemanly criticism, but hokum for all that.[1] The offices of that disgusting paper, as you know, are peopled with very old gentlemen who carry no literary credentials but a pocket Tennyson and a long ruler—the ruler to rap all originality over the knuckles, & the Tennyson as an infallible criterion by which to test everything they review, from 'Chaucer to Ezra Pound'. They were particularly unfair with you; your book, in spite of its little horrors and 'Helens' & 'Black Masses' & 'Possessions', was worth more than the few niggardly lines they devoted to it, & the few patronising remarks about 'youthful freshness' & 'the uncomplicated daring of youth'. 'Lack of experience' had to come out, of course, it's a wonderful fall-back. But even in detail the so-called criticism was hopeless: what 'impulsive mannerism' is there in that very pleasant phrase 'grandly frail', which is an ordinary figure of speech (I can't remember the name) to be found in any English textbook. The dig at Mr. Newbury was justified, of course, it was a very easy dig to make; but the anonymous review certainly didn't do you justice. My Dad read your book & liked it very much. He thought it was nearly all fresh and lovely. 'Graceful skimming' was his phrase, I think, &, on the whole, it's very apt. But you aren't going to skim any more. Today's poems—at least they are today's poems to me—are incomparably better. I wish they could have been printed, too.

MS: Buffalo   *SL(R)*

GEOFFREY GRIGSON
[?April 1934]   5 Cwmdonkin Drive Uplands Swansea

Dear Grigson,

Thank you very much for writing. I'm sorry we could not meet for lunch, but your illness was a very real excuse. I shall be in London in about a month's time when I hope we can meet again. I'll let you know when I'm coming up.

I wonder whether it would be possible for you, when you are fit and about again, to see whether there is any chance for me to do some review work. I hope you won't mind me asking you this, but things are not going

---

[1] *Symphony For Full Orchestra*, just published, had been reviewed in *The Times Literary Supplement*.

too well with me at present and I'd welcome any sort of journalistic work at all.

New Verse was awfully good this month, and I was pleased to see Carlos Williams given one in the eye.[1]

The poem you said you'd read and tell me about is incomplete in the version you have. I enclose the complete poem.

Yours Sincerely,
Dylan Thomas

MS: Texas   *SL*

GEOFFREY GRIGSON
[April or May 1934]   5 Cwmdonkin Drive Uplands Swansea

Dear Grigson,

Thank you for your letter, and for the promise of the books for review.

I am enclosing a new poem which I hope you will be able to read, and which I hope will interest you. I think it is a little better than the others you have of mine. I will be very interested to see what you say about them.

I will be up in London at the end of May. I hope we'll be able to meet then.

Yours Sincerely,
Dylan Thomas

MS: Texas

PAMELA HANSFORD JOHNSON
Wednesday May 2 [1934]

<u>Very Early</u>

I have decided not to get up today, to lie serene in my bed and write of the things that go round me, the shapes of shadows on my mountainous knees, the curving of my immaculate breast and the life in my ever-scribbling fingers. I have put on nice new pyjamas, so this is going to be a pleasant day, and perhaps I shall not think of worms at all but only of the sun that I'm sure is shining in the curious world outside, and of other equally lazy people who, too, from the white islands of their beds are writing to ones they love on the commercial sea. In peril on the commercial sea. What is this death, this birth and apparent pain, this glib

---

[1] The April issue, reviewing Williams's *Collected Poems*, 1921–31.

love, this rush to the head of so many extraneous creatures of the air that crowd my words and never let me stop a sentence at a nice, rhythmic stop? Don't tell me.

Which I think is about as nice an opening to a letter as any as I can think of. And having told you that I intend to spend the whole day in bed, I now contradict my own slothful intention and pull the sheets back. I shall go out immediately and commune with the sun—yes, I have established the fact: the sun is shining most strongly—or, on second thoughts, retire into a blowsy world of papers and pencils and write weak odes to a literary parhelion.

Now it's very obvious that I shouldn't begin to write so early. Half in, half out of sleep, I can't possibly write anything but a lot of high-falutin nonsense. Most words are Boojums at eight o'clock. And I can never say, 'Hark, hark the Snark' until at least after breakfast.

Well, why am I writing now? *You* have already risen and are staring, not very intelligently, at the stories of sudden death in the Express. Or perhaps it may be later than I think, and you are buying your cigarettes at the shop where the girl who thinks me jolly would be very much surprised if, tousled and red-eyed, livered and lachrymose, I was to walk in now. Or perhaps you are sitting in the bus, passing Chelsea or Kronsky, and wondering what the hell rhymes with piano. And here *I* lie, in a lukewarm bath of half-slumber, with the unpolished taps of words turned full on. Yes, why? I wanted to tell you the most remarkable dream I dreamed last night, in which I was climbing ladders all the time and waving to Pamela-faced horses on the top of asylum towers. But when I started to put the dream in order, it sounded Double Dutch, or, at least, Double Hatch, to me.

After Breakfast

It is still too early to be intelligent. Sometimes I think it always is, and that about fourteen o'clock I might really get up and say something brilliant. But anyway you wouldn't like me if I did, and the hankering after cleverness is the hobby (wrong word introduced for the sake of the alliteration) that, theoretically, I most abhor. I should like to indulge in a rapid rifle rattle of Oscar wit—not necessarily concerning Oscardom (Pouff is the sweetest thing)—and say new clever things about sex and moths and hipbaths and all other luxuries in this breadandbutter world.

The mention of Oscar reminds me of Oscar Browning, that divinely blueblooded snob of the Oxford nineties. The last incident about him I read yesterday—I wish I could say I'd read it Gomorrah—in a book called 'Swan's Milk' by Louis Marlow. I'll repeat the very simple story, but first explain that Oscar was a little, very old, bald don, of the sort who always stops—in hopes—to read the writing on public lavatory walls. Oscar and another man were sitting on a mountain side, talking. 'What is the difference between a bob and a shingle?' the old don enquired. 'There's not much difference, only a shingled head looks like a boy's, behind.' 'A boy's behind,' roared Oscar, 'A boy's behind. How can I sit here and listen to your obscene observation. A boy's behind. I've never wanted to see a boy's behind. Any other simile. But a boy's. . . .' And in sheer joy he kicked a little dog who happened to be near them right over.

That's all. And that's enough for an hour. I want to read the crime page in the Telegraph. And I have, too, a violent desire to draw pin-men.

Noon

Or, at least, somewhere near noon. It's the word that attracted me. Have I ever told you of the theory of how all writers either work towards or away from words? Even if I have, I'll tell it to you again because it's true. Any poet or novelist you like to think of—he either works *out of* words or in the *direction of* them. The realistic novelist—Bennett, for instance—sees things, hears things, imagines things, (& all things of the material world or the materially cerebral world), & then goes toward words as the most suitable medium through which to express these experiences. A romanticist like Shelley, on the other hand, is his medium first, & expresses out of his medium what he sees, hears, thinks, & imagines.

A nice, true chunk of dogmatism, superbly inapt on such a May morning.

I have noticed in my last few letters—you are guiltless, as usual—a tendency to write a lot of immaterial matter, and then lump in all the actual replies at the end. So that half of your pages go uncommented, though never, my darling, unread. Let me be a model letter-writer for once, & reply to your letter page by page in strict order.

Our Future

I believe with all my heart that we'll live together one day as happily as two lobsters in a saucepan, two bugs on a muscle, one smile, though never to vanish, on the Cheshire face. But I will never exhaust *my* flow of pessimism, for, sadistically, it gives me a delight, or a pain and a delight mixed in one, to imagine the most dreadful things happening to us, to imagine a long future of bewilderment and disillusionment ending in Tax Collectors (I never want to hear their bloody names again) matchselling, and sterile periods of the production of cracker-rhymes that we, in our hopeless megalomania, will imagine as the disregarded fruits of genius. That one day you will vomit at the sight of my face, and I at the tones of your voice. That I go nuts and you go gaga. So let me occasionally chime in with a deep chord of misery, & throw myself over an abyss of hopeless and quite unnatural speculations as to the future of two small and harmless persons who, in accordance with everything god has said or has been said to say since the beginning of the world, love and want each other.

May 29

Is a date that has become very important on the calendar. I will, unless everything goes wrong and the winds of circumstance blow me helter-skelter in my pyjamas over the Adriatic or the Caribbean, be seeing you then, and the twenty odd days to go will be more turtle footed than any twenty days have ever been.

When I said that I must have something definite in mind when I come up, I did not mean that, otherwise, I should be starving all the miserable day in the bewidgeoned park. Those days are not yet; they're just held in store. No, what I meant was the utter boredom I'd endure between the times of goodbye and halloa to you. So something definite there must be—Vicky's proud party, or a futile interview with an uncaring [*word omitted*], or even a few luncheon appointments with bad poets. I'll write and arrange something with somebody, and probably the result will be as vague as that.

Trouble at home. What a mild, mad phrase. No, no, there's none, or, at least, none that matters. But my father & mother are going to leave here about the end of June & go to live in the country, God-knows-where.[1] I won't go to the country. I'll come to town. And it will need a very philanthropic deity, indeed, to tell me what I do or where I sleep or even—if it wasn't for you—why, why. I won't stay with my sister, either. I am going to find a high, conventional garret, there to invoke the sadistic Muses, get a little drunk on air, and wave my hand to you over the Dome.

Your Stories

'Headline' was good. 'Buried Treasure' was good. And there's a big bit that's good in 'A Man Had A Monkey'. Obviously I like it less than the other two, but the theme is pretty, and the working out, with the exception of a part of the Divine Comedy at the end, sufficient. A very guarded opinion that I at once upset by saying, in my most fruity manner, how, after even the first rough reading, the lump rose obediently in the throat. My objections to the end are these—objections, quite unusually, concerned with the matter and not the treatment. Your God (in the story) is, admittedly, the God of the myth and the fairystory, but there is no reason to make him a silly God, or to make Gabriel a bad book-keeper. All the details of the sentimental murder of the monkey would be known in heaven. God proclaimed sentence on the monkey-keeper in a most unjust & ungodly way. If the monkey hadn't been within earshot, the most terrible things might have happened to the man. And there is never a miscarriage of justice in the heaven of the fairy books. The monkey should leap on to God's throne and pull at His sleeve *before* sentence was pronounced. Otherwise, it's silly, & God is even sillier. '. . . and he was dreadfully afraid. But suddenly there was a clashing in the branches . . . etc.' O.K.

[1] It was 1937 before D. J. and Florence Thomas left Cwmdonkin Drive for a village outside the town.

And the other thing: no elephant could deafen Gabriel unless he was a white one. I understand why you wrote the passage about Gabriel stopping his ears. But it won't do.

With pruning & the removal of some of the too many & too emotional adjectives ('Silver' clashing, for instance, in my first objected-to paragraphs) the story might easily be as lovely as Anatole France's 'My Lady's Juggler', a story that, in no way disparagingly, it at once brings to mind.

On points of writing alone, I have a few more things to quarrel with, & especially the very first paragraph of all which is written most carelessly and incompetently. Your 'he's' & 'them's' are terribly misleading. The punctuation doesn't help, either. *Who* earned enough money? Napoleon & Charlie Chaplin? . . . so that people would laugh at *whom*? The tail, the beast, the *pollened* head? Or the man & his monkey? To collect pennies for *whom*? I understand it, of course, but it's most clumsily ambiguous.

'Pollened' is pretty unnecessary. 'Its head on his breast' is enough. And surely the man is an Italian. Even if he wasn't, he wouldn't say 'Old chap' to the monkey—You seem very fond of putting these prep-school endearments & colloquialisms in the mouths of nearly all your characters. I remember the little Annie who called her husband 'a silly ass', & the father in the Tallboy Terror who said the most unspeakably Poonah things.

Oh, my dear, their 'hairy nudity'. How *can* you speak of such things. Why not 'the hirsute appendages on their ungarmented forms'? or something equally as dreadful.—'Where his friends chattered together & swung on the trees, untrammelled by velvet jackets & hateful gold braid'. I'm not suggesting that as a substitute for your too heavily adjectived paragraph, only removing a few of the adjectives to let you see for yourself how much better it sounds & looks when it is more simple & unaffected.

The monkey's 'brittle' bones are not wanted either. The monkey's bones are enough by themselves.

'Impart' is a bad word. Be simple, dear, with a simple story, & let the monkey try to 'give' his warmth to the man.

'That was deeper than the forest trouble' is too easy & conversational. 'That was deeper than the troubles of the forest' . . . that isn't good, I know, but it isn't as slipshod. You'll find a better phrase than that.

'Old chap' appears again on page 3. So does 'beastly'. I think he'd say 'nasty clothes', just as if he were talking to a very little child.

'Old chap' again at the foot of the same page. Bai Jove, old horse, this bally diction is enough to put you under the weather, what?

'Winnowed like mustard seed' is too flowery. It's out of the very appealing naiveté of the rest.

The rest is slight and lovely. I have no complaints. I can only sit back & read it & like it very much, & envy you for a gift of sweetness in writing that is more valuable in the end than all the loud & strident sournesses of the rest of us.

I'll read this again. This is, perhaps, the first prose piece of yours that I would willingly print in any prose anthology—with the adjectives, or some of the adjectives, removed, & the heavenly injustice rectified. Yes, you *are* going to write good stories, very good stories. You've written one now, slight as it is. But it's no slighter than 'My Lady's Juggler'. And that's a story that will last, as yours might last. Go on, my Pam, go on. The sky's the limit.

Referee Poets. No. 2[1]

Thank you for your abortive list of poems. I disagreed heartily with you. 'We See Rise The Secret Wind', 'In Me Ten Paradoxes', 'The Eye of Sleep' & 'Thy Breath Was Shed' are all very bad indeed.[2] I have rewritten 'The Eye of Sleep' almost entirely, and it is now a little better, though still shaky on its rhythms and very woolly as to its intention (if any). But I know how hard it is to make any sort of comprehensive list for anyone else.

I am going to include some poems which have been printed, so 'Boys of Summer', though altered & double the length, is to open the book. Other poems are:

'Light Breaks Where No Sun Shines'. 'Before I Knocked And Flesh Let Enter'. 'No Food Suffices' (revised). 'When Once The Twilight Locks' (revised). 'Our Eunuch Dreams'. 'A Process In the Weather'. 'The Force that through the Green Fuse'. 'Where Once the Waters Of Your Face'. 'That The Sum Sanity' (revised). 'Not Forever Shall the Lord of the Red Hail' (revised).[3] And about six or seven others I am still in the process of pruning and cutting about. You say Vicky's obstinate. Well you know I am, too. And nothing that I don't want goes in.

Red Book[4]

So that's where I left it. I was despairing of it. You are an angel not to read it. I confess that if you had left your book somewhere, & told me implicitly not to touch it, the first thing I would do when your back was turned would be to peep, with a nasty, aren't-I-a-lad expression, into the pages. But I believe you, and I am glad you haven't read it because it contains more nonsense to the square inch than most wards in a home for people who imagine they are Bath buns or postage stamps or maypoles etc.

I wish I could have disguised myself as an Old Girl—pince-nez, warts, & thin vowels are essential, I suppose—and come to hear your impassioned reading. Did you read your Symphony? If you intend to some

---

[1] Thomas was the second of the *Referee*'s prize poets, with publication of his book guaranteed. It appeared at the end of 1934 as *18 Poems*.

[2] Of these four Notebook poems, only 'The Eye of Sleep', rewritten as 'I fellowed sleep', appeared in *18 Poems*.

[3] Of the ten poems in this group, three were not used in *18 Poems*: 'No Food Suffices', 'Not Forever Shall the Lord of the Red Hail' and 'That The Sum Sanity'. The last is a distant echo of Thomas's first *Sunday Referee* poem, 'That sanity be kept'; in its revised form it was printed in the *Swansea and West Wales Guardian*, 8 June 1934.

[4] Probably the 'red notebook' containing stories, now at Buffalo.

other time, a good idea would be to cultivate—if that is [the word] and I'm sure it isn't,—a violent indigestion before beginning. Think how easy the timpani would be then. But I'm afraid you want artificial teeth to do full justice to the harp. What is it like, really, reading your own poems to a set of polite people who, in all probability, imagine a trochee to be a new sort of lawn game? Were you nervous? I hope you were, you bitch, for you shouldn't read poems to Old Girls. I've a good time [mind] to ferret an Old Boys' Society, & read them the waxiest & wombiest efforts that I've got.

Answers. And Tit Bits

Play was 'Strange Orchestra', which we've done before.[1] I played, as usual, a degenerate artist. But my drawings were good. One was a large abstract, done mainly in furniture varnish, titled from the Revelations: 'The Star Called Wormwood'. And the other two were early Victorian pastels of nude women rolling about in fields. A few of the audience were quite horrified, the con-Genital idiots!

I can't think what plays we could do, but I think we'd be funniest as the Macbeths. But in our prospective society, I refuse to play incestuous fathers all the time. Let me have a change now and then, and play a homosexual butler. You, my dear, shall play whores & whores only. 'Sex', by Mae West, may be a good Starring Vehicle for us, though I refuse to appear without my trousers in more than two acts out of the three.

Would you like to play Mrs Alving in 'Ghosts'. I'd love to play Oswald, even though he is your son. We'd give them neurosis with a capital F.

I'll look up some plays, & show them to you when I come up. I'm enclosing a poem[2] and a story. Darling, will you type the story for me so that I can send it to Lovat Dickinson's.[3] Perhaps you won't like it very much, but I refuse to anticipate that. Tell me what you think of it. Damn the details; just tell whether, as a whole, it's at all successful.

The poem is, I think, the best I've written—I've said that to you about a lot of mine, including all sorts of wormy beasts. It may be obscure, I don't know, but it honestly was not meant to be. It's too—I can't think of the word—for any thing but New Verse to print. I'll get Grigson to do it. But it isn't Grigson's opinion I want. It's yours. And what are these 'new standards' you've arrived at. I hope they aren't too high.

Only about an hour ago, a boy of fate, disguised as a telegraph messenger, came with a wire from 'New Stories' accepting my 'Enemies'.[4] It was accepted by another paper a month or two ago, but

---

[1] A slip or a deception—the play was *Hay Fever* (see letter of April 25). Earlier in the year Thomas had been dismissed from the lead part in a Little Theatre play, *Martine*, because at the dress rehearsal he popped out to the bar once too often. Thereafter he did little acting.
[2] Probably 'If I was tickled by the rub of love'.
[3] Lovat Dickson (b. 1902), author and publisher, was managing director of Lovat Dickson Ltd, publishers, 1932–8. The story was 'The Visitor'; Johnson's diary notes that she typed it on May 6.
[4] Published in *New Stories*, June/July 1934.

refused at the last moment because of the word 'copulation' on the last page. Now 'New Stories', has it, copulation & all, & is to print it next month.

Try 'New Stories', 118 Banbury Road, Oxford. Address it to E. J. O'Brien—of the 'Best Short Stories of the Year'.

Money

Short stories of the sort I write hardly make anything. 'New Stories', for instance, perhaps the best story journal of the lot, doesn't pay at all. And poetry wouldn't keep a goldfinch alive. Novels and popular, narrative stories are the things. I'm damned if I'm going to write for the Strand, even if I could, which I very much doubt, and novels are a long and arduous business. Besides, it's no use writing a novel merely for the sake of writing one. You have to have something to say that only the novel can express. My novel—I've done the first chapter—will be, when and if I finish it, no more than the hotch-potch of a strayed poet, or the linking together of several short story sequences. I shall scrap it in a few days. No, novels aren't for me—yet. So what's the alternative? Six months ago I'd have suggested the docks or the oven with the greatest equanimity. But now I've got to live. It's when I'm with other people more than when I'm by myself that I realise how much I want you and how very far away you are from me. I'm willing to work. I do work, but in an almost anti-mercenary direction. Which is no good at all for you or me. Something has to be done, but Christ knows what it is. And Vicky can't help. He can do little more than keep himself alive, & that not very comfortably. And the arty people I know are almost as broke as I am. There are all sorts of things I could do. I could get in with a bad repertory company in Coventry, or some place like that—I forget the exact place. But that's as far away from you as ever & quite futile. A man wants to take me for a long trip up the Mediterranean, and I could go to Russia with a Welsh Communist organisation. All very nice, but what the hell's the good? I might have a fairly good time, but I'd make no money at all, and if I thought about you when I was standing on the dockside at Odessa I'd break my heart. So something has to be done. And with that nice, comfortable platitude, I sink back into a usual lethargy and continue to write of my uncommercial maggots.

Percy Droppeth Again[1]

No more Percy again. I haven't got the time. This has got to go by the Last Post. Percy, the ubiquitous, the inscrutable, & the entirely bafty, will have to wait. But he'll come. What a profoundly unamusing book we might make out of him. I wonder how much madness the British reader takes to his ounce of nonsense. Can you imagine the Times Supplement reviewing 'The Quality of Percy'? 'This bafty book. . . .' 'Conglomeration

---

[1] The 'Rev Percy' began as a character in games of fantasy that Dylan Thomas and Dan Jones played.

of youthful horseplay, senile smut, & lunatic obscurity'. Mr. Gerald Gould . . . 'Hotcha!'. No, I can't imagine it, either.

By the way, raw carrots are splendid. But raw potatoes are bloody. I've given them up, anyway, and had breadandmilk for supper last night. It tasted pretty loathsome, but I got it down somehow & pretended it was good. No more yapping at my diet. My darling Pam, you don't eat half enough yourself. I won't be satisfied until we play a rousing game of hockey together. And, after the match, we'll retire into the woodshed—where all dirty things happen—& commit fel-o-de-se.

Again I haven't replied to half your letter, & again I've left too many things unsaid. I don't think that I've said I love you. But I do. Oh I do. Goodbye, Pamela, & write soon, very soon.

Dylan XXXXXXX
a magic number, dear

MS: Buffalo   SL(R)

PAMELA HANSFORD JOHNSON
May 9 '34

Yesterday I received from Southampton a small, round tin of Tooth Powder, enclosed, in an explanatory note, at the request of a Mrs. Johnson of Battersea Rise. 'Eucryl destroys germs in every part of the mouth.' Was that the intention of your mother's much-to-be-thanked request? Or perhaps you sent it after my ringworm poem, in order that I may clean my mouth out with great thoroughness? Give my love to your mother, and thank her for the Powder. Whether it will destroy the germs or not, I cannot possibly say. I hope not. I admire germs. And, if I remember, I shall bring a few more than usually bawdy paragraphs into this letter to satisfy their lecherous itches.

And, while I remember, too, let me raise one nasty growl about your unparalleled bitchiness in pinching my letter to the Neuburg. I wrote a stony, non-committal letter to him, received your pathetic appeal, and immediately tore the old effusion up and posted off a charming, Micawberish affair. And don't you go about jeering at my Old School Tie. I hate Old School Ties. I haven't got one. I shall now attempt to light a Russian cigarette in a most rakish manner, and look all sexy at the mantelpiece. But it doesn't work. I am fated to be British under my Russian exterior. But don't always point at my Tie. Just pretend it isn't there. Anyway, it was a sweet letter, and, if nothing else, I meant what I said about Pamela Johnson, though if I had had any idea that she would see the letter, I would have introduced a long and dirty paragraph all about her nasty little moist-nosed muse.

Again I am unwell. Melodramatic introduction, reminiscent of some wheezy Shylock, to a page of remorse and self pity. But no, it shall not be. Even more melodramatic. Sir Jasper Murgatroyd enters through the trapdoor with a snarl, and immediately opens his waistcoat and distributes, from his navel, Empire Marketing Board pamphlets on 'The Caul of the Colonies'. To put it plainly—it is an intellectual impossibility to put anything plainly—I feel about as much use as [*seven words are deleted, the last two of them* Nudist Colony] (a sudden puritanism makes me delete this. Very indecent). (I am trying very hard to deny the Tooth Powder, and to devote all my bawdy and soul to the composition of Old Tin Kettle innuendoes. But it fails. This May morning is un-naturally church. The birds sing the Ave Maria. My germs tell me that Ave Maria sounds like a sexual disease. I whisper 'Poonah' to them, and display an invisible gout. They vanish.) But I am ill, ill as hell. I have had a headache for a fortnight, and haven't slept for longer than that. I've lost all hope of ever going to sleep again. I lie in the dark and think. I think of God and Death and Triangles. I think of you a lot. But neither You nor the Triangles can make me sleep. I've drugged myself up to the eyelids. I have a little box of tablets with an instruction on the cover not to take, on any account, more than three. I take nine, and still I remain awake. I have tried everything. I have tried getting drunk. I have tried keeping sober. I have counted sheep and bathchairs. I have read till I can't see any more. I have tried completely under the bedclothes & on top of the bedclothes, right way up, wrong way up, with pyjamas, without pyjamas. A good idea, of course, is to gas yourself just a *little* bit. But I can't think how that's going to be done.

No more. Darling, send me to sleep. No more. Perpetually pathetic, these daft little notes of mine can serve no purpose but to show you, again and again, how much I need you.

And no Mediterranean for me. I'd love the sun, and I'd love the places the sun would take me to. But it's all useless, for, when I came back, I'd be just where I was before I went away—a little less pale perhaps, but as green as ever as to what I must do in this dull, grey country, & how one little colour must be made out of you and me. The chromosomes, the colour bodies that build towards the cells of these walking bodies, have a god in them that doesn't care a damn for the howls of our brains. He's a wise, organic god, moving in a seasonable cycle in the flesh, always setting and putting right what our howls at the astrologers' stars and the destiny of the sun leads us on to. If we listen to him, we're O.K. And he tells me, 'Don't you go away now. You stick to your unamiable writings and your never-to-be-popular morbidities. You stick as near as you can to what you love.' So no trampsteamer up a blue sea for me. Give me Pamela & a Chatterton attic.[1] Enough for the likes of me, and too much, too, for God knows why she loves this idiot writing & writing, precious as a herring, on this Old School paper.

[1] Thomas Chatterton (1752–70), precocious and impoverished poet, whom Wordworth called 'the marvellous Boy'. He committed suicide.

It must be this ecclesiastical morning that drives me into such stagey melancholia. And so, by cunningly sitting in a room looking over the east of Swansea chimney pots, I avoid the sun and all the priestcraft of May. I sit and devour the brick walls with my eyes, hoping to draw out a little of the masons' opium that, hot from their foul pipes, cemented these breeding huts together. But the room is stuffy, filled with the tobacco smoke it shouldn't be filled with & my naughty thoughts that leap, like Tom Warner's,[1] from clinical observatories in Vienna to syphilitic cabarets in Buenos Aires, from Builth Wells to Chimborazo, from the altitudes of poetical ideals to the rhyming of 'catalepsy' and 'autopsy'.

I shall have nothing to send you. The old fertile days are gone, and now a poem is the hardest and most thankless act of creation. I have written a poem since my last letter, but it is so entirely obscure that I dare not let it out even unto the eyes of such a kind and commiserating world as yours. I am getting more obscure day by day. It gives me now a *physical* pain to write poetry. I feel all my muscles contract as I try to drag out, from the whirlpooling words around my everlasting ideas of the importance of death on the living, some connected words that will explain how the starry system of the dead is seen, ordered as in the grave's sky, along the orbit of a foot or a flower. But when the words do come, I pick them so thoroughly of their *live* associations that only the *death* in the words remains. And I could scream, with real, physical pain, when a line of mine is seen naked on paper & seen to be as meaningless as a Sanskrit limerick. I shall never be understood. I think I shall send no more poetry away, but write stories alone. All day yesterday I was working, as hard as a navvy, on six lines of a poem. I finished them, but had, in the labour of them, picked and cleaned them so much that nothing but their barbaric sounds remained. Or if I did write a line, 'My dead upon the orbit of a rose', I saw that 'dead' did not mean 'dead', 'orbit' not 'orbit' & 'rose' most certainly not 'rose'. Even 'upon' was a syllable too many, lengthened for the inhibited reason of rhythm. My lines, *all* my lines, are of the tenth intensity. They are not the words that express what I want to express; they are the only words I can find that come near to expressing a half. And that's no good. I'm a freak user of words, not a poet. That's really the truth. No self-pity there. A freak *user* of words, not a poet. That's terribly true.

> 'I'll not be a fool like the nightingale
> Who sits up till midnight without any ale,
> Making a noise with his nose,'

is a quotation I write down for no reason at all. Neither do I feel it to be correct. For I'll be a fool like the hyena, sitting up till dawn without any pleasure, making a noise with his guts.

[1] A Swansea friend, later a musician.

This is out of mood with the day. I should be writing some sunny paragraphs, imagining in the words for you a green and blue expanse of Welsh country where the cattle, in accordance with all conventions, 'low', where the lambs 'frisk', and the glassy streams 'babble' or 'tumble' according to the rhyme. I'll walk this afternoon, and, perhaps, in the late night, when I write to you again, the nearsummer loveliness will have gone into me so deeply that all the clowning and the pretentious stomachraking of the last two pages will be nothing but an echo that refuses to 'ring' in your ears or an odour that refuses to 'waft' to your nose.

But, before I go out, very lonely and quite twice as pale & haggard as usual—I hardly weigh anything at all, eight stone or under now—, into my Gower bays, there are several matter of fact things in your last letter which I want to answer.

Now Orage,[1] though a very pleasant and a very sincere man, is known to be almost entirely lacking in taste. He runs the literary sections of the New English Weekly by a system of filing. He has in his office literally hundreds of poems and short sketches and stories. Most of them are bad, but that doesn't matter. It's quantity with him, not quality, that counts. And week by week one or two of those stories and poems are taken down from their dusty shelves and printed. You just wait your turn, and then in you go. So there's really very little satisfaction in having anything printed in Orage's paper. He doesn't pay *at all*, and the standard he sets is so low that it's hardly flattering to be accepted by him. He goes in for mediocrity. 'Headline', whatever its faults—and I begin to suspect that its main faults, at the moment, may be my fault—is not mediocre, and not original enough—in subject, at least,—to startle him into an acceptance. I've no idea where you can plant 'Headline'. Its matter, I should imagine, would be too ordinary for 'New Stories', which deals with rather out-of-the-way affairs. 'The London Mercury' might like 'A Man Had A Monkey', though I believe they keep you waiting rather a long time before they reply. The 'Everyman' prints stories. So does 'John O'London'; but, for the last, the more conventional the better. I'll have a look at some more of the magazines littered about the house. I can't remember the name of the story, but the one about the watch, the little girl, and the nasty old gentleman, is more of a *commercial* effort than any I can think of of yours. And, though you'll probably squeal to heaven at the suggestion, you might do worse than send it to a paper such as 'Nash's'. There are scores of papers like that, above the standard of the 'Strand' & 'Pearsons', that *might* stretch their standards of taste sufficiently to allow admittance to your cheery little story. And have you sent any poems to J. C. Squire? And have you sent to Harriet Monroe?[2] And what about a mild (very mild) poem to Frank Kendon, of John O'London's. He printed a terribly weak, watery little thing of mine—I've

---

[1] A. R. Orage (b. 1873) edited the *New English Weekly* until his death in November 1934.
[2] Harriet Monroe founded *Poetry* (Chicago) in 1912 and edited it until her death in 1935.

never shown it to you—last week (Saturday May 5).[1] These do seem dreadfully lowbrow suggestions. But they're not derogatory. Far from it. But you've struck such a curious *medium* in your poetry lately that publication becomes very difficult; there are so few medium papers left. By that I don't mean 'middlebrow' or anything like that. But you've brought 'conventional' poetry, descendent from Tennyson & the middle Victorians, to a point of near-perfection, and any modern, even any *alive* influence, is absent. So that editors of most periodicals are rather troubled at your poetry, for most of the editors (&, unfortunately, the editresses) look at the influences first and the individuality afterwards. If a poem, in the John Donne descendency, is fairly good, they print it; if very good, in the Tennyson descendency, they refuse to. What they never realise—they cannot, of course, being, principally, caterers for the fashionable taste of the moment, and a taste which has spat Tennyson out & sucked up the good & the bad of John Donne in large mouthfuls—is that the convention, the heredity, of the poem doesn't matter a farthing. It's the individuality of the poet, an individuality that owes nothing to the Jacobeans or the Victorians, that really matters. If you, still (& inevitably) retaining the old Johnson individuality, were to tack on to your poems the conscious influence of Donne, Tourneur, Traherne or Manley Hopkins, you'd get published all over the place & be the moment's wow in every public salon. But you're not going to do that, because you realise that it's worthless, & that what Jack Common (entirely ignorant of everything outside intellectual socialism) refused for the Adelphi is far more valuable than most of the Donne-fathered babies he lets discharge inside his nice yellow covers.

I like your new poem, very much as the Toothy Beth (what happy little jingles you could write about a Toothy Beth) would like it. I like it, but can't say much more about it. There is usually some phrase, or simile, or line, or even stanza to which I object, or in which I find sometimes a purposely rough image I imagine to be unsuccessful because it is not smooth enough & sometimes a little gush-bubble that a rude snarl of mine can prick to nothing & sometimes a precious word (a 'burgeon' or a 'pinguid') which revolts against my waxy ear and my urny taste. But, in 'Sarcophagus', I can find nothing except a desire to be liked. And I fall to desire, as always, liking it with a toothed inarticulateness. It's a bit harmless, a little bit thin, I think. I see no vast reason why it should have been written. But written it is, and read it have been, and like it I do. I'm not usually as dumb as this over a poem of yours. But, really, I've nothing at all to say about it. It's there, just there, and I like it. For which brilliant piece of criticism I shall be awarded the Neuburg biscuit—a weekly prize for the longest nothing in the vaguest words.

H. Corby seems a dirty boy.[2] But you're too old a bird to be stoned by

---

[1] 'Dare I?', a shortened version of a Notebook poem that later had its missing stanza restored, became 'Ears in the turrets hear', and survived to reach *CP*.

[2] Herbert W. Corby was another of the *Sunday Referee*'s poets. He also wrote articles for the paper.

him. I think I should like to quarrel with H. Corby about the Justification of The Phallus In Architecture, or The Influence of Sodomy On Wickerwork. What a perverted time we boys would have.

Is, by the way, the Babs of the skyblue jumper the same Babs Ross who sometimes decorates the Poet's Corner with her sweet little name? Anybody who can write a poem & put Babs under it deserves a pat on the back. I lift my hat. Three moths and a woodpigeon, one calling your name, fly out. Ach, it is always the same. These woodpigeons. . . . !

And now, before I get any archer, & start to crack very weak jokes about plums, let me go out for my much-talked of walk. Goodbye till tonight, my dear.

Morning. Sunday 13.[1]

But the night never comes. And two loose days have passed since I wrote those last ink words. They were loose days, and I accept the reprimand—before it comes—with a bowed head and a dim, canary mouth. I don't know why I do it. It's silly and childish, but somehow inevitable, especially on a sunny Saturday evening in a seaside village where, most of the afternoon, I had lain in the sun, trying to colour my face and look out-of-doors.

I hate the little, minor disturbances of the world—the forgetting of letters, the losing of papers, the tiny falls, mishaps & disappointments which crop up, regular as the suicidal wish, each gassy day. Last night, in the deserted smokeroom of a seaside pub, I found myself suddenly cornered by three repulsive looking young men with coloured shirts, who asked me, in a most polite & Turpin way, for my cigarettes. Since they all looked *exactly* like Wallace Beery in one of his less debonair moments, I gave them my cigarettes and enough money to buy three pints of beer. They then smiled—or rather showed me about ten (or less) broken teeth (between them)—and persisted in drinking their illgotten beer in front of me & making rude remarks about the length of my hair. Now, I don't mind their communist ideas, or even the practice of them. But why *my* cigarettes, *my* beer, & *my* funny hair? It's little incidents like that that make one feel very weak & small in a country full of strong barbarians. Before they left me—probably to intimidate another lonely little person—they told me what was apparently a dirty story in Welsh. That was the last straw, & later the sun went out.

This morning, looking at Vicky's noncommittal remarks about Dylan Thomas, the experimentalist, I found myself wondering who this sadnamed poet was, & whether he had any separate existence from the sadder person, of the night before, bullied out of his lawful cigarettes by three strongmen & falling back, in the event of his comic cowardice, on to a stony pile of words. And why should this experimentalist be given so many lines in a national newspaper, & my Beery-mouthed desperadoes be consigned to the mortality of a letter page?

[1] In *SL*, the text from this side-heading to the end turns up in the wrong place, attached to another letter.

Anyway, I'm not an experimentalist & never will be. I write in the only way I can write, & my warped, crabbed & cabinned stuff is not the result of theorising but of pure incapability to express my needless tortuities in any other way. Vicky's article was nonsense. If you see him, tell him I am not modest, not experimental, do not write of the Present, and have very little command of rhythm. My Pegasus, too, is much, much more spavined than that of A. L. Basham,[1] who is too selfconscious, or Pamela Johnson, whose latest published 'Poem' is sweet, girlish drivel.

Tell him, too, that I don't know anything about life-rhythm. Tell him I write of worms and corruption, because I like worms and corruption. Tell him I believe in the fundamental wickedness and worthlessness of man, & in the rot in life. Tell him I am all for cancers. And tell him, too, that I loathe poetry. I'd prefer to be an anatomist or the keeper of a morgue any day. Tell him I live exclusively on toenails and tumours. I sleep in a coffin too, and a wormy shroud is my summer suit.

> 'I dreamed the genesis of mildew John
> Who struggled from his spiders in the grave'

is the opening of my new poem. So there. But I don't like words either. I like things like 'ungum' & 'casabookch'. XXX, for you, my bleeder.

All of which, I think, must be owing to the condition of the liver. But never forget that the heart took the liver's place.

My novel, tentatively, very tentatively, titled 'A Doom On The Sun' is progressing, three chapters of it already completed. So far it is rather terrible, a kind of warped fable in which Lust, Greed, Cruelty, Spite etc., appear all the time as old gentlemen in the background of the story. I wrote a little bit of it early this morning—a charming incident in which Mr. Stipe, Mr. Edger, Mr. Stull, Mr. Thade and Mr. Strich watch a dog dying of poison. I'm a nice little soul, and my book is going to be as nice as me.[2]

New story about Mae West: Mae West visited a farm while on a tour through the West States, & was taken around the farm by a handsome young farmhand. They came across a bull making love to a cow. 'Tell me,' said Mae West, 'How does the bull know exactly when the cow is—sort of—wanting to be made love to?' 'Waal,' sd the farmhand, 'It's all a matter of smell with these here animals.' Later they came across a ram and a ewe, also in a Lawrencian attitude. And on asking the same question, Mae West received the same answer. As the farmhand saw her to her car, she turned round & said: 'This has been a real swell day. Say, you must come up and see me sometime—when your catarrh's better.'

Which leads me, quite naturally, to the end of this ridiculous letter. [*Some words are deleted.*] (Sorry. Had to cross this out. It was indecent.) I love you, Pamela, more every day, think of you more every day, and want

---

[1] A. L. Basham was the third and last *Referee* poet to have a book sponsored.
[2] Some of these characters with anagrammatic names occur in Thomas's story 'The Holy Six'. See, in the next letter, Thomas's description of 'my novel of the Jarvis valley'.

to be with you more every day. Don't take much notice of my rantings
and rumblings, and less of that horrid poem I sent you last week. I love
you and love you. I only believe in you. Nice, round Pamela, I love you.
All the time. Always will, too. Write very soon and keep me alive. Sorry
for all my letter. I'm not too well—perhaps it's that. You don't mind how
daft the letter, do you? If it's the mask I know, never lift it, my
twiceblessed. Love, & the crosses I can't write because there's not room
enough. P.S. What do you want for your birthday? Books? Rings?
Wurlitzer Organ?

[*On a separate sheet*:][1]
And now goodbye. I seem to be getting back into my old letter mood,
and don't really want to stop writing. But I have to stop sometime, and
I've already delayed this letter longer than I wanted to. Reply in a very
few days, will you. And do be honest. Remember, I'm very fond of birds
(Damn, that again!). Yes, do write back soon. Wave your hand to your
mother for me, and kiss yourself goodmorning and goodnight.

Dylan

MS: Buffalo   *SL(R)*

PAMELA HANSFORD JOHNSON
May [about 21, 1934][2]   Laugharne

I am spending Whitsun in the strangest town in Wales. Laugharne,
with a population of four hundred, has a townhall, a castle, and a
portreeve. The people speak with a broad English accent, although on all
sides they are surrounded by hundreds of miles of Welsh county. The
neutral sea lies at the foot of the town, and Richard Hughes writes his
cosmopolitan stories in the castle.[3]
I am staying with Glyn Gower Jones.[4] You remember I showed you one
of his bad poems in the Adelphi. He is a nice, handsome young man with
no vices. He neither smokes, drinks, nor whores. He looks very nastily at
me down his aristocratic nose if I have more than one Guinness at lunch,
and is very suspicious when I go out by myself. I believe he thinks that I
sit on Mr. Hughes' castle walls with a bottle of rye whiskey, or revel in
the sweet confusion of a broadflanked fisherwoman.
Incidentally, I showed him some of your poems, your latest poems.
And he couldn't understand them at all. An ardent admirer of the
Criterion, he fails to understand you. And it's quite true. You are getting
pleasantly obscure, and much of what you write at the moment must

[1] The final paragraph may belong to another letter.
[2] This is the letter that acquired the wrong text in *SL*; see note, page 133. It was also given
the wrong date, 'May 11'. Whit Monday was May 21.
[3] See page 188.
[4] Glyn Jones at that time used the pseudonym 'M. G. Gower'.

seem quite mazy and difficult to almost anyone except myself. But then the reason is obvious. I, too, am mazy and difficult. We both are in our fleshly lives. And let me remind you that you will find my body damnably difficult to dispose of. 'That particular one' (your Bluebeard words) has found a widow. I will never find anyone except you. The only solution will be a little poison in my cup. Even then there would be the phantom Thomas, head under arm, three mackintoshed, weakchinned and blowsy, seeking you out and groaning his disembodied bawderies in your ear. Or, of course, you could garotte me as I nibble at my vermicelli.

(Rose plot,
Fringed pool,
Ferned garotte.)

I seem always to be complaining that I cannot fit the mood of my letters into the mood of the weathered world that surrounds me. Today I complain again, for a hell-mouthed mist is blowing over the Laugharne ferry, and the clouds lie over the chiming sky—what a conceit—like the dustsheets over a piano. Let me, O oracle in the lead of the pencil, drop this customary clowning, and sprinkle some sweetheart words over the paper, (paper torn slyly from an exercise book of the landlady's small daughter). Wishes, always wishes. Never a fulfilment of action, flesh. The consummation of dreams is a poor substitute for the breathlessness at the end of the proper windy gallop, bedriding, musical flight into the Welsh heavens after a little, discordant brooding over the national dungtip.

My novel of the Jarvis valley is slower than ever.[1] I have already scrapped two chapters of it. It is as ambitious as the Divine Comedy, with a chorus of deadly sins, anagrammatised as old gentlemen, with the incarnated figures of Love & Death, an Ulyssean page of thought for the minds of the two anagrammatical spinsters, Miss P. & Miss R. Sion-Rees, an Immaculate Conception, a baldheaded girl, a celestial tramp, a mock Christ, & the Holy Ghost.

I am a Symbol Simon. My book will be full of footlights & Stylites, & puns as bad as that. Kiss me Hardy? Dewy love me? Tranter body ask? I'll Laugharne this bloody place for being wet. I'll pun so frequently and so ferociously that the rain will spring backward on an ambiguous impulse, & the sun leap out to light the cracks of this saw world.

But I won't tell you my puns, for they run over reason, and I want you to think of me today not as a bewildered little boy writing an idiot letter on the muddy edge of a ferry, watching the birds & wondering which among them is the 'sinister necked' wild duck & which the 'terrible' cormorant, but as a strong-shouldered fellow polluting the air with the smell of his eightpenny tobacco and his Harris tweeds, striding, golf-footed, over the hills and singing as loudly as Beachcomber in a world rid of Prodnose. There he goes, that imaginary figure, over the blowing mountain where the goats all look like Ramsay MacDonald, down the

---

[1] The imaginary 'Jarvis hills' and 'Jarvis valley' occur in early stories. The novel was never written.

crags and the rat-hiding holes in the sides of the hill, on to the mud flats that go on for miles in the direction of the sea. There he stops for a loud & jocular pint, tickles the serving wench where serving wenches are always tickled, laughs with the landlord at the boatman's wit, ('The wind he be a rare one he be. He blows up the petticoats of they visiting ladies for the likes of we. And a rare thirst he give you. Pray fill the flowing bowl, landlord, with another many magnums of your delectable liquor. Aye, aye, zor'. And so on), and hurries on, still singing, into the mouth of the coming darkness. Or he hies him manfully to the Hikers' Hostel, removes his pimples with a bread knife, and sprinkles a little iodine over the one and forty bats that ring the changes in the Hikers' belfries.

But the eye of truth, tired of romancing, turns back with a material squint on my self, and marks the torture in my too-bony hand and the electric livingness in the bodies of the goldfish I carry in the lining of my hat. Pamela, never trust the goldfish in the lining. They dribble lead over the nice, new felt. And their molten excreta drops, with the noise of the drums in Berlioz, on to the open skull.

I am tortured to-day by every doubt and misgiving that an hereditarily twisted imagination, an hereditary thirst and a commercial quenching, a craving for a body not my own, a chequered education and too much egocentric poetry, and a wild, wet day in a tided town, are capable of conjuring up out of their helly deeps. Helly deeps. There is torture in words, torture in their linking & spelling, in the snail of their course on stolen paper, in their sound that the four winds double, and in my knowledge of their inadequacy. With a priggish weight on the end, the sentence falls. All sentences fall when the weight of the mind is distributed unevenly along the holy consonants & vowels. In the beginning was a word I can't spell, not a reversed Dog, or a physical light, but a word as long as Glastonbury and as short as pith. Nor does it lisp like the last word, break wind like Balzac through a calligraphied window, but speaks out sharp & everlastingly with the intonations of death and doom on the magnificent syllables. I wonder whether I love your word, the word of your hair,—by loving hair I reject all Oscardom, for homosexuality is as bald as a coot—, the word of your voice, the word of your flesh, & the word of your presence. However good, I can never love you as earth. The good earth of your blood is always there, under the skin I love, but it is two words. There must be only half a word tangible, audible, & visible to the illiterate. And is that the better half? Or is it the wholly ghostly part? And does the oneeyed ferryman, who cannot read a printed word, row over a river of words, where the syllables of the fish dart out & are caught on his rhyming hook, or feel himself a total ghost in a world that's as matter-of-fact as a stone? If these were the only questions, I could be happy, for they are answered quickly with a twisting of sense into the old metaphysics. But there are other and more dreadful questions I am frightened to answer.

I am whimsy enough today to imagine that the oyster-catchers flying over the pearlless mudbanks are questioning all the time. I know the question and the answer, but I'm going to tell you neither, for it would make you sad to know how easily the answer drops off the tip of the brain. Fill up the pan of the skull with millet seed. Each seed shall be a grain of truth, & the mating grains pop forth an answer. (Bugger me black.)

I wish I could describe what I am looking on. But no words could tell you what a *hopeless*, fallen angel of a day it is. In the very far distance, near the line of the sky, three women & a man are gathering cockles. The oyster-catchers are protesting in hundreds around them. Quite near me, too, a crowd of silent women are scraping the damp, gray sand with the torn-off handles of jugs, & cleaning the cockles in the drab little pools of water that stare up out the weeds & long for the sun. But you see that I am making it a literary day again. I can never do justice [*the words* in my precious prose *are deleted*] to the miles and miles and miles of mud and gray sand, to the un-nerving silence of the fisherwomen, & the mean-souled cries of the gulls & the herons, to the shapes of the fisherwomen's breasts that drop, big as barrels, over the stained tops of their overalls as they bend over the sand, to the cows in the fields that lie north of the sea, and to the near breaking of the heart as the sun comes out for a minute from its cloud & lights up the raggèd sails of a fisherman's boat. These things look ordinary enough on paper. One sees them as shapeless, literary things, & the sea is a sea of words, and the little fishing boat lies still on a tenth rate canvas. I can't give actuality to these things. Yet they are as alive as I. Each muscle in the cocklers' legs is as big as a hill, and each crude footstep in the wretchedly tinted sand is deep as hell. These women are sweating the oil of life out of the pores of their stupid bodies, and sweating away what brains they had so that their children might eat, be married and ravished, conceive in their wombs that are stamped with the herring, &, themselves, bring up another race of thickhipped fools to sweat their strength away on these *unutterably* deadly sands.

But now a piece of sun comes out again. I am happy, or, at least, free from this morning's tortures. Glyn has gone fishing, and in another half hour the 'Three Mariners' will have undone their waistcoats. I shall drink beer with the portreeve,[1] & no crimping pussyfoot shall say me nay.

I forgot to bring your letter with me. It lies locked at home in the Pamela drawer. Its memory makes Laugharne a bit brighter—but still not bright enough—and it closed with the only words that should ever close a letter. But I can't remember many of its details. I'll reply to them again, or perhaps they can wait till I see you again. I shall look out for your tail-less story. I forgot to bring 'Anna' too. It is the best story you have written. You are becoming very competent, dear, and your stories are all your own. There are many things for me to say about 'Anna', but they, too, must wait.

Oh hell to the wind as it blows these pages about. I have no Rimbaud

---

[1] Laugharne is an ancient borough, and its mayor is called a portreeve.

for a book or paper rest, but only a neat, brown rock upon which I have drawn three very ferocious travesties of your face—one eyeless, one toothless, & all entirely bloodless. Oh hell to the wind as it blows my hair over my forehead. And woe on the sun that he bloody well shines not.

Soon I see you. Soon I kiss you hullo.

It's getting cold, too cold to write. I haven't got a vest on, and the wind is blowing around the Bristol Channel. I agree with Buddha that the essence of life is evil. Apart from not being born at all, it is best to die young. I agree with Schopenhauer (he, in his philosophic dust, would turn with pleasure at my agreement) that life has no pattern & no purpose, but that a twisted vein of evil, like the poison in a drinker's glass, coils up from the pit to the top of the hemlocked world. Or at least I might do. But some things there are that are better than others. The tiny, scarlet ants that crawl from the holes in the rock on to my busy hand. The shapes of the rocks, carved in chaos by a tiddly sea. The three broken masts, like three nails in the breast of a wooden Messiah, that stick up in the far distance from a stranded ship. The voice of a snotty-nostrilled child sitting in a pool and putting shellfish in her drawers. The hundreds and hundreds of rabbits I saw last night as I lay, incorrigibly romantic, in a field of buttercups, & wrote of death. The jawbone of a sheep that I wish would fit into my pocket. The tiny lives that go slowly & liquidly on in the cold pools near my hands. The brown worms in beer. All these, like Rupert Brooke, I love because they remind me of you. Yes, even the red ants, the dead jawbone, & the hapless chemical. Even the rabbits, buttercups, & nailing masts.

Soon I see you. Write by the end of this week.

Darling, I love you.
XXXX

MS: Buffalo   SL(R)

PAMELA HANSFORD JOHNSON
Sunday morning [May 27 1934][1]   in Bed

Question One.   I can't come up
        Two.   I'm sleeping no better
Question Three. 'No' I've done everything that's wrong
        Four.   I daren't see the doctor
Question 5.   Yes I love you

I'm in a dreadful mess now. I can hardly hold the pencil or see the paper. This has been coming for weeks. And the last four days have completed it. I'm absolutely at the point of breaking now. You remember

---

[1] Johnson's diary for May 28 records 'appalling distressing letter from Dylan'. The letter is scrawled in pencil; everything about it seems designed for maximum effect. The housewife who is the likeliest candidate for the part of scarlet woman says it isn't true.

how I was when I said goodbye to you for the first time. In the Kardomah[1] when I loved you so much and was too shy to tell you. Well imagine me one hundred times worse than that with my nerves oh darling absolutely at the point of breaking in little bits. I can't think and I don't know what I'm doing   When I speak I don't know if I'm shouting or whispering and that's a terrible sign. It's *all* nerves & no more   But I've never imagined anything as bad.

And it's all my own fault too. As well as I can I'll tell you the honest, honest truth. I never want to lie to you. You'll be terribly angry with me I know and you'll never write to me again perhaps   But darling you want me to tell you the truth don't you

I left Laugharne on Wednesday morning and went down to a bungalow in Gower. I drank a lot in Laugharne & was feeling a bit funny even then. I stayed in Gower with Cliff, who was a friend of mine in the waster days of the reporter's office. On Wednesday evening [. . .] his fiancée came down. She was tall & thin and dark with a loose red mouth & a harsh sort of laugh. Later we all went out & got drunk. She tried to make love to me all the way home. I told her to shut up because she was drunk   When we got back she still tried to make love to me wildly like an idiot in front of Cliff. She went to bed and Cliff and I drank some more and then very modernly he decided to go & sleep with her. But as soon as he got in bed with her she screamed & ran into mine

I slept with her that night & for the next three nights   We were terribly drunk day & night   Now I can see all sorts of things. I think I've got them.

Oh darling, it hurts me to tell you this but I've got to tell you because I always want to tell you the truth about me. And I never want to share   It's you & me or nobody, you & me & nobody. But I've been a bloody fool & I'm going to bed for a week   I'm just on the borders of DTs darling, and I've wasted some of my tremendous love for you on a lank redmouthed girl with a reputation like a hell. I don't love her a bit   I love you Pamela always & always   But she's a pain on the nerves. For Christ knows why she loves me   Yesterday morning she gave her ring back to Cliff.

I've got to put a 100 miles between her & me

I must leave Wales forever & never see her

I see bits of you in her all the time & tack on to those bits   I've got to be drunk to tack on to them

I love you Pamela & *must have* you   As soon as all this is over I'm coming straight up. If you'll let me. No, but better or worse I'll come up next week if you'll have me. Don't be too cross or too angry   What the hell am I to do? And what the hell are you going to say to me? Darling I love you & think of you all the time. Write by return   And don't break my heart by telling me I mustn't come up to London to you becos I'm such a bloody fool.[2] XXXX Darling. Oh Darling.

MS: Buffalo   *SL*

[1] Kardomah Ltd ran a chain of cafés.
[2] Thomas went to London on June 13, stayed two weeks, and was forgiven.

TREVOR HUGHES
[7 June 1934]

Dear Trevor,

. One day, with all the provocation in the world, you will spurn forever my unorthodox and unpunctual advances and break up into a million fragments the friendship that still lies between our spasmodic bursts of correspondence. For I am the most unreliable friend that ever was, but, far from glorying in my conventional disregard of the decent limits and conventions of friendship, I am heartily ashamed of it and make an effort now to stir out of stupor and to write what I hope—unfortunately I remember saying this before—will be the first of a new and protracted series of confessionals.

The last time I wrote to you was soon, though not soon enough, after our parting at the Lyons' Café of the Clerkly Slaves and the appointment, which, of course, I failed to keep, at the Tavern of the Long Hair and the Flowing Tie. And in that letter, I remember, was a frank, though perhaps misguided, criticism of your story, a number of weak apologies, and a promise to write again directly upon receipt of your answering letter. Your letter came, and only today, on the seventh of June, do I prepare to reply. Postpone again the spurning and breaking, and do please regard the shortness of this letter as nothing but a timid fear upon my part that my name at the foot of the page will no longer hold its accustomed magic in the dens and quagmires of your abominable Lane.

Now, Trevor my lad, how is the world misusing you, and are your metaphysics still, like mine, neatly and surgically wrapped in a wadding of darkness? Here there is still no light, only a new mile of suffering murk added to the horizon, and a fresh acre of wonder at this rotten state that might easily and sweetly be changed into the last long acre where the dead breathe for the first time. But how goes it with you? Is there an arc of light over St. Paul's, a new-gutted twinkling in the stars of the electric sign, a stronger tide of words, or a repeated sea more dismal than the Sargasso, more heavenly sounding than the Bosphorus? Here I am getting older and no wiser, and have lately become entangled with an erotic girl with whom I indulge in unrepeatable displays of carnality. In *your* tight-tided little island, does the hank of bone and the curled slit play its hot, customary part?[1] You—who said once that you should have been canonized in accordance with your principles—are you lately become a celibate to whom the lifting of skirts is no more than the lifting of skirts? I am looking forward to the day when Mr and Mrs Hughes, in their two backed beast, face the double faced world. That way, perhaps, lies your salvation

---

[1] Explicit sexual detail is rare in Thomas's letters. Perhaps he had been sexually involved for the first time. A poem written not long before (30 April 1934 in the Notebooks) observes,

> 'This world is half the devil's and my own,
> Daft with the drug that's smoking in a girl
> And curling round the bud that forks her eye.'

and mine, though I doubt whether I, personally, could remain sober and faithful for more than a week on end.

Such is our weakness, comrade. In our anatomical creature, we see the creature of the material world as weak and struggling as ourselves. But, day by day, I realize more that, together, we could work out our separate providences, and reach, at least some kind of heaven up a ladder of words.

So write soon to me, before I see you on my next visit to London which will be in the next week or two.

I will not apologise again for all that needs apology, but will content myself with knowing that, to me and, I hope, to you, the mere composition of this letter means more than all the apologetic stupidities I could put together for somebody else.

Dylan

MS: Buffalo

EDITOR, SWANSEA AND WEST WALES GUARDIAN[1]
June 8 1934[2]

TELLING THE TRUTH TO THE PUBLIC
EXPOSE HUMBUG AND SMUG RESPECTABILITY

Sir—In this overpeopled breeding box of ours, this ugly contradiction of a town for ever compromised between the stacks and the littered bays, the Philistines exercise an inevitable dictatorship and regard the first glimmerings of a social intelligence and the first signs of a godly abhorrence of the parochial diseases much as the black man must have first regarded the features of his lily-faced brother.

You have most worthily demonstrated the fact that a local newspaper need not exclusively confine itself to the printing of photographs of our more bovine notabilities; the detailed reports of crimes which, in a less criminal state of society, would be unnecessary; insipid gossipings on the topographical positions of vanished streets and the references in bad novels to our God-chosen town; the retelling of old jokes; running commentaries on the gradual break down of the parish pump; and the useless quibblings between Christ-denying Christians, irrational Rationalists, and the white-spatted representatives of a social system that has, for too many years, used its bowler hat for the one purpose of keeping its ears apart.

But the colour of a shirt counts little to the man who has no shirt on his back, and the musical heaven after death harped on by the gentlemen

---

[1] A weekly newspaper, more radical than most, that survived for a few years in Swansea. Thomas was under the influence of Bert Trick, the left-wing grocer.

[2] *SL* dates it 14 January 1934 in error.

with the harmonium is a poor substitute for the man whose heaven on earth—warmth, clothes, food, a woman, and may be, children—is denied him on all sides. You can do more than merely allow the amateur and professional politicians of the town to display their bad manners in public. It is within your power to force up to the very limits of censorship, upon all your readers some little consciousness of the immoral restrictions placed upon them, of the humbug and smug respectability that works behind them all their handcuffed days, and to do this, not from any political bias, but from the undeniable conviction that the divinity of man is not to be trifled with, that the manna of God is not the lukewarm soup and starch of the chapels, but the redhot grains of love and life distributed equally and impartially among us all, and that at our roots of being lies not the greed for property or money, but the desire, large as a universe, to express ourselves freely and to the utmost limits of our individual capabilities.

Fascism would sprout to life like a flower through a coffin's cracks, watered by the excreta of the dead, the droppings of the political dead, the spittle of the Anti-Christs who have crucified Him and His children since the kiss of a man who wanted thirty pieces of silver in order, perhaps, to bribe one of the councillors of Jerusalem with a sack of coal or a cask of wine, or, as a member of the Jerusalem Road Improvement Committee, to buy a row of houses that the committee had decided to knock down for extension purposes. It would still stink of the weeds of this decomposing system of society, and all the tails of all the black shirts in the world would not wipe away the mud and the black and blue bruises from the well kicked bottom of the British public.

That we know. The shirts are changed, but the masks remain, hiding the riddle faces of those to whom the beauty of the tangible world approximates to the individual leisure for observing it. To them there is no world that is not to be touched and felt or sensed by the ambiguous senses of the maltreated body. To them the individual is a factor towards a state, and still an intricate machine for work that sells its sweat and muscle or else starves and is broken down. To them the individual is not a world, a structure of bone, blood, nerves and flesh, all made miraculous by the miracle of the mind, but a creature that works for the profit of its fellow creatures so that it may drag out its days and eat what is provided it and be buried at its own expense.

Fascism would clear the working man's house of bugs and attempt to provide him with a little more of what he should never have been deprived of; the divine right to live, regardless of his own working capacity.

Fascism would do this and more, so that he might work the harder and be dragged deeper into a false state of security and a blasphemous content, with his position at the very bottom of an anti-religious world of class.

That we know. It is within your power to force the consciousness, of that, and the hate of that, upon a thousand brains, and to show, through the medium of that consciousness, that the beautiful world has been made foul by the men who have worked against men, by the devil in man which has worked against the God in man.

Teach to hate, and then to believe in the antithesis of what is hated.

Yours etc.

Swansea   DYLAN THOMAS

EDITORIAL NOTE.—Mr. Dylan Thomas is a contributor of literary articles and reviews to the 'Morning Post' and the 'Listener' (the official organ of the BBC), and is also a contributor to 'New Verse' and 'New Stories'. A volume of his poems will shortly be published. He is a Swansea man and a member of the Little Theatre.

SL

GLYN JONES
[?early July 1934]   5 Cwmdonkin Drive Uplands Swansea

I have no possible excuse this time; no yellow letter weeks old in my pocket to pardon—in some respect, at least—the interminable time I have taken in replying to your letter, thanking you for the returned manuscript of 'Uncommon Genesis', and commenting upon our double show in the recent New Verse.[1] No excuse except that of laziness, a thing I would be heartily ashamed of if it were not for the summer weather, the pressure of commissioned prose, and the state of torpor which, as you know, is inevitably the rest [?result] of a London visit.

I had three weeks in town, saw Richard Rees again, and many other editorial gentlemen who, so far, have been unable to comply with my very reasonable—& soon very necessary—desire for congenial employment. I had a certain amount of good luck though, planted some poems, found an agent[2] who will take all my prose, and was commissioned—money, unfortunately, on delivery—to write a long novel all about my Jarvis valley. I've done a few thousand words already. About a 100,000 are needed. Work for the winter.

After reading your poem in New Verse I came to the very vain and boastful conclusion that it was strongly influenced by myself. Other people noticed it, too, though whether wrongly or rightly I cannot say. I didn't like it very much. I didn't like my own poems either. Do tell me if I was more conceited than usual in imagining the poem of Glyn Jones to be indebted—indebted, probably, for its worse points—to Dylan Thomas.

Have you written to the Rhondda woman yet?[3] If not, let me see the

---

[1] The June issue.
[2] The firm of Curtis Brown.
[3] Probably Margaret Haig, Lady Rhondda (1883–1941), wealthy daughter of a Welsh coal owner; she was proprietor and editor of the weekly magazine *Time and Tide*.

letter before you send it, will you? I might want to add a pathetic appeal for a job at the end of it. I'd take a job anywhere now, because, although I have plenty of work to keep me infernally busy for months, there is no immediate money in it. My dad is retiring at the end of this term, and after that I face the bitter world alone.[1] Are there any possibilities in Cardiff? I'd do anything, but am unfit for most things, my only qualifications being a Heart of Gold and a willing and discursive pencil.

'Uncommon Genesis' I have cut by at least half. It is now quite good. My agent—God, that sounds good—has it now.

When are you coming down to see me? Any Saturday will suit me perfectly, and I'll be really delighted to see you. What about this Saturday? The arrangements are in your hands entirely. Bring down one of your more arty friends if you want to. As far as Hart goes, this is Liberty All.

Dylan

Write soon, tell me when you're coming down, and do please understand that laziness is the only reason I haven't written many times & at much greater length than this.

MS: Carbondale

PAMELA HANSFORD JOHNSON
[about 3 July 1934]

Good morning. I hope it is morning with you. If not, good morning still. The sun in my heart comes up like a Javanese orange:—for similar images compare any poem in the Poet's Corner. I am at my open window again, looking out now on boys with red hair playing cricket. As always at this magically, *and* dirtily, casemented window, I am happy and aloof. Yes, I can think of you doing your usual things in your usual house, imagine your [?tottering] up the Rise and your burning Minor in the bus.[2] But I, to you, move in a fabulous, Celtic land, surrounded by castles, tall black hats, the ghosts of accents, and eternal Eisteddfodau.[3] Come down to see *me*, but come, my love, in the summer when we can move from this North London stuffiness near to the sea, and lie about on large cliffs by small villages, and fix my moustache not on a rolling, public bowl but on the edge of each private wave. To compensate for my disadvantage over you, here is an ambiguous, and totally inadequate, outline of my house and district. G.W.R. station. Shabby, badly built streets. Unutterable melancholy blowing along the tramlines. Quarter of an hour's tram ride

[1] D. J. Thomas didn't retire until the end of 1936.
[2] De Reszke Minor was a brand of cheap cigarette.
[3] An eisteddfod is a Welsh musical and literary gathering; 'eisteddfodau' is the plural.

up a long, treed road. A square, a handful of shops, a pub. Up a treed hill, field on one side, houses on the other. Near the top of the hill a small, not very well painted, gateless house. Large room, smaller room, study, kitchen. Four bedrooms, w.c., lavatory. Space at back sufficiently large for wash-house, clothes line, deck-chair and three sparrows. Private school in field opposite. Nice field. Tennis court above. Very nice, very respectable. Not much traffic. Lot of sparrows. My own room is a tiny, renovated bedroom, all papers and books, cigarette ends, hardly any light. *Very* tiny. I really have to go out to turn round. Cut atmosphere with book-knife. No red cushion. No cushion at all. Hard chair. Smelly. Painful. Hot water pipes very near. Gurgle all the time. Nearly go mad. Nice view of wall through window. Pretty park nearby. Sea half a mile off. Better sea four or five miles off. Lunatic asylum mile off. Workhouse half a mile off. All this sounds depressing, but you must come down. And come down soon, as soon as you can. If it's hot and summery we *can* have a wonderful time. And if it rains, we can fug all day and all night with the greatest pleasure in the world.

You asked about Dad. He's no better, and has to see his London doctor even more often. My mother is weak but still garrulous. You won't like her. She talks too much, too often, and too unintelligently for it to be possible for you to like her. But she's very kind and would love to see you. So explore this Welsh darkness, my darling. I may even take you to Laugharne, which is the nearest approach under the sun to a Stygian borough.

Is This Political Work?

If you read the newspapers, you'll see that Swansea is the centre of all revolutionary activities this week. It is the week of the trial of Tom Mann and Harry Pollitt, whose trial has been framed-up by the police and the local authorities.[1] I have just left the Socialist Party, and offered my services to the Communists. I *was* in time for Mosley's meeting,[2] and was thrown down the stairs. No harm done, however. I have just completed a seditious article attacking the shirted gentleman, having discovered, quite by accident, that he is the biggest owner of slum property in Birmingham. Cha!

Old Stiffened Bowels-Gore is a dirty but comic boy.[3] Don't choke him off yet. There must be a certain amount of pleasure for him in chattering about genital organs to unknown and invisible young ladies. He's far enough away. Tell him he can write as freely as he likes—the dirt-box — and enjoy his little bit of Stockport filth. Then, when the letters grow too

[1] Harry Pollitt, general secretary of the Communist Party of Great Britain, and Tom Mann, a veteran Party member, appeared at Swansea Assizes on July 3 charged with making seditious speeches in the South Wales coalfield. They were found not guilty next day.

[2] Sir Oswald Mosley, the British fascist leader, held a rally at the Plaza Cinema, Swansea, on Sunday July 1. Thomas was not thrown down the stairs.

[3] Johnson had received (she wrote in her diary) a 'peculiar letter from a curious poet' in the north of England, whose name Thomas parodied as 'Stiffened Bowels-Gore'.

verminous, write back and tell him what he can do with his book on Lawrence. Or tell him to devote his phallic energy to poor old Hannah. Still, his letter is a nasty piece of work. He's the [?best] example of an 'in-and-in' I've ever heard of.

Your poem is good, and promising. It is careful, well modulated, and, fortunately, neither too sweet nor too simple. I don't know about the sixth line of the first verse, which sounds something like the opening line in a London Mercury sonnet.[1] And the seventh and eighth line of the second verse are quite bad. The poem is intelligent, and has many beautiful phrases. 'The blood was love.' 'The funnel of the tempers.' The lost Atlantis line is a successful surprise. On the whole, it's one of your best poems. Obviously much care has been taken with it, and if these remarks do sound un-naturally guarded it is because your poetry is changing so definitely in attitude, and is becoming so much more intense and muscular, that I am frightened to say much for fear of interrupting its progress. I always knew you had a splendid poetry in you; now it's forming itself. My influence, obvious mainly in lines five, ten, and thirteen, and, perhaps, in the construction of a few other phrases, will drop away and leave your verse naked and itself. Progress from this, but don't, as in the lines of the 'stucco wall' & the 'line of lamplight', sink to an easy, impressionist objectiveness. Both these lines could have appeared in Rupert Brooke's 'Great Lover' catalogue, and have no place in a poem such as this. Not much of a comment on the poem, I'm afraid. But what it promises is so good that I daren't say anything more. Go on, work on from this. Condense even more. Oh, I forgot, line nine is bad, too. Another item in the Rupert catalogue. The rest—too good for me to spoil, and an incalculable improvement on nearly all that is printed in 'Symphony'.

I admire the Obituary, too. You could write in many directions. This is a good piece of impromptu writing. Thank God, in your Poem you've found the one direction for you. Go ahead, lidy. All the juiciest coconuts is at the top.

Your story is as lovely as all the last stories you've sent me. You've got a style and a matter of your own. Little as they are, I can't think of anyone's stories printed today that are better. You are bloody good, you know. I'm sending the story back, just a little bit sub-edited, but I want you to send it back to me again. Reasons for sub-editing: 'Returned the pressure' is far too cold a phrase. 'Quick' is unnecessary and spoils the sound of the sentence. 'Broken the ice' is very hackneyed, &, again, doesn't add anything. 'Blade of grass' is simpler & more effective than a 'green blade.' The descriptive sentence isn't needed, and I don't like fruit on the sky. 'The man's' sleeve is false. So is 'Hell'. You know what's wrong with 'choking bliss'. I don't know why, but, really, the name of the boy is unimportant. Obviously she won't go to see him again. He comes

---

[1] Under Squire's editorship, the magazine was not keen on 'modernist' verse.

& he goes, &, as it's the girl's story, it's better that his shadow should be nameless. 'Fretting' is one of your blasted words I can't bear; 'quieten his fingers' is good. Of course he looked at his watch, & not at his boot. Why mention it? 'Defensive fury etc'—either Ethel M.[1] or David H., I don't know which. To shout 'something' is rather slack, & an avoidance of an issue. Who cares about the bus-conductor? 'Darkness' & 'aloneness' in one sentence sounds horrible. 'The man,' drat him, again. 'From the darkness of a forgotten past' sounds like Corby & his scientific skull. What part of the woman's anatomy is her 'bed'. She kissed the woman on the bed. I don't like sentences that have the slightest suggestion of ambiguity.

Now, my dear, what are you going to do with this and with the rest of your really splendid stories? Either buck your agent up, or take them away from him. Anyway 'Procession' & this are entirely your own property. Send them to Hamish Miles, & ask him to consider them either for Life and Letters or New Stories. Both these are stories as good as any I've read for years. You've got nearly everything that Katherine Mansfield possessed, & a good deal more. Again let me remind you of the position of the coconuts. Go on, go on, my darling lady.

All the editing in 'Suddenly A Woman' *is* worth abiding by. Just with those few phrases—the phrases & words I have blackened—thrown out, the story is *perfect*. O.K., love.

I have just finished a review for the Adelphi. God, some tripe is published. Out of seven books sent by Rees only two are worth anything. The other four are unbelievably bad. Excerpt from 'The Selected Poems of Charles King':

> 'Thou camest from the Paradise of Love,
> A fondling in the dew-drops, out of Time,
> When far in Being's arcane Hesperid-grove
> Strayed Monna Lisa with her Prince of Rhyme.'

Excerpt from Frank Kendon's 'Tristram'.

> 'The thirsty greyhound drew his leash
> Tighter about Sir Tristram's wrist;
> He heard a noise of rising water:
> The dog should wet its thirst, at least.'

Excerpt from 'Singing Waters' by Ian Dall:

> 'As might a butterfly when first
> It from the dark cocoon does burst,
> He rises from the rippled ring
> To joy of rhythmic uttering.'

[1] The novelist Ethel M. Dell? Or the novelist Ethel Mannin?

And a poem by Sydney Salt, one of the highbrows of Majorca:

Seeing Goya.

'Goya shot a few bullets through the sky.
So did Dostoevsky—who else?
Hungry men these, who knew the meaning of lean.'

What a life is the life of a hack reviewer. Thank God the others, William Soutar & William Montgomerie (Squared Circle) are very traditional & very competent. Sydney is nuts.

I'm enclosing a short story. I've been a bit tired, & this is a recreation story. Don't be too hard on it, & if there's any merit in it all perhaps you'll type it out for me darling? I'll have a poem to send you next time. It's too hot to be very fertile. I don't know how you manage it. I think I must be very lazy.

In my next letter, too,—it should, I know, be in this, but I've put the damned papers very carefully away and can't remember where—I'll send the rest of 'No More Canary Wine'. It's highly mannered, but will grow out of that, and should be a rattling good story.

Is the finger better? Have it cut off if it hurts much more. I should love you with only four fingers on one hand.

I miss you. I miss you terribly. I think of you, love you, and look at your picture which I've taken out of my little locked drawer and put on the ledge over my table. Oh, darling, darling, you're such a long way away. I should like to be sticking my moustache on every milestone between us.

XXX

It won't, it can't, be long.
Send me Pieta.
Tell me how goes my Son of Kong?[1]
Give my love to your mother.
And take *all* my love for yourself.

XXX

And if you talk again of the beastly young men who have been in love with you as 'the others', I shall do something hideous & horrid with the sharp insides of grandfather clocks.

X

MS: Buffalo   SL(R)

---

[1] The 1933 film *King Kong* was much talked about. In Pamela's diary (20 August 1934), Dylan was 'Baby Kong'.

EDITOR, SWANSEA AND WEST WALES GUARDIAN
July 6 1934

THE REAL CHRIST—AND THE FALSE

Peculiar Heavens

CREATED BY LITTLE ORATORS

Mr. Dylan Thomas, the literary critic and poet, writes:

Since my last letter, when, with as much forceful imagery as the law of censorship allows me, I spoke of the party to which Mr. Mainwaring Hughes[1] lends, if nothing else, a sense of humour and a clean dickey, I have listened to a Christian orator promising his audience a celestial mansion on the condition that they give themselves to Christ, and asking them to be content, while on the earth, with any sort of insanitary hovel, ragged garments, and bad and meagre food that the powers of the land feel it fit to provide them.

While admiring the sincerity of the orator, and envying his mastery of the accordion, I could not help wishing that he would utilize his power of expressing such morbid convictions, his clear diction, and very effective histrionics, for the purpose of providing his Christ with a flat-iron instead of a harp, and for impressing upon those who sniggered around him the fact that the essence of Christianity is a product of good, red, living vitamins rather than of a sticky balsam for embalming the bodies of the dead.

For his Christ is clothed in a shroud. The wounds are still bleeding, the cry of despair and abnegation still on his colourless lips. His Christ, like an ethereal sexton, sits waiting in the clouds for man to die. The orator, and his bannered boys, forget that the boulders at the gate of the tomb were thrown aside, and that the raised and living Christ came out like a man from anaesthetic, a symbol of life, a reawakened, revolutionary force, not a walking corpse with the words of a dead message stale and yellow on his mouth.

Michael Angelo's Christ of the Last Supper is full-mouthed, with a bellyful of wine and chicken. (It is very pleasant to reflect that he would be ineligible for the British Union of Fascists.) The orator's Christ is a pussyfoot and a vegetarian, and what is more, a Deity superbly indifferent to the crimes of His children against His children, to the blasphemous blackening of the air as an English Bishop buys foreign controlled armament shares, as men of culture and integrity are thrown penniless out of their own land by a megalomaniac drunk on words and blood, as Sir John Simon[2] pulls another feather from the Angel of Peace.

Can this timid emblem of suffering stare around at our contemporary world, and, sickened of the waste and murder, the obscene hypocrisy of

[1] Mainwaring Hughes, a coal merchant and town councillor, was a leading local member of the British Union of Fascists.
[2] Sir John Simon (1873–1954) was British Foreign Secretary, 1931–5.

those war-mongers and slave-drivers who venerate His name and void their contagious rheum upon the first principle of His gospel, afford no more proof of His living energy and His Messiahdom than the mere offer of a heavenly accommodation (h. and c., cherubs, every godly convenience) at the end of this giddy life?

The heaven of the capitalist is best described by Richard Aldington:[1]

> 'It was like a crematorium
> Or rather a cadaver factory,
> Where every day
> Millions of people were consumed to smoke.
> Out of ten thousand towering chimneys
> Gushed black greasy smoke
> That whitened to a cloud of bank notes.
> All the angels drove to work in tanks.
> Far above them the mystic symbol,
> Made of dazzling electric lights,
> Ran about the sky and changed its colours:
> More and more and more for ever,
> Holy, Blessed, Glorious, Mass Production.'

UNIFORMED ANGELS

In the heaven of the Fascists the uniformed angels parade every morning, making the customary salute, before the golden throne. The humbler angels are kept serenely in their places. There are no intellectual angels. The black Jehovah, very naturally, distrusts intellect. And only the Best Books are read. There are organised sports, and even the cherubim are forced to show, by their prowess in swinging on the parallel bars and in improvising knuckle-dusters with three pennies, how eminently qualified they are to organise the paradisaical rank and file. The anthem of their heaven is, of course, a setting of that famous poem:

> 'How odd
> Of God
> To choose
> The Jews.'

But the heaven of the religious orators is more infernal still, a sublimated charnel-house, foul as a morgue set at the end of a slum near the parade of policemen, unsavoury old women, and drinkers of methylated spirits, a dismal place full of young men singing Welsh hymns in suspiciously high voices, and blind old men dabbling their hands in the blood of the crosses that stand up all over the place like so many scarlet pylons.

Which is the heaven of the living men. We shall not for the promised

---

[1] Richard Aldington (1892–1962), poet, novelist and editor. The poem Thomas quotes (in a condensed version) is a section from 'A Fool i' the Forest'.

residence in any of those cloudy regions, bow down contentedly before the twisting makers of laws and moneys that provide us with the fag ends of existence on the earth. It's heaven on earth or no heaven. Neither a Christ of cloud nor a Deity that the moths have been at, is a Saviour for us. Our symbol of faith must be a naked life, not a pale cross of death done up in a mummy blanket and surrounded by the Pyramid walls of an established stupidity.

DYLAN THOMAS

Swansea

JOHN LEHMANN

From the 1930s, John Lehmann (b. 1907) was a leading figure in literary London, as poet and editor. With Denys Kilham Roberts he edited *The Year's Poetry* for 1934 (which contained Thomas's 'Light breaks'); for 1935 ('Especially when the October wind'), and for 1936 (three further Thomas poems).

[?July 1934]   5 Cwmdonkin Drive Uplands Swansea

Dear Mr. Lehmann,

Thanks very much for the note and the letter. I enclose three poems. The first, beginning, 'I see the boys of summer', was published in the June New Verse. The other two are unpublished. I send you these three as they more or less go together, being based on something of the same idea and in chronological order. I am having a book of poems brought out in a few months, and, I suppose, the first two of these poems, at least, will be printed in that book. If you like the poems at all, I hope that fact won't prevent you from possibly accepting them.

I was asked to mention the names of some of the periodicals I've contributed to during the last twelve months: Adelphi, New English Weekly, New Verse, Sunday Referee, John O' London's, Listener, and a few Welsh papers which aren't of much literary interest.

I could, if you wish, send you some more poems. I do hope you'll let me know.

Yours Sincerely,
Dylan Thomas

MS: Brick Row Book Shop, California

JOHN LEHMANN
[?July 1934]   5 Cwmdonkin Drive Uplands Swansea

Dear Mr. Lehmann,

Thanks very much. I am glad that you are going to use a poem of mine. 'Light' was, as probably you know, printed in the 'Listener', to whom the only acknowledgement belongs.

I do not want my age to be published, of course. For purposes of arrangement *only*, I was born on October 27, 1913.

I shall be in London for the August Holiday Week, and, perhaps, for a little longer. If you are not away during that time, would it be possible for me to meet you? Perhaps we could have lunch together?

Yours Sincerely,
Dylan Thomas

MS: Texas

GEOFFREY GRIGSON
[?July 1934]   5 Cwmdonkin Drive Uplands Swansea

Dear Grigson,
    Thanks for the note.
    I have no poems at all at the present moment, or at least no poems which I should care for you to see. I hope in a few days to be able to send you two new poems, though.
    I enclose my answers to the questionnaire.[1] I'm afraid they sound rather priggish in places, but I couldn't avoid it. They make me sound, too, very contented with my work, which I am certainly not. If they are not what you want, or are too long, I'll be quite willing to do another set of answers.
    You asked me to remind you, some time ago, about the books for review. I've been doing a certain amount of reviewing lately, & would be very pleased if you could, as you promised, send a few volumes along.
    I'm sorry to have no poems ready. I'll send you some during the week, if I may.

Sincerely,
Dylan Thomas

I hope to be in London about the middle of August. I was up a little time ago, but heard that you were away on holiday. I was sorry to miss seeing you.

MS: Texas   *SL*

PAMELA HANSFORD JOHNSON
July 20 '34

    Your letter made me very happy, too. I am listening to Monteverdi's Ballet of the Ungracious Ladies. And that is very happy music, in spite of

---

[1] Published in *New Verse*, October 1934, as 'Answers to an Enquiry'. Thomas said his poetry was 'the record of my individual struggle from darkness towards some measure of light'.

Pluto and a coloratura Venus. I have only just finished reading 'The Stranger' of Algernon Blackwood—a very happy story, in spite of the ghost. I am smoking a good Turkish cigarette, and have pinched a glass of invalid port from my mother's bedside. Your letter is on the table in front of me, and, later in the night, Comrade Trick is coming to take me to a Fascist demonstration. Nothing much could be better. Your presence would make everything all right. Through the body of words I tickle you a courteous salute under the chin. You now have a long white beard, and I find myself tickling General Booth of the Salvation Army. But these little snags of vision are to be expected. Yesterday I divined the position of a garden slug. There, under that particular tuft, that small square of soil (I said) lies a fat slug. I dug up the tuft, and there the slug lay, smiling like Mona Lisa. I now add to my list of recondite & entirely uncommercial attainments that of being able to unearth slugs at any given moment. If we ever possess a parrot or a canary, my gift will be distinctly useful. If not, it can still be used as a method of bridging over any awkward pause in the conversation. 'Find a slug for the gentleman.' 'Certainly, my dear.' And, so saying, I produce from the potato bed a black, juicy specimen with a long mane.

Your pun on the first line of James Joyce's little lyric has been very much appreciated by a select section of my friends. How very apt that the book from which that particular lyric (this sentence I challenge you to beat for literary coyness) is culled, should be called Chamber Music. Can *I* be vulgar for a moment, too? I heard a funny story yesterday about a man with three testicles. This man, this very odd man, went into a public house and called a drink. Then, after a few drinks, he turned round to the company in the bar and said: 'I bet you a pound note that me and any other bloke here have got five testicles between us.' At this, of course, there was much merriment, and the bet was taken on. 'Him and me,' said the very odd man, pointing to a little fellow in the corner. 'Now we'll go into the other room, and then you can come in one by one & see that what I've said is true.' Just as he reached the door of the other room, the little fellow from the corner followed him & whispered softly in his ear, 'I say, mate, I hope you've got four. I've only got one.' I think that's a very funny joke. It doesn't look very funny written down, but just you try it on the right company!

Back to the land now. No more talk of gangrene and sexual aberrations. I'm enclosing a new story, 'The Vest'[1] which will provide all that is needed of violence and general nastiness (General Nastiness of the Fifth Buffs).

Your Stories
Neither of them are as good as the last few you've sent me. 'The Old Mrs' is rather badly written all through, although the theme and the

[1] First published in *Yellowjacket*, May 1939.

working out of it is good. Incidentally, the punctuation in both stories is abominable, and makes nonsense of many, too many, of the sentences. But all I said in my last letter about the merits & the attitude of your stories applies to 'The Old Mrs' & 'Magnificat'. Everything in them, except the actual writing, is as good as in 'Pietà', 'Anna', & 'Suddenly A Woman'. I've hacked them about a bit, as usual, though not in the Old Mrs, at least, with very much effect. In 'The Old Mrs' you are frequently very slipshod in expression. 'Anyway', 'To be literal', 'Metaphorically speaking', 'For all that', 'The Devil to pay' and other abominations of style are littered along the pages. The story is too realistic, too human in a John Bull sense, for me to be able to criticise it as thoroughly, or, rather, with as much possible insight, as a story that is more severely psychological—'Suddenly A Woman'—or more fanciful & mysterious — 'Anna'. I don't know much about human beings. Only the exceptions interest me. I dislike people as a whole, & the Man in the Street is evil when you take him out of the Street. So, biased and not very competent, I do not find the 'Old Mrs' half as interesting a story as 'The Two Gardeners', or as fascinating—in a literary sense—a character as our little Minnie or our ugly Clara. But from the point of view of *writing* alone, there's a lot to quarrel with in this domestic tragedy.

Reason for Quarrel & Pencilling
First pencilling. The opening sentence had to be altered to get over the wretched paragraph on page three: 'She arose, preparatory to . . . sleep.'
Second Cliché. Unwarranted cliché too.
Third I've protested before at your habit of making a very simple operation, such as this, into a vague colloquialism. 'As she was dried' is what you meant & what you should have put.
Fourth 'Shrivelled' is too decorative, too descriptive, an adjective. 'Empty' is literal.
Fifth Colloquialism, again.
Sixth Horrible. 'To be literal'. Chk! Chk!
Seventh One of your damned colloquial 'anyways' again.
Eighth Precious affectation. Bad Viola Price.
Ninth This is purely a suggestion. The Harmonium, as the dead husband's musical instrument, seems to me a truer choice than the piano.
Tenth No reason to mention this at all.
Eleventh I like 'Aces'. You shouldn't have cut it out. It links together the actions of seeing the girl & buying from the girl.
Twelfth Not 'dived', darling. The poor gentleman wasn't a performing seal.
Thirteenth Ugly word. The rather frigid correction I've made seems to be more in keeping with the impersonal, &, itself, rather frigid, nature of Maggie's romance.
Fourteenth 'She blushed' is enough. You don't blush 'coldly', & 'hotly' is a real Ethel M-ism.

Fifteenth The slice of Mrs Leach's life is not essential. I still don't like your efforts at the colloquial speech of the Lower Classes.

Sixteenth Just to get over the cutting out of Mrs Leach's monologue.

Seventeenth Horrible. 'Metaphorically speaking.' Chk! Chk!

Eighteenth See reason number Eight. When you decide to write badly, then...

Nineteenth Bloody colloquialism that looks, & is, cheap & hindering.

Twentieth Just another suggestion. 'You be careful, that's all' seems to me to be enough. It implies the mysteriousness with which old ladies—as far as my very little knowledge of old ladies goes—invest the most ordinary platitude.

Twenty First The ironic 'rather beautifully', is obvious in the rest of her conversation. You needn't comment. (That's a nasty thing to say, too.)

Twenty Second Clumsy sentence. And marred, as you so often mar a sentence, by that infernal dash '—' of yours. The dash, except in very special cases, is a sign of carelessness, or of ignorance of punctuation. In your case it's just damned carelessness. And there are dashes all over the story.

Twenty Third Exactly the same reason. It's so simply avoided by a full stop & another capital letter.

Twenty Fourth Untrue psychologically. I hate idiomatic speech of this sort.

Twenty Fifth An Ethel M. trick. Very much unworthy of you even in your most pedestrian—or, if you like, realistic moments.

Twenty Sixth I've altered the last sentence to get over the obviously necessary deletion of the clumsy 'that, though she was showing etc' sentence.

And that's a hell of a lot of hacking, isn't it? But I'm sure it's justified. As you'll see, I've done my best, too, to do something with the punctuation. Have a look, when you're typing the story again, at the commas I've introduced. You'll be able to correct them a bit. At the moment they're not too good, as I've got a special punctuation of my own. But your commas in this story are planted just where you like & not where the sense or the construction dictates.

Go carefully through the punctuation, do cut the worst of the things I've mentioned, stick to the last sentence, &, if you like, prune the whole thing even a little more. *Then* send it to your agents. It will probably be good. Emotionally, it's good even now. And the motive is *remarkably* good. But in places it's shoddy, definitely shoddy, a very second-rate example of your work. It is, perhaps, more saleable a story than 'Anna' or 'Pietà'. But it hasn't got as much of the you—the literary you, now, not the flesh & blood—that I love.

In case I haven't told you before: I love the other *you* too. I love you, my darling.

Magnificat is, to my mind, a better story, but that is, perhaps, because it is less real than the other—less real, that is, than the world of regular appointments & cafés & cinema foyers, a world that I, caught between two foyers, regard as *less* real (& so do you) than that of divine madnesses, milk-suckled dolls, & petty crucifixions. The main fault of the story lies, again, in the actual writing. I don't know, but perhaps you are writing too fast. Not too much—no-one can ever write too much, & it's an absurd lie to say that by writing 'too much' it is possible to write oneself out—but too quickly. The theme, the motive, is again very effective. Clara is a dramatic figure of some importance, and Mr. Calder is a good symbol. But there are patches of shoddiness, and far too many sentences, badly punctuated sentences, too, of the same construction. But this, in spite of the things I'll point out & which you are really fully aware of, is a true story in that it is a story that is true to yourself. Even if you are truly despicable, the truly despicable writing of your stories is worth-while & very essential. As it is, you are lovely (I'm awfully biased in that respect), & *each*, each single, unlovely sentence (by unlovely I do not mean conventionally ugly or anything at all like that) is a lie to your loveliness & is unworthy of you. Don't say I expect too much of you. I expect only what I know you are capable of producing. This applies all ways. Now to the story. I won't, as in the criticism of the 'Old Mrs', give a detailed list, but only point out some of the more obvious & the more debatable things. To begin with, Clara wasn't a daily help, because she 'slept in'. 'Architects paraphernalia' I object to for the same reason that I objected to 'the drying business' in the other story. The *fact*, the fact that Mr. Calder did keep architectural implements in the top room, is mentioned towards the end of the story. 'Sullen Clara was' is a magazineish inversion. Almost a perversion. So 'one day Clara found herself a young man', did she? What a horrible transformation of sex! 'Jealousy was a ball of flesh in her throat' is a good example of figurative language gone wrong. In this tale, anyway, figurative language is *not* wanted. Not f.l. of this sort, at least. 'She mottled with anger' reminds me of another character of yours who also attempted to imitate the Big Bad Wolf. The dashes—the damned dashes that I'm employing now—I won't comment on. I don't like the idea of Kitty meeting her father at the bottom, but that's because I've got a nasty mind. The trouble is that so many other readers have. The picture of Mr. Calder sucking his cold pipe (Clara, apparently, had put the matches in the soup) brings to mind the picture of the Poona father in the 'Tallboy'. It's just such a damned foolish, &, as regards the story, unnecessary thing, that that old war-horse would have done. And Mr. Calder, apart from that, & in spite of the very little time & space you devote to him is by way of being a genuine creation. Now I'm very dubious about the end of the story. It's right that a star *should* fall, & it's pretty certain that a star *did* fall. But should you mention it? Yes, perhaps you should. I've suggested an alternative end sentence, cutting out the possibly melodramatic touch of the 'rattling windows'. It's only a suggestion, but have a look at it. If nothing else, it might suggest a better end to your mind.

This is what I meant by too many similarly-constructed sentences: 'She bent down and, scraping her fingers under the dresser, examined it closely.' 'She would run up to her room and, burying her face in the pillow, dream of her wedding day.' 'The preacher told the story once again and, as Clara heard of the sorrows etc, she felt the tears fall on to her folded hands.' And so on, right through the story. Use that construction if you like, but *do* put a comma after the first 'and'. Always. Otherwise the sentence doesn't make any sense.

You do work, darling, don't you? You're going to be prodigiously pro-lific one day. And I shall smart with shame as I produce one obscure line to your twenty equally obscure & equally good lines, & one story to your seven. Go on working. Produce as much as you like but don't work too fast. And heed your Uncle Dylan when he points out the obvious faults, even though he himself goes on writing stories like 'The Vest'. 'The Vest', by the way, you mightn't like at all. Tell me what you think of it, & don't spit at it at once because it's nasty. There's a lot of nastiness in the world, and I must use my dung-fork now & then. By my next letter I hope to have another story ready to send you. If you can, type out 'The Vest' for me. Don't hurry about it, though. I've got agents now, too—theirs are the last few letters you've re-directed to me—& they want some stories of mine. Curtis Brown. They seem very good.

I'm going to write to Neuburg to-day, Sunday, asking him about my bloody book. I won't be very rude, I promise you. He is a little swine, though, isn't he? I can understand why he doesn't love me any more. But surely he hasn't given up loving you. He mustn't do that, he's such a nice little badger. (I've read a book on the life of the mole. You wouldn't believe! He's a horribly lecherous little thing. O Mole Mio.)

'Flower', by the way, in my 'All all and all'[1] (Bradawl, Nuttall, & Bugger-all) is a two-syllabled word.

Ha! 'Teredo' is an old one on me. I wrote a poem in 1933 beginning

> 'Half is remembered since your halfhands' knocking,
> And ten teredo fingers bored the womb'

Why don't you call your cat 'Egypt'? This is good Shakespeare, & good felinology. Or why not 'Dda', in memory of Hywel Dda,[2] a Welsh prince, who introduced the first law for the protection of cats? The rest of the names that I can think of are inevitably bawdy.

More (for no reason at all) of my long-postponed Political Corners*

An economic system (he barked) must have an ethical sanction. If it can be forced home on the consciousness of people that the present economic system is ethically bad, the seed has been planted that may in time grow into a fine revolutionary flower. Convince people that a thing

* I'm very fair, anyway. I mark this section so that you can skip it.

[1] 'All all and all the dry worlds lever', soon to appear in *18 Poems*.
[2] 'Hywel the Good', a Welsh king of the tenth century.

is bad, and they are ready to listen to a reasonable plan for its overthrow. There is and always must be a stream of revolutionary energy generated when society is composed, at top and bottom, of financial careerists and a proletarian army of dispossessed. Out of the negation of the negation must rise the new synthesis. The new synthesis must be a classless society. But there is no great future for a political party based solely on the claims of the workers, as human labour in industry is almost obsolescent. The negation has emerged, & the future of politics must be in the synthesis of production & consumption. There is no use in the ownership of a national plant unless, there is sufficient financial credit to make it function. The control of money—that is banking, credit, consumption—is the only key to the communal State. Industry is capable of giving the community a high standard of living, and it is only a faulty monetary system which prevents industry from delivering the goods. Aggregate prices are higher than the aggregate of communal incomes & wages. The monetary & credit system is only a system of book-keeping or accountancy. What is required is not a bloody revolution but an intellectual one. Alternatively, there is the confiscation of property by force. The revolutionary political parties are not in common agreement on that point. The Communist Party, with the faint endorsement of the I.L.P., advocates force to reach power. The Socialist League, the New Socialist Party, the orthodox Labour party believe in first attaining constitutional power and then putting their policies into practice. If constitutional government cannot, in the space of a year after the next General Election, fulfil their policies, then a united front must be made, the army and the police force must be subdued, and property be taken by force.

No-one can be neutral, neither worker, intellectual, nor reactionary, for the composition of the classes has changed. The class-struggle is primarily the intellectual struggle, and, however remote it may seem from the economic process, it is nevertheless conditioned by it. All that matters is the right and the wherewithal to live, and all that remains is to discover, not by hypothecating, but by the trial experiment of constitutionalism, & then, if that fails, of force, the most scientific way to introduce the new society. The governing principle must be that of consumption. The worker is only a factor in production, & nearly an obsolete factor at that. But a consumer is a perpetual factor in any society. All society ceases to be class-ridden when treated purely as a primary body of consumers. The most efficient and just organisation is under the direct control of the State. Those controlling the State shall earn, in consumer-credit, no more than the worker who controls the drains of the State. Private profit must end. Reserves against depreciation must be the only charge on industry.

The release of humanity from toil is overdue. Long hours & low wages are anachronistic. The whip of poverty can only flog a dead horse. The shout of the ring-master is a dead language. Our heritage is machine-made leisure. We have the desire, the means, & the opportunity, but not the common & united front that is not frightened, if the ballot and the pressure of constitutional government fails, to advocate, & practise, the last reserve of communal force.

The State of the future is not to be an economic despotism or a Christian utopia. It is the state of Functional Anarchy.

And a fol dol dol and a reel of cotton. So much for that. I'm preparing a paper on Functional Anarchy from which, with the permission of my readers, I shall quote in my next open letter to the constituents of the Battersea ward.

This is a mess of a letter, too. It dribbles and mouths all over the place like Maurice Chevalier. I'll blame it on the weather which is an unhealthy mixture of blues and grays. As soon as I finish this letter, I'm going to sit in the sun and watch a county cricket match. Even degenerates like myself have that old True-Blue urge which naught can vanquish. I am looking for my School Tie which is, I believe, acting as a sort of strap around a pile of pornographic literature lent to me some months ago by a small man on the sands. I am also practising, in a low voice, how to say, 'Well played, sir,' & 'Demmed bed luck' when a ball hits the wicket-keeper in the pelvis. Happy, funny, bloody, wicked, dirty, beautiful world o'mine. Oh why aren't I with you, my darling?

And of course I'll see you before your holidays. I'll be up in August. And don't forget about Wales.

Write soon and write much. Tell me again you love me. I love you so much. Tell me all there is to tell. Go on working hard. Don't draw moustaches on my photograph. Give my love to your mother. Do make another burn-mark in the Chelsea Bells.[1] Have a drink for me. And kiss me good morning before I gird up my loins and go. All possible love whateffer. Do call your cat 'Egypt'.

Dylan

XXX. Sometime in August. (I think I shall have someone to sit (again) on my face so that, meeting, you won't recognise me, and we can start being in love again. A dirty desire.) I love you. Bloody-face loves you.

MS: Buffalo   *SL(R)*

TREVOR HUGHES
[? summer 1934][2]   5 Cwmdonkin Drive

Dear Trevor,

I have the villain of a headache, my eyes are two piss holes in the sand, my tongue is fish-and-chip paper. Dan Jones is staying here for a few days, and last night and the night before we wasted our substances and distended our bellies with low company. It's difficult to write, because the

[1] The Six Bells, a Chelsea pub.
[2] There is no reliable clue to when the letter was written, but its manner suggests it was at least as late as this.

bending of the head hurts like fury. And my hand ain't what she was. Oh, woe, woe, woe, unto Mumbles and the oystered beer. Dan is playing very weak music. I wish I loved the human race, but ghouls, vampires, women-rippers, deflowerers of weeny infants, warted soaks, pimps, and financiers pass by the window, going God knows where or why, in a dream up and down the hill. It isn't a silly face, it's a purposeful face, with a big vein of rottenness, an almighty canker, growing under the nose. The horrid moustaches of the human face: dripping with last twelvemonth's tears and beer, stained with egg, cows' kisses, udder- rubbings, and night custard.[1] The teeth, the werewolf's teeth, big as gob-stoppers, windy teeth, full of holes, just like Ramsay MacDonald,[2] crunching on the Paste and Putty of Our Hearts—what utter snobs we are to imagine that the card-shapes under our waistcoats hold more of beauty and sensitivity than the little cupid abortions of gelatine beating under a whore's shirt. Look at the notices in tram cars: Spitting on Christ prohibited. In the parks: Do not walk on God. What shall it be? Jew's mucus or gentile's praise? Ripeness is all—all balls. We're over- ripe, we night-walkers, cunt-stalkers, wall-chalkers. The women of the world, perpetually out of perspective, cry, Focus, Focus. Is it our fault that we misinterpret them? Perhaps we've got to be superstitious, natural, supernatural, all one huge satanic process. Our words—'give me a half-pint, a Hovis, a book by Paul de Kock,[3] and thou, thou old lavatory chain'—are spells to drag up the personified Domdaniel pleasure.[4] Everything we do drags up a devil. Last night, Dan and I, none too brightly, for the womb of the Mermaid was empty, and the radio-gram blaring, discovered we had too little feeling. We almost lost our tempers, proving how unfeeling we were. The petty emotions, hates, loves, and spites, we said grandly, were nothing to us. We were artistic Ishmaels, and we scorned with a ha and a ho the lusts that shot up bushes, burning like cantharides, all over the waterless places. Sex was an instrument to annoy women with, and the anachronistic loyalties, faithfulnesses, holy-desires, gratitudes, mercies and charities were no more than words to cover over the evil intentions of our inferiors. (Because they are inferior, these blubbery-eyed old men, stiff-dickied, these shop-assistants with their ingrown virginities priced at 1/11¾, these frigging boys, these wailing mothers, & disappointed communists; and God help our godheads if we can't play Christ, and Christ was always the white sheep among the black, the superior, the natty gent in a tramps' ward.) We started to remember old cruelties, the purposeful raising of desires in girls we knew & the purposeful unsatisfying of them, the tongue-cuts, the embarrassments, the ungrateful things we had done, the muck we'd uttered with our tongues in our cheeks. Our lowest

[1] Thomas had a long-running fantasy about this imaginary beverage, whose properties were both magical and obscene.
[2] James Ramsay MacDonald, Labour Prime Minister of the National Government, 1931–5.
[3] Charles Paul de Kok (1794–1871), French writer, supposedly indecent.
[4] Daniel Dom, an apocalyptic figure in early Thomas writings, notably in the story 'Prologue to an Adventure'.

feelings, when we sit drunk-maudlin, holding a whore's hand, are the highest feelings of the maggoty men around us. Artists don't have to die etc. They crucify themselves etc. All the old bullshit.

Why am I writing this? Is it to show the futility of effort? Are you playing Freud to me as I tell you that, like Havelock Ellis, I bore holes in the floor to piss through, or cut a pigeon's throat as I copulate? I don't know why or what, but last night we, who had no feelings, spoke passionately, waving our arms in the air, saying, Desire is Nothing, as we stroked her buttocks, saying, Hunger is Vanity, as we swilled and wallowed, damning the conventions as we took a bus home and lied when we got there. Why I am writing this is uselessness. Stop it. I can't shout, like Lawrence, of the red sea of the living blood. Why can't I put a message in a parcel? There's muck in the soul of man, and a devil in his loins. God was deposed years ago, before the loin-cloth in the garden. Now the Old Boy reigns, with a red-hot pincers for a penis. Here's to him. But the sun's shining, there's a froth on the park trees, mother has made welshcakes, I've got a large Players, & my shoes are off. Take now content, no longer posturing as raped and reaped, the final emblem. Very contented, I promise to write again soon. And soon I'll be seeing you. Sadder than ever before, with a cough and a headache, I say, Goodbye, Trevor, mind Anna & the blue trees. Like a devil, too, I wave my pincers at the stars.

Dylan

MS: Buffalo   *SL*

GLYN JONES
[?early August 1934]   5 Cwmdonkin Drive Uplands Swansea

Nearly every note I scribble to you seems to start off with an apology. I'm becoming fatalistic, and have given up excuses. But I'll make an exception in your case, and hasten to assure you (*not* one of my favourite idioms) that I only received your letter today. I've been away off & on for the last week, & everything has become rather jumbled. I *am* going up to London very soon, but, at the moment, I can't tell the exact date —whether it will be towards the end of this week or at the beginning of next or what. When—definitely—are you going up? Write soon and tell me, won't you? Even if our days of departure can't be fitted in any way, we'll both be in town some time next week. Now give me the name of your Gower-st hotel or boarding house, so that I shan't miss you. In return I'll give you my telephone number (I've forgotten it for the moment) *at* the house *at* which I shall be staying for some of my visit.

A perfectly bloody note, I admit. Don't take any notice, or not much notice, of the Pateresque idiom employed throughout. Write soon & tell me your plans. We'll have, if nothing else, a few days together anyway. I want to see the Covent Garden Ballet? Do you?

Dylan

P.T.O.

I nearly forgot to tell you: I was severely rated by my family after you left at the end of your door-step visit some weeks ago, and am commanded to write a public apology (it's a bloody funny world, I never seem to do anything right, and what I do do right I forget) for my apparent, but totally unintended rudeness in not extending an invitation to your people to come in & have tea. It didn't matter if they'd had tea, or didn't want tea, or didn't want to come in, or were anxious to get home—I should have asked you to ask them. This isn't the commanded apology. This is quite private & sincere. Your car had gone half way down the hill before I realised. I was awfully muddled at the time, trying to think out a rhyme for 'badger'—with one result, a vulgar half-rhyme.

Give my regards to your people. And when you're all in Swansea again, you damn well have to come in and nibble a bit of bun even if you're all crammed up to the eyes with food and looking for a place to get sick.

So long.

Dylan

MS: Carbondale

GEOFFREY GRIGSON
[?early August 1934]   5 Cwmdonkin Drive Uplands Swansea

Dear Grigson,

Here are the two poems I said I'd send you. I hope it's not too late. More especially, I hope you like the poems. They are both very recently writ-ten. Do let me know if it is too late, as I may be able to do something else with the poems. But I hope, again, that you'll like them and be able to print them.

I'm coming up to town at the end of this week. Will you be away then?

Sincerely,
Dylan Thomas

MS: Texas   *SL*

GLYN JONES
[?early August 1934]   5 Cwmdonkin Drive Uplands Swansea

I have been waiting, and am still waiting, for a letter from London that will definitely decide my day and hour of departure. The letter has not yet come. If it does not arrive by Monday or Tuesday, I shall be leaving G.W.R. Swansea at 7 a.m. If the letter does arrive after this note is posted, I may be going up any time between now & then. All horribly vague, &

insufficient excuse for you to return to Cardiff. You carry on from North Wales, Glyn, and I'll give a ring to the Garth Hotel early on Thursday morning—about nine o'clock, before you go out. I'm sorry but I don't know what the devil my phone number is, & shan't know now until I reach town. But a ring at nine o'clock Thursday morning to the Garth Hotel will find you, won't it? I'll be seeing you. Is there going to be anybody with you? I'll be alone all the day time every day. I will, as I said before, be seeing you. Good luck to your North Wales trip.

Dylan

MS: Carbondale

PAMELA HANSFORD JOHNSON
2nd August[1] [1934]

Excuses
    This letter is short and late for two reasons. First, I have been waiting until today for a reply from Gertrude Stein, hoping, that as a result of her letter, I should be able to come to town very soon, and with a good, if futile, excuse. Second, I turned out for a cricket team on Tuesday evening, finished with the remarkable analysis of 34 overs 60 odd runs & 3 wickets, 1 innings 0 runs, 2 dropped catches, & have been a physical wreck ever since, tortured with rheumatism & a stiff right arm. The Stein letter arrived this morning. To all intent it was quite bloody, but it furnishes an excuse of sorts, and I shall be in London on Wednesday or Thursday of next week. The Stein has, apparently, nothing to do with the bicycles which are owned by a Mr. Magnus Cohen.[2] There's nothing in it for me, of course, but I'll have a peep at him, &, perhaps, sing a few snatches of the Horst Wessel song outside his office door. I have given up my cricketing career, & can now cheat at Mah Jong with a dexterity worthy of Mr. Arthur Waley himself.[3]

Agents
    What a beautiful word, too. Think of Rodin's 'Pinker', and the natural annoyance following their mistake in not attempting to *make* saleable what is only unsaleable to a mind counterfeited with slush magazine stories will fade into a proper perspective. As it is it's all right. Pinkers[4] will sell 'Headline' & the poem for you, & *you*, eventually, will sell the

---

[1] Thomas wrote '2nd July' in error.
[2] Some joke or fantasy concerning a non-literary Stein seems to be intended.
[3] Arthur Waley (1889–1966) was an authority on Chinese literature.
[4] James Brand Pinker founded a New York literary agency.

rest. That's the worst of being 'classy'. You have to look awfully high all the time. You won't ever be *very* popular, but, dear! dear! you will be loved. Curtis Brown's don't like me very much either. I think they've got morbid minds, for the first two stories they are sending out are 'Martha' & 'The Vest'. Now if they want smutty stories . . .

Jokes

The mongoose was appreciated. Have you heard of Mae West's Trunk Crime? 'Come up & saw me sometime.' Isn't Baffy a lovely word? It's a better name than Taffy for your cat.

Virginity

A criticism not a physical discussion, although the criticism is dreadfully short. I can't do justice to it in a few lines. Further nagging will follow. Yes, I don't like Kensington. The story's too human for me. It's very clever but it's too feminine. It's a minor affair in every sense of the word, and the actual writing appears rather too casual. The theme, again, is good. All your themes are. And there's a very strong end. But it is—it has to be, I suppose—too commonplace for me to like it as much as your others. I hope the next story will be a little more imaginative. The nature of language, not the language of nature, for you! 'Anna'. 'The Gardeners'. Even 'Hidden Treasure' (with some alterations) are all truer to you because they are bothered less with the actions of human feet & hands & more with the action of the imagination.

Vicky

Ironically following Virginity. I'm glad he still loves us. I'm glad, too, that he hasn't been able as yet to get my book published, for I want to cut some of the poems out & substitute some of the later ones. He *is* the King of the Poet's Corner. Those six poems of his contained all the faults & merits of his literary 'brats'. In those six poems he showed himself as he really is. Good for him.

Entertainment

I'll be in time for the first Prom.[1] I know you don't like the first Proms, but they're playing some of the Planet music. Till Eulenspiegel, & two Bach string preludes. Let's go, shall we? I like the noise & the tobacco smoke & the young men with beards & the young women with the London Mercury under their arms.

Heil!

Of course. Young Freddy is the ideal Fascist novitiate. I should have seen that. He's perfect. I suppose we will go to Vicky's one evening? I hope he'll be there. I'm doing a new series for the local socialist paper: a series on Intellectual Revolution. I've got some lovely articles to come: on 'Censorship', 'Sex Ethics', 'Blood & Force', 'The Marxian Brothers',

---

[1] The Promenade Concert was on Saturday August 11.

'State Nurseries', & 'The Sin of Patriotism'. You should see the letters I'm receiving. I had one from 'Mother Of a Boy Scout'.

Beer

It wasn't a very good parody, was it? It certainly made me laugh though, and some of Herr Mittelbrau's lines were better than the originals. I've written a reply, but I've lost it. If I find it, I'll bring it up & you can give it to Kalie to give to him. 'Light', incidentally, is to be published in 'Poems of the Year', an anthology brought out by the Bodley Head in opposition to Thomas Moult's horrible 'Best Poems'.

New Poem

I enclose my new poem. I hope you'll like it. It's going in New Verse this month.[1] I took a long time over it, &, at the moment, anyway, I'm a little bit pleased with it. Not much—just a little bit.

The Sweetest Thing

I do love you, Pam, but I'm not going to tell you in this letter. I'm to see you in a few days. I'm so happy to think of that that my rheumatism vanishes. X

Cruelty

Have you seen the Spectator review of 'Symphony'. In case you haven't, I enclose it. Good God is all one can possibly say. Vicky deserves every word of it, of course. But you don't, my darling, & Vicky shd be publicly horsewhipped for insulting your book as he did with his asinine compounds & his lack of tact. Now, my darling, don't let the review annoy or worry you. Show it to Vicky, & I hope it annoys & worries *him*. I know you worry like hell when someone—not me, of course, for I am a privileged person—slates you. But who cares? It doesn't matter. I think it's a very funny review, anyway. He must have enjoyed himself writing it.

And now goodbye. Write to me by Monday or Tuesday. Give my love to your mother, & do thank her for the trouble she has taken in the cyclists' cause.

I'll be with you so soon. Goodbye & all the love in the world.

                                                            XXX Dylan

MS: Buffalo   *SL(R)*

---

[1] 'If I was tickled by the rub of love' appeared in the August *New Verse*. But Thomas had already sent her that poem. This one may have been 'Half of the fellow father as he doubles' (retitled 'My world is pyramid' for *18 Poems*), which *New Verse* published December 1934.

TREVOR HUGHES
Wednesday [?August 1934]   53 Battersea Rise London SW 3[1]

Dear Trevor,
   All the apologies in the world would be, I know, quite unavailing. It
wasn't until this evening that I realised what a prize bugger I have been. I
stayed in the Fitzroy until about half-past seven this evening, saw no sign
of you, wondered why on earth you hadn't arrived, for you are, as a rule,
as punctual & as conscientious as I am not, & then was conscious of a
faint and rather terrible suspicion. Was I too early, too late? No, that
wasn't it: six it was all right. Then I took a disconsolate & suspicious
bus-ride back to Battersea. Then Pamela, who acts in a vaguely sardonic
secretarial capacity to me, distrusting me—in that sense, at least—as
much as you do, looked up her little diary & found—as I had been vaguely
terrified—that *Tuesday was the night. Will* you accept the apology? It's
damnably true, & I know what hell it is sticking lonely in the Fitzroy for
an hour—I've done it myself. I know. Do please accept it. I wanted like
hell to meet you & to drink bad beer with you & be as scatter-brained &
egotistic as ever to your burning silence. I'm going home Tuesday. I
think. Will you meet me Monday. *Not* in the Fitzroy. We daren't trust
that again. *I'll* come to meet you outside Baker Street at six. Monday. If
you feel it worth it, do write and confirm it. Pamela sends you her love.
She likes you almost as much as I do.

                                                        Dylan

MS: Buffalo

GEOFFREY GRIGSON
[?August 27 1934][2]   53 Battersea Rise (at the moment) S W 11

Dear Grigson,
   I know you'll excuse this note, but it is quite essential that I take
advantage of the offer you made, I think seriously, last week. I can't go
back to Wales yet, for even the foundations of the Old Home seem to be
crumbling. If I had realised at tea yesterday that things were really as bad
as they are, I wouldn't have had to trouble you with this undignified note.
My world of good, dying fathers and bad, female poets is proving
affectionately unstable. I don't mind the Garret and Crust at all, but I'd

---

[1] The Johnsons' house in south London (the postal district was SW 11; SW 3 is Chelsea).
Thomas was in London, staying with Pamela and her mother most of the time, from
August 10 to September 15, when the Johnsons returned with him to Swansea, and stayed
at the Mermaid Hotel for two weeks. In London, Thomas is known to have met Trevor
Hughes on Monday August 20. So—if he was not telling the truth about 'going home
Tuesday'—this letter may have been written the previous Wednesday, August 15.

[2] Johnson's diary, Sunday August 26: ' . . . he left me to go to Grigson's for tea & didn't
come back [till 1.10 am]. So dispiriting.'

much prefer to borrow some money and to postpone such a conventionality. Again I apologise for the substance and the mood of this.

Five o'clock, Wednesday?

> Very sincerely,
> Dylan Thomas

MS: Texas   *SL*

GLYN JONES
[autumn 1934]   5 Cwmdonkin Drive Uplands Swansea

Dear Glyn,

As usual I am apologising, &, as usual, there is every excuse for my delay in writing to you. I only arrived home from London a few days ago; I had been up there ever since I was there with you—a long and, comparatively, worth-while stay. Mother had forgotten to readdress your last letter, & it was waiting, all virgin & unopened, for me.

Yes, certainly let's go to see Caradoc,[1] & the sooner the better, as I intend returning to London—permanently, then—in about a month. By the way, Geoffrey Grigson is very interested in you and your poetry. When are you going up to town again? He wants to meet you and to introduce you to some others of the New Verse people.

And what about coming down to Swansea on Saturday? Can you manage this Saturday? If you can't, let me know when you can come down. I hope it'll be soon. The Aberystwyth date depends, of course, on you.

Write soon, explaining your Caradoc &, don't forget, your Swansea plans.

And don't be too
annoyed at the
(really) unavoidable
delay in writing.

> Dylan
> (Good for New Stories. When?)

MS: Carbondale

PAMELA HANSFORD JOHNSON
[October 1934]

P.S. Jumper at end of week (mother).

Book It And See

First of all, to reply to the short letter marked Bloody private and

---

[1] Caradoc Evans (1878–1945), who outraged the Welsh establishment with his novels and stories. When Jones and Thomas visited him in Aberystwyth that autumn, he gave them tea and friendly conversation.

confidential. Runia seems to have given you a fairly correct summary of the correspondence between us. Another letter—written by Neuburg & Runia in collaboration, actually in different sorts of ink—came later, explaining very carefully a number of things that I can't understand at all, and asking—as you intimated—for a poem for this Sunday's Referee. Why, do you know? I suspect vaguely Caponeish measures. Vicky is, I believe, putting me on the spot, though what spot, & why, God alone knows. My letters, as perhaps Runia told you, demanded the return of my book.[1] But I'm no more likely to get it than I am to find Gibbon's History of Christianity in my navel. Only force remains. No, I can't seriously adopt the idea of a second selection of even more immature & unsatisfactory poems. I find, after reading them through again, that the poems in Vicky's confounded possession are a poor lot, on the whole, with many thin lines, many oafish sentiments, several pieces of twopenny Christ, several unintentional comicalities, & much highfalutin nonsense expressed in a soft, a truly soft language. I've got to get nearer to the bones of words, & to a Matthew Arnold's hell with the convention of meaning & sense. Not that it matters, anyway. Life is only waves, wireless waves, & electric vibrations. Does it matter, my little radio programme from Battersea, that the high or the low tension runs down? I have, of course, in the weakness of my spirit, sent some clumsy poem for the Referee.[2] But, blast, I will be firm, & the October date still stands. Much thanks for the Bloody private low-down. Yah for Neuburg & his literary thieves' kitchen.

House Lend A Little Chairful

In reference to my prospective studio. Janes[3] and I will be coming up definitely about the second week of November, by car fortunately, bearing with us typewriters, easels, bedclothes, brassières for lady models, & plum-cakes for Nelson's lions—a cherry or two for Eros, a copy of the London Mercury for Nurse Cavell. We want a room about fifteen shillings per week: it must be as large as possible, larger if possible, unfurnished, with good light. Preferably gas: electric is bad for our sensitive eyes & complexions. But don't worry about looking for one: we will procure one, even if it is a little out of Chelsea. But you might keep your eye open; one eye. Have you a mattress & a chair either to give or sell to two poor, unrecognised geniuses? I don't want to take a mattress

---

[1] Thomas was disenchanted with the *Sunday Referee* over his forthcoming book of poems. The newspaper wanted a publisher to share the cost, but was having difficulty finding one. Johnson's diary, Friday October 19: 'Worrying calls from Runia [Tharp] re Dylan's book which necessitated me writing him a second letter.'

[2] 'Foster the light' appeared in the *Sunday Referee* on October 28.

[3] Alfred Janes (b. 1911), the Swansea painter, first met Dylan Thomas through Dan Jones, and was a lifelong friend. In 1934 he had just left the Royal Academy school and taken a flat in Redcliffe Street, near the Fulham Road. He and Thomas moved in on November 13.

up, it's too big, & I don't want to buy one because I'm frightened of getting rabies or ringworm. Don't throw any old furniture over the neighbours' walls. It would be vitally useful to us. If you have a fairly large & dirty table you don't intend taking with you, store it somewhere, & I'll buy it from you. Don't forget, my prospectively philanthropic clother & furnisher of the artistic poor! Table, mattress, chair! I don't want to buy them from a second-hand shop, owing to the possibility of disease; I would, if you had them, like to purchase them from No. 53 (going—gone) Battersea Rise.[1]

The Hart, My Lord

Your letter does read as though your nerves had been chewn by a dog. Why, o neurotic, this sudden tremble? Don't tell me. The wholesale effect of years' official labour. The reaction of liberty.[2] And so on through all the psychological text phrases to an unenviable end. Condole with your mother for me; if her nose troubles her, remove it. It would not be uncharitable to say that she would not miss it. Nevertheless, condole; read her 'Pursuit' in a baritone voice; put my letters in her tea. And, for yourself, Take The Philosophic View. Look at the gallons of stars, the London infinity, & what is an over-pumping heart? (These things are easy to say: I have just spilt the ink on my hand, & am cursing God.) Be better, darling, but don't worry about being better. If we die, here are two nice epitaphs:

> Here lies the body of Pamela J.
> You can kick in her ribs, there's nothing to pay.
> Here lies the body of Dylan M. T.
> You can trample his balls. He don't care a d—.

Cruel, you aver? But then, but then, isn't the world cruel, Mrs. Matthews?

(Here too lies the body of Meriel Right,
With teeth in her buttocks, & serve her right.)
But she's a nice girl, & that serves her right, too.

Pursuit

Well, I wouldn't chase it. I'd let the damned thing go. Blood on the raspberry to it, for all I care. I think it's lousy, just lousy. There's no merit in it at all: it's coy, it's turgid, it's affected, it's nauseating. I cannot, I am afraid, approve of the New Manner, which seems to me to be a bloodier way than ever of linking together Old Mannerisms. No, I mean, you just

---

[1] The Johnsons were to move from Battersea to a flat in Chelsea.
[2] Johnson had left her job at the bank and was writing her first novel.

can't go on like that. It's criminal. I know you're not well, but you can't blame the poor thing on a too-rapid heart. Sorry to be so rude. I can't give any constructive criticism.

On A Testicle Made For Two

Your insertion of the word 'testicles' at the foot of a page entitled 'Blast & Fugger' has rather puzzled me. I don't know whether you were being merely low, (come out of the wood, girl, if you are, & let's be really indecent), or whether you were using that very nice word merely as a swear-word (If so, I congratulate you. I'd never thought of it) or whether there was some deeper, & more sinister, significance. I'd rather believe in the second theory (testicles as a term of disapprobation). The first theory belies your dainty character, & the third gives rise (ha, phallic!) in my mind to many disturbing ideas: you aren't, by any chance, turning male, are you? I do hope not. I've always wondered why you won't come to bed with me; it just seems silly to me, but now I am beginning to wonder. What with these sinister references (Did you know that in Ancient Mexico there was a Court Dignitary Called the Keeper Of The Imperial Balls? I didn't) & the nail-cum-penis dream that perplexed you so much some time ago, who knows? Tell me the dreadful truth. I'm sure I don't like little boys in That Way.

John O'London's Circumcision[1]

A definite success. There were thirty five people in the audience, that's all, and thirty of them were women. But what women! All of a dim, uncertain age, most of them virgins, & all with some smattering of Freud & Lawrence. The chairman, a big-bellied bore, introduced me as a Young Revolutionary (I was becomingly clad in red) who was tackling A Difficult & Courageous Task. I then gave them the works. At the beginning there was a frozen & horrified silence, but eventually I induced a few titters, &, at last, real, undeniable interest. A glassy look came into the eyes of the spinsters. I put in several wise-cracks, & ended with 'Let Copulation Thrive'. Then the ladies, in one solid mass, bombarded me with questions. In the Communist Erewhon[2] I had dealt with, would there be no perversions? What we consider as perversions, I replied, (excuse the novelette form of this report) are, for the most part, healthy & natural bypaths of sexual life. How could a woman defend her honour in

---

[1] The John O'London's was a literary society in Swansea. Trick left an unpublished account of the proceedings which says there was a 'stunned silence'. Thomas's subject was allegedly 'Pornography and the nineteenth-century novel'.

[2] *Erewhon*, the imaginary land of Samuel Butler's satire (1872). It is an anagram of 'nowhere'.

such a State? Tin drawers, I replied with Ready Humour. Do you believe
in preventatives? The day, I replied, that legalised birthcontrol & clinical
abortion come into practice, will go down as a French Letter day in the
annals of history. And so on for two hours, until middle-aged ladies, who,
before that night, would have blushed or been horrified at the mention of
pyjamas, were talking gaily about whirling-sprays, Lesbianism, sanitary
towels, latrines, fornication & other everyday & normal things. Trick
made a nice little speech about the inevitability of Revolution, a gentleman defended repression with a very blood-shot eye, Janes made a joke
about gallstones, & the meeting closed. God knows what we've done to
those ardent & earnest ladies, but I hope it hurts. The more I see of Wales
the more I think it's a land entirely peopled by perverts. I don't exclude
myself, who obtain a high & soulful pleasure from telling women, old
enough to be my mother, why they dream of two-headed warthogs in a
field of semen. (I heard, later, that a committee meeting has been held, &
that care must be taken in the future as to who is invited to lecture.
Those bloody women woke up in the cold light of morning, & regretted
those few hours of—if nothing else—verbal freedom.)

Last week-end I spent in Aberystwyth with Caradoc Evans. He's a great
fellow. We made a tour of the pubs in the evening, drinking to the eternal
damnation of the Almighty & the soon-to-be-hoped-for destruction of the
tin Bethels. The university students love Caradoc, & pelt him with
stones whenever he goes out.

I have nothing to send you (except a pound of love), but have nearly
finished a short story. I am working very hard on a poem: it is going to be
a very long poem; I've completed fifty lines so far; it is by far the best
thing I've done; I don't suppose I'll have finished it even when I see you;
but you shall read what there is of it then.

How much more of your novel? Of course, I want to see it all before
Pinkers have it.

Now love & goodbye, more love than goodbye, for I'll see you soon. But
write soon & much, & do, my darling, get better for me. I don't like to

think of you ill. (And you, very naturally, don't like being ill.) Don't forget any old furniture—especially mattress, table, & chair. Give my love to your mother.

Love again, & a terrible lot of it. XXXXXX

Dylan

MS: Buffalo   *SL(R)*

ERICA WRIGHT (T. S. ELIOT'S SECRETARY)
Sunday [4 November 1934]

Dear Miss Wright,
Thanks for your two letters. In reply to the first: I intend coming up to London in about ten days' time. And, for the second, I can only say that the arrangements are, very unfortunately, out of my hands.[1] A wire was sent to me on Saturday, saying that a publisher was to start—whatever 'start' means—on Monday, if Mr Eliot was still undecided.[2] I'm writing back today to say what you told me. And that's all I know about it. Mr Eliot hasn't written yet, but I expect I may hear from him [*Thomas typed* 'Him', *then overtyped a lower-case* 'h'] tomorrow. I wish I knew more about all this than I do. I'll try, anyway, to stop whatever mysterious decisions *are* being made.

Yours very truly,
Dylan Thomas

MS: Valerie Eliot

GEOFFREY GRIGSON
[November 1934]   5 Cwmdonkin Drive Uplands Swansea

Dear Geoffrey,
I've been meaning to write to you for the last month, and was awfully glad to get your letter. In answer to your questions: (a) I am in Wales, (b) I'm coming to London in about ten days, (c) I *have* been on the Balearic

---

[1] Miss Wright wrote on November 1 to say Eliot 'hopes that you will not make any decision about the publication of your poems before hearing from him'.
[1] The *Sunday Referee*, afraid of losing their prize poet, moved at last. As a result, Eliot returned Thomas's poems to Neuburg on November 5, 'with great regret that you are unable to allow us to keep [them] for further consideration'. Eliot said later that he regretted having been 'so fussy' about Thomas's work – 'one ought to have accepted the inferior with the first-rate'.

Islands occasionally, (d) I've died once or twice, too, (e) I am never lascivious. Penniless I retreated from London, and penniless I return. I've been staying all over the place, with Caradoc Evans in Aberystwyth, with an indulgent but ailing mother, as now, with a large lady and her hotel on the Gower Peninsula, and in a cottage in Carmarthenshire, glorying in the name of Blaen Cwm, where I lived on carrots, (no, that's not quite true, I had onions as well). But in ten days or less I'll be taking a room with another bloated aristocrat in town. I hope I'll see you and Norman[1] very soon.

Have you seen Pope Eliot lately. He's doing funny things with my book. Three or four days ago his secretary sent me a letter by express post—I don't quite know what express post means, but you have to pay sixpence to the boy at the door—asking me to make no arrangements until I had heard from the Pope himself who was writing that evening. What earthly arrangements could I make? And I'm damned if he's written. I remember somebody telling me once that she had used a poem of mine as a sort of funnel to put in a bottle, as a sadistic doctor wanted a sample of her urine. Do try to find out if the entire staff of Faber and Faber are doing similar things with my twenty poems.

Of course you can use any poems of mine you want to. I've written a new one—bit better than the others, I think—which I enclose. Perhaps you'd like to use that too, or instead.

Thanks very much for the promise of the books. But it's hardly worth sending them if I'm coming up in ten days, is it? Do let me have some then, though. I'm relying on reviews to ensure the carrots and onions.

Yours,
Dylan

Do you think it would be better if the enclosed poem were not divided into stanzas? I've tried it that way, but it seemed more obscure.

Ross-Williamson of the Bookman has given me some reviews. Do you think Janet Adam Smith[2] would too if I wrote her a nice, cooing letter?

MS: Texas   *SL*

---

[1] Norman Cameron (1905–53), poet and advertising copywriter. A friend of Grigson, he kept a brotherly eye on Thomas during the latter's first years in London.
[2] Janet Adam Smith (b. 1905), author and journalist, was assistant editor of the *Listener*.

Success and Marriage
1934–9

The publication of *18 Poems* in an edition of 250 copies, just before Christmas 1934, caused sufficient stir in the narrow-drawn literary circles of the time to make Dylan Thomas a 'name' among a few influential critics and readers. Two years later *Twenty-five Poems*, though more guardedly received, added to his reputation. Much of this time was spent in London, but he rarely had a fixed address, and his parents' house in Swansea remained his real base. His tiny earnings for stories and poems, supplemented by borrowing, with Cwmdonkin Drive available as a refuge, enabled him to lead the casual life he desired. In the spring of 1937, following D. J. Thomas's retirement, his parents moved to a smaller house, and shortly afterwards, Thomas married Caitlin Macnamara, whom he had met the previous year. They lived either at her mother's house in the New Forest or in the small town of Laugharne, on the coast of West Wales. Their first child, Llewelyn, was born in 1939. Poverty had become a practical problem, rather than an appropriate condition for a poet. Thomas was beginning to earn a little more from his writing. But it was a precarious existence.

A. E. TRICK
[December 1934]   5 Redcliffe Street London SW10

Dear Bert,

   This seems a nice and suitable time to write the letter that I know I should have written at least a week ago. The Sunday Referee has done us both quite proud, although personally I do not think that Neuburg chose the most flattering passages of either your letter or comrade Thompson's. Your criticism was good, and naturally I agreed with every word of it: it contained, expressed in a beautifully condensed way, what you and I have discussed for so many hours. And win the prize—what is the prize, by the way?—it bloody well should. Comrade Thompson wrote at far greater length than you, explaining subtleties in my bad poem that I was and still am not aware of. And your Oxford cum Vanoc[1] letter was just as good; I heard two anarchistic gentlemen arguing vigorously over it in a café last night.

   There is no news, or there is all news. The city goes on, myself now a very insignificant part of it. I live, with Janes, just off the Fulham Road, on the borders of Chelsea, Fulham, South Kensington, and Brompton, in a large room with a bathroom and sort of inferior wash up adjoining. This is the quarter of the pseudo-artists, of the beards, the naughty expressions of an entirely outmoded period of artistic importance, and of the most boring Bohemian parties I have ever thought possible. Slightly drunk, slightly dirty, slightly wicked, slightly crazed, we repeat our platitudes on Gauguin and Van Gogh as though they were the most original things in the world. There are, of course, scores of better people that I do meet, but these little maggots are my companions for most of the time. I think I shall change my digs quite soon.

   Another Swansea boy—hark, hark the parish pump—lives in the room above us. He is Mervyn Levy,[2] a small and cunning Jew who does small and cunning drawings, and, at the present, does not work in the Royal College, Kensington. This bloody land is full of Welshmen, and, day by day as I feast my eyes upon their mean and ungenerous countenances, I feel more like Caradoc whose books are, in a small circle at least, becoming a highbrow success owing to my uninterrupted praise of them.

[1] A letter from an H. Thompson was mentioned in the Poet's Corner on November 11. On November 25 the *Sunday Referee* published a letter from Trick, in reply to an article about pacifism by the political correspondent, 'Vanoc II'.
[2] Mervyn Levy (b. 1914), artist and entrepreneur, was at school with Thomas and remained a friend. His drawings of Thomas are in the National Portrait Gallery and the National Library of Wales.

I am not at the moment working very hard; I find it difficult to concentrate in a room as muddled and messy as ours is nearly all the time; for yards around me I can see nothing but poems, poems, poems, butter, eggs and mashed potatoes mashed among my stories and Janes's canvases. One day we will have to wash up, and then, perhaps, I can really begin to work. As it is, most of the more recent stuff that I brought up with me has been accepted in various periodicals. A new, very highbrow magazine called, very originally, 'Art' is to print my 'Burning Baby'[1] in its first quarterly number, January 1935, the Adelphi is printing my 'Tree' this December, the next 'Criterion' is printing my 'The Visitor'—that is in the middle of this month—New Verse is printing a long poem which you have in your cuttings book and also a review, slating, of Spender's new poem 'Vienna', and my book of poems will be out before Xmas.[2] I have hopes, too, of a publisher, probably Boriswood, publishing my stories in the spring. To continue this egoistic survey, I have met a number of new notabilities including Henry Moore, the sculptor, Edwin and Willa Muir, Wyndham Lewis, and, certainly not least, Betty May.[3]

Betty May is, as you probably know, an artist's model who has posed—perhaps that is not the most correct word—for John, Epstein and the rest of the racketeers. She wrote a book, too, describing herself as 'The Tiger Woman of Paris'. At least she didn't write the book, she sponsored it; it was written really by Gilbert Armitage[4] for the sum of £40. I am going to write an article for her, under her name, for the News of the World. My payment will not be monetary, but, and although she is now not as young as she was, that will not matter.

Now how does your world go? Has the Guardian reformed and started to print your nasty little nigglings again? And what are you doing all these long winter nights: writing propaganda? propagandish poems? indignant and abusive letters? or reading more of those damnable facts that you manage to extract from all sorts of seditious quarters? I kept the Daily Worker Princess Marina Supplement for you, but, as usual with all such things, I went and lost it. It was a special and particularly seditious pamphlet abusing the whole of the Royal Family and exhibiting almost bawdy cartoons of our 'Enemy the King'.[5] Very good. London was hell on the day of that Royal Ramp, the streets crowded enough to be almost impossible to walk in, the whole of the traffic disorganised and the pubs open to eleven all over the city. There were women and their babies—I

---

[1] 'The Burning Baby'—inspired by the nineteenth-century Welsh eccentric, Dr William Price, who cremated the body of his illegitimate child on a hillside—upset publishers and printers for years, although the small-circulation magazine *Contemporary Poetry and Prose* published it in May 1936.

[2] David Archer of the Parton Bookshop had put up £20, the *Sunday Referee* £30, and the book came out on or about 18 December 1934.

[3] Edwin Muir (1887–1959), writer and critic. Betty May, the so-called 'Tiger Woman', artists' model and one-time friend of Aleister Crowley.

[4] Armitage was a well-connected literary journalist.

[5] Princess Marina married the Duke of Kent, 29 November 1934.

saw them—who waited all night outside the Abbey, keeping those perishing children in the cold and fog for at least forty hours. I told Norman Cameron about it and said that they all should be put in lunatic asylums. He said that there was no necessity; all that needs be done is to keep them in England. Isn't this letter well typed?

Write to me soon, telling me all that you know I would like to know, all about the Guardian and sedition in general. As this is the first letter it must not, according to the rules of etiquette, be too long. There, you liar, it isn't etiquette I'm worrying about, it's just sheer laziness.

Give my regards to Mrs. Trick junior and senior and to Miss Trick whose poems, so Vicky tells me, are by far the best and the most sincere that he receives.

Write soon. And don't forget: all the news.

Dylan

I came across yesterday, in the possession of a fellow whom I don't know & can't borrow from, the first *real* literature of Fascism & Nazism. It is called 'Might is Right' & was printed in Australia in the 1890's. The author is called Ragnor Redbeard. If you can by any method, get hold of it.

MS: Ohio State University   *SL(R)*

GLYN JONES
[December 1934]   5 Redcliffe Street London SW10

Many thanks for the letter, and many apologies that you should have had to write the first letter since I came up to town about a month ago. I seem to have been very busy and have written only two letters home during the whole time. I haven't written to any friends at all, and hope that they know me well enough by this time to realise that it's no more than a lazy carelessness on my part—though a lazy carelessness is bad enough, God knows.

Very, very glad to hear that you are coming to London about Christmas. I am looking forward to seeing you and to introduce you to Grigson. I am, as I think I told you when, during the famous Caradoc expedition, we last met, staying with a painter called Janes. We possess one large room in a quiet street in South Kensington—in South Kensington, that is officially, but we are near Chelsea, Fulham and Brompton. Everything is in rather a mess, but if you don't mind that, and I don't somehow think you do, then I do really wish you would sleep with us. Janes spends most of his time indoors and cooks his own meals, but I have most of my scanty meals in cafés—scanty not for the reason of utter penury, although I have had and do have and am having at the moment a particularly lean period, but for the sake of the demon alcohol who has become a little too close and heavy a friend for some time now. Pile in with us, will you? We shall also have the greatest pleasure in providing quite nice breakfasts free of all charge. Does that induce you? Yes, of course it does. So when are you definitely coming up? I'm not, I don't think so at the moment at least, going home for Christmas. My book of poems is coming out then, and I hope to make just sufficient money to keep me happy for the few most important days of the holiday.

So you've been reviewing Edith Sitwell's latest piece of virgin dung, have you?[1] Isn't she a poisonous thing of a woman, lying, concealing, flipping, plagiarising, misquoting, and being as clever a crooked literary publicist as ever. I do hope you pointed out in your review the real points against the book (you did, I know, but I like being dogmatic)? The majority of the book was cribbed from Herbert Read and Leavis,[2] actually and criminally cribbed. She has misquoted Hopkins at least twenty times, reprinted many poems without the permission of publisher or poet. Yes, that was my poem all right, reproduced without my name, misquoted at the end, and absurdly criticised. I duly sent my protest to Gerald Duckworth and he replied to the effect that so many protests of a similar sort had been received, that he could as yet do nothing about it. It is being hoped that he will have to withdraw the book. I *would* like to see your review of it.

What news there is can wait until I see you. Let it be soon, and don't forget to let us know when that will be. You stay with us, of course.

Dylan

Excuse me typing this, but I have only just found my pen & ink.

MS: Carbondale   *SL*

GLYN JONES
[Christmas 1934]   5 Cwmdonkin Drive Uplands Swansea

Dear Glyn,
I'm so bloody sick of apologising to you in every one of the too few letters that I write you that today I refuse to So Humble myself. Ach!

Now this is the position: I, unfortunately, have to stay in Swansea until Saturday, as then my sister & brother-in-law are returning to London & will give me a commodious and entirely inexpensive ride. I suggest—& I have already explained it to Janes, my partner—that you stay the nights you are in London—the nights I am not—in 5 REDCLIFFE St; there will be an entirely empty & quite pleasant bedroom at your disposal, & Janes

---

[1] Sitwell's book *Aspects of Modern Poetry*, published by Duckworth, was savagely critical of *New Verse*, and used Thomas's poem 'Our eunuch dreams' as one of its bad examples. She added insult to injury by not mentioning Thomas by name.

[2] F. R. Leavis (1895–1978), the rigorous literary critic.

will see to your little wants & to your larger wants, such as breakfast etc. You'll find him a very nice chap, &, of course, expecting you. I'll see you, then, on Saturday evening. To get to REDCLIFFE St, you take a 14 bus from Piccadilly (marked Putney), which goes up the Brompton Road, the Fulham Road, & stops outside the Redcliffe Arms at the corner of Redcliffe Gardens. Walk up Redcliffe Gardens on your right, & there, after a few street turnings, lies the ancient baroque architecture of my residence. Don't forget—No. 5. Now do be an angel, & do what I say. On Sunday we'll go to the Grigsons' house in Hampstead.

(I've lost your home address, & only hope that the vague marks I have made on this envelope will be satisfactory to the postman.)

Cheers.

Dylan

MS: Carbondale

GLYN JONES

[Christmas 1934] (Another version of previous letter. See Appendix 2.)

CHARLES FISHER[1]

[early 1935]   5 Redcliffe Street SW10

Dear Comrade Fisher,

Thank you very much for your letter to which I would have replied sooner had it not been for about twenty reasons: the abominable cold cramping the fingers, elongating the sweet hours of bed, and forcing, eventually, the tired half sleeper to erect a small fire in an insufficient grate; the sin of laziness, cancelling the positive virtue that regards sin and virtue lazily, equally and equably; the lack of ink, my tame harridan having, bless her breasts, spilt the contents of a full bottle on the linoleum; the worries of a life that consists, for the most part, in building the brain on paper and pulling down the body, the too small and too weak body to stand either the erection of a paper brain or the rubbing of saloon counters; the pressure of words; the lack of stamps; flu in embryo, a snotty, chicken-faced foetus swimming, very red, behind the nose; and another twelve reasons, all too complicated to go into at the moment. The ink still staining the linoleum, and my harridan asleep, I have to type this letter. The keys are cold.

You asked me to tell you about my theory of poetry. Really I haven't got one. I like things that are difficult to write and difficult to understand;

[1] A colleague and close friend of Thomas on the *South Wales Evening Post*, Fisher was later a journalist in Canada.

I like 'redeeming the contraries' with secretive images; I like con-
tradicting my images, saying two things at once in one word, four in two
words and one in six. But what I like isn't a theory, even if I do stabilise
into dogma my own personal affections. Poetry, heavy in tare though
nimble, should be as orgiastic and organic as copulation, dividing and
unifying, personal but not private, propagating the individual in the mass
and the mass in the individual. I think it should work from words, from
the substance of words and the rhythm of substantial words set together,
not towards words. Poetry is a medium, not a stigmata on paper. Man
should be two tooled, and a poet's middle leg is his pencil. If his phallic
pencil turns into an electric drill, breaking up the tar and the concrete of
language worn thin by the tricycle tyres of nature poets and the heavy six
wheels of the academic sirs, so much the better; and it's work that
counts, madam, genius so often being an infinite capacity for aching
pains.

About manuscripts. I'm very pleased and glad that you do want a
manuscript of some poem of mine, and I'll try to let you have what you
want. But my method is this: I write a poem on innumerable sheets of
scrap paper, write it on both sides of the paper, often upside down and
criss cross ways, unpunctuated, surrounded by drawings of lamp posts
and boiled eggs, in a very dirty mess; bit by bit I copy out the slowly
developing poem into an exercise book; and, when it is completed, I type
it out. The scrap sheets I burn, for there are such a lot of them that they
clutter up my room and get mixed in the beer and butter. Now what
can I send you? A typed copy? Shall I write some out for you? or preserve
from the waiting fire the next batch of almost illegible sheets? Anything
you like. I am at your service.

Write again soon. I write so few letters, and like writing them, even if
my style is a little too heavy footed. Give my regards to Mr. Job; prevent
Mr. Hatcher from taking too many Woolworth waitresses to the cinema
and from inviting little girls up dark lanes to show them his stamp album;
plant a rose in Reuben's hair; remember me to Bill Latham and to Tom
Lucy; and tell Eric that Henekey's devastating cider now costs two pence
halfpenny a glass.

Dylan

PS. The manuscript, whatever it will be, I'll send on to you when you tell
me what you want. I can't give you the exercise books, for they contain
the only copies I possess.
PPS. What are *you* doing with yourself? Do you write at all now, that is
apart from the daily hack work?

MS: the recipient   *SL*

MORTON ZABEL[1]
[?February 1935]   5 Redcliffe Street London SW10

Dear Mr. Zabel,
    Thank you for your letter which was sent on to me by the 'Criterion'.
    I'm afraid I can't suggest titles for the two poems you've decided to
keep for publication. Would it be possible to use the first lines as titles?
    You very kindly asked me to let you see some more poems. Here are
three very new ones.
                                        Sincerely yours,
                                        Dylan Thomas

PS. If you like the new poems, and decide to keep them, perhaps the first
lines, as in the case of the other two, had better be used as titles.
                                        D.T.

MS: University of Chicago

A. E. TRICK
Tuesday [?February 1935]   5 Redcliffe Gardens London SW10

Dear Bert,
    This is only the second letter I've written since I came to this very Big
City, and it should have been at least the tenth; I've had such a lot that I
wanted to say to you, and, now that I do sit down and attempt to tell you,
I can't remember a damned thing. Before I try to remember, anyway,
thanks for the review in the Guardian and for your Trickish letters in the
Post. What a swine Hughes is, isn't he? have you ever read such mannered blarney in your life?[2] Bud and blossom be ——. What's he think
I am? Something in a vase or a horticultural exhibition? I liked your review
immensely, but then I'd seen it before; but who *is* responsible for the
proof correcting? And what did the last sentence mean? Who is the
crowner of hacks? By the way, what did you think of Vaughan Thomas's
article?[3] It was quite, or even very, flattering, and, I suppose consequently, I liked it. It appeared pretty intelligent, too; I'm meeting him
one day this week, or rather one evening, when we intend to have a peep,
in our country cousin way, at the Literary Great in the Cafe Royal.
Thanks for sending Mewis's letter along; I haven't replied yet, and
haven't had time either to write something smutty for his sensational
speech in the J.O.L. meeting. He told me that you, from the depths of an
abusive and economic imagination, conjured up several wisecracks for

[1] Morton Dauwen Zabel was editor of *Poetry* (Chicago) 1936–7. The letter is annotated in
  another hand, 'Feb 9/35 retd new mss'. The magazine published no poems by Thomas
  until 1937.
[2] Thomas was offended by a fulsome review that Trevor Hughes had written of *18 Poems*.
[3] A. Spender Vaughan-Thomas reviewed *18 Poems* in the *Herald of Wales*, 12 January 1935.

the Social Menace and the Dowdy Lady ('I got a son at sea', you remember) to writhe at and object to. I hope they had more crack in them
than wisdom; be a dynamitard, if that's spelt correctly, and blow the
retired sea captain, Weeping Willy, and the ingrown virgins sky high and
with as much rude and illbred noise as possible. I still think of that
evening with a faint glow of 'something attempted obscenely, something
dung', and remember your muddly boots with pride. Have you attended
one of those highbrow salons again? No, of course you haven't; I was
forgetting that there is now probably a subdivision of the Society called
'The Anti-Thomas And Trick League', presided over by a backbiting
eunuch and a couple of embodied maidenheads.

London is good; Porth is better; and the nostalgia of open and grassy
spaces is, as they say in sentimental diaries or even dairies, strong upon
me. I go my way, and the rest of London go theirs. All London is out of
step, except me. My book is selling well. A few complimentary reviews
have appeared, and Edwin Muir is to write another in the Listener in
about a week or a fortnight's time. My chest, he complained, is bad, and
my nose runs. Janes has got a rash. There are mice in my room. Work is
sporadic. Two and two are still, to my disordered muse, five or even six,
and algebra is the study of curves. I'm working on a story to be called 'The
Lemon' which will probably be given the raspberry by every self or
public-respecting editor in London; and I have just finished two poems
which are, I hope, to appear in the new New Verse, Uncle Geoffrey
permitting. Some rude reviews of mine you'll see in the Feb Adelphi, and
also a review of my own book (what a thrill of pride overcame me when I
put those long wished for words on paper) by Rayner Heppenstall[1] who is
a nice little Yorkshireman with an aptitude, even an obsession, for
singing Yorkshire songs about the Seven Immoral Joys of the Holy
Mary—at least he sings them when he's drunk, and drunk he was when I
first met him.

Celebrities I meet often and too often, they being a lousy set on the
whole, or off it. Herbert Read, Grigson, Cameron, the Muirs, and
Heppenstall are the best. Racketeering abounds, and the only racket a
comparatively honest person such as myself can belong to is that of the
squash racket; squash 'em right, and left, that's the motter.

'The Duchess of Malfi' is now on in town, and this evening,
Wednesday, I am to see it for the second time. You remember how much
you liked it when you read it first; well, it's a hundred times more
thrilling and more beautiful on the stage, and, although the London
production is rather thin blooded and Bloomsbury aesthetish, the play
comes over and survives all sorts of bad acting; it's the greatest tragedy
since Shakespeare—no, but perhaps Webster's White Devil is better still;
I believe people are negotiating to have that put on eventually in the
Embassy, Hampstead.

If these films come your way do see them: Morgenrot, the German

[1] Rayner Heppenstall (1911–81), novelist and poet; after 1945 a radio producer/writer.

Nazi propaganda film about submarine warfare, The Forbidden Territory, a sort of Boys' Own Paper version of an anti Soviet message, The Thin Man, which has probably been to Swansea and is the best American film I think I've seen, and any of the new Walt Disney's, especially 'The Orphans' Benefit'.

Since I've been in London I've come into contact on a number of occasions with intellectual communism and communists, with A. L. Morton, editor of the Daily Worker, Cockburn, proprietor, with a youthful notoriety, Esmond Romilly, editor of the schoolboys' communist monthly, Out of Bounds, and with all the pseudo-revolutionaries such as John Lehmann, John Pudney etc.[1] And I dislike all of them. Not so much as persons; most of them, I'm sure, would be quite kind to dumb animals; but *as* revolutionaries and as communists, for, born in fairly wealthy middle-class or upper middle class homes, educated at expensive prep schools, public schools, and universities, they have no idea at all of what they priggishly call 'the class struggle' and no contact at all with either any of the real motives or the real protagonists of that class struggle. They are bogus from skull to navel; finding no subjects for their escapist poetry, they pin on a vague sense of propagating the immediate necessity of a social conscience rather than the clear sense of expressing their own un, pro, or anti social consciousnesses. The individual in the mass and the mass in the individual can be made poetically important only when the status and the position of both mass and individual are considered by that part of the consciousness which is outside both. I shall never, I hope, be mixed up in any political ramifications of literary, or pseudo literary London; honest writing does *not* mix with it; you can't be true to party *and* poetry; one must suffer, and, historically, poetry is the social and the economic creed that endures. I think I'll be able to send you some more inflammable literature during the week.

Yes, on deep consideration, Porth *is* better. Some people have invited me to spend part of the summer with them in the hills of Derbyshire, and I think of accepting. Conditions have more to do with writing than I realised; it may seem affected, but I do really need hills around me before I can do my best with either stories or poems; the world here is so flat and unpunctuated, like a bad poem by K. J. Raine. I'm moving from be-artised (in two senses) Chelsea soon anyway, and will let you know my change of address. There are all sorts of plans in my head: Derbyshire, Ireland, East End tenement, Richard Hughes in Laugharne (he's invited me), and even a short tramping existence around England. And I don't know what's going to happen yet.

This is a Me letter; so let yours be a Your letter, telling me all about your political naggings etc. What are you reading now? If possible, get

[1] A. L. Morton wrote for, not edited, the *Daily Worker*; Claud Cockburn was the paper's diplomatic correspondent, not its proprietor; Giles Romilly had run away from his public school the previous year, aged fifteen, to campaign against private education. John Pudney (1909–77), novelist and poet, in 1935 on the staff of the BBC.

hold of Fontamara,[1] by whom I don't know, which is a very good novel of the kind you like. Bernard Brett's 'The Irreconcilables' is quite good, too. Have you bought a copy of my poems yet, you dog? I haven't got a copy to send you, although, God knows, you deserve one as much as, more than, almost anybody. I might have a new book this year, but I don't know yet. Tell me what people in Swansea think of the poems, if they think anything at all.

How is Mrs. Trick junior? And Mrs. Trick senior? Remember me to Pamela,[2] and tell her that Uncle Neuburg considers her the brightest and the most originally promising of all his juvenile poets and poetesses. He wants a poem from her soon.

Don't be as long in writing a letter as I am. I'll really be expecting one next week. Make it as long as you like, or as long as I like, which is even longer.

Dylan

MS: Ohio State University

GLYN JONES
[March 1935]   5 Cwmdonkin Drive Uplands Swansea

Dear Glyn,

As you see, the trials of life have proved too much for me, the courts have found me guilty, and, rather hollow eyed and with little real work to my credit, I've returned home for a few weeks' holiday. I'm leaving, I believe, in the first week of April, but for the country then, and not for London—: Surrey, Cheshire, Derbyshire, I don't know which. It's very lonely here in Swansea, and the few old friends I have spend their days in work and their evenings in indulging in habits which I've had quite enough of—at least temporarily. As it is, I'm working on some short stories, but I don't know whether they're any good, and I would like you to have a look at them. Do you feel like coming down one Saturday before I go? There are crowds of things for us to talk about, and far more peace and comfort than we had in the pubs & that wretched room of mine in London.

How are you getting on? Have you sent any poems to Geoffrey G. yet? What about your story of the workman shitting over the cliff? The Adelphi hasn't printed the other story yet, has it? Has Pope Eliot replied? And all sorts of other questions.

And now I remember one of the main points of this letter. Some weeks ago in the gossip column of the South Wales Evening Post, there was a

---

[1] *Fontamara*, by the Communist Ignazio Silone, first published in Britain in 1934, is about the ravages of Fascism in an Italian village.

[2] Trick's daughter Pamela was five years old, and had a vivid turn of speech. An obscure phrase in Thomas's poem 'My world is pyramid', 'What colour is glory?', is said to be hers.

paragraph to the effect that Richard Hughes, in a long conversation with the gossip-writer about modern poetry, had said how much he admired my poems.[1] That definitely gives us an introduction to him, doesn't it? What do you say if I write him a note, asking whether we could call & see him in his Castle one week-end? If your car is still alive, we could run down to Laugharne, visit him & his beard, & then either return to our homes—these things could be settled later—or stay with our relations around Llanstephan. I think we'd have an interesting time. I won't write to him, of course, until I hear from you.

Levy, by the way, who now has very fierce black whiskers almost down to his middle, sends his greetings to you, & is going to try to get hold of you when he goes back to Cardiff at Easter. Will you be there then? *His* address is still 5 Redcliffe Street.

Drop me a line soon. I feel quite keen about visiting Richard Hughes.

Yours,
Dylan

P.S. Roger Roughton[2] also wishes to be remembered to you. He's just left for America.

MS:Carbondale   *SL*

PAMELA HANSFORD JOHNSON
[?early March 1935][3]   5 Cwmdonkin Drive Uplands Swansea

I've retired home, after a ragged life, for a few weeks' rest before I go to the country for the summer. I should have written what's much too long a time ago, because there's so much to explain and so much that, perhaps, will, and should, never be explained—it means such a lot of belly rubbing and really tearful apologies on my blasted part. But never mind that. Britons never will be slaves, and I'm a rat. I saw Janes before I left London, and he told me that he had had tea with you and that you were working hard on your new novel. He said, though, that you were having rather a lot of trouble with it. Would you like me to go through, in my usual nagging way, what you've written so far? You know—to say, 'No, no, no, this can't be, too lush, too lush', & 'This is impossible', & 'Cut, cut, cut'. Etc. I'd really like to; you write better when you've got someone to stand behind your shoulder sneering when you go purple & using a cruel pencil

[1] 9 January 1935.
[2] Roger Roughton, Communist and literary journalist, edited *Contemporary Poetry and Prose*, 1936–7. He committed suicide in 1941.
[3] Johnson wrote in her diary on March 7: 'Letter—of all Things, from Dylan, who is in Wales & repentant. I wish he hadn't written.' Their relationship cooled quickly once Thomas was living in London. In January 1935 she had written in the diary: 'Says he loves me but can't resist Comrade Bottle.' But Thomas continued to visit her and to write, spasmodically, for another year.

over your choicest peacock-greys. Would you like me to repeat my usual & my 'This Bed' sub-editing?[1] If you would, and you still aren't too angry with me for all the silly and careless things I've done, send the MSS to me at home, & I'll send it back very soon & very carefully gone-through.

Love to your mother and—always—to you.

Dylan

MS: Buffalo   *SL*

RICHARD HUGHES

Richard Hughes (1900–76) was already an established author. He lived in some style at Laugharne Castle, a house built amid the ruins, overlooking the estuary.

[early April 1935]   5 Cwmdonkin Drive Uplands Swansea

Dear Mr. Richard Hughes,

As I'm going to spend this coming week-end in Llanstephan, I wonder whether I could call and see you some time on Saturday (6th)?[2] Only a few days ago I was shown an old cutting from a local newspaper in which you said that you'd read some of my poems. That does give me some sort of introduction, doesn't it, however vague? I was in Laugharne in the late summer, but the ferryman, who knows everything, told me you were away, and so I didn't batter at the Castle gates. I do hope I'll be able to see you this time.

Sincerely,
Dylan Thomas

MS: Indiana

MICHAEL ROBERTS[3]
Sunday 7th [envelope postmarked April 8 1935]
5 Cwmdonkin Drive Uplands Swansea

Dear Michael Roberts,

Sorry I haven't been able to reply sooner, but the Parton Bookshop redirected your letter to me only a few days ago.

---

[1] Pamela Hansford Johnson's novel, *This Bed Thy Centre* (the title suggested by Thomas), was published in 1935, followed the next year by *Blessed Above Women*.
[2] 'Saturday April 6' fits the calendar.
[3] Poet and journalist (1902–48). He edited *The Faber Book of Modern Verse*, 1936, which included two Thomas poems.

Very pleased you intend including me in the anthology. No, the American rights haven't been sold, of course.

Is the anthology coming out soon? I'll be sent proofs, I suppose?

Thanks very much again.

Sincerely,
Dylan Thomas

MS: Berg

DESMOND HAWKINS

Hawkins (b. 1908), later novelist, critic and broadcaster, reviewed Thomas's *18 Poems* for the magazine *Time & Tide*. When he became literary editor of *Purpose*, he wrote to Thomas, inviting him to contribute.

15.5.35   Three Gates Higher Disley Cheshire[1]

Dear Desmond Hawkins,

Thank you so much for your letter. Of course I remember you well. And thank you for your criticism in Time and Tide. I've been so unwell during the last month or two that I haven't been able to write to you about it, but I do appreciate all the kind things you said. On the whole the literary weeklies have treated that book of mine in a very gentlemanly way, but, apart from your review and one other, there were no constructive comments. Those privately coded blocks of feeling, derived from personal, unpoetical, or even anti-poetical, complexes must certainly be done away with before I write any more—or, at least, before I write any better, and I must do something about my policeman rhythms.

I'm so glad to hear that you've got the opportunity of publishing uncommercial and 'tolerably specialised' criticism, and I'd be awfully pleased to do anything I could. I don't know whether I'm capable of even a 'tolerable' specialisation. Poetry, Jacobean and Metaphysical, and music, minus the more intricate technicalities, mysticism (honest), and psychology (abnormal for preference) are, for Purpose's purpose, about the only things I appreciate sufficiently. Perhaps I can do something for you on those lines?

I'm staying in Cheshire until the end of the week, and then returning to London for some days. Somebody told me you were living in the country, but, if you happen to be in town when I am, perhaps we could meet somewhere—'somewhere' inevitably means a pub—and talk over things. If that's not possible, will you let me know before Monday?

[1] A cottage in the Peak District where Thomas stayed for a month with a friend of Norman Cameron, a young history lecturer, Alan Taylor, and his wife Margaret. Taylor, later A. J. P. Taylor the historian, thought Thomas a sponger, and took against him from the start. His wife thought Thomas wonderful, and became a devotee and patron.

And, of course, I'd be delighted to send you or, preferably to give you, some poems.

Sincerely,
Dylan Thomas

MS: the recipient

A. E. TRICK
[summer 1935]   Glen Lough Co. Donegal Meenacross Lifford

Dear Bert,

Is it any good telling you that, for the last three months or more, I've been meaning and meaning to write a long letter to you, a sort of self-explanatory monologue and travelogue, an unnecessary lecture on the ways of a Welsh poet in the amazing world? I've been meaning to ask Twentieth Century all about the economic ruptures, and whether the Guardian had managed to invent a truss for them yet, to learn about the new Vanocs of Socialism and the bollocks of the old gang, to inquire, very politely and sincerely, into the questions of health, work, and happiness. But I'm never very hot on meaning: it's the sound of meaning that I like, and so the long letter remained unwritten, the months moved on, and I shifted from the Derbyshire peaks to the London saloons, from the upper reaches of the Thames to the edge of the Atlantic without saying hallo or goodbye to you. How is the family? How is the small world? (It's the big world, really.) What have you been reading and doing? Does John J. still dance with the skeleton? Has the corpse of Mainwaring H. sprouted rhubarb yet?[1] How many times have you lectured on 'The Syphilisation of Man' to the ingrown virginities of the prig-squared Circle? Tell me all about everything. I'm ten miles from the nearest human being (with the exception of the deaf farmer who gives me food), and, in spite of the sea and the lakes and my papers and my books and my cigarettes (though they're damned hard to get, and I've few left of them) and my increasing obsession with the things under the skin, I'm lonely as Christ sometimes and can't even speak to my Father on an ethereal wave-length. I came here—'here' is a cottage studio, once owned by an American artist, perched in a field on a hill facing a lot of wild Atlantic—with Geoffrey G., but he's gone back to town.[2] And here is a wild, unlettered and un-frenchlettered country, too far from Ardara, a village you can't be too far from. Here are gannets and seals and puffins flying and puffing and playing a quarter of a mile outside my window where there are great rocks petrified like the old fates and destinies of Ireland & smooth, white pebbles under and around them like the souls of the dead Irish. There's a

---

[1] Mainwaring Hughes of Swansea.
[2] The studio, formerly a donkey-shed, had been used by the American artist Rockwell Kent. Grigson took Thomas there for a rest cure, and stayed a couple of weeks. When Thomas left, he walked off without paying the farmer, Dan Ward, which offended Grigson and may have begun their estrangement.

hill with a huge echo; you shout, and the dead Irish answer from behind the hill. I've forced them into confessing that they are sad, grey, lost, forgotten, dead and damned forever. There are St. Bridget Shapes crossed in the rafters of my cottage, and these Shapes are to keep away what and who should be kept away. You are superstitious here or mad, whimsy or barmy, and the blood sports are bloody sports, but I can break a trout's neck now as skilfully as Geoffrey (who gave me the killing rod) but with more conscience. My days these days are planned out carefully, or at least conveniently, to the clock I haven't got (if time is the tick of a clock, I'm living in a funny dimension, in an hourless house): I rise at nine, I breakfast and clean up till ten, I read or write from ten till one, I lunch at one, then I walk over the cliffs to the sea and stay or walk about there till half past three or four, then tea, after tea I write until the early dusk, then I climb over the hills to the high lakes and fish there until dark. Back. Supper. Bed. I have a little illegal poteen whiskey with my supper, and I smoke black shag in a bad pipe. One day a week I shall walk ten miles to Glendrumatie where there is a shop and a porter bar. It rains and it rains. All the damned seagulls are fallen angels. Frogs and storms and squids and clegs and mutton-birds and midges and killing beetles. Dead sheep in the bracken.

But this is by no means a despondent letter. Words are coming nicely, and the rain can't get in through the roof. I have a blazing turf fire, and the only sound is the sea's on the million stones. I have a beard, too, a curly, ginger growth, neatly irregular, sweetly disorderly. I'll keep it for good, I think, or long enough, anyway, for the Tricks & the Thomases & my Mumbles Mermaid (bless her hair and her tail) to admire and finger it. I have my homesicknesses, but they vanish all right, like all the thoughts of permanency, and the Uplands and the Park go up in a wet smoke. In my sicker moments I think of me writing by my gas-fire opposite the tall, Greek nudes, of walking past your shop to the trainstop, and rattling along to a beery and fleshly Oystermouth,[1] of walking to your house in the Sunday rain and sitting by the fire until we've set the whole world straight, and the whole Welsh world is dark. But I wouldn't be at home if I were at home. Everywhere I find myself seems to be nothing but a resting place between places that become resting places themselves. This is an essential state of being, an abstraction as concrete as a horsefly that's always worrying the back of your neck, plaguing and bothering before it draws blood. I'm at home when the blood's spilt, but only until the pricked vein heals up again, and my water and sugar turn red again, and the body and the brain, all the centres of movement, must shift or die. It may be a primary loneliness that makes me out-of-home. It may be this or that, & this and that is enough for to-day. Poor Dylan, poor him, poor me.

I wish I could provide you with notes on the financial, political, economic, industrial, and agricultural conditions of this lazy and vocal

---

[1] Oystermouth is part of the Mumbles, Swansea.

land, but my powers of natural observation, never very clear, would gain me less Marx every day. I find I can't see a landscape; scenery is just scenery to me; botany is bottomy or Bottomley, Horatio obliqua;[1] little He wotted when he made the trees & the flowers how one of his Welsh chosen would pass them by, not even knowing that they were there. My own eyes, I know, squint inwards; when, and if, I look at the exterior world I see nothing or me; I should like very much to say that I see *everything* through the inner eye, but all I see is darkness, naked and not very nice. What can be done about it? The birds of the air peck my moustache. Idly I shoo them aside, engrossed in thoughts concerning the spiritual anatomy of the worms of Donegal. This is a poor, dirty land, and the pigs rut and scrabble in the parlours. There are few political feelings in the West, though most people seem to favour a mild Republicanism. My deaf farmer believes in fairies, and burns a red lamp under a religious magazine reproduction of somebody's hideous head of Christ; even his calendars are Christian: I always expect to find a cross in the soup, or find a chicken crucified by skewers to a fatty plate.

Have you heard from Fred Janes? He's living higgledy piggledy in a ruin and a riot of a Kensington studio with Levy, the bearded, and a couple of other irresponsible and wildly conventional painters. He might be re-turning to Swansea soon; London's lousy in the hot weather, and Fred loves Gower like a Rhossilli rabbit. He might, too, bring Scott,[2] a little beard, with him. That'll be nice; Scott's well worth knowing, and Fred is more seriously *and* comically metaphysical than ever.

I've stayed with Dan Jones in Harrow for a few days. He reads all the time, and is cleverer than ever. But his mind's in a mess, for he doesn't know any direction, he isn't sure either of music or writing, though he does both competently and often brilliantly. I wouldn't be surprised to see him turn into a first-rate literary critic, producing a standard study of 'A Comparison of European Literatures'. He has all that Jamieson had, with more wit, more sensibility, and, within his time limits, a far more comprehensive erudition, [. . .] but I like him.

Trevor Hughes, of the undiluted letters, is no nearer the looney bin, but the smell of the padded cells is floating about his nostrils. He has lately become a friend, counsellor, & admirer of Pamela J., who has spurned me as a small, but gifted, Welshman, of unsocial tendencies & definitely immoral habits. Her last novel has sold well, & is now in a fifth edition. Her next honourable addition to the shelves of libraries & the welfare of widow wombs is to be called 'Blessed Among Women'.

The rest of my acquaintances are very much as usual, thank you. Geoffrey G. has a small daughter, Caroline, & a new hedgehog. Norman Cameron has a book of poems appearing very soon. And my next poems

---

[1] Horatio Bottomley (d. 1933), journalist, MP and fraud. Thomas, who rarely employed a Latinism, seems to be using this one to suggest deviousness.

[2] The painter William Scott (b. 1913) lived with Thomas, Janes and Levy at a new address, Coleherne Road.

will be published by Dent.[1] Now the news fades, the rain is coming heavily, and I'm going to make myself some creamy tea. I'll write more, & more interestingly I hope, after the creamy tea. Good-bye, as is said, (and that's a foul thing to say), for now.

For now was a long now, and it's morning again, with the wind sweeping up from the sea, and a straight mist above the hills. I've had breakfast, built a tiny stone bridge over the stream by my front door, fallen twice in the muddy gutters by the side of the stream, and banged my thumb with a hammer. In half an hour or less I'm going to work on my new story, 'Daniel Dom'. Did I tell you about it when I saw you last? It's based on the Pilgrim's Progress, but tells of the adventures of Anti-Christian in his travels from the City of Zion to the City of Destruction. I've been commissioned to write it, but I won't be given any money until the first half a dozen parts or chapters are completed. The agents are rather frightened of blasphemous obscenity (and well they might be), and want to see how clean the half dozen chapters are before they advance me anything. The poor fish don't realise that I shall cut out the objectionable bits when I send them the synopsis & first chapters, & then put them immediately back. I've finished John's story, too; it's called, 'Cora, The Vampire'. I'll send it to you to show to John once I've had it typed. Do you still take New Verse? A long poem of mine will be in the next one— (consternation!).[2]

I don't know how long I shall be here; it all depends on how the silence and the loneliness attack me. I had thought of staying here until September, but the hot months are long months, and, though I can't say I like my fellows very much, and though my social conscience is becoming more flea-bitten every day, I can't indefinitely regard my own face in the mirror as the only face in the world, my beard as the only beard, my undisciplined thoughts as the only thoughts that matter under the sun, or the lack of light, and as the thoughts that revolve the egg-shaped earth. I will want more than an echo, sad, grey, lost, forgotten, & damned forever, to answer me in August, & more than the contaminated sheep to rodger on the high cliffs. But, if I can, I'll stay here until September, come home for a few weeks, & then return to London; when the season commences, I hope to have a certain amount of dramatic criticism, or, if that sounds too pompous, a little free entertainment on the stage & a little free love off stage from any publicity-seeking actresses I can find. It's fairly honest to be a dishonest critic of a corrupted, commercial theatre—as the best socialists suck all they can from the jaundiced arseholes of an anti-socialist state.

Before I say goodbye, I must tell you about Vicky Neuburg. He's got a new residence in North London, a crazy room full of books, kippers & warming-pans, a hot-as-hell conservatory with a fountain pool full of

---

[1] After some ups and downs, the firm of J. M. Dent published *Twenty-five Poems* in September 1936.

[2] August/September issue, 'A Poem in Three Parts' (later called 'I, in my intricate image').

goldfish, & a jungled garden where members of a strange Neuburgian clan, The Circle (I think) of Creative Art & Life, meet, talk, jibber, froth, prowl, & presumably do their poetical best to fornicate, among the rushes and wormy ferns. The Creature himself—I must tell you one day, if I haven't told you before, the story of how Aleister Crowley turned Vicky into a camel—is a nineteenth-century crank with mental gangrene, lousier than ever before, a product of a Jewish nuts-factory, an Oscar Tamed. Runia Tharp is a believer in the voice of nature, and cages a fart in the bath under the fond delusion that it resembles, in pitch & tone, the voice of some Wordsworthian spirit invoking a horsefly. Rest In Purgatory.

Write soon & at great length, telling me all there is to tell of everything in which you know I'm interested—personal things, impersonal things, local politics, news, views, & all the etceteras you can think of.

Give my love to everybody—even Mrs. Waldron. (I saw a seal like Mrs. Waldron yesterday.)

Yours,
Dylan

MS: Ohio State University   *SL*

JOHN LEHMANN
3 August 1935   Glen Lough Meenacross Lifford Co Donegal

Dear Mr. Lehmann,
So sorry not to have replied before. I've been moving around rather a lot, and my letters have got muddled. I haven't written very many poems lately; the problems of where on earth to live, and, even more important, how on earth to live anywhere, have been too difficult; but I'm enclosing six fairly recent ones, one of them a hundred lines long, you might think it better to choose from than from any of those in my book. You'll have to excuse my handwriting; I don't think there's a typewriter nearer than Belfast.

Would it—I don't suppose for a moment it would—be possible that the publishers might advance me my payment *before* publication, *soon*? I need it like hell, and more urgently.

Anyway, here are the poems. And apologies again for delay.

Sincerely yours,
Dylan Thomas

TS: J. M. Dent

JOHN LEHMANN
August 14 1935   Glen Lough Meenacross Lifford Co Donegal

Dear John Lehmann,
   Thank you very, very much indeed. I doubted the possibility of an
advance from Lane, and I certainly didn't expect you to advance anything
on your own account.[1] It was very, very kind and thoughtful of you. I
needed the money urgently—to pay my debts here and return to England.
Thank you again. I hope to pay you back quite soon.
   A letter was forwarded to me yesterday from Kilham Roberts, explaining that you hadn't been able to get hold of me, and telling me again
about the Year's Poetry. You'll be letting him know, I suppose, that
you've got my address.
   I shall be here only a few weeks more, but anything addressed to me c/o
Norman Cameron, 49c British Grove, will always be forwarded on.
   If you don't like the poems I've sent you, I could let you have one or
two more.

                              Very sincerely yours,
                              Dylan Thomas

TS: J. M. Dent

DANIEL JONES
Tuesday August 14 1935   Glen Lough Meenacross
            nr. Glencolumkille Lifford Co Donegal Irish Free State

Addressed, unavoidably, to Fred [Janes].
And to be read either late at night or
when at least *half* tipsy.

   This is the first long letter I've ever written to you. I'm not much good
at writing letters, I can't strike the, if I may coin a phrase, happy medium
between trying to be funny, not trying to be funny, and trying not to be
funny. I can't write as I talk—thank God I can't talk as I write, either —
and I get highflown and flyblown and flyfaultin if I try very consciously
not to be self-conscious. Take me as I come—sounds like Onan—and
remember the dear dead days that had to have a gallon or two of nonsense
(often awfully good nonsense) or parch. This is written for two main
reasons: first, because I've been socially rude, (*you* can't talk), and Goat
has probably shown her horns and Bear has growled and the jealous Hook[2]
been haughty as wadding ever since I said, 'Yes, ten o'clock outside the

---

[1] John Lane of the Bodley Head published *The Year's Poetry*, the publication concerned in
   this and the previous letter.
[2] Goat, Bear, Hook: fantasy-names for members of Jones's family.

Queen's Hall,' and then, doom on my roving scrotum, found a Jewess with thighs like boiled string and got drunk and woke up with a headache and a halfpenny and a button. It was, if I may coin a phrase, the same old story. You, I know, didn't care a seal or a fig when I flouted (that's a word I haven't used for years, have you?) the conventions and didn't even apologise. My excuse for not apologising is that you're so hard to get hold of, Harrow's will-of-the-wisp, Pinner's Sibelius (I'm still the Swan of Tawe). Give what is proper to give, anyway, to Goat and Hook and Bear, and tell Jumbo, 'There is an indiarubber police-force in Archix.'[1] Make up what story you can to explain my sins away; they won't believe it; on the last morning-after, Bear said 'whiskey' in a clear voice, and then leered. The second, and the most important reason for my writing is: I never can believe that the Warmley[2] days are over—('just a song at twilight when the lights Marlowe and the Flecker Beddoes Bailey Donne and Poe')[3] —that there should be no more twittering, no more nose-on-window-pressing and howling at the streets, no more walks with vampire cries, and standing over the world, no more hold-a-writing-table for the longest, and wrong adjectives; I can't believe that Percy, who droppeth gently, can have dropped out of the world, that the 'Badger Beneath My Vest' and 'Homage to Admiral Beatty' are a song and a boat of the past; that Miguel-y-Bradshaw, Waldo Carpet, Xmas Pulpit, Paul America, Winter Vaux, Tonenbach, and Bram, all that miscellaneous colony of geniuses, our little men, can have died on us; that the one-legged grandmother — remember the panama-hat-shaped birds, from the Suez Canal, who pecked at her atlas-bone—doesn't still take photographs of Birmingham; that the queer, Swansea world, a world, thank Christ that was self-sufficient, can't stand on its bow legs in a smoky city full of snobs and quacks. I'm surer of nothing than that that world, Percy's world in Warmley, was, and still is, the only one that has any claims to permanence; I mean that this long, out-of-doored world isn't much good really, that it's only the setting, is only supposed to be the setting, for a world of your own—in our cases, a world of our own—from which we can interpret nearly everything that's worth. And the only world worth is the world of our own that has its independent people, people like Percy, so much, much more real than your father or my mother, my Jewess or your girl on the roof, places and things and qualities and standards, and symbols much bigger than the exterior solidities, all of its own. Didn't we work better, weren't poems and music better, weren't we happier in being unhappy, out of that world, than in—not even out of—this unlocal, uncentral world where the pubs are bad and the people are sly and the only places to go are the places to go to? I think it is the same with you, though it's so long since I've seen you, dry months, too, that you may be,

---

[1] Jumbo was Jim Jones, Dan Jones's elder brother. Archix was an imaginary country.

[2] Dan Jones's house in Swansea, before the family moved to London.

[3] Thomas is using the names of poets to produce a punning version of the lyric, 'Just a song at twilight/When the lights are low,/And the flick'ring shadows/Softly come and go'.

though you couldn't be, all different, all older, in your cat's lights more learnèd, even Harrowed to some sort of contentment, never regretting for one moment the almost-going of Percy's celestial circle. No, that couldn't be; that world *does* remain, in spite of London, the Academy, and a tuppenny, half-highbrow success. I never thought that localities meant so much, nor the genius of places, nor anything like that. I thought that the soul went round like a Gladstone bag, never caring a damn for any particular station-rack or hotel-cloakroom; that gestures and genius made the same gestures in Cockett and Cockfosters;[1] didn't we look at our geniuses and say, 'We're taking you somewhere else to live, but we won't part.' I placed my hand upon my heart and said that we would never part; I wonder what I would have said had I placed it on my head. So on and on; like an unborn child in the city I want to get born and go to the outskirts. Here in Ireland I'm further away than ever from the permanent world, the one real world in a house or a room, very much peopled, with the exterior, wrong world—wrong because it's never understood out of the interior world—looking in through the windows. This sort of nostalgia isn't escapist by any means, you know that; just as the only politics for a conscientious artist—that's you and me—must be left-wing under a right-wing government, communist *under* capitalism, so the only world for that WARMDANDYLANLEY-MAN must be the WARMDANDYLAN-LEY-WORLD under the world-of-the-others. How could it be escapism? It's the only contact there is between yourself and yourselves, what's social in you and what isn't—though, God knows, I could shake Bram's intangible hand as seriously as the hand of Dean Inge, and with far greater sense of reality. Even surrealism, which seemed to have hopes and promise, preaches the decay of reality and the importance, and eventual dominance, (I don't like those words however much I try to look on them coldly), of unreality, as though the two could be put in two boxes: isn't Percy flesh, bone, and blood, isn't Evangeline Booth a shadow, isn't Percy a shadow, isn't Evangeline flesh, bone, & blood, isn't Percy flesh-bone-& blood-shadow, isn't Evangeline flesh-bone-and-blood-shadow, isn't Percy-Evangeline flesh bone and blood?—and so on and on. I'm not going to read this letter over afterwards to see what it reads like; let it go on, that's all; you don't mind the dashes and the hyphens and the bits of dogma and the brackets and the bits of dog-eaten self-consciousness and the sentimentality because I'm writing by candlelight all alone in a cottage facing the Atlantic. From the WARMDANDYLANLEY-WORLD I'd no more think of writing this letter than of using words like 'Proust' and 'flounce' and 'akimbo' and 'schedule' and 'urge' when talking in that W-W; I wouldn't have or need to; this is only covering old ground in words and phrases and thoughts and idioms that are all part of that world; it's only because, now, here in this terribly out-of-the way and lonely place, I feel the need for that world, the necessity for its going on, and the fear

---

[1] Suburbs of Swansea and London.

that it might be dying to you, that I'm trying to resurrect my bit of it, and make you realise again what you realise already; the importance of that world because it's the only one, the importance of us, too, and the fact that our poems and music won't and can't be anything without it. Soon I'm going out for a walk in the dark by myself; that'll make me happy as hell; I'll think of the almost-but-never-going-gone, and remember the cries of the Bulgarian scouts as I hear that damned sea rolling, and remember the first world—where do they pretend it is, Waunarllwyd?[1]—as I stand under an absurdly high hill—much too high, our world has its hills just the proper, the *nice*, length (I'm arching my index-finger & thumb and joining them tastefully)—and shout to it, 'Go on, you big shit, WARMDANDY-LANLEY-WORLD has a hill twice as beautiful and with a ribbon and bell on it, & a piece of boiled string on the top, if the WARMDANDYLANLEY-MAN wants it like that'. And I'll finish this when I come back.

[*New page.*] But it was so late when I came back that I padlocked out the wild Irish night, looked through the window and saw Count Antigarlic, a strange Hungarian gentleman who has been scraping an acquaintance (take that literally) with me lately, coming down the hill in a cloak lined with spiders, and, suddenly very frightened, I hurried to bed. This is written in the cold of the next morning, the Count is nowhere to be seen, and it is only the thin mouth-print of blood on the window pane, and the dry mouse on the sill, that brings the night back. It's hard to pick up the night threads; they lead, quite impossibly, into the socket of a one-eyed woman, the rectums of crucified sparrows, the tunnels of coloured badgers reading morbid literature in the dark, and very small bulls, the size of thimbles, mooing in a clavichord. At least, they lead to absurd things. Where was I last night? Feeding my father with hay? offering Hook a newt in a bluebag? I was talking about worlds. We must, when our affairs are settled, when music and poetry are arranged so that we can still live, love, and drink beer, go back to Uplands or Sketty and found there, for good and for all, a permanent colony; living there until we are old gentlemen, with occasional visits to London and Paris, we shall lead the lives of small-town anti-society, and entertain any of the other members of the WARMDANDYLANLEY-WORLD who happen to visit the town; Fred will be a greengrocer, painting over his shop, Tom an armyman with many holidays, Thornley a nearby vicar, Trick a nearby grocer, Stevens a bankmanager with holidays, Smart a bankmanager with holidays, and the rest of our vague WARMLIES this and that all over the wrong world.[2] Mumbles, and the best saloon bars in Britain, will be open for us all night. And Percy will come drooping slow there. Yeats never moves out of his own town in Galway, Sibelius never out of Helsingfors. So Jones and Thomas, that well-known firm of family provisioners, shall not move out of their town. So be it.

---

[1] Waunarlwydd (the correct spelling) is another part of Swansea.
[2] Fred Janes's father was a greengrocer. Thornley Jones wrote music. Alan Stevens worked in a bank, and so did P. E. Smart.

But now of course all the things are different; we must peck on and snoot away in an unlovely city until we can manage our own fates to a Walesward advantage. If you and the menagerie stay on in Harrow, I shall, in the winter, come and lodge near there, too, and go up to town only once or twice a week. We shall twitter. That, at least, is practicable. And Harrow, hell with such a nice name, shall shine like a star, and the maidenheads fall like rain.

I am working hard here, and have got lots of new poems. I want you to see them, I want you to tell me a lot about them before my new book[1] comes out at Christmas.

Write before I leave here on the thirtieth of August, a long, careless letter.

All the love of one WARMDANDYLANLEY-MAN to the other one.

MS: Texas

ROBERT HERRING[2]

[summer 1935]   Glen Lough Meenacross Lifford Co Donegal

Dear Mr. Herring,

Very many thanks. I'm glad you liked the poem, and hope that the story will prove printable, too.

As to payment, it would really suit me better if a cheque could be sent on earlier than is usual. You did mention that possibility, although I quite understand that nothing definite can be arranged yet.[3]

Thanks for the good wishes. I hope I'll be allowed to contribute again.

Yours sincerely,

Dylan Thomas

From September on, my address will be 5 Cwmdonkin Drive, Uplands, Swansea. It will, at least, always find me.

MS: Carbondale

---

[1] It was 1936 before *Twenty-five Poems* appeared.
[2] Robert Herring (1903–75) edited the magazine *Life and Letters Today* from 1935 to 1950. In December 1935 it printed the first seven sections of the 'Altarwise by owl-light' sequence, which Thomas had been working on in Ireland. The Spring 1936 issue carried his story 'The Lemon'. See letter to Desmond Hawkins, page 203.
[3] The letter is annotated in another hand: '£5 for Story & Poem'.

DESMOND HAWKINS
16th Sep '35   5 Cwmdonkin Drive Uplands Swansea

Dear Desmond,

Are you annoyed at not hearing from me? The truth is that from the time I left you until the day before yesterday, when I arrived home, I've been on the blindest blind in the world and didn't know what day it was or what week or anything, lost most of my little property, including many, to me, valuable papers, and, what is worse for me, my job on the Morning Post.[1] I can only excuse myself by pretending that it was practice for the more alcoholic pages of our King's Canary.[2]

I don't remember whether you gave me the completed list of names of characters or not, and if you did I lost them. So, before I can begin my part, do send the full list along. I'll be able tomorrow, when my hand doesn't shake so much, to work on the opening pages but I can't do much without all the Chapfork Benders etc. So send 'em soon. We must—and the lord knows it's my fault alone—get to work.

What about the poems? Have you, as I thought you might, decided that the shorter one is better for your purpose?

Write & tell me anyway. And I'm so sorry for the delay.

Yours,
Dylan

P.S. Do you remember Fluffy, the chorus-girl with glasses? It was mostly her fault, the nice, nice bitch.[3]

MS: the recipient

GEOFFREY GRIGSON
[?September 1935]   5 Cwmdonkin Drive Uplands Swansea

Dear Geoffrey,

I'm an old twicer, aren't I? Here I lie, lily-faced between the sheets, looking like Shelley and the Three Little Pigs rolled into one, very pretty in my white pyjamas, with a droshki cough. Thanks so much for your letter, dear Doctor, and I'm so glad the Morning Post has taken me back without a scolding.[4] I promised to explain to you what happened and why

[1] Thomas had been reviewing thrillers for the strait-laced *Morning Post* since Geoffrey Grigson, its literary editor, hired him at the start of the year.
[2] *The Murder (or Death) of the King's Canary* was to be a satirical detective story, poking fun both at the genre and at thinly disguised literary figures. The 'Canary' was the Poet Laureate. Over the years Thomas had different collaborators for this laborious joke. In the second paragraph, 'Chapfork Bender' = Stephen Spender.
[3] Thomas and Hawkins had met her at one of their haunts, The Marquis of Granby.
[4] This sounds like the reviewing job that Thomas thought he had lost when he wrote to Hawkins on September 16. But he may have been sacked and re-hired more than once, and the dating of this letter to Grigson is uncertain.

after I left you in London, but now I try to I can't. I drank the night custard of the gods, but they must have been the wrong gods, and I woke up every morning feeling like hell in somebody else's bedsitting room with concealed washbasin. This morning I have battled with a venomous doctor who wanted me to go places with him and do things, but, old Terry,[1] I won by a short lung. I have to stay indoors for six or eight weeks, during which time I feel sure I'll be able to work hard and well. So do send me thrillers, and I promise the most satisfactory reviews. But, for the love of the great grey cunt of the world, don't tell the details of my present indisposition to anyone but Norman the Nagger: they might ruin my lecherous chances.[2] No, I shan't begin dying yet. I've lived a bit quicker than lots of people, so I *can* begin five years under the scheduled time. But that gives me nearly ten years, and, lo there Sadokiel[3] (tell Normal that, it's nice to be quoted), that embryo you told me about is going to produce many strange and good things.

So send the thrillers and love to you, Doctor Terry.

Love to Normal, too. I'll be writing to him.

                                                         Carlos

MS: Texas

RICHARD CHURCH

Church (1893–1972) was a poet and novelist who worked as a civil servant before joining J.M. Dent as poetry editor in 1933. Letters from him to Thomas in the Dent files show him striving to be fair to poems which were not to his old-fashioned taste.

8th October '35   5 Cwmdonkin Drive Uplands Swansea

Dear Richard Church,

Thank you for your letter.

I shan't be in town until the first week of November. Shall I call in and have a talk with you then? I'd be up sooner, but this wretched illness of mine keeps me indoors. I'd have replied sooner, too, but I don't seem to be able to concentrate. These are passing troubles, and in a very few days, I hope, I can get down to sub-editing my poems.

Here, anyway, are most of the manuscripts. I haven't titled any of

---

[1] 'Dr Terry' was one of Thomas's nicknames for Grigson.

[2] 'Norman the Nagger', 'Normal' on other occasions, was Norman Cameron, whose attitude to Thomas was equivocal, as in his poem that Thomas's enemies like to quote, 'The Dirty Little Accuser' ('When he quitted a sofa, he left behind him a smear./My wife says he even tried to paw her about'). Whether Thomas was really suffering from gonorrhoea, as he implies to Grigson, is an open question.

[3] Thomas is quoting from a poem by Cameron, 'The Successor', about a high priest, Sadokiel.

them. The first poem, divided into six parts of fourteen lines each, (each to be printed on a separate page, for, although the poem as a whole is to be a poem in, and by, itself, the separate parts can be regarded as individual poems) is so far incomplete; there will be at least another four parts.[1]

I hope you'll like this poem, incomplete as it is, and the others. I'll be able to type out & revise the rest quite soon.

Cameron has just sent me a copy of his book.[2] It is awfully good, isn't it?

I'm looking forward to seeing you at the beginning of November when we can talk over most of the details.

Yours sincerely,
Dylan Thomas

MS: J. M. Dent

NANCY and HAYDN TAYLOR[3]
October 27th 1935 [Thomas's 21st birthday]

Dear Nancy and Haydn,

Thank you both very much. It is nice to be remembered, especially at such an important, if I may coin a phrase, cross-road in life's journey.

The family lawyers, Paff, Grabpole and Paff have just departed; there's been a little bother, you know, over the transferring of the estate. Later on this evening I'm going down to the Marlais Head to give a formal address to the tenants. They're to present me, I believe, with a platinum walking-stick, complete with bell. Lord Hunt-Ball has given me a glass-tube for holding tiny flannel shirts. Lady Utterly has presented me with a wooden leg.

Thanks again for the present. I bought a grey hat and a book of ballads. I also have a tweed suit covered in coloured spots, a new mackintosh, new shoes, a book, new trousers, a pullover, & no hope for the future.

There's no news. I'm working moderately hard, and Dad has a very painful throat.

I'm coming to town for three days in the first week of November, and am already preparing my small jar of red paint.

The tenants are clamouring. I must go.

Love,
Dylan

MS: Haydn Taylor

[1] 'Altarwise by owl-light', which eventually had ten sections.
[2] *The Winter House.*
[3] Thomas's sister and brother-in-law.

DENYS KILHAM ROBERTS
28.10.35   5 Cwmdonkin Drive Uplands Swansea

Dear Mr. Roberts,
   Here are the corrected proofs.
   Poem[1] was printed in New Verse and in my Eighteen Poems, (Parton Press).
   Poem In October[2] was printed in the Listener and in Eighteen Poems.
   I was born 27th October, 1914.

Yours truly,
Dylan Thomas

MS: Texas

DESMOND HAWKINS
1.11.35   5 Cwmdonkin Drive Uplands Swansea

Dear Desmond,
   A very short note. How are you? Thanks for last letter.
   Can you come and have a drink next week? A morning drink if possible—say 12 o'clock in the Marquis on Tuesday or Wednesday morning? I'm up for about four days. We can discuss much belated Canary then. I've done a first bit but it's lousy, and I'm rewriting it. May have it ready. Hope so.
   Now as to the poem for Purpose. Do for sweet Christ's sake use the one beginning Foster the Light, nor veil the cunt-shaped moon. The fact is: I was having a poem done in the coming Life & Letters, & had a letter from R. Herring to-day saying the poem had just been printed, owing to my abominable carelessness, in the Oxford Programme. As Life & Letters is just going to press, he wants another poem pronto.[3] All I have are passages of that long thing I gave you beginning, Altarwise by owl light in the bleeding house. So do, do, Desmond, use the Foster rather than the Altar. (That is, of course, if you'd intended using either.) After all, you see, L & L have paid me a fiver already for the poem they now can't print. What an existence. Excuse haste & violence.
   Drop me a card, if you can, by Monday first post saying whether you're going to meet & — & when.

Yrs Dylan

---

[1] Probably 'I, in my intricate image'.
[2] 'Especially when the October wind', not the piece now known as 'Poem in October', written nine years later.
[3] *Programme* had published 'How soon the servant sun' and 'A grief ago' in issue No. 9, 23 October 1935. *Purpose* didn't publish 'Foster the light'.

Nice poem in S. Bookman. What shall we call him: Writhing Codd, Ruthven God?[1]

MS: the recipient

ROBERT HERRING
[November 1935] [incomplete][2]

[...] I'm enclosing it—or them—in the hope that you will like it, despite its obscurity & incompleteness. It's the first passages of what's going to be a very long poem indeed, but each section is a more-or-less self-contained short poem; if you think they're nice, you can use one, or two, or all, or whatever you like of them—calling them 'Passages Towards a Poem' or 'Poems for a Poem', whichever seems to you least precious [...]

I've just looked at the ms I'm sending you. It's smudgy & smells of all sorts of things. Sorry. And there are review scraps on the back. Can't be helped.[3]

RICHARD CHURCH
9 12 35   5 Cwmdonkin Drive Uplands Swansea

Dear Richard Church,
    Thank you for your letter, and for the candid criticism of my poems.[4] I do appreciate the trouble you have taken to make your attitude towards these poems quite clear, and am glad that you value my work highly enough to condemn it when you find it—though wrongly, I believe—to be influenced by such a 'pernicious' experiment as surrealism. Far from resenting your criticism, I welcome it very much indeed, although, to be equally candid, I think you have misinterpreted the poems and have been misled as to their purpose. I am not, never have been, never will be, or could be for that matter, a surrealist, and for a number of reasons: I have

---

[1] Ruthven Todd, poet and journalist. After Dylan Thomas's death he was commissioned to write the official biography. He produced a manuscript, but it was never published.

[2] The text is taken from a dealer's catalogue, where it is abridged as shown.

[3] See previous letter.

[4] Church had written (November 26): 'I believe that poetry should be simple as well as sensuous and beautiful ... It should be the expression of the poet's personality after the conflict and not during the conflict ... With these axioms, I look upon surrealism in poetry with abhorrence ... I am distressed to see its pernicious effect in your work, because I believe you to be outstanding amongst your generation ...'

very little idea what surrealism is; until quite recently I had never heard of it; I have never, to my knowledge, read even a paragraph of surrealist literature; my acquaintance with French is still limited to 'the pen of my aunt'; I have not read any French poetry, either in the original or in translation, since I attempted to translate Victor Hugo in a provincial Grammar School examination, and failed. All of which exposes my lamentable ignorance of contemporary poetry, but, surely, does disprove your accusations. As for being 'caught up in the delirium of intellectual fashion of the moment', I must confess that I read regrettably little modern poetry, and what 'fashionable' poetry I do come across appears to be more or less communist propaganda. I am not a communist.

I hope you won't object, but I took the liberty, soon after receiving your letter, of writing to a very sound friend of mind and asking him what surrealism was, explaining, at the same time, that a critic whose work we both knew and admired had said that my own poems were themselves surrealist. In his reply he told me what he thought the principal ideas of surrealism were, and said that surrealist writing need not have any 'meaning at all'. (He quoted some dreadful definition about 'the satanic juxtaposition of irrelevant objects etc'.) I think I do know what some of the main faults of my writing are: immature violence, rhythmic monotony, frequent muddleheadedness, and a very much overweighted imagery that leads too often to incoherence. But every line *is* meant to be understood; the reader *is* meant to understand every poem by thinking and feeling about it, not by sucking it in through his pores, or whatever he is meant to do with surrealist writing. Neither is the new group on which I'm working influenced, in any way, by an experiment with which I am totally unfamiliar. You have, and no doubt rightly, found many things to object to in these new poems; all I wish to do is to assure you that those faults are due neither to a delirious following of intellectual fashion nor to the imitation of what, to my ignorance, appears a purposely 'unreasonable' experiment inimical to poetry.

In conclusion, I have quite a number of poems simple as the three you liked, poems, to my mind, not half as good as the ones you cannot stand for. Do you wish me to send those on to you, or would you rather me wait until we can discuss everything when I come to town in the early new year?

Again, I trust you will not find this letter pretentious or impudent. I have thought a great deal about what you said in your letter, and my only excuse for the possible pretentiousness of my reply is that I really do want to realise that you have—my obscurity is to blame—misinterpreted the purpose of my obviously immature poetry, and attributed to it experimental absurdities I hardly knew existed.

Yours sincerely,
Dylan Thomas

MS: J. M. Dent

PAMELA HANSFORD JOHNSON
[?December 1935][1]

Hullo Pam,

I haven't written to you for such a long time that I'm tired of waiting for your reply; and neither has mother, catering for her invalids, including Arthur now, the pleasant uncle,[2] answered your nice letter to her; and dad only answers bills. What a family. We all have our little aches, we moan, we plug ourselves with patent medicines. Dad has a new pain (isn't this lovely ink, it's called Quink) in the eye, mother has indigestion, Arthur has rheumatism and a cold, I cough. When *you* wrote last you were dying, almost cuddling the long, black guardian worm who is the exclusive death-property of the Johnsons. Are you better, my rose, my own? And you aren't cross with me? No, of course you aren't, my mole, my badger, my little blood-brown Eve. (That's how I feel.) But this is a shoddy letter and I'm not going to finish it—just to spite myself. I haven't written a word—except for incompetent thriller reviews—since I came home. Not even a letter. I feel too weak and too tired.

But here's a true story: Tom Warner is learning short-hand. On Monday he wrote the word 'egg' all day. On Tuesday he wrote the word 'kick' all day. On Wednesday he decided to revise Monday's work, sat down, and wrote 'eck'.

Tom plays the piano for Heather on Friday nights. It's driving him mad. He has to play Ketèlbey and Irving Berlin and selections from talkies.

It's no good. I can't write. I shall put this in an envelope and then sit looking at the fire. I love you. I am a blue-green buzzard and my name is Dylan.

MS: Lady Snow's estate

RAYNER HEPPENSTALL[3]
31st December 1935   5 Cwmdonkin Drive Uplands Swansea

I owe you a lot of apologies, five shillings, and a long letter. I haven't got enough news to make a long letter, I certainly haven't five shillings,

---

[1] Thomas wrote occasionally throughout 1935 and into 1936, and this letter may be the one whose receipt was noted on 11 December 1935. But it could be earlier or even later. It is one of two letters (the other dated 6 August 1937) that came to light among the papers of Lady Snow (her second marriage was to the writer Lord (C. P.) Snow) in 1984. During her lifetime she said she owned 'a hundred letters' from Thomas. The total at Buffalo is barely thirty, counting all the fragments. Her executors have no information.

[2] Arthur, a brother of D. J. Thomas, worked on the Great Western Railway, as their father had done.

[3] See note, page 184.

but I do apologise for my delay in answering your letter, quite half of which I nearly understood. Green ink makes everything illegible, anyway, but your handwriting makes even a simple address look like a nice Sanskrit poem. From what I could gather, you'd come back either from the Rectory or the Fitzroy and were gassed hard. Purposely you were in a strong, and came out only for impudent purposes. What a time you've been having. But thanks again, I'm frightfully glad to hear from you. I never think of cider without thinking of black eyes, and the mere mention of Clerkenwell brings back the years like the smell of old violents (what I meant to type was old violets, but I'm damned if I'm going to cross anything out). Now, on the last day of the year, I am sitting more or less seriously down to type you a long delayed, but now most seasonable, letter. I'm typing because my own handwriting is bloody and my hand shakes.

As, with lynx eyes, you'll spot, I'm taking a rest at home far from the beards and bow ties, and will be here until the end of January. Let's meet when I come back to town and, over beer, roar our poems at each other like little Bellocs, and stamp up Bloomsbury, waving our cocks.

I had a letter a little time ago from Oswell Blakeston,[1] and he said he'd met you and a new black eye of yours in, I think, the Café Royal. He said that you had said you were now entirely tamed and pugnacious no longer. But do be pugnacious once more, just once more, and attack G.E.G.[2] like a bloodhound. I like him as a chap, but he's a mean little, cheap little, ostentatiously vulgar little, thumb-to-my-nose little runt when he tries to be funny at the back of New Verse. I've never read such a hideous, ineffective piece of invectory, malicious, Beachcomberish balderdash as his ten nasty lines about your poems.[3] They were really disgusting, and nobody could have any patience with them. How is the book doing, by the way? I don't read many periodicals now and have seen very few reviews. I see you're writing for Oswell's supplement in Caravel, too. Do you know anything about Caravel? I've never, in my ignorance, heard of it before.

I spent most of the summer in Donegal and did a lot of good work there, but a wave of rather alcoholic laziness has set in since and I am only just beginning to put words together again. The poetry machine is so well oiled now it should work without a hitch until my next intellectually ruinous visit to the bowels of London. I want to go abroad this summer but I don't know where. Do you know anything about Spain? Can you get along without Spanish and without money? (The same applies to any country and I'll probably end up in a bedsitting room off the Fulham Road.)

But why Kilburn, Rayner, of all places? Why not a much cheaper place in the East End? If you don't object to vermin you can get a palace of a flat

[1] Oswell Blakeston (1907–85), writer and painter.
[2] Geoffrey Grigson.
[3] *First Poems*.

near London Bridge for about [?12 shillings; *Thomas typed* L2 shillins] a week. Come and live in Limehouse with me, and write books like Thomas Burke.[1]

I told you there was no news. I live a comfortable, sheltered, and, now, only occasionally boozy life in Swansea, along with Fred Janes. I'm writing a very long poem—so are you, if I read your letter correctly—and a number of dream stories, very mixed, very violent. There is much to be said, if I may coin a phrase, for leading the conventional life. (But when I think of it, I always have, for the shabby drunkenness of upper Chelsea was even more conventional than this.)

Write a letter sometime and tell me what you're doing.

Good luck, and plug Grigson.

Yours,

Dylan

MS: Texas   *SL(R)*

FREDERIC PROKOSCH[2]

[?winter 1935/6]   5 Cwmdonkin Drive Uplands Swansea South Wales

Dear Frederic Prokosch,

I should have replied months sooner, but I've been ill and away. Thank you so much for writing. I've put down the first things I could think of in the book you sent me. I'm glad you liked some of the poems in it. I liked your poem in New Verse immensely. Don't forget you promised in your letter that you'd send me a copy of your novel when it appeared.

I think the first and the eleventh are the best poems in my book.[3] I don't care much for the last one, the one you said you liked; it's a mechanical thing, and there are lots of near-Swinburne in it. Dent's are bringing out some more poems in the spring. I'll ask them to send you a copy.

Thanks again for writing. Did you get my address through David Gascoyne?—his name's on the envelope. And do you ever come to England?

Sincerely,

Dylan Thomas

The book's in a separate envelope.

MS: Texas

---

[1] Thomas Burke (1886–1945) wrote *Limehouse Nights*.
[2] American poet and novelist, b. 1908.
[3] 'I see the boys of summer' and 'When, like a running grave'.

DENYS KILHAM ROBERTS
[?winter 1935/6] (Encloses proof of poem. See Appendix 3)

RAYNER HEPPENSTALL
January 6th 36   5 Cwmdonkin Drive Uplands Swansea

Thanks for letter. I'll write a good reply in a few days. For the moment
excuse this nasty little note, but I've got to tell you immediately what I
forgot to tell you before. When I wrote to you I meant to say: Don't be
cross because I've used your name in some letters from the West Wales
and Swansea Guardian to London publishers. I was asked a few weeks ago
to run a weekly book column for the W.W.G.,[1] and I thought it would be a
Good Thing if I managed to delude publishers, when writing to them and
asking them for review books, by telling them that some literary blokes
with Names would be possible or/and occasional contributors to the
column. So, most illegally, I used your name and Blakeston's. I let
Blakeston know yesterday, and you today—I should have let you both
know days ago, of course, before the publishers could ring you up and find
out my little lies. But I forgot. You don't mind, do you? It can't do you any
harm, and it might do me some good. I didn't, of course, expect you to
review for this unknown paper, and used your name only as a Bluff. So,
again, don't be cross. Actually, if you ever want a couple of books, I'll do
my best to get hold of them for you.
    Best wishes etc, and I'll be writing.

                                        Dylan

Where is Mortimer Market?
And the East End is on, as far as I'm concerned.

[*There is a small drawing of Thomas, arms spread. From his mouth
emerges a balloon with the words*, 'Don't lock me up, Messrs Cape'.]

MS: Texas

---

[1] Thomas introduced a column called 'Books and People' in the *Swansea and West Wales
  Guardian* on January 17, and contributed to it once thereafter.

EDITH SITWELL

The poet and critic Edith Sitwell (1887–1964), having savaged Thomas in a book in 1934 (see note, page 180), had changed her mind. Her belated review of *18 Poems*—and of the poem 'A grief ago', published in *Programme*, October 1935— was to appear in the *London Mercury* for February 1936.

17th January 1936   5 Cwmdonkin Drive Uplands Swansea S. Wales

Dear Miss Sitwell,
   I wouldn't be able to thank you enough for your letter, so I won't try, but I loved it and appreciated it, and I'll owe you a lot always for your encouragement. No, of course, I don't care a damn for an audience, or for 'success', but it *is* exciting—I suppose it's the only external reward—to have things liked for the reasons one writes them, to be believed in by someone one believes in who's right outside the nasty schools and the clever things one (me) doesn't want to understand, like surrealism and Cambridge quarterlies and Communism and the Pope of Rome. And yes God does permit everything, and health's only a little thing, and to the devil anyway with 'personal troubles' which *are* the devil—(mine are only the indescribably mean naggings of having absolutely no money at all, for I live on my few poems and stories and you know what that means, and a few rowdy habits, and the very insignificant melancholies of 'things not coming right' etc, and really nothing very much more). I'm a very happy sort of bird, and I don't care much.
   How I would like you to be able to do something about those new poems of mine, because there are quite enough to make a small book and I would like to have nothing more to do with Richard Church. I've a contract for poems with Dent's, but if Church dislikes my surrealist imitations so strongly that he'll be willing to break the contract—and I think he does hate them and will be willing—could I let you know then and would you help me? It *is* kind of you to suggest wanting to help them be published.
   I don't think I should have mentioned that I was eighteen when I wrote that Welsh-starch-itch-trash poem;[1] it sounded like an excuse, but it wasn't because I'm twenty one and the same excuse would apply to every line I write. I know, though, that you didn't take it as an excuse—and anyway why should I talk about that silly poem? Why, by the way, Miss Sitwell, are people of my age—and I would say that when I know that age doesn't matter a bit in poetry, (does it?)—so terribly frightened, in their talk and letters, of being solemn and earnest for one moment? I know I am.
   And I'm going back to London in the middle of February (I shall beard the Church then) and will try my *hardest* to manage to stay there until the first few days of March, because I want so much to meet you. My

[1] 'Our eunuch dreams', the poem that Sitwell castigated. He must have written her a previous letter.

address is Swansea until about the seventeenth of next month.

Again, I won't try to thank you, because I couldn't enough, for your advice and help and encouragement.

Yours very sincerely,
Dylan Thomas

MS: Berg

DESMOND HAWKINS
18th January 1936[1]   5 Cwmdonkin Drive Uplands Swansea

Dear Desmond,

I should have answered you such a long, long time ago that, in spite of my natural good manners, it's hardly worth apologising, is it? I am sorry, anyway, and I'm not dead—(I had my suspicions yesterday morning, though).

Thanks for Purpose; I liked the reviews and I'm so glad you said a few words about Cameron's poems—his book's been horribly neglected from what I can see from the periodicals that come into my Swansea retreat, ('retreat' it is, from the onslaught of my London enemies, from that ghoul of a Marquis—though here, admittedly, there's the very devil of a Mermaid). And I always like Porteus, don't you?[2] (Though G.E.G. isn't all that good.)

Going to soak the Bookman for a guinea? I don't know if it'll like advanced young men now that Ruthven Todd's been given the push. He (Todd) is probably nice and is coming to London some time this month. I'm nice, too, but I won't be back until the middle of February—for a couple of weeks or more then, so let's meet. Let's meet in a pub like the Plough, or even somewhere in the East, but not in that bunch of Charlotte-street baNinas.[3]

You did tell me—I mean, I didn't dream it, though thank God my dreams of that Papal paper are very rare—that you were going to do a fiction review for the Criterion, didn't you?[4] That's fine. I must write a novel quickly for you to review it. (And the King's Canary shall *not* die. We'll have a shot at it, blast us we will.)

About poems: I don't know that I've got anything much good at the moment, but I probably will have by the time I see you. I'm working hard enough but so slowly, & a lot of my time for the last week or two has been spent in preparing a smug paper for the L.C.C. Institute of Education. You're not in a vast hurry for poems, are you? I'll be in town

[1] Thomas wrote '18th February' by mistake.
[2] Hugh Gordon Porteus, writer and critic.
[3] A word-play on Nina Hamnett.
[4] T. S. ('Pope') Eliot edited the *Criterion*.

not later than February 17, & will send you a postcard, with dates for you to pick from—as many as you like—a week before that.

Best wishes
Dylan

Remember me to Porteus if you see him. I'd like to meet him again very much. Couldn't we arrange a mild, or a bitter, night out all together?

MS: the recipient

EDITH SITWELL
24th January '36   5 Cwmdonkin Drive Uplands Swansea

Dear Miss Sitwell,
  This is horrid paper; I had some Sweet Nell of Old Drury Bond but I've lost her. Thank you so much for your letter, and of course I'd love to dine with you on the 18th at your club and come to your party. It's kind of you and nice of you to ask me. The one person I know, and only slightly, is David Higham[1] who arranged the Dent's contract for me. I'm looking forward a lot to being taken round to Duckworth and Bumpus. (No, I don't know Mr. Wilson.)[2] Are you sure you really don't mind taking all this trouble? I'm so very grateful to you. You must have listened to a great deal of the woes of young poets. And to take a regular job is the most sensible suggestion in the world. I would willingly and gladly, but have, apart from the little writing, reviewing, hack journalism, and oddjobbery I've done, hardly any qualifications. But you shall have all my confidences when we meet. They look depressed on paper, and I'm not. (If there's been too much talk of 'the woes' in my letters, it's because it's been raining every time I've written to you. It always rains in Swansea.) I do hope your arrangements won't fail you, and that I shall meet you on the 18th & the 19th.

Yours very sincerely,
Dylan Thomas

MS: Berg

[1] David Higham led an exodus from the firm of Curtis Brown in 1935 and set up a new literary agency, Pearn, Pollinger & Higham. Thomas was wobbling between the old firm and the new.
[2] J. G. Wilson ran Bumpus, the booksellers.

ROBERT HERRING
30.1.36   5 Cwmdonkin Drive Uplands Swansea

Dear Robert Herring,
   I'm sure the worst will happen; it always does; I shall get blind. So let's
meet, shall we, on my first day in town? the 10th. Shall we meet
somewhere in the evening: I mayn't be up for lunch. You can tell me all
about Miss S. She isn't very frightening, is she? I saw a photograph of her
once, in medieval costume. And thanks a lot: I'd like very much to dine
on the 20th. Don't bother to write, unless, of course, you *aren't* free on
the 10th. I'll ring you in the afternoon to fix the time and pub. I shan't
wear a gardenia but I am short with bulging eyes, a broken tooth, curly
hair and a cigarette. Otherwise I am respectable enough even to go into
Oddenino's (That's not a suggestion for a meeting place, but the Café
Royal is, I believe, barred to me, and anyway I prefer places with things to
spit in). Do you ever see Oswell Blakeston by the way? If you do, wave
your hand at him for me. I hope to have a drink with him next month.
And if you *aren't* free, then do suggest any other day after the 10th.
                                         Yours sincerely,
                                         Dylan Thomas

MS: Texas   *SL*

DESMOND HAWKINS
1.2.36   5 Cwmdonkin Drive Uplands Swansea

I'm coming to town on the 10th, this Monday week. What about meeting
Tuesday the 11th, Wednesday 12th or Thursday 13th morning
in—say—the Plough[1] between 11.30 a.m. and mid-day? Drop me a card &
tell me; and if you know a better pub around the district—O.K. Discuss
everything then. Sorry to scribble such a tiny note but I *must* have a shit.
                                         Yours,
                                         Dylan

MS: the recipient

DANIEL JONES
6.2.36 [on the envelope: 'oh so urgent']   5 Cwmdonkin Drive

RA. On this most significant notepaper[2] I write to Warmley's Bigwig for

---

[1] The Plough was near the British Museum. Writers and editors drank there.
[2] The paper has heavy horizontal lines.

the first time since August 1935. There wasn't any need for me to write
and say 'Ra, Maestro' when you carried off the Musical Biscuit of the
Year, because you knew I wasn't exactly displeased about it.[1] I'm coming
up to London on Monday (the 10th). How do I get hold of you? Write
quickly & tell me. We must meet (we most certainly must meet. There
are 350 things I want to tell you). Tom is here with me at the moment,
cutting a horn lesson to make 3/- illegally. Can't write. Notes between
Warmlies are barmy. Great Men (and the whole point is, of course, that
we mean it) must *meet*. And soon. Don't forget. Write before Monday.

Love,
Dylan

MS: Texas

RAYNER HEPPENSTALL
6.2.36   5 Cwmdonkin Drive Uplands Swansea

I do hope this finds you, because when you wrote last you said you might
be sacked from your Soho home at any moment. You wrote a nice, sad
letter, do you remember, just after that Blairy man had let into you with a
metal shooting stick? And you had a cold and were hard up and hadn't got
any food—only lots of stamps. When I read the letter I had a cold and a
hangover and rheumatism in the elbow, 3/1d between me and a big place
quite near called Tawe Lodge;[2] and I couldn't write seriously, and I didn't
want to see Shirley Temple, and all my friends were dead. And aw what
the hell anyway was just what I felt. Now I'm better, no hangover, no
cold, no rheumatism, 3/2d, and a short story—called most beautifully
'The Phosphorescent Nephew' finished, typed, and accepted by a half-
doped American editor.[3]
    I'm coming to town on the 10th, this coming Monday. Do let's meet
during the week. And let's make it the morning, shall we, because I think
I've found a small, fluffy thing and I want it in the evenings. What about
Wednesday morning—provisionally? But you make the date. Where shall
we meet? Shall I ring your bell (if you've got a bell), or what about a clean
pub with no beards in it? Let me know before Monday if possible. I
haven't seen you for months. Are you clean-shaven? Looking forward etc.

Yours,
Dylan

MS: Texas

[1] Jones had won the Mendelssohn Travelling Scholarship.
[2] The Swansea municipal 'workhouse', for paupers.
[3] The story has not been identified.

OSWELL BLAKESTON
[?March 1936]   Cwmdonkin Drive Uplands Swansea

Dearest mouse my dear,[1] You're awfully lucky, you and the little whisker friends, all smug and slimy, listening to Cocteau & Burns and Naylor & Allen behind the skirtingboard.[2] Nobody ever heard of a Mouse Menace, you are not a national danger, and people write poems about you and call you slinkie and nice and velvet. You'd be safe even in Chicago, where they'd give me a fifth leg. Every year sixteen thousand London brothers & sisters cornered caged and killed. They brought out an Act to destroy me in nineteen nineteen, when I was only five years old. But they give me a week! I haven't seen you for so long, not since we spent an evening in not going to the Queen's Hall, and not since I left you, outside the Café Rat, very rudely for a sillie. I'm coming back, travelling under the seat all the way, nibbling brown paper, at the beginning of next month. Will you meet me? And this time I'll promise not to be bad; I'll powder my snout and not run after hen-rats. And will you send me more of my fan-mail sometimes? I'm so unpopular these days, whenever I switch on the wireless, it's an interval. I was abominable about the B.B.C. But I'll get what's coming to me: when I die I'll go to hell; and it'll be Rat Week always.
    Much love to you, very much, Oswell.

                                                    From
                    [*the letter is signed with a self-caricature*]

MS: Texas   *SL*

ERIC WALTER WHITE[3]
8.iii.36   5 Cwmdonkin Drive Uplands Swansea

Dear Eric Walter White,
    I am, by accident not by nature, so abominably rude and unreliable that I have to spend the best part of the first week after my regular short visits to town in writing frantic letters of apology. Before these regular short visits, I work out my plans in the most pleasant detail: almost every day is arranged so that something nice happens in it. And then, when I do come to town, bang go my plans in a horrid alcoholic explosion that scatters all my good intentions like bits of limbs and clothes over the doorsteps and into the saloon bars of the tawdriest pubs in London. I *was*

[1] Both Blakeston and his friend Max Chapman, painter, have described brief sexual encounters with Thomas in the early London days. Rodents obsessed Thomas, and were part of some shared fantasy.
[2] Gramophone records: Jean Cocteau reciting poetry; George Burns and Gracie Allen, American husband-and-wife comedians; Naylor, an astrologer, reading horoscopes.
[3] Eric Walter White (b. 1905), arts administrator and writer.

looking forward to meeting you and to being taken to hear music; but minor nastiness followed rudeness (ringing you up, for example, and then not appearing) and I heard no music at all and I failed to meet you. It would bore you to death to hear all the reasons, but I do really and deeply apologise for my behaviour.[1]

I'm returning to town in about a fortnight, before I go into the country to work, and nothing so silly shall happen again. Will you have a meal with me then and let me apologise personally? Do say yes.

Yours very sincerely,
Dylan Thomas

MS: the recipient   SL

WYN HENDERSON[2]

9.3.36   5 Cwmdonkin Drive Uplands Swansea

Darling (Dylan) Darling (Dylan again) Wyn, and Oswell (if he's about),

How nice of you to purr about me after dinner, two fed, sleek cats rubbing against the table legs and thinking about a scrubby Welshman, with a three-weeks-accumulated hangover and a heart full of love and nerves full of alcohol, moping over his papers in a mortgaged villa in an upper-class professional row (next to the coroner's house) facing another row (less upper) and a dis-used tennis court. It was a lovely rolling letter, out of the depths of dinner, and a winy mantle of love hung over it, and thank you a lot, Wyn and Oswell.

Wyn privately: As your mascot and very welcome guest, I'd love to come to Cornwall more than anything else: it sounds just what I want it to be, and I can write poems, and stories about vampire sextons deflowering their daughters with very tiny scythes, and draw rude little pictures of three-balled clergymen, and go [to] pubs and walks with you. It's all too lovely to be good; and I'd enjoy it so much. I'm coming to town in about a fortnight: I've got to meet a few publishers and try to get money from them as I haven't any, and, I believe, to read some poems over the wireless. That won't take long: the publishers will (probably) pretend to be deaf, and the wireless will break down. If you are gone by then, chugging into Cornwall, shall I follow you and will you meet me, me lost, me with beer in my belly and straws in my hair? And if you haven't chugged away, but are still rampaging in Bloomsbury (or where-ever you rampage mostly) we can go together, can't we? And that will be

---

[1] They were supposed to meet on February 20 at the Reform Club, after Thomas had been to a cocktail party at Edith Sitwell's. He didn't turn up, but telephoned to suggest they meet at a restaurant instead. He didn't turn up there either.

[2] Wyn Henderson (1896–1976), occasional journalist and publisher, friend of many poets and artists. She had a cottage near Land's End. Thomas met her through Oswell Blakeston. It was probably Norman Cameron's idea that he take refuge in the country.

nicer still. (This letter, Wyn dear, is too excellently phrased. But I've just finished writing a story called The Phosphorescent Nephew; and whatever I do now, bugger me it's literary.)

So thanks, Wyn, for the invitation. I do hope you won't be gone when I come back to London—even though you have to go away and leave me there temporarily—because there are lots of little things to talk about.

Much love to you, (and to old Slime, the State Parasite).

Dylan

MS: Texas   *SL*

ERIC WALTER WHITE
March 13th 36   5 Cwmdonkin Drive Uplands Swansea

Dear Eric Walter White,

Of course I wasn't appalled, I was awfully pleased to get your letter and forgiveness so soon. I hope you're feeling better and are out of bed.

Yes, it was rather risky fixing an appointment immediately after a party, though E. Sitwell's party was very sedate and had more dukes than drinks. I'm so sorry the reference to my 'explosion' made you feel old and sad, but with most members I know of the generation before mine, it seems mostly to be a matter of constitution rather than inclination, and Norman Cameron, with whom I stay when in town, and whom you probably know, is always telling me, 'Just wait till *you're* past twenty five.'

And the Fitzroy and the Running Sore shall be barred; I know a good pub in the Bayswater Road and one in Paddington, but the ones more central seem nearly all spoilt now. There used to be that lovely one in Wapping, looking over the river, until the beards went there. I think the Plough's safe these days, and the one Younger's house in Mayfair is quite clean up until about 8-30. Anyway, we'll see, shall we?

Here's one of the two copies left (to my knowledge) of my poems. A chap here was keeping them in the vain hope that they would one day reach a fabulous price, but I told him not to be silly, and he gave me this one back quite willingly—he hadn't read it anyway. Thanks a lot for wanting it, though three-quarters of the poems are awfully young and awkward as you'll see.

I hope to see you soon.

Best wishes,
Dylan Thomas

MS: the recipient

DESMOND HAWKINS
[March 1936]   [Swansea]

Dear Desmond,

It's funny about ram. Once I looked up an old dictionary and found it meant red, but now I can't find it in any dictionary at all. I wanted ram in the poem to mean red *and* male *and* horny *and* driving *and* all its usual meanings. Blast it, why doesn't it mean red? Do look up and see for me.[1]

I'll be in town for about four or five days from the week-end of March 28 on. Monday's the 30th: what about our beer party Monday, Tuesday, or Wednesday? Do you think you could arrange it? I'll be going, on Thursday I believe, to Cornwall for the spring. (We moneyed poets. And do I get half a guinea for my ram-rose?)

I hope the Pope consents: I've never seen him human, only in his office telling me 'And what is more, surrealism is a dead horse'.[2]

What happened in Church?

Yours,
Dylan

MS: the recipient

RICHARD CHURCH
17th March 1936   5 Cwmdonkin Drive Uplands Swansea

Dear Richard Church,

I'm so sorry to have delayed sending my poems to you.[3]

I have been thinking about them a good deal, and about what we said when we last met. I promised to send two lots of poems, one lot containing the recent things, most of which you've already seen, and one of more-or-less simple, unambiguous poems. But I don't think now that that's a very wise plan—or, to my present way of thinking, a very honest one. Just as you, as you said, would consider it almost dishonest to publish poems you could not explain to those people who might buy them, so I feel it would be dishonest of me to attempt to get published a complete book of 'simple poems': I shall always go on trying to write simple, unambiguous things, but they can only be a very little part of my

[1] Hawkins planned to publish 'Find meat on bones', but wanted to know what 'ram' meant, in Stanza 3: 'A merry girl took me for man,/I laid her down and told her sin,/And put beside her a ram rose.' The poem appeared in *Purpose*, April/June issue, 1936.
[2] Thomas was introduced to T. S. Eliot at one of the beery Plough lunches later that month. H. G. Porteus, another of the circle, who was present, says that Thomas and Eliot 'then both departed, fairly tanked up', for the lunch described in Thomas's first letter to Vernon Watkins.
[3] A form letter from Dent dated March 19 acknowledged receipt of 'the manuscript entitled TWENTY-THREE POEMS'.

work ('my work' sounds awful, but it can't be helped). What I want to do is to include a certain number of these 'simple poems' in each collection of new poems I, God willing, might publish in future years. The same with this present collection.[1] As you'll see, most of the poems are the very recent ones you have, in the past, objected to—along with ones much less difficult. I should not like the simples or the not-so-simples to be published separately: after all, they were written more or less at the same time and do, together, represent my 'work' for the past year and more.

If, after this final reading—and believe me I'm not being snooty at all—you come to the conclusion you could not honestly print them in your series, am I at liberty to try to have them published elsewhere? I hope, of course, most sincerely, that you will be able to publish them: if not, the day *may* come when none of my poems will be indecently obscure or fashionably difficult.

> Yours sincerely,
> Dylan Thomas

MS: J. M. Dent   *SL*

GEOFFREY GRIGSON
Sunday [?March 1936]   Cwmdonkin Drive Uplands Swansea

Dear Geoffrey,
Thanks so much for the books. I'm coming up to town tomorrow, for about 3 days, before going to Cornwall. 3 days with N, of course.

Shall I ring you up? I haven't seen you for months. Can't we have a drink together, and grieve?

About books, too. I'm a good chap now, and will always do them regularly, pronto, and properly, for as long as you want me to.

And has Fanny left you for ever and ever? Going to tell Terry about it.

Thanks about books—again.

> Love to you Doc.

MS: Texas

---

[1] *Twenty-five Poems* (1936) contained seven poems that could be called 'simple'. Six of these were written between March and August 1933, *before* the group of 'anatomical' poems that formed the core of *18 Poems* (1934). What appealed to Church was a style that Thomas had already abandoned.

RICHARD CHURCH
[April 1936]   Polgigga Porthcurno Penzance Cornwall[1]

Dear Richard Church,
   I am so sorry that I failed to call in and see you when I was in town, but
I was there only a very few days and then not feeling particularly well or
editorworthy. I'm hoping to recover some of my lost good health in the
country and to do some serious work.
   So far I'm afraid I've no other poems to add to the ones already in your
possession, or none, at least, with which I am pleased enough as yet.
   Have you come to any decision as to the fate of the poems? I do
apologise for my delay in writing, and hope that you'll let me know some
time the result of your re-reading.

                                        Yours sincerely,
                                        Dylan Thomas

MS: J. M. Dent

DESMOND HAWKINS
Sunday April 11th [1936]

Dear Desmond,
   Address above. It's sunny all day here, and rat to your nasty grey
London. So sorry you couldn't make it last Monday; we might have got so
pleasantly pissed and played darts again. See you when I come back in
about seven weeks' time. Do send that ten bob on: I've finally let the M
Post down, and have nothing to live on now. Curse.[2]

                                        Yours
                                        Dylan

Address isn't above, it's below: here:
Polgigga, Porthcurno, Penzance, Cornwall. That isn't three places, it
really is my address.

MS: the recipient

---

[1] Wyn Henderson's cottage was in the village of Polgigga.
[2] The newspaper printed a review article by Thomas on March 27, then nothing more until
    it carried two final articles, August 28 and September 11.

T. S. ELIOT
12th April 1936   Polgigga Porthcurno Penzance Cornwall

Dear Mr Eliot,
   Thank you so much for the note. I should have replied before, but I've
been trying to settle down here and, after being so messy in London, it
takes a long time.
   I've got some new poems, but I'm not really certain about them, and
don't at the moment think they're good enough to send you. Anyway, I'm
going to work hard on them and see what happens. I've been writing quite
a lot of stories lately. Would you care to see the very latest one? It's called
'The Orchards', and I'm enclosing it. Perhaps you won't like it at all;
nobody's seen it to tell me anything about it, and it may be all wrong. I do
hope it isn't because I've spent a long, long time working on it. Even if
you can't use it—and I hope you will be able to—a lot—would you tell me
something about it?
   I'm looking forward to another little beer party with Hawkins and
Porteus. Are you coming along?
                                   Yours sincerely,
                                   Dylan Thomas

MS: Valerie Eliot

VERNON WATKINS
Thomas's friendship with the poet Vernon Watkins (1906–67) began in 1935,
when Watkins, who lived near Swansea on the Gower Peninsula, read *18 Poems*
and went to see him. Watkins, eight years older than Thomas, had published
nothing at the time (his first book, *Ballad of the Mari Lwyd*, appeared in 1941).
After a severe mental breakdown in 1927—he revisited his old school, attacked
the headmaster and was held in a nursing home for a considerable period—he
worked as a bank clerk in Swansea for the rest of his days, a literary and
intellectual fish out of water. Both Dylan and Caitlin, misinterpreting his gentle
air, thought he had homosexual inclinations, and were surprised when he
married. His widow Gwen Watkins, who regards Thomas as a ruthless exploiter
of his friends, has written of her husband: 'Dylan was his *alter ego*: when he
supported, protected, admired Dylan it was because of the life he had never lived
himself.'

Monday [postmarked April 20 1936]
                                   Polgigga Porthcurno Penzance Cornwall

Dear Vernon,
   Perhaps it's a bit late to say Sorry for not having let you know I couldn't
come to see you that particular Sunday—whenever it was—and to tell

you how much I missed you and the unwonted walk and the toasted
things for tea and the poetry after it; but I want to say Sorry, and I hope
you'll forgive me, and I hope, though that's the wrong way of putting it,
that you missed your hearty, Britain-chested, cliff-striding companion as
much as I did. I had crowds of silly, important things to do: pack, write
formal letters, gather papers, and catch the Sunday night train; and I
didn't get out of bed until all those things had to be scamped through.
Now in a hundred ways I wish I hadn't come away; I'm full of nostalgia
and a frightful cold; here the out-of-doors is very beautiful, but it's a
strange country to me, all scenery and landscape, and I'd rather the bound
slope of a suburban hill, the Elms, the Acacias, Rookery Nook, Curlew
Avenue, to all these miles of green fields and flowery cliffs and dull sea
going on and on, and cows lying down and down. I'm not a country man; I
stand for, if anything, the aspidistra, the provincial drive, the morning
café, the evening pub; I'd like to believe in the wide open spaces as the
wrapping around walls, the windy boredom between house and house,
hotel and cinema, bookshop and tubestation; man made his house to
keep the world and the weather out, making his own weathery world
inside; that's the trouble with the country: there's too much public world
between private ones. And living in your own private, four-walled world
as exclusively as possible isn't escapism, I'm sure; it isn't the Ivory
Tower, and, even if it were, you secluded in your Tower know and learn
more of the world outside than the outside-man who is mixed up so
personally and inextricably with the mud and the unlovely people
—(sorry, old Christian)—and the four bloody muddy winds.

I was in London for just over a week, and the same things happened
there that always happen: I kept roughly a half of my appointments, met
half the people I wanted to, met lots of other people, desirable and
otherwise, and fully lived up to the conventions of Life No. 13: promis-
cuity, booze, coloured shirts, too much talk, too little work. I had Nights
Out with those I always have Nights Out with: Porteus, Cameron,
Blakeston, Grigson, and old Bill Empson[1] and all—(Empson, by the way,
has been very kind to me in print, in a review of the Faber anthology,
saying, quite incorrectly, though than which etc. there could be nothing
nicer for my momentary vanity, that little or nothing of importance,
except for Owen and Eliot, comes between Eliot and ME. Ho! Ha!) Also I
had lunch with Pope Eliot, as I said I would have; he *was* charming, a great
man, I think, utterly unaffected; I had a spot of rheumatism that day, and
nearly the whole time was spent in discussing various methods of curing
it, ('I think it was in 1927 I had my worst bout, and I tried Easu Ointment'
etc). I left London with Life No. Thirteen's headache, liver, and general
seediness, and have by this time thoroughly recovered.

Polgigga is a tiny place two miles or less from Land's End, and very near
Penzance and Mousehole (really the loveliest village in England). We live

[1] The poet Sir William Empson (1906–84).

here in a cottage in a field, with a garden full of ferrets and bees. Every time you go to the garden lavatory you are in danger of being stung or bitten. My hostess, or what you like, has unfortunately read too many books of psychology, and talks about my ego over breakfast; her conversation is littered with phrases like narcissist fixation and homosexual transference; she is a very simple person who tries to cure her simplicity by a science which, in its turn, tries to cure the disease it suffers from. I don't think that's my phrase, but here in this Freudian house it's truer than hell. One day, though never in a letter, I must tell you the whole silly, strange story behind all this—this most irregular, unequal Cornwall partnership; I don't think for a moment that you'll enjoy it, and I know that you'll agree with me how wrong, if there can be any values here, I was to begin it. But I *shall* tell you, probably when I see you in the summer—a summer I'm looking forward to a lot. The one thing that's saving me—saving me, I mean, not from any melodramatic issues but just from sheer unhappiness—is lots and lots of work. I'm half way through another story, and have more or less finished a poem which I want to send you when I'm better pleased with it. But here again I'm not free; perhaps, as you said once, I should stop writing altogether for some time; now I'm almost afraid of all the once-necessary artifices and obscurities, and can't, for the life or the death of me, get any real liberation, any diffusion or dilution or anything, into the churning bulk of the words; I seem, more than ever, to be tightly packing away everything I have and know into a mad-doctor's bag, and then locking it up: all you can see is the bag, all you can know is that it's full to the clasp, all you have to trust is that the invisible and intangible things packed away are—if they *could* only be seen and touched—worth quite a lot. I don't really know why I should be unloading any of this on you, and probably boring you—no, that's wrong, you couldn't be one of the bored ones of the world—at the same time. But you are—even if only momentarily—the one happy person I know, the one who, contrary to facts and, in a certain way, to circumstances, seems to be almost entirely uncomplicated: not, either, the uncomplication of a beginning person, but that of a person who has worked through all the beginnings and finds himself a new beginning in the middle—I hope, for your today's happiness,—a beginning at the end. That's not clear, of course. You might, and would, I know, if you could, help me by talking to me. I don't fear—we talked about it, do you remember—any sudden cessation or drying-up, any coming to the end, any (sentimentally speaking) putting out of the fires; what I do fear is an ingrowing, the impulse growing like a toenail into the artifice. Talk to me about it, will you—it's probably a terrible task I'm trying to drag you into—in any way, any words. And tell me what you're doing and writing. I'll write you again soon, a clearer letter, less face-in-the-earth, less eye-in-a-sling.

Yours always,
Dylan

God, I almost forgot.

Are you rich temporarily? Would you like to lend me some money, a pound or, at the very most, two pounds? I have a beastly, vital debt — rather a lot—to pay in the next few days; I've got together most of it, but not quite all, and all has to be paid. I can—if you *are* penniful temporarily, and, if you're not, do forget it and go on writing the long letter you're going to write to me—let you have it back next week certainly. Of course you don't mind me asking you, but if you're broke or holiday-saving, I can get a few pounds elsewhere—though not, Mr. Watkins, with such lack of embarrassment as I can ask you for it.

Yours always again,

D.

[*Pencil P.S.*]

   Did the snaps—I bet they didn't—come out well, or at all?

MS: British Library   VW

ELFRIEDE CAMERON[1]
25th April [1936]   Polgigga Porthcurno Penzance Cornwall

Dear Elfriede,

   Wyn is not quite my cup of nightcustard:—(difficult English idiom, cup of tea). When we booze it's all right, but when we don't she talks about Books and Havelock Ellis and the frustrated ego. (Then I'd like to slap her across the tittie with a hard-boiled ego.) I'm enclosing a little drawing (very refined line) of her & me. But I do manage to do a little work, and I'm sending you a poem I've written here, a poem about the same Long Gentleman (you ask Norman) who shared his bed with grapefruit and windscreens and everything. I'm going to do a story too—a nice one you'll like, with no worms or bellies, but all about a man who was unanimously elected by the Board of Skeletons to act as referee for three seasons in the cricket matches of the dead: they play with bits of each other in Dead Cricket, with shin-bone and eye-ball, and all. I'm going to try to write it anyway, if Wyn doesn't take me out too much to introduce me to busmen. I know I don't need much encouragement to whack the bottle bang, but I should always try to stay, when away from the intellect-ruining city, in company that gives me no encouragement at all: then I have only myself to blame when I'm a Bad One. That's very common-sense; I wish I hadn't come here; this is a little London, even though the Out-of-Doors is lovely and there's lots of Nature about. I don't like the big, natural spaces between houses much, but Cornwall's a nice, nice county as the exterior world goes, and Mousehole is the best village. I

---

[1] Norman Cameron's first wife; she was German.

want to live there (Mousehole), not with our Wyn but cosy and cheaply with something dumb and lovely of my own choice, with a woman who hasn't been psycho-analysed or rodgered by celebrities. Wyn at her best's at her booziest, when she sings her simple song about the Sparrow:

> There was a bloody sparrow
> Flew up a bloody spout,
> Came a bloody thunderstorm
> And blew the bugger out.

I think that's awfully good; I say it about twice a day and laugh and laugh; but perhaps it's not so funny.

How are you? Get better soon, won't you, and full of health and unwheezy. Are you still red in bed, or pale and lazy downstairs, or making a German beast of yourself in the country—striding all over the awful Out-of-Doors in creaky-leather shoes? Are you going to write to me, and tell me about yourself? I don't think I've got any news or gossip or dirt—apart from lots of silly stories about Havelock Ellis, about what scent he uses on his handkerchief and why he makes his female visitors drink so many cups of tea. And David Archer[1] is leaving London; his mother has given him a riding jacket to go to Durham in, but he has not arrived there yet. People, apparently, are coming quite openly now with handcarts to take away the few remaining books from his shop; David is furious because somebody has the idea of turning the shop into a café. He, David, told me in a letter that Gladstone used to come to the shop, but I think that he was boasting a little. It rains here all day, even better excuse for Wyn to take me fugging in the Logan Inn (where Norman is a most attractive person, very drunk, very Fascist, and who wishes to be remembered to you). I have met the Mousehole people, the whimsy Veronica with her lame leg called Gilbert, & the bloated McColls, and the self-eaten postmaster, and I hate them all.[2] Wyn has a new dog aged ten weeks which I hate more than anybody: last night late, it jumped on to my bed, sat on my face, pissed on my chest, and bit my belly. I am going to kill it with a little axe. Get all well again quickly, Elfriede. Am I going to stay with you some time? Sorry this is a dull letter, but I've got bees in the brain because I was Bad yesterday.

All my love,
Dylan

MS: Sir Theodore Brinckman

---

[1] David Archer, d. 1971, once described as 'a left-wing Bertie Wooster', came from a well-to-do Wiltshire family, spent his inheritance running the Parton Bookshop, and so helped publish *18 Poems*, and died penniless. He published other poets besides Thomas, among them David Gascoyne, George Barker and W. S. Graham.

[2] Veronica Sibthorp (previously McColl, later Armstrong: she was married three times) (1908–73) came from a wealthy family, as did Archie McColl, her first husband. John Waldo Sibthorp, whom she married about 1932, was a printer, and had been one of Wyn Henderson's lovers. Veronica had a crippled leg, which she referred to as 'Gilbert'. At

DESMOND HAWKINS
25th April [1936]   Polgigga Porthcurno Penzance Cornwall

Dear Corkpins,

Did you get my letter? I've been expecting to hear from you. Don't the firm of Daniel send their contributors copies of their journals? Or do they just send them a bag of healthy nuts and a dirty post card in Basic English? The Editor knows where to ram my rose. And Purpose owes me twenty pints.[1]

Are there any Purpose books for me to review? My Morning Post is broken; now I stand naked in Cornwall with no Conservative erection. Have you any books on Music or Magic you'd like to give me? Have you reviewed Harry Price? (He sounds like Purpose's cup of tea.) Would you like some ha ha dirt on Beverley Nichols's Gods and Public Anemones?[2]

And do you remember talking to me about Time and Tide? Would it be wise for me to write to them for reviews, mentioning old Corkpins? Or could you do some back-stairs work? I used to sleep in Lady Rhondda's Valley. Really I do need review work more than ever before. Has the Literary Review any books for me? And is it to print my story?

Do write and answer soon. I want books, books, books, any sort from anywhere. Books, books. (God, I'll have to learn to read. I wish you could review books by stars alone.)

Seen David Archer? Roger R.[3] tells me that David's mother has sent him a riding-coat to go to Durham in, but that he hasn't arrived there yet; that people are now coming quite openly with handcarts to remove all his books; that he says Gladstone used to call at his shop; (but nobody believes that, that's boasting).

If we ever—and we must—write the Canary, I've got some nice true stories for it about Havelick Pelvis. I met a woman down here who used to stay in his house a lot; she says that every morning of the first few weeks of her first visit he came into her bedroom with a cup of tea; when she'd finished it, he gave her another and asked her, 'Now do you want to make water?' Then he'd give her another cup of tea and ask her, 'Surely now you want to make water.' Then he'd give her another cup of tea and hold the chamber pot up invitingly and say, 'Now surely you must make water now.'

about the time of this letter she was having an affair with Thomas, as was Wyn Henderson. Her third husband, the painter John Armstrong, is said to have made her destroy letters from Thomas; two that survive are in this collection, but they were not written until 1939.

[1] In the 'Canary' fantasy 'A. Desmond Hawkins' became 'B. Osmond Corkpins'. *Purpose* was published by C. W. Daniel & Co.
[2] Harry Price (1881–1948), occult author. Beverley Nichols (1898–1983), popular author.
[3] Roger Roughton.

Don't forget: do write and tell me about reviews.

Yours,
Dylan

MS: the recipient

RICHARD CHURCH
1st May 1936   Polgigga Porthcurno Penzance Cornwall

Dear Richard Church,

I am so very, very glad that you are going to publish my poems.[1] Knowing how you feel about their obscurity and (occasional) wilful eccentricity, and about your own obligations, both as a publisher and a poet, to the public you have already created by bringing out the work of so many of the more Intelligible Boys, I do appreciate your decision to let me and that public 'face each other'. I can only hope that the poems will, in some little way, justify the faith you have in them—a faith, perhaps, that goes against judgement.

In less than a month I shall probably be able to let you have the other half dozen poems you need: two new ones, completing the long poem of which you have the first eight sections, and four younger ones selected and revised.

I'm very glad too that you liked my story in *Comment*.[2] I've had quite a lot of stories of more or less the same kind published lately, and have got together enough to make a book. I know you don't publish short stories at all; if you did, I should certainly have sent the book to you to look sternly upon. (I'm afraid I can't make good sentences on a typewriter.) At the moment I'm vainly squinting around for some innocent publisher who doesn't mind losing money on twenty difficult and violent tales.

One day I hope, as you suggest, to write a story about my earlier world; but I don't feel sure enough of myself to attempt it yet in the form of a novel. What I have been thinking of lately is a book about Wales with a slender central theme of make-belief, a certain amount of autobiography, and also a factual Journey of the more popular kind (the Bad Companion's English Journey, Muir's Scottish one, etc).[3] It's difficult to write about this in a letter, but I should, when I come back to town in a month's time, like to talk it over with you. Could we arrange to have a meal together? I'll let you know the exact date of my return. I'm sure that if you would be

---

[1] Church had written on April 28: '. . . Still I cannot understand the meaning of the poems, but in this matter I have decided to put myself aside and to let you and the public face each other.' Church asked for half a dozen more poems to 'add to the bulk'.

[2] 'The Dress'. *Comment* ('Incorporating Poets' Corner') had been started by Victor Neuburg and Runia Tharp; the *Sunday Referee*'s poetry period was over.

[3] J. B. Priestley, whose novel *The Good Companions* appeared in 1929, published his travelogue *English Journey* in 1934. Edwin Muir's *Scottish Journey* was published in 1935.

kind enough to talk over this Welsh idea with me, it would clear up nearly all the vaguenesses and leave me something practical and (almost) commercial to work upon.

Do excuse this very loosely written letter.

And thank you again for all your encouragement.

Yours sincerely,
Dylan Thomas

MS: J. M. Dent   *SL*

OSWELL BLAKESTON
May 4th [1936]   Polgigga

Darling Slime,

I'm out of circulation too, with a swollen throat and a pint-sized headache, a jumping hand and not half enough air in my lungs. I'm not sober either, or at least not so much that you'd point after me in the street and say, There goes a sober man. I think you are the nicest person in the world, and I think I'm the wickedest rat in the wrong world too. I've been here weeks, in this little London to me, and I haven't said Hullo to you: I've heard you're swollen and ill and I haven't even had the Welsh, the worst, decency to say Sorry, so sorry, to you; to say, Oswell, nice, you know how much I do like you, you know what a Bad One I try to be and what a Good One I am really. Thank you for the Nott letter. I think of you a lot, more than you know old dirty, but I never seem to try to tell you that I do. Spit on me because I'm awful. This is Dylan Sacrifice Day. And how are you now, poor poisoned and bottom-burned Oswell, Simon, & Dewsbury,[1] king girl, friend of all boozy poets (and me too)? Do get better soon; mus Slimus shan't become extinct; get better and healthy and pretty again; you mustn't swell. I know you want to know if I'm happy with Wyn, and I am in some ways because Adie is good and gentle, (Wyn sent her away to stay with the beery and nice McColls, but asked her to come back because I missed her such a lot), and because the country, as open-air goes, is very grand. And Wyn, when she boozes, is a person I like, but, when she's drinkless, she's booky. Now she's taken a hill house in Mousehole, and we move there in a fortnight. Then I'm coming back to London for a very tiny time before returning for the summer. Meet me, won't you, and we'll both be stronger and better and we'll rampage everywhere. Get well. My love to you, Dylan.

MS: Texas

---

[1] Pseudonyms that Blakeston was using.

T. S. ELIOT
6th May 1936   Polgigga Porthcurno Penzance Cornwall

Dear Mr Eliot,

I am so very glad that you were interested in my story and that you're going to print it.[1] If I have some poems during the next few weeks, may I send those as well for you to read? I'm able—so far—to work hard and regularly here, and should certainly have something to show you in a short time.

I know this is very irregular, and I know that English periodicals never pay on acceptance but only on publication. But do you think it would be possible for me to be paid for my story in advance, or, failing that, to be paid *something*, however little? I feel rather silly and nervous asking this, but it really is extremely urgent to me. I've never been in a worse fix for money than I am now—and that means a lot, because I live by the poems and stories I write and am consequently nearly always penniless. But this time I have to find money somewhere, and in a very few days. The only way I can think of is to try to obtain in advance payment for the few recent things of mine that have been accepted but not yet printed.

I do hope you don't mind me asking this. I'll quite understand, of course, if the Criterion isn't able to pay any contributor in advance; though I really hope it is.

Again, I'm so sorry about this letter; honestly I wouldn't have written hadn't it been so terribly important to me.

Yours very sincerely,
Dylan Thomas

MS: Valerie Eliot

FABER & FABER
14th May 1936   The Queech Raginnis Hill Mousehole Cornwall

Dear Madam,

Thank you for your letter. I am returning to town next week, and shall be delighted to accept Mr Eliot's invitation to the Criterion Evening.

Yours faithfully
Dylan Thomas

MS: Valerie Eliot

---

[1] The *Criterion* published 'The Orchards' in July 1936. It is the story where the joke name 'Llareggub', made famous by *Under Milk Wood*, first appeared.

GEORGE REAVEY[1]
17th June [1936] [postcard]   5 Cwmdonkin Drive Uplands Swansea

I didn't see you (I think) at the Surrealist party to ask you about the Poetry
Reading on the 26th.[2] I see my name's down on the little notice. That
means I'm definitely invited to read, doesn't it? I'd love to, of course. I
don't quite know what stuff to choose, though. I'm coming up to town on
the Friday morning (for the weekend). Could you spare half-an-hour
sometime that day—before the reading—to look through some stuff with
me? You'll know what'll go down best. I've got a little chunk of prose & a
new poem [that] might do. But we'll see—if you *can* spare that half hour.
Let me know all about it, won't you? Best wishes, Dylan.

P.S. I owe you a whole £.

MS: Harvard

JOHN JOHNSON[3]
June 18th 1936   5 Cwmdonkin Drive Uplands Swansea

Dear John Johnson,
   I'm so sorry I haven't replied to your letter before this. I was in London
some days ago, but had unfortunately left your address behind, and I
didn't know any quick way of getting hold of it. I shall be back in town for
the weekend of the 26th of this month. Could we have lunch, or a
lunchtime drink, together on Saturday 27th, or on Monday? Do let me
know, won't you?
   Thanks for writing, and for the nice things you said. We can talk about
plays and things when we meet—if, as I hope, we do.
                                        Yours sincerely,
                                        Dylan Thomas

TS: Thomas Trustees

---

[1] George Reavey (d. 1976), critic, poet and translator. He was connected with the Europa
   Press, and spent much of his time in Paris.
[2] The International Surrealist Exhibition was held in London at the New Burlington
   Galleries, June 11–July 4, attracting much publicity and derision. The associated reading
   featured Paul Éluard reading his poems in French; translations of his poems by, among
   others, Samuel Beckett, Reavey and David Gascoyne; and poems by assorted
   non-surrealist writers, including Thomas.
[3] John Johnson, later a literary agent, was then assistant editor of *Life and Letters Today*.

JOHN JOHNSON
[late June 1936] (Postcard, arranging meeting. See Appendix 4.)

RICHARD CHURCH
22nd June 1936   5 Cwmdonkin Drive Uplands Swansea

Dear Richard Church,
    All my apologies. I *am* so sorry about this very rude delay. I found that
my housekeeper in London had forgotten to send the poems along to you
that evening before our last meeting; and I looked through them again
and thought them lousy. Now I've polished them up and worked hard at
them, though two I had to scrap entirely. I'm enclosing five: four you
haven't seen before, and the fifth is a slightly altered version of a poem
you already have.
    For purposes of acknowledgement: The poem beginning 'And death
shall have no dominion' was printed in the New English Weekly; the
ones beginning 'Today, this insect, and the world I breathe' and 'Then
was my neophyte' are to be printed next month in Purpose; and the last
two sections, IX & X, of my long poem are to be printed next month in
Contemporary Prose and Poetry.
    Do forgive me for being so long in sending them. I haven't, actually,
been at all well, and am about to go into the country again—the only
place for me, I think: cities are death.
    By the way: after reading my long letter indignantly denying certain of
your critical charges, you'll be amused to know that I'm reading some
poems to the Surrealist Exhibition on the 26th of this month—(though I
haven't discovered why I am).

                              Sincerely yours,
                              Dylan Thomas

MS: J. M. Dent

J. M. DENT & CO
1st July 1936   5 Cwmdonkin Drive Uplands Swansea

Dear Sir,
    I agree that the simpler form of the acknowledgement of the periodicals
in which my poems were printed is advisable.
    As to the other matter: if you omit the numbering of the poems, are
you going to use the first line of each poem as its title (as I did, for what I

thought would be reasons of convenience, in the list of contents)? I have not otherwise titled any of the poems, and would not like to have to do so. If you think the method of first-line titling would be best, then of course it's o.k. with me.

As I've taken out some of the poems from the first collection Mr. Church saw, and put in others, the book can't be called Poems In Sequence any longer. I want it called by the number of poems there are in the book: 30 Poems (or whatever it is; I've lost count, having reshuffled them such a lot).

There are, incidentally, now ten sections of the work in progress which makes the last poem in the book, and not eight as you said on the sheet which I am returning.

Yours truly,
Dylan Thomas

MS: J. M. Dent

RICHARD CHURCH
1st July [1936]   5 Cwmdonkin Drive Uplands Swansea

Dear Richard Church,
   I shouldn't be sending you this I know but I've lost the letter accompanying the enclosed form. I'm afraid it's awfully unsatisfactory, but I really can't put anything else down. And the title can't be Poems in Sequence any longer, as I've reshuffled all the poems, taken a few out and put a few more in, before I suggested that title. I want it to be called, as I think I mentioned when I saw you, just the number of poems there are in the book (another thing I don't know, as I've sent the poems in batches and in such a muddly way).

Yours sincerely,
Dylan Thomas

MS: J. M. Dent

NIGEL HENDERSON[1]
7th July 1936   5 Cwmdonkin Drive Uplands Swansea

Dear Nigel,
   Thank you so much for the papers; I've been working on the poems and I've burned the indiscretions. I should have written and said thanks weeks ago, but I mislaid your address, and the letter you wrote has been chasing me all over the place; it arrived this morning. Sorry you didn't

---

[1] Wyn Henderson's younger son. He was connected with the fashionable Group Theatre, which produced 'committed' plays.

give me a nudge at the exhibition; it wasn't earnest conversation really; probably little jokes.

About the Group Theatre: I had some drinks with John Johnson about ten days ago, but hadn't anything much to offer him. I've been thinking of doing a Horrible play, mostly in prose with verse choruses and have got bits of the story mapped out; but I would like to meet Doone[1] before I get down to it, as, without *some* sort of promise that it will be performed, I don't feel like devoting a lot of time to it at the moment—I can't as a matter of fact, because I've to review lots of crime stories in order to buy beer and shirts and cigarettes.

I'm coming up to town at the beginning of August. If you're about then, perhaps we could fix a Doone, you and me meeting? And if you've got a green hat of mine, do be an angel and send it along; it rains here all the time, and my brim's coming off.

I'll drop you a line as soon as I know definite London dates.

Thanks again,
Yours,

only source: SL   Dylan

RICHARD CHURCH
10th July 1936   5 Cwmdonkin Drive Uplands Swansea

Dear Richard Church,

Thank you for your note. I'm glad you think the first line method of indexing is satisfactory.

But I don't really like POEMS IN PROGRESS as a title; I don't think I understand what it means anyway. The last incomplete poem in the book, consisting of 10 separate poems, is in itself a work in progress; to call the whole book POEMS IN PROGRESS would rather complicate things wouldn't it? I rather like the uniformity of 18 POEMS as a first book and 30 POEMS (or whatever it is) as a second. If you don't like a numerical title, I personally should prefer just POEMS or NEW POEMS, however dull that may sound. But it's 30 POEMS (or whatever it is) that I'm fondest of. However, you know best, and I leave things to you. I hope you don't use POEMS IN PROGRESS though.

Yours sincerely,
Dylan Thomas

[*a drawn line connects the words* NEW POEMS *with this postscript*]

which, of course, sounds too important

MS: J. M. Dent

[1] Rupert Doone, instrumental in founding the Group Theatre in 1932, was responsible for most of its productions.

RICHARD HUGHES
14th July 1936   Cwmdonkin Drive Uplands Swansea

Dear Richard Hughes,
   I'm going to Fishguard by car tomorrow, and passing awfully near
Laugharne. I do hope you'll be there because we—that's painter Alfred
Janes and me—would like very much to call on you.[1] We shall, shall
we, some time in the afternoon? Hope I shan't miss you as I did last
time.

> Yours sincerely,
> Dylan Thomas

MS: Indiana   *SL*

JOHN JOHNSON
15th July 1936   5 Cwmdonkin Drive Uplands Swansea

Dear John Johnson,
   Thanks for your letter. I was very sorry, too, that we didn't have more
time together, but it was—this is my weekly sorry day—all my fault
really. I should have had a proper lunch with you, not a few bolted drinks
with Betty Boop.[2] I always find Lunch in London a deliberate lie; next
time we meet, let's make it Drinks.
   I hope I'll be able to start a play quite soon; and I realise, of course, that
there can't be a guarantee of production. So glad, though, that you're
going to help make things easier.
   I'll send you the stories, sixteen of them. Four or five of them
sentimental and possibly worthless—I hope not, because I think they are
readable at least—, at the beginning of next week. I'm going away this
morning to stay very richly with Richard Hughes in a castle, otherwise I
could send them off earlier. Hope this isn't too long a delay. And thanks

---

[1] Earlier in 1936, Thomas had met the woman he was to marry, Caitlin Macnamara, when
    she was with the painter Augustus John. In July, John and Caitlin were staying with
    Richard Hughes in Laugharne, which was probably Thomas's reason for calling. He and
    John had a row and scuffled outside an hotel before the end of the day. Caitlin has said that
    she regarded John, who was thirty-five years her senior, as 'a dirty old goat'. He was
    certainly keen on her, and jealous of the poet he had introduced. An undated letter from
    John to Caitlin is with the Veronica Sibthorp papers at the National Library of Wales. 'I
    hope you haven't caught any more diseases from Dylan or others,' it says. 'Keep the fun
    clean also your quim my little seraph . . .'
[2] Betty Boop was a nubile film-cartoon character, created (1930) to publicise the Boop-
    Boopa-Doop song. According to Johnson, Thomas meant Caitlin.

so much for wanting to take this trouble over them. But I doubt if an established, commercially established, publisher would be very keen; some people consider the stories dirty and, occasionally, blasphemous —which they probably are. But you shall see anyway, and thanks again for wanting to.

I think I'll be in town some time in August; let you know beforehand and we'll have some drinks.

Yours,
Dylan Thomas

TS: Thomas Trustees   *SL*

DESMOND HAWKINS
[?1936]   5 Cwmdonkin Drive

Dear Desmond,
A thousand, if I may coin a phrase, apologies. I've only just reached home.
These are the only pomes I seem to have. Hope I'm not too late, & that one of them will prove (see 'if I may' at the top) satisfactory.
I'll write a letter very soon.

Yrs
Dylan

MS: the recipient

DENYS KILHAM ROBERTS
[?summer 1936] (Sends poems to. See Appendix 5.)

JOHN LEHMANN
17 August 1936   Cwmdonkin Drive Uplands Swansea

Dear John Lehmann,
I'm sorry about the delay in answering your card; it wasn't readdressed here until today, as the fellow with whom I share my London address has been away on holiday.
I agree, of course, about your printing the poems. I do hope, though, that all the editors decide on printing either 'A grief ago' or 'Then was my

Neophyte', as I think the other poem they have in mind, 'From love's first fever', is awful.[1] However, anything's all right with me.

Yours sincerely
Dylan Thomas

TS: Thomas Trustees

DESMOND HAWKINS
21st August 1936   Cwmdonkin Drive Uplands Swansea

Dear Desmond,

I'm not dead or poxed—much—or paralysed or mute; just depressed as hell by this chronic, hellish lack of money; it's the most nagging depression, and is always with me; night and day in my little room high above the traffic's boom I think of it, of possessing it in great milky wads to spend on flashy clothes and cunt and gramophone records and white wine and doctors and white wine again and a very vague young Irish woman whom I love in a grand, real way but will have to lose because of money money money money.[2]

I was in London three weeks ago over the bankholiday, behaving so normally that I'm still recovering; I knew it was useless trying to get hold of you in holiday time; I stayed out of the silly neighbourhood, in Chelsea with my Ireland. I may be coming back in September.

No, no titles, (though I like Sunset over Nigeria, and you can use that if you like, or Necrophilia in Mumbles).[3]

Betty? Pfff. She gives *me* a pain in the appendix. (And is it only appendix?)[4]

Remember me to your baby. I'll write it a dirty poem when it's older.

Love, Dylan

MS: the recipient

DESMOND HAWKINS
27th August 36   Cwmdonkin Drive Uplands Swansea

Dear Desmond,

Look, have you still got a copy of that story of mine about the looney-

---

[1] *The Year's Poetry, 1936*, published 'A grief ago', 'From love's first fever' and 'Where once the waters of your face'.
[2] Caitlin Macnamara.
[3] Hawkins had asked for something better than first-line titles.
[4] A West End shopgirl, briefly on the scene.

bin: Uncommon Genesis it was called, but I want to rename it just The Woman And The Mouse. I've lost my manuscript copy, and I must include the story in a collection I'm hoping to get published soon.[1] If you have, will you send it along as soon as you can? You shall have it back, for whatever curious purposes of your own, as soon as I've typed it out again. I'm hoping to be in London for a few days next week: mainly to sit for a drawing for a frontispiece for a book which I've been half commissioned for.[2] But it all depends on m

o

n

e

y,

money, [a line is deleted]
Could P. pay me a quid for those two poems now?

Soon I'll really have to make a horrid little law of my own that all poems by me, Rat Thomas, have to be paid for on acceptance, not on publication. [a line is deleted]. No, but cross my chest, for anybody's sake see if P. will pay me now. It's absolutely essential—if you like words like that—that I do get enough money by the beginning of next week to take me up to town and keep me there for 2 or 3 days. When this drawing is done, I'm sure my proposed book—Welsh Journey—will be immediately commissioned. I'm writing little belly-whine notes to all the few editors (including Corkpins himself) who owe me pennies for stuff of mine they've accepted but not yet printed. And unless these editors (including Corkpins) fork out, I shall have to cancel my visit, my drawing, and any prospects I may have of being given enough by a trusting publisher to undertake at once my Celtic Totter. So do have a shot to get me that quid, or whatever it is. If all the few editors will do their short share, I'll be able to buy a pretty ticket and come right up. Looking forward to almost seeing you.

Dylan

MS: the recipient

JOHN HADFIELD (at J. M. Dent)
1st September 1936 (Encloses photograph. See Appendix 6.)

<hr>

[1] Published in the quarterly review *transition*, Fall 1936, as 'The Mouse and the Woman'.
[2] See the letter to Church, page 227.

EDITH SITWELL
2nd September 1936   Cwmdonkin Drive Uplands Swansea

Dear Miss Sitwell,
   I know I couldn't have expected you to answer my letter of so many
months ago. I was dreadfully rude, not turning up and everything, and I do
understand about your not answering my silly letter of apology. But I
hope you aren't cross with me really, and I really do want you to believe
that I regret—as much as anything in the world—not having continued
the friendship I think we began. Will you meet me again, in spite of
things? You're still a great encouragement to me—& always will be—& I
do appreciate it.
                                        Yours very sincerely,
                                        Dylan Thomas

MS: National Library of Wales   *SL*

GEOFFREY GRIGSON
[?September 1936]

Dear G.
   Thanks again for the books.
   I can't send any new poems now, as Dent has brought out my book —
which had unpublished ones I wanted you to see—unexpectedly.[1]
   I liked the German poem. I'm trying to learn a little German myself.
Here's something I made of it: I found it awfully hard, & had to para-
phrase in bits. But all the meaning & the flatness and the metre & things
are there.[2]
                                        Love,
                                        Dylan

MS: Texas   *SL*

DESMOND HAWKINS
[September 1936]

Dear D,
   Look: Dent has just brought out my book—unexpectedly. I didn't think
it was coming out for weeks. It contains the two poems you've got to

---

[1] *Twenty-five Poems* was published on 10 September 1936. It was hardly unexpected.
[2] The poem was by Wilhelm Busch, the 'German Edward Lear'. Thomas's translation, made
    from a literal crib supplied by Grigson, consisted of twelve couplets, beginning, 'The
    Elephant one sees afar/Goes for a walk in Africa.' On the back of it Grigson has scrawled
    'DYLAN, MY GOD'. Ferris's biography wrongly connects the poem with another letter.

print in Purpose, I mean that you're going to print in Purpose. What does [a] careful editor do about things like that, do you know?

Love,
Dylan

MS: the recipient

CAITLIN MACNAMARA

Born in London (in 1913) of Protestant Irish parents, Caitlin was one of three sisters. Her father, Francis, thought himself a poet, hobnobbed with artists, and abandoned his family. Caitlin—the first syllable is 'Cat', not 'Kate'—was fiery and self-assured. She had been a dancer and had lived in Paris. See note, page 234.

Sunday [card, postmarked 19 October 1936]

Darling, thank you for your long lovely letter and the handkerchief which isn't a handkerchief at all but my very very favourite scarf which I wear all the time—and for the photograph. I like you when you climb, but I'm awfully prejudiced, I like you when you do anything, (and that's quite separate from loving you altogether). This squiggle is only to tell you that I've almost finished a letter for you and a nice story, but that I won't be able to send them off until tomorrow: I have an ill father who's horribly fond of talking about death, so I sit and read to him. I love you, it's almost too wonderful (to me) to say; but I want to say it and I want to say it and I am saying it—: I love you; and we'll always keep each other alive. We can never do nothing at all now but that both of us know all about it. You can do anything & be anything, so long as it's with me. This, as you might gather Miss Macnamara, is from Dylan—& God, he must be with you soon XXXXXXXXXXXXXXXXXXXXXXXXXXXXXXXX

[*typed in the margin at right angles to the text are the words*: The Elephant. *Beside them is written*: This hasn't got anything to do with anything: it was typed on the card when I bought it. That's silly.]

MS: Texas

DESMOND HAWKINS
22nd October 1936   5 Cwmdonkin Drive Uplands Swansea

Dear Desmond,

YOU PURPOSE PEAPOTS OWE ME A QUID FOR THOSE TWO POEMS. How are
you? Try to remember to keep some lunch dates free for me when I come
up to town in about a fortnight's time. I've got some new poems and some
new jokes and some new diseases, I'm feeling fine.

A WHOLE POUND YOU PEAPOTS. IN THE HUMAN INTEREST[1]—MY EYE.
MONEY, TINKLY MONEY, FOR GOD'S SAKE.

I'll let you know exactly when I come up more or less TINKLE

Dylan

(From Dylan Thomas, author of Two Poems in the September–
December 1936 issue of Purpose, C. W. DANIEL & Co)

MS: the recipient

E. AND J. MUNRO[2]
10th November [?1936]

Are you coming along tomorrow night? I'm dim, but I hope so.

Dylan

TS: Thomas Trustees

JULIAN SYMONS[3]
10.11.36 [postcard]   5 Cwmdonkin Drive Uplands Swansea

Thanks for writing; it's nice to hear that you're bringing out a magazine,
and I'll be delighted to send you something. I haven't got a poem at the
moment; I expect that I'll have one finished in a week or ten days; by the
end of this month certainly. That's not too late, is it? I'll send it along as
soon as possible.

Yours sincerely,
Dylan Thomas

MS: Texas

[1] W. Symons, editor and proprietor, wrote his editorial under this heading.
[2] Unidentified correspondents.
[3] Julian Symons (b. 1912), novelist and poet. The magazine was *Twentieth-Century Verse*,
first published January 1937. Thomas contributed 'It is the sinners' dust-tongued bell.'

JULIAN SYMONS
16 11 36 [post card]   Cwmdonkin Drive Uplands Swansea

Glad to hear the end of the month isn't too late for a poem; and very
pleased you're going to review my book: I do hope you like it.[1] I've had
the oddest set of reviews, and I've been called everything from a literary
Marx Brother to a Roman Catholic.

I'd rather not review Auden; I'm not close enough to him, he's not
sufficiently my cup of tea, for me to enjoy his new poems very much or to
talk about them constructively (with a few exceptions, especially the
prologue); and I know he's far, far too good for me of all people to attempt
to be destructive. But thanks very much.

Best wishes,
Dylan Thomas

MS: Texas

CAITLIN MACNAMARA
[?late 1936]

Nice, lovely, faraway Caitlin my darling,
    Are you better, and please God you aren't too miserable in the horrible
hospital? Tell me everything, when you'll be out again, where you'll be at
Christmas, and that you think of me and love me. And when you're in the
world again, we'll both be useful if you like, trot round, do things,
compromise with the They people, find a place with a bath and no bugs in
Bloomsbury, and be happy there. It's that—the *thought* of the few, simple
things we want and the *knowledge* that we're going to get them in spite
of you know Who and His spites and tempers—that keeps us living I
think. It keeps *me* living. I don't want you for a day (though I'd sell my
toes to see you now my dear, only for a minute, to kiss you once, and
make a funny face at you): a day is the length of a gnat's life: I want you
for the lifetime of a big, mad animal, like an elephant. I've been indoors
all this week, with a wicked cold, coughing and snivelling, too full of
phlegm and aspirins to write to a girl in hospital, because my letter would
be sad and despairing, & even the ink would carry sadness & influenza.
Should I make you sad, darling, when you're in bed with rice pudding in
Marlborough Ward? I want so very much to look at you again; I love you;
you're weeks older now; is your hair grey? have you put your hair up, and
do you look like a real adult person, not at all anymore beautiful and
barmy like the proper daughters of God? You mustn't look too grown-up,
because you'd look older than me; and you'll never, I'll never let you,

----

[1] *Twenty-five Poems.*

grow wise, and I'll never, you shall never let me, grow wise, and we'll always be young and unwise together. There is, I suppose, in the eyes of the They, a sort of sweet madness about you and me, a sort of mad bewilderment and astonishment oblivious to the Nasties and the Meanies; you're the only person, of course you're the only person from here to Aldebaran and back, with whom I'm free entirely; and I think it's because you're as innocent as me. Oh I know we're not saints or virgins or lunatics; we know all the lust and lavatory jokes, and most of the dirty people; we can catch buses and count our change and cross the roads and talk real sentences. But our innocence goes awfully deep, and our discreditable secret is that we don't know anything at all, and our horrid *inner* secret is that we don't care that we don't. I've just read an Irish book called Rory and Bran, and it's a bad charming book: innocent Rory falls in love with innocent Oriana, and, though they're both whimsy and talk about the secret of the language of the hills and though Rory worships the moon and Oriana glides about in her garden listening to the legendary birds, they're not as mad as we are, nor as innocent. I love you so much I'll never be able to tell you; I'm frightened to tell you. I can always feel your heart. Dance tunes are always right: I love you body and soul:—and I suppose body means that I want to touch you & be in bed with you, & I suppose soul means that I can hear you & see you & love you in every single, single thing in the whole world asleep or awake.

Dylan X

I wanted this to be a letter full of news, but there isn't any yet. It's just a letter full of what I think about you and me. You're not empty, empty still now, are you? Have you got love to send me?

MS: Maurice Neville

GLYN JONES
[December 1936]   5 Cwmdonkin Drive Uplands Swansea

Dear Glyn,
   I was very glad to hear from you; it's been such a long time; and, though I knew more-or-less that a letter to your school address would still find you, I was for some reason really dubious about writing: you seemed to have vanished so successfully into Cardiff and marriage that I wondered whether you were cross with me in some vague way about a vaguer something or other that I may have said or done. I'm awfully pleased to know it's nothing like that; I think we both must have been just careless. How are you? I see you quite a lot in the Adelphi, but have you given up Grigson's paper and the rest? I hadn't heard about the book of stories: that's grand. What's it going to be called? I believe I've met Hamish Miles once. (bald?)

And about the review:[1] of course I didn't think it was unfair; it's about the best I've seen of the book, and it helped me a lot; it really *was* constructive; I never knew, for instance, that I was such a numerical demon. And I agree with what you said about some of the poems being 'tidy enough' but so weak in contrast with some of the earlier bits of explosive bombast; that's true, and perhaps I was silly in allowing those 'tidy' poems to appear more as a concession to obscurity-decriers than anything else. You're the only reviewer, I think, who *has* commented on my attempts to get away from those rhythmic and thematic dead ends, that physical blank wall, those wombs, and full-stop worms, by all sorts of methods—so many unsuccessful. But I'm not sorry that, in that Work in Progress thing,[2] I did carry 'certain features to their logical conclusion'. It had, I think, to be done; the result had to be, in many of the lines & verses anyway, mad parody; and I'm glad that *I* parodied those features so soon after making them, & that I didn't leave it to anyone else.

But, personally, I'm sorry you didn't mention the one particular poem in the book—'Then Was My Neophyte'—which I consider the best. Nobody's mentioned it; perhaps it's bad; I only know that, to me, it is clearer and more definite, & that it holds more possibilities of progress, than anything else I've done. But thanks a great, great deal for your review. I'm afraid I shan't be in London on the 12th; I've been home here for nearly two months, & shan't be returning until the middle of next week. *If* you're still up, my address will be 27 St. Peter's Square, Hammersmith, W.6. I don't know the telephone number but you can get it from Directory Enquiry; it's Cameron's flat, but, as he's just moved in, I don't suppose his name will be in the book. And anyway, if you *won't* be up then, could you come down & see me for the day in the New Year? I'll be home most of January. Or could I come up & see you? I'm looking forward to either—very much.

Yours,
Dylan

MS: Carbondale   *SL*

T. A. SINCLAIR
20th January 1937   Cwmdonkin Drive Uplands Swansea

Dear Sir,

Thank you so much for asking J. M. Dent whether the line 'Once in this *wind*' was not a misprint for 'once in this *wine*'.[3] Of course it is, though no-one at all, including myself, spotted it. I'm letting Dent's know at

[1] In the *Adelphi*, December 1936.
[2] The 'Altarwise by owl-light' group.
[3] In 'This bread I break'.

once. Thanks again. I *do* appreciate the fact that someone has read my
poems so carefully.

                    Yours sincerely,
                      Dylan Thomas

I apologise for the delay in answering you: I've been away, and most of my
letters were unavoidably not forwarded to me.

MS: Texas

OSWELL BLAKESTON
27th [January 1937?]   5 Cwmdonkin Drive Uplands Swansea

[*the head of the letter has four ragged circles, inscribed respectively:*
'original genuine rat print' '& this' '& this' '& this']

Hullo dear Oswell,
    I *am* glad you've let me know you are back in London again and so
much better. I didn't know where you'd been mousing, or I'd have inked a
whisker and written to you, sniffed all my little sewer newses and
included a cheese-eye view of my Swansea nest; I'd have told you how an
awful lot of my family (all looking exactly like me, very dirty, broken-
toothed, smelling of armpits and yesterday's poems and things) had taken
a summer cruise to Tristan da Cunha; & how other members of the
family (from the black branch) had invaded London, drunk all the inkpots
dry in some East-End warehouse-offices, and lived for a long time on
brown paper: this was reported in the Daily Telegraph last week, and I've
pasted it in our album. And about our album: we get a lot of fan-mail;
there was a letter from a Retired Lieutenant in the Daily Telegraph a few
days ago, advising some agricultural correspondent not to get rid of all the
Rats in his farm-fields as, as soon as the Rats have been stamped out,
enter Adders in hundreds. So if you ever cast me out, you'll have a
dreadful snake in my place, all puff and hiss.
    Where have you been? And who's who now? I don't like your young
men very much; I think you'll be able to write a naughty book and call it
slime and punishment.
    If I can, if money allows me, I want to come up to town next week; I
must come up to see about a book, a Journey through Wales, I want to,
and think I shall be, commissioned to write; and to have a frontispiece
drawing of me done by old Augustus (type Moose) which will, shifty
agents tell me, almost ensure that publishers will kiss my ears and drown
me in milk and pounds. If you have a green-backed drop of milk you
could, or would like to, spare me, I think I'd be able to rat my way about
and claw up a little more and buy a ticket to London, and bite through the

skirting-boards into the publisher's little room and frighten him into giving me a nice commission—which would mean drinks and taxis and ridiculous food for you and me and other needy animals. But if you can't and haven't, don't worry a bit. You aren't an inadequate mouse. You're the best mouse: rats are dirtier and uglier and live on the little balls of fluff and dust between their toes. *If* I can manage, by some means or another, to come up to town next week, shall we—one night—get helplessly drunk?

Love
Dylan

P.S. I've got nothing to send *you*:—only a little piece of cheddar left over from tea.

MS: Texas

DAVID HIGHAM
9th February [1937]   5 Cwmdonkin Drive Uplands Swansea

Dear Higham,
   I do, really and deeply, apologise for my rudeness in not replying to your last letters. I've been ill, off and on, but not ill enough, I admit, to excuse my rudeness. I think the real reason why I haven't answered you before is that I felt—and still feel—ashamed, ashamed, that is, about all this nonsensically careless business of my book of short stories. It's quite true what you heard: that Spenser Curtis Brown had my stories, sent them to Church (who, incidentally, was forced to refuse them), and has now given them to Frank Morley.[1] It came about in—my fault, of course—a vague and weak way: Curtis Brown wrote to me quite a time ago, enquiring about my stories and asking me to send them to him. I sent them, more or less without thinking, though obviously I should have — and should greatly have preferred to—let you have them once they were ready. My capacity for even the simplest business undertaking is negligible; it sounds as though I'm trying to plead the notorious vagueness of the Dreamy Poet Type B classified by Punch, but really I'm a complete nitwit when it comes to replying to people, organising anything, making any sort of deal, keeping my tiny affairs in order, and even, in this shame-making case, just sending to *one* agent the very little, and very uncommercial, work I do. None of that vagueness is a respectable excuse, I know; but my new resolutions are for Punctuality and Order, and I *will* keep them.
   As for this project that I should do a book about Wales:—I am very keen about it, and feel pretty sure that I could make a good job of it too. What I

---

[1] A director of Faber.

wanted to do was a Welsh Journey, from the top of the agricultural North to the Rhondda Valley, a Journey suggested by Priestley's and Muir's though, of course, owing nothing to their method of approach, being far more personal and intimate: not a series of generalisations about Wales, or a survey of its position today, or a Nationalist tirade, or a naturalists' rambling-tour, or an historical textbook about harps and castles, but an intimate chronicle of my personal Journey among people and places. I should want to do the Journey alone, some times on foot, sometimes by bus or train, having a more-or-less definite route but being at liberty any time to interrupt it when any especially interesting incident, or people, or place, appeared. That is, I should map out for myself a set number of towns or villages on the Journey from North to South, which I'd regard as my brief headquarters; what route I would take between those headquarters would be decided by what incidents arose, what people told me stories, what pleasant or unpleasant or curious things etcetera I encountered in the little- known villages among the lesser-known people. This is all very vague, and is meant to be. I purposely do not want a too-definite or binding plan to be put before a publisher; I want the Journey to be individual and informal; neither quite a picaresque travel book nor a personal journey, but a mixture of both; and certainly not a Journey that blusters about the Open Road. It's difficult to explain, but somehow I feel certain it can have a commercial interest for publishers. (Augustus John will do a frontispiece for it—a portrait of me—and, if I can make him, some drawings. But the frontispiece is certain. I know lots of newspaper people in Wales, too, and can get as many photographs as are needed.) What I had in mind was that I should be paid expenses, preferably weekly, for the length of time the journey takes—expenses enough to pay my travel and accommodation bills (£5?)—which should be anything from two to three months. I realise that even a publisher favourably inclined might hedge a bit at undertaking to dole out expenses like this on a project which I am able to describe only so vaguely; and it occurred to me that perhaps he would pay my expenses for, say, *one* month, give me time to write up fully the chronicle of that one month's Journey, and then read it and see whether it's good enough to warrant him going on paying expenses for the rest of the time needed to complete the book. (I don't know whether I'm making myself clear; I know I'm writing very clumsily today.) Naturally I'd rather that some nice publisher would guarantee to pay expenses for the whole 2 to 3 months; but I know absolutely nothing about how far publishers allow themselves to go on a thing like this. I could, if necessary, draft out a rough map of the route I'd like to take. I intended calling on—and, in some cases, staying with a number of Welsh and anglo-Welsh writers and painters who live in Wales—Richard Hughes and Caradoc Evans for instance—and of getting some Welsh sketches from Cedric Morris, the painter.[1] I can't think of anything else at the moment.

I shall be in town next week for some days. Perhaps, if we met, I might be able to explain this Welsh project a little more clearly; at least I can

---

[1] Sir Cedric Morris (1889–1982), painter, of Sketty, Swansea.

try. Do let me know whether you'll be able to see me then, any time during the week, and whether this Journey business is, as I ignorantly believe it to be, of some practical value.

And, before I forget, Simon and Schuster of New York say they are interested in my work. Do you think it advisable to get in touch with them about 25 Poems?

Sincere apologies again for my rudeness and carelessness.

Yours sincerely,
Dylan Thomas

MS: Texas   *SL*

DAVID HIGHAM
11 2 37   5 Cwmdonkin Drive Uplands Swansea[1]

Dear Higham,

Thank you for taking my long delayed letter so nicely. I'm coming up to London tomorrow, but will be there only a few hours before going on to Cambridge; I'm returning to London on Wednesday: could we meet sometime in the morning? I'll ring you up anyway on that morning, and find out. I wish it would be possible for us to meet somewhere outside; I get more terrified of offices every day. But, again, I'll find out when I ring you. And I do hope there'll be something a bit definite about the Welsh book.

Yours,
Dylan Thomas

MS: Texas

CAITLIN MACNAMARA
Wednesday [April or May 1937]   59 Gt. Ormond St W1 (HOL7701)[2]

Caitlin Caitlin my love I love you, I can't tell you how much, I miss you until it hurts me terribly. Can you come up to London before I go to Wales

---

[1] The last letter Thomas is known to have written from his childhood address. His father had retired from the Grammar School at the end of 1936, and in the spring moved to Bishopston, on the edge of Gower.

[2] This was the Sibthorp address; Thomas may still have been involved with Veronica, the woman he had met in Cornwall. In later years she let it be known that he had wanted to marry *her*. Another affair had been in progress with an American woman, the writer Emily Holmes Coleman, fifteen years older than Thomas, who had been married and had a child; she had also been in a mental hospital. Both these 'older women', of a kind that appealed to Thomas, were displaced by Caitlin. David Gascoyne's *Journal 1936–1937* records meeting Caitlin on 13 April 1937 ('My first impression was of a hard innocence') and continues: 'Until quite recently, Dylan has been living with Emily Coleman who was "in love" with him. Yesterday or the day before, he confronted her with Caitlin M, whom he announced his intention of marrying almost at once.'

again, because I think I shall have to be in Wales a long time, a couple of months almost; I've been in a nursing home with bronchitis and laryngitis or something, no voice at all, no will, all weakness and croaking and spitting and feeling hot and then feeling cold, and I'm about now but quavery and convalescent and I must see you. I haven't seen or written to you or let you know I'm alive—which, at the moment, and remembering neurasthenically my days of almost-death, I don't think I was—since Wednesday, the 21st of April, when I lost you in the morning, found money, and shouted on the wireless.[1] Darling, you mustn't have been angry with me for not writing my love, my love which can't ever move but is growing always; you must not have disbelieved, for one little split hair of the day or night, that day and night I think of you, love you, remember everything all the time, and know forever that we'll be together again—& Christ knows where—because it must be like that. But I don't want to write words words words to you: I must see you and hear you; it's hell writing to you now: it's lifting you up, (though I'm sure I'm not strong enough), and thinking you are really my flesh-&-blood Caitlin whom I love more than anyone has loved anyone else, & then finding a wooden Caitlin like a doll or a long thin Caitlin like a fountain pen or a mummy Caitlin made before the bible, very old and blowable-away. I want you. When you're away from me, it's absolutely a physical removal, insupportable & irreparable: no, not irreparable: if I lost a hand when you weren't with me, when you came back it would grow again, stronger & longer than ever. That's my cock words again, though all it means is true as heaven: that it's nonsense me living without you, you without me: the world is unbalanced unless, in the very centre of it, we little muts stand together all the time in a hairy, golden, more-or-less unintelligible haze of daftness. And that's more words, but I love and love you. Only love, and true love. Caitlin Caitlin this is unbearable. Will you forgive me again—for being ill and too willy-minded & weak and full of useless (no God, not useless) love for you, love that couldn't bear writing even if it could, to write & say, I'm dying perhaps, come & see me quickly, now, with some gooseberries and kisses for me. I'm not dying now, much. If you're where I'm writing to—please everything you are—can you telephone here? And come up? & be with me somewhere, if only for an only I don't know how long? Please, Caitlin my dear.

XXXXXX
Caitlin

Dylan   X   Caitlin

Dylan

I have to be abstemious.

MS: Maurice Neville

[1] Thomas was booked to make his first radio broadcast, from the BBC studios in Swansea, reading poems and discussing 'Life and the Modern Poet'. At the last minute he asked to do it from London instead, then vanished from the studio without leaving a script for their files: 'a very serious matter', the BBC kept telling him.

D. J. AND FLORENCE THOMAS (his parents)
June 10 [1937]   c/o J W Sibthorp Mousehole Cornwall

Important Letter

Dear Mother & Dad,

There's no doubt whatever that I've been a careless, callous, and quite unreasonable person as regards letting you know about myself since I left you at the beginning of April, and, as usual, I've no excuse, and you know me well enough to realise that if I did genuinely have one I wouldn't be long in explaining and elaborating it. Since I last wrote, and that was much too long ago, I've been working hard, but not too productively, have secured a little, but not extravagantly much, money on advance for the Welsh masterpiece, and have—I'm not sure how much of a shock this might be to you —during the last three days moved on to Cornwall for a little—I can't actually call it a holiday—change of sorts and of weather and of companions. I intend, things which I want to explain permitting, to stay here until the end of June, and then return home for a while—to see mother and you—before continuing the rest of this daft & postponed journey of mine. I'm staying here with Caitlin Macnamara (whose writing on the envelope mother'll probably recognise) in a cottage lent to me by a man called Sibthorp; the address isn't really Mousehole, but, as the postal system here is so bad, I've been told that a Mousehole address is far easier & quicker to write to. The cottage is in Lamorna Cove, a beautiful little place full of good fishermen and indifferent visitors. I suppose that I'm piling on the shocks and surprises in this very late letter, but I must tell you too that Caitlin and I are going to be married next week by special licence (I think that's what they call it) in the Penzance registry office.[1] This isn't thought of—I've told mother about it many times—speedily or sillily; we've been meaning to for a long time, & think we should carry it out at once. Everything will be entirely quiet & undemonstrative, two of the villagers here will be witnesses, and neither of us, of course, has a penny apart from the three pounds which we have carefully hidden in order to pay for the licence. We'll stay on here until the end of the month, then for a time Caitlin will go home to Hampshire & I'll come back to Wales until I can make just exactly enough money to keep us going until I make just exactly enough money again. It may, & possibly does, sound a rash and mad scheme, but it satisfies us and it's all we ask for. I do hope it won't hurt you; though I know I'm a thoughtless

---

[1] Dylan and Caitlin were not married (by special licence) until July 11. This was a Sunday, and the registrar at Penzance would have needed persuading to open the office for their benefit. Why they should have gone to this trouble, when they had been on the point of getting married for a month, isn't clear. D. J. Thomas would have liked to stop what he thought was an unsuitable union. In June he had enlisted the support of his son-in-law, Haydn Taylor, who telephoned the registrar. But there was nothing to be done, and a letter from D. J. to Taylor on June 25 shows him already resigned to 'the mad scheme', since 'the young irresponsibles are bent on their supreme act of folly'.

letter-writer & (this sounds like a novelette, doesn't it?) a pretty worthless son. I want you to know now & forever that I think about you every day and night, deeply & sincerely, and that I have tried to keep myself, (& have succeeded) straight & reasonable during the time I've been away from you: a time that seems years, so much has happened. I'm completely happy at the moment, well-fed, well-washed, & well looked-after. It's a superb place —the haunt, unfortunately, of aged R.A.s and presidents of West Country Poets' Rambling Clubs—and a delightful cottage, and weather full of sun and breeze, and I'm so glad mother's being well again, & I send her all my love. Do you mind, but I've got to ask you to do a few things for me, simple things and, to me, very necessary ones: could you send on some clothes, my green suit, a shirt or two, one of the pairs of shoes I've left, & those dark gym-shoes. I've had to buy an extra pair of flannel trousers, but I'm still a little short of clean and changeable things. Is it too much to ask, on top of all I ask you—& on top of what so rudely I rarely acknowledge? I would be so grateful, & I mean that with all my heart. I'll write again tomorrow, because then I'll know the exact Penzance date. I'm terribly terribly without money, so can't phone or get up to Penzance to find out: Rayner Heppenstall, who's staying with his wife a few miles away, is going to lend me a few shillings tomorrow, & I can then see to the few essential things.

Please write to me quickly; I would appreciate, so very much, you sending clothes & letters; and I'll try to be much more explicit & less (I should imagine) sensationally full of Dylan-life-altering news when I write tomorrow.

All my love, apologies, & hopes,

Dylan   X

MS: Haydn Taylor

DAVID HIGHAM
14th June [1937] for the moment at Oriental Cottage Lamorna Cornwall

Dear Higham,
Letters only just this moment forwarded; I've been honeymooning I think, and haven't yet done enough mss to send you. It's getting too personal & not enough Welsh: I've had to scrap lots. But it's coming, dear God, it's coming, & I faithfully promise you shl have it very soon. I *do* want money too, so I *must* work hard.

Yes, happy thank you, sunburned & steady-handed.

Sincerely,
Dylan Thomas

MS: Texas

NANCY and HAYDN TAYLOR
Sunday [postmarked June 20 1937; no stamp]
                    Oriental Cottage Lamorna Cove Nr Penzance Cornwall

Dear Nancy and Haydn,
  I heard from my late London address that you had been ringing up
during the last week to try to get hold of me, and that you'd heard—from
father, I suppose—of my plans for a pleasant and eccentric marriage. The
people in the London address told me that they had carefully been evasive
in their replies to your questions about my whereabouts as they didn't
know whether or not I wished them, for whatever strange reasons I might
have had, to be broadcast. Father may have told you my Cornwall address, but, in case he didn't, here it is. It's a borrowed cottage with a
jungle garden and three lavatories, and is only a few miles from where I
stayed last year. But I don't imagine that that's of any interest. I lead a
most mysterious life, on the surface; actually, it is the almost inevitable
life of any penniless drifter with a liking for odd places and odder people,
very few regrets about anything and no responsibilities. You mightn't
agree with 'no responsibilities', considering that I'm so very nearly married, but Caitlin is—whether that's a fortunate thing or not in the opinion
of others—sufficiently like myself to care little or nothing for proprietary
interests and *absolutely* nothing for the responsibilities of husbandly
provision. It will not yet, of course, be possible for us to live together all
the time, & we'll go away whenever we feel like it or—& this will be,
until the days of our comparative prosperity, which still would mean a
genuine but never-yet wretched poverty, more frequent—whenever it is,
from the point of view of money or/and accommodation, essential. (I'm
sorry about these tortuous phrases, but I've just been reviewing, with
unction, cunning, & entire literary dishonesty, a book on Social Credit &
the Economic War.) Incidentally, I'd like to explain about my not returning home the day after Nancy and I met at Paddington Station: the lent
pound note I gave back to the original lenders, my own expected cheque
did not arrive for several days, & by that time I was again in debt for
almost the complete worth of the cheque. It was unfortunate in some
ways, but good in others, as, had I not been in London when I shd
officially have been working at home, this lovely three-lavatoried cottage
would never have been mine for the summer, Caitlin & I would not have
come to a decision so quickly, and (perhaps, but I think it unlikely,
bloody unlikely) another social catastrophe would have been averted. So
much for that. I'm sending this letter of explanation to your Laleham
cottage, as I haven't had any news about your moving. I hope it reaches
you. As a gesture, Christian, gentlemanly, ladylike, sisterly,
in-law-brotherly, friendly, & (in face of your obvious distrust of what
could be, & has, by father, been called 'this lunatic course of action')
congratulatorily from a married couple of some years' standing to two
younger persons about to embark on the voyage of legal matrimony,

would you like to slip me a couple of quid? I'm afraid the last few words are a sorry come-down after the grandiloquence of my previous circumlocution, but I do, actually, want to buy a hell of a lot of things almost at once, &, though father's been desperately kind & sent me five pounds last week with sort of resigned wishes for my happiness, I'm still really short of the bare amount I need. This is a letter of apology, explanation, defence (though not apologetic) and cadgery. I'll always be grateful if the cadgery succeeds, honestly grateful. Anyway, write to me very soon: I'll pay every intention to the advice etcetera that I anticipate from so many family counsellors & despairers. But in seriousness, you could help me with very little. And with less than very little, I now put down my pen and hope this leaves you. Forgive this ill, & too-often facetious letter; the best thing that can be said about it is that none of it is blarney.

Love to you both,
Dylan

MS: Haydn Taylor

DAVID HIGHAM
Friday [July 2 1937]   Oriental Cottage Lamorna Cornwall

Dear Higham,
I'm glad the Curtis Brown business is over at last. When Faber has finished looking through my MS, could you return it to me just for a few days? There are several details I want to correct, etc.
More personally: do you think it would be possible for you to get a little money—however little—out of Dent for me almost immediately? That may sound rather startling, perhaps, considering that I haven't supplied any of the required words yet; the book's in a hell of a mess, disheartening me, but I know it will come all right. But the trouble is that I have no money at all—literally none, no cigarettes, too little food on a diminishing credit—to live anywhere at all to continue writing. It's almost impossible to knock this stuff into shape—a book, that will eventually, I'm afraid, not contain many references to Wales—with all these mingy worries nagging on all sides.[1] If I can't obtain some money by early next week, I'll have to move from here to nowhere: and in nowhere I can obviously do nothing. Do please try to raise me a little money, even five pounds, from Dent. I'd be more than grateful, it would, cheaply here in the country, keep me going for some time, and I could again, I'm sure,

---

[1] The 'Welsh journey' book was never written.

work hard and well. Sorry for the wheedling, slightly desperate, note, but it can't be avoided.

I hope you cán write quickly.

Yours,
Dylan Thomas

P.S. The Best Short Stories people are printing a story of mine in this year's collection. It wouldn't, I suppose, be possible for you to get me paid by them in advance? Not that I'm hopeful.

MS: Texas

DAVID HIGHAM
Tuesday [July 6 1937]   The Lobster Pot[1] Mousehole Cornwall

Dear Higham,
So glad Faber want the story for their Welsh book. And of course I accept.

I hope you've received my pathetic, and now even more disastrously important, letter. As you see from the address above, I've had to move from Lamorna, and I shan't be able to stay here long without some almost immediate money. It's hard to work at all under these conditions.

'The Orchards' is going to appear in the Faber Book of Modern Stories, too, isn't it?[2]

Yours,
Dylan Thomas

MS: Texas   *SL*

DAVID HIGHAM
Tuesday (July 13 1937)   Lobster Pot Mousehole Cornwall

Dear Higham,
Thanks very much indeed for getting hold of all that money for me so promptly. Dent's *are* good to me. Those cheques did a lot of good, and have temporarily made us safe.

I'm afraid that, owing to the muddle about my changing addresses so often, my acknowledgement of O'Brien's letter—Best Short Stories— didn't reach him until the book had gone to press. So that's three guineas

---

[1] The Lobster Pot was a restaurant and guest-house, run jointly by Wyn Henderson and Max Chapman. There was an adjoining cottage; Dylan and Caitlin lived in it before and after their marriage.
[2] Faber published *Welsh Short Stories* and *The Faber Book of Short Stories* in 1937. 'The Orchards' appeared in both.

I won't be having. Nelson, however, are doing an anthology of poetry very soon, & have agreed to pay me a few guineas for one from my first book. They might, do you think, hand over the money to you beforehand?

I'll let you have back the book of short stories manuscript not more than a week after I receive it.

Thanks again.

Yours,
Dylan Thomas

MS: Texas

VERNON WATKINS
15th July [1937]   Lobster Pot Mousehole Cornwall

I'm sorry that this is such a
short & inadequate letter: I'll
do much better next time.

Dear Vernon,

If, in some weeks' time, you see a dog-like shape with a torn tail and a spaniel eye, its tail between its legs, come cringing and snuffling up Heatherslade gravel,[1] it will be me; look carefully at its smarmy rump that asks to be kicked, its trembling, penholding paw that scribbles, 'kick me', in the dust. It will deserve your anger. But, really, the Grief of the Sea[2] was this: I was fooling about with a copy of the poem, playing the pleasant, time-wasting game of altering, unasked-for, somebody else's work; and then, when I met Keidrych with the manuscripts I had collected, blindly and carelessly I must have included among them the for-my-own-benefit, not-to-be-shown copy instead of the original. I hope you forgive me: that's the truth. I was worried when I saw the first number of Wales, with that Thowdlerized version in it, and should, anyway, in a few days have sent off an explanation to you. Further than that I Cannot Go, but you may still kick me when we meet in Pennard again—and I'm hoping that will be soon.

Yes I thought 'Wales' was good, too. I had actually very little myself to do with the editing, though when Keidrych goes up to Cambridge next year I shall probably—and with you as colleague, or whatever it is, if you'd be—take it all over. And no more Nigel Heseltine[3] when we do: he

---

[1] Watkins lived with his parents on the Gower coast, above the little bay called Heatherslade.

[2] Thomas had made some changes to the proof of Watkins's poem 'Griefs of the Sea', which appeared in the first issue of the magazine *Wales*, whose editor was Keidrych Rhys.

[3] Nigel Heseltine was seen (if not by Thomas) as a promising young writer of the period, publishing stories and verse. But he made a career as an economist, working overseas. His father was Peter Warlock (Philip Heseltine), the song composer.

can crawl back into the woodwork, or lift up his stone again. And wait until you see a review by Margiad Evans of Glyn Jones's stories in the next number: I told Keidrych, quite truthfully, that it read as though Miss Evans were being raped in the Blue Bed[1] as she wrote the review.

My own news is very big and simple. I was married three days ago; to Caitlin Macnamara; in Penzance registry office; with no money, no prospect of money, no attendant friends or relatives, and in complete happiness. We've been meaning to from the first day we met, and now we are free and glad. We're moving next week—for how long depends on several things, but mostly on one—to a studio some miles away, in Newlyn, a studio above a fish-market & where gulls fly in to breakfast. But I shall be trying to come home soon for at least a few days, along with Caitlin: I think you'll like [her] very much, she looks like the princess on the top of a Christmas Tree, or like a stage Wendy; but, for God's sake, don't tell her that.

Write as soon as you can, and bless me.

Love to all the family.

Yours always,
Dylan

MS: British Library   *VW(R)*

PAMELA HANSFORD JOHNSON
6th August 1937   Fradgan Studios[2] Newlyn Penzance Cornwall

It was very very nice of you to write, I'd been wanting to hear from you. I'm a long way from everywhere, in a high huge haystack of a studio over the harbour, full of worries and happiness lazing away all the writeable days, writing an occasional bad love poem of the sort that begins, 'It was not love until you came', drinking scaly beer in the pubs near the Fish Market, counting Caitlin's change—if any, fighting with primus-stoves, spending the rent. Caitlin can only cook one thing, and that is Irish bread which requires a very special type of oven, unobtainable in England; she drinks a lot though, so we eat in the morning as we're too unsteady in the evening to open the tins. (That isn't altogether true: I've managed to finish two stories which are unlike anything I've ever seen, and a satanic Horliquinade[3] just like something I never want to see.) I can now light old Etna, the primus, without burning more than two fingers and an eyelash, and can be left alone with the methylated spirits. If I'm reformed, it isn't noticeable. Newlyn is famous for its fleas and Dod Proctor:[4] I go to bed

[1] Glyn Jones's book, being reviewed by Margiad Evans, was *The Blue Bed*.
[2] Max Chapman had a studio there.
[3] Presumably a pun on 'Horlicks', the bedtime drink.
[4] Mrs Dod Proctor (1892–1972), painter, who lived in Newlyn for many years.

with the former, and could with the latter. Caitlin was very rude yesterday to the Proctor woman who's thin and red-tipped and shiny. As we were leaving her house, the Proctor said, 'Wait a minute, I must powder my nose'. And Caitlin said, 'Why don't you put it in a bag?' There has been a young rash of poets, lately; you can buy a surrealist in Mousehole—an artists' village full of fishermen—for a couple of whiting; Rayner Heppenstall, very nice man, newly married, came down for a religious gloom; Oswell Blakeston, coming out of the well to work, has done little more than sit about on his headquarters; Philip Henderson has gone rugged in a wee wee Wendy bungalow next to a bird-hospital run by a marionette-maker. There are Teas, Christian Science & literary, and folk dancing and punch-&-judy shows for adults. A young man living in Truro, got hold of my address somehow & invited himself over. I couldn't read his signature, & when I opened the door at tea-time there was a bright brand-new pig standing there who said his name was Thuel Roskelly.[1] There weren't any acorns so we gave him whiskey and it made him drunk and after he'd snorted a lot and rubbed his back—covered, undoubtedly, with short stiff hairs—he said he was a poet, that he wrote in Comment, had met Victor B & thought him conventional, said he himself couldn't write very well but that he was practising hard and would in time be able to fart in tune. He was very odd. He slept on the sofa after that, so we tip-toed off and left him shaking himself like a cocktail, with snores and hiccups. When we came back, he'd gone. The air here is very invigorating and there is a splendid view of the English Channel.

Last week, a man [called] Mulk Raj Anand[2] made a big curry for everybody about. The first course was beans, little ones. I ate two and couldn't speak. A little man called Wallace B. Nichols,[3] who has made a small fortune out of writing epic poems on people like Cromwell and Nelson and Mrs Elsie Guddy, took a whole mouthful and was assisted out. He writes for the Cornhill. After the main dish, which was so unbelievably hot that everyone, except the Indian, was crying like Shirley Temple, a woman, Mrs Henderson, looked down on to her plate & saw, lying at one corner of it, a curious rubbery thing that looked like a red, discarded french letter. In interest, she picked it up and found it was the entire skin from her tongue.

It's terribly hard, Pamela dear, to thank you for all the nice things you said in your letter. All I can say is that I'm happy, very happy indeed. We are poor as the mice that live in our clothes cupboard, and have no prospects of anything but a short, irresponsible, & happy life of poverty. That's sententious.

I'm so glad you're happy too. And there's nothing again for me to say about that. We know each other very well. I'll call with Caitlin as soon as

---

[1] Thuel Roskelly was a young poet and journalist.
[2] Mulk Raj Anand (b. 1905), Indian novelist.
[3] Wallace B. Nichols (b. 1888), novelist and poet.

we get back to town, and we'll all get plastered. You said you wanted to send us something: that's lovely. I asked Caitlin, & she doesn't know what. We live day-by-day, buying just enough food to last the day, buying a new towel, if we can, when the old one gets talkative, buying soap when we offend each other. What we want to do, & have been unable to do, is to buy a bigger lot of small things so that they'll be there when we want them. So, if you can & if you like, you can send me a pound with a long newsy letter. That is not the correct thing to ask, I suppose, but it's the thing everybody forgets. You can't eat cut glass or drink decanters or wash with a silver spoon. Very incorrect, but we know each other very well. If you can, too, But the newsy letter, *yes*! My love to Mrs J. Say, 'Well, old man, we both asked for it, eh?' to Neil[1] for me. And love & happiness to you.

Dylan

MS: Lady Snow's estate

EDITH SITWELL
20th August 1937   Fradgan Studios Newlyn Penzance Cornwall

Dear Miss Sitwell,
    Before anything else, I want to thank you with all my heart for your great generosity and graciousness. Caitlin and I thank you for the lovely present with which we bought all sorts of things we wanted, from knives and towels to a Garbo picture, and paid off the clamourers. And to the man who gave me the present you enclosed, all I can say is thank you. I shan't ever be impertinent about his name, but I shall always think of him with gratitude. He must be a kind, splendid person.
    And now I want to apologise for this apparently very rude and dis-respectful delay in answering and acknowledging your present and letters. I'm awfully bad with letters, I know, but I couldn't be unmannerly, or unappreciative, enough to let a reply like this linger on through slackness or carelessness. For the last ten days I've been in and out on the Newlyn fishing-boats, making a little money, and have hardly been on shore at all during the daytime. I've just been snatching a few hours of sleep when I can, too utterly tired in head and every limb to write even the shortest sentence of gratitude for all you've done and are doing for me. This sounds weak, but it honestly is true. Sometimes over twelve hours, on a rough sea, in a twelve-foot boat. My job's over now, and I can start thinking again, not moving all the time in a kind of fish-eyed daze.
    It's wonderful of you to take all this trouble about trying to get me some work. I'm sure, aren't you, that something must come out of it.

[1] Pamela Hansford Johnson married Gordon Neil Stewart in 1936.

Almost above all, I should like some connection with the BBC. I've done one broadcast, of my own poems and of a few poems by Ransom[1] and Auden, on the West Regional programme, and I was told that it went down quite well. That was late in April this year, but no-one's got in touch with me since. I love reading poems aloud, and I do hope Mr. Maine will succeed in making the BBC interested enough to let me read some more. Oh those little ninny five-minute readings with a death at the end of each line. I wouldn't mince, anyway. I should enjoy very much reading some of Sacheverell Sitwell's poems, if the BBC, & he, some time allowed me: it's great and grand aloud, isn't it? pillars and columns and great striding figures through a microphone. I'm writing today to Peter Quennell,[2] though I know him very slightly from parties, and I'll send Miss Reynolds my three or four new poems. A friend of mine is typing my new story, and, as soon as it's finished, I'll send it to you along with the poems. I do so much want you to read them; I'm not sure of them at all; I hope you'll tell me all about them; sometimes I'm afraid they caricature themselves.

Life here has at last become too much, even for us who don't demand grand comforts. With smells from the fishmarket in front of us and dust from the coal-yard below us and flies from the dump behind us, we might as well live in the street. Our studio's haunted, too, and last month the landscape painter next door hanged himself from the rafters. So we're going to go to Wales for some time, to my mother's house, sailing around to North Devon in fishing-boats & working our way, as best we can, across to Swansea. It shouldn't take us more than a week. We start about September 1st. I do hope this change of address won't be awkward if any of the people you've asked to help me want to get in touch immediately. My mother's address is MARSTON, BISHOPSTON, near SWANSEA, Glamorgan.

It's impossible for me to tell you how deeply I appreciate your kindness, and value your friendship. I'll always remember it. Caitlin thanks you very much for your message. She's looking forward to meeting you. I hope we all can meet in London, soon. And I hope sincerely that your friend in Paris will get better.

All my gratefulness &
apologies,
Yours very sincerely,
Dylan Thomas

MS: Texas

---

[1] John Crowe Ransom (1888–1974); Thomas always wrote 'Ransome'.
[2] Peter Quennell (b. 1905), author and historian.

GEOFFREY GRIGSON
September 7 [1937]   Marston Bishopston Glamorgan

Dear Geoffrey,
    Here are the hundred words, though I don't know if it's the sort of thing
you want.[1]
    No, I haven't gone back into the grass. I spent the summer in Cornwall,
and was married there. I'll give you a ring, if you like, when we're in town
at the end of the month and we can meet and make a noise. If you like.
                                                        Dylan

Good luck to Auden on his seventieth birthday.

MS: Texas

DESMOND HAWKINS
[1937 ?September]   Marston Bishopston Glamorgan

Dear Desmond,
    I haven't seen you for a year, or perhaps more. Where are you living now and
how are you? I'm coming to London at, I think, the beginning of next month.
We must meet, there must be such a load of gossip for us both, and stories, and
intimate literary secrets. I've been in Cornwall all the summer, met
Blakeston there who said you were turning up to stay outside Penzance. You
didn't though, or did you? I'm beautifully married, and how's your daughter?
Let me know your town days, I'm looking forward to a big beery lunch with
you. If you want a poem or a dirty crack, you've come to the right shop.
                                                        Love,
                                                        Dylan

MS: the recipient

DESMOND HAWKINS
[1937 ?September]   Marston Bishopston Glamorgan

Dear Desmond, progenitive man of letters,
    My wife is Irish and French, you haven't met her, she is two months
younger than I am,[2] has seas of golden hair, two blue eyes, two brown

---

[1] *New Verse* for November was an 'Auden Double Number'. Thomas contributed one of
'Sixteen Comments' ('I think he is a wide and deep poet . . . He makes Mr Yeats' isolation
guilty as a trance'). 'Seventieth birthday' was a Thomas joke: Auden was thirty.
[2] Caitlin was actually ten months older.

arms, two dancing legs, is untidy and vague and un-reclamatory. I am lost in love and poverty, and my work is shocking. I can let you have one longish and very good poem, unprinted, for an immediate guinea. It is this week's masterpiece, it took two months to write, and I want to drink it.[1]

I'm a bumpkin, too, and my news is stale as New Verse. I haven't been in town since May, but I'm going up next week to try to write some quick advertisements for petrol and make enough money to buy my wife a ping-pong table.[2] We competed, the week before last, in the Swansea Croquet Tournament, and only lost by one hoop.

If you want that poem, it's yours for a pound. I've come down one shilling, and it's forty lines.

Can you be in town Friday, Saturday, Sunday or Monday of next week? Goodbye & good luck, cradle-filler.[3]

Dylan

MS: the recipient

JULIAN SYMONS
22 October [1937]   Blashford[4] Ringwood Hants

Dear Julian Symons,
    When does the next number of 20th Century Verse appear? I can send you a longish poem in about a week. So sorry not to have answered your last letter: I've been changing addresses so often & so quickly I haven't been able to attend to anything.
    And can you let me have Ruthven Todd's address?

Sincerely,
Dylan Thomas

MS: Texas

VERNON WATKINS
[postmarked October 25 1937]   Blashford Ringwood Hants

Dear Vernon,
    Thank you for the poems. I like them all. My respect for them is always

---

[1] An early version of 'I make this in a warring absence'. See the succeeding letters. The poem eventually appeared in *Twentieth Century Verse*, January/February 1938.
[2] Norman Cameron, an advertising copywriter, may have found some freelance work for Thomas.
[3] Mrs Hawkins was expecting a second child.
[4] Blashford is a village in the New Forest. Caitlin's mother, Yvonne Macnamara, lived there in a house that was formerly a pub, the New Inn.

increased when I read them again, and in typescript. 'Mana' is magnificent, especially the fourth verse. At the moment, I think it's your best short poem. I still don't like the first line. Perhaps I never mentioned it, but from the beginning, from the first time I saw the poem shaping, I've felt the line to be wrong, disliked 'fabled'—not because it is used as a verb, but because of its position—and felt uneasy about the rhythm. The rhythm is one that I myself have used to death, and my feeling against it is perhaps over-personal. The line is so stridently an opening line: tum tum tum, all the wheels and drums are put in motion: a poem is about to begin. I see the workman's clothes, I hear the whistle blowing in the poem-factory. And one other line I think is bad: 'Laid in the long grey shadow of our weeping thought'. This, to me, has far too many weak words. They are weak alone, & weaker when added together. They do not cancel each other out, though, but elongate a thin nothing: a long, grey, weeping sausage. But that's fancy talk. What I mean is, the whole line seems a kind of tired indrawing of breath between loud & strong utterances. And I've always disliked the weak line. I admit that readers of complicated poetry do need a breather every now and then, but I don't think the poetry should give it to them. When they want one, they should take it and then go on.

. I don't know yet what I'll read at the Cardiff lecture, but I'll let you know beforehand: the Ballad certainly, After Sunset probably, one or two of the lyrics in 'Wales', and, perhaps, either Mana or Griefs of the Sea. And an Auden, a Ransom, maybe Prokosch.

This is a very lovely place. Caitlin & I ride into the New Forest every day, into Bluebell Wood or onto Cuckoo Hill. There's no-one else about; Caitlin's mother is away; we are quiet and small and cigarette-stained and very young. I've read two dozen thrillers, the whole of Jane Austen, a new Wodehouse, some old Powys, a book of Turgenev, 3 lines by Gertrude Stein, & an anthology of Pure Poetry by George Moore. There are only about 2,000 books left in the house.

My poem is continuing. You shall have it next week. Regards to your mother & father. Remember me to Francis[1]—to whom I *must* write. And have a nice week-end.

Dylan

[*four lines of verse are deleted*]

This was a quotation from the new verse of my poem, which I've thought better about.

MS: British Library   *VW*

---

[1] Francis Dufau-Labeyrie, a French friend of Watkins. Later he translated Thomas's *Portrait of the Artist as a Young Dog.*

JULIAN SYMONS
28th October 1937   Blashford Ringwood Hants

Dear Julian Symons,
  Thank you for Todd's address. I'll let you have the poem very shortly;
and no, of course I don't mind it being held over until December.
  I'm afraid I couldn't write anything about Lewis;[1] I haven't read
enough, and I'm not an admirer. I'm looking forward to reading the
number, though.
  That sounds a splendid idea—the stories by poets. I hope it comes off,
and I'd like you to use a story of mine very much.

                                              Sincerely,
                                              Dylan Thomas

MS: Texas

DESMOND HAWKINS
30th October '37   Blashford Ringwood Hants

Dear Desmond,
  No, my goodness, I had no letter from you. No-one can have forwarded
it from Wales. I am staying here near the New Forest, and am too broke to
move. By crook I got from Wales, as I told you I would, but not to London.
Here I feel planted for ever, or until next week. As soon as we're in
London, I'll let you know. Thank you very much for the week-end
invitation. I accept with pomp. The poem I have to revise. I thought it
was perfectly correct—as to detail—before I read it again early one
morning. Then I saw that the third verse, which dealt with the faults and
mistakes of death, had a brilliant and moving description of a suicide's
grave as 'a chamber of errors'.[2] I'm now working hard on the poem, and it
should be complete in some days.
  Lately, I've been receiving strange requests from magazines: first, for a
kind of obituary notice, for New Verse, on Auden, or perhaps a tribute on
his seventieth birthday; second, for a valuation (Symons's word) of
Wyndham Lewis, for 20th Century Verse; third, for a description of my
most recent trauma, with, if possible, ancestral symbols, for 'transition';
& last for a contribution to a special number of Henry Miller's 'The
Booster', 'completely devoted to The Womb'.[3] Do you think this means,
at last, that I'm a man of letters? The only contribution to give Mr.

---

[1] Wyndham Lewis. See next letter.
[2] 'I make this in a warring absence', Stanza 6, has the phrase, 'the room of errors'.
[3] The writer Henry Miller (1891–1980) was invited to help run *The Booster*, formerly the
   magazine of the American Country Club in Paris. Later it was renamed *Delta* and had a
   brief life as a literary journal.

Miller, anyway, is a typewritten reply to the effect that I too am, passionately, devoted to the womb. And you, Mrs. Dyer. Looking forward to seeing you.

Love, Dylan

MS: the recipient

VERNON WATKINS
13th November   '37   Blashford Ringwood Hants

Dear Vernon,
   Thank you for the new version of 'Mana'. I think it's very right now, don't you? I never really care to suggest actual, detailed alterations in anyone else's poem, (in spite of the apparently contradictory evidence of 'Griefs of the Sea'), but I'm glad you did alter the first line—(here-it-comes-boys)—and that line in the middle—(now-boys-take-a-deep-breath).
   Here, after so long, is my own new poem.[1] I hope you'll like it. I've used 'molten', as you suggested, but kept 'priest's grave foot', which is not, I'm sure, really ugly. In the last line of the seventh verse, you'll notice—'a man is tangled'. It was weeks after writing that line that I remembered Prokosch's 'man-entangled sea':[2] but I don't think any apologies are necessary, anyway. Lines 4 & 5 of the last verse might, perhaps, sound too fluent: I mean, they might sound as though they came too easily in a manner I have done my best to discard, but they say exactly what I mean them to. Are they clear? Once upon a time, before my death & resurrection, before the 'terrible' world had shown itself to me (however lyingly, as lines 6 & 7 of the last verse might indicate) as not so terrible after all, a wind had blown that had frightened everything & created the first ice & the first frost by frightening the falling snow so much that the blood of each flake froze. This is probably clear, but, even to me, the lines skip (almost) along so that they are taken in too quickly, & then mainly by the eye.
   I wonder if you would type a couple of copies of the poem for me — there's no typewriter within miles—and let me have them as quickly as you can. I must get the poem off, and soon, because I need, terribly urgently, the little money it will get me.
   News, though not much, when I write again. And I'll write when I send off the poem to Eliot—(I want the Criterion to do it). Don't forget, will you? And much love to you.

Dylan

[1] 'I make this in a warring absence', also called 'Poem (for Caitlin)' on first publication. The *VW* note calls it 'Poem to Caitlin'. This is confusing, since a different poem, 'Unluckily for a death', had the title 'Poem (to Caitlin)' on first publication.
[2] In Frederic Prokosch's poem 'The Baltic Shore'.

P.S. It's a full stop after 'ice' in the last verse.
P.P.S. If I come to Cardiff to lecture—which is financially improbable —
I'll try to spend the night at Swansea. And see you, of course.
P.P.S. Since writing this, I've done another little poem:[1] nothing at all important, or even (probably,) much good: just a curious thought said quickly. I think it will be good for me to write some short poems, not bothering about them too much, between my long exhausters.

MS: British Library   *VW*

VERNON WATKINS
[Postmarked November 20 1937]   [Blashford]

Dear Vernon,
    Thank you so much for the typewritten poems. I agree with you entirely as to the (apparently) hurried ending of my sixty-line-year's work, and will alter the middle lines of the last verse.[2] This should take me until Christmas, and my present to you will be, inedibly, the revised and final copy. About go-cripple-come-Michaelmas I'll write next time. It looks & smells good. At the moment, though, I have another favour to ask. In ten days' time I am to give a reading in the London University, reading alone with no commentary. I scrapped the Cardiff lecture, as I had prepared no grave speech and did not feel like travelling 200 miles just to recite, in my fruity voice, poems that would not be appreciated & could, anyway, be read in books. The London affair, however, is at the request of a vague friend, & will have to be fulfilled. I shall read you, me, Auden, Ransom, Prokosch, Yeats. I have plenty of me at hand, several of you, & enough Auden. Will you assist me, tremendously too, by telling me what of Yeats to read and—this is the favour, the tiresome favour—copy out for me the poems you choose?
    This house is stacked with books, but all prose, and I have brought nothing with me but a few Penguin Shakespeares and a pocket dictionary. I know it's a bother for you, but if you could type for me—say, half a dozen Yeats (middle & late, including, if you think it as good as others, the one ending 'A terrible beauty is born', & the ones I know so little & that one you have read me)—it would be kind and splendid. It's too much to ask you also to copy out one Prokosch, but, if you have some spare minutes, could you do it? I want the reading to be of poems not *too* well known—with Yeats's exception, & Prokosch, I believe, is still only known as a dilettante name—outside the Criterion & one or two other papers of an established snob-appeal. The programme, roughly, I have in mind is: 'Dead Boy' & either 'Captain Carpenter' or 'Judith'—of Ransom; 'Prologue' & 'Ballad' of Auden; one good Prokosch; at least three

[1] 'The spire cranes.'
[2] 'I make this in a warring absence.'

Yeats; that tiny poem by Antonia White; John Short's Carol; Gavin Ewart's 'sexual insignia' poem; your Ballad of the Rough Sea, Griefs of the Sea, & Mana; my new poem, & two of the poems at the end of my last book. I shall read for, probably, 3/4 of an hour, explaining, of course, that my reading is not supposed to prove anything, and that my selection is based on nothing but a personal liking. The details of the programme I may alter. Anyway, do try to copy out those things as quickly as possible. I began this letter two days ago, & then, owing to the arrival of all sorts of odd people here, put off sending it until to-day. Now the time I have before the reading is alarmingly short; I've just realized the date to be the 27th. This is rudely rushing you, but could you type the Yeats—&, I hope very much, a Prokosch by about Wednesday. It's blackmail to say I'm relying on you, but I crookedly am. I respect your judgement, & your typing. Love & admiration as always.

Dylan

MS: British Library   *VW*

HERMANN PESCHMANN[1]
21st Nov 1937   Blashford Ringwood Hants

Dear Mr. Peschmann,
   Thanks for the letter. I'm sorry it isn't possible for me to speak to your Society this year: the worst of having such frequently changed, & always indefinite, addresses is that all one's letters go astray. I should be glad to come along one Monday or Wednesday early in January: perhaps we can fix a definite date some time soon.
   And thank you very much for forwarding my letter to Anna Wickham.[2]

Yours sincerely,
Dylan Thomas

MS: Philip Skelsey

LAWRENCE DURRELL[3]
[?December 1937]   Blashford Ringwood Hants

Dear Lawrence Durrell,
   I would like to have seen you too, after that first short meeting in

---

[1] Critic and anthologist, after an earlier career in business. An extra-mural tutor in literature, he ran a poetry club at Goldsmiths' College, 1936–9.

[2] Anna Wickham (Edith Alice Mary Harper) (1884–1947), poet, feminist, bohemian; she committed suicide. A notice in the hall of her house in Hampstead said, 'Saddle your Pegasus here'.

[3] Lawrence Durrell (b. 1912), not then established as a novelist, lived mainly outside England, in Paris and the eastern Mediterranean.

Anna's house,[1] in a clean pub with an evening before us and pockets jingling and lots of fire and spit and loud, grand affectations and conceits of Atlases and London coiling and humming: but Caitlin and I went away in a pantomime snow, thrown out at midnight, and we spent the night very coldly and trained back without tickets to charity in the morning. Now *this* warmth is ending, and we'll train back without tickets to London and live there in a bad convention. I think that England is the very place for a fluent and fiery writer. The highest hymns of the sun are written in the dark. I like the grey country. A bucket of Greek sun would drown in one colour the crowds of colours I like trying to mix for myself out of a grey, flat, insular mud. If I went to the sun I'd just sit in the sun; that would be very pleasant, but I'm not doing it, and the only necessary things I do are the things I am doing. Unless by accidents, and my life is planned by them, I shall be nearer Bournemouth than Corfu this summer. It will need a nice accident for us to live anywhere; we are stages beyond poverty; completely possessionless; and we are willing but angry; we can take it, but we don't want it. I liked your Stygian prose very very much, it's the best I've read for years. Don't let the Greek sun blur your pages, as you said it did. You use words like stones, throwing, rockerying, mossing, churning, sharpening, bloodsucking, melting, and a hard firewater flows and rolls through them all the time. . . . And it's so brave too; you used the sudden image of Christ with incredible courage. I mean to borrow the typescript of the Black Book as soon as I get to London.

But I wonder what Anna will make of Miller's books. I know her well. Morals are her cup of tea, and books are just beer: she swallows them down without discrimination of taste or body or brew, and judges them by the effect they have on her bowels. For her a good book produces a bad poem from her, containing an independent moral judgement, but the poem could really have been written without the book. And I think it insulting to books to take them as a purgative in order to void material which, with a little constriction of the muscles, could have been voided anyway.

My own book isn't nearly ready. I am keeping it aside, unfinished, and writing off, now, the things that would be detrimental to it if I were to continue. You said on the back of the envelope that you wanted a poem for a special number;[2] I have one I can send, but Miller, in his letter, said he did not know when the two prose pieces of mine would appear, owing to some unexplained difficulties, and it's rather silly, isn't it, sending you stuff to keep and not to print. But do tell me; I'd love to send you the poem of course.

Sincerely,
Dylan Thomas

MS: Carbondale   *SL*

[1] Anna Wickham.
[2] The reference is to *Booster*, later *Delta*, which Durrell helped Miller to edit. Two Thomas poems and a prose piece appeared in *Delta* in 1938 and 1939.

HERMANN PESCHMANN
January 3 1938 (About the date of a poetry reading. See Appendix 7.)

GEORGE REAVEY
January 3 1938   Blashford Ringwood Hants

Dear George,
   I shan't be in London until the end of next week. We were, as you
know, staying with Anna Wickham, but a difference of lack of opinion
made us return to the country. I'm afraid I can't yet find a copy of 'The
Orchards'. It was printed in the Criterion, & reprinted in The Faber Book
of Modern Stories & Welsh Short Stories (also published by Faber). I
haven't a copy of any of these books, otherwise I'd tear the story out. I'm
writing today to my home in Wales, asking if there is, by any chance, a
copy there. That's the best I can do: I never manage to keep the manuscripts of anything I write.
   I'm enclosing a list of names to send to about the guinea edition.[1]
Something should definitely come from some of them. I'll write you if I
think of any others.
   Is it possible for you to write about the details of the book you
mentioned in your note & on the telephone? Or would you prefer to leave
it until I come back to town? Anyway, do let me know.

                                                       Yours,
                                                       Dylan

MS: Harvard   *SL*

DAVID HIGHAM
8 January 1938   Blashford Ringwood Hants

Dear Higham,
   I'm glad Reavey's been reasonable. Yes, £20 was what was paid to me, I
remember now.[2] Formally, I approve that the rights revert to me provided
that should the book be published elsewhere Reavey be repaid. Is that
correct?
   With regard to the book & Church. I should rather like to select the
stories to include in the new book myself, but perhaps Church should be
sounded on this. Will you find out *exactly* how many stories he requires

---

[1] George Reavey and the Europa Press were supposed to be publishing a collection of stories
by Thomas, *The Burning Baby*, in both a limited and a popular edition. After many
tribulations, the book failed to appear.
[2] Apparently a payment for *The Burning Baby*.

to make the new book the required size? I suggest five.[1]

Augustus John suggests that the portrait frontispiece should be done in colour. This is quite an expensive process, of course, but wouldn't it be worth it? It would sound, and look, good. Will you mention it to Church when you talk to him about the other things?

I hope the Oxford Press will stump up soon. Everything's getting dreadful again.

What there is of my family is well & strong.

Yours,
Dylan Thomas

MS: Texas

REV. KENNETH THOMPSON[2]

13 I 38   Blashford Ringwood Hants

Dear Mr. Thompson,

Thank you for writing. I believe I should apologise to you, too, for I don't think I answered your last letter, a long time ago. I'm really sorry if I didn't: I had no means of getting in touch with you, as I'd unfortunately lost your address: Earl's Court was all I could remember.

And thank you for telling me about Hartcup. I wrote to him today, asking him if he'd like to send me some poems. I hope he will.

And I hope, too, that we'll be able to meet some time again, in Swansea or in London.

Best wishes,
Yours sincerely,
Dylan Thomas

MS: Bodleian Library

DAVID HIGHAM

January 19 1938 (About money etc. See Appendix 8.)

JULIAN SYMONS

20 January 1938 Saturday. (Hopes to send poem. See Appendix 9.)

JULIAN SYMONS

[?January 1938]   (Sends copy of poem. See Appendix 10.)

---

[1] A second book, to include prose and verse, was planned by Dent. This became *The Map of Love*, published 1939.

[2] Unknown correspondent.

HERMANN PESCHMANN
Feb 1 '38   Blashford Ringwood Hants

Dear Mr Peschmann,

Thank you for the letter. I'm glad my visit went so well, & hope I'll be able to come again.

You say you want to know what the poem (in Twentieth Century Verse) is 'about'.[1] There I *can* help you, I can give you a very rough idea of the 'plot'. But, of course, it's bound to be a most superficial, &, perhaps, misleading, idea, because the 'plot' is told in images, & the images *are* what they say, not what they stand for. Still, I hope this is of some assistance, even if not especially for your review. (Could you, by the way, send me a copy of that New English Weekly? I'd be very grateful, because I'm out of touch with everything here.)

Sincerely,
Dylan Thomas

The poem is, in the first place, supposed to be a document, or narrative, of all the emotional events between the coming and going, the creation and dissipation, of jealousy, jealousy born from pride and killed by pride, between the absence and the return of the crucial character (or heroine) of the narrative, between the war of her absence and the armistice of her pre-

Stanza 1 sence. The 'I', the hero, begins his narrative at the departure of the heroine, at the time he feels that her pride in him and in

Stanza 2 their proud, sexual world has been discarded. All that keen pride seems, to him, to have vanished, drawn back, perhaps, to

Stanzas 3 the blind womb from which it came. He sees her as a woman
& 4 made of contraries, innocent in guilt & guilty in innocence, ravaged in virginity, virgin in ravishment, and a woman who, out of a weak coldness, reduces to nothing the great sexual

Stanza 5 strengths, heats, & prides of the world. Crying his visions aloud, he makes war upon her absence, attacks and kills her absent heart, then falls, himself, into ruin at the moment of

Stanza 6 that murder of love. He falls into the grave; in his shroud he lies, empty of visions & legends; he feels undead love at his

Stanza 7 heart. The surrounding dead in the grave describe to him one manner of death and resurrection: the womb, the origin of love, forks its child down to the dark grave, dips it in dust, then forks

Stanza 8 it back into light again. And once in the light, the resurrected hero sees the world with penetrating, altered eyes; the world that was wild is now mild to him, revenge has changed into

Stanza 9 pardon. He sees his love walk in the world, bearing none of the murderous wounds he gave her. Forgiven by her, he ends his

---

[1] 'I make this in a warring absence'—in the January/February 1938 issue as 'Poem (for Caitlin)'.

> narrative in forgiveness:—but he sees and knows that all that has happened will happen again, tomorrow and tomorrow.

MS: Texas   *SL*

VERNON WATKINS
7th February [1938]   Blashford Ringwood Hants

Dear Vernon,
   I haven't written to you for such a long time. I don't know, even, if I thanked you for the typewriting of those Yeats, Prokosch, & Watkins poems. If I didn't, I'm ashamed. And, ashamed or not, thank you very much. And for the jack-in-the-box at Christmas: it frightened us all: we opened it late at night, when we were very delicate, and leapt to the ceiling like Fred Astaire.
   I was in London last week, and read some poems to night-students of the university. I didn't like the people at all; some looked like lemons, and all spoke with the voices of puddings. I detest the humility I should have, and am angry when I am humble. I appreciate the social arrogance I have in the face of my humility. I bow before shit, seeing the family likeness in the old familiar faeces, but I will not manure the genealogical tree. Your poems, Ballad, Mana, Griefs, Sunset, were more successful — from the point of controversy afterwards—than any I read. By a few, your poems in 'Wales' have been admired: The Sunbather, in particular, got them on their backs. Will you send me any new poems there are? I shall probably be addressing, from my canonical chair, more earnest suckers next month; & I'd prefer them to suck up something valuable.
   I've been writing some poems, but they're away, in the house of an enemy, being typed. They're matter-of-fact poems, & illogical naturally: except by a process it's too naturally obvious to misexplain. Rhymes are coming to me naturally, too, which I distrust; I like looking for connections, not finding them tabulated in stations. A sense of humour is, I hope, about to be lost: but not quite yet: the self-drama continues: bluff after bluff until I see myself as one: then again the deadly humour. But don't bother about this understated difficulty. Send me poems, & I'll send you some. Mine—not through humility or knowledge of less competence—will be more unsatisfactory. At the moment I am, in action, a person of words, & not as I should be: a person of words in action.
   Here's a photograph, taken by a woman near us. It's one of many: this is the toughest. Why I want you to think of me—photographically, when I'm not about—as a tough, I don't know. Anyway, it's very big; you can write a poem on the back, or draw whiskers on it, or advertise Kensitas[1] in the front window.

---

[1] Kensitas cigarettes.

My love to you, my regards to your family, & write soon. I hope to see you before the summer. Caitlin is well, happy, & dancing.[1] I miss you.

Dylan.

MS: British Library   *VW*

CHARLES FISHER
11th February 1938   Blashford Ringwood Hants

Dear Charles,

This is mostly to ask you if you could find out Dan's address for me. Tom, I suppose, knows it. I've been in London a lot since I saw you last, and meant to have a nostalgic re-union with Dan, but all I knew was that he lived in Sherwood Ho., Harrow, which didn't seem right. I'm going back to town at the end of next week, so could you let me have the address quickly? It would be very nice of you, and I'll leave you a sycamore tree in my will as soon as I've uprooted it from my wife's mother's garden. I miss our old meetings. Here, apart from Caitlin and a few very immediate people, there's no-one to talk to easily except Augustus J., who can't hear. Swansea is still the best place: tell Fred he's right.[2] When somebody else's ship comes home I'll set up in Swansea in a neat villa full of drinks and pianos and lawn-mowers and dumb-bells and canvases for all of us, and the villa shall be called Percy Villa. I have been writing quite a lot, being locked in a room every morning with beer & cigarettes and the implements of my trade. I've been lecturing, too, to classes of London University. My stories are appearing next month, under the title of 'The Burning Baby: 16 Stories', published by the Europa Press of Paris & London, and in 2 editions—a general one, and a limited signed one, dear me. And my next book will be that reversed version of Pilgrim's Progress, & will appear with the Obelisk Press, Paris.[3] Publicity over. Give my love to the boys—I can't write to them, because I don't know their numbers or roads—& when you write tell me how they are & what they're doing, & what you're doing and how you are. Don't forget the address, will you?

Love,
Dylan

MS: the recipient   *SL*

[1] Caitlin was fond of dancing, and would have liked to make it a career.
[2] Unless otherwise indicated, 'Fred' in a Thomas letter is always Alfred Janes, as 'Dan' is Daniel Jones, 'Tom' is Tom Warner and 'Vernon' Vernon Watkins.
[3] 'Prologue to an Adventure'. It was never more than a short story.

JAMES LAUGHLIN

James Laughlin (b. 1914, three days after Thomas), was the founding editor and president of New Directions Publishing Co. in the U.S., which in 1936 (to the alarm of his wealthy family) set out to publish avant-garde writers. Laughlin has also written poetry of his own. He remained Thomas's American publisher to the end.

15 February 1938   Blashford Ringwood Hants

Dear Mr. Laughlin,

Thank you for writing, and for offering to send me a copy of the last New Directions Collection, which I would very much appreciate. No, I haven't as yet an American publisher, but I have an agent here who is, I believe, in touch with one in connection with my two volumes of poems, 18 and 25. Next month a volume of my stories, 'The Burning Baby', is to be brought out by the Europa Press of London and Paris. Would you be interested in that volume for America? If so, do let me know when you send along the Collection. I have also a number of new poems that have appeared only in some English magazines, not in a book of mine. Would you care to see those? I should like to get them printed in America, but do not know what periodicals to send to.

Yours sincerely,
Dylan Thomas

MS: the recipient

DENYS KILHAM ROBERTS

26 February 1938 (Permission to anthologise two poems. See Appendix 11.)

HENRY TREECE

Poet and critic (1911–66), an enthusiastic exponent of the romantic 'Apocalyptic' movement, which was a muddled reaction against politics in poetry that developed towards the end of the 1930s. With J. F. Hendry (b. 1912) he edited *The White Horseman*, a collection published in 1941. His modest study of Thomas, *Dylan Thomas. 'Dog Among the Fairies'*, was not published until 1949.

[February or March 1938]   Blashford Ringwood Hants

Dear Mr. Treece,

Thank you for your letter. Reavey told me, when I was in town last month, that you were writing a book about my poetry, and that he believed a section of it had been printed; but he was vague about names and dates, and I had no means of getting in touch with you. I think the information actually surprised me more than it must have surprised Richard Church[1] who is, without due respect, a cliché-riddled humbug and pie-fingering hack, a man who has said to me, when I told him I was starving, that a genuine artist scorns monetary gain, and who later confessed, with a self-deprecatory shrug and a half-wishful smile that has brought tears to many a literary society, to a slight jealousy—'we're not so young as we were, you know'—of the vitality of modern youth. He thinks like a Sunday paper. I can see him telling you, with that pale, gentle, professional charmer's smile, placing together the tips of his thumb and index finger, as if to express some precise subtlety, 'It is perhaps just a *little* too early, don't you think?' If the information had been less surprising, I would have felt ashamed, it was not a thing I expected, then or ever; two small books of verse have never, to my knowledge, produced, in their writer's lifetime, a book of explanation and assessment by another writer, nor has such an adequately small reputation as mine needed an analysis of it to make it bigger. But this is not to say that I personally consider it inadvisable to write such a book as yours, and it would be unnatural of me not to be pleased and grateful. I am very much pleased, and I hope you *will* finish the book. Whether there is a place for it, and whether this is the time to place it, I can't be expected to know. I should think a publisher might be induced to take it, and I've no doubt that all the papers and magazines that have reviewed or discussed my books will take good notice of it; also a small book would be brought out cheaply, and a number of people, I should think, would get hold of it if only in order to attack the idea of such a book being written. That is, I don't quite mean that the idea of the book will be unpopular, but many of the Church-minded fogies will, with kindly condescension, 'regret' its appearance so early—I can hear them peep-peeping—in a young man's career. Will you send me a copy of the first chapter in the New English Weekly?[2] I'd be very grateful. I can't make any real, practical suggestions yet, for obvious reasons; but I should like to read some of what you've already done, and then, if you'd let me, I'd like to write at length. I could send you all the new work I have, and other sorts of material. And I'll see, of course, that you're sent a copy of my short-story book next month. Do write soon, as I will be changing my address. And do please understand that I myself think the book a grand idea, but that it should be continued only if *you* yourself, scorning the pooh-poohers and youth-talkers, the hedging ill-wishers and gassy jealous-mongers, think it interesting and advisable. It isn't for me to say anything but thank you, to promise you wholeheartedly all the assistance you may want of me, and to repeat my own belief in the eventual success of such a book:—(This,

---

[1] When Treece approached Church, the publisher suggested that a book-length study of Thomas might be premature.
[2] 28 October 1937, 'The Poetry of Dylan Thomas. An Assessment'.

again, is no more than natural conceit; my opinion as to the advisability of having a book written about my own work is bound to be too prejudiced to be of worth to you.) Best wishes, and

Yours sincerely,
Dylan Thomas

MS: Buffalo

JULIAN SYMONS
[March 1938]   Blashford Ringwood Hants

Dear Julian Symons,
   It's in order, isn't it, for my Poem (for Caitlin) to be printed in a Paris periodical? I want it to appear in the Booster, which hasn't any English circulation. I'll see, of course, that an acknowledgement is made.
   I've just been sent a couple of poems by Meurig Walters, & hear you've got some of his.[1] I do hope you'll be able to print one. I think they're very strong & original, don't you?

Yours,
Dylan Thomas

MS: Texas

MEURIG WALTERS[2]
March 10 1938   Blashford Ringwood Hants

Dear Meurig Walters,
   I only want to say how much I liked your 'Rhondda Poem' in the last number of 'Wales', and how very good I think it is. I wrote to Julian Symons, of '20th Century Verse', about it, asking him whether he'd seen it and, if so, didn't he agree that he should get in touch and ask you whether you'd contribute to his paper. And he told me he had some poems of yours already, and is going to print them soon. I'm looking forward to them with great interest.
   My admiration for that one poem and for all [that it?][3] promises, for its energy and roughness, its freedom from the traditional corruptions of 'taste' and 'beauty', and from that holy trinity of the English writer, memory, evocation, and nostalgia, is very genuine, and I just had to write

---

[1] See next letter.
[2] Meurig Walters (b. 1915) was at theological college when he wrote 'Rhondda Poem', and has spent most of his life as a Presbyterian minister.
[3] The page is badly creased.

and 'congratulate' you—a word I do not really like using—on the liveliest contribution that has appeared in 'Wales' and one that proves yet again its indispensable function.

Sincerely,
Dylan Thomas

MS: National Library of Wales

GEORGE REAVEY
14 March [1938]   Blashford Ringwood Hants

Dear George,
  Keidrych Rhys tells me you've sent him circulars about the book. What about sending me a few to post around? Did you get my last note? Have you got in touch with John?

Yours,
Dylan T

MS: Harvard

CHARLES FISHER
March 16 '38   Blashford Ringwood Hants

I'm very busy writing, & I'd like to
send you my new poem when it's
finished—next week. Send me
something you've done.

Dear Charles,
  Thank you for the news, and the address, and the fact that you all miss me a bit. I've been in London, but only for a short time, and couldn't get in touch with Dan. And since I returned I've been very busy failing to make money. I may get a job on the BBC: it all depends on the BBC. It was nice to hear of your play, and Fred's fishes, and Tom's sonata. You talk, by the way, about Ifor Davies as though I knew him. I don't. Wish him a symphony for me. Murder of the King's Canary: I'd very much like to do it with you because I've got lots of new ideas which I'm too lazy to tell you at the moment. Will it go as a radio play? I'd like to make it, with you, into a novel, make it the detective story to end detective stories, introduce blatantly every character & situation—inevitable Chinaman, secret passages etc—that no respectable writer would dare use now, drag hundreds of red herrings, false clues, withheld evidences into the story, falsify every issue, make many chapters deliberate parodies, full of

clichés, of other detective-writers. It could be the best fun, & would make us drinking-money for a year. Write some time & tell me how you feel about it; I hope to be somewhere about Swansea in the early summer, and we can discuss it properly then.[1]

Love to all the boys, & to yourself.

Dylan

MS: the recipient

DESMOND HAWKINS
March 16 1938   Blashford Ringwood Hants

Dear Desmond,

It was very very nice to hear from you, and very wicked of me not to have congratulated you on your safe delivery. I have just been reading a book by Dr. Carlos Wms, D.D., B.O., full of medical details, and I know what you must have suffered. In your sweet mirth, as T. E. Brown says in my favourite poem, God spied occasion for a birth;[2] and who knows what little Hitler rocks dreamily at your feet as you, at your littered desk, sit destroying a reputation with one critical hand and tossing off your Grigson-pipe with the other.[3].

The poem that was meant for your stupendous number—there isn't, I suppose, a spare copy?—died, twisted in its mysteries and I am trying now to bury it in another poem which, when completed, I shall send to you along with a photograph of Caitlin and myself breeding a Welsh Rimbaud on a bed of old purposes and new directions.

Answering your questions:

The Europa press belongs to George Reavey, that sandy, bandy, polite, lockjawed, French-lettered, i-dotted, Russian t'd, non-committal, B.A.'d, V.D.'d, mock-barmy, smarmy, chance-his-army tick of a piddling crook who lives in his own armpit. He diddled and swindled me, the awful man; I will get him to send you a review copy, *and* a photograph of his headquarters if he isn't sitting on them.

I am staying here charitably until next week when we go to London again with a pick and axe for the gold pavements. I am working busily on

[1] Fisher had succeeded Desmond Hawkins as the *Canary* collaborator.
[2] Thomas is mocking the schoolmaster poet T. E. Brown (1830–97), chiefly remembered for the poem that begins, 'A garden is a lovesome thing, God wot!'. The poem Thomas quotes is 'Between Our Folding Lips':—
    '. . . We love, God makes: in our sweet mirth
    God spies occasion for a birth.
    Then is it His, or is it ours?
    I know not—He is fond of flowers.'
[3] Desmond Hawkins thinks that this obscure joke may have had something to do with Geoffrey Grigson's alleged dislike of pipe-smoking. But 'tossing off' means masturbation.

some new stories; I want to write a whole lot like that one you liked about Grandpa, stories of Swansea and me.[1] I don't, by the way, think that that story is better than the one in the Faber book, or than others in my Europa mistake:[2] these stories are more than 'free fantasy': they do mean a lot and are full of work.

Croquet is over; it's all shovehalfpenny & skittling squirearchy now; we've a rolling road here & an old inn and a wind on the heath. To heel, to hounds, to hell.

Do you ever see the little quarterly, 'Wales'? There's good writing in it. You might drop it a poem, care of me; it prints those English outsiders as well; and it pays nothing, on publication.

Shall we ever see you in London? Perhaps, later, when your moving's over, you'll invite us for a week-end? We are quite good, and hate babies.

Write soon; I'll send you a pretty poem.

Love,
Dylan

MS: the recipient

ROLAND PENROSE[3]
21 March 1938   Blashford Ringwood Hants

Dear Roland,

Of course you may count on my support, and I'll send you a story or a poem when it's needed. I don't, I suppose, get paid for a contribution? That sounds extremely mean, but I write so slowly and produce so little that it's essential—considering the fact that I try, though always without success, to exist on my writing—I have a little money for anything of mine that is published. I really am in a very bad, distressing position now, living on charity, unable to buy for myself even the smallest necessary luxuries, and having little peace of mind from those most small and nagging worries to work as well and carefully as I should like. I may have to stop writing altogether very soon—for writing is obviously full-time or not at all—and try to obtain some little, sure work. I'm sorry to write as meanly and wretchedly as this, but the way in which I'm forced to live has begun to colour everything. But, of course, if the Gallery Bulletin[4]

---

[1] 'A Visit to Grandpa's' had just appeared in the *New English Weekly*, of which Hawkins was now literary editor. It was the first of ten stories, conceived as a book (eventually *Portrait of the Artist As A Young Dog*) and written in 1938 and 1939. Thomas saw it as 'a provincial autobiography'.

[2] The projected 'Burning Baby' book.

[3] Sir Roland Penrose (1900–84), authority on art; in 1938 a surrealist painter.

[4] The magazine of the English surrealists.

can't pay, I'll still be very pleased to send you a poem or some prose. Best wishes,

Yours ever,
Dylan T

TS: *Thomas Trustees*

VERNON WATKINS
[postmarked 21st March 1938]   Blashford Ringwood Hants

Dear Vernon,
    Many thanks for your letter, and for the poems before. We are not going to Ireland, and we will try to be in Gower some time in the summer. The reason I haven't written for such a time is not because I found nothing to say about your new poems, but because I have been in London, in penury, and in doubt: In London, because money lives and breeds there; in penury, because it doesn't; and in doubt as to whether I should continue as an outlaw or take my fate for a walk in the straight and bowler-treed paths. The conceit of outlaws is a wonderful thing; they think they can join the ranks of regularly-conducted society whenever they like. You hear young artists talk glibly about, 'God, I've a good mind to chuck this perilous, unsatisfactory, moniless business of art and go into the City & make money'. But who wants them in the City? If you are a money-&-success-maker, you make it in whatever you do. And young artists are always annoyed and indignant if they hear a City-man say, 'God, I've a good mind to chuck this safe, monotonous business of money-making & go into the wilderness and make poems'.
    Poems. I liked the three you sent me. There is something very unsatisfactory, though, about 'All mists, all thoughts' which seems—using the vaguest words—to lack a central strength. All the words are lovely, but they seem so *chosen*, not struck out. I can see the sensitive picking of words, but none of the strong, inevitable pulling that makes a poem an event, a happening, an action perhaps, not a still-life or an experience *put down*, placed, regulated; the introduction of mist, legend, time's weir, grief's bell, & such things as 'which held, but knew not her', the whole of the 13th line, 'all griefs that we suppose', seem to me 'literary', not living. They seem, as indeed the whole poem seems, to come out of the nostalgia of literature; the growth is not, like, say, Rossetti's, a hothouse growth, but one that has been seeded from a flower placed, long ago in the smelling and blowing and growing past, between pages. A motive has been rarefied; it should be made common. I don't ask you for vulgarity, though I miss it; I think I ask you for a little creative destruction, destructive creation: 'I build a flying tower, and I pull it down'. Neither—a phrase we used once, do you remember?—could I call this an

'indoor' poem; one doesn't need the sun in a poem to make it hot. But—though this [is] silly—it is a poem so obviously written in words; I want my sentimental blood: not Roy Campbell's blood, which is a red & noisy adjective in a transparent vein, but the blood of leaves, wells, weirs, fonts, shells, echoes, rainbows, olives, bells, oracles, sorrows. Of course I can't explain my feelings about the poem, except, sentimentally speaking again, to say that I want a poem to do more than just to have the appearance of 'having been created'. I think, of the poem, that the words are chosen, & then lie down contented with your choice.

'Was that a grief' has a lot more vulgarity in it, breaches of the nostalgic etiquette. There are, too, I think, stalenesses: 'a later threnody', 'in the years to be'; awkwardnesses: 'Next from blood's side, with poppy's nonchalance'; weaknesses: 'Their fingers frail as tendrils of light's flower'. Stale, because the words come, not quite without thinking, but without fresh imagining: down they go, the germ of what you want & what is yours ready-folded in a phrase not yours and that you don't need. The awkwardness of 'poppy's nonchalance' is obvious: it sounds like a man with a lisp & a stutter trying to gargle. And weak, because that particular alliterative line is too easily-taken, a 'breather-between' energies. But I like the poem greatly, your 'grand lines' in the 4th verse are as grand as they could be. And all of it has your own peculiar power of minute concentration: the immense, momentous scrawl on the leaf.[1]

I've always liked your ballads very much, & so far—inevitably—the ballads & lyrics mean more to me than the long & complicated poems. Will you let me send the Collier ballad to Robert Herring?

Here are 4 poems, two short simple ones, done fairly quickly, a conventional sonnet, and one I have spent a great deal of time on.[2] The typewriter I generally use has been taken from me. Could you type these out for me? I very much want to send them away some-time at the end of this week and sell them for a mouse's ransom.

I haven't finished the World story[3] yet, but I'm working on a series of short, straightforward stories about Swansea. One has been finished & published, & I'll send you a copy when I have one: which will [be] in a few days.

Don't be too harsh to these poems until they're typed; I always think typescript lends some sort of certainty: at least, if the things are bad then, they appear to be bad with conviction; in ordinary mss. they look as though they might be altered at any moment.

---

[1] The Watkins poems that Thomas is discussing were later published with the titles 'Call It All Names, But Do Not Call It Rest', 'The Windows' and 'The Collier'.

[2] 'O make me a mask', 'Not from this anger', the first part of 'After the funeral' and 'How shall my animal'.

[3] According to Watkins, 'In the Direction of the Beginning'. This ornate piece in Thomas's 'prose-poem' style consists of a single very long paragraph and was published in the magazine *Wales*, March 1938, as 'fragment of a work in progress'. But Thomas got on with his autobiographical stories and left the other unfinished.

Write soon & send a poem.

Love,
Dylan

P.S. About 'blowing' light in the last verse.[1] Can you think of anything better? Do try.

MS: British Library   *VW*

HENRY TREECE
23 3 38   Blashford Ringwood Hants

Dear Henry Treece,

I wanted to write as soon as I had your long, explanatory letter and the first chapter of the book, but I suddenly became very busy trying to make enough money to let me be busy in peace. Now, having failed utterly to rake in or stave off, surrounded by the noises of disruption and ejection, at last and again on the doorstep, facing a butterless future, I can reply to you at ease.

Do you, I wonder and hope not, know what it is to live outlegally on the extreme fringe of society, to bear all the responsibilities of possessionlessness—which are more and heavier than is thought, for great demands are made of the parasite, and charity, though soon enough you can learn to slip it on with a pathetic feeling of comfort, is a mountain to take—and to live from your neighbour's hand to your mouth? I have achieved poverty with distinction, but never poverty with dignity; the best I can manage is dignity with poverty, and I would sooner smarm like a fart-licking spaniel than starve in a world of fat bones. A poem, obviously, cannot be begun with the strength and singlemindedness it demands and deserves unless there is enough money behind it to assure its completion: by the second verse the writer, old-fashioned fool, may need food and drink. I know I will be paid—and how well, how well—for a poem when it is finished; but I do not know how I am going to live until it *is* finished. If I am going to live on writing any longer, I shall have to give up living; or write in a vacuum. Now I go without cigarettes, the tubular, white ants, in a smoking, swarming country. I feel in the position of the professor who was seen far out in the sea, spluttering, struggling, waving his arms and crying, 'I'm thinking, I'm thinking'. People on the beach, who knew he was always thinking, did nothing; and he sank.

Yes, I have seen my poetry called 'considerable' and 'important', and so it is to me. I am not really modest at all, because, putting little trust in most of the poetry being written today, I put a great deal in mine. Today the Brotherhood of Man—love thy neighbour and, if possible, covet his

---

[1] In *CP*, the penultimate line of 'How shall my animal' is 'You have kicked from a dark den, leaped up the whinnying light'.

arse—seems a disappointing school-society, and I cannot accept Auden as head-prefect. I think MacNeice[1] is thin and conventionally-minded, lacking imagination, and not sound in the ear; flop Day-Lewis;[2] and Spender, Rupert Brooke of the Depression,[3] condemns his slight, lyrical, nostalgic talent to a clumsy and rhetorical death; I find his communism unreal: before a poet can get into contact with society he must, surely, be able to get into contact with himself, and Spender has only tickled his own outside with a feather. And who is there? George Barker,[4] perhaps, with his hysterical persecutions and after-midnight revulsions? Gascoyne, with his Man's Life Is This Meat, and needing a new butcher, with his lobster on a bald head and his indigestible Dreams of Isis and peachmelbas? You mention Cameron and Madge.[5] Cameron's verse has no greater admirer than myself, and I respect Madge's verse, though with complete lack of affection. But when you say that I have not Cameron's or Madge's 'concentric movement round a central image', you are not accounting for the fact that it consciously is not my method to move concentrically round a central image. A poem by Cameron *needs* no more than one image; it moves around one idea, from one logical point to another, making a full circle. A poem by myself *needs* a host of images, because its centre is a host of images. I make one image,—though 'make' is not the word, I let, perhaps, an image be 'made' emotionally in me and then apply to it what intellectual & critical forces I possess—let it breed another, let that image contradict the first, make, of the third image bred out of the other two together, a fourth contradictory image, and let them all, within my imposed formal limits, conflict. Each image holds within it the seed of its own destruction, and my dialectical method, as I understand it, is a constant building up and breaking down of the images that come out of the central seed, which is itself destructive and constructive at the same time.

Reading back over that, I agree it looks preciously like nonsense. To say that I 'let' my images breed and conflict is to deny my critical part in the business. But what I want to try to explain—and it's necessarily vague to me—is that the *life* in any poem of mine cannot move concentrically round a central image; the life must come out of the centre; an image must be born and die in another; and any sequence of my images must be a sequence of creations, recreations, destructions, contradictions. I cannot, either—as Cameron does, and as others do, and this primarily explains his and their writing round the central image—make a poem out of a single, motivating experience; I believe in the single thread of action through a poem, but that is an intellectual thing aimed at lucidity through narrative. My object is, as you say, conventionally to 'get things

[1] Louis MacNeice (1907–63), poet and radio playwright. Thomas invariably wrote 'Macneice'.
[2] Cecil Day-Lewis (1904–72), poet and novelist.
[3] Norman Cameron is said to have coined the phrase.
[4] George Barker (b. 1913), poet and author.
[5] Charles Madge (b. 1912), poet and sociologist.

straight'. Out of the inevitable conflict of images—inevitable, because of the creative, recreative, destructive, and contradictory nature of the motivating centre, the womb of war—I try to make that momentary peace which is a poem. I do not want a poem of mine to be, nor can it be, a circular piece of experience placed neatly outside the living stream of time from which it came; a poem of mine is, or should be, a watertight section of the stream that is flowing all ways; all warring images within it should be reconciled for that small stop of time. I agree that each of my earlier poems might appear to constitute a section from one long poem; that is because I was not successful in making a momentary peace with my images at the correct moment; images were left dangling over the formal limits, and dragged the poem into another; the warring stream ran on over the insecure barriers, the fullstop armistice was pulled & twisted raggedly on into a conflicting series of dots and dashes.

All this, of course, is not a comment on your chapter, but only a most unsuccessful attempt, again, at 'getting things straight' for myself. As for helpful comments, I'm afraid I have none. I shall be very interested to read your chapter on Hopkins's influence, because I have read him only in the most lackadaisical way; I certainly haven't studied him, or, I regret, any other poet. The comparison with the Surrealists should give you a lot of scope, especially if, as I'm sure you do, you think it little more than a highbrow parlour game. I haven't, by the way, ever read a proper surrealist poem, one, that is, in French from the Breton boys. I've seen some translations by Gascoyne, but they were worthless.

Before I forget: New Directions, America, is going to publish both my books of verse and my book of stories, and also the long story I have been working on lately.[1] It's the intention of New Directions to 'build' me in America; advanced writing apparently sells very well over there, they're such culture-snobs; and I should think that, in some little time, the end of this year perhaps after my books are published, there would be no difficulty at all in finding a small, snob publisher to do your book: it could later be done in England. I really think it would be more successful, to begin with, brought out that way.

I want to send you the dozen or so new poems I've written and a bundle of reviews, but I will have to wait until they are forwarded to me from my last lodgings. Here, however, is one very new poem, which I consider—at the moment—to be more satisfactory as a whole than anything I've done. I hope you can understand the handwriting, I've no typewriter.

I'm sorry I can't suggest anything; if I do think of anything helpful I'll write it down and send it to you immediately; and the other manuscripts won't, I hope, be long coming. My book of stories has been delayed, owing to the printers turning shy and calling certain paragraphs obscene; I

---

[1] The first New Directions book of Thomas's writings was published in 1939. In 1938 *New Directions in Poetry and Prose*, an annual anthology edited by Laughlin, published the 'In the Direction of the Beginning' fragment.

understand new printers now have it in hand, and it is to appear on the
1st of April. I'll send you a copy, of course.

I have, suddenly, thought of a very little something, but it is a point,
probably, that you have touched on, or are going to touch on, incidentally:
the question of religion and the supernatural in my poetry. I know there is
something I should like to write you about those questions: shall I?

I am sorry not to be able to stamp this letter. My wife and I are here
completely alone, and have no food and no money at all. Neither shall we
have any until the end of next month. Until then, quite honestly, we
starve. That is easy to write, but all the world's hells to know.

Yours very sincerely,

Dylan Thomas   SL(R)

MS: Buffalo

HENRY TREECE

[?late March 1938]   Blashford Ringwood Hants

Dear Henry Treece,

This is to thank you, deeply, for your presents; for I shan't regard them as
anything else. I, too, will send you a present one day, and may you welcome
it as gratefully as I did yours. The cigarettes tasted better than any I've ever
had; I am, by preference, a chainsmoker, though usually all the links are
missing. I am not hurt, I do not lift the nose, nor call you Boy Scout: Thank
you very much for sending me two such very nice things; and I am grateful
to you always. (It is more than a romantic fallacy to say that only a garret-
poet can produce the immortal line; it's a realistic lie. One can write on bare
nerves, but not on an empty stomach; the 'impulse' of a poet is not affected
by hunger & squalor, but the 'craft' needs time and concentration which a
man nagged by hunger cannot afford to give it.)

I'll write *very* soon with, if possible, more suggestions & mss. Please
don't bother to return anything I send you. Do you want the chapter
back?

This is only a note of thanks, but the word is not 'only'.

Sincerely,

Dylan T   SL

MS: Texas

JAMES LAUGHLIN

March 28 1938   Blashford Ringwood Hants

Dear Mr. Laughlin,

Thank you for writing, and for sending me the books; they interested
me very much indeed, and I thought they were splendidly produced. I
appreciate deeply the kind things you said about my work. I have, of
course, no hesitation at all in accepting your offer of American
publication, and in letting you have not only the books I have published

in England but also the books that I am writing and shall write in the future. I should like you, that is, to be my American publisher for good and all.

About the books of mine that have been printed over here: my first, 'Eighteen Poems', which had a considerable success in its way, was brought out by the Parton Press; the copyright is mine, and you can have the book whenever you like. (Details about sheets—and some, I think, may have been printed already, in preparation—can be gone into later, can't they?)

My second book, 'Twenty Five Poems', was published by J. M. Dent. I did not, by the way, know I had any American agents; in fact, I have not, and I have never heard of Ann Watkins Inc. The agent in England who handled my 'Twenty Five Poems' was David Higham, of Higham, Pollinger, and Pearn, 6 Norfolk St, Strand, London; Watkins Inc. *may* do their work in America; I just don't know.[1] Neither have I heard from Watkins Inc. about your publication terms. Will you get in touch with Higham? I am writing to him by this post. I am quite sure there will be no possible difficulty in getting them to arrange for you the American rights, etc. of the Dent-published book. Dent has not, of course, any claim to the American copyright; my contract with them is for the British Empire alone.

My third book, 'The Burning Baby: Sixteen Stories', will appear on the first of May—it should have appeared sooner, but there was some un-avoidable delay owing to the printers turning shy of some particularly harmless passages—from the Europa Press.[2] I have already written to George Reavey, of that Press, telling him to correspond with you immediately, and suggesting to him, as you said in your letter, that he should, right away, print 500 sheets for you. That matter should be easily settled. Reavey's address is: Europa Press, 7 Great Ormond St, London W.C.1.

Now comes the most difficult, and to me the most desperately im-portant, part of this letter. I must say, straight away, that I *must* have some money, and have it immediately. I live entirely by my writing; it can be printed only in a small number of advanced periodicals, and they pay next to nothing, usually nothing. I was married recently—against all sense, but with all happiness, which is obviously more sensible—and we are completely penniless. I do not mean that we just live poorly; I mean that we go without food, without proper clothes, have shelter on charity, and very very soon will not have even that shelter. I have now less than a shilling; there is no more to come; we have nothing to sell, nothing to fall back upon. If I can be tided over for a little time, I think I will be able to work hard enough to produce poems and stories that will provide some kind of food and shelter. If not, there is no hope at all. I apologise for this recital, but every one of my hopes is based on the possibility that New Directions may be able to give me an advance on royalties: on royalties, perhaps, for books to come as well as for the books already published and

[1] Ann Watkins & Co, a New York agency associated with Pearn, Pollinger and Higham.
[2] The printer decided the text was obscene. See page 303.

which are, apart from certain arrangements, outside my province, with Reavey and my agent Higham, already yours. I will, of course, sign a contract with you stating that *all* my books, past, present, and future, are to be published by you—if you want them—in America. If New Directions cannot see its way clear—and it's all extremely irregular, I know, and must be very annoying to you—to give me an advance on royalties now, before even the books have been published in America, I am more than willing to dispense with my future royalties and take whatever sum you can give me for the complete American copyright of all books I shall write. For what I need now, and more urgently than I can tell you, is money to continue living. And, unfortunately, money *at once*: that is the important thing. I hope to finish a long prose work soon, perhaps next month—that is, if I can procure lodgings and buy necessities, for we must leave this address the moment we can buy a railway ticket to anywhere —and have it published in London in the autumn. That book, too, I can deliver, and will deliver, to you quickly as some further exchange for the advance I hope to the lord you will be able to forward me when you receive this letter, this unavoidably miserable letter for which I again apologise. I had hoped to write all this in a businesslike manner, but I failed. I failed because, although I know nothing about the business of publishing or the agreements that can be made between publisher and author, I know enough to realise that my most sincere appeal for an immediate advance on the work you wish to publish is unorthodox and, possibly, insolent. I am sorry I had to write this, but I am forced to do away with dignity and formality, and ask you this question: Can you, at once, give me money for which, in return, I promise you all the work I have done and will do? I wish very much to be published by you. I hope, beyond all things, that you will answer me. I'll try to make my next letter to you a less wretched affair than this.

Yours very sincerely,
Dylan Thomas

MS: the recipient   *SL*

MEURIG WALTERS
28 March 1938   Blashford Ringwood Hants

Dear Meurig Walters,
   I was glad to hear from you that you were glad to hear from me; it was kind of you to talk so kindly about my letter which was, after all, the very smallest tribute I could pay to a poem that immediately struck me as one of the most original I had read for a long time; and it was encouraging to me to know that my encouragement to you was not misinterpreted as an act of senile condescension but taken simply for what it was: the congratulations and best wishes of one young man who writes a lot of poetry to another young man who writes little—on his own statement—but who is going, I hope, to write a lot more.

Glyn Jones—I haven't seen him for 2 years—was biographically correct: I am 23, married, from Swansea, and without property. I have been living out of Wales now for about a year, but not through choice; I hope at Easter to be somewhere near Swansea. We must arrange to meet.

I have just written to Keidrych Rhys suggesting that a mass-poem — though that's an ugly name—should be written by all the contributors to 'Wales'. That is, that each person should write a verse-report of his own particular town, village, or district, and that all the reports, gathered together, should be made, not by alteration but by arrangement, into one long poem. The poem would be called Wales, & wd take a whole number of the paper. The poem would be written by *all* the writers concerned, & not by individuals. If the idea comes to anything, I hope you will take charge of the Rhondda report.[1]

Please do write again. I shall be very glad to see any poems of yours, new or old.

Sincerely,
Dylan Thomas

MS: National Library of Wales

MERVYN PEAKE[2]
[?March 1938][3]   Blashford Ringwood Hants

Dear Mervyn:

Do excuse this delay: my addresses are in a muddle, as always, and I never know what charitable home I may be trying to park myself in next. I hope your show went well, and I wish very much I could have seen it: I saw some splendid notices. Nothing we planned seems to have gone right, that visit to Wales for instance, and it is all my fault; I feel I can't go on with the idea of a Welsh travel book; for one thing, Rhys Davies has just done it, and a feeble job it was.[4] But I'm trying to do a series of stories about Welsh people,[5] and I'd like to show you one or two of them when we can get together in London—which I hope will be very soon—for you to see if you could, or would like to, do anything about drawings for them some time.

And the crazy book, yes, yes, of course. I *do* wish I could have seen the new drawings. I'm looking forward a lot to getting down to that book — though, now, I have no idea of what the story would be. Have you?

[1] The Mass-Observation movement, described at the time as 'a technique for obtaining objective statements about human behaviour', had a bizarre offshoot in attempts to write poetry by committee. Charles Madge, a founder of M-O in 1937, organised the 'Oxford Collective Poem', which took twelve undergraduates a month to research and write. *New Verse* published it in May 1937. *Wales*'s reply was never written.

[2] Mervyn Peake (1911–68), writer and painter.

[3] Peake's 'show', referred to in the letter, was an exhibition of line drawings at the Calmann Gallery. Maeve Gilmore, then married to Peake, wrote in *A World Away* (1970) that, on the day of the private view, 'Hitler marched into, oh God, was it Czechoslovakia? or was it Vienna?' Only Austria was properly invaded in 1938. Hitler entered Vienna on 13 March.

[4] Rhys Davies (1903–78), novelist, published the descriptive *My Wales* in 1937.

[5] *Portrait of the Artist as a Young Dog.*

And have you seen a little quarterly called 'Wales' that prints poems & stories, fairly experimental, by Welsh people writing in English? Have you got a poem you could send me for it: I'm a kind of literary adviser to the thing. I hope you have.

I'll ring you as soon as I get to town.

Yours,

MS: *University College, London*   Dylan

VERNON WATKINS
April 1 38   [Blashford]

Dear V:

The mouse is released, the cheesy bandits have nibbled off, there are squeaks of jubilation, and whiskers glint in the sun. Thank you very much indeed for the present; it came when we had no tubular white ants to smoke, when we needed them passionately; now we've got antheaps, and this evening we go to the pictures, and your closeup shall be brighter than any.

I liked your two words, and am keeping both. I'm as sure now as you are of the 'lionhead', and 'whinnying' is certainly far better than my word and may—I am coming to think it is—be the best.[1] I'm so glad you liked the poem, I had worked on it for months. The opossums are unsatisfactory, I know.[2] Before your letter came, I had cut out the ubiquitous 'weather' from the anticlimatic poem, and am revising it all; I will conquer 'rebellion in'; and 'eyed' tongue shall, momentarily, become 'lashed'.[3] The poem in memory of Anne Jones[4] I am completely rewriting; and again the 'weather' shall drop out: I'm making it longer and, I hope, better than any of my recent simple poems.

In one thing you are still wrong: 'poppy's nonchalance' is bad; it cannot be anything *but* bad; and I refute *your* criticism from the bottom of my catarrh. 'In the years to be' should, of course, stand; I was silly, and perhaps priggish, to call it a catchphrase; there is no reason why it shouldn't be and no reason that you should not revitalize it if it were; I've got one of those very youthfully-made phrases, too, that often comes to my mind & which one day I shall use: 'When I woke, the dawn spoke'.[5] You are right to write poems of all kinds; I only write poems of allsorts, and, like the liquorice sweets, they all taste the same.

---

[1] In *CP*, 'lionhead' occurs in 'How shall my animal' ('That melts the lionhead's heel'), as does 'whinnying'; see postscript and note, page 280.
[2] Watkins had referred to the one long and three shorter poems sent by Thomas (letter postmarked March 21) as an 'opus' and three 'opossums'.
[3] In *CP*, 'O make me a mask' has 'The bayonet tongue'. But the words 'rebellion in' were not changed.
[4] 'After the funeral.'
[5] A later poem by Thomas begins, 'When I woke, the town spoke'.

I've just read a poem in an American paper, that I think's very good:
Evening Prayer:
[*by Robert Fitzgerald, later collected in* In the Rose of Time. *Omitted here*].
I'm looking forward very much to seeing you.
And thanks again,

Love, Dylan & Caitlin

MS: British Library   *VW*

VERNON WATKINS
[?April 1938]   Blashford Ringwood Hants

Dear Vernon,
In haste. Thank you for the letter & the revised poem; I shall write
tomorrow evening—so that perhaps our letters cross—about this & the
Broken Net. Now here is the Anne Jones poem, & now I think it is more
of a poem; will you type it for me?[1] I knew it was feeble as it stood before,
& the end of it—that is the part that becomes the new brackets—was too
facile &, almost, grandiosely sentimental. (By the way, when you type it,
will you spell Anne as Ann: I just remember that's the right way: she was
an ancient peasant aunt.) I think there are some good lines, but don't
know abt the thing as a whole.
News—I have a little—& criticisms etc in tomorrow's long letter. You
don't mind typing for me, do you? I'm looking forward to what you say
about the poem. But—again—don't read it till it's typed.
The 38th line may seem weak, but I think I wanted it like that.
Anyway. . . .

Love to you

MS: British Library   Dylan   *VW*

GEORGE REAVEY
Sunday [early April 1938]   Blashford Ringwood Hants

Dear George,
About the American negotiating: James Laughlin IV, of New Directions, wrote to me last week; he wants to be my publisher in America,
and do all my future books as well. I'm going to sign a contract with him
some time. But about the 'Burning Baby': Laughlin had heard that the
Europa Press was doing it, & asked me to suggest to you right away that
you consider printing 500 sheets for him. Laughlin was leaving America
last week, & can be got hold of c/o American Express Co. Paris. I think,
don't you, it's a good idea to get done by 'New Directions'? They've

---

[1] 'Broken Net' was a Watkins poem. 'Ann(e) Jones', i.e. 'After the Funeral', was nearing its
final form.

published Cocteau, Miller, Stein, Saroyan etc., & make nice books. (Laughlin sd he wanted to get in touch with the Europa Press quickly; he wants to bring out *a* book of mine this year.) In the event of New Directions doing the 'Burning Baby', I get, don't I—and that, for me, is the most important thing, because I am penniless—a separate advance royalty from them? I'm going to, anyway: I just have to.

I hope there's not going to be too much complication about getting the John portrait; I know it's in his London studio, but he's terribly careless. I suppose, if the worst comes, the book can come out quite well without him.[1] I shall probably be seeing him in a few days, & I'll try to get things straight then: but I know that he's going to leave all the business of photographing, block-making etc. to you.

Film rights? Yes, of course you can handle them for me, but, Christ, how could *those* stories be filmed? Shirley Temple as the Burning Baby? Don't forget the Laughlin.

Yours,
Dylan

MS: Harvard

RICHARD HUGHES
[?April 1938]   Blashford Ringwood Hants

Dear Richard Hughes,
    Caitlin and I are spending Easter in Wales, and some time of it near Llanstephan. Will you be at Laugharne then? And if so, may we call and see you?
    We are hoping very much to rent a cottage for the summer, somewhere in Carmarthenshire. Do you know of any likely places cheap enough for us? If you do happen to know of anywhere, or know anyone who might know, we'd be very grateful if you'd tell us, when—as we hope—we can meet you again.

Sincerely,
Dylan Thomas

MS: Indiana

GEORGE REAVEY
[?April 1938]   Blashford Ringwood Hants

Dear George,
    Sorry not to have written before. I've been away, and neither did I know about the A. John portrait. The very good one he did, like a bloody fool he burnt while drying it in front of the fire for a final sitting, and he's only just finished another one. He's taking it with him to London today. His address is: Park Studio, Pelham St, South Kensington. He will have a good man he knows to photograph it, but knows nothing about how to get a

---

[1] Augustus John's painting was eventually used for *The Map of Love*.

block made. Will you get in touch with him about it? He'll autograph 50 copies. What sort of blurb do you want me to do? Is it necessary to have a blurb at all? Wouldn't just, 'This is the first collection of prose by D.T.' do as well as anything? I don't like the usual sort of inadequate and mis-leading summary that appears; I myself am obviously not going to write a eulogy; and it isn't for me to write any sort of critical preface. I'd much prefer the stories to speak for themselves. You asked about reviewers. The papers that have noticed my work at length have been New Statesman (Stonier), New English Weekly, Times Lit Sup, Observer (Henry Warren), Criterion, Time and Tide, Spectator, Western Mail, Cardiff, South Wales Evening Post, Listener, Telegraph, Life and Letters, all of whom should obviously be sent review copies. But I suppose you know all about that. Anyway, do send some to Welsh papers too. Oh yes, and to Seamus O'Sullivan of the Dublin Review: that's got a good circulation I think. I can't think of any more names; actually, the list I gave you was of people who might be persuaded to buy the limited edition. Henry Miller wants a copy, and says he'll show it to lots of people and try to make them buy it: but I wouldn't know about that.

You wanted excerpts from reviews. Here are some. There are lots more but I haven't got them. Perhaps you can find some knocking about in old papers. Do write to me soon and tell me how things are progressing.

Yours,
Dylan

MS: Texas

GEORGE BARKER
4th April [1938?]   Marston Bishopston Glamorgan

Dear Barker,
  It was nice to get your letter. For some reason we never seem to have met—I saw you in Archer's once, and at a boozy party—but I hope we'll be able to when we're both in London. I hardly know any verse-writers at all; I know the one who looks as if he'd had an unfortunate sexual experience under the sea; and the one with little red pig eyes and a private income; and Norman Cameron and Desmond Hawkins of whom I'm very fond. But all my friends are failures, I think the glories of the world are mingy, and the people I know and like best—hack Fleet streeters, assistant assistant film-producers, professional drunks, strays and out-laws, who are always, & always will be, just about to write their auto-biographies—are too big to want them or to get them. I'm only saying this, in a first letter to you, because I liked very much the idea of an exchange of verse epistles between us, and I think it would be amusing to begin by talking about ourselves and our friends. Who'll start? I wish *you*

would: an epistle about where you live, what you do, all the why's, objects & near people. And what about the form? Wouldn't it, don't you think, be best for us both to use the same form, blank verse or some variety of stanza? I can see a lot of good, pleasant things coming out of this. We might publish them? Anyway, do write & tell me things, tell me whether *you'll* start the exchange. I go away walking tomorrow, but your letter will be forwarded from this address. And I'll be in town in June.

Best wishes,
Dylan Thomas

MS: Texas

JAMES LAUGHLIN
April 25 1938   Marston Bishopston Glamorgan South Wales

Dear Laughlin,
   Have you heard yet from the Europa Press? Reavey has not written to me. He is probably in Paris, being tasteful, noncommittal, and useless.
   I hope next month to be able to move to a cottage in a Welsh fishermen's village. It will be completely peaceful there, and I should be able to work without these bloody nagging worries that make any sort of concentration impossible. But of course my moving there, and my living & working, depends on what money I can scrape up, or have scraped up for me. I do hope to God that you can keep to your promise of sending me some, soon, early in May. I'm reckoning entirely on it. The rent for the cottage is nearly a pound a week, that is, nearly 5 dollars. Food is cheap there, & we'll be able, I hope, to buy enough. But the rent, without your help, is right out of our reach. I'm sorry to have to rely on you so much, especially as you've had no work of mine yet; but, as you know, you can have all I'll do; & I *must* be paid immediately for it: some advance, I mean. It's a pity I've got to write to you like this.
   When you write, do tell me when you are arriving in London. I should very much like to be there to meet you; actually it's rather important that we should meet for arrangements etc. But now all that matters to me is moving to that little village & trying to live there.
   Henry Miller, himself a poor chap, is getting some of my new prose printed in France, but I shall make nothing out of it.[1]

---

[1] The Parisian *Delta*, under Lawrence Durrell, published 'Prologue to an Adventure' in the Christmas 1938 issue.

I hope I'll be hearing from you very soon.

Sincerely   (& with apologies
for all this money talk; but it *is*
urgent, & I do hope as heartily as
you do that steel begins to boom)

Dylan Thomas

MS: *the recipient*

MEURIG WALTERS
26th April 1938   Marston Bishopston near Swansea Glam

Dear Meurig Walters,
     Thank you for the letter and the poems. I want to write a long letter
about it and them, but this is only a hasty note. I've just arrived here, and
I shall stay until May 1st. Then I'm going to Laugharne—do you know it?
It's between Pendine and St. Clears, ten miles or more from Carmarthen
—for the summer. I wonder when we could meet. I can't come to the
Rhondda, I'm afraid, because I never have any money. But if you can
come to Swansea before May 1st, or to Laugharne (which is far more out
of the way) any time after, I'd like to meet you very much. Do let me
know. Perhaps we *could* see each other in Swansea? Any pub or place. If
that can't be managed, I'll write my long letter sooner.

Yours,
Dylan Thomas

P.S. Several other contributors to 'Wales' live in Swansea, & we could
meet them: Vernon Watkins, John Pritchard,[1] Charles Fisher, etc.

MS: *National Library of Wales*

JAMES LAUGHLIN
[?May 1938]   Blashford Ringwood Hants

Dear Laughlin,
     Thank you very very much for the twenty dollars. I'm glad you told me
how things are with you. This will get me and my wife to Wales, where I
come from; there I hope we can live cheaply in the deep country; and next

---

[1] John Prichard (b. 1916), another Swansea friend, published stories and poems. Thomas
   usually misspelt his name.

month's twenty dollars—it's good of you to spare and promise so much when you're near broke yourself—should keep us going if we eat and drink carefully. I must get to London to meet you in May. Yes, I know I'll never make much money if I stay honest, but then I don't need much; I like money, I like the way it crinkles, I like good food and too much drink; but what I really want is just enough to keep me warm and living so that I can go on with poems and stories.

I've written to the Europa Press about those sheets, but Reavey is somewhere in Paris and won't be back until after Easter. I'll write to you as soon as I hear from you, *and* get him to write. How long will you be in England, and where, if anywhere, do you intend staying? You might care to find a temporary place with me. But that can wait too. Don't get butchered before we meet; two pals of mine are lost in Spain already. Thanks again; now we can eat.

Dylan T

MS: the recipient

GEORGE REAVEY
[early May 1938]   Gosport Street Laugharne Carmarthenshire Wales

Dear George,
    This is my new address. How is the book getting on? Any proofs coming soon? James Laughlin asked me to tell you not to forget about the sheets. *Let me know a few things.*
    Sorry to have missed your party for Beckett & the other man (That's the painter, isn't it, whose work we liked so much?). We haven't been in London together since we last saw [sic], & it isn't likely I'll be up before my book comes out: I'll be up then for a drink with you.
    Regards to your wife.

Yours,
Dylan

MS: Harvard

JAMES LAUGHLIN
May 7th 1938   Gosport Street Laugharne Carmarthenshire Wales

Dear Laughlin,
    Thank you for the cheque. Your letter was forwarded rather late. It will help me a great lot. I've managed, as I think I told you in my last note, to

get a fisherman's cottage, furnished, here in a very odd town; and if I can raise enough regular money to live on I should be happy and contented. This is a good place, undiscovered by painters, and, because the sea is mostly mud and nobody knows when the water will come in or go out or where it comes from anyway, with few sprinkling trippers or picnickers. It's a sociable place too, and I like that, with good pubs and little law and no respect. I hope you can come here to see me. There's a spare bedroom for you. I too hate London, and it would be better in every way for us to meet here. If you can manage it, I'll tell you, in my next letter, how to get here. It won't cost much to come down from London.

About my book of stories and their commercial possibility in America. The stories aren't as esoteric as you might imagine. Some of them are pretty straightforward, & I think one or two, God help me, are straightforward pretty. I know it's not a very good book, but it's got things moving and happening, it isn't dead meat, it isn't dished-up Joyce, it's not heavy or soulful. Reavey is printing about a 1000 copies for England, but I don't believe he knows how to sell anything except a false personality. He's tucked up under his own armpit & looks at the world around him through a moist clump of ginger hair. He does *admit* bad taste, he's above commerce (but not so far above that he can't swindle his authors, who are a puny lot anyway and cultivate their wet dreams). The dark, struggling world with its riches, hostilities, bitches, unjustices, obscene middle-age, is a tasteless joke to him: 'oh, *must* you bring up the world again? that living dodo?': a deprecatory hem, a slight, supercilious Cambridge titter, a ringed and dainty gesture copied from some famous cosmopolitan bumboy, a deadfish smile, a tinkle in a sherry glass that is never filled up more than once, a drawing of well-decorated blinds, a discreet itch in the cock, a little bed-niggling, a short sleep with carefully surrealist dreams, & the stupidity, poverty, insanity, enmity, of the great world that holds the world of Reavey like a flea's shit in a whalebed, is dismissed again for ever, counted as nothing. (Though I don't know why I should trouble to write all that.)

And yes yes what a grand, comic heroism it is, this glandular, neural importance of ours, this fighting and entering, denial, acknowledgement, and annihilation. How I hate those words. How I hate to know what we're doing—Don't show my V.C. to the visitors, Willie,—to put down immodestly the facts of our own naked heroism. And every time we're given a little medal for it we nearly get sick with glory and hate and *shame*. But I know I shan't go down; I've got that heroism, too, and badly. I think that this *churning* matters, I shall go on writing what's wanted even though it won't ever be. We all may be wrong, but it's still the charge of the light brigade, the Battle of the Boys of the Light. Oh the lovely melodramatic heroes. On, on, money to right of them, fame to the left, an income, a new suit, a special party, 'Tell me Mr. Gluepot how did you start writing? do you believe in the feminine verse-ending? is Europe at the Crossroads?', lobster for tea, champagne every night, a niche in Letters, and an everlasting hole in the earth.

You say I will find you sentimental, grossly contrived, & blundering. You will find me sentimental too, vague, conceited, cowardly, proud, very ordinary, all appetite & no belly. I'll tell you all about the things in New Directions, with arrogance, vehemence, but don't believe me. I'm very sincere but I rarely know what I mean, & my attitude is a loud mixture of great tolerance & great intolerance.

No, I can't translate. I'm without education, I left a smalltown school when I was 15 or so. I do some hack reviewing occasionally, but either slate or praise the books too much for my reviews to be used regularly. The standard of reviewing is mediocrity, and—tum tum the Boys of Light—I refuse to judge by it.

I'll try to get a copy of my 2nd book of poems for you. And I'll write a letter to Reavey's armpit and tell it that the wide world outside wants to know about sheets.

Here's a new poem, just finished. I'm sorry not to be able to type it. Before you read it properly, will you type it out yourself? I think typescript gives a manuscript some finality and completion.

And don't forget: try to come here after Pound.[1]

Thank you again, very much.

Dylan Thomas

MS: the recipient

KEIDRYCH RHYS

A key figure in Anglo-Welsh writing, Rhys (b. 1913) founded the literary magazine *Wales* in 1937 and ran it (with interruptions) until 1959.

May 8th 1938   Gosport Street Laugharne Carmarthenshire

Dear Keidrych,

We've taken a fisherman's cottage here for the summer. Hope you'll come and see us sometime soon. Together we might make an attack on Squire Hughes and get him to put up some money.[2] I'm afraid I can't, at the moment, raise anything. Is it true that the Parton Bookshop has gone bust? And have you really lost £80?

I'm not going to do a review of Heseltine's nonsense. It's just a Violent Rain in the neck to me.[3] If people were making a great blather about Heseltine, saying that these poems were good or anything like that, I'd like to say, in print, that I think them bad; but as no-one cares a bit, why should I bother. I'll send the pamphlet back, if you like, for someone else to do.

[1] Laughlin, who published Ezra Pound, was on his way to see him in Italy.
[2] Richard Hughes was a potential source of extra finance for *Wales*.
[3] *Violent Rain* was Nigel Heseltine's first book of poems.

Heseltine should receive the recognition due to him: complete silence. I'm not going to mention him again ever in a letter to you.

What did the Criterion say about *Wales*?

I had a sweet letter from Meurig Walters. He said that he knew his poems weren't very hot yet, but, after all, he'd only written about 10 and he couldn't expect to be perfect.

What are you doing in Leeds? Do you want a Wales contribution from me? Write soon, & don't forget to look us up & stay a bit.

Love,
Dylan

MS: Carbondale

HENRY TREECE
16th May 1938   Gosport Street Laugharne Carmarthenshire

Dear Henry Treece,

I've been moving house. That is, I've left, with trunks and disappointment, one charitable institution after another and have found and am now occupying, to the peril of my inside and out, my rheumatic joints, my fallen chest, my modern nerves, my fluttering knitted pocket, a small, damp fisherman's furnished cottage—green rot sprouts through the florid scarlet forests of the wallpaper, sneeze and the chairs crack, the double-bed is a swing band with coffin, oompah, slush-pump, gob-stick, and almost wakes the deaf, syphilitic neighbours—by the side of an estuary in a remote village. (The village also contains bearded Richard High-Wind Hughes, but we move, in five hundred yards, in two or more different worlds: he owns the local castle, no roof and all, and lives in a grand mansion by its side and has a palace in Morocco: these legendary possessions were acquired half by whimsy, half by influence. I could beat out an elfin cadence with the best, be naughty, delightful, naive, adult, shrewd, bewitching and pawky about children—'He has the fairy alchemy':—H. Wolfe[1]—but all the influence I could raise wouldn't buy me a paper-bag of trippers' shit from Merlin's cave.) And that is my excuse for not writing, for not thanking you for the Hopkins chapter[2] or enclosing the mss I promised. It's taken such a time to settle down and up. I hope you'll forgive me. I was much impressed by the Hopkins chapter, which means I enjoyed it and thought much of it was true. What a lot of work you've put in. I never realised the influence he must have had on me. As I told you before, I have read him only slightly. I have read far more Francis Thompson. I've never been conscious of Hopkins'

---

[1] Humbert Wolfe (1885–1940), poet and senior civil servant.
[2] Chapter 5 of Treece's book about Thomas was called 'The debt to [Gerard Manley] Hopkins'.

influence. As a boy of 15 or 16, writing in all sorts of ways false to myself, composing all sorts of academic imitations, borrowing sometimes shamelessly and sometimes with the well-suppressed knowledge of a pretence to originality, I find—from looking over many hundreds of those very early poems—that there was, and still is, to me, not a sign of Hopkins anywhere. (And I *had* read him then, as I had read a great deal of poetry, good and bad; or, rather, I had read *through* his book.) The people most to be found in those early poems were, I think, the Elizabethans and George Peele, Webster and, later, Beddoes, some Clare (his hard, country sonnets), Lawrence (animal poems, and the verse extracts from the Plumed Serpent), a bit of Tennyson, some very bad Flecker and, of course, a lot of bits from whatever fashionable poetry—Imagists, Sitwells—I'd been reading lately. But out of all that muddle, some poem-sections of which I enclose unaltered, I see no Hopkins. You might see it; you've already proved several things to me in that extraordinary chapter. Sometimes, I think, the influence of Swinburne is more obvious than that of Hopkins in a couple of the quotations from my poetry that you use: 'All all and all the dry worlds couple',[1] for instance. This is rhythmically true, at least.

Very much of my poetry is, I know an enquiry and a terror of fearful expectation, a discovery and facing of fear. I hold a beast, an angel, and a madman in me, and my enquiry is as to their working, and my problem is their subjugation and victory, downthrow & upheaval, and my effort is their self-expression. The new poem I enclose, 'How Shall My Animal', is a detailed enquiry; and the poem too is the result of the enquiry, and is the furthest I can, at present, reach or hope for. The poem is, as all poems are, its own question and answer, its own contradiction, its own agreement. I ask only that my poetry should be taken literally. The aim of a poem is the mark that the poem itself makes; it's the bullet and the bullseye; the knife, the growth, and the patient. A poem moves only towards its own end, which is the last line. Anything further than that is the problematical stuff of poetry, not of the poem. That's my one critical argument, if it can be called that; the rest is a poetical argument, and can only be worked out in poems.

I've been looking through some old reviews, hoping to find some vague material for you. Desmond Hawkins' review of 25 Poems in the Spectator was one of the best, I remember, but I haven't a copy of it. He said several very good, clear things. Here are a few reviews which might give you some opportunities for remarks etc. There's no point in sending you ordinary, straightforward damning or congratulatory reviews, is there—This is great, This is punk. Stephen Spender, by the way, said in a review of the year's poetry some time ago—in the Daily Worker—'The truth is that Thomas's poetry is turned on like a tap; it is just poetic stuff with no beginning nor end, shape, or intelligent and intelligible control'.

---

[1] The poem is 'All all and all the dry worlds lever', but 'lever' becomes 'couple' in the third stanza.

Do you think that's worth mentioning and refuting? It's a belief held by many fancy poets like Spender. (I should like to know, too, how much that complete bit of nonsense was caused by a review I once wrote for New Verse of Spender's 'Vienna' operetta. Have you a copy of that review?) I know that you wouldn't want to introduce into your book any particular bickering, but Spender's remark is really the exact opposite of what is true. My poems *are* formed; they are not turned on like a tap at all, they are 'watertight compartments'. Much of the obscurity is due to rigorous compression; the last thing they do is to flow; they are much rather hewn. Now Spender himself has no idea of form; his poetry is so much like poetry, & so remote from poems, that I think most of his work will become almost as unreadable as the worst of the Georgians—& very soon.

Another remark I came across in a review—by Julian Symons of Hart Crane[1] in 20th C. Verse—is: 'No modern poet except Thomas is, for me, more affecting, more able to twist words to the shape of the reader's tears.' Are you going to mention Hart Crane? Three or four years ago, when I first knew Norman Cameron, he told me that the most obvious modern influence in my poetry *was* Crane, a friend of his. And he was astonished, and at first unbelieving, when I told him that I had never heard of Crane before. He showed me some of his poems then, and I could certainly see what he meant: there were, indeed, two or three almost identical bits of phrasing, and much of the actual sound seemed similar. Since then I've read all Crane's poems, and though now I see the resemblance between his poetry and mine to be very slight, I can understand that some people might still think I had come under his influence.

You ask me about the Middle Ages. I know nothing about them. You must remember I've had no education—I left a provincial secondary school when I was 15 or so—and I've never read anything except in Modern English. Also, I can't read French, although I've often been called an imitator of the surrealists etc. I'm looking forward to the chapter on surrealism, and the 'straight' poems.

I want to let you have this very inadequate letter straight away. There's been too much delay between our writing, but it was all my fault and now I'm settled, however precariously, once again. I'm not enclosing in this letter a selection of very early poems; I'll try to get them typed tomorrow & will then send them off straight away. I haven't forgotten about religion & the supernatural, but it seems to me now like an essay that has to be written so it will be better if I say what I think about it, at random, informally, from time to time. One of the times will be when I send off the typed poems, tomorrow or the day after. Again, forgive me. I've got a lot of material about—reviews, about 10 exercise books full of poems,[2] a few articles on poetry etc.—and they only need a little weeding & cutting

---

[1] Hart Crane (1899–1932), American poet; he committed suicide.
[2] Only four exercise books, containing about 200 poems, are known to exist; they are at Buffalo.

before I can let you have them. If you've got any questions that might have arisen from the chapters you've done or from the plan for the rest of the book, do let me know.

All Best Wishes,
Dylan T

MS: Buffalo   *SL*

JAMES LAUGHLIN
May 17 1938   Gosport St Laugharne Carmarthenshire Wales

Dear Laughlin,
   Very glad to hear that you will come down to Wales to see me. I suppose it will be early in June.
   And glad that you liked the poem I sent you. I enclose two others. When is the 1938 New Directions[1] to appear? I haven't much new stuff yet, apart from the 3 poems you now have of mine. 4 short poems are coming out in Poetry, Chicago—not because I like the paper but because it pays.[2] If your number comes out late in the year, I should have one or two poems and some prose by then. I write extremely slowly: a poem may often take 2 months.
   Auden is, I think, 31. I am 23. I don't know Auden, but I think he sounds bad: the heavy, jocular prefect, the boy bushranger, the school wag, the 6th form debater, the homosexual clique-joker. I think he sometimes writes with great power: 'O Love, the interest itself in thoughtless heaven, Make simpler daily the beating of man's heart.'[3] I can't agree he's as bad as MacLeish.[4] He's overpraised of course. I've added my own little dollop of praise in a number of New Verse devoted entirely, with albino portrait and manuscript, to gush and pomp about him. He's exactly what the English literary public think a modern English poet should be. He's perfectly educated (& expensively) but still delightfully eccentric. He's a rebel (i.e. an official communist) but boys will be boys so he is awarded the King's Medal; he's got a great sense of Humour; he's not one of those old-fashioned, escapist Bohemians (which means he doesn't get drunk in public, that he dresses like a public school-master not like a 'silly artist'); he follows his own ideas truly of the brotherhood of man, 'Love thy neighbour and, if possible, covet his arse', but there's no hanky-panky about him; he's a man's man. He's just what he should be: let him rant his old communism, it's only a young man's natural rebelliousness,

---

[1] *New Directions in Poetry and Prose.*
[2] *Poetry* (Chicago) published 'When all my five and country senses see', 'O make me a mask', 'Not from this anger' and 'The spire cranes' in August 1938.
[3] The opening lines of W. H. Auden's poem 'Prologue'.
[4] Archibald MacLeish (1892–1982), American poet.

(& besides, it doesn't convert anybody: the awarding of conservative prizes to anti-conservatives who are found to be socially harmless is a fine, soothing palliative, & a shrewd gesture. And, incidentally too, the rich minority can always calm down a crier of 'Equality For All' by giving him *individual* equality with themselves).

About Higham. I am writing to him. He has handled only one poetry book for me, '25 Poems', which Dent published. He has had nothing to do with the handling etc. of either my first book of poems or my book of stories. I shall be telling him that—apart from '25 Poems', for which he still manages the *minute* royalty arrangements between me & Dent (about 10 shillings every quarter)—I don't require any more the services of an agent. Neither do I. I shan't, whatever Higham hopes, be producing a novel, now or at any other time: only obscure poems & imaginative prose, & over those, as he well knows, he needn't bother a bit.

Looking forward to seeing you soon.

Dylan T

MS: the recipient

HENRY TREECE
June 1st [1938]   Gosport Street Laugharne Carmarthenshire

Dear Henry Treece,
    I think Edith Sitwell would be very pleased to read the book. I don't know if she likes me, personally, now, or not. I have the idea she's offended, but this may be incorrect. I wrote her some two months ago at her Paris address, but have had no answer; perhaps she's away, perhaps the letter hasn't been forwarded, perhaps the address is dead, perhaps she has been insulted by my very long delay in replying to her letters, perhaps she too has gone lazy or bad-mannered (this I doubt extremely). Anyway, she still likes my work and she'll undoubtedly like yours, and her London address, which won't be dead unless this Girton & county and deaf middle-aged ladies' institution has been raided, is care of The Sesame Club, 49 Grosvenor St., W.1. The Paris address is 129 Rue Saint-Dominique, VII. About her review, & the subsequent letters, in the Sunday Times,[1] some of which you said you might mention or include:—She makes a few interesting misreadings, or, rather, half-readings. She says the 'country-handed grave' in my poem A Grief Ago is 'that simple nurse of grief, that countryman growing flowers and corn'. My image, principally, did not make the grave a gentle cultivator but a tough possessor, a warring and complicated raper rather than a simple nurse or an innocent gardener. I meant that the grave had a

[1] Sitwell's review appeared on 15 November 1936.

country for each hand, that it raised those hands up and 'boxed' the hero of my poem into love. 'Boxed' has the coffin and the pug-glove in it.

Edith Sitwell's analysis, in a letter to the Times, of the lines 'The atlas-eater with a jaw for news/Bit out the mandrake with tomorrow's scream,' seems to me very vague and Sunday-journalish. She says the lines refer to 'the violent speed and the sensation-loving, horror-loving craze of modern life'. She doesn't take the literal meaning: that a world-devouring ghost creature bit out the horror of tomorrow from a gentleman's loins. A 'jaw for news' is an obvious variation of a 'nose for news', & means that the mouth of the creature can taste already the horror that has not yet come or can sense it coming, can thrust its tongue into news that has not yet been made, can savour the enormity of the progeny before the seed stirs, can realise the crumbling of dead flesh before the opening of the womb that delivers that flesh to tomorrow. What is this creature? It's the dog among the fairies, the rip and cur among the myths, the snapper at demons, the scarer of ghosts, the wizard's heel-chaser. This poem is a particular incident in a particular adventure, not a general, elliptical deprecation of this 'horrible, crazy, speedy life'.

You say you intend showing the book to Michael Roberts who will be 'sympathetic towards us'. You are not treading on my corns when you call Roberts a good Thinker, but I personally can do without his condescension. He commented in the London Mercury that 'it is a pity D.T. should sometimes give the impression of using a large & personal vocabulary merely to make a schoolboy exhibition'. The phrase I object to is not 'a schoolboy exhibition', for I'm not afraid of showing-off or throwing my cap in the air, but 'It's a pity'. What function has this patronising 'pity' in criticism? Do I need a critic to weep over my errors of taste? Let him point them out, tell me, if he likes, how to rectify them; but, for Christ's sake, not sympathise.

Yes, I should certainly write to James Laughlin of New Directions (Norfolk, Connecticut). I've had a lot of letters from him lately about plans for publicity for my stories and poems in America, & I know he'll be very interested in your book. He seems genial & very earnest and has been giving me small sums of money regularly, though now they've ceased. He talks about 'his' poets; and takes an avuncular interest in obscurity.

I wonder whether you've considered writing anything—perhaps only a few paragraphs—about the Welsh-ness of my poetry:—this is often being mentioned in reviews and criticisms, and I've never understood it. I mean, I've never understood this racial talk, 'his Irish talent', 'undoubtedly Scotch inspiration', apart from whiskey. Keidrych Rhys—editor of the very good little magazine 'Wales'—always has a lot to say about it. He's an ardent nationalist, and a believer in all the stuff about racial inspiration etc. If you felt like it, you might drop him a line (c/o J. F. Hendry, 20 Vernon Road, Leeds) & tell him about your book and ask him what he thinks about the Welsh in my work. Anyway you'll get back a long & interesting letter: he's the best sort of crank.

I know little Dyment.[1] He's a harmless twig, not worth shaking off.

Yes, the oompah *is* a swing-band term. I enclose a glossary from a story in a swing magazine: Black Trumpet.

And Hughes is still a jive-man. His stories, I think, are mediocre: his verse negligible: his demon, whimsy (see any conversation in H. W. in Jamaica, & especially the last sentence in the book).[2] Of course I get more out of life than he does. My envy may be rancid, but my faith is the best butter.

I think the method you adopted in the Surrealist chapter—the clearing away of superficial misconceptions by attack and contrast of quotations—is the only effective one, and I thought the whole chapter extremely well argued & formed. You know Gascoyne's poem in a very early number of New Verse, that begins something like 'White curtains of tortured destiny'? There are some lines in that I feel sure you could make use of, lines far more engaging and precociously lunatic than any in his Magritte poem. I've nothing to argue about in this chapter, &, apart from that Gascoyne poem for quotation, no suggestions. It's a fine piece of work, & has convinced me once again that my own sane bee in the bonnet can never be a pal of that French wasp forever stinging itself to a loud and undignified death with a tail of boiled string.

Did you tell me, in an early letter, that you might spend some of your summer holiday in Wales? Why not come & see us here? There's room for you, & food.

Yours,

Dylan T.

I'm looking forward to the other chapters, & will try to let you have the poems I promised you—early ones—very soon. They're not being as easy to arrange as I imagined.

MS: Buffalo   *SL(R)*

JAMES LAUGHLIN

June 1 1938 (Instructions for Laughlin, now in England, on how to reach Laugharne. See Appendix 12.)

---

[1] Clifford Dyment (1914–71), poet and film writer; Richard Church was fond of his work, and published his first book of poems, *First Day*, in the same series as Thomas's *Twenty-five Poems*.

[2] Richard Hughes's novel *A High Wind in Jamaica* was published in 1929.

D. S. SAVAGE[1]
10 June [1938]   Gosport Street Laugharne Carmarthenshire S Wales

Dear D. S. Savage,
  Just had your note about the Partisan Review. I'll be delighted to send a couple of poems, in a few days when they've been typed. It doesn't matter if the poems have been printed before, recently, in English magazines, does it?

With best wishes,
Yrs truly
Dylan Thomas

MS: Texas

GEORGE REAVEY
16th June 1938   Gosport Street Laugharne Carmarthenshire

Dear George,
  I am sorry to hear about the complications; I rather thought it was some stupidity on the part of the printers that had caused this delay. Will you tell me which are the stories, or sections of stories, to which most objection is taken? The only story I can think of which might cause a few people a small and really unnecessary alarm is The Prologue To An Adventure; this I could cut out from the book, and substitute a story about my grandfather who was a very clean old man.[2] If, however, objection is taken to the book as a whole, then your suggestion of publication first in Paris seems very sensible. I was approached by Lawrence Durrell, for the Obelisk Press, some time ago, and I am pretty confident that, through Durell and Miller, it would publish the book. That is, unless you have other Paris plans. To publish first in America doesn't seem so good to me, as Laughlin does not want to bring the book out there until a book of my poems has been published and until he has managed to establish for me a small American reputation. I don't think either that a collection of opinions from 'responsible' people should be used except as a very last chance. As to your suggestion of publishing the first edition at a guinea, I know nothing: is the alleged obscenity any less harmful at a guinea? and would a guinea book sell at all?
  I had a letter from John this morning. What a muddler he is. He says now that he is dissatisfied with his portrait of me, & would like to do another:—we may as well wait until the Religious Tract Society offers to publish The Burning Baby. But I'll find out what I can from him when he comes down here next week.

---

[1] Derek Stanley Savage (b. 1917), poet and author. Savage contributed to the American magazine *Partisan Review*, and in 1938 compiled a 'little anthology' of British poets for it. The other poets he chose were Roy Fuller, Julian Symons, Keidrych Rhys, David Gascoyne and George Barker.
[2] 'A Visit to Grandpa's.'

There is no contract between me & the Parton Press as to my 18 Poems. The book, as you know, was published by David Archer, then in charge of the Press, & the copyright is mine. I lost badly on that book, owing to my ignorance & Archer's vagueness: I was given, in small irregular sums just about the time of publication, no more than £4 or £5, & have not received a halfpenny royalty although the book, for poetry, has sold, since 1934, remarkably well. The profits of the book—at the beginning at least, when reviews would sell it—just went straight to help Archer's personal debts. Since then, although many copies have been sold, I know, I have heard & had nothing at all. So if new arrangements are to be made, I think I should be given a fair lucrative deal. Are you prepared to give me money? When, & how much? I think the book, given some new publicity, wd sell quite well again. Auden's first poems in their new, stiff-covered edition went, as you remember, splendidly: & that was before he was the comparative best-seller he is today.

I won't be in London for some time, as I cannot afford the fare. Let me know news (if any) about the book, & (very soon if possible) about the 18 Poems. Unless I can manage to cut out the offence in my stories, Paris publication seems to me best, though I am getting heartily fed-up with all the bother and can't, at the present moment, see why I should extend your publishing rights to 2 years; if you fail to do anything with it in the stipulated time, I may as well have a shot at it myself. I want the book published soon, because I need urgently the little it will make me. This is not a definite refusal of your suggestion for extension, but is certainly what I feel like now.

> Sincerely,
> Dylan T

MS: Harvard

HENRY TREECE
16 June 1938   Gosport Street Laugharne Carmarthenshire

Dear Henry Treece,

I'm very glad indeed that you both will come and spend some time with us in the summer; any time, for any time. I warn you that our cottage is pokey and ugly, four rooms like stained boxes in a workman's and fisherman's row, with a garden leading down to mud and sea, that our living & cooking is rough, that you bathe or go dirty; you will find my wife extremely nice, me small, argumentative, goodtempered, lazy, fumbling, boozy as possible, 'lower middle class' in attitude and reaction; a dirty tongue; a silly young man. I hope you like drinking, because I do very much and when I have money I don't stop. There are three good pubs here, the best bottled mild in England, and no prohibitive drinking hours;

there are walks, & boats, and nets to pull, and colossal liars to listen to. There is a double bed in one room, two single beds in the other; you can sleep in the double bed, or in the two beds, or sandwiched in a single one. There is an earth lavatory and it smells like a shithouse. Welcome; & let me know when. (By the way, what do I call you? Throw your Treece away.)

   This is a bad time for me again, and I can't buy a stamp for you. I haven't a single penny, or halfpenny, or filed French slot-coin. Smokeless and breadless, we face a bad weekend. We wait for shillings which we have no right to expect. Bitter, cruel Laugharne; my pipe is full of buttends from the grate, my table crowded with the dead ends of poems, my head full of nonsense. The sun is shining on the mud, my wife is out cockling, I am writing to a critic in Northumberland, a little girl has called with buns, I say, 'No buns', though all my everlasting soul shouts for them and my belly is turned by the sight in the kitchen of two poor dabs we caught, two out of all the breeding monsters in the sea, with a broken net yesterday. Last week I finished a long story about my true childhood, and here's a letter from Life & Letters saying they will print it and pay for it in September.[1]

> O Chatterton and others in the attic
> Linked in one gas bracket
> Taking Jeyes' fluid as narcotic;
> Drink from the earth's teats,
> Life neat's a better poison than in bottle,
> A better venom seethes in spittle
> Than one could probe out of a serpent's guts;
> Each new sensation emits
> A new vinegar;
> Be a regular
> Fellow with saw at the jugular.
> On giddy nights when slap on the moon's mask
> A madman with a brush has slapped a face
> I pick a stick of celery from the valley
> I find a tripper's knicker in the gully
> And take another nibble at my flask.
> What meaning, voices, in the straight-ruled grass,
> Meaning in hot sock soil? A little cuss
> Can't read sense in the rain that willy nilly
> Soaks to the vest old dominies and drunks.
> Dissect that statement, voices, on the slabs.
> Love's a decision of 3 nerves
> And Up or Down love's questions ask;
> On giddy nights I slap a few drunk curves
> Slap on the drunk moon's mask.

[1] 'The Peaches', another of the *Portrait of the Artist* pieces. It appeared in October.

> Rape gulp and be merry, he also serves
> Who only drinks his profits
> And would a-wooing go around the graves.
> Celibate I sit and see
> Women figures round my cell,
> Women figures on the wall
> Point their little breasts at me;
> I must wait for a woman's smile
> Not in the sun but in the dark;
> The two words stallion and sterile
> Stand in a question mark.
> The smiling woman is a mad story,
> Wipe it away, wipe a crumb
> From the preacher's table.
> I offer you women, not woman,
> A home and a dowry:
> 3 little lusts shall your dowry be,
> And your home in a centaur's stable.

That's better; but the trouble is I can quite easily feel like that these days, & when I said my head was full of nonsense I meant it. I'm an expert at aping my own moods; now I could wear Dowson's invisible hat, & my throat can encompass Chesterton's dead rattle; John Gawsworth's[1] sanitary towels float down the air like red snow.

When I mentioned Life & Letters, I thought that that paper might easily be interested in any chapters of yours you might like printed separately. Herring's a friend of mine, more or less, & why not write to him? And do tell me what poem, or piece of poem, you'd like me, for a footnote, to analyse in detail? I'll send you some things very soon, & try to answer your questions. You might send me the 'straight' chapter some time. Apologies for muddled letter, for the lack of a stamp.

Dylan Th

MS: Buffalo   SL(R)

D. S. SAVAGE
28 June [1938]   Gosport St Laugharne Carmarthenshire

Dear D. S. Savage,
    Here's one of the poems I promised.
    When I wrote before, I forgot that I had promised to New Directions

---

[1] John Gawsworth (T. I. F. Armstrong) (1912–70), writer and eccentric.

nearly all my new poems:—N.D. is going to publish my two poem books in the U.S.—for that yearly anthology of theirs. So this is the only one I can spare. It hasn't been published anywhere in England yet, & if it is it will only be in some small, non-U.S.-sale paper like 20th Century Verse.

But I think you said that contributions weren't too late by August 1, and if I finish a new poem before then, shall I send it along?

Sincerely,
Dylan Thomas

MS: Texas

JAMES LAUGHLIN
28 June [1938]   Gosport Street Laugharne Carmarthenshire

Dear Laughlin,

I was extremely sorry you could not come to Wales; our cottage was brushed and cleaned and lardered; I wore a fresh shirt and red trousers.

I received an order from Miss Swan; she is very kind, and must be charming.[1] There was difficulty over her address, and though I have written to several addresses there has either been no answer or the letters have returned 'unknown'. Would you forward this letter to her as soon as possible? I do not, on any account, want her to think me ungrateful for her generosity and the nice things she said about my poems. I have asked her if she would send me her poems, and if she would like to see mine. You won't forget this letter, will you? A little regular assistance is almost more than I can hope for, but I still do hope.

You ask me if I have been published in America? Only in transition (when it had, as it still may have for all I know, an American address) & in Poetry. I have been asked for a poem for an English number of the Partisan Review, and shall send them one. There will still be over half a dozen poems—not counting those in preparation—for the New Directions anthology when they are needed. 'Poetry' published a poem of mine in their English number, edited by Auden and Michael Roberts, last year, & were supposed to have printed in their May number (as I think I told you) 4 short new poems you haven't seen. Whether the poems appeared in the May number or not I don't know.[2]

I have no new poems completed yet, but will let you have them in time. And I am now more than halfway through that long piece of prose I mentioned to you in a previous letter; it would do best, I think, as a separate pamphlet, but you shall see & tell me what you think.

[1] Emma Swan, of New York City, who sent Thomas money over the years. New Directions published her poetry.
[2] See note 2, page 299.

Do I leave the editing of my 2 books—the selection of 30 of the best poems—to you? I'm quite prepared to, of course.

Reavey—do let me know what you think of him, especially after my malicious analysis—wrote a few days ago to say that he was having trouble with the printers over my stories, and that he has been warned by a solicitor not to think of publishing them, as they stand, in England. I replied and told him that if the alleged offence was contained only in isolated passages I wouldn't have any honest qualms about cutting them out. But the little weazel hasn't answered me, & might be cooking up all sorts of plans. You said it was not honest of me to conceal from you the fact that Reavey had the American rights of my stories; I was not *concealing* it from you because I didn't know the fact existed: the contract was rushed through and gabbled over, Reavey taking quick advantage of my vagueness and stupidity. I'm not in the habit of concealing, dishonestly, facts about my small & uncommercial work; usually I'm cheated myself.

I hope your publicity campaign's getting under way; & I'm looking forward to the contracts that you said you would soon be drawing up. I'll write and tell you when anything happens, & keep you posted with my new work. If there are any other questions, do please ask me. Apologies for the long delay.

Best wishes,
Dylan T

Please remember Emma Swan's letter.

MS: the recipient

VERNON WATKINS
5th July [1938]   Gosport St Laugharne Carms

Dear Vernon,
   When are you and Francis, or you or Francis, coming here again? Come soon. My mother wrote to tell me that she'd seen you, & that you told her you hoped we weren't too tired when you arrived that Sunday. Of course we weren't. It's always lovely to see you. I've nearly finished my story,[1] & you must see it & read it in detail & tell me where I am too extravagant.
   Harvard University wrote to ask me for something for their special magazine in honour of Eliot—just a paragraph or two of what I think of him, his writing, his religion, his influence, etc. I've written a heap of notes, none of which seems really satisfactory. Do please tell me a few

[1] 'One Warm Saturday', according to Watkins.

things, just as you helped with that little Auden appreciation. Just a few comments or notes.

Don't forget to come soon.

Love,
Dylan

MS: British Library   VW

HENRY TREECE
6th or 7th July [1938]   Gosport Street Laugharne Carmarthenshire

Dear Henry,

I should have written ten days ago and acknowledged your kind and welcome bungift, six days ago and acknowledged the chapters, and should have answered immediately your short note about August 2. But rudely I've put all off, wanting time to read the chapters carefully, to write about them, to analyse a poem, to answer your questions, so that I could send one long, full letter. Even now, when I do write at last, these ambitions are only partly realised and still full of holes, and the analysis, Freud help it, must wait until next time. I'm working, hard for me, though there's very little to show for it: some incomplete prose about a dwindling woman, a tame poem, a taste of nice words in the head.

I'm especially glad you can come to stay for August week, as this is the week of great celebration here: a carnival with queen, a regatta with prizes, a dance with soaks. Laugharne—pronounced Larn—will be almost gay and certainly crowded. The High Wind blows its trumpet, few that can walk from their houses will walk back, there will be speechmaking, drunkmaking, sickmaking, Mr Watts the draper will undoubtedly shit his trousers, and we must all dress up. Perhaps it won't be like that at all, but it is a good week for a visit anyway. I'd been hoping that, by the time you arrived, we would have been in our new house, but that's unlikely now. I don't know how you get from here to Harlech, but I know you can quite easily; North Wales is just a bit further on, one way or the other. And I don't know how you get to Laugharne from Northumberland; somehow, I do know, you must get to Carmarthen or to Tenby: we lie about midway. From London it's easy (but unhelpful): Paddington to Carmarthen direct: half an hour's busride from there. There is no railway station here, but we have a nice townhall. From where will you travel? (And no, before I forget, I wasn't in Baker-St. Post Office Christmas 1936. Were you in the Knitted Buoy department of Llantrisant Naval Museum on Mother's Day? Why Baker-St?)

I thought the Straight-Poems chapter was convincing and concise. Do I understand, from your Eliot quotation at the head of the chapter,[1] that the

---

[1] 'The progress of an artist is a continual self-sacrifice, a continual extinction of personality . . . Poetry is not a turning loose of emotion, but an escape from emotion; it is not the expression of personality, but an escape from personality.' (T. S. Eliot, *The Sacred Wood*.)

poetry in these straight poems is a calculated escape from the personality-parade of my loud and complex poems? I don't know if they are at all, and I really don't see how they could be; I wrote them, most of them anyway, quite a long time before the other poems in the 25 volume. The straight poems in '25' were, indeed, with a very few exceptions—I'll be able to show you all dates when we meet, but I can't now remember the exceptions because I haven't got copies of the two books—written before most of the poems in the '18' volume. But I don't want to muddle things now; we can go together over all my manuscripts (if you care to, of course) and see properly how these poems do genealogically work. It might have very curious results. Both books contain poems written over about 8 years; there is no definite sequence. I have a great deal of material still, in mss books, to shape into proper poems; and these I will include, quite vaguely, (that is: without considering an easily marked, planned, critical 'progress') in future published books. But we can talk about this. (Those above are teastains.)

I was interested in what you said about my lack, except in that little finger-poem,[1] of any social awareness. I suppose I am, broadly, (as opposed to regimented thinkers and poets in uniform) antisocial, but I am extremely sociable. But, surely it is evasive to say that my poetry has no social awareness—no evidence of contact with society—while quite a good number of my images come from the cinema & the gramophone and the newspaper, while I use contemporary slang, cliché, and pun. You meant, I know, that my poetry isn't concerned with politics (supposedly the science of achieving and 'administrating' human happiness) but with poetry (which is unsentimental revelation, and to which happiness is no more important—or any other word—than misery):—(I'll elaborate that, if you'd like me to. Not that it's obscure, but it may, in some way, be helpful to add to it.) But the idea you gave me was that you actually consider me unaware of my surroundings, out-of-contact with the society from which I am necessarily outlaw. You are right when you suggest that I think a squirrel stumbling at least of equal importance as Hitler's invasions, murder in Spain, the Garbo-Stokowski romance, royalty, Horlick's, lynchlaw, pit disasters, Joe Louis, wicked capitalists, saintly communists, democracy, the Ashes, the Church of England, birthcontrol, Yeats' voice, the machines of the world I tick and revolve in, pub-baby-weather-government-football-youthandage-speed-lipstick,   all small tyrannies, means tests, the fascist anger, the daily, momentary lightnings, eruptions, farts, dampsquibs, barrelorgans, tinwhistles, howitzers, tiny death-rattles, volcanic whimpers of the world I eat, drink, love, work, hate and delight in—but I *am* aware of these things as well.

Another very small criticism: in your Introduction you say that I 'do not, like other poets of (my) age, lean over gates, seeking kinship with daffodils & sheep'. Do you mean other poets of my age-in-years, of my

---

[1] 'The hand that signed the paper', perhaps written with Hitler in mind.

generation, or of my century? I ask you, what other poets of my age —
excluding people like Gawsworth, who are not poets at all but just
bearded boils in the dead armpit of the nineties—*do* lean over gates? It's a
crack at young Georgians, not at New-Versers, intellectual muckpots
leaning on a theory, post-surrealists & orgasmists, tit-in-the-night
whistlers and Barkers, Empson leaning over his teeth to stare down an
ice-cold throat at the mathematical mystery of his doom-treading boots,
Grigson leaning over his rackets to look at his balls, Cameron riding on
the back of neat graves. And, actually, 'seeking kinship', with everything,
daffodils, sheep, shoehorns, saints, bees, and uncles is exactly what I *do*
do. I think, with all due lack of respect, that it's a futile crack anyway.

It's nearly post-time and I've done almost nothing except get noisy
about very little matters. I think I'm putting most of my comments &
criticisms off until August. But I'll write soon, properly soon, with more
about these chapters: I took several notes which need only a little
filling-out to make a long, vulgar, enthusiastic, argumentative letter
proving nothing at all. Write when you can. I'm returning the Introduction.

Yours,
Dylan T

I haven't, of course, read the chapters you've sent me in any order, but,
from what I have read, it seems to me that you've quoted that make-it-
clean-boys part of my Answers to an Enquiry about ½ dozen times.[1] This
is probably due to the irregular way I've read. How does the plan of the
book stand now? I'll certainly let you have a poem-analysis for a footnote,
and more material you'd care to use may come out of our future joint
examination of piles of mss.

Dylan

MS: Buffalo   *SL(R)*

WYN HENDERSON
13 July 1938   Gosport Laugharne Carmarthenshire

Darling Wyn,
Norman[2] and his new Dutch girl—there's a nice girl too, perhaps —
came down last weekend, full of love and London chatter and drink and
money. Norman told me that you were working hard for my book of
stories. I'd been worrying about them, wondering what was happening

---

[1] In the *New Verse* 'Answers to an Enquiry' (October 1934), Thomas wrote, 'Whatever is
hidden should be made naked. To be stripped of darkness is to be clean', in answering
'Yes' to the question, 'Have you been influenced by Freud and how do you regard him?'
[2] Norman Cameron.

and going to happen, fearing the subterranean, and sub-human, activities of ginger George;[1] but now, to me, everything's grand. Thank you very very much; why didn't I ask you about the stories in the first place; thank you for working for them; I do hope you succeed in making the meanies realise I'm not a smuthound. Norman also said that you had, or were trying to get, a lawyer's list of words, phrases, or sentences to which objection is taken. I wrote to mangy George, asked him to get a list, told him I was willing, within reason, to cut anything out, that I deprecated Paris publication; but filthy, armpit-loving, rude-eyed George never replied. The only thing to excuse him would be a business head, for he has no gifts, no charm, no merit; but he's apparently learned only trick A: how to cheat poor young men of pennies, piss in cripples' trays. Are you working independently? Can I help in any way? I wish you could write to me. I should have written to you a long time ago.

Soon, in the beginning of August, we hope to move from this ugly, furnished fisherman's cottage to a tall and dignified house at the posh end of this small town, and are busy trying to collect, piece by piece, po by washstand, furniture from friends & relatives. Rent is a mystery certainly, food is a luxury almost. Caitlin—who sends much love to you—is going to have a baby: most likely in January: it's a very nice mistake, and neither of us worries at all.

Norman said you were busy these days? What else do you do? Write soon. Give our love to Ian & Nigel,[2] and of course to yourself: lots. And thank you again.

Dylan
& Caitlin

MS: Texas

GEORGE REAVEY
[July 1938]   Laugharne Carmarthenshire S Wales

Dear George,
I've been expecting to hear from you.

I was told that Wyn Henderson has been interesting herself in the welfare of my stories. I wrote to her; she said she was compiling, for my benefit, a list of legally objectionable phrases etc. Also that you now definitely intended publishing, first of all, a small, expensive, signed edition in Paris. Is that true? And then a bowdlerised English version. I'd be pleased, and surprised, to be told something about this: before the book comes out, if possible.

[1] George Reavey.
[2] Wyn Henderson's sons.

Augustus John says that a portrait of me is now ready. You can get a photograph of it, if you care, without difficulty.

Henry Miller says the Obelisk Press is keen to get the stories. He'd like to know if, when, & how.

Dylan T

MS: Harvard

VERNON WATKINS
Wednesday [postmarked July 14 1938]   Gosport St Laugharne

Dear Vernon,
We'll be able to come up to Bishopston this weekend.
Is Francis coming here on Thursday? We've had no word yet.
News when we meet. Think about Eliot for me.
Are you listening-in tonight?

Love,
Dylan

MS: British Library   *VW*

CHARLES FISHER
Friday [?July 1938]   Gosport St Laugharne Carmarthenshire

Dear Charles,
We ½ expected you on Saturday, & on Tuesday too. Sorry we weren't awake and up personally to see to breakfast and your departure. Hope you'll come again, and spend the night. Hughes is back now, & we may all go up there for dinner & pull his beard. Also we must get started on the Canary. Dorothy Parker called *her* canary Onan. See you perhaps tomorrow? We were run up to Swansea last night to see the fight, but you weren't—as you probably know—in the Singleton. Have you heard anything about the wireless set? We've found a large room now for Caitlin to dance in, & all she needs is music. Don't forget, will you? If you *can* come down tomorrow, don't bother to inform us beforehand: we'll be around.

Love,
Dylan

MS: the recipient

HENRY TREECE
24th July [1938]   Laugharne Carmarthenshire

Dear Henry,

Thank you for the cutting. I disagree that it's a great pity Roberts[1] gossips to newspapers: it's very revealing, he loves all that sort of publicity (though he'd chuckle at it in public) and I think it shows him up beautifully. He certainly is not the popular conception of a poet, nor any other conception either; he's a professional prig, and dry as dust in the place where he isn't damp. I heard him once sneering at the 'childish' idea of poets wearing long hair and corduroy trousers; and if that's not childish, what is? He said Eliot, who was a good poet, dressed and looked like a business man; of course Eliot does, because Eliot is a business-man, and a prosperous one. Empson, Bottrall,[2] MacNeice, & others have professional jobs, & dress to fit them; other poets (or not) are advertising writers (Quennell, Cameron, Tessimond[3]), reporters like Madge, booksellers, clerks; they all wear the uniform of the work that pays them. I like very much the idea of poets dressing professionally, if they are poets alone. I dislike 'he's a poet but he dresses like an ordinary chap'; I like, 'he's an ordinary chap but he dresses like a poet'.

Am I sensitive about my age—in years? (I'm not, by the way, younger than Chatterton when he died: he was 18). I don't really feel sensitive at all about it; and the only thing that, naturally, annoys me is the gossip of another generation: I belong to my own, generation and gossip. Myself in 10 years bores me now, but then I suppose I shall be just as interested. The best moment, & the one it is least possible to realise, is this: 5 to 12 on Sunday morning, 24th July 1938. I'm sensitive, & hackle-raising, only, perhaps about every moment, younger or older, that isn't this.

The drawing of yourself has a very big nose. But in your letter you said you were keeping it to the grindstone. No drawing of my own could do justice to my particular baby bulbousness; I look like an Aryan Harpo bitten by wasps, and the moths have been at my teeth.

I'm glad that Laughlin, in spite of his 'premature' babbling, will do your book in America. He is running some sort of a small publicity racket out there now: advertisements & readings on the radio etc. He should, he tells me, be ready to do your book next summer.

Keidrych Rhys came here a few days ago; I asked him about your letter to him, but he said he'd never received it. I've asked him anyway to write to you.

Yes, I know the London Bulletin. Reavey's announcement of my stories for June is incorrect. He's had a lot of trouble with solicitors or lawyers, & it is now impossible to print the stories in England in their present form.

[1] Michael Roberts.
[2] Ronald Bottrall (b. 1906), poet and administrator.
[3] A. S. J. Tessimond (1902–62), poet and advertising copywriter.

A small, expensive edition will be done in Paris first, then a purged one here. I hate the Paris idea, but Reavey bought out my copyright.

We're looking forward to your visit on August 2nd. When you write again, before that, address the letter just to Laugharne, no special address, as we are moving into another house during the next few days & I'm not quite sure what it's called. Just 'Laugharne' will reach me.

Best wishes,
Dylan

MS: Buffalo

D. S. SAVAGE
Sunday [July 1938]   Gosport St Laugharne Carmarthenshire

Dear D. S. Savage,
  Sorry to bother you, but it's about that poem of mine for the Partisan Review. Do you remember I told you that New Directions was going to publish several new poems of mine this year? Well, I've just had a letter from them & they say *they're* going to use the poem—'How shall my animal'—that I sent to you. Is it too late to ask you to change the poem in your possession for another, the one I enclose? If it is too late, do let me know quickly and I shall write to New Directions telling them not to use the poem. That, however, takes time, so I thought it best to write first to you, hoping you'll be able to change the poems.
  This is a lot of bother about a very small matter, but it's no fault of mine. Sorry.

Yours sincerely
Dylan Thomas

MS: Texas

JAMES LAUGHLIN
July 27 1938   Sea View Laugharne Carmarthenshire S Wales[1]

Dear Laughlin,
  Before anything else: Would you mind substituting this enclosed poem for 'How shall my animal', which you were going to use in the new New Directions.[2] It's a livelier poem anyway, but I find too that it's one the

---

[1] A thin six-roomed house, rented from the Williams family, who more or less ran Laugharne.
[2] *New Directions in Poetry and Prose*, 1938, published three Thomas poems: 'How shall my animal', 'In memory of Ann Jones' and 'I make this in a warring absence'.

Partisan Review is going to use: and they, unfortunately, had the poem before I sent it to you. It's a pity our very first bit of business together, however simple, should be complicated like this, however simply. I only hope this request for substitution isn't too late. If it is, nothing fatal has happened—there is still time to explain to the Partisan people—but I'll be glad if I am in time. I'm an unbusinesslike bugger but getting better.

And now: I can't properly understand all the contracts. One I do understand, & have signed and enclosed it. I'll fire along to you everything I do, right away. But the long contract, about me being the author and proprietor of a work entitled 'Poems', isn't clear to me. I'm author and, I gather, proprietor too, of the '18 Poems'; but am I proprietor of the '25 Poems'? I don't know. I've lost the contract between me & Messrs. J. M. Dent: if I ever read it. I know Dent's haven't got any American rights to my book, but can I call myself proprietor? Have you, by the way, ever written to David Higham, of Higham, Pollinger & Pearn, London, who was, for that book, '25 Poems', alone, my agent? Until I get a little elucidation, from you or him, I can't clearly sign that contract. Or the other contract either. All the contracts please me, except as to that one detail: I promise you all future books etc. All that I agree to. But I must know whether I am the proprietor of that one book. And, too, if Higham must still be my agent, *everywhere*, for that book. I've tried, in previous letters, to make this clear to you: that I'm not clear at all about '25 Poems'. I'll sign, of course, because I want you to publish in America everything I do & have done. But I'm not intelligent about things like this, & they must be explained to me simply. Sorry again about this bother, but I obviously can't—as I did once—sign without understanding. Neither can I, *yet*, send back signed those receipts for the £8, or 40 dollars, you sent me: because they say you have the right to publish *all* my books in America, & I don't know—I know there are no American rights, but nothing else—about the '25 Poems'. Do write soon.

Glad everything else is going well: propaganda etc. And I hope the broadcasting is a success. You're getting on well for me; I wish I was better, & clearer.

Reavey is talking now about a Paris edition first of my stories, followed by a bowdlerised English version. There again I know nothing: he sends me cryptic notes & no explanations.

Best wishes. Thank you for forwarding the letter to Emma Swan. She has again sent me a little money.

Dylan T

P.S. I'll have some new stuff to send you soon.
P.P.S. Are you going to try to get published in American magazines all my stories? and poems? I mean the stories & poems in your possession, that have been published in English magazines? That's fine.

MS: the recipient

JAMES LAUGHLIN
28 July 1938   Sea View Laugharne Carmarthenshire S Wales

Dear Laughlin,
   In yesterday's letter I forgot to enclose this (I hope) substitution poem.
Here it is now. Does my probable stupidity as to your contract annoy
you? I look forward to you writing.

                                        Best wishes,
                                        Dylan T

Henry Treece tells me that you were quite keen about his book about me.
He's coming down to spend a holiday with me next week: he's a total
stranger to me, by the way.

MS: the recipient

CHARLES FISHER
Thursday [late July 1938]   Sea View Laugharne Carmarthenshire

Dear Charles,
   We've moved house & tilted our noses. Our previous house, once a
palace, is now that cottage. How we ever existed there is beyond us. Here
we could have two bedrooms each, which is quite useless.
   Will you give Tom this note.
   When are you coming to see us. Henry Treece is down next week to
stay. Come along & meet him? Bring some poems.

                                        Love,
                                        Dylan

MS: the recipient   *SL*

CHARLES FISHER
Monday August 8 1938   Sea View Laugharne Carmarthenshire

Dear Charles,
   Sorry—we all were—that you couldn't come down on Saturday. Treece
and his abominable girl are going away tomorrow morning, but can you
still visit us Tuesday? We'll expect you. Bring Fred if you can. But bring
yourself and poems, jokes, & bits of play.

                                        Love,
                                        Dylan

MS: the recipient

T. S. ELIOT
23 August 1938   Sea View Laugharne Carmarthenshire

Dear Mr Eliot,
   I am applying to the Royal Literary Fund for a grant of money because
of my present desperate position and because my wife is soon going to
have a baby. We have no support at all apart from my earnings as a writer,
which are extremely little, and I hope the Fund will see that my cause is
deserving. I'm told that in my application I should give the names of two
or three well known writers who will say a word for me. Could I please
use your name, which would be of very great help? As far as I can gather,
all you would have to do—if you did agree to help me in this way—would
be to answer the enquiries of the Fund trustees and to say that, in your
opinion, I was deserving of their charity. Without some such immediate
grant I will have to give up the house that with difficulty we rented and
furnished here & take again to lodgings and running from debts and
instability and less and less opportunities for doing my own work. But
above all I have to consider the welfare of my wife and her baby, and I do
very much hope that you will allow me to use your name.
                                          Yours sincerely,
                                          Dylan Thomas

MS: Valerie Eliot

JOHN DAVENPORT

John Davenport (1908–66) was a pugnacious critic and literary figure, subject of many
anecdotes, who lives on as a character in other writers' reminiscences but never wrote
a book of his own. He was more affluent before the Second World War than after it,
scouting for stories for a film company and (according to his own unreliable account)
writing, or perhaps not writing, a script for Robert Donat in Hollywood.

24 August 1938   Laugharne Carmarthenshire S Wales

Dear John,
   Thank you for writing. Of course your messages weren't delivered,
though Norman and Augustus have both been here to see us, flashing
rolls. We hope to be in Hampshire in October, to stay a little bit before
our saint or monster,[1] and then we must meet. Unless you have a car and
drive one day to Wales: we can put you up somehow any time.
   About my books of poems. New Directions is or are, as far as I know,
going to publish them both in America; or, rather, one book with nearly
all the poems in it. Also, as far as I know again, the stories. This as far as I
know nonsense is due to a disagreement between myself and James

[1] The child that Caitlin Thomas was expecting.

Laughlin (of New Directions) as to the honesty, or fairness, of the contracts he has sent me to sign. He gave me, when I was broke and hungry, eight pounds, which I regarded foolishly as a present. Later, he sent me a contract to sign that said that the eight pounds was an advance on royalties to be earned by the books which I had, in my gratitude, only promised him.[1] Now I am asking for a proper advance—some lump sum is utterly essential to me right away—or I shall take away the books. If he refuses, hums and ha's, I'll send, with great pleasure, everything to you. Thank you a lot.

The English publication of my stories is in a far worse mess, and I can get nothing clear from Reavey who is certainly not my dream, either, of a literary businessman. I write pathetically to George, but he just won't answer. Publication, he has condescended to tell me on a postcard, of the stories as they stand would lead to imprisonment. What he will not tell me is the particular words, phrases, passages to which objection is taken; these my scruples will allow me to alter without hesitation; but how do I know, without being told, what words etc. the dunder printers and lawyers think objectionable: piss, breast, bottom, Love? I understand, from someone else (Wyn Henderson), that George is going to get the stories done by a Paris smut press first, then allow the lawyers he has apparently consulted to castrate them for English publication. I just sit and hate. Nobody tells me anything. (There will be, Laughlin says, no difficulty about American censorship.)

I am writing, at the moment, a letter of appeal to something called the Royal Literary Fund, asking them for an immediate grant of money to help me live and help me pay for the care of Caitlin and child. This Fund moves slowly, slower than we grind, and I don't hope much from it. But without its help, without some grant—and I am a deserving cause, I have no support at all apart from my earnings as a writer, which won't pay for napkins and doesn't for our food—we are more desperate than you could realise. Do you know of any Society etc. that might give me some little grant, some little immediate living money? And do you know what 'well known writer' would support my bread and butter application? I'm writing to Eliot, but I must, to satisfy these charitable meanies, have some more names.

I'll let you know what happens about New Directions. Thank you again. Regards to you both.

Yours,
Dylan T

I didn't know my '25 Poems' were out of print. I could get you a personal copy, though, if you want one, I'm sure.

MS: Texas

---

[1] Thomas's letters to Laughlin don't bear this out.

ROYAL LITERARY FUND[1]
26.8.38   Sea View Laugharne Carmarthenshire S Wales

Dear Sir,

I am writing on the advice of Mr. Denys Kilham Roberts to ask if I am eligible for a grant from the Royal Literary Fund.

I am 23 years old, and married. I have been trying to live by my writing for five years, and have lived in poverty nearly all that time. So far I have had to be content with poverty, and have always been fortunate to have just enough food and to have a room to work and sleep in. But now my wife is going to have a baby, and our position is desperate. I cannot provide her, by my very small earnings, with the care she needs; and my own health—my lungs are weak—does not let me take, even if it were offered to me, regular employment outside the country. My one hope is that I should be considered deserving enough for a literary grant that would enable me to continue working and to care well for my wife during her pregnancy and afterwards. We have no support at all, apart from what my writing brings us; and my writing is printed mostly in uncommercial magazines.

Mr. Kilham Roberts told me that I should give the names of a few wellknown writers who will support my application. I am sure that, among others, Mr. T. S. Eliot, Mr. Cyril Connolly,[2] Mr. Richard Church, Mr. Richard Hughes, Mr. Charles Williams (of the Oxford University Press), and Mr. W. H. Auden—though I have not written personally to all these gentlemen—would support my claims.

I have published two books of poetry: '18 Poems', in 1934, '25 Poems', in 1936, and a book of my short stories, 'The Burning Baby', is being printed at the moment. I am a contributor to many English and American periodicals, including 'The Criterion', 'The Listener', 'New Verse', '20th Century Verse', 'Contemporary Poetry & Prose', 'New Stories', 'Poetry (Chicago)', 'John O'London's Weekly', 'New English Weekly', 'Life and Letters To-Day'. I have reviewed regularly for the 'Morning Post', and for 'The Adelphi', and contributed reviews to 'The Spectator', and 'Time and Tide'. I am reviewing now, though unfortunately without payment, all novels for the 'New English Weekly'. My work has been represented in most recent anthologies of poetry, including 'The Faber Book of Modern Poetry', 'Poems of Tomorrow', 'The Modern Poet', 'Poems of Today', 'The Year's Poetry' for 1934, 1935, 1936, 1937, and in 'The Faber Book of Modern Stories', and 'The Best Short Stories of the Year'.

My work has been reviewed at length in many periodicals: 'The Sunday Times', (a long review by Miss Edith Sitwell), 'The New Statesman',

---

[1] The Fund, which has existed since 1790, helps authors whose work is of 'approved literary merit' with grants when they fall on hard times. Thomas was quick to detect its hint of charity for the deserving poor.

[2] Cyril Connolly (1903–74), critic and editor, notably of the magazine *Horizon*, 1939–50.

'Time and Tide', 'The Spectator', 'The Listener', 'The Criterion', 'Life & Letters', 'The London Mercury'.

A book about my work—'Dylan Thomas: An Introduction' by Henry Treece—is to be published shortly.

My need is urgent. I do most sincerely trust that I am eligible for a grant, and hope to hear from you. Do please tell me if there are any other details you could wish me to supply.

Yours truly,
Dylan Thomas

MS: Royal Literary Fund

JOHN DAVENPORT
31st August 1938   Laugharne Carmarthenshire S Wales

Dear John,

Thank you very much. What a list of the boys, the nibs of the P.E.N. Club,[1] pipesucking, carpetslippered, New Statesman in pocket, 'Mr Y has timbre', symposium contributors ('I write in white ink, in a kneeling position'). How can I choose from such richness, rule out a Strauss for a Guinness?[2] No, but I leave it to you if you don't mind choosing, because perhaps you know what sort of writer the Royal Literary Fund will have most faith in. I myself have written to Eliot (who has replied, & has already written 'strongly' to the secretary) and to Connolly, who hasn't yet replied (is he in England, do you know?). I should think the more, and the generally better known, names the better. Huxley?[3] He's famous and respectable, isn't he? but I doubt very much that he knows my name. Does that matter? I heard from the Secretary this morning; he said that his committee doesn't meet again until October, a cold & cheerless way off, so he intends to approach the Government on my behalf for an immediate spot. To do this, he needs, *at once*, a few letters 'authenticating the merits' of my case. So the point is: which of the names you suggest—(it really is terribly kind of you to take this trouble)—would be most likely to write, of their own initiative, an immediate brief letter okaying me? Would it be better to try to choose a few names that have been known to like my poems? or would some of the eminent say, if you asked them, a couple of nice words in a short letter, just for friendlinesses sake and the brotherhood of Art? Of the names you wrote down, I'm known to John Hayward—I mean by 'known' that I know I'm known to them—E. J. O'Brien, Calder Marshall, Collier, Spender, Empson (though I

---

[1] P.E.N. ('Playwrights, Poets, Essayists and Novelists') is an international organisation for writers.

[2] Probably the authors Ralph Straus and Bryan Guinness (Lord Moyne).

[3] The author Aldous Huxley.

think he's in China, isn't he? and I must have, in my favour, some *at-once* responses), Aaronson, Quennell, Rickword.[1] But I should think more-or-less middleaged people would be safer. It would be grand if you'd write to 3 or 4 of these, telling them about things & asking them to write as soon as possible a short letter to

> H. J. C. Marshall
> Secretary Royal Literary Fund
> Y. Gell
> Trelyllyn
> Nr. Towyn, Wales.

How quickly I get money—and God how much I need it—depends on how quickly any of these people will write an 'authenticating' letter.

That was news about Laughlin who, when he came to England in June, wrote telling me that only the huge price of a railway ticket from London to South Wales prevented him from coming to interview me culturally. Pigiron duke[2] sounds good, and I'll probably try taunting him with it if he still sticks by his disgusting idea of a business advance of £8. He's boosting me now in America, gave a broadcast last month which would have been a joy to hear. In an American paper—I've forgotten which—he wrote an article about me & said that I had the medieval mind. He proved this (a) by a line of mine, 'May fail to fasten with a virgin o', which he said was 'ballad in origin' and had something to do with raggletaggle gypsies o, and by which I meant a circle, a round complete o, and (b) by my use of the word 'denier' which he said was an ancient coin and which I meant to be a person who denies.

I've just had, from Reavey, at last, a lawyer's list of the objectionable words, phrases, passages & whole chunks in my short stories. The word 'copulation' (used by me in reference to a tree, most innocently), 'pissed', (I said that a man spitefully pissed against the wind in order to wet somebody behind him), 'All Pauls Altar', the actual description of a murder committed by a naked woman (especially the phrase 'her head broke like an egg on the wall'), 'the holy life was a constant erection to these gentlemen', and about 20 long passages, none in the least way tittivating, none using obscene words, none evasively or circumlocutionarily to do with fucking,—all have to go in the English edition. And anyway I'd rather tickle the cock of the English public than lick its arse, which is what even this small and comparatively unimportant piece of unjust censorship would have me do.

Thank Clement[3] very much for her offer of infant clothes, which Caitlin would love to accept. There won't be any need until about the end

---

[1] John Hayward, critic. Edward J. O'Brien, short story anthologist. Arthur Calder-Marshall and John Collier, authors. Edgell Rickword, poet.
[2] The Laughlin family firm made steel.
[3] Clement was John Davenport's first wife.

of the year, before which perhaps we'll see you. It's very kind of her. Our thing, we hope, won't be too monstrously small or big for the clothes. Write soon & tell me what members of the troupe will perform for me. Thanks again v. much.

Love to both,
Dylan

MS: Texas   *SL(R)*

ROYAL LITERARY FUND
31 August 1938   Sea View Laugharne Carmarthenshire

Dear Mr. Marshall,

Thank you very much for your letter, and for replying so quickly.

Here is the application form. I haven't, in the fifth question, made any reference to the fact that my wife soon will have a child. Question seven I could answer very simply, but, as regards question eight, I haven't kept an exact record of my extremely small earnings.[1] The little money I've received during the last year, and that has somehow kept us alive, has been given to me by a few friends who are, themselves, unfortunately, not well-off and who obviously can't be expected to give me anything more.

In the list of published works I'm not required, am I, to put down all the poems and stories of mine that have appeared in periodicals and anthologies? I mentioned those in my first letter to you.

About Regulation number II.[2] I have written to several people, asking them for their support for my application, but so far only Mr. T. S. Eliot has replied, saying that he 'will be glad to write strongly in my favour'. He is staying now in Cardiganshire, and I am asking him to send a letter directly to you.

You were kind enough to suggest that, as your Committee does not meet until mid-October, you would approach the Government on my behalf and try to arrange some immediate help: I would be very very grateful if you *would* do that, for October seems, to me in my desperate state, with inevitable debts mounting, a long way off, and I have no idea how, without some such assistance, we can continue living until then. The last thing I want to do—and the first thing I will have to do unless some immediate money can be granted—is to give up the house that we have, with difficulty, half-furnished here and to be forced to move about again hopelessly and helplessly from lodging to lodging. Without some sort of permanent place to live in, without the certainty of regular food &

---

[1] Thomas wrote: 'Literary earnings during the past year: under £30.'
[2] 'No Application for a grant shall be entertained . . . unless accompanied by letters from two or more respectable persons authenticating the merits of the case.'

shelter, my own work, necessarily difficult because of its experimental nature, is almost impossible to concentrate upon.

I have written for copies of my two published books of poems; they should arrive here the end of this week and I shall send them on to you at once. Both books are, I believe, difficult to obtain, although they went into two editions. My own copies I was forced to sell some time ago to a man who collected first editions and who offered me a little more than their original cost.

The third book, of stories, will not be ready until the autumn; owing to some difficulty of censorship—the book was actually finished at the beginning of the year—it will appear first in France, then in America (with New Directions Ltd.) & then in England where the Europa Press will publish it. I am afraid that my published work, as you will see it, is very small, for most of my poems and stories, and all that I have done since the publication of my last book—including a long story to appear in the September Life & Letters To-Day, & a poem in the September Criterion—has come out in periodicals.

Thank you again. Mr. Eliot's letter should arrive in a day or two; also, I hope, some supporting letters from other writers.

Yours sincerely,
Dylan Thomas

MS: Royal Literary Fund

HENRY TREECE
September 1 1938   Sea View Laugharne Carmarthenshire

Dear Henry,
Every apology, true and false, for not having written before. The Old Master[1] stayed on several more days after you left for Harlech; his varnish was cracking visibly; he left us bloated, and dumb from his deafness; then a friend of mine, a Jewish funny drawer with lots to do and say, hitchhiked here from London, on his way to Ireland.[2] He stayed on, occupying all my time in ways you know by now and Caitlin's in the ways a male pig expects, for over a week until my motherinlaw and a neuter friend came for a holiday in the pub. Now they're all disappeared, & I'm forced to work; thank God the sun has gone in and I needn't go out; we've nothing left but our wits and paper. Please forgive me. I really have had no time even for politeness—and anyway I know you too well now to need to be polite—and certainly not for a long letter. The only things I've written have been letters to the Royal Literary Fund, asking them for a grant, and to some respectable persons—Mr. Eliot and minor deacons

---

[1] Augustus John.
[2] Mervyn Levy.

—asking them to support my application. What I need now urgently is some small regular income; the garret's repugnant; I can't keep a steady head and wag a wild tongue if worry like a bumbailiff sits silently nagging by my side. Poverty makes me lazy and crafty. I'm not a fineweather poet, or a lyrical tramp, or a bright little bowl waiting for the first fine flush, or a man who cuts his face with a grand phrase while shaving; I like regular meals and drink and a table and a ruler—and three pens. Eliot has supported me strongly—he's staying in Wales now, 30 miles from here, and is coming For Tea,—and the Fund secretary is, apparently, going to apply for me to the Fascist Government. Mr. Chamberlain is crazy about modern verse, and I shall send a photograph of myself, in bowler and gasmask, rhyming womb with tomb.[1]

This is only a note to let you know I'm alive, & to apologise, and to say how much we enjoyed your staying here & how much we hope you'll come & stay again & that we'll meet again soon. Little awkwardnesses may have arisen—you took the up path, I took the Brown[2]—but they weren't I hope, anything serious; & one day I'll walk 10 miles with you, & you shall sit 10 hours in a saloon chair with me. Perhaps none of us got really going; in your short stay I had toothache, headache, hangover, rheumatism, & seasickness, & was all the time perfectly healthy; Nelly had a bad Welsh cold. I hope she's better now. Over this weekend I'll write the good letter, with analysis etc. That's a promise.

I asked John about a drawing; he'll do it when he comes back from France in the autumn. If he does it quickly, in one go, it should be good, & might help the commercial success of your book.

More very soon. Terribly sorry about his rude delay.

Love,
Dylan

Caitlin wishes all the right things for you & Nelly.

MS: Buffalo   *SL*

VERNON WATKINS
Sunday [?September 1938]   Sea View Laugharne Carmarthenshire

Dear Vernon,
Thanks for the letter & the poem which I like immensely now, after many readings; it's one of the very best, & I'll write more about it soon to you (& about 2 others I've got) or read it over with you when we meet.

Here are 2 short ones of mine, just done.[3] Could you type them properly

---

[1] Neville Chamberlain was Prime Minister of the right-wing 'National' Government. Gas masks were in the news as fears of war continued to grow.
[2] Brown's Hotel, the Laugharne pub favoured by Thomas.
[3] Identified by Watkins as 'The tombstone told when she died' and (probably) 'On no work of words now'.

for me? In the ballad-like poem I'm not *quite* sure of several words, mostly of 'great' floods of his hair. I think it's right, though; I didn't want a surprisingly strong word there. Do tell me about it, soon.

What about a weekend here? There's plenty of food, beds, & welcome. Come by bike. What about next weekend? Let me know.

Love,
D.

MS: British Library   *VW*

ROYAL LITERARY FUND
15th September 1938   Sea View Laugharne Carmarthenshire

Dear Mr. Marshall,

I'm naturally very sorry indeed that your efforts to obtain some temporary help for me, prior to the meeting of your committee, have failed. Thank you very much for your kindness, and for the trouble you have taken.

I hope that by this time you've received a letter from Mr. Eliot. I've asked some other writers to send you a letter on my behalf, though, as I asked for their help urgently, I gave them your Welsh address.

I have written to the Cymmrodorion Society, not mentioning your name or the name of the Society. Thank you for the address. I'll let you know what happens, though I'm not at all optimistic about this. My position now, as you will hardly need to know, is far more desperate than ever & I cannot continue for long.

Here are my two books of poems. I have been a long time getting hold of them.

I do not think I told you, by the way, that my new book of poems is almost ready to send to a publisher. I hope it will appear next spring. I am working very hard.

Yours sincerely,
Dylan Thomas

MS: Texas

JOHN DAVENPORT
23 ix 38   Laugharne Carmarthenshire

Dear John,

It's disappointing of course, but I expected it. I know that tolerant sadness, that liberal shrug in the rustling gloom; I've heard 'rather a forlorn enterprise' (resigned but still whimsical), 'there it is what can we do' (palms lifted, ash dropped on the untidy waistcoat drooping on a wrong button), 'we're only the intelligentsia you know' (arch, self-deprecatory and twisted smile), 'yes, Spain is terrifying' (serious suddenly, the eyes studiously dilated) echo, like the pad of old slippers in a room carpeted with the competition-pages of the New Statesman, on late summer evenings when nostalgic Hampstead lies half asleep in a briar cloud and the air is full of the soft cries of reviewers and the gentle choosing of books. I react like Beachcomber, and could raise up my club Lewis.[1] The little pessimisms of these Boots-minded[2] thrush-watchers—, calculated to make appear difficult the too-easy occupation of writing,—could drive me to not drinking. When does anyone 'establish his claim to be a professional writer'? When he makes enough money not to want assistance? Are my needs less because I'm young? Must I live celibate on bread and poems until my Novel is Accepted? Anyway, something may come, I suppose, of this lion-prodding; I'd like to print the growls. Eliot and Charles Williams—he's very respectable *and* enthusiastic—have written letters for me. Will *one* of the people you've approached do anything? I hope so. The 'exceptional circumstances' must be stressed. And about what, if anything *does* happen, will the Fund slip over? Any idea? Do write if there's any news, or if there isn't.

Dylan

Haven't managed to get 25 Poems yet. My new book of poems is almost ready. I've no idea who to give it to; I don't like Dent's.

MS: Texas   *SL*

VERNON WATKINS
Monday [postmarked October 14 1938]   Sea View Laugharne

Dear Vernon,
  I'm sorry not to have written before, I've been awfully busy with my own work, with reviewing, & muddled up with trying to get money from a sinister philanthropic society. Here's my new big poem and—with no anger at all—the Hardy-like one.[3] I considered all your suggestions most carefully. A 'strange & red' harsh head was, of course, very weak & clumsy, but I couldn't see that the alliteration of 'raving red' was effective. I tried everything, & stuck to the commonplace 'blazing',

---

[1] J. B. Morton's predecessor as 'Beachcomber' at the *Daily Express* was D. B. Wyndham Lewis.

[2] Boots Library was one of several commercially-run 'circulating libraries' that had to be popular to survive.

[3] The 'Hardy-like poem', discussed in the first paragraph, was 'The tombstone told when she died'. The 'big poem', discussed in the second, was later called 'A saint about to fall'.

which makes the line violent enough then, if not exactly good enough, for the last. In the last line you'll see I've been daring, & have tried to make the point of the poem softer & subtler by the use of the dangerous 'dear'. The word 'dear' fits in, I think, with 'though her eyes smiled', which comes earlier. I wanted the girl's *terrible* reaction to orgiastic death to be suddenly altered into a kind of despairing love. As I see it now, it strikes me as very moving, but it may be too much of a shock, a bathetic shock perhaps, & I'd like very much to know what you think. No, I still think the womb 'bellowing' is allright, exactly what I wanted; perhaps it looks too much like a stunt rhyme with heroine, but that was unavoidable. 'Hurried' film I just couldn't see; I wanted it slow & complicated, the winding cinematic works of the womb. I agree with your objection to 'small'; 'innocent' is splendid, but 'fugitive' & 'turbulent' are, for me in that context, too vague, too 'literary' (I'm sorry to use that word again) too ambiguous. I've used 'devilish', which is almost colloquial.

As to the big poem—only provisionally called 'In September', & called that at all only because it was a terrible war month—I'm at the moment very pleased with it, more than with anything I've done this year. Does 'Glory cracked like a flea' shock you? I think you'll see it *must* come there, or some equal[ly] grotesque contrast. The last line of the 2nd verse might appear just a long jumble of my old anatomical clichés, but if, in the past, I've used 'burning brains & hair' etc too loosely, this time I used them—as the only words—in dead earnest. Remember this is a poem written to a child about to be born—you know I'm going to be a father in January—& telling it what a world it will see, what horrors & hells. The last four lines of the poem, especially the last but two, may seem ragged, but I've altered the rhythm purposely; 'you so gentle' must be very soft & gentle, & the last line must roar. It's an optimistic, taking-everything, poem. The two most important words are 'Cry Joy'. Tell me about this, please, very soon. I'm surer of the *words* of this poem than of the words in any recent one. I want mostly to know what the general effect of the poem is upon you (though of course you can criticize, as you like, any detail).

Sorry you couldn't come this weekend. Do try to come next. I'm afraid we're much too poor to be able to come up to see you for a long time. So do your best.

All love,
Dylan

[*The following poem was sent on a separate sheet of paper. It was printed that winter, in the magazine* Seven, *but not thereafter in Thomas's lifetime.*]

I, the first named, am the ghost of this sir and Christian friend
Who writes these words I write in a still room in a spellsoaked house:
I am the ghost in this house that is filled with the tongue and eyes
Of a lack-a-head ghost I fear to the anonymous end.

[*On reverse of envelope:*]
Can you send me a typed copy of the long poem?

The word is OGRE, not orge or orgy &, as Prichard would say, I'll listen to no criticisms of it.[1]

MS: British Library   VW

JOHN DAVENPORT
14 October 1938   Laugharne Carmarthenshire S Wales

Dear John,

No grant was made me. My literary claims 'were found not strong enough for the purposes of this society'.[2] Who *do* they give their money to? I'm an excellent and most disturbing case. Must you be a Georgian writer of belle-lettres, suffering in Surrey? Must you be in the evening of your days, with nothing to look forward to but nostalgia, borrowed copies of new books about Wilde, and inclusion in any Gawsworth anthology of the unburied dead? Or is the Royal Fund available only for successful writers having a bad year? Only *recommended* this year by the Medium Book Society! Poor chap, send him a large cheque and a luncheon invitation from a publisher's nark; let Miss DuMaurier[3] knit him a smoking-coat, & don't forget the special, indelible inkstains. But I'm furious. And after Miss Sitwell wrote two pages to the secretary, too. You don't know, do you, any rich person I can try now? I'll dedicate my next poems to him, & write a special sponger's song. Can't I live even on the immoral earnings of my poems? No, but there must be someone, somewhere in England, who'd like to do a poet a good turn, someone who wouldn't miss just enough money to ensure me peace & comfort for a month or two to get on with the work I'm in the middle of now & which I so much want to finish. All my hopes were in that Royal set-up, & now we'll have to abscond from here, as from everywhere else I've ever lived in, leaving, this time, a house full of furniture we had the devil of a lot of cringing trouble to obtain. Thirty bloody pounds would settle everything. If you know any rich chap fond of a jingle, who knows his Peters & Quennells, do let me know at once. Otherwise it'll be traipsing again, no stability at all, no hope, and certainly no work. Try to think of some sap, some saint. There's no reason why I should bother you like this, but here

---

[1] In the poem 'On no work of words now'. Watkins had typed it.
[2] Among those who wrote to support Thomas as a worthy cause were T. S. Eliot, Edith Sitwell, Charles Williams, Walter de la Mare and John Masefield. Writing to H. J. C. Marshall in 1941 (when a second Thomas application was successful), the author Frank Swinnerton said: 'As I remember it . . . one member of the Committee [probably S. A. Courtauld] read aloud as gibberish one of his poems; and he was turned down because he was only 25 . . .' Courtauld was a businessman. Thomas was 23, not 25.
[3] Dame Daphne du Maurier, novelist.

I can't get in touch with anybody with more money than a betty with no cunt or more generosity than a fucked weazel.

Yours,
Dylan T.

I'm putting in a poem, someone just typed a few copies of it.

MS: Texas

BBC [R. G. Walford, Copyright Section]
14 October 1938   Sea View Laugharne Carmarthenshire S Wales

Dear Sir,
   In reply to your letter of the 12th, I authorise the broadcast of my poem 'The hand that signed the paper' in the programme on October 18th, and agree to the fee of one guinea which you proposed.

Yours faithfully

TS: BBC, from original letter in Legal Section

BBC
14 October 1938   Sea View Laugharne Carmarthenshire

Dear Sir,
   I enclose the confirmation sheet, agreeing to broadcast on October 18, etc.
   I received a letter today from Broadcasting House, Manchester, inviting me to read a poem at the same date & time; but this letter says that the rehearsal & performance will be from London. My five minutes (stipulated in your agreement) is obviously part of the programme 'The Modern Muse', but the difference of place (London & Manchester) mentioned in the two letters, yours and Mr. Bridson's from the North Region, has confused me a little. I hope you'll clear up these small difficulties by return.[1]
   I am now living in Laugharne, outside Carmarthen, and your letter was sent to my old Swansea address. My fare, I am afraid, would have to be paid from Laugharne to Manchester, & not from Swansea. Also, owing to

[1] 'The Modern Muse. A Recital of Contemporary Poetry' was broadcast from the Manchester studios, 10.30 pm, October 18. Those who read their own poems included Spender, Auden, MacNeice, Kathleen Raine and Charles Madge. Thomas read 'The hand that signed the paper'. Michael Roberts presented the programme; D. G. Bridson produced it.

my circumstances, I find it necessary to have to be given the railfare & subsistence allowance *before* I travel.

Sorry if these questions & demands are troublesome, & hope you'll be kind enough to explain etc. by return.

Yours faithfully,
Dylan Thomas

MS: BBC

BBC
15 October 1938 (Accepts fee for poem. See Appendix 13.)

HENRY TREECE
[mid-October 1938]   Lyulph's Tower Ullswater Penrith[1]
                                       Not my address. Still in Sea-View.

Dear Henry:

If it wasn't that I know bitterly how wild it makes a man or a Caitlin, how it puts into the head a sense of injury that was perhaps not there before, I'd say Now don't be huffy. Of course—as you should know; am I a quivering bundle of temperament, all wind and wet conceit that I can imagine I could, even if I wanted to, be rude to my equally unconceited, un-nonsensical friends—I haven't any wish not to fulfil my promises, not to write you lots of times and lots of pages. It's only that I'm lazy about writing, and deeply depressed. You mustn't be offended because I'm a lazy pig—(I know, I bitterly know, 'who's offended, damn your presumption, jerry-headed conceit that makes you think your lack of writing can offend me'; & that's true, but I always mean one way less than I say & the other way more; it is my everpresent conscience, concealed under a Punch humour, that forces me to make each fact dubious, to attempt to add suspicion to straight details)—I've wanted to write so often, have thought about you, what you're doing and why, and several times have written Dear Henry down, stared at the paper, sunk into coma, picked my nose & made a small salt meal, though there were many things to tell you and, even then, many apologies to make. I'm depressed about facts, which no-money makes dubious; debts are climbing, tradesmen barking, the Government is too busy, the Royal Literary Fund regards my literary claims as insufficient (you have, I think, to be a Georgian, a writer of faded belles-lettres), we will have to abscond from here one day next week, leaving a furnished (now much better, & more fully, furnished than

[1] Lyulph's Tower was a house that Richard Hughes sometimes borrowed.

when you were here) house behind, a lovely town, some friends. At least, if not absconsion, a holiday from debts; and that will not pay them. We will go to Swansea for a week or two, then Hampshire. (On this Tuesday, the 18th, I'm going to Manchester, to broadcast with Auden, MacNeice, Spender etc. in a programme, called The Modern Muse, compered by M. Roberts. I suppose it would be quite impossible for you to meet me in Manchester that evening? I know only that you're North, I've no idea where. If you could, come to the B.B.C. offices.)

Now about your last, full letter: It was odd to hear that Donald Duck of the New English Weekly has decided that I'm too young for your book. He wrote me last week, saying he had met you, that he would encourage the book all he could, & also that I was a swell reviewer. He was enthusiastic, quacked for pages. What did he tell you? He must change his mind very quickly; & what a mind, too! Having Gawsworth to edit his anthology! Gawsworth would be a standing joke if he weren't completely supine. I'm glad Seven is doing the surrealist chapter; they want one or two new poems of mine to go in the same number with it; I sent some short ones yesterday, but it may be too late. Your offer—which I should have thanked you for a long time ago—of a percentage of anything that comes from your book is terribly generous. It *was* nice of you to think of it, and I accept it very gratefully. I hope we'll both make out of it, and be able to meet to spend. I'll try to be in London at Christmas; you must meet some of my disreputable friends; I have one of the best collections. Caitlin won't be with me; she looks increasingly robust & our little half-formed monster is kicking & smiting.

There haven't been any visitors here for some time now, & we live very quietly. We have a supper a week with the Hugheses, & they have one here. I am writing poems, & will send them to you as soon as they are typed. One, I think, is as good as anything I've done: a longish poem to my unborn child. You shall see it next week. I want to post this off now, because it's late & I'm going to Swansea tomorrow morning & then on to Manchester. This is the first of a regular series of dull letters. And I've nearly finished for you an analysis of two poems.

Yours ever,
Dylan

I'll send, too, the address—when I can find it—of a new American quarterly edited by Ransom. The first number appears in December. They want new critical work.

MS: Buffalo   SL(R)

VERNON WATKINS
[postmarked October 19 1938][1]   Sea View Laugharne Carmarthenshire

Dear Vernon,

I'm going to Manchester on Tuesday to take part in a programme, that will be broadcast on the National, sweetly called the Modern Muse. About 10.30 at night. Don't forget to listen in. I'll probably read one, at the most two, short poems of my own, &, for that alone, the journey wouldn't be worth while; but I may as well go up to meet Auden, Spender, MacNeice, Day-Lewis & some others who'll be there; Minnie Roberts is compering, which is just about his job. I'll tell you all about it in Swansea, for I'll come back there on Wednesday. Looking forward to seeing you.

Thank you for typing the poems, & for the things you said. I agree that 'carbolic' & 'strike' cd be bettered,[2] but, at the moment, I'll just leave them; I may be able to go back clearly to the poem some time soon, but I'll publish it now as it is in Life & Letters, & then, we'll see. Glad you liked the straight story;[3] I'm doing another now: illuminated reporting.

That hymn must be great in the original, I wish I could read German.

Love,
Dylan

MS: British Library   VW

CHARLES FISHER
21 October [1938] [card]   Sea View House Laugharne Carmarthenshire

So sorry if our sudden change of plans put you out at all. I found suddenly that I had to broadcast—I don't know whether you heard it—with Auden & some others from Manchester, on the Tuesday you were going to collect us. This meant a little money, and that money will keep us for some more days in Laugharne. We'll have to spend, in the future, such a long time with parents that we think it wiser, if only for their sakes, to live for as long as possible on & by ourselves. Can we, in spite of this small muddle, ask you again: and ask you soon?

I've got several new poems to show you. My new book of them is almost ready. It's to be called 'In the Direction of The Beginning', for it will include the long story by that name.[4] Looking forward to showing things to you.

Love,
Dylan

MS: the recipient

[1] This was the day *after* the broadcast.
[2] 'A saint about to fall' has the phrase 'the carbolic city' and the line 'Strike in the time-bomb town'.
[2] Probably 'The Peaches', just published.
[3] That story was not included, and the book was called *The Map of Love*.

VERNON WATKINS
[card, postmarked October 24 1938]

                           [*note at side:*] This poem's just a statement, perhaps.

This very short poem is for my birthday just arriving.[1] I know you'll hate the use of the 'Forever' line, but there it is. I scrapped the poem beginning with that line long ago,[2] and at last—I think—I've found the inevitable place for it: it was a time finding that place. I'm pleased, terribly, with this—so far. Do tell me, & type please. In the first version I had 'like a stuffed tailor'. I think stuffed is wrong, don't you? Try to read the end of the poem as though you didn't know the lines. I do feel they're right. In the old 'Forever' poem they were completely out of place—& the rest of the poem wouldn't stand without them. So bang went the whole poem, obviously, & here at last is what it should be.

MS: British Library   *VW*

D. S. SAVAGE
Oct 24 [1938]   Laugharne Carmarthenshire S Wales

Dear D. S. Savage,
    Thank you for the letter.
    The bother about the poems for New Directions and The Partisan Review has been settled. New Directions have persuaded Partisan Review to print another poem, & have themselves kept the one I originally sent to you.
    I don't know what poem I could send for the broadsheet series; I'll try to write something specially for it, but if that doesn't come off I'll let you see a selection of recent poems. Good luck with the series. What sort is it going to be? Woodcut nymphs?

                                    Best wishes,
                                    Dylan Thomas

PS. Will you let me know the closing date? If the first broadsheet, & if the first is to be mine, comes out early December—how much time does that give me?

MS: Texas

---

[1] Thomas enclosed 'Birthday Poem' (in *CP* as 'Twenty-four years'). His twenty-fourth birthday was October 27.
[2] The abandoned poem, beginning 'For as long as forever is', was probably written in 1936. Texas has a twelve-line draft, reproduced in Ferris's biography.

DAVID HIGHAM
27 Oct '38   Sea View Laugharne Carmarthenshire

Dear Higham,

I must apologise for my very long delay in writing to you & in answering your letters. Actually, I never had a letter from you about Laughlin: it must have gone astray in one of my previous, too temporary addresses. It was not laziness, really, that kept me from writing: I've had a very hard time lately, & have been trying, in all sorts of ways, with guile & charity, to set up a house & to live in security. This has almost succeeded, though not quite.

First of all, about the Dent's book. I tried to do it as agreed—a travel book—and failed. Now I'm trying to make it a semi-fiction, semi-autobiographical book, each chapter a short story. One of the stories appeared in the October Life & Letters To-Day. This is rather a big undertaking, & is taking time.

I've nearly got ready my new book of poems, to be called 'In The Direction Of The Beginning'. W. H. Auden tells me that the Hogarth Press, of which he is one of the new advisers or directors, would be very glad to see it and almost sure to want to do it. Is that a good idea, do you think? He also told me—how officially, I don't know—that he thought they'd give me an advance of £50 on receiving & accepting the mss. Even if Dent's *did* want to do this book, I'd prefer it to be published *outside* a series.

I'm enclosing 2 of Laughlin's contracts. Richard Hughes has added a few notes & objections to the first contract, and I can't add much to them.

The contract about 'option & right to publish in U.S.A. any book or books which I shall write or have written' doesn't seem any too good to me. Laughlin says 'in consideration of sums received in advance on royalties', & these sums were two cheques for £4 each, and I can't regard that as anything but a very small advance on the one book of Poems. I think it a good idea for New Directions to do the one book of Poems, as, anyway, nobody else seems to want to do them, & as N.D. has a small but good reputation for modern verse.

My book of stories, 'The Burning Baby', which Dent's refused, & which I eventually gave to the Europa Press because I was sick of the book, is apparently having quite a lot of trouble. No printer'll touch it:—obscene. Now they're thinking of doing it in Paris, which sounds a smelly idea but, perhaps, the only one practicable.

I do hope you'll let me know what you think about these things, & that you'll forgive me for all my past carelessnesses.

Yours sincerely,
Dylan Thomas

MS: Texas

T. ROWLAND HUGHES[1]
2– October 1938[2]   Sea View House Laugharne Carmarthenshire

Dear Mr. Hughes,

Mr. Bridson, of the North Region, told me to get in touch with you. I mentioned to him, just after broadcasting in a programme of his, that I wanted to read some more poems. He said that Cardiff was obviously the place for me to do it from and that you were the person to whom I should write. I've broadcast a few times before; I had quarter of an hour for poems of my own from London about eighteen months ago, and recently took part in a programme, The Modern Muse, from Manchester.

One idea that I had was to be asked to broadcast a short series of readings from the work of Welsh poets, or poets of Welsh ancestry, who wrote or write in English: from Vaughan to Edward Thomas, Wilfred Owen, W. H. Davies, & the younger men, contributors to the periodical 'Wales' & to most of the verse periodicals published in London & abroad, who are now making what is really a renaissance in Welsh writing. I don't think anything of the sort has been done before on the air, and I know that there are a great number of people in Wales who are extremely interested in the development of Anglo-Welsh poetry & who have far too few opportunities of hearing that poetry read.

I should be very interested to hear what you think about this, and I do hope that one reading, at least—if not a whole series—could sometime be arranged.

If you find the suggestion at all suitable & to your liking, would there then be the question of an audition? I think Mr. Bridson, or Mr. John Pudney of London, would be kind enough to support me about that. I have done some reading for both of them.

> Yours sincerely,
> Dylan Thomas

MS: BBC

T. ROWLAND HUGHES
November 3 '38   Sea View House Laugharne Carmarthenshire

Dear Mr. Hughes,

Thank you for writing, and for passing my letter on to Mr. Watkin Jones.[3] I hope something comes of my suggestion. Yes, I know that W. H. Davies & Huw Menai etc. have given readings of their own work, but I'm

---

[1] Hughes produced 'features' (documentary programmes) for the BBC's Welsh Region in Cardiff.
[2] Second numeral illegible. Received by the BBC November 1.
[3] Alun Watkin Jones produced talks programmes at Cardiff.

sure there hasn't been any comprehensive broadcast of Welsh–English poetry, no—silly word—survey.

I don't think I'd be able to do one of those long dramatic programmes in verse; I take such a long time writing anything, & the result, dramatically, is too often like a man shouting under the sea. But if you'd let me know a little more about these programmes—length, subjects unsuitable, etc—I'd like to have a try. It sounds full of dramatic possibilities, if only I was.

I should like very much to call & see you & talk over these things & others when I am next in Cardiff, which I shouldn't think will be for a long time— unfortunately. And I hope if you're in this part of Wales, you'll call & see me.

Yours sincerely,
Dylan Thomas

MS: BBC

JOHN DAVENPORT
4 November 1938   Sea View Laugharne Carmarthenshire

Dear John,

How very very nice and kind of you. That five pounds helped an *awful* lot, and now our debts are almost all paid off. We want to leave, the middle of this month, to stay in Hampshire, and perhaps now we'll be able to leave owing nothing, which will be grand. Thank you so much.

Last night we went to Hughes to dinner—you know he lives here, don't you; in the ruined castle—and he gave me a great lot of his prize bitter and this morning I don't know what I am. I've heard nothing yet from the Royal Literary Fund. Are they *definitely* reconsidering their decision? How did you work it? When you said they gave away forty five thousand a year, didn't you mean four to five? I'm waiting anxiously, twitching every time the postman walks over the cockles to our door.[1]

A couple of weeks ago I read some poems on the wireless in a programme called The Modern Muse. All the boys were in it, and what a mincing lot we were. Did you hear it? All the poets were born in the same house, & had the same mother too.

I'm sending a copy of 25 Poems, but I couldn't get a first edition. Will this do?

The monster clothes came this morning. Can any child be small as that? Thank you, Clement. Caitlin's writing a note.

Is Chippenham full of bedroom suites? And is it far from Fordingbridge, because we'll be there—or very nearly there—in a fortnight & we must meet.[2] Let me know.

---

[1] The path to Sea View was strewn with cockle shells.

[2] Davenport was moving to a house near Chippenham, in southern England. Augustus John lived at Fordingbridge; Thomas's mother-in-law, Mrs Macnamara, lived at Blashford, not far away.

Did you like the poem I sent you? I think the Hogarth Press, under John Lehmann, is going to do my new book: it's called 'In The Direction of The Beginning'.

Thanks a lot. This letter's very weak because of bitter but my gratitude isn't.

Love to both
Yours
Dylan T

MS: Texas   *SL*

JOHN DAVENPORT
[card, postmarked 21 November 1938]   Blashford Ringwood Hants

This is only to let you know that we've moved at last, for a bit, to Hampshire. Augustus drove us up but now we're getting better. We won't be able to come & see you for a while as we're broke. If you could call here, let me know anytime. Thank you for the postcards. Nothing yet from the Royal Literary Fund. More when there's news or when I meet you.

Dylan T

MS: Texas

KAY BOYLE[1]
[?November 1938]   Blashford Ringwood Hants

Dear Kay Boyle,
    Nicholas Moore[2] wrote to me today, enclosing your letter to him. I've written back to him, telling him that I haven't got a novel but that a book of stories of mine may be free in a few days. New Directions wanted to do it, but I'm quarrelling with them about terms etc, and it will probably end up in refusal all round. But just as I posted the letter to Moore, I realised that I'd been wanting to write to you for a long time, without knowing your address. Ever since you published Monday Night. I thought that was a very grand book indeed, and I wrote a review of it—a meagre little one, it had to be—which I do hope you saw. This is a fan letter. You haven't got a greater admirer than me.

Dylan Thomas

MS: Carbondale

[1] Kay Boyle (b. 1903), American novelist and poet, then living in Europe. Her novel *Monday Night* appeared in 1937.
[2] Nicholas Moore (b. 1918), poet; he edited the magazine *Seven*.

DAVID HIGHAM
November 24 1938   Blashford Ringwood Hants

Dear Higham,

I'm sorry not to have answered your last letter before this. It really wasn't just another bit of my carelessness, for I *did* intend to write at once but I didn't have the chance: I've been moving—but I'll be at this address over Christmas—halfstarving, worrying, and escaping from things. [*In the margin:* tradesmen, not things of the spirit.] Also, I was trying to finish my story so that I could let you have the whole manuscript at once. The story is, I'm afraid, taking longer than I thought, and getting to be a much bigger work. So I'm sending you all the poems and (roughly, though probably quite a bit over) half the story. The story, as I'm working hard now, I'll finish by Christmas. You'll see that some of the poems fit in with ideas in the story, and the whole thing does, I believe really, make a comprehensive book, not—as perhaps the suggestion of a book of poems *plus* a story might imply—a hotchpotch. I enclose separately a synopsis of the story, making clear in it where this present manuscript breaks off. It may be a little unfortunate—but surely not so that it will affect consideration—that this manuscript *does* break off at a rather violent part of the story. The rest, I can assure those people on Dent's who thought my Burning Baby stories too violent—is fit enough for any obscure-minded baby to read. The portrait of me by Augustus John, which was promised for the Wales book, could be used as a frontispiece for 'In the Direction', couldn't it? John has done a new portrait, which would reproduce excellently, and he is willing to let it be photographed anytime. Do let me know what you think. Is there—and this is very very important to me, as my wife is going to have a baby at the beginning of January and that means a lot of expense, and I am entirely without support—the chance of getting that £50, or some of it at least, on the strength of this manuscript? It isn't complete, but what the book will be like as a whole can easily be visualised. I *must* have some sort of an advance before Christmas.

About Reavey and the *Burning Baby*. He may have told you that he had everything in connection with the stories in hand, but that isn't so. He can't get it printed, as it stands, in England, and Laughlin, who wants to do it in America, doesn't intend even to think about publishing until late next year or the year after. That's far too far away. Reavey is now, as far as I can gather, thinking of doing it in Paris first and getting me to cut out the naughty bits afterwards. His contract with me says that unless he's published it, or has got the publishing of it under way, within a year of the signing of the contract—then the book comes back to me. The contract was signed last December. Nothing practical seems to have been done yet. Some time ago, he wrote me asking me to allow him a further year to try to get it published—and asking me to write down my agreement with that so that he could add it to the contract. I refused. Could you get in touch with him and tell him that, when the contracted year is up, I want the stories back. Then I could get down to the job of 'cleaning' them up so that, after all, perhaps they could be done by a reputable publisher.

I hope to hear from you. Especially about that £50. Something really is essential.

Apologies for the delay.

Yours,
Dylan Thomas

P.S. The Hon. Secretary, Miss M. Gulick L.R.A.M. 15 Belgrave Road, S.W.1., has written to me on behalf of the Association of Teachers of Speech and Drama, saying that their Individualist Choir, who won the first place in Choric speaking at the Oxford Festival this year, when my poem 'And Death Shall Have No Dominion' was one of the poems 'set', have been invited by H.M.V. to make a record, & they want to recite my poem on it. Can't we get a fee out of them, for the Festival performance of my poem & for this recording? These people can't do what they like with poems without paying the author.

MS: Texas

JOHN DAVENPORT
25 Nov [1938] [card]   Blashford Ringwood Hants

Augustus can't drive us over, he's in one of his States, & in bed. But I've just been awarded the Oscar Blumenthal prize for poetry, so there, and can pay you a visit when it's most convenient to you. Tell me when & how.

Dylan

MS: Texas

LAWRENCE DURRELL
30th November [1938]   Blashford Ringwood Hants

Dear Lawrence Durrell,
  It's nice to hear from you and I'm glad you'll be in England and we *must* meet. I've been living in Wales up until this last week, now I'm here. I'm afraid I can't come to London: no money at all. But this place is much nearer London than my old address; it's about 2½ hours in the train, fare 18/- return. I do hope you can manage to come down. I've forgotten the route; the thing to do is to ring up the Southern Railway, Waterloo

Station, & find out about Ringwood, Hampshire. I know, though, that 18/- is right. I'm quite near here to your auntie in Bournemouth.

Could you get me a copy of the Black Book?[1] I'll give you all I've written in exchange, odd poems, small books.

Hoping to hear from you.

Dylan T

MS: Carbondale

DAVID HIGHAM
December 3 1938   Blashford Ringwood Hants

Dear Higham,

Thank you for your note. I hope Dent's agree.

I can't find anywhere my contract with Reavey: it was given to me last year when I was living nowhere in particular & that's where I seem to have left it. If I do come across it, I'll send it to you immediately. Otherwise, might Reavey, do you think, send me another copy? Sorry for this.

Yours,
Dylan Thomas

I've just won the Blumenthal Prize for Poetry in America. Worth £20. Is that of any value, apart from the lovely money? I mean, will a thing like that help to influence Dent's or anyone else? I don't suppose so.

MS: Texas

D. S. SAVAGE
December 10 1938   Blashford Ringwood Hants

Dear D. S. Savage,

Will you forgive me for not writing before? I had the chance of going pleasantly away for a few days, & have only just returned. And, more importantly, will you—or can you, after this lapse of time—forgive me if I do not say anything more about your poems except that I like some of them? I have tried to make honest sentences, but they were all too vague; & the more detailed praise or criticism of a particular poem isn't any good for your present publishing purpose. It is useless, & probably boorish-sounding, to say, with truth, that some of the lines I like immensely &

[1] Durrell's novel *The Black Book* was published in France and the US in 1938, but not until 1973 in Britain.

that the seriousness of your poems seems to me always admirable. But that is all, apart from remarks about actual poems in detail, that I *can* say. I do wish you every success with this book—which, if ever I have a chance to review it, & I certainly might have if only for a small-circulation paper like the N.E. Weekly, I shall really try to say a lot of things about &, somehow, to make up for the apparent, but quite unmeant, rudeness of this apology.

I hope you will write to me soon.

Congratulations on the 'Poetry' award. It was a very nice present, wasn't it?

> Yours,
> Dylan Thomas

MS: Texas

DAVID HIGHAM
December 10 1938   Blashford Ringwood Hants

Dear Higham,

Sorry not to have answered at once; I had the chance of going away for a few days, & have only just come back to find your letter.

I'm glad about the Dent acceptance of the poems, & I'm all for it, of course. Do you know why Church wants to see me? I don't want to see him. But I suppose there's some reason. Tuesday or Wednesday this coming week would suit me all right; so would Thursday or Friday, if it comes to that, but I'd prefer the beginning of the week if that's possible. You'll see that I get my expenses *beforehand*, won't you? Otherwise, I couldn't move.

I've sent letters to the addresses in which my Reavey contract might be found, & am waiting for answers. I'll let you know at once.

Thank you for getting Miss Gulick's reply.[1] Have to be content with that problematical guinea.

Yes, the anthology rights of my poems published by the Parton Press *are* free. The copyright of those poems is, anyway, mine. No contract was drawn up at all. What do the Oxford U.P. want with Poem Two? For an anthology?

By the way, I haven't been paid yet by Penguin Books for their inclusion of 2 poems of mine in the 2 volume Century's Poetry, edited by Kilham Roberts. The anthology seems to have been out for some time.

> Yours,
> Dylan Thomas

MS: Texas

[1] See letter dated 24 November 1938.

C. H. FORD[1]
December 14 [1938]   Blashford Ringwood Hants

Dear Mr. Ford,

Thank you for your letter. I'm very glad that you recommended me, in the first place, to Laughlin, and that you like my poetry. I have a new book coming out next spring, which I hope you'll be able to get hold of—if you don't, let me know. Rather different sort of poems, many of them. I hope you'll like them as much.

And thank you for the collaborated poem. I like bits of the language, but it didn't seem to make anything. It was very nice of you to ask me to collaborate, but I don't want to. I think a poet today or any other day is most pleasurably employed writing his own poems as well as he can. With all due lack of respect, I believe this chainpoem to be a pretentious, and lazy, game.

                                    With best wishes,
                                    Dylan Thomas

MS: Texas

VERNON WATKINS
December 20 1938   Blashford Ringwood Hants

Dear Vernon,

It's almost too cold to hold a pen this morning. I've lost a toe since breakfast, my nose is on its last nostril. I've four sweaters on (including yours), two pairs of trousers & socks, a leather coat & a dressing-gown. Who was the French poet who had alphabetically lettered underpants, & wore every one up to H on a cold morning?

I've just come back from three dark days in London, city of the restless dead. It really is an insane city, & filled me with terror. Every pavement drills through your soles to your scalp, and out pops a lamp-post covered with hair. I'm not going to London again for years; its intelligentsia is so hurried in the head that nothing stays there; its glamour smells of goat; there's no difference between good & bad.

I went to see Dent's—Church, really—about a new book. I'm making it an odd book: 15 poems & 5 stories: all to be called In the Direction Of The Beginning. It may look a mess, but I hope not.

It was a great pity we didn't manage to get down to Bishopston before coming here for Christmas and birth; it's been a long time since seeing you, and I want your new poems. Please write quickly, *for* Christmas, with them & news. I'm enclosing a little new poem; been doing several little ones lately; send you them all soon.

[1] Charles Henri Ford (b. 1913), American writer, artist and film-maker.

Thank you for 'Poem In the Ninth Month'.[1] It's fine. I'll use it, of course. And sorry about that bracketed line in the birthday poem, but, until I can think of something else or feel, it will have to stay. I thought your alternative line clumsier & more bass-drum (rather muffled, too) than mine. I do realise your objections to my line; I feel myself the too selfconscious flourish, recognize the Shakespeare echo (though echo's not the word). If ever I do alter it, I'll *remember* your line.[2]

Was the American anthology you mentioned one edited by Norman McCaig? I've sent him something. Will you let me see the revised 'Room of Pity'. And the Yeats poem, please.

This morning the secretary of the London Verse-Speaking Choir—I think it was called—rang me up & asked me whether I could attend the final rehearsal, before making an H.M.V. record, of their speaking of my 'And Death Shall Have No D'. I said I couldn't, so there & then the Choir recited it to me down the telephone. Oh dear. Picked voices picking the rhythms to bits, chosen elocutionists choosing their own meanings, ten virgins weeping slowly over a quick line, matrons mooing the refrain, a conductor with all his vowels planed to the last e.

Caitlin's very strong & well & full. She sends love. So do I, as you know. My silence is never sulks. Remember me to your father & mother. Regards to Dot & Marjorie. Have the best Christmas.

Last year at this time Caitlin & I were doing an act in a garret. This time we're just as poor, or poorer, but the ravens—soft, white, silly ravens—will feed us.

Yes, I wish I was in Swansea sometimes too.

Ever,
Dylan

We've got a Monopoly set. Apparently the Monopoly manufacturers have made a new game, called—I think—Families. It's all to do with ages, & the point is not to die.

MS: British Library   *VW*

JOHN GOODLAND[3]
December 22 [?1938]   Blashford Ringwood Hants

Dear John Goodland,
    I was interested to hear about Apocalypse, and I'll be glad to see the

---

[1] Watkins's suggested title for 'A saint about to fall'. Thomas used it for magazine publication but not thereafter.
[2] The line, the second in 'Twenty-four years', was: '(Bury the dead for fear that they walk to the grave in labour.)'. Thomas didn't change it.
[3] John Goodland (1919–78) started *Seven* with Nicholas Moore when both were at Cambridge.

manifesto when you can send it along. I don't know what to say about your kind invitation to me to contribute, except that, anyway, I haven't started writing a word about Crane[1] yet, and I write very slowly. I couldn't possibly get any material at all ready by January 1. By the end of January, perhaps, I shall have finished a long story on which I've been working, off and on, for over a year. But that, apparently, would be too late.

It isn't for me to criticise, not having read the manifesto nor knowing what you mean by apocalyptic writing; but many of your suggested contributors are, I am certain, by any definition, among the least apocalyptic writers alive; and that says something. (Of course, if you announce well beforehand a symposium of apocalyptic writing, you'll have almost every hack poet, hitherto content with imitations of the queenly social verse, with forced echoes of a schoolboy enthusiasm for jokes and bums, with stupidity about sanity, whipping himself into a false delirium, snatching—in case the apocalyptic game flourishes—at the chance of a frenetic reputation, downing Auden on a pylon for Blake on a bough.) Also, you suggest Read to write the preface if Yeats isn't willing. A preface by Read is suicide; as soon as he gives a 'movement' his good wishes, it dies with indignity; his name on the cover of a new book or magazine establishes its good taste and failure; he has supported, with condescension and theoretical nonsense, almost every popular-at-the-time dud from Blunden to Dali, but the worst of it is that he has also lent his support to some honest writers and writing; he can't always miss, and the good have to suffer with the bad.

I hope you'll let me know more about the definite closing date etc.

Yours sincerely,
Dylan Thomas

MS: Texas

LAWRENCE DURRELL
28 [?December 1938]   Blashford Ringwood Hants
                                       Tel: Ringwood 110

Dear Lawrence Durrell,

I couldn't reply before because I've been spending Christmas in a neighbouring house & the letters weren't forwarded.

I'm very glad you & Miller are in London, and I'm looking forward very much to seeing you. Thanks a lot for the pound.

You're sure, are you, that you couldn't manage to come down here? I've got the willies of London & it makes me ill as hell. But if you can't

---

[1] Hart Crane.

possibly, then of course I must come—& thank you for your invitation. I mustn't miss this chance of seeing you both, & God knows when, if ever, I'll come to Paris. And how long are you going to be in England? I could get a lift up next Monday to London. Is that too late? Let me know quickly, won't you? If you could come down here, you could be put up somehow of course—& I'll send you the pound back beforehand, & any other money I might have. But, anyway, I'll see you all.

Best wishes to yourself, your wife, Miller, Perlès.[1] My wife sends hers.

Dylan T

MS: Carbondale

VERNON WATKINS
29 December 1938   Blashford Ringwood Hants

Dear Vernon,
    What a lovely Compendium. We play all the games in turn. Halma is a demon's game, but one called Winkle's Wedding is too young and sounds like a mass-poem written by adolescents in Roughton's dead paper.[2] Did Families exist? I had a stocking this year, full of sweets and cigars and mouth-organs and cherry brandy. Thank you also for the pretty croquet card. I wish there was something to send you, apart from my love & the small poem I forgot to enclose last time. Before I forget: there's a new periodical, Poetry (London) which promises to be, if nothing else, well produced. A monthly. Edited by man or woman called Tambimuttu.[3] Contributors, God bless them, to the first number will have their names *engraved* on the special souvenir cover. Will you send it something? It may be honest; if so, it shouldn't want to pack its pages with the known stuff of the known boys; a new paper surely should give—(say)—Barker a rest: he must be very tired. The address of Tambimuttu is 114 Whitfield St, London W.1.
    Is Fig still with you, and how was your holiday? Ours was long and weakening, with parties, charades, and too much. Now we reform again; I have a study with the door compulsorily locked and no thrillers allowed inside; there'll be nothing to do but poems.
    Congratulations on the magnificent Yeats poem: so few faults in such noble danger; the fine feeling constant.[4] That may be smug to say, but I'm sick of avoiding clichés of appreciation & expressing a large like in small,

---

[1] Alfred Perlès, writer, friend of Henry Miller.
[2] Roger Roughton's *Contemporary Poetry and Prose* ceased publication in 1937 after ten issues.
[3] See page 361.
[4] 'Yeats in Dublin.'

tough terms. I think it's one of your most truly felt poems; that's not to say that other poems of yours are not true or felt, but only to say that the purity in it is never less than the poetry. What a poem for the old man after that historic interview. In another letter later I'll tell you the few things in the poem that are, to me, uneffectively understated: one or two instances, especially in the reported speech, when understatement is an excess & moderation, economical sobriety, a wallow. But now I want only to tell you how moved I was by the poem, & how much I admire it.

This is quick thanks. My little news must come with my Yeats' grumbles.

Write soon.

Dylan

Caitlin sends her love, too, to all of you.

This Cwmdonkin poem—minus pandemonium[1]—*must*, please, be typed before read. Don't send me a copy. I've got one. There's a fullstop after 'kill' in the 6th line.

MS: British Library   *VW*

HENRY TREECE
31 December 1938   Blashford Ringwood Hants

Dear Henry,
    Your indignation shames me. In the note of December 19th, it's Ever, Henry. Between that time and the 30th a poison has worked, a bird has told you, and Yours Sincerely, Henry Treece stares and floors me. I had your nice last letter in Laugharne, and was proud and glad to have it. You liked me as a man but did not admire me—(the past tense is open to correction)—which is just as it should be; I have the same feelings about myself. My selfish carelessness and unpunctuality I do not try to excuse as poet's properties. They are a bugbear & a humbug. The selfish trouble is that I myself have had to put up with these seriously annoying faults for so long that I've almost come to think other people can bear them. I am the one who wakes up nearest to myself, and the continual horror that comes from the realisation of this individuality has made me almost to believe that the reactions of others to my horrible self—that would not be itself did it not possess the faults etc. that make me now write this simplified confession of complicated egoism so untidily—are small enough, in comparison, to be counted as the others' loss or to be beaten down by one unsulky thought. But of course I apologise, & sincerely. My silence is never the result of promises for noise. My every intention to be in London over Christmas was kicked in the wish by the thought of

[1] 'Of Pandemonium in Cwmdonkin Park'—the park near Thomas's childhood home—is a line in a Watkins poem. The poem Thomas sent was 'Once it was the colour of saying'.

[becoming] a father. We were taken away from Laugharne with a rush, & never seem to have recovered. I don't know why your letter returned 'unknown', unless it was a post-official hint at the subsidence of my already rickety reputation. Perhaps this letter to you will be returned, marked 'No Such Person'. Nothing is above red ribbon except a heart.

Answering your first letter: I won't sign, with or without argument, the Apocalyptic Manifesto.[1] I wouldn't sign any manifesto unless I had written every word of it, and then I might be too ashamed. I agree with and like much of it, and some of it, I think, is manifestly absurd. That's not giving my own variety of bird to a thing over which you & others have spent considerable time & thought; it's only to say that the language of such documents is strange to me, that organic reality is all my cock. I cannot see how Auden is unaware of Donald Duck, unless Donald Duck is supposed to be a symbol and not a funny bird. Donald Duck is just what Auden is aware of. To him (Auden), *what* this problematical squirrel of ours stumbles over is more important than the squirrel act of stumbling. Auden often writes like Disney. Like Disney, he knows the shape of beasts—(& incidentally he, too, might have a company of artists producing his lines)—unlike Lawrence, he does not know what shapes or motivates these beasts. He's a naturalist who looks for beasts that resemble himself, and, failing that, he tries to shape them in his own curious image. The true naturalist, like Gilpin, offers his toe to the vampire bat; Auden would suck the bat off. I liked very much your reasonable contradiction of the quotation from Marx. But it's all rather like flogging a dead force. Another thing that's admirable is the insistence, without irrational prejudice, on man's dissolution. I like the title: 'Apocalypse: The Dissolute Man': more than yours. But this isn't the time to argue with a statement of belief in which I mostly believe but with which I cannot sympathise wholly (or even dissolutely), owing to my own dogma of Arrogant Acceptance. If I'm given time—you know I write slowly, & not too often to be interfering—I'd be very glad to write for Apocalypse, whole or corner. I'll try to write something about Crane, but it will come slowly. That's not, I know you know, an affectation. Would you like that chunk of prose I was working on—copying out, once, in affectedly microscopic writing—in Laugharne? The first half is finished. And I'll have a poem, not a very long one, completed by the middle of January.

I shan't quarrel now—this is meant, however misguidedly, for a patching-up letter—with your promise of Apocalyptic 'publicity'. Don't you believe me when I say that I don't want to be publicised? Or don't you? I have all the publicity that my small output deserves, and because some other people's small output has more & undeserved publicity, should I worry? Publicity will not get me more money; the little work I produce is paid for as highly as the rags I contribute to can afford. Publicity would not increase my output—indeed, the opposite—nor

---

[1] Thomas's attitude to the 'Apocalyptic' movement lacked enthusiasm, but he never managed entirely to dissociate himself from it.

would it make it saleable to better-paying magazines, nor would it make pay at better rates those magazines that still would print me.

About the manifesto quotation from that letter of mine. Don't you think, looking at it coldly, that its effectiveness (if any) would be increased by cutting out '... but I *am* aware of these things as well'. Surely, my conscious catalogue implies that? I think those last few words —whoever wrote them—sound smug. Imagine me suggesting that I *was* not aware of Oxo, Damaroids, & Bunny Austin. Can't you end the quotation at '... tick & revolve in'? Please; & that is, too, if you have to use the bit of silliness at all.

I'd written half this letter when I heard from Henry Miller who'd come to London for a few days; & luckily I managed to get driven to see him. Also I met that sap Goodland the blue-&-water-eyed contact-man, yesman, no man. I just missed the other boys, Cooke,[1] Moore, etc. They're better than Goodland?

I *have* reminded John of the picture. He now has two portraits finished of me. One I'm going to use in my next lot of poems; the other John is entirely willing to let be used in your book. An expert photograph will have to be taken of it; your publishers will, of course, have to see to that. I'm working on an analysis of a few of my poems *now*, but there have been so many interruptions lately. Now they are over.

I'm glad to hear you're getting married so soon. Remember us to Nellie. And are we seeing you this summer? Thank you for your open house. You know about ours too.

Write soon. This has been an awkward letter to write. I'm sure all our next letters will be easy. Regards from Caitlin.

Yours sincerely,

Dylan Thomas

Ever,

Dylan

MS: Buffalo   *SL*

LAWRENCE DURRELL
[?early January 1939]   Blashford Ringwood Hants

Dear Lawrence,

Thank you for the pretty picture. And thank you and Nancy for giving me such a nice time in London. I wanted to write before, but I've been feeling flabby and careless. What happened to you on the Geographical morning? I waited in the stated pub, leaving only for a few minutes to go to the pub opposite. It was all a pity; I lunched with Cameron, & you

---

[1] Probably Dorian Cooke, a poet of the period.

should have too. How did Miller get on with him? Goodland's blue eyes make me belch.

I liked Miller enormously,[1] as I'd always expected I couldn't do anything but, and you must please keep him to his promise of coming to stay, in the spring, in Wales, in the live quiet. We all, I hope, had too little time together. And there's time to put that right. Will you write, and will Miller write?

To you & Nancy,
Dylan

MS: Carbondale

'POETRY' (Chicago)
January 5 1939 [?incomplete][2]

You asked me about reviewing Delmore Schwarz's book. Though I'd like very much to read it some time, I wouldn't like to write about it. I try to get as much reviewing work as possible, but only novels, the lighter the better, for money. But thank you for asking me. I want to send you some general critical prose this year.

Yours sincerely
Dylan Thomas

GEORGE BARKER
January 6 1939[3]   Blashford Ringwood Hants

Dear George Barker,
   Do you feel like forgiving me for the months and months delay in answering your letter and acknowledging your poem? I've got hundreds of excuses, most of them genuine, and I'll tell you them all if you want me to or are forgiving enough to listen. But what I want to know is: are you in Dorset now, & would you be in to me if I came across from here with Augustus John, with whom I'm staying? This week-end or some-time, or early next week? I should very much like to see you, apologise, & talk more about the epistles.

Best wishes,
Dylan Thomas

MS: Texas

[1] In Durrell's account (*Poetry London–New York*, No. 1, 1956), he brought Miller to London, and invited Thomas to a dinner party. Thomas failed to appear, then telephoned from a nearby pub, where Durrell found him, 'too frightened to move'. Durrell persuaded him to go and meet Miller.
[2] The text is from a bookseller's catalogue.
[3] Thomas wrote '1938', but the date was almost certainly 1939.

VERNON WATKINS
Sunday [postmarked January 8 1939]   Blashford Ringwood Hants

Dear Vernon,

I was told you telephoned. Caitlin and I didn't get back until fairly late, and as you said it wasn't a call of life & death, we took you at your word and didn't worry. I'll ring you one night. It will be nice to hear you again, those soft Cambridge accents sliding from Wales. Thankyou.

Since you've apparently been taking lessons from John Prichard in refusing to accept adverse criticism, I shall make my grumbles about your good Yeats poem illegible to invisibility. Here come the grumbles, hot, strong, and logical, but you can't see them. Incidentally, the effectiveness of a history of conversation is determined by selection. Though the statements are word for word, the words are still wrong in the poem. You can say to me that effectiveness is less than truth; I can only say that the truth must be made effectively true, and though every word of the truth be put down the result may well be a clot of *truths*.

I'm glad you liked my last poem. I shan't alter anything in it except, perhaps but probably, the 'close & cuckoo' lovers. The 'dear close cuckoo' lovers is a good suggestion.[1] I can't say the same for 'halo for the bruised knee & broken heel' which is esoterically *off* every mark in the poem. I see your argument about the error of shape, but the form was consistently emotional and I can't change it without a change of heart.

Last week I went up to London to meet Henry Miller who is a dear, mad, mild man, bald and fifty, with great enthusiasms for commonplaces. Also Lawrence Durrell. We spent 2 days together, and I returned a convinced wreck. We talked our way through the shabby saloons of nightmare London. I saw, too, Cameron who has written a good poem, John Goodland who has no merit, & a man dressed in brown paper.

We still play with the Compendium, & are now the very disappointed owners of brand-new Milestones which is a kiddies' mixture of Ludo & Happy Families & quite without the subversive, serious charm of Monopoly. A woman bought the set for us, so it really was lucky you didn't.

I'll tell you when the great birthday comes. We're waiting now. Caitlin had very few angles before, but now she has none. The word is mellow.

We'll be back in Wales, I hope, at the end of February. Certainly in March. Laugharne will be beautiful in the Spring. You must come often. We'll learn, perhaps, to sail together. Love to your family, &, of course, to yourself.

                                                            Dylan

I'll write a better letter soon, with a poem.
But you must write too.
Do you know which stories of mine Francis has translated? A chap called

---

[1] The poem was 'Once it was the colour of saying'. 'Close and cuckoo lovers' became 'cold and cuckoo lovers'.

Constantine FitzGibbon[1]—you saw his translation of a little poem in 'La Nouvelle Saison'—wants to do my 'Lemon' story. Is Francis doing that?

MS: British Library   *VW*

CHARLES FISHER[2]
[January 1939]   Blashford Ringwood Hants

We hope to be back in Laugharne
at the end of February. Don't forget
us then: Liberty and Calamity hall,
where a naked man may bury his
towels in peace.

Dear Charles,
  I was glad to hear from you; living is even more miserable for all your absences; I should have written a long time ago to find out how all that curious collection is carrying on in the last days of the fall of the British Empire, but I am fat and slothful, sentimental and unscrupulous, a bag of a boy in the flush of his pulled youth. This flat English country levels the intelligence, planes down the imagination, narrows the a's, my ears belch up old wax and misremembered passages of misunderstood music, I sit and hate my mother-in-law, glowering at her from corners and grumbling about her in the sad, sticky quiet of the lavatory, I take little walks over the Bad Earth. Our baby should be born at the end of next week, we wait and it kicks. Lack of money still pours in.
  And I'm glad you're all working, on levitation, rainbow's promises, the drama, & Sketty organs. I heard last week from Bob Rees, who said that he wrote to Fred to find out my address and that, to his great surprise, he got a real letter back from the old umbrella himself. Bob says that he's going to write a book one day, to be called 'The Life and Letter of F. Janes'.
  Will you give me, some time, Dan's new address? I still feel Warmley.

Love to you all,
Dylan

Only source: SL

---

[1] Constantine FitzGibbon (1919–83), author, was an American who became an Irish citizen. He was later a friend of Dylan and Caitlin, and wrote the first biography of Thomas.
[2] Charles Fisher has mislaid the MS since he supplied it for *SL*.

HENRY TREECE
January 26 1939   Blashford Ringwood Hants

Dear Henry,

Thanks for the good letters.

And straightaway I must say that I haven't got anything for 'Seven'. Half a poem's on my table, and that's all. I'm sorry my name has to remain on the cover, but, after all, I had not promised to contribute to this number. 'Apocalypse' is a different affair, isn't it? I mean, surely 'Seven' hasn't taken that as a new name? Actually, I still have that large chunk of prose I told you about, and from which I read you bits, but that's got to be bought. I've spent so much time on that that I don't part with it except for real money; and I'll stick to that even if it prevents the thing ever being printed. It applies to my promised contributions to 'Apocalypse', too. From now on, I'm going to be paid, & paid fairly, for every line of mine that's printed. Cash-minded Dylan, that's me—if you know the reference. I'll sell 'Seven' seven pages of glamorous prose. Any offers?

Glad you're feeling better now. I'm not feeling better. I'm worried and lazy and morose, I've got a hundred headaches and a barbed mouth, I hate every living person with the exception of a Mrs. Macarthy who lives in Chelsea. I can't write this letter.

Keidrych is hysterical. Why should I be interested in the blurb for Glyn Jones's book in America? And why, anyway, should he send it via Lincolnshire? He's always doing things like that; once he sent me a lot of used stamps and the bibliography of Arthur Machen.

Thanks for the warning about our literary friends' correspondence circle. I don't want to hurt anybody—much. But Goodland *is* a sap, 19 or 90. His blue eyes are pools of piss—aristocratic piss. He's got fallen arches in his mouth. You say that he might have been frightened of me? Of me? I'm like a baby in the dark.

More when I feel good. Caitlin is still waiting, the baby's overdue by 3 days. No worry, though. She sends her regards to you & Nelly.

This letter's really to tell you about 'Seven' & me. More, about me, when I don't feel so sick & angry.

Love,
Dylan

& more soon, too.

MS: Buffalo   *SL*

JOHN DAVENPORT
30 Jan 1939   Blashford Ringwood Hants

Dear John,
   Sorry, but I didn't send off those stories as I said I would & as I wanted
to, very much, for advice. Caitlin had to go to Poole Hospital yesterday
evening, is now in The Labour Room, & I'm waiting. I'll ring you up
tomorrow, Monday, & tell you what there is to tell. And I'll send the
stories too. I'm worried & in a bit of a muddle about everything.

                                      Love to Clement & yourself
                                                           Dylan

MS: Texas

VERNON WATKINS
1 February 1939   Blashford Ringwood Hants

Dear Vernon,
   This is just to tell you that Caitlin & I have a son aged 48 hours. Its
name is Llewelyn Thomas. It is red-faced, very angry, & blue-eyed. Bit
blue, bit green. It does not like the world. Caitlin is well, & beautiful. I'm
sorry Yeats is dead.[1] What a loss of the great poems he would write. Aged
73, he died in his prime. Caitlin's address—if you would like to send her a
word—is Maternity Ward, Cornelia Hospital, Poole, Dorset.
                                         Our love to you,
                                                           Dylan

MS: British Library   *VW*

VERNON WATKINS
Saturday [February 1939]   Blashford Ringwood Hants

Dear Vernon,
   A very short letter to thank you for your letters to Caitlin and me about
our mumbling boy. He's in the room with me now, making noises to his
fingers, his eyes unfocusing, with his red skull half-covered in golden
cotton. He & Caitlin came back from hospital today. She's well.
   Here's a new poem.[2] Tell me: is it too short? do I end before the point?
does it need more room to work to a meaning, any expansion? I intended

---
[1] Yeats died January 28.
[2] 'Because the pleasure-bird whistles.'

it as a longer & more ambitious thing, but stopped it suddenly thinking it was complete. How do you feel about it? And what about a poem from you? Write very soon.

Ever yours,
Dylan

Have you ever seen such insulting rot as that written about Yeats in the respectable Sunday newspapers.

MS: British Library   *VW*

LAWRENCE DURRELL
Sunday [?February 1939]   Blashford Ringwood Hants

Dear Lawrence,
   Thank you for your letters, and your writing. All at sea on the BB. I'm sickened & excited. If you want—& you say you want—& I believe you—a poem for the new Delta, why not the one you like in the paper of Tambimuttu's, that distinguished Celanese?[1] If not—and perhaps, I hope, as well—here's a new short poem. And I'd rather have the 7/6 than a book-token. My bowels need more than consonants & vowels. When you like, and sooner. Oh, a boy, by the way & the womb. Llewelyn. The homage of his father. You say I'm obscurely worried, but it's too obscure to worry about. I kick against my prick. Everything's OK except why. But is the spring promise of coming to see us in Wales still good? You & yours & Miller. Write soon.

Dylan

MS: Carbondale

JULIAN SYMONS
Feb 5 1939   Blashford Ringwood Hants

Dear Julian Symons,
   Sorry for the delay & for the single poem; meant to send you a couple. I haven't been able to work during the last week because of my new, red son. Hope this will do.

Dylan Thomas

MS: Texas

[1] The first issue of *Poetry* (London), February 1939, printed Thomas's 'A saint about to fall'.

DAVID HIGHAM
20 February 1939   Blashford Ringwood Hants

Dear Higham,

I'm sorry to be so long returning these stories and suggesting, for
Dent's, the ones which I should like to be included in my book of verse
and prose. But I've been trying hard to raise enough money to keep my
wife and son going for the next month or two, and unsuccessfully. Now
I'm relying entirely on Dent's. They've got the mss of the poems, and
here are the stories. Of the stories I suggest The Orchards, The Enemies,
The Map Of Love, A Prospect Of The Sea, and The Visitor. Those are all
stories to which no objection, other than literary, could be taken, and
anyway they're the best—especially in a book also to contain poems.
Church has, among the mss of the poems, part of a prose-piece called 'In
The Direction Of The Beginning'—a title I originally intended as the title
of the whole book. I have, however, been considering this piece, and have
now decided to make it part of a much longer work which I want to
spread over many months to come. But that decision doesn't alter the
book: there are still sixteen poems and five stories; and two poems, now
finished but not polished up enough yet, to be added. So that Dent's *have*
the whole mss of the whole book, only not yet finally arranged in
order—surely a small consideration considering that the book will not be
published until after the spring. (Church can, of course, choose other
stories from the enclosed collection if he wants to, but I'm sure my
choice is right for the purposes of this book.) And, having the mss in their
hands, can't they be persuaded to give me the £30 promised on 'completion of Mss'? If they *can't* be persuaded, then I'm sunk. And this is no
begging or joke. I can't return with my family to Wales until some
important debts there, principally for rent, have been settled; and there's
no money, other than Dent's promised money, coming to me in the
world. Do please do your very best for me. After all, here is the book they
wanted. The John portrait they can photograph any time they want to—I
have all his permission. (By the way, have you heard if they'll do it in
colour or not?) And the only thing left to do is to arrange the order of
contents. I have, I know, altered the original idea of the book by wishing
to cut out the prose-piece already in Church's possession, but I must do
that, and five stories and eighteen poems—the two extra ones will be
ready and typed by the end of the week—is quite as big a book as Church
said he wanted. Please, Higham, do try to get that advance *immediately*.
We've got to move, and we can't until our Welsh village has been pacified
financially. I can rely on you, I know, to do your best for me as quickly as
you can.

                                              Yours,
                                              Dylan Thomas

RICHARD CHURCH
22 February 1939   Blashford Ringwood Hants

Dear Richard Church,
    Sorry not to have got in touch with you for so long.
    Higham now has the complete mss. of my short stories and I've told
him which stories I confidently suggest for inclusion in the prose and
verse book. Perhaps you have already seen Higham, and he has explained
to you that I wish to cut out the incomplete prose-piece called 'In The
Direction Of The Beginning'. I know this will alter the plan of the book,
but, I think, alter it for the best. That prose-piece would, I believe, when
complete, overbalance the poems and the rest of the stories—by
hysterical weight, not by value. I intend now making it quite a long thing,
say about the length of Petron, and then I'm sure it would be better to
publish it by itself.
    If you look at the stories I've suggested, you'll see I had some trouble
over the names of the characters. It's fairly unimportant, I suppose, but it
should be settled. The name originally used in 'The Orchards' story was
Peter, the same as in 'The Visitor', but, on rereading, I took a dislike to
the name. It applied more to a character in a slick, fashionable story, and
seemed out of place in short imaginative stories or fables. What do you
think? I've changed the name in 'The Orchards' but not in 'The Visitor':
so that you can see how they compare. Do tell me. Perhaps even 'Marlais'
seems an affected choice of name; it was the only one I could immediately think of, being my own.[1]
    I hope very much, that's putting it weakly, that Dent's may be
persuaded to give me my advance for this book now. It is complete, and
only needs arrangement. I've a family to support, and nothing to support
it with—just nothing. I do need that advance at once, if I am to keep my
wife and son well if only for a short time, and hope you'll help me to
get it.

                                    Yours,
                                    Dylan Thomas

MS: J. M. Dent

DAVID HIGHAM
25 February 1939   Blashford Ringwood Hants

Dear Higham,
    Very glad to have your letter & the contract. I knew you'd manage
things for me. Thank you.

[1] The names remained Peter ('The Visitor') and Marlais ('The Orchards').

Here's the contract, initialled.

What a hole there's going to be in my £50.[1]

Have Dent's come to any conclusion yet about the John portrait? Do they want written permission for reproduction from John? It isn't necessary, but I can get it if needs be. What about colour?

Thanks again.

Yours,
Dylan Thomas

MS: Texas

KEIDRYCH RHYS
Tuesday [?February 1939]   Blashford Ringwood Hants

Dear Keidrych,

Thanks for the reviews etc. (And I'm looking forward to the editorial note you spoke about.) I'll see what I can do with these, & show them to some people. But my influence, as you know, is very small indeed. About editorship: please, I'd rather *not* go down, printed, as co-editor—though I'd like very much to have a look at the stuff beforehand, if you feel like sending it. This number 6/7 is *your* making, and it would be too late now for me to argue against any of the chosen, and advertised, contributions.[2] But in future numbers—if there are any, & by God there must be—I should be very pleased to do something more constructive than merely to grumble at you while you do all the work. But, really, there's no point at all in me having anything official to do with this new, already prepared, number. Though if you want, in spite of that, a hand with comments & reviews *for* the number, do let me know; I'll do anything you like. What splendid notices 'Wales' has had, by the way. Surely those, handed to the right person, should mean something.

Again—and I'm sorry that all my recent letters seem so disagreeable—I won't write to Barker asking him for a poem. One of the outstanding things about 'Wales' is that, so far, it has not printed one of Mr. Barker's masturbative monologues—as every other verse-magazine of our time has done, with disgusting frequency. And I think 'Wales's' standard should be upheld.

More soon; & please write too.

Dylan

MS (photocopy): Thomas Trustees

[1] £20 of the first £50 for *The Map of Love* had to go to George Reavey, to repay the *Burning Baby* advance.
[2] Issue No 6/7 of *Wales* was dated March 1939.

VERNON WATKINS
Wednesday [postmarked March 3 1939]   Blashford Ringwood Hants

Dear Vernon,

Very short note. I've got to do the proofs of my new book of poems this week, & I'm thinking of putting in this poem just finished. Please, can I have a quick criticism.[1] It's deeply felt, but perhaps clumsily said. In particular—is the last line too bad, too comic, or does it *just* work? Have you any alternatives for the *adjectives* of that last line?—you see obviously what I *mean*.

Terrific hurry to get this in time for post.

Hope you're well. Back in a fortnight. Letter much sooner. Caitlin & Llewelyn well. Hope you are.

My love,
Dylan

MS: British Library   VW

JULIAN SYMONS
March 3 1939   Blashford Ringwood Hants

Dear Julian Symons,

Thanks for the magazine, and for the congratulations on the birth of my son. Do I get my guinea? Him and me need it. I'll try & send along another poem soon.

Yours,
Dylan Thomas

MS: Texas

DAVID HIGHAM
March 3 1939   Blashford Ringwood Hants

Dear Higham,

Thank you very much for the speedy cheque. Things are a bit easier now.

Here's the contract signed by me, with the extra initialling.

You forgot, by the way, to enclose the counterpart of this contract signed by Dent.

I'm seeing John today, and I'll get a note from him then authorising reproduction of his portrait.

---

[1] The poem enclosed was '"If my head hurt a hair's foot"'.

I've seen a review of 'The Year's Poetry. 1938', edited by Denys Kilham Roberts & published by the Bodley Head. It is supposed to have published several of my poems[1]—Roberts asked for them & accepted them months ago—but so far I've had no copy of the book or cheque, & never received proofs. I wonder whether you could enquire for me some time. Thank you again for all you've done.

Yrs,
Dylan Thomas

MS: Texas

DAVID HIGHAM
March 4 1939   Blashford Ringwood Hants

Dear Higham,
I agree with you, of course. Ten years is an absurdly long time, and during which I may write my Gone with The Wind. And I approve, of course again, of your decision to be firm about five years or f-all. And 60 dollars, as you reasonably said, is not a sufficient consideration for a 50 years option: just over, possibly, a dollar a year.

If Laughlin doesn't agree to your terms, can we try another American publisher right away. The little tyke has no legal right to get his 60 dollars back if we do. I've had several letters from American publishers, wanting to see my work, especially prose—Simon and Schuster were the most enthusiastic; extremely so. Also, I heard from Kay Boyle today that a friend of hers, Caresse Crosby Young, has come to Europe to look for books, as she is going to work with a N.Y. publisher. Kay Boyle has boosted me to her.

Thank you for the Dent-signed contract.

Yours,
Dylan Thomas

MS: Texas

RICHARD CHURCH
March 4 1939   Blashford Ringwood Hants

Dear Richard Church,
I've been asked to write, by next Wednesday, a descriptive note of 200 words for my book of poems and stories. I haven't had a reply yet to my

---

[1] The book contained one Thomas poem, 'In Memory of Ann Jones'.

last week's letter to you about the choice of stories—I do hope you'll be able to accept mine—and about my wish to cut out that long prose fragment. I do hope you'll tell me what you think about these things before I write the note.

I shan't finish that fragment for quite a long time; I've decided to make it far fuller & to put in much more detail etc. Is there any point in publishing, in this new book, the fragment as it is now? Anyway, I still think, don't you, that its title should be kept as the title of the whole book, whether the fragment is omitted or not. It does apply to most of the poems & stories in the book.

I'm having the 2 extra poems typed, & will send them along Monday or, at the latest, Tuesday.

I'm looking forward very much to hearing from you.

Best wishes,

Yours,

Dylan Thomas

MS: J. M. Dent

M. J. TAMBIMUTTU

A modest poet, Tambimuttu (1915–83) made his name by publishing others in his magazine *Poetry*. He was born in Ceylon, and sometimes told people he was a prince there. In the United States after the war he ran the short-lived *Poetry London–New York*, but his heyday was the war years, his habitat Soho and Bloomsbury.

March 5 [1939]   Blashford Ringwood Hants

Dear Tambimuttu,

Thanks for your cheque and for the first number of your beautifully produced magazine. The print's always a pleasure to read, even if some of the poems aren't. That's no sneer, believe me. I congratulate you a lot on the handsomest 'intelligent' poetry magazine I know of, and on the courage of your unfashionable introduction. I do understand that you have an extraordinarily large circulation, and that you can't, for that reason, weigh the paper down with too much difficult verse—and I'm not suggesting that the best is difficult, only that most of the best today is bound to be. I suppose there is, there must be, some reason why John Gawsworth, F.R.S.L., should appear with, say, MacNeice. I think that to include Gawsworth—I mean nothing personal—that leftover, yellow towelbrain of the nineties soaked in stale periods, in a magazine most of whose contributors are, at least, and if little else unites them, nostalgic for nothing but a better *present*, is overdoing your ostensible wish to make 'Poetry' readable to a great number of people on first sight. (I agree, incidentally and only just, with a possible editorial policy which takes the view that if a number of people will only buy the magazine for the not-so-good verse that attracts them easily and immediately, the good verse may do its work on them in spite of themselves and the magazine may prosper.) I *can* see the point in beginning a new magazine with an easily conventional lyric or two, especially if the (problematical now, no fingerpointing offence) editor's real favourites of poems which appear later in the number contain such words as Marx, copulation, and pylon, words very likely, and rightly likely, to put off bookstall tasters. But whether robins, rills, and Mercury woodcuts work the other way I wouldn't know. Please don't take this as a badtempered letter. I want, as much I think as you do, to see 'Poetry'—it's needed alright, verse magazines in England are very sad—grow into something extremely entertaining and popular. Poetry editors are mostly vicious climbers, with their fingers in many pies, their ears at many keyholes, and their tongues at many bottoms. *You've* shown, in your introduction, how much you believe in the good of poetry and in the mischief of cliques, rackets, scandal schools, menagerie menages, amateur classes of novitiate plagiarists etc. More subscribers and power to you. But one trouble I see is that, in an attempt to include many sorts of poetry, you're liable in the end to sacrifice poetry for variety. I know that you dislike as much as anybody whose dislikes have not been patterned for him, the sort of anthology that begins by saying, 'In this we aim to represent every school of contemporary poetry', and the sort of gushing, inaccurate, Professor Daisy textbook beginning 'It is now apparent that there were at the introduction of the twentieth century five poetical channels of thought.' To try, in paper or book, to represent the whole 'field' of contemporary poetry is to take a turd's eye view. Surely the only thing an editor can say about this particular point is, 'This paper's going to print the best poems that are sent to it, and let the contemporary field disappear up its own pansies'. (This may be irrelevant arguing, and I'm sure is badly put.) I lent 'Poetry' yesterday to the butcher's son here, so haven't got it by me to write you in detail about the poems—as you suggested I should try to do. I'll try in a later letter. Just received yours this morning. I heard one of your broadcasts, hope you'll be talking again soon. Lord, what a difficult business it must be, running a poetry paper: and afterward what heavy enthusiasm or condemnation from small and amateur pontiffs like me. Don't take too much notice, only my sincere congratulations. I'm afraid I don't know when I'll be in London again, I can't afford to take a penny bus most days. But when I'm up, I'll let you know at once. Best wishes,

Dylan Thomas

I'll send my poems by Wednesday. Thanks for the extra time you're allowing me.

MS: Texas   *SL*

RICHARD CHURCH
8 March 1939   Blashford Ringwood Hants

Dear Richard Church,
  Thank you for your letter.
  I enclose three more poems. The sonnet I am not sure about, it seems
mechanical. What do you think? We do want as many poems as possible,
don't we?
  I'm extremely sorry you do not want to include the story, 'A Prospect
Of The Sea', which is one of my own favourites. If I removed, or toned
down to complete harmlessness, its 'moments of sensuality', would you
then consider again its inclusion? I very much hope so, though of course
your decision is final.[1]
  I agree with your suggestion of 'The Map of Love: Verse & Prose' as the
title.
  The additional poems I should like to be included somewhere about the
middle of the collection, where you think fit, but not at either end.
  And I don't really think that I agree with 'The Dress' coming at the very
end of the prose? (I suppose the verse will come first in the book? That
certainly seems the best.)
  I think 'The Dress' is too pathetic a note to end the book with. I suggest
'The Orchards'—but again, it is not a very important point, and I leave it
to you.

                                        Sincerely,
                                        Dylan Thomas

P.S. Here also is the 200 word blurb. I couldn't do one, & got a friend of
      mine to help. Is it what you wanted?

MS: J. M. Dent

A. E. TRICK
[March 1939]   Blashford Ringwood Hants

Dear Bert,
  This is to tell you, with variations, what I'm sure you must know by
now: that I'm the father of a son named Llewelyn, aged six weeks, a fat,
round, bald, loud child with a spread nose and blue saucer eyes. His full
name is Llewelyn Edouard, the last being a concession to Caitlin's French
grandfather; but in spite of this he sounds militantly Welsh, and, though
this is probably national pride seen through paternal imagination or

---

[1] Church had written on March 6 to complain that 'A Prospect of the Sea' had 'moments of
sensuality without purpose [and it] brings us near the danger zone'.

viceversa, he looks it too. Before anything else, before apologies, re-criminations, and news, how are your wife, Pamela and Kerith? Please do remember me to all of them, though Kerith I suppose, remembers me as nothing but a shifting blur with a mop on top.

For well over a year now, we've failed to keep in touch with each other: was it my fault or yours? Mine, perhaps—I'm careless, I know, and appear rude but never feel or mean it—though you've not written either. I hear nothing from the boys—is Fred still pineappleing and knifing, con-summating in the cinema, expressing down Walters-road with his head full of fruit and stars, has Tom erased himself completely yet?—so, nothing about you. Though, I'm set in a life now, two stone heavier but not a feather steadier, though never again will I fit into Swansea quite so happily and comfortably as I did—for I'll be a hundred jokes and personal progressions behind all my friends, I'll be almost a dead face, or worse still a new face, in which nothing will interest them but the old shades and expressions—I'm strong and sentimental for the town and people, for long virulent Sundays with you and scrapbooks and strawberry jelly at the end, for readings and roarings with all the grand boys. I'm not meaning to talk like an ancient village outcast; no more than two years separate me; I'll be all the summer, and every summer I hope, in Carmarthenshire. But one small, close society is closed to me, and the social grief is natural. We're all moving away; and every single decisive action happens in a blaze of disappointment.

What's been happening to you? How are the Townhill[1] and Council schemes? Here in this flat, narrow chested and vowelled county, full of fading squires, traditional English romantic outlaws, sour gentlewomen and professional ostriches, I long for my old, but never properly mounted, soapbox of bright colours, and my grand, destructive arguments learned so industriously and vehemently from you on winter evenings after Cwmdonkin sonnets and Lux to sweet ladies—you gave my re-belliousness a direction, and on the black, back-to-the-wall umbrella-man's Day[2] I'll have you to blame, which will be a small recompense.

We come back to Wales in the first week in April, to Laugharne where we rent—though the landlord would disagree—a crumbling house, and to Swansea for a day or two to let my mother see Llewelyn in all his shit, sweetness, and glory. I must see you then. You'll recognise me by belly, black hat, and a nostalgic flavour of the Uplands.

And I want you to see my new poems, which will make a book in the summer. Not quite a book, for the whole thing is called 'The Map of Love' and has fifteen poems and seven stories. Old stories mostly, but cut and pruned to buggery or sense.

---

[1] Townhill, a working-class suburb, was built as a public housing project between the wars.
[2] The 'umbrella man' might be Neville Chamberlain (he always seemed to carry one), and the 'Day' the coming war.

I've got so many questions to ask you that I'll keep them all until we meet. Do write a little soon and let me know how things are and what you are doing.

Love,
Dylan

MS: Ohio State University   *SL*

DESMOND HAWKINS
March 12 1939   Blashford Ringwood Hants

Dear Desmond,
   I'm very rude but please forgive me because I didn't mean to be. I've been away from this address, haven't been doing any work, and letters have got muddled. I *did* receive your note about a poem, but I hadn't got one: I'd sent away the only one I had a few days before: I wish you'd been able to give me a little notice. But no blame on you about anything: it's I'm Uncle Dirty. And I tried to do something with that left-over lot of books, but it was so flimsy I couldn't make an entertaining article out of it. I'm wanting very much to review some more, & punctually: give me the closing date. Thank you, Desmond, I hope you'll send them along soon. Has the N.E.W. reviewed 'Bitter Victory' by Louis Guilloux—the best modern novel I've read, I think anyway at the moment. No, perhaps not that, but very grand. Has your novel been reviewed in the N.E.W.? Or could I have it? I've seen some very pretty words about it. Best luck with it.[1]
   Dent's are bringing out my new poems, plus ½ dozen stories, in the summer, under the name 'The Map of Love'. Do get hold of a review copy.
   My son is almost as big as me, but not quite: you'd hardly recognise me. I've put on over 2 stone and am a small, square giant now. Let me have the books soon. Apologies again. Give me the news.

Dylan

MS: the recipient

DESMOND HAWKINS
16 March [1939]   Blashford Ringwood Hants

Dear Desmond,
   Waiting for the two promised novels. I'll include a Caldwell review, though it's a weak book. 'Bitter Victory' by Louis Guilloux is published

---

[1] Hawkins's first novel, *Hawk Among the Sparrows*, had been published.

by Heinemann. If you can get me a copy—mine's a library one—I can promise you & the publishers to do a full, praising review.

I'm sorry your book's been reviewed already in the N.E.W. If you'll send me it, I can certainly do a notice of it in *Seven*, if nowhere else. But *Seven*, I'm afraid, is a quarterly, & the Spring number's just come out.

When you see my new book, 16 poems & 7 stories, you'll be disappointed, perhaps,—or perhaps really my violence wasn't much good either—by the choice of stories. Blame that on dirty Church, not on me. I gave him a heap of stories to select from, & he wdn't include one that had 'its moments of sensuality'. A few of the stories were written when I was five or six years younger, & are sure to look tame. That man's a pale beast.

What's your son's name?

Dylan

MS: the recipient

VERNON WATKINS
[postmarked March 20 1939]   Blashford Ringwood Hants

Dear Vernon,

I didn't write sooner because I thought I'd be returning. Now I know it'll be April 6 or 7 when we drive back to the best places. We'll be in Bishopston one day at Easter, the boy with us.

I agree with every word you wrote abt my poem.[1] The 2nd person speaks better than the first, & the last line is false. I haven't been able to alter the first part, & will have to leave it unsuccessful. The last line is now: 'And the endless beginning of prodigies suffers open'. I worked on from your suggestion.

I'd like to go over the final proofs of all the poems with you, but that won't be for a few weeks. Some weeks. Did I tell you the book, which will be priced at 7/6 and have a John frontispiece portrait, includes 7 s. stories as well? All unviolent ones. Church refused to pass the best, 'P. of the Sea' because of its 'unwarrantable moments of sensuality'—the fish. Perhaps I'll make a little money from this book: I think a lot of 'readers' prefer to pay 7/6 for a book to 3/6.

Does Dot know Lawrence's 'Kangaroo' poem? Send her my love. The favourite meal in Australia—'The Ritz couldn't do you better my boy' an Australian told a man I know when he was out there—is a very underdone steak with an over-poached egg on top, followed by a cup of tea.

News when we meet. Quite a lot too.

Love from us,
Dylan

MS: British Library   *VW*

[1] '"If my head hurt a hair's foot"'.

DAVID HIGHAM
21 March 1939   Blashford Ringwood Hants

Dear Higham,
   Here is, at last, the authorising note from John. This is what was
wanted, isn't it? The portrait's in the Nicholson Gallery—Bond St?—&
the people there know all about the fact that Dent's want a reproduction
of it.
   Yes, do please keep the remaining stories of mine for the time being.
   Anything about The Year's Poetry?

                                                    Yours,
                                                    Dylan Thomas

MS: Texas

DESMOND HAWKINS
March 25 1939   Blashford Ringwood Hants

Dear Desmond,
   This is only to tell you how much I liked the novel. Will it be too late to
say things about it in the next *Seven*? I mean, will it do any good to the
sales etc then? Anyway, I want the Opportunity of stating publicly my
Appreciation and excitement. There were a few things I disagreed
with—towards the middle, when you dealt with Ellen & Milly and their
boys, you changed the style of writing too drastically I thought, even
though I liked what was going on very much—but mostly nothing but
congratulations on one of the best first novels etc. How good to see &
hear and feel, too, the real romance of the out-of-town middleclass; the
half-finished buildings, the last bus home. Oh, I thought the vicar was not
a success—the only one who wasn't completely useful to the book. But
Mrs S.[1] You know such a lot about women, Mr. Hawkins, you *must* be a
pansy.

                                                    Claps & best wishes,
                                                    Dylan
How abt my review books? Nothing's come yet.

MS: the recipient

---

[1] Mrs Sparge, a character in Hawkins's novel.

FRANCES HUGHES (MRS RICHARD HUGHES)
March 29 '39   Blashford Ringwood Hants

Dear Frances,

We're coming back next Wednesday, the fifth, I think, of April, and we're looking forward to it a lot. No more muggy south, narrow vowels, flat voices, flat chests, English Riviera, and housefulls of women. We want to see again the dilapidated Roman emperors, the giant liars and big women of Laugharne, Mrs Peounds and Peounds, the petrol-drinkers and bee-swallowers. It's very damp here. We're being driven down, but not by Augustus. He's coming later in the month, as soon as, or before, we can arrange Llewelyn's christening. He's out and more or less about now, though Mavis's wedding put him back a few beds. We saw the newsfilm of the departure from the registry office, and Augustus, blowing clouds of smoke, hopped in the first car before bride or groom could get in.[1] Caitlin says that she's written to Mrs Williams—we had, apparently, no difference with her, it was laziness that put her off writing—to ask her to prepare and air a bit before we return; and she asks you, please, will you see that Mrs Williams does it & have a look yourself too. (The house must be full of mice by this time, but of course you can't do anything about that.) Love to you and Diccon from Caitlin and me.

                                                              Dylan

MS: *Indiana*

LAWRENCE DURRELL
[?March 1939]   Blashford Ringwood Hants

Dear Lawrence,

I forgot to thank you for the pound, crisper than celery and sweeter than sugar oh the lovely sound, not through ingratitude, it's as welcome as a woman is cleft, but through work (half a poem about energy), sloth (in a chair looking at my feet or the mirror or unread novels or counting the patterns on the wc floor to see if I can work out a system for my football pools or watching my wife knit or dance), depression (because, mostly, there weren't more pounds from more people), small habits (from bar-billiards to broadcast talks, slick-bonneted Hampshire roadhouses and socialist teas), love, unqualified, the nearness of Bournemouth, colds and pains in the head and your Black Book about which more in another and longer letter. I liked too very much your eggy poems in Seven. Thank you for the Emily Brontë poem: I thought at first sight it was a rejected

---

[1] Mrs Mavis de Vere Cole, widow of a famous practical joker, Horace de Vere Cole, married the archaeologist, Dr Mortimer Wheeler, on March 16. Between marriages she had had a child by Augustus John.

manuscript of mine: a great likeness, and yes I can read nearly every word of it.[1] Why are you still in London, has somebody moved Corfu? And do you want another poem from me, for seven shillings and sixpence? Regards to your wife and muse, to Heppenstall if you see him and not to Goodland.

Dylan

MS: Carbondale   *SL*

HENRY TREECE
[March 1939]   Blashford Ringwood Hants

Dear Henry,

Sorry not to reply sooner. I'd decided, until your postcard this morning, not to write a word for some weeks, not a word of anything. It wasn't a moral decision: I wanted to go and play billiards at the conservative club, etc.; all day long. But I'll have to do that little analysis now before you shame me to incoherence, and certainly before your marriage upon which I congratulate you with all the sincerity of a smug, happy, penniless husband and father. I'll finish over this weekend the strongly promised stuff.

I don't know why you have to work yourself up into such an indignant rage when you say that you won't pay me for the analysis. Nobody asked you sir. It never occurred to me.

Of course I don't associate you with Goodland. You're my friend.

I hadn't heard about the anthology.[2] Naturally I'd like to contribute to most things you're likely to do or intend doing, but I won't have anything much *to* contribute for some time. All my new poems belong to the book which Dent's are bringing out in the summer definitely. Your anthology couldn't appear before then, and obviously the same poems couldn't appear in both things. I'll have a few poems I suppose, but I'll have to get them published in magazines—if the anthology isn't under way by that time—as soon as they are completed because I need every halfpenny. I have nothing with which to bring Llewelyn up—he's six or seven weeks old. Nothing is O, not an inadequate income. Is the anthology Apocalyptic?—whatever that means. Barker's paralytic. He should be indecently buried. He grows worse every fake fit and crud of midnight spunk.

I saw your *Seven* article, and I'm looking forward to seeing another one in Poetry. Glad the first one was disliked by Grigson & Symons. What a

---

[1] Durrell, visiting the British Museum, had seen an autograph letter by Emily Brontë and been struck by the similarity between her writing and Thomas's. He sent Thomas a facsimile postcard.

[2] See page 373.

fancy magazine Poetry is with its wig-and-scroll cover, treesnaps, and woodcunts, Barkers, whistlers, pukers, masturbative monologues, Tambimuttu—although I admire the courage of the queer introduction —wetting his Celyonese, Spender with life still Nestling on his lips. The postwar man, as Tambimuttu might have said in his first Indian letter, struggling for watered spirits. The English poets now are such a pinlegged, nibcocked, paperhearted crowd you could blow them down with one bellow out of a done lung. I'm not taking, conscientiously, the inverted attitude, even if it isn't inverted, that insists on the worthlessness of the intelligentsia and the great qualities of those outside it, especially as I am living now—but not for long, Laugharne in April—in the country where the English romantic outlaw is at his loudest in praise of characters and soil—'I wouldn't share a piston with Stephen or Wystan but I'd roll in a sewer with Jan and Bill Brewer'—and I suppose that in finding my sympathetic friends where I mostly do I'm at last on my own level. Don't get me wrong, I'd always prefer to see a street full of lords to a street full of other unemployed. Not that this matters.

Don't worry that anyone else will get hold of your letters: I have no clique, no correspondence club. You know how I live—I'm not, I hope, sentimentalising over this point, over other points I am happy to any time—and that life doesn't contain letter or culture snooping. What you say to me is safe from any but my own misinterpretation.

I'll write more when I send what you want. Sorry about the flimsy delays.

Dylan

MS: Buffalo   *SL(R)*

ALLEN TATE[1]
March 30 1939   Sea View Laugharne Carmarthenshire

Dear Mr Tate,
    Thank you for writing. Here are two poems. Both have just been printed in English periodicals, but you said that didn't matter. If neither of these is suitable, I'd like to send you some more.

Yours sincerely,
Dylan Thomas

MS: Kenyon College

[1] Allen Tate (1899–1979), poet and editor. He was probably seeking poems for the *Kenyon Review*, with which he was associated, and which published '"If my head hurt a hair's foot"', Summer 1939.

DESMOND HAWKINS
[April 4 1939][1]   Laugharne

Dear Desmond,
  Forgive all sorts of things. I wish this was a livelier review, I don't feel
so hot yet but will be in a few days. If the Caldwell review, and a meagre
one it is, is too late now or not good enough, do cut it out. Writing soon.

                                                          Dylan

MS: the recipient

KEIDRYCH RHYS
[?April 1939]   Sea-View Laugharne Carmarthenshire

Dear Keidrych,
  We came back a fortnight ago. We're expecting you. Any time, the
sooner the better. What about this week? Plenty of room here. We'll talk
about everything then. No, my letter in 'Poetry'[2] wasn't meant for
publication & *certainly* didn't refer to you; [...] and [...] were two in
particular.

                                                    Love,
                                                          Dylan

MS: Texas

M. J. TAMBIMUTTU
[?April 1939]   Sea View Laugharne Carmarthenshire S Wales

Dear Tambimuttu,
  I liked the second number of Poetry very much. I hope you weren't
offended by my first letter, to which you never replied; I thought, at the
time, that it may have sounded rather offensively dogmatic. I'm afraid I
haven't anything for the May number, but I'll send you my new poem as
soon as it's ready.
  Am I to be paid a guinea for my poem in the second number?[3] I do very

---

[1] Dated by Desmond Hawkins at the time.
[2] Tambimuttu printed some of Thomas's March 5 letter in the April issue of *Poetry*
   (London). The people Thomas named to Rhys are still alive.
[3] "'If my head hurt a hair's foot.'" Issue dated April 1939.

earnestly need it, not having a single penny now. *Please* send it as soon as you can.

Sincerely,
Dylan Thomas

MS: Carbondale

VERNON WATKINS
[April 1939]   Laugharne

> I was too late for the shops in Swansea
> & couldn't get a Life & Letters. I shall in Carmarthen
> tomorrow. Is there any other good news?
> Laugharne is, I've found out,
> D.C.

Dear Vernon,

Godfather by proxy you shall be, and I'm very glad you can be. As to a gift: honestly don't worry about that, we've just had a big gift from you. Is the wireless set, please, *A.C.* or *D.C.*? The expert here can't tell & daren't test it until he knows for certain; he might blow it up. It was grand to see you, and you must come down soon, a very soon weekend. Until today it's been wonderful here, & we've driven all about Carmarthenshire in the large car you saw. We're still, of course, without a penny. I'll bring the last batch of proofs to you as soon as they come; or you spend a critical day with them here. We were sorry to miss your mother. Don't forget about the wireless.

Love,
Dylan
& from Caitlin & Llewelyn

MS: British Library   *VW*

DESMOND HAWKINS
Mayday [1939]   Laugharne Carmarthenshire S Wales

Dear Desmond,

Thank you for the letter. The Date came and went, but still I was not well enough even to blow down a Todd. Now I've nearly finished the review, which I will post tomorrow morning from my bed of asthma. And

I want to do a nice lot of work for you. Do you want an article on Miller? Forgive this ill shit.

My regards to your enviable wife and delicious children.

Dylan

MS: *the recipient*

HENRY TREECE
[?May 1939]   Laugharne Carmarthenshire

Dear Henry,

Congratulations on your marriage. Late, of course, but true. Our son is screaming outside the window; because this is scrappy and dim blame him. Thank you both for the cake; Caitlin ate it immediately. I'd heard about Hendry's anthology before you wrote, from Keidrych who was here some weeks ago being consciously queer and talking little magazines until the air was reeking full of names and nonsense and the rooms packed to the corners with invisible snobs. But I didn't know that you were handling it with Hendry, I'm glad you are.[1] (What, by the way, is Hendry's criticism like? His poetry seems to lack it.) I can't keep up with the quarrels that surround Seven, Delta, & the rest, and only hope that you can work them out to our advantage: to provide one magazine that publishes without venom but with some point. About my own contributions to the anthology: I haven't got anything new—all I've been working on are straightforward stories, sold now for large (to me) sums to Life & Letters and Story—but you can, naturally, reprint what you like. When is the anthology appearing? My own book, under the title of The Map of Love, comes out on the 1st of August. By that time I should have a new poem, & may have, though it's unlikely, finished an article on Miller that I've been preparing since he first hit me in the belly. Sorry to be so unhelpful. I've done nothing yet on Crane; there's not, in an isolated article, much to say, (I think) and it's better to read him. Print, of course, your article in 'Poetry'. How could the publicity offend me? Only one thing: do, for friendship's sake, cut out that remark of mine about 'I have a beast & an angel in me' or whatever it was: it makes me sick, drives me away from drink, recalls too much the worst of the fat and curly boy I know too well, he whose promises are water & whose water's Felinfoel, that nut-brown prince.[2] (But no beer-talk, that makes one sicker: Bellocy Bill & Squire John, Bless the bed that I piss on; Novelists neuter,

---

[1] J. F. Hendry edited *The New Apocalypse* (1940). It included a Thomas story, 'The Burning Baby', and poem, 'How shall my animal'. Other contributors were Nicholas Moore and Treece.

[2] Felinfoel is a make of South Wales beer.

Catholics chancred, Fill the fucking flowing tankard; O Georgian blotters and cricketing sops, You'll never catch me on the hops etc.) At this moment your letter, with blank postcard, dropped through the door. I found sinister the absence of any comment on my cowardly delays, but thank you very much for being so good with me, so consistently good in spite of what must seem my arrogance and selfish irresponsibility. If your & Hendry's anthology is appearing in July—that is, before my own book appears—then it's no good you printing much of mine that will be in my book. The contents of my book should come as new to people who buy it—most of the stuff's been in little magazines, but not many people read them—& for them to be printed (I mean, for many of them to be printed) in an anthology brought out almost simultaneously with my own book is obviously absurd. (That's very loose writing, the baby's louder, I hope the meaning is clear.) I suggest therefore that you reprint no more than one of my newer poems—either 'A Saint About To Fall', which came out in the first number of Poetry, or 'How Shall My Animal', a copy of which I'll enclose—and one story, 'A Prospect Of The Sea' which is *not* appearing in my book but which Life & Letters printed some time ago. I think it's about my best story to date; Church refused to let me include it in 'The Map of Love'—16 poems & 7 stories—because it has 'moments of undeniable sensuality'. You'll have to ask Herring, I suppose, for permission, which of course he'll give; sorry I've no copy at all of the story: could you get one direct from Herring, do you think, & charge it, if necessary, to Apocalypse—is that the finally decided title?—accounts? I wish I had something fresh to send you; if I do, shortly, you shall have it.

Tell me the new gossip soon. Caitlin and I are well and strong now, happy here as always among friendly people, and in debt to many of them. Is Nelly well? Our regards. I doubt very much that we'll be able to move out of Laugharne this year, in spite of your nice invitation to us. I'd love to move North, though, for a week or two. Are you coming here? There's room and welcome always, you know that. We work, play darts, don't read enough, spend a couple of evenings a week with the hospitable but whimsy Hugheses. I get stouter, burlier, squarer every day: 12 & a ½ stone now. We have a few visitors, Keidrych, Vernon Watkins; Roughton is coming down soon, probably for Whitsun; there's a possibility of Miller in the summer, though what a city-hound like that will do here God knows. No, no truculence now, hardly ever disgruntled. Tell me the names of the new rackets and the number of balls. It'll be nice to hear from you. I've kept to the last the shocking admission that I can't—at the moment anyway—write those analyses you want me to, & which I want to do too. By can't I mean just that: the words won't come: I've tried a hundred times, & have never got further than the lines of a new poem or a series of completely sidetracking ideas. But I'll go on trying. Tell me about your book.

Dylan

DAVID HIGHAM
May 11 1939   Sea View Laugharne Carmarthenshire S Wales

Dear Higham,
    The Marked Proof of my Dent's book came today. I'll be returning it this week. My contract says, '£20 will be paid the Author on his passing the proofs for press'. Is returning the Marked Proof passing the proofs for press? If it is not, would it be possible—unorthodoxly I suppose, but my need is very urgent—for you to get Dent's to give me £5 advance on that £20 which should soon be forthcoming anyway. My need is urgent because on this coming Saturday, the 13th, I'm to pay a bloody tradesman's bill or County Court proceedings will be taken. Do you think—you've been frightfully good before—you *could* make Dent's let me have a £5 by Saturday. This is a rush, I know, & I'm not too optimistic, but I do need the stuff. If not by Saturday, could you, do you think, manage it quickly?
    Dent's will be pleased to hear that my Welsh book, a sort of provincial autobiography, is coming on well. Instalments of it have been printed in the New English Weekly & in Life & Letters To-Day: a new bit will be in the July Life & Letters.[1]
    Any news about the other things I asked you?
    Sorry for this money bother.
                                        Yours sincerely,
                                        Dylan Thomas

MS: Texas

VERNON WATKINS
[May 1939]   Laugharne

I'm sending this to your office
because I've got the idea,
wrong perhaps, that you leave
before the first post arrives.[2]

Dear Vernon,
    Glad you're back from Paris. Waiting to hear everything. Herring wrote me & told me you'd been to see him. Impression? Proofs of my poems just come. One poem I want to rewrite, *with* your assistance; but I must do it quickly.[3] Can you come down Saturday—for, if possible, the weekend?

---

[1] 'Old Garbo'.
[2] Envelope addressed to Watkins at Lloyds Bank, St Helens Road Branch, Swansea.
[3] 'When all my five and country senses see.'

Please try, I need your help a lot. It really is important to me.

This Saturday, 13th, of course.

Love from us all,
Dylan

P.T.O.

Bring your masque. Herring wants me to write about it for the July number.

We haven't had the wireless set up in our house yet. It's still in Billy Williams's—he's the local electrician. He wanted me to get hold of the set's book of instructions for him, or, at any rate, a little 3 plug lead which is supposed to go in at the back of the machine but which wasn't among the parts you gave me. Billy says the set, *without* this little plug thing, will go beautifully in the day-time but makes a bad noise as soon as the Laugharne electric power is started. The plug thing will cut out the bad noise. I meant to ask you about this before, but you were away.

MS: British Library   *VW*

VERNON WATKINS
[postmarked May 12]   Laugharne

Dear Vernon,

I don't know if you leave Pennard before the first post comes or not. In case you do, there's a note from me waiting you in your Bank. This is an extra note—because if, & I hope terribly that you can, you do come, you might want to let your people know *not* by telephone alone, & get a few things, pyjamas perhaps. By 'come' I mean come to Laugharne—as the other note will tell you. I need you urgently to rewrite a poem with me that belongs to the final proofs of my book which have to be sent off almost at once.

Love,
Dylan

MS: British Library   *VW*

VERNON WATKINS
[?May 1939]   Sea View Laugharne

Dear Vernon,

I don't think I ever wrote to you after you sent the magazine with your Yeats poem in it. Sorry. I liked the poem, of course, and it seemed more closely worked than what I remember the first version to have been. Hughes & I read it together. Did you, by the way, like Hughes? He did you, very much.

Here's my new poem.[1] I hope you'll think it's good; I'm extremely pleased with it at the moment—it was written in a very enjoyable mood, (or any other better word) of surly but optimistic passion—though it is, as you'll see, in places a little awkward. I am not sure of the word 'animal' in the last line but one of the first stanza; it says more or less what I mean, that the rails, the frame if you like, of the bed of the grave is living, sensual, serpentine, but it's a word I've used perhaps too often.

'Crotch'—last line, third stanza—I've also used, once fairly startlingly, but I'm afraid the word is quite essential here. Or so, at the moment, I think. The last two lines I can see you disliking, especially the crude last lump. But that sudden crudeness is (again) essential to the argument, to, if you don't mind, the philosophy. Perhaps I should, or could, have found a stronger & nobler adjective for the light, to be in greater opposition to the very real crudity of the lump of the earth. And is the internal rhyme in the last line but one effective? I think so. Do let me know what you think of the poem, & soon, if you can.

Love,
Dylan

Don't bother too much about other details in it; apart from what I've mentioned, it's the spirit of this poem that matters.

MS: British Library   *VW*

JOHN DAVENPORT
May 11 1939   Laugharne Carmarthenshire S Wales

Dear John,
   It's good to hear from you, I'm very sorry too we never met again in the Fitzroys of Salisbury—(I looked about, after you'd told me of Salisbury's literary reputation, & saw crowds of New Forest writers, some tweed and briar, some lankly titled, many going sandalled after Russian tea)—or that we couldn't afford to move across to each other. Yes, of course, Caitlin and I will be looking forward a lot to your all coming here, & make it soon. How is Roger, I haven't seen him for two years or less, he was magnificently prosperous when I did see him, and dressed, I was glad to see, like a capitalist.[2] I say come soon because I'm going to be summoned for a few small debts and unless something happens I shall spend Whitsun picking opium. I haven't dared answer the door all this week; who knows what wired fortunes I've missed that way, invitations to sherry and princesses with Tredegar,[3] fan-mail from Dowlais. When we

---

[1] An early version of 'Poem (to Caitlin)' (= 'Unluckily for a death').
[2] Roger Roughton.
[3] The second Viscount Tredegar, Evan Frederic Morgan (1893–1949) was a writer, and had money. He is said to appear in Ronald Firbank's novel, *The Flower Beneath the Foot*, as an eccentric Englishman from Wales, the Hon. 'Eddie' Monteith, who joins an archaeological expedition to Sodom.

stayed with you in Marshfield[1] I was richer than I had ever been, I may have spoken scoffingly of small sums, my vistas were misproportioned, even my mind rustled and clinked. Now, at my lowest, I'd sell my soul to Tambimuttu—have you seen his 'Poetry' magazine, Barker's masturbative lack of elegy, Gawsworth's Foreskin Saga, Celanese love-songs? I'm so penniless—the stamp on this letter's stolen—that I'm thinking of trying to work out a small income for myself on these lines: to get as many people as possible, people, that is, of assured incomes and some little interest in whether I do or not avoid the debtors' jug, to promise to send me five shillings (5/-) a week each; if I could get ten people, we'd flourish. I've thought of a possible few, including yourself and Norman, and what do you think of the idea? I've done nothing, except this letter, about it yet. It's not as crazy as it may sound; I do very much want to go on working here, but I find it very hard when I can't go out in the street for fear of a woman with a shilling owing to her chasing me into the mother sea. As I can't make money by what I write, I think I should concentrate—Miller, incidentally, believes in this too, as you may have found out—on getting my living-money from *people* and not from poems. Do tell me what you think. But it's all a plan for the future, it would take some time to get started; now, now I'm trembling for Saturday which is the final day.

Yes, I believe, too, that Durrell, a very pleasant chap, is over-rated, but I can sympathise with the people who did boost up the Black Book so vehemently when it appeared because the first reading of it does, I think, shock you into emotional praise; it is, on the surface, so much *cleverer* than Miller, and anyway many reviewers of the Black Book hadn't, remember, read a line of Miller before. Durrell's verse is a bad show-up or down; but I think Miller's city nightlife is new and tremendous. We can agree when we meet. My book 'The Map of Love' is due in August; definitely, a notice appears in the Dent's summer catalogue. There wasn't any need after all for us to have gone through the stories, for fish-like Richard Church did the simplest thing by cutting all the best stories out. The ones left are, mostly, very tame, & there will only be the poems—the book is 17 poems & 8 stories—to save it. One story had 'its moments of sensuality', so out it went.

Caitlin and Llewelyn are strong and well. I hope you all are too. Write soon, & come here soon. My love,

Dylan

A few of the people I've thought of approaching about my five bob fund are: Edith S., Norman, John Davenport, Richard Hughes here, Lynette Roberts,[2] Peggy Guggenheim,[3] Augustus, Robert Herring. But of course

---

[1] Davenport's house was in the village of Marshfield.
[2] Lynette Roberts (b. 1909), a writer; later she married Keidrych Rhys.
[3] Peggy Guggenheim, the American art collector and patron.

they won't all agree. I want more possibilities for this Trifling Subscription.

MS: Texas   *SL(R)*

JOHN DAVENPORT
[?May 1939]   Laugharne

Dear John,
   This is a small note to thank you a great lot for the cheque & the names. The cheque saved us; it was marvellously kind of you; Caitlin & I are grateful. No dank debtors' walls obscure us, the fawning tradesmen doff their horns. I'll draft a letter for the fivebob fund & let you have it, it's grand to have your assistance. A witty letter, do you think? I'll write very soon. Or a straight-from-the-shldr? Love to you all, Caitlin sends hers too. Thanks again, John. And try to come here soon.

                                                                                          Dylan

MS: Texas

VERONICA SIBTHORP[1]
[spring 1939]   Laugharne Carmarthenshire S Wales

Darling Veronica,
   This is the first letter between us for nearly a year, and we should all have our nails pulled out for it, and how are you and where are you? I've been once in London since we saw you last, and then for two days at Christmas: I ran into sinful Wyn,[2] nearly knocked her down, and she told me you spent your life doing crosswords, which seemed very odd and our Inventions is a better game. Will this reach you? If it doesn't, you won't know so I'll write again to Upper Berkeley Street or chase you through Archie[3] through the Etonian Register or Conjugal jails. Please answer, it's terribly foolish us not writing and trying to meet. Caitlin had a baby in January, a son called Llewelyn now weighing one stone, with my Greek nose and chiselled chin. I wired you then, to Berkeley Street, but perhaps I got the number wrong or perhaps you weren't there, because the post office people returned it. And, as soon as they returned it, I should have written to Lamorna, but I got singing drunk for a fortnight and have been

---

[1] See note, page 225.
[2] Wyn Henderson.
[3] Archie McColl, Veronica Sibthorp's first husband.

lazy and careless almost ever since. Last week we christened the baby, Augustus was here, you should have been too. Augustus could not follow the service, although he had the text, and broke in with the refrain 'I desire it' at intervals. I wish you could come down here for a holiday or longer. Can you? We've got two spare rooms in this crumbling house by the sea, and mice alone occupy them. Be a bigger and better mouse for us. You'd love it here; the beer and the people, the house and the sea, are all very posh in a good sense. I do hope you can afford to come, it's not really very far by train—because that was the reason, wasn't it, that stopped you coming last year. Regular lack of money flows in for us still, we are always with nothing but arrogance, guile, and hope. I'm just about to pawn, for debts and the demon alcohol, a silver christening present to Llewelyn. Little, as they say, the poor boy wots. We still, of course, have the itch and have grown quite attached to it, but, if you have lost it, you needn't worry about getting it again when, & if as I hope, you come down here, for all except our bedclothes conceal nothing worse than moths and mice's breath. How are Archie and Jake?[1] I'm a huge thing now, 12½ stone, and my eyes are finally Sprotted. We *do* want to see you; try to see us, & write very soon. Love from Caitlin, & from me, Dylan.

This was bound to be a little letter, because there's so much news & so much nice nonsense that we have to meet to tell it.

MS: National Library of Wales

DAVID HIGHAM
14 May 1939 (Proofs returned to J. M. Dent. See Appendix 14.)

J. M. DENT
May 15 1939 (Sends photographs of himself. See Appendix 15.)

DAVID HIGHAM
May 16 1939 (Thanks for cheque. See Appendix 16.)

[1] 'Jake' was John Sibthorp, Veronica's second husband.

J. M. DENT
May 25 [1939]   Sea View Laugharne Carmarthenshire

In Reference to 'The Map of Love'
Dear Sir,
    In answer to your wire just received: the reading of the last words of
line 14 and the first words of line 15 on page 112 is: 'be swallowed down
on to a hill's v balancing on the grave' etc.[1] The isolated letter, in case my
handwriting's bad, is v, vee, the letter between u and w. *Not* a capital
letter. In its context, its sense is: a triangular hill is turned upside down &
looks like the shape of the letter v. (If you call that sense)

                                        Yours truly,
                                        Dylan Thomas

MS: J. M. Dent

CHARLES FISHER
Wednesday June 14 1939   Seaview Laugharne

(pigeon fucking begins)

Dear Charles,
    Yes, of course, Tuesday. I've been hoping you could come down soon;
and it's nice very nice, to hear that Fred and fat Tom will be with you. It's
a woe or so ago, if I may quote from a wellknown sheepchaser, since I last
saw Tom.
    I won't have a story but I've got one new poem: The G.O.M., Grand
Ovary Manica, at his most secretive.
    Our baby's getting devilish; I wish we had a *huge* pusher for him.
    Keidrych and I are giving a broadcast soon. Tell you about it when we
meet.

                                        I remain your
                                        humble savant
                                        Dylan

TS: J. M. Dent. Charles Fisher no longer has the MS.

[1] In the story 'The Orchards'.

VERNON WATKINS
[June 1939]   Sea View Laugharne

Dear Vernon,

I don't find your way of criticizing at all irritating; you know that. It's the most helpful there is for me, and I want it to go on. About many suggestions of yours we'll always, of course, disagree, especially when they seem completely to misunderstand my meaning; but, as nobody else has done,—though this is a late and wrong place for a recommendation of your complete intellectual honesty, a thing we needn't talk about—, without rancour, affectation, or the felt need to surprise. I think you are liable, in your criticisms of me, to underrate the value—or, rather, the integrity, the wholeness—of what I am saying or trying to make clear that I am saying, and often to suggest alterations or amendments for purely musical motives. For instance, 'Caught in a somersault of tumbled mantime' may (and I doubt it) sound more agreeable—we'll leave out any suggestion of it sounding inevitable because it is, however good the implied criticism, a group of words *outside* the poem—to the 'prophesying ear' than 'In an imagining of tumbled mantime', a line I worked out *for* its sounds & not in spite of them.[1] My criticism of your critical suggestion in this instance is that your 'ear' is deaf to the logic of my poem;

> 'Caught in a somersault etc etc
> Suddenly cold as fish'

is an ambiguous tangle, very like nonsense. (I know your suggestion was not meant to be the last substitutive word for my first words, but was meant mainly to suggest further things, allway pointers, to me myself; but the suggestion still does, I believe, show the way your criticism often works: towards the aural betterment (ugh) of details, without regard for their significance in a worked-out, if not a premeditated-*in-detail*, whole). This is certainly one critical way, but when it suggests 'withered' for 'sheeted', in the last line but one of the first stanza, *I* suggest it cuts across the poem and does not come out of it. It is a poet saying 'This is what I would have done'; not a critic saying, 'This, I think, is what the poet should have done'. I suppose, argumentatively, not randomly speaking, that all criticism which is not an analysis of reasons for praise must primarily be suspicion; and that's stimulating. Nothing but the inevitable can be taken for granted, and it always excites me to find you dealing suspiciously with a word, a line, that I had, in a naturally blind or artificially blinkered moment, taken, myself, with too much trust, trusting too much the fallible creative rush of verse—small or large rushes of verse—that comes, in many cases, between the mechanical

---

[1] The poem is 'Unluckily for a death'. The *CP* version is much altered from the version Watkins first saw; the line 'In an imagining of tumbled mantime' was one that disappeared.

preparations for that (in a way) accidental rush. (Woolly writing, I'm afraid; hope the meaning comes clearly.) With your annoyance at the word 'chuck' I agree; and my use of it is sentimental. I have tried 'cast', but that is too static a word; I'll find what I really want. And, yes the poem did appear to tire of itself at the end—: (by the way, I resent that 'tire of itself' idea, which arrogantly supposes the self-contained *identity* of the poem even in its forming phases; the poem is not, of course, itself until the poet has left it). The jingle of 'abide with our pride' I'm retaining; I wanted the idea of an almost jolly jingle there, a certain carelessness to lead up to the flat, hard, ugly last line of truth, a suggestion of 'Well, that's over, O atta boy we live with our joy'; a purposeful intolerance—no, I meant an intolerance on purpose—of the arguments I had been setting against my own instinctive delight in the muddled world. Whether that intolerance, carelessness, etc. is *poetically* effective is another kettle of wishes.

It is very fine news of the masque, and Caitlin and I will be there.[1] We will try to bring Hughes too. Why don't you write to him? You want a big audience, of word-boys as well as theatre boys. Who have you asked? I shall do a review for Life & Letters, but after the show you must let me read the masque. We'll be there for the First Night, I hope.

We want a little poem for Llewelyn.

Love till we see you; and before and after. Can you come & see Norman Cameron? He'll be down for a weekend soon, I'll let you know when.

Write soon. Here is a new short poem, nothing very much.[2]

Dylan

The word I used too much—'sucked'—is here bound, I think, to be.

'Desireless familiar' is a phrase in my 'Orchards' & what caused me to write the poem. The best thing is, as you'll perhaps agree, the simple last line of the middle bit.

MS: British Library   *VW*

JOHN DAVENPORT
23rd June 1939   Sea View Laugharne Carmarthenshire

Dear John,

Norman says he's coming here the same time as you: June 31st, next weekend. Hope that's definitely fixed. We're looking forward to you very much. Is Roger driving? Norman, I suppose, can stay for the weekend only; it will be lovely if *you* can stay longer—it's too far to come for such

---

[1] *The Influences*, to be performed by Swansea Little Theatre. The Thomases didn't get there.

[2] 'To others than you.'

a short time. There's plenty to do here, and even if there wasn't there would be. I've been writing quite hard, got a couple of stories and a couple of poems, plans and beginnings. I've done [one] or two drafts of a 5/-letter—I should have written to you before, but surprise tiny money momentarily wiped out the future; now the nasty future *is*—and I want to go over them with you, if you will, and we'll Get Down and Organise. I want to hear about the Miller visit—fuck fuck fuck—too. Grand to stay with you when he was there (or when he wasn't). I'm going to broadcast poems in August, let you know when—breathless boom boom boom. How is Clement? Caitlin's strong and the baby's piercing. Lots to tell you, not important but jolly. Write to confirm the 31st: we'll be terribly disappointed if you don't all come.

General love,
Dylan

MS: Texas

J. M. DENT & CO.　　　　　　　　　　　　　Sea View　Laugharne　Carmarthenshire
29 June 1939

Dear Sir,
   Thank you for the proof of the wrapper for my book, which I return.
   I suggest that you cut out the statement from the Manchester Evening News, on the back flap. This seems a very dim and tame blurb, and very flat after the praise of the other notices quoted. If you would care to, you could use instead these remarks from a notice in New Directions, America, 1938:—'It is no exaggeration to say that his name is on the tongue of every young poetry reader in England. His poetry is verbal sculpture—almost fiercely strong'. If you don't want to use that, I think the Manchester Evening News remark shd still *not be allowed to stand*; the Evening News is not a paper famous for the value of its literary opinions; & anyway it's a feeble blurb.

Yours faithfully,
Dylan Thomas

P.S. There was a most complimentary review in the Specatator just after the book was published, though I'm afraid I haven't got a copy. Perhaps you can find it; I know Dent's sent me a copy of it through their Press Cutting Agency.

MS: J. M. Dent

VERNON WATKINS
[early July 1939]   Sea View Laugharne

Dear Vernon,
  This is to tell you, with great regret, that we *may* not be able to come to
your play. If Hughes can come—he's not sure yet, he may have to go to
London—then we'll be able to; if not, not. I thought I'd have some money
this week, but bills took it at once & now we couldn't afford to go to
Carmarthen even. But *if* Hughes can go, he'll take us & then everything
will be all right. I'd hate to have to miss the play, more than I can tell you.
Cameron was supposed to have come here last weekend, but cdn't manage it. Instead, Roger Roughton drove John Davenport down in an impossibly luxurious car; they returned yesterday. I hope very very much to be
able to see you on Thursday night; and we *will* try. But if we can't, you
must get the Theatre to give us a private performance later on.

Love from us both,
Dylan

MS: British Library   *VW*

W. T. DAVIES[1]
July 5 1939   Laugharne Carmarthenshire

Dear W. T. Davies,
  Keidrych may have told you that Taig,[2] of the Swansea Little Theatre,
intends taking a theatre in London for a night or two at the end of
September, and presenting there poems by Welshmen writing in English.
Watkins' Masque will probably be included. The poems aren't necessarily
to be dramatic, but the audience will be given something to occupy their
eyes without sacrificing their ears. All kinds and numbers of speakers
will be used. Taig hopes to have some London Welsh actors to read some
of the poems. I'm collecting lots of poems together for Taig and myself to
go over in more detail—though all the dramatic ideas that come out of
the poems, the dramatic possibilities rather, will be Taig's. Would you
care to send along a selection of your own poems? I want to include as
many *Wales* contributors & supporters as possible. I'd be glad of your
help.

Yours sincerely,
Dylan Thomas

MS: National Library of Wales

[1] W. T. ('Pennar') Davies (b. 1911), writer and clergyman.
[2] See page 399.

JOHN DAVENPORT
[?July 1939]   Sea View Laugharne Carmarthenshire

Dear John,
   About Thomas Flotation Ltd:—I wrote to Norman, asking him if he'd give 5/- a week, and he said yes. But his business mind got working, and he suggested: 'the best arrangement for you might be to open a bank-account into which all your sponsors could put a series, say, of monthly post-dated cheques; and John (as he lives in your direction) might act as a funnel'—that, I think, was the word—'if he would be so obliging'. Do you understand that, apart from 'funnel'? Norman says, and vaguely I agree with him, that 'it's too much of a bother for people to send you 5/- every Friday'. What arrangement could be made? Does Norman suggest that these post-dated cheques—why post-dated?—be put into your account? If so, why need I have an account? If they're all put into mine, how are you a funnel? I'm writing to Norman again, but I'd like your views. Surely there must—if people can't be bothered with sending 5/- a week—[be] some very simple method of them sending it to me monthly? The trouble shouldn't begin with that, but with getting these sponsors Thomas-minded. So far only 3 have definitely said yes: you and Roger and Norman. Will *you* ask Peggy G., Guinness, & Redgrave,[1] none of whom (apart from a few envious minutes with Guggenheim) do I know at all. And will Roger ask Penrose? I'll write to Penrose myself, but I think it would be a good idea for Roger to begin. I'm feeling rather miserable at the moment, my head is bloody & bowed, because I can't get this scheme working at once. I do so much need it to work, we're awfully in debt. Sorry, John, to have to ask you so much; I wouldn't if I didn't know that you really wanted to help, & that you had helped such a lot before & so kindly & nicely. Try to send off to those people soon; & then perhaps you can tell me when I should write to them myself. Are there any other names? Like a fool, I lost your first list—though I remember that I didn't know personally many of the people you suggested, & that it would have been too odd perhaps for me to have written to them directly. I've got to get 12 chaps. I'm writing today to Augustus, & asking him to ask Evan Tredegar.[2] Though I don't expect much from that. This scheme has got to get going now; & I'm relying on you a hell of a lot.
   We were very very sorry you couldn't manage to come back to Laugharne. I didn't tell too many funny stories, did I? Caitlin thought you might have been bored that last cockle evening. We'd love anyway to come & stay with you soon & have lots of music and things. I've nearly finished a nice new poem I'll send you. Love to you and Clement. Is Roger back with you yet? Caitlin sends love to you both.
                                                                    Dylan

[1] Probably Bryan Guinness, and the actor Michael Redgrave.
[2] Lord Tredegar.

I want to know something definite about 5/- arrangements—bank accounts, postdated cheques, funnels, how people are to send to me —before writing to Sitwell & a few others. And, I want to write to them soon. Try to puzzle something out.

MS: Texas

JOHN DAVENPORT
[?July 1939]   Sea View Laugharne Carmarthenshire

Dear John,
    Norman asks me to send this letter of his on to you: an explanation of the funnel-&-cheque letter. The arrangement he suggests means a lot of bother to you; I hope you think it's a good suggestion—though it depends on the various sponsors (so far, *definitely* four only)—and that the trouble won't be too awful. If the trouble is, & you don't feel up to it, then I must think, or ask someone else to think, of another arrangement. What do *you* think?
    Love to Clement & you from us both.

                                                     Dylan

MS: Texas

W. T. DAVIES
July 1939   Sea View Laugharne Carmarthen

Dear W. T. Davies,
    Thank you for your letter. Yes, Keidrych Rhys told me about the plan to form a literary society in Wales, but he was vague as to its ideas. And so am I, still. Can I ask some questions first? How is it intended that the young Welsh writers should get together? Is there any suggestion of trying to have an actual Group premises in Swansea or in some other convenient centre? Or of arranging regular conferences? I can certainly see, if not the need for this, the enjoyment to be got from gratifying the wish for that need. That may sound disagreeable; if it does, it's only because group, conference, manifesto, are words for things to be suspected—suspected of giving too many opportunities for official rigamarolling, high-sounding 'party' pronouncements, etc—unless one knows something quite definite about the reasons behind the desire to arrange them. In what manner could the proposed society 'substitute energy and responsibility for the dilettantism and provincialism of life and literature in Wales'? And what does it mean? Does it suggest that a

literary society, by being honest and energetic and having as some of its members responsible artists—by 'responsible' I mean here artists who know what they are doing and who go on doing it faithfully to the best of their ability—could strengthen and further the work of its writing members? Or are you suggesting that it could 'give weight' to the work of Welsh writers, that is: that it could influence, by its solidity and (if you like) responsibility, readers in Wales to give a wider and more careful attention to the work of those writers? I doubt if any literary society could, in our time, do this second thing: (that's very arguably open); but I do believe that, through regular discussions, readings of papers and creative work, young Welsh writers could possibly be encouraged to experiment further & not get tired or disillusioned, and that perhaps a new passion and tolerance could be brought to their thinking about and creating of a living literature in this mismanaged, discouraged, middlebrow-beaten, but still vigorously imaginative country. (I'm talking as one of the young writers and can therefore, perhaps, be excused these pompous, old man's phrases.)

Would the society include writers in Welsh and English? Is Welsh Nationalism a part of the proposed Manifesto? And when do you think that a few people could meet and talk about 'policies'? I'm very interested; what I've said is a sign of my interest, not a quarrel, of course, with you or with the tentative ideas advanced in your letter. I hope you'll write again.

Yours sincerely,
Dylan Thomas

MS: National Library of Wales

W. T. DAVIES
[July 1939]   Sea View Laugharne Carmarthenshire

Dear W. T. Davies,
    Thank you for writing such an interesting and persuading letter. I still don't like the idea of societies, groups, manifestos. I don't think it does any harm to the artist to be lonely *as* an artist. (Let's all 'get together', if we must, and go to the pictures.) If he feels personally unimportant, it may be that he is. Will an artistic milieu make his writing any better? I doubt it, I'm afraid. God, inspiration, concentration (cool, hot, or camp), John O'London's, opium, living, thinking and loving, hard work, anything you like, may or may not do that. It—the milieu, the organisation for responsibility, though that's an unfair phrase I admit, may make him realise—perhaps, in an extremely lonely case, for the first time—that there are others like himself, other perplexed people who are trying to write as well as possible and to attach an importance to writing. But the

result of a consciously-*made* intelligentsia may be to narrow, not to widen, the, if you'll excuse me, individual outlook; and instead of a lonely man—and writing, again, is the result, as somebody said, of certain favourable bad conditions—working in face of an invisible opposition, (the crude opposition, of family, finance, etc. that says 'writing is a waste of time' & 'why don't you do something worth-while' has always, surely, had to be disregarded) there may be just a group of condoling, sympathy-patting, 'I was always bullied at school', 'So was I', 'Down with the philistines', 'They don't understand a poet', mutually acknowledging, ism and isting, uniformed grumblers making a communal opposition to a society in which, individually, they feel alone and unimportant. I'm selfish enough not to feel worried very much about the writer in his miserable artistic loneliness, whether it's in Wales or Paris or London; I don't see why it should be miserable anyway. I think that to fight, for instance, the fascism of bad ideas by uniforming & regimenting good ones will be found, eventually, to be bad tactics. I'm not suggesting for a second that that is what you are suggesting; this rather silly letter is less an argument against your arguments than the expression of my own possibly old-fashioned romantic feelings. Don't take any of it too seriously—not, I suppose, that you would—and let me say that I'd be very pleased indeed to become a member of the proposed society, though a quarrelsome & reactionary one, if that does not mean I have to sign any manifesto. I do appreciate that you aren't wasting time, and lots of good may come out of the plans. I hope it will. Perhaps we will be able to meet some time. Is Mountain Ash far from Swansea? I'm staying in Swansea—Marston, Bishopston—until next Wednesday. Anyway, best wishes & excuse much of these tantrums.

Dylan Thomas

MS: National Library of Wales

HENRY TREECE
[July 1939]   Sea View Laugharne Carmarthenshire

Dear Henry,

I was glad you wrote to me, I like hearing, and I'd feel, I know, very angry if you wrote to me as badly and as irregularly as I do to you. I mean always to send you regular letters full of news and opinions, but what happen are occasional flat bits of grumbling and promises, fully felt and meant, of small worth for your book. And, though I want to be bright and full of opinionated news, this letter won't be any better either, for I'm deep in money troubles, small for some, big as banks for me, my debts are rising, it's raining, my new troubles and poems won't move, and what have I got to sparkle about I'd like to know? We've been staying for a fortnight with my father and mother, who are nice, warm-hearted people forced, by silliness and an almost hysterical greed for safety, to be so penny-cautious, so impatient for my success, (which means for me to have money, a position, and property), that I could run right out and exchange all my happiness for something entirely useless like an old bird-bath or a book of MacNeice's poems. Money and property I should like, but my life's set now towards not getting them. My father's house is stuck on a crowded piece of beautiful landscape—This Way to the Cliff Scenery—and surrounded by 4000 Territorial soldiers. Girls hot and stupid for soldiers flock knickerless on the cliff. We're returning to Laugharne tomorrow. There are only 50 soldiers there. What are you doing for your country? I'm letting mine rot. A girl I knew, sweet and reckless, is Captain Mabel now. Liberals are talking of Hitler's unscrupulous sincerity. MacNeice on the radio asked F. R. Higgins on the radio, and both, if you ask me, were pissed, 'Would it be honest of me, in the present state of the world, to go and live in a little cottage in Ireland and let war and its rumours roar?' (I distrust people who question their own honesty; such people walk critically behind their actions, observe the action of writing a poem before the poem itself; wherever you go and whatever you do, your honesty, or lack of it, goes, and acts, with you.) A schoolmaster in Wales wrote asking me if I would join a Society of Welsh writers and help to attack and crush provincial dilettantism and the feeling of unimportance and loneliness which young provincial writers are, he says with knowledge, possessed by. (If they feel so unimportant *as* writers it is perhaps because they are; and loneliness, from anything except friendship, hasn't hurt anybody.) A speaker on the wireless said that English dogs don't like foreigners. My liver's rebelled against me, and I have sudden attacks of overwhelming temper, blood rises to my head, and I stamp my little feet. Are you happy in your new state and house? We'd like to visit you—Caitlin and the baby are well—but won't be able to until we can find travelling and during-Lincolnshire money, which may never be. The little I get goes, after a few pleasures, to tradesmen and two landlords. We must, I suppose, live. And I do get little; I'm hoping to sell some new straight autobiographical stories in America for a whole pile of England-trotting money; I'm hoping for retaining money from Dent's. My book comes out on the 24th of August, but I've had all that matters from that and now there are only reviews to come. Have you found a paper to review it for? What about, if nothing with a larger circulation is willing to let its poetry go to anybody who likes poetry ,— the dramatic critic of the Times for 30 years has just confessed in a book of memoirs that he always loathed the theatre—the New English Weekly? I should like very much to see your article in MacDiarmid's paper.[1] Could you send me a copy: if you have only one, I'll return it quickly. I'm sure, by the way, that the Oxford University Press, however

---

[1] The poet Hugh MacDiarmid (Christopher Murray Grieve) (1892–1978) edited the quarterly *Voice of Scotland*.

kind, will not do your book; Charles Williams, who works for it, is a friend but he could not, only 2 years ago, persuade, by any means, the Press to publish my poems; they mightn't be inclined to bring out a book of criticism about work they did not 'see fit to' print themselves. Why won't Symons publish it? He's produced some books, hasn't he: Confusions about Symons by X etc.? Will you send me your long poem? Our handshakes to Nelly.

Love,
Dylan

I've got quite a lot to tell you. Next letter, soon. The baby Llewelyn is singing & eating paper, I can't think now of anything but that. Let me have your news.

MS: Buffalo   *SL(R)*

DAVID HIGHAM
[July 1939]   Sea View Laugharne Carmarthenshire

Dear Higham,
     Any news of Laughlin?
     This is an urgent, and despairing, too, plea for money. Do you think you could persuade Dent's to give me some immediately? Is there, do you think, a possibility of getting Dent's to make out a contract for future books of mine—on the lines of Laughlin's proposed contract, covering the next five or more years, but obviously not so mean and ridiculous a one? I would willingly, of course, if you thought it wise and worth-while, let Dent's have first option, or anything else, on all my future work if only they would advance me some money now before it is too late—that is, before I am made to leave, as I certainly *will* be made to leave, this house and town. I am very much in debt here, to landlord and tradesmen, for about £30 altogether, and unless I can begin, at least, to pay off the debts at once, I'll have to move, and move God knows where because, without a certain amount of credit, I can't possibly be expected to carry on week by week or even day by day. I am working a lot now—have more than ten poems towards a new miscellaneous book such as the one Dent's are bringing out next month, and several stories towards the Welsh autobiographical book for which Dent's have given me half the advance. But unless I have some money at once I'll have to shift house, which means shift from a house to no house, and get in such a mess of living again that it will be impossible to work on anything. Can you get from Dent's either some more of the advance money still coming to me for the Welsh book not yet completed, or some money as well as a retainer for the promise of my future books? Next year I shd have two new books (including the

Welsh one) ready, the second being another selection of prose and verse similar to 'The Map of Love'.[1] And I think that, given some security, and being allowed to go on living here, I'll be able to produce a lot of stuff and work far faster than I have in the past. I find it *extremely* difficult to keep a wife and a child, but the difficulty has now reached a point when only an immediate sum of money, £30, to cover my pressing debts can save me from being chucked out, my books and bits of furniture and beds being taken away, and my work, present and future, being hopelessly spoiled and interrupted. I wouldn't write this unless there was nothing and nobody else for me to ask. I have tried to live without requesting anything further from Dent's, and without troubling you any further—for you have already done a lot for me, though not as yet, I'm afraid, greatly to your advantage—but now I just must get money, and at once. Will you see Dent's, will you tell them what I have told you in this letter? Publishers do, sometimes, give retainers to their authors, don't they? I don't mind what it is—retainer, or contracted promise for all future work—but I must have money for my debts or have everything taken away from me and be quite homeless. I hope you will do your best for me, I know you will, and see how really serious this is for me.

Yours sincerely,
Dylan Thomas

Would it be advisable for me to come up—(though, on my own account, I couldn't)—to see you & Dent's about all this?

MS: Texas

JOHN DAVENPORT
August 1 [1939]   Sea View Laugharne Carmarthenshire

Dear John,
   What about a line on my flotation fund and old Pawk's suggestions?[2] I'm lost without your support. Was Laugharne too much or too little? Augustus wrote to say he wouldn't be here until the autumn. Charles Morgan[3] is staying with Hughes and we're going along tonight to be dazzled. Some man is going to take a London theatre for a night or two in September and give, among other things, dramatic performances of my poems. I'll be there full of cracks etc. Shall we see each other in London?

[1] No such book appeared; instead, the war came.
[2] Norman Cameron.
[3] Charles Morgan (1894–1958), novelist and playwright.

Can I peep inside your club, just a peep? Do let me know something. Recently I may as well have been writing to a malting-house.[1]

Love to you & Clement
from us both. Dylan

MS: Texas

KEIDRYCH RHYS
[August 1939]

Dear Keidrych,

I'm returning the BBC script. We'd better pacify Mr. Watkin Jones and agree to his alterations.[2] Will *you* make them, in accordance with what he said? I leave it to you, you'll know best: just make it clear that you're talking about English poetry by Welshmen when you refer to the un-cultivated tradition, & not talking about their precious Welsh poets. After all, it's the *English* poetry we're bothering ourselves about in this programme; poetry *in* Welsh can be left alone, as far as our talk goes that evening. You should be able to alter the questioned paragraphs very easily. And 'world at large' is a more understandable phrase, I think, than 'the outside world'. But do what you think best. We (or you, rather) *must* alter these 'objectionable' phrases; it's worth agreeing with their piddling suggestions in order to get across what we really want to. I may myself, later & with, probably, the disgust of Mr. Jones, change one of my selected poems; but that can be left until the rehearsal.

Does Harry Roskolenko *pay* for contributions to his anthology?[3] Must they be unpublished poems, or just poems unpublished in America? I don't know Laura Riding, & I think that if she has refused to contribute nothing will make her change her mind.

[*in margin*: Don't forget to answer this, will you?]

I'd like to meet Saroyan.[4] Is he in London?

MS: Texas

---

[1] Davenport's address was The Malting House.
[2] The programme was to be called 'Modern Welsh Poets'; Thomas would read, Keidrych Rhys would discuss. Someone with a long memory at the BBC wrote on the correspondence in thick blue pencil: 'We *must* have this man's script before he appears in the studios.'
[3] Harry Roskolenko (1907–80), American writer and editor.
[4] William Saroyan (1908–81), American writer.

BBC
[August 2 1939]   Sea View Laugharne Carmarthenshire

Dear Sir,
   I'm enclosing the reply sheet you sent me on July 31, and I should like
to say that I'm afraid I will need my actual travelling expenses to be paid
me, out of the 5½ guineas, *before* the day of the broadcast, as otherwise I
may not be able to afford, that day, to travel at all. I hope this isn't
inconvenient; I wouldn't insist on it unless it was really necessary.[1]

                                        Yours faithfully,
                                        Dylan Thomas

MS: BBC

DAVID HIGHAM
August 3 1939   Sea View Laugharne Carmarthenshire

Dear Higham,
   Thank you very much indeed for acting so promptly and so well for me. I
agree that Dent's have been really generous; and, of course, as I said in my
wire this morning, I accept all the proposals most readily. I'm especially
glad—apart from the promise of an immediate £30, which is terribly
welcome & urgently needed, even before the contract is completed —that
the proposals for the two prose books didn't specify that either had to be a
novel: for if they had, I'm afraid I'd have had to swear it all off. Both books
will probably be stories of some kind or another. The periodical payments
will help me greatly. *Thank you* again for all you've done.[2]

                                        Yours sincerely,
                                        Dylan Thomas

Any Laughlin news? Or are you waiting until my 'Map of Love' comes
out? Surely we can get an American publisher to tackle that. I've had a
number of v. good American reviews & criticisms lately & a couple of
articles on my poems have been published.

MS: Texas

---

[1] The 5½ guineas (about £5.75) in the contract was to include travel expenses to the
Swansea studio on September 6.
[2] Thomas apparently received £30 in August and a further £40 before the end of the year, as
well as regular payments of £8 a month that began in September and continued through
most of 1940. Neither book was written in the form (or during the period of time)
anticipated.

J. M. DENT
August 11 1939   Sea View Laugharne Carmarthenshire

Dear Sir,

I'm glad to hear that my book, The Map of Love, is coming out on the 24th, and that my own copies are on the way.

You ask me to suggest the names of any periodicals that might not be on your review list. I think that *Seven* might be very useful, it has an important circulation in Oxford and Cambridge and other university towns etc. It is edited by Nicholas Moore whose address is: 68 Chesterton Road, Cambridge. Also, though this is quite possibly on your list, *Wales*, which has a wide following here. Edited by Nigel Heseltine[1] from Cefn-Bryntalch, Abermule, Montgomeryshire. I was one of the founders of this paper & will have an interesting, if nothing else, notice. Also Hugh MacDiarmid's quarterly, *The Voice of Scotland*, which is read by the whole of the Scottish National Party & also by nationalists in Wales & Ireland.

I don't know if you send review copies to the U.S.A., but 'Poetry, Chicago' has given me quite a lot of attention, including one of their yearly prizes, lately. Anyway, I hope you will be able to send to *Seven*, *Wales*, & *Voice of Scotland*: they're all worth it, I'm sure.

                                    Yours faithfully,
                                    Dylan Thomas

MS: J. M. Dent

DESMOND HAWKINS
14th August 1939   Sea View Laugharne Carmarthenshire

Dear Desmond,

Nice to hear. I've been back in Wales a good, in many ways, time now, since April. Too long not to know anything about you. Honestly, Tambimuttu had that buttu of a poem at the time I promised you one; and now of course I've nothing. I've got a short story, but it's longish, about the length of the straightforward stories I've been printing recently (if you saw them) in Life & Letters: perhaps 4000, or a bit under. No good? I'm trying to make my living out of straight stories now; I've got a contract too, & must finish a book of stories by Christmas. Auto-biographical stories, Provincial Autobiography, Portrait of the Artist as a Young Dog, or something like that. Have you, as we boys are always asking each other, got far with your novel?

I'm very glad you're doing my book for the Spectator, and that you like it. There could have been a better selection of stories, I think, but Church

---

[1] Heseltine had taken over some of the editing from Keidrych Rhys.

was timid. I know that many of the poems are difficult, and will be called, though not by you, surrealist. (Aren't they, by the way, using 'surrealist' a bit more sparingly now?) I am trying hard to make them less Hide-and-Seek-Jekyll: (cf. your notes on mixed personality in the Spectator once). Few are stunt poems (cf: 'Fog has a bone' in my last lot).[1] And the best are deeply emotional. That said, I agree that much of the poetry is impossibly difficult; I've asked, or rather told, words to do too much; it isn't theories that choke some of the wilder and worser lines, but sheer greed. I'll try to answer, in a discursive way, your questions and natural bewilderments. There isn't anyone living I wd rather write a review of me than you. (For that, which is very true, please substitute *magnificent* for every *interesting*.)

I. Or Nuts to You. Poem 13.[2] 'Nut', yes, has many meanings, but here, in the same line as 'woods', I can't really see that it can have any but a woody meaning. The actual line is a very extravagant one, an overgrand declamatory cry after, in my opinion, the reasoned and quite quiet argument of the preceding lines. The *sense* of the last two lines is: Well, to hell and to death with me, may my old blood go back to the bloody sea it came from if I accept this world only to bugger it up or return it. The oaktree came out of the acorn; the woods of my blood came out of the nut of the sea, the tide-concealing, blood-red kernel. A silly, far-fetched, if not, apparently, far-fetching shout—maybe—but, I think, balanced in the poem.

II. Here I can't get which poem you mean, so I'll take both. First of all, the 3rd & 4th line of poem one (January 1939).[3] Perhaps these lines should have been put in a pair of brackets, but I think that brackets often confuse things even more. The poem begins with a queer question about a bird and a horse: because one thing is made sweeter (qualify this word) through suffering what it doesn't understand, does that mean everything is sweeter through incomprehensible, or blind, suffering? (Later, the poem has a figure in it standing suffering on the tip of the new year and refusing, blindly, to look back at, if you like, the *lessons* of the past year to help him; and the case, which is really a case for a prayer, begins to make itself clear.) Then I, the putter of the question, turn momentarily aside from the question and, in a sort of burst of technical confidence, say that the bird and beast are merely convenient symbols that just *have* to suffer what my mood dictates, just *have* to be the objects my mood (wit or temper? but here 'mood' alone) has decided to make a meal upon and also the symbolic implements with which I cut the meal and objects up. Loose and obscure explanation; but writing freely like this is the best way, I believe, to get the stuff across, by writing around the difficulties & making notes on them.

---

[1] 'How soon the servant sun.'
[2] 'On no work of words.'
[3] 'Because the pleasure-bird whistles.'

III. The next things you wanted to discuss were stanzas three and four of the poem (page 4) beginning 'I make this In A W.A.' (Work of Art, Workshop of Agony, Witbite of Agenwar). The stanzas are a catalogue of the contraries, the warring loyalties, the psychological discrepancies, all expressed in physical and/or extra-narrative terms, that go towards making up the 'character' of the woman, or 'beloved' would be wider & better, in whose absence, and in the fear of whose future unfaithful absences, I jealously made the poem. I didn't just say in one line that she was cold as ice and in the next line that she was hot as hell; in each line I made as many contraries as possible fight* together, in an attempt to bring out a *positive* quality; I wanted a peace, admittedly only the armistice of a moment, to come out of the images on *her* warpath. Excuse me, but this note I wrote for a my-eye essay by H. Treece may as well come in now: 'I make one image, though "make" is not the word; I let, perhaps, an image be made emotionally in me & then apply to it what intellectual and critical forces I possess; let it breed another; let that image contradict the first, make, of the third image bred out of the other two together, a fourth contradictory image, and let them all, within my imposed formal limits, conflict'. A bit smug, and old stuff too, but it applies here. And the conflict is, of course, only to make peace. I want the lasting life of the poem to come out of the destroyers in each image. Old stuff again. Here, in this poem, the emotional question is: Can I see clearly, by cataloguing and instancing all I know of her, good and bad, black and white, kind & cruel, (in coloured images condensed to make, not a natural colour, but a militant peace and harmony of all colours), the emotional war caused by her absence, and thus decide for myself whether I fight, lie down and hope, forgive or kill? The question is naturally answered by the questions in the images and the images in the questions—if the vice-versa makes any different sense. Yes, the syntax of stanza 3 is difficult, perhaps 'wrong'. *SHE* makes for me a nettle's in-nocence and a soft pigeon's guilt; she makes, in the fucked, hard rocks a frail virgin shell; she makes a frank (i.e. imprisoned, and candid and open) and closed (contradiction again here, meaning virgin-shut to diving man**) pearl; she makes shapes of sea-girls glint in the staved (diver-poised) & siren (certainly non-virgin) caverns; *SHE IS* a maiden in the shameful oak—: (here the shameful oak *is* obscure, a mixture of references, half known, half forgotten, nostalgic romantic undigested and emotionally packed, to a naughty oracle, a serpent's tree, an unconventional maypole for conventional satyrate figures). The syntax *can* be allowed by a stretch or rack-stretches; the difficulty is the word Glint. Cut out 'Glint' and it's obvious; I'm not, as you know too well, afraid of a little startling

* negate each other, if they could; keep their individualities & lose them in each other.
** This is adding to the image, of course, digging out what is accidentally there on purpose.

difficulty. Sorry to be so conflicting and confusing; I hope this is the only method, though: this rambling and snatchy expansion.

IV. Poem 5. This is a very decorative poem, a poem, if you'll pardon me, on stained glass.[1] There are many ornamental designs, but all, I hope, utilitarian. And I really can't get down to explaining it; you just have to, or just don't have to, let the poem come to you bit by bit through the rather obvious poetry of it. It's not a really satisfactory poem, but I like it. The blue wall of spirits is the sky full of ghosts: the curving crowded world above the new child. It sounds as though it meant the side of a chemist's bowl of methylated spirits, & I *saw* that too and a child climbing up it. (There's a pretty fancy the stout young gentleman has. I'm 12 and a ½ stone now, by the way, a bull of a boy.)

V. *On the angelic etna of the last whirring featherlands.*[2] I wanted to get the look of this stanza right: a saint about to fall, *to be born,* heaven shifting visionarily under him as he stands poised: [*interpolation, linked to the word* visionarily, *which is circled:* changingly, the landscape moving to no laws but heaven's, that is: hills moving, streets flowing etc] the stained flats, the lowlying lands, that is, *and* the apartment houses all discoloured by the grief of his going, ruined for ever by his departure (for heaven must fall with every falling saint): on the last wave of a flowing street before the cities flow to the edge of heaven where he stands about to fall, praising his making and unmaking & the dissolution of his father's house etc—(this, as the poem goes on to talk about, is his father-on-the-earth's veins, his mother's womb, *and* the peaceful place before birth): Standing on an angelic (belonging to heaven's angels & heavenly itself) volcanic hill (everything is in disruption, eruption) on the last feathers of his fatherlands (and whirring is a noise of wings). All the heavenly business I use because it makes a famous and noble landscape from which to plunge this figure on to the bloody, war-barbed etc earth. It's a poem written on the birth of my son. He was a saint for a poem's sake (hear the beast howl).

All very unsatisfactory. I wrote it down hurriedly for you: not so much to try to elucidate things but to move them about, turn them different ways, stir them up. The rest is up to you.

Oh yes, *hyleg.*[3] It's a freak word, I suppose, but one or two every now & then don't hurt: I think they help. It was what I wanted & I happened to know the word well. I dessay I could explain this selfishness at intolerable length, but I want you to have this scribble right away.

If you want the story—you *can* pay a bit?—let me know. If you give me a little time, I'll try to do a poem specially.

Dylan

If I can I'm going to be in London at the end of the month.

MS: the recipient

[1] 'It is the sinners' dust-tongued bell.'
[2] 'A saint about to fall.'
[3] *O.E.D.*: '*astrol.*: ruling planet of a nativity.'

J. M. DENT
August 22 1939 (Asks for more copies of *Map of Love*. See Appendix 17.)

NANCY PEARN[1]
22 August 1939   Sea View Laugharne Carmarthenshire

Dear Miss Pearn,
   Thank you for your letter. I'm very glad that you and David Higham are
glad about the Dent arrangement. I'm extremely fortunate, and am very
grateful to you both.
   Is Higham back yet?
   And do you know when my first payment—for the month of
August—of £8 is likely to come to me? There's not much of the month
left; and I'd relied on having that payment to cover certain commitments
—that's a grand way of putting it—that I wouldn't have undertaken
hadn't I thought I'd be, for me, very rich before September. Do you think
you could find out if it *is* possible for me to be paid *this* month's payment
this month?
   Yes, I see a good deal of Richard Hughes. He's just left for a holiday in
North Wales.
   Thank you again.

                                   Yours sincerely,
                                   Dylan Thomas
MS: Texas

THOMAS TAIG[2]
23 August 1939   Sea View Laugharne Carmarthenshire

Dear Mr Taig,
   Here is a selection—out of a great wad of material—of poems that
might be suitable for some kind of dramatic presentation.[3] There's lots
too much, of course, but you need a lot, don't you, to read over? I
suggest—unless you think that alternative scheme, of putting on a
certain number of different poems every night or every few nights, is
better —that as few *poets* as possible should be chosen. Some of Glyn
Jones would be excellent material, I should think; and Alan Pryce-Jones's

---

[1] Of Pearn, Pollinger and Higham.
[2] A lecturer at Swansea University College, and active in the Little Theatre. The poetry-
reading event planned by Taig is described in Thomas's letter dated 5 July 1939.
[3] With the letter are four poems copied out by Thomas: his 'Ears in the turret hear' and
'Find meat on bones'; 'Voyage' by Alan Pryce-Jones, and 'Landore' by George Woodcock.

poem 'Voyage' seems, to me, grand for your purpose. I've included a few more-or-less-journalistic poems about distressed Wales: you could probably make a fine thing of 'Rhondda Poem' & 'Landore'. I've included, too, several of my own; I do hope you'll be able to give me the opportunity of reading: I enjoy reading poems aloud so much, & have got to understand most of the poems turned out nowadays by Our Young Welsh Poets. But we must meet soon; I hope we can as soon as you return. If you'd like a larger selection of poems, or more poems by chaps I've meagrely represented here, do write & tell me please.

I hope everything goes well. I've written to a few people & will let you know at once what does, or doesn't, happen.

Yours,
Dylan

I haven't included anything of Vernon's: mostly because the big number of the show is his Masque, & otherwise because I haven't much suitable of his at hand. We can get hold of one of his excellent ballads, though, if you like, later.

The 2 numbers of Wales I enclose for Idris Davies's two prose poems: Shadows & Cakes, & Land of My Mothers. Bits of these, anyway, might be very effective.

MS: Sir Theodore Brinckman

VERNON WATKINS
[postmarked August 25 1939]   Sea View Laugharne

Dear Vernon,
   Sorry not to have written before. I've been busy—over stories, pot-boiling stories for a book, semi-autobiographical, to be finished by Christmas—lazy —messing about in the sun and pub—and worried, by the nearness of this monstrous and still incredible war. No, my book couldn't have come out in a viler month; almost as bad as some woman I was told of who published her first (&, since, her only) novel on the day of the opening of the General Strike & did not have one single review or advertisement (no papers were printed for a week); & not one single copy of the book was sold. I haven't seen Hawkins's Spectator review yet; hope to get it sent on in a day or two. I saw the imbecile Western Mail with striking, if podgy, photograph.
   Your Masque I left with my father in Bishopston. Can you call there for it, or shall I write to him asking him to send it on to you?
   [. . .] has been staying in Llanstephan, very near. We saw him a few times [. . .] [he] is all right, but weak; insipid, perhaps; his gentleness has grown in like a soft, jelly-like nail. 'Of course, there's much to be said,' 'You should see both points,' 'No offence meant but.'

This war, trembling even on the edge of Laugharne, fills me with such horror & terror & lassitude that I can't easily think about the London programme. I've selected a good number of poems—including some by Alan Pryce-Jones which, in their very worldly & wellbred way, are really beautiful. None by you. You can either send a ballad or two direct to Taig, or wait until we all three meet. Perhaps the last would be the best. I didn't want to select anything of yours without your approval, and anyway I haven't much of yours at hand. Taig suggests only 20 minutes for the short poems; I say at least ½ hour. But everything—including all our happiness—depends on Hitler, Poland, & insanity.

I'm afraid I shan't be able to come Swansea way for a while. If there's no war I'll be broadcasting, with Keidrych, from Swansea on the 6th of September, 6.40 to 7. Could we meet you in Swansea afterwards for a drink? I think I'll try to return to Laugharne that same evening.

Laugharne is a little Danzig.

Wish I could see you soon. When can you come down?

Caitlin & Llewelyn are well. Love to you from us,

Dylan

Regards to your family.

MS: British Library   *VW(R)*

NANCY PEARN

[late August 1939]   Sea View Laugharne Carmarthenshire S Wales

I'm writing a short note
to Richard Church

Dear Miss Pearn,

Sorry to pester you like this about the Dent's 8 quid due to me *this month*, but I need it most urgently. I know it's difficult to do things in this vile crisis, but it's just because of that vileness that I do need, so badly, the promised money. I haven't anything to buy anything with (not even envelopes), &, even here, all sorts of preparations are necessary — being made officially necessary too. As I don't intend fighting anyone, my position is being made most uncomfortable: and a little money would, at least, ease it. Please do try to buck Dent's up *immediately*.

Yours,
Dylan Thomas

It must be hell in London.

MS: Texas

D. J. THOMAS
August 29 1939   Sea View

Dear Dad,

Grand, *magnificent* dictionary. A lovely surprise. Thank you very very much for it. I will take good care of it and use it often. It is a most valuable thing for me to have; & it appears to be an extremely good dictionary too. Immediately, I looked up all sorts of obscure words: & the result couldn't have been better. Exciting to open the important-looking parcel this morning, & find just what I have been wanting. Thank you for the dedication too; I'm glad you enjoyed the *Map of Love*. Do please tell me what you liked best in it, & what seemed most difficult & unattractive. I haven't yet seen the Spectator review, though Vernon wrote to tell me it had appeared & was 'good & sensible'. I saw Fisher's article, which was really about how well he knew me. I haven't seen any other reviews. Was there one in the Observer? I couldn't get hold of it last Sunday.

Yesterday I had the first work done on my teeth: 4 fillings. There is one extraction to come—an unnoticeable stump at the back—& about 6 more fillings. Then, with care, my teeth should last me for good. I wasn't hurt, although, because the teeth needing repair were scattered all about my mouth & not in a cluster, no injection could be made.

These are awful days & we are very worried. It is terrible to have built, out of nothing, a complete happiness—from no money, no possessions, no material hopes—& a way of living, & then to see the immediate possibility of its being exploded & ruined through no fault of one's own. I expect you both are very anxious too. If I could pray, I'd pray for peace. I'm not a man of action; & the brutal activities of war appal me—as they do every decent-thinking person. Even here the war atmosphere is thick and smelling: the kids dance in the streets, the mobilised soldiers sing Tipperary in the pubs, & wives & mothers weep around the stunted memorial in the Grist.[1] Our own position is, *so far*, quite comfortable.

I hope you enjoyed your queer, lackadaisical day here—in spite of bookshelves & Polly's snailing—as much as we did. If there's no disturbance before September 6, I hope to see you in Swansea on that day. We must make arrangements later.

Thank you for everything you brought us on your visit. We were really grateful, although, perhaps, we found it difficult to say much.

And thank you greatly for the very fine dictionary. I am proud to possess it.

I hope mother's well, or better than she has been.

Love to both of you
from us both,
Dylan

[1] The memorial is a market cross; the Grist is the part of Laugharne at the foot of the hill, by the shore.

This shd have been posted yesterday, but just before the post went I found I hadn't any envelopes—& wasn't in time. Sorry.

DESMOND HAWKINS
29 August [1939]   Sea View Laugharne Carmarthenshire

Dear Desmond,
   Are you going to use that story? When—war permitting—does Purpose come out? I may have a small poem for it. If you don't want the story, do send it back quickly as I can get some money for it immediately: & Christ, do I need it.
   Haven't seen your review yet.

Love,
Dylan

W. T. DAVIES
30 August 1939   Sea View Laugharne Carmarthenshire

Dear W. T. Davies,
   Thank you for your letter, and for the poems you sent. I should have acknowledged them sooner, but I've been in rather a muddle and this bloody war buggers the orderly mind.
   It's very doubtful if Taig's programme will come off—or on—this next month. If it does, your 'Siege' will be included. I would have included more—or suggested for inclusion—but all the short poems must be packed into half an hour & that doesn't really allow a chap to be represented by more than one poem.
   I was interested to know further things about the Society; and of course I'll still be a member even if I am too snooty to sign the manifesto.
   You said you might be in Carmarthenshire the end of this month. Do call on us, please.

Yours,
Dylan Thomas

VERNON WATKINS
[September 1 1939]   Sea View Laugharne

Dear Vernon,
    War seems to have begun. But do come on Sunday, if you can. With
Taig too. Any time? Will you make it lunch? If so, arrive by one, please.
Perhaps you can let us know—phone—in the Saturday evening.[1]
    What are you going to do in the war? I can't kill & so, I suppose, will
have to join the dangerous RAMC.
    Looking forward to you.
    Keidrych & Heseltine—nasty Heseltine—came down yesterday. Went
back this morning.
    Love to you & family from us.

                                                          Dylan

MS: British Library   *VW*

DAVID HIGHAM
September 1 1939   Sea View Laugharne Carmarthenshire

Dear Higham,
    Here's the Laughlin contract, signed.[2] I must say that 60 dollars as an
advance seems meagre & unsatisfactory to me—£12 or £13, isn't it?—but
I am sure you have done the very best possible.
    Yes, of course I approve of your permitting Chatto's to have my poem
for their anthology.[3] No, the Parton Press have no interest in anthology
rights.
    This bloody war won't stop Dent's monthly allowance, will it?

                                            Yours sincerely,
                                            Dylan Thomas

MS: Texas

[1] Germany invaded Poland on Friday September 1. Britain declared war on Sunday
September 3.
[2] Probably for *The World I Breathe*, poems and stories.
[3] Probably *A Book of Modern Verse*, 1939, which included 'The force that through the green
fuse'.

A Writer's Life
1939–49

The Second World War made the publishing of books and magazines more difficult, and interfered with the livelihood of many 'literary' writers. Thomas, who was determined to avoid military service, spent the early part of the war drifting from place to place, but later found work writing scripts for the propaganda films then being mass-produced in London. In the middle years of the war he wrote little or no serious verse, but made up for this with a dozen or more poems in 1944 and 1945; some of them made vivid use of images from air raids. A year after the war ended, *Deaths and Entrances* (1946) was well received. Thomas was now a notorious literary figure: drinker and half-hearted womaniser, as well as craftsman obsessed with his vocation. To some he was a scrounger and a liar, but he had loyal friends as well as brigades of hangers-on. As a freelance writer he appeared to be successful. He wrote, read and acted for radio, and worked on film scripts; the immediate postwar years were spent mainly in Oxfordshire, within easy reach of London and the broadcasting studios. He attracted loans (rarely repaid) and gifts from friends and patrons. None of this gave Thomas the freedom from debts and anxiety, which—he complained—stood between him and his work. In 1946, 1947 and 1948 he wrote only one poem, 'In country sleep'.

DESMOND HAWKINS
September 3 1939   Sea View Laugharne Carmarthenshire

Dear Desmond,

Yes, terrible terrible. Being my hero, my chief concern, too, is to keep out of death's way. And no, I don't know what to do either: declare myself a neutral state, or join as a small tank.

Hope you do my story, I want a pound badly. I liked your review very much, and thank you. I want to see Muir's review, too. Hope he agrees that the poems, as a whole, are better than any I've written. But a filthy time for a book. Only my Aunty Polly's bought one, I think.

And I want a pound quickly, too. No, sorry the short poem isn't finished yet. If it is, you must have it straight away.

                                                            Dylan

MS: the recipient

DAVID HIGHAM
11 Sept 1939   Sea View Laugharne Carmarthenshire

Dear Higham,

I wonder—without bothering you too much—whether you could find out for me, from Dent's, whether they are going to send me the press-cuttings about my new book as they did about my last one? I've heard that several reviews have appeared, but I take no papers. It is, apart from anything else, very useful to me to see what things the reviewers say.

I'm extremely glad that you believe my Dent's monthly-arrangement is bound to continue.

                                                            Yours,
                                                            Dylan Thomas

MS: Texas

GLYN JONES
11 September 1939

Sea View   Laugharne   Carmarthenshire

Dear Glyn,

Thank you for the Miller book back. I'm glad you enjoyed most of it, and I mostly agree that it is not the super book I sometimes blurb it to be to fellows who haven't read it. As writing, it *is* unoriginal, but it has, sentimentally speaking, more guts & blood in it than new English prose books have. The only recent prose I've had as much pleasure out of, loud meaty pleasure, has been another American book—Nightwood (far different, with original writing too).[1] I remember you said, in Laugharne, that you hadn't read it: would you like to? I like the *idea* of Miller's anti-literature, but it is a pity he writes, so often, in the old literary way to try to achieve it. He's always got the same cracks to grind, but, after all, good fucking books are few & far, & if you look at *Tropic of Cancer* as the best modern fucking book, & not—perhaps my sincere enthusiasm misled you—as a universal life-&-death book, then I know you must enjoy & admire it enormously. (The adverb is also, I notice, on the back of the book.) Yes, it is, to date, his best *book*, but passages from *Tropic of Capricorn* which I've read in magazines are really much better, wider, less repetitive, & contain the best descriptions of America I've ever read. But I'm too annoyed & unsettled to write clearly, even about Miller's books which I do know well & feel about clearly. I want to get something out of the war, & put very little in (certainly not my one & only body). I'm trying to get some profitable civilian work; that will probably be impossible. Does your School go on? Do tell me what you intend doing when, after registration, you are called up? Prison & the Medical Corps are both disagreeable to me. Regards to your wife, from us both.

Dylan

I want to see your review in Welsh Review. Will it appear now?

MS: Carbondale   *SL*

DAVID HIGHAM
12 Sept 1939 (Sends unspecified forms. See Appendix 18.)

[1] Djuna Barnes, *Nightwood*, published 1936.

SIR EDWARD MARSH[1]
September 14 1939   Laugharne Carmarthenshire S Wales

Dear Sir Edward,
   I am writing to you, a patron of letters, to ask for any help that you may
be able to give me. You may have read some of my work, or heard it
spoken of. If not, I can refer you to Miss Edith Sitwell and Mr. T. S. Eliot,
who will tell you that I am a poet of some worth and deserving of help. I
have a wife and a child and am without private means. For the last few
years I have been earning just enough money to keep my family and
myself alive by selling poems and short stories to magazines. These
sources of income are now almost entirely dried up. It has occurred to me
that you, with your connections with the Government, might be able
to obtain some employment for me, either in the Ministry of
Information—though that, I am told, is overrun with applicants,
stampeded by almost every young man in London who has ever held a
pencil or slapped a back—or elsewhere, any other place at all. I have been
a journalist and an actor in a repertory theatre; I have broadcast, and
lectured. I am 25 years old.
   I suspect that this letter is one of many similar that you are receiving,
and must apologise for giving you this additional trouble.
   I have never, even in my most desperate moments, begged or attempted
to seek any employment outside my own limited and underpaid profession. But now I must have work—I want to be able to go on writing,
and conscription will stop that, perhaps for ever—and I beg you to help
me.
   I would very much like to give you, if you wanted it, any information
about me and my work. Or I could, again if it was needed, attempt to
come to London.

                                        Yours sincerely,
                                        Dylan Thomas

MS: Berg   *SL*

JOHN DAVENPORT
14 September 1939   Sea View Laugharne Carmarthenshire

Dear John,
   Although you haven't answered any of my letters since you came down
here in June—and one of the letters was important, about the 5 bob
flotation scheme which has now come to nothing; I don't know if it
would have come to anything even if you *had* helped me—I'm still trying

---

[1] Sir Edward Marsh (1872–1953), scholar, civil servant and epicure.

to get a word out of you, and this time again writing for advice or assistance. If you don't answer, I shall know Something is Wrong, though I shan't know what the Something is, unless, as I said before in one of my letters-to-the-void, you were so unspeakably bored with your visit that you've decided not to speak. It's this War. I am trying to get a job before conscription, because my one-&-only body I will not give. I know that all the shysters in London are grovelling about the Ministry of Information, all the half-poets, the boiled newspapermen, submen from the islands of crabs, dismissed advertisers, old mercuries, mass-snoopers, and all I have managed to do is to have my name on the crook list and a vague word of hope from Humbert Wolfe.[1] So I must explore every avenue now, I can't afford to leave an Edward Marsh unturned. Because along will come conscription, and the military tribunal, & stretcher-bearing or jail or potato-peeling or the Boys' Fire League. And all I want is time to write poems, I'm only just getting going now, and enough money to keep two and a bit alive. The only thing I can do, apart from registering myself on the official list of writers to be kept available for possible abuse by the government, is to write to people, friends and acquaintances or just people who might be able to help, and to ask them, on knees not yet broken, whether they can give me a job or suggest to whom or what I should apply. For my little money-sources—(apart from anything else)—are diminishing or dying. Soon there will not be a single paper paying inadequately for serious stories & poems. Do you know of anything for me? I can speak & act too. Does the film-world want an intelligent young man of literary ability, 'self-conscious, punch-drunk', who must (for his own sake) keep out of the bloody war, who's willing to do any work—provided of course that it pays enough for living? I'm not expecting plums from the war—after all, they must go to the kind of chaps who refused to give me anything out of the Royal Literary Fund — but I do want something. Will you tell me if you know of any chances, if, in your clubman rambles, you meet persons who might be just even likely to consider me for some job, if there is, to your knowledge, any vacancy in films of any sort, and, most important, if you are willing, after such a long silence, to try to help me? Otherwise, I don't see how I am to continue here, or anywhere else, even for a very short time. As soon as war was, bills were popped in; the attitude of the tradesmen is changing rapidly; there's a great difference between a rich pacifist & a poor coward. Is it worth, (do you think, & also, of course, if you are willing to think), my coming to London to pull, lick, and see? Please write to me.

Love from us both to you both,
John & Clement,
Caitlin & Dylan

MS: Texas   *SL*

---

[1] The poet Humbert Wolfe was a senior official at the Ministry of Labour, a useful man to know at the start of a war.

DESMOND HAWKINS
Sept 14 1939   Sea View Laugharne Carmarthenshire

Dear Desmond,
  So you've been trying to pull strings too, have you, you old racketeer?
You should be ashamed: go on and fight for culture like a fool: don't
attempt to get anything out of the fucking war. I wrote to Mr. Humbert
Wolfe, and what does he do but send me a copy of a letter he wrote to you.
So you were there first; alright, then, I shan't tell you the famous man *I'm*
writing to. (If he sends me a copy of a letter to you, we may as well send
out circulars signed with both our names.) But do you think there's any
possibility at all of wheedling oneself—whining, under protest—into any
governmental job. I wrote to Norman Cameron who told me that every
literate or semi-literate party-goer in London is stampeding the Ministry
of Labour, willing to do anything from licking stamps & bums to writing
recruiting literature or broadcasting appeals for warm bodies to become
cold. The question of conscience *can*, apparently, be ignored, even among
our honourable intelligentsia. And what work would there be, even if we
did manage to fawn in, in the Government? Principle prevents us, I hope,
from propaganding; I personally know nothing of any foreign language
except a very little about the sanitary-towel of the gardener's wife & a few
Welsh dirty words. I can't decipher anything, not even poems. What I'm
doing is writing urgent & bad-tempered letters to everybody who has ever
said publicly that I am a better poet than Alfred Noyes, & telling them
that, unless someone does something soon, there'll be one better-than-
Alfred poet less, that the Armed Forces are not conducive to the creation
of contemplative verse, and that all my few sources of income are drying
up as quickly as blood on the Western Front. Though it will probably
leave my correspondents unmoved, there is nothing else that I can think
of to do. The Army Medical Corps is presumably admirable, but I don't
want to help—even in a most inefficient way—to patch poor buggers up
to send them out again into quick insanity and bullets. Have you any
suggestions? I know you must be trying, too, all that you can think of.
(The literary Left, I suppose, is having a loud whack at the Nazi nightmare; or can it do its work better in safety? Auden is in America, isn't he?
And the very best place, too, for a militant communist at this time.)
Come & stay here, completely out of harm's way, and help compose
letters to the Big Boys. It's speed that counts now; jobs must be obtained,
or exemption promised, before conscription & military—'what would
you do if you saw a soldier raping John Lehmann?'—tribunals. And
what—as a matter of interest—did you reply to Wolfe?
                                          Love,
                                          Dylan

MS: the recipient

JAMES LAUGHLIN
15 September 1939   Sea View Laugharne Carmarthenshire S Wales

Dear Laughlin:

That was an awful bother with agents and contract, but it was taken right out of my hands—I have to show all business dealings to them—and it's settled now and that's alright.

40 poems, you say, and 10 stories. Right. But perhaps you could allow just one more story. I've gone carefully through all my prose, and the eleven I have chosen do seem, to me, pretty unalterable—that is, I shouldn't like any one to be omitted. Simple sentimental stories, melodramatic stories, apocalyptic stories, all the kinds I write and have written are represented.

I hope you like my selection of poems. If, by any chance, you want to substitute one poem for another, do let me know, won't you? But I do think I've chosen the best: by the simple process of not allowing the worst.

Reavey, as you might have heard, was unable, owing to the squeamishness or carefulness of printers, to bring out my book of stories, and J. M. Dent's bought the mss. back from Reavey and included some of the stories in a prose-&-verse book of mine, *The Map of Love*, which they have just published.

You will see that I have given the numbers, & pages on which they are to be found, of all 40 poems. You have my first two books, & I'm enclosing the proof-sheets of the third (corrected).

You may have copies (in magazines) of some of the selected stories, but I'm enclosing more copies of them anyway. Do you mind, some time, returning these magazine copies?

I suggest—and I am sure you too have decided on this—that the poems come first & the stories second.

As to the arrangement of the poems: do you think it would be best to print them in strict chronological order (with a note saying, at the beginning, that the first group are from a book published in 1934, the second from a book in 1936, the third in 1939)? Or do you think it would be more effective to print the 1936 & 1939 poems first, in the order in which they appear in the books, & then print the 1934 poems? I am in favour of the first arrangement, but it is, after all, up to you. What I would *not* agree with would be to print the poems just anyhow (according to editorial taste), with no mention of their dates. (And no aspersions against your taste.) The stories you can arrange as you like, though obviously *The Enemies* must come some time before *The Holy Six*, which is a kind of continuation.

I think that 'The World I Breathe' is a good title. I've been considering 'These Ancient Minutes', (from the poem on page 19 of 25 Poems).[1] What do you think? I don't mind which.

---

[1] 'Hold hard, these ancient minutes in the cuckoo's month.'

One story, 'The Prospect of The Sea', which I believe to be one of the best, is not among the selected material I am suggesting & sending. I'll post it to you tomorrow: I know where it is, but I can't get hold of it today.

Would you like me to send you, for any publicity purposes, extracts from reviews of the 3 books in the English press?

The fragment, 'In The Direction of the Beginning', which you printed in N.D. 1938 must not, by the way, be included, as it is the beginning of a new book not yet finished (a book I shall send to you next year).

I think that's all for the moment. Any questions?

Do write to me soon.

> Best wishes,
> Dylan Thomas

Will you, if you see him, tell Kenneth Patchen[1] that I am writing to him this week, & that I'm sorry for the delay. It's this war you might have heard.

MS: the recipient

SIR EDWARD MARSH
September 19 1939   Laugharne Carmarthenshire S Wales

Dear Sir Edward,

I know you'll forgive me for not replying at once to your very kind letter and for not thanking you, very sincerely, for your gift. A friend called here and drove me to see my father: I don't often have the chance of seeing him, as he lives fifty miles away and we're both too poor to move much, and I stayed with him until yesterday. Your letter was waiting for me. It was most generous of you to assist me. I had, as you knew and said, no thought at all of asking anything other than advice, but I am very grateful and your gift was welcome indeed and will help us *considerably* over a bad time.

I was afraid that the Ministry of Information would be crowded with staff and that it would be useless for me to apply, but I must thank you for mentioning my name there. I do hope that, if anything does come to your notice, you will let me know. For the present I can only wait; and will, if necessary, when the time comes, register myself as a conscientious objector and see what national work I will be directed to do by the tribunal.

> Thank you again.
> Yours sincerely,
> Dylan Thomas

MS: Berg

[1] Kenneth Patchen (1911–72), poet, was published by New Directions.

DAVID HIGHAM
21 September 1939   Sea View Laugharne Carmarthenshire

Dear Higham,
    Thank you for enquiring about the cuttings. A pile have already been
sent to me from Dent's.
    It is indeed extremely unlikely that I shall do any work of national
importance, & Dent's can continue to pay me without fearing that the
Government is making me a profiteer. I am, as you might have seen from
my letters, an objector.

                                        Yours,
                                        Dylan Thomas

MS: Texas

JAMES LAUGHLIN
22 Sept 1939   Sea View Laugharne Carmarthenshire

Dear Laughlin,
    Here's the other story I promised. I hope you'll be able to include 11
stories in the book; otherwise I think that the *Burning Baby* is, perhaps,
the one to omit.[1] Certainly not this tale.
    Hope to hear from you soon.

                                        Yours,
                                        Dylan Thomas

You will, whatever else, see, won't you, that it is made clear which
groups of poems belong to the certain dates.

MS: the recipient

DESMOND HAWKINS
24 September 1939   Sea View Laugharne Carmarthenshire

Dear Desmond,
    I've filled up that questionnaire from David Higham. A lot of good will
come from that. My only special qualification I put as reading poems
aloud. Not 'If' to the troops, either. I've no wish to propagandise, nor to do
anything but my own work. I'm Mr. Humanity and can't kill or be killed
(with my approval). Like you, I shall wait, register as as an objector, and

---

[1] *The World I Breathe* was published on 20 December 1939, and included 'The Burning
  Baby'.

see. Chapel Wales is down on conscription alright, but my objection can't be on chapel-religious grounds, and I'd have little support. What have we got to fight for or against? To prevent Fascism coming here? It's come. To stop shit by throwing it? To protect our incomes, bank balances, property, national reputations? I feel sick. All this flogged hate again. We must go on with our out-of-war life. It's a temptation, in the pubs, on Saturday nights, in the billiard saloon, to want to allow myself to get that fuggy, happy, homosexual feeling and eat, sleep, get drunk, march, suffer, joke, kill & die among men, comrades, brothers, you're my pal, I'm with you son, back to back, only die once, short life, women and children, here's a photograph of my wife, over the bloody, down the bloody, here's to the bloody, shit and blood. But the temptation's not too strong, and the sanity of the imagination is. I'd like you very much to send me your collected advice; there must be lots of tips. Thank you for your letter. Write soon.

Dylan

Tell me, please, about my story & Purpose. I haven't got one penny, and unless Purpose can send me a quid or 30 bob straight away I must send that trivial story to Herring.

MS: the recipient

DESMOND HAWKINS
[Sept/Oct 1939]   Laugharne

Dear Desmond,
   Sorry to rush you: but what about the pacifist tips and the fate of my story? The local PPU reply was very vague.[1]

Dylan

MS: the recipient

VERNON WATKINS
Thursday [postmarked September 29 1939]   Sea View Laugharne

But is there
any reason
against you
coming down here in the weekend?

Dear Vernon,
   We were all ready to come when bills came too, and, to our disgust, we

---

[1] Hawkins had advised him to contact the Peace Pledge Union.

felt we should pay them at once with the money we were intending for our Swansea visit. We did. Caitlin and I were very sorry to miss Dot once again. Just as we're about to come, we have a wire from you saying 'Dot is here', & our plans, quite soon after, are changed. Just as we used to leave the day before she came.[1] All that's unfortunate & accidental, as you might know: we'd love to see you & Dot right now but we have to stay here with a baby and a new kitten called Pussy. I hope a lot we can come to see you soon. Write to me. Poems? I want to have everything (except aeroplanes)

> Love, to all,
> Dylan & Caitlin

MS: British Library   *VW*

A. E. TRICK
29 September 1939[2]   Sea View Laugharne Carmarthenshire

Dear Bert,

And I never managed to see you in Swansea after all. I was there for a few days about 2 months ago, but stuck all the time in Bishopston pennilessly. I didn't write asking you if you could come down to see *me*, because I didn't know when my pennilessness would end and allow me suddenly to come to Swansea and Brynmill for the day. The state did not end, and hasn't ended yet. Now it's harder than ever, poor or not, to move from this cockled city even to Carmarthen overrun with soldiers and war urgers and rememberers. I wish it were possible for you to visit us: Laugharne is sweet and quiet, and our house big enough to conceal all the Tricks in the world. How are wife and children? Tell Kerith I agree with him when he said 'Damn that' about my being a poet. Damn it forever, it makes uncomfortable life even harder and bonier and gives a poor man a wild beast for a conscience.

How does the body-snatching go? Be quick, there'll be less bodies soon. I live from poem to mouth, and both suffer. Now I am trying to complete, by December, a book of short stories, mostly pot-boilers, called, temporarily, 'Portrait of the Artist as a Young Dog: stories towards a Provincial Autobiography'. They may be amusing eventually, but the writing of them means the writing of a number of poems less; they're all about Swansea life, the pubs, clubs, billiard saloons, promenades, adoles-

---

[1] Dot was Watkins's sister. It was a standing joke that she and Thomas always missed one another by a day.
[2] Thomas wrote '1929' by mistake.

cence in the suburban nights, friendships, tempers, and humiliations. The book is on contract: I get too little regularly for the job: I am commissioned to write another prose book by the middle of next year, but there is, apparently, no clause in the contract forbidding obscenity and I'll give Dent the whole fucking works.[1] Hope you get hold of my autogeographical book; you knew all the stories, but the poems were new. I'd love to know what you think of them.

Llewelyn is bursting with energy; soon he probably *will* burst. He's 8 months, just 8 months, old now & has the familiar Thomas puffed innocence about him, lollypop eyes, and nose that looks to heaven. His eyes are blue. If I can find one later, I'll send a photograph of him discussing philosophically with himself the alternatives of crowing or blowing.

As one Daddy to another, what are you doing in the War? I'm very puzzled. When it is necessary, I am going to register as an objector, but also, because I want to get something out of the mess if possible, I'm trying to get a mild job, in the film-writing racket, before conscientous-registration is forced on me. My little body (though it's little no longer, I'm like a walrus,) I don't intend to waste for the mysterious ends of others; and if there's any profiteering to be done, I, in my fashion, wish to be in on it. But my natural, &, to me, sensible, greed & opportunism will unfortunately come to nothing; I'm sure of that: I know a few wires but they only tinkle when I pull them. So I'm afraid that I shall *have* to take the Tribunal. Is there any possibility of getting a soft job in Swansea? I don't know how you feel about all this, but I can't raise up any feeling about this War at all and the demon Hitlerism can go up its own bottom: I refuse to help it with a bayonet. To talk about keeping Hitlerism out of this sink of democracy by censorship and conscription, mystery-mongering, umbrella-worship, atrocity-circulation, & the (thank God mostly unsuccessful *so far*) * [*circled addition*: * how long?] fostering of hate against a bewildered, buggered people, is only to encourage the rebellious pacifism of anti-social softies like myself. *Write soon* and tell me all about the War: I've only my feelings to guide me, & they are my own, and nothing will turn them savage against people with whom I have no quarrel. There's a need now for some life to go on, strenuously & patiently, outside the dictated hates & pettinesses of War, & that life I, for my own part, shall continue to support by my writing and thinking & by living as coolly, hotly, & as well as I know how.

Our love to you all,
Dylan

And do tell me all the news too. I miss the boys & the smoky nights. Here everything is so slow and prettily sad. I'd like to live in a town or a city again for a bit. Let there be one town left, & we'll fill it with ourselves.

MS: Ohio State University   *SL(R)*

---

[1] Thomas may have been looking ahead to *Adventures in the Skin Trade*, the book he began to write the following year; Dent were duly disturbed when they saw the result.

VERNON WATKINS
September 29 1939   Sea View Laugharne

Dear Vernon,

I haven't written all this month because there's been no news of any
importance—only the War—and I've been busy, too, with my innocent
stories. I've written to a few people, asking them about the difficulties,
you know which ones, but nothing has come of it, and I intend registering
as a conscientious objector as soon as necessary.

I suppose you've heard that Keidrych is to be married in Llanstephan
next Wednesday.[1] She's a curious girl, a poet, as they say, in her own
right, with rich Welsh parents in South America (oil-diving or train-
wrecking) and all the symptoms of hysteria. She was here a few days ago
& she said that Life was too hard for an artist and I said that for 'an artist'
of the sort she meant nothing was too hard, and she burst into tears and
told Keidrych to protect her. Keidrych was asleep on the settle at the
time. I don't suppose you'll be able to come to the wedding, which is a
pity because we will make a party to go over to Ferryside and get silly.
Send your rice anyway. Keidrych's parents are making difficulties [...] are
talking of disowning their only son & won't attend the ceremony. I am to
be best man. Have you got a respectable suit you can lend me, or, rather,
trust me with? I'll return it, unegged, straight after the wedding—the next
day, really, I can't undress in the church porch. I shall hardly ever, if ever,
need a respectable suit again & it would be silly of me to put myself in
more debt by getting a new suit for this one remarkable occasion. You're
the only chap about my size. Two men could go in one of Hughes's suits,
though he has offered me one with tails. (that looks like rails, doesn't it?)
I'll take great care of it if you would lend one? Caitlin, who has a very odd
creation to wear, with different coloured sleeves & frills,—she had it
made some time ago, by mistake—promises her personal supervision of
the suit. And its neatly-packed, punctual return.

I don't know if anyone else will be there. Nasty Heseltine perhaps —
though he's trying to be a bomber. Some glamorous friend of Lynette's
(that's the girl). One uncle of Keidrych's [...] Mrs Williams from the pub
here. Llewelyn, unavoidably.

My Collected Works—or, really, 40 poems & 12 stories—are to be
published in America in December with the pathetic title of 'The World I
Breathe'. I objected to the title, but was told it would sell like cakes there.
It's a title, I believe, based on Gone With The Wind. Did you read my
'Cough' story in Life & Letters?[2] The others in my coming book are all
like that, though not exactly. Your *Rough Sea* looked splendid. I read it
aloud again & woke the baby.

Have you seen Taig recently? Is there a chance of the show coming off
this year?

[1] To Lynette Roberts.
[2] 'Extraordinary Little Cough.'

Caitlin (and I) wants to tell Dot that she is very something or other not to come down and visit us & stay with us for as long as she can bear it. September is by far the loveliest month here. Make her come, please. And when are you coming. I haven't seen you for more than a day & a bit for more than a year or more.

Do see if you can lend me a suit. All care and gratitude too. I've only got a pair of baggy trousers & a damp leather coat.

Love to you,
Dylan

Regards to your family.

MS: British Library   *VW(R)*

VERNON WATKINS
Sunday [postmarked October 8 1939]   Sea View Laugharne
                                                      Carmarthenshire

Dear Vernon,

First: many, many thanks for the supersmart suit in which no moth-holes could be seen and which suited me, apart from a hesitation at the waist, very well indeed. I looked neat, clean, and quite prosperous. It's grand of you to let me keep it: I am now ready for all sartorial occasions, so long as at some of them I can appear in jersey & corduroys & at others in a smart brown suit, slightly open in the middle, with its pockets full of rice.

Perhaps you've been seeing Keidrych; when he left us, he didn't know whether they were going to Swansea or Cardiff; but I imagine Swansea won. If you have seen him, you know all about the wedding; if not, I can tell you that it was distinguished mostly by the beauty of the female attendants, the brown suit of the best man, the savage displeasure of Keidrych's mother, & Keidrych's own extremely hangdog look & red-rimmed eyes:—he reminded you of all the old marriage musichall jokes in the world: I've never seen any one so miserable. The female attendants were really lovely to look at—it wasn't just my spite. There were two & Caitlin, all with long curly hair, black, gold, & silver. The clergyman was illiterate & apoplectic.

We're hoping to come to Bishopston for a few days very soon: mostly to have a bath, as there's no water in Laugharne & I smell like an old beaver. I'll try hard to get there: it'll be good to see you again & talk & listen.

Thank you again, &
our love & mine,
Dylan

MS: British Library   *VW(R)*

HENRY TREECE
13 October 1939   Sea View Laugharne Carmarthenshire

Dear Henry,
   This is a very short note to say how sorry I am for the long delay in writing and to promise a long news letter this week. There's plenty to tell you. I've got out of the habit of writing letters, but I must write to you. I'm fairly busy all the time writing sentimental stories for a kind of provincial autobiography I'm doing for Dent's & which has to be finished by Christmas: not a serious book. I think it's about time that I produced a purely-entertainment book now; a series of obscure poems is too much & too thick.
   I haven't been sent, yet, any of the monthly magazine reviews—which are bound to be the most full and intelligent. Life & Letters, Wales, etc. have delayed their reviews. Here however are a few daily & weekly ones, for what worth they are to you. Return them sometime. The Cutting Agency shd be sending me some more soon, & I'll let you have them at once.
   I'd love to see the Adelphi & Welsh Nationalist reviews of yours: I'm afraid the Agency won't send me those, they're very uncommercial papers. Could you let me have copies for a day or two? I'd be very very grateful. Here's the Voice of Scotland: sorry, again, it's so late.
   I'm compiling an article to be called Objection to War—the objections of writers etc. who will *not* assist the war in any way. Just General objections not wanted.
   Can you suggest anybody?
   I'll be writing with full news & arguments.
   Regards to Nelly, from us both.

                                        Dylan
Thanks for the cheque.

TS: Thomas Trustees. MS letters to Treece are at Buffalo and Texas, but this is not among them.

LAURENCE POLLINGER[1]
14 October 1939   Sea View Laugharne Carmarthenshire

Dear Mr. Pollinger,
   Here is the Dent's contract, initialled & signed.
                                   Yours sincerely,
                                   Dylan Thomas

MS: Texas

---

[1] David Higham was in the Army, and Laurence Pollinger looked after Thomas at the agency for the next six years.

DESMOND HAWKINS
14 October 1939   Sea View Laugharne Carmarthenshire

Dear Desmond,

Thank you for the tribunal talk. I'll be wary.

I wrote to the Welsh secretary of the Peace Pledge Union. He said that membership of the PPU would be an advantage, as tribunals are often impressed by the fact that one is associated with people of similar opinions. But it wouldn't be of much help to say one joined the PPU in October. Anyway I'd prefer to be alone. You know, don't you, that a written statement will have to be sent in first, & then read aloud by the objector. If I write a statement soon, in preparation, I'll send you a copy for criticism etc. And you do the same. This Welsh secretary man says that he does not think it advisable—unless one is quite inarticulate—to be represented by a lawyer. I'm getting in touch with a barrister I know, just in case, & will tell you if he tells me anything interesting. I'm trying hard to think of respected gentry to get testimonials from. I know one defrocked bard.

This Welshman also says that, in his opinion, a few testimonials as to my literary capabilities, invaluableness and/or etc would be of great assistance too—as well as testimonials as to my sincerity & hate of killing. Any very respectable literary testimonialist that you can think of? *Do tell me a few people.*

I'm afraid I couldn't with honesty *plead* as a Christian, although I think I am one.

Yes, please, I should like to do some reviews of novels. Any chance of getting some of the novels about Wales that are coming out now—in particular, 'How Green Was My Valley' by Richard Llewelyn (Michael Joseph)? I could do a snappy article. But any novels will do.

Wales will do that little story of mine.[1] Sorry about *Purpose*.

Dylan

Oh, I forgot. I'm thinking of compiling for *Life & Letters* a thing called 'Objection to War'. Objections, not generalised but whole-heartedly practical, of various people, mostly writers. *Not* a Pacifist, pro-Russian, Mosleyite or literary peace-front, but the individual non-party non-political objections of people like you & me. I think, at this time, when many people who appeared trustworthy are turning out as penny heroes, guttersnipes, rattlesnakes, mass-minded fools or just lazy buggers, it would be valuable. Will you write your Objection—to war, to this war, to any war—briefly. Will Barker write too? I'm getting in touch with him. *Life & Letters* will give the Objection a few pages. Write soon.

Dy

MS: the recipient

[1] 'Just like Little Dogs.'

GLYN JONES
October 14 1939   Sea View Laugharne Carmarthenshire

Dear Glyn,
   I've thought of compiling, or some other word, an article to be called
Objection to War which I hope Robert Herring will print. A collection of
individual nonpolitical (but political opinions can colour what they like)
objections to war, this war, any war. Objections mostly from writers. Will
you write your objection, briefly, and let me have it? I don't mean the
thing to be any pacifist united front, but merely the individual views of
several people put together. Now, when so many hitherto trustworthy
people are ratting, backing out, being heroic or lazy, I think it would be
good to have printed, in a good magazine like Herring's, the sincere
objections of people who help to keep papers like Herring's going. Will
you do this?

                                                   Love,
                                                   Dylan

Sorry I lost your address.
Can you give me Rayner's?
I had a quick glimpse of your
Welsh Review review, but haven't had a
copy yet.

MS: Carbondale

GLYN JONES
27 October 1939   Sea View Laugharne Carmarthenshire

Dear Glyn,
   Thank you very much for the letter, and for the statement which I
thought was grand, just the thing for this intended collection & probably
far more suitable than a possibly seditious article such as the other one
you talked about. I'm writing to Rayner & to Savage, & will be seeing
Keidrych tomorrow. I've had a little thing from Desmond Hawkins, &
expect to hear soon from Barker, MacDiarmid, & H. Read. I do hope
Herring *will* print them.
   I'm glad your book's coming out—the poems. The Fortune Press do
them nicely, don't they? And thank you a lot, I'd love to have a copy. I'm
looking forward to it.
   I'm afraid there's little chance of us coming to Cardiff for a while: I
can't move an inch now. I'm broker than I've ever been—which means
I'm ordinarily penniless but also in debt. I wish to the lord it were

possible to get something out of Wales. Things are getting worse here every day.

Love to you & family,
Dylan
& Caitlin

I'd like to send you the more-or-less complete edition of my poems which New Directions are publishing in December.

MS: Carbondale

RAYNER HEPPENSTALL
27 October 1939   Laugharne Carmarthenshire S. Wales

Dear Rayner,
  Glyn Jones gave me your address. How are you? I've wanted to write to you for a long time, but for the moment let me ask you this.
  I'm trying to get together, for publication in any unsqueamish paper (preferably Life & Letters To-Day), a collection of objections to war from writers mostly of our age. Not just general objections, but the statements of fellows who aren't going to support the war at all. I don't know how you stand now, but, if you do thoroughly object and intend to stay by your objections, will you write your reasons in a fairly brief statement?—in any way you like, of course. I think the publication, especially in a widely circulated popular-literary magazine such as Life & Letters, will, or might, do, at this time, a lot of good. This is not meant to be a Peace Pledge front, it's no party or union thing at all, just the statements of individuals. Whatever your feelings, do write anyway. I'd love to hear from you. I've had statements from Glyn Jones, Desmond Hawkins, Keidrych Rhys, MacDiarmid, and hope to have them from Barker, D. S. Savage, Durrell, & others. Any names to suggest? This, my dear old Rayner, is no racket, & I don't care a bugger how well or not the chaps write. Objections from *individuals.* Be in the army & see the next world.

from Dylan

MS: Texas

D. S. SAVAGE
27 October 1939   Sea View Laugharne Carmarthenshire

Dear D. S. Savage,
   I'm trying to get together a number of statements of objection to war
from young writers. These I want to get printed in Life & Letters Today:
or, if they become squeamish, in some smaller, independent paper. I don't
know how you feel about this, so, in a first letter, will only say that the
objections must not be just *general* ones:—'war is bloody, criminal, &
absurd, everybody knows that, & I object to it heartily but I suppose I
shall have to do something when the time comes'. Now, more than at any
other time we have known, *definite* objections are needed. If you intend
not to support the war and to take no part in it, will you write, fairly
briefly, your reasons?—in whatever way you like, of course. I have
written to several people, and have had statements of objection, so far,
from Desmond Hawkins, Glyn Jones, Keidrych Rhys. I've been promised
statements, too, from Barker, Heppenstall, N. Moore, MacDiarmid, and
others. Any names—whether or not you yourself are a thorough objector
—you can suggest? I needn't tell you that, if you are an objector, the fact
that you contributed to a thing of this sort, in face of public opinion, and
against most even of the intelligentsia, will *not* be in your disfavour if, &
when, you appear before a tribunal. Glyn Jones told me that he believed
you stood with us. I do hope so. Write to me, if you will, anyway.

                                           Yours,
                                           Dylan Thomas

MS: Texas   *SL*

DESMOND HAWKINS
Nov 2 1939   Laugharne Carmarthenshire

Dear Desmond,
   In your last letter, which I had Friday, you said the novels from the
New English would probably have reached me by that time. Not a sign of
them—though what sign they are supposed to make I don't know. Will
you see what's happened? I want a fortnight to do them in—& *from* the
date they arrive.
   By the way, do you know what periodicals there are nowadays which
print longish stories? I've got a good one, & I want some crinkly for it.

                                           Dylan

Rayner Heppenstall tells me his novel 'The Blaze of Noon' is due out now. I don't know the publishers. Do you think I could have it for review?

MS: the recipient

RAYNER HEPPENSTALL
November 2 1939   Laugharne Carmarthenshire S Wales

Dear Rayner,
  I am not 'making a stand against war'—which I doubt was the expression I used; if I did use it, it was for convenience quickly and not for argument, not to be offered as an expression of my own thinking or feeling for you to put into inverted commas and throw back to me; certainly not as a militant priggishness. I am banging no drum for a Right, right, left, or wrong; I am not forming fours to oppose sixes and sevens—to 'justify my existence' (back the phrase comes, dolled up in selfconscious punctuation. I too can recognise a cliché & must let you know, as you let me know, that I recognise it as one) but to prolong it. In asking you to 'contribute to my symposium' I was merely asking you, as a man I know who writes, to let me have your individual objections to war; these objections, if they existed, could take any form; I was not attempting to form a common or rarefied front or backside; because I thought people might like to read them, I set out to collect individual objections from some of my friends & acquaintances. Also, of course, because I wanted to read them; I wanted to know what my friends and acquaintances are going to do when they are told by the State to fight not their enemies. My own 'stand' is a sit, and it will be on my own sit me down.
  I'll certainly use your 'bit of nonsense'—which is what I do believe it to be—and thank you for bothering. Your question, 'who's to stop me letting my rifle off up the colonel's arse?', has only one answer: 'Plenty of people'.
  And it's no use telling me, with heavy underlining, that you <u>won't</u> have an <u>attitude</u> to the war, much less to WAR. I don't care a bugger whether you won't or will: I wanted to know if you objected to war & why & whether you were going to 'serve' or not. My curiosity, I imagined, might have a journalistic interest. Others might like to be told that the only pacifists you come across are sexual perverts (crossed out & tut tut) or elderly ladies worried about dividends. You must have been living in a curious world—and there's no reason why you shouldn't have—to come across no other kinds of pacifists. Those are the kind that Beachcomber hopefully imagines make up the whole 'forces for peace' in this country. Perhaps the only socialists you come across are teetotal fruitarians.
  When you come to talk about one's duty as a writer, then *one* can only

say that his duty is to write. If to undergo contemporary reality to its most extreme is to join in a war—the evil of which is the war itself & not the things it is supposed, wrongly, to be attempting to exterminate—against people you do not know, and probably to be killed or maimed, then one can only say flippantly that the best poems about death were always written when the poets were alive, that Lorca didn't have to be gored before writing a bullsong, that for a writer to undergo the utmost reality of poverty is for him to starve to death and therefore to be, as a writer, useless.

Three more reasons of yours why you will probably join up are, to me, even more doubtful; and by that I mean that the honesty that made up those reasons is in doubt. You say you may join up because you *could not* cash in on the Ministry of Information. Does that mean you *can* not? Is it any worse to receive a good salary for muddling information, censoring news, licking official stamps, etc. than it is to kill or be killed for a shilling, or less, a day? You say you *could not* work on the land as one of a chaingang. Again, I do not see how that is any worse. One large lot of people is nearly always as 'congenial' as any other lot, & the matey folk-warmth of the trenches can only make for hysterical friendships, do or die companionships, the joking desperate homosexual propinquity of those about to die: the joy of living and dying with a Saturday football crowd on an exploding ground. You say you *could not* languish like a martyr in jail. Why a martyr anyway? The only reason one will go to jail is if a tribunal refuses to register one as an uncondition[al] objector & then if one will not do the services, substitute for military service, which the tribunal enforces. The individual can do what he likes: whatever he does, he is punished. I wanted to know which punishment *you* preferred.

How is the nest of fairies? Dan Jones told me something or other. Nice to hear you're having a baby. You or Margaret? Take no offence, Mr. H., but you said in your letter that you were pregnant. I'll get the Blaze of Noon, if I can, for review in the New English Weekly.

I'm living extremely quietly here, with Caitlin & Llewelyn. No money, of course, and we can't, even if we wanted to, move. I've nearly finished a book of straight, autobiographical stories: Portrait of the Artist As a Young Dog. Dent's give me a little miserable allowance which pays for cigarettes, lights, & coal. We're always warm, but badly in debt.

If you see Dan Jones ever, ask him to write. He's one of my oldest friends, but [...], and I like him a *lot*. He was down here in the summer, drinking & posturing.

Will you be in London in December? I hope to come up for a week. And is Durrell there too? I'd like to see you very much.

Love to you & Margaret.

Dylan

I'll let you know the hour of my birth after I see my mother. The date is 27 October, 1914. The place, Swansea.[1]

MS: Texas   *SL(R)*

DESMOND HAWKINS
Saturday [November 1939]   Sea View Laugharne Carmarthenshire

Dear Desmond,
    The review. Is it too long? Perhaps my autobiographical introduction should be cut, I don't know.[2]
    Can I have Rayner Heppenstall's Blaze of Noon? I've read some of it, & want to give it a good notice.
    And have you, by any chance, a copy of Purpose with Muir's review of my book in it.[3] Laughlin of America wants some good review extracts for preliminary publicity to my American book coming out sometime in December.
    I haven't numbered the pages of this present review consecutively, in case you want to chop it about. Hope it can stand. It's not v good but I'll get better when I get more into novel-reading—I'm out of practice.

                                                                    Dylan

MS: the recipient

HERMANN PESCHMANN
November 6 1939   Sea View Laugharne Carmarthenshire

Dear Mr. Peschmann,
    I don't suppose you've kept them for a moment, & I certainly don't blame you, but:—have you, by any chance, got those few random notes of mine that I used when I talked, a couple of years ago, to Goldsmiths' College? Perhaps you remember them:—notes about Hardy etc. I'm preparing a paper for a Cambridge lecture, & those old notes may help a little. Sorry to trouble you, & if you haven't the notes it doesn't matter a bit.

                                                            Best wishes,
                                                            Dylan Thomas

MS: the recipient

---

[1] Heppenstall was interested in astrology.
[2] The review, 'Novels and Novelists', appeared in the *New English Weekly* on December 14, and included notices of books by Frederic Prokosch and Dorothy Parker.
[3] Edwin Muir, reviewing *The Map of Love*, October–November issue.

VERNON WATKINS
Monday [November 1939]   Sea View Laugharne Carmarthenshire

Dear Vernon:
   I'm going to talk to the English Club at Cambridge on December 7. Not talk, but read poems. I want to read one of yours—what do you suggest?—and some of the very last Yeats, some of those lovely poems you said down here a few months ago when we were walking down a hill. Could you copy a few of those Yeats out for me—& also one or two recommended poems of your own. I'm going to read some Hardy, one Ransom, one Hart Crane, one Auden, one Spender, some Henry Miller, a bit of Nightwood, one or two of my own, one decorative Wallace Stevens.[1] Any suggestions? Would you like to copy out a few odd poems, anybody's? But anyway do send the Yeats, & yours.
   News in another letter.

                                        Love,
                                          Dylan

MS: British Library   *VW*

JAMES LAUGHLIN
Nov 8 1939   Sea View Laugharne Carmarthenshire S Wales

Dear Laughlin,
   Thank you for your letter. And thank you too, very much, for the cheque. I'm looking forward to having a copy of N.D. 1939, and also to seeing Patchen's new book. It's very kind of you to promise to send it to me.
   Here are 2 reviews of *The Map of Love.* Read's review is particularly good, & I hope it's not too late for you to be able to use extracts for advertisement.[2] Will you send back Seven—it's the only copy I have — along with the other magazines I asked you to return when you had finished with them?
   No, I haven't been told to fight yet, &, when I am told I shan't. Though whether it's going to be more hell as an assured objector than as a bewildered fighter, I don't know.

                                        Best wishes,
                                          Dylan Thomas

MS: the recipient

---

[1] Wallace Stevens (1878–1955), American poet.
[2] Herbert Read in *Seven*, Autumn 1939. He wrote: 'It contains the most absolute poetry that has been written in our time.'

VERONICA SIBTHORP
November 8 1939   Laugharne Carmarthenshire S Wales

Darling Veronica,
    It's nice to know where you are, even though you say no news and may
be staying with Aleister Crowley and Thuell Roskelly. You never answered my last chatter letter which was an answer to your letter saying
you would be able to come down to see us very soon. That was months
and months ago. Now comes a brief note saying nothing out of, if I may
coin a, the blue. What have you been doing all the time? How are Archies
& Jakes[1] and their mistakes? Have they married them? Write, please, a
long letter; and in return I'll send you, as soon as I can get hold of it, a
copy of my slim volume. At the moment I've only got my own love-
stained copy which I've lost. I'll try to be brave enough to write to
Dent's—to whom I owe a book—and ask them to send you a complimentary copy with a view to you reviewing it in the Taltz Mill Times.
Is that really the name of the house? O Christopher almighty who sees
each Robin fall, Pooh to you and Pooh to me and swing on my tilty ball.[2]
Llewelyn our son is a nice boy: you must come & stay with us, do, and
we'll all play with the woozikins. (Oswell & Max,[3] by the way (of all
flesh) send me occasional letters still, with cigarette-cards of Hedgerow
Horrors from Player's: signed Sister Bats, or Brother Badgers, whatever
the card may be. We laugh until we die.) Caitlin, who is well & strong &
who just, a few minutes ago, bounced the baby's head on the brick floor
like a ball, sends her love & would love to see you: I am trying to finish,
by Christmas so that we may spend a Christmas not to be remembered,
my adolescent autobiography entitled Portrait of the Artist as a Young
Dog. It will, I hope, be out next spring. My only War joke is that I have
been thinking of volunteering as a small tank. Really, I am going to do
nothing at all. Do tell us everything you know about everything: we're
miles from anywhere or anyone here, and sometimes, on lucky days,
we're miles from where we are. More elbow to the Power of Love. Write
soon.

                                        My love to you,

                              xxxxx   Dylan   xxxxx

MS: National Library of Wales

---

[1] Archie McColl; John (Jake) Sibthorp, who knew Aleister Crowley.
[2] Veronica Sibthorp's third husband, John Armstrong, lived in Essex, at Tilty Mill House,
     presumably the address from which she wrote to Thomas.
[3] Oswell Blakeston; Max Chapman.

VERNON WATKINS
Nov 10 1939   Sea View Laugharne Carmarthenshire

Dear Vernon,

Thank you a great lot for the present—for the poem and the money. I liked both immensely. The poem, I think, is altogether successful.[1] And thank you for the great Yeats poems; I'll read them all, of course. The poem of yours that you sent with them is a serious failure, I think—I mean it is a serious poem which fails. *The Windows*, I can't say much about it here and now, but I'll be coming to Swansea at the very beginning of December, all being well & I'd like very much to go through it with you then. The fifth verse particularly struck me as ugly & over-worked. The whole poem, to me, creaks & blunders, although some isolated bits I like & remember. It's altogether too ponderous & stuffy for me; it *is* a camphored elegy—mothballs. But don't mind my rudeness, I'll tell you my real & detailed objections to the poem later. They might amuse you anyway. This is a dirty note—I can't find a pen. Better one coming *before* we meet, & that should be on the 1st of December.

Thank you again for the terribly kind postal order, the Yeats, The Windows (an admiring boo from me) & Life & Letters which I thought had only your poem to redeem it this month; but what a grand redemption.

> Very much love to you
> from
> Dylan

Love from the family to yours.

MS: British Library   *VW*

JOHN DAVENPORT
16 November [1939]   Sea View Laugharne Carmarthenshire

Dear John,

We're going to be able to get away from here, which is killing us a bit this winter, for a week in December, might go to Ringwood, and would be delighted to be invited to stay with you for a day or two. My previous letters weren't answered, and this is a last request for a little word. It would be nice to have somewhere to go; & we'd like to see you. Do you know Frederic Prokosch's poem, The Dolls? I've seen it in lots of anthologies lately. Do try & get hold of it for Spender-voice reading. I've done an almost *exact* imitation of it which you might like: but you must see the original by its side:

[1] Watkins's 'Portrait of a Friend'.

The Molls

I found them lying on the floor,
Male shapes, girl-lipped, but clad like boys:
Night after night their hands implore
Emetic Percies for their joys.

They retch into my secret night
With stale & terrifying camp
And offer as the last delight
A crude, unhappy, anal cramp.

Gently they sigh to my behind
Wilde words, all buttered, badly bred,
And when I dream of them I find
Peacockstein's poems on my bed.

The real last line of the poem is: 'Small tears of glass upon my bed'. I couldn't beat that & didn't try.

Love to all,
Dylan

MS: Texas   *SL*

D. S. SAVAGE
24 November 1939   Sea View Laugharne Carmarthenshire

Dear D. S. Savage,
  So very sorry. Yes, I did get your letter and the admirable peace offering. And I thought I *had* acknowledged it, so perhaps it's my letter that's gone astray. But most likely I'd meant to write, thanking you, & then thought that I'd posted what I'd never written. But, anyway, thank you now: the contribution to my intended peace demonstration was grand. I'm very glad, personally, that you feel like that. So do I. I was going to come to Cambridge early in December, & was looking forward to meeting you. The university English Society asked me to speak there, & I said yes — providing you pay my expenses. Then they pleaded poverty, the rogues & liars, & wanted to postpone the meeting, or whatever it was going to be. Fuck them all. Sorry to miss you—I did hope we could have arranged to meet, if only for a drink.
  I'll let you know more about this peace thing when it gets going—not many people have replied yet. Thank you for suggesting some names—I've written to Miller.

Yours,
Dylan Thomas

MS: Texas

RAYNER HEPPENSTALL
Nov 27 1939   Laugharne Carmarthenshire S. Wales

Dear Rayner,
    Just to let you know that I was born *about* 11 p.m. Monday October 27
1914.
    This would look a very curious note to someone who didn't know why
I was telling you.
    Hope to see you soon.

Ever,
Dylan

MS: Carbondale

VERNON WATKINS
30 Nov 1939 (Asks him to forward letter to Taig. See Appendix 19.)

LAURENCE POLLINGER
December 9 1939   Sea View Laugharne Carmarthenshire

Dear Mr. Pollinger:
    I'm enclosing the manuscript of my new book: a book of autobiographi-
cal stories called, for the moment, 'Portrait Of The Artist As A Young
Dog'. About 55 to 60,000 words. My contract of 12th of October this year,
says that, on the receipt of my manuscript, to be delivered before December 31 (not less than 50,000 words), Dent's will let me have at once the
£45 advance which is the balance due to me in accordance with a contract
of March 7, 1937. Will you see to it that Dent's do let me have this money
immediately. I am writing to Richard Church about details of the book,
but I do not suppose that he is responsible for paying out the money. I
must have the £45 *before* Christmas. Actually I need it on the 20th, to
pay off large & pressing debts. I don't see why there should be any
difficulty about this, do you? Please do stress the urgency of this, to
Dent's. Before Christmas. On the 20th.
    Do you think you could also buck them up, unless you've already got
it, about my December cheque. I'd like to have that always in the first
week of the month. I rely on it to live.

Yours sincerely,
Dylan Thomas

TS: J. M. Dent. The MS is not with the Higham material at Texas.

HENRY TREECE
13 December 1939   Sea View Laugharne Carmarthenshire
[*in the margin: Sketch of a man in a hat. Below:* I don't know why I
cramped this so much. Does it mean that I always sleep on the edge of the
bed? Or perhaps the grandmother I secretly lust after had one eye.]

Dear Henry,
   I wish I could be up in London Christmas week, when you're there: I
haven't seen a town for 12 months. But I'm afraid we have to spend the
holiday with parents, Caitlin's or mine, in Hampshire or Swansea: probably Swansea, with Vernon Watkins and other queer men for company.
Do you know Vernon's poetry? Sometimes it is, I think, very good.
Always unfashionable, but I don't mean that that's why it's good. How
are you and Nelly? Perhaps next year, before being conscripted, I may
manage to come up to see you. I hope so. Do you? About this anthology
for the Virginia Spectator: I think you'd better count me out. I don't like
the company—in print, I mean—of Moore, Cooke, Heseltine, and anyway
I'm not an advanced writer in the way that the inclusion of those names
suggests. Besides, I've nothing new except straight stories. When is your
book coming out in America? Do let me see it. Merry Christmas, and
love. There's no news I can remember for the newsy letter I want to write,
so I'll have to make up news and write to you quickly. This is only an
answer about Virginia.
                                                   Dylan
[*on the envelope:*]
So very sorry. Just found this in a drawer. Thought it was posted 10 days
ago. Try to make up for this by writing soon & at length, with poems etc.
                                                   Dylan T

MS: Texas

CHARLES FISHER
[December 1939]   Sea View Laugharne Carmarthenshire

Dear Charles,
   I did enjoy hearing from you about yourself and the local lads with
whom, in the intervals between Fitzrophobia, attempted 19th century
dissipation, artgraft, amateur poncing, I condescended to muck pro-
vincially about. But the lads themselves are splitting up, perhaps even
cracking up. Vernon should write the Glamorgan Lad and tell how, one
by one, we reach the gallows, the marriage bed, the grave,[1] Harrow,
Windrush, or the Air Force. I'm coming to Swansea, to swell your

---
[1] Thomas was thinking of A. E. Housman's ballad sequence, 'A Shropshire Lad'.

numbers, in Christmas week, or, if I happen to see an old blind lady crossing Laugharne High Street and I rush to her aid and later she turns out to be Lady St. Clears and leaves her fortune to the last person who did her a service, earlier. I am, at last, fed up with this retreat, the day has come, the castle and the pretty water make me sick. I want to see our beautiful drab town, I want to have smuts in my eye in Wind Street, I want to hear the sweet town accent float into my ears like the noise of old brakes. Keep some days for us when we arrive; show us round the town; reserve two seats (and one seat specially sawed down) in the Kardomah my Home Sweet Homah. Perhaps Mabeley will be about too, unless he's almost a Warden.[1] I'm glad the Spy Service didn't take you: you would always have given up your papers to Dolores (the password is cocksnap, knock a hundred times on the onionseller's door, his name is Tabash, call him Dickinson) even if they were the wrong papers. I like your standard war joke; you should give the healthier-looking waitresses white feathers. I'm not doing anything about the war; resigned to personal neutrality, I wait until I am called up, and then I will probably scream and wheedle and faint.

There's a story of mine about me and Dan in the December Life & Letters, by the way.[2]

See you all, or both, soon. Love, to you & Fred.

Dylan

We never see the Keidrych Rhyses now. I'm number one on the list, Mrs. R's list, of people who have a bad effect on hubby. That's what she thinks. I tell him bad things about poetry; such as that his isn't poetry at all.

MS: the recipient   *SL*

VERNON WATKINS
December 13 1939   Sea View Laugharne Carmarthenshire

Dear Vernon,

What do I want for Christmas? Oh, that's nice. I want a war-escaper—a sort of ladder, I think, attached to a balloon,—or a portable ivory tower or a new plush womb to escape back into. Or a lotion for invisibility. I don't want a cathedral—you said I couldn't have one—so can I have a dear book? If you like best giving toys or games, could I perhaps have The New Yorker Annual (published by Hamish Hamilton at, I believe, ten & six) which is all funny drawings, half a game, half a book? I should like that very much indeed.

---

[1] Part-time air-raid wardens were being recruited in thousands.
[2] 'The Fight.'

As for Llewelyn, a poem in his stocking is more than he deserves — unless you think, as I think, that everybody deserves everything or nothing. And if you want to add a croaking duck or floating frog, that'll be lovely, the boy is no zoologist and likes, better than anything else in the world, sucking. I can't pretend that he will admire the poem, even if it's grand which I hope and wish, but we will. We send our love, and will be coming up next Thursday. My sister is going to drive us. Of course we're looking forward to seeing you: a silly way of saying we'd fly up if we could, before that. But there will be Christmas Eve for us, and we'll smoke your ridiculous cigarettes and buy bathfuls of cointreau, bitter, biddy, or ink. For you this Christmas a record: which? The land, the air, Elizabeth, Trouts or Surprises? Thank you for the New Yorker Annual.

Dylan

I'm so glad you liked the fresh, Dan story. I've finished the book now and have nothing to do but wait for Swansea, marble-town, city of laughter, little Dublin, home of at least 2 great men.

MS: British Library   *VW*

LAURENCE POLLINGER
29 [probably December 1939]   As from
Marston Bishopston nr Swansea

Dear Pollinger,
    Thank you for getting the Dent's cheque through so quickly. I'm v grateful. Sorry not to have acknowledged it before.
    I wonder if you'd ask Dent's what so far are the sales of my Map of Love. I asked once before, but someone forgot to tell me.
    Some of the stories I've included in 'Portrait of The Artist As A Young Dog' I want to sell to American papers—New Directions have just brought out my book there, & it would probably be a good time, and the stories, as well, might appeal to some of the better-paying magazines there.[1] Shall I send the stories on to you when they are typed?

Yours sincerely
Dylan Thomas

MS: Texas

<hr>

[1] The *Portrait* book was not yet published, either in Britain or the U.S. The book that had just appeared in the U.S. was *The World I Breathe*.

LAURENCE POLLINGER
Jan 3 1940 (He is staying at Blashford. See Appendix 20.)

LAURENCE POLLINGER
Jan 10 1940   Blashford Ringwood Hants

Dear Pollinger,
    Thank you for getting the sales of *Map of Love*. I shall blame the war for
them.[1]
    The Dent's cheque has arrived: very punctual.
    No, New Directions has not had any sort of a copy of *Portrait of The
Artist As a Young Dog*. Do they want one straight away? I haven't got a
duplicate typescript, nor a typewriter, and I can't afford to employ a
professional. So *what can be done*? I've got copies of a few of the stories
which I'll send on to you once I return to Wales—for magazine selling in
America.

                                    Yours sincerely,
                                    Dylan Thomas

MS: Texas

VERNON WATKINS
[postmarked January 30 1940]   Blashford Ringwood Hants

Dear Vernon,
    Thank you for typing the poem. And for wanting to get Llewelyn
something for his birthday. That's tomorrow. I wish I could have written
to you, asking, from him, what he wanted before this, but we've been
staying with Joey the ravisher. You will be interested to know that she is
appearing in a pantomime—Cecil Beaton's snob show for the troops —
dressed as a scarlet & gold satin admiral. She'd knock you cold. Caitlin
says that Llewelyn needs most of all: undervests and/or nappies. Is that
too dull? she asks. Perhaps it would be easier for her to get them in
Ringwood—unless you feel strong enough to ask for such things in the
Kiddies' Department, and anyway it's difficult to tell you what size he is.
So, if, again, you don't think underwear a very happy present for a one
year old boy, perhaps you'd like to send a little bit of What Matters on to
Caitlin [*marginal note:* I'm not sure if these negatives make sense] &
she'll buy the things & you shall see Llewelyn in them—if you've got
eyes that penetrate outer wrappings, or even if Caitlin shows you—when

---

[1] Pollinger had written that sales were only 280 copies, adding, 'Pretty discouraging, eh?'

we return to Bishopston in about 10 days time. Llewelyn says Ta to you—*and* ba, da, ma.

I agreed with your criticism of the 'lubber crust of Wales' but have, so far, done nothing about altering it. Gaels is good, but that sounds to me facetious.[1] Actually, although I thought the pun out quite coldly, I wanted to make the lubber line a serious one, and I'm glad that you like it apart from its joke. I'll tell you, later, what I do about it: I shall probably use Gaels, anyway. Now I'm working on a new poem, a poem which is giving me more pleasure than I've got out of any work for months, or even years.[2] Yes, the Lawrence calling-up-of-memory in the kangaroo lines was intentional,[3] but if in any way it seems feeble, perhaps a little tame, in such a poem (strenuously resisting conventional associations) then, of course, I must change it. I'll let you know when I come back to the poem. As it is, changing only the word 'Wales' I might print the poem in L & Letters just as it is, alterable bits & all; & then work on it later. I see nothing silly in that. I didn't like much 'I do not regret the bugle I wore' but its omission makes the end too vague. I'll either retain the line or alter it—alter it, that is, in a worked-on version later. I'll send you the new poem v. soon. I've just finished my Portrait . . . Young Dog proofs. Out in March. I've kept the flippant title for—as the publishers advised—moneymaking reasons. I'll be writing when the poem's finished. Love, & thanks for poem, criticism, & godfatherliness.

D.

MS: British Library   *VW*

J. M. DENT
30 Jan 1940   New Inn House Blashford Ringwood Hants

Dear Sir,
    Here's the corrected marked proofs.
    In the tablet opposite title page I've put down my first book, 18 Poems, which was not produced by Dent's but by a private firm—& is now out of print. I don't know what the rule of the House is, but I should v much like this title to be included.

Yours truly,
Dylan Thomas

MS: J. M. Dent

---

[1] The poem was 'Once below a time'. The line in question remained 'Up through the lubber crust of Wales'.
[2] 'There was a saviour.'
[3] In 'Once below a time', a passage in the second stanza, which includes the line 'From the kangaroo foot of the earth', has a faint echo of D. H. Lawrence's poem 'Kangaroo'.

LAURENCE POLLINGER
Jan 30 1940[1]   at New Inn House Blashford Ringwood Hants

Dear Laurence Pollinger,

Here are 9 stories—from my Portrait of Artist As Young Dog book—for you to send to your American branch to distribute among magazines there. Do you think some of them will appeal to good-paying papers? I do hope so, & I hope the American branch will try: I'm tired of appearing in American highbrow papers that pay with love & stamps. I think some of these stories might go down well commercially.

I'll send you on a complete spare proof copy—corrected—of the book, for you to send to New Directions, in a few days.

Somebody told me, by the way, that, if an author's name was down on that Ministry of Labour list your office sent around to its people—the official questionnaire—it would be unlikely that he would be ordinarily conscripted into the Army. Is that true? I doubt it. I'm due to be conscripted in a few months' time, & by Christ I want to avoid it. Do please tell me about this.

                                        Yours,
                                        Dylan Thomas

MS: Texas

DESMOND HAWKINS
Jan 30 1940   at Blashford Ringwood Hants

Dear Desmond,

Terribly sorry about the lateness of the review. To make up, in some way, may I give this story to the New English? Five bob, if they can afford it, just so that I can keep up to my promise to myself that I wouldn't write anything for nothing ever any more. If they can't, okay.

Do write to me.

                                        Yours,
                                        Dylan T

MS: the recipient

[1] Thomas wrote '1939' by mistake.

VERNON WATKINS
Feb 3 1940   Blashford Ringwood Hants

Dear Vernon,

Thank you—Caitlin is writing separately—for the present for Llewelyn, who is an intolerable dandy and shames his stained and smoky father. He also had a suit from grandparents, and a musical box, and the most menacing, lunatic doll, half Mervyn Levy, half Harpo Marx, that I have ever seen—with a twitching head and revolving ears—and some napkins and barley sugar and a cake (with one candle) which his cousin ate.

For 'I do not regret' in my much discussed poem[1] I have put 'Never never oh never to regret the bugle I wore' (all one line), so that the repetition, the pacific repetition, of 'I would lie down, lie down, lie down and live' is loudly and swingingly balanced. When you see the poem again, I think you'll like the alteration.

I'm glad Herring is going to print some Llewelyn poems. Little the little one knows. Our family is very proud of the poems.

The dim snaps were liked a lot.

Is Dot still with you? We will miss her easily this time. Our love to her & you, and all.

                                        Dylan

P.S.
This all is
shockingly late
because Caitlin
thought I'd
posted it &
I thought she
had. Also
I've been in
bed for 3
days—just
up now—with
a huge cough &
cold.
Write soon, & I
will too.

MS: British Library   *VW*

---

[1] 'Once below a time.'

DESMOND HAWKINS
Feb 13 1940   Blashford Ringwood Hants

Dear Desmond,
I sent you a short story a few weeks ago, for the New English Weekly.
Do you or they want it? If not, *do chuck it back.*[1] Someone may pay me
for it.
I'm going up to London this Thursday. Any chance of seeing you?

Dylan

MS: the recipient

LAURENCE POLLINGER
13 Feb 1940   at Blashford Ringwood Hants

Dear Laurence Pollinger,
Here's the proof copy for New Directions.[2]
I haven't got my New Directions contract at hand, but I remember that
no detailed arrangement for payment of royalties, advance etc on my new
books was mentioned. A new contract was to be made for each book. I
should like you to stress to New Directions, when you send off these
proofs, that, if they accept the book, I require a decent advance on
royalties. On the first book of mine that they printed, I was advanced £10
only, which was absurd. But it was an 'advanced' book mostly, & as this
book should be much more popular I obviously expect better treatment.
James Laughlin will, of course, send his draft of a contract (if he takes the
book) directly to you; so please don't forget a nice advance sum.
Dent's cheque just arrived. Thank you.

Sincerely,
Dylan Thomas

MS: Texas

---

[1] No story appeared in *New English Weekly*.
[2] *Portrait of the Artist as a Young Dog*, which New Directions published in September
1940.

LORNA WILMOTT[1]
28 February 1940   c/o New Inn House Blashford Ringwood Hants

Dear Lorna Wilmott,
   Thank you very much indeed for lending us your flat. We left London yesterday, Tuesday, but in such a hurry that I forgot to call at the delicacies shop and leave the key. I hope that, if you did return to London yesterday, it didn't make any trouble. Actually, we found the front door open every night, &, though we closed it, someone else always opened it again. So I don't think my carelessness could have kept you out of your own flat. We left so hurriedly, & with so little time to think, that we mayn't have tidied everything up. I hope not, though, and I hope too that you won't think we're too messy. It was very kind of you. I do hope we'll all be able to meet when we come up to town next.

                              Yours sincerely,
                              Dylan Thomas

MS: Rupert Shephard

JAMES LAUGHLIN
March 5 1940   Laugharne Carmarthenshire S Wales

Dear Laughlin,
   I've just remembered that, very rudely, I haven't yet acknowledged my book, which you sent me. Or the Virgil ode.[2] I thought you made a marvellous job of the book: probably the handsomest I'll ever have, unless, as I hope, you'll do another of mine. The paper & the print and the cover, I liked everything a great lot. You sent me only one copy, and we'd arranged that I be sent six. Do let me have the others soon, because I want to give them away as presents. The book's much admired, and I must give copies to friends. Please don't forget. How is it, or was it, selling? And what kind of reviews did it, or didn't it, have? Could you send me some

---

[1] First wife (now deceased) of the painter Rupert Shephard. They were friendly with the Thomases, both of whom Shephard painted in Laugharne, at Sea View (the paintings are in the National Portrait Gallery), early in 1940. Shortly afterwards Thomas was in London, seeking work that would keep him out of the Army, and Lorna Wilmott let him borrow her flat. She and her husband returned to find that Thomas and friends had pawned gramophone, typewriter, cutlery, family silver and fur coat. Shephard says that the episode took place in April 1940, and that Thomas's 'very feeble little letter', complete with false date, was written as part of a retrospective attempt to cover his tracks. When Lorna Wilmott wrote threatening to tell the police, Thomas sent a telegram saying, 'Call off hounds, will restore everything'. After much trouble, most of the effects were recovered.
[2] Laughlin had translated Virgil's Fourth Eclogue and used it on a New Directions Christmas card.

copies of the reviews, or at least of some of them? I do *very much* want to see them. If you don't want to part with the actual reviews, knowing my carelessness—although I do promise that I would return them very quickly—perhaps you wouldn't mind copying out a few of them, or bits of them: the most interesting fors and againsts. By this time, you'll probably have received a corrected proof copy of my book of straight auto-biographical stories. Do you like & want it? It's just about to appear over here; the publisher's very hopeful of it. I'll send you copies of its reviews straight away. Did Patchen ever get the long over-literary letter I sent him? I'd like to hear from him again. Is he still with you? I shall be conscripted in about a month now, and am worried. I won't fight, and I don't want to object. Wish I was well out of it. Do write to me, & don't forget the other five copies of my book or—if you'll be kind enough — some copies of reviews. I'll send reviews of Portrait of The Artist As a Young Dog as soon as they come out.

> Best wishes,
> Dylan Thomas

MS: the recipient

VERNON WATKINS
March 6 [1940]   Blashford Ringwood

P.S. The Virgil ode[1] I said I was
  enclosing won't fit in the
  envelope. Sorry, I'll buy
  a big envelope this week.

Dear Vernon,
  I'm so glad you liked my lyrical poem, that you thought it was one of my best.[2] I'll think of 'stupid kindred', which is right, of course, in meaning and which prevents any ambiguity, but kindred seems a little pompous a word: it hasn't the literal simplicity of hindering man. No, I can't see 'seep' with dust, & unless a better word can be made will remain true to 'fly'. But about line 3 of the last verse, you're right as can be and somehow I must make 'death' the second word. I'll let you know what I can work out. I like the word 'blacked', by the way, in spite of its, in the context, jarring dissonance with 'locked'. I had, quite apart (that is absurd, I mean secondarily to) from the poem, the blackout in mind, another little hindrance on the scene, & the word seemed, to me, to come rightly. But I'll think about it. Your criticism's always terribly suggestive, & in that particular 'death line' you showed quite clearly to me the one

---

[1] See preceding letter.
[2] 'There was a saviour.'

big misbalance in the poem. Ta. I'm writing an awkward, satirical poem about war-time London now: a kind of elaborate, rough, angry joke which Keidrych would like a lot. You shall see it, of course; you might like it too, with all the proper reservations: I had to have a change after my austere poem in Milton measure.

And now I want very much to see the long-waited-for Ballad.[1] Would it be too much work for you to copy me a copy? I thought I'd be back in Wales early this month, but I may have to go up to London to see about a possible, but very improbable, job that would keep me from pleading or soldiering. To do with films: I shan't get it. But if I do have to go up to town, it means I shan't be home for a bit of time & I must see the Ballad before that. Do, please. I'm glad you're happy from it. It must be very good.

Has Life & Letters come out yet? I haven't been sent my copy. Thank you for wanting to give Llewelyn the quid from the Llewelyn poems. But Caitlin says he's got plenty of clothes now; and if you'd like to send me the quid, or 14/- of it, you'd save us losing our bed. The bed on which you have slept in Laugharne is being bought on hire-purchase from a shop in Swansea, at 7 bob a month, and we owe them 2 months on it—no, 3 including this, I forgot—and they're going to do something cruel with solicitors unless we pay immediately. And I'm without a penny and hopelessly in debt, here as well as in Laugharne. I think it would be very nice for Llewelyn's poems to save our bed. (Our cardboard bed, do you remember it?) Llewelyn's bronchitis is better, and today he is out in the sun. I'll send you my awkward poem in a day or two. But let me have the ballad. I'll recite it to the collected household. Caitlin's mother is waiting, too, to read the poems to her grandchild: I have only the prologue with me here. I'm enclosing Laughlin's Christmas card.

> Love to you from Caitlin & me,
> & to your family

Since this—I lost the post—I've been reading the (my) poem very carefully, and have made these slight but, I think important (relatively) alterations: '*And laid your cheek against a cloud-formed shell*'. This harder word, 'formed', balances the line, avoids the too-pretty internal rhyme of 'laid' & 'made', & stops the too easy flow, or thin conceited stream.

To avoid ambiguity, & also the use of the word 'kindred', I've turned 'his' in line 6 of verse 2 into 'that'.

In the last verse, the 3rd line now is: 'Brave deaths of only ones but never found', which I believe to be right. Do look at it carefully. For 'fly' in last line but 2 of last verse I have now 'ride'. I'm sure of that: it's mysteriously militant, which is what I wanted.

MS: British Library   VW

---

[1] Watkins's 'Ballad of the Mari Lwyd'.

LAURENCE POLLINGER
March 6 1940   Blashford Ringwood Hants

Dear Pollinger,
    Sorry I missed you in London.
    Would it be asking too much of you *not* to take out the three quid I owe
your firm from my about-to-come March cheque? I want very much to return
to Wales, and am relying on the Dent money to get me there. Minus the three
quid, I'd have only four and a bit left, which isn't enough to take myself &
family back & settle up the few odds & ends I have to before going. Perhaps
you could deduct what I owe you either from my April cheque or from any
American money—I'm looking forward to having Laughlin's offer—that
might come before then? I hope you can do me this favour.
    Thank you for your kindness in town.
                                                    Yours sincerely,
                                                    Dylan Thomas

MS: Texas

STEPHEN SPENDER
March 7 1940   Blashford Ringwood Hants

Dear Stephen,
    Thank you for writing, and for having written to Marsh. I thought he
could do nothing for me, so I was not disappointed. I'll have a medical
examination when I have some money, and try to get a certificate.
Augustus John has told me that Kenneth Clark, of the National Gallery,[1] is
in charge of some film board, and tries to help young men who paint or
write; he, John, is writing to him for me. Do you know Kenneth Clark, or
know anybody who knows him and might press my claims or whatever is
the right thing to do? I hope you do: I'm in such a hurry, and anyway I want
a job. Thank you so much, as well, for writing to Eliot: I hope Faber will let
me do the selection.[2] Here is a poem you might like to use, or anyway read.
    I'll send along another—if you don't, or even if you do, like this one—
when it's finished. Probably at the end of next week.

                                                    Yours,
                                                    Dylan

Don't forget to try to do a little Clarking around for me, if you can.

MS: Harvard

[1] See page 446.
[2] Perhaps *A Little Book of Modern Verse*. Anne Ridler edited it for Faber in 1941.

VERNON WATKINS
[March 1940]   Blashford Ringwood

Dear Vernon,

Thank you so much for the bedsaver; it has. Lovely of you, and one day I will buy you a bank all for yourself.

I've no news. We're just hanging on here until I hear, or don't, from London where I *may* be offered a job, though it's improbable.

I've not finished my satirical poem yet, & have, for the want of satirical feeling, left it for a time to begin an ambitious new poem. Sorry you can't send the Ballad, I must see it soon.

Thank you—I nearly forgot—for Life & Letters; mine came today. The Llewelyn poems were appreciated by everyone; I liked, myself, the Dalai Lama poem particularly. Apart from you & me, I didn't like much in the number, & thought Glyn Jones's story affected & imitative. Peter Helling's got something, hasn't he? Why no Caradog? 'Got something', my God. Am I trying to be a Little Master.

Thank you again, & love from the both of us. News, I hope, soon; & we're longing to return. South England is a flat green plate covered with soldiers.

                                                Dylan

MS: British Library   *VW*

LAURENCE POLLINGER
March 13 1940 (Asks for money. See Appendix 21.)

VERNON WATKINS
March 19 [1940]   Blashford Ringwood

Dear Vernon,

Here's my 100 line satirical poem.[1] I'm sure you won't like it. Or am I sure? It isn't, by a long something, your favourite kind, but you like all kinds and may appreciate—(not the word)—this half-comic attack on myself. I've got very little to say about it myself: you'll see the heavy hand with which I make fun of this middle-class, beardless Walt who props humanity, in his dirty, weeping, expansive moments, against corners & counters & tries to slip, in grand delusions of all embracing humanitarianism, everyone into himself. The first 'Cut' in the last verse

---

[1] 'The Countryman's Return.' Published in a magazine, *Cambridge Front*, Summer 1940, but not thereafter. *VW* gives the text.

is, of course, cinema. And a loud Stop. The heaviest satire against myself (or the figure I have made myself into) is in the 7th to the 13th line of the last verse. Then, in the very last part, by a change of rhythm I try to show the inevitability of my unrepentance of the charges that the rollicking attack has made. The whole thing's bristling with intentional awkwardnesses, grotesque jokes, vulgarities of phrasing; but I know it *is* a whole thing, & that's *something*. Tell me. I shan't alter much of it anyway: it's not the sort of poem to try to polish; in fact, I've tried to avoid most slicknesses, which might have come so easily. This proud talk is only because I've just finished.

I may be back on Thursday, unless I'm called to town. I'll let you know.

My love,
Ever,
Dylan

Could you type all this? I've no-one else to help me in *any* way about poems.

MS: British Library   VW

SIR KENNETH CLARK[1]
25 March 1940   Laugharne Carmarthenshire S Wales

Dear Sir Kenneth,

I wonder if you got my letter of just over a week ago? I sent it to a Portland Place address, which Augustus John had given me, and which was in the telephone book. Augustus wasn't sure, though, whether you still lived there. If you have had my letter, I apologise for bothering you again; but I daren't take the chance that you have [?not] had it. I do hope this reaches you through the Ministry of Information; I wanted to write to your private address, because you must be bombarded with letters at the other place.

Augustus said he'd written to you and talked to you about me, about my chances of getting a job, any kind of job I'm capable of doing, to avoid conscription. And he told me that you'd said you'd look out for a job, but that, anyway, you didn't think I would be conscripted. In my letter, which perhaps has gone astray, I asked you if you'd be kind enough to tell me how probable my exemption was, and, if it wasn't very probable, could you help me to get some work, which would exempt me? I'm to register on April 7, which leaves me hardly any time, and if I do have to register it will have to be as an objector. I don't want to do that, because,

---

[1] Kenneth Clark, (1903–83), later Lord Clark, art historian and writer, in 1940 at the Ministry of Information.

though I will not fight, I am perfectly willing to do some kind of work; and I think it would be wasteful and silly for me to be made to work at something I know absolutely nothing about and at which I would probably always be inefficient. Augustus told me, too, that you knew some of my writing. I've got a year's work planned out, I'm halfway through a long book, and I do very much want to go on with my work. Conscription, or objection, must, I know, stop that work altogether—objection too, because I hardly think a tribunal, especially in Wales, would pay much attention to my nonreligious, nonpolitical reasons. I know it's presumptuous of me, as a complete stranger to you, to worry you with my worries, but I've no-one at all to turn to, no-one to advise me, and very little time left. Also, Augustus said that you were very willing to help me; and I shall be grateful for ever if you can.

I wrote my first letter to you from Hampshire, where I was staying, and asked you if you could arrange to meet me in London; if there would be a reason in my coming to London; if you would care to see me. I waited in Hampshire until the end of last week, hoping to hear from you, but now have had to come home to Wales. Will you let me know if I shall come to London to see you? Or, anyway, tell me about the possibilities of exemption or any kind of exempting work? I wish I could have made this letter shorter. I do hope you will answer me.

Yours sincerely,
Dylan Thomas

Only source: SL

SIR KENNETH CLARK
April 1 1940   Laugharne Carmarthenshire S Wales

Dear Sir Kenneth,
  I don't know which of my two rather silly, and almost duplicate letters, you got first, but thank you very much for your answer. I quite understand that jobs can't be found—I wasn't asking for a bogus job; quite willing to work at almost anything—for every poet and painter and dancer: it was just that Augustus had given me a little personal hope. I also asked Herbert Read to write you a line for me, and by this time you've probably received it. I didn't know then that getting a job was quite hopeless, and I'm sorry to bother you with these odd recommendations etc. I'll join up, now, with my age-group, and trust to God and other people that I may get a noncombatant job within the army. My great horror's killing.

Thank you again,
Yours sincerely,
Dylan Thomas

TS: J. M. Dent

LAURENCE POLLINGER
4th April 1940 (Any money from America? See Appendix 22.)

LADY CLARK
4 April 1940   Laugharne · Carmarthenshire S Wales

Dear Mrs. Clark,
    Thank you for your letter. I'm very grateful to Sir Kenneth for trying to get me exempted; I know it must be almost impossible now, but it's grand he had a shot at it.
    I should very much like to join your friend Captain Cazalet's lot[1]—I couldn't quite read if you wrote 'battery', and, if you didn't, I don't know if it's the right word—and it would be a nice consolation to be among people I knew slightly, etc. And thank you for writing to him to see if it's possible. If it *was* possible to get in there, would it also be possible, do you think, to get—eventually, of course—a nonfighting job: anything, dish-warden, dishwasher, latrine minder? There must, surely be little jobs in the army, like cook or storeboy. If there's a chance of that, I should far far prefer to be in Captain Cazalet's problematical battery than among complete strangers. *Far.* Do let me know, soon, if you can, whether or not I can join them.

                                    Yours sincerely,
                                    Dylan Thomas

TS: J. M. Dent

LADY CLARK
12 April 1940   Laugharne Carmarthenshire S Wales

Dear Lady Clark,
    Thank you a lot for sending on Captain Cazalet's letter. You've been most kind to me. This is certainly a great help. I've written to Captain Cazalet, and, if that suits him, will go to see him next week.
    I'm glad you like my new book. I've just started a kind of sequel to it—hope I'll be able to get a little time to finish it too.
                            Thank you very much again
                                    Yours sincerely,
                                    Dylan Thomas
TS: J. M. Dent

---

[1] Victor Cazalet, one-time Member of Parliament, who organised his own unit of anti-aircraft gunners, 'Cazalet's Battery'.

JAMES LAUGHLIN
April 15 1940   Sea View Laugharne Carmarthenshire S Wales

Dear Laughlin,

Thanks for the letter; and for the Nation review: far more sensibly serious or vice bloody versa than most I get in England. Yes, please do send on some other reviews as they come, I want very much to see them.

I'm glad you liked my Portrait of the Artist As A Young Dog,[1] and that you want to do it. I hope you can get an answer soon from Dent's about sheet prices, because I want to arrange a contract with you quickly as I must have some money. Since the war, all my little sources of money have dried up, I haven't seen one penny now for over a month and am living on suspicious credit, I'm badly in debt and there's nothing at all coming unless it is from the American sale of these new stories. Do, please, see if you can settle with Higham, Pollinger and Pearn to arrange an advance for me straight away. Things haven't been worse ever.

The stories from the Portrait by the way, have been sent by Higham, P and P to Ann Watkins, who's trying to place them. So it's best not to try to have them placed twice.

I'm sending some new poems to the Southern Review.

Not many reviews of the Portrait have come along yet; the weeklies and monthlies haven't had time, and it's only the once-a-week book pages of government newspapers that have noticed it so far. On a separate sheet I'll copy a few bits from them, but probably they won't be much good. As soon as serious reviews appear, I'll send them on.

I thought I had sent Herbert Read's review, in the little paper Seven, of my Map of Love, but you said it hadn't reached you so I'll also copy out some of it. Read told me that he wrote about me in the Kenyon Review *before* reading the Map of Love, and that if he'd read it then he'd have altered much of what he said.

Doings and plans: I'm writing poems, trying to keep small wolves from the door and trying not to think of the Big Bad Wolf. I registered on April 6 on the military register, and will, if I pass the medical test, join an anti-aircraft battery early next month. Alone, I would object, but there is almost no chance of my being exempted by a Carmarthen chapel-headed tribunal and the most that I could hope for would be civilian non-combatant work: this would pay me nothing, and my family would be left destitute. By going into the army, I can keep them in food, & shelter them. Or the dear government can. I am disappointed that I cannot object, because the Germans are not my enemies, I do not want to die or kill, freedom's only a word and I'm a thinking body. Sentimentally, I prefer to be in the army than in the pacifist camps, to be among other poor buggers having a bad time. I shall be an abominable soldier. I hope I

---

[1] The book had been published in Britain on April 4.

shall have enough cynicism to carry me through, but all I can feel are personal loves and hates.

I had wanted to write a sequel to the Portrait: a year in London, but written as a continuous story: the flight into another convention: a proper city book, and far free-er in style than the slight, 'artful' other stories.[1] But this will have to wait, I write very slowly & need quiet & will be able to do very little in the army; after the war after the after lord god almighty perhaps I won't want to do that book at all, and am writing poems now to get them, excuse me, off my chest while there's a chest to get them off from.

I'll send some poems for the next number of N.D. before the army calls and snivelling I obey, and perhaps you'd like to use one of the Portrait stories too: I think the last one's best.

Do try to arrange some advance soon.

Dylan Thomas

Tell Patchen to write.

MS: the recipient

STEPHEN SPENDER
May 6 1940   c/o Marston Bishopston nr Swansea Glam

Dear Stephen,
    Just to let you know that this will be my address for a couple of weeks— in case anything comes, & lord it *must* come—out of the letters you terribly kindly wrote for me.[2] This is my father's house & it's very awkward to stay any length of time, so I do hope the patrons unbutton quickly.

    I went, by the way, to have another army medical examination, this time in Wales, & was found to be Grade III, which will keep me out of all the main army nastinesses and perhaps out of the army altogether.

Yours,
Dylan

MS: Harvard

GWYN JONES[3]
May 6 1940   c/o Marston Bishopston nr Swansea

Dear Gwyn Jones,
    Excuse my not answering before: I've been away.
    I'm very glad you're going to include my story 'The Tree' in your

---

[1] The 'city book' was *Adventures in the Skin Trade*.
[2] Spender had enlisted the help of Herbert Read, the critic, and Henry Moore, the sculptor, in raising money for Thomas.
[3] Professor Gwyn Jones (b. 1907), writer, translator and Norse scholar.

Penguin anthology,[1] and of course you may do so and I hereby give *my* formal assurance about copyright. The story was published by Dent.

I don't suppose there's a chance, is there, of my getting the four guinea fee beforehand? Do you think you could try for me? I'm in a very tough spot at the moment, I've had to take my family away from home until I can get enough money to pacify the tradesmen, and every penny I can get in advance for work I do want badly. And after all, the Penguin's very rich. Anyway, will you have a shot? It means a lot to me.

I hear they're doing a play of yours in the Swansea Little Theatre next week. Are you coming along to see it? If you'll tell me the night, perhaps we could meet afterwards. I hope so.

Yours sincerely,
Dylan Thomas

MS: the recipient

STEPHEN SPENDER
13 May 1940   c/o Marston Bishopston nr Swansea Glam

Dear Stephen,
Thanks for the letter, I do know it isn't an easy job for you to work out and carry out this appeal. But I misled myself and you when I told you that, as the medical board had graded me 3, I wouldn't be called up for a long time. I've been told now, authoritatively, that grade 3 people will be called up exactly the same time as the other, 1 & 2, people in my age-group—though, of course, for different work: mostly, I gather, noncombatant. It was the first kind of excitement following the result of the medical examination that led me to wish-imagine I wasn't, therefore, wanted for the army. But in your letters, surely none of these details need be gone into: the fact is that I *shall* be called up when the rest of my age-group is.[2] That can be said truthfully and simply; whether I'm called up to fire bullets or peel spuds doesn't, for the sake of this appeal, make much difference, does it? I didn't realise, anyway, that the whole grounds of your appeal would be that I was being called up. I thought that the filthily desperate state of my money life at the moment was the important reason for help. You asked for a few particulars:—

I've had to sneak my family away from our home in Carmarthenshire, because we could no longer obtain any credit and it was too awful to try to live there, among dunning and suspicion, from hand to mouth when I

---

[1] In the event, *Welsh Short Stories*, edited by Gwyn Jones, printed Thomas's 'A Prospect of the Sea'.

[2] Thomas was not called up. Whether he avoided military service by guile or incapacity has never been established. He told Dan Jones that he did it by turning up drunk for medical examinations.

knew the hand would nearly always be empty. I've had to leave all our books and clothes, most of my papers etc., and unless I pay our most important debts quickly, everything will be sold up: the beds & china & chairs & things that we've managed, with difficulty, to collect over three years. Now, until some money comes, we're staying here in my father's house: he's a very poor man and finds it, himself, hard to live: we're almost an intolerable burden on him, or, rather, we will be very very soon. I'm writing only poems now, those extremely slowly, and can expect very little money for them. I do not want to write another straight prosebook yet; it would eventually get me some money, I suppose, but it would mean ten or more poems less, which, I think, would be sad and silly for me. And when I am called up, if only to be latrine-minder, I shall obviously have less and less time in order to gain me even a few occasional pounds. My wife & myself have not a private penny. I do, a lot, want to return to Laugharne, Carmarthenshire, pay our debts, find ourselves in our own home again, live there working quietly until I am needed; & then to leave my family there, knowing they are, at least, clothed and housed. My debts amount almost exactly to £70. If I could get £100, I could settle everything & make a new start there: ensure food for the two others for a long time to come. If I cannot pay these debts & have a little to live on, there's no hope at all: everything we have collected and built up will go & I do not see where & how my wife & child can merely live. I cannot go away, leaving them nothing but debts & their lodging in another's poverty. I'd sooner die with them, & this little money worry is making a nervous fool of me when I want to be, and can be, solid and busy.

Thank you & Herbert Read & Henry Moore. I do hope something will happen from your kindness. And I hope this letter explains.

Yours,
Dylan

MS: Harvard

PETER WATSON[1]
June 2 1940   Laugharne Carmarthenshire S Wales

Dear Peter Watson,

Thank you very much for sending on the two cheques.[2] I never thought I'd have so much, and was frightfully pleased: I'll be able to settle everything now. As you see, I've gone back to this place.

You said, by the way, that the £10 cheque came from Lady Clark.

[1] Co-founder (with Cyril Connolly and Stephen Spender) of *Horizon*.
[2] Part of the response to Spender's appeal.

Should I thank her personally? I can't, of course, thank any of the others because I don't know who they are.

Yours,
Dylan

MS: Harvard

STEPHEN SPENDER
June 4 1940
[extract from letter written at Laugharne][1]

... The results were wonderful ... life's quite different now, and I'm beginning to work like a small, very slow horse.

SIR EDWARD MARSH
4 June 1940   Laugharne Carmarthenshire S Wales

Dear Sir Edward,
    I've just been given the names of the very generous subscribers to Stephen Spender's fund for me. Thank you, greatly, for your kindness. The result of the appeal was wonderful, I had never hoped to receive such help. It has made every difference to me, settled all my debts and enabled my family to go on living here certain of food and shelter for a long time to come. For your grand help in the past and now, I shall always be grateful.

Yours sincerely,
Dylan Thomas

MS: Berg

LAURENCE POLLINGER
4 June 1940   Sea View Laugharne Carmarthenshire

Dear Mr. Pollinger,
    I wonder if you could get Dent's to send me on the rest of the reviews of my last book. They've been very good about it, & you sent me a lot from

---

[1] Spender had this letter in 1976, when the extract was copied, but doesn't know where it is now.

them about 2 months ago—or less. But I know that several more have come out lately. I find the cuttings of great value, & *would* like to see them.

I know this isn't the time to think about poetry-publishing now, but would you sound Dent's as to the possibility of reprinting, some time, my *18 Poems*, which was originally published by The Parton Press. The copyright is mine. I'm wanting to know about the possibility of this, as a man called Tambimuttu, editor of some Poetry magazine & beginner of some small press, has asked me whether he can republish the poems in a very cheap edition. And obviously I'd prefer to have Dent's do them—for, say, 2/- or 2/6. I think they'd sell: I'm often having enquiries about them.

Yours sincerely,
Dylan Thomas

MS: Texas

VERNON WATKINS
Tuesday [?summer 1940]   Laugharne

Dear Vernon,
  TA for the great pound. I heard it singing in the envelope.
  Be an R.A.F. officer. You're too senile to be made to fly, and there's obviously more time to write poems when you're an officer than when you're creeping round corners slow as snails on your motorised scooter.
  Ring up Laugharne 3 and say that you'll come *this* weekend. We want you to very much.
  TA again, & be sure to come down, please.

Love
Dylan

MS: British Library   *VW*

VERNON WATKINS
[postmarked June 5 1940]   Sea View

Dear Vernon,
  The first word since the death of our date in No. 10,[1] when pimples would have put us in our places—though I think Caitlin would have frightened them, not frightened them away, perhaps, but certainly made

---

[1] A pub near the Swansea town centre.

each blush. What a lot of pities we never could arrange longer and noisier evenings: noisy with our own poems, and even with poor Yeats's or done Pound's. ('Well, what do you think of Paradise Lost?' 'It was the title got me.') But we had our moments, I heard Baille's Strand and two, at least, fine ones of your own, we heard Figaro and 'I am' very very high up in the Empire roof, Beethoven accompanied our croquet, you nearly caught us napping on the Worm[1]—and what would a stranger, hearing suddenly, make of that?—and, of course, we carefully missed Dot. Is she still in Pennard? Give her our love and tell her that God must consider us allergic: we don't. Can you come down here soon? You & Dot? You? We've distempered the rooms & made a cosy home: come and sit down, talking, on our deceptive chairs, and lie in the stormy bed of which Llewelyn now, most indirectly, owns half a leg—it was the proceeds of a poem to him, do you remember, that saved it.

Here's a poem.[2] I showed you the beginning, or *a* beginning, months—is it?—ago in Laugharne. Tell me straight away. I consider, at the just-finished illusionary glowing moment, it's good. I've never worked harder on anything, maybe too hard: I made such a difficult shape, too. Points: (1) I want a title for it. Can you suggest? Modern Love?[3] Wd that be affected? I've often wanted to use other people's titles, & once began my Ode On The Intimations Of Immortality. It is a poem about modern love. For some reason, I wrote a note under the poem in my copybook:

All over the world love is being betrayed as always, and a million years have not calmed the uncalculated ferocity of each betrayal or the terrible loneliness afterwards. Man is denying his partner man or woman and whores with the whole night, begetting a monstrous brood; one day the brood will not die when the day comes but will hang on to the breast and the parts and squeeze his partner out of bed. Or, as a title, One Married Pair. It's a poem of wide implications, if not of deep meanings, and I want a matter-of-fact, particular title.

(2) 'Helled and heavened shell'. Is this too clumsy? I like it, but it may be. (3) The longest line in the last verse: is this too—prosy? I wanted a very direct statement, but perhaps this straggles.

Write soon & tell me about yourself your poems & this.

Love,
Dylan

Will you type the bleeder? It's not so easy to type either. Hope you can see the arrangement of the length of lines.

MS: British Library   *VW*

---

[1] Watkins and Thomas were once nearly cut off on the Worm's Head.
[2] 'Into her lying down head.' The version that Thomas enclosed, printed in *VW*, differs from the *CP* version.
[3] 'Modern Love' is a poem about an unhappy marriage by George Meredith (1828–1909).

SIR HUGH WALPOLE[1]
8 June 1940   Laugharne Carmarthenshire S Wales

Dear Sir Hugh,
  I suppose that Stephen Spender has told you by this time of the terribly
good result of his appeal for me; he raised more lovely, important money
than I'd dared to hope; people's kindness has changed everything for me
except the war: now I can live here, working, for as long as I'm allowed,
with certain food and shelter for a long time for my family, and sure small
luxuries. Thank you, very much, for your generosity. It was very good to
think that you wished me so well, and I'll always be grateful.

                                          Yours sincerely,
                                          Dylan Thomas

MS: Texas

CLEMENT and JOHN DAVENPORT
June 8 1940   Laugharne Carmarthenshire S Wales

Dear Clement and John,
  I don't know if you're still in Marshfield: Roger told me in a letter just
about Christmas that you might be moving. How are you both?
  The author Hughes here is going to Bath, he's on the Admiralty now.
His wife wants to go with him. There's nowhere to stay in Bath. I told her
you lived—or used to live—a few miles outside, and she asked me to ask
you if you'd think of—if only for a week—swapping houses, hers for
yours. A week would do fine, or any time longer. She's got a nice house: I
hope it's possible for you to come, though I don't suppose it is. Do let me
know.

                                          Yours,
                                          Dylan

MS: Texas

[1] Sir Hugh Walpole (1884–1941), novelist.

JEAN OVERTON FULLER[1]

19 June 1940   Laugharne Carmarthenshire S. Wales

Dear Miss Fuller,

I hadn't heard anything about Vicky and Runia[2] for years, until a fortnight ago. Then Pamela Johnson wrote to tell me that Vicky had just died. I was very grieved to hear it: he was a sweet, wise man. Runia's address is 84 Boundary Road, N.W.8. At least, I suppose she's still there: I wrote her a letter, but haven't had a reply yet: probably she's too sad to write.

Yours sincerely,
Dylan Thomas

MS: the recipient

JAMES LAUGHLIN

20 June 1940   Laugharne Carmarthenshire S Wales

Dear Laughlin:

Thanks for the last letter you wrote dated exactly a month ago. Yes, do try to speed the agents on the new book contract so that I can have some money. It's getting harder to live here. And what bits there might be from the first book—as you suggested there might by now—I can do with. Hope the agents have heard from Dent's.

Here are some more bits from English reviews. A few new ones, and old ones I found. Some of them may be of use to your collection: how's it getting on? I don't quite understand what it is to be. Copying these reviews out makes me feel like a crab; and certainly no good.

Let me have, please, some American reviews to make me feel worse. I've only had that one in the Nation—was it?—and particularly want to see Aiken's.

I'm not in the army yet. I was passed unfit. I've got an unreliable lung. But I'll probably be used for something. Anyway, we're all in it. Or will be soon. No bombs here yet. Twenty miles away, though, last night.

I'll type some new poems today and let you have them separately. For Partisan Review, or whatever you think best. For the New Yorker, perhaps the poem beginning: 'There was a saviour'. What do you think?

Don't forget money. Try to make it soon.

Yours,
Dylan T

MS: the recipient

---

[1] Jean Overton Fuller (b. 1915), author, was a member of Victor Neuburg's literary circle in the mid-1930s. Her book *The Magical Dilemma of Victor Neuburg* deals with the period, as well as with Neuburg's involvement with Aleister Crowley.

[2] Runia Tharp, Neuburg's companion.

LAURENCE POLLINGER
22 June 1940   Sea View Laugharne Carmarthenshire

Dear Laurence Pollinger,

Here is a copy of *18 Poems*. I hope you can persuade Dent's to republish it. If they will republish, I suggest that I add *ten recent*—& *unpublished*, except in magazines—poems, which should help the sale. Auden did the same with his republished first poems (Faber) & the result was very successful: more for the money, & a fine contrast of the new & the old. I do think this would make a good book.

I can, if necessary, send along some reviews of *18 Poems*; by Edwin Muir & others; for the (possible) book jacket.

You will see that the *18 Poems* were published by the Parton Bookshop and the Sunday Referee. All this means is that the Sunday Referee, who were then running a weekly Poets' Corner or something silly like that, helped, a little, to finance the printing of the book. No contract was made, & the Referee, of course, took no royalties &, for that matter, no interest. The Parton Press no longer exists, & the copyright of the poems is mine. I made no contract, either, with the Parton Press. I can get, if Dent's should want it just for safety, a note from the chap who used to run the Parton Shop & Press corroborating me.

I'm not in the army—yet. I took Higham's advice & went before the military board who found me 3. Whatever that will come to mean.[1]

No word from America? I heard from Laughlin a week or two ago. He said that he was trying to find out at what price Dent's would make sheets, of the *Portrait of the Artist as a Young Dog*, for him, but that Ann Watkins & Co. hadn't given him, up to May 20, any reply. I hope this can be speeded up a bit; I need money.

Try to press these 18 Poems plus 10 new poems on Bozman,[2] won't you?

Yes, thank you. Dent sent on the rest of the reviews. Some very nice, some snooty.

                                        Yours,
                                        Dylan Thomas

MS: Texas

---

[1] Higham was unable to remember, thirty-five years later, what his advice had been.
[2] E. F. Bozman (1895–1968), editor-in-chief at J. M. Dent.

FRANCIS BRETT YOUNG[1]
4 July 1940   Laugharne Carmarthenshire S Wales

Dear Mr. Brett Young,
  Stephen Spender has just sent me the wonderful result of his appeal for
me. Thank you very much indeed for your generosity. I had never hoped
that the appeal would be so successful. Now I have been able to get out of
miserable debt, and begin again with money behind me. People's
kindness to me, a stranger, has altered everything, made me happy, &
allowed me to begin my own work again, knowing that knocks, bills,
tradesmen and a hundred impossible calls will not interrupt at every
second or nearly so. Thank you very much.

Yours sincerely,
Dylan Thomas

MS: University of Birmingham (UK)

LAURENCE POLLINGER
[late July 1940][2]   at The Malting House Marshfield
nr Chippenham Wilts[3]

Dear Laurence Pollinger:
  I'm sorry that Dent's won't do the Eighteen and Ten poems.[4] I haven't
any work fit for them to see yet, other than poems, as I find I have to
rewrite the short novel I have been working on. There should be enough,
in revised form, for Dent's to see quite soon.[5] This isn't an easy time to
work in, and I find I have to revise thoroughly everything I do. But there
will be some stuff. It's coming on.
  I think that Laughlin's royalty offers are bloody, and his idea of an
advance preposterous. 50 dollars, about twelve quid, for a whole book of
stories that might sell very well in America, in spite of what dear little
Laughlin says, seems to me to be absolutely unfair. I'm sure another
American publisher could be made to offer a more honest advance than

---

[1] Francis Brett Young (1884–1954), novelist.
[2] The letter was received on July 30.
[3] John Davenport's house, a handsome building in the main street of Marshfield (which is
     in Gloucestershire; the postal town was in Wiltshire), was briefly a refuge for writers and
     musicians in the first summer of the war, while the Battle of Britain was being fought over
     south-east England.
[4] In 1942 Thomas sold the rights in *18 Poems* to the Fortune Press, who reissued the book
     that year. The rights had to be repurchased in 1949, before Dent could plan the *Collected
     Poems*.
[5] Dent were asking for the prose book that was due to be delivered at the end of June. The
     unfinished 'short novel' (which was to remain unfinished for ever) was *Adventures in the
     Skin Trade*. All Thomas's references to 'novel' and 'prose book' over the next few years are
     to the *Adventures*.

that. However, I'll probably have to sign Laughlin's filthy contract as, oddly enough, I can't live without money in my pocket. And the stopping of Dent's monthly cheque will just about make me sign my entire future writings away for a guinea.

No news, I suppose, from Ann Watkins about placing the stories in American magazines? If she can't do anything with them soon, I should like to have them back as John Collier has written to me from America to say that he thinks he can place some of the stories himself.

Yours sincerely,
Dylan Thomas

MS: Texas

MISS M. CRANSTON (Pollinger's secretary)
Aug 6 1940 (About anthology permissions and money. See Appendix 23.)

VERNON WATKINS
8 August, I think [1940]   at The Malting House nr Chippenham Wilts

Dear Vernon,
It shows what a terribly long time we haven't written each other: I've been here for nearly 2 months, and you still think I'm in Laugharne. So I can't come this weekend, however much I want to, and I do want to very much. What a sensational postcard you sent me, & only comfortable, wild Pwll Du on the front. Dot going to Japan & you joining the army; dear God. Have you joined, or are you conscripted? Do tell me everything about it. And why a motorcycle driver?[1] I know what your motor-driving's like from Pendine sands. I'm not going to say *you're* barmy, but the chaps who engaged you to drive on the public roads must be very strange little men with curling beards & tall white hats. But I want to know *all* about the decision & mystery. Please write soon.

I'm staying here in John Davenport's house. He's an amateur writer & musician, extremely able, weighing nineteen stone. It's a big house, full of books & pianos & records. There are lots of other people staying here too: Lennox Berkeley, Arnold Cooke (who remembers you very well at Repton. Do you remember him?) who are both professional composers, Antonia White, and William Glock.[2] Aren't they nice names? Davenport

---

[1] Watkins had applied to join the Army's field security police.
[2] Sir Lennox Berkeley (b. 1903), composer. Arnold Cooke (b. 1906), composer. Antonia White (1899–1980), writer. Sir William Glock (b. 1908), musician, later the BBC's Controller of Music.

& I are writing a fantastic thriller together,[1] so I haven't done a poem for a long time although there are 2 I want to write badly: both nightmares, I'm afraid. Oh Europe etcetera please do be bettera.

A great old friend—he's neither great nor old—came for last weekend: Jim Thornton. And his wife. I gave him your address. Perhaps you've heard from him by this time. I hope so.

The other Llewelyn poems are in Life & Letters, are they? I'll get a copy. I want to see them a lot. Llewelyn is with Caitlin's mother at the moment, but we'll have to have him back soon because we both miss him, especially Caitlin.

I don't know what my own plans are. I want a job very badly, because I haven't a penny: quite as a matter of fact, not a penny. If you ever have 5 shillings you hate, I shan't. I've applied for a BBC job, but I think my lack of university will spoil it. It wd be a very well paid job, but boring: making preces (I mean summaries) of the world's news for Empire bulletins.

Caitlin & I go bicycling nearly every day. I love it. I wish you could come here, I wish I cd see you. Do write straightaway & tell me the whole stories.

I'll write a long letter by return.

Love from C & me,
Dylan

Remember me to your pa & ma, please

MS: British Library   *VW(R)*

J. ROYSTON MORLEY, BBC
August 20 1940 [telegram]

SCRIPT ARRIVING PADDINGTON BETWEEN 2.30 AND 3
WEDNESDAY AFTERNOON SORRY FOR DELAY. DYLAN THOMAS.

Original: BBC

J. ROYSTON MORLEY[2]
Wed [August 1940]   Malting House Marshfield nr Chippenham Wilts

Dear Morley,

Here's nearly all the abomination. The last bit of a scene—about a typed page—I'll send on tomorrow: you'll have it first post Thursday. If

---

[1] The *King's Canary* spoof. Davenport had replaced Charles Fisher as collaborator.
[2] John Royston Morley, then at the BBC, had known Thomas before the war. As editor of a literary magazine, *Janus*, he printed a story by Thomas, 'The Horse's Ha'.

this stuff is really *too* bad, do tell me straight away.[1]

On the telephone you said this morning that we'd arranged to have lunch Thursday. Was it just a slip? Friday you told me was the best day to come. I'll ring you Friday morning.

Do have this typed before you read it: it will look a little less bloody.

> Yours
> Dylan Thomas

MS: BBC

BBC
21 August 1940   at The Malting House Marshfield Gloucester

Dear Sir,

I agree to the fee of 12 guineas for the broadcast of my script on the Duque de Caxias; and with the script rights you detailed.

I should be very glad if I could be paid the fee fairly soon—I have written the script & delivered it—as I have already had to make one journey to London in connection with the script & will have to make another journey tomorrow. I can't really afford these visits.

> Yours faithfully,
> Dylan Thomas

MS: BBC

VERNON WATKINS
[summer 1940]   Malting House Marshfield nr Chippenham Wilts

Dear Vernon,

God, yes, how awful it must have looked. But I didn't get the 2 quid. Mad things have been happening to letters: I've lost one before, about 3 weeks ago. I think this house must be marked, & the letters opened. Really. The house, as I told you, is full of musicians, all are young men, not one is in the army, one has a German name, there *was* a German staying here some time ago, and there have also been five lighting offences in about six weeks. Perhaps a lucky censor got your lovely present. I am so sorry, for you & for me. 2 crinklers. And at bank-bombing time too. I thought that your not answering my letter was because you'd

---

[1] Morley had commissioned a short script about the Duque de Caxias, to be broadcast to Brazil. This was the start of Thomas's career as a scriptwriter.

been hijacked into the army. I couldn't realize *you* were waiting for an answer from *me*.

I can't imagine Gower bombed. High explosives at Pennard. Flaming onions over Pwlldu. And Union Street ashen.[1] This is all too near. I had to go to London last week to see about a BBC job, & left at the beginning of the big Saturday raid. The Hyde Park guns were booming. Guns on the top of Selfridges. A 'plane brought down in Tottenham Court Road. White-faced taxis still trembling through the streets, though, & buses going, & even people being shaved. Are you frightened these nights? When I wake up out of burning birdman dreams—they were frying aviators one night in a huge frying pan: it sounds whimsical now, it was appalling then—and hear the sound of bombs & gunfire only a little way away, I'm so relieved I could laugh or cry. What *is* so frightening, I think, is the idea of greyclothed, grey-faced, blackarmletted troops marching, one morning, without a sound up a village street. Boots on the cobbles, of course, but no Heil-shouting, grenading, goosestepping. Just silence. That's what Goebbels has done for me. I get nightmares like invasions, all successful. (Ink gone)

I saw, and of course liked for I'd known nearly all of it before, the Llewelyn poems. Have you any time for writing now? Will you let me see something new? I've collaborated in a detective story and am just about to begin a short story. I do scripts for the BBC, to be translated into, & broadcast to, Brazil. I've got an exciting one to do next, on Columbus. But I haven't settled down to a poem for a long time. I want to, & will soon, but it mustn't be nightmarish.

I just looked again at your last letter, and you said in it that bombs were falling on the cliffs. I hope they missed you. Where is the nearest air-raid shelter? Singleton? You must run very fast. In this house Caitlin & I have our bedroom on the top floor, and so far we haven't got up even when the German machines are over us like starlings. But I think we'll have to, soon. My mother wrote & told me that people are sleeping on the Gower beaches, in barns and hedges. I went to see a smashed aerodrome. Only one person had been killed. He was playing the piano in an entirely empty, entirely dark canteen.

What are our Swansea friends doing? Is Fred still crossgartering fruit and faces? drilling? objecting? I don't hear from him ever. Life & Letter, of course. My father said he saw him in an airbattle over the town, standing in the middle of the street, his long neck craned.

I don't know at all when we'll be back in the ruins. I'll have to go to London so often, once—& if ever—this job gets really going. I'd love to see you before you undrive your motorcycle. No chance of us meeting in London? We've never done that. That would be lovely.

Write soon. Forgive this unavoidable & rude-appearing delay. Sorry, very sorry, sorrier than I can tell you, about the death of the pounds.

---

[1] From the summer of 1940, Swansea suffered frequent air raids at night.

Lower me immediately on the equinoctial list of dislikes.

> Love from Caitlin & me.
> Remember me to your people. I hope the
> bombs won't touch the croquet lawn.
> We must all play next summer.
>
> Dylan

MS: British Library   *VW*

VERNON WATKINS
[summer 1940]   [postmarked Chippenham]

Dear Vernon,

It was lovely to hear from you. Thank you for the rest of the lost present. It was needed, alright: by others. I'm in debt, & need my job quickly. Perhaps we're both marked. You translate Hölderlin & swear in German to the Home Guards; I have no visible means of support, & have been known to call the war bloody and silly. I hope there's a special censor for our letters: a man who keeps a miserable family on the strength of attempting to decode our innocent messages.

I hope Dot will like Japan. Would she care for me to write to Empson, asking him for addresses of some of his friends? He was there for years, & knows a lot of people. He'd like to. Old Japanese professors. Pale tea & poetry afternoons. I wish we were going there too, I could do with a bit of inscrutability. Europe is hideously obvious and shameless. Am I to rejoice when a 100 men are killed in the air?

Is the Pioneer Corps non-combatant? Was Fred happy about it?[1] Do you know his address? I'd like to write to him, even tho he won't answer. I'll enjoy seeing his war-pictures: the veins of a leaf that blew from a shelled tree; the crisscrosses on the head of a spent bullet. He should do widespread camouflage work, & make Oldham look like the back of a herring.

I can't do much work, either. I go for long bicycle rides, thinking: 'Here I am on a bicycle in a war.' I play whist with musicians, & think about a story I want to call 'Adventures in the Skin-trade'. I've finished my poem about invasion, but it isn't shapely enough to send you yet.[2]

Caitlin dances every day in a private Roman Catholic chapel.

Remember me to your mother & father.

Don't forget: cover the croquet lawn, bury your poems in a stout box, & don't stare at the sky too much. The wrong wings are up there.

Thank you again. I'll come to Wales soon.

> Love,
> Dylan

MS: British Library   *VW*

[1] Fred Janes had joined the Pioneer Corps.
[2] 'Deaths and Entrances.'

LAURENCE POLLINGER
[summer 1940] (Returns U.S. contract. See Appendix 24.)

BBC
28 x 40 (Seeks payment for 'Columbus' script. See Appendix 25.)

JOHN LEHMANN
11 Nov 1940   c/o Malting House Marshfield Chippenham Wilts

Dear John Lehmann,
    I'll be very glad to be a contributor to the Penguin New Writing.[1] Thank
you for writing. I haven't finished any new stories yet, but I hope I will
have by the time you've fixed the publishing details.
    I'm glad you like my Portrait of the Artist as a Young Dog. I'm going to
start soon to write a continuation of it: one long story about London.

                                        Yours sincerely,
                                        Dylan Thomas

MS: Texas

M. J. TAMBIMUTTU
Monday 11th Nov '40   Malting House Marshfield
                                        near Chippenham Wilts

Dear Tambimuttu:
    Sorry I wasn't able to reply before. I haven't been at any of the addresses
you wrote to, & some of them were very slow being forwarded.
    And I'm sorry I haven't a poem for the November number. The last
poem I did I've just sent away somewhere else: before hearing from you.
It's a pity; I should like very much to be included.

[1] The influential *Penguin New Writing* first appeared in 1940, the idea suggested by the
periodical *New Writing* which Lehmann edited from 1936.

I'll certainly be able to send you a poem or two for the Jan 15th number. I'm glad you're beginning again.[1]

Good luck,
Dylan Thomas

MS: Texas

BBC
24 November 1940   The Malting House Marshfield Gloucestershire

Dear Sir,
I shall be glad to accept a fee of twelve guineas for the feature programme on the march of the Czech Legion across Russia in the last war, which is to be broadcast in your Overseas programmes.

I have not, by the way, been paid yet for a programme I did several weeks ago on Christopher Columbus, broadcast Overseas. The sum Mr. Harding[2] and I had agreed upon was fifteen guineas, as the programme lasted nearly an hour. I should be extremely grateful if you could arrange to have this paid me.

Yours faithfully,
Dylan Thomas

MS: BBC

ROYSTON MORLEY
24 Nov 1940   The Malting House Marshfield Gloucestershire

Dear Royston Morley,
Thank you for your letter. It'll be nice doing another programme. I'll remember what you said. I haven't got much interesting material yet— can't find, in Bristol, any books in which the march is fully written up— but I'm writing to the Czech Legation. If you do happen to come across the name of any book or article, do let me know.

Best wishes,
Yours sincerely,
Dylan Thomas

MS: BBC

---

[1] After the first three issues in 1939, *Poetry* had failed to appear.
[2] Archie Harding was a BBC features and drama producer.

ROYSTON MORLEY
[?1940]

Dear Morley,
   The last page. Is this kind of propaganda too sticky? I hope to be able to know soon much more exactly what's wanted. Could I have a script to do without battles, d'you think? Or perhaps with only 20 or 30?

Yours,
Dylan T

MS: BBC

LORD HOWARD DE WALDEN[1]
24 December 1940   c/o Marston Bishopston Gower
                                                      near Swansea Glam

Dear Lord Howard
   I've just posted to you, separately, a copy of my American book. I thought it had been sent a long time ago, but I found it at the bottom of a suitcase I was packing this morning before leaving here. It's very very careless of me, and I think it must look ungrateful too. And it can't even reach you for Christmas; it'll have to be a very small thank-you for the New Year.
   I've left the place I was staying at in Wiltshire for many weeks now, as the friends who were putting us up couldn't afford to any longer. We — that's my wife & myself and our son—must leave here too, straightaway, because this is my mother's house and she can't afford us either. We can put the baby with someone, and then go to London which is the only place I know where there are a couple of friends with spare rooms.
   You said, in your letter, that you hoped you would be able to help me again sometime; and I'm desperately sorry that the sometime I do need help again should be so very soon after your last great kindness. I'll understand at once, of course, if you're quite unable to spare anything, at this ghastly time, to someone who can have no claim at all upon you and to whom you've been so good already and so recently. All I can do is to tell you how I'm fixed. We are now quite homeless. What I need is just enough to let me look around for a cottage somewhere in Wales where we can begin again to try to live and work alone. We could, perhaps, get along for a little time in London—I don't know how—but obviously couldn't have our baby there. I have begun a prose book, and will be paid for it quite well when it's finished, but I must have somewhere to live quietly until it is. And I don't think London—even if we could manage to exist there—is the right place. There's sure to be a cottage in Pembrokeshire or

---

[1] Thomas Evelyn Scott-Ellis, 8th Baron (1880–1946), patron of music and drama in Wales. The family has Welsh connections.

Carmarthenshire I could hire cheaply, but as it is I can't even go to look for it let alone pay the first month or so's rent. I believe my book could be good, and I want to write it more than anything else in the world. I'm not in debt now—your cheque settled most of that months ago—so that we could begin without any arrears and shadows, if we *could* begin.

If you were able to help me, I should like very much for you to consider it as a loan to be repaid on the finishing of my book. And, please, I don't mean that to be presumptuous or impertinent. Perhaps I would be able to repay the loan even earlier, as I'm trying to put my case in front of the Royal Literary Fund who have refused me, in the past, on the grounds, mainly, that I am not old enough to need support.

Will you write to me? Your letter will be forwarded to London from this address.

I'm really deeply grateful to you, and I hope you like some of the things, in the American book, that you haven't read before.

I'm enclosing several poems done during the last six months. I hope you'll be able to find enough time to read one or two of them anyway.

Yours sincerely
Dylan Thomas

MS: Texas

JAMES LAUGHLIN
25th December 1940   c/o Marston Bishopston near Swansea S Wales

Dear Laughlin,

It's my Saviour's birthday today, and I'm reminded of what's owed to me. You never sent my six authorised copies of the Portrait of the A as a Y.D. Nor the reviews of The World I Breathe (which I particularly want to see; Aiken's[1] very much so), nor the pamphlet you were bringing out. For my side of it, did I ever acknowledge the cheque on advance of royalties for the Portrait? I've got an idea I didn't, owing to the bombs. Anyway, thank you. Will you send your things along as soon as you can? I'd like to hear from you, too.

Fortunately I'm not in the army yet. I've been living in London,[2] which is

---

[1] Conrad Aiken, American author, in *Poetry* (Chicago).
[2] Thomas's movements, never easy to follow, become baffling in wartime. He wrote fewer letters than before, and shuttled between Wales and London, seeking work and dodging bombs. Constantine FitzGibbon and others think he was writing scripts for propaganda films—his bread and butter for several years—from 1940. Theodora FitzGibbon says (in her autobiography *With Love*) that Thomas went to see Donald Taylor of Strand Films on 8 September 1940. But the scriptwriting came a year or so later. Once he began work for Strand, Thomas was paid £8 or £10 a week, which doesn't agree with the Welsh-bound poverty evident in his 1941 letters. See his letter to Vernon Watkins, page 493.

exciting, and writing a few poems and trying to get hold of some money. Hope to hear soon.

Yours,
Dylan Thomas

MS: the recipient

SIR HUGH WALPOLE

27 December 1940   temporarily c/o Marston Bishopston Gower
Glamorgan

Dear Sir Hugh,

I'm trying to get a grant from the Royal Literary Fund. I tried about two years ago, but I'd published only two books then and the granters didn't think that that was enough or that the books were good enough. Now I've published three more, and I've been told my chances are much better—if I can get one or two strong recommendations. You were extraordinarily kind to me when Stephen Spender was collecting some money for me once, and I wonder if you'd be kind enough to help me again by writing a little letter saying that I deserve a grant.[1] The committee—who've been acquainted with the details—are bound to see that I need money, but it's going to be harder to persuade them that my poems and stories are worth it.

Perhaps you'll wonder why I'm broke again after Stephen's fund. All that that collected went almost at once on old debts for rent & tradesmen, and I've been living since then with some friends who can't afford us any longer. Now we're homeless. I must look for a cottage but can't travel to look and couldn't pay a week's rent if I found one. I was going to go into the army, but the Medical Board rejected me at the last moment. I've begun a prose book but it'll take a good time to finish & I've nowhere to live & nothing to live on until it is.

If you could spare the time to write a letter I know that it would have a tremendous influence, and I'd be very very grateful. The address is: H.J.C. Marshall Esq. Royal Literary Fund, Stationers' Hall, E.C.4.

I'm awfully sorry to bother you. I wouldn't if my need wasn't great to me.

I'll always appreciate your kindness.

Yours sincerely,
Dylan Thomas

MS: Texas

---

[1] Walpole obliged with a letter to say he thought Thomas 'a genuine and promising poet with, I think, a touch of something like genius'.

H. J. C. MARSHALL (Royal Literary Fund)
January 1 1941   c/o Marston Bishopston near Swansea Glamorgan

Dear Mr. Marshall,

Mr. Astbury,[1] whom I saw some weeks ago, has just written to tell me that you are willing to put forward to the Committee of the Royal Literary Fund a further application on my behalf.

The Committee did not grant my previous application, and you told me, in a letter, that their main reason was that I had not produced enough literary work of sufficiently high merit. I had then published only two books. Three new books of mine have been published since, however: two in England and one in the U.S.A. The titles of my books are:

18 Poems   (1934)
25 Poems   (1936)
The Map of Love   (1939)   (Poems & Stories)
Portrait of the Artist As A Young Dog   (1940)   (Stories)
The World I Breathe   (1940)   (Poems & Stories).

I am collecting another book of poems—which should be ready in the spring of this year—and have just begun a long prose book.

I am married, and have a son aged two.

For the last six months we have been staying with some friends who can no longer afford to support us. Now we are quite homeless and haven't one penny. We are staying temporarily with my father, who is a poor man and not really able to feed, even for a short period, three more mouths. We have nowhere at all to go when we leave here, which must be very very soon.

I need urgently to find somewhere in the country, rooms or a cottage, where I can keep my family and work on the prose book I have just begun. I have a contract with J. M. Dent's, and will be paid for this book when it is finished, but I do not know how or where to live while I am writing it nor how to support my wife & son.

I am medically exempted from the Army because of my lungs.

I have written already to Sir Hugh Walpole, Mr. J. B. Priestley, and Mr. Edwin Muir, asking them if they would be so kind as to recommend my work to your Committee, and I will ask some other writers too to say a word for me.

If they are needed, I could send you a selection of press cuttings about my work; also some articles on it which have been printed in periodicals recently.

My need is really great. I do not see how we can continue to live unless I am given some support. If I can be given money enough to feed and shelter us & to enable me to work hard without the ceaseless worries caused by our homelessness and pennilessness, I know I can produce two books this year: poems & prose. I want to write these books, and to feed

---

[1] B. E. Astbury, of the Charity Organisation Society.

and shelter my family while I am writing them, more than anything in the world.

If you want any other details about me or my work, I shall be very glad to send them to you.

Yours sincerely,
Dylan Thomas

MS: Royal Literary Fund

JOHN DAVENPORT
Jan 8 1941   c/o Marston Bishopston Glamorgan

Dear John,

I had a telephone by my side last night so I had to ring you up. It was lovely to hear Clement. It was good to see you in London too, and I liked the Queens lunch with rednose and his belonging girl, and shabby humped elegant Pulham,[1] and barmy Archer[2] apologising for eating, and us, and port and mussels. It was grand, just like the old times we never really had together in London. But the second meeting was an absolute daze to me, and I slept in the dark bombed room like a pig and I was obstreperous and over-confidential, closing one eye, and weepy and repetitive, during the moments awake. I hope I wasn't too much for you, for a rather sinister countryman in his town club, menacer of Churches,[3] of devious and improbable connections, living up to de Walden's income, the largest host in London. 'So this is what they call a host. I'd forgotten.' Remember that architectural beard at the beginning of the 4 hour lunch? I rang you up the next morning, but you'd gone with Dawes to the country, so we went after lunch, travelling for about nine hours, and some officers in the restaurant car thought I was a spy—me—and asked to see my identity card which I didn't have all because I wore a black hat and because a young Welsh boy in naval uniform was sitting opposite me, copying out his poems on small bits of paper and handing them to me slyly across the table.

After buying a few useless things—did Clement get her salonscene ?—the Watson money[4] disappeared, quick as a sardine, and we've been cooped up here, in little, boiling rooms, for nearly three weeks, quite broke, waiting for the second instalment: or, anyway, waiting for little sums to carry us over while we wait. Today the pipes burst, and Caitlin, in a man's hat, has been running all day with a mop from w.c. to flooded

---

[1] Peter Rose Pulham, painter and photographer.
[2] David Archer.
[3] No doubt a gibe at Richard Church.
[4] Peter Watson of *Horizon*. The magazine published the poem 'Deaths and Entrances' in January.

parlour, while I've been sitting down trying to write a poem about a man who fished with a woman for bait and caught a horrible collection.[1]

I finished the Czech script, three weeks late, and sent it on to Morley with a rude note, as though it were his fault. The script uses five announcers, and if Archie Harding doesn't fall for that I'll lie down with his wife's hobby. 'War. The shadow of the eagle is cast on the grazing lands, the meadows of Belgium are green no longer, and the pastures are barbed with bayonets. War. War.' Five announcers, and a chorus of patriots crying 'Siberia', 'Freedom of Man', 'Strengthen us for the approaching hour' like a bunch of trained bulls.

I told Clement on the telephone that we were thinking of going back to Laugharne to live, for a time; sharing a house there with the owner of the buses, the garage, the pub, the electric plant, the cockles, and, no doubt, eventually, us. As soon as I can I'm going down to inspect. Perhaps you & Clement will come to see us, once, and if, we're settled?

I know I did apologise, in town, for my not writing after that morning rush away from Marshfield, but I haven't apologised to Clement. All I can say is: I was very muddled and unhappy, and didn't feel a bit like having any contact at all—until the muddles were straightened in my head — with anyone in the place where for so many months I had been so happy.[2] You gave me a wonderful time; the summer talked itself away; and our book was the Best of its Kind or unkind, and Arnold and Lennox and Eric Dawes were fine new friends, and I loved our Club of Bad Books, and Antonia, buttoned, unbuttoned, dame, flapper, was always a charmer and a caution. I had the nicest, fullest time for years. Thank you both.

If I can—and Clement said I may—I'll try to come to Marshfield next weekend. We must do the last pages of the Canary then, and have it published quickly and make some money and enemies.

I heard yesterday from Frank Swinnerton[3] about my application to the Royal Literary Fund. He's on the Committee, but won't be able to attend the January meeting although he's written a letter supporting me. Priestley & Walpole have also written.[4] But Swinnerton says I must try to canvass some of the other members so that they'll appear at the meeting and squash the opposition of the older boys who would rather give

---

[1] 'Ballad of the Long-legged Bait.'
[2] Perhaps Thomas was distressed because that summer he detected Caitlin in a love affair. She was infatuated with one of his acquaintances, and arranged to spend the night with him at a Cardiff hotel. Covering her tracks by visiting Thomas's parents in Swansea, she sold some of the household effects at Laugharne, bought pretty clothes with the proceeds, and went to the assignation. (It ended farcically, by Caitlin's account: 'We just lay there and nothing happened'.) Thomas, left behind at Marshfield, found out, probably from his mother, that a night was missing from Caitlin's itinerary. They had violent rows, and for a while he refused to sleep with her.
[3] Frank Swinnerton (1884–1982), novelist.
[4] The novelist J. B. Priestley (1894–1984) wrote to Marshall (January 6) that he thought it unfair of them to have refused Thomas in 1938: 'his work may be difficult, obscure and not to the taste of most of the Committee, [but it] is taken very seriously by the younger critics'.

compassionate help to a poor old bedridden girl who once wrote an ode to the Queen than to an unintelligible young man who should be earning his living by bum or stamp licking, national service, family name etc.

He tells me to write immediately to de la Mare,[1] J. C. Squire, Alec Waugh.[2] The main thing is to write very quickly, to get them there for the meeting rather than to get them to write a few words; & I haven't any of their addresses. Could you drop a line to Waugh and/or Squire? Where could I get hold of de la Mare? It's a bother for you, I know, but if I can get a grant straight away I'll be able to settle my debts. If I don't get a grant, the debtees will have to wait until my Watson comes in. Swinnerton seems to think that de la Mare (who we must have in our parodies, by the way) and Sir Frank Knight wd go *specially* to the meeting if they were given enough warning. Can you help?

How are Clement's angels and devils? Kingsmill-shockers?[3] horned or Samite Davenports?

My mother says she re-addressed several letters to Marshfield *before* Christmas: a registered couple of quid, a tiny cheque from the College of Wales. And you said there were one or two things, askings for anthologies, from America. Do forward them if you can find them, John, as we want the little sums dreadfully to carry us over until Watson & grant. As it is, we can't go out in the evenings at all, can't go to Swansea, buy fags, see a film.

I told Vernon Watkins about Arnold wanting to set songs. Would Arnold like to still? I'll get Vernon to send some if he does.

Much love to Clement, Arnie blarney, and you.

Dylan

MS: Texas   *SL(R)*

H. J. C. MARSHALL
9 Jan 1941   c/o Marston Bishopston nr Swansea Glamorgan

Dear Mr. Marshall:

I hope you received my letter early last week, in which I applied for a grant from the Royal Literary Fund. I have been worried about it, as Stationers' Hall, E.C.4. didn't seem a detailed enough address, although it was the one Mr. Astbury gave me.

I omitted, in that letter, to say this:

After being rejected by the Army, for which I volunteered, I tried hard

---

[1] The poet Walter de la Mare (1873–1956) supported the application, but with less enthusiasm: the obscurity of Thomas's poems ('which personally I think is rather excessive') restricted their appeal to a narrow audience.
[2] Alec Waugh (1898–1981), novelist.
[3] Hugh Kingsmill (Lunn) (1889–1949), author and journalist, another occupant of Thomas's derisive gallery of 'men of letters'.

to get some work of national service, and, when that failed, mainly owing to my illhealth, I tried to get work of any kind. I tried to get into the monitoring service of the BBC, for example,—a job that illhealth wouldn't bar me from—but my application wasn't answered. So I realised that I would have to live, & to support my family, entirely on my writing. And only when we found ourselves homeless, and without any money at all—as we are now—did I turn to the R.L.F.

I'm mentioning this because I do think that the Committee should know that I *have* tried to make my living by non-literary work, as most young writers have done in the past, and that I still hope I may find some national work to do. My troubles are now immediate—I do not think we can stay here more than another week, and, after that, there is nowhere for us at all—and that is why I am asking the R.L.F. for a grant.

I would very much appreciate it if you would let me know whether my previous letter, and, of course, this letter, have arrived safely.

Yours sincerely,
Dylan Thomas

MS: Royal Literary Fund

JOHN DAVENPORT
16th January 1941   c/o Marston Bishopston nr Swansea

Dear John,
Sorry not to be able to manage this weekend to finish off the book and see to the collecting & sending here—or somewhere else—of our goods. I've just heard from Laugharne that there are some other rooms vacant there, and that we should go down to have a look at them, and to reserve them if they're all right, before soldiers or evacuees come along. I must go; although there's no chance yet of my doing anything but promising to take the rooms 'sometime', even if they were entirely suitable.

I've written to de la Mare. No answer yet. Thank you for wiring. I'm glad you think you've roused Squire & Waugh.

The cheque was kind and grand. It will take us to Laugharne & perhaps pay a first instalment on the possible reservation. What writing? It's the only money I've had since Christmas.

About money, all I can say is, quoting, more or less, your letter: If, and when, I get money from any of my possible sources, I do really feel that you ought to have some of it. I'll try, as soon as, and if, the money comes, to give you a share of it; and of any other monies, soon or future, that might, and will, I hope, be coming. That *is* all I can say, apart from: whatever, of course, comes from our joint book shall be all yours. Now, I have in the world only some of the fiver, most of it, you sent me, and a few dim possibilities. I've Caitlin to keep, and a home to find, and Llewelyn to take away at once from Ringwood. We *must* leave here by the beginning of February; it's extremely awkward staying here at all. My gratitude to you & Clement is not 'dim or fading', and soon I hope I'll be able to show you practically. All I don't want you to imagine is that, having partially helped to impoverish you, I am now living in a conscienceless luxury. I am penniless & homeless. Asking me for money seems a not very kind joke now. *My* responsibilities, too, are growing & heavy. I do appreciate your position, John, and I'm sure you'll appreciate mine. All I can do now is to wait & hope. I want to pay you just as much as I must keep Caitlin, Llewelyn, & myself. I hope I can do both, & soon too.

Love to Clement. Remember me to Arnold again.

Dylan

MS: Texas

H. J. C. MARSHALL
16th Jan 1941   c/o Marston Bishopston nr Swansea S Wales

Dear Mr. Marshall,

Thank you for the form. The post had been held up, and the first form arrived only a day or two before the second.

I am sending you two of my last three published books under separate cover.

I see that you have marked clause I of the Regulations.[1] I understood that the first long letter I sent you—plus the added note of January 9—would be sufficient; but if it isn't, I would be grateful if you would let me know, so that I can detail again the causes of distress etc.

Yours sincerely,
Dylan Thomas

MS: Royal Literary Fund

H. J. C. MARSHALL
17 Jan 1941 (Sends three books. See Appendix 26.)

---

[1] The applicant was required to write a letter 'stating the *causes of his (or her) Distress* . . .'

JOHN DAVENPORT
27 January 1941   Marston Bishopston Swansea

Dear John,

No, the sneer wasn't justified. My silence has been accidental, not a dignified or otherwise reproof for your Financial Times. We had to go to Laugharne, to see about lodgings for the future, and we've only just come back, having failed to find them. Before I went, I wrote you a letter in answer to your first long one, and caught a bus in such a hurry that I had to leave the letter to be posted by someone here. It wasn't posted. I enclose the letter, with apologies for the silly, careless delay.

Thanks v much for writing to Sir Frank. I enjoyed his knightly note to you. What is he: author or gentleman? To me he said only that I could take his support for granted—(but not along the street?)—and that my handwriting had almost ruined his already failing eyesight. De la Mare has also promised support at the Meeting of the Burke & Hare Peerage. And, thanks, too, for talking to Alec Waugh. I don't know how I've 'offended him in some way', considering that I've never met him. I offend enough people I meet, especially my friends, without giving annoyance to total strangers. I'm glad he wrote to Marshall, but I hated his note to you: 'advise Dylan to write more stories and fewer letters.' I should like to write to the Petroleum Department—what's he doing there? gathering material for another oily novel?—advising 'Alec to write fewer stories and more letters', always supposing that there could be anyone who wanted to receive them. When I want advice from Alec Waugh, I'll go to his brother.[1] Perhaps I did write to too many English authors, but it was at Swinnerton's suggestion; and Swinnerton, by this time, must know the English Literary Scene like the back of his crossed palm.

As you'll see from the delayed letter, I have already surrendered to you all problematical rights & monies of the Canary without a tail. So that leaves a sum which, in time, I hope to be able to pay off.

I'm thinking of trying to live, eventually, somewhere in Cornwall. Come to St. Ives & see the bigbrimmed ghost of Laura Knight,[2] the flesh of Lamorna Birch,[3] the absence of flesh of Dod Proctor, and the authentic hole in the wall where Wallace B. Nichols pulls the glowingly alive pageant of history out of his little ear. I know a man who keeps a pub in St. Ives, and might stay there.

I'll try my best to come along on February 7. If I can't come, it will only be because I can't move from here—here where it is growing more

---

[1] Alec Waugh wrote to Marshall to 'strongly support' the application, adding, 'I don't like his work and I don't like anything I hear about him as a person. But he is producing work that is respected by people competent to judge . . .'.

[2] Dame Laura Knight (1877–1970), painter.

[3] Samuel John Birch (1869–1955), painter, adopted the name 'Lamorna' from the Cornish village where he worked.

intolerable every minute—or can only afford to move Caitlin & myself to another temporary lodging.

I've asked Vernon, whose poems Faber's might be doing in the spring, to send Arnold his songs. Less lumbago to Arnold.

Yours ever,
Dylan

MS: Texas

LAURENCE POLLINGER
27 Jan 1941   c/o Marston Bishopston nr. Swansea Glamorgan

Dear Pollinger,
   Many apologies for not writing sooner. Everything's been very muddled for me, and I've been living, or trying to live, all over the place for several months now. I hope to have those books ready to send you soon. As soon as, in a less temporary home than this, I can get down to finishing them.
   Will you send, in the future, whatever is to be sent to me c/o the above address? *Not* Marshfield, Chippenham, which is now a dead address.
   I wonder if you could find out for me how my 'Portrait of the Artist' went, as regards sales? And whether there's any money due to me on it yet? I need all I can get, badly.

Yours,
Dylan Thomas

MS: Texas

M. J. TAMBIMUTTU
19 February 1941 (Sends poems by Veronica St Clear Maclean. See Appendix 27.)

H. J. C. MARSHALL
2 March 1941   c/o Marston Bishopston nr. Swansea

Dear Mr. Marshall,
   Sorry not to have acknowledged the R.L.F. cheque before.[1] I've been away from this address, and the letter wasn't forwarded.
   Thank you for the trouble you've taken.

Yours sincerely,
Dylan Thomas

MS: Royal Literary Fund

[1] The Fund made a grant of £50.

JOHN LEHMANN
13 March 1941   Marston Bishopston nr Swansea

Dear John Lehmann:
   Thank you for writing, and for wanting to know about my new book.
I'm afraid I haven't got anything much of it done; I'm still looking for
somewhere to live on extremely little—do you know of anywhere?—and
have been so homeless and penniless and uncertain lately that I've only
been able to write little bits of the story; I hope very soon to find a place
to live in, really to live in for perhaps even two months, and then I can get
it going. I'll let you know as soon as there's enough to print. I'm very glad
you want it for New Writing. Staying, on sufferance, with parents and
unfortunate friends, wanting to get away but quite unable, it's hard, I
find, to settle to writing anything continuous.
   And I'm very glad that you want to print some of the stories from
Portrait of the Artist As A Young Dog. I wish I had sent some of them to
you in the first place. I'd like, a lot, to see them come out in New Writing.
Will you let me know which ones you're thinking of printing? I'm sure
Dent won't raise any objection. The book sold hardly at all. Three or four
hundred copies, I think. And if Dent do agree, any chance of a few quid
soon?
   I don't know when I'll be in town next, but I'll drop a line to Atheneum
Court when I do come. I'd like to see you.

                                        Sincerely,
                                        Dylan Thomas

MS: Texas

CLEMENT DAVENPORT
April 2 [1941]   Marston Bishopston Glamorgan

Dear Clement,
   Sorry to write only when we want things. I owe you and John a letter or
letters, among other things. But I'm awfully busy with a long poem, and
I've just borrowed this typewriter to type out the never-ending Canary,
God moult it, and I'm helping about the house, shuffling and breaking, and
I think that unless I'm careful and lucky the boys of the Government will
get me making munitions. I wish I could get a real job and avoid that.
Clocking in, turning a screw, winding a wheel, doing something to a cog,
lunching in the canteen, every cartridge case means one less Jerry, bless all
the sergeants the short and the tall bless em all blast em all, evenings in the
factory rest centre, snooker and cocoa, then bugs in digs and then clocking
in and turning and winding and hammering to help to kill another stranger,
deary me I'd rather be a poet anyday and live on guile and beer.

In the pink bedroom we slept in and stored apples in and knocked about, you'll find unless they've moved a number of, I think, red small exercisebooks full of my old poems and stories. Would it be a lot of trouble for you to send them to me? I mean, will you? I've got a chance of selling all my mss,[1] for about the price of two large Player's after the next budget, and it's easier, and more honest too, to send the real mss rather than to copy out the copies in different coloured inks and with elaborate and ostentatiously inspired corrections. Will you send them here, and not to Laugharne as we haven't reached there yet though we should very shortly. I've got to send them off in the next few days. Thanks very much.

How's everything? Give my love to Arnold, if he's still with you, and tell him that the weather down here is quite middling and sometimes we have rain and sometimes we don't. I'm going to write to him soon, too. Love to yourself,

Dylan

I'm sending a note to John the same time as this.

MS: Texas

JOHN LEHMANN
April 3 1941   Marston Bishopston Glam

Dear John Lehmann:
I'm very glad Dent's okayed the stories for New Writing. Hope I'll get my 75% in time.

I don't know what to put in Notes on Writers, about myself. Will just this do: '26 year old poet & short story writer, born & living in South Wales. Author of 18 Poems, 25 Poems, The Map of Love, Portrait of the Artist As A Young Dog, and, in America, The World I Breathe, a collection of poems and of several stories not published in the English volumes. Contributor to periodicals in England, U.S.A., South America, & France.'

It's very feeble.

Yours,
Dylan Thomas

MS: Texas

[1] See page 480.

BERTRAM ROTA
8 April 1941   Marston Bishopston Glamorgan

Dear Mr. Rota,[1]

Thank you for your letter. I am very interested in selling my manuscripts.[2] The trouble is that most of my poems I write into exercise books,
and that each exercise book contains a lot of poems, including utter
failures that I shall never print. The same goes for my stories. If you
would care for me to send a few of these books along, I'd be delighted. I
think it would be a pity to disfigure the books by tearing a few poems out.
I do not know, of course, if there would be a market for such work in
bulk, as it were. Will you let me know soon? I should like to sell them, if
possible, as I am in need of money.

In the meantime I enclose, for your offer, a small group of manuscripts:
five poems and a story.

Yours very truly,
Dylan Thomas

PS. I have almost completed what I think is my best work so far: a long
Ballad, which *Horizon* is printing next month.[3] The manuscript of that,
comprising a great deal of drafts, corrections, & alterations, is certainly
the most interesting I have. Perhaps you would tell me if you'd like to see
this, too?

D.T.

MS: Texas   *SL*

CLEMENT DAVENPORT
23 April [1941]   Marston Bishopston Glam

Dear Clement,

Sorry not to have thanked you before for sending on my manuscript
books. I wanted to write to you from Laugharne, and so put it off every
day. Now we won't be in Laugharne until, definitely, the end of the
month. No, May the second. Caitlin says: Will you send the gramophone

---

[1] The name of Rota, a London dealer in books and manuscripts, had been removed from the
MS before it reached Texas.

[2] Thomas sold Rota the core of his early manuscripts, in the form of four exercise books
containing poems, and one with stories. Other similar notebooks with early poems are
known to have existed; they may have been lost before this date, although they must still
have been in his possession a couple of years earlier, because he incorporated Notebook
poems, otherwise unknown, in the *Portrait* stories. Rota sold the five notebooks, together
with other manuscripts, to the Lockwood Library of the State University of New York at
Buffalo. The library paid Rota just over $140. Whatever Thomas received, it was less than
that.

[3] 'Ballad of the Long-legged Bait.'

& the records on to her, c/o Laugharne Castle, Laugharne, Carmarthen-shire, because she says how nice it would be to have it there when we arrived.[1] Will be very grateful. How are you? and how is John? I haven't heard from him yet. Vernon Watkins hasn't heard from him either, and wants to know very much if John still wants him to go up to talk in Repton.[2]

I envy you terribly the dream of Mexico City. All I can see is a high-explosive factory on the horizon. I met a man yesterday who worked in a high-explosive factory in the last war, & he said, 'Oh, don't you worry about it. Everything's all right. I lost the sight of my right eye but I got the O.B.E.'

Love to Arnold, to whom I still haven't written a promised letter, if he's still with you.

Love to you from Cat & myself. Will we see you one day?

Dylan

MS: Texas

BERTRAM ROTA[3]
[1941] [fragment]

[...] I mean, not that the poems are good or bad, but only that they show the growth of poems over a period of just more than a year, one extremely creative, productive year, in all their stages and alterations, and—in many instances—show how a quite different poem emerges, years later, from the original. [...] The majority of them have not been printed anywhere yet, though I'll quite probably print some of them in my next collection due some time this year[4] and in altered form perhaps in future books. [...]

---

[1] The Thomases had arranged to stay with Frances Hughes in Laugharne. Richard Hughes was away at the war.
[2] Repton was the public school where Watkins had been educated. Davenport, no longer affluent, probably taught there for a few terms. He taught at Stowe for a year from autumn 1941.
[3] This extract is taken from Thomas's letter that accompanied the MS poems sent to Rota, who quoted it when he wrote to Charles D. Wood of the Lockwood Memorial Library, Buffalo, 1 September 1941.
[4] No new collection of poems appeared during the war.

JOHN DAVENPORT
25? April 1941   Marston Bishopston Glam
Dear John,
    Deeply, really distressed to hear about poor, dear, old Roger.[1]
Although I hadn't seen him for more than two years, and wasn't likely
to see him for years to come, if ever, I've always known that he was
about somewhere with his little eyes and his cigarette, calm and treble
in the middle of the crumbling system; I knew that he was always
somewhere, perhaps driving a Bugatti with the radio full on, or riding a
ladies' broken bicycle. It was nice to know that one always *could* see
him. Now I find that, straightaway after your letter, I miss him an awful
lot. I can understand how upset you are. You won't forget, will you, to
let me know how he died, and as much of the why as we'll ever be able
to know.
    There won't, I suppose, be a single obituary line anywhere. I think we
should do something, John. It may be silly, but I think it would be right. A
letter—New Statesman?—saying that there are so many deaths now that
the death of Roger Roughton will perhaps pass unnoticed, and that we,
the undersigned, don't want it to. We could say that his paper[2] was the
most lively & original for years and years. We could say just a few things
about him, his work for the Communist Party, his publishing, his parties,
his poems, himself. And get a few chaps—Bert Lloyd, maybe Enoch
Soames, & Henry Moore, you'll know who to get—to put their names.
What d'you think? You'll know better than I would. Roger shouldn't be
allowed to pass out, in the middle of a bad war, in dirty Dublin, without
his friends publicly recording it and their gratitude to him. We should do
it quickly, too. Do let me hear from you very very soon.
    I've nearly finished the Canary typing now. I'd have been quicker, but
have had to borrow Vernon's typewriter for short, irregular periods. Can
you send me, or ask Clement to send me, the last few pages of the last
part? Do you remember, we did a little that pre-Repton weekend? In
small exercise books. I wrote about half a dozen pages, nearly up to the
Blackpool dinner from which Chronos escapes. The exercise book is
probably in the pub room somewhere. When I've finished all the typing,
& the quick end of the book, I'll write or wire you, & then perhaps you'll
be able to ask me up to Repton & we can correct it all.
    I told Vernon that a stamped envelope to him had probably been on
your desk for weeks. He quite understood. Faber's are bringing out his
poems this year. I'm very glad. Provisionally titled 'Gratitude of a Leper',
though I'm not quite sure myself.[3]
    I've just finished my ballad. Too late, unfortunately, for the May
Horizon. It's about 220 lines long, a tremendous effort for me, & is *really*

---

[1] Roughton had committed suicide in Ireland.
[2] *Contemporary Poetry and Prose.*
[3] It appeared as *Ballad of the Mari Lwyd.*

a ballad. I think you'll like it. At the moment, I think it's the best I've done.

I'll write to Antonia today about the script. Thanks.

Sorry not to have written before, about a number of things. I'll get them in order, and tell them to you very soon. Now I want to get this off, so that we can pay our tribute to Roger.

I wish I knew what your life in Repton was like. Mine here is almost intolerable. We're leaving on May 2 to stay some weeks in Laugharne. Caitlin thanks you very much for the gramophone, and for the arrangements you're making. She's having a worse time here than I am; at least I have my corner and my web.

Love from us both.
Dylan

MS: Texas   *SL(R)*

BERTRAM ROTA
May 5 1941   Laugharne Castle Laugharne Carmarthenshire

Dear Mr. Rota:

Can you tell me what modern novelists' first editions are worth selling now? I should like to get rid of some of mine, which include William Faulkner, Richard Hughes—High Wind in Jamaica, and the plays—H. G. Wells—first private printing, in New York, of the Country of the Blind—Evelyn Waugh etc. But I have a lot of first edition novels, and would be very glad to hear which names might fetch money nowadays. I'd also be exremely obliged if you would tell me whether you would be prepared to buy any of them. I shall send you, if I may, some more of my own mss very shortly.

Yours sincerely,
Dylan Thomas

I am not sure if I acknowledged your last letter, and the enclosed money. I have been moving to the above address since then, and may have forgotten. Anyway, thanks very much.

TS: J. M. Dent. Anthony Rota, Bertram Rota's son, doesn't know what became of the MSS of this and another Thomas letter, dated June 3, after his father's death.

ARCHIE HARDING (BBC)
May 6 1941   Laugharne Castle Laugharne Carmarthenshire

Dear Mr. Harding:
  Thank you very much for your long, and extremely helpful, letter about
the amount of backing the B.B.C. could give me if they were questioned
by the Ministry of Labour as to whether I was doing any work for you that
could be called valuable. I understand, naturally, that you could not
support me *in full*; but what you said in your letter, and what you said
you could say to the Ministry of Labour if necessary, will, I hope, do the
trick:—that is, keep me for a while longer out of the factories.
  Thank you for sending on the reports from the Czech Legation. I'm
afraid I found them pretty useless: just dry accounts, with no personal
detail to speak of, of the taking of towns and military positions. 'Then we
took Omsk and Tomsk and Bomsk. We lost 40 wagons and 3 men. This
was in April.'
  I have added one scene to my previous script, but really cannot see how
to add any more. The only things I could add would be figures and place-
names. The Czech officers who so very kindly wrote their reminiscences
have apparently so little dramatic feeling that they could make their
reminiscences of Dunkirk as uneventful as a meeting of the Coke Board.
  I hope the script is not too unsatisfactory.
  Thank you again for your letter. I apologise for not answering before
but I have been moving about a lot, trying to find somewhere to live, and
have only just managed to settle down here for a few weeks.

                                        Yours,
                                        Dylan Thomas

MS: BBC

M. J. TAMBIMUTTU
May 21 1941 (Wants payment for a poem. See Appendix 28.)

VERNON WATKINS
22nd May 1941   Laugharne Castle Laugharne Carmarthenshire

My dear Vernon:
  It's been a long pause. And, apart from the loss of your company, a
great, sighing relief. I hope we can stay here for a good bit: I have the
romantic, dirty summerhouse looking over the marsh to write in, and

Caitlin an almost empty, huge room to dance in. Also, we have lots of records now, and we hear, quite often, another word than 'ration'.

Is Dot home? Our love if she is; or isn't, of course, though it is hard to think with affection of someone in S. Africa. Or to think, perhaps I mean, without envy.

My prosebook's going well, but I dislike it. It's the only really dashed-off piece of work I remember doing. I've done 10,000 words already. It's indecent and trivial, sometimes funny, sometimes mawkish, and always badly written which I do not mind so much.

Any more about your leprous collection? Perhaps the volume should be surgically bound. I do hope it comes out this summer, just before the gas.

When can you come down? There's no room in this house—there are 10 children under 10—but there is in the pub, cheap. Write quickly, and say. You must; we must see you before your new 'Confession of a Dirt-Track Rider'. Because we'll never come back to Bishopston, God's least favourite place. Write this week. Thank you for everything you gave us on our long visit. A little money has arrived for me since your last pound for the road; now that has gone. But anyway we can get so very few cigarettes down here. None now for days. I have taken to biting my nails, but they go down so quickly, and one has only 10.

Well, well, look at the world now.

Love,
Dylan

MS: British Library   *VW*

LAURENCE POLLINGER
May 23 1941   at Laugharne Castle Laugharne Carmarthenshire

Dear Laurence Pollinger:
    I am so sorry—mostly, I'm afraid, for myself—that I never managed to send on any of the promised books. Something went wrong with the lot of them, and the prose book, the novel, I scrapped entirely just a short time ago. Now I have started it again, and it seems to be going really well. But I do want some money to carry me over while I am completing it. Would you be so kind as to find out from Dent's whether they would be prepared to give me an advance—they owe me 40 quid, don't they—on receipt of not less than *ten thousand words* and a *detailed synopsis* of the rest. It would be ordinary novel length. When I saw you last year, you did, I believe, tell me that you thought a forty quid advance on such an instalment would be possible. Or have things changed since then?
    If you could possibly get them to agree, I'd revise and type ten thousand words straight away and let you have them.

I do hope you'll do your damndest for me.

Yours sincerely,
Dylan Thomas

I shall be at the above address for some weeks.

MS: Texas

VERNON WATKINS
28 May 1941   Laugharne Castle Laugharne Carmarthenshire

My dear V:

Thank you for the letter with Jammes in it.[1] And the round silver trash. Filthy, damned stuff, the halfcrown was the only lovely money I'd seen for a week and more. And it's still all I've seen. This is getting ridiculous. The joke has gone too far. It isn't fair to be penniless *every* morning. Every morning but one, okay; but no, *every* morning. If you do have a tiny bit to spare, whether it clinks or tinkles, let alone rustles, *do* send it, Vernon. This is absurd. Anything, bled boy, leper, from a penny to a pound. My head's been whirling with wondering how to get twopence, fairly or foully, to put on this nearly a letter. If I fail, it must go naked. Here we are, safe and quiet, and should be happy as cabbages, but it's hard—for me—without a single hour's, halfhour's, minute's, going out in the long, social evening. So if you can don't forget, oh quickly quickly don't forget. I get in such a nagged, impotent, messy state when I'm like this; sit and snap and worry all day; can't be easy, can't work hard, just sit by myself saying 'Fuck it' in a flat voice. I *do* like that wonderful independence of being able to walk across the road *any* time and buy an envelope or some Vim. Don't forget, like lightning, yours ever,

Dylan

My dear V:

I liked the translation enormously much. What a poem! Of course, 'behoves' is right. I read it aloud, slowly, to Caitlin. The music is beautiful. Two possible exceptions: 'poverty' and 'limpidity' so close together; and 'infatuated flies'. Especially the alliteration seems uncertain to me. I'm going to read it again in a minute. Get on with your slow giant Sleeper, I loved the bulls I saw for a moment on the typewriter. And the opening, old lines. You must—can you?—finish it this month, because of the advent of mechanical death. (What a lot of trouble it would have saved if We had sunk the Hood and They the Bismarck). I'm glad you wrote, telling the officials you can only just turn on a bathroom tap. Be a

[1] Watkins's translation of a poem by Francis Jammes.

censor: pry and erase. Don't be a cyclist or a parachutist or a mine-tester or the first man on the *very* edge of Dover cliffs.

No, I couldn't do that Ackerley article.[1] I'm not going to talk about poetry now that I have had to, temporarily, stop trying to write it. Besides, he would not print one's truth, because it *would* blast the B.B.C. and every other government institution.

My ballad will be in the June number of Horizon. They haven't printed it nicely: it's in double columns. They wanted more space for an article called 'Whither Solidarity?' or 'An Analysis of Prokosch's Rhythm In His Middle Period'.

My novel blathers on. It's a mixture of Oliver Twist, Little Dorrit, Kafka, Beachcomber, and good old 3-adjectives-a-penny belly-churning Thomas, the Rimbaud of Cwmdonkin Drive.

I was terribly sorry you didn't come down last week-end. It would have been really good. Come down *as soon as* you can. Bring Dot if she's about & will come. Give her our love. I'm afraid I won't be able to meet you in London, or to meet you anywhere further away than walking distance from here. I wish we could meet in the bombs there. But visit us, please.

See if you can squeeze another drop from your borrowed-to-death body. I'm not going to tell you how grateful I am and have always been; or how vile I feel when I ask you again. Really vile. Weazels take off their hats as I stink by. No, I am sorry. I have no right. I hope I am spoiling nothing. It is just that I am useless, & have nowhere to turn.

I have told Caitlin about Kierkegaard, & he will be sent on,[2] with thanks for him, & love, when we are bloated enough with pennies to be able to bluster into the p-office & say, 'Post this, you fool. *All* of it. *All* the way.'

Remember us to your mother & father and Dennis.[3] Tell him all the boys here fight with hatchets.

Love,
Dylan

MS: British Library   *VW*

BERTRAM ROTA
June 3 1941   Laugharne Castle Laugharne Carmarthenshire

Dear Mr. Rota:

Thank you for your letter and for the catalogue. I have some of the things you seem to be requiring, but haven't got them out of storage. I am enclosing a few volumes—one or two of them rather badly looked after,

---

[1] J. R. Ackerley (1896–1967) was literary editor of the *Listener*, 1935–59.
[2] A borrowed book that Watkins wanted back.
[3] An evacuee from south-east England, living with Watkins's parents.

I'm afraid—which I hope you'll be able to give me a price for, soon. They aren't much, I know. And I'll send others on later, along with some of my own mss.

Yours sincerely,
Dylan Thomas

TS: J. M. Dent

LAURENCE POLLINGER
9 June 1941   Laugharne Castle Laugharne Carmarthenshire

Dear Pollinger:
   Did you get my letter? About the novel? I've written separately to Richard Church, but have had no answer yet. I do hope you'll buck Dent's up for an *immediate* advance. I now have over 15000 words to show them, which I'll send you as soon as I know what they are prepared to advance.[1]

Sincerely,
Dylan Thomas

MS: Texas

M. J. TAMBIMUTTU
June 9 1941   Laugharne Castle Laugharne Carmarthenshire

Dear Tambimuttu,
   Thank you for the post-dated guinea; and sorry to have been a bother about it, but even in a castle one must eat and smoke. I suppose.[2]
   I hope number six goes well, though I'm not looking forward to Treece's article after his ridiculous overpraise of Read[3]:—

---

[1] Dent disliked what they saw of *Adventures in the Skin Trade*. An editor wrote to Pollinger on July 10: 'This material is not good enough; and we would like you to put this fact plainly before the author. It seems to us that Dylan Thomas has reached a crucial point in his literary career. He made a flying start, and there has been no lack of recognition of his uncommon talent . . . In our view, however, he has not maintained the position which he gained by his early work.' The letter quoted some damning comments by the firm's readers—'more coprolitic than ever, and seems to be quite without intellectual control . . . Thomas cannot build a literary career merely on the miniature furore created by his early work . . . Unless he pulls himself together he is going to fizzle out as an author most ignominiously . . .' Dent said they still had faith in his future, but 'it seems to us that he is now slipping into a state of literary irresponsibility'. One assumes Pollinger didn't pass on such painful opinions to his client.
[2] Issue No. 6 of *Poetry* (London), May/June 1941, printed 'Love in the Asylum'.
[3] In 'Herbert Read — A Salute', *Poetry* (London) No. 4, Jan/Feb 1941.

'*All* Elizabethan tragedy, *all* the colour and violence of the ballads,' or whatever the words were, in some such ice-cream line as 'O O Antonio'. I think the article did Read a disservice, for the natural reaction to it was ridicule and that, unfortunately, might embrace Read's own dull, honest poetry too. If someone says a line is better than Shakespeare, and it's really just an ordinary, pleasant line, one's inclined, I think, to pass over the ordinary pleasantness of it by attacking the humbug, or gutter eye, that sees it as superb. I hope Treece doesn't say that there's *all* metaphysics in some ordinary line of mine. Although I am a friend of Treece's, I think he is a loud and brawling hypocrite. This isn't for print; I don't like magazine quarrels, I can have as many as I like outside. Also I think it's a mistake for one young poet to shout at length, in print, about the works of an almost exact contemporary, good or bad. Young poets don't want praise, they want money. Treece has been climbing for some years now, and he isn't even in sight of the ladder yet. And he's surely old enough now, you'd believe, to realise that he won't get anywhere up those snob-snotted rungs by licking the bums of his creative friends or by describing, incorrectly, the contours of them for the benefit of other blind and mouthey climbers.

I don't think it's a bad thing to be a climber, so long as you make sufficient entertaining noises as you slime your way up. Grigson did make some sort of simian show, but you can't see Treece for the wood, the numb and solid wooden front against all sensitivity or intelligence.

A thing I don't like about 'Poetry', now that I'm feeling like this, is its plague of dedications: 'For Nigel', 'To Nicholas', 'From Basil', and the letters with all the Christian names and the back-pats and kicks. It's too much like 'Hi Gang' on the wireless. The intimate magazine should be circulated only among the family, and I'm damned if I belong to your family or Nigel's or Basil's. The public's got a right to demand that its entertainment should be public; and if the public likes all this matey to-you for-you we're-all-poets-together hugging and buggering party exhibition, then the public, as nearly always, is wrong.

What I do like about 'Poetry' is some of its poems; which is as it should be. Let's have less about them and more of them.

I'll write again when I get number six. Best wishes for it.

> Yours,
> Dylan Thomas

Sorry, I haven't got a copy myself of my 18 Poems. And I'm sorry some cad removed yours, but if your copy was inscribed by me to Runia—an old friend—then some cad must have removed it from her.

Yes, I'd love to send you some drawings, or illustrations. I'll have a shot right away.

MS: Texas   *SL(R)*

VERNON WATKINS
Sunday 21 June 1941   Laugharne

My dear Vernon:
   It was very nice seeing you those days. I loved Rilke and the scrabbling in
the shrubbery and your Sea Music. I wish you could have stayed longer.
Sorry for being so huffish and insultable that last night: you know how it is.
   Ackerley has been in Laugharne for the last 3 days; or four. Funny, after
our talking about him. Someone who stayed here last year told him about
the place; he'd never heard of it before. He was sorry to miss you, here and
in London: I told him you'd been in London & that you missed him here
by one day only. He's quite a charming man, rather grey and tired, with a
nice smile and a lazy, affected, very pleasant voice. About 50. He said he
liked your poems a great deal. Most of the time he was here he spent
doing great walks, but I met him every evening in the pub and he came to
the house for drinks.
   Here is a tiny poem I've just done. Not very well formed; just a poem
between bits of my unfortunately forced novel, a breathing space between
mechanizations; & I think I agree with you about that destination phrase.
   Do write soon; and tell me about going to London. We're just the same.
                                        Love,
                                          Dylan
                                            Poem on back.

[*Written on back of letter: first verse of 'The Marriage of a Virgin = On
the Marriage of a Virgin'.*]

MS: British Library   VW

VERNON WATKINS
[July 4 1941][1]   Laugharne

Dear Vernon:
   A wonderful surprise present. Thank you. I could buy Laugharne, but it
would be ostentatious.
   A great pity you couldn't come this weekend. Beforehand I miss you.
And you'd have had the pleasure of Hughes's company. He's been aloofly
here for some days. I don't know what he does on the Admiralty, but I can
imagine him being introduced: 'Ah, Admiral, and here's Hughes, Richard
Hughes, you know, our Out of Contact man.'
   I'll try to come down next weekend, and thank you. If I don't it will be
because I'm in London; or, of course, because Marjorie's with you. I must
go to London quickly, to see what honey of a ministerial job is open for a

---

[1] Thomas wrote: 'Friday June 4 (?)41'. June 4 was a Wednesday; July 4 was a Friday. On
balance the latter seems more likely.

man of the strictest obscurity and intemperance: £1000 a year, excluding tips, bribes, blackmail, bloodmoney, petty cash, and profits realized by the sale of female clerks into the white slave traffic and the removal of office furniture.

I look forward to the new poem.

I'll write as soon as I know about my London visit.

Anyway, next weekend or the weekend of the 20th.

> Thank you again,
> Love,
> Dylan

I'm enclosing the short, now finished, poem.[1]

MS: British Library   *VW*

VERNON WATKINS
Tuesday [?1941]   Laugharne

Dear V.

Here are two poems of very different kinds. That is to say, here are two poems. Do tell me at *once* what you think of them. I am a bit dubious about 'Through ruin' in the third line of the sextet. Originally I had 'All day.'[2]

Looking forward to the weekend. As I told you, the only 2 things that will prevent me coming are London & utter poverty (in which I am now, having to borrow 2 1/2d for this stamp). But I do want to come. I'll ring up either on Thursday evening or Friday morning. What's the trainfare?

> Much love,
> Dylan

MS: British Library   *VW*

VERNON WATKINS
Wednesday [?1941]   Laugharne

Dear Vernon:

Thank you for the lovely weekend. A pity we couldn't have done more, but I liked very much what we did. I *must* have a copy soon of the Foal which I remember, lots of it, by heart on a first hearing: nothing, perhaps, to old Datas Watkins but a great deal for me. I hope the Money poem goes

---

[1] 'On the Marriage of a Virgin'.
[2] One of the poems enclosed was 'Among those Killed in the Dawn Raid was a Man Aged a Hundred', which contained the words 'through ruin', later removed. The other was 'The Hunchback in the Park'. 'Dawn Raid' was published in *Life and Letters Today*, August 1941.

well, and probably 'Earth-winged mortal' is right. It's just that to me it doesn't express the meaning you originally told me.[1]

Thank you for the croquet & the poems & the kindness & the money; and thank your mother for me, very much, for the superabundance of far-too-good-for-the-war food. Remember me to your mother & Mr. Watkins & Dennis.

Yo— etc Lederer came down with me for 2 days & is returning tomorrow. He *walks*. A nice boy, but terribly affected in many ways. Dante is boring. Eliot is dry. Gorki is a journalist. But I think that what he really thinks, & will one day be brave enough to say, is simple, unaffected, & right.

Thank you for 'Assembling'. Of course.

A proper letter soon when I know more plans. And I hope I can send you a poem soon.

I liked everything.

Love,

Dylan

& Caitlin

& Llew

MS: British Library   VW

CHARLES FISHER

July 15 1941   Laugharne Castle Carmarthenshire

My dear Charles,

While looking through a drawer to find something—it was not my drawer so I did not know what the something would be though I hoped for tinned food—I came across an old letter of yours to me, and with your home address which I'd lost. It really took the wind out of my sails (I was a yacht at the time), finding your handwriting in somebody else's drawer where peas at the very least should have been. It was like, not very much like, I admit, burgling a safe and finding an old friend inside it not a day older than one foot two. I thought I'd better write at once, before I found a drawing of Fred's (Still Life: One Egg. June 1936–June 1940) behind the hatrack in the music room or a manuscript of Tom's (Mabinogion, a Tone Poem for Horn and Kardomah) behind the butler in the cook's room. Especially as there is no music room and no butler and the only hatrack is a bust of Dante on which some child has written 'Odd Job'.

I saw too little of you in Swansea last time; hat and moustache for half a quick evening among the good-shows of the young lieutenants and Peggy and Betty and Babs the dancing dailies. I remember reading some of

---

[1] 'Foal' and 'Money for the Market' are poems by Watkins.

my unfinished Ballad—the whole is coming out in this month's Horizon—in a thick, confidential voice, being bought two pints at a time, giving my belly what-for; but the date we made for later I forgot at once, and spent the next evening trying to be in three Gower pubs at the same time, waiting, wondering which of them I had arranged to meet you in, then remembering too late that the meeting was to have been in Swansea, a large town. After months and months, and if you remembered the date yourself, forgive me, and do write.[1]

I think that quite soon I'll be made to do work in a factory, so this is my last bit of as much freedom as one can expect to enjoy without any money. I haven't seen a coin for weeks. Do they still sing as you spend them? Jesus, I loathe my poverty. Caitlin will, I hope, be able to stay on here while I am being thrown to the high explosives. My upper lip is a board, but still I am very miserable.

I'm writing, now, a long story about London, called 'Adventures In The Skin Trade'. Miller and Wodehouse.

Do you know Tom's address? I want, through him, to find where Daniel is, that Lost Tribe in himself.

Tell me how you are, what you're doing, and be good to the Generals.

Love,
Dylan

And just a poem, finished today.

MS (incomplete): the recipient   *SL*

VERNON WATKINS
28 Aug 1941   c/o Horizon 6 Selwyn House Lansdowne Terrace WC1

My Dear Vernon,
    A tiny note to tell you where, if you write, I can be got hold of. It's only a forwarding address, I haven't moved into the editor's chair. The place I'm staying in in London with Caitlin is closed after tomorrow or Friday and we haven't yet found anywhere new. We've been having an awful time, and I have felt like killing myself. We arrived with no money, after leaving Llewelyn in Ringwood, and have had none since. In Laugharne that was not so bad. In stinking, friendless London it is unendurable. I am still looking for a film job, & have been offered several scripts to do 'in the near future', which might mean weeks. In the meantime, we sit in our bedroom and think with hate of the people who can go to restaurants. Have you written? Frances Hughes has, as yet, forwarded no letters. I would have written to you long before, but have been too miserable even

---

[1] To this point, the only source is *SL*. Charles Fisher's MS begins at page 2; he no longer has page 1.

to write Poem at the top of a clean page and then look out of the window at the millionaires catching buses. Are you, I don't hope, in the army? Write soon. Soon perhaps this will have been worn away, hunger, anger, boredom, hate and unhappiness, and I will be able to write to you about all the things we have always had, and will always have, to talk about together. We are prisoners now in a live melodrama and all the long villains with three halfpence are grinning in at us through the bars. Not the best bars either. Bless you,

Dylan

MS: British Library   *VW*

JOHN LEHMANN
[?summer 1941]   c/o Horizon

Dear John L.
   Here are the proofs. Sorry so late. You wanted me to say something about the book as a whole. Will just this do?
   'A Fine Beginning' is the first chapter of a novel in progress to be called 'Adventures In The Skin Trade'.[1] The novel is a semi-autobiographical continuation of 'Portrait of The Artist As A Young Dog' and takes the principal character of that book of stories up to the age of twenty.

Dylan T

MS: Texas

BBC
[?1941] (Returns contract from 'Mars Hotel, Frith St., Soho'. See Appendix 29.)

JOHN SOMMERFIELD[2]
6 January 1942[3]   Strand Film Company[4] Filmicity House
                                              5a Upper St Martin's Lane London WC2

Old John,
   My first letter, too. After all these pints. It was better than a Pimm's to hear from you, and especially to hear that you'll be in London so thirstily

---

[1] It was published in Lehmann's *Folios of New Writing*, autumn 1941.
[2] John Sommerfield (b. 1908), novelist and documentary-film writer. He was in the RAF.
[3] Thomas wrote '1941'. Sommerfield has no doubt that it was the following year.
[4] The Strand Film Co, where Thomas was now on the payroll as a writer/director, made documentaries for the Ministry of Information.

soon. I look forward, my constitution is not so happy. And get me here, will you, TEM. 1891, as quickly as you can once they let you out. We'll make a date straightaway, for that moment. Why can't you desert for a bit? Or is this scrap and scribble bluepencilled? We'll choose a good — qualified—place, but that doesn't mean we won't visit all the qualified bad places too. Glad you liked my winter verses, very quickly produced from my tame Swinburne machine, and don't forget: TEM 1891, or above address, and we'll be quietly noisy together for as long as you like and we can. All my lack of news *then*. Caitlin sends best love. Send ours to Molly.

I'm still helping to produce those things that Beachcomber calls the series of priggish, facetious shorts extolling the virtues of sad girls in unfitting uniforms and the vices of happy thinking, moving, and x-ing — the word I must use. How are you?

Always,
Dylan

MS: the recipient

OSCAR WILLIAMS

The American Oscar Williams (1900–64) wrote poetry but was best known as an anthologist. He acted as an unofficial literary agent for Thomas, selling manuscripts as well as poems.

April 5 1942   13 Hammersmith Terrace London W6[1]

Dear Mr. Williams:

I got your second letter—thanks very much—but I'm afraid your first *must* have gone down. I'm glad you want to use some of my poems in New Poems 1942. Looking forward to seeing it.

Horizon will be sending on those signed sheets. When I signed them, only Spender & Empson had been there before. I hope the other chaps you want are obtainable. Rodgers[2] is somewhere in Northern Ireland.

I'm sorry, but I believe my signature got a bit strange at about the 50th sheet. I'd forgotten everything about the person whose name I was signing, and eventually even his name. The weather, or war, or London, perhaps.

---

[1] Sir Alan Herbert, the author, lived next door. The Thomases borrowed a studio through the intercession of John Pudney, the Herberts' son-in-law.
[2] W. R. Rodgers (1909–69), poet and radio scriptwriter, was a Presbyterian minister in Northern Ireland before joining the BBC.

I haven't any new poems at the moment, as I'm working on a long story which takes most of the time that's left over after half-earning a daily living in a film company: a company that works on shorts for the Ministry of Information. When I have some, I'd be glad to send them along.

Delighted to hear from you.

Good luck.

Dylan Thomas

MS: Harvard

BBC

20.5.42   13 Hammersmith Terrace W6

Dear Sir,

Enclosed, the signed copyright form. I hope the cheque for the agreed amount can be sent on very quickly, as I am trying to settle all my accounts etc. before moving. I would appreciate it this week if possible.

Yours faithfully,
Dylan Thomas

MS: BBC

RUTH WYNN OWEN

Ruth Wynn Owen was an actress, originally from North Wales. Thomas met her in Bradford in 1942 when she was with a touring company, and he was making a film documentary about the theatre in wartime. She has said that she fell in love with him but refused to become his mistress.

[?May 1942]   [headed paper: Strand Film Co, etc]
as from 13 Hammersmith Tce W 6

no, not any longer after Saturday.
So will you—if you will
write, please—please write
to the film address.

Your letter—thank you very, very much for it; I was terribly glad to hear—came just after I had been seeing you on the films, you with your wand, showing a ladderless leg in the wings. You looked, if I may or mayn't say so, pretty good to me, and I wish you were in London, where even the sun's grey and God how I hate it, and not in Preston with a lot of sillies. I do hate the life here, the grey gets in your eyes so that a bit of green nearly blinds you and the thought of the sea makes you giddy as you cross the road like a bloody beetle. You wrote to me on a moor, and I write to you in a ringing, clinging office with repressed women all around punishing typewriters, and queers in striped suits talking about 'cinema' and, just at this very moment, a man with a bloodhound's voice and his cheeks, I'm sure, full of Mars Bars, rehearsing out loud a radio talk on 'India and the Documentary Movement'. I wish I were on the Halifax moor talking to you, not to dishonest men with hangovers. Perhaps I shall be able to give a long-postponed talk to the Cambridge English Society during the week of June 8, which would be wonderful because perhaps you don't work all day and perhaps you would come out with me, walk somewhere, watch me drink a pint, and talk and talk and talk. Would you like that? If you would, then I could try very hard to come up for a day. Let me know will you?

You said you wrote a bad letter, and you wrote a lovely one, though too short. I said, horribly, that I wrote a good letter, and I'm almost inarticulate. What's a good letter anyway? To put down a bit of oneself to send to someone who misses it? To be funny and selfconscious or selfconsciously formal, or so very natural that even the words blush and stammer? I only know I'd prefer to talk to you, but as I've got to write because you're a million miles away, in the mild and bitter north, [at the head of second page: terribly late letter] then I must write anything, anything or everything, just as it comes into the thing that keeps my collar from vanishing into my hat. First, how very very odd it was, coming across you out of the blue, out of the black, out of the blue-and-black bruise of a smutty town at the end of a witless week, when everything had gone wrong, had gone wrong, as I didn't know then, only to come extravagantly right. I saw, suddenly, a human being, rare as a Martian, an actual unaffected human being, after months and months, and years indeed of meeting only straw men, sponge and vanity boys, walking sacks full of solid vinegar and pride, all the menagerie of a world very rightly at war with itself. (And now even the ink is spitting.) I felt, at once, so at ease with you that I can still hardly believe it.

Thank you for saying about Llewelyn. He's going away, tomorrow, for a few weeks to his grandmother, quite near Salisbury. Just outside Fordingbridge. I have to move from Hammersmith Terrace, and am trying to get a house in St. Peter's Square to share with some people who have furniture. You don't know, I suppose, anyone who has any furniture stored in London and who would want to give it a good home? The only things I have are a deckchair with a hole in it, half a dozen books, a few toys, and an old iron. These would not fill even a mouse's home. It is very good sometimes to have nothing; I want society, not me, to have places to sit in and beds to lie in; and who wants a hatstand of his very own? But sometimes, on raining, nostalgic Sunday afternoons, after eating the week's meat, it would, however cowardly, whatever a blanketing of responsibility and conscience, be good to sprawl back in one's own bourgeois chair, bought slippers on one's trotters. But to hell with it, I want to talk about you, I know too much about myself: I've woken up with myself for 28 years now, or very nearly. But I can't write about you—and now the spitting pen is broken and the ink over documents ostentatiously and falsely called Important—because, though I feel much, I know so little. So goodbye for a time, and the smaller the time the better—at least for me. You will write? And I will see you?

love,
Dylan

MS: the recipient   *SL*

RUTH WYNN OWEN
Monday July 6 1942   [headed paper, Strand Film Co etc]

My Dear Ruth,
    A very tiny note to thank you most properly and deeply for your lovely letter. A tiny note because I'm just off to Scotland. I'll be back in about a week. I want to write a full, long letter full of love and nothing, and I will from perhaps the wet, never-so-good-as-I-probably-think Highlands. I couldn't manage Cambridge, mostly because, as you told me, the boys had come down. I shan't tell you how much I am looking forward to seeing you when you come to London in 14 days' time. I shan't but I'd like to. Let's paint this foul town the colour we like the best.

X
Dylan

MS: the recipient

CAITLIN THOMAS
Sunday [?1942][1] [incomplete]   84 Old Church St S W 3

Caitlin,
    I love you.
    I am desperate without you. I love you, more and more and more the longer I am without you. I cannot go on without you, for you are forever too wonderful and I can only say Cat my darling you are my sweetheart

---

[1] The date could be 1942 or 1943, and in any case is before the birth of the Thomases' second child, Aeronwy, in March 1943. Caitlin was often in Wales, either in Laugharne or with friends in Cardiganshire, where she may have been at the time of this letter. Thomas went down when he could.

and nothing can come between us. God, Catly, if only I could see you now. I want to touch you, to see you, you are beautiful, I love you.

Why I had not written was because of money,

[four pages, 2 to 5, are missing]

money that the Accounts deducted; so that, if you still want me, which is unlikely, and if the presence of Elizabeth etc. does not overcrowd the house, I could come down on this Tuesday. Will you wire? Wire me at the office: Strand Films, 1 Golden Square, W.1. Or to the office telephone number: GER 6304. As soon as you get this letter. And tell me if you want me to come down. I can't describe to you, I never will be able to describe to you, how much I love you, my own wife and Llewelyn's mother, my own Caitlin, and how much I want to see you terribly terribly soon. Forgive. How can I tell you the kind of money panic I got into? You weren't there to hold me & tell me, every day you went further as I could not write, I don't know *why* I thought I couldn't write & tell you the truth. I am telling you the truth now. And I love you so very much that even in writing gabblingly, desperately, like this, I can somehow come near you and kiss your heart.

Please, my very own dear, tell me that you want me to come down. It is the only thing on the earth that I have to look forward to. And if, because of the other visitors, I cannot come down this week, wire all the same & tell me when I can. I saw the Roberts this morning who told me they have written to you to say that *they* cannot come go down [*sic*] to Wales for another week. Perhaps you may think it best—if you want me to come, and, O my darling, please do—for me to come with them: that is, if I can. But I want to come as soon, as soon as I can: if ever I can now, but I know that I must be with you, live with you, always. Why I wired to say that I could come down *this* weekend was that I had heard that Taylor[1] was returning and I knew he would, at once, straighten things out. But, when he returned, he asked me to stay on until Tuesday to do some small special job. And I couldn't refuse. Then, at the end of the small job, I have to do another, longer one; but this he has agreed to let me take away with me for a week to do. I could come to you now. I love you. I love you. Love me, Caitlin. You will always be my

[end of page 9]

MS: Maurice Neville

---

[1] Donald Taylor was managing director of Strand Films.

CAITLIN THOMAS
[undated fragment, probably wartime][1]

[*page headed 3*] that I could borrow. I was ashamed to write without sending anything to keep you going on—I know you will say I am a bloody fool, but you know too that that, justly bugger me, is what I unfortunately am—and, as the days went on and I could not write, I became desperate, I became ill with wanting you, with being ashamed that I could not write, with being ashamed that I was too much of a money headed fool to write, with thinking of you 200 miles away thinking that I had, as you said, a

MS: Texas

RUTH WYNN OWEN
28 August 1942   Talsarn Cardiganshire[2] as from Strand Films [etc]

Ruth my dear,
   I missed you; and I think that I must have willed myself to miss you that night after the theatre; not of my thinking self, whatever that vain, paste and cotton-wool wad of my self may matter, for I tried hard to reach the Salisbury or the stagedoor; I think I must have willed my lateness and weakness, willed it because, simply, I was ashamed of my hysterical excitement of the wet-eyed and over-protesting night before. I remembered losing my head in Piccadilly, which left very little for my heart had gone two months ago, gone into your by-me-unkissed breast. And you'll have to forgive now, along with my tears, protestations, and denials, my almost archly over-writing writing in this late, loving letter. I can be natural—my behaviour, then, in the black streets was as natural as my too-much drink and my giddiness at seeing you again allowed me—but perhaps my nature itself is over-written and complicate me out of this, you Ruth in a well. Was there something a little clinical in your attitude, or was it my windy head that blew your words about and got me dancing with love and temper among the bloody buses? I'm sure, and this isn't a mockmodest wish to be stroked back into vanity, that you were all right and I was all wrong. I had time wrong, I was thrusting its hands, instead of letting it move passionately gently until we could in time's good time be as near as we wished and we must. So forgive me: I'll follow

---

[1] This item may belong to the previous letter. Texas acquired it about 1958 with the collection owned by T. E. Hanley of Pennsylvania.
[2] Talsarn was the remote village where Caitlin Thomas and sometimes her husband stayed with a family from Swansea that he had known since childhood. Food rationing was less noticeable in the countryside.

the ticking old fossil until it's the Now Now hour, I'll follow it through the provincial towns and sail with it under the stagey bridges.

Believe me, I love you too.

And when will you be back in London? I shall go back from Wales on Tuesday. Will you wire me? I think that is the best: everything that comes here is unopened except bottles. And if you don't, or forget to, I will phone the stagedoor. We must find each other again and when we meet again I'll be more controlled and, indeed, even sane.

The cocks are crowing in the middle of the afternoon, and the sun is frying.

Will you trust me?

It is grand and lovely to have known you for even a little for such a little time.

I hope you are well and I know you are sweet and more than sweet to *me*.

When we are together next, let it be on your whole free day or at least on your whole free evening. Time will not let me say or ask more than that.

Dylan

MS: the recipient

T. W. EARP

Tommy Earp (1892–1958) was an art critic and hard drinker; Thomas was very fond of him. They shared the crossword puzzler's weakness for smart anagrams and double meanings. Among the topical ingredients in the verse that begins the letter, 'Timothy Jenkins' was a joke version of the name of a Russian general, Timoshenko.

30 August 1942   Gelli Talsarn Cardiganshire
                                  as from Strand Films [etc]

Dear Tommy:
On-and-on General Bock is driving a wedge among pincers,
Timothy Jenkins feints on the flank and the rouged Duke is wan,
The war is sweet with the summer breath of the panzers
And the dehydrated choirs of day welcome the dawn.

As I tossed off this morning over Talsarn Bridge to the fishes,
At war myself with the Celtic gnats under a spitfire sun,
Reading that twenty poems make fifteen cartridge cases,
Commandos are trained to be cannibals and bombs weigh a hundred ton,

Poison is dropped from the sky in the shape of hipflasks and cheque-
books,
Pigs can be taught to firewatch and hens to lay handgrenades:
O the summer grew suddenly lovely as the woodland rose in a phalanx
And the painted privates I thought were bushes moved in their Nash
parades.

I have been here for over a week with Caitlin, with milk and mild and
cheese and eggs, and I feel fit as a fiddle only bigger; I watch the sun from
a cool room and know that there are trees being trees outside and that I do
not have to admire them; the country's the one place you haven't got to
go out in, thank Pan. I missed you last Friday, and was not in time, (as I
thought, up until the last moment, that I would be able to catch the
Thursday-night train), to let you know. I hope you did not wait nor were
cross, and that the Monico made up for the lack of green tooth and pot
belly, for the absence of one ventripotent scortatory Krut.[1] I'm returning
tomorrow, Tuesday, and will be in London until Friday night. Can you
come up during the week, or on Friday? A visit will make up for London
after Wales. I want to bring my bit of a novel with me, and let's try the
Ladder & the Jubilee and have a gala climb, without banting and
unanned.[2] I do hope you can manage it. Will you write or wire?

Ever,
Dylan

MS: Ohio State University   *SL*

LAURENCE POLLINGER
19 Jan 1943[3]   Strand Film Co 1 Golden Square W1

Dear Laurence Pollinger:
Sorry not to have got in touch with you for so long. So many reasons for
my carelessness about this & about so many other quite urgent things; so
many reasons, & all too dull to bother you with.
About the new poems Laughlin is bringing out in America.[4] They are,
so he told me some months ago, only a very small collection of poems
that have appeared, since my last book, in periodicals here & in America.

---

[1] Del Monico, where Earp had been waiting for him, is a pub in Soho. 'Ventripotent' means
gluttonous, 'scortatory' means fornicating. 'Krut' might be an anagram for 'Turk', but in
any case means Thomas.
[2] Ladder, Jubilee: drinking clubs. 'Banting': John Banting was a painter and illustrator.
'Unanned': which 'Ann' is undiscoverable.
[3] Thomas wrote '1942' in error.
[4] New Directions published *New Poems*, seventeen Thomas poems, in February. The series
was 'Poets of the Year'.

They are to make up a pamphlet, or more-or-less a broadsheet, in a series rather insolently called 'Poet of the Month'. In no way can the little selection be called a *book* of poems; and I see no point in letting Dent's have a copy as there are far too few poems for them to make a commercial book out of it. I would prefer to wait a short time until I had added to the little American broadsheet the rest of the poems I have written & written in periodicals since my last Dent-volume appeared.

Agree terms with Laughlin, certainly; & I hope you can get the cheque through as soon as possible. Will you let me know—at the above address, which will always find me now as I have turned into a script-writer — what happens?

Sorry again for my long absence from any correspondence with you.

Sincerely,
Dylan Thomas

MS: Texas

CAITLIN THOMAS
[1943]   8 Wentworth Studios SW3[1]

Monday, in misery in our leaking
studio, among vermin and falling
plaster & unwashed plates.

My Own Caitlin, my dear darling,
It's never been so useless and lonely away from you as it is this time; there is nothing to live for without you, except for your return or when I can down to Laugharne which must, somehow, be this week because I love you far more than ever and I will not exist without your love and loveliness, darling, so please write and tell me you miss me, too, and love me, and think of us being, soon, together for ever again. By the time you get this, you'll also have got, I hope, *a bit more money* which I will wire either tonight or tomorrow morning. I could not send any more on Friday as there were so many things to pay; & some rent, too.

There is *nothing* to do without you; so terribly terribly sad to come back to our empty barn, lie all night in our big bed, listening to the rain & our mice and the creaks & leaks and the warnings;[2] so sad I could die if I hadn't got to see you again & live with you always & always, when I woke up without you, think of you hundreds of miles away with

[1] The Thomases occupied this unglamorous Chelsea apartment (in Manresa Road) at intervals from mid or late 1942. Visitors remember Caitlin's vegetable stew bubbling on the stove when she was there, and squalor when she wasn't.
[2] 'Warnings' in those days meant air-raid warnings.

Aeronwy Lil[1] at your breasts that I want to kiss because I love you, my Cat. I hope to God I can come down for 2 or 3 days at the end of the week.

Last night I called on pudding Vera who has been in bed for over a week with apathy and illusions and who said she'd written to you about Gelli.[2] She did not know you were in Laugharne,[3] & when I told her she said could she spend a week or a bit *in* Laugharne with you before going on *with* you to Gelli for a week or a bit? And I said I'd tell you, I knew nothing about it.

How is it in Laugharne? Tell me everything; and especially that you love me & want me as I love & want you now, at this moment, and for every moment of my life & yours always. How is Frances, Mrs Wood (?), & Ivy?[4]

I have seen some, not too many, of the usual people: Dan. The Rat who has now sold everything in his den or hole except that double revolting bed. My office horrors. Nobody I want to see at all because there is only one person I ever want to see and that is you darling oh oh darling I love you I want to be with you.

I'm going to the Chelsea tonight. Alone. And then back to think about you in bed. Give my love to Aeronwy. Every bit of my love to you, every substance & shadow of it, every look & thought & word. Oh I hate it without you.

xxxxxxx
Dylan

PS I work in Elstree,[5] have to leave Chelsea frightfully early. I hate Elstree & Chelsea, too; very much. I have seen one or two films, halfquarrelled again with J. Eldridge,[6] & over-wound the clock which I shall take to a man.

PSS What do you want me to send you? Books? Shawls? Skirts? Napkins? Cloak? Shoes I see on the floor? I'll send money anyway, and, I hope to God, myself. Kiss me. I'll say your name *very loudly* tonight as I put out the light.

PSSS Are you going to go over to Blaen-Cwm again? I'll write to them tomorrow.

PSSSS No more, dear, until I send a few pounds.

OH DARLING.   X

MS: Maurice Neville

---

[1] Aeronwy was born in London, 3 March 1943.
[2] The house in Cardiganshire.
[3] Caitlin was staying with Frances Hughes.
[4] Ivy Williams of Brown's Hotel.
[5] Strand Films used studios at Elstree.
[6] John Eldridge directed films for Strand.

HERMON OULD[1]
31st May 1943   [headed paper: Strand Film Co etc]

Dear Mr. Ould,
    Thank you for your letter. I am most interested in the scheme of Mr.
Olaf Stapledon's enquiry and in the statement you enclosed, and I will
try, as soon as possible, to send along what I myself think about them.
    I would also like to become an ordinary member, and would be grateful
if you would tell me the exact procedure.

Yours truly,
Dylan Thomas

MS: Texas

CAITLIN THOMAS
Thursday [? 1943]   King's Arms Stirling Corner Barnet Herts[2]

Darling:
    Darling:
        Caitlin my dear dear Cat.
    It's awful to write to you because, even though I love writing to you, it
brings you so near me I could almost touch you and I know at the same
time that I *cannot* touch you, you are so far away in cold, unkind
Ringwood and I am in stale Barnet in a roadhouse pub with nothing but
your absence and your distance, to keep my heart company.
    I think of you always all the time. I kiss my uncharitable pillow for you
in the nasty nights. I can see you with our little Mongolian monkey at
your breast; I can see you in that unfond house listening with loathing to
the News; I can see you in bed, more lovely than anything that has ever
been at all. I love you. I love Llewelyn & Aeronwy, but you above all and
forever until the sun stops and even after that.
    And I cannot come down this weekend. I have to work all day Sunday. I am
working, for the first time since I sold my immortal soul, very very hard,
doing three months' work in a week. I hate film studios. I hate film workers. I
hate films. There is nothing but glibly naive insincerity in this huge tinroofed
box of tricks. I do not care a bugger about the Problems of Wartime Transport.[3] All I know is that you are my wife, my lover, my joy, my Caitlin.
    Oh Cat darling I miss you too much to bear.
    Come Back on Wednesday. I'll send you another inarticulately loving

---

[1] Hermon Ould was general secretary of P.E.N., the writers' organisation. Thomas was
elected to membership two years later, on 2 May 1945, but there is no further trace of him
in P.E.N. records.
[2] Barnet is near Elstree and the film studios.
[3] The film was probably *Is Your Ernie Really Necessary?*, its title a parody of the wartime
slogan, ' Is your journey really necessary?' It was filmed but not released.

letter tomorrow, with some money. You should have it by Saturday morning.
No, it's better that I wire the money so that you can have it for the weekend.
Even though I dislike Blashford very much, I envy it because all my love is
there with my children and with you.

Come back on Wednesday. *Please.*

I haven't been in London at all as I have to start working unlikelily early in
the morning & carry on until six o'clock.

I love you more, even, than when I said I loved you only a few seconds ago.

I think I can get [. . .] a little part in this film: a tiny part as a pudding-faced
blonde sloth but I shan't tell her that.

Write to me telling me two things: that you love me & that you are coming
back on Wednesday which is like a day full of birds & bells.

I am writing on the back of a script by Mr. J. B. Priestley. But that doesn't
spoil what I have to say to you. I have to say to you that I love you in life &
after death, and that even though I drink I am good. I am not drinking much. I
am too lonely even for that.

Write.

Give my love to the pigmy baby & kiss Llewelyn on the forehead for me.

Touch your own body for me, very gently. On the breast & the belly. My
Caitlin.

Your
Dylan
X

MS: Maurice Neville

T. W. EARP

July 1 1943 [incomplete]   Ger. 6304 [the Strand phone number]

Dear Tommy:

When next shall we stumble to the stutter of our lewis-gun carols
From bombazine-bosomed bar to a bliss of barrels,
Two period percies friscoed with ladders and banting,
Two spooned swiss pillars, tumble falsetting and ranting?

O when, marcel-bound, shall we ruth our swine's way to the many-johned
Penny-fond antelope's cavern from the royal back-bar of beyond,
Or, sinister self-mabuses ripe for the phelan of the withy,
Peggy-legged limping in bottle-dress be hooved from the Wardour-street
smithy?[1]

MS: Ohio State University   *SL*

---

[1] A crossword-puzzle poem. Line 1 is a pun on the Lewis Gun, a type of machine-gun, and
Lewis Carroll. Line 3, 'ladder' is the Ladder Club and 'banting' is John Banting again. Line
4, 'swiss' is a Soho pub known as 'the Swiss', and 'spooned' indicates what to expect
next, a slip of the tongue that will turn 'swiss pillars' into 'piss swillers'. Line 6, the
Antelope is a Kensington pub. Line 7, *Dr Mabuse* was an early horror film. Line 8,
FitzGibbon says there was a drinking club in Wardour Street run by a woman called
Smith. And so on, and so on.

WYNFORD VAUGHAN-THOMAS[1]
[?September 1943]

This is, I think, the first time I've written to you—treasure the paper, boy!—and, oh, for what a reason. I'm whimpering in bed, with mumps and gout, the music-hall duo, and cannot work and am, quite suddenly, utterly without money and horribly in debt. My face is a sad bladder and my big toes full of teeth. And tradesmen bludgeon the door all day and summonses fall like grouse. There is no one here to borrow a mite from [...] and I am writing to ask you if you could temporarily (oh cringing word) help me with a little money however little. If you can I will send you a cheque post-dated eight weeks hence when I begin again to write film-scripts in London where, God, I must spend the winter. Snarl and throw over the Devonshire Castle[2] if you must, but try your best, and do not think too hardly of your lumpish and gehenna-toes Dylan.

MS: the recipient

RUTH WYNN OWEN
September 19 1943   Carmarthenshire
                                  as from Strand Films 1 Golden Square W1

Ruth, my Dear,
  It's over a year, I think, or know, since I wrote to you with my heart on my sleeve; now the shape of the hidden heart is arrowed, bloody, with a children's on-a-tree inscription under it: X loves Y, though those aren't the names. I've been in Wales for some weeks now, and have had time and a rinsed head enough to be able to write what I want. In London, I mean to write you every day, but the laziness, the horror and selfpity, that London drizzles down on me, stop everything but the ghost of a hope that perhaps you will ring, will drop a postcard to say you have come to town and would like to see me, or, ghostliest of all the half-hopes, that you might turn the corner of a street I am walking and that all the traffic will stop and the sirens suddenly sing sweetly, At last! at last!
  Not that I had any right to think that you might write me, ring me, meet me; it was my turn, but I was too cowardly to go on, thinking that you might tire or say, forever, go away and no more.
  But I want to forget the falsities and lazinesses and evasions and pretences of the oh-dear-crying past—oh, the mountainously pretentious want—and to say only what I think and feel now at this moment which,

----

[1] Wynford Vaughan-Thomas (b. 1908), broadcaster and writer; he is from Swansea. He says he received the letter 'just after I returned from reporting the raid over Berlin in September 1943'. He sent £10.
[2] A London pub.

deep down, has been the same long moment for a year and more. But why do you want to hear from me? and how do I know that you do? I don't know, but I hope. Will you write and say that you still want to hear? to see me? And come to London—I'm going back tomorrow—or let me come to you. I can come anywhere. At any time. Tomorrow.

Thank you for your card at Christmas. Such a nice, prim, nothing-at-all remark it is—'thank you for your card at Christmas'—to end an inarticulate little letter on; because I must end, because I do not yet know if, after such a silent time, you want me to go on or want to see me. Perhaps you've forgotten. I am short, snub, unsteady, moles on my cheek, in a check suit. Of you I have only the still picture from the silliest film in the world, which is still the best film for the one reason that it allows me to send you now, with all my heart, my love.

Dylan

MS: the recipient

T. W. EARP
4 October 1943   Strand Film Co 1 Golden Square W1

Dear Tommy,
   Your letter to me, when I was in Wales, was waiting for me, too late, when I came back from Wales; and, since then, I have not heard a word from you or seen you, and London is empty of everyone except the unseeable ubiquitors, our gumfed Allies.

   When are you coming up next? I hope it's very soon. Bill Gaunt[1] wants to make a bad day for all three of us. Anyway, we must have a good bad day. Please do wire or write. Can you bring some Pera?[2] I am pretending to be busy now.

Yours
Dylan

MS: Ohio State University

CAITLIN THOMAS
[?1943]   [headed paper: Strand Film Co etc]

My dear darling:
   It's the same; but true again. True as God, even though the ink, for some reason, has changed. But if we're to spend the rest of our life in

---

[1] William Gaunt (1900–80), painter and writer.
[2] Anagram of 'Earp'.

Wentworth Barns, let us at least pay to have Van and Grada on the telephone. It's hell trying to get hold of you, to tell you, Cat, that I couldn't get home—home, Wentworth, but still our big gay bed—because, if I had done so, it would be only for quarter of an hour or less. I'm tangled with doctors and M and B; one doctor is facing me as I write.[1] I left Barker after a few minutes: he'd had a letter from Donald making a date for next week, so that he felt he needn't come along to get messed about *before* then. I am going, as you know, to meet another doctor—someone called Peter Gorer—at the Gargoyle[2] at 7 o clock tonight; I won't be finished until 6; and it would, however, my darling, lovely to come back before then, [be] useless, unprofitable, (from the point of view of us being together), and just silly. I will stay in the Gargoyle until 7.45 (quarter to eight) & then taxi back. *Unless*, unless, Cat, you can come up to the Gargoyle for a drink before that. I'd love you to, not because of the horrid, low-ceilinged, devil-enveloping Gargoyle Club itsbeastlyself, but because you and I have not been together—even for a moment, apart from badly-acted Chekov—for what seems months & months. So if you can, please come along to the above horrible Gargoyle on, or after, just after, seven; & then we can go and have a look at the big naughty world of the Café Royal or the Wheatsheaf, just for a tiny bit before going back together. If you can't, or if you dislike me, I'll be back just after eight. Do what you like. Only remember I like you. I am sorry to write to you only by such plutocratic methods as messenger-boy-sending. I love you.

Dylan

Our money will be up tomorrow early evening at the same time as my not-enough-pittance comes. Dear Cat.

MS: Maurice Neville

T. W. EARP
Friday [?1942/3]   [headed paper: Strand Film Co etc]

Dear Tommy,
  I hope that a week today'll see you in Finch's with Normal and me; and many apologies for having been late & self-fuddled after my rover's Jamboree last Tuesday, the Tuesday the Gargoyle was so usually foul, Tennant[3] trembling in the twenties, and Caitlin and myself still

---

[1] 'M and B' was the popular name for one of the early antibiotics, manufactured by May and Baker. Thomas was working on *Conquest of a Germ*, a film released in 1944.
[2] The Gargoyle Club, above a printing works in Soho, was opened in 1926 by David Tennant as a non-profit-making venue for writers and artists. By the 1940s there was less culture and more drinking.
[3] David Tennant (1902–68), a younger son of the first Lord Glenconner.

boycotted and scouted after our paid-in-the-bowel sing-sing, our brownied-off boy and girl bushranging, round the nightclub log. And I don't forget lovely Virginia[1] having arrived in at the back door of a foreign society from the front door of the Parson's house. I saw you go in a daze of night, and could not remember if I had made our next Friday appointment, for by that time I was odd God wot and all I could think of, nearly, was how quickly to get out after getting another in: one of those brandy-and-milk-and-thunders. So please do write. By another post as they say I am sending you the very hard to read because of the typewriting and crossing out only copy of the first half or so of the comic novel I've been telling you about for too long.

Yours ever,
Dylan

MS: Ohio State University

T. W. EARP

23 12 43   Film Centre 34 Soho Square W1

Dear Tommy,
   I did get your letter at the address you find, and I find, though differently perhaps, it hard to credit; but a day late. Letter or message would, I think, arrive even on time at my older, above, address, rather than at that House I try to visit only on money-for-jam-and-ham-days.[2] I missed the Hole;[3] and missed you, too, on returning, after about an hour of recrimination, not self, to Sloane Square that last happy stagger.
   Thank you for the Chinese Serenade, Yai Sigh, sing low, prang gong, ring high, me too in admiration and in pride at being present at that excellent poet's appearance.
   What a pity you can't manage Boxing Day (which was *not* at Basingstoke). If, however, you feel that we could meet in any town between Salisbury & your nearest, ring me at East Knoyle 83.[4] I'd jeep along at once.[5]
   Will you be in London soon? I hope v much.

Dylan

MS: Ohio State University

[1] Mrs Tennant.
[2] Perhaps Filmicity House, one of Strand's addresses. Does 'jam-and-ham' mean that the Accounts Department was there, paying him for writing commentaries that 'hammed it up'?
[3] 'The Coal Hole' was a popular pub in the Strand.
[4] David Tennant's country home was at East Knoyle, in Wiltshire. Thomas used to stay there.
[5] Thomas couldn't drive.

DONALD TAYLOR[1]
Monday morning. 11 [?1943]   8 Wentworth Studios Manresa Rd
                                          off King's Rd Chelsea

Dear Donald:
  I was going to hold up M & B anyway, in spite of Elton's demands,[2] as you suggested; but now the holding-up's unavoidable for a day or two as I've got laryngitis or bronchitis or asthma or something: a complaint, whatever it is, that makes your chest like a raw steak, prevents breathing, & produces a food-losing cough. Caitlin's going to leave a message for Elton this morning.
  I tried to get hold of you Saturday in order to take you at your word about money. Five pounds was sent by Davies, but that had to go immediately on rent, debts, etc; the other salary money, which didn't, of course, arrive, was to have kept us for the rest of the week. I'm seeing an income-tax man tomorrow who will, I hope, be able, quickly, to arrange that I'm paid my ordinary salary 'pending I.C. discussions.' In the meantime, would you, as you said, lend me the salary-making-up money? I do need it so urgently.
  I phoned Paddock (is that his name? I forget for the moment) & have sent the ms along. He sounds very promising.
  When I received my fiver—from Ossy's own hands, as everything must now pass through him—I was told that a Parish memo had arrived to state that taxis should not be taken on jobs, people shd be interviewed in the office and not taken out to lunch, regular hours observed etc—*when can I resign, please?*
  Do hope you can send that dough along by hand. Sorry to be a nuisance.

                                                      Dylan

MS: Buffalo

MAJOR PETER BAKER[3]
[?26 January 1944]   Film Centre W1

Dear Peter Baker,
  Here is the manuscript of the first thirty thousand words of the novel

---

[1] Thomas's employer at Strand Films.
[2] Sir Arthur Elton was supervisor of films at the Ministry of Information.
[3] Presumably the Peter Baker (d. 1966) who became a publisher after the Second World War, and was Conservative MP for South Norfolk from 1950 to 1954, when he was gaoled for forgery. But in January 1944, Baker, an acting major in the Royal Artillery, was a prisoner of war. The letter, at Buffalo, is only a typescript, so the correct date could have been miscopied. A more likely date would be January 1946, when Baker had just started his Falcon Press. But 'Film Centre' had ceased to be a Thomas address by 1946. Baker's father, also a Major Baker, was general manager of Ealing Films. Unfortunately his first name was Reginald.

we were talking about.[1]

This represents roughly a half of what the whole novel will be. It may look a little formless now, but actually the whole conception of the book is made to a most formal pattern.

It might be worth while my saying in a few lines what happens in the rest, the unwritten, as yet, part of the story. The hero, as you will notice is in the gradual process of losing his clothes; and as the story progresses so he loses more and more clothes, bit by bit. He loses these clothes through a series of incidents and in a number of places that are not connected by content or atmosphere with any of the incidents that came beforehand. That is, he does not progress through any ordinary drunken romantic picaresque movement, but through all kinds of sober, grisly, embarrassing, mortifying, but always readable, I hope, adventures in the wilderness of London—from Kilburn to Cockfosters.

Eventually, of course, he winds up without any clothes at all, and finds himself outside Paddington station a moment before dawn. Standing there naked, having had every garment fall from him simultaneously with the acquisition of every new experience, he wonders: 'Now I am here, outside Paddington station, just from where I began my pilgrimage, as naked as the day I was born. What'll happen to me? Will a very rich woman in a Rolls-Royce and a fur coat pass me by in the almost dawn, stop her chauffeur, and befriend me and lard me with charity and nymphomania? Or will a policeman pick me up for indecent exposure, my having shed all the skins of my semi-proletarian, bourgeois, provincial upbringing? Or will a romantic tart clutch me to her used bosom, in the Catholic tradition of Francis Thompson? Or will, when dawn breaks, I see everyone walking about the streets, going to work, conducting traffic, going about their daily dulness, as naked, as utterly naked as I?'

That's how the book will run. Sorry if it sounds pretentious, but it's difficult to summarise the plot of something that's supposed to be nasty *and* funny.

Will you write me at the above address when you've read this; and I do hope you can do something about it.

Details, if any, until then.

Sincerely,
Dylan Thomas

TS: Buffalo   *SL*

---

[1] *Adventures in the Skin Trade.*

JOHN BAYLISS[1]
[?1944]   64 Grove Park Road Chiswick W4

Dear Mr. Bayliss:

Have I written to you? I know I did write, but have I posted it? If not, do please accept my apologies. Everything's in such a muddle here, as you probably saw even from the outside of the vicarage. Do use those two poems of mine that you want. On the same understanding as the other contributors of course: drop of royalties, if any.

Sorry I was away when you called. Call in if you're round here again, won't you?

Yours sincerely,
Dylan Thomas

T. W. EARP
[postmarked 1944 ?Feb 9]   Far End Bosham Sussex[2]

Dear Tommy:

Everything went wrong last lost London meeting. Jobs came up and Tennant fell down and I couldn't reach the Ladder and Tennant couldn't remember if it was the Ladder we were to reach and I looked-in at the Antelope and it drawled with moustaches. An awful day. Now we're moved to a house in Bosham—very nice, too, looking over water and perhaps Russell Flint[3]—but I'm keeping the Manresa Studio on. I'll be up in London twice or more a week, but always on payday Fridays. Let me know, at Film Centre 34 Soho Square, when you're coming up. We must meet.

Almost as important—but perhaps a thing to be talked about when we meet in London—is that Petersfield is on the main London line from Bosham. Isn't Petersfield your market-town? And I would, I would like to meet there one morning.

Please don't forget to write. We have a dog now.

Dylan

MS: Ohio State University   *SL*

---

[1] John Bayliss (b. 1919), writer and editor, serving in the RAF, was compiling an anthology that appeared yearly (as did many others, to circumvent the wartime ban on new magazines), *New Road*. He had visited a vicarage in Chiswick where Thomas was staying. The poems, published in the 1944 volume, were 'Dawn Raid' and 'On the Marriage of a Virgin'.

[2] A bombing campaign on London, the 'Little Blitz', began in January 1944 after three years of relative freedom from air attack. The Thomases moved to a cottage at Bosham, on the Sussex coast, for several months.

[3] Sir William Russell Flint (1880–1969), painter, best known for his watercolours.

T. W. EARP
[postmarked April 13 1944]   Far End Bosham Sussex

Dear Tommy,

Very very disappointed I couldn't manage our Petersfield meeting. Donald wired urgently for my help on the rebuilding of Coventry Cathedral, so I had to hurry up and help him rebuild it in Henekey's.[1] I do hope the wire, my wire, reached you before you started out.

When can the next date be, in Petersfield? Tuesday would suit me, this coming Tuesday, admirably, at the same time, 12.20, in church or pub opposite. Would it suit you? There'll be no cathedral-call this time; a country-town few hours would be very pleasant.

I'm looking forward, so is Caitlin, to your coming down here. I have found some nice places, and there are no Pauls or Ninas, however goodhearted, at all: only the worst people I've ever met and not to talk to. Grand if I could bring you back here with me after Tuesday's Petersfield.

Write or wire about Tuesday.

And will you ask May, please, about Bosham, and send her my love?

I have poems to bring on Tuesday, and hope Pera has been busy too.

                                          Yours,
                                          Dylan

MS: Ohio State University   *SL*

T. W. EARP
Sunday 15 or 16 April '44   Far End Old Bosham Sussex

Dear Tommy:

It was distressing not to meet you so many times. I can't remember in detail how we missed each other so successfully; once, I think, I wired confirmation of a wrong Petersfield date too late, and, by going to town, missed your wire confirming the right one. Then I was sent to Coventry, a visit of a few days which confused things for many more, and went to a wedding, and had such a fall into melancholy I couldn't even get round to Lysol or the utility blade but could only whimper in bed and fail to understand detective stories. In one communication you too hinted at the coming on of coma from which I hope you've now recovered enough to meet either this Tuesday or this Friday. On Tuesday I shall be, anyway, but with hope, in Mooney's Cambridge college[2] from half past twelve. On Friday I can be anywhere you like at any after-twelve time if you'll write,

---

[1] Thomas was working on a film about the much-bombed city of Coventry called *Building the Future*.

[2] One of the 'Irish houses', London pubs run by the J. G. Mooney company.

or wire, before then to Bosham. But Tuesday will be best, of course, because it is nearest.

Here is a poem in three parts. One part, the second, I've already shown you in London when I probably forgot to mention that it was incomplete. Also another short poem. I would love to hear what you think about them when, at last, our bi-paths join in some coal-hole, some cheese-hole, or in any other reputable and, almost essential, acquaintanceless sewer.

Yours,
Dylan

MS: Ohio State University   *SL*

M. J. TAMBIMUTTU
[?1944][1]   [headed paper: 24 Culross Street W1]

Dear Tambi,
My price has gone up, you mink! It's *thirty* shillings now.

Yrs,
Dylan

MS: Carbondale

LAURENCE POLLINGER
Wed 28th June 1944   Gryphon Films[2] Verity Films
                                  Filmicity House 2–6 West Street WC2

Dear Laurence Pollinger:
Sorry not to have answered your letter before this: the letter about James Laughlin of New Directions and his wish to know what the hell I'm doing.

I'm glad Laughlin's working towards plans for the issue of my first American book, THE WORLD I BREATHE, in a cheaper form. Does this mean any money for me? Hope very very so.

Incidentally, I have never had my agreed-upon so-many copies of the pamphlet (Poet Of The Month) NEW POEMS that he published fairly recently.

---

[1] *Poetry* (London) printed two Thomas poems in April 1944.
[2] Gryphon was the successor to Strand, and had ambitious plans to make feature films. Donald Taylor was still in charge.

I haven't a new *book* ready for him, but I have got some work on the way. Perhaps you will tell him that I shall finish a short novel this year: the novel [*six words are deleted:* Dent turned down some time ago:] ADVENTURES IN THE SKIN TRADE. Just in case he wants to mention it in some advertisement of his. And there will be a new collection of poems but probably this won't be much good for him as quite a number of them will have already been published in the NEW POEMS pamphlet. How many I can't know until I am sent my copies of the pamphlet.

I'm writing films now, and have almost completed a feature film based on the lives of Burke and Hare. This film will be put into production by the Gryphon Films, for which I work, some time this year; but I do think that it might be a good idea to publish the script separately, perhaps with an introductory essay. I'll let you have a copy of the script very soon.[1]

I shall also send you a book of poems, for Dent's. Can you tell me what advance I can expect on a book of poems from J.M.D.? Ordinary poem-book length. Size of my TWENTY FIVE POEMS, about. I'd like to know what I could expect so that I can plan my financial embarrassments for the winter.

Hope to hear from you, and sorry about my delay.

Sincerely,

MS: Texas   [*no signature*]

T. W. EARP
12 July 44   Hill Cottage Hedgerley Dean near Slough Bucks[2]

Dear Tommy:

Haven't seen you for so long. When will you be up, or are the flying bombs keeping you out of town altogether?[3] I don't go up myself unless there's a real reason. Give me a real reason to come up next week. Can you make it Monday or Tuesday or Wednesday? I'm going to Wales for a few weeks quite soon and *should* like to see you before I go. Could you come to Wales? Anyway, let me know at the above, Donald's, address whether you can come to town next week. We must meet, if you can come, in an underground bar: Ward's, Piccadilly; Coal Hole; Falstaff; Piccadilly Hotel American Bar; or any other really low place you can think of. Hope to hear.

Yours
Dylan

MS: Ohio State University

---

[1] Taylor never succeeded in making the film, *The Doctor and the Devils*. Thomas's script ('from the story by Donald Taylor') was published in 1953. A version (written by Ronald Harwood) was in production in London in 1985.
[2] Another temporary address, this time west of London.
[3] Attacks by the pilotless weapons began in June and drove a million people out of London.

VERNON WATKINS
27 July 1944   Blaen Cwm Llangain near Carmarthen

Dear Vernon,

I didn't think it was so long since we saw each other, or since I wrote to you. We were three months in Sussex, and two months near Beaconsfield.[1] So it's nearly half a year and what a year and what a pity and what the hell. We must (always my fault that we haven't) write regularly to each other now, if only to report that a little tepid blood is still trickling, that there is still a faint stir somewhere in the chest, that we can still put pen to paper, paper to bottom, thumb to nose, the world to rights, two & two together, put and take.

The Sussex months were beastly. When it wasn't soaking wet, I was. Aeroplanes grazed the roofs, bombs came by night, police by day, there were furies at the bottom of my garden, with bayonets, and a floating dock like a kidney outside the window, and Canadians in the bushes, and Americans in the hair; it was a damned banned area altogether. They worshipped dogs there, too, and when a pom was born in one house the woman put out the Union Jack.

Near Beaconsfield, where Chesterton sat on his R.C.,[2] it was better. We stayed with a man who runs the film company I fool for, and the country was green and okay, but the well-off people were dry and thin and grieved over their petrol-less motorcars and played bridge like ferrets, and the poor snarled and were all named Body.

Now we're with my mother and father in Llangain, near Llanstephan where everyone goes into the pubs sideways, & the dogs piss only on back-doors, and there are more unwanted babies shoved up the chimneys than there are used french letters in the offertory boxes. It's a mean place but near Laugharne where we will go next week.

Is Dot in Carmarthen? Let me know. We'd love to see her.

I've found that I can do most of my filmwork outside London, (which soon will be shelled terribly by things that scream up into the stratosphere, passing the queen bees, and then roar down on to Manresa Road),[3] and so we are looking, again, for somewhere to live in the country. In Laugharne, if possible. In Wales, preferably. And we'll stay here, getting on my father—for he's one bald nerve—until we find a house, a flat, a room, a sty, a release.

By the way, I have a new complaint. Itching feet. There is nothing to see, the feet just itch. I have to take my shoes off many times a day and rub my soles with my socks. Ask Dan if he knows what it is—he's learned in little woes. How *is* Dan? I'd write to him but have lost his

---

[1] With Donald Taylor, whose house 'near Slough' (see previous letter) was also near Beaconsfield.

[2] A pun. The author G. K. Chesterton (1874–1936) had lived at Beaconsfield. He was a convert to Roman Catholicism. 'Sat on his R.C.' sounds like 'sat on his arse'.

[3] There were rumours in London of forthcoming attacks by German rockets.

address. Ask him to write to me; I feel very Warmley to him all the time, and would very much love to hear.

Here is a poem (printed in 'Our Time') which perhaps you haven't seen.[1] I didn't print the Lorca lines above the poem. Will you tell me about it? It really is a Ceremony, and the third part of the poem is the music at the end. Would it be called a voluntary, or is that only music at the beginning?

Keidrych & Lynette are in Llanybri. I always knew Keidrych was a turnip, and now there are little turnips growing all over his top. Lynette, who cannot read Welsh, is revising the standard nineteenth-century book on Welsh prosody, and also annotating a work on the Hedgerows of Carmarthenshire. I hope she becomes famous, & that they will name an insect after her.

I am writing poems, and have three new ones I'll send you when they are typewritten and after I have heard from you about the Ceremony.

Write very soon, please, & tell me everything.

Love,
Dylan

MS: British Library   *VW(R)*

VERNON WATKINS
26 August 1944   Blaen Cwm Llangain near Carmarthen

Dear Vernon,
    I'm so very glad that you are going to Pennard on September 2nd, and that Gwen[2] is coming down too and that we shall be able to see both of you. Do you think that you could come to Carmarthen town to meet? It's only an hour by bus from Swansea. We would come to Pennard but it's a nuisance taking the baby on crowded buses and my mother is never very well and it's rather a strain for her to look after Aeronwy for a whole day. If you come to Carmarthen we could meet in the Boar's Head or somewhere and have some beer in a corner and a long lunch. So please do try. I'll look forward to hearing from you. Bring a poem. I've just finished two poems, one over 200 lines and I'm excited by it. The other is a Laugharne poem: the first place poem I've written. I'll bring them both along.[3]
    We may be living in New Quay in a week or two, & are trying to get a house. If we do—the house will be right on the sea—you *must* come

---

[1] 'Ceremony After a Fire Raid.'
[2] Gwen Davies, Watkins's fiancée.
[3] 'Vision and Prayer' and 'Poem in October'. Thomas was enjoying a new burst of creativity. Blaen Cwm, where most of 'Poem in October' was probably produced, was the family cottage where he had been writing poetry since adolescence.

down to stay after you are married. Or before, of course, but I mean as a special bit of holiday. Caitlin sends her love to both of you. And mine is sent always.

Dylan

No word from Dan. Do you see him? Or will you send his address?
I saw Mervyn Levy. He's stationed at Llangennech.
Keidrych is living in Llanybri again, but I don't see him much.
Our dog has got mange.
Aeronwy cannot walk but she climbs rocks.
And of course we are coming to your marriage, in our brightest colours.

MS: British Library   *VW*

VERNON WATKINS
Wednesday [August 30 1944]   Blaen Cwm Llangain near Carmarthen

Dear Vernon,

A complication. On Monday Sept. 4 we are moving into a new house—we call it a house; it's made of wood and asbestos—in New Quay, Cardiganshire. It's in a really wonderful bit of the bay, with a beach of its own. Terrific. But it means that we're much further from Carmarthen. Now how can we meet? Can you come down here? You said you didn't want to spend your leave outside Pennard, but couldn't you spare us just *one* night in New Quay? We would love it so. Anyway, write. After Monday, our address will be Majoda, New Quay. The name is made of the beginnings of the names of the three children of the man who built the questionable house. I may alter the name to Catllewdylaer.

Here is a new poem.[1] It's a month & a bit premature. I do hope you like it, & wd like very much to read it aloud to you.

Will you read it aloud too? It's got, I think, a lovely slow lyrical movement.

Write as soon as you can.

We must all meet.

Love,
Dylan

In the poem, I notice, on copying out, that I have made October trees bare. I'll alter later.[2]

MS: British Library   *VW*

---

[1] 'Poem in October'; it celebrates Thomas's thirtieth birthday.
[2] 'Bare' became 'winged'.

T. W. EARP
September 1st 1944   Majoda[1] New Quay Cardiganshire

So much Meux has flowed under the bridges
You could drown London town, which would be just,
Since we met in the spring and drank religious.
If we don't meet again I shall throw away my trust.
And bitter's gone up and bombs have come down
Since Pera and pal like a pair of mouse
Squeaked in the liquorish wainscots of the town
And thumbed their whiskers at Philmayicity House.[2]
It's a long way from London, as the fly bombs,
And nothing of Donald's guile can lug me
Away from this Wales where I sit in my combs
As safe and snug as a bugger in Rugby.
We've got a new house and it's called Majoda.
Majoda, Cards, on the Welsh-speaking sea.
And we'll stay in this wood-and-asbestos pagoda
Till the blackout's raised on London and on me.
But meet we must before the dove of peace
Drops in my eye his vain and priggish turd,
And England's full of cultural police,
(For you, at once, a sentence of three months Heard,
For me a year on bread and de Polnay, Peter),
And verse inspectors kick up a mingy din
Demanding, at pistol point, to read your metre,
And oh the significant form troops mincing in!
How shall we meet, then, since countries lie between
The Rimbaud of Ockham and Swansea's Villon?
O fly the miles in Stephenson's machine
And spend a month with
                              Yours ever
                              Dylan

MS: Ohio State University   *SL*

---

[1] See previous letter.
[2] Filmicity House had been one of Strand's addresses. Other parts of the pun might be Phil May, the cartoonist; Philip Lindsay, the writer, who worked for Strand; Earp's wife, who was called May. In line 1, Meux is a brew of beer. Line 21, Peter de Polnay, novelist. Line 26, Earp lived in a house in Hampshire called Ockham Cottage.

DONALD TAYLOR
4th September 1944   Majoda New Quay Cardiganshire

Dear Donald,

Here is Resistance:[1] or, at least, the commentary minus the concluding chorus (I'll explain that in a moment). Writing it was made more difficult by my not knowing for what countries the film is intended, nor whether it will be shown before the war is over or after. I have worked on the assumption that it *will* be after—or, anyway, after all the chief countries of resistance have been freed; and so the Resistance story must be told in the past tense: 'we were free; we were occupied; we were maltreated; we made sporadic attempts at revenge; for these we suffered; we learnt that Resistance must be organised; we became a movement; we became an Army; we fought and won. Now we are free again.' Following that rough line, I have, as you'll see, stopped short at 'we won.' I wanted to hear from you before writing the short section of 'now we are free again': to hear whether the treatment is in accordance with the plan we roughed out together. I haven't put in any visual indications at the side of the commentary. You know all the material there is at hand, and I, of course, don't. When the 4th Voice begins there is, I remember, a Russian resistance-meeting sequence which would go well. I don't know if you agree, but I haven't *mentioned* underground press, telephone-exchanges etc but have indicated, perhaps sufficiently, in the commentary towards the end where the press etc shd be seen.

Do let me know if it's at all satisfactory: and what to write at the end. Just the 'now we are free again' stuff?

Anyway, I do hope it is something to work on. It is in a sufficiently loose form for me to be able to change it around drastically at a moment's notice.

Looking forward to hearing from you.

I've found a bungalow right on the Atlantic, with a beach of its own, & moved in today. Want a holiday? Tell me when you need me in London. I pay my own fare, of course.

Waiting to hear to work to do anything.

Ever,
Dylan

On reading through, I see a couple of rather too-literary phrases which I shall cut out in next (& final?) version. 'Steely sea,' for instance. Out!

MS: Texas

[1] Thomas enclosed a seven-page MS headed *The Unconquerable People*, written for four Voices in fiery prose or perhaps verse:
'. . . Men cannot chain / forever the fury of Man / against their evil / though they break his bones. / Resistance began. / Resistance began / clumsily, hastily, with a knife in the dark . . .'

LAURENCE POLLINGER
Sept 12 1944   Majoda New Quay Cardiganshire

Dear Laurence Pollinger,
    I was glad to hear that Laughlin of New Directions wants to bring out a
Selected Volume of my stuff. Yes, please do go ahead & draw up a
contract with Laughlin. Is a 'flat 10%' good? What's it mean, really? Any
advance?
    I'll be sending along a new book of poems for Dent's next (I hope)
week.[1]
    Has Laughlin answered you about my enquiry as to what has happened
to my copies of *New Poems*?[2] I've never seen a single copy. Do ask him to
let me have some, will you?

                                          Sincerely,
                                          Dylan Thomas

MS: Texas

DONALD TAYLOR
19 Sept 44   Majoda New Quay Cardiganshire

Dear Donald,
    Wonderful news—or half-news. I have my fingers, legs, and eyes,
crossed.
    Do write or wire me once you know the best/worst.
    I hope you're not quite so penniless, & in debt, as I am, but, anyway,
the dough from B & H will be, I'm sure, welcome.[3] And oh the difference
to me!
    I've read through Resistance many times and added a valediction. I
can't do more until I know more of your, & M.O.I., reactions. Your wire
about it was so hopelessly muddled by the P.O. people here that all I
could clearly make out was that you hoped the MOI would consider
making a more ambitious film than they'd intended. This commentary
can be expanded, contracted, rewritten or thrown away & started again at
a moment's notice, as you know.
    Do tell me: has V.2. really arrived? Here there are rumours.[4] I'm
coming up, unless you call me earlier, at the end of the month. Want to
discuss many things urgently.

                                          Ever,
                                          Dylan

[1] The volume being planned was *Deaths and Entrances*.
[2] The 'Poets of the Year' volume, published 1943.
[3] 'B & H': Burke and Hare (the film about the body-snatchers) = *The Doctor and the Devils*.
[4] German rockets, 'V2s', began to bombard London in September.

You'll notice I've suggested that we cut out the opening lines 'We were free'. Surely, 'we' weren't?

MS: Texas

PETER LUNN LTD[1]

20 Sept '44   Majoda New Quay Cardiganshire

Dear Sir,

Thank you for your letter of the 15th.

I am very interested indeed in the idea of editing, and writing the commentary for, the book of photographs you mention.

I shall be in London at the end of the month—on the 28th, I think—and will be staying up for some time. If you would write me, making an appointment for any day after the 28th, I should be grateful.

I could, if it was really urgent, come up a few days beforehand. Anyway, I hope you'll let me know.

Yours faithfully,
Dylan Thomas

MS: National Library of Wales

T. W. EARP

[postmarked 21 September 1944]   [Cardiganshire]

> Dear Tommy, please, from far, sciatic Kingsley[2]
> Borrow my eyes. The darkening sea flings Lee
> And Perrins on the cockled tablecloth
> Of mud and sand. And, like a sable moth,
> A cloud against the glassy sun flutters his
> Wings. It would be better if the shutter is
> Shut. Sinister dark over Cardigan
> Bay. No-good is abroad. I unhardy can
> Hardly bear the din of No-good wracked dry on
> The pebbles. It is time for the Black Lion
> But there is only Buckley's unfrisky
> Mild. Turned again, Worthington. Never whisky.

---

[1] A small publishing firm that wanted Thomas to write an illustrated book about the streets of London. It had been impressed by captions he wrote for a feature in the magazine *Lilliput*.

[2] Line 1, Earp lived in a village called Kingsley. Lines 11 and 12, Buckley's is a Welsh beer, as Worthington is an English. Line 17, parch, a Welsh clergyman, literally 'reverend'.

I sit at the open window, observing
The salty scene and my Playered gob curving
Down to the wild, umbrella'd, and french lettered
Beach, hearing rise slimy from the Welsh lechered
Caves the cries of the parchs and their flocks. I
Hear their laughter sly as gonococci. . . .
There slinks a snoop in black. I'm thinking it
Is Mr. Jones the Cake, that winking-bit,
That hymning gooseberry, that Bethel-worm
At whose ball-prying even death'll squirm
And button up. He minces among knickers,
That prince of pimps, that doyen of dung-lickers.
Over a rump on the clerical-grey seashore,
See how he stumbles. Hallelujah hee-haw!,
His head's in a nest where no bird lays her egg.
He cuts himself on an elder's razor leg.
Sniff, here is sin! Now must he grapple, rise:
He snuggles deep among the chapel thighs,
And when the moist collection plate is passed
Puts in his penny, generous at last.

On Saturday Augustus comes, bearded
Like Cardy's bard, and howling as Lear did.
A short stay only but oh, how nice. No
One more welcome than the oaktrunked maestro—
No-one but you who'll never come unless
I send the million-miscarriaged Welsh Express,
A train of thought run on wheels within wheels.
But on October 1 I show my heels
To New Quay, Cards, and then shall brave V.2.
And come to London. Remember me to
May. Is there a chance of one I never see
Coming up, also? Write me: Ever,

                                                    D.

MS: Ohio State University   *SL*

PETER LUNN LTD
25 Sept 44 (Confirms meeting on September 29. See Appendix 30.)

PETER LUNN LTD
6 October '44   Guild House 2–6 West St London WC2

Dear Sirs,
   Re Book on Streets. I am in receipt of your letter of October 6 and
confirm that the terms contained in it are in accordance with our
arrangements.[1]
   I hope that it is possible for me to let you have the completed manuscript in about three months.

                              Yours faithfully,
                              Dylan Thomas

MS: National Library of Wales

DONALD TAYLOR
[?October 1944]   Majoda New Quay Cardiganshire

Back in the bosom, repentant and bloodshot,
Under the draper-sly skies,[2]
I try to forget my week in the mudpot
And cottonwool it in lies:

'I do not, my dear, pretend that I mastered
Altogether the intemperate vice.
I may in the Gargoyle have fallen down plastered,
But I did see my publishers—twice.

You wouldn't believe me were I to aver
That I never went out 'on the bust'.
You'll pardon the phrase? Ah, thank you, my dear,
And I did see an editor—just.

Now let us be frank. I behaved, I'm afraid,
Like a squalid and tiddly dunce.
But I really was brave in that *terrible* raid,
And I did make some money—once.'

Dear Donald,
   I'm sending you the words for 'Our Country'.[3] I took away a typed copy

---

[1] Thomas was paid an advance of £50.
[2] Cardiganshire people, the butt of many Welsh jokes, are supposed to have a sly streak, and
   also to thrive as drapers.
[3] Another rhetorical film for the Ministry of Information, released in 1944. Texas has
   Thomas's eleven-page MS.

but, as most of the corrections to be made were only of punctuation, I made such a mess of the typesheets I decided to write out the whole thing afresh. Going through it, as I did, carefully, it's my opinion that it may be a mistake to have the words printed in the premiere programme. For two reasons. First: the cuts you made in the verse-commentary, which, from the point of the film, were essential, did destroy some of the continuity of the verse *as verse*. The words were written to be spoken & heard, & not to be read, but all the same there was in the original version—before your most necessary cuts—a literary thread, or, at least, a sense-thread, which is now broken. And, second: I think that, to many people, a reading of these words before the film will presuggest an artiness that is not, I think, in the film. If, for instance, Alf Burlinson, who is loud in his praise of the film and of the verse (inseparable, we hope), had first of all seen the words written or printed down his reactions to the film would, I think, have been different. Written down, the verse looks a little chaotic—as it's bound to be. And, to Alf & others, 'modern'. Heard spoken to a beautiful picture, the words gain a sense & authority which the printed word denies them. I don't make myself very clear, but these are two quite relevant points. If you *are* going to print the words, perhaps Miss Harrington, who now knows my kind of punctuation or lack of it, could do them? Anyway, whatever you think best is alright by me.

I am just starting to go through 20 Years[1]—the book, John's selection of passages, & my own notes. I shd start on the real work this week.

I hope to hear from you soon about B & H. Passed? Hope to God so as the money I collected in London is all gone in debts. And new ones are rising.

I enclose, for your private interest, Watt's letter on the Dickens script.[2] Not much there, once it has been threed up. Could you return it some time?

> Yours ever,
> Dylan

Thank you for London kindness & help with the scrappy Streets synopsis. I saw some of Banting's suggested drawings for it. Very nice. Very sweet. Very unsuitable.

P.S. On page 6 of the 'Our Country' verse: I know that the place-name Shipbourne is wrong, but can't remember what was right. It might have been Shibbon. Perhaps Colin could find out if there *is* such a place as Shibbon-in-Bredon, for I seem to remember that the penultimate line of the list of place-names was only one word. May be wrong, though. Anyway, Shipbourne is wrong.

MS: Texas

[1] A film was projected (but never made) based on Maurice O'Sullivan's book about the Blasket Islands, off the south-west tip of Ireland, *Twenty Years A-Growing*.
[2] A film on the life of Charles Dickens that Thomas was to write with Philip Lindsay. It was not made.

VERNON WATKINS

TO BE READ FIRST

28 Oct 1944   as from Majoda New Quay Cardiganshire

My dear Gwen and Vernon,
   What on earth can you think of me?[1] It is the last, last, last thing of all—on top of all the other things—that the hasty letter I should scribble in such a panic to you, while on the train away from London where we never met, should remain unposted until today: 26 days after your wedding. I have no excuses, but that I was so flurried and anxious, so tired, so miserable, that I put the train-letter into my pocket, arrived in New Quay after an 8 hour journey, imagined, in a kind of delirium, that it was posted, & then waited, perhaps without much hope of ever hearing, to hear from you that, though I was not forgiven, my explanation was understood. What can you think of me? Today I found the letter, crumpled, unposted, in my overcoat. Please, please do try to understand. I shall let you have these two letters now, & a poem I meant also to send weeks ago,[2] without another word of apology or abasement. All our love to you both, for your happiness forever.

Your worst man,
Dylan

[Sent with letter dated 28 October 1944]
The Train to Wales, 1.30 Wed.

On Not Turning Up To Be Best Man
At The Wedding Of One's Best Friend

Reeking & rocking back from a whirled London where nothing went right, all duties were left, and my name spun rank in the whole old smoky nose, I try, to a rhythm of Manchester pocket-handkerchers, and Conk him on the mousetrap, Conk him on the mousetrap, from the London-leaving wheels, to explain to you both, clearly & sincerely, why I never arrived, in black overcoat & shiny suit, rose-lapelled, breathing cachous & great good will, at lunch and church. But the train's stacked tight, I'm tabling a bony knee for this little pad, and am stuck, in the windy corridor, between many soldiers, all twelve foot high & commando-

---

[1] Thomas had failed to appear at Vernon Watkins's wedding in London, where he was supposed to be best man, on October 2. According to Gwen Watkins, Vernon said, 'That's the end of Dylan as far as I'm concerned.' But when this letter arrived, he was quick to forgive. The enclosure, written in pencil on well-creased paper, has many alterations; Mrs Watkins thinks its appearance was faked, to make it look as if it had lain in Thomas's overcoat pocket for weeks.

[2] 'Vision and Prayer'.

trained to the last lunge of the bayonet. It's not easy to think, or write, or be, and my explanations, true as air, sound, when I try to marshal them, like a chapter of accidents written in a dream by a professor of mathematics who has forgotten all formulas but the wrong one that 2 & 2 make 5. First, then, I arrived in London on Thursday & was sent straightaway, that is, on Friday morning, to Coventry: the City of Coventry, where the company who pay me occasionally are making a film called 'Building The Future', a subject on which I particularly should have no say. In Coventry I arranged to catch a train back on Sunday night, which would carry me to London in time to meet you both at the station. That train, owing to no fault of my own but to callous & diffident members of the hotel staff, who did not trouble to get the train-times straight, but only late, I missed. There was no other train until the next morning, which was Monday, & that train would reach London at an hour just convenient for me to be able to get into a cab & race for the church. I could not, at that hour of Sunday night, reach my office to leave a message for someone there to spend Monday morning ringing up you & your people & making my—by this time—frantic excuses; I could, in-deed, have reached the office by telephone, but there would be no-one there to answer, except some celluloid rat or other. So I waited until Monday morning & then, before catching the train, rang up the office & told a secretary girl to ring Charing Cross Hotel straight away, get in touch with anyone called Watkins, & explain the whole position to him or her. I had not, myself, got the time to ring up Charing X Hotel, as it wd take hours, & as my call to the office could be, & was, made Priority, thereby saving those hours during which, by the nicotine-stained skin of my few teeth, I caught the wedding-going & troop-crammed horribly slow train. On arriving in London I managed, by the fervour of my heart only, I am sure, to snatch a cab. I sat back, wheezing, in it. 'Where to?' the driver said. And—this is the real God-help-me—I couldn't remember the name of the church. It was after half past one. I looked in all my pockets but had left your last letter, I suppose, in wood-&-asbestos Majoda, New Quay. I tried, in my head, every church name I knew. I explained to the driver: 'A Church in the City. Very old.' Suddenly something came & I said, 'I think it's Godolphin. Or something like that. Yes, Godolphin.' We went to the City, the driver was dubious. We asked policemen: they were certain. By now, after two, & you too, I feared & hoped, married without my presence but with all my love, I went back to the office to find the secretary-girl out for lunch & the few people still there surprisingly cool and ignorant of all the infernal muddle that had been clotting up the wheels of the world for over a day. There was nothing to do. When the girl came in I asked her, though I was terrified to ask, if her little side of the whole business had gone well. She had tried the Charing X Hotel all the morning. The Watkins were out. She had left my name. The Watkins were out.

Later that evening, feeling wretcheder than ever before, alone in my beast of a studio, I remembered the church. Of course I remembered the church. Not Godolphin but St. Bartholomew the Great—too late! O what a prize of prize pickles & I'll understand always if you never want to see me again. I know this hasty jumble can't explain all the somersaulting & backspinning of circumstance against my being where I most wanted to be: at your wedding. God bless you both, & do try to forgive me.

All my love,
Dylan

MS: British Library   *VW*

T. W. EARP
28 October 1944   Majoda New Quay Cardiganshire

Dear Tommy,
  I came up to town for a week but it was sudden and accidental and I made no arrangements & hoped to see you only by hanging about some of the places in which sometimes we hang about together. But at the end of November, when I can move next, we must & will meet. I'll send you a string of wires beforehand, none of them contradictory. Oh I do wish you & May could come down here before then—won't you ever?
  I've just had a birthday & here is a poem.[1] I hope you'll read & like.
  Tell me about it when you write; & write soon.

Yours,
Dylan

MS: Ohio State University

DONALD TAYLOR
28 October 1944   [headed paper: Gryphon Films etc]
                              as from Majoda New Quay Cardiganshire

Dear Donald,
  Now who could be writing to *you* from Gryphon? Why, bless my soul, it's the little Welsher. This is only to thank you for your wire, and to tell you that though work on *20 Years* has been going so slowly & badly that at one time I thought we'd have to alter the title to *40 Years*, now I believe I can get ahead with it properly. Reason for the badness & slowness is that this little bungalow is no place to work in when there's a

---

[1] 'Poem in October'.

bawling child there, too: the rooms are tiny, the walls bumpaper-thin, & a friend arrived with another baby with a voice like Caruso's. Now, however, I have just taken a room in a nearby house: a very quiet room where I know I can work till I bleed. So little's been done on 20 Years—I've spent my time running out to look at the sea, away from the greater sea of noise within—it's not really worth discussing or sending. But now I shall get down to it with axe, concentration, and blow-lamp.

I hope the censors have finally come to heel. Let me know what happens from time to time about all our films, made, halfmade, unmade, readymade, secondhand, if you can.

A very nice fellow here, who runs a Nautical School, asked me how to get 16 mm films to show. All kinds: they're tough boys. I asked him to get in touch with you, who would—I hoped—tell him, in turn, who to get in touch with. Hope you can help him.

The Dickens terms are indeed scandalous. I would like to have nothing to do with them at all—they really are almost insolently puny—& I won't if some other book-money I'm expecting comes along before the contract. Otherwise I'm afraid I'll have to sign as even the preliminary £20, which is all I'll get out of the first £100, will settle a debt & take this bungalow for another three months. I hope not to have to sign, though, damn their meanness.

How are things? Have a drink for me, only make it beer, as a new resolution, now a fortnight, nearly, old, has banned all other drinks—for a long time, I trust & believe.

Ever,
Dylan

Will write again soon, with *much more encouraging* Twenty Years news.

MS: Buffalo   *SL(R)*

LAURENCE POLLINGER
28 Oct 44   Majoda New Quay Cardiganshire

Dear Pollinger,
Enclosed title page of book of poems. Forgot to put it with the manuscript which I hope now is in your hands—along with explanatory letter.[1]

Yours sincerely,
Dylan Thomas

P.S. Have just received the copy of *New Poems* and Laughlin's letter. I'll reply personally to Laughlin, at once. Would you send the remaining

---

[1] *Deaths and Entrances* was not published until 1946, when it included poems still unwritten in October 1944.

presentation copies of *New Poems* to me here at New Quay? I want to make some alterations in them before sending them on to friends.

MS: Texas

VERNON WATKINS
Nov 15 1944   Majoda New Quay Cardiganshire

Dear Vernon,

I was so very pleased to have your letter last week, your letter this morning, and, best, yours and Gwen's (even in 1980) pardon. I can now take my head out of the grubby lining of my overcoat pocket, where I have been keeping it for weeks along with a beetle, something that looks like porridge and smells like the Underground, and an unposted letter. I can take my head out now and face the perpetual rain.

I like your address, especially if it is Story Stratford. What kind of a house have you, or is it a room, or rooms, or a flat, or the use of somebody's old larder to live in? I should like very much to visit you, if I may, if Gwen will bury her sten-gun in the garden before I come, one day, soon, in December. Caitlin and I are going to London the first week of December. Caitlin will leave Aeronwy with her mother, at Ringwood, and we will probably stay in an hotel for a week or two. Caitlin hasn't had a holiday away from Aeronwy since Aeronwy appeared with pain and trumpets. So we want to go to cinemas & theatres and eat nice spicy meals and meet you and Gwen and go to see paintings and drink in the Eight Bells and Claridges like improper people and sneer at the V.2. and come back here for Christmas. (I didn't tell you that Vera Phillips, now [...], for she has married a man called [...] but who, for years, we thought was called Waistcoat, is living in the next bungalow to us on this ratty cliff. She lives alone except for her baby daughter who is five months old and, during all that time, has screamed only twice. Vera says it is because of character. We say it is because of laziness. Vera lives on cocoa, and reads books about the technique of third-century brass work, and gets up only once a day to boil the cat an egg, which it detests.) So we must meet in London. Is it possible for you & Gwen to have leave together & come up and see a play in a theatre, or outside a theatre, with us? And a real meal, not a crawl on bent minds round the Tambied pubs?

Has Dot told you yet that we met in Cardigan, filthy town, for a, on my part, rather rambling hour? I had been to a farmers' fair. Dot looked awfully well, and was lovely to meet. I hope I'll see her again when she comes billeting.

I am so glad you liked the 'Vision & Prayer' poem; and that the diamond shape of the first part seems no longer to you to be cramped & artificed. I agree that the second part is, formally, less inevitable, but I cannot alter it, except, perhaps, in detail. I will read the very last line again, & see what, if anything, can be done about the stresses. I haven't a copy of the poem with me but, as I remember, I liked the last line *for* the awkward stressing, for the braking, for the slowing up of the last two same-vowelled words (I wrote 'birds' instead of 'words'). But I'll read the whole poem again, most carefully. Yes, the Hound of Heaven is baying there in the last verse, but, at the moment, and again from memory, I don't remember seeing any Hopkins after the poem was finished.

I'll look out for the David poem[1] in the Listener, if I can get a copy from our newsagent who closes nearly all day and sells, I think, only the Western Mail and ink.

Here is a poem of mine which I started a long time ago but finished very recently, after a lot of work. This poem, the Vision & Prayer, & the birthday poem are coming out together in the January Horizon.[2] I hope you'll be able to get a copy & see them in pretty print.

How is Dan? Is he a new father? Do you see him? Send him my love, if you do.

And love from Caitlin & myself to you and Gwen.

Ever,
Dylan

MS: British Library   *VW*

LAURENCE POLLINGER
17 November 44   Majoda New Quay Cardiganshire

Dear Laurence Pollinger:
    You'll have received, I hope, my wire before this, accepting Dent's offer and asking you to get the agreement sent to me for signature as soon as possible. I'm glad you will be able to arrange for the £50 to be paid upon delivery to Dent of my signed copy.[3] So do please let me have the agreement very quickly. I must have the £50 on or before the 24th of this month. That is a very fateful date.

    I was hoping for a larger royalty, and would, I know, have been able to get a substantially larger one from Nicolson and Watson.[4] Probably not on such good royalty terms, but, then, I never expect my poems to sell very much. Immediate money is, at this stage, what I need for work done. However ...

[1] Watkins's poem 'Reprisals of Calm'.
[2] The January 1945 *Horizon* contained 'Holy Spring', which was enclosed with the letter, and 'Vision and Prayer'. The 'birthday poem', 'Poem in October', was in the February issue.
[3] The publisher's contract for *Deaths and Entrances* is dated November 24.
[4] A small firm of publishers with whom Thomas had had dealings.

I shall look forward to hearing from Church about those 'points of detail' you mention. And also to seeing a specimen of the 'small and attractive format' in which my book will be published. But the latter can wait until I come up to town the first week of December when, I hope, we can meet. I will ring you then. I do hope you'll be able to spare a few minutes to come out and talk over a drink, as even the friendliest office drenches me with dread.

About Mr. Gottlieb:[1] I am sure I have behaved naughtily, but I could not, really, wait for un-naughty arrangements to be made. I was then, as ever, and as, again, particularly now (until the coming of Dent's £50 which *must* be before the 24th), tangled in debts, and Mr. Gottlieb's ready cheque book tempted me too much. I will bring up his letters of contract and agreement to show you.

About Laughlin: there is no point in sending him a duplicate complete typescript of *Deaths & Entrances* as at least half of the poems in it appeared in the New Directions publication of *New Poems*. Several of the poems Laughlin published I have, for the Dent's book, extensively revised, but not *so* extensively as to warrant their publication, in America, *as* new poems. The best thing to do, I should think, would be to wait until I have another half dozen poems to add to the ones, in the Dent book, which have not appeared in *New Poems*.

I am writing to Laughlin about the *Selected Works*, answering all his points. I shall, at the same time, enclose the additional poems, included in Deaths & Entrances, for him to see. He can then decide whether he would prefer to include these in the *Selected Works* or wait (as I have suggested above) until there are sufficient new poems added to them to make a separate new book worth while. However, again . . .

I shall definitely ring you when I'm in town early in December.

And I await eagerly the Dent agreement to sign.

Yours sincerely,
Dylan Thomas

MS: Texas

JOHN BAYLISS
25 Nov 44   Majoda New Quay Cardiganshire

Dear John,

Thank you for the copy of New Road, I was very glad to have it. I haven't read much of it yet, but it seems a fine job. It was good to see Antonia White's poem reprinted, I had been trying to remember it all on and off for years.[2]

---

[1] Gottlieb, of Peter Lunn, had commissioned the 'Book of Streets'.
[2] The Antonia White poem was 'Epitaph'. The 1944 number of *New Road* contained, besides two poems by Thomas (see page 513), poems by Vernon Watkins and John Ormond (Thomas).

Sorry I haven't a story; I haven't written one now for a long time, but I shall try again soon and if it works I'll send the result along. I'm writing filmscripts for a living & the time—the work time, I mean—left over from that I try to spend on poems: a miserable arrangement, which should be reversed. But I *have* collected a book of poems together & Dent will be bringing it out early next year at the very sane price of 3/6: it'll be called Deaths & Entrances: I hope you'll manage to get a copy.

I'll see what I can do about a story in the next month, if that's not too late, but I can't promise anything for the only stories I've written since the war, & very few, have been straightforward anecdotes (not, I'm glad to say, of the 'Then he downed a bloody pint, see' kind). Be seeing you some day.

> Yours,
> Dylan

MS: Texas

VERNON WATKINS
Tues Nov 28 44   Majoda New Quay Cardiganshire

Dear Vernon,
  I hope you find the poem visible this time.
  I will be in London from December the first: for, say, ten days. (Though I don't know why, 'say'.) Will you wire me, any day after the first, at GRYPHON, 2–6 WEST STREET, W.C.2, and say when you & Gwen can come up. I suggest either Monday, Dec. 4, Tuesday, Dec. 5, or Wednesday, Dec. 6. I suggest one o'clock (1 p.m.) as the time, and the Back Bar of the Café Royal (table facing the door) as the place. If you can meet *there*, at *that* time, on *any* of the three days suggested above, your wire need contain only the one word—Monday (or Tuesday, of course, or Wednesday)—and I shall be there—(Back Bar of the Café Royal, table facing door, one p.m.)—henna'd, camelia'd, & smelling of moths.
  I shall buy the December Horizon for your poem. How big is it? Send, by rail, or carrier pigeon, or in a plain man, a prose summary of all your poems and a pocket bicycle and a machine for draining witches and oh God help me I should never write letters after lunch: I am whimsical, I am porky, there are peas in my ears & my smile is gravy.
  Yes, we could see 'Night at the Opera', I should love that, or a murder film called 'Laura', or even Henry V.
  I am *very* frightened of the rockets.
  There is no news here: a woman called Mrs. Prosser died in agony last week, there has been a coroner's inquest on a drowned coastguard (verdict suicide), Vera's cat was wounded by a rabbit trap & died, all night long we hear rabbits shrieking like babies in the steel jaws in the hedges, Caitlin

killed five mice in one day by traps, but, still, I am quite happy and am looking forward to a gross, obscene and extremely painful middle-age.

Did I tell you I was going to Ireland early next year: to an island off Kerry? Well, I am, & I shall tell you about it when we meet.

Wire me after the first, at the unlikely address of GRYPHON, 2–6 West St., W.C.2.

Love to you both from Caitlin & myself.

> Ever,
> Dylan

MS: British Library   *VW*

D. GOTTLIEB (Peter Lunn Ltd)
19th December 1944   [headed paper: Gryphon Films, etc]

Dear Mr. Gottlieb,

After our explosive interview on the telephone this morning, I have thought it best to write to you this brief and sincere explanation of my point of view, while apologising for my rudeness and carelessness in not replying to your correspondence and for the shifts and evasions that my laziness and neurotic fear of telephones and telegrams have reduced me to.

In our letters of contract and agreement, there is no mention made of any definite date upon which the manuscript is to be delivered.[1] But we did have a verbal understanding to the effect that I would endeavour to produce some work—part, if not whole—by the 6th of January 1945. This I will still endeavour to do, and have every hope of succeeding on or near that date. The work I have so far done is only in form of notes but these I hope to resolve into something concrete by or near the verbally agreed date.

I hope this may be satisfactory to you and that my not replying before may be forgiven.

> Yours sincerely,
> Dylan Thomas

MS: National Library of Wales

---

[1] All Thomas ever produced was a three-page synopsis headed, 'A Book of Streets. Words and Pictures about Streets. Streets in London.'

OSCAR WILLIAMS
31 December 44   as from Gryphon Films Guild House
                                            2–6 West Street London W

Dear Oscar,

The signed anthology for 1942 has arrived, and the Man has come Towards me.[1] Thank you very much for both. I haven't yet read more than a scattered few of the poems in your own book, stopping with delight and surprise at many knock-me-down lines, and shan't try to write anything to you until I have read the whole book carefully, and more than once, through from torpedo to cloudburst. Of the 1944 anthology I like a great deal. I like all that I have read of Alfred Hayes: has he had a book out there? And Shapiro's poem, and most of W. R. Rodgers's, and, as always, the lovely poems of my friend Vernon Watkins (who certainly should be published in book-form in America). And much more, of course. I don't agree with you at all about Timothy Corsellis, and think that you have anthologised, in Henry Treece's poem, two of the worst lines since man began to write:

'And the green shark-cradles with their swift
Cruel fingers setting the ocean's curls.'[2]

Treece has written his own criticism in one almost comparably bathetic line: 'In the beginning was the bird'.

Oh yes, and while I'm feeling like that, let me curse you to the company, eternally, of novelists and actors for tacking on to the end of my poem, 'When I Awoke' the last verse of my poem, 'On A Wedding Anniversary'. I do not like either poem, but they *are* better apart. I expect a printed apology and an orange.

I am looking forward to a few cheques from magazines to which you sent my new poems. Thank you so much. I'm very glad to be able to send things to you, knowing that you'll get them printed. I am extremely poor at the moment; there is no chance of getting any money out of poetry in this country, no Guggenheims, no literary dibbers, only a few magazines, which pay nothing or a pound, and a handful of greyfaced young men with private incomes, weasely habits, and no inclination to give one anything but melancholia or dysentery.

I'll try to write something on war and poetry during the next week, but can't promise anything. I shan't know until I start writing whether I have any clear ideas on this, or on any other, subject. I prefer what I think about verse to be *in* the verse.

I meet Dunstan Thompson sometimes in London, and find him quite charming.[3] I asked him what you yourself were like & he made an elegant

[1] Williams's first book of poems was *The Man Coming Toward You*.
[2] From Treece's poem 'The Dyke Builder'.
[3] Dunstan Thompson (b. 1918), American poet and traveller. In 1944 he was in the U.S. Army, stationed in Europe.

movement of his long sea-green hands, signifying, to me, nothing but the efforts of a man to play the flute without using his mouth.

Thank you, again, for the books & the good wishes, & for sending my poems around.

It is the last evening of the bad year and I am going out to celebrate myself sick and dirty.

Make what you can of 1945.

I shall try to write soon, sending the letter by airmail (or in a sealed man).

Yours,
Dylan

MS: Harvard   *SL*

D. GOTTLIEB
3rd January 1945   Majoda New Quay Cardiganshire

Dear Mr. Gottlieb,

Thank you for your considerate letter and for your acceptance of my apologies for behaving in a quite uncivilised manner.

I'm afraid I have nothing of consecutive value to send you by the suggested near-date of January 6th, owing more to domestic troubles beyond my control—my wife has influenza and I am trying to combine the duties of housekeeper and children-minder along with my own work —than to the difficulty, however pleasurable, of the job itself. I suggest that we move the date forward one month: to the end of the first week of February. The plan for the book that I had started work upon I've decided to scrap, as a much better plan came to my mind; and this change necessitates far more work & will result, I think, in a far more original book. Roughly, my plan is this: to call the book *Twelve Hours In The Streets* and to take the life of the streets from twelve noon to twelve midnight. Thus the street can fit the hour, and vice versa; streets that to my mind, & perhaps to the minds of many others, recall instantly some specific hour of day or night will fit naturally, & not artificially, into the structure of the book. And the whole might well be an imaginative, picaresque perhaps, cross-section of the life of the English streets for a whole modern day. (There is a *kind* of Elizabethan analogy to this in Nicholas Breton's 'Elizabethan Day' reprinted in Dover Wilson's Penguin book on Elizabethan England.)

I hear that Banting's drawings were considered too gay for such a book as I have in mind; & perhaps this is so. Have you another illustrator in mind?

I hope to hear from you soon.

> Yours sincerely,
> Dylan Thomas

I should add that I am, of course, as desirous as you of having the book published in the early, rather than in the late, part of 1945 (other conditions, as you say, permitting) and that I intend working on nothing else for the next month.

> DT.

MS: National Library of Wales

D. GOTTLIEB
6 February 1945   Majoda New Quay Cardiganshire

Dear Mr. Gottlieb,
   Thank you so much for your letter of January 6th. I would have replied sooner, but I was waiting—rather vainly, as it happened—for my nasty attack of gastric 'flu to disappear—a 'flu I caught from my family (as I think I told you my family was suffering from, the last time I wrote).
   I came up to London last month, with the intention of seeing you and talking over the book with Games, but, almost as soon as I was up, I got caught with this annoying trouble & was forced to travel back, through snow, in an ice-bound train, in order to get a little nursing attention from an already flu-fed-up family.
   I hope to come up to town in about 10 days time—when I will ring you at once &, I hope, arrange for a lunch & discussion as soon as it suits you.
   I have one or two new ideas which I think are essential to the artistic success of the book.

> Regards,
> Yours sincerely,
> Dylan Thomas

MS: National Library of Wales

T. W. EARP
6 Feb '45   Majoda New Quay Cards

Dear Tommy,
   Very deeply sorry to have missed you in the Bell, that Monday. I was, strictly, in bed, in Chelsea, in London, in pain, with gastric flu; and alone, so that I could not get to the telephone to leave a love and a sorry message. I came back, as soon as better, here, in order to get nursed and

cursed. How is May? I still hope you and she may be able to get down here soon, when May can travel. We may, by that time, have a better (or worse) house, near here. Write when you can, and do tell me about the enclosed poems:—I enclose them in case, as rightly, you have not seen the January Horizon. One, the triangular looking poem (though badly typographed here) I have shown you the beginning of.[1] Now the beginning is different, & the rest, which you have not seen, obviously so. All regards from us both, and *please* don't insult us by not visiting us very soon.

Dylan

MS: Ohio State University

DONALD TAYLOR
8 February 45   Majoda New Quay Cardiganshire

Dear Donald,
  I feel very badly about it that our conversation some evenings ago should have disturbed you, and I do apologise now and immediately, knowing that the disturbing influence was, however it sounded, quite unintentional. I can only say that I'd just come out of a gastric chamber, had had a few hurried drinks to see if I were still alive, and then spoke to you, not in a quiet box as I usually do when I ring up, but against a background of maudlin sea-captains and shrewd, if stunned, travellers in petrol. One ear was hearing you and the other ear busy shutting out the buzzing of those Cardy drones, and I spoke, I know, hurriedly & stupidly. Please take no notice of what I said about Labour: I'm proud to be asked to try to do the script: my only fear is that I shall not do a very good job of it: I am not, as you know, politically very acute, and will have to rely, as always, upon emotionalism. But I will send off the opening sequences in a few days, and you will be [?able to] tell from them whether I should go on alone with the scripting or whether I should work at it closely with you and, alone, do only the dialogue (whose indications we could map out together) and the descriptive-visual writing. Another reason for my unfortunately—and, again, really unmeant—disturbing conversation, was that I was enormously pleased by the good news of the 'Suffer Little Children' film,[2] and very very keen on getting on with it at once. I know the short films have to be done, and I am sorry that I gave the impression of wanting to get away from them; it is, of course, the big-scale film of ideas that we both wish to work at, work hard & work soon, but 'Labour', too, is a job of work and I have, in my proper self, no intention of trying to

---

[1] 'Vision and Prayer.'
[2] *Suffer Little Children*, alternatively *Betty London*, was to be a feature film, the kind that Donald Taylor hoped to produce after the war. It was not made. Some of Thomas's dialogue is said to have been used in a Diana Dors film, *Good Time Girl* (1948).

escape it. I do want to say again that I think 'Suffer Little Children' a superlative idea, and I am longing to talk about it in detail and around it, to discuss it at great length with you, and to work upon it as soon as possible & to produce the completed script more quickly than any other we have done.

I'll come up as soon as you want me, but you will have the opening Labour sequences in your hands first.

Sorry again.

What news of B. & H.? I think I forgot to tell you the new name I had thought of for Dr. Robert Knox: *Thomas Rock*. This is very near, in vowels & general feeling, to the original, and does, I think satisfy Bridie's[1] complaint: it does sound the name of a man who could be very distinguished & great in science. What do you think?

Let me know if you wish me to ring you again soon; & this time I shall choose the privacy of a public booth not the propinquity of a public bar.

Ever,
Dylan

I have just finished reading—and will send on under separate cover — the autobiography, called *The Islandman*, of Tomás Ó Crohan (The Blaskets, 1856–1937). It is *the* very first book about the Blaskets, written in 1926, published 1929. Ó Crohan was, apparently, a great & famous man, a Celtic scholar & authority, & lived all his 81 years on the Blaskets. It is most extraordinary that O'Sullivan makes no mention of him: he was, of course, very much alive on the Island *all* the time O'Sullivan was living there; it is also very odd that George Thompson should study Irish under a boy like O'Sullivan when there was already on the Island an acknowledged (by Yeats & everyone else interested in the folklore & the language) Irish scholar & taleteller.

There is no mention, either, of O'Sullivan in Ó Crohan's book.

'The Islandman', 'Twenty Years', and Robin Flower's own book—the 'West Island' is it—represent all the available written literature of and upon the Blaskets; literature, that is, of general appeal, for there must be many, & probably untranslated, essays & papers on folklore, dialect, etc. etc., written by visiting scholars. But we should be able, from those 3 books, to tell the story of life on the Island *in its entirety*. I do not suggest that we use the actual material of Ó Crohan's & Flower's books, but that we study them as background. I should very much like to see a copy of Flower's when I come up to town.

D.

MS: Buffalo   SL

---

[1] James Bridie (1888–1951) wrote a comedy about Burke and Hare, *The Anatomist* (1930). Taylor had been in touch with him to allay fears of plagiarism.

JAMES LAUGHLIN
10th February 1945   as from Gryphon Films [etc]

Dear James Laughlin,
   I haven't written to you for a very long time.
   I got your letter, dated Sept. 18. '44, which first mentioned the volumes
of SELECTED WRITINGS you were bringing out in your New Classics
Series, and I was proud and glad you were going to do a volume of mine.
   I've been all those months replying because I couldn't find anyone here
who could really do the job you wanted—'a sort of "warm" account of
what you yourself are like, what you are working toward in your poetry
and that sort of thing'. The main difficulty was that the people who do
know what I'm like don't know what I am working toward in my poetry,
and don't care anyway. And most of the people here who write about
poetry can't tell one person from another. So I was glad to hear today from
Pollinger that you had found your own man over there, J. L. Sweeney, to
write the introduction, and that the personal account is necessarily cut
out as Mr. Sweeney & myself are unknown to each other except through
our writing.[1]
   Have you any idea when the book will be coming out? And do you want
a portrait for it? I seem to remember, in another, now unfortunately lost,
letter, that you did mention it. If you do, will you tell me and I'll have a
new photograph taken by a good man in London and sent to you immediately. Only for God's sake, please don't use any of the two or three
old portraits that Oscar Williams dug up out of somewhere and has used
in his Poems of The Year series. All those were at least five or seven years
ago, and I'm much fatter and coarser now: and that, if my face is to appear
at all in the Selected volume, is how it should look.
   You asked me to tell you what I consider are my best 20 odd poems, my
best 4 stories, and the 2 best chapters of the autobiographical Portrait.
   These I have written down on a separate sheet, enclosed,[2] and I do very
much hope you will be able to stick fairly closely to it. They are my
considered opinions after re-reading all the stuff. (But don't let that worry
you.) Pollinger also told me today that he had himself written to you,
explaining that I had no new stories I thought worth including in the
Selected volume but that there were a few new poems I wish most
urgently to be included. These I enclose—they are coming out sometime
in American periodicals—and have also written their titles down in my
enclosed list of personal choices for the volume.
   My opinion as to what is my best mayn't, on the whole, agree with
yours & Sweeney's. Will you tell me, before publication, which you both
have chosen? I shan't, of course, mind a bit: I'm probably blind about
most of the poems; the only ones I feel most strongly about are the last

---

[1] John Lincoln Sweeney (b. 1906), author and curator; member of the English faculty at
   Harvard.
[2] The list was sent with the letter of February 16.

nine from the books, & the four new ones; but that's probably because they *are* new.

I hope to hear from you soon, though I don't know how long air-mail letters take these days.

Do forgive me for not writing before this: I've been very busy at my wartime job, which is writing filmscripts, and also trying to think of someone who could, as you asked, do the introduction. If you *did* want a personal note to add to Sweeney's introduction, I should suggest either Vernon Watkins, whose poems you probably know & who was brought up in the same town as me, or one of my best friends T. W. Earp, who is quite well known here as a painting critic and a general dear old talking body about the place.

Will you give my regards to J. L. Sweeney, whose job I don't envy a bit?

> Wishes,
> Yours,
> Dylan Thomas

I should like to come over to the States after the war for a few months. Any chance of getting a job to keep me while over there? Reading, talking?

A note about the typography of the poem *'Vision and Prayer'*.

In the corrected proofcopy—corrected, that is, in detail—I am enclosing, the lines are not spaced as they must be. The point is that each stanza of Part One starts, in the first line, with one beat and goes up to nine beats in the ninth line, & then decreases regularly down to one beat again. Up to line nine, each line should be one exact space to the left of the preceding line, the line above it, & should then decrease space by space. (Sorry this is so confusing to write down; it's simpler to explain in conversation to the printer; but you probably get it anyway). Thus, each stanza of Part One should look like this, as far as possible.

There must be no variations in the straight diamond lines of the left hand side of the poem, as—in the proofcopy—there are in, for example, lines 6, 7, 8 of stanza one.

Who

Are you

Who is born

In the next room

So loud to my own

That I can hear the womb

Opening and the dark run

Over the ghost and the dropped son

Behind the wall thin as a wren's bone?

In the birth bloody room unknown

To the burn and turn of time

And the heart print of man

Bows no baptism

But dark alone

Blessing on

The wild

Child.

is a bit nearer to what I want. I wish I had a typewriter here, I could show you exactly. But I'm sure you get it now.

In Part Two of the poem, the lines should go—absolutely symmetrical again—from nine beats in line one to one in line nine & increasing to nine in line seventeen: a complete reversal of Part One.

Sorry to bother you.

Dylan T

Looking again at my copying out of stanza one I see that I've made a balls of it, but I know you see what I'm after.

MS: the recipient

JAMES LAUGHLIN
16 Feb '45   as from Gryphon Films [etc]

Dear Laughlin,

Here is my suggested—& very shakily suggested—list of contents for the Selected Writing volume.[1]

Hope you've had my long letter & enclosed poems, or, anyway, that they arrive the same time as this.

I'm more & more doubtful about the *beginning* of my list.

Yours,

Dylan Thomas

---

[1] *Selected Writings of Dylan Thomas* (New Directions, 1946) included the material on Thomas's list, plus a further twenty-five poems and stories.

POEMS

[*in the margin:* From 'The World I Breathe' and 'New Poems']

I See The Boys Of Summer In Their Ruin
The Force That Through The Green Fuse Drives The Flower
When Like A Running Grave Time Tracks You Down
I In My Intricate Image Stride On Two Levels
A Grief Ago
Then Was My Neophyte
Sonnet IX
Sonnet X
I Make This In A Warring Absence When
It Is The Sinners' Dust-Tongued Bell Claps Me To Churches
The Spire Cranes. Its Statute Is An Aviary
After The Funeral, Mule Praises, Brays
How Shall My Animal
A Saint About To Fall
If My Head Hurt A Hair's Foot
There Was A Saviour
Among Those Killed In The Dawn Raid
Love In The Asylum
Ballad of The Long-Legged Bait
Deaths & Entrances.

[*in the margin:* Unpublished in Book Form in America]

Ceremony After A Fire Raid
Holy Spring
Vision and Prayer
Poem In October.

PROSE

[*in the margin:* From 'The World I Breathe']

The Orchards
A Prospect Of The Sea.

[*in the margin:* From 'Portrait of the Artist']

The Peaches
One Warm Saturday.

MS: the recipient

BBC
16 Feb' 45 (Sends bus-fare details. See Appendix 31.)

VERNON WATKINS[1]
26 2 45   Majoda New Quay Cards

Dear Vernon,

I was very very glad to hear and see from you; it's been a long and complicated time since we disappointingly met, and I'm happy and relieved to think that the offence, (for my lost, preoccupied manner must really have been that), I gave when we did meet in that gabbling drink-grey crush, the worst of the town, has, if never to be forgotten utterly, lost some disfavour,. (I have just been writing at length to Llewelyn, on the occasion of a fall from a tree and a split tongue, and the effort of not talking to a boy of six has made me adopt the claptrap periods of a leader-writer under gas.) I have found, increasingly as time goes on, or around, or backwards, or stays quite still as the brain races, the heart absorbs and expels, and the arteries harden, that the problems of physical life, of social contact, of daily posture and armour, of the choice between dissipations, of the abhorred needs enforced by a reluctance to 'miss anything', that old fear of death, are as insoluble to me as those of the spirit. In few and fewer poems I can despair and, at rare moments, exult with the big last, but the first force me every moment to make quick decisions and thus to plunge me into little hells and rubbishes at which I rebel with a kind of truculent acceptance. The ordinary moments of walking up village streets, opening doors or letters, speaking good-days to friends or strangers, looking out of windows, making telephone calls, are so inexplicably (to me) dangerous that I am trembling all over before I get out of bed in the mornings to meet them. Waking to remember an appointment at X that coming evening is to see, before X, galleries of menacing commonplaces, chambers of errors of the day's conventions, pits of platitudes and customary gestures, all beckoning, spurning; and through, over & out of these I must somehow move before the appointment, the appointment that has now become a shining grail in a dentist's surgery, an almost impossible consummation of illegal pleasure to be achieved in a room like a big gut in a subterranean concentration-camp. And especially, of course, in London. I wish that I could have met Gwen 'properly,' and glad that she wanted to; I was 'myself' in the sense that I was no-one else, but I was broken on a wheel of streets and faces; equally well, I may be just as broken in the peace—what peace?—of the country, hysterical in my composure, hyena-ish in my vegetabledom. I

---

[1] Not in *VW*: Gwen Watkins found the letter in a kitbag after her husband's death. She suggests that Thomas's statement in it of his difficulties with 'the problems of physical life, of social contact', constitute 'his real letter of apology for letting Vernon down [at the wedding]—real, in the sense that he is now telling the truth'.

will, if I may, try to come to stay in the pub in Stony Stratford[1] when next I come to London: but oh the bony cupboards and traps and vats before that.

I wish I could see your new poems. The translation in Horizon I did, & remembered much of it; it was beautiful.

I am glad Francis[2] is alive, well, and happy.

I have lost Dan's address again. Will you tell him that we are not going to Ireland for a long time, perhaps not even this year, as another film has risen out of some fool's mind and must be written so that we can eat and tremble at the approach of each quiet, unsensational & monstrous day? The studio is being carefully looked after. I'll write to Dan this week & will send the letter to you.

Love to you and Gwen from us both.

> Ever,
> Dylan

I wish I could understand your letter from Heatherslade. It was dated the 24th, which was Saturday, but said that you were afraid we would be unable to meet as you were leaving on Friday. If that was not also, and unfortunately, typical of myself, I should say it was a piece of genuine-accept-no-other Vernon.

Don't mind this silly letter. It was lovely to have yours.

MS: British Library

LAURENCE POLLINGER
24 March 45 (Sends letter to be forwarded to Richard Church. See Appendix 32.)

DONALD TAYLOR
Tuesday March 28(?) 45   Majoda New Quay Cards

Dear Donald,
   Today, limp in the hut, watching the exhausting sea, lost in our Betty —Betty dark?—drowned in our Sophie—Sophie fair?[3]—but writing little until tomorrow, first, cold thing in the morning, with the dew on the grass, and the Captains in bed, and the trees talking double rook. I was so very sorry you went back. Did you get a sleeper? And even the Captain is gone, with all his wheezy rumbling as though he were trying to bring up

---

[1] Vernon and Gwen Watkins, both in the armed forces, were billeted at Stony Stratford, Buckinghamshire. Both worked at Bletchley Park, the code-breaking centre. So did Captain Dan Jones.
[2] Francis Dufau-Labeyrie.
[3] Betty and Sophie were characters in the projected *Suffer Little Children*.

from his cavernous inside a very old, rusty, seaweedy anchor. Frank sparkles still, but the Lion lies down.[1] This is only to say (1) I hope you'll be back soon, (2) I *do* hope you can, somehow, manage a little money this week, by some not-so-Verity ruse,[2] (3) I'll work as hard as I know on the synopsis or whatever we call it, as long as we call it good, and (4) Please don't forget to have a shot at doing those 'personal' thousand words for the introduction to my American Selected Writing. Let me see what you bang out. If you're too busy, I can ask Tommy E. to do something, but I hope you aren't. You've got Laughlin's letter, haven't you? He wants the thing very, very, very soon. Let me know.

Tomorrow morning I shall be fit as a tuba again, and will work, work, work,

Ever,

Dylan

MS: Buffalo   *SL*

VERNON WATKINS
28 March 1945   Majoda New Quay Cardiganshire

My Dear Vernon,
    Lovely to hear from you. I'd have written before this but am, unfortunately, caught, however innocently—and it will [be] the sweet job of the defending counsel to impute guilt to my every innocent thought and action—in a Case of Attempted Murder, Caitlin, I, and three others being the attempted murderees (though that isn't quite right, as we certainly didn't attempt to be murderees). [...], though that's not what I call him, started a fight in the local hotel, in which I took a small part, lost, returned home to the bungalow next to mine, and, when I also had returned home and was talking to Caitlin & 3 others, fired many rounds from his Sten gun through our paper-thin walls, missing us by inches and Aeronwy by feet. It's all very nasty, and I'm as frightened as though I had used the Sten gun myself. He also had a hand grenade. He is now on bail—the first stage of the case coming off next Thursday, the 5th of April—and Caitlin and I go to bed under the bed.[3] The last letter I wrote

---

[1] The Black Lion, the local pub.
[2] 'Verity' was a film company associated with Gryphon.
[3] The man involved, who is still alive, was a Captain in the British Army. He was married to a childhood friend of Thomas, and was not long back from a gruelling tour of duty in Greece, where he had been dropped behind the German lines. For more than a year he had trained partisans and taken part in sabotage attacks. The trouble at New Quay began with a brawl in the Black Lion between the Captain and some film people, friends of Thomas. No doubt everyone had been drinking too much. The shots, about eighteen rounds from his automatic weapon, were certainly fired, at and in the bungalow. Thomas behaved coolly, the Captain went away, and the police were called. On April 12 the local magistrates sent him for trial. At Lampeter Assizes in June the Captain said that 'the whole affair was a bluff'. The judge suggested there was no evidence of attempted murder, and the jury found him not guilty. Thomas told marvellously embroidered versions of the story for years.

to you, at Pennard, told of my daily terrors, my everyday traps & pits etc. I'm sure you thought I was exaggerating. At debts' and death's door I now stand with a revolving stomach, waiting for V.1000[1] and the Bubonic Plague.

I'm so delighted you and Gwen are going to have a child this summer. Do give Gwen my congratulations; you yourself shd have received mine as soon as I opened your letter, by telepathic pigeon.

How are you both? I miss seeing you, but then I have missed seeing you properly for—what is it—years; at least, since we left our studio, where we did have some proper evenings. The war's over soon, let's see each other then, a lot. You'll be going back to Swansea, of course. I want to stay in Wales for a bit, too. The Irish trip is off until the summer, & perhaps until even later.

Give my love, when you write, to your Mother and Father. My Father is awfully ill these days, with heart disease and uncharted pains, and the world that was once the colour of tar to him is now a darker place.

I'm sending some new poems. The long one doesn't, I think, come off, but I like it all in spite of that. It isn't really one piece, though, God, I tried to make it one and have been working on it for months.[2] Do tell me all you think of it, and of the others. And do let me see some of your new poems, please. Write very soon.

Love from both to both,

Ever,
Dylan

Urgent Postscript

James Laughlin, of New Directions, America, who is going to bring out a book of mine, 'Selected Writings', in America, wants, from a friend of mine over here, a short, 'personal introduction' to the book, of *not more than 1000 words*. There is a 'critical introduction', but that Laughlin is having written by an American, J. L. Sweeney. Laughlin has just written to me to say that he must have this 'personal' thing *at once*. Could you do it, or, rather, would you like to do it, or, rather, have you got time to do it, or, again, could you make or find time to do it. What Laughlin means by a 'personal introduction' is, roughly, this—I quote from memory as I haven't got the letter here—:'an idea, in non highbrow language, of what you yourself are really like; a human portrait of the poet written by a close friend of his or by one who has known him for a long time.' You'll have to excuse phrases like 'non highbrow language', 'human portrait', etc, but what he really wants is clear, I think. American readers of poetry seem never to be really satisfied unless they have portraits—photograph or words—of the writers; and they like them as candid and intimate —

---

[1] An uneasy joke about a successor to 'V2', the German rockets.
[2] The long poem was 'A Winter's Tale'; the others were 'The Conversation of Prayer', 'This Side of the Truth' and 'A Refusal to Mourn the Death, by Fire, of a Child in London'. *VW* has details of small variants from the *CP* versions.

comic, if you see me that way, & you must do, sometimes—as possible. To me, of course, that introduction coming from you, as my friend and as—we've both said this, with a kind of giggling gravity—the only other poet except me whose poetry I really like today—would be the best in the world. Let me know if you would do it; and, if you would, could you do it *terribly* quickly and let me have it so that I can send it off almost at once. It's a lot to ask, and you hardly ever write prose, but.... Well, I'll hear from you. We know each other by doing so many things together, from croquet to bathing (me for the first time) in the icy moon, poetry and very high teas, getting drunk, reading, reading, reading, sea staring, Swansea, Gower, Laugharne, London ... I've written thousands of letters to you; if you've kept some you could use what you liked to help build up this 'human portrait' of this fat pleader,

Dylan

Write very soon.

MS: British Library   *VW(R)*

GWYN JONES
28 March '45   Majoda New Quay Cardiganshire

Dear Gwyn Jones,
   I should have written long before to say how glad I was to meet you that booming afternoon in Carmarthen, and to thank you for the copies of *Wales* which I have now read from eagle to Corona.[1] Who is William Morgan? I liked his Working Day poem very much indeed. I'd not seen any of Alun Lewis's Indian poems before, and could see, as you said, his death walking through them.[2] I think your goodbye to Caradoc was fond and just.[3]
   Are you staying in Aberystwyth for a few weeks? I hope to come along soon, and am looking forward to a few drinks in the town with you. At the moment I am caught in a policecourt case; someone fired a Sten gun at us; I hope he missed.

Best wishes. Yours,
Dylan Thomas

I'll write you a note a good time beforehand about meeting in Aberystwyth.

MS: the recipient

[1] The magazine was not *Wales* but the rival *Welsh Review*, which Gwyn Jones edited. The cover featured a small dragon that might have been mistaken for an eagle in a poor light. 'Corona' was a fizzy drink, made in Wales, that loyally advertised at the back of the magazine.
[2] The Welsh poet Alun Lewis died accidentally while in the Army in 1944.
[3] An obituary of the writer Caradoc Evans.

OSCAR WILLIAMS
March 28 '45 _   Majoda New Quay Cardiganshire Wales

Dear Oscar,

Many thanks for the letter and for Poetry's cheque. I'm very glad you don't mind sending my stuff to the magazines. Here are another five poems: one longish one, four short ones.[1] The longish one, I'm glad to say, has taken a great deal of time and trouble, and has prevented me from writing filmscripts on Rehabilitation, Better Housing, Post War Full Employment, etc. for the socialist film department of the Ministry of Information. If it surprises you that the Ministry, or any Ministry, should have a socialist department, I can say that none of the scripts approved by that department get further than the next where they are shelved among a million dead ideas and periodically reshuffled by dead young men with briar pipes that are never lit in the office but which they always have protruding from their mouths like the cocks of swallowed bodies. By such so-quickly-to-be-buried work I earn enough to live on if I do without what I most like. So I'd love a little ladleful from the gravy pots over there—a lick of the ladle, the immersion of a single hair in the rich shitbrown cauldron—though naturally I expect nothing. It is very very good of you to try to fish something up for me. In this country, it would be the skull of a boiled fawner who, smelling the gravy steam, fell in and died, to the especial pleasure of his mother who had borne him piping. The war, they say, is all over bar the dying; and, when it is, I want to come over to America. How could I earn a living? I can read aloud, through sonorous asthma, with pomp; I can lecture on The Trend of Y, or X at the Cross-roads, or Z: Whither? with an assurance whose shiftiness can be seen only from the front row; I can write script and radio films, of a sort; I can—and so on with the list that could be, and is, supplied by every person fit for nothing but his shameful ability to fit into the hack ends of commercial, intellectual, or personal, advertisement. I hope you'll get the five poems printed. Perhaps 2 or 3 of the short ones together in one magazine? You know. I hope you like them, or some of them. I've forgotten if the address you have of mine is the one at the top of this letter or the one of the Gryphon Film Company. If it *is* Gryphon, please do use that when—and I do hope you do, soon—you write. That is more-or-less permanent. The Welsh address I leave, for nowhere, some time in June. My poems are coming out this spring and, though by that time you will have seen all the poems in it—several, however, in very altered versions —I'll send it on at once. I'm looking forward to yours, and to the War Poets. Laughlin is bringing out a 'Selected Writing' of mine—when, I don't know—with a critical introduction by J. L. Sweeney. Though I know his name, I don't know his writing. It is very lovely here; I have a

---

[1] The 'longish one' was probably 'A Winter's Tale'. *Poetry* (Chicago) published it in July. Three other poems (see page 548, note 2) appeared in quick succession in issues of *The New Republic*.

shack at the edge of the cliff where my children hop like fleas in a box—in London, the only remaining flea-circus I have seen is pushed about the streets in one half of a child's pram—and my wife grumbles at me and them and the sea for the mess we all make, and I work among cries and clatters like a venomous beaver in a parrot house. A letter full of nothing.

Yours,
Dylan

MS: Harvard   *SL*

DONALD TAYLOR
Tuesday [April 1945]   Majoda

Dear Donald,

I'm sorry that my telephone calls are always about the same dear little thing, but I can't help it. I just can't get straight, ever since five pounds was, quite justly, deducted from my weekly pay: the week you were down. I really am in a mess, and am likely to get in more of one. And I must say that I *can't* live on eight pounds a week. Can't. Ten is hard enough to get on with, with a pound worth about eight shillings, but eight pounds is impossible, and I don't know what to do. If only somehow one could manage until this film is sold—as it really should be, it seems to me to have everything. But on eight a week, one can't. It means I cannot do anything that requires more than about a pound; I can't get Llewelyn down for this incredible April, I can't buy a pair of trousers though my bum is bare to the sun, I can't join a library, & I *shouldn't* even smoke. All the eight, or even, really, the ten does, is to pay rent, food, oil, & coal. Enough? No, Christ no. There are a hell of a lot of other essential things, and I can't get them. And, once in debt for anything over a pound or so—as I am, as I am—that debt can never be paid, and grows & grows into proportions beyond any hope. All this is, I know, familiar to you; but things have reached a climax for me, & I can't go on with this amount of money. I don't know what the hell to do, & wish to the Lord we could fix something together. I've got such great faith in the films we'll make together, it seems so silly to be grumbling about money now when, soon, we should be crinkling all over. But there it is.

I hope the script will be finished in a week.[1] The trial, necessitating my getting my mother here from another county to look after the children, hindered it a lot;[2] as all this petty hell about money is still doing. But I do think: a week. I'll send it off with notes; there are, I think, 4 or 5 sticky constructional points, but I have only in one case altered a constructional

---

[1] 'Suffer Little Children.'
[2] Thomas gave evidence when the Captain with the machine-gun appeared before the local magistrates.

detail from our original. I have, too, cut out the jewels in the empty house that B. & S. & the boy break into. It seems to be too forced, too much of a coincidence, that Betty's downfall shd come, both times, through jewels left so *absurdly* open for anyone to take. So I think that just 'breaking & entering' is enough to send B. & S. to School for three years. Other suggestions etc. I'll write about at length when I send the complete MS.

Sorry for most of this letter, but I had to say it. And I still don't know what to do.

Ever
Dylan

MS: Buffalo   *SL*

VERNON WATKINS
April 19 45   Majoda

Dear Vernon,

It was so good of you to write that little personal—what?—thing, then, so quickly and so very nicely. Just, I should imagine, what New Directions want, and I have sent it off *just* as it is, not even altering 'good' to 'great' or putting in a paragraph about my singing voice or horsemanship.[1] Thank you a lot. It did, I know, sound rather awful: Write about me. If you had asked me to do it about you, I think I should have pleaded everything from writer's cramp to never having met you except in the dark, & then only once. I'm so glad you wrote the last bit about the poems: how you so much more liked the latest to the earliest. Wouldn't it be hell if it was the other way around, and the words were coming quicker & slicker and weaker and wordier every day and, by comparison, one's first poems in adolescence seemed, to one, like flying-fish islands never to be born in again? Thank God, writing is daily more difficult, less passes Uncle Head's blue-haired pencil that George Q. Heart doesn't care about, and that the result, if only to you and me, is worth all the discarded shocks, the reluctantly-shelved grand moony images, cut-&-come-again cardpack of references.

And I'm very glad you liked the new poems I sent, especially A Winter's Tale. I won't be able to test your suggestions for myself until I have the proofs back from Dent: I seem to have lost other copies. My book should be out this spring, costing, luckily, three and six so that perhaps lots of people can buy it and pass it on.

Yes, Captain [. . .] has nearly put me off drinking, though, indeed, the night of the shots of the dark I had drunk only some bottled cider and talked morosely to retired sailors in dusty corners, provoking nobody, so I thought.

---

[1] When *Selected Writings* was published in the U.S., it had the introduction by Sweeney, but not the 'personal' note by Watkins.

I do hope I see you soon in Stony Stratford. I am going to London the end, perhaps, of next week.

Thank you again for the little personal what; it was, I thought, nice, funny, and, as far as I know, right.

I'll write again, very soon, and more.

Love,
Dylan

MS: British Library   *VW*

LAURENCE POLLINGER
27 April 45   Majoda New Quay Cardiganshire

Dear Laurence Pollinger,
   Very sorry not to have answered your letter of Feb. 6 about Laughlin's edition of *Selected Works*. I thought I *had* answered: I should have my head read: my books won't be.

   I've sent the poems—the additional poems for the *Selected Works*—on to Laughlin direct, & have had a letter back from him.

Yours sincerely,
Dylan Thomas

MS: Texas

VERNON WATKINS
May 21 1945   Majoda New Quay Cardiganshire

Dear Vernon:
   Lovely to hear from you. I wish I could come to Pennard to see you, but I am broke & depressed & have just returned from London & hated it more than ever & though it is lovely here I am not. Oh, I do wish *you* could come down here. There is room, rest, food, & sea. Can't you?

   Dot is engaged to—who? I couldn't read. *SANTI?* Never heard of him, if that is the name. Write clearly & jog my old man's memory. Where did I live with him, & when? Has he two names? What nationality is he? Give me clues, I'll give you the frankest low-down in the world. Anyhow, I hope Dot will always be happy.

   Just a tiny note. I'm worried about things. I think I'll walk & grieve and scowl at the unmitigated birds—the first adjective, of any kind, I cd think of.

   Can't you come down? *Try.*

My love, & Caitlin's, to your people and yourself.
Write soon with S. clear & clued.

Dylan

MS: British Library *VW(R)*

UNKNOWN WOMAN[1]

May 21st 1945   Majoda New Quay Cardiganshire

I'll send away, at once, the poems you sent me, to the few editors I know:
Herring first, then Cyril C., then Muir of Orion—though you probably
know him as well as I do—, then Quennell of Cornhill; and will let you
know. Here I am efficient. There, inefficient but not poppycock, or, at
least, not very much, and what there was was not directed at—if that's
what you do with poppycock—anything that matters. I liked all the
poems, but am not going to say anything about them yet because I am
down, down, down among the live men, drowned in writs, terrified of the
past, the knock, the crunch on the gravel, even the baying of the sea a
little distance from my hand. I missed you, in fact, in theory, in every
way, dearly. Next time I'll see more of you, may I? Have you got any more
that I am allowed to see? No laughing at you, now or ever. The opposite,
which isn't crying. Are you being a subconscious girl for Donald? He is
cross with me, I am cross with him, but we will live to kill another pig. It
is very quiet here; only the hunting noise of the hard-away sea, the
throbbing of tractors, the squealing of rats and rabbits in the traps, the
surging of seagulls, thrushes, blackbirds, finches, cuckooing of cuckoos,
cooing of doves, discussion of works, crying of babies, blinding of wives,
sputtering of saucepans and kettles, barking of dogs, voices of children
playing trumpets on the beach, bugling of sea cadets, naying, chucking,
quacking, braying, mooing, rabbit-gunning, horse trotting, scraping of
magpies on the roof, mice in the kitchen: an ordinary day, nature serene
as Fats Waller in Belsen. I'll be up again in about a month. I hadn't your
address, knew it just as Charlie, Highgate, or I would have written.
Horror came over me, and I went into a basement. How are you? Believe
me, I will write soon, and tell you about the poems.

Love, always,
Dylan

---

[1] The letter, probably to someone connected with Strand or Gryphon Films, was sold at
Sotheby's, London. An unreliable typescript copy, from which this text is taken, was later
made by a dealer.

CAITLIN THOMAS
Sunday night [June 24 1945]   26 Paulton Square SW3[1]

My dear my dear my dear Caitlin my love I love you; even writing, from a universe and a star and ten thousand miles away, the name, your name, CAITLIN, just makes me love you, not more, because that is impossible, darling, I have always loved you more every day since I first saw you looking silly and golden and much much too good forever for me, in that nasty place in worse-than-Belsen London, no, not more, but deeper, oh my sweetheart I love you and love me dear Cat because we are the same, we are the same, we are the one thing, the constant thing, oh dear dear Cat.

I'm writing this in bed in Constantine's and Tony's at about one o'clock Sunday morning—I mean after midnight. You are the most beautiful girl that has ever lived, and it is worth dying to have kissed you. Oh Cat, I need & want you too, I want to come to you, I must be with you, there is no life, no nothing, without you: I've told you, before, in the quiet, in the Cardy dark, by the sea, that I adored you and you thought it was a word. I do. I do, my love, my beautiful. I can see your hair now though I can't see it; & feel your breasts against my stupid body; I can hear your voice though you aren't speaking except to—who? Mary? Bloody Mary?[2] Did you see the thing in News of the World?[3] 'Among those not to be congratulated after the trial were Cat Thomas & her vile Dylan who loves her so much he is alone alone in a big room in London in England and yet he lets her live 300 miles away.' Oh, be near me, tonight, now, Sunday, 300 miles away. I kiss you. I love you.

I'll try to come back Wed or Thur but may have to put it off until the end of the week. I've been told of a few flats & houses & am looking for them. Now I must try to sleep because I can only say I Love You My Own Heart My Little One Caitlin my Wife and Love & Eternity.

                                        X   Dylan

Monday morning.
Still in bed. About eight o'clock in the morning. Found it terribly hard to sleep. Said your name a thousand times, my little dear. In a few minutes I'll get up and go to work: to write, still, about Allied Strategy in Burma: oh why can't they get someone else.

Tony has promised that *she* will look, for us, at the few addresses of flats I've been given. I'm thinking it is by far the best thing to get a very

---

[1] Constantine FitzGibbon, then serving in the U.S. Army, and his wife Theodora (sometimes 'Tony' or 'Toni') lived in part of the house, which was owned by the writer Maurice Richardson.

[2] Mary Keene, wife of the film director Ralph Keene, was staying at Majoda with her baby, and had been there on the night of the shooting.

[3] The *News of the World*, reporting the Captain's acquittal on June 24, began its report, 'Officers and civilian friends congratulated a captain in the Royal Engineers renowned as a guerrilla and sabotage expert in Greece after he stepped from the dock . . .'

temporary furnished flat—however not nice—rather than an unfurnished one; so that we can leave it any time we raise enough money to go to America. I'll let you know if anything comes of it. I've been doing very little except work with Eldridge & Donald; anyway, I've only been here two days. Leaving you was like cutting my body in half; and yours. I LOVE YOU. That's as sure as the earth's turning, as the beastliness of London, as the fact that you are beautiful, as that I love Aeronwy and Llewelyn too—Caitlin my own my dear—Wire me TEM 5420 to say if you want to speak on the telephone to me. I'm going to the Zoo tomorrow, with a Lilliput photographer, to write captions for his pictures: What Animals Think. I don't know if it's Brandt;[1] rather hope not. If they commission me straight away, I'll send on half the money. I think, by the way, that our court expenses will be sent to me at Majoda. If they are, you'll be okay. Wire or phone me about it. I'll come back as soon as I can: certainly this week. I am longing for you. That's such a little understatement. I want you. You're the whole of my life. The Rest is nothing. Believe me, Cat, forever, and write or wire & phone & let me hear your voice because I love you. I want to be in your arms.

Always & always and always & always

X
Dylan

MS: Maurice Neville

SHEILA SHANNON[2]

5 July 45   Majoda New Quay Cardiganshire Wales

Dear Miss Shannon,

Your letter asking me about those two poems was, as you thought, waiting for me here at home. In case spoken consent to your including them in your anthologies isn't enough, here it is in writing. Grand: print what you like of mine.

I hope to see you some time again. Perhaps we could have lunch? I'll ring when I get back to town.

Yours sincerely,
Dylan Thomas

MS: National Library of Wales

---

[1] Bill Brandt.
[2] Sheila Shannon was helping to edit two anthologies published by Frederick Muller, *Soldiers' Verse*, which included Thomas's 'The hand that signed the paper', and *Poems of Death*, which included 'And death shall have no dominion'.

OSCAR WILLIAMS
July 30 1945   as from Gryphon [etc]

My dear Oscar,

Many thanks for many things.

For the cheques from periodicals, they couldn't have been more welcome, they seethed in their envelopes, which sounds like Lawrence, and burst in a shower of drinks and cabrides and small hospitalities to the dour and filmy mackintoshed bar-flies who work, or don't, with me.

For the anthologies, all of them so heavy and in such large lovely type, so dear, and with such lovely ladies and gentlemen to be seen out at the back: all portentously smoking (the pipes of bedpan), prinking, profiling, horizon-eying, open-collared and wild-haired in the photographer's wind, facing America and posterity and the music, shy as professional novelists caught accidentally in an arc-lamp, framed against rock and ruin, musing in cactused, glass-haired, first-editioned, (oooh, Cyril, a Kafka's missing), Paul-Kleed brown studies, some smelling visibly of just-a-little-rice-and-bamboo-shoot-dish-my-wife-found-in-Mexico, or of peanut butter and homebrewed cider, some painted, some by painters, some by themselves, some just painted, one self-drenched and solemn under a coat of Celtic jam, one bow-tied to his explosive cross, the pin-up poets, oh how I love you all.

For your own book of poems. You've let down your hair hard and loud on the one real ground, and sometimes you fall over it into a boiling black Belsen of your own. The poems never relax or play fair or explain or whine about their condition or are ashamed, but conduct their prolific unpretty lives in front of the nose of your nerves. They are pieces that fly, hot and violent and exuberantly unhappy, off a poem in the making. The wheels go round, crying, protesting, denying, on rails that are laid out only as the wheels express towards them. The rules, the form, spring up urgently as the temper of making needs them.

For your letters, too long unanswered but cherished next to my heart, hair, identity disk, razorscar from a Poetry Tea, the tattooed hoofprints of Dali's mother—It is hysterical weather where I am writing, Blaen Cwm, Llangain, Carmarthenshire, Wales, in a breeding-box in a cabbage valley, in a parlour with a preserved sheepdog, where mothballs fly at night, not moths, where the Bible opens itself at Revelations; and is there money still for tea? My son, in the nonstop probably frog-filled rain, is performing what seems, from this distance, to be an unnatural act with a beaver. Looking closer, I see he is only destroying his sister's doll—the little pixie. I can hear, from far off, my Uncle Bob drinking tea and methylated spirits through eighty years of nicotine-brown fern. My father, opposite, is reading about Hannibal through a magnifying glass so small he can see only one word at a time. I could lie down and live with Hannibals. And my wife is washing an old opera.

For the crust you offer in America. It is already nibbled, and I am the mice. Hands, and teeth, across the ocean.

For reading this.

Next morning. Still raining, and not daffodils. A farmyard outside the window, sows and cows and the farmer's daughters, what a day of dugs. I've been reading all Lawrence's poems, some aloud to no-one in this bombazine room, and liking them more & more. Do you remember:—

> O the green glimmer of apples in the orchard,
> Lamps in a wash of rain!
> O the wet walk of my brown hen through the stackyard!
> O tears on the window pane!
>
> Nothing now will ripen the bright green apples
> Full of disappointment and of rain;
> Blackish they will taste, of tears, when the yellow dapples
> Of autumn tell the withered tale again.
>
> All around the yard it is cluck! my brown hen.
> Cluck! and the rain-wet wings;
> Cluck! my marigold bird, and then
> Cluck! for your yellow darlings.[1]

Yes, there's his brown hen cluck in the gambo-swished mud,[2] scratching for Christ, cackling in droppings, Gladys's pet lamb-now-sheep follows here maaa-ing for poor, unloved Gladys's unmade milk, an Italian prisoner is scraping hay off a hedge, one Fontamara-brown-sly-innocent eye in the back of his head fixed on her black bloomered bottom as she bends to scatter grain for the yellow darlings. The rainy robin tic tac at the pane. Over the hill, the hoarse noise of a train carrying holes to Hugh's Castle. Near, a grey gulled estuary, and sheepshanks, corpses of cats, cowteeth, bottles of ether, jellyfish, frenchletters, indecipherable messages in jars (the secret of the Marie Celeste, the Number of the Beast, the name of Cain's wife, pyramid riddles, Tibetan acrostics, next year's newspapers) on the foreshore. I'm trying to establish my geography. Up the hill-lane behind this house too full of Thomases, a cottage row of the undeniably mad unpossessed peasantry of the inbred crooked county, my cousins, uncles, aunts, the woman with the gooseberry birthmark who lies with dogs, the farm labourer who told me that the stream that runs by his cottage side is Jordan water and who can deny him, the lay preacher who believes that the war was begun only to sell newspapers which are the devil's sermon-sheets, the man who, when his pony could work no longer because of old age, hanged it on an apple-tree to save a bullet, the woman who cries out 'Cancer!' as you pass her open door.

I should have written long before this, but couldn't bring myself to write only Thank you so very much for distributing my poems and for the sweet money, or to send you grunts of salutation from my trough. I have

[1] From D. H. Lawrence's 'Ballad of Another Ophelia', slightly misquoted.
[2] A gambo is a cart.

been trying to find out what legal etc. complications I will have to go through before leaving this country for America. First of all, because I have no financial independence, I have to be assured—or, rather, the American Embassy over here will have to be assured—that, on arriving in America, there is a job, or there are jobs, waiting for me; that I will not become a liability to the United States. There must be a sponsor, or sponsors, who will sign a declaration saying that I & my dependents will *not* be allowed to become liabilities. So what is my first step? The American Embassy has given me several printed forms to be sent to whoever I imagine will employ me in the States & guarantee me a living. If I send those official forms to you, could you do anything about them? That is, could you approach TIME—whom you suggested as possible employers, if only for part of my time—and get some definite promise, however small, from them? If that *could* be arranged, then, after the returning to the American Embassy here of the signed 'We-won't-let-the-bugger-starve' declaration, and after the final examinations, interviews, and okayings, physical & political, I could sail within three months. So that, supposing with your help some job, appointment etc. could be fixed, I should be able to arrive, a Migrained Father, in the early spring of next year. I have not yet written to Theodore Spencer,[1] because I have lost your letter with his address in it, and with the particulars of the work he might be able to give me in Harvard. Also, I did not quite know how to approach him. I have found that he is an old friend of a very old friend of mine here, Augustus John, who sends him every greeting and asks him to do what he can. Perhaps Augustus has already written, I wouldn't know, when I saw him last he was chasing a woman in uniform through the Zoo, horned & goat-bearded. If Spencer could assure me — that is, again, if he could assure, on a form I could send you to send him, the Embassy here that Harvard will engage me in any lecturing or librarying—of some work, it would work wonders. Otherwise, a patron would do just as well, to say that he will look after me & mine in luxury, New York, or even in a kennel, Texas. I should most like to read, library, or lecture at Harvard. Time & Harvard. A promise of work from T & H from next spring on would settle, I think, everything—apart from money to travel with, & this I must try to rake up from the gutters in which I pretend to work. I'm asking you a lot, causing you bother, heaping responsibilities on your shoulders, prematurely crust-gulping. Will you do what you can? If you say yes, I will send the Embassy forms to you straightaway. I shall not write to Spencer until I hear from you.

I should bring my wife, my son aged now 6½, my daughter aged now 2½. Their names are Llewelyn and Aeronwy. *They are quite nice hell.* My wife's name is Caitlin, she is Irish. We would all come together because I do not want to return to this country for a long time.

The rain has stopped, thank Jesus. Have the Socialists-in-power-now

---

[1] Theodore Spencer (1902–49), poet and critic, member of the Harvard faculty.

stopped it? An incometax form flops through the window, the letter box is choked with dockleaves. Let's get out, let's get out.[1]

Later. I have been out. I went to the Edwinsford Arms, a sabbath-dark bar with a stag's head over the Gents and a stuffed salmon caught by Shem and a mildewed advertisement for pre-1914 tobacco and a stain on the wall, just above my head, that I hoped was beer. I had some beer with a man who said he was shot in the groin in the last war, and who, unable to have a woman ever since, blames it on the dirty Jews. He said, 'Look what they did, the moochin',[2] and showed me a scar on his calf. I said that I thought he said he had been shot through the groin. 'And the calf, and the calf', he said in a terrible temper. 'And the calf, the bloody yids.' He is an official in some Department—a Department set-built for the early German films—that investigates the authenticity of discharged soldiers' pension-claims. 'Every time I see "Psycho-neurosis" on a discharge paper, I say, Lead-Swinger.' He told me the best way to boil lobsters, which was detailed and painful. I told him Norman Douglas's recipe for raping a dog: Catch the dog, open the drawer of a desk, put the dog's head in the open drawer, and then close the drawer. He told me how he had once made a child of six dead drunk. It began to rain again, great wrathful drops. We parted enemies. I rode back on a bicycle through the justice-must-be-done-let's-rain-on-sinners rain, and the bicycle wheels through the pools & slush on the roads asked the same monotonous & inane questions as the boiler-pipes once asked Gorki: Have you got any rubber? Do you want some fish? Cows under crying roadside trees, looking over the estuary, weed and webfoot mud, waited for Royal Academicians. Snails were coming out; a P.E.N. Club of slugs crossed the road; Manchester, Manchester, fetch a pocket handkercher, said the engine over the hill; you could hear little boys in desolate back-gardens facing the depressed water slapping each other on the stomach.

And back to a cardtable holding up a jamjar full of cigarette-ends, the rough draft of a ten minute film on the Kitchen Front, your War Poetry anthology, a spool of film showing a pair of hands over a sink, Why Birds Sing, Llewelyn's stampalbum, a large sheet of paper with the first line of a poem at the top: 'O'. I must, this week, at this table, finish the Kitchen Front, write a broadcast talk to be called 'Memories of Christmas' for the Children's Hour, write a begging letter to a Sir, write another line to come after 'O', fill up my £1000 People's Crossword, observe ill-nature, stop doodling, be natural, not sniff, not put ash in my coatpocket, remember that we all are brothers—'but not a trace of foul equality, nor sound of still more foul human perfection. You need not clear the world like a cabbage patch for me. Leave me my nettles, let me fight the wicked, obstreperous weeds myself, & put them in their place. I don't at all want

---

[1] The result of the first postwar general election in Britain, announced on July 26, was an overwhelming victory for the Labour Party. Thomas expresses the middle-class fears of rampaging socialism that were abroad in 1945.

[2] 'Mochyn' is Welsh for 'pig', colloquially 'dirty pig'.

to annihilate them, I like a row with them, but I won't be put on a cabbage-idealistic level with them.' I don't agree. Judy O'Grady and the Colonel's Lady and Lamarr Hedy and the Workers' Mayday, we're all bothers and blisters under unoriginal sins. For Whom Omar's Bowl Tells. The Censury of the Common Man. All Men My Enemas. O God, O Aren'tweall.

I liked the War Poetry immensely. Everything I liked, much I didn't know. I could have done with some Lawrence, though.

> Surely you've trod[den] straight
> To the very door!
> You have surely achieved your fate;
> And the perfect dead are elate
> To have won once more.
>
> Now to the dead you are giving
> Your last allegiance.
> But what of us who are living,
> And fearful yet of believing
> In your pitiless legions?[1]

But, probably no, he is too unequal. Thank you for the *two* copies, one for each eye. And I don't like the verses I have quoted above, either. Some of the contributors' views on War & Poetry I was glad to read; by others, especially by Treece's, appalled. War can't produce poetry, only poets can, and war can't produce poets either because they bring themselves up in such a [?way] that this outward bang bang of men against men is something they have passed a long time ago on their poems' way towards peace. A poet writing a poem is at peace with everything except words, which are eternal actions; only in the lulls between the warring work on words can he be at war with men. Poets can stop bullets, but bullets can't stop poets. What is a poet anyway? He is a man who has written or is writing what he, in his utmost human fallible integrity, necessarily communal, believes to be good poetry. As he writes good poetry very rarely, he is most often at peace with the eternal actions of words and is therefore very likely to be caught up in any bang bang that is going. When he is fighting, he is not a poet. Nor is a craftsman a craftsman. I think capital-lettered War can only in subject matter affect poetry. Violence and suffering are all the time, & it does not matter how you are brought up against them. And so on. But this is all vague and loose, like myself this rainy moment, and all I want to say before we bid a reluctant farewell to colourful Carmarthenshire is: Thank you again for books, periodicals, letters, cheques, friendship, and the help I know, I hope, you will give me in trying to get to America—which can succeed only if the authorities are informed that a position or positions—cut-glass for job or jobs—is or are

---

[1] From D. H. Lawrence's 'Obsequial Ode'.

waiting me in America, in your more-than-European idealism, like a be-aureoled bleached skeleton hovering its cage-ribs in the social heaven, beneficent. Lawrence again; oh leave me, you talking prick; oh to be where the Lady Loverlies shatter and the blackguards ride no more. Write soon.

Dylan

[On reverse of sheet: a drawing of three men in tall hats, fighting.]

MS: Harvard   SL

LORRAINE JAMESON[1]
4 August 45   Blaen Cwm Llangain near Carmarthen

Dear Miss Jameson,

I'm so sorry not to have replied sooner to your letter. I've changed my address, and the letter has only just been forwarded to me.

Thank you for wanting me to do something else for the Children's Hour. I think 'Memories of Christmas' a perfectly good title to hang something on, and I'll get down to it soon.[2] Is there a closing date? If I have any other ideas, I'll let you know.

I wonder whether you'd be interested in my reading a short story of mine—'A Visit to Grandpa's—that was included in my book of stories called 'Portrait of the Artist As A Young Dog' (Dent)? I'm afraid I've no copy of the book or the story, but perhaps the BBC Library has—though I doubt it. Anyway, if you could get hold of it & read the story, perhaps you'd let me know what you think? I think it would go well, very well.

Thanks again, & apologies for the delay.

Yours sincerely,
Dylan Thomas

MS: BBC

[1] Lorraine Jameson ran the 'Children's Hour' programme at the BBC in Cardiff.
[2] Thomas had read a radio talk, 'Reminiscences of Childhood'—a revised version of a broadcast on 14 February 1943—in Children's Hour on 21 March 1945. Jameson's suggestion (on July 17) that he write about 'Memories of Christmas' was to prove lucrative after Thomas's death. In 1950 he combined the 1945 radio talk with a 1947 article that he wrote for the magazine Picture Post, 'Conversation about Christmas', to produce 'A Child's Memories of Christmas in Wales' for an American magazine. As 'A Child's Christmas in Wales' this probably has come to appeal to a wider audience, both in print and as a recording, than anything else he wrote.

J. M. DENT
8 August 45   as from Gryphon [etc]

Dear Sir,

I must apologise for not having returned the proofs of my book of poems—'Deaths & Entrances.' I see they were sent to me on 30th of May, but they have only just been forwarded. I will correct them & send them on in a few days. I do hope this very long delay will not prevent the book being published this year.

Apologies again for being, unavoidably, a nuisance.

Yours truly,
Dylan Thomas

MS: J. M. Dent

CAITLIN THOMAS
[1945 ?mid August]   M[ervyn] Peake's flat

My dear
My Caitlin
    darling more times than ever before to me, I love you. And this time has seemed the very longest since we haven't been together all the time, since I've had to leave you alone, or with parents, for weeks & ten-days and eternities:—the *very* longest; I have never missed you more nor loved you more, and every long night without you has been sleepless and fear-filled, and I've cried to be with you. I've said to you, all these hours away, Oh be around the next corner, Caitlin my own, climb up the stairs of the next bus I'm in, be waiting, somewhere, somewhere very near, for me. But I knew you were in a hutch in a field, so far away, with two neurotics & a baby and a dog, bound to Daddy-likes-his-dinner and eternal after-noon walks.[1] I do, I do, I do think of you all the time. And I love you. I've been having an awful time, too, looking for a house, a flat, a room, a hole in the wall. One excellent thing *might* happen. I said 'House news tomorrow I hope' at the end of a money wire, but the news is put off till next week. It's a house about 30 miles from London, near Bovingdon, in Herts, & we could have it free for 3 months, furnished. Isn't *that* better than me having to jog back & forth to you in Wales, every few days or so it seems, & better, much better, for you? But God knows, nothing might happen. And there's the *chance* of a flat somewhere in Chelsea, very small. Nothing else, & they're both chances.
    I hung on because all V.Day Week was impossible to travel. You had to

---

[1] Caitlin was at the Blaen Cwm cottage with her parents-in-law.

get to the station last night to get a train next morning. The second V.Day I've not had the luck to avoid: London was terrible, terrible, terrible.[1]

And I've no extra money. No house, as yet, no money, as yet. But good chances of money, at least, from the BBC. But *that's* not much good if we can't live in , or near, London to do it. It's acting in plays, especially verse plays for the Empire Service: & they pay well.

So I'm not much good to you, coming home, (not home), but I hope, oh God I hope, you'll say you *are* & kiss me. I want you holding on to me, & me on to you. I love you I love you I love you dear sweet Cat, dear mine.

Think that I think of you.

Feel that we know each other forever.

Know that I love you.

Tomorrow I'll see you, poor & a bit dirty but oh so glad.

X

       & to Aeron   Dylan

MS: Maurice Neville

VERNON WATKINS
22 Aug 45   Blaen Cwm Llangain nr Carmarthen

My Dear Vernon,

How happy and glad Caitlin and I are that Gwen and you have Rhiannon. Every love and good wish for ever and ever from us both to the three of you. There could never be fonder and truer parents, and never more loving well-wishers. This isn't word day. God bless you all.

               Dylan

MS: British Library

DAVID TENNANT
28 August 1945   as from Gryphon [etc]

My dear David,

Across the counties, from mean, green, horse-thieving Wales, I raise one Playercoloured aspen hand to salute and supplicate. The last time I saw you, you had just gone from the Prince of Wales, and who am I to

---

[1] 'VE Day', 8 May 1945, had marked the end of the war in Europe. 'VJ Day', victory over Japan, was Wednesday 15 August, but there was a two-day public holiday, the Wednesday and the day after.

blame. The rest of the day was dark, shot with fire, a humming-top of taxis and glasses, a spinning sight of scowls and leers seen through the wrong end of a telescope made of indiarubber, a rush of close-ups, strange mouths and noses flattening themselves on one's own in places that seemed to be now a turkish bath, now a lavatory, now a gymnasium for midgets, bar, hothouse, hospital, knockshop, abattoir, crematorium, revolving cathedral and, at last, a bed only an inch from the ceiling. I'm coming to town again on Thursday, and would love to see you. This time I shall be collected, calm but gabbling, a patient on a monument: beer only, for me, for weeks, for health, forgive me, for Christ's sake, for sanity, four freedoms. Can you ring me? A City, or at least a Fleet St. morning would be lovely. Do you know of any flat, small house, in London or fairly near that I could rent? I am getting desperate now. We *have* to move. There has never been, for me, anything more urgent than this. I have to find somewhere to live in, if only for a few months. Do you know of anybody? Would you ask some of the people you see? God, I'd be grateful. I'm going out of my mind here, and can do no work. There *must* be somewhere. Do do, do do do ask and see for me, David. I can't go on like this, travelling eight hours to spend a weekend with Caitlin. We must be somewhere fairly near London, if not in it. This is the supplication I referred to at the beginning. Can you, will you, help in any way by asking any who might know, who could know, who would be kind? It is spoiling everything, having nowhere permanent to live. I want so much to work, and cannot without some certainty of surroundings. A house, a flat, two rooms. I have managed to write one new poem and will bring it up to show you when we meet, I think you will like it, it's a poem for evenings and tears. I shall look forward to you ringing. Don't forget, please. Let's hug the counters of nasty reporters' pubs, and drink to the Only Atom. I think I could lie down and live with men, they are so unplacid and so unselfcontained, they sweat and whine about their condition; I like that. I'll be, I hope, seeing you soon. Do your best for me, about finding some hole in the wind to lay down my two heads.

Everything to you.

Dylan

Only source: SL

DONALD TAYLOR
Tuesday [?1945]   [Wales]

The postman knocks. By Cain, he knocks once more!
I spring from bed. Then, rising from the floor
Where I have fainted, rush to the door and fall
Again. Youth, what a joy is youth! The hall

Is dark with dogs. They bite me as I pass.
My dear dumb friends! I'll put some powdered glass
Today in their Bob Martin's. That'll teach
Them manners. And now at long last I reach
The dog-and-child-chewed mat and find?—yes, yes!—
A bunch of letters from the far U.S.
Ah, what epistolary pearls unseen
Blush in these envelopes! what hippocrene!—
'Be my pen-pal' from Truman. Or 'Dear Friend,
Shall we arrange a *personal* Lease-Lend?'
From Betty Hutton. Or 'Will you play for me
An Air on my G. String?' signed Gypsy Lee.
Or 'We salute you, Script-King!' from MacArthur,
Hecht, and Wilder. Or a plea to bath her
From Miss Colbert. But, alas, vain hopes!
There's nothing in those Sam-stamped envelopes
But a request to write on 'Whither Art?'
For 'Cyclorama', 'Seed', 'Rubato', 'Fart'
'Prognosis', 'Ethic', 'Crucible', and 'Clef'—
And other small reviews that pay sweet F.

In other words, none of the money I expected to come did come, and I am broke and therefore unable to buy a ticket to come to London. Can a few pounds expenses be arranged somehow and wired on to me on Wednesday? My own expense account is fairly clear, and I could settle up with the accounts department when I arrive. I should very much like to come up on Thursday, the first train, arriving lunchtime. *Can* it be managed? I'll ring you Wednesday afternoon. But, if possible, I'd like to have the expenses (?) wired before that, as the Thursday train leaves 7.30 in the morning. Sorry to be such a nuisance. I very much want to discuss this film with you—or, rather, the tentative idea I've been working a bit at. And there are tons of other things. No V. Days. All work and discussion. Hope you can send on the fare etc.

Ever,
Dylan

MS: Texas

T. W. EARP

28 Aug 45   as from Gryphon [etc]

Dear Tommy,
    I'll be in London from Friday, August 31st, for a week. Can we meet? Will you let me know, by wire, phonecall, note, or sealed man, when and where? It's been a long time.

Anyone want to let a house in your district? We're getting desperate.
I hope May is better.
Perhaps we could have a Hants tiny party this time?

Ever,
Dylan

MS: *Ohio State University*

FRANCIS BUTTERFIELD[1]
[?1945]

Dear Francis,
   Just as Caitlin was about to send off her letter to you, this Electric bill
came. I suppose it's a bill that Fred Brown owes: it certainly has nothing
to do with me, as I haven't been in the studio for over a year. Will you
hand it on to Fred & get him to settle it? Or arrange it somehow—to hell
with old bills that are no concern of mine, I've enough new ones that are.
   I'll be up in about a fortnight. Hope to see you.

Yours,
Dylan

MS: *Eric Barton*

CAITLIN THOMAS
Thur [?September 1945]   Gryphon Guild House

My darling dear, my own, my poor, beautiful Caitlin, this [is] only a little
note because I want you to have this money straightaway. I have been
waiting every day for money to come from the BBC; it still hasn't come;
this was a cheque from the agents for poems in anthologies. I will send
the BBC money as soon as it comes. I love you forever, &, though I
thought last time, & the time before that, that I never in all our lovely life
together missed you [?so] desperately, & loved you more dearly, this is
the worst time of all, I love you & need you, dear my dear & think of you
in that grave & look around me at mine. I am terribly sorry not to have
sent you money sooner; I had none. I hope this will help, & there shall be
more. The Electricity Summons, supposed to be paid by Fred months ago,
I [?telephoned] Fred about this afternoon & [?will get] the money at once
from him & send it off to the electric buggering people. There are 2
chances of a house, & I have had a message from Miss Griffiths we met in

---

[1] The letter was found in the grate of the house in Twickenham where Butterfield, a
painter, died.

Llanstephan asking me to ring her at home this evening. Perhaps she will have something definite, please our Lord & preserve our sanity. Do not be too depressed, my sweetheart, though you've every right to be. I shall be back on Monday, arriving in Carmarthen at six. I should love you & love you & love you to meet me. I hope to God I shall be able to say, We can go up to town almost at once. Donald is going on holiday—*not* to N. Quay—& I needn't return anyway for a fortnight. But I told him, quite definitely, I wouldn't return at all unless there is a house but would live in Majoda again. I love you. I am so glad you liked the two broadcasts. Do listen on Sunday at 11 p.m. & less than a day after I shall be with you, my true love until death & forever afterwards. I want to hold you & kiss you. Kiss Aeronwy for me. Say that you love me. Wait for me. I love you & though I am wild unhappy think of you every second. You are everything that is good. I love you.

Dylan

MS: Maurice Neville

T. W. EARP
Monday [postmarked September 3 1945]   Gryphon

Dear Tommy,
    Too gastric to write anything except 1 o clock Wednesday at the Salisbury will be fine & lovely.

Ever,
Dylan

MS: Ohio State University

LORRAINE JAMESON
12 Sept '45   Blaen Cwm Llangain near Carmarthen

Dear Miss Jameson,
    Thank you for your letter. I'm sorry you had such difficulty getting hold of my book of stories. I'm sure you're right, & that 'A Visit To Grandpa's' is not really suitable for children. Thank you, though, for mentioning it to Aneirin Davies.[1] I should like very much to read it from the West Regional one evening, & will give Aneirin a ring next week.

---

[1] Aneirin Talfan Davies, talks producer at the Cardiff BBC.

I've been away for a little time, but shall get down to writing 'Memories of Christmas' straightaway, & will send it on in plenty of time—I hope.

Yours sincerely,
Dylan Thomas

MS: BBC

A. J. HOPPÉ[1]
18 September 1945   as from Gryphon [etc]

Dear Mr. Hoppé,

I am returning herewith the corrected proofs of my book of poems, 'Deaths and Entrances'. Thank you very much for sending on the new set of proofs; I'm afraid I made a terrible mess of the other two.

And you'll see that I've made, and am making, a nuisance of myself over these proofs. Let me try to put my points in order.

(1) The poem on pages 16 and 17 I have completely rewritten, retaining only the title line and one or two others.[2] The poem in its final, revised form—exactly the same length as the original—I am enclosing.

(2) The poem on page 32 is substantially altered. In form, it is now three stanzas of four lines each.[3]

(3) I have crossed out the poem on page 36 *entirely*, and am substituting another, and shorter, poem—'*In My Craft or Sullen Art*'—which I enclose.

(4) The poem '*Vision and Prayer*' on pages 43–50 is not set typographically as I wish and as I tried to explain in a letter to my agents which was forwarded to Mr. Richard Church. I am enclosing a copy of the Sewanee Review, in which the poem is printed *exactly* as it should be. I do hope, & beg, that the poem will be printed in the book just as it is in the magazine.

(5) I am enclosing a further poem, '*Fern Hill*', not so far included in the book, which I very much *want* included as it is an *essential* part of the feeling & meaning of the book as a whole.[4]

As so much re-setting etc. will have to be done anyway, I do most earnestly hope that '*Fern Hill*' can be included in the book. I myself would be very unsatisfied were it omitted. (I realise, naturally, that it should have been sent along in the first place with the others, but it was not at that time completed.)

---

[1] Hoppé was a director of J. M. Dent.
[2] 'Unluckily for a death.'
[3] 'On a Wedding Anniversary.'
[4] The poem was written at Blaen Cwm in the summer; see letter to Edith Sitwell, page 582.

(7) I have not corrected the title-page as the numbers will nearly all have to be altered if, as I very much hope, 'Fern Hill' can be added to the book.

I'm sorry there has been such a delay in my returning the proofs, and that such an amount of additional work—for which, of course, I will pay—is involved.

I am sorry too that I cannot send the revised form of 'Unluckily For A Death', & the substitute-poem, 'In My Craft or Sullen Art', in typescript. I am on holiday in Wales & far away from typewriters.

I am looking forward to hearing from you, and apologise again for all inconveniences etc.

Yours very truly,
Dylan Thomas

MS: J. M. Dent

FRANCIS BUTTERFIELD
Friday 21 [?Sept] '45[1]   Blaen Cwm Llangain near Carmarthen S Wales

Dear Francis,
    Caitlin and I are sending up some things to London—a trunk or two and a single bed among them—which we want temporarily put among our other things in the studio. A van is bringing them up from Wales this coming Wednesday (26th), and will deliver them at the studio sometime late afternoon. As I don't suppose you'll be in then, would you tell the van Hengelaars that a van *will* be arriving then & that the few things are to be put in the studio? I don't know how the key-arrangement is now, but in case it's altered since my time & the key no longer hangs on a string through the door, would you—if there is a new key—let the van Hengelaars have it on Wednesday afternoon so that the vandriver can shove the stuff in without any bother?

    This note *might* be unnecessary; we might be in London before then, staying temporarily with Toni and if we are will look out for you around Chelsea. I hope to see you very soon anyway, about a couple of things. Where d'you go? The Black Lion?

Ever,
Dylan

MS: Eric Barton

[1] September matches day with date, and is the best candidate.

LORRAINE JAMESON
25th September 1945   [headed paper: Gryphon Films, etc]

Dear Miss Jameson,
   Here is the script of 'Memories of Christmas', which you invited me to do. I do hope you like it.
   I've been sent a contract, applying to the story alone, for 'A Visit to Grandpa's', which is also, so my Agent's note said, to be included in the Children's Hour, but I've had so far, no contract about my reading of it. I want, of course, to read the story, and the 'Memories of Christmas', myself.
   Will you write and let me know?

Yours sincerely,
Dylan Thomas

MS: BBC

ANEIRIN TALFAN DAVIES[1] –
28th September 1945   [headed paper: Gryphon Films, etc]

Dear Aneirin,
   Thank you for your letter. I should like very much to record that story of mine called 'A Visit to Grandpa's'. I've had a contract about the copyright of it, from the B.B.C., but I gather it was for the Children's Hour. Still, I'd rather me read it than anybody else. Could I do that and then talk with you about some of the other broadcasts that you suggested? There is one that I have already sent to Miss Jameson; and I agree with you that a talk in justification of 'penny horribles' would be lovely to do. So if you would let me know I would be very grateful.
   Do you ever come to London nowadays? My telephone number is TEMPLE BAR 5420.
   Best wishes,

Yours,
Dylan Thomas

MS: BBC

[1] Talfan Davies wrote to Thomas on September 25 to say he wanted to record 'A Visit to Grandpa's'. He asked for more scripts because Thomas's last talk (presumably 'Reminiscences of Childhood') had 'taken very well with our listeners. I wonder could you repeat the miracle with a talk on a Welsh country village? Or does this idea appeal to you?—a talk in justification of "penny horribles"—"The Magnet" and so on. I think I heard you once defend this type of literature for children . . .' The talks were never written.

A. J. HOPPÉ
28th September 1945   [headed paper: Gryphon Films, etc]

Dear Mr. Hoppé,

Thank you for your letter. I think the poem 'Vision and Prayer' must be set-up as it was in the Sewanee Review. I wish it were easier for me to say that I should like the book to be kept to its sixty-four pages, but I'm afraid that I can't think how four pages could be well omitted. If it is any help, the poem called 'On a Wedding Anniversary' could be cut out, but that, after all is only one page, so, if you don't mind, the best thing seems to me that 'Vision and Prayer' should be printed as in the American magazine and that the further additional poem 'Fern Hill' should be put at the end of the book.[1]

You said that you would be prepared to do that, if necessary, and I would be awfully glad if you would.

Yours sincerely,
Dylan Thomas

MS: J. M. Dent

A. J. HOPPÉ
6 Nov 45   39 Markham Square London SW3[2]

Dear Sir,

Here enclosed are the corrected *final* proofs of my book of poems Deaths & Entrances. Thank you for printing the poem as it is on pages 43–54.[3] I do hope something can be done about page 45.

Yours faithfully,
Dylan Thomas

MS: J. M. Dent

LORRAINE JAMESON
7th Nov '45   39 Markham Square Chelsea London SW3

Dear Miss Jameson,

Thank you for your letter of October 23, which has just been forwarded to me, saying that my talk on 'Memories of Christmas' will be used in the Children's Hour on Sunday December 16 at 5.15 p.m.

[1] 'On a Wedding Anniversary' wasn't deleted. 'Fern Hill' was printed as suggested.
[2] The Thomases had found a flat at this address.
[3] 'Vision and Prayer.'

I shall be in London all December, & would very much appreciate it if you could, as you suggested, arrange for me to broadcast from here.

Apologies for the unavoidable delay in my answering your letter, & I hope it hasn't inconvenienced you too much.

Yours sincerely,
Dylan Thomas

I wonder if it would be possible for me to have a copy of my Christmas script sent to me, at the above address, before the broadcast? I haven't got a copy, & should like to have a look at it before reading it.

MS: BBC

BBC
November 10th 1945   39 Markham Square SW3

Dear Sir,

I regret not having been able to answer your contract letters of 23rd October and 1st November concerning the two scripts on, 'Augustus John' and 'Nationalism in Poetry.'[1] Illness prevented me from answering, as, unfortunately, it also prevented me from writing the script on John—as, perhaps, you might have heard by this time.

I do not quite know, therefore, what position this leaves me in. In your letter of November 1st, you said that though six guineas is actually your standard rate for a 10-minute talk that is not read by the author, you felt that, in my case, a higher rate—that of seven guineas—should be paid. As, unavoidably, I failed to turn out the script on John, I wonder whether the seven guinea rate still applies for the script I am in the process of writing on Nationalism in Poetry. I should be very grateful to hear from you, and to sign a new contract for the Nationalism talk, and apologise for any inconvenience caused you by my delay in answering your letters.

Yours sincerely,
Dylan Thomas

TS: BBC (copy made for Legal Section)

---

[1] The Augustus John script was commissioned for a 'Famous Contemporaries' series in the BBC's Eastern Services. 'Nationalism in Poetry' was for the Belgian Service.

ANEIRIN TALFAN DAVIES
Nov 11 '45   39 Markham Square Chelsea London SW3

Dear Aneirin,
   I've only just found your letter dated 29th Sept; I must have put it aside,
meaning to answer it directly, and then mislaid it in the bother of
moving. The above is now my address, and *not* c/o Gryphon Films.
   You said in your letter you were hoping to come to London before long,
and that then I could record 'A Visit to Grandpa's'. I do hope I haven't
missed you. Will you let me know?
   I haven't written the penny-horrible script yet but will get down to it
next week.
   How are you?

                                      Yours,
                                      Dylan

MS: BBC

LORRAINE JAMESON
30 Nov [1945] [postcard]   39 Markham Square Chelsea London SW3

Sorry not to reply before to your letter of 26th. Yes, 11.0. a.m. December
6th at Broadcasting House, London, will be fine for me to record my
Children's Hour talk, 'Memories of Christmas'. Shall I receive further
notification or shall I just turn up? If I don't hear from you, I'll turn up
anyway.[1]

                                      Sincerely,
                                      Dylan Thomas

MS: BBC

BBC
November 30th 1945 (The Hindustani Service, the Belgian Service and
Augustus John. See Appendix 33.)

---

[1] Unknown to Thomas, the head of Children's Hour in London had insisted that he be
prerecorded—'As you are aware,' he told Cardiff, 'there is tremendous risk in taking Dylan
Thomas "live" in the programmme for reasons which I do not think I need enlarge upon.
He is notoriously tricky . . .'

BBC
Nov 30 '45 (Returns contracts. See Appendix 34.)

MAURICE CARPENTER[1]
[?1945]   39 Markham Square SW3

Dear Maurice,
  Sorry not to have answered before, but thanks a lot for the poem which
I liked on a first reading and want to read many times again.
  About this poetry reading. Is it the one I got a letter about from J. P.
Tredgett, Croydon, a reading to be given at the Ethical Church on January
21? It sounds a bleeder. Do give me a ring and tell me: any time before
eleven in the morning.
  Thanks again for the poem. See you soon. Best wishes New Year etc.

                                                        Dylan

MS: National Library of Wales

CYRIL CONNOLLY
Dec 5 1945   .   39 Markham Square SW3

Dear Cyril,
  Do you remember our conversation if that is the word in the Gargoyle
some nights ago about fifty pounds that I think you said you thought I
should have for my poem but for your fear that I should spend it?[2] Spend
it of course I would, but certainly not all on what I don't know why I
shouldn't spend it on anyway. I'm so much in worry and debt that the
money would be wonderful *now*. Without it, or some other, I shall have
to leave here for nowhere: our landlord's a vampire and strangers call
every day baying. Is there any chance? If not of that, then of something
reasonable down for future poems all of which you may have? Every day
is worse and worst. Do try, please.

                                                        Ever,
                                                        Dylan

MS: McFarlin Library, University of Tulsa

---

[1] Poet and critic.
[2] Perhaps 'A Winter's Tale', which appeared in a special French issue of *Horizon*.

OSCAR WILLIAMS
December 5th 1945   39 Markham Square Chelsea London SW3
                                                                        England

New address, for as long as
I pay the rent to our vampire,
the only one that garlic does
not keep off.

Dear Oscar,

In front of me, two unanswered letters from you dated October 2 and November 1. Behind me, two months when there was nothing in my head but a little Nagasaki, all low and hot. I've lurched and boasted and lied through eight weeks of my allotted spin, at war with the lining of my stomach. Now I have won and am ill at peace again, in bed with a poultice called Mrs Hyam, I can write to thank you for your letters and their bangs of good news and to try to answer all the importents in them.

Poems   Here is the signed form ('authorizing', my my!) about the nine poems you want for the Scribner anthology.[1] I hope, if this is too late, that you took my authorisation for granted. For you, for Poetry, and for money, I'd sign up for the Dynamos.

Also, here are two new lyrical poems which I hope you'll send to the magazines. I like the long one, and may be given an Horizon award for it.

And about awards: Thank you, an awful lot, for getting the Levinson Prize from Poetry (Chicago) for me. I'd love to see it and stroke its little front: the cheque's, not Poetry's[2]—I know what's in front there. Will it come one day? No sign of the cheque yet, nor any official notification. 'View' has written asking for poems. Who's View? I didn't gather from their letter that they'd like the two poems I [sent] you. They sounded as though they liked their poems inside out. I like to see the outsides of poems, knowing there's an inside in.

George Barker and I read some poems on a platform yesterday to twenty or so communists and a couple of people. He sends his love.

I do quite a lot of reading of poetry on the radio here. I've read a lot of Elizabethans lately, & Lawrence, and Hardy. And some of my own next week. Do you think there will be any chance of my reading verse, or prose, on the American radio? I'm quite good; at least I'm often allowed to do it, though late at night: at hours carefully arranged so that no-one can be offended except those who like hearing verse read aloud and who also like going to bed early.

America: My Going, or Coming, To It

After much formfilling and dirty-questions-answering at the front door of the American Embassy, I am now going to try the back, hoping that consular Sweeney is in residence. The position, so far, is this: I must

---

[1] *A Little Treasury of Great Poetry*, published 1947.
[2] The prize was worth $100.

have, or the American Embassy must have, a letter or letters from responsible people, or authorities, or institutions etc, in America to say that I am being *invited* to America to take up a position as X, Y, or Z. And the more pompous the position (or 'appointment', I think, is the better word) can be made to sound, the better. Lecturer, adviser, critic, etc. is the kind of thing, I believe, that gets them. Yes, the letter or letters must invite me to take up an appointment, on my arriving in the States, with, or under, the signers of the letter or letters. This straight letter approach is better than the ordinary formfilling which relatives & near friends etc. are usually asked to do. The letter, or letters, can either, formally, invite *me*, or, formally, tell the Embassy that I am being invited. If this invitation is found to be genuine—as, *of course*, it will—then they'll see about granting me visas. These will have to be special visas. Or, alternatively, I take out immigration papers, insisting, I trust, that I can return to this country. But the thing is: LETTER, or letters, STRAIGHTAWAY. Can you get this done? You said, in yours of Oct. 2, that J. L. Sweeney 'has promised to do something very definite about getting me here.' And that you are to 'bring the forms to be filled by him, and that Something Will Be Done.' Your capitals. Okay and marvellous. Does that still stand? If so, (pray God), you have only to tell J. L. Sweeney that a letter from him or from someone else important has to be written to me or the Embassy inviting me to a post, position, appointment, or bit of money, in the States, and the worst may be over. I haven't written to Theodore Spencer or to Professor Morrison. Should I? Or should you again—I'm relying entirely on your kindness and on our transatlantic friendship—tell them the position. Anyway, so far as I can see it, one single good, important-sounding invitation will do. Once over there, I can try, with God's help & yours and the help of any old poetasters etc. to get other positions, appointments & other money (films, radio).

(I think, incidentally, I shall be fixing up, for an American publisher, with Reynell & Hitchcock who have written very sweetly & whom I have just answered.)

So my future is in your hands. BUT DON'T WORRY. Next: The visas obtained one day next year perhaps, how the hell do I raise the passage fare (one way) for myself and wife & two children? Maybe I can do something about that this end. Maybe. I'm not thinking of *that* yet. I'm just rushing down, I hope not too incoherently, the *real important things*.

Now I'm going to airmail this off at once, and wait, shaking, to hear from you, J. L. Sweeney, & anyone else who wants me to come, poor sod.[1]

I'll write another letter, about other things, once this is mailed. Take my usual flowery letter as being written.

Ever,
Dylan

MS: Harvard

---

[1] The plans came to nothing, and it was more than four years before Thomas reached the promised land.

MARGARET TAYLOR

Margaret Taylor (1905–80), who claimed Celtic origins, was brought up by British parents in India, and then in an English convent. She married the historian A. J. P. Taylor in 1931. Taylor has written that he disliked Thomas almost from the moment he met him in 1937. Mrs Taylor, on the other hand, was inordinately fond of him. She had a little money of her own, and after the war began a career as patron of the poet that was of great benefit to the Thomases but had disastrous consequences for her marriage. She wrote poetry.

[?1945]   Holywell Ford. Guests' Bedroom[1]

My dear Margaret,

I was so glad to be allowed to see the poems and to keep them for such a long time: too long a time, perhaps, though we did talk about them for a little and (on my part) a mostly inarticulate minute. I kept them so long, not because I had nothing to say about them but because I had so much. I find it awfully hard to say, about another's poems, just 'I enjoyed them', or 'I didn't like them', or, humming and ha-ing, to mumble something about 'the influence of X' or how much 'you could learn from Y'. The only way I know to talk about poems—another's poems—(unless they are *all* perfect, which means unless they are written in Heaven with a Gabriel-winged-Waterman dipped in nectar and God's blood)—is to try to go through them in detail for sound and shape and colour. The *meaning* of a poem you cannot, as a poet, talk about in any way constructively: that must be left to theoreticians, logicians, philosophers, senti-mentalists, etc. It is only the *texture* of a poem that can be discussed at all. Nobody, I think, wants to talk, either, about how a poem *feels* to him; he finds it emotionally moving, or he doesn't; and, if he does, there's nothing to discuss except the means, the words themselves, by which this emotional feeling was aroused. It is, of course, far easier to point out what one disagrees with than it is to comment sensibly upon what one finds good. One disagrees with a line of poetry because one discovers, immediately or after re-reading, that it is not inevitable, it could be changed, the wrong words have been used or the right words in the wrong order, indeed one changes them about in the mind as one reads; but when the inevitable line appears, what is there to say? The music is made, the magic is done, the sound and the spell remain. This is only a (I'm afraid) repetitive, pedantic, platitudinary preliminary (God help us) apology for the few comments I want to make on each of the poems. I'm very conscious of how little, if at all, I can help to make these poems, or your future poems, nearer, in texture and intensity, to what you yourself would wish them to be. I can only burble, like an old bird with its beak

---

[1] A house in the grounds of Magdalen College, Oxford, of which Taylor was a Fellow. Apparently the Thomases first stayed at the house itself. In the spring of 1946, Mrs Taylor persuaded her husband to let the Thomases occupy a damp summer-house near by, on the banks of the Cherwell. It had gas and electricity but no water, which had to be fetched from the house.

full of bias and soap; and you can but curse yourself for ever having given your poems to such a turgid rook.

[*See Appendix 35 for about 2000 words of commentary on thirteen poems by Mrs Taylor, omitted here.*]

Thank you for letting me have the poems, and I hope you found *something*, of even the frailest value, in all these argeybargeying pages of Sneezer's Manual.

May I see some more poems when they are ready?

Love to you,
Dylan

I haven't read this over, so you must forgive, please, all the slips & redundancies etc.

MS: Texas   *SL(R)*

AILEEN GOLDMAN[1]
January 12 1946   Holywell Ford Oxford

Dear Mrs. Goldman,
    Thank you very much indeed. I was delighted to have your letter, and so glad you liked my talk on 'Holiday Memories'. It was most kind of you to write. It's one thing to be moved by a broadcast—though that too rarely, I find; it's quite another thing to be moved to write to the chap who did it. I'm proud to think that the talk, or essay, or story, or whatever it is, did really mean something, at least to one listener. No, two: I was forgetting your son, whom I'd like to thank separately for having recommended it to you in the first place.
    Thank you, again. I hope to do another South Wales 'Memory' quite soon; and I hope, too, you'll be able to hear it.

Yours sincerely,
Dylan Thomas

MS: Texas

---

[1] An admirer in Manchester.

JOHN DAVENPORT
February 13th 1946   Holywell Ford Oxford

My Dear John,
  Wd you do me a favour? Could you send on the enclosed letter to
Norman? Or if you haven't his address, do you know who would have?
It's rather urgent, in a way. I'll tell you when we meet.
  And let's meet soon. I'll ring Bush House next week. Probably Tuesday
morning. And hope you're about. Terribly sorry to have missed you last
time. I rang your office. E. Lutyens told me I had lost £500, but I think
that was malice.[1]

                                          Love,
                                            Dylan

MS: Texas

T. S. ELIOT
24 March '46   Holywell Ford Oxford

Dear Mr Eliot,
  Thank you for sending me the letter about Ezra Pound. I return it,
signed.
  And thank you for letting me have that dreadful, unutterably moving
statement made by Pound's attorney.[2]

                                          Yours sincerely,
                                            Dylan Thomas

MS: Valerie Eliot

DAVID HIGHAM
March 25 '46   Holywell Ford Oxford
                                                       Ox: 47549

Dear David,
  Thank you for your two letters, March 5th and 13th. I would have
answered them straightaway, but I've just had a short spell in hospital[3]
—since seeing you, but nothing, I assure you, to do with that —and am
only now about again. It was very nice to see you again after so long.

[1] Norman: Norman Cameron. Bush House: a BBC building, where Davenport was then
  employed. E[lizabeth] Lutyens (Mrs Edward Clark) (1906–83): the composer, a friend of
  the Thomases.
[2] The poet Ezra Pound (1885–1972), charged with treason against the U.S. for wartime
  broadcasts from Italy, was deemed unfit to stand trial on February 13, and committed to
  an asylum.
[3] St Stephen's Hospital. He is alleged to have been suffering from 'alcoholic gastritis'.

(1) I have a copy here of your letter of Feb. 21st, about the Mondadori proposal; but I know nothing more about it than is contained in your letter. I should, of course, like to be published in Italy, and especially in a de-luxe edition such as you believe Mondadori to be proposing.[1] Can you go ahead and find out whatever there is to be found? And might there be some real money.

(2) About the BBC and your talk with Nancy Pearn about improving prices for my work there. I am writing to the BBC, (Contracts) as you suggest, to notify them that from now on all my financial arrangements with them are to be arranged with you. I'll send the letter off today. I (a) gather that this—i.e. the financial arrangements to be taken over by you—applies also to my work *as an actor* reading the work of others. (b) Contracts for my work as an actor have in the past been sent to me from the Talks Department. But the Dramatic Dept. obviously pays higher fees. How does Equity fit, or not fit, in with this?

(3) About your talk with Bozman concerning the book to be called provisionally, either *Top Hat & Gasworks* or *Bob's My Uncle*. I note that Bozman agrees the book might well consist of BBC childhood reminiscences plus short stories, straight & fantastic. I'll get together, from the BBC & odd periodicals etc, all the material there is to hand as quickly as possible, & let you have it with an indication of what I intend to add.[2]

(4) Good news, to me, about the new edition of *Deaths & Entrances* of 3,000;[3] and also the binding of the sheet stock of the *Young Dog* book, the *Map of Love*, & the *25 Poems*. How soon do you think you can touch Dent's for some more money for me on account of the new printing of Deaths & Entrances?

Hoping to hear from you soon.

Yours,
Dylan

MS: Texas

T. W. EARP
Tuesday March 26th 1946   Holywell Ford Oxford

Dear Tommy,

Will you write to me some time at this address? If you give me, say, 2 days' notice, I can come up any day you like. And then we'll both have trains to catch and maybe that'll be good though at the moment I can't think why. Anyway, it's been a long time and let's meet in ... Coal

---

[1] No such edition seems to have been published.
[2] The book didn't appear until after Thomas's death, and then became two books, *Quite Early One Morning* and *A Prospect of the Sea*.
[3] *Deaths and Entrances* had been published on February 7.

Hole?—anywhere in town when you come up please. Only 2 days' warning, and up I come from bore's hill,[1] out of hospital fresh as a fresh as a

Yours
Dylan

MS: *Ohio State University*

EDITH SITWELL
Sunday March 31st '46   c/o A J P Taylor Holywell Ford Oxford

Dear Miss Sitwell,
   It's nine or ten years, I think, since I last met you, though we did write some letters after that; it is, anyway, a long long time, and all that time I've very much missed being able to write to you occasionally and to send you poems and to ask you about them, for I value, with all my heart, what you have said about them in the past. I find it so easy to get lost, in my actions and my words, and I know that, deeply lost so many times, I could have, through writing to you and through your writing, come somehow out and up, so much less sufferingly than I did, into the miraculous middle of the world again.
   I think that, in some way, I offended you, through some thoughtless, irresponsible written or spoken word, on some occasion, those nine or ten years back. And I can't forgive myself that I can't remember what, exactly, the offence was, how crude or ignorant. Whatever it was, it seemed to stop, as though for ever, our writing to one another, let alone our meeting. May I say, now, as I know I should have said many years before, how sorry and, inarticulately, more than that, I am that some minor (oh, I hope so, minor) beastliness of mine, presumption, conceit, gaucherie, seeming-ingratitude, foul manner, callow pretension, or worse, yes, indeed, or far worse, interrupted our friendship, just beginning, and lost for so long, to me, the happiness and honour of being able to send my work, as it was written, to you, and to write to you of the never-ending-circling problems and doubts of craft and meaning and heart that must always besiege us. If my apology, true as my love of your Song of the Cold, reads to you as stiltedly as, quickly writing, it sounds to me, I'm sorry again and can only say how hard I find it to move naturally into the long silence between now and nine beautiful, dreadful years ago.
   I'm daring to write to you now because I have been reading, in Our Time,[2] your passages, or message, about my new poems, all those words

---

[1] Boars Hill is a residential district favoured by Oxford elders.
[2] *Our Time* ('incorporating *Poetry and the People*'). Sitwell reviewed *Deaths and Entrances* in the April 1946 issue.

glowing out of the paper like caves and eyes, full of understanding and mysteries:—though that may sound, God knows, affected, but how can I say how profoundly I was moved by the expression of your profound & loving understanding of the poems I've worked upon for so long and through so many giant and pygmy doubts, high and low darknesses, ghastly errors and exaltations? The poems you liked least were of course the worst in the book: they were worked at intermittently, out of changing values, there was no cohesion in them, poems of bits, or bits of poetry sliced off at the intellectual end of a series of conflicting, locked, and lost-before-they-were-begun, arguments. 'Paper and Sticks' was a 'light relief' where none was wanted; and I am always light as a hippo. But your quickening to the best of the poems came across to me like a new life of sympathy and mystery; to share the joy you express at the joyful poem, Fern Hill, is a new joy to me, as real as that which made the words come, at last, out of a never-to-be-buried childhood in heaven or Wales.

I hope you will write to me, forgive me for a long-gone never-meant boorish blunder or worse. Am I better now, I can ask only the never-telling tides of war and peace and duties around me? I hope you will let me meet you again.

For months and months and grey months I've been basemented in London. Now we can stay here, in a kind of summerhouse by the river, for a few green months (I trust). We are so miserably poor, blast and blast it, but the spring's singing all over the place, and, between scraping and hacking and howling at my incompetence, I've time to listen and, soon perhaps, to work again. 'Fern Hill' was the last poem I've written, in September, in Carmarthenshire, near the farm where it happened. I want very very much to write again. And I should like to write to tell you how I fell about all your poems written during the war, if one day I am forgiven and I may. There is no: 'There is no need to say what I feel about poems whose beauty is true and strange and clear to all *and* the blind'. There's always need to say what great work means to one man, how your creation of revelation and his revealed acceptance meet in a point—did Yeats say it?—of light.

But I've written enough and too much—pass over, if you can, all the tongue-knotted awkwardnesses, these stammers for nine years back —and I must wait now hoping, all the time, to hear from you.

Yours sincerely,
Dylan Thomas

MS: Texas

DAVID HIGHAM
April 5 '46   Holywell Ford Oxford

Dear David,
   Thank you for yesterday's letter. I'm delighted you managed to get
Dent to make the £24 odd up to £50.[1] Can you really get the cheque as
quickly as possible? I've just been sent urgent school-bills etc for loud &
all too quickly growing children, & must pay them *at once*. I *do* hope you
will be able to: otherwise I'm sunk.
   Thanks again.

                                                        Yours,
                                                        Dylan

MS: Texas

MAURICE CARPENTER
April 5 1946   Holywell Ford Oxford

Dear Maurice,
   Nice to hear from you. And I'm glad you've managed to get a 2 page
May Day space for poems. I'm awfully sorry, but I haven't got a poem.
The one I mentioned on St. Patric's night has become very odd & foggy;
and I'm afraid there's no chance of finishing it under a couple of weeks.
   I hate the title Flame Bird, and don't like The English Helicon. I like, as
a title: 'Danger Men Writing'.
   Hope to see you soon. Thank you a lot for what you said about Edith
Sitwell's review. There's a new edition of my poems—3000—being
printed now.
   Give me a telephone number, if there is one. I come up once a week,
but not on a fixed day.

                                                        Yours,
                                                        Dylan

MS: National Library of Wales

---

[1] A payment for *Deaths and Entrances*.

'JOHN'[1]

April 5 '46   Holywell Ford Oxford

Dear John,

Thanks for the letter. I'm sorry, but I haven't a poem at all. When is your *final* date? If it's a reasonable way off, I might be able to finish, in time, one I'm trying to work on now. If it isn't, I'm glad you invited me anyway, and I hope you'll get a good page together.

I haven't been able to get to Dublin yet, but I hope this spring. I'd cut my toes off to go.

Yours,
Dylan

Do you ever come up to Oxford? Do drop me a line if you do. We're here for quite a bit, I think.

MS: Texas

NANCY PEARN

April 15 '46   Holywell Ford Oxford

Dear Miss Pearn,

Thank you for your letter of April 11th; I'd have answered at once, but have been in town.

I'm glad that you have made the Features Contract department agree to pay at the rate of 33 & ⅓ per cent above the standard rate as arranged with the Authors' Society.

I note also the payments due to me for the use of 4 of my poems in the Italian Service on 10th April.

The letter I'd thought I'd send to the Talks Contract Dept authorising the BBC to deal with you on this side, I mislaid somehow & am writing to them again & will post it with this letter.

Yours sincerely,
Dylan Thomas

MS: Texas

BBC

15 April '46 (BBC Talks contracts should go to his agents. See Appendix 36.)

---

[1] Unidentified recipient. It is not John Lehmann, John Bayliss, John Ormond or Sir John Waller. It might be the late John Pudney.

JEAN LEROY[1]
15 April 1946   Holywell Ford Oxford

Dear Miss LeRoy,
    Thank you for your letter of April 12.
    I see that the Head of the Talks Contract Dept. of the BBC says that I do
not qualify for professional actor's fees when I read other people's work
on the air, but that 'naturally all fees are subject to negotiation.'
    Yes, I have already done two of the three readings you mention, in the
'Book of Verse' programmes, & will be doing the third tomorrow.
    I see that the BBC have sent you the three contracts with them,
proposing a fee of 5 guineas plus 13/2 fare from Oxford to London for each
broadcast; & you want to know how these fees compare with the ones I
have been paid for similar jobs in the past. For all 'Book of Verse' programmes I have, in the past, received 5 pounds each.
    I think we shd accept this difference, don't you? I'm urgently in need of
the money & further discussions will probably make little or no odds. So,
if you think it advisable, I say go ahead & collect what they offer. But
what d'you think?

                                            Yours sincerely,
                                            Dylan Thomas

MS: Texas

W. EMLYN DAVIES[2]
April 26th 1946   Holywell Ford Oxford

Dear Emlyn Davies
    What a wonderful gift. A very, very lovely book, eye-and-I delighting,
and, to me, a great tribute. I shall always keep and treasure it. Dent's
didn't send it along until last week, and then I was away. I came back to
find this burningly good present waiting. Dent's had kept it in their office
for days, to show everyone; they wrote to tell me, as indeed they should
write to tell you, however well you *must* know it, what a splendid piece
of craftsmanship they thought it was, and how much everyone there
appreciated it. No-one can appreciate it as I do, except perhaps my
children when they're old enough. And no, they couldn't either.
    Of course I remember you, and well, though it was such a short
friendship owing to all kinds of reasons—mostly, I think (and hope) to my
going away. It's strange to think of you living in the house where I was

---

[1] Jean LeRoy became an executive of Pearn, Pollinger and Higham after the war.
[2] Emlyn Davies, a schoolmaster, moved to 5 Cwmdonkin Drive in 1937, when the
    Thomases left, and lived there with his family until his death in 1973. He used compasses
    and coloured pens to make abstract 'calligrams' or patterns: in this instance to illustrate
    Thomas poems.

born. If I come to Swansea, as I certainly shall do one day, though, as you probably know, my mother and father are now in Carmarthenshire and I have very few home associations in the town, may I call and see you?

A very good friend of mine lives in Swansea; he's just returned after five and a bit years in the Air Force: Vernon Watkins. Do you know him? I'm sure you know some of his poems. He lives at 131 Glanmor Road, Sketty. If you don't know him, I wish you would. I'm writing to him, and may I give him your address too? He has great powers and profound poetical sincerity, an ear for all music and a tongue against all humbug; he's a pretty marvellous chap, but don't tell him I said so.

It would be silly to say that I'm glad you like my poems; glad's a spindly little [word], and there is no such thing as 'like' in the splendidly loving care of your beautiful penmanship. But I am glad, anyway. Glad that you remember that evening, years ago, in Cwmdonkin Drive. Glad to think that the first printed poem of mine, Light Breaks, must have said to you what it meant to me.

My wife, whose name is Caitlin, wants to say with me again: Thank you for the book.

> All good wishes,
> Yours,
> Dylan Thomas

MS: H. W. E. and A. G. Davies

VERNON WATKINS
April 27th 1946   Holywell Ford Oxford

My dear Vernon,

There's never been such a long time between our letters, and I hope, atom willing, there won't be again. (Somewhere in the wet Magdalen trees a bird makes a noise exactly like Doctor Ludwig Koch.) It's been my fault of course, that goes without whining, but I'm heavy with reasons like Doctor Magnus Hirschfeld. Right below where we live—it is, I think, a converted telephone kiosk, with a bed where the ledge for directories used to be—there is a vole-run. (Do not tell this to Fred who said that I could not speak for half a minute without mentioning vermin or Dracula, and that was five years ago.) The run is so narrow that two voles cannot pass each other. Suddenly, an elderly, broad vole with a limp came quite fast down the run from the left just as an elderly, broader vole with a limp came from the right. From where I am sitting, expectantly nervous and ill like patients on an imminent, I could see what the voles were thinking. They never stopped running as they thought, as they neared one another. Who was to turn back? should they both turn back? should they fight, kiss, call it a day, lie down? They never stopped their limping running as I saw and heard the decision made. With a wheezing like that of a little otter, with a husky squeaky updrawing of shining arthritic legs, the elderly broader limping vole jumped over the back of the other. Not a word was said.

We've been here about six weeks, just behind Magdalen, by river and vole-run, very quiet, Aeronwy in a day-nursery near and sleeping in the next-door house or house-proper, Caitlin and I going our single way into the vegetable kingdom. I haven't worked for a long time, apart from reading, every week, over the air to the Indians: an audience of perhaps three, and all of them bat-or-Tambi-voiced. I'm reading Hardy on the ordinary service on May 19th. Probably about eleven at night. Try to remember to listen. I've written a long comic poem, not to be published, to keep the uttermost cellarmen of depression away and to prevent my doing crosswords.[1] I've written a few pieces, nearly all quotations, for the Eastern radio, on Edward Thomas, Hardy, and some others. And I'm going to do a programme on Wilfred Owen: though all my job is the selection of the poems for professional readers to (badly, usually) read, and the interpolation of four-line comments between each. I'd love to see your essay on Owen. Could I? I'd be very careful with it and return it spotlessly unAeronwied. And I want to write a poem of my own again, but it's hard here with peace and no room, spring outside the window and the gascooker behind the back, sleep, food, loud wireless, broom and brush all in one kiosk, stunted bathing-hut or square milkbottle.

About Owen: Siegfried Sassoon has a lovely chapter about him, completely new, in his latest book, Siegfried's Journey. You would like it very much.

It's strange to think of you, and Fred, and Tom sometimes, in Swansea again. How is that blizzardly painter, that lightning artist, that prodigal canvas-stacker? Has he reached the next finbone of the fish he was dashing off before the war? Please give him my love.

And Cwmdonkin Park. I wish we were there now. Next month sometime I'm going down to see my mother, who has been very very ill, outside Carmarthen, and will stop at Swansea on the way back? Have you a little sheetless, must be sheetless, dogbox with nails for me to sleep in? Any shelter for a night? Unless you've been mending the roof. Then we could, maybe, all spend one evening together, wipey-eyed, remembering, locked in these damned days, the as-then-still-forgiven past.

You and Fred and Tom and, shame, no Dan whose future's stranger than ever, his multiplying harassed women trailing children like seaweed, his symphonies shouldering out in his head to unplayable proportions, his officer's trousers kept up now by three safety-pins. And me too: I had a little time in hospital but I'm out again now and fit as an old potato.

Love to you all, Gwen, Rhiannon, yourself, from Caitlin, Llewelyn [in

---

[1] The poem is unknown.

margin, arrowed from 'Llewelyn': in Cornwall for a month], Aeronwy and myself. Please do send a photograph of Rhiannon. And the Owen?

Dylan

MS: British Library *VW*

DAVID HIGHAM
April 27th 1946 Holywell Ford Oxford

Dear David,

Same wolfish cry, I'm afraid, for money, though I need it really for other wolves. I wrote to Miss LeRoy telling her that, as far as I was concerned, the extra bit she'd obtained for me for reading poetry on the radio was acceptable. That immediately covered three small contracts. There were, too, a few other BBC copyright fees that had come or were coming. Also, there may be a few other bits and pieces.

I'm really in a hell of a way for money at this *very moment*, fearing that cheques may even be returned to my landlords unless I bung in something to the bank at once. That's bad enough, indeed it's fatal, but there's worse which wouldn't, I know, interest you: I mean, the worse is embarrassingly intimate. I can hear it howling now from 50 miles away. You said, in your last note, when sending me your pro-Dent's cheque for £50, that that left me £16 still in your debt. Could you, oh please, take the £16 off our next piece of real or real-ish money and let me have some now, straightaway? I can't write URGENT big enough; there isn't enough paper in Oxford to contain the letters.

I've got quite a lot of those stories—provisionally 'Bob's My Uncle '— together, & a friend of mine is trying to collect the rest out of miserably forgotten advanced quarterlies etc. I'll let you have, *quite* soon, what there is plus indication of additions.

But, immediately, it is, on my word, a desperate matter of having money. Will you see what you can do?

When—as I hope to God—that's somehow settled, I should very much like to see you for a few minutes about films.

And excuse this franticery.

Yours,
Dylan

MS: Texas

GODFREY THURSTON-HOPKINS
April 27th 1946 (Sends information about printed version of 'Memories of Christmas'. See Appendix 37.)

JOHN ORMOND [THOMAS][1]
30 May 1946   Holywell Ford Oxford

Dear John Ormond Thomas,[2]

I think I owe you two apologies.

First, for being so unhelpfully, even helplessly, comatose when you and the Picture Post photographer came along to that Time for Verse reading on May 19th. I had a really sickening bout of gastric 'flu, and only wanted to lie in a corner, whimper, and die: I don't know how the hell I managed to read aloud at all; I know I couldn't speak. And God knows what the pictures looked like. If they're *too* frightful, I do hope you can take them again. Patric Dickinson's always about at the BBC, and I'm more than willing and will co-operate to the extent of as many grimaces and standings-on-the-head as you like. Could one see what was taken before, if ever, they appear? I really *don't* want to appear as a liverish, green, sulky, hunched and glazed man—as most often I am very well indeed, and suffer from nothing more than the occupational complaints of nervousness and high blood-pressure. Do let me know.

And the other thing is, that I was introduced to you wrongly; or, rather, not rightly enough. I caught, on our first and second meeting, only the words 'Thomas' and 'Picture Post'. And it wasn't until I got home, after the photographic evening, and read your preliminary letter that was waiting for me there, that I knew really who you were. You must, after our letters etc. of the past, our common town and school background, and, of course, my knowledge of your poems, have thought me offensively rude. Do forgive me. Perhaps we can meet one day, in Fleet Street, for a drink or six?

Don't forget to drop me a line, if you can, about the photographs; and, if possible, let me have a shuddering glance at them before they appear.

                                               Yours,
                                               Dylan Thomas

MS: the recipient

[1] Poet (Cholmondeley Award, 1975) and BBC film producer (b. 1923), of Swansea, who had corresponded with Dylan Thomas before they met. His later films include studies of Thomas (*A Bronze Mask*) and Vernon Watkins (*Under a Bright Heaven*). In 1946 he was a writer on the staff of the magazine *Picture Post*. 'Time for Verse' was a BBC series for which Dylan Thomas often read. Patric Dickinson was the producer. The article that appeared in *Picture Post*, 'A Nest of Singing Birds', 10 August 1946, featured a number of 'BBC' poets.
[2] Now known as 'John Ormond'.

HARRY KLOPPER
May 30th 1946   Holywell Ford Oxford

Dear Mr. Klopper,

Thank you for your letter, and for letting me see the nine short poems from your long poem to be called 'The Vision'. I meant to reply long before this, but have been away. Do forgive me: the delay wasn't caused because I could think of nothing to say about your poems, but because I had too much to say and too little time to sit down and say it. Even now, I'm very much rushed for bread-and-butter work, and can put down only a few short and, I'm afraid, inadequate comments on the poems. Perhaps, if you'd be kind enough to let me see the second part of the long poem, when it is finished, I could write my own, frankly personal, impressions of it at greater length.

Let me say, first of all, that I do appreciate the difficulties you must feel in writing poetry in a, comparatively, recently acquired language, especially when you are, as you mentioned in your letter, cut off from all literary activities. This last, in the case of a poet writing in his native language, might indeed be more of an advantage than a hindrance; but, in your case, I can see that it must be grievously hard not to be able to share, with anyone sympathetic to the writing of poetry, in some discussion of the problems that arise out of it. I can imagine that one of the gravest disadvantages you encounter is that of feeling yourself—even though temporarily, and at inevitable moments of depression and self-mistrust —incapable of appreciating how an ordinary reader of English poetry would react to the texture and movement of your words, not to their meaning (for the meaning that any poetry can convey is common to all readers and writers in every language) but to the *stuff* itself out of which the poetry is made. Though you may be certain of the logical development of the argument of each poem, you are, I believe, *un*certain of the *feel* of it. Too often, unmarried words limp together towards the consummation of the last line, only to find it entirely unsatisfying, unrewarding of the intellectual passion that had forced them towards that end.

All I can say that might be interpreted as even remotely constructive is that you must endeavour to feel and weigh the shape, sound, content of each word in relation to the shape, sound, content etcetera of the words surrounding it. It isn't only the *meaning* of the words that must develop harmonically, each syllable adding to the single existence of the next, but it is that which also informs the words with their own particular life: the noise, that is, that they make in the air and the ear, the contours in which they lie on the page and the mind, their colours and density.

So that in these poems—no, not individual poems but pieces of poetry moving towards a poem—I see that the abstract words rarely harmonise, or live together, with the concrete. In piece I, for instance, the 'avarice of shuffling feet' is, to me, quite discordant. I always feel that one should be very reluctant of putting down any abstract words at all, or at least of abstract words that one has not previously, or is not going to later, define. I believe, referring to the line in piece I, that it is better to put down an avaricious word, an avaricious image, than the vague abstraction, the undefined word that means so many different things to so many different people. That is, to put down something like 'where all the shuffling feet are misers' (that's only the first tentative suggestion that came into my head) rather than 'the avarice of shuffling feet'. I admit this is an absurd suggestion: I'm not attempting to rewrite your poem, God forbid, but merely to instance, concretely, something of what I mean by saying that the juxtaposition of a vague word and a particular word is, to me, nearly always unsatisfactory.

Later, in the second piece, I confess that I can never make anything much of such a phrase as 'the measureless depth of fears'. I like, in poems, to be told why or how this 'depth' is full of fears, and even exactly what the 'depth' is. Such a line as 'the untellably deep, squid-crowded sea' would, in spite of its impromptu silliness, mean more to me.

Certain lines of the second piece I like; and the repeated lines, though they do contradict what I said about the juxtaposition of vague and particular, are moving.

The opening of piece III seems, to me, to be intellectually confused, the images mixed in some sort of evocative pudding.

It is, of course, far easier to point out what one disagrees with than it is to comment sensibly upon what one finds good. One disagrees with a line of poetry because one finds that it is *not* inevitable, it could be changed, the wrong words, quite simply, have been used; but when the inevitable line appears, what is there to say? The music is made, the magic is done, the sound and the spell remain. And so it is easy for me to say that I find most of piece IV unreal: the words speak to a dictionary-in-the-head, even to a dictionary of synonyms for I do not believe the words to be exact, to be 'just'.

But pieces VI and VII, because the words are objects, make an immediate impact. 'Yes', one says, 'this is what it is about; he is looking through windows at the rocks; I can understand, I think, his grief and transitory omnipotence.'

And I think the rhythms of *all* the pieces could be tautened; but that tautening will emerge itself as each word is valued according to its individual life.

But how little I can help you! How profoundly difficult it is! I can only burble like an old bird with its beak full of bias and soap; and you can but curse yourself for ever having given your poetry to such a turgid rook.[1]

Send me some more any time you like, and believe me that, in spite of what I have said or only half said, I was grateful to you for having read them.

---

[1] Thomas used the same sentence in a letter to Margaret Taylor, page 578.

And do let me know if you want the poems back.

Yours sincerely,
Dylan Thomas

MS: Carbondale   *SL*

JEAN LEROY
May 30 1946   Holywell Ford Oxford

Dear Miss LeRoy,

Yes, I agree to the BBC fee of 5 guineas and 13/2 fare—retrospectively
—for my 7-minute reading in 'The World Goes By' series recorded on May
6th.

Incidentally, a travel voucher for return fare from Oxford to London for
my participation in a 'Time for Verse' programme on May 19th I never
used, having mislaid it & bought a ticket myself. Now I've found the
voucher and enclose it. Perhaps you can get the BBC to cancel it and
allow me the return fare in exchange?

Last Monday, the 27th, I went up to London to take part in a ½ hour
programme on the National Insurance Bill[1] (fee 7 guineas & 13/2 fare).
You had already sent me notice of the engagement. In London, I found
that the programme had been put off a *week before*, and that, owing to
some hitch of a newly-engaged secretary's, it had been forgotten to notify
me of the postponement. The producer, R. D. Smith, wired his apologies
afterwards, but I had *wasted* a whole day and been forced to pay travelling
expenses etc. *for* that day. I don't know what the BBC ruling is in cases
like this, but I do hope you can get me, at least, my out-of-pocket
expenses. Okay?

Yours sincerely,
Dylan Thomas

MS: Texas

DAVID HIGHAM
June 10th 1946   Holywell Ford Oxford

Dear David,

Hindle, of Henry Holt,[2] told me he'd had a talk with you about my
publishing-position in America; and that you believed *New Directions* to

---

[1] Probably a dramatised documentary.
[2] A firm of American publishers.

have an option on my next books. I told Hindle that I'd unfortunately mislaid my last *N. Directions* contract, but that *I* believed I was entirely free of them after the publication of my *Selected Writings*, which shd be out any time now. And I promised Hindle that I wd let him know *definitely*, by the time he returned at the end of this week, whose belief was correct: yours or mine.

Can you dig up the Laughlin contract & find out, for good & all, whether we did allow him option on any future work of mine—and, if so, on how many books? I do hope *I'm* right, & that I'm no longer bound to that mean Laughlin. Even if I am, Hindle says that Holt will try to get me away from *N. Directions*. But until it's known, obviously he, Hindle, can't make any actual offer for future work. Could you let me know very soon?

No news yet from Harper's magazine, I suppose, about my proposed visit to, & article on, Puck's Fair?[1] If they don't want it, is there any English newspaper or magazine?

Yours
Dylan

MS: Texas

DANIEL JONES
Monday June 24 '46   Holywell Ford Oxford

My dear Dan,
    I've only just got, dear God, your letter.
    I've been in London & Birmingham and jeopardy & hazard.
    I'm eely and oily.
    I'm hot trottered toast.
    I'm my cup of toe.
    I hate the earth: oh to hell with that incommensurable cowpad.
    Cleopatra smells of Marmite.
    Come again, King Cain, and have a cosh, I'm Abel.
    It was terrible to miss you. I wanted so much to help with mothers, aunts, children, luggage, eartrumpet.
    In my reeking way, I'd forgotten you were going so soon.
    I'm weevil.
    I haven't forgotten the other help and shall send it as quickly as possible. Or, best, give it to you here.
    I had a job every day to do, last week, shouting 'Hi' in the North & 'Varlet' in Portland Square.[2]

---

[1] Puck Fair is a modest Irish bacchanalia held every August at Killorglin, Co. Kerry. *Picture Post* advanced £50 in the hope of an article. Thomas went to Kerry but wrote nothing.
[2] Thomas was busy at various BBC studios, acting and reading poetry.

How long will you be in Swansea? *Will you write by return?*

And this is important. When can you *come, alone or with your piece of Exeter oatcake, to Oxford?* It *must* be in the next fortnight. Margaret Taylor, my hostess, has an empty (but for 5 children) house for a fortnight and sends an invitation: there's a big bedroom waiting, & three lavatories.

I have a cricket bat & a hard ball and a choice of lawns.

I wish beyond anything you would come.

I have a room in Magdalen to read, write, dance & destroy poems in.

I am negotiating the purchase of a barrel of Flower's Best Bitter.

There is a grand piano, a harpsichord, & a large library of records (*with* gramophone).

We are on the river, & there is a punt.

I shall have some money.

Will you write at once?

Caitlin is looking forward very much to seeing you & Irene; or you alone; or Dan first & then Jones after.

If you cannot *possibly* come, I will try to come to Swansea.

[*A sentence has been deleted:* But, for the next few weeks, I have to do a few hours' work every day, & I know I will not work in Swansea.]

But for the next few weeks I think it will be difficult for me to move all that way from London, as I am waiting for a job.

Oh, it *will* be good here if you come.

My love for always, & my truly deep apologies for not being able to come down with them, to your mother & Aunt Alice. I am so glad they are home again, at last.

And I *will* see them soon.

But we *must* be here first.

I shall sharpen the cricket-bat in anticipation.

We have a tame robin, & the swan calls on Mondays.

Love from your old friend,

Dylan

By return, write.

And all regards to Vernon & Fred.

MS: Texas   *SL*

ALEC CRAIG[1]

July 2 1946   Holywell Ford Oxford

Dear Alec Craig,

Thank you for your nice letter, & for what you said about my reading at the Wigmore Hall.

---

[1] Alec Craig (b. 1897), author, ran a poetry circle.

I'd like very much to come & read again at Bayswater.

Monday, Sept. 10, will suit me perfectly well.

I see you want me to read for 2 sessions. Again, I'd be delighted.

Let's fix up a place for meeting before the reading, shall we, a little later on.

Hope to hear from you soon.

Oh, by the way: could I, on the 1st occasion, read the poems of *other* poets?

Sincerely,
Dylan Thomas

MS: Thomas Trustees

JOHN ARLOTT[1]
Monday 22 July 1946   Holywell Ford Oxford

My dear John,

I forgot, last Yeatsday, entirely, to ask you to have lunch with Margaret Taylor, Roy Campbell, & myself—& any young man of Margaret's—on Wednesday of this week, the 24th, at the White Tower, Percy St. It's Margaret's lunch & she's very keen on it. She wants us to meet about a quarter to one in the Wheatsheaf pub next door.

I had to tell Margaret T. that I'd asked you, as she'd been at me to do so for days & days. So, if you can't manage it, will you ask—as a special favour—Sylvia to wire deep regrets for inconvenience etc. to Margaret at Holywell Ford tomorrow, Tuesday.

Sorry to be such a nuisance, but I *had* to tell Margaret I'd asked you & you'd said yes. I've put you in a false position, but it's only a tiny one, I hope. Will you do it for me? That is: either turn up—the lunch will be good—or wire apologies, impossible, sudden call to work etc. to Margaret. I hope you can manage it, of course.

I hope you get this note before you go Test-wards. If you do, will you leave all information & details with Sylvia or at the reception-desk on TUESDAY. I'll be in town & I'll ring Sylvia. If there's no reply, I'll call at Oxford St.

But do your best. I'll be seeing you Friday.

Ever,
Dylan

MS: the recipient; but all the letters to Arlott are taken from typescripts.

[1] John Arlott (b. 1914), author and cricket commentator. Arlott, a policeman who joined the BBC as a producer, was responsible for many of Thomas's verse-reading programmes, especially for the Eastern Services.

JEAN LEROY
July 22nd 1946   Holywell Ford Oxford

Dear Miss LeRoy,

Sorry not to have answered your enquiries about the 30 minute BBC Feature Programme for the *This Is London* series. But I am very glad to hear that the BBC are now going to pay forty (instead of thirty) guineas for *one* broadcast use of my script.[1]

Incidentally: surely your information that the script was broadcast in the African Service on Friday, July 12, is wrong? I didn't hand in the script until late on Thursday the 11th. And also I was the narrator, myself, in the recording of the script on Monday July 15th. You *must* be wrong; but if, by some most improbable chance you aren't, then I need to be paid for *two* broadcasts: the July 15th recording was, I gather, for the North American etc service.

And, incidentally again, I've not yet had word of your receiving an actor's contract for me for my part in that recording of the 15th.

But this is what I'm really writing about:—I'm going away to Ireland for a holiday on August 4th. And I must have, well before then, the outstanding money due to me from the BBC.

This outstanding money now includes:

1) *20 guineas* (plus railway fares) for programme on *Wilfred Owen* recorded June 19.

2) *15 guineas* for *Time For Verse* broadcast July 15th.

3) *40 guineas* for *This is London* recorded July 15.

There are also: *7 guineas* (plus fare) for my part in *Book of Verse* in the Far East Service on July 18; and *7 guineas* (plus expenses)—this is the usual fee, at any rate—for my part as narrator in my script recorded on July 15th.

But for these two last, I have not yet heard of your having had contracts sent to you.

It is items 1) 2) and 3) that are, to me, enormously important. Without them I can't go away.

Will you, *please*, collect those *three* outstanding fees for me *straightaway*. There is such little time. I will be so grateful.

I'll give you a ring, tomorrow, Tuesday, to see if you've had this letter and to press its urgency even further.

And a last, tiny thing. I didn't use my BBC travel-voucher from Oxford to Birmingham for a broadcast on *Lord Byron*, in the Midland Regional, on July 16th—(cheque for broadcast already received). I was working in London & had to travel from London to Birmingham, having left the

---

[1] By now Thomas was in demand for many kinds of radio work. For 'This is London', a series broadcast overseas, he wrote *The Londoner*, an account of a day in the life of a working-class street. Although plainly written, it points towards the fantasy of *Under Milk Wood* a few years later. 'It is a summer night now in Montrose Street,' says the closing passage. 'And the street is sleeping. In number forty-nine, all is quiet. The Jacksons are dreaming.'

voucher in Oxford. I return the voucher herewith, hoping—though only dimly, not at all urgently—that the BBC will accept it and refund me the railway fare. Will they do that, I wonder?

But urgent, really, are the seventy-five odd quid. Which I *must* have almost straightaway.

I'll be ringing you.

Yours sincerely,
Dylan Thomas

MS: Texas

LAURENCE GILLIAM[1]

July 23 '46   Holywell Ford Oxford

Dear Laurence,

Thank you very much for your letter. I was sorry about the recording-car for Puck Fair, but I knew it was terribly short notice.

I'm so glad you liked the 'Portrait of a Londoner' programme, and I'll let you know some script-suggestions as soon as I can. If, in the meantime, you think of any that I could have a shot at, I'd be very grateful.

But I'll be suggesting something very soon anyway.

Yours,
Dylan

MS: BBC

LORRAINE JAMESON

July 23 1946   Holywell Ford Oxford

Dear Miss Jameson:

Thank you for your letter of the 17th. I hope this answer won't be too late: your letter's only just been forwarded to me.

Yes, I should like very much to do a Children's Hour talk for the next quarter's programmes. (I didn't know, by the way, that Aneirin Davies had left Talks, and was expecting, a long time ago, to hear from him.) But I think 'Penny Dreadfuls', as a subject, would be a little too narrowing: I've forgotten nearly everything about them. I suggest a talk on memories of books I read as a young boy: this would include Penny Dreadfuls, & Chums & Tiger Tim's Weekly & the B.O.P. & the Magnet & the Gem

---

[1] Laurence Gilliam (1907–64) was Head of Features in BBC radio, an innovator who filled his department with poets and journalists. He had written to say that the London programme was 'a most sensitive and successful piece of radio'.

etc., but also Henty & Marryat, Swiss Family Robinson, Jules Verne, Water Babies, etc etc etc: a talk, of course, not overmuch keeping to its subject and certainly not just a literary record: just a bit of nostalgic knockabout.[1]

Can you give me a dead-line date for receipt of the M.S.? Any other suggestions for further talks—Children's Hour or not—would be most welcome.

Yours sincerely,
Dylan Thomas

MS: BBC

VERNON WATKINS
26th August 1946   Blaen Cwm Llangain near Carmarthen

My dear Vernon,
   I'm a little nearer Swansea, anyway, and I hope to see you and Gwen and Rhiannon at the end of this week or the beginning of next. I'd have written from Ireland but I didn't take letters or anything with me and couldn't remember your address. V. Watkins, Swansea, looked presumptuous. Ireland was lovely. We spent all our time in Dublin and in Kerry. We ate ourselves daft: lobsters, steaks, cream, hills of butter, homemade bread, chicken and chocolates: we drank Seithenyns[2] of porter and Guinness: we walked, climbed, rode on donkeys, bathed, sailed, rowed, danced, sang. I wish you'd been there. I didn't write anything, but here in Wales I will—all about Ireland. It'll be lovely to see you all, and so soon. I'll let you know exactly when.

Best love,
Dylan

MS: British Library   *VW*

JOHN ARLOTT
26th August '46   Blaen Cwm Llangain near Carmarthen

My dear John,
   I tried to get hold of you as soon as I got back from Ireland but you were always out. I don't know if you'd written while I was away, because my letters haven't been forwarded yet:—I expect them tomorrow. I should,

---

[1] The talk was not written.
[2] Prince Seithenyn was the legendary Welsh drunkard whose lack of vigilance let the sea breach a dyke.

anyway, have given you my Irish address. I saw Reggie Smith, and was so disappointed I wasn't there for the Lawrence programme. Ireland took all my money in the world—and some of other people's money, too—so I *must* get as much work now as I possibly can. Will you help? Any scripts and/or readings you can manage will be terribly welcome. I'll do you a script in a few days if you can get me one, or can come up to town for a reading at a day's notice—provided the BBC will pay expenses to & from Wales. I have to spend 10 days or a fortnight here with my mother, who is ill, and after that will go back to Oxford. Do your best for me, please, John: I'm in a real spot and simply must have a lot of work to do. How did the Lawrence go? Ireland was grand: I ate myself daft, but have now recovered. When do you go abroad? Hope to hear from you very soon. And *any* work: the bigger, of course, & the higher paid, the better.

Ever,
Dylan

MS: the recipient

DONALD TAYLOR
26th August 1946   Blaen Cwm Llangain near Carmarthen

Dear Donald,
   I haven't written to you for many months. I realised that, if ever there were any news to tell me, you would write. I'm here for a week or so, and, in this tremendous quietness, feel lost, worried about the future, uncertain even of now. In London, it doesn't seem to matter, one lives from day to day. But here, the future's endless and my position in it unpleasant and precarious. Do write and tell me if there are any hopes of our ever selling our pictures, old or new? I've reached a dead spell in my hack freelancing, am broke, and depressed. A word would help.

Yours,
Dylan

MS: Buffalo

UNKNOWN
28th August 1946   as from Holywell Ford Oxford

Dear Sir,
   I am sorry not to have answered, before this, your letter of August 9th. I've been away.

By all means, send me your manuscript book of plays; I'll be pleased to read them and, if I can, comment on them. But I should warn you that I know nothing whatsoever about Welsh History: perhaps your plays will help to fill a lamentable gap in my already gap-filled knowledge.

Yours sincerely,
Dylan Thomas

MS: Carbondale

E. J. KING-BULL[1]
28th August 1946   as from Holywell Ford Oxford

Dear Mr. King-Bull,
  Thank you for your letter of the 23rd of this month.
  The new series of poetry broadcasts,[2] which are to form part of the new 'Third' Programme beginning at the end of September,[3] does indeed sound elaborate and ambitious. I hope it has every good luck.
  I should be most glad to be one of the poets in the series, and thank you for wanting me to be. And I should, I think, be very happy collaborating with G. W. Stonier.[4]
  You suggest that, once I accepted the invitation generally (which I do), the three of us might meet soon for lunch and get down to it. I'll be back from holiday in about a week's time. Shall I give you a ring, then, or drop you a card? My address, for the next week, is: BLAEN CWM, LLANGAIN, near CARMARTHEN. After that, as above. If I don't hear from you while I'm in Wales, I will, anyway, get in touch with you as soon as I return. I'm sure that the three of us could beat four programmes into shape in a very short time.

Yours sincerely,
Dylan Thomas

MS: Texas

[1] Eric James King-Bull was a BBC producer.
[2] 'The Poet and His Critic.' See letter to King-Bull, page 608.
[3] The BBC's Third Programme, so called because it supplemented the existing domestic channels, 'Home Service' and 'Light Programme', set out to be cultural and élitist; at one time it was proposed to call it 'The Arts Programme'.
[4] George Stonier, writer and critic.

MISS PEARCE (at Pearn, Pollinger & Higham)
28th August 1946   Blaen Cwm Llangain near Carmarthen

Dear Miss Pearce,
   I've just got your letter of August 21st. In it you say that you have arranged for me to take part in the programme, *COMUS*, to be broadcast on Monday, Sept. 30th from 9.45 to 10.45 p.m.—rehearsals 28th Sept, 29th Sept, 30th Sept, times & studios for these rehearsals to be arranged.
   The fee offered, you say, is 12 guineas plus 15/- fare & £2 subsistence.
   Yes, do accept the proposal on my behalf, but: is the 12 guinea fee offered that which is offered to actors and not just to non-acting readers? I do a great deal of BBC readings, and have been trying for some time to get my position straight. 12 guineas for a programme which necessitates rehearsals on 3 days does not seem particularly generous to me. I have been told by a BBC producer with whom I am in touch that he is trying to get better fees for non-acting readers—needless to say, I cannot tell you his name, as the producers are not supposed to talk to the people they employ about money—and I would be very much obliged if you could find out how my 12 guinea fee compares with the fees offered to acting-readers. But, in any case, accept this. I should only like a little investigation to be done on account of future work.
   I shall be at the above address for another week. After that, the address is, as usual, HOLYWELL FORD, OXFORD.

                                        Yours sincerely,
                                        Dylan Thomas

MS: Texas

DAVID HIGHAM
29th August 1946   as from Holywell Ford Oxford

Dear David,
   Thank you for asking Ruthven[1] to dig up my old stories. I'll get busy and do my share, too, though what I must really do is to start writing a few new stories to add to the old ones. And I will.
   My address, until Sept 7th, is Blaen Cwm, Llangain, near Carmarthen, Wales. But any ordinary communications, if there are any, can wait for me at Oxford.
   I enclose a letter from Harper you might think worth answering for me. Is it?

                                        Yours,
                                        Dylan

MS: Texas

[1] Ruthven Todd.

MARGARET TAYLOR
29th August 1946   Blaen Cwm Llangain near Carmarthen

My dear Margaret,
    It was lovely to have your letter. But it was sad to miss you in Wales;
and this is the second time, for we called at Laugharne, once, just after
you'd gone. One day, how odd and good it would be to spend together, in
this timeless, drizzled, argufying place, some very unOxford days. I wish
New Quay had had more sun for you, though Jack Pat loves it as it is for
then he has his guests all trapped and cosy in his godly grot. Time has
stopped, says the Black Lion clock, and Eternity has begun. I'm so glad
you met and like Dai Fred who bottled your ship. Did you come across
Dewi, the battery-man? Evan Joshua of the Bluebell? The Norman you
know is New Quay's noisiest and least successful fighter; every summer
he starts a fight, & every summer some tiny little ape-man knocks him
yards over the harbour-wall or bang through the chemist's window. Did
Mrs Evans the Lion twitch, wink, and sip? Did Pat bring his horse in the
bar? Jack the Post is an old friend: he once married a pretty widow in
London & everything was fine, he said, except that wherever they went
they were followed by men in bowler hats. After the honeymoon, Mrs
Jack was arrested for double bigamy. And all the husbands appeared in the
court and gave evidence as to her good character. But I do hope you and
Alan and Giles and Sebastian[1] enjoyed some bits of the rainy time. I'd be
so ashamed, after our lauding, if the place had let you down with a wet
Welsh bump. Did you meet Taffy Jones, the stuttering ace? He's not very
nice. Or Alistair Graham, the thin-vowelled laird? Was the red plywood
bungalow, where we lived for a year and where the machinegun incident
took place, pointed out to you? I should have told you to take Sebastian to
the back room of the Commercial public house, where there are two very
large & very fine coloured prints of Louis Wain cats: do you know his
cats? Very alive and odious, capering, creeping, sneaking, ogling &
dancing, arch as Eliot's.[2]
    We had breathless days in Ireland: four in Dublin—oh the steaks, the
chickens, chocolate, cream, peaty porter, endless blarney of politics never
later than 1922—& the rest in Kerry, all wild sea and hills and Irish-
reeling in kitchens. And a day on the Blasket: a very calm day, they said:
the wind blew me about like a tissue-paper man, and dashed us against
the donkeys.
    We'll be staying here for another week, though I've got to go to London
on Sunday to read in the Time for Verse programme at 10-30. Do listen if
you can. Val Dyall and I are reading sea-battle poems: 'Of Nelson and the
North', Tennyson's 'Revenge' etc. But we'll be in the studio when you
come back from France. I can't tell you how much we're looking forward

---

[1] Margaret Taylor's husband and their sons, Giles (b. 1937) and Sebastian (b. 1940).
[2] T. S. Eliot's book of children's verse, *Old Possum's Book of Practical Cats*, was published
in 1939.

to being there again. We love it; and can never thank you both enough for having let us descend on you, you being so kind every way. Let's have some little journeys, foot and bus, round Oxford when you come back, please. We've hardly been on any; & perhaps September will be good.

Roy Campbell told me, when I saw him for a moment in London on the way here, that he likes Robert's reading very much. He wants us to read in a programme together, soon: a Milton programme, I think. Robert's done some work for him—and very well—already.

Aeronwy, in a fortnight with the Leahys, has developed a powerful, whining Oxford accent: and not the musichall sort.

Thank you for forwarding my letters. Could they go on being forwarded until the end of next week? But if it's a trouble, with you away, let them stay till we come. So many were out of date, but I only lost one job, and that a perniketty one.

I do hope you have a lovely holiday in France.

And we'll see you soon, which will be splendid.

                    Love from us both.

                                        Dylan

I'm glad about the Lyric man; & thank you. Will he write to me?

MS: Texas

DONALD TAYLOR

23 9 '46   Holywell Ford Oxford

Dear Donald,

    Thanks for writing.

I'm up in town at least two days a week, doing things for the BBC—and will be able to make quite a good thing of it.

If you ever come up nowadays, do let me know, at this Oxford address, & perhaps we can meet & have a drink.

I should like to talk about, among other things, turning B & H into a full-length radio play—they want them now, however experimental or unsqueamish, up to an hour and a half—for the Third Programme.

Pleasant to meet again anyway.

Love to your family.

                                        Dylan

MS: Buffalo

JEAN LEROY
Nov 6th 1946   Holywell Ford Oxford

Dear Miss LeRoy,

I see from your letter of the 5th that you've accepted, on my behalf, two invitations from the BBC: the first, to play in two live performances of *In Parenthesis*; & the second, to play the chief part in two live performances of *Aristophanes*.[1] And the fees you have accepted are twenty guineas *inclusive* for each.

I think these fees absurd; and though I've previously agreed with the producers of these two shows to play in them, I really do object to accepting the money offered.

Take *Aristophanes*. There are 3 whole days' rehearsals, plus one rehearsal from 2 p.m. onwards, *plus* two one-hour-&-a-half performances. Thus, four whole days (minus one morning) are to be spent on this show. Living in London for four days will cost me at least five pounds. Add to this my railway fare, & it works out that for four whole days work, including two live performances, I am offered about £14: £7 for each long feature performance, in which I am the principal character.

The same, except that I am not in this the principal character, applies to *In Parenthesis*.

Perhaps the trouble is that I am still being booked through Talks Dept. If that's so, it really must be seen to at once. In these two shows, & in very many others, I am a radio actor & *must* be contracted through Drama Dept.

But, even for Talks, £20 *inclusive* for 4 whole days' work is unacceptable. Absolutely unacceptable.

I do hope you'll do something about it straightaway.

Yours sincerely,
Dylan Thomas

MS: Texas

DAVID HIGHAM
23 11 46   Holywell Ford Oxford

Dear David,
    Re letter re Vogue.
    Sorry, but I was away and got your original letter of the 4th of

[1] *In Parenthesis*, the allegory by David Jones, had been adapted for radio by the BBC's Douglas Cleverdon; Aircraftman Richard Burton, waiting to be demobilised from the RAF, was also in the cast. 'Aristophanes' was 'a panorama of Aristophanic comedy', *Enemy of Cant*, by Louis MacNeice.

November—asking me to get hold of a copy, for Vogue's American editor, of my BBC script on *Memories of Bank Holiday*—too late to do anything about it. So glad you managed to get the *Listener* to her.

Re second par. re the possibility of my writing an article for English *Vogue*: I've had a letter from Audrey Withers wanting to fix up a meeting to discuss the article, & I think it's probably best for me to answer her myself as the next week or ten days are in a hell of mess for me with lots of jobs big & little:—but I'll be able, with a bit of fiddling, to fix a meeting.

Nice to be so busy—(I suppose).

Will get down to Dent book *very* soon.[1]

Yours,
Dylan

MS: Texas

JAMES LAUGHLIN
Nov 24th 1946   Holywell Ford Oxford

Dear James,

I'm so sorry we didn't manage to have, together, quieter drinks, or less, or more, and that, before you went off to Paris, we hadn't advanced very much my America-ward plans. What I do really remember is that you did promise to look out for a house in the Adirondacks where I could live for some time with my wife & two children; and that pretty soon. Of course I believe your promise, but this letter's only to tell you again that I want to be writing—poems, stories, scripts—and broadcasting—poems, stories, scripts,—and that I must be fixed up, somewhere in the country, up the hills, and fairly near a city (New York, in this case) before I can. So this is only to tell you (again) that I am very much relying on your true and proper promise. All I write in America is yours for America, (and I want, and mean to, write a lot), but until that is settled I have no intention of writing anything at all. I think I can, from this side, with the active help of Edith Sitwell, manage to get jobs—lecturing, reading, etc—to be awaiting me in America. But from *your* side, and from you personally, I want to know that there is *immediate temporary accommodation* for the four of us (Dylan, Caitlin, Llewelyn, Aeronwy) when we arrive in New York, and a house in the country for us pretty soon afterwards. I hope I'm not being dictatorial. What I want to say, again, is that I want to work a lot and very much, but that those things have got to be seen to (as you promised) before I leave here.

And the other importance: Even if, from this side, Edith contrives to

[1] Probably the projected collection *Bob's My Uncle*.

get for me a few American lectures etc, I still won't have the money to take the four of us on ship, plane, raft, or even by carrier pigeon. Caitlin is insisting that I write to you in this way: if she did not insist, I would still be writing this way. I hope that we, together, have a successful author-and-publisher existence: but it *must* be in America, and it *must* be through you. Can you write, or cable, me as soon as possible. These, to be dull, are the facts once more:

(1) I want to come early in the New Year to the States.
(2) I will not come unless I bring my family with me.
(3) I need the money to take us over.
(4) I want somewhere temporary for us to stay when we reach N. York.
(5) I want somewhere, after that, preferably in the hills, and certainly in the country, where we can live.
(6) Where we live must be somewhere near whatever place you think that I best can earn my living (mostly by broadcasting) in.
(7) I want to write a lot.
(8) What I write is, by our agreement, yours without any condition to print, publish, in America.
(9) And this, most importantly, must be soon.

Please, James, what can you do about it? And, please, make it quick. I hope to see you soon—but not here. And this, on my heart, is urgent. Don't forget.

Yours,
Dylan

MS: the recipient

CAITLIN THOMAS
Monday afternoon [December 2 1946]
as from Garden Flat 45a Maresfield Gardens Hampstead[1]

Darling my dear darling Cat, my love, I love you for ever, please my sweet think of me I love you Catty darling I love you. I'm writing this, very quick, very short, in the bloody BBC Maida Vale Studio where Louis's *endless* play is going on. And tonight—8.30 about—I'm reading Edith's vast bad poem.[2] Try to listen, dear. It *was* recorded, but I'm going to do it, 'live', again. Here's a tiny cheque. I daren't do any more until I get the letters sent to me (c/o Bill) that I hope are in Holywell Ford now. Please *do send* them, Cat my beautiful darling. Then I can send another cheque immediately. I don't want to phone because of maudlin Magdalen

---

[1] The address of friends, W. R. (Bill) McAlpine and his wife Helen.
[2] Thomas read Edith Sitwell's poem 'The Shadow of Cain' on December 2. The 'endless play' was MacNeice's *Enemy of Cant*.

Maggie. Will you phone me before you take Aeron (how is she?) to school? About 9-ish. HAM 1483 (Bill's number). I love you I love you I love you.

Dylan   XXX & all in the world

Back Thursday afternoon. But do, dear, phone *tomorrow morning* about 9.

MS: Maurice Neville

E. J. KING-BULL
December 26 1946   Holywell Ford Oxford

My Dear King-Bull,

A very late indeed, but most sincere, apology for not turning up, as I promised, and as I so much wanted to, at our Earp meeting.[1] I got caught up, inextricably, with three dull, but urgent, things; and wasn't free until nearly three. That's no excuse—I could have rung. Please do forgive me. And thank you, a lot, for such a gentle reproof in your nice letter. I do hope you enjoyed Tommy E's company. I'm sure he'll do a thorough, and entertaining, job. I'm writing him by this post. He hasn't yet got in touch with me.

You ask whether I've any suggestions for readers. I think, emphatically, no woman. I can't, offhand, think of one poem of mine that needs a woman's voice; any poem, indeed, that wouldn't positively be better off for not having a woman's voice (I think I was caught in negatives, then, but you know what I mean). I think *two* men, don't you? I suggest, for one, John Laurie:—he does know my poems, though I can't tell if he'd care to read them aloud. I do really want a *masculine* voice. David King-Wood, as well? I don't, of course, know what poems Tommy E. is choosing, but for some of my poems I think Laurie's voice most suitable. And he's awfully intelligent.

You ask, too, about a copy of my 'Twenty Six Poems'. You mean, 'Twenty Five Poems', don't you? I've borrowed a copy from a friend, and am sending it, today, to T.W.E.

When is the first date of the series?

I'll give you a ring, if I may, as soon as I'm in town next.

And thank you very much for not being cross about my failure to turn up that day. I *did* miss it so much.

Dylan T

---

[1] The meeting was to discuss Thomas's contribution to 'The Poet and His Critic'. Each poet in the series was examined in four programmes, which contained examples of his work, together with critical appreciation and the poet's reply; they were expansive days for radio culture. T. W. Earp was to be Thomas's critic. In the event, due to the bitter weather and power shortages of early 1947—which shut down the Third Programme for two weeks in February—and to Thomas's illness, only three of the four programmes were broadcast.

P.S. Again about readers: I have a friend, W. R. MacAlpine, 45a Maresfield Gardens, Hampstead, N.W.3., who knows more about my poems than I do and who reads them, aloud, extremely well. He has an Irish accent. Perhaps you'd think of trying him out?

MS: Texas

T. W. EARP
[about December 26 1946]   Holywell Ford Oxford

My dear Tommy,
   After months and months and months and months, I failed to turn up to meet you. Half it was that Commander King-Bull frightens me, and half that I got held up in rehearsals for the part of a raven, and the bit of reason over was drink.[1] I was terribly, deeply, sorry to miss you. But I'm so glad you're willing to do those Critical Scripts. I had a note from K-Bull saying you had no copy of my '25 Poems'. Neither have I, but I borrowed one for you on big promises that it would be looked after (no Empson eggs between the pages) and returned. Have you got all the other books —particularly 'The Map of Love', which is hard to get hold of, and which has some of the poems I'm fondest of? When can we meet? Let's make it soon, and before the first broadcast. Will you wire me? I'll come up at once to town and turn up too early and wait biting my legs to the quick. So many things to tell you. I have missed you a great deal. Caitlin sends her love to you and May. So do I. Please wire soon as you can. What about Henekey's Holborn to meet in next week?
                                                          Yours,
                                                          Dylan

MS: Ohio State University

JOHN DAVENPORT
[?December 1946]   [headed paper: TELEPHONE MESSAGE] 3.30

Dear John,
   Terribly sorry missed you today: I had an idea I'd, myself, look for that abominable briefcase. So I went round, feeling hopeless, with Louis's Pinkerton clueing, found it. I'll write to the cops tomorrow, putting them off. Hope to see you just after Christmas in London. Many thanks. I'll get that poem shipshape for Jan 1.
                                                          Yours ever,
                                                          Dylan

[1] Thomas played a raven in *The Heartless Giant*, 'a Norwegian fairy story', by Louis MacNeice, broadcast on December 13.

Can't wait. Have got to catch 4.45 Padd for Oxford where, tomorrow, I pick up Llewelyn to take him to that Ringwood hell-hole.

MS: Texas

ARKIN COURTS & CO[1]
January 10 [1947]   Holywell Ford Oxford

Dear Sir
    I enclose cheque for Fifty Six Pounds. I hope this covers the claim and the costs and that further proceedings will now be stayed.

                                            Yours faithfully,
                                            Dylan Thomas

MS: National Library of Wales

GRAHAM GREENE
[?late December 1946/early January 1947]   At Holywell Ford Oxford

Greene was a director of Eyre & Spottiswoode, the publishers, and also was known for his interest in the cinema; Thomas was hoping he might publish *The Doctor and the Devils*. Margaret Taylor had made the initial approach.

Dear Graham
    Thank you so very much for troubling about all this. I fear two things: first, that the script's no good, and second that, even if it were, it would be impossible to release it from whoever owns the copyright.
    I looked the script over again—and it looks amateurish: the dialogue's over wordy, and the construction badly needs pulling together. Probably a good subplot's needed; probably nothing is needed but 'No!'
    Anyway, I'm so grateful to you for telling Margaret—whose idea it was that I should dig it out of justified darkness—you'd read it.
    Will you let me know?
    I'm so sorry to have missed you & Walter Allen[2] that morning some weeks ago. I found I had to work in Maida Vale that morning: too far to come to town.

[1] A firm of solicitors who had issued a writ on behalf of John Westhouse, a firm associated with Peter Lunn Ltd, when it became obvious that no 'Book of Streets' was forthcoming. Thomas had eluded the writ since the previous May. It was served early in January 1947, as he left the BBC after reading 'A Visit to Grandpa's'. The letter is in another hand, with Thomas's signature appended.
[2] Walter Allen (b. 1911), author and journalist.

And thank you very much for sending 'The Little Kingdom' & Mervyn Peake's Grimm. Lovely drawings. I haven't read the Emyr Humphreys yet.[1] It was terribly kind of you.

I do hope we can meet soon.

Yours,
Dylan Thomas

MS: Sir Theodore Brinckman

GRAHAM GREENE[2]
[? 1947] [incomplete?]

The brief and, I'm afraid, ignorant history of a script, tentatively called 'The Doctor & The Devils', about Dr. Knox, the Edinburgh anatomist and Burke & Hare, the murderers.

This script was written by me when I was employed as a script-writer by a small company called Gryphon Films which was formed as a result of the dissolution of the documentary-making Strand Film Company.

The director of the Gryphon unit was Donald Taylor. (His private address is Hill Cottage, Hedgerley Village, near Slough, Bucks.) He resigned from Gryphon Films at the same time as myself: September, 1945, just as the Film Producers' Guild Ltd was being formed.

Gryphon Films had its offices in Guild House, (which now houses the Film Producers' Guild), St. Martin's Lane, W.C.2., and was somehow financially connected with Verity Films Ltd., which is still there. I do not know any details at all of the financial connection between Gryphon & Verity. But Donald Taylor, under whom I directly worked and on whose orders I wrote 'The Doctor and The Devils' must know. I have always been under the impression that the copyright is his.

Some of the research necessary for the scripting of this film was done by a member of Gryphon Films. And I also worked upon the preliminary roughing-out of the script with Taylor who took, throughout, a lively producer's interest.

The script was shown to a couple of wellknown producers, or companies, who—so I gather, but only at secondhand as Taylor told me little or nothing once the script was finished—were most enthusiastic about it and wished to do it but refused when Taylor demanded that he should direct it himself. I have, as I said, no firsthand proof of this.

I do know that Michael Redgrave, who read it, was extremely keen to play in it.

I also know that the script was sent to James Bridie whose play, 'The

[1] Emyr Humphreys (b. 1919), novelist. *The Little Kingdom* was his first book.
[2] Graham Greene's MSS of this and the next letter were loaned and copied for *SL*. Greene no longer has them, and assumes they are lost.

Anatomist', is on the same subject. Taylor wished to have it clear in writing that the script owed nothing to the play and that should the script be filmed Bridie could in no way object. Bridie replied satisfactorily.

When the script is seen, and if it is thought to have cinematic possibilities, Taylor is, of course, the one man to approach on the question of copyright.

Dylan Thomas

Only source: SL

GRAHAM GREENE
January 11 1947   Holywell Ford Oxford

Dear Graham,

Thank you such a lot for your letter. And, please, forgive me for not having answered it straightaway. I've been working in London, and very muddled too about where to live—here is feverish—and how and why. And about many other things, one or two of which I want to worry you with if you don't terribly mind. I know you're so busy, as publisher, writer, man and all, but if you could, though I've no right in the world to ask you, help, I'd be grateful always. I'm so sorry Margaret Taylor nagged you about the filmscript over Christmas: I only heard afterwards how she had written and phoned and plagued and plugged, all through kindness towards me I know; I didn't realise she was making such a business of it. I felt and feel, vague and nervous about it myself, and about sending it to you and trying to make some of my problems, if only for a moment, yours.

But, first, thank you very very much indeed for reading the script. I am so glad you liked it—if anyone could *like* such a nasty thing. And for writing to say what you thought about it. And for getting in touch with Michael Redgrave: it's good to think he hasn't forgotten the script & still wants to do it, in spite of the old B picture and Tod Slaughter's Plans.

About publishing the script. I'm pretty sure Dent's wouldn't touch it with a pole, and I'd very much like you to do it. But the question of copyright remains, of course, the same as when I wrote you about Donald Taylor and the other complications.

What I want, *frightfully urgently*—and this is the chief of the worries I want to worry you with—is some money for or from it or the chance of getting some, and ever so quickly, I can't tell you how quickly I need it, some money from Rank. I've got a pile of doctors' bills for Caitlin and for my son Llewelyn who is never, I'm sorry, well; and a looming writ; and another one on the doorstep. I'm in a hell of a mess. And *now*. So what I want to ask is, is there any chance of Rank & his boys giving me some money at once, either on account of this script or on account of another script I could—and very much want to—write for them? I know that 'The Doctor & The Devils' might never, because of horror & copyright, ever be produced. But I should like it to be regarded as a *sample of what I can write for the films*. I want, naturally, to write a hundred-times-better script, and I'm sure I can. I can write other than horrible stories, and I want to. Would there be anything in the suggestion that I cd write a *film specially for Redgrave*? Would the reading of this D. & D. script make it clear to Rank and boys that I am capable of writing for the screen? and, if so, would they think of giving me some money, or putting me under contract?

On top of bills & writs, all howlingly pressing, I must get out of here & find somewhere else to live at once. And that will take money, which I haven't got. All I earn I spend & give to past debts. I'm in a mess all right. But I *know* I could write a good new script. And I wish Redgrave & Rank would pay me to do it.

Sorry about this breathless letter. Shall I ring you next week? and can you help, with the film boys, in any immediate way? Thank you again for your letter.

Yours,
Dylan Thomas

Only source: SL

URSULA KEEBLE[1]
January 11 1947   Holywell Ford Oxford

Dear Mrs Keeble,
   Thank you very much for your letter of the [7th] suggesting that I might be interested in doing a poetry programme for one of the English Series (Dept. of School Broadcasting) in the Summer Term, 1947. I am indeed interested, and would be very glad to do a programme. I could discuss the details with you any time you like—either at B.H. or by correspondence. I haven't any definite ideas at the moment, but am very keen to try to put poetry over to these rather 'hostile' children:—or is that too harsh a word? I look forward to hearing from you, and shall in the meantime try to think up as many ideas and approaches as possible.

Yours sincerely,
Dylan Thomas

MS: BBC

---

[1] A BBC producer in schools broadcasting. A programme was scheduled for June but never made. Mrs Keeble wrote in an office memo, 'I feel that we cannot pander to his artistic temperament any further, and must give him up as a bad job.'

D. J. AND FLORENCE THOMAS
January 12 1947   Holywell Ford Oxford

Dear Mother and Dad,

I haven't written since before Christmas: it seems years ago. So much, and nearly all petty, has happened, so many plans made and broken. I wish I had written much sooner, to wish you a peaceful and well New Year, but I've been busy as a hive and mostly in London where, without a headquarters, I find it hard, even impossible, to settle down at borrowed desk or friend's table to write. Every proper wish now, though so late, and I *do* hope to see you soon. I'm glad you're back home; it's wicked weather to move about in. But I'm sure Hetty & Ken were awfully good and kind. How is Arthur?[1] I haven't seen him since—was it in London, when he & you came up about poor Will? How long ago? Will you send him Caitlin's love, and mine, when you write?

We had rather a gay and noisy Christmas here. Oxford's a very sociable place on occasions like that, and we went to several parties. We had Christmas Day lunch very quietly, just Caitlin & Aeronwy & myself in our snug summerhouse: we ate the biggest of the two delicious and tender chickens Mother sent, and a rich dark pudding made us by the Taylor cook, Florence, whose [...] baby is due any day now, and a bottle of caustic red ink called Algerian wine. Aeron had some crackers. She loved her teaset and gives an assortment of dolls & bears daily parties. She had quite a lot of presents altogether, including a tricycle from us, books, a little mangle, a Noah's Ark, a golliwog, and a stocking full of nonsense and tangerines. Then Christmas Day Dinner with the Taylors, with turkey. Boxing Day dinner with some friends of ours here called Veal — he's a young composer, and son of the University Registrar—and Saturday dinner with a Corpus Christi don called Stahl, & his wife. Our second fat and luscious chicken we added to the Veals' table. One of our troubles here is that we can't invite anyone back; so instead, we took along a few things to their flats, rooms, or houses. The day after Boxing Day I had to go to London to give my after-the-news talk.[2] A lot of people found the talk eccentric; perhaps it was; it wasn't, certainly, what most people expected to hear after the news. I've had quite a big post from it: half of it enthusiastic, the other half calling me anything from obscurantist to poseur, surrealist comedian to Bedlamite. The Manchester Guardian reviewed it very cheeringly; the News Chronicle with boos.

On New Year's Eve we went, with lots of other people, mostly BBC, to the Chelsea Arts Ball at the Albert Hall. Never been to it before. 5000 people there, all in fancy dress. A tremendously bright affair. I went as a Chinaman, Caitlin as a grand Spanish lady. It really was very exciting: wonderful to look at: all the boxes round the great hall packed with

---

[1] Hetty and Ken were family friends. Arthur, D. J. Thomas's brother.
[2] 'The Crumbs of One Man's Year.'

pierrots, ballerinas, costermongers, Elizabethans, pirates, courtesans, tigers, Dutch Dolls, empresses, clowns, & the huge floor rainbowed with dancers. Valentine Dyall and Michael Ayrton—do you ever hear him on the Brains Trust?—were two of our company.

The day after that Dyall & I took part in 'Richard the Third' on the Overseas Service of the BBC. Eastern & Overseas Services I now do quite a lot of work for: scripting, acting, & reading. They do a potted Shakespeare play a week. Last week it was Titus Andronicus, which I'd never read and probably never will read again,—but it was great fun to do. There was a very fine actor, George Hayes once of the Old Vic, playing Aaron the damned Moor.

Last week I read my story 'A Visit to Grandpa's', too. Did you hear it? 10-30 pm on Wednesday, in the Home Service.

I haven't many reading engagements for the near future. I'm talking about Sir Philip Sidney on the 24th, from the West. Can you get that? It will be repeated later in the Third Programme. And, for the Shakespeare series I mentioned, I'm arranging the programme on 'Merchant of Venice'. But that's impossible to hear in England, without a short-wave set. I've finished, & recorded, the first of two programmes about Oxford —the first was an exchange programme with Princeton USA—and very soon will be able to do my 'Return Journey—Swansea' programme. A day in Swansea, & the rest in Blaen Cwm.[1]

Did I tell you about the opera-libretto I have been asked to write? A full-length grand opera for William Walton.[2] I have to turn out a very rough synopsis before I am definitely commissioned. This I hope to do next week. Michael Ayrton, who will do the decor, & I are going, on Wednesday, for a few days, to Gravesend, Tilbury, & all around there, as I want to set the opera in a near-docks area.[3] A very modern tragic opera, in the bombed slums of wharfland. If this ever comes to anything, it will be the biggest English operatic event of the century. Really it will. A whole Covent Garden season in 1949 is contemplated. If, & when, I am commissioned to write the libretto, I should be able to stop doing any other work & devote about six solid months to it.

I've got a new book out in America: 'Selected Works'. I've had some good American notices—I enclose one from the New York Times. Can you return it afterwards, as I'm trying to file all American stuff for future use, when, one day, we go across there—but so far only one copy of the book which I can't, at the moment, find. As soon as other copies come, I'll send you one at once. It's a nice-looking book.

Do you ever listen to the series 'Poet & Critic' on the Third Programme? I'm the next Poet, the Critic being T. W. Earp. There'll be either

---

[1] Thomas's feature-programme about the poet in search of his lost youth was researched in Swansea in February, and broadcast from Cardiff in June.

[2] Sir William Walton (1902–83), composer.

[3] Michael Ayrton (1921–75), painter and designer. Thomas's libretto was not written.

three or four programmes, half an hour a week. Starting the end of this month. I'll let you know exact dates later.

As to domestic news: we're well on our way to getting a cottage here, in Magdalen grounds. But I shan't know finally for about six weeks. It will be fine, if it works. The cottage is an old mill-house, on the Cherwell, surrounded by gardens. It is Magdalen property, and, *if* I get it, it will be on a very long lease and at a very small rental. It will be a proper home for us. In the meantime: at the beginning of February, Caitlin & I think of moving to Richmond, to share a house—a big house—with Helen and Bill, the people we went over to Ireland with last summer.[1] It's a house just by Richmond Bridge, right on the river. I do hope you'll be able to come & stay with us in it in the early spring. There's tons of room, & it's extremely comfortable. I'll tell you more about this—an almost certain plan—later on. Our idea is to share both the Richmond house & the Oxford cottage with Helen & Bill, one part of the mixed family being, probably, 'in residence' in Oxford while the other part is in our 'town house'. The Richmond house belongs to Helen, so our rent will be most reasonable. It's all pretty ambitious, but may come off.

Caitlin & I are going to lunch with Edith Sitwell in London tomorrow. She's on her way to Switzerland.

Last weekend, we went down to Ringwood & brought Llewelyn back with us for a week or so. He likes it here, with the two small Taylor boys. It's Giles's birthday-party today, Sunday, & there's a hell of a row going on all over the house. They're playing Murder, by the sound of it. Llewelyn's very pale and frail, but full of life. Caitlin's taking him, this week, to see a Dr. Walker here, a famous children's specialist. He's been suffering all the winter from asthma, and he's frightfully nervous too and has a peculiar way of walking. If the Doctor says he needs a change of climate—which the Bournemouth Doctor recommended—Margaret Taylor has, voluntarily, promised that she will pay to send him over to, & keep him in, a kind of holiday-school in the Isle of Wight for about 3 months. But we'll know the Doctor's opinion on this on Wednesday. Whatever happens, we're [?not] going to allow Llewelyn to go back to Ringwood for any length of time. He *must* have the company of children of his own age, & also he *must* get away from the flat, damp New Forest district.

Llewelyn's a great reader. He reads everything, except poetry which he 'hates'.

And now I can't think of anything else. Oh yes: interest has been revived in my filmscript. Did I ever thank Dad for sending it on? Anyway, thank you now, very much.

Caitlin will write this evening. Thank you for all the Christmas presents. I can't tell you how welcome they were. And for the pound, which filled Aeron's stocking full. Llewelyn was awfully pleased, too, by his Christmas gifts from you. I wish you could see him, & hope that you soon will.

[1] The McAlpines.

I'll write later, with news of Llewelyn's Doctor & whether he'll be sent to the I. of Wight or not. And etcetera & etcetera.

Please write and tell me something, as soon as possible.

All love from
Caitlin & myself,
Aeronwy & Llewelyn,
Dylan

MS: Thomas Trustees   *SL*

KATHLEEN GURNER[1]
March 1 1947   Holywell Ford Oxford

Dear Miss Gurner,

Thank you very much for your letter, & for enclosing the schoolgirls' letters. I did enjoy reading them.

About my poem 'October', which appears in '18 Poems'. Of course you have *my* permission to use in it the series of anthologies of poetry for use in schools which a cte of the Training College Association is bringing out. But I'm afraid there are difficulties. The Fortune Press, which brought out my '18 Poems' some years after they were originally published, are making things difficult about copyright. Indeed, I believe they are trying to sue my agents. But this is something I understand little about & want to know less; so I'm sure the best thing for you to do, if you still want the poem in spite of these complications, is to write direct to my agent, telling him that you have my own permission to use the poem. He'll know what to say then about the legal position. He is David Higham, of Pearn, Pollinger, & Higham, 39–40 Bedford St. Strand. W.C.2.

Sorry about this bother. And thank you again for writing & for sending me those letters.

Yours sincerely,
Dylan Thomas

MS: Texas

CHARLES FISHER
March 1 1947   Holywell Ford Oxford

My dear Charles,

Me too. I've thought, very often, during the last years, of writing, sending the letter somehow care of someone in the Army or in Swansea,

---

[1] Letter addressed to her at Goldsmiths' College, University of London.

but it came to nothing but 'My dear Charles' and a case-book doodle. The moment we met, when Dan was with me, in the Gargoyle, blew away like a butterfly cork, & I lost, or forgot, your address. So now I know where you are, and that's fine: I can write again & hope you'll write. Any sense or nonsense.

I went to Swansea a fortnight ago, for two nights, saw Fred, Vernon, Walter Flower, John Prichard, Bill Henry, Mrs Giles of the Singleton, the Borough Architect, and Mr Ernest Davies who wears very high collars, is, unlikelily, a fashion-designer, unless he was pulling my leg with a crane, and makes, out of cardboard & cellophane, very tiny naked women who do a kind of arthritic can-can when he lights a match behind them. Fred, I was astounded to see, was painting a rather careful picture of two herrings; Vernon, you would never believe, was writing a poem about spiritual essences; Walter, you'd hardly credit it, told me stories about councillors & trout.

Caitlin & Aeronwy & Llewelyn and Brigit and Tobias[1]—the last two are not really mine—and me are going to Italy, for six months we hope, in a month's time, where I hope to write poems, after a year's stop, which I will send to you. I have just had mussel-poisoning. All around us here, where we live by the river, frenzied voles are climbing the trees after the birds' bits. I have a black eye, too, which seemed to grow in the night. There is no news.

Write soon and tell me your no news. It was lovely to hear from you.

Ever,
Dylan

MS: the recipient

T. W. EARP
March 1st 1947   Holywell Ford Oxford

My dear Tommy,
Thank you so much for your letter.
The people who told you about my health, when you were last in London, were *all* correct, & at the same time. I was roaringly well, then, some minutes after, a little mewling ruin. I would very nearly run down one street, to cringe, very nearly on my belly, up the next. In Finch's I was a lion; in the Duke of York's a piece of cold lamb with vomit sauce. Now I [am] back in ordinary middle health again, headachy, queasy, feverish, of a nice kind of normal crimson & bilious. I think that I am nearly well enough not to have to go out this morning in order to feel well enough to

[1] Tobias was the son of Brigit Marnier, Caitlin's sister.

work this afternoon: a preposterous process, as it means I go to sleep with my face in the pudding & wake up sticky & fretful & bite my nails to the shoulder-bone. I hope, very much, that you are well too. I liked the first & second do's on me, & am looking forward to the third tonight which will be your fourth. I mean, the third section, supposed to be my reply, will now end the series. The Commander[1] writes to tell me that, owing to rushed Third Programme planning, your 4th (now 3rd) section is cut to 15 minutes, which means the loss of 'Fern Hill' & 'Vision & Prayer'.

I found the greatest difficulty in writing my piece, & have become rather hysterical in my generalisations. My references to your critical remarks are warm-hearted and dull. So am I.

Write me when you'll be in London, and, unless some film-work I am rushing at the moment in order to get some money for Italy prevents me, I'll be there, fit as a fuddle.[2]

It was a great pleasure to me to hear you on the wireless; and thank you, very deeply, for all the extremely kind & penetrating things you said.

I hope to see you very soon.

Yours ever,
Dylan

MS: Ohio State University   *SL*

MICHAEL AYRTON
March 16th 1947   Holywell Ford Oxford

Dear Michael,

I've let you down, and myself, and even if you can never forgive me, and I don't see why you should, will you bury a hatchet in a glass with me? I'll ring you at the end of this week, and get a nasty answer.

The books are being sent off this afternoon. I should have written the thing at once. I'm sorry.

I hope your show went well. Is it still on? I should like a long peep. I saw Martin Boddey,[3] for a few stolid, comfortable minutes, the first day, and he said a lot had sold. I'm so glad.

A tree fell, last night, on our roof: a fir-tree.

Yours ever,
Dylan

TS: Thomas Trustees

[1] E. J. King-Bull was a former naval Commander.
[2] Edith Sitwell had decided that America, which Thomas was still anxious to visit, was not a wise choice for a poet who drank too much. She headed a committee of the Society of Authors that awarded travelling scholarships. It gave the whole of its 1947 grant, £150, to Thomas. The formal decision was taken on March 26, and linked with 'a strong recommendation' that 'his travels should be in Italy rather than anywhere else'.
[3] Martin Boddey was a singer.

VERNON WATKINS
March 16 1947   Holywell·Ford Oxford

Dear Vernon,

It was lovely, all those weeks ago in the snow, to see you and talk and laugh, Bush, water-pistol, Fred (Fish) Janes, and all. I was sorry not to be able to come out to Pennard on my last evening: I lost the address, and had to go and see a master from the Swansea Grammar School to find out how much of the school was burned. 'Bloody near all', he said; then, with a nasty sigh, he added, 'All except Grey Morgan'.[1]

Thank you very much for wanting to buy Llewelyn a book for his Christmas Birthday. I'd like him to have a Bible too. But I'll ask him, in a minute—he's downstairs, playing Demon Rummy—and I hope he won't say Arthur Rackham [Ransome?] who he thinks is the best writer in the universe except the writer of the Dick Barton series.

God brought a new one out of his bag of storms last night, tore down the trees and dropped one on our roof, flooded the only path, drove the voles to the trees, broke a window, sent Caitlin flying. I'd like to see Pennard now.

My Swansea programme was postponed because of fuel & weather, too little one, too much other, and can now be heard on April 2nd.[2]

We go to Italy on April 8, but not to Florence: to a village near Rapallo. I shall ask about Pound.

I want very much to come & see you after April 2nd—the broadcast is from Cardiff—and will wire you at once if I can.

I'm looking forward to hearing 'Mari Lwyd' on Thursday. I'm one of the readers. I hope you won't mind too much.

Llewelyn's just sent his love, thanked you very much, and said:

I *do* hope I can see you soon.

Give our love to Gwen and Rhiannon.

                                            Ever,
                                            Dylan

MS: British Library   *VW*

D. J. AND FLORENCE THOMAS
[about April 11 1947] [postcard]   From Villa Cuba San Michele di Pagana
                                                      Rapallo Italy

Arrived here a day ago, after fearsome three days travelling with Caitlin, Brigit, Llewelyn, Aeronwy, and Tobias. One night in Milan. Rapallo is

---

[1] Thomas had been in Swansea to research his radio script *Return Journey*. The Bush was a pub in the High Street. J. Grey Morgan was headmaster of the Grammar School, badly damaged in a 1941 air-raid—'. . . the echoing corridors charred where [young Thomas] scribbled and smudged and yawned in the long green days . . .'

[2] *Return Journey* wasn't broadcast until June 15.

very beautiful. Blazing sun, blue sea & sky, red, pink & white villas on fir-treed hills, orange-groves, olive-trees, castles, palaces. Our hotel small, v. pretty, fifteen minutes from Rapallo. Please write to above address. I am writing full letter this afternoon. All love to both from us all. I hope to God Dad's better.

X Dylan

D. J. AND FLORENCE THOMAS
11th April 1947   Villa Cuba San Michele di Pagana Rapallo Italy

Dear Mother and Dad,
.I don't know which will arrive first: this letter, or a postcard of Rapallo. But the object of both is the same, and a pretty obvious one too: to tell you that we have all—Caitlin, Brigit, Llewelyn, Aeronwy, Tobias, & myself—arrived safely in Italy after three days' travel. Three very exhausting days. We had booked through from London to Rome—you *have* to book sleeping-reservations a long time ahead—before we knew where we were going. And so when we decided on Rapallo, we still had to travel on the Calais–Milan–Rome express, which meant that we had to go through Switzerland. If we had booked through to Genoa, we would have missed the whole Swiss loop. We'd have shortened the journey by a day. But it couldn't be helped. One of the nuisances was that our baggage got left behind at the Swiss–Italian frontier, and Caitlin & I had the hell of a job next morning, while Brigit looked after the three children, of chasing the baggage through the bowels of Milan station, endlessly interviewing bureaucratic officials in a jumble of languages, queueing up before wrong ticket-offices, bribing the Customs with English cigarettes, changing pound-notes into Black Market lire, dragging the children out of the hotel into rude & reckless taxis, & *just* managing to catch the train. Milan is a giant, nightmare city. The snow & the rain had just ceased before we arrived—a day or two before. The immensely long, wide streets, which run the entire length of the city, or seem to, were bakingly hot & dusty, clanking with great, packed, racing trams, buzzing with little toy motor-bikes; there were stop-me-&-buy-one bicycle-boys selling, not ice-cream, but bottles of Chianti, & set-faced sinister armed policemen. Brigit stayed in the hotel, and Caitlin & I went round the city & the cafés in the boiling sun, speaking our lame Italian. I have a dozen phrases, half probably wrong; Caitlin makes long & impressive-sounding speeches, which few can understand. But I hope we will pick up a working vocabulary fairly soon. Nouns I can remember; grammar, no. I shall have to learn it the dull way, I'm afraid, through a text-book.

The worst part of the journey was the shortest: from Genoa to Rapallo: an asthmatic train creeping & bumping over the bridges, over the bridges just erected or actually in the process of being erected. Nearly all the bridges along the Italian Riviera were blown up, but whether by the Germans or by the British I have not yet been brave enough to ask, or linguistically capable of asking.

San Michele is about a mile outside Rapallo: half way between Rapallo & Santa Margerita: not far from Portofino. It's a lovely village. Our little hotel—expensive; we can't stay *here* long—is right on the sea; our bedroom balconies are over the water. High hills above the village, covered with villas, fir-trees, olive-trees, wonderful villas, pink, red, white, turreted, pinnacled, baroque Christmas-cake; the sea's bright blue, the very bright blue sky cloudless. It's so lovely, lying by the sea in the sun; incredible after this winter. I wish you could both be here. Do please write soon, very soon, and tell me how you are. Especially Dad. The last time Mother wrote, he was ill again, and in pain. I do hope, above everything, that he is better now. Do let us know at once, now that you have our (temporary) address. It seems all wrong, us here in the great sun, on the Riviera, & Dad ill, who would, I'm sure, feel so much better for a complete change of climate.

We walked to Rapallo this morning, but didn't have much time there. The front is all enormous, expensive hotels & cafés, packed with the rich: like Nice, or Mentone. But the little of the town itself that we saw is heavenly. Max Beerbohm lives here, though I don't know where; in some wonderful villa up in the olive groves, perhaps. Here Ezra Pound used to live; here it was he went mad too.

I had a letter from Edith Sitwell this morning, who is mostly responsible for us being able to come here. She is the chairman of the Authors' Society Travelling Committee, which occasionally gives writers money to move about. Talking about money: the Bank gives you nine hundred lire for a pound; the Free Market, as it is known, gives you eighteen hundred. This part—indeed, much of the North, I think—seems well off for food. We have had excellent food, superlatively cooked, for the last two days: dinner being some form of very good spaghetti in a rich sauce, followed by white meat, artichokes, spinach, & potatoes, followed by bread & cheese (all kinds of cheese; my favourite gorgonzola), followed by apples or oranges or figs, & then coffee. Red wine always with the meal.

It's lovely to see the oranges growing around us.

Write soon, & so will I. Next week I am going, alone with Caitlin, to Rome, to see about British Council lectures. I have also an introduction to one of the heads of Italian films, an American Russian Jew. I'll let you know what happens.

Now write soon, & tell us everything. I hope to God Dad's better. All with me send their love. And I send all mine.

Dylan

EDITH SITWELL
11th April 1947   Villa Cuba San Michele di Pagana Rapallo Italy

My dear Edith,

I owe you such a great deal of happiness, and so many apologies. First of all, let me thank you for persuading us to go to Italy, and for helping, wonderfully, to send us. I do not know how long we will be able to stay—perhaps for only a short time—but I am grateful to you every warm, blue minute, every orange and olive tree, every fir on a hill. And, second, let me, please, say how sorry I am, and how angry with me Caitlin is, for not having answered at once, except by cold telegram, your two letters, one of business, both of friendship. I wanted not to answer until the purpose of the letters was achieved, and I could say, writing in the sun, how fine & alive it was to be in the sun and how I and Caitlin thanked you for it & for everything. I should have written at once; this letter will take days & days to reach you; but I did so want it to come from here.

I was very, very sorry not to see you again in London. I had to go, for one thing, to Wales to read a script about childhood, which I hope, a lot, you will be able to hear. It will be on the Home Programme, under the title of Return Journey, but I am afraid I do not know when. It will be quite soon. I *did* want to see you again. Are you better now? You were ill at that lovely banquet after that over-long reading. Will you write a letter here, and tell us?

I went to see Denys Kilham Roberts, and got from him a letter to the Bank of England asking them, on behalf of the committee of the Travelling Fund, & of the Authors' Society, please to allow me to have, in Italy, that £150 on top of my ordinary, legal £75 allowance. It was then too late to do much about it, but I hope to hear, any day now, from *my* bank who are dealing with it for me. Kilham Roberts' letter seemed, to me, a model of tact and persuasion. I hope the Treasury is susceptible.[1]

We spent one night in nightmare Milan, which I enjoyed horribly, and came on here, over blown-up bridges, in a lame train, the children dirty, exhausted, excited, too many. But here is beautiful; the little pension's like a clean, pink ship in the sea. Everybody is kind, and oh the nice wine.

But, even if we could—the pension's expensive—we wouldn't want to stay on here for more than a couple of weeks. Rapallo *is* a Riviera rich holiday-place, isn't it, and we, I think, don't want to holiday but to stay, to live for a bit. I want, above all, to work like a fiend, a *good* fiend. And the pretty pension on the legendary water is *terribly* temporary. We want a small house to fill, cook in, work in, where the children can be noisy, where we can make a rhythm and a way of our own. Anywhere. Not at all necessarily by the sea. Osbert said, at that unforgettable after-Canticle supper, that he could write, perhaps, to find out whether, somehow, it would be possible to find a house somewhere that I could borrow or

---

[1] Exchange Control made it illegal to move money out of Britain without official permission.

cheaply rent. I know he meant it, but I did not know if he would want me to write to him about it. So I haven't written. Shall I, do you think? I am writing, now, only to you, not to Osbert or to Sacheverell who, also, said that maybe he could help to find us a place of—for a time—our own. Shall I write to Sacheverell too, do you think? Or would you ask them again? I do not know what is best. A house, any kind, anywhere, would mean very very very much now.

And in the meantime, the sun *is* heaven. I'm going to walk to Santa Margarita tonight. Thank you because we are here. When I can write anything, I'll send it to you, if I may.

I have lost my copy of my Reply to T. W. Earp in the Poet & Critic broadcast series, but have written to King-Bull asking him to send a copy, urgently, direct to you.

I am *intensely* proud that you are writing an essay on my poems. I want to write so much better poems, though. Now, and all the time.

I will write again, very soon.

Love from Caitlin & me,
Yours ever,
Dylan

MS: Texas

E. J. KING-BULL
[April 1947]   Villa Cuba San Michele di Pagana Rapallo Italy

Dear King-Bull,
    Would you do me a favour? Edith Sitwell has just written me asking for a copy of my Reply to Tommy Earp, the last in the Poet & Critic series about me. I haven't got a copy. Could you send her one, to Renishaw? She says she wants it urgently, as she's writing an essay about my poems for, I think, New Writing: & in a hurry.[1] I'd be awfully glad if you could.
    Here I feel hot & lovely, though I look just hot.
    Thank you so much if you'll do that.
    How are you?

Dylan

MS: Texas

[1] 'Comment on Dylan Thomas' by Edith Sitwell appeared in *The Critic*, Vol 1, No 2, Autumn 1947.

MARGARET TAYLOR
12th April 1947   Villa Cuba San Michele di Pagana Rapallo Italy

My dear Margaret,

I was profoundly sorry not to see you; up to the last grey, ruinous moment I thought that, somehow, I could return to say au revoir, thank you for too many thousand things to count, above all your loyalty to me when I was wretched, ill, mean, drawn taut, lost, utterly unworthy of faith or affection, of anything but a kind of kicking pity. I wanted to thank you for your more than kindness to Llewelyn and Aeron, whom you helped to make well; to Cat and me, whom you housed when we were in a sick muddle; to me, to whom you were almost gentle. I do hope that you can help us to find a house in or near Oxford, so that we can see each other again. I want, so much to come back to Oxford. Oh, anywhere a house. I am lost without one. I am domestic as a slipper, I want somewhere of my own, I'm old enough now, I want a house to shout, sleep, and work in. Please help; though I deserve nothing.

The journey was first good, then baddish, then disastrous, then good again, then bad. The disaster happened at the Swiss frontier, when we lost our luggage. We should not have gone through Switzerland anyway. We found the baggage at last, after eternities deep, deep down *under* Milan station, through Ufa corridors, in Kafka cells and temples of injustice. Our lack of Italian helped. In steel-barred rooms, where Mussolini personally had whipped and interrogated, we faced row after row of tiny, blue Customs-officers in wide hats, who smoked our cigarettes, spilt sugar on the clothes, joked at a great speed, ogled Caitlin, and cut our luggage labels off with scissors.

San Michele is a very pretty village; the sea's blue under our balcony; there's a wind, but the sun's hot; our pension is small, sweet, dear; there is lots of food & wine. The front at Rapallo, a mile away, is far too much of a rich playground, with enormous hotels, women from Phillips Oppenheim,[1] international millionaires, &, this morning, us. But the town behind the swagger front is full of most lovely houses, cafés, chianti, gorgonzola, markets, orangetrees. We are going to Portofino tomorrow. I do not know if I can start working here. There is no escape in a small hotel from the too many children. And besides, we must live in the country. This is sophisticated as Nice.

Caitlin & I will go to Rome next week to see film-&-British Councilmen.

Write & tell me Nish-news. How are you? Don't, don't be unhappy, please. Write soon. And you will help about a house, won't you? I am as homely as a tea-caddy, but have no pretty pot.

Thank you, dear Margaret, for everything.

Yours ever,
Dylan

---

[1] E. Phillips Oppenheim (1866–1946) wrote romantic mysteries.

Caitlin sends her love. Could you, do you think, send a couple of thrillers or a magazine? I am forced to read poetry only.

Write soon,
D.

MS: Texas   *SL*

DAVID HIGHAM
24 April 1947   Villa Cuba San Michele di Pagana Rapallo Italy

Dear David,
My bank has just told me that it has obtained the authority of the Bank of England to transfer that Authors' Society £150 to me in Italy. Good. My bank also tells me that, as I drew out so much to pay for passages etc, I am much poorer than I thought & they cannot transfer to me more than just £50. Bad. You see, I had paid in, as soon as I received it, the Authors' Cheque, & then drew on it. So will you please do what you said you could do: get £100 from Dent, for the Guild Books thing,[1] & push it into my bank (whose address Mr. Webb has) *straightaway*? I'd be enormously grateful. Then the bank could send me the £150, & I could stay on.
Heard anything from Taylor (Donald)?
It's very lovely here; I'm working on a long poem.[2] I hope Ireland was good too.

Yours,
Dylan

MS: Texas

RONALD BOTTRALL[3]
25th April 1947   Villa Cuba San Michele di Pagana Rapallo

Dear Ronald,
A very brief note. Will you, very much please, forward the enclosed letter, as soon as possible, urgently, to Maniani? From someone in your most pleasant party, Praz I believe, I got one version of his name and address. From Osbert Sitwell, who wired me this morning, another. Praz[4] (is that the name of the sidewhiskered chair-lover?) wrote down: Maniani, 6 Via Nibby, Roma. Osbert wired: Gino Magnani Rocca Via Antonio

---

[1] A paperback edition of *Portrait of the Artist as a Young Dog.*
[2] 'In Country Sleep.'
[3] Bottrall was the British Council representative in Rome.
[4] Mario Praz, critic and author.

Nibby 16 Roma. Could you, from telephone book and staff, find out his correct name & address & *send off the letter at once, please please?*

I'm going to Florence on Monday and will see Francis Toye,[1] *if possible.* Then I'll write to you again, with worries & questions.

Thank you for being so nice to us in Rome.

I will see you again, for more niceness, shortly.

Yours,
Dylan

MS: Texas

D. J. AND FLORENCE THOMAS

May 5th 1947   Villa Cuba San Michele di Pagana Rapallo Italy

Dear Mother and Dad,

Since writing last, Caitlin and I have been to Rome & to Florence—not on the same visit. In between whiles, we came back to Brigit, Llewelyn, Aeronwy, and little Tobias: all of them fat and contented by the sea in the sun.

Rome is a frightful journey from Rapallo. All travelling, over any distance, is bad. There are few trains or buses, and all the bridges have been blown up, or nearly all, either by Allied bombers or by retreating Germans. We went by bus to Rome: four in the afternoon till eight the next morning. And a damned uncomfortable bus too. The children could never have done it in one go. Rome was, I am glad to say in my little travelogue letters, Rome. We stayed in the oldest hotel in the city, directly behind the Pantheon. We had about five days there altogether, but, most of the time, just wandered round rather than going on vast exhausting tours of inexhaustible galleries & churches. We did spend one morning in the Vatican City, dizzily moving down marble miles, craning and panting in the Sistine Chapel which is more wonderful than I could have believed, staring down from a great height into St. Peter's itself, from huge cool galleries that seemed the size of public squares and corridors like the terraces of gods. We met a great number of people, writers, painters, musicians, mostly through the good offices of the British Council who, housed in the Palazzo di Drago or Palace of Dragons in the Street of Four Fountains, give sumptuous parties, in tapestried rooms, to visiting intellectuals. The Council, whose director in Rome is a poet, Ronald Bottrall, whom I knew in London, gave a very good party for us; and after it we had the addresses of many people whom we met on subsequent days. They all talked English, which is shaming to foreigners who can only just catch buses, order wine, & count their change in

---

[1] Francis Toye had been director of the British Institute in Florence.

Italian. There was one American writer, Frederic Prokosch: has Dad read any of his novels? The one or two I've come across are very good. One most learned scholar, Mario Praz, author of 'The Romantic Agony' & an authority, abroad, on English metaphysical poets. I made a couple of film contacts—nasty word—but they have, so far, come to nothing. It was very lovely strolling about Rome in the bright bright sun. We couldn't face the bus back, and flew from Rome to Genoa in an old army-plane: nearly everybody got very sick. The dock-front of Genoa is marvellous. Such heat and colours and dirt & noise and loud wicked alleys with all the washing of the world hanging from the high windows. We were there only a few hours, but the next day I took Brigit and Llewelyn there—it's an hour and a half from Rapallo—while Caitlin looked after the small children. Llewelyn was very excited, and ate much glorious ice-cream in garish cafés & felt like hell returning in the bus.

Then four days later, Caitlin and I went to Florence: not such a bad journey: 8 hours by bus through wonderful country. We stopped at Pisa, saw, of course, the Leaning Tower, & then, in Florence in the evening, met a lot of young Italian poets to whom, from Rome, we had introductions. Again, we were terribly lucky in our hotel, right in the centre of the city, in the Cathedral square, by the great Dome, and the Baptistry, and Giotto's Belltower. Next morning, we met, by accident, in a sidestreet, Stephen Spender, who was there, just like us, only for a few days. We had lunch & dinner together. We saw the Pitti Palace & the Uffizi. I'd just been reading Romola,[1] and could follow the city, almost, from my memories of that. The lovely, more than lovely, Ponte Vecchio was left untouched by the Germans, but the other lovely bridges were blown to hell, and also the little hanging houses round the Ponte Vecchio, old as Dante.

And the next day we rented, until the end of July, a little house some five miles from Florence, up in the hills, looking over the city, among pines and olives, beautifully green and peaceful, a cool, long house with a great garden & a swimming pool. The rent, in English money, was £25 for 2½ months. If my money holds out until the end of July, we will, I know, be peaceful and happy there. The garden is full of nightingales and orangetrees. There are vineyards all around us. We move there next Monday, May the 12th.

The address is:

> Villa del Beccaro,
> Mosciano,
> Scandicci,
> Florence.

From there I will write again, at length, & tell you how we fare.

We *do*, with all our hearts, all of us, hope Dad is better & that Mother is

---

[1] *Romola* (1863), a novel by George Eliot, set in fifteenth-century Florence.

able to carry on. Mother, in her letter, says the sun was shining. I hope it will be a lovely summer.

We are all well. Llewelyn is a fat boy now, but he misses the company of English boys of his own age to play with. He reads a lot. Now he is reading the Three Musketeers, in tiny print, in the same edition I read it in. Nelson's Classics, I think.

This afternoon, they are all out in a rowing boat in the still blue bay. I can see the boat from our window.

I'll let you know all about food etc. in my next letter.

The English tobacco situation is dreadful, isn't it. Here, there are nothing but Black Market cigarettes. We bought a pile of coarse black tobacco from a sailor in Genoa, and are rolling that.

Love from all to both. Caitlin is writing. And you, please, write soon.

> Best love,
> Dylan

P.S. When I can buy a big envelope, I will send on some American reviews of my Selected Writings, which Laughlin of New Directions has just forwarded.

MS: Thomas Trustees   *SL*

D. J. AND FLORENCE THOMAS
[card, postmarked 19 May 1947]

This is our house. Really, it's a hundred times nicer than this picture, which gives little idea. It's on the hills above Florence, some five miles away or more from the centre, from the great Cathedral dome which we can see from the sunbathing terrace above our swimming-pool. And I hope that sounds grand enough. It's a very big villa, with huge rooms and lovely grounds, arbours, terraces, pools; we have a pinewood and a vineyard of our own. There are cypresses and palms all around us, in the wide green valley below with poppies among the vines and olives, and in the higher hills. Our garden is full of roses. Nightingales sing all night long. Lizards scuttle out of the walls in the sun. It is very lovely. I am writing a long letter, which may arrive the same time as this. We all send you our fondest love.

> Dylan

MS: Thomas Trustees

MARGARET TAYLOR
May 20th 1947   Villa del Beccaro Mosciano Scandicci Florence

My dear Margaret,

At last we've found, in pinewoods on the hills above Florence, a house until the end of July. The pooled ponded rosed goldfished arboured lizarded swinghung towelled winetabled Aeronshrill garden leads into our own (dear God) olives and vines climbing to a mutes' conventicle, a Niobe's eisteddfod, of cypresses. What seem to be armoured belligerent emerald wasps bang and bully the bushes; one-noted birds blow their brains out in the pines; other very near birds, which I can see, birdily fox me with very distant cries from the wrong trees. I can smell the sun. There is a swimming pool into which I have been only once—by mistake. Caitlin, Brigit, and the children are seals and newts there. Mosciano, the nearest village, is thin and tall, shouldered like Peter Quennell against the church. (The Marquis of Q I met in Rome. Recovering from a prolonged debauch in London, he was spending, at the expense of an airways company for whom he was writing a travelogue, a week with the British Ambassador,[1] drinking, by the gallon, grappa, which, to me, tastes like an axe.) Florence sparkles at night below us. In the day we see the Dome. It is perhaps five miles away. To get to the city we suffer by trap and tram. But there's so little need to move. The pinehills are endless, the cypresses at the hilltop tell one all about the length of death, the woods are deep as love and full of goats, the house is cool & large, the children beastly, the wine ample, why should I move at all until July the 31st. And then to the lovely unfound house in Oxfordshire, the house built round the desk you bought me? Oh I *do* hope so. And thank you thank you for the desk.

Did you receive the postcard, overcheerily scribbled with messages, after a big red dinner, by Caitlin, Natasha, Stephen and myself?[2] Stephen was very gay, Natasha British as a hockeystick: I hadn't seen her like that. In flatheeled shoes she thumped the hot Florence pavements, gawky as an Arthur Marshall schoolgirl, shouting English, elbowing the droll Florentines from her gym-knickered way. I have met many of the young intellectuals of Florence, who are rarefied and damp: they do not write much but oh how they edit! They live with their mothers, ride motorscooters, and translate Apollinaire.

And thank you, so very much indeed, for the books and papers which came to Rapallo and which were terribly welcome, all of them, Sunday papers, thrillers, Listeners. And for your lovely letter and for all it said. Do, do write again, and soon. Tell me all your news.

I wish I had heard you read my poems, and Vernon's, and Alun Lewis's, and Roy's 'Skull In the Desert'. I wish I had heard you reading, on the Macedonian lake, from my orange stamp-book. And the changing fish

---

[1] Peter Quennell comments that he was neither recovering from a debauch nor writing a travelogue for an airline.
[2] Natasha Litvin, pianist, Spender's second wife.

and the living fossils of that deepest legendary water! God's pulling your leg.

It is all so widely quiet here, and the valley vining away to the church towers. In the next room, in her rest hour, Aeronwy is singing an obscene song. Brigit's Tobias, a spotty frog-boy, is screaming in the lavatory. Llewelyn, in the garden, is trying to cut a boat out of a pinecone with a breadknife and has several fingers left. Brigit is superintending the screaming of the boy-frog. Caitlin has shut herself away and is learning Italian—undoubtedly by looking through the window at the trees. I am sitting in a half-shuttered room over the vineyard, writing to you who are in Oxford, and thanking you for everything always, and sending my love.

Write soon.

I read anything in English.

Yours ever,
Dylan

MS: Texas   SL(R)

BILL and HELEN MCALPINE
May 20th 1947   Villa del Beccaro Mosciano Scandicci Florence

My dear Helen and Bill,

I'd written much, much sooner—did you get a postcard?—but waited until we had a house of our own to write from. Up to now, we've been staying in hotels and pensions: expensive and unsatisfactory. And the Riviera sea was too tidy. Now, on the hills above Florence, some five miles from the centre, we have found a lovely villa in the pinewoods: beautiful, nightingaled gardens, cypresses, pillared terraces, olive trees, deep wild woods, our own vineyard and swimming pool, very tasty. There is a big room waiting for you. The cellar is full of wine. We live on asparagus, artichokes, oranges, gorgonzola, olive oil, strawberries, and more red wine. We have the villa until the last day of July. Can you come? We'd love it, so much. Write at once, and forgive this delay. Best love from Cat and me.

Yours ever,
Dylan

I will let you know all, if any, details when you write.
I am writing poems.
Are you married?
Brigit's son Tobias has just fallen in the swimming pool.
Have you got your passports? Do hurry.

D.

MS: Buffalo   SL

R. B. MARRIOTT[1]
May 24th 1947   Villa del Beccaro Mosciano Scandicci Florence

Dear Marriott,
   So sorry not to have been able to answer, long before this, your letter of
March 27th. I've been abroad for some time, and changing my addresses
frequently, and letters follow me like incompetent snails.
   I'm glad you've been asked to write about me for the Western Mail—it
has dealt filthily with me in the past, mostly through reviews of A. G.
Prys-Jones who merely pins on a few irrelevant labels, surrealism, etc.,
raises nonconformist hands and misquotes—and for a South African
paper, and also to broadcast to France. Perhaps, so much time has gone,
the articles and broadcast are over. If they're not, and I could be of any
help by answering questions in a letter, please do write again—and I'll do
my best.

                              Regards,
                              Yours sincerely,
   TS: J. M. Dent   Dylan Thomas

DAVID HIGHAM
May 24th 1947   Villa del Beccaro Mosciano Scandicci Florence

Dear David,
   This is only to give you our new address, which we hope to be at until
the end of July. After that, unless a miracle happens, we'll have to come
back to England. I hope to finish a radio play by the end of our stay here.
But more about that later. The long poem is coming on slowly. No
Donald Taylor news as yet?[2]

                              Yours,
   MS: Texas   Dylan

JOHN DAVENPORT
29th May 1947   Villa del Beccaro Mosciano Scandicci Florence Italy

My dear John,
   This pig in Italy bitterly knows—O the tears on his snub snout and the
squelch in the trough as he buries his fat, Welsh head in shame, and
guzzles and blows—that he should have written, three winevats gone, a
porky letter to Moby D. or two-ton John; but with a grunt in the pines,
time trotted on! The spirit was willing; the ham was weak. The spirit

[1] Raymond Bowler Marriott, journalist, later drama critic of *The Stage*.
[2] Thomas still had hopes of *The Doctor and the Devils*, whether as book or film.

was brandy: the ham was swilling. And oh the rasher-frying sun! What a sunpissed pig I am not to dip a bristle in Chianti, and write. I have so many excuses, and none at all. A few days ago I climbed a tree, forgetting my shape and weight, and hung this shabby barrel from a branch by my white padded mitts: they were torn neatly up the middles. Also, very slowly, I am trying to write a poem , moping over it every afternoon in a room in the peasant's cottage: our little spankers make so much noise I cannot work anywhere near them, God grenade them. It was so good to hear from you, and to know you will be in Florence in July. Of course you must stay with us, but I had better explain that we are some miles from Florence itself, up in the hills. To get to the city, we go by horse-&-trap to Scandicci and then suffer in the tram for twenty-five minutes. One can order a car from Florence, but it costs about 3000 lire—thirty shillings. But we will, of course, manage somehow. We are all looking forward to you *enormously*. Will Rodney be with you?[1] If he has his car, everything will be so easy. If he hasn't, it won't be such a problem anyway. We are in very beautiful country, and there is lots of room and wine in the house. No, I don't know Edward Hutton, but we were going to see him when we first came here: he wanted to let half his villa to an English or American family. We have got to know lots of the young intellectuals of Florence, and a damp lot they are. They visit us on Sundays. To overcome the language, I have to stand on my head, fall in the pool, crack nuts with my teeth, and Tarzan in the cypresses. I am very witty in Italian, though a little violent; and I need space. Do you know anybody in Florence nice to have a drink with? I met Stephen Spender there a few weeks ago. It was very sad. He is on a lecture-tour. It is very sad. He is bringing the European intellectuals together. It is impossible. He said, in a lecture I saw reported: 'All poets speak the same language.' It is a bloody lie: who talks Spender?

I am going to write to Higham about Phillips & Green; this week. Thank you for sending Green's letter.

Write soon. It will be lovely to see you here. Love to all from us all here. And to Tommy, if you see him, to whom I must write.

I don't know what my plans are yet; they depend on money, and not on mine. We have been offered a house in Parma when we leave here on July 31st, and I should like to go. Also, the Oxford Taylors have wired about taking us a house in Witney, to which, I suppose, we'd have to return. It's very difficult. I am going to write a radio play when this slow poem is finished. How are you? Give Kingsmill[2] a punch for me.

Yours ever, & see you soon.

Dylan

MS: Texas   *SL*

---

[1] Rodney Phillips was financing a literary magazine, *Arena*, and Davenport was to be one of the editors.
[2] Hugh Kingsmill.

MARGARET TAYLOR
[2 June 1947]   [telegram from Scandicci]

LETTER ARRIVED HOUSE SOUNDS LOVELY PLEASE TAKE IT
MANY THANKS WRITING FULLY. DYLAN.

Original: Texas

MARGARET TAYLOR
June 4th 1947   Villa del Beccaro Mosciano Scandicci Florence

Dearest Margaret,
   How wonderful you are to me, and to us all here. I drink to you—or, I
have just drunk, because it is elevenses on a sizzling day—in our red, acid
wine which bites nice holes; but the spaghetti, later, will cover the holes
like elastoplast. Thank you, so very much, for the telegrams about the
Thomas Manor,[1] the books, the papers; and the letters. It is so good to
hear from you, to know that you will write again, to wait for the postman—a small woman, who walks twenty miles a day and whistles uphill
in the sun—and your handwriting. I liked *all* the books: The Hole In The
Wall (like Jacobs in hell), Dialstone Lane, Deadlier than the Male,
Almayer's Folly, the Tolstoi, the thrillers & the Onion. (Thrillers kill me
in this house, at night; huge birds, like Crow but which I hope are owls,
beak at the window and whoosh; mice behind the walls squeak round in
their divers' boots; men in distant cottages cry Ho; someone teehees in
the electric light bulb every time I turn the page of some unconvincing,
semiliterate blood—ooh! there's a tap dripping in that drawer—and
thunder). The book Graham published (did you read it?) seemed to me
really convincingly nasty: I shall never go to Joe's Club again, or Sam's, or
the Free Lance, or the White Monkey, or the M.L., or the Horseshoe, or
Peggy's, or Ma Hibbs': I shall even carry my knuckledusters into the
National Liberal.[2]

---

[1] To house the Thomases, Mrs Taylor had bought a cottage with the deceptive name of The
  Manor House, in the village of South Leigh, Oxfordshire. When they returned from Italy,
  she rented it to them for a pound a week.
[2] All the places mentioned were drinking clubs, except the National Liberal, of which
  Thomas was, improbably, a member.

Our plans for the future: turmoiled. We have been offered, I think I told you, by Gino Magnani Rocca, who came to Oxford, a composer, a friend of Lizzie's,[1] a house near Parma, big, cool, green, when we leave here at the end of July. But by that time, or before, our money will have run out, & I cannot get any more. The British Council in Rome will lend me only the money for our fares back. So we may be returning, some brown, one scarlet, at the beginning of August: not the right time at all. If we do, do you think our Manor will be habitable? Cookable in, I mean? And with water? We'd go to see my mother in Wales for a week or two, we always do in August, but after that ...

Do write soon again. There are so many things. I love hearing from you. I rely on you, your help, your letters, so, so much. Do you mind this pin-nib? Can you read me?

And Aeronwy loved her animal book, & Llewelyn his Alice. They are falling in the pool at this moment; not the books. Aeron's making a noise like a female parrot locked in a room with Heath.[2] Caitlin is cutting something with a scythe. Brigit is resting; Tobias is kicking her. This afternoon I go on writing my poem, which is the slowest in the world.

Do you remember André Frenaux, who came with another Frenchman & a wife one evening to Holywell Ford? He recited a poem of his. I met him in Florence, & he spent two nights here, reciting a poem of his. He is like a fat owl, though lively, & very charming.

What are you writing for Roy?[3] And when, and what, do you read? I wish you were reading on the Overseas programme, which I can get here on a cross wireless that spits.

And the papers full of Xwords and cricket scores! O my liver and lights, my bird in three letters, my Wisden teeth!

And now the house, the home, the haven, the pound-a-week Manor! Thank you with all my heart, from the depth of my teapot, from the marrow of my slippers warm before the fire, for finding a house for us. It is what I most want. It sounds *good*. 20 minutes from Oxford, ten from Witney, a Free House in the village, a kind old couple, fields, a garden: all I want's a new body and an alchemist's primer. Will you come often, very often? I am so happy and glad about it.

RENT Shall I send, to you, a couple of months' rent in advance? Or more?
KITCHEN Will the Electric Company lend us electric stove, etc, as they did to the Little House?
BATH Will it be terribly hard to get?
WATER Is there water? Can it easily be fixed?
FURNITURE Will you tell me when you have taken it? Then I can write to my mother who will, at once or as soon as it can be arranged from there, send on some furniture, some good, big, ugly things, dressing tables, dining table, etc, which she has for us?

[1] Elizabeth Lutyens.
[2] Neville Heath, sadistic murderer, had been tried and hanged the previous year.
[3] Roy Campbell.

LET Can I get the house for a long time? I want to send Llewelyn to school either in Witney or in Oxford, & Aeronwy somewhere near, and work at my crochet there.

I am so glad about it; and so profoundly grateful to you. It means a heaven of a lot.

I am so glad you are seeing Roy, and dear Reggie, and Bertie,[1] and the ship-launching turtledove, and unconquerable Lizzie out of the Pit.[2] Do you like Parry? And how is the green & beige, brilliantined tapeworm in the Little House? Not a word about him. Does he have mincing, sibilant gin-giggles every night? And do the all-too normal voles approve?

I am looking forward such a lot to your next letter. And to all your letters. For the house: bless you for ever. It's made me so happy.

Now it is cold-lunch time, gorgonzola, wine, strawberries. Two foreigners—I think they must be Italians—are being loud, & perhaps indecent, on our seesaw. There is one thing: I *can* say, in Italian, 'Do not be indecent on our seesaw'. The opportunity to say it is rare.

And thank you for everything.

There's a cheque with this for school-car, gas, etc, mentioned in your last letter.

> Yours ever,
> Dylan

MS: Texas

D. J. AND FLORENCE THOMAS
June 5 1947   Villa del Beccaro Mosciano Scandicci Florence

Dear Mother and Dad,

How are you both? It's a long, long time since a letter came from you; or is [it] that time moves so slowly here and one looks forward as much to the postman? or postwoman, rather, a little woman, too, who walks about twenty miles a day, up & down these steep Florentine hills, in the baking sun. Whatever it is, we do want to hear from you soon. Letters from England seem to take, on the average, five days to get here.

I hope it is sunny in Carmarthenshire. I read in the Sunday papers Margaret Taylor sends me that it's going to be a wonderful year for fruit in England. Here we have had strawberries and cherries galore, lemons, and oranges from Sicily—too early for the more Northern oranges. Peas, beans, asparagus, artichokes. I don't know if we'll be here for the peaches. We do very well indeed for food, though it isn't cheap, by any means. You

---

[1] 'Reggie': R. D. Smith, another BBC producer. 'Bertie': W. R. Rodgers.
[2] Elizabeth Lutyens's dramatic work, *The Pit*, was given its first performance in London on 18 May 1947; Parry Jones sang the tenor part. According to Lutyens, Thomas had been paid £50, years earlier, to write the words, but failed to deliver. W. R. Rodgers did it for £5.

can get *anything*, if you have the money. Not as in England. Recently there was an English Exhibition in Rome, organised by the British Council, to show what goods etc. England was producing, what films it was making, pictures painting, books writing, etc; and how much food it was eating. One person's total rations for a week were exhibited.[1] And the reaction, even among the intelligent visitors, was: 'Yes, I see. That's the amount of sugar, or butter, or tea, one person's allowed in England. And very small too. How much does he have to pay for Free Market sugar, butter, tea, etc?' And everybody downrightly refused to believe that *that* was the amount you got, that and no more, and that you could not buy any more. They just did not believe that the Black Market in England is a tiny affair. In Italy, it is the White Market that is the tiny affair. The ration for cigarettes is 15 a week, I think. At *every* street corner, in *every* town, men, boys, & women, sit with great trays of cigarettes, English & American the dearest & the most popular. (We smoke the cheapest, rough Italian cigarettes: Nazionali, all stamped as the property of the Italian State. These we buy openly illegally at any shop, at any corner, for about 1/2 for twenty—twice the legal price.) Vegetables we get from gardens here, but they aren't cheap either. The pound is worth, officially, 900 to 1000 lire; but by some wangling I cannot follow, the Bank will give you about 2000 lire for it. If you walk down the street, however, you will be stopped by any amount of touts and offered—at the present moment—2,450 for it. Into whose hands the English Pounds & the 'hard' currency Swiss francs and Swedish money go, I don't know. Some speculators are hoarding them against preposterous inflation. It is almost impossible to achieve any money perspective here. A big glass of good wine costs 20 lire, about 2½d. A small bottle, less than half a pint, of extremely thin beer costs about 60 lire. The horse & trap we go in down the hill to Scandicci costs 350 lire each way. Sugar costs about 10/- a pound. I don't know offhand the price of rice & spaghetti, but I do know that the poor can afford to buy only the rationed amount per week, which is minute; & spaghetti is their staple dish. Nor can they buy more than the rationed amount of bread & flour: also tiny. And not only the real poor. It applies to the professional classes too. Only the profiteering rich, the already rich with well protected money, & foreigners can buy the goods with which the shops are stacked. And English foreigners, at any rate, not for long. The Americans, of course, can bring as much money as they like into the country. I hope to be able to last out, financially, until the end of our tenancy here: that is, the last day of July. But it won't be easy: neither Caitlin nor Brigit is a good manager. And, after the 31st of July, unless a miracle happens, we return. The best news is: We have a house. Margaret Taylor, a great friend to us, has found it. It is in South Leigh, which is 25 minutes by train from Oxford, 10 minutes from Witney. Eynsham is 2 miles away. Bablockhythe about 3½. South Leigh

---

[1] Rationing of some foods in Britain continued into the 1950s.

is on the branch line which runs from Oxford to Yarnton, Eynsham, Witney, Bampton, & on up the Thames past Kelmscot to Lechlade. The house is called South Leigh Manor, but Margaret says that its name must *not* give me a dream picture of a moated, mullioned grange with coats of arms etc., but that obviously the Manor itself has vanished long ago and the house must be the old farmhouse that belonged to it. Its rent is £1 a week plus a couple of shillings a week rates. It has three bedrooms, two rooms downstairs, a tiny kitchen, & a washhouse where Margaret proposes installing a bath. It has a good garden in front & a bigger piece at the back. It is down a small farm drive. Attached to the house at the back is a cottage inhabited by an old couple who work for the neighbouring farmer —but looking the other way, and quite apart. The village is very small: one shop, one church (Margaret says it is lovely), one pub, and this a Free House. But Witney, quite big, is only 10 minutes away. The house is 5 minutes from the station. I think we are very fortunate. Margaret has been going around by car for nearly 2 months, looking all over Oxfordshire, and this was the *only* place. She says she is going to move our Wentworth Studio pieces into it very soon; they are stored with her at Holywell Ford. All except the big bed, the beautiful studio bed, which, as I think I told you, was stolen by our tenant. Also Margaret has several bits & pieces for us. Now as to the furniture in Waunfort. Shall I let you know as soon as Margaret lets *me* know that she has settled about the house? and can Hobbs then [move] the furniture to Oxford, picking up Margaret on the way? You must let me know what Hobbs will charge, and I will send a cheque. We need, of course, every stick of furniture, every cup or frying pan, we can lay our hands on. We will be starting, once again, with no utensils or anything; I'll write to you about all this immediately I have definite information from Margaret.

I think I told you, before, that an Italian composer, Gino Magnani Rocca, whom we met in Oxford—he is a friend of my friend Elizabeth Lutyens—has offered me part of his country house near Parma, after July, & is coming to Florence this month to see me & to talk about it. But obviously I cannot go there without money. Anyway, there is almost a stronger reason for our returning to England after our stay in this villa. Llewelyn *must* go to school; he *must* be with English boys of his own age. I'm afraid here he is getting very fed-up. There is so little for him to do, with only grown-ups and two small, bawling children. And, God, how they do bawl. They are, I'm afraid, bad for each other. Aeronwy is once more rather fractious and hysterical. There would be *so* much for Llewelyn to do with a boy of his own age here. The woods are beautiful; the garden one of the loveliest I've seen. There are wild groves and streams: paradise for cowboys & indians. But he can't play all day alone. He reads a great deal: Dickens, Marryat, Arthur Ransome, Encyclopedias, Captain Cook's Travels, Stevenson, & anything he can find here, thrillers included. But he can't read all day, either. He makes elaborate paper games of his own. We have just hired a wireless, & he footles with this, getting the BBC Overseas Service mostly—but it doesn't come through very well. It's not much of a life for him, though he is very well now, and brown, and fattening out. On Sundays, a family from Florence come out for the day with their two little boys: the man is editor of a literary quarterly here, and has translated lots of my poems. But the language barrier prevents Llewelyn & his boys really getting together.

It is terrifically hot to-day: ever since June began. It is useless to try to do anything between midday and 4 in the afternoon. And it will get hotter day by day. Florence lies below us, through the vines & olives, in a rippling haze.

Today there is a fiesta in Mosciano, & Brigit & Caitlin & the children are going. I am going to work. I cannot work usually in this house, even though it is large. Aeronwy & Tobias make a terrible din together, though Aeronwy is good enough by herself. So I work in a room in the peasant's cottage which is part of this estate: a good room, small & plain, looking into a wild wood. I am working on a long poem, but so slowly. And after it is finished, I want to write a radio play. Has my Swansea broadcast been on yet? I know it's due some time in June. Do tell me about it when you hear it.

My 'Portrait of The Artist' book of stories is also due this month on every bookstall in the shilling Guild edition. 50,000 copies to begin with.[1]

I enclose a few American cuttings.

Can you give me Nancy's address when you write? She wrote to me very nicely, but I lost the letter & want to reply.

How is Idris? Remember me fondly to him.

Is Mabli a home dog again? Write soon.

And, so far as I know, & I hope, we will be seeing you, as usual, in August.

Caitlin is writing. She sends her love.

And all my Love,
Dylan

PS. I'm sorry: I can find only one American cutting, after all, from the best of the American University-sponsored quarterlies, the Southern Sewanee Review. Others when I can find them.

PPS. I have just had sent to me—Margaret again—'The Hole In The Wall' by Arthur Morrison, & W. W. Jacobs' 'Dialstone Lane'—both in the new Century Library. Both excellent. Also a very good thriller—'Deadlier Than The Male' by Ambrose Grant. Worth reading.

MS: Thomas Trustees   *SL*

---

[1] The book wasn't published until March 1949.

DONALD TAYLOR
June 7th 1947   Villa del Beccaro Mosciano Scandicci Florence

Dear Donald,

I was very disappointed not to meet you that day, so long ago now, in the National Lavatory Club:[1] I should have rung you to try to fix another date, but was whisked off by trolls. And I should have written, too, long before this, but have been soaking up the sun here, moving around a bit, and trying to work. We are staying high up in the hills above Florence, among vines & pines and olives & cypresses, and living extremely quietly, though the children would turn paradise into a menagerie —which perhaps it is—and I have a floating stomach because of too much oil. Are you in England? I hope Germany's over, for you. I had a letter today from David Higham, who said the film-agreement[2] was still being drawn-up by you and whoever-it-is, and that Dent's are going to publish the script. He has not yet arranged terms with Dent. About the version of 'Doctor & Devils' which is now with Dent: that is, I gather the copy you gave Higham. Is it the best version for publishing? i.e. is it the one with most descriptive writing? If it isn't, do you think you could send Higham the longer version straightaway? It will not affect the terms he will arrange with Dent's, who have taken the script on the version they were given, but they may as well have the longer version as soon as possible. Higham also said you would write a short introduction about the B & H Case & the history, such as it is, of the script. That's grand. Have you gone into the question of reproductions of Trial Documents, drawings of B & H, of Edinburgh, of Tanners' Lane, etc.? And do you think these really necessary? They might help.

I am probably coming back to England the first week in August; lire will almost surely have run out by then. I have got a cottage in South Leigh, about 25 minutes by train from Oxford, but of course shall be in London a lot. Do you think the film-agreement will be completed by that time? And do you want me to do any work on the script while it is in production? I'm afraid I shall be quite broke again when I return, and living on bits of broadcasting etc.

Do write, when you can.

And are we ever going to write a script together? A really good one, completely our own? I hope so. I do hope so.

There's a recorded thing of mine being broadcast on June 28, on the Home Programme, which I *would* like you to hear.[3]

The heat is sizzling, the wine overpowering, the villa enormous. We have no visitors, but one has invited himself in July. One guess; J. Davenport. My, he gets around. Our hill will kill him. One postwoman's died already this year (though it wasn't really the heat: a house fell on her).

---

[1] The National Liberal Club.
[2] See letter of June 14 to Higham.
[3] A repeat broadcast of *Return Journey*. But it was on the Third Programme.

Have you Ambrose Grant's 'Deadlier Than The Male'? Not half as good as Patrick Hamilton, but still good.

Looking forward.

Yours ever,
Dylan

MS: Buffalo

JOHN ARLOTT
June 11th 1947   Villa del Beccaro Mosciano Scandicci Florence

My dear John,

Thank you for writing. It was very good to hear from you. Though I hear your voice every day: from Trent Bridge, at the moment. You're not only the best cricket commentator—far and away that; but the best sports commentator I've heard, ever; exact, enthusiastic, prejudiced, amazingly visual, authoritative, and friendly. A great pleasure to listen to you: I do look forward to it. Here, in the hills above Florence, I lead the quietest life I ever remember leading: it is sizzling hot, the hill to the nearest village is a spinebreaker, I am far too limp and lazy to go often to Florence, and I can work only in the early mornings and evenings: never my best time: I'm used to working from after lunch until pub-time, which in the country used to be about seven. Here I drink in the garden, alone or with Caitlin: we have no social life: I am a sun vegetable: I live on red wine, cheese, asparagus, artichokes, strawberries, etc. The etc. is usually more red wine. We have our own vineyard. The villa is enormous. So, probably, am I, after two months. I'm coming back in August: if the lire last till then. I was given some travelling money by the Authors' Society; otherwise I'd have been back long ago. And I'll be broke when I return, so any bits of booming—I heard Rape of Lucrece today; is Shakespeare over? and what is the next series?—narrating, etc., will be very welcome. Also, I'd love to write any programme you think I could do: *and, scrupulously, on time.*

Yes, of course I'd love some dollars, but I have so far, no poem. It would be useless giving you a chunk of the long one I'm twisting and gnarling: it's got to be read as a whole. If I do manage to write any short ones in between, I'll send them to you straightaway.

I can't afford to go to Venice. I've spent some time in Rome, in Genoa, in Siena, and on the Riviera. But now I can just afford to stay here on my sunburnt behind. I *would* like to go to Venice though. Perhaps I can seduce your girl: or am I the wrong shape?

I'll be ringing you in August. Love to you & your family. Remember me to Val, when you see him. My daughter has fallen in a cactus bush.

Yours,
Dylan

MS: the recipient   SL

HERMANN PESCHMANN
14 June 1947   Villa del Beccaro Mosciano Scandicci Florence Italy

Dear Mr. Peschmann,
    Thanks for the letter, and, again, for the invitation.[1]
    Though it seems, now, such a terrible long way off, what about the first
date you suggest? Monday, September 15th. Perhaps you'd let me know.
    And what about a reminding p.c. nearer the date—though perhaps we
shall meet before then in the George. Anyway, I'll look forward to coming. And would much rather be put up—which is very kind of you—than
take the last train back.
    I'd like to read poems by other people, too, if I may. More of them than
of me.

                                        Yours sincerely,
                                        Dylan Thomas

MS: the recipient

DAVID HIGHAM
14th June 1947   Villa del Beccaro Mosciano Scandicci Florence Italy

Dear David,
    Thank you for your letter of the 9th of June. *The Doctor & The Devils*.
Yes, please go ahead with the agreement.[2] It seems satisfactory.
    I have written to Donald Taylor, but perhaps you would drop him a line
too. I may have got his address wrong: I put Hill Cottage, Hedgerley
Village, near Slough, Bucks. I asked him about his introduction to *D. &
Devils*, and also about some prints he had of Burke & Hare at the trial, of
the School of Surgeons, of Doctor Knox etc. Also—&this is important, I
think—I asked him to send you, at once, the other version of the script:
the one with more descriptive writing. Dent should be given a chance,
obviously, of seeing both versions & printing the one they like best. So
would you send him a word about it?
    And what about *Doctor & Devils* in America? I don't think it's up
Laughlin's street, but he should have first refusal. Or should we wait,
before sending it to America, for Taylor's introduction?

                                        Yours,
                                        Dylan

[1] Thomas was to read at the Reigate Poetry Club. He cancelled the engagement at the last
    moment, but read there about a year later.
[2] Taylor was selling the film rights of *The Doctor and the Devils* to Gainsborough, a
    subsidiary of the Rank film organisation. He agreed to pay a proportion of the money to
    Thomas, who later received £365 in twelve monthly instalments.

P.S. Could I have a few copies of the Guild Book edition of my 'Portrait of the Artist As A Young Dog' sent to me when it comes out?

MS: Texas

JOHN GAWSWORTH
[card, postmarked 18 6 47]

Dear John,
    Here's permission to print a digest of my broadcast, *In The Margin*,[1] in the Literary Digest. And thanks. Sorry I haven't got any new poems at the moment, but hope to have one or two soon. I'm having a long holiday over here, returning in the autumn. How are things?

Yours,
Dylan Thomas

Any little fee for the digest can be sent, please, to Holywell Ford, Oxford.

MS: Buffalo

MARGARET TAYLOR
20th June 1947   Villa del Beccaro Mosciano Scandicci Florence

My dear Margaret,
    Parcels, books, magazines, papers, and lovely letters arrived, safe as houses, safe as our house to be for which never, till kingdom or atom come, can I thank you enough. 'A Child of the Jago' is savage and black and satisfying, like a rape in the Blackwall Tunnel.[2]
    This is only a little letter, and I'll write another, longer one this weekend, full of the almost nothing we do every day and how we like it. This is only to tell you about the beautiful parcels we'd be lost without, and the letters that mean so much. You are meeting so many people, and so many good ones. Good Bertie, still making his Ulster parish calls on an invisible bicycle.[3] And cornucopian Rosamond. Has she given birth to Day-Lewis yet?[4]

---

[1] This was the series title. Thomas's contribution, 'How to Begin a Story', appeared in the *Literary Digest*, Autumn 1948.
[2] *A Child of the Jago* (1896), a novel by Arthur Morrison, is a violent tale of London's East End.
[3] W. R. Rodgers.
[4] C. Day-Lewis, the poet, was the lover of Rosamond Lehmann, the novelist, during most of the 1940s. They didn't have a child, as Thomas seems to suggest.

I do like the sound of Mr. Hall, & Mr. Bob Russell, & the woman of 'San Remo', and 'The Retreat'. And yes, in spite of your most true and convincing exhortations to us to stay on in Italy, we have to, and will, come back in August. We'll have, for one thing, no more money by the end of July, and no way of getting any. I'll have to borrow, as it is, from the British Council to buy our return tickets. And, too, I want to get Llewelyn to school, and among boys of his own age and language again. For all its sun & splendour, and food and woods, this, with no children but our own Aeron and unpleasantly spoilt Tobias, is no place for him. For little children, yes. And heaven for us, who love to do nothing in the sun. But the days are swelteringly long for a friendless boy, and utterly without incident. His company is necessarily adult—which was so wrong when he lived with Cat's mother—or shrilly infant. How nostalgically he talks about Giles and Sebastian: the happiest time he ever spent was when he stayed with you and us and them. *So we'll return early in August.* Where will you be in August? We *must* see you before we go to Wales to see my mother. And then we'll want to come back to Oxfordshire in early September. There'll be so many hundreds of things to do for our house before then; and we must meet, in London or in Oxford or in both, and do, quickly, all we can. I want very much to see you apart from anything, from house, from bath, from windows & surveyors.

I am so smart in my Oxford clothes.

Poor Ruffini. The letter about him, the Rapallo pension has only just forwarded. Cat has written to his father.

I have written a hundred lines of a poem.

Today we have visitors from Florence: a brood of translators & their wives, & one American professor. I can hear them gaggling. I haven't gone out yet. Or perhaps it is frogs and cicadas, one with an American accent.

What a miserable little letter. I'll write on Sunday, among the bells.

God bless you. Write very soon.

Dylan

MS: Texas

RONALD BOTTRALL
June 20th 1947   Villa del Beccaro Mosciano Scandicci Florence

Dear Ronald,

Thank you for, quite a long time ago now, forwarding my letter to Gino Magnani Rocca, a charming man, and for your note.

We found a villa here, on the hills over Florence, soon after seeing you—and how nice it was to see you—in Rome. Good country, big house, our own wine, a swimming pool (into which I have been only once, by accident), nightingales bawling their heads off, neighbours who do us with great charm, and eight miles away, by rack cart and iron maiden tram, Florence, which I don't like a lot. I mean, I like the people I don't know in the streets, but not the writers etc, who are nearly all editors, I meet in the cafés. So many live with their mothers, on private incomes, and translate Apollinaire. They talk of 'letters'. Montale[1] seems to be an exception, but smug, with his English horse or Sloane-street wife, warmed slippers, dry wit, like old Ryvita, aloof tolerance, cigarette-holder, and private God laid on. And why is the British Consul called, so nearly, Greenlees? It's confusing. And he's a porker. But of course there are pleasant ones; there must be; I wish I knew them.

Did an acquaintance of mine, from Paris, André Frenaux, call on you? I gave him your name and the Council address.

Two things, one of them extremely important, to us, and most urgent. The unimportant first. I've been asked to give, on the Florence radio, a reading of poems, by English poets, written in, or about, or connected with, Italy. Can you suggest some names and poems. I'm illread. I said, Browning, Shelley, (but what Shelley?), Pound (if they'll let me), D. H. Lawrence. What about others, lots of others to select from? Landor? I have no books here. I'll be awfully grateful if you can help.

And now the expressly urgent thing. It's money. We have this villa until the end of July, and hope, somehow, to last until then. And, at the very beginning of August, we must return to England. But we have no return-tickets, and no money to pay for our fares. Indeed, we haven't, really, enough money to last until the end of July. And I want to, I must, get the train-and-boat tickets *now*. Presumably a great lot of people will be travelling in August, and I should book as long ahead as possible. From England, I booked nearly two months ahead. And the tickets *have* to be for the beginning of August, the very beginning, as we shall be homeless and penniless. I want to borrow £100. I can give you a cheque for this immediately, though that, I suppose, is illegal. Legally, I can pay £100 into the British Council when I return to London; or into your English account, if you keep one now. There are six of us, and £100 will just buy the tickets and leave enough over for travelling and incidental expenses —The incidental expenses will all, I'm afraid, have to go on things smashed by children in this furnished villa. I want to be able to go to Florence *straightaway* & book our tickets for the first day, if possible, of August. We'd travel from Rome. (Incidentally, will you be in Rome at the very end of July? I do hope so.) There's no need for me to tell you how deeply important all this is to us. And until it's settled, & I have the tickets-to-England safe, I shall feel, as I do now, unsettled & rather miserable. If I can give you a cheque here in Italy, all the better. But, otherwise, I'll write a cheque, to you, or to the British Council, *as soon* as I arrive in London. Edith told me I must rush to you as soon as any really urgent need arose. And here I rush.

[1] Eugenio Montale (1896–1981), poet and critic, 1971 Nobel Prizewinner.

Need I come to see you in Rome to deal with this (unfortunately) breathless bit of business? or can it be done by letter? I don't want to move if I needn't, as I'm trying to work hard, & regularly.

I met Stephen Spender in Florence, as perhaps he told you. You are lucky: you must have had him for days.

Do write as soon as you can. I'm sorry this is nearly all about money.

Unless I can get tickets *at once*, I may have to wait in Rome, without any money, in August, for weeks. So please. And thank you a very great deal.

Caitlin and I both send our love to you and your wife.

Yours ever,
Dylan

And the English–Italy poems.
Any not-translation Rossetti?
Byron?
Yeats? I seem to remember some.
Swinburne?
Any Bottrall?

MS: Texas

DONALD TAYLOR
[card, postmarked June 27 1947]

Thanks so much for the letter. You sound frightfully busy. I'm looking forward to meeting you, as many times as we can, early in the autumn, and to hearing some prison stories. Good news about The Importance of Being Earnest. You've probably had a note from Higham, whom I asked to write to you about which version. Dent's will want to go ahead with printing almost straightaway. So let Higham have The Business of Death, though we'll keep the other, D & D, title. Hope the contract's completed by end of July! This is our villa, but it's nicer than this. We are all devoured by mosquitoes. We are going for a week to the island of Elba. Good luck in the Shetlands, if you get there with all the children. I'll get in touch as soon as I get back.

Ever,
Dylan

MS: Buffalo

D. J. AND FLORENCE THOMAS
30 June 1947   Villa del Beccaro Mosciano Scandicci Florence

P.S. Can't find the Spectator cutting. Will look again.

Dear Mother and Dad,
    Thank you for the long letter; I was so glad to get it, but distressed to
hear that Dad was again so ill and suffering. I hope, with all my heart, he
is better now, or, at least, that there is not so much pain. Caitlin, sending
her love, hopes, too, he is a little better. It is dreadful, all this distance
away, to think of him so ill; and for there to be nothing that one can do.
Perhaps the good weather is some little help. Is it still good weather? I
haven't heard the English radio news for a week or more. We get the
Overseas programme quite well on our hired set, and I manage to hear a
few programmes I like: the Eric Barker ones, and the Books of Verse; half
hour readings & interpretations, which aren't heard at home but which
are mostly very good. They're the series I contribute to a lot, in London. I
couldn't hear my Swansea broadcast. It seemed to go well. I've had a few
letters forwarded, & one tiny clipping (enclosed) from the Spectator,
which Margaret sent. Did I tell you, by the way, that Dents are publishing
that Burke & Hare script early next year? Also that my new book of
stories is almost ready; will be quite ready, I hope, by the end of this year.
I haven't got a title for it yet. The long poem I am working on here is
going very slowly indeed. Now the heat is so intense I can work, properly,
only a couple of hours a day. My regular time, from, roughly, 2–6, is quite
hopeless. The nights are almost intolerably muffling, airless, mosquitoed.
I can't budge out of doors after midday, & try to work in the evenings,
behind shutters. But the whole 24 hours are hot as hell; and the children,
I'm afraid, are rather wilting under them. In Florence, to which I had to go
a couple of days ago, the heat's like a live animal you fight against in the
streets. No one moves who hasn't got to. Here we are in the hills, but
wish we were far far higher. If only the sea ran up the mountains! Our
swimming pool is a blessing; Caitlin, Brigit, & the children are in & out
all day, like seals. It has just gone midday; I'm writing, in my pyjamas, in
a shuttered room, with a flask of fresh wellwater at my side; and sweat is
running down my face. *Everybody* has a siesta after lunch; the shops in
Florence close from one to four in the afternoons. There's fruit about —
peaches and apricots—but the Sicilian oranges are finished. There are
lemons, too, & soon will be plums & pears, in a week or less. Will you
have lots of apples? I read somewhere it's going to be an apple-record year
in England. Hope so.
    Now: about our returning, and our coming down to see you. We hope
to return in the first days of August, but have no proper plans as to what
to do when we reach London. We should very much like to come down to
Blaen Cwm, as we always do, but are worried that Dad's health is not up
to it. Caitlin would help Mother all she can, of course, & I'll do every-

thing I can—especially as I hope to have some more money than usual—but we mustn't land on you, with noise & children, if it's going to be a nuisance now that Dad is so frightfully unwell, & in pain, again. The strain of our visit might really harm him. I could come down myself for a week, after seeing Caitlin & the two children safe somewhere. But I must hear from you about that. And, please, under no circumstances whatever, (if that's grammatically right), say 'Yes, come', if Dad isn't fit enough to receive us. To say nothing of Mother.

Our house-to-be in South Leigh won't really be ready until September, though we could move in, in a rather camping way, earlier than that. Electricity can't be laid on till September; but Margaret has got hold of lamps & an oil stove for us. About furniture: Margaret says to do nothing about getting your furniture from Wales until we have seen the house & have seen what furniture she already has for us. So we will go to see it as soon as we get back, & then write, or tell you, fully. I realise that Hobbs will have to be given plenty of notice beforehand.

Margaret has invited Llewelyn to stay in Oxford [*the page has been cut*] [...] 2 boys until they go to France for a [...] know he would like [...] famous Dragon School in Oxford. He'll be fixed in some good place, anyway. He wants schooling, & the company of boys of his own age, more than anything else in the world. And wants it immediately.

We are getting frightfully short of money here; otherwise I would take the family to the island of Elba for a week or so, which, I am told, is cheap and beautiful. And, by the sea, there is always something for children to do. Here, Llewelyn, in particular, is getting restless &, in the boiling sun, listless too. And we are all bitten, by flies, ants, & mosquitoes. But I don't see how I'll be able to manage it. No film job has turned up; & only one broadcast, from Florence, which pays very badly. There'll be no work to do in July. Everything closes, for the summer. I'm hoping to hear from the British Council. It's such a nuisance, having a little money in the Bank in England & not being able to cash a cheque here. However.

Write soon. Tell me how Dad is. Tell me about August.

[*page incomplete*]

MS: Thomas Trustees

T. W. EARP
July 11 1947   Villa del Beccaro Mosciano Scandicci Florence

My dear Tommy:

> In a shuttered room I roast
> Like a pumpkin in a serra
> And the sun like buttered toast
> Drips upon the classic terra,

Upon swimming pool and pillar,
Loggia, lemon, pineclad pico,
And this quite enchanting villa
That isn't worth a fico,
Upon terrace and frutteto
Of this almost a palazzo
Where the people talk potato
And the weather drives me pazzo—

I am awfully sick of it here, on the beautiful hills above Florence, drinking chianti in our marble shanty, sick of vini and contadini and bambini, and sicker still when I go, bumpy with mosquito bites, to Florence itself, which is a gruelling museum. I loved it in Rome, felt like Oppenheim on the Riviera, but we have been here, in this villa, two months and I can write only early in the morning, when I don't get up, and in the evening, when I go out. I've wanted to write to you, and have longed for a letter from you. We're coming back, some brown as shit, some bleached albino, one limp and carmine, all broke, early in August. Will you be in London, or visiting? I do hope we see each other often this autumn. I am told the bitter's better, and I will be writing a filmscript to buy same. We *really* do have an enormous swimming pool (into which I have been only once, by mistake), and our own vineyard, olives, mosquitoes, and small Italian mice with blue chins. I have written a longish poem which I'd like to send you when it is typed by an Italian professor of English in Florence. I asked the professor about Elba, where we thought of going, and he said—it was the first remark I heard him make—'Plenty di fish-dog'. He translates Henry James and Virginia Woolf. Give my love to May and to yourself. Write when you can, before August if possible, and tell me where, if you're in London, as you said, last time we met, you might be, I can write. Now I am going out to the cicadas to shake my legs a bit.

In the very opposite of haste,
Dylan

MS: Ohio State University   *SL*

MARGARET TAYLOR
July 11 1947   Villa del Beccaro Mosciano Scandicci Florence Italy

My dear Margaret,
   Parcels, books, magazines, letters,—how many, how often, how good. You are the best friend that a stout—oh, I'd love some—temporary exile could hope to have; and better than I deserve, for I do not write half enough to you, though always I am wanting to spider-cover a hundred bedsized sheets with news and moonshine. Thank you for 'The Vet It

Was That Died', and 'Poison in Jest', and 'High Table', and 'Keynotes'—a nineties Katherine Mansfield—and 'Ladies In Crime', and the Statesmen, Spectators, Tribunes, and soft Punches. I read Punch from the first advertisement for Old Skipper Tobacco and First Eleven cigarettes, through comic servants, zurring farmers, dropped aitches, motherly bodies, dear old parties, to the last advertisement for Three Nuns' Whiskey. It's rolling on croquetlawns in Wilts with Low Church curates called Sidebotham, or breathing deep the smell of lawnmowers, vicar's shag, rainwet marquees, hot deckchairs.

Helen and Bill,[1] hotfoot, gooseberry-eyed, worn-tongued, all ears, in literary London, cannot tear themselves away and will not be visiting. Bill is too busy pushing a peanut with his nose up a long, long hill, and Helen is helping: she cannot provide a peanut, but by God (who is, Bill has discovered, 'intellectually muscle-bound'), she can blow! She can puff!

And John D. can't come until the end of July, which is too late.

I wish you were coming.

I have written today to the Telephone Manager at Oxford. I want a telephone very much:—not that I think that Christ will ring.

And, yes, I shall keep the ditch as clean as clean, as pure as Stafford Cripps[2] (from whom salt comes).

Llewelyn has been sent, by Caitlin's mother, far too many books for us to be able to carry back. So he is making parcels of them, addressed to himself, and sending them to Holywell Ford. Will you keep them for him? Then he will pick them all up when we move to South Leigh.

What was the hitch-in-the-house, too silly to tell me, that needed a spade-chinned lawyer to clear up? Will you tell me, one day?

Llewelyn's education. It is lovely of you. He can go to Witney Primary County School for a term, and try, then, to get into Magdalen School. I'll see Mr. Stainer, and Mr. Busby. And Aeronwy can go to Witney too. Llewelyn is forgetting all he learned. Aeronwy has forgotten everything except songs about little white Jesus. I am so glad Llewelyn will go to Magdalen.

Thank you very much for your invitation to him to spend a time with Giles & Sebastian before you go to France. He would like it a lot, but I think he wants to go to Hampshire as soon as we return to get together old books & games to bring to the new house.

And, anyway, we will not be able to travel to England until after the 5th of August. Probably the 7th. Every place is booked till then. But I'll be back in time to see you before you go away. And, after you return, we'll be very near.

My mother has written to me to say that some furniture is waiting, in her cottage, ready for my (or your) word to have it vanned to South Leigh.

---

[1] The McAlpines.
[2] Sir Stafford Cripps, Labour politician, had the reputation of being irritatingly upright.

There is one bed only, a kitchen table, a dining table, some chairs, two dressing tables. Odds & ends. Mostly odds.

I must see the house before I go to see my mother. (My father is very ill again.) And before the house, you. I shall wire as soon as we reach London.

Caitlin will buy a nice Italian purse as soon as she goes to Florence.

My poem, of 100 lines, is finished, but needs a few days' work on it, especially on one verse. Then I'll send you a copy. The manuscript is thousands & thousands of foolscap pages scattered all over the place but mostly in the boiler fire. What I'll have to send you will be a fair copy. I think it's a good poem. But it has taken so long, nearly three months, to write, that it may be stilted. I hope not. I want, as soon as the last revision is made, to write, quickly, some short poems. I can't think of anything else; which isn't, of course, true. I mean, when I think, I think of the poems I want to write; not of their shape but of the feeling of them, and of a few words. But I can, in this blaring sun, creaked round by cicadas, write for so little of the day. By eleven in the morning I am limp as a rag or Stephen's rhythm. And I can't work again till the evening, when I want to go out. My social life: damp litterateurs pedal from Florence; neighbouring labouring men come in to dance; we walk, with Guido the gardener, or Eddo the tractor driver, or others with shining hair and blue cheeks, to village cantinas. The nearest café, at Mosciano, is no café but a wine-counter in a packed, tiny, fly-black general shop. Sometimes, an Australian professor comes from Florence to shout Dinkum and Good-oh in the garden. A Harvard professor of Romance languages came with rimless spectacles and no lips, and was nasty. Luigi Berti, a translator, editor, and expert on English literature, visits us on Sundays. He comes from Elba. He said—it was the first English statement I heard him make—'In Elba oo veel lak der skool di fishdog'. Or, 'In Elba you will like the schools of dogfish'. He translates, for a living, Henry James, Virginia Woolf etc.

Good old Normal. I can see his voice now.

I had a letter, about my Swansea broadcast, which I'm sorry you wouldn't hear, from the old lady who kept the sweetshop when I was a child. She said, Fancy remembering the gobstoppers, and the sherbet-suckers, and the penny piece-packets, and me, Mrs Ferguson. And a letter from the very old lady who ran the Dame School where I learned to do raffia work. She said, 'I think I must be getting old, but I don't like children very much these days.'

Has Lizzie been, drunk, and gone? I hear John Arlott's voice every weekend, describing cricket matches. He sounds like Uncle Tom Cobleigh reading Neville Cardus[1] to the Indians.

Is your house empty at last?

I'll send my poem this week. It isn't the one whose beginning I showed you.

---

[1] Neville Cardus (1889–1975), music critic and writer on cricket.

I haven't thanked you for the plumbers, for the Dali bath, drains, pole-talk, & everything. But I thank you all the time.

I don't think we'll be able to go to Elba. We are down to our last ten pounds, & the British Council will give me none. Luckily, I can get my bank in England to forward, through Cooks, a voucher for return tickets. But I don't know how we carry on until August 7th. We leave here on July 31st. If you don't mind, perhaps you could put, in your next letter, five one pound notes which I shall pay you when we return. There is little chance of ordinary-looking letters, so long as they are *not* registered, being opened. Unfortunately, five or ten pound notes, which take so much less room, are not negotiable here.

I shall be seeing you now, soon, if only for a little time.

                                                        Dylan

MS: Texas

BILL and HELEN MCALPINE

July 14 1947   Villa del Beccaro Mosciano Scandicci Florence

My dear Helen and Bill,

What a really big pity, and everybody waiting, from the torpedo lizards in the hairy pool—remind the gardener to change the water!—to the pickaxed and pneumatic-drilled mosquitoes in the guest's bedroom —remind the parlourmaid to take the bottles and the gorgonzola off the bed! We had planned such a lot of things to do, and all with wine: picnics, prickstrips, titlicks, nipsicks, gripwicks, slipthicks, tipsticks, liptricks, etcetera etcetera, parties, expeditions. Perhaps we can all come to Italy next year, and do things on a pig scale.

We are trying to arrange to spend our last weeks here in Elba, but have nearly exhausted our money and are twisting for more. We return on August 11th, and will be in London on the 13th. Will you be at home? And can you put us and our bags up for one night? Llewelyn, the next day, will go to his grandmother in Hampshire, & Cat, Aeron & I will go to Wales to see my mother for a fortnight. Then we return to a house Margaret has found us, in South Leigh, half an hour from Oxford: near Witney: small and a bit battered, but right in a village and in good country. I hope you'll be coming down, a lot, to see us there. We *are* looking forward to seeing you, so much, and having beer and words: no, not having words.

The first two parts of my poem are finished. I'm working on the third. It's not as long as it sounds. I'll show it to you, please, when I come back.

The Best to John.

What a pity you couldn't come.

Llewelyn is teaching English to some little girls nearby. As I write, in the garden, I can hear them doing their lessons, very loud: Funny bloody fart, funny bloody fart.

I do hope you'll be able to put us up that one night: we'll be rather lost. Are you writing stories, Bill? I hope there's a lot for me to read.

Love, from both to both,
Dylan

MS: Buffalo   *SL*

D. J. AND FLORENCE THOMAS
19 July 1947   Albergo Elba Rio di Marina Isola d'Elba Livorno Italy

Dear Mother & Dad,
We leave the Villa Beccaro tomorrow, Monday, for the island of Elba. And, above, is our address until the 10th of August. Elba is 12 hours by train & boat from Florence, but there are several changes: which, un-usually, is a good thing, for we will eat at the towns at which we stop. Elba is a much larger island than I'd always imagined: someone told me it's as big as the Isle of Wight. We won't be staying at the principal town, Portoferraio—almost certainly misspelt, as our atlas is packed—but at a small fishing village recommended to us by a man in Florence, a trans-lator & editor of a literary quarterly, whom we have grown to know quite well. He and his family will be in Rio di Marina too. The hotel, or boarding house, where we'll be staying, is so small that it can take no other lodgers but us. There are only 3 bedrooms, & these our large family will fill. It'll be nice, though, having an hotel to ourselves. And it is, as Italian prices go, quite cheap. I didn't think we'd be able to go to Elba at all, but a man in Florence, who works for the Italian Radio & is going, in October, to the Italian Section of the BBC in London, helped me out (quite illegally) with money. If he hadn't, we'd have been in rather a mess; because we can't get a train for England until August 11th—& our tenancy expires here on July 31st. The children, Llewelyn especially, are very very keen on going to the sea again. There'll be lots of sailing & fishing, and—which the Riviera dismally lacked—sandy beaches to play on. The heat will almost certainly be too intense for me to be able to do much, if any, work, so I too shall sprawl in the sun & go out in little boats. I'll have to work like hell when I get back. I've written nothing since I've been here but one longish poem. And I'd intended to write also some stories & a radio play. My Swansea broadcast, by the way, has had a great reception: many, many letters, from Swansea people, from Welsh exiles, from Mrs Hole, of Mirador, & Mrs Ferguson, the Uplands sweetshop, & Trevor Wignall, the old sporting journalist from Swansea,

and several producers on the BBC. Also some good press notices, three of which I enclose. I want very much to write a full-length—hour to hour & a half—broadcast play; & hope to do it, in South Leigh, this autumn.

I've been expecting a letter from you every day. I *do* hope no letter doesn't mean that Dad is seriously unwell again. Please write as soon as you can: I am very anxious for news of you. And we want, so much, to know if Caitlin, Aeronwy & I shall come down to Blaencwm for the second half of August. I wrote you about it in my last letter, saying that we wouldn't all come unless Dad were fit enough to have visitors —including such a rowdy visitor as Aeron. Llewelyn will go, when we return, to Blashford for a fortnight: mostly to collect his books & games to bring them, in September, to S. Leigh. So do write, please. Did I tell you that Llewelyn will be able, once he is 9 years old, to go to Magdalen School in Oxford: which is owned & governed by the College, & is said to be one of the finest schools in the country? We're very lucky, through the Taylors, to be able to get him in. And there are all kinds of special advantages connected with Magdalen College—use of its grounds, river, etc—and special scholarships from School to College, provided by an ancient Magdalen grant. Until he is 9, Llewelyn will go, from S. Leigh, to Witney County School; attached to the School there's a nursery school for Aeronwy.

Helen & Bill McAlpine, who were supposed to visit us here, had to call off at the last moment.

Tonight, to finish our supply of wine here, we are inviting the neighbouring peasants in. There will be music—fiddles & accordions—in the garden.

No other news. This is a dull letter. It's only to give you our new address, & to ask you please to write soon & tell us how Dad is & how you both are & whether we shall be seeing you in August. Caitlin & family send their love. All mine.

Love,
Dylan

MS: Thomas Trustees

DAVID HIGHAM
July 19 1947   (Sends Elba address. See Appendix 38.)

D. J. AND FLORENCE THOMAS
23rd July [1947] [postcard]

We came to this strange town yesterday. If you don't get my letter before, our address until August 10th is:—Albergo Elba, Rio Marina, Isola d'Elba,

Italy. I might have given it to you wrongly in my letter, before we reached here. It's the 2nd largest place on the island: 27 miles, the length of the island, from where Napoleon was exiled. There are about 5,000 people here, living by fishing & mineral mining. It's not strictly beautiful, but it's odd & exciting. Very very hot and blue, wonderful bathing. A world by itself. I'll write a letter tomorrow. Love from all of us.

Dylan

MS: Thomas Trustees

MARGARET TAYLOR
[July 23 1947] [postcard]

Arrived here yesterday. Very strange town, second largest on Island of Elba. Our address is: Albergo Elba, Rio Marina, Isola d'Elba, Italy. It's very very hot, dusty, tortuous, grey & blue, full of fishers and miners, strong wine, music at night. That's all I know so far. Tomorrow we going all over the island. Our train leaves August 11th. We'll just be able to see you before you go to France.

Dylan

MS: Texas

BILL and HELEN MCALPINE
[card, postmarked 26 July 1947]

A message from Albergo Elba, Rio Marina, Isola d'Elba, Italy. Lucky Napoleon! This is a most beautiful island; and Rio Marina the strangest town on it: only fishermen and miners live here: few tourists: no foreigners. Extremely tough. Something like a Latin Cahirciveen.[1] Notices 'Fighting Prohibited' in all bars. Elba cognac 3d. Of course, no licensing hours. Bathing wonderful. Regret your absence. Looking forward letter. Returning August 11th.

   Love to both from all.

Dylan

Only source: SL   *SL*

---

[1] A town in south-west Ireland.

BILL and HELEN MCALPINE
August 1 1947   Albergo Elba Rio Marina Isola d'Elba Livorno Italy

My dear Helen & Bill,
   What a nasty, really nasty, business for you. [...] I always loathed. I do
hope things work out as well as they can. I'm terrified of courts. A clever
solicitor could make me confess to being Jack the Ripper. As a witness in
a Juvenile Court in a case of the alleged dodging of tricycle tax, I would
see the shadow of the Black Cap and the smile of the American Army
hangman, Sergeant Dracula. I'm sorry, too, for [...], living with that
viperish, Byron-skulled necrophile. Our best wishes for the most
favourable conclusion to a sordidness caused by kindness. One moral
is—you must only be kind to us, in future.
   Elba is a wonderful island. One day we will come here together. Rio
Marina is a communist town: communism in Italy is natural, national,
indigenous, independent. And the green and blue transparent yachted
winkled and pickling sea! We are rarely out of it, except to drink, eat,
sleep, sing, fuck, walk, dance, ride, write, quarrel, climb, cave & café
crawl, read, smoke, brood, bask in the lavatory over the parroty fruit-
market. There is no winter in Elba; cognac is threepence a large glass; the
children have web feet; the women taste of salt.
   We go back to Florence on the 9th of this month, and leave for home on
the 11th. I will wire you as soon as I know the time of our arrival in
London. It will be very grand to stay with you, once more, for a couple of
days.
   We look forward to you both enormously.
   Again, may the trouble not trouble you too long, or too deep. Tonight
there is dancing in the streets.
   And all our love.

                                                                    Dylan

MS: Buffalo

MARGARET TAYLOR
August 3 1947   Albergo Elba Rio Marina Isola d'Elba

My dear Margaret:
   The heat! Old Elbanites on their flayed and blistered backs whimper
about the heat. Sunblack webfooted waterboys, diving from cranes, bleed
from the heat. Old scorched mineral-miners, fifty years in the fire, snarl
at the heat as they drag the rusty trolleys naked over the skeleton piers.
And as for us! The children all sun-and-sea-rashed, Brigit peeling like the
papered wall of a blitzed room in the rain. And I can hardly hold this pen

for the blisters all over my hands, can hardly see for the waterfalls of sweat, and am peeling too like a drenched billboard. Oh, oh, oh, the heat! It comes round corners at you like an animal with windmill arms. As I enter my bedroom, it stuns, thuds, throttles, spins me round by my soaking hair, lays me flat as a mat and bat-blind on my boiled and steaming bed. We keep oozing from the ice-cream counters to the chemist's. Cold beer is bottled God. If ever, for a second, a wind, (but wind's no word for this snailslow sizzle-puff), protoplasmically crawls from the suffering still sea, it makes a noise like H.D.'s poems crackling in a furnace.[1] I must stop writing to souse my head in a bedroom basin full of curded lava, return fresh as Freddie Hurdis-Jones in Sodom, frizzle and mew as I sit again on this Sing-Sing-hot-seat. What was I saying? Nothing is clear. My brains are hanging out like the intestines of a rabbit, or hanging down my back like hair. My tongue, for all the ice-cold God I drink, is hot as a camel-saddle sandily mounted by baked Bedouins. My eyes like over-ripe tomatoes strain at the sweating glass of a Saharan hothouse. I am hot. I am too hot. I wear nothing, in this tiny hotel-room, but the limp two rivers of my Robins'-made pyjama trousers. Oh for the cyclonic Siberian frigidity of a Turkish bath! In the pulverescence of the year came Christ the Niger. Christ, I'm hot!

But the Island I love, and I wish I were not seeing it in one of the seasons of hell.

Today is Sunday. On Thursday we go back to Florence, which is said to be hotter. On Monday, we catch our incinerator home.

Thank you, so much, for the £5. I hope you got my euphemistic wire. It was so welcome. And more, perhaps in the post now, will be welcome, welcome again. You are good to, & for, me. And the house! You find it, furnish it, scythe the garden, soften the bureaucrats; we are known, before we go, to the coaled & carred publican. Salute Bob Russell!

I will ring you as soon as we get to London, on the evening of the 12th or the morning of the 13th, and we will meet.

My brains are hanging out like a dog's tongue. I must go, looking for God, ice, impossible air, blister-biting blimp-blue bakehouse sea.

Till the 13th, about, goodbye.

I have altered several words in my poem.

Dylan

MS: Texas   SL

---

[1] Hilda Doolittle (1886–1961) wrote poetry under the initials 'HD'.

DAVID HIGHAM
August 6 1947   Elba

Dear David,
    I never received your note of 17th June with enclosed specimen page for
Doctor & The Devils. But I like, certainly, the idea of printing the
continuity matter in ordinary type, not in italics, so that it reads like a
story.
    Has Donald Taylor sent you the other version of the script? It is
important that Dent sees that before going on setting up.
    I'll be back in London, I hope, on the 13th of August, & will ring you.
Perhaps we shd have a few minutes together.

                                                              Yours,
                                                              Dylan

MS: Texas

JEAN LEROY
19th September 1947 (About a BBC fee and expenses. See Appendix 39.)

DAVID HIGHAM
19 September 1947   Manor House South Leigh Witney Oxon

Dear David,
    Sorry, but I have only just returned from town to find your letter of the
10th trying to arrange a lunch between Bozman and myself for last
Wednesday. I had a note from Bozman today, saying he would be in
Oxford on Saturday the 27th, and I shall meet him then without fail.
    Very glad that Roberts of N and Watson proved amenable, and that
Dent are prepared to advance the necessary money to repay him. Never
no more.[1]
    I see from the last accounts-statement sent to me by you on September
17, that I have received, as my share re film rights 'The Doctor And The
Devils', the sum of £91.5.0. And then occur the words: '3 instalments'.
Does that mean that the £91 odd pounds constitute the *first* of *three*
instalments? And that my whole share is eventually to be only
£273.15.0? I thought Taylor promised something in the neighbourhood of
£400. I shall see him about this anyway. But DON'T tell me that the £91
constitutes the whole of the *three* instalments. If—and there bloody well

---

[1] Nicolson and Watson had bought the rights of *Adventures in the Skin Trade* years earlier.
Dent were now buying them back on Thomas's behalf.

should be—there are another two instalments, each of £91 odd due to me, when will they be paid? At what intervals? Can you find out? I may not be able to see Taylor for a week.

The Atlantic Monthly, who are printing my new poem[1]—you sent on to me a request from the editor—have sent me the enclosed two Exemption Certificates, to be returned, signed, at once.[2] I enclose the covering letter also. I haven't completely filled the forms, as I did not know what to put for the address of 'trustee or agent'. Does that mean literary agent, too? And if so, would you fill it up? If I should put only my own personal address, would you mind filling that up and bunging the things off straightaway? Thanks.

I'll let you know what decisions, if any, Bozman and I come to when we meet.

Excuse the typing. I can use only one finger of my left hand.

Yours,
Dylan

MS: Texas

GILBERT PHELPS[3]
September 24th 1947   Manor House South Leigh Witney Oxon

Dear Gilbert,

Hundreds of apologies, all real, all late, for never having written from Italy about the Lawrence programme and about the poems and stories you were kind enough to let me read. I did enjoy them, a lot, and think it absurd they are not being published all over the place. There are so few magazines that pay anything and that get to enough people. Life & Letters, ed. Robert Herring, 430 Strand, W.C.2., is independent, I think, and imaginative. And what about a story to Argosy, which often prints intelligent ones and pays well too. I can let you have quite a long list of American little reviews, if you like, though probably the best are Partisan Review, Accent, Kenyon Review, and Sewanee Review. Give you the addresses when I can find them in the as yet unsorted muddle after moving into a new house: a fiveroomed cottage, lightless, waterless; the address is a credit-snarer.

I must apologise very much, too, for failing to return the mss. And I'm afraid I won't be able to for another week or so. They are with my own papers in a suitcase still in Italy, along with other vital luggage, which

---

[1] 'In Country Sleep', in the issue of December 1947.
[2] The certificates were necessary to avoid tax being deducted, in the U.S., from Thomas's earnings on work sold for him by Williams.
[3] A BBC talks producer. He had sought Thomas's advice about some of his own writing.

dirty Thomas Cook & Son Ltd. should have brought over for us but forgot, the international bleeder. As soon as the luggage comes, I'll send all your things off. Do try to forgive me.

About the Lawrence script. Yes, thank you very much, I should like to do it sometime very much. When will you be in London next? Will you drop me a line. I come up at least once a week. We could talk about all the things. Looking forward.

Excuse this dreadful typing. I've broken my right arm, can't write, and have to type with one left finger.

Yours
Dylan

Regards to
your
wife

MS: the recipient

JOHN DAVENPORT
September 24th 1947   The Manor House South Leigh Witney Oxon

My dear John,
    The above my permanent address, until they find us out. Do please forgive my not writing. I can only tap with one finger of my left hand on this decrepit engine. And sorry about no copy of my poem—tossed off in Florence one evening, between a Mass of Life and a little Crucifixion in oils—but found Roy Campbell had the last copy, which he was dragging around the thin puce belfries of the Third Programme. Roy had been the only person I had told, after lunch that day, that you were going to ask Redgrave if he, Redgrave, might think, some time or another, of reading it if he liked it. Some of the words swirled into Roy's babble-box, a little of the highly hypothetical information strayed into that vague and thorny veldt, and the result must have been what Redgrave heard from the BBC: that he was quite definitely reading my poem. Do apologise to him for me, will you? I quite certainly had not misguided the BBC on purpose, nor mentioned R's name but in private maybe-ing conversation. I shall be in town next Wednesday lunch: a week today. Could we meet? twelve or twelve-thirty? pub, Lib or Authors? I'd love to. Last time there were so many people, and I myself was just about an inch and a half above the ground: I mean, in the air, not sticking out.

    I'm so glad you thought of getting a copy of my little egg from Normal.

    I have rather a good film idea, which also might interest Redgrave: a dark and fantastic romance of the German 1830's.[1] I'll try to type out a

---

[1] *The Shadowless Man*, a script based on a nineteenth-century German story about a man who sold his shadow. It was written in collaboration with Margaret Taylor, but never filmed.

readable synopsis once I CAN USE TWO LEFT FINGERS AND HAVE A NEW RIBBON. Absolutely unexplained capitals!

Drop a line about Wednesday, can you?

Our Manor is a cottage, but only five minutes from Witney and exactly twenty five by train from Oxford. Do come down. Only one small single spare bed so far, but I think the new Davenport, that sveltie, could manage quite comfortably. One weekend snag is that the pub isn't open on Sundays; but others are only two miles off.

DO forgive me for not having written long before.

Love,
Dylan

MS: Texas   *SL*

R. N. CURREY[1]
25th September 1947   Manor House South Leigh Witney Oxon

Dear Ralph,

Many thanks for Indian Landscape, and for your letter. I've had time only to read a few of the poems, and enjoyed them enormously, even more than I guessed I would—and that after reading, and liking so much, several scattered ones during and since the war. Those I have read seem to me right, true, just, exact, and exciting, and I'm looking forward, a lot, to reading them all.

About your Arlott Poetry Magazine: of course you may use my Fern Hill poem, and thank you for wanting to use it. I'd be glad to read it myself, but don't know how John Arlott will feel about this, as I have read the same poem in another of his programmes. However ... drop me a line if you both decide to want me to read it.

Hope to see you soon. At the Liberal, perhaps?

Yours
Dylan

and excuse long
delay.

MS: the recipient

---

[1] A schoolmaster and poet (b. 1907) who also broadcast. His book *Indian Landscape* had just been published.

DAVID HIGHAM
October 7th 1947   Manor House South Leigh Witney Oxon

Dear David,
   First of all, to tell you what Bozman and I talked about, unless he has
already got in touch with you.
   A book of poems, 1934–1947, and to include two new long poems
hitherto unpublished in England, for next spring. This depends, of course,
on whether the Fortune Press business can be settled satisfactorily before
then.[1] I hope indeed that it can, and that you can soon start contract
arrangements with Dent.
   The Doctor And The Devils: Thank you for your note about this. I have
not yet got hold of Donald Taylor, but hope to see him in London this
week. Dent want to make a big thing of this, with a lot of publicity. And
to introduce it in a new way.[2]
   My old, half-finished novel, *Adventures In The Skin Trade*, which
Dent, with raised hands, refused to touch a few years ago, and which I
then gave, under that ridiculous contract, to Nicolson and Watson,
Bozman wants now to see again. He will give me, quickly, a final decision
upon it; if Dent will do it, please go ahead, David; if not, then let us try to
sell it, in its incomplete form, reputably, and not, as I did, by back doors
and Tambis.[3] When Nicolson and Watson, on receipt of Dent's cheque,
returned you the two contracts I had signed, did they also return the
manuscript of the first half of *Adventures In The Skin Trade*, which I had
given Tambi? If they did not return this, would you ask N. and W.
straightaway for it, so that it can be shown very soon to Bozman? If
Bozman doesn't want it, please bung it off somewhere, so that I can get
some money and, thus encouraged, finish it. I think Graham Greene
would be interested in it: more than anyone else, I should think. N. and
W. have the only available copy at the moment.
   Stories: Bozman favours the idea of putting the old fantastic stories, the
new more-or-less naturalistic ones, *and* the Childhood Memories etc I
did for the BBC, all into one book, and not to publish, even with good
drawings, the Memories as a small single volume. I agreed. These stories
to be collected together and arranged by me *as soon as possible*.[4]
   It is, then: *Doctor and Devils*, if the Fortune Press business is cleared,
and the *Poems 1934–1947* for next year, as early in the year as possible;
and the *Stories* to follow. *Adventures*, when handed over to Bozman, to
be given a quick decision upon—though, really, speaking for myself, I
would rather Graham publish that particular one.
   And now, lastly and quite as importantly, MONEY. I've done it again.

[1] Fortune Press had bought the copyright of *18 Poems* in 1942. Thomas bought it back in
   1949. But no book appeared until *Collected Poems* in 1952.
[2] This was the film script in book form.
[3] Tambimuttu had editorial connections with Nicolson and Watson.
[4] For whatever reason, this failed to happen.

With a little money behind me, I've settled in a nice new house, bought a few things for it, behaved a little extravagantly,— and now, yesterday morning, comes a letter from the bank saying that, not only am I not as well off as I imagined but that I am overdrawn and, unless something happens immediately, several cheques, made out to local tradesmen, will be returned. If they are returned, it will ruin us for ever in this village. Quite literally. It's enormously important, in a narrow tiny community like this, to keep frightfully well in with everyone, especially tradesmen, farmers, publicans etc. And unless you can pay in for me, at once, a cheque from Dent, we will forever be *out* with the tradesmen, farmers, publicans, etc. to all of whom I have given cheques.

So. You said, previously, that Dent will give me a hundred pounds advance on *Doctor and Devils.* I know there is, as you wrote me, some small stickiness about this from the film end, but Taylor assures that it will all come right. Can you get that hundred pounds *at once*, and send it to my bank. It really is a question of about two days. In about two days' time, unless they get a cheque, they will return those damned cheques and bugger us up here for all time. I have wired to the bank saying money is on its way. Please help. If Dent can't give the hundred for D. and D., then perhaps for something else. QUICKLY PLEASE. I shall ring you on Thursday morning, from London.

Yours very urgently
Dylan

It's damnable, after, to us, a momentary affluence, to return to the old hand-to-mouth day-to-day living; but it would be worse if the hand refused to give the mouth anything at all. So do, please, get that hundred, David. Bozman seemed extremely friendly, & optimistic about the future.

MS: Texas

DAVID HIGHAM
7th October 1947   Manor House South Leigh Witney Oxon

Dear David,

I've remembered one thing since writing you, so urgently, earlier this morning. About Donald Taylor and my share in the film rights of The Doctor And The Devils. Your secretary wrote to me, in your absence, on September 22 and told me that Taylor proposes to pay me my total amount of £365 in twelve monthly instalments. I have received, in one lump, the first three instalments. Could the next nine instalments be paid to me, as proposed, *strictly* once a month and not in irregular lumps. That is to say, can I be assured of a monthly cheque on a definite day of the month? This would ease matters for me considerably, and assure our rent etc. for the next nine months. I'd be very grateful if you would arrange this on a proper stated day of the month monthly basis.

Yours,
Dylan

But the really frightful *urgency* of my earlier letter this morning remains unabated.

MS: Texas

DAVID HIGHAM
12 Nov 1947   Manor House South Leigh Witney Oxon

Dear David,
    I've just got home to find Bozman's letter re *Adventures In The Skin Trade*, and also your note about it.
    I shall write to Bozman, today, and tell him that I don't agree with his ideas about the book and intend to finish it, as I planned, symbolism and all, in the form of a short novel. So would you show what there is of it to Graham Greene—also telling Graham that there is a *strict* plot behind the book, that it is all planned out, and that, if he feels any interest in it, I should like very much to discuss the *rest* of the book with him. I don't want any one reading it to think of it as just a fragment of comic romantic taradiddle without a real structure & purpose.[1]
    Perhaps if you'd let me know when Graham's had it, I could give him a ring about a lunch date? What d'you think?

Yours,
Dylan

MS: Texas

JEAN LEROY
12th November 1947 (About sundry BBC fees and expenses. See Appendix 40.)

---

[1] Dent relinquished their interest in the book, and Graham Greene offered £200 for it on behalf of Eyre and Spottiswoode, who seem to have paid half. But the book remained unfinished, and the £100 was ultimately repaid and the rights reverted to Dent.

MR TURNER
Dec 30th 1947   (Replies, to unknown correspondent, about prose books
he has published. See Appendix 41.)

ROY CAMPBELL
30 Dec 1947   Manor House South Leigh Witney Oxon

Dear Roy,
   Thanks for the postcard. You said, 'what day suits you best to do 3 & 4
Instalments of the W. H. Davies *next* week?' You meant, didn't you, the
week beginning Monday Jan. 5th? If so, *Monday 5th* itself would suit me
fine. Any time you say. And what about *Tuesday 6th* or *Thursday 8th* for
Instalments 5 and 6?
   Please drop a line, or wire, me here if this suits.
   Had a good Christmas? My inside feels like a flooded tin-mine.
   Caitlin sends love to all. So do I.
                                                      Dylan

MS: BBC

JEAN LEROY
30 Dec 1947   Manor House South Leigh Witney Oxon

Dear Miss LeRoy,
   The enclosed BBC cheque—for what I don't know, unless for the 2
instalments, already recorded, of the serial story, Autobiography of a
Super-Tramp; perhaps you could find out?—was, for some reason, sent to
me. Could you have it paid in, and a cheque sent to me as soon as
possible, please? I'm dead broke after an exhausting Christmas.
   Best wishes for New Year,
                                          Yours sincerely,
                                          Dylan Thomas

MS: Texas

JOHN ORMOND
Dec 30 1947   Manor House South Leigh Witney Oxon

Dear John,
   What about my cheque? Can you hasten it up? I'm dead broke after a

loud, wet Christmas, and relying on P.P.[1] Do your best—*as soon as possible. URGENT.*

See you, I hope, in London sometime next week.

Yours,
Dylan

MS: the recipient

DAVID TENNANT
Feb 7th 1948   Manor House South Leigh Witney Oxon

My dear David,

Alas! I lost my little notebook in which I had written down, at Virginia's invitation, the date of your party; and your letter, travelling via Roy Campbell, took days & days: the little romp in East Knoyle was over, when the letter came. We were both very very disappointed, but thank you both so much for asking us: we wanted, such a lot, to have a few little quiet innocuous drinks and demurely to throw an armchair or two. I do hope you'll give another party one day. And I do hope to see you soon. Have you regular London days? so that we could, maybe, meet on one of those mornings and begin our decline together—with or without Tommy Earp, as the case may be. Tommy's address is: 4 High St. Alton. Hants.

Yours ever,
Dylan

TS: J. M. Dent

CAITLIN THOMAS
Sunday [?January or February 1948]   Blaen Cwm Llangain

Caitlin, my own, my dear, my darling whom I love forever: Here it's snowbound, dead, dull, damned; there's hockey-voiced Nancy being jolly over pans and primuses in the kitchen, and my father trembling and moaning all over the place, crying out sharply when the dog barks— Nancy's dog—weeping, despairing. My mother, in the Infirmary, with her leg steel-splinted up towards the ceiling and a 300 lb weight hanging from it, is good and cheerful and talks without stop about the removed ovaries, dropped wombs, amputated breasts, tubercular spines, & puerperal fevers of her new friends in the women's surgical ward. She will have to lie,

---

[1] 'Conversation about Christmas', in *Picture Post* dated December 27. John Ormond had proposed he write it; the fee was £50.

trussed, on her back with her leg weighted, for at least two months, and then will be a long time learning, like a child, to walk again. The doctors have stuck a great steel pin right through her knee, so that, by some method, the broken leg will grow to the same length as the other one. My father, more nervous & harrowed than I have ever seen him, cannot stay on here alone, & Nancy cannot stay with him,[1] so she [will] take him back with her to Brixham [to][2] stay, until my Mother can leave the Infirmary. My Mother will therefore be alone in the Infirmary for months. No-one here will look after the dog Mably, & Nancy cannot take him back to her tiny cottage as she has, already, a Labrador retriever: they didn't know what to do but to have Mabli destroyed, which is wrong, because he is young & well and very nice. So I have said that I will take him.

My darling, I love you. I love you, if that is possible, more than ever in my life, and I have always loved you. When you left, going upstairs in the restaurant with that old horror, I sat for a long time lost lost lost, oh Caitlin sweetheart I love you. I don't understand how I can behave to you senselessly, foully, brutally, as though you were not the most beautiful person on the earth and the one I love forever. The train hourly took me further & further away from you and from the only thing I want in the world. The train was icy, and hours late. I waited hours, in Carmarthen Station in the early snowing morning, for a car to take me to Misery Cottage. All the time, without stopping, I thought of you, and of my foulness to you, and of how I have lost you. Oh Cat Cat please, my dear, don't let me lose you. Let me come back to you. Come back to me. I can't live without you. There's nothing left then. I can't ask you to forgive me, but I can say that I will never again be a senseless, horrible, dulled beast like that.[3] I love you.

I am leaving here, snowbound or not, on Tuesday, & will reach London early Tuesday evening, with bag & Mably. I could come straightaway to you if—if you will have me. Christ, aren't we each other's? This time, this last time, darling, I promise you I shall not again be like that. You're beautiful. I love you. Oh, this Blaencwm room. Fire, pipe, whining, nerves, Sunday joint, wireless, no beer until one in the morning, death. And you aren't here. I think of you all the time, in snow, in bed.

Dylan

MS: Maurice Neville

---

[1] Thomas's sister Nancy, now divorced from her first husband, Haydn Taylor, was living with her second husband, Gordon Summersby, in Brixham, Devon. She had gone to Blaen Cwm to look after her father while her mother was in hospital in Carmarthen. Florence Thomas's injury, and her husband's increasing ill-health, made life difficult for Dylan and Caitlin through much of the year.

[2] The paper is badly creased.

[3] Dramatic quarrels between the two, accompanied by blows, became a feature of their lives. The rows alternated with dramatic reconciliations.

JOHN ORMOND
6 March '48   Manor House South Leigh Witney Oxon

Dear John,
A coincidence. I'm going down, with Caitlin, to spend a week in
Laugharne—from March 29 (Easter Monday). Half for holiday (undeserved),
half to see my mother in Carmarthen hospital—(she's broken her thigh).

Laugharne, as you know, I lived in for several years, sometimes with
Richard Hughes. I know the little town intimately, and everyone in it,
including the Portreeve (this time, a publican friend) and officers. (My
photograph, even, looking repellent, is hung on the walls of Brown's
Hotel.) It's an extraordinarily interesting place, and unique; the ceremony
of Beating the Bounds is, so far as I know, practised nowhere else. The
town would make lovely pictures (especially from the tower of the
Castle, and from St. John's Walk).

As I am going to Laugharne for a week on the 29th, would you ask Tom
Hopkinson[1]—showing him this letter, if you like—if he would care for
me to write an article: about the town itself, the Portreeveship (though
that's not the word), the inhabitants, the customs including the Common
Walk, etc. I really do know it intimately, love it beyond all places in
Wales, and have longed for years to write something about it. (A radio
play I am writing has Laugharne, though not by name, as its setting.)[2]

If Tom Hopkinson would care for me to do this, could I be paid my
expenses? I'm terribly hard-up, and was going, with difficulty, to borrow
enough money to take me down & keep me in the hotel for a week. I can
promise no repetition of the disastrous PUCK FAIR VISIT! Indeed, I do so
much want to 'pay a tribute' to Laugharne.

Let me know. If Tom H consents, the photographer need not, of course,
be down there the same time as myself. (The Common Walk, as you say,
doesn't take place till Whit Monday.)

Anyway, do ask about this, and let me know when you can.
See you soon?

Yours,
Dylan

MS: Texas

EDITH SITWELL
March 15 [1948][3]   Manor House South Leigh Witney Oxon

My dear Edith,
I've been away, and have just seen your wire. So sorry.

[1] The editor of *Picture Post*. No money was forthcoming in advance, and the article was not
written.
[2] The early stages of *Under Milk Wood*, though it had not yet acquired that title.
[3] Thomas wrote '1947' by mistake.

No, of course I'll try to read the Smart, but I'm afraid I'll fail *miserably*. Thank you so much for suggesting an alternative. I shouldn't really, have bothered you with my fears about the Smart—(though they *do* exist. It's a wonderful poem).

Thank you *very* much for inviting Caitlin & me to lunch with you Wednesday 31st, too. It sounds so mysterious. We'd love to come, & look forward to seeing you a lot.

Only a very hurried note because I'm going to London almost at once to see about writing a film.

It will be lovely, for both of us, to see you so soon.

Did I thank you for my copy of 'Cain'?[1] I do now, anyway, most gratefully. Will you write soon? perhaps?

Love,
Dylan

MS: Texas

VERNON WATKINS
April 17 48   Manor House South Leigh Witney Oxon

Dear Vern,

I'm going to write an enormous letter, very soon, to make up for this long long but never unthinking silence. I haven't written a letter longer than a page for oh dear! years, I think. And I'll send my new poem too. The long one in Horizon had 16 misprints, including Jew for dew.[2] They are bringing out the poem as a broadsheet, to placate me, though I'm not cross.

This is only to say, *Of course*, please use my Man Aged A Hundred in your Old Age programme, and I'm glad and proud you want it, and that I shall definitely be one of the readers in the programme.[3] I'll love that.

Will you write & tell me when you will be in London, before or after Paris: preferably both. And I will come up, and we'll meet and talk and blare & whimper.

We're going to Paris at the end of May, for the British pretty Council. Wish it was when you were there.[4] We are staying, for no reason, at the Hungarian Embassy. Or perhaps I am someone else.

Llewelyn (to go, next term, to Magdalen School), Aeronwy, Caitlin, &

[1] Sitwell's *Shadow of Cain* ('Edith's vast, bad poem' as he called it to Caitlin) had been published in book form.
[2] 'In Country Sleep', in the December 1947 issue.
[3] Watkins was compiling a BBC programme of prose and verse.
[4] Watkins was to read a paper on Yeats in Paris. Thomas was to read poetry there for the British Council, but the reading was cancelled.

me, who are all well, send our love to Gwen, Rhiannon, Gareth and you. There's names!

See you soon, and I'll write *enormously* soon, too.

Dylan

MS: British Library   VW

AILEEN GOLDMAN
April 17th 1948   Manor House South Leigh Witney Oxon

Dear Aileen Goldman,

Thank you, very much indeed, for your very very nice letter: I'm so pleased you liked the readings from 'Autobiography of a Super Tramp'. It's a lovely book, isn't it, and I'm glad I was allowed to make it known to such lots of people who had missed it before, and also to recall it, and try to bring it to life, to people who already knew & loved it. (On one of the readings, the 13th I think it was, I was suffering from gastric flu, and it sounded like it too, or even worse. I hope you missed that one, or blamed your set for bad reception.)

And thank you very much for saying you want to hear me broadcast again. I shan't be doing much for some time, as I am busy on film-scripts, having just finished a version of 'No Room at The Inn' and just started a filmstory about the South Sea Islands, called 'The Beach at Falesá', based on a short story by R. L. Stevenson.[1] But I shall do an occasional broadcast: my next is in one of the 'Time for Verse' programmes, on May 9th. I do hope you'll be able to hear it.

Thank you, again, so much, for writing. Delighted to get your letter.

Yours sincerely,
Dylan Thomas

MS: Texas

AUDREY WITHERS[2]
April 20 1948[3]   Manor House South Leigh Witney Oxon

Dear Miss Withers,

Every apology under the sun, and I abase myself, I knock my head on the stones, I cut out my lying tongue. I can't do it. I just can't finish this

---

[1] A new and lucrative career, writing feature films, had opened up briefly for Thomas. The domestic film industry enjoyed a few good years after the war. Thomas did some work for British National, rewriting dialogue; *No Room at the Inn* was one of the pictures. *The Beach of Falesá* was the first of three films he worked on for Gainsborough; the script was later published (New York, 1963; London, 1964). His remuneration for the *Falesá* script consisted of £250 at the outset, £20 a week for ten weeks' work, and £250 on completion. The other two scripts carried similar fees.

[2] Audrey Withers was editor of the British *Vogue*, 1940–61.

[3] Thomas wrote 'May 20'. Someone, presumably the recipient, has altered this to 'April 20'.

damnable London article. I never knew it wd be *quite* so difficult, to try to rewrite something half from memory. Phrases I had used in the lost original kept floating up and then drifting away, tangled my brains, stopped me from scribbling anything new. I would have been better advised by myself had I begun afresh, taking no notice of old semi-remembered words and ideas; but now it is too late. Did my agents tell you? I gave, while hurrying to the train for Wales, my handwritten ms. to a most trustworthy friend to post, who has since told me that she, for the 1st time in years, got herself politely tipsy at a party of little, damp writers, went home, haphazard, in a taxi, and left my stuff on the seat or floor. I'm so dreadfully sorry for all the inconvenience my careless trust in a hitherto most trustworthy friend has caused you. I do not suppose you can ever let me write for you again; but do you mind if some time soon, I send you an illustratable article, all written, typed, completed? Try to forgive me. Honestly, I *have* been trying to finish this London piece, but the vanished original is far too distracting, and I would be days & days trying a new angle altogether and new words.

My most Spaniel-like apologies, & very sincerely.

Yours,
Dylan Thomas

MS: New York University

CORDELIA SEWELL[1]
April 21st 1948   as from Manor House South Leigh Witney Nr Oxon

My dear Cordelia,
Re. our conversation tonight on the telephone. You said that you agreed that my Mother and Father should, on Wednesday, the 28th April, come along to your cottage. My Mother will have to sleep, and stay, in the downstairs bed. I am assuming that the rent of your cottage is three guineas per week, & am enclosing cheque for one month from Wednesday the 28th April. You will, by this time, have talked to Caitlin & worked out various things. The 'various things' include, naturally, your coming & going: Mary (ours, that is, Caitlin's, Mary) will look after my M & F & me, and Caitlin will be to and fro helping them (and you) as much as we can.

Yours ever,
Dylan

MS: National Library of Wales

[1] Cordelia Sewell was a friend of the Thomases, and had a cottage in South Leigh.

CAITLIN THOMAS
Thursday [probably April 22 1948]   In the Train to Brixham
[*written on reverse of letter from David Higham dated April 19 1948*]

My own Cat my darling whom I love forever, my dear,
    I'm writing this in the long train. Five hours of it. Steamed pig-fish and
dripping cabbage and soapsud lager for mock-lunch. Three sleeping bores
in the carriage, one with a bucket mouth. I tried to go yesterday, but was
not called early enough, by Eileen, to catch the eleven morning train,
which is the only good, or even reasonable, one. I phoned Nancy last
night. My mother is coming out of hospital this coming Wednesday. No
woman has been found. She & Dad, in an ambulance, will be coming to
us on Wednesday. I also, as you probably know by this time, rang up
Cordelia. Her cottage will be free—except for occasional visits by her &
Black Beauty—on Wednesday, when Nicola & Vee return to school. So I
am going to take the cottage temporarily for my people. Mary will have to
look after them all. She can, aided by us. Please say you think this is a
brilliant idea. I think it is. I will leave Brixham Saturday morning & be
back in sweet Sow Lye Saturday night.[1] I love you more than ever. I think
of you all the time. I love you, my dear dear. Here is an open cheque for
Mags or [*illegible—?*Alice] Green to cash. I love you with my heart & my
head & my body.

                                                                    D.
If you want to ring me, the number is: BRIXHAM 3318.   D.

MS: Maurice Neville

KATHLEEN GURNER
April 27 1948 (Gives permission for anthology use of poem. See Appendix
42.)

ROBERT POCOCK[2]
[?29th] April 48[3]   Manor House South Leigh Witney Oxon

Dear Bob,
    11.30 George this Saturday. Nicholson's XXXXX or Younger's Scotch.
Lunch upstairs if greedy or faint.[4] Cricket, Oxford v. Gloucester. In the
evening, in Witney, Cordelia and two odd friends, the Colgroves, will

---

[1] 'Sow Lye' is a surviving form of 'South Leigh'.
[2] A BBC producer and friend.
[3] '29th' is crookedly written and could be some other date.
[4] The George is in Oxford.

probably come with their van and take us to some country houses —public. My father & mother arrive to stay with us on Friday, which will imprison Caitlin, but she will be with us at least on Saturday morning. The landlord of the Fleece has nearly lost his eye, our dog Mabli has eczema, our cat Satan had mange and is now dead, Caitlin has gone to London with Margaret Taylor & left me quite alone, the house beer has run out, I am 3 weeks behind with my filmscript, not having started it yet, my gas fire has just exploded, I have flooded the kitchen with boiling soup, I am broke, Caitlin has taken the cigarettes, I was suddenly sick in the middle of the night, Phil has just sent me his 25 shilling book about Hampton Court, rabbits have eaten the lettuce, and seven cows, who have opened the gate, are trying to get into the lavatory. There is no news.

Ever,
Dylan

MS: Texas   *SL*

GEOFFREY GRIGSON
29 April 1948   Manor House South Leigh Witney Oxfordshire

Dear Geoffrey,
   I didn't get your first letter, nor the one to Glyn Jones. Your letter, April 18, has just reached me. I've had lots of addresses lately. Yes, of course, do use the poem from my Eighteen Poems. What are you editing? Another Stuffed Owl?[1] I don't know Glyn Jones's address, but a letter sent c/o Gwyn Jones, Hillside, Bryn-y-Môr Road, Aberystwyth, would be sure to get him.
   Yes, I'm alive all right. And you?

Yours,
Dylan

MS: Texas

DAVID HIGHAM
May 3 '48   Manor House South Leigh Witney Oxon

Dear David,
   No, Donald Taylor hasn't paid anything at all to me direct. I wondered what had happened. *Do* please go ahead with the *extraction*. I am, curiously enough, broke.

---

[1] *The Stuffed Owl*, 'An Anthology of Bad Verse', edited by D. B. Wyndham Lewis and Charles Lee, was first published in 1930.

About Denys Val Baker and his using my poem 'In Country Sleep' in his Little Reviews Anthology. Okay, of course, and thanks for getting a little more from him than he wanted to give, but, please, *insist* on my having a *proof* sent to me. The poem, as printed in Horizon, had something like *16* misprints, and that is the copy Val Baker will use.

Yours,
Dylan

MS: Texas

DAVID HIGHAM
14 May 1948   Manor House South Leigh Witney Oxon

Dear David,
   Thanks for yours of 13th, and for straightening things out with Andrews (who's a marvel, to get it down to £85).[1]
   I enclose, signed, the authorisation you wanted.

Yours,
Dylan

No word from Donald Taylor?

MS: Texas

C. GORDON GLOVER
May 25 1948   Manor House South Leigh Witney Oxon

Dear Gordon,
   Thanks for 'A Poet In A Pub'. The titles you boys think up![2]
   Just a few points.
   I am 33, not 31.
   I don't think I used, of my father, the words 'the finest Shakespeare reader of his day'. The phrasing seems foreign. If anything like it *is* needed, couldn't it be: 'a great reader-aloud of Shakespeare'? or something like that? As it stands, the phrase could mean that, of all people of this time who read Shakespeare, he was the most indefatigable, omnivorous,

---

[1] Leslie Andrews, an accountant, had given this estimate of Thomas's liability for arrears of income tax. He was brought in after Margaret Taylor visited David Higham the previous January, to discuss the growing muddle of Thomas's tax situation: for the first time in his life he was earning substantial fees as a freelance, and needed to provide against the Inland Revenue's day of reckoning.

[2] Glover, journalist and broadcaster, had interviewed Thomas, and sent him the draft of an article for the magazine *Band Wagon*.

etc. etc. I meant only that his reading aloud of Shakespeare in class seemed to me, and to nearly every other boy in the school, very grand indeed; all the boys who were with me at school, & who have spoken to me since, agree that it was his reading that made them, for the first time, see that there *was*, after all, *something* in Shakespeare & all this poetry; and a great number of boys have gone on reading poetry *after* school life, because of those readings. I think that a phrase such as I suggested above would cover this point.

I would not be surprised—you are quite right—if people said I was a sort of modern Villon. But my lack of surprise would be caused *not* by the fact that I think I resemble, in any way in the world, a sort of modern Villon, but because I am used to listening to balls. I am about as much a modern Villon—I cannot, incidentally, read French—as I am a modern Joanna Southcott, Raleigh, Artemus Ward, or Luther.

I wasn't at Mrs Hole's kindergarten with either Dan Jones or Fred Janes (n, not m), whom I met later.

Do you think the extract, about 'Break break break', from my autobiographical sketches,[1] is confused by mixing it up with words not in the extract? Or not? I don't, myself, think that a reader would know that this extract came from my book; or, alternatively, I think that the reader would think the whole thing, including your interpolations, came from my book. It's very tiny, anyway, & doesn't really matter. Just a little point, sir.

It is true to say that I often cover perhaps a hundred sheets of paper in the construction of one poem. But what I said was, that I often covered more than a hundred sheets of paper with drafts, revisions, rewritings, ravings, doodlings, & intensely concentrated work to construct a single verse. Nor is this anything to be proud, or ashamed, of; I do not think any better of a verse because it takes weeks, and quires, to complete it. It is just that I work extremely slowly, painfully, in seclusion.

It was Aeronwy who was born in a blitz—as though it mattered!—not Llewelyn, who anticipated the war by more than 6 months.

Do, please, for old crimes' sake, cut out my spontaneous, and quite unbelieved-in, disparagement of village cricket. It was something I said for something to say. I'd be *awfully* pleased to see *all* references to cricket omitted. Let's leave cricket to Jack Squire; I have no ambition to join his jolly Georgian squirearchy.[2]

Finally, as a 'Profile', your admirable article should, I think, have taken, however parenthetically, other aspects of this impermanent, oscillating, rag-bag character into consideration: aspects, I admit, of which you, with

---

[1] 'The Fight', in *Portrait of the Artist as a Young Dog*:
   Dan kicked my shins in the silence before Mr Bevan said: 'The influence is obvious, of course. "Break, break, break, on thy cold, grey stones, O sea".'
   'Hubert knows Tennyson backwards', said Mrs Bevan, 'backwards.'
[2] Another disparaging reference to the poet John Squire, whose school of rural writers was sometimes guyed as 'the Squirearchy'.

great good luck, could have little first-hand knowledge: my basic melancholy; sullen glooms and black studies; atrocious temper; protracted vegetable comas; silences and disappearances; terror of death, heights, strokes, mice; shyness and gaucheness; pompous, platitudinary, repetitive periods of bottom-raking boredom and boorishness; soulburn, heartdoubt, headspin; my all-embracing ignorance; my still only half-squashed and forgotten bourgeois petty values; all my excruciating whimsicality; all my sloth; all my eye!

I enclose the article, with many thanks. What a fellow I sound! Thank God I don't have to meet myself socially, listen to myself, or, except when reluctantly shaving, see that red, blubbery circle mounted on ballooning body, that down-at-soul hick, hack, hock-loving hake which now inscribes itself,

Yours ever,
Dylan

MS: Texas

HERMANN PESCHMANN
23 June 1948   Manor House South Leigh Witney Oxon

Dear Mr. Peschmann,
Forgive my not answering your letter before this: I've been away on various jobs about the country, and on arriving home found my family all measled, and had to cook & char.

Thank you for inviting me to contribute a brief prefatory note to your anthology—which, by the way, I wish the best of luck.[1] But do you very much mind if, with reluctance, I say I'd rather not? I know your anthology's going to be very good; it isn't that; it's just that I'm laying off making any pronouncement about modern poetry, any comment, even, for the time being: for many reasons: I'm afraid this sounds more pompous than any pronouncement would, but I do hope you know what I mean. I'm not writing any poetry myself these days, & don't feel qualified to write about anyone else's.

I still feel very guilty, by the way, about that disastrous non-turning-up at your society. I hope to make up for that one day, if you still want me to.

Yours sincerely,
Dylan Thomas

MS: the recipient

---

[1] *The Voice of Poetry*, 1930–50 (Evans, 1950).

HERMANN PESCHMANN
[?summer 1948]   Manor House South Leigh Witney Oxon

Dear Mr. Peschmann,
   Sorry for the delay: I've been away.
   Formal consent to print my four poems in your anthology, okay by me.
But do you mind getting in touch with my agent, David Higham, of
Pearn, Pollinger, & Higham Ltd., 39–40 Bedford St., Strand, London WC2,
because I'm in a bit of a mess over copyright, especially that to do with
the Fortune Press.
   Thank you for your invitation to me to come along to the Reigate
Poetry Club, in spite of my lapse last time. This time *definite*. Can you,
sometime, fix an October date?

                                   Yours,
                                   Dylan Thomas

MS: Texas

MRS F. I. WEBLEY
June 25 1948 (Declines invitation to speak. See Appendix 43.)

DAVID HIGHAM
25 June 1948   Manor House South Leigh Witney Oxon

Dear David,
   As you see, from the enclosed, I want to open a quarterly credit account
with Blackwell's.
   Will you support me as a reference?
   If so, will you either send enclosed back to me or bung it along to
Blackwell's?
   Hope you don't mind. If you do, doesn't matter. Let me know, though.

                                   Yours,
                                   Dylan

MS: Texas

JAMES LANGHAM[1]
5 July 1948   Manor House South Leigh Witney Oxon

My dear James,
Please forgive me. The most awful, but obvious, things happened, and I couldn't get out of bed—no, not if *two* of you were waiting for me—till the afternoon.

I am coming up to London again early this week, & will ring you at once. It won't be too late?

Yours ever,
Dylan

MS: BBC

CAITLIN THOMAS
Sunday [?summer 1948]   [South Leigh]

Caitlin my darling, my own dear love, I love you forever & ever.

How are you? I think about you *all* the time, every every hellish second here.[2]

And it *is* hell here, too. Margaret has driven my father nearly mad since we left, patronising, lecturing him on art & music, letting the house get filthy and children-scrabbled.

And since I came back on Friday night, she's been alternately duckeying and weeping.

Mary loathes her too, & is waiting for you—as I am doing, my dear, all night & day.

I am keeping away all I can, writing letters in the bedroom.

Yesterday, SHE asked me: Do you want me to go? and I couldn't say Yes, I was feeling too ill.

Were you ill too?

Oh, dear, my dear, come back on Monday. SHE will go then.

Alan came out yesterday on his bicycle. I didn't see him. He saw HER going on her way to Mrs. Green. There were SCENES on the road.

And the bitch was red-eyed all evening, while my father talked about saucepans & operations and I trembled.

Come back, my love.

There are lots of huge lettuces, & I love you.

Love to Aeron, Llewelyn, & your mother etc.

Have you enough money?

I shall have to go town *twice* next week, over films, but will soon be settling down to writing them.

[1] A BBC producer.
[2] Caitlin and the children were with her mother, presumably in Hampshire.

Oh Christ, it's awful here without you.

All the love
I have,
Dylan

MS: Maurice Neville

HARALD SVERDRUP[1]

[1948]   Manor House South Leigh Witney Oxon

Dear Mr. Sverdrup,
    Sorry not to have answered before.
    My house here, though with such a dignified address, is a poky cottage full of old people, animals, and children. And everyone I want to meet, I have to meet outside somewhere: generally, and preferably, in a pub. So can we meet one evening in Oxford in the bar of the George? It's large and impersonal, nobody cares what you do or say, and the beer is better than usual. Monday or Tuesday of next week would be fine for me. About 7 o'clock? Can you let me know? If neither evening suits you, let's fix one at the end of next week. I look forward to hearing from you. I shan't by the way be able to do anything about taking part in a BBC discussion as I am nearly drowned under film work and daren't take a day off for some weeks.

Yours sincerely,
Dylan Thomas

MS: the recipient

SYDNEY BOX[2]

26 July 1948   Manor House South Leigh Witney Oxon

Dear Sydney,
    Perhaps you'll have heard, by this time, from agent Pollinger, that I shan't have to do that Welsh film I mentioned after all for Ealing: terms were no good, & time too short.[3] So if you'd care for me to start work for you as from *August 1*, rather than from *September 1*, as previously agreed, I'd love to.
    Belatedly, I'm sending you, by separate post, 'Forgotten Story'. Done

[1] Harald Ulrik Sverdrup (b. 1923), Norwegian poet, and translator of some of Thomas's work, then living in Oxford.
[2] Sydney Box (1907–83), film producer, then with Gainsborough.
[3] See letter dated July 27 to Clifford Evans.

anything about it yet? I'd like to work on it, and, very much so, on that episodic idea, 'Me & My Bike'.[1]

And, last: though that hunk of work I did on 'Beach of Falesá' is not a shooting script, could I get the £250 that is still owing to me as the last instalment? I'm really broke: down to very small postdated cheque.

Hope to work with you soon.

Yours,
Dylan

MS: Texas

RALPH KEENE[2]
27th July 1948   Manor House South Leigh Witney Oxon

Dear Bunny,
Thank you for letter and Revised Outline of *Me & My Bike*.

I don't know if *you* know, but it seems as though I shan't be doing this script for Ealing after all: disagreement on terms & on length of time (absurd) allowed for writing.

I have written to Sydney, telling him this, and saying also that I could start work for him, if he wanted it, as from August & not, as arranged, as from September. If he agrees, I could, perhaps, begin work on *M & M B* almost straightaway. There is, of course, *The Forgotten Story* as well, but he may have done something about that. I like that too.

But I'm *extremely* keen on the Bike. For me, as a supposedly imaginative writer, it's got wonderful possibilities, and I feel very enthusiastic about it. Sydney's carte blanche as to freedom of fancy, non-naturalistic dialogue, song, music, etc is enormously encouraging.

Yes, & whether I begin work for Gainsborough in August or September, I'll have a shot at one of the sequences almost straightaway: I've a lot to do, judging, my God, Poetry Festivals, & Third-Programming this week, & August Bank Holiday I devote to grossness. But after that, I'll get down to work at once: i.e. on Tuesday or Wednesday 2nd or 3rd of August. I've no preconceived ideas, but am so delighted with the *whole* idea that I hope to be able to produce something on the lines we all want.

I'll get in touch with you when anything has happened.

Yours ever,
Dylan

MS: Texas

[1] *Me and My Bike*, the idea for which may have been Thomas's, was to be a 'film operetta'. The finale would be a cyclist pedalling into heaven to a chorus of bicycle bells. Only the opening sequence was written. This was published after Thomas's death, and formed the basis of a television film by Derek Trimby for BBC Wales.
[2] 'Bunny' Keene, a film director, then with Gainsborough.

CLIFFORD EVANS
27 July 1948   Manor House South Leigh Witney Oxon

Clifford Evans (1912-85), the actor, had written a film story, and thought that
Thomas might write the script. As a result Thomas attended conferences at the
Ealing film studios. But the producer disagreed with him over ideas and finance.
The film was later made as *A Run for Your Money*.

Dear Cliff,
    Disaster & apologies.
    First disaster: the Saturday evening appointment I failed to keep. I had
to go, that day, to the hospital in Oxford to see about moving my mother,
who's got a broken leg there. It was an awful rush, and I scribbled a wire
to you and gave it to the station-porter here, a most reliable man except
every now & then. That was one of the then's. Two days ago, he found the
wire under a pile of Goods Vouchers on the station desk, apologised, and
bought me a pint. I'm really deeply sorry, not being so irresponsible as all
that, whatever They (whoever They are) might say.
    Second disaster. I heard, through agent, that Ealing was offering me
£250 for a full treatment, this to be done under a month, the starting date
to be that on which we met, with Frend, in Ealing (or perhaps a day after, I
can't, for the moment, find the agent's letter).
    I wrote back to the agent, saying that he & I had agreed that I should work
on this film for Ealing only if Ealing paid me what Sydney Box was prepared to
pay me: i.e. £1000 for a shooting script. Also, I said that I *would* be agreeable
to do a treatment only if I were given more time and, consequently, more
money. To this, the agent replied that he had got in touch with Ealing who, on
hearing that I had not accepted the £250 & the time-limit, considered the
matter closed and would make other arrangements. That's the story from my
side. And I was going to write to you in detail about it.
    In the meantime, I've heard that my agent, on receiving the definite
CLOSURE from Ealing, had written to Box to say that I could begin work
for him (Box) as soon as he (Box) wanted.
    So there it is, and I think that's where it will stand. I wanted, a lot, to
work with you on *Nightingales*. But I told the agent, quite frankly what I
thought: that the time allowed—it would have worked out at just over a
fortnight, considering that we'd written nothing for nearly a couple of
weeks after meeting, with Frend, in Ealing—wasn't enough to do justice
to the story in. And I'm sure I was right.
    It's a stupid mess, isn't it?
    I'll ring you when I'm up next. Are you going down to Ealing August
Bank Holiday week? Anyway, I'll know when I ring—which will be, I
hope, on Thursday or Friday of this week. I *was* looking forward, too, to
our couple of Welsh days.

                                        Yours ever,
                                        Dylan

MS: Clifford Evans's Estate

SYDNEY BOX
August 5 1948   Manor House South Leigh Witney Oxon

Dear Sydney,
    Thank you a lot.
    I've heard from Jan Read[1] & from Bunny too, and I expect my agent will
be hearing about contracts etc. soon.
    So glad to work for you from August 1.
    I'll have a shot, straightaway, now the holidays are over, at one of the
sections of 'Me & My Bike', & will, anyway, be seeing Bunny about it
early next week.
    Have good times away.

                                        Yours
                                        Dylan

MS: Texas

JEAN LEROY
6 Aug 48   Manor House South Leigh Witney Oxon

Dear Miss LeRoy,
    Re your letter Aug. 5.
    Yes, please do accept BBC fee of 6 guineas for my 'part' in programme
'Looking At Britain' recorded on July 30.[2] Best payment I've received: 2
short lines of verse spoken without rehearsal! More jobs like that.

                                        Yours sincerely,
                                        Dylan Thomas

MS: Texas

JOHN LEHMANN
7 Aug '48 [postcard]   Manor House South Leigh Witney Oxon

Yes, please, of course use my poem 'Fern Hill' for the English number of
'Prisma'.[3] Shall one see a copy one day? Like to.
                                        Yours,
                                        Dylan

MS: Texas

[1] Jan Read was a script editor at Gainsborough.
[2] The programme, about Radnorshire, was for the Overseas Service.
[3] *Prisma* was a book of contemporary verse that Lehmann was editing for the British
    Occupation authorities in Germany.

DAVID HIGHAM
Tuesday [August] 10 '48   Manor House South Leigh Witney Oxon

Dear David,
    Thanks for yesterday's letter. I enclose signed approved letter.
    I'm very glad Laughlin's bringing out a special limited selection.
Sounds very fine.
    BUT   This is extremely important.
    I myself have no copy of my SELECTED VERSE which Laughlin
brought out. I had my proper number of author's copies, but gave them
away at once. Looking into a friend's copy the other day, I was horrified to
see a number of glaring misprints: real stinkers: things like, in a love
poem, 'coal' for 'cool'. And in another poem, one he will certainly reprint,
one whole line left out, making havoc of rhythm & meaning. Mistakes all
over the place.
    So, please God, before he, Laughlin, brings out this special edition, &
before he reprints SELECTED VERSE, I *MUST* have *PROOFS*.
    Riddled with mistakes.
    Will you let Laughlin know *at once.*
    He mustn't print or reprint until these awful errors are rectified.
    It's a bit late in the day, isn't it? But it's got to be done now.

                                        Yours,
                                        Dylan

MS: Texas

JEAN LEROY
20 August 1948 (Instructs her to accept work. See Appendix 44.)

JOHN DAVENPORT
26 August '48   Manor House South Leigh Witney Oxon

My dear John,
    I feel furtive & guilty about missing our last date at the Savage. As,
perhaps, you noticed, I was not myself when we met in the Authors' and
went out for wine; I wrote the Savage time down in my little book, and
lost, later, my little book, my hat, my train, and had only a mist for
memory. Then I should have written, but, at home, full of remorse, I
could only potter gently in the garden, whimper, and hide, behind the
runner beans, from tradesmen. Please forgive me.

And thank you very much for putting me up, with Parry as seconder, for the Savage.[1] In a year, then, unless I am blackballed by Sir Jack or Kingsmill, I can give up the National Lavatory and be bad in worse company.

The Stahls have gone to France, won't be back for three months. In case letters are forwarded to them, I will write their address at the end of this, when I get to a telephone book.

I'm terribly sorry to hear about the money trouble. I cannot, at this moment, help in any way, and am, this morning, going to try a post-dated cheque at the village grocer's: well post-dated too. I haven't yet had my Gainsborough contract to sign, and have been living on little bits from the BBC. That's one reason I haven't been up to town. Also, an emissary of a man from whom I borrowed largely while in Italy has come to London—to the Italian Section, Bush House—and he wants, dear God, to meet me very soon. I am sunk. If the Box contract comes quickly through I shall save a little bit for you—very little it'll have to be, I'm afraid — before it all goes to Signor Furio Bianchini.[2] The box on which I write is vulgar with bills. Llewelyn must have a complete set of school-clothes for Magdalen C.S. next term. Caitlin wants a pressure-cooker & a night-gown. My mother & father will, I think, always be with us. I have given, months ago, a postdated cheque for £70 to Margaret Taylor, which is due September 1st. I am to go to read in the Edinburgh Festival on the 4th, & must hire a suit. Last week I fell down & broke my front tooth & have to have it taken out in Oxford by a German dentist called Mr. Pick. I wish you could come down for a few days: there's room, free, in the village. I do really wish so. I'll ring you at Bush House next Wednesday, and try to meet. Hope to God you can clear the bums. At the bottom of the garden, a man, at 3/- an hour, is digging a new shitpit & will dig on, he says, until he reaches water. By that time I shall owe him this house, which is not mine. Love to all & to you. I do look forward to seeing you.

Ever,
Dylan

MS: Texas

CAITLIN THOMAS
[?late August 1948]

My darling own dear dear Cat,
I love you for ever & ever & think about you all the time always asleep

---

[1] Thomas was elected to the Savage Club (popular with writers and actors) in 1949. 'Parry': Parry Jones, principal tenor at Covent Garden.
[2] Thomas borrowed £179 from a Mr Treves in Florence and Elba the previous year. The money was still unpaid in 1950.

& awake. I am sorry, my sweetheart, that these cheques are so late: I had no time, from the BBC, to get to Bank between 10 & 3. I go to Edinburgh Saturday morning. I love you.

Be well, be good, be mine, dear

MS: Maurice Neville

JAN READ (Gainsborough Films)
September 9 1948 [telegram from Witney]

SORRY LATENESS REPLY BEEN EDINBURGH FESTIVALLING WHAT ABOUT CONFERENCE TUESDAY WEDNESDAY OR THURSDAY NEXT WEEK PLEASE WIRE MOST CONVENIENT. DYLAN THOMAS.

Original: Texas

JOHN PURVES[1]
23rd Sept 1948   Manor House South Leigh Witney Oxon

Dear Mr. Purves,

Enclosed, at last, your book. You have every reason to cherish it; it's a most remarkable collection; and I can imagine how you must have felt when you thought that a nasty man, me, had lost it.

I can't tell you how upset I was to realise how much I had upset you by my irresponsible carelessness; and I can only hope that the recovery of the book, all safe & sound, will perhaps help you, if only a little way, towards—one day—forgiving me.

The facts are simple. In a violent hurry to catch the London train, I gave both wire and parcel to the maid. She sent the wire, and brought the parcel back with her & put it on my desk. She is methodical in everything, even in her forgetfulness. I should never have entrusted her with so valuable a commission, but usually she is extremely able.

Since the sending of the wire, but not of the book, I have been partly in London and some of the time travelling about the country for the filmcompany who tolerate me; and no letters or wires were forwarded, as I had no fixed address.

Returning home yesterday, I found all your urgent letters and distressed, and distressing telegrams, and found the unfortunate truth out at once.

[1] John Purves was a university lecturer at Edinburgh who collected literary autographs.

Nothing I can say can compensate for the anxiety I have caused you. But I would like you to believe that I am deeply sorry and regret, very bitterly, my unthinking carelessness.

I was very glad to be asked to write a poem in your book, among such distinguished company.

I offer every apology.

Yours sincerely,
Dylan Thomas

MS: National Library of Scotland

GRAHAM ACKROYD[1]
24 Sept 1948   Manor House South Leigh Witney Oxon

Dear Graham Ackroyd,

Very sorry not to have answered your letter long before this. It was a long time being forwarded, I've been away, and I'm afraid I could read only about half of your handwriting. This is difficult to write mainly because I couldn't get, from what I could read, the general idea. It's going to be a comic novel? My Long-Legged Ballad, brash, barging, & violent as it may be, isn't a comic poem, though it *has* been laughed at; and I don't want bits of it to be used as chapter-headings for a book that's meant to make you laugh. This may sound priggish. The Ballad is a serious sexual adventure story; and I can't see how bits of it can add to a story about an eccentric puppet maker & his family buggering about and turning a bloody village upside down. Can you tell me more about the story, *your* story, please.

As for your p.p.s., which you've probably forgotten, I could read so little of this that all I gathered was: the puppet maker's youngest daughter, a fast from flaying the harp up school, wanted to read my old Ballad at the Oxford Festival, and that, for some reason, the great moment of her life was when I, God help me, visited her father for ship you are the custard only.

You will, I'm sure, understand that, although I am not one to stand on a non-existent dignity, I can't give permission for you to write into a novel such jabberwock sentences as I could translate.

Will you, in capitals, or on typewriter, tell me more about the novel, please? tell me what on earth, or sea, my Ballad, a serious, if chaotic, poem, has got to do with such antics as I can decipher? and finally tell me what queer ideas the youngest daughter might have about me, and in

---

[1] Graham Ackroyd (b. 1920), later a painter, was hoping in 1948 to be a writer. The novel, afterwards destroyed, was about a young poet's encounters with eccentrics.

what character & in what capacity and to what length am I supposed to visit her no doubt delightful father?

Yours sincerely,
Dylan Thomas

MS: Texas

JAN READ
September 30 1948 [telegram from Chiswick]

STUFF ARRIVING MONDAY SORRY DELAY. DYLAN THOMAS.

Original: Texas

JAN READ
7 Oct 48   Manor House South Leigh Witney Oxon

Dear Jan,
  Hope you've got revised script of *Falesá* by now.
  When you read it, you'll see, (I trust), that I've followed the main line of the suggestions on which the three of us agreed, and have tried to re-member, & interpolate, all the chief points. One thing you'll notice is that I have cut out altogether the *two other traders* and stuck to one alone, calling him by the name of one of the other traders, Johnny Adams. This, I think, simplifies matters. We talk now about only *one* person whom we never see; our plot works back only to the *immediate* prede-cessor of Wiltshire. Perhaps you will think that the omitting of the French Priest's suggestion of 'poison', & the putting-in, instead, of 'driven mad with fear', lessens the tension: that Case *should* be rumoured as a murderer early on. But I can't agree with that; and think, anyway, that it's an improvement to cut out as many invisible characters as possible.
  As you'll see, I've cut all the introduction-by-the-waterfall cock about Uma. I've cut the Long Randall-&-burial-alive flash back. I've cut Namu, the renegade pastor.
  I want to apologise for the dialogue I have given the French priest, & also for not attempting his real French. I am shockingly bad at French – English broken dialogue, & worse at the French original.
  Apologies, also, for the long delay. I'm engulfed, as ever, in domestic mishaps & sicknesses.

I hope you & Ralph & I can meet soon: there'll be lots of things to disagree with in this version.

Yours,
Dylan T

MS: Texas

FRANCES HUGHES
October 10 1948   Manor House South Leigh Witney Oxfordshire

Dear Frances,

Thank you for your letter.

I'm giving this to Margaret Taylor to give to you in Laugharne. Unfortunately, I can't get away myself; I'm trying to write a musical comedy film, and am weeks behindhand. Margaret Taylor has come to Laugharne to see if she can find out, for me, exactly how the Starke-Hughes-Castle[1] case is going, and what chance there is of my getting the house for some years, and, if I did manage to, exactly what financial commitments I would be held to. Do, please, help her if you can. I can't explain my 'longing' to have the castle any more clearly than I did in my letter to Diccon.[2] I want very much to live in Laugharne because I know that there I can work well. Here, I am too near London; I undertake all sorts of little jobs, broadcasting etc., which hinder my own work. In Laugharne if I could live there, I would work half the year on my film-scripts, and half on my own poems and stories: cutting out all time-wasting broadcasts, articles, useless London visits.

I realise that there's a great difference between owning and renting a house, and that Mrs. Starke can be a querulous & annoying person to be tenant of. But, still, if anyone, *not* Mrs. Starke, is going to live in the castle, I'd like it to be Caitlin and me. So will you please, for both of us, let Margaret Taylor know how things stand? And if we *could* get the house, we'd like to buy, rent, or whatever, what furniture there still is in the Castle: that is, of course, if you are not going to take it away.

Anyway, we hope and we hope.

Caitlin's love,
Yours ever,
Dylan

Only source: SL

[1] Mrs Starke owned, or had owned, the house known as Laugharne Castle. There was a long-running row about alterations that Richard Hughes wanted to make.
[2] 'Diccon': Richard Hughes.

MARGARET TAYLOR
Thursday evening [?October 1948]   Manor

My dear Margaret,

Your letter, just arrived by winged messenger, has set us dreamily
grinning, hopelessly shaking our heads, then beaming and gabbling
together again as we think of the great house at the end of the cherrytreed
best street in the world, bang next to the Utrillo tower, with its wild
gardens and owly ruins, the grey estuary, forever linked to me with
poems done and to be, flat and fishy below with Tom Nero Rowlands, the
one last fisherman, who hates the water, trudging through it like a
flatfooted cat; saying to ourselves, 'No no no, do not dream of it, never for
us too ugly too old', and then once more saying, not too loudly, 'Perhaps
and perhaps, if we try, pray, whisper, fear the God, abjure drink and
fighting, be humble, write poems, do not bite our nails, answer letters,
collect the fallen apples for economical pulping into glass jars, do not
throw her crutches at my mother, be good, be patient, sing, love one
another, ask God for peace, perhaps and perhaps one day one day the owly
castle and the noble house will be ours for some of the seven most
heavenly years since pride fell.'[1] Oh the kitchen for cooking & eating, for
thinking Breughels! the room to the left as, praise be, you enter the house,
that room for music and Caitlin dancing! the nursery for Aeronwy, that
we must have more children to fill! the bedroom looking up at an
unbalanced field, the field of infancy where even now we are all running
so that, writing this in the rain, I can hear all our thin faraway children's
voices glide over the plumtrees and through the ventilation skull-holes of
this window! and the other bedroom looking out, happy as hell, at the
clock of sweet Laugharne, the clock that tells the time backwards so that,
soon, you walk about the town, from Browns to the gulls on the Strand, in
the only Garden Age! the long cool once Dufy-hung living room: the only
room in the world rightly described as one for living, and, at its end, the
gravel path to the brass cannon pointing, as all cannons should point,
uselessly out at the estuary air! the room, the velvet, padded room
upstairs where poems are waiting like people one has always loved but
never met, and O to sit there, lost, found, alone in the universe, at home,
at last, the people all with their arms open! and then, but only through
my tears, the hundreds of years of the colossal broken castle, owls asleep
in the centuries, the same rooks talking as in Arthur's time which always
goes on there as, unborn, you climb the stones to see river, sea,
cormorants nesting like thin headstones, the cocklewomen webfoot, &
the undead, round Pendine head, streaming like trippers up into seaside
sky, making a noise like St Giles Fair, silent as all the electric chairs and
bells of my nerves as I think, here, of the best town, the best house, the

---

[1] Thomas's hopes of being able to live in Laugharne Castle were premature. That winter
Margaret Taylor found them the Boat House instead.

only castle, the mapped, measured, inhabited, drained, garaged, townhalled, pubbed and churched, shopped, gulled, and estuaried one state of happiness!

Shall I tell you what I think when we meet? I have plans and stratagems, dreams & details, a head herring'd with ideas, I am weak and ruthless and exultant about this. I would do anything. I will. To Caitlin, it is as adorable and as impossible to conceive as it is to me!

Oh, *let's* do what we can, I had to write this to you.

And we'd like to come out on Saturday.

Dylan

MS: Texas   *SL*

SYDNEY BOX
Nov 7 1948   Manor House South Leigh Witney Oxon

Dear Sydney,

Sorry you were too busy for me to be able to see (and worry) you last Wednesday at the Studios. Perhaps, anyway, it would have been better for me to write.

The small (but not to me) point I wanted to see you about was, I'm afraid, a money one.

I'm in debt £150 to my bank. Until I pay them that sum, they will allow me to cash no more cheques. Until that sum is paid, I cannot carry on domestically day-to-day nor can I attempt to live normally on the weekly salary I get from Gainsborough.

So: My contract says I am to be paid £500 on the completion of each of this year's two scripts I do for you. Would it be possible for me to get £150 of this £500 on advance now? If it isn't possible, I'm sunk. Really sunk. One & all.

Please do what you can. And every apology for the embarrassing bother I'm making. But I can hold out against tradesmen etc (& the bank) only a few more days.

I do hope to see you for an unfinancial drink one day.

And, please, this nonsense is urgent.

Yours ever,
Dylan

MS: Texas

JEAN LEROY
Nov 16 1948 (Instructs her to negotiate better BBC contract. See Appendix 45.)

JAN READ

Nov 16 48   Manor House South Leigh Witney Oxon

Dear Jan,

Thank you for the copy of the 1st draft of 'Rebecca's Daughters'.[1]

I've now read all the stuff you gave me about the subject but haven't yet started getting down to the writing. I'll be doing this next week.

So glad Sydney was amused by the first chunk of *Me & My Bike*. I look forward to hearing more about it. Bunny wrote & said he was very Keene[2] on going on with it as it is.

See you soon.

Yours

Dylan

MS: Texas

HERMANN PESCHMANN

Nov 16 48   Manor House South Leigh Witney Oxon

Dear Hermann,

So sorry not to have written before. And sorry we missed you on our way back from Brighton: we had some friends with us, and were rather a large party (though we could indeed have tried to bring you & your wife over for a drink in Reigate or elsewhere). Brighton went very well, and noisily.

About the Anna Wickham poem: I'm sorry, but I've scrapped all my notes including, accidentally, most of the poems I'd so laboriously written out. But you can find the poem in Richard Aldington's massive new anthology.[3] I'm afraid I don't know if it was pre-1930—the poem, I mean—but I rather think so.

Thanks for the newspaper extract.

Regards to you both.

Yrs

Dylan

MS: Texas

---

[1] *Rebecca's Daughters*, based on material already owned by Gainsborough, was about the raids on South Wales tollgates in the 1840s, by bands of men dressed as women and led by a mysterious 'Rebecca'. It was the third and last of the Gainsborough scripts Thomas worked on.

[2] 'Bunny' was Ralph Keene.

[3] *Poetry of the English-speaking World* (1947).

JOHN DAVENPORT
17 Nov 1948   Manor House South Leigh Witney Oxon

My dear John!

O God, what a pickle, and I'm entirely useless. If only if only I could raise *ten* pounds, ten mean little pounds, to help you whom I owe so much from the past. If only, just for our sake, I could raise a guarantee from someone else. But my lady-patron no longer pays, at least not in money; a night at the opera, yes, ballets & cocktails whenever, but not one more crisp crunchy note can I drag from her unloved breast. My *own* foreign debt is pressing; the unanswered letters of the Italian lender grow briefer and less English. I have already borrowed in advance from my fee for my next unspecified filmscript in order to unfreeze *my* bank account so that I can write little overdraft cheques to tradesmen & the publican. And, crowning all this, Brigit's & Caitlin's mother & Brigit herself who is living with her have only this week written to say they are penniless and that they must appeal to rich, cigary filmtycoon *me*.

I am so sorry, John, that my letter to you is as full of woes as you to me. A wretched answer. I would to God I could send a better one. But I had to tell you how things are with me; if only they were one inch better, I could send some contribution. But all is stony here, & Christmas coming.

Can Helen & Bill McAlpine do nothing? They are the only people I know who might help. Augustus? Oh, but you must have gone through all the possible names in your great unhappy head, my beamishless boy. And flippancy doesn't help. Would you care for a drink on Friday lunchtime? I'm in town to wheedle. Henekey's downstairs 12.30 or 1? I'll ring & see anyway. I can at least buy some flat yellow pints, and we can whimper together. I'd love to see you. Why does your trouble coincide with mine? When I last saw you, at Brighton time, I was rolling in ready cash. Now I have to roll on credit. There's nothing here to sell. My soul's sold, my wits wander, my body wobbles, Aeronwy is too young, I won't let Caitlin, the only pictures on our walls are from Picture Post, our dog is a mongrel, our cat is half a mouse.

Small cheer for the needy in the old Manor House.

If you tackle McAlpines, do so quickly: they leave London next weekend to take a cottage in this cowpad village.

I have not yet managed to see Sidney B about our working together. He is always out, or out to me, or showing his great teeth to Rank. But I may see him Thursday evening.

I will ring on Friday morning. I do hope we can meet.

All my apologies for so abysmally failing you.

                                        Love,
                                        Dylan

MS: Texas   *SL*

VERNON WATKINS
Nov 23 48   Manor House South Leigh Witney Oxon

Dear Vern,
    Thank *you* for coming to the lunch. It was lovely to see *you*. Thank you for writing and for remembering the book. Last week I bought it and left it, *at once*, in a cab. Before I had opened it. I left also Robert Graves's Collected Poems, Betjeman's Selected Poems, two library books about sudden death, somebody else's scarf and my own *my own* hat. Now I must wait till Christmas to read you. 'Cave Drawing', & 'Llewelyn's Chariot', I have, and one of the Carmarthen poems in an anthology. But I want all. I'll ask your godson about an annual when he comes back from school. It's games morning. He hates it, can't kick or throw. All he can do is dribble. Also he draws good engines, likes arithmetic, says Yah about poems, & Wizard about aeroplanes, Dick Barton, Up the Pole,[1] tinned spaghetti, walnuts, and the caravan where I now, dear help me, work.[2] Nothing happens to me. I go to London and bluster, come back and sigh, do a little scriptwriting, look at an unfinished poem, go out on my bicycle in the fog, go to London & bluster. Mervyn Levy wrote to me yesterday. I wish Fred would write. I would to him if I had his address. And to Dan. My mother's no better, and will probably have to go to hospital again very soon. My father's better & naggier. I wish you had heard my story about Rhossilli. I wish I were in Rhossilli.[3] I wish we saw each other oftener. Next Spring we will, in Laugharne and in Swansea. I'm so cold this morning I could sing an opera, all the parts, and do the orchestra with my asthma.
    Write soon. Love to you all from us all.

Ever,
Dylan

MS: British Library   VW

GRAHAM ACKROYD
November 24 1948   Manor House South Leigh Witney Oxon

Dear Graham Ackroyd
    I do apologise for not having answered your most understandable letter of nearly two months ago. I mislaid it, difficult though that was. Thank you very much for it.
    Permission for poem etc. granted. I look forward to reading some Todd.

---

[1] Popular radio programmes.
[2] Margaret Taylor provided a caravan in the garden for Thomas to escape to.
[3] Thomas read his story, 'Extraordinary Little Cough', about a childhood camping holiday in the Gower village of Rhossilli, on the radio on October 27.

(And I like the idea of the young man who is writing Todd's Life *and* Works. I wish someone would write *my* works. Then I could go out on my bicycle.)

I hope you write again, when you've got time and some railway posters.[1]

Yours sincerely
Dylan Thomas

MS: Texas

JEAN LEROY
25 Nov '48 (Queries BBC payment. See Appendix 46.)

JEAN LEROY
Dec 6th 1948 (Thanks her for arranging fee. See Appendix 47.)

JOHN GAWSWORTH
7 Dec 48   Manor House South Leigh Witney Oxon

Dear John,
    Awfully sorry, I've got nothing for your first number, really nothing, no poem nor prose. Soon, when I start writing again, I'd like very much to send whatever-it-is along. All the time now, I'm filming & radio-ing, reading, & worrying:
    I got the L.D.[2] (& cheque), thanks.

Yours,
Dylan

MS: Buffalo

JAN READ
13 Dec 48   Manor House South Leigh Witney Oxon

Dear Jan,
    I hope that, by this time, you'll have heard from my agent Pollinger.

---

[1] Stung by references to his handwriting, Ackroyd had replied on the back of a poster.
[2] *Literary Digest.*

This is only a personal note to thank you for the tone of your letter to Pollinger, and to assure you I am now working *hard* on Rebecca, having somehow managed to tidy over my domestic crisis, & will send it along as soon as possible.

Apologies all round, to Sydney & Bunny.

Yours,
Dylan Thomas

MS: Texas

VERNON WATKINS
13 Dec 1948   Manor House South Leigh Witney Oxon

Dear Vernon,

Lovely book.[1] Thank you very very much. I am reading it from the beginning, some every night, slow & light & lifted. I saw the review in the Times Literary Supplement & liked its praise but not all its detail; & pre-'Raphaelitism' is barmy. I'll write again when I've read all the (to me) new beautiful poems. How good you really are!

Llewelyn's Annual: he says there is something called 'Science & Wonder' (Number 2. Very important, number 2.) Or anything, and he thanks you from his rag-&-bone shop.[2]

All well but poor and tired here. I am sorry, I do not mean my mother is well, poor thing, she's as ill as a ward.

Love to all from us all,
Ever,
Dylan

MS: British Library   *VW*

DAVID HIGHAM
Dec 21st 1948   Manor House South Leigh Witney Oxon

Dear David,

Please forgive delay. I have been in an accident, was knocked off my bicycle by a lorry, and have badly broken arm & ribs. Also feeling shocked & bruised all over & have a wonderful black eye.

Thank you very much for at last successfully effecting an agreement with the Fortune Press. I enclose Dent's agreement, signed.

I can't, at the moment, find Laughlin's copy of my *Selected Writings* to

---

[1] Watkins's *The Lady with the Unicorn.*
[2] W. B. Yeats, 'In the foul rag-and-bone shop of the heart' ('The Circus Animals' Desertion').

send on, proof-corrected, being too full of pain-killer to think or re-member clearly. But I hope to be better tomorrow and will find the book & send it at once on.

I wonder if you would do me a favour. I should write separately to Pollinger but feel too battered to do so. Could you tell him of my accident & ask him whether he thinks he should let Gainsborough know, as I'm afraid my filmwork will be held up for—in the doctor's opinion—10 or more days. Whimpering, I now lie down.

Yours,
Dylan

MS: Texas

ROBERT MACDERMOT[1]
10 January 1949   Manor House South Leigh Witney Oxon

Dear Robert,

Thousand apologies for not having answered at once your December letter about *Peer Gynt*. I've been laid up after an accident, with broken shoulder & ribs, too bloody and bowed to write a word or think of anything.

Thanks a lot for wanting me to do a new version of *Peer Gynt*. I really would *love* to, above anything, a great & favourite play, but I just daren't. I'm long behindhand with a filmscript for Gainsborough, and won't be able to finish it for the next three weeks or a month. Which makes it, to my grief, impossible to turn out a *P.G.* by the end of February.

I suppose you must now hand it to another chap—but if there ever was a chance of your postponing it, & of letting me have a shot in the Spring, I'd be more than delighted. Much more.

By the way, isn't 8 weeks a *madly* short time for anyone—I don't know a syllable of Norwegian[2]—to produce a really good version of a great play?

Do think of me in the future whenever anything as exciting as that turns up, will you, please? I *would* like to write for Television.

I've never seen a Television show. Could I come along as a silent, out-of-the-way looker-on one day?

Thanks again.

---

[1] MacDermot, the head of BBC television drama at a time when the service was more of a curiosity than anything else, had written to Thomas (20 December 1948), 'How allergic are you to *Peer Gynt*? I ask because we want to do a full-scale television version of it in late March or early April.' He wasn't happy with existing versions; nor was the producer, Royston Morley. This was the same Morley who commissioned programmes for Brazil early in the war. (In 1947 he had had plans for a TV adaptation of Euripides' *The Trojan Women*. Thomas was said to have been 'interested', though nothing happened.)

[2] Thomas wrote 'Norweigan' in all his letters about *Peer Gynt*.

All the best wishes for New Year,

Yours,
Dylan

MS: BBC

DAVID HIGHAM

Jan 20 1949   Manor House South Leigh Witney Oxon

Dear David,

Since my enclosing note this morning, sent with the *Mardersteig Proofs* & the corrected copy (to be returned to me) of the New Directions *Selected Writings*, I have come across a copy of the poem, unpublished in book form, which Laughlin wants to include in the Mardersteig edition.[1] So he needn't bother about the Atlantic Monthly: here is the poem.

Yours, ·
Dylan

MS: Texas

ROBERT MACDERMOT

26 Jan 1949   Manor House South Leigh Witney Oxon

Dear Robert,

So glad you have been able to postpone the production of *Peer Gynt* until, probably, the Autumn.

And I should be delighted to have a shot at the adaptation & to try to deliver it by the end of May. My cautious words 'have a shot' and 'try to deliver' I use because I have never tried anything of this sort before, have a great admiration for the play & no Norwegian, and am very awed by the task ahead of me. But I'll do my very best.

As a matter of fact, there is in Oxford now a young Norwegian poet, Harald Sverdrup, whom I've met lately because he is preparing a talk on my poems, and translations of them, for the Norwegian section of the B.B.C. He seems a very nice chap & has marvellous English. Should I sound him out next week—when I meet him—about the possibility of his helping me—at any rate, in the first stages.

---

[1] A small issue of an *ad hoc* volume of Thomas's verse, *Twenty-six Poems*, printed by the Officina Bodoni, the hand press founded in Verona by Giovanni Mardersteig. James Laughlin and J. M. Dent were the publishers. The book is dated December 1949, issued the following year.

You will, anyway, won't you, be able to give me a literal translation and also let me have from the library all the available translations for reference?

I'm sorry this letter is, again, so late. I'm terribly busy on a script for Gainsborough, and that reminds me: About my terms! My agents, Pearn, Pollinger, & Higham, will be getting in touch with you and/or your copyright people & I'm going to instruct them to ask for a *really* good fee. It's a terrific amount of work, and extremely difficult too. Also, it will mean my setting aside work on another filmscript—and Gainsborough pays very well. So my agents will want all they can get, and more.

Do let me know what you think of the idea of attempting to co-opt the Norwegian poet, please.

And when shall I come up to see you or Royston?

Yours,
Dylan

MS: BBC

E. J. KING-BULL
26 Jan '49   Manor House South Leigh Witney Oxon

Dear King-Bull,
Thanks for the letter. And for the commission. I understand now quite what is wanted: whether I can provide it is another matter. I'll try my best. And I'll get my agents to attack the copyright people straight away.

I shan't be able to get down to it for some time, though. I've got a filmscript in hand, and also am about to prepare to work on *Peer Gynt* for television. But I think I should be able to put something across the *Plain Dealer* by, as you suggest, mid-April.[1]

Perhaps we can have a word about it, over a drink in London, when I'm about to start on it & when I've got hold of a copy and read it several times—including backwards?

Yours,
Dylan

MS: BBC

JEAN LEROY
26 January 1949   Manor House South Leigh Witney Oxon

Dear Miss LeRoy,
The BBC has approached me about two programmes.

---

[1] See next letter.

First: Robert MacDermot, Head of Television Drama, has written asking me if I would do a new version of 'Peer Gynt', based on a literal translation from the Norwegian. This is for a full-scale television production in, probably, the autumn. And they would like, if possible, to have my version by the end of May.

I have written to Mr. MacDermot, telling him that I should like, very much, to do it, but that it entails a great deal of work of a high and concentrated order, as well as much & careful reading of all existent versions in English and, probably, some initial work with a Norwegian translator. This being so, and also considering that I am under contract to Gainsborough Films and therefore will have to work *doubly* hard, I told MacDermot that I would need a good deal of money and that my agent would press like the devil, for the very maximum (and more) that Television can pay. So will you get in touch with them, please, and start this devilish pressing straightaway? I look forward, a lot, to having a bash at it, but obviously cannot do so, in light of my other work and of my film obligations, unless it is made *really* worth my while.

Second: E. J. King-Bull, of the Third Programme, has asked me to make a 'treatment', for the Third, of Wycherley's 'The Plain Dealer'. What he requires is a 'personality treatment' of the play, including adaptation and cutting to a programme period as near to ninety minutes as possible. In King-Bull's words: 'Your interpolatory passages should either hasten or elucidate action which it would be tedious to broadcast, or point your general statement on whatever content of the play you choose to emphasise. Although there ought not to be more than a smallish proportion of exposition by you, it should maintain the personality stuffing and not often be mere "cut-to-narration"'.

Anyway, you'll be gather[ing] from King-Bull's rather curious phrasing, that it's quite a lively task. *And*, again, one that should be handsomely paid. Not only do I edit, adapt, & cut the play, but I introduce it, personally, on the microphone, and, throughout the play, interrupt, interpolate, & comment in my own sweet fashion. Thus the commission entails my working as editor, adapter, writer, and broadcaster. Will you see what money they offer—and then damn-near double it?

Hope to hear from you soon, & also that I've made things clear.

Yours,

Dylan Thomas

P.S.   It is, of course, the Peer Gynt that is the *big* job.

MS: Texas

HECTOR MACIVER[1]
17 February 1949   Manor House South Leigh Witney Oxon

Dear Hector,
I've often meant to write. But what's the good of meaning? (as your Dylanttantes might say).

I'll write at once to J. M. Dent, asking them to send to you, from me, what in-print books of mine they possess. All, I think, are in print, except the first one and that soon should be: there's been some legal bother about it, something I don't understand about copyright. Anyway, some copies of the others will be reaching you. And I will not draw nasty pictures on the flyleaves.

Really I did mean to write, to thank you for whisky and ale, but work and sloth alternately kept me busy and then I lost your address. I wish I could speedily return to Scotland: here it is low and sodden, moley and owly, rheumatic, cloddish, gustless. In the Spring, we go to Wales to live, in a house on an estuary.[2] That will be nice, I do so hate it here in this toadish dungwilted valley among slow rabbits & sly cows. Oxford is near, but full of young men. Our pub is cold, and wild with dominoes.

I wish you would come South. If ever you do, do write or wire and I'll puff up to London full of the worst intentions. I appreciated a great deal your room, spirit, & company.

MacDiarmid is coming to lecture to the Oxford Poetry Society next month. Or is supposed to come. A party is being arranged.

I am working on a film which is trying to kill me.

Write when you have time & inclination. Anyway, to tell me if the books have arrived safely. And how they could arrive unsafely I don't know, unless a censor opens the parcel & Lallans them.[3]

It was good to hear from you.

                                              Yours,
                                              Dylan

MS: National Library of Scotland

JEAN LEROY
17 Feb 49 (Welcomes proposed *Plain Dealer* fee. See Appendix 48.)

[1] Hector MacIver (1910–66), Scots teacher and writer. Probably Thomas met him during his visit to Edinburgh the previous year.
[2] Mrs Taylor had bought the Boat House for £3,000.
[3] 'Lallans' means Scots dialect, as revived for literary purposes.

CAITLIN THOMAS
Saturday   6 o'clock [March 5 1949]   Hotel Flora Praha[1]

Darling my dear Caitlin whom every moment—away from or with her—I love more, my sweetheart Cat: I love you.

I arrived in Prague about 24 hours ago, was met at the airport by an elderly woman & a young man who took me at once to a reception in the House of Parliament where hundreds of Czechs, Slovaks, Russians, Rumanians, Bulgarians & Hungarians were drinking wine. After, dinner: really incredibly bad food but nice people. After that a party to say goodbye to two Greek film-men who were returning to the Greek War. Today, hours of Congress & translators. Lunch with an old Czech friend of Norman Cameron's. After, more Congress & each guest made a speech. Including me. Tonight, a Smetana opera. Tomorrow, more speeches, and a broadcast. I love you. All this has nothing to do with writing—I mean, all this multilingual congressing. But Prague is so beautiful. And bitingly savagely cold; you, my love, would die of it. Tomorrow, I shall buy a small fur hat here. All the insides of buildings are very very warm. I have, in spite of all these appointments, a terrible loneliness. Even in 24 hours. And I want to be with you. Do not be too sad; though it is stupid of me to say, Don't. But please don't be, my own Caitlin. If I can get a seat in the plane, I will fly back on Wednesday. If not, the next day. Nobody here so far allows me to go into a café, pub, or dive. They prefer parties in the home. We don't agree. But they are a wonderfully friendly people. I do do hope we can come here together. Keep well. Give my love to A & L. And to you, my lonely love, my true self, my undying faith, every dear wish. I think only, dream only, *am* only you. Oh, Cat.

                                        X   Dylan

MS: Maurice Neville

MARGARET TAYLOR
[card, postmarked Prague, March 1949]

My hands are so dirty, excuse this scrubby note. I have just come, bludgeoned & flummoxed, from a Congress in 6 languages. [?Tonight] I go to the [?]. Cold & beautiful [?], but the lager thin.

                                        Dylan

MS: Texas

---

[1] Thomas was one of many writers invited by the Czechoslovak Government to see a Writers' Union inaugurated.

ELWYN EVANS (BBC)
14 March 1949 (Declines invitation to talk about [Gerard Manley] Hopkins. See Appendix 49.)

JEAN LEROY
March 14 1949 (Accepts improved *Plain Dealer* offer. See Appendix 50.)

JEAN LEROY
March 18 1949 [telegram from Witney][1]

PLEASE ACCEPT PEER GYNT OFFER AND OBTAIN HALF IMMEDIATELY THANK YOU VERY MUCH DYLAN THOMAS.[2]

---

[1] Copied in 1975 from the original at David Higham Associates, now missing.
[2] The fee offered was 250 guineas (£262.10s).

Ways of Escape
1949–53

In the spring of 1949 the Thomases moved back to Wales, to the Boat House at Laugharne, bought and nominally rented to them by Margaret Taylor. Soon after, their third child, Colm, was born. The return to Wales, which Thomas seemed to anticipate as a solution, had little or no effect on the deepening chaos of his domestic life. He began to write poetry again, and worked, in the end successfully, on the 'play for voices' that became *Under Milk Wood*. But his life with Caitlin was stormy, and he was either unable or unwilling to make any serious attempt to live within his income. An invitation to read poetry in New York City led to a three-month tour of North America, when, for the first time, he had a taste of popular fame, and earned nearly £3000. The money went on expenses or otherwise ran through his fingers. The United States became, like the Boat House, a place of intended escape that led him back only to himself and a conviction that his powers were failing.

E. J. EVANS
8th May 1949   The Boat House Laugharne Carmarthenshire

Dear Sir,

Please forgive my not having answered your letter before this. I have just come back to Wales to live, and letters have been misforwarded.

I shall be most grateful if you will include my name in the list of those who are supporting the appeal to the Prime Minister for a Civil List Pension to be awarded to Huw Menai.[1] I have the greatest admiration for him—though I do not know him personally—for his work, and I think the Port Talbot Forum is to be congratulated on its sponsoring of the appeal —which I do most sincerely hope will succeed.

                              Yours faithfully,
                              Dylan Thomas

TS: J. M. Dent

DAVID HIGHAM
9 May 1949   The Boat House Laugharne Carmarthenshire

Dear David,

Very many apologies for not having sent back the Fortune Press agreement long ago. As you will see from the above address, I have moved back to Wales, & unfortunately forgot to leave a forwarding address in the South Leigh post-office so that nothing was sent to me here. I've arranged things with the P.O. now. But, for the future, my permanent (as possible) headquarters is as above. Enclosed, the Fortune agreement.

I also enclose letter & contracts from Columbia Records Inc., N.Y. These will explain themselves. If you think the contracts satisfactory, will you send them back to me to sign & I will send them to you, signed, by return.[2]

I hope to get a real *lot* of work done here, & have already started. I must get a book ready this year.

---

[1] Huw Owen Williams (1888–1961), poet. E. J. Evans, of Port Talbot, had asked Thomas for his support.
[2] Columbia were issuing an album of records, of poets reading their own work, under the title 'Pleasure Dome'. Thomas's contribution was to last five minutes.

I will try to come up to London abt once a month, & will let you know beforehand so that, if possible, we can meet for a few minutes to discuss things.

Apologies again for great delay.

Yours,
Dylan

MS: Texas

DAVID HIGHAM
9 May 1949   The Boat House Laugharne Carmarthenshire

Dear David,
I want to buy some review-clippings from an American Literary Clipping Service. I enclose the forms as sent to me. The Service tells me they have, already, 70 American reviews awaiting me. I should like to buy what they call '250 Economy' clippings for 14 dollars, but do not know how to send the money to America. Can it be done by your office through Ann Watkins, & the price deducted from some future cheque of mine? I hope so. I shd very much like to see those 70 reviews.

Incidentally, I have been asked to America to lecture this coming autumn or next spring;[1] perhaps we can discuss this when we meet, as I hope, next month.

Yours,
Dylan

MS: Texas

MARGARET TAYLOR
Tuesday [postmarked May 11] [1949]   Boat House

My dear Margaret,
I should have written. I have been meaning to write each day. I've been wanting to write, but have put it off and off. Oh, all those bells were cracked long ago! They ring like dustbins! But it's true that each day since coming to this place I love and where I want to live and where I can work and where I have started work (my own) already, I've been saying to my contemptible self, You must write to Margaret at once to say that this is *it*: the place, the house, the workroom,[2] the time. I can never thank you

---

[1] See page 708.
[2] The Boat House is below a cliff, almost at sea level. Thomas's workroom was a small hut, a former bicycle shed, adjoining the public path that ran along the top of the cliff.

enough for making this fresh beginning possible by all the trust you have put in me, by all the gifts you have made me, by all your labour & anxiety in face of callous & ungrateful behaviour. I know that the only way to express my deep deep gratitude is to be happy & to write. Here I am happy and writing. All I shall write in this water and tree room on the cliff, every word, will be my thanks to you. I hope to God it will be good enough. I'll send you all I write. And ordinary letters too, full of trees & water & gossip & no news. This isn't that kind of letter. This is only the expression of the greatest gratitude in the world: you have given me a life. And now I am going to live it.

Dylan

MS: Texas   *SL*

DAVID HIGHAM
May 16 1949 (Sends signed Columbia contracts. See Appendix 51.)

ELWYN EVANS
May 21 1949   The Boat House Laugharne Carmarthenshire

Dear Mr. Evans,

   Thank you so much for your letter. I have, as you see, moved back to Wales to live, and I hope I'll be able, now, to broadcast occasionally in the Welsh Home Service.

   And I *would*, sometime, like to do that proposed talk on Manley Hopkins, but I daren't undertake any new work like that—for even a 15 minutes talk on a poet would take me a long time to write—for some time to come. I don't suppose you'd like me to give a reading from some poet connected with Wales—say Edward Thomas, or W. H. Davies? I'd love to do that—particularly Thomas—& could make a good selection with just a few notes or comments.

   Probably that isn't the sort of thing you want at all. In which case, I'm awfully sorry—& I do hope one day I can write a talk for you.

Yours sincerely,
Dylan Thomas

MS: BBC

WILFRED GRANTHAM[1]
28 May 1949　　　　　The Boat House　Laugharne　Carmarthenshire

Dear Mr. Grantham,

I owe you very many apologies for what must seem my appalling rudeness in never having acknowledged your letters about the previous scheduling of *The Plain Dealer*. I didn't receive your telegrams until well after the time you wanted the script, as I had been away from this address, moving all over Wales so that no letters or anything could be forwarded. And then I fell ill, & still am ill. But these miserable facts are, I know, no excuse for not having word sent to you. I can only say that I felt, & feel, so perfectly bloody that I just groaned at all my obligations & put my head under the blankets.

And now, the worst thing is that I really *dare* not promise my adaptation by June 9th. I can try, here in bed, to write but am so uncertain of my insides that I may fold up halfway through. Please do try to accept my apologies, difficult though that is in face of all the bother (& worse) that I have caused you. I *hope* to be fit again *very* soon, & to send you the script next month; but I daren't take the risk of promising it by this new date, & then, perhaps at the last moment, failing you. I hope this is clear, if regretful: I am full of doctor's dope.

And I do hope that the BBC will be lenient enough to give me a later date for this job—a job I very much want to do.

More apologies are useless, but, though unsaid, are nevertheless most genuine.

Yours sincerely,
Dylan Thomas

MS: BBC

JOHN MALCOLM BRINNIN
May 28 1949　　　　The Boat House　Laugharne　Carmarthenshire　Wales

Brinnin (b. 1916) was a poet and lecturer who in 1949 became director of the Poetry Center at the Young Men's and Young Women's Hebrew Association, New York City. An admirer of Thomas's work, one of his first acts as a patron with a purse was to invite him to read at the Center, for a fee of $500; he also offered to help arrange other readings. It was the invitation that Thomas had been hankering after since 1945.

Dear John Malcolm Brinnin,

Let me first of all apologise for not having answered your letter long before this.

---

[1] Grantham was the BBC producer now in charge of the *Plain Dealer* project. Thomas had been paid part of the 100-guinea fee for adapting the play and acting in it. No script was written.

Secondly, thank you most sincerely for your letter.

And thirdly, accept with great pleasure the invitation of the Poetry Center of your institution to come to the United States to give a reading of my poems.

About the first: I've been changing addresses, a lot, lately, and mail has been erratically forwarded. I had your letter only last week—but even then I should have answered it at once.

About the second: I feel extremely honoured to be the first poet to be invited from abroad, who was not already a visitor, and delighted too. I've wanted, for some time, to come to the States, and there couldn't be a pleasanter way of coming than this.

And about the third: I should like to come to New York to give my reading early in 1950, probably in January or February. I should be only too glad to accept your sponsorship and to read in other places, including California.

Now about the financial side of it: I quite understand that you, as a non-profit-making organisation, must work on a modest budget, and, apart from transatlantic expenses, I should be prepared to accept, for my reading at your headquarters in New York, any fee that you yourselves think adequate. I must, however, point out that I have no private money, that I will arrive in New York with almost none and therefore must, by other arrangements made by you, make money immediately. I myself am very inefficient at arranging any financial details, but I am seeing my London literary agent next month & will ask him to get in touch with Ann Watkins Ltd of New York, with whom he is associated: she will then get in touch with you.[1] I hope, also, that Ann Watkins will be able to fix up a few other jobs for me, outside of your sponsorship, so that I shall be able to bring back some money to England. I mention this—that I must bring back some money to England—because, in order to come to America, I shall, of course, have to refuse literary and broadcast commissions here for some months. And when I return to England, I shall be, more or less, starting off again, picking up scripts etc. here & there.

I hope I'm not writing confusedly: I've had influenza, and am full of injections.

I should like to stay in the States for about three months.

Does that cover most of the points? I hope so. And I hope I'll hear from you soon again.

And, again, apologies for this overdue reply; & many many thanks for the honour you have paid me.

Yours sincerely,
Dylan Thomas

MS: Delaware   *SL*

---

[1] Brinnin acted as agent and took a percentage of earnings from the first tour. In his *Dylan Thomas in America* he pointed out that the costs he had to meet from his own pocket, such as phone calls and telegrams, meant he received only token payment.

DAVID TENNANT
July 3 1949   The Boat House Laugharne Carmarthenshire

Dear David,
  That was wonderfully good of you. It has made a chunk of peace. I can now go out without my mask. Thank you sincerely, David. I'm sorry your land's unsteady too, and doubly grateful that, at such a time, you could throw me such a big bit of the landslide. It's sweet to be able to go out in the daytime again. I have got terrible pains in my big toe, which I am too poor to call gout but which feels very much like it. And it also hurts to pee, about which I dare not think at all. I wish one day you could come down to this part, a lovely part. There are three herons now in front of my window, all looking like Edith Sitwell. I have to come to London next month, for a broadcast, for only 2 days, & will look in, hoping very very much that you will be there. Thanks again, and for always. It has made an enormous difference.

                                             Yours,
                                             Dylan

TS: J. M. Dent

ELWYN EVANS
July 3 1949 (Promises copyright details for reading. See Appendix 52.)

DAVID HIGHAM
July 8 1949 [telegram from Laugharne][1]

LETTER IN POST EXPLAINING PEER GYNT ABSURD SITUATION
DYLAN

---

[1] Copied in 1975 from the original at David Higham Associates, now missing.

DAVID HIGHAM
July 9th 1949   The Boat House Laugharne Carmarthenshire

Dear David,
    Peer Gynt.
    I was told of no dead-line date.
    I have received, from Miss Ramsden, a literal translation of only *two* of
five acts. Am I to learn Norwegian & translate the other three acts for
myself?
    And, most important of all, I should like to bring this to the attention
of the B.B.C.:
    Louis MacNeice is translating a work of similar stature to Peer Gynt:
Goethe's Faust. For this, the B.B.C. has allowed him one whole year,
during which time no other work is expected from him. On top of a
special fee, he is, for that year, paid his usual B.B.C. salary, which means
that he is not obliged, for that year, to do any other work.
    I, on the other hand, am expected to produce a five act play in a few
months, for a fee not sufficiently large to allow me to devote *all* my time
to this work. Far from it. And now the B.B.C. is cutting up rough at a time
when not *half* of the literal translation has been given me.
    I bring in MacNeice's case only because I think that the BBC is treating
him fairly and can expect a thorough & painstaking job. Peer Gynt is just
as difficult to work upon as is Goethe's Faust. Both are enormous plays.
Why should one have to be scamped through insufficient money & time?
    Perhaps I should have insisted, earlier, on a long & elastic period of
time in which to do this work. But certainly I have to insist now. I cannot
begin to work upon the play until the whole literal translation is in my
hands. And then, by the very magnitude of the job, it is bound to take a
long time.
    Also: MacNeice is translating Faust in the only way possible for a non-
German scholar. He is going through the text, line by line, word by word,
with the German expert who is supplying the literal translation. Only in
this way can he appreciate the texture of the German; & do justice to its
word-music.
    Maybe it is not in order for me to parallel MacNeice's case with mine.
But I am certain that the way he is working upon Faust, & the time he is
allowed for that work, & the money he is paid, should also be the way in
which I shd work upon this important & complex play.
    If the BBC decide to cancel my contract, then they must. And somehow
we must pay them back the £150 I have been advanced. But if they think
that someone else can trot out a translation in the very short [?space] of
time they have allowed me, then they must, of necessity, be content with
an inferior job.
    Perhaps you can convey to them some of these—to me—most
justifiable points?
    And forgive me if I am, for once, riding a high horse.

I *want* to do Peer Gynt. But it *must* take a *long* time. It must because it is a great play, and I am not prepared to hack it out to a ridiculous time limit.

Hoping to hear from you, & to see you later in the month.

Yours,
Dylan

MS: Texas

ELWYN EVANS
13 July 1949 (Sends Edward Thomas script. See Appendix 53.)

JEAN LEROY
15 July 1949 (Accepts Edward Thomas fee. See Appendix 54.)

HECTOR MACIVER
15 July 1949   The Boat House Laugharne Carmarthenshire

Dear Hector,

Thank you for the school magazine. I was sorry to see no picture of you in charge of any athletic group, but enjoyed the 'Chant' and 'A Group of Trees'. K.M. certainly has something there; and the echoes, though I cannot place where they come from, seem to me not unpleasant. But, indeed, he might be very good. The Anonymous author of 'Chant' I would, myself, take to be a far older boy with a taste for Scotch, though I may be entirely wrong. I read the Rector's letter, and am delighted not to be in his school.

Did the books from Dent reach you safely? Do let me know some time. If they didn't, I shall write Dent an indecent, but icy, card.

I don't know if I can be in London at the end of the month, but, if I can, very certainly will. *Would you send me a line to say when & where you'll be?* I'd like to know beforehand so that I could try to get a little job to do in London on or about that date to pay my fares & some, at least, of my expenses.

I am writing this with a vile Biro junior which cuts through paper & table-top, spits greased mock-ink at shirt, eye, and wall, and whose writing fades, sometimes conveniently, almost at once.[1]

---

[1] Ballpoint pens were coming into general use. Some of Thomas's letters, written with early models on cheap paper, are difficult to read.

My study, atelier, or bard's bothy, roasts on a cliff-edge.

My wife is just about to go to the infirmary to have a Thomas. There are not enough of them already.

And now I'm going to greet the unseen with some beer.

Don't forget the postcard.

Yours,
Dylan

I've just realised that I have a broadcast to do in Cardiff on July 29th, and could, if you were in England, join you in London on the 30th.

MS: National Library of Scotland

DAVID HIGHAM
15th July 1949   The Boat House Laugharne Carmarthenshire

Apologies for this dreadful Biro pen

Dear David,

Thank you for your long, & lucid, letter of the 13th.

I do agree that what we really want is a little more consultation, between you & me, before I commit myself to any major job with a time-limit on it. And in the future I'll see to it that we do have a chance to confer.

But now I'm afraid that, in spite of the BBC postponing their limit to Sept 30, I still have to say that I can't do it. The last 3 acts have just arrived from Miss Ramsden: I couldn't do the vast amount of work on them that is necessary in 2½ months. I had begun to do preliminary work on Act One when your letter came. And I *had*, on the original receipt of the first 2 acts, written to Miss Ramsden about them.

Would the BBC allow me to keep Miss Ramsden's translation & work on it when I can throughout this year, setting no time-limit but allowing me to do the best job I *can* do on it *in my own time*? I should be most grateful if they could.

About the return of the money: I do not see how, at this moment, the matter can be arranged. Gainsborough Films still have £150 coming to me, but I would rather let them pay me this in due course rather than ask them, officially, now. I can, however, try unofficially, myself, through Ralph Keene.

I am just beginning the 1st treatment for Gainsborough of a technicolor film of 'Vanity Fair'[1] (with, dear God, Maggie Lockwood) & there shd be lots in that eventually. But at the moment I don't see where the money to refund the BBC is to come from. My wife is just about to have another

---

[1] A project to film *Vanity Fair*, starring Margaret Lockwood, on which Thomas did some work.

baby—it is a few days overdue[1]—and I'll need all I can get. What do you think?

I hope to be able to see you next week.

Yours,
Dylan

MS: Texas

WILFRED GRANTHAM
July 15 1949   The Boat House Laugharne Carmarthenshire

Dear Mr. Grantham,

I'm sorry as anything, but the reason you've had no word from me of the 'Plain Dealer'—&, what is worse, no script—is, still, this persistent gastritis of mine which I'm about to have X-rayed for many an ulcerous fear.[2] And I daren't promise it by August 15th in case I'm whizzed away to hospital. It's not such a long job, I know, but I do feel so bloody. I hope that, again, the BBC will be lenient with me & not, yet, demand back the half of my fee which I have already been paid. I may, indeed, be able to do the job by the required date, it may take a very short time to do, but what is that to the planners? I apologise for this useless letter, & plead for leniency.

Yours sincerely,
Dylan Thomas

MS: BBC

JOHN DAVENPORT
30 July 1949   Boat House Laugharne Carmarthenshire

My dear John,

Arrived back, rather bruised, to find the financial situation here far worse than even I, in my tearful jags of the last week, cd have imagined. They've stopped sending coal, & will, any moment, stop sending milk: essential things in a baby-packed, freezing house. I'm summonsed for rates. No more meat. I cannot write a cheque, of course, so that we are—for the first time for years—literally without one shilling. Four cheques

---

[1] The child, a boy, was born at Carmarthen, 24 July 1949. He was named Colm Garan; the second name is Welsh for 'heron'.

[2] It was becoming harder to distinguish Thomas's bouts of genuine ill-health from the excuses for editors that increasingly he had to make. By now the BBC was very suspicious of him.

have been returned from the Savage, but without savage comment. And my father is dangerously ill with pneumonia; and I've had some sort of breakdown. Christ!

So if you do ever come across anyone—*excluding* Tony,[1] to whom I write separately, & about a different matter—with a single fiver to spare, it would make a difference. Or suggest anyone to whom I could write. The Tony-Liddel-Bank thing will work some time, for I shall be forced to go to America, God help me, my breakdown, & my guts, but it's *now*, at *once, temporarily*, the nine quid for milk, the ten for coal, six for builder, eight for summons, without mentioning cigarettes for Cat, sweets for Aeron etc. If you do see anyone interested, *please*, old boy. For any amount. To be paid after America. Can you also, please, send me Wyn Henderson's address?

How are you?

I'm on the *rim*.

Thanks to Marjorie[2] for her dinners & kindnesses.

Love,
Dylan

Am sending letter to Tony (which is only to corroborate the Liddel arrangement) care of you.

MS: Texas

MARGARET TAYLOR
Friday August 5 49   Boat House

My dear Margaret,

I haven't been up to the main street for over 2 days, ever since coming back, via Swansea & Vernon, from Cardiff. And your registered letter — though there *was* no letter, only those great green things I hadn't seen for so long—had arrived before I called at Brown's this morning. There I heard that you'd left me an urgent message to ring you: but this morning it was days too late, & so I must inadequately write. I hope the message wasn't terribly, [?stranglingly] important. And thank you ten times for this morning. I didn't know what to do, & one of the main reasons I didn't go out was fear of debts snapping at my heels. Thank you a great deal, & once I am again out of the money-wood, in the straight & pounded clear—though it will, as I said in nasty London, be ten weeks—may I be able to repay some of my now almost national debt to you.

Caitlin is awfully well. I do hope you got her letter. She gave me, just before leaving hospital, several letters—to ·mothers, sisters, &

---

[1] 'Tony' was probably an affluent acquaintance, introduced several years earlier by Mervyn Levy, with whom Levy served in the Army.

[2] Davenport's second wife.

yourself—to post, but only yesterday I came across, in a pocket packed with fag-ends, a letter to Ringwood. I trust that was the only one that missed the letterbox.

Colum[1] Garan—Welsh for heron. Did Cat tell you?—looks just like any other baby I've seen, skinned and fragile, though Caitlin says he looks just like my father. Apart from the baldness, I see no resemblance.

Swansea was very noisy. Dan, Vernon, Fred, & I are to do a halfhour broadcast together from Wales some time next month. I'll let you know when, in case you can pick up the station which is mostly preacher & choirs.

I'm writing this in the heaven of my hut. Wild day, big seas for Laugharne, & the boats of the Williamses lurching exactly like Williamses.

Write soon. I have no news. I am beginning to work hard again. Llewelyn goes to Lundy next week.[2]

And the thanks I can never express, again, for the help by which I can do the shopping, pay the girl, walk out at all into the best town.

> Yours ever,
> Dylan

MS: Texas

G. V. ROBERTS
5 August 1949 (Accepts invitation from Tenby Arts Club. See Appendix 55.)

PRINCESS CAETANI[3]
6 August 1949   The Boat House Laugharne Carmarthenshire

Dear Madame di Sermoneta,
    I am very very sorry not to have answered, long before this, your letter of the end of June. I didn't want to say that I could send you a poem until I was quite sure I could; and I wasn't sure until I finished, only this week, the poem I enclose.[4]

---

[1] Thomas often wrote 'Colm' as it was pronounced.
[2] Thomas's sister and her husband were living on Lundy Island, in the Bristol Channel.
[3] Marguerite Caetani (1880–1963), also known as the Duchess of Sermoneta. As Marguerite Chapin of Connecticut she married the Italian Roffredo Caetani, Prince of Bassiano, in 1911. A patron of the arts, she published many important writers in two literary magazines that she financed and edited, *Commerce* (1924–32) and later *Botteghe Oscure*, which means 'dark shops' and was named after the district of Rome where she lived.
[4] 'Over Sir John's hill', published in *Botteghe Oscure IV* (December 1949). The Boat House faces the hill, half a mile away across the sands. Thomas wrote the poem, his first for two years, to celebrate his return to Laugharne.

The cheque you so very kindly sent on account of the poem—which I should, of course, have acknowledged—was more welcome than perhaps you could imagine. I had, myself, been ill and was, and am, in debt; and the cheque did really help. I would be most grateful if I could be sent any more small amount of money that is, maybe, due, on the poem, as soon as possible: I have a just-born new son, & there are so many things that are needed. I hope that this doesn't sound too grasping, especially after your first kindness and after my carelessly not replying to it.

Can I print this poem separately in an English magazine, or does your review also circulate in England?

Thank you very much for sending me a copy of the review, which had some magnificent poems.

Yours very sincerely,
Dylan Thomas

MS: Camillo Caetani Foundation

DAVID HIGHAM
Monday [mid August 1949] The Boat House Laugharne Carmarthenshire

Dear David,

Thank you very much indeed for the arrangement you have managed to make by which, for seven weeks, I can be paid £10 a week.[1] And for the first cheque. I haven't written before to acknowledge this, but did send a wire, fully approving the idea, last week—I do hope you got it, otherwise you must think me more careless than I really am.

I hope, by the end of the 7th week—or is it eight weeks? I'm writing this on the sand in the sun, & your letter isn't to hand—that I shall [have] finished my final script for Gainsborough & that, if only temporarily, my financial position will be upright again.

In the meantime, those cheques of £10 a week will save our lives. Thank you for making them possible.

I hope to see you soon, in London, but not until the script is finished.

Thank you for the Caton agreement,[2] which arrived separately.

Yours,
Dylan

P.S. I hope Mrs Taylor, for all her kindness, is not becoming a nuisance.

MS: Texas

[1] Higham had withheld money from tax demands which may have proved less than anticipated.
[2] The repurchase of rights in *18 Poems* for £150. N. Caton was a director of Fortune Press.

PRINCESS CAETANI
11th October 1949   The Boat House Laugharne Carmarthenshire

Dear Madame di Sermoneta,
    If I were to write down the number of apologies I owe to you, it would
sound, I'm afraid, all too false and ridiculous:— nobody, one might think,
could say that he was sincerely sorry so many times and still be sincere
about it. So let me, for the moment, apologise only for not having
answered your letter of September 23rd, nor acknowledged the very kind
and very welcome cheque enclosed in it, nor even replied at once to your
note of October 4th. There are lots and lots of reasons for all this
appallingly rude delay of mine, but all so small, and contradictory, and
confusing, I hardly dare name them. The letter to Witney, Oxfordshire,
was long being forwarded to the above address in Wales, which is where I
live; I have been away from home, unnecessarily broadcasting and
lecturing; I have been ill, and depressed; I have missed the times of the
post; I have carried letters around in my pockets for days; I have had so
many really small, difficult, pokey, little jobs of work to do I have spent
my time trotting and braying from one to the other and back again like a
donkey stung by wasps. And there [are] many many more equally trivial,
but momentarily insurmountable, obstacles to prevent my just being able
to sit down calmly for a minute and write to you and thank you and to
hope that we *will*, somehow, in spite of all the time that has frittered
away, be able to meet in London before you leave.
    You said, in your note of the 4th, that you wd be staying in London at
least a fortnight. When—if you know it now—is the *really* last day on
which we could meet? The 19th & the 20th are impossible to me: I talk to
two Welsh societies on those dates—and about God knows what.
    But I do so hope that somehow I may be able to come to London & meet
you after that, or just before. Nothing is easy. This is eight hours from
London. I am tangled in hack-work. Depression has me by the ears. And
there are other reasons too, locusts of them. But, perhaps, it *may* still be
managed.
    I am very glad you liked the poem I sent you. Alas, I have not finished
another: these damned little fly-paper jobs I have to do keep me stuck
from my work. But when I manage to finish the poem now half completed, it is yours to print. And thank you for what you said about the
other poem.
    Perhaps, if I'm ever forgiven, I shall hear from you soon about the
possibility of our meeting?
    And a sea of sorries again.

                                        Sincerely Yours,
                                        Dylan Thomas

MS: Camillo Caetani Foundation

DAVID HIGHAM
11 Oct 1949   The Boat House Laugharne Carmarthenshire

Dear David,

Thank you for your summary of the points we discussed in your office.[1]

I enclose the first letter I had from John Malcolm Brinnin in America. The second I can find nowhere. All I remember of the second letter was that it said the fee for my recital at the headquarters of the Y.M.Y.W. Hebrew Association wd be 500 dollars: inclusive. This was written after I had said I would go to read there. I should very much like to know if the 500 dollars is supposed to include my fare out to the States. And also, of course, I must be absolutely sure of several other really worth-while engagements there before I *do* go. I want to come back to England with some dollars. Also, as I told you, I want to take my wife. I hope Ann Watkins is dealing with these points now.

Has that income-tax £10 a week I was receiving now come to an end? I didn't receive the usual letter & cheque today. I hope to God it hasn't: I can't continue without it: bills are *piling* up here: the worst bill is £50 for school- fees: and I'm afraid I was extremely optimistic when I said I would finish V.Fair ten days from our last meeting. It is going very stickily at the moment—though soon will, I hope, race ahead. *Do* please see what can be done: either a continuation, somehow, of that tenner a week or a possible advance on the Verona-printed poems (which I see advertised for February publication in Dent's catalogue. At the price of £5.0.0. Who'll buy?). Really, it's urgent.

No other point that I can think of.

Yours,
Dylan

MS: Texas

JOHN DAVENPORT
11 Oct 1949   Boat House Laugharne Carmarthenshire

My Dear John,

A scruffy note from a scruffy man. And, too, to tell you that I *haven't* finished that poem I promised for Arena: [*in margin*: Next number of Arena for certain] there's lots of work to do on it, and, instead of doing it, I've been getting on with my awful script,[2] broadcasting from Swansea

---

[1] Higham had tried to construct a plan of action for the conventionally successful freelance writer that he hoped Thomas had inside him, struggling to get out. It included *Vanity Fair* ('to be finished in about 10 days'), *The Plain Dealer* ('not to take more than a month'), *Peer Gynt* ('to be ready by the end of the year'), the U.S. visit (followed by 'a full year at your own work so far as possible, beginning with the completion of the *Skin Trade*'), 'the small effort required to collect material for the book for Dent', and Thomas's radio play.

[2] The slow-moving *Under Milk Wood*, still a long way from acquiring that title.

with Dan Jones & the boys[1]—Dan conducts the London Philharmonic in a performance of his 1st Symphony in the S'sea Festival of Music next week; this week, Wed or Thur, is conducting three tone-poems of his on the Welsh Regional (three!)—and being a pest up the wilds here, Mydrim, Brechfa, & Marble Town. But, as soon as I finish it, I'll send it to you, Jack, & Randall whom I thank, v much, for their wire to which I should have replied had not etc.[2]

I'm sorry I saw so little of you in London last, which sounds a compliment but is really a grief. I may be up in a fortnight & will write, ring, or just glaze in.

Ever,
Dylan

MS: Texas

JOHN DAVENPORT   Boat House Laugharne
[?1949]

Dear Comrade,[3]

I was sorry to miss you when I was up in the smoke last week, I was quite looking forward to a good chat about Arena in the 'local', but you know how it is, I got caught up with rewording a petition against decadent tendencies in the cultural field, I expect you'll be having a copy to sign any day now, I hope you'll agree with subsection 4, it was my idea, I had the hell of a job getting it past, I can tell you, they thought it was a bit individualist, but that's them all over. Bert and I had a regular square-up, but he came over to my way of thinking once we got down the old Coal Hole, I had him almost laughing at the end. 'You poets'll be the death of me,' was all he could say. There's more to Bert than meets the eye, I happen to know as a matter of fact he often listens to the Third but for Christ's sake don't let on I told you, he's as sensitive as a kid about being tough and anti-pansy—remember when he threw his beer all over that chap with long hair in that boozer near Kew Gardens? Mind, I don't say he didn't deserve it, but it's his own hair, I said, remember, he can do what he likes with it so far as I'm concerned. But here I am rambling on, & there's work to be done. I've got a little meeting in the back room of Brown's tonight, Ivy Williams is going to be chairman, you wouldn't think she was with us, would you? She's hot, I can tell you. We're trying

[1] 'Swansea and the Arts', a discussion—carefully scripted in advance—with Thomas as presenter. The others taking part were Vernon Watkins, John Prichard, Dan Jones and Fred Janes. Recorded at Swansea October 6, broadcast (Welsh Home Service) October 24.

[2] Jack Lindsay and Randall Swingler were the editors (with Davenport) of *Arena*, 'a literary magazine interested in Values'.

[3] Some of Thomas's friends have claimed him as a serious socialist. But he was happier parodying the Left than supporting it.

to organise a Left Library in the snooker room, I know it sounds small beer, but by God you don't know this burg or do you? It's true bloody blue to the core, even the workers vote Liberal and as for listening to a word against *dear* Winston—a chap almost knocked me down last week for saying this was a slave state, and he was only a lorry driver, too, earning four quid odd, it's uphill work down here I can tell you, and there's hardly any time left to get on with the old poetry. But still I've got a new one ticking over, it's going to be something pretty big, I hope, a kind of colloquial Lycidas set in the Rhondda valley.

I'll be painting London red again—& do I mean it—on Jan second. See you then.

Dyl

MS: Texas   SL

JAMES LAUGHLIN
October 13th 1949   The Boat House Laugharne Carmarthenshire
                                                                        Wales

                                                  (Thomas-hunting begins)
Dear Jay,
   Have you heard that I'm supposed to be coming to the States in February 1950? I've been asked, by John Malcolm Brinnin—what's he like?—to read, grandly and solemnly, like a man with the Elgin marbles in his mouth, poems to the Y.M. & Y.W.H.A. at New York on, I think, February 23. Brinnin said that he could also fix up a few more readings in various parts, including California. Do you know of any people, places, institutions, etc. from whom or which, by reading aloud modern British poems and a few, as few as possible, of my own, I could get a handful of dollars? Ann Watkins is seeing to the Brinnin side: which, if his letters are any proof, is what he has. Perhaps, if anything occurred to you, you could have a word with, or drop a line to her? I'd be very, very grateful. I want to stay in the States for three months. And I want to be able to return to England with some money so that I won't, at once, have to chase again the hackjobs by which, dear Christ, I live, have at once to set into motion again the insignificant, wheezy little machines that sausage out crumbs and coppers for me, scriptlings, radio whinnies. I don't want to find myself in New York with only two or three scantily paying engagements in front of me, and to return as broke as when I arrived. We have a new, three months' old son. I would, naturally, have to support him, my other two children at school, and my wife, for the three months of my absence. I should like to be able to bring my wife with me. Would that be possible, do you think? I don't want to load you with all my worries and apprehensions, but whom else do I load? The idea of the

States puts the fear of Mammon in me, though I very much want to come. Briefly, can you help, in a practical way, to alleviate the worries of my visit? How, I don't know. But do write and tell me something soon, if you will. Maybe I should be writing like this to Brinnin, not to you. But you I know, all nine feet of you, as I remember, and me in my abbreviated coat, and Godfrey Winn popping out like a Jill in the Box.[1] If I cannot bring my wife, then I must leave with her money enough for three English (or Welsh) enormously costly months! And how the hell am I to do that?

Here, we can nearly carry on by my drivelling for films & radio. Without me, the Boat House sinks, the cormorants have it. Indeed, I can hardly, now, walk up the main street of this sad, lovely town without the bowler-hatted shags at my throat and ankles.

So please do write. Suggest what you can. Say what you like.

I have a couple of poems; and a few autobiographical sketches which, perhaps, you could try to place for me in the commercial magazines. I'll send them on when they are found, washed, and typed.

There are, I suppose, no chances of a reading on the radio? Why should there be?

I want to enjoy my visit, and come back rustling, if wobbly.

Yours,
Dylan

MS: the recipient   SL

JOHN DAVENPORT
13 October 1949   The Boat House Laugharne Carmarthenshire

Dear John,

I've only now remembered that I addressed my yesterday's letter to you at Rossetti Mansions. It might not reach you. This, then, to make doubly sure, is to apologise for the fact that I haven't yet completed the promised poem for Arena, and to say that it will be ready for the next number and that the fee will be at least one crippling port, large, in the Savage or the Authors' now that Kingsmill is dead and being cut by Dickens. And please to thank Jack & Randall for the telegram, and yourself, of course. Things are appalling here, which can only mean one thing. Bills and demand notes, at me like badgers, whoosh! up the manholes, or gathered, grinning and panting round my bed, odiously familiar, like the little hyenas in Paphnutius's cell.[2] It is bad in a small community where everything is known: temporary insolvency goes the glad rounds as swift as a miscarriage. I owe a quarter's rent on my mother's house, Llewelyn's school fees (for last term), much to each tradesman. Yesterday I broke a

[1] Godfrey Winn (1908–71), popular columnist.
[2] St Paphnutius, an Egyptian monk, much persecuted.

tooth on a minto. There are rats in the lavatory, tittering while you shit, and the official rat-man comes every day to given them tidbits before the kill. Unfortunately for my peace of mind, the rat man has only one arm. [...], the biggest prig in Wales, is coming to see me on Saturday about something priggish, with his [...] and his thirstlessness, looking about him, prigbrows lifted, in my fuggy room like an unloved woman sniffing at the maid's linen on the maid's day out. I am three months behind with my filmscript, a year behind with Peer Gynt. I have the hot & cold, rose-flush comings & goings after elderberry wine last night in a hamhooked kitchen with impossibly rich, and thunderingly mean, ferret-faced farmers who dislike me so much they treat me like a brother. At last the National Insurance has caught up with me who has never put a stamp on his card, having no card. If you see anyone likely, pinch his boots for me. I cannot come to London to hunt, for obvious reasons. Indeed, I dare not step out. This morning I had a toadstool for breakfast, and Caitlin called me a guttersnipe, though there seemed to be no connection. I'm sorry to write you such mournings. See you at the barracudas.

Love,
Dylan

MS: Texas   *SL(R)*

JEAN LEROY
16 October 1949 (Accepts Swansea programme fee. See Appendix 56.)

PRINCESS CAETANI
2nd November 1949   The Boat House Laugharne Carmarthenshire

Dear Madame di Sermoneta,
   I did enjoy, very much, meeting in London, though, to me, the meetings were all too brief and few. That, I feel, is entirely my fault. In London I am flustered, excited, unable to concentrate; I am so nervous, usually for no reason, that my nervousness too often turns to unintentional rudeness; I am stupid, shy, and garrulously arrogant in turn; all I seem to want to do is to get away from where I am and from what I am doing, however much I might like where I am and what I am doing; I can almost never say what I really mean to say; I am out of my world —though what that world may be, God knows—altogether. And it is for these reasons, and for many others, I am sure, which I am not, myself, perceptive enough to see, that our meetings *were* so brief, so very few.

So let me apologise, from this calm distance from London, for what must have appeared to be my vague and pointless behaviour and—what is worse—my ingratitude.

I wanted to talk to you about your magazine, and to hear you talk about it; I wanted to discuss with you several things in it that seemed to me to be of particular interest; I wanted to suggest to you the names of a few little-known English writers whose work I thought you might like to see.

And, instead of that, all I could do was to talk, disconnectedly, about myself, scatter you with ash, gollup your whisky-&-soda, make an inexact arrangement with you about a short story of my own, and then rush off into the London night I loathe.

But let me, anyway, and in writing, try to make exact the position of the story which I am to write for Botteghe. The next story I write is to be given to you immediately. In our conversation—if you can grace with that word a jumble of ineptitudes from myself and some kind words from you—you gave me no time-limit by which the story should reach you. If you care to give me a rough time-limit, I shall abide by that. The story I will try to make as good as I can.

And you, do you remember, agreed to pay me, in advance, for that story, the sum of £100. And there is, of course, no further money than that due to me from Botteghe for that story.

You gave me a cheque for £50, and said that you could send on the remaining £50 very soon.

I hope I am right in my interpretation of our agreement.

And now I come to the most shamefaced part of this shamefaced letter.

I need that other £50 so very desperately, so very quickly.

When I came home, thank God, from London, I found my wife ill, really ill, with worry over the summonses for debt that had been pouring into the house during my absence. The amount needed to clear them is, to us, enormous, insurmountable. But if I *could* possibly have that £50 *straight, straight* away, I could at least settle the most urgent and virulent debt of all.

I apologise for the horribly stilted manner in which I am writing to you. I, too, am too sick with money to feel, for a moment, free.

But all I mean is, I'm in a hell of a hole. I see no way of getting out of it. But that other money, if sent to me at once on the wings of the dove of the Air Mail from whatever country you are in, *would* help. (I was, of course, too careless, too conscienceless, to enquire from you where you were going when you left the Connaught Hotel. I can only hope this letter reaches you very soon.)

What self-pity I drench these pages in! How ghastly to read they must be! But all I can say, in any possible extenuation, is that, in all my moneyless days, I have never been more hopelessly engulfed in debt, that we can't sleep, and I can't work.

When I see you again, if ever, I can tell you, perhaps, what the hellish circumstances were. Now, however, there is no past tense: the hellish circumstances just *are*.

Thank you for your kindness in London.

Yours sincerely,
Dylan Thomas

MS: Camillo Caetani Foundation   SL

BBC
November 7th 1949   The Boat House Laugharne Carmarthenshire

Dear Sir,

I'm afraid this is a very bothering request, but I do hope you can help me.

A few years ago—perhaps in 1944, or 1945—I broadcast a talk, for the Welsh Children's Hour, called '*Memories of Childhood*'. To the best of my recollection, I broadcast it from Carmarthen, Mr Aneirin Talfan Davies producing.

Now I am making a collection, for publication in book form, of many of my old sketches and stories, and would like, very much, to include this particular one. Unfortunately, I have lost my only copy, and am wondering if you could dig out, from BBC files, the copy I used when broadcasting.

I'd be enormously obliged if you could help me. My publisher is waiting to get on with the book.

Yours faithfully,
Dylan Thomas

MS: BBC

HELEN and BILL MCALPINE
Saturday 12 Nov 49   Hut on Cliff

My dear two, Helen & Bill,

First, before apologies, messages of love, questions, and our tiny news, how more than pleased we are that the job's in the Billy-bag.[1] How sensible of them to recognise, when they saw him, the proper man. I'm always surprised when a bloody Body shows any sense at all. And how glad, too, will be your age-old friends in the township when, this Saturday night, I tell them in the great shining bars, the chromium Corporation, the Cross Club ('Dancing to Romaine & her Music'), the Back Room

---

[1] McAlpine was a scientific officer with the British Council.

Hotel. But nobody could be as delighted as I am. Except Caitlin. Congratulations from my dirty eyrie, from the Columed house, from all the statues of the herons: relations on a monument.

How is the wrist? I can't say Helen's wrist, Bill's job, when I'm writing to both of you. I must suppose that you are one and the same person: you are a scientific officer, you fell arse over tip while skating, you have been writing stories, you are grieved because you cannot use your sewing machine, you old bisexual you. You are plastered, your wrist is plastered. How long will it be before you can type and stitch, button your flies and your brassiere? Does it INTERFERE? Send details at once, preferably illustrated, in plain envelope.

How are the stories? Is the book of them ready yet? And are there any new ones I could be sent?

And can you both manage to come down here for Christmas? We want you to, very much. And so does everyone else. Not a day potters by but I'm asked news of you, I'm commanded to send wishes, greetings, amiable insults, coarse remarks, love. Phil, Marie, Driver Raye, Frank who lays eggs with his mouth, Fleming, Tommy (Nero) Rowlands, Ivy of course, Texan Ebie,[1] Dynamo Bill, Banjo Ned, the Irish teetotallers, fiend Aeron, Colum if he could, Llewelyn from his presumably masturbative dormitory, Jack Pierce, Billy Thomas, my father ('This is the end of civilisation!'), my mother ('Now don't think I'm interfering, dear, I just happened to be looking out of the window as you fell down Brown's steps'), people whose names I don't know, Tommy Gravel-Voice Williams, Up-it-Comes Gilbert, Ted and Norma (whose name should be spelt with a low whistle), Ivan, Shee, little battered men on Friday nights, the lecherous and patricidal ferrymen, dumb barber, all, all say, 'when are they coming down again?' and do not need to explain who they mean. I forgot wren-legged Tudor; he too. So if you can come for Christmas, not only the Boat House but all the barmy town will cheer and drink your health, happiness, and unique contribution, if I may phrase it so, to the life of lazy Laugharne. Send answer by return, preferably on an incredibly obscene postcard, preferably of blonde Lesbians, preferably in sexicolor.

Early this week, Ebie, laying his pistol down, and I went to Whitland Mart and bought three geese & a turkey. (Alas, only one goose is mine.) All alive. The buying took fifteen minutes, just after lunch, but, oddly, we didn't return till midnight, the birds in the boot savage and famished. Now they all live on the lawn back of Brown's, leering into the kitchen. We buy them Black Market grain at [...] St. Clears: also, little wicked chops, but those for us. We had a very farmerish day, and came back covered in manure, slapping little sticks against our thighs, talking turkey and a lot of cock. Ebie didn't get up till teatime next day, and then rushed off to be given medicine by his fancy woman, [...]. Next day he didn't get up at all.

---

[1] Ebie (variously spelt) and Ivy Williams kept Brown's Hotel.

My American plans are going ahead. I'm to read in the Museum of Modern Art, New York, & the Library of Congress, Washington, and several other places. I've been given a flat for my New York stay, in the centre of the city. The Gotham Book Mart is giving me a party on my arrival. I'm also to give a broadcast, & to spend a week at a Massachusetts Women's College oh my. I'm going to try to take Caitlin with me. Brigit has promised to have Colum for the 3 months, if necessary, and maybe Nancy & Gordon will take over the Boat House and look after Aeron, the innocents. So really all that stands in our way is money and red-tape permission. I hope Cat can come. She won't stay on in Laugharne if I do have to go alone, but can't think where to go. If I can't get permission to take her, perhaps she & Helen could fix up something together? Cat still isn't well, gets thinner and more nervous every day. I wish and I wish to God she would be well again. America may help, though it's a queer place for a rest-cure.

I wish I had been to Burton, and to the Goose Fair. The ear-rings are *very* nice.

This morning, a photographer, John Deakin, came down from London to take pictures of me for the new American magazine, terribly tasty, terribly glossy, rich as rich, he says, called Flair. He told me he has seen a dummy of it. Its manifesto is written in white ink on silver paper. The captions to some of its photographs are invisible; heat has to be applied to the blanks before the words appear. The cover is by Cocteau. Deakin, [...], took pictures of me in a high wind in the church cemetery, one of them inside the railings of a tomb,[1] my hair, uncut for months, either completely covering my face (I think he liked that) or blown up like a great, dancing, mousey busby. I look forward to seeing the pictures.

I have finished my poem, a hundred lines, but it may need a second part to it.[2]

Write soon & tell me everything. Our love to Fred. And very much to you both.

                                        Dylan

MS: Buffalo

---

[1] Thomas seems to be standing in the grave, with leaves to his waist, staring at the camera. It is among the best-known photographs of him.

[2] 'Poem on his birthday' was the only newly-written work of this length. If this is the poem meant, it was the second he had written since returning to Laugharne (the first was 'Over Sir John's hill'), and celebrates his thirty-fifth birthday, which was October 1949. But it was incomplete, and was not finished and sent off for publication for another two years. In November 1949 Thomas was also working, with difficulty, on 'In the white giant's thigh'. He told Vernon Watkins it took him three weeks to write the opening line.

JOHN MALCOLM BRINNIN
November 23 1949   The Boat House Laugharne
                                   Carmarthenshire Wales

Dear John Malcolm Brinnin,
   First of all: Many apologies for this month-long delay in answering
your extremely nice and helpful letter. My lying cable said, 'Letter in
mail'. And I did intend to write at once, but had to go away, felt suddenly
ill, clean forgot, put it off for a rainy day, was struck by lightning, any or
all of these. And your cable about a second reading, my wife mislaid,
found only this morning in a mousenest handbag.
   Thank you profoundly for your letter. I can't tell you how pleased I am
that you should have suggested you look after my American readings. I
can think of nothing more sensibly pleasant. What an abominable phrase!
Nothing I have ever enjoyed has been sensibly pleasant. I mean, I can
think of nothing better. I was very nervous about my visit: that is, about
the arranging of readings to make some money. I should have made a
mess of things. My life here, in the deep country, is incredibly complicated; but, in a city, I spin like a top. And procrastination is an element
in which I live. Thank you, very much indeed, for having, in the first
place, made my visit possible, and for wishing to work with me. Naturally, I understand about the fee for expenses; I couldn't, anyway, allow
you to work with me if you did not take a percentage. And the 15 per cent
you mention is very, very moderate for all the troublesome work you'll
have to do. I feel relieved now; and can face the whole undertaking with
only quite minor paralysis.
   It's very very good of you to lend me your New York apartment for my
stay there.[1] And the idea of a little rest cure in Saratoga Springs is also
appealing: I think I shall need it.
   As to the number of readings: you say that you will be able, you think,
'to arrange for, at least, fifteen engagements, and, very likely, considerably more'. How many jobs do you think I should do? I don't want to
work my head off, but, on the other hand, I do want to return to England
with some dollars in my pocket. And, of course, I want to get around the
States a bit. I'll have to leave this to you. I have been asked to be one of
the Kemball-lecturers-for-the-year at Mount Holyoke College,
Massachusetts, at a fee of 150 dollars. I think I should accept this, don't
you? And would it be possible to give a reading somewhere else near there
—boring two birds with one stone? I should say, sometime in March for
Holyoke. But you will know when to fit it in. I shall write today, to
Holyoke, accepting, and saying that you will get in touch with them
suggesting some dates, most possibly in March, which might be convenient for them. I enclose the Holyoke letter. Is that all right? Also: the
Watkins agent has been writing to Robert Richman, of the Institute of

---

[1] Thomas stayed in hotels in New York City, and with Brinnin in Massachusetts.

Contemporary Art, about a reading & a lecture in Washington; together with a suggestion about a reading at the Library of Congress. I enclose Watkins' letter, to Richman. Would you care to write to Watkins about this? and arrange what you think best—if anything. I must say Richman wants a hell of a lot of the profits. I hand the baby over, with bewildered gratitude.

I should, incidentally, like *very* much to go to California.

I hope, I do hope, that in *most* of the cases you *will* be able to arrange that travelling expenses be paid in addition to the fee. It seems very important. And that leads me to the trickiest, to my mind, problem of all: Treasury permission from here to go over to the States. *And* the money with which to travel. I've no idea how to approach the Treasury about this, or what U.S. Departments I must approach. No idea in the world. Can you help in this? It's a kind of bureaucratic nightmare: *why* are you going? *who* wants you to go? *What* will you do when you get there? *Are* you a Communist? *Do* you have clean thoughts? And the question of travelling money: I want, if possible, to go by plane, not liking the big dull sea except to look at. This costs in English money about £80. How many dollars that is, since the devaluation of the pound, I have no idea.[1] I presume that the 500 dollars you offer me, through the Poetry Center, *includes* my travelling expenses to America. Is it possible for you to let me have an advance cheque to pay for the plane journey? And soon! I say 'soon', because I know I should book a plane trip well in advance. Whether you can or not, I've no way of telling—until you write. Do write quickly about this important point. And also about the Treasury etc. formalities, or what you know of them. I dare say my London literary agent can help a bit, but he's a stiff sod and frightens the life out of me: I believe he is always waiting for an Enormous Novel, which he won't get.

I *do* wish we could talk these things over a drink.

Lloyd Frankenberg[2] has written to me, saying that he is to be in charge of a series of Poetry Readings at the Museum of Modern Art, & wanting me to give one. He said that, when he knew the dates & the fees, he would get in touch with the Watkins agents. I shall now write to him & tell him that, for my visit, you've very kindly undertaken to act as my agent etc. and will he arrange this through you.

About the readings themselves: Is there any strong reason why my readings should all be devoted to my own work? I most sincerely hope not. What I should like to do, more than anything else, is to read from a number of contemporary British poets, including myself. I far prefer reading other chaps' work to my own: I find it clearer. An hour of me aloud is hell, & produces large burning spots in front of the mind.

Will you be seeing Laughlin? He wrote to me about the same time you did, saying that 'to make any real money for you, things will have to be

[1] The sterling exchange rate, fixed at £1/$4.03 since the early days of the war, was changed to £1/$2.80 on 18 September 1949.

[2] Lloyd Frankenberg (1907–75), poet.

done hard and tough and business-like'. I hope you're an adamantine tartar. Laughlin also suggests that 'it might be well to get up a variant programme in which you would read the classic English poets'. What do you think? Personally, I shall be glad to read *anything*—& will certainly do my best to make it entertaining—except poems in dialect, hymns to Stalin, anything over 500 lines. Dare I, in my Welsh–English voice, read any American poets to American audiences? Over here, when I give broadcast readings, I quite often read some Ransom. But, whatever your opinion, I do very much want to read from *other* contemporary British poets. At the mere thought of reading only myself, I begin to feel hunted, invisible trolls shake hands with my Adam's apple.

There are so many urgent matters in this letter, I shan't now burden you with any more but will wait for your reply.

Very many thanks again, for what you have done and will do, for the apartment, for all the friendliness.

I hope to see you a few days before the 23rd of February, in N. York.

Laughlin says there will be a party for me at the Gotham Book Mart as soon as I get there: I shall polish up my glass belly.

With best wishes,
Yours sincerely,
Dylan Thomas

Will you, anyway, get in touch with Jay Laughlin who, I'm sure, will be very helpful about lots of things. He said, in his last letter, that he'd be going into details with Watkins & seeing what, between them, they could cook up. Perhaps he can cook up something with you now. About MONEY, pretty money.

MS: Delaware   SL

ANNA MILL[1]

Nov 23 1949   The Boat House Laugharne Carmarthenshire Wales

Dear Professor Mill,

Please forgive me for not having answered, much sooner, your letter of October 22nd: it has—blame the Post Office—only now been forwarded from my old address.

Thank you very much indeed for the Department of English's invitation to me to be one of your Kimball lecturers for the year. I'm delighted to accept it.

I shan't be in the United States until the end of February: I give a

---

[1] Professor in the English Department of Mount Holyoke College, Massachusetts.

reading in New York on the 23rd. So, would some date, most convenient to you, early in March be suitable? Mr. John Malcolm Brinnin has very kindly undertaken to act as my agent in the arrangement of American engagements, and I have today written to him to ask him to get in touch with you, as soon as he can, about the matter of the date.

I should certainly prefer to give a reading than to speak on English poetry. Could I be allowed to make my reading a small personal anthology of the work of contemporary British poets, including some of my own? I very much hope so.

Thank you, again, very much for your letter, and for the invitation. I look forward to my visit.

I hope you will be hearing from Mr. Brinnin very shortly.

> Yours sincerely,
> Dylan Thomas

MS: Mt Holyoke College

JAMES LAUGHLIN

Nov 23 1949   The Boat House Laugharne Carmarthenshire Wales

Dear J,

Thank you, a lot, for your nice letter. It's good to think I have a friend your side, helping to Cook Things Up.

Perhaps Brinnin has already got in touch with you, and told you that he's undertaken to act as my agent, for readings etc., for my three months' visit? It seems quite a wise move; he says he's capable of looking after all details, of getting jobs and collecting the dibs, which I'm certainly not. I *do* want to dig up a few lucrative readings, as well as to get around and, in my mazy way, enjoy myself. I've asked Brinnin to see you, & be a co-Cook.

My wife, incidentally, won't be coming over, or trying to come over, after all. Since the birth of our last son—4 loud months now—she's been most unwell. All she wants is a long and sun-soaked rest cure, which is hardly what she would get in New York in February. If I can possibly manage it—it is only the tiny problem of Money—I'd like to send her, for 3 months, to Italy. She likes the little island of Elba, where she can live very well and cheaply. That would be nice. It is only money I have not got. (I have half a novel. Well, nearly half. The novel will not be more than 70–80,000 words. You wouldn't, I suppose, like to give me an advance on that? Well, I can but ask.)[1]

---

[1] The ever-unfinished *Adventures in the Skin Trade*.

I hope you won't have gone on your European trip before I arrive. I'll try to get to New York about February 20. That is, if Brinnin, on behalf of the Y.M. & Y.W.H.A. Poetry Center, can advance me, from my 500 dollars for my first reading, enough for my plane fare. I don't want to, unless I have to, go by boat. I like it up in the air, having frequently lived there.

No, I haven't enough poems for a new book. Not for a year or more. I'll be publishing a collection of stories & sketches here in England, but several of the stories you've already printed, old ones, in The World I Breathe: J. M. Dent considered those particular ones to be, in parts, obscene. Now that I am better known here, they don't seem to mind so much. And the other stories & sketches that will make up the English book won't be enough to make a separate American one. I'll be sending some sketches to you for you to—as you very kindly suggested—bung across to Watkins to sell with aggression to the richer periodicals, I hope.

I'm having a tough time here at the moment. I want to write only poems, but that can't be. Never have I wanted to more. But debts are battering at me. I cannot sleep for them. Quite a moderate sum would clear them up & make the tradesmen twinkle. I wish I could sell my body to rich widows; but it is fat now and trembles a little. I'm sick of being so damned & utterly broke, it spoils things. I want to build poems big & solid enough for people to be able to walk & sit about and eat & drink and make love in them. Now I have only the scaffoldings of poems, never being unbadgered enough to put up roofs & walls. My table's heaped with odd lines, single words, nothing completed. (And this letter did not, oddly enough, begin as a whine of my woes.)

I hope Brinnin will keep you informed as to what arrangements he is making for me.

I look forward to my visit, to meeting you again. I like the idea of the Gotham Book party. I should like to go to New Orleans, but I suppose it is too far.

Is there anyone I should write to? Is there anything I should do? Oh, helpless baboon!

Thanks for Ruthven's address. Good old Ruthven, as you say. But I won't stay with him. Brinnin is lending me his apartment. Good old Brinnin, too.

What else? I can't think. I'm cold, it's raining on the sea, the herons are going home, the cormorants have packed up, I must go and play darts in the cheerless bar, put my flat beer on the slate, listen to talk about swedes and bulldozers, Mrs. Griffiths's ulcer, what Mr. Jenkins said to Mrs. Prothero who is no better than she ought to be, the date of Princess Margaret's birthday, the price of geese, Christmas coming—oh, horrid thought! No presents for the unfortunate, importunate, devilish, trusting children! No Scotch or puddings or mincepies or holly! Just cold bills on toast, boiled writs, summonses on the spit!—the deaths of neighbours, the infamy of relations, the stature of Churchill, the invasion of water voles!

If you can help Brinnin in any way, I know you will.

Yours ever,
Dylan

I'll send odd sketches along when typed.

MS: the recipient   SL

PRINCESS CAETANI
24th November 1949   The Boat House Laugharne Carmarthenshire
Wales

Dear Madame di Sermoneta, (is that what I *should* call you? You have so
many names)

Please forgive me for this long delay in answering your very pleasant
letter and acknowledging, with a thousand thanks, your generous and
most welcome cheque: I have been away, giving readings of poems (not
my own) to various societies in Wales and haven't had time to write a
word. The cheque helped, greatly. I can see now over the boiling edge of
my debts. Thank you, for replying so graciously, and so soon, though you
were ill in bed. I do indeed hope you are well again, and back in Rome.

I see that you are wanting the story by March the first. And March the
first it will certainly be, if I am not, before then, popped into the cooler,
peeled, pipped, and sliced.[1] I have the skeleton of a story now, but so
unpleasant that it should perhaps remain in its cupboard. I'll see. But a
story, anyway, will come.[2] And, later, a poem. I am glad you like Fern Hill
best of my poems to date. I also used to like it, & think it was among the,
say, half dozen of mine which came nearest to what I had in heart and
mind and muscle when first I wished to write them. I do not, now, read
any of my poems with much pleasure, because they tell me I should be
writing other poems *now*; because they say I should work on poems every
day; because, when I see all their faults, I think that in the new poems I
should be writing, *those* kind of faults, at least, would not occur again;
because, falling so short of the heights I had wished them, they are cruel
and not-to-be-gainsaid reminders of the fact that only through un-
ceasingly devoted and patiently passionate work at the words of *always*
new poems can I ever hope to gain even an inch or a hairslength. I do not
like reading my old poems; because I *am* not working on new poems;
because I must earn my living by bits and pieces of forced prose, by

---

[1] Phrases were worked over, as in so many of Thomas's letters. A draft version at Indiana
has, 'if I am not, before then, stoned to death by tradesmen', with 'tradesmen' crossed out
and 'writs' substituted.

[2] *Botteghe Oscure* published four poems by Thomas before his death, but only one prose
work, part of the then unfinished *Under Milk Wood*: 'Llareggub, A Piece for Radio
Perhaps', April 1952.

exhibitionist broadcasts, by journalistic snippets; because, nowadays, I can never spare the time to begin, work through, and complete a poem *regardless* of time; because my room is littered with beginnings, each staring me accusingly in the eyes.

Next year, in February, I go to the U.S.A. to give readings of poems and, I hope, to earn some dollars to bring, rustling, home. I shall spend 3 months there. Have you any friends there you would like me to see, or rather, whose addresses you would like to give me? I shall be going to, I believe, Washington, California, Massachusetts, as well as New York. But I know very few Americans.

And, when I return in the spring, I think I shall be offered quite a good job on the B.B.C., taking over Louis MacNeice's job when he goes, as British Council representative, to Athens.[1] This would entail only a few broadcast scripts for me to write, which I will enjoy, and those to be as imaginative & experimental as I like. So, perhaps, in the coming year my most horribly pressing problems will be solved. I now have only to live through the next few months, which include Christmas. And how I am to do that, I've no idea in the whole world.

I am glad you will be spending some of the summer in England, and that we can meet then somewhere in the country. I shall look forward to that, very much.

So thank you again.

It's a fine life, if you don't weaken.

Your letter helped me.

> In all friendship,
> Yours sincerely,
> Dylan Thomas

MS: Camillo Caetani Foundation

SL

MARGARET TAYLOR
Nov 28 1949   City of Dreadful Night[2]

My dear Margaret,

Sorry not to have written over the weekend, as I said I would when we talked indistinctly on the telephone: on Saturday night I fell down again and cracked some ribs, how many and how badly I won't know till I'm Xrayed tomorrow. Don't tell Miss Isaacs, who thinks that I am rarely perpendicular. The pain is knifing, I cannot sit or lie, and I bellow. I wake the baby with my bullshouts. I cannot sleep. I can hardly write: this is

---

[1] MacNeice went to Athens; Thomas didn't get his job.
[2] 'The City of Dreadful Night', a poem by the Scotsman James Thomson (1834–82); in it, the poet seeks 'dead Faith, dead Love, dead Hope'.

written as I hang off a bed, yelling. Also I have gout in my toe, phlegm on my lungs, misery in my head, debts in the town, no money in my pocket, and a poem simmering on the hob. Caitlin is thin and pale, Aeron raucous, Colum okay.

Thank you for your letter. Perhaps something will come one day from the University of Wales, though I am not popular with the authorities, being non-Welsh speaking, non-rationalist, non-degreed, non-chapelgoing, & not to be trusted. It is very good of you to try.

I have the distinct possibility of being given a good job when I return from America—I can tell you about it later—and I am not over-worrying about next year. It is, as always, NOW that matters: NOW and approaching Christmas for which we are able to make no preparations & during which we will be penniless. I wish to the Lord I could finish this wretched script. I had decided, quite sternly, to finish it this week—I cd do it in ten days, anyway—but conveniently, and nastily, fell down. Week after week I have put it off, pulling out a poem instead once I got into the littered, great hut. Perhaps, when the hospital men have bound my diaphragm up tight, I can still get down in a fury & finish it. But, if not— & I may, after all, break my neck as a final procrastination—then these ravens are without Elijah.

I don't think Caitlin is coming to the States with me. It would be difficult, expensive, and, I think, bad for her. She wants a long & utter rest. New York, & huge journeys across the subcontinent, cold winter, parties, won't give her that. She would like to go to Elba, where it is cheap to live. But, now, the cheapest mouse-box is a Ritz to us.

Of course I should like to meet Glen George. When? Where? I'll be in London, ribs allowing, 12, 13, 14 December, to be a Raven in Louis's 'Dark Tower'.[1] A Raven: oh caw, what irony! Would you want me to meet him in London? or in Wales? I could go to Aberdare from here, if you thought it wise, if Glen George would like it, if I could afford it. I am still mobile—though down down in the sad world: and now I really do know that the earth is flat.

A dim bulbed letter. I hope you are well, & the little girls. We would have liked to come up for Christmas, but I couldn't stay in H. Ford. It is going to be chaotic, and worse, here.

Write about Aberdare.

My poem is now 80 lines long.[2]

Ever,
Dylan

MS: Texas

---

[1] *The Dark Tower*, a Louis MacNeice play for radio.
[2] Presumably 'Poem on his birthday'.

DAVID HIGHAM
December 1 1949   The Boat House Laugharne Carmarthenshire

Dear David,
    America:—
    I'm intent on going now, and had better straightaway acquaint you
with what has been happening.
    John Malcolm Brinnin has written to me at length, suggesting that he,
as a wellknown lecturer, literary journalist, etc., in the States, and as
Director of the Poetry Center of the Y.M. & Y.W.H.A. of New York,
should become my secretary and agent for my stay there. He offered me,
as well as his own peculiar knowledge of the American literary scene (if
you'll excuse me), with particular reference to its poetry, a flat, or
apartment, in the centre of N. York and a country cottage some little
distance out in which to relax (or recuperate). He said that the Lecture
Agencies, which prefer novelists anyway, have nowhere near his own
acquaintanceship with the institutions etc. which like poets, and would
take, for their services, anything up to 40%. He, although he would do it
for friendship, as a fellow-poet (dear God!), cannot afford to do so, &
would have to ask 15% of what I make on my appearances as a reader and
lecturer. I cabled back & agreed, realising that Ann Watkins Inc are
primarily literary agents, and believing that Brinnin will really do a good
job for me. (I hear extremely well of him from Laughlin.) Brinnin wrote to
me today, saying that he had already 'committed me to, or penultimately
arranged, visits to (beyond the initial two Poetry Center readings)
Harvard, Library of Congress, Bryn Mawr, Vassar, Amherst College, University of Chicago, Iowa State University, University of Michigan, Wayne
University, Detroit, Smith College, Holyoke College, Massachusetts,
etc.' And he says he can arrange as many readings elsewhere as I am
prepared to give. These alone, on top of the reading (or readings) for the
Museum of Modern Art, as mentioned in Lloyd Frankenberg's letter,
make, for me, the prospect of my visit *extremely* worth while.
    I wrote to Brinnin, before his letter arrived today, asking him to let me
know, as soon as possible, what were the Treasury, Passport, etc. formalities through which I would have to go. And I expect to hear from him
soon. But I should also like to have a clear word with you about all this. I
understand *nothing* of it. Nothing at all. But surely a letter from Brinnin,
acting as my secretary & Lecture-agent, and detailing all the
arrangements he has made with such eminently respectable &
excellent-sounding institutions such as Harvard, Vassar, Bryn Mawr,
Museum of Art, Library of Congress, would mean something to the
Treasury & to all the bureaucrats concerned? I shall be in London at 4.30
p.m. on the 11th of December, and will stay on the 12th, 13th, & 14th,
rehearsing for a broadcast play of MacNeice's. So could I, either on the
11th, or at some lunchtime on any of those other days, meet you so that I
can get some of my most pressing problems ('Where do I go to?' 'What do I

have to say?' etc.) straight, or straighter? I must, I suppose, hurry everything up, as visas, travel-tickets, etc., cannot be too easy to procure.

Incidentally, MacNeice has written me a private, off-the-cuff letter, though on behalf of Laurence Gilliam, asking me whether I would like to take his (MacNeice's, of course) job over, on the BBC Staff, when he leaves to be British Council representative in Athens sometime in the New Year. I replied, enthusiastically, yes. MacNeice said I would get the same salary as himself, would not be expected to produce the scripts I write (so long as I *do* produce them), and could do most of my work in Wales. It sounds, doesn't it, ideal. It will be imaginative scripts, *of my own*, that will, on the whole, be required. I am only hoping that the job will be open for me until I return from the States at, probably, the end of May.

Let me know what you think of my *firm* decision to go to America. And when you can see me to advise me, if you will, about all the technicalities of Treasury & travel.

I enclose, signed, the 4 Exemption Certificates you sent.

Yours,
Dylan

MS: Texas   *SL*

LORRAINE DAVIES[1]
1 Dec 1949   Boat House Laugharne Carms

Dear Mrs Davies,
Thank you very much for your letter. I do apologise for all the trouble my request is causing. I wouldn't have bothered you had there been any other copy in existence. It's a piece of luck [for] me that the discs weren't destroyed.

Thank you again, & I'll expect the teledephonication—what is the word?—in about a fortnight. It's extremely good of you.[2]

Yours sincerely,
Dylan Thomas

MS: BBC

---

[1] Lorraine Jameson, who produced Thomas's 'Children's Hour' broadcasts, was now married.
[2] The BBC had been unable to find a copy of the script Thomas wanted: his childhood reminiscences, presumably in Version II. But the recording had been kept, by mistake. A 'telediphone' was the BBC's word for a script transcribed from a recording.

SELDEN RODMAN
December 6 1949   The Boat House Laugharne Carmarthenshire Wales

Dear Selden Rodman:
   Many, many thanks for your letter, your wonderful invitation, and the
100 Modern Poems. I know your and Eberhart's *War and the Poet*, but
neither of your other anthologies.[1] I'll try to get hold of them when I reach
New York. I've had time to read, in a hurry, only a few beautiful
strangers: Ransom's Blackberry Winter, Lowell's 'Where the Rainbow
Ends,' and 'The Raid' by William Everson, whom I've never even heard of.
So much of Beyond Frontiers is new to me. This *is* a book.
   Haiti ... You could seduce me to visit Haiti easier than winking. I love
and long to go. But the dates are damnable. I'll be in New York at the end
of February. I'm booked up for readings right through March and early
April—J. M. Brinnin's fixing these up for me. So I've no chance of coming
to Haiti while you are there. When do you return? I don't think I'll leave
the States till the end of April. Will we be able to meet in N. York? I do
hope so. And does the Haitian invitation stand for another year? If my
wife and I manage to come to the States in 1951, can we—if we can raise
the money—come then to the island? Impossible to tell you how much I
should like that.
   How long does it take—N. York to Haiti? Even now, *perhaps*,
somehow, I can manage a little time.
   Will you write? Anyway, with luck we'll meet some time in April.
Thank you again.

                                        Sincerely
                                        Dylan Thomas

TS: J. M. Dent

JOHN DAVENPORT
[30 Dec 1949][2]   Boat House

Dear John,
   Another point I forgot in my first letter:
   You know when I was up last, at the end of my visit, I said 'To hell with
America, to hell with my visa', and lurched home. Well, now it's quite
obvious I have to go to America, so my visa's vital. The plane ticket, for
Jan 20,[3] has just been sent to me. That doesn't give long for me to get a
visa, especially as I can't come up to London at once because I have no

[1] Rodman, a writer and critic, and the poet Richard Eberhart edited *War and the Poet* (New
    York, 1945). Rodman's *100 Modern Poems* (New York, 1949) included two poems by
    Thomas.
[2] Thomas wrote '30 Jan', but 30 Dec is more likely.
[3] Thomas meant Feb 20.

money at all. Do you know of any high-up American who might help with getting a quick introduction to the American Consul or who might help speed things up? Sorry always to be wanting so much from you, & giving so little back. Just if you *do* happen to know how to quicken the visa-problem.

The problem of how I get to London to see the Consul remains.

Caitlin's just come in with the insuperable grocery bill for 2 months.

Love,
Dylan

MS: Texas

CAITLIN THOMAS
(??1949) [on a fragment of paper; perhaps a postscript]

I love you
I'm hysterical & foulmouthed
All the baby's faults are mine not yours
I love you forever
You are all right

X
Dylan

MS: Maurice Neville

C. J. CELLAN-JONES[1]

10 January 1950   The Boat House Laugharne Carmarthenshire

Dear Mr. Cellan-Jones,

I owe you so many apologies I don't know where to begin, but as I must begin somewhere let me please say, shaggy forehead to ground and tail wagging in a desperate effort at propitiation, how very very sorry I was not to have been able to answer at once your kind and charming, censorious and forgiving, letter—which I did not deserve a bit but which I was deeply delighted to have. (Looking back, for a second, at what I've written, I see that an unfriendly eye—a Swansea doctor's eye, for instance —could interpret me as meaning that I think I did not deserve your

---

[1] A surgeon, secretary of the Swansea branch of the British Medical Association, at whose annual dinner, on 20 October 1949, Thomas was to have been guest of honour. His narrative of what kept him is a sanitised account of a drinking expedition with friends that ended, as he says, in Bristol.

censoriousness. That is far from the case. Indeed, I thought that your remark about having wished, on October 20th, to murder me in cold blood to be little short, or shorn, of lamb-like. I should have wished upon myself the Death of a Thousand Cuts; and especially if I were a surgeon.) But I'm apologising now, in the first place, for what must have seemed to you the final rudeness, the last straw, if you'll forgive me, that breaks the Cellan's back: I mean, the fact that I did not acknowledge straightaway your incredibly lenient letter of nearly a month ago. I plead that the collected will of the members of the Swansea Branch of the British Medical Association, working by a clinically white magic known only to their profession, drove me, soon after my inexcusable nonappearance at their Annual Dinner, into a bog of sickness and a cropper of accidents from which I have not yet fully recovered. The first effect of this malevolent mass medical bedevilment I experienced a week after the Dinner when stopping, heavily disguised, at Swansea in order to try to learn how really execrated I was in the surgeries and theatres, the bolus-rooms and Celtic lazarets, of a town I can approach now only in the deepest dark and where certain areas, particularly around the Hospital, are forever taboo to me. I felt sudden and excruciating pains, and when I whimpered about them to a friend he said: 'Whatever you do, don't you get ill in Swansea, it's more than your life is worth. Go in with a cough and they'll circumcise you'. So I knew what the position was, and I took my pains home. But even at home, word of my unworthiness had reached the doctors' ears, and I was treated like a leper (fortunately, a wrong diagnosis). Ever since then I have felt unwell. A little later I had an attack of gout—undoubtedly the result of some Swansea specialist sticking a pin into a wax toe—and a little later still was set upon by invisible opponents in the bogled Laugharne dark and fell down and cracked my ribs. So that when your very nice letter was forwarded to me—needing medical attention, naturally I could not spend Christmas in Wales whose every doctor loathed my every rib—I was in bed, in London, feeling like hell, unable to write a word, unable even to answer you, to thank you for your forgiveness and for all you said about my part in 'Swansea and the Arts'. I want to thank you now, belatedly but most gratefully, for that letter. And I do hope you understand why I did not acknowledge it long, long before.

This leads me to try to make an apology for a far more serious breach of courtesy and good faith, and one of which I am profoundly ashamed. I felt, and knew, it to be a great honour when I was invited to be your chief guest and to propose the British Medical Association at your Annual Dinner. I looked forward a very great deal to that evening, though not without much knocking at the knees, and wrote a long, but not, I hope, too ponderous, address, and demothed my monkey-suit, and borrowed some proper shoes, which hurt, and went up to London a few days before, on a radio job, with all the good intentions in the world. The evening of the 19th, when about to set out for Paddington, an acquaintance of mine said: 'I have a new, a very fast, sportscar, a present from my mother '—who should know better—'and I will drive you down to Wales like winking. We will spend the night at Bristol'. The car *was* very fast, he *did* drive like winking, and we *did* spend the night at Bristol. Just outside Bristol, he drove his car into a telegraph post and buckled it, which I hope drove his Mother mad. And we spent the night, sick and shaken, in a hotel that frowned at our bruises and blood; and when I crawled out of bed, on the afternoon of the 20th, I could not find my acquaintance—the police, I was told, had called to see him—nor his buckled car in which I had left my bag in which I had left my strenuously worked-upon address, my suit, my borrowed hurting shoes. I looked round several garages: it wasn't there. And I was far too timid to dare to enquire at the police station the whereabouts of car, acquaintance, bag, suit, address, or shoes. And, anyway, by now, it was too late to catch a train which would get me to Swansea in time to deliver, in the suit I hadn't got, the address I couldn't find.

I should, I know, have informed you of this sad, sordid story the very next day. But I put such a confession off and off and off until it seemed too late to matter: by this time, I realised, I was among the doomed.

Written down cold, months after, it does, I agree, sound a thin tall story. The unfortunate fact is that I am one of those people to whom these stories really do happen.

I do hope you will be able, somehow, to accept this preposterous excuse, although it is so very lately given.

And I hope you will be able to convey my most heartfelt apologies to your colleagues for all the inconvenience, and worse, caused by my failure to attend their Dinner.

And I hope, last of all, that because one Welsh writer has proved himself unworthy of the honour they were so generous as to bestow upon him by their invitation, they will not, in future, think that no Welsh writer can be trusted. No Welsh writer can.

Thank you, again, for your letter and for the very kind things you said: I hope, one day, that I shall deserve them.

Yours very sincerely,
Dylan Thomas

MS: James Cellan-Jones   SL

PRINCESS CAETANI

12 January 1950   The Boat House Laugharne Carmarthenshire

Dear Madame Caetani,

How extremely nice of you! Madame Subercaseaux sent us that lovely New Year's 'token'—and what an insufficient word that is—some time last week, and it arrived, not out of the blue, but of the pouring black. It arrived just at the very moment that the darling Bank wrote to me and said I must cash no more cheques, for however tiny amounts, until an overdraft (quite insurmountable) is paid. It arrived when I hadn't enough to buy cigarettes—what Lawrence called 'those tubular white ants'—and without these I feel naked and lost. It arrived when it was welcomer than the sun—and what a way to talk about money! Anyone would think that one couldn't get on without it! Thank you, most really, for your goodness. We are trying to live on that 'token' now—and that alone —until my raked and weather-sloshed, leaking, creaking, bit of a boat limps home. Thank you again, and for your sweet letter.

And thank you for promising me to send me letters to your sisters in New York & Washington. I shall be in New York on or about the 20th of February, and in Washington sometime in March, when I read poems at the Library of Congress. And I will certainly, with your letters and your permission, look them both up. And I will try not to be arrogant and awkward and unpleasant, as I was with you—but those apologies are over now, and next time we meet I shall, I hope, and since your recent letters, be at my ease with you, & therefore simple and natural. I shall like to meet your sisters. Are they like you? And, yes, I shall be going to Harvard; and so perhaps I can meet your friends there? I'm not sure if I go to Princeton, but I shall know when I reach New York and then, if I may, I shall write to you.

My story for you is only ½ completed. I have been worrying so much lately, about all the usual things with one or two miserable additions, that I've found it hard to sit down every day in peace (as I must, if I'm to do my best) and write, without the little, prodding devils of responsibility at work behind my eyes. One of my newest worries is: how my wife is to live while I am away. This is a lonely place, & she has no-one to help with the children. I should like her to take a holiday somewhere, in the sun. She would like to go to Elba, which we love, but that is impossible. Somehow, I must claw up enough money just to keep her here—our house is warm & comfortable, and at the water's edge—until I return maybe with dollars enough so that, for some months, I need do nothing but write my own poems & stories.

It's a flat, dull day, with grey rain oozing like self-pity: in fact, a day like this letter. No more of it.

I will try, very hard, to finish the story before leaving—though, indeed, I cannot leave until my wife is provided for. But something will happen. It always does. And often it is nasty. (I said, 'No more of it'. And here the pity again is galloning down the drab sky.)

Please don't forget—I know you won't—your letters to your sisters.

I have about 40 readings to do in the States, which will keep me tearing busy.

Yes, I am frightened of drink, too. But it is not so bad as, perhaps, you think: the fear, I mean. It is only frightening when I am whirlingly perplexed, when my ordinary troubles are magnified into monsters and I fall weak down before them, when I do not know what to do or where to turn. When I am here, or anywhere I like, and am busy, then drink's no fear at all and I'm well, terribly well, and gay, and unafraid, and full of other, nicer nonsenses, and altogether a dull, happy fellow only wanting to put into words, never into useless, haphazard, ugly & unhappy action, the ordered turbulence, the ubiquitous and rinsing grief, the unreasonable glory, of the world I know and don't know.

Write soon, when you can; and forgive, if you can, the agitation of my letters, which is caused only by the superficial worries of mouth-to-mouth living & day after day; and thank you, with all my heart, for your New Year's gift and for the affection of your letter.

Yours sincerely,
Dylan Thomas

MS: Camillo Caetani Foundation

SL

'CYRIL'[1]
January 31 1950   Boat House Laugharne Carmarthenshire

Dear Cyril,
   Davenport told me, a few weeks ago, that the Hulton people would give me, in advance, £50 for an article which I'd write about the USA on my return. Is that true? And can you get it for me? And can you, please, get it at once? I'm desperate here, & for the first time for years have not got one single shilling. Coal & milk are both cut off, hell in this weather in this baby-packed house. I must get them put on again, & pay other terrible debts. Can you get the Hultons to send me £50 advance *at once*? I'll write them a lovely article. Can't tell you how wretched things are. It's all happened at once. There isn't even enough food in the house.

Yours ever,
Dylan

You *must* believe me.

MS: Carbondale

---

[1] Unidentified recipient, presumably on the staff of a magazine.

JEAN LEROY
31 January 1950   Boat House Laugharne Carmarthenshire

Dear Miss LeRoy,
   Sorry not to have answered your letter of January 18th about my
reading my poem Fern Hill, on February 16, in the Home Service Schools
transmission. I think the terms are very generous, but I'm afraid I can't
fulfil the engagement. As a matter of fact, I didn't know I'd been asked to
do it: certainly I haven't by letter. I'd like to do it very much, but I'm
leaving for America a couple of days after the 16th, & have a lot of things
to settle down here, & a trip to London just at that moment would do me
no good.
   By the way: I see, from a letter of yours of January 27th, that the BBC
will be rebroadcasting a selection, on the Third, of poems read by me, and
you include a list of those poems & also the copyright charges the BBC
will pay me. This rebroadcast is dated for February 7. Will you, please, see
that the cheque for this is sent to me here, at the above address, & not to
my Bank, with whom I am having a little overdraft trouble at the
moment?
   Thank you so much: it's quite important to me.
                                        Yours sincerely,
                                        Dylan Thomas

MS: Texas

PRINCESS CAETANI
12 Feb 1950   The Boat House Laugharne Carmarthenshire

Dear Madame Caetani,
   This is only a very [?short] letter, to thank you, very much, for writing
those notes to your sisters and to Archibald MacLeish. If things go well, I
hope to be able to see them next month. It was awfully kind of you to
write to them. And, too, to think of sending my wife a cheque on
February 15: it will mean a very great deal to her, and she is as grateful to
you as I am: if that is possible.
   I am supposed to travel on the 20th. My visa is not yet through, though
I have hopes of it tomorrow. All depends on that and on my ability to get
enough money, before I go, to pay some outstanding, and howling, debts,
and to leave, with my agent, a weekly sum for Caitlin & the children.
That I have some chance of getting, from my publishers.
   The only address I have, in the States, so far, is: c/o John Malcolm
Brinnin, Valley Road, Westport, Conn. I shall be headquartered—and

probably hanged and drawn as well—in New York, but that address will always find me.

I shall certainly try to see Samuel Barber, whose music I love—especially, perhaps, his setting of 'Dover Beach'—and Richard Wilbur.[1] Thank you, a lot, for their addresses.

I am, I think, supposed to be at Princeton on March the 6th, and I would indeed appreciate a word, to his friends, from your friend the attaché at the American Embassy in Rome. Though perhaps I have left things too late?

Perhaps I have left everything too late, & may never go at all. I have been too horribly worried to see, in the proper way, to all the necessary forms. And then my father has become dangerously ill, & there is only my mother, an invalid, to look after him. And now the damned roof is leaking all over this letter. I feel like an expurgated page of a Russian novel.

If I do get to the States, I will write you a long, long letter. And I hope to be able to correct my story for you there, & send it on. Forgive its lateness.

I wish you were to be in America.

Many thanks again for all, from us all. I shall, visa & money or not, write you very soon.

Yours,
Dylan

MS: Camillo Caetani Foundation

BILL MCALPINE
Sunday 12 Feb 50   Boat House

My dear Bill,

I was right, I knew, to run to you weeping when things did, really, get too much. All the thanks there are, from Cat & me, for your kindness & quickness in helping us at one of the lowest—no, the very lowest, I think—downs of our seesaw life.

Now to say: Forgive me, Bill, for not writing immediately to thank you very very deeply. I've been in such a stygian depression, and so desperately flustered about visas, passports, inoculations, summonses, clanging overdraft, tradesmen, my father, Cat for the future, I couldn't do anything straight; I couldn't even write you back, as soon as your help came. Forgive me.

Tomorrow I go to Cardiff to get, I hope, at last, my American visa. To get to Cardiff, I had to borrow from my mother: you'll realise from that that I'm still in an awful state of suffering brokeness. If the visa's okay—I

---

[1] Richard Wilbur (b. 1921), poet.

expect nothing to turn out well—I will try to borrow money in Cardiff to go on to London to see a bankmanager to try to cash a postdated cheque. That sounds impossible, but I have got a plan afoot. I *can* do it, if the visa is okay. I think so, anyway. Then—after all these if's—I return to Laugharne to settle up vast bills & to try to provide for Cat when I am away. I have my plane ticket: for the 20th. If, if, if, if, visa & bank work out, then Cat & I will come to London to stay the weekend in Margaret's London house, where she wants to give a little Sunday party before I fly on Monday. If, if, if, if, visa & bank *do* not work, I shall have to fly anyway: but out of the window, into the sea.

Cat wrote a long letter to Helen today. Maybe it will arrive the same time as this. Presumably your old address forwards letters.

If I *am* in London this Tue or Wed, I'll ring the B.Council & try to find you.

My father is off the danger list. He had pneumonia as well, &, though the muck on the lung has not cleared up yet, the Doctors are optimistic. He is starting to grumble, though very weakly.

Thank you again, Bill, & I hope I see you very soon.

Keep your prayers crossed for us.

Ever, to you both,
Dylan

MS: Buffalo

CAITLIN THOMAS
[February 1950]   Savage Club 1 Carlton House Terrace
London SW1

Darling I love you, darling.

Things have gone all right. Visa & bank okay. Am seeing posh dentist[1] tomorrow Wednesday so cannot come back at once. Will catch sleeper-train on Thursday night.

Here is 10 pounds. Will you please, my love, collect my suit from cleaners & send it *at once* to above address. Then I can be in Picasso play.[2]

I love you.
Thursday night.

X
Dylan

MS: Maurice Neville

[1] Thomas had bad teeth. The American novelist Peter de Vries, who caricatured him as McGland in *Reuben Reuben*, made McGland commit suicide on hearing that he must have all his teeth out.
[2] A one-night performance of *Desire Caught by the Tail*.

CAITLIN THOMAS
Saturday Feb 25 '50[1]   [headed paper] Midston House 22 East 38th Street
New York 16

My darling far-away love, my precious Caitlin, my wife dear, I love you as I have never loved you, oh please remember me all day & every day as I remember you here in this terrible, beautiful, dream and nightmare city which would only be any good at all if we were together in it, if every night we clung together in it. I love you, Cat, my Cat, your body, heart, soul, everything, and I am always and entirely yours.

How are you, my dear? When did you go with Ivy back to Laugharne? I hope you didn't racket about too much because that makes you as ill as racketing makes me. And how is my beloved Colum and sweet fiend Aeron? Give them my love, please. I will myself write to Llewelyn over this weekend when I temporarily leave New York and go to stay with John Brinnin—a terribly nice man—in his house in the country an hour or so away. And how are the old ones? I'll write to them, too. I love you, I can see you, now this minute, your face & body, your beautiful hair, I can hear your lovely, un-understandable voice. I love you, & I love our children, & I love our house. Here, each night I have to take things to sleep: I am staying right in the middle of Manhattan, surrounded by skyscrapers infinitely taller & stranger than one has ever known from the pictures: I am staying in a room, an hotel room for the promised flat did not come off, on the 30th floor: and the *noise* all day & night: without some drug, I couldn't sleep at all. The hugest, heaviest lorries, police-cars, firebrigades, ambulances, all with their banshee sirens wailing & screaming, seem never to stop; Manhattan is built on rock, a lot of demolition work is going on to take up yet another super Skyscraper, & so there is almost continuous dynamite blasting. Aeroplanes just skim the tips of the great glimmering skyscrapers, some beautiful, some hellish. And I have no idea what on earth I am doing here in the very loud, mad middle of the last mad Empire on earth:—except to think of you, & love you, & to work for us. I have done two readings this week, to the Poetry Center of New York: each time there was an audience of about a thousand. I felt a very lonely, foreign midget orating up there, in a huge hall, before all those faces; but the readings went well. After this country weekend, where I arrange with Brinnin some of the rest of my appallingly extensive programme, I go to Harvard University, Cambridge, Boston, for about 2 days, then to Washington, then back to New York, then, God knows, I daren't think, but I know it includes Yale, Princeton, Vassar—3 big universities, as you know, old know-all,—& Salt Lake City, where the Mormons live, & Notre Dame, the Jesuit College, & the middle West, Iowa, Ohio, Chicago—& Florida, the kind of exotic resort, & after that

---

[1] Thomas flew to the U.S. on February 20, and was there for just over three months. In Brinnin's account, he spent the first few nights at the Beekman Tower Hotel, but was asked to leave, presumably for drunken behaviour, and moved to Midston House.

the mere thought makes my head roar like New York. To the places near to New York, Brinnin is driving me by car; to others I go by myself by train; to the more distant places, I fly. But *whatever* happens, by God I don't fly back. Including landing at Dublin, Canada, & Boston, for very short times, I was in the air, cooped up in the stratosphere, for 17 hours with 20 of the nastiest people in the sky. I had an awful hangover from our London do as well; the terrible height makes one's ears hurt like hell, one's lips chap, one's belly turn; and it went on forever. I'm coming back by boat.

I've been to a few parties, met lots of American poets, writers, critics, hangers-on, some very pleasant, all furiously polite & hospitable. But, apart from on one occasion, I've stuck nearly all the time to American beer, which, though thin, I like a lot & is ice-cold. I arrived, by the way, on the coldest day New York had had for years & years: it was 4 above zero. You'd have loved it. I never thought anything could be so cold, my ears nearly fell off: the wind just whipped through that monstrous duffle. But, as soon as I got into a room, the steamed [heat?] was worse: I think I can stand zero better than that, &, to the astonishment of natives, I keep all windows open to the top. I've been, too, to lots of famous places: up the top of the Empire State Building, the tallest there is, which terrified me so much, I had to come down at once; to Greenwich Village a feebler Soho but with stronger drinks; & this morning John Brinnin is driving us to Harlem. I say 'us', you see: in the same hotel as me is staying our old New Zealander, Allen Curnow, & I see quite a bit of him.[1] I've met Auden, & Oscar Williams, a very odd, but kind, little man.

And now it must look to you, my Cat, as though I am enjoying myself here. I'm not. It's nightmare, night & day; there never was such a place; I would never get used to the speed, the noise, the utter indifference of the crowds, the frightening politeness of the intellectuals, and, most of all, these huge phallic towers, up & up & up, hundreds of floors, into the impossible sky. I feel so terrified of this place, I hardly dare to leave my hotelroom—luxurious—until Brinnin or someone calls for me. Everybody uses the telephone all the time: it is like breathing: it is now nine o'clock in the morning, & I've had six calls: all from people whose names I did not catch to invite me to a little poity at an address I had no idea of. And most of all most of all most of all, though, God, there's no need to say this to you who understand everything, I want to be with you. If we could be here together, everything would be allright. *Never* again would I come here, or to any far place, without you; but especially never to here. The rest of America may be all right, & perhaps I can understand it, but that is the last monument there is to the insane desire for power that shoots its buildings up to the stars & roars its engines louder & faster than they have ever been roared before and makes everything cost the earth & where the imminence of death is reflected in every last power-

[1] Allen Curnow (b. 1911), New Zealand poet.

stroke and grab of the great money bosses, the big shots, the multis, one never sees. This morning we go down to see the other side beyond the skyscrapers: black Harlem, starving Jewish East Side. A family of four in New York is very very poor on £14 a week. I'll buy some nylons all the same next week, & some tinned stuff. Anything else?

Last-minute practicalities: How does the money go? Have any new bills arrived. If so, send them, when you write (& write soon my dear love, my sweetheart, that is all I wait for except to come home to you) to the address on the kitchen wall. I enclose a cheque to Phil Raymond, & an open cheque to Gleed; pay that bill when you can.

Remember me. I love you. Write to me.

Your loving, loving Dylan

MS: Maurice Neville

D. J. and FLORENCE THOMAS
Sunday 26th February 1950   [headed paper: Midston House etc]

My dear Mother & Dad,

How are you both? How are you keeping, Dad? Get stronger every day, please, so that when I come home to Laugharne, you'll be up and about and able to join me for one at Phil's. And Mother, too, by that time, must be spry enough to be able to run, like a goat, down the Boat House path. I was very sad to leave you at such a moment, with Dad so weak & with Mother not fit to do all the little things for him that must be done. I was very sad, driving away that morning, leaving you & Laugharne, but it had, God help me, to be done.

Caitlin's told you, I suppose, about our London visit and Margaret's house and party at which such a lot of old—& some new—friends turned up, so I won't add anything to that. Helen & Bill, by the way, send their fondest regards to you both.

The plane trip was ghastly. It seemed to go on for ever, and all my 30 fellow passengers seemed either actively unpleasant or moronic. The plane was stiflingly hot, & there wasn't any of the usual slight plane ventilation because of the height we travelled: in the stratosphere. We couldn't put down at the airport in Newfoundland because of icy weather conditions, so had to land somewhere in Canada. We got out for an hour: the cold was unbelievable, all the airport ground crew dressed up like Hudson Bay trappers and beating their great grizzly-bear-gloved hands together & stamping on the snow. And when we did, after several stifling eternities spent high as the moon, arrive in New York, it was to find it one of the coldest days there for years: when we got off the plane, it was four above zero. Luckily I'd rather the cold than the heat, and my old duffle-coat was very helpful. John Brinnin, my agent, a terribly nice man,

met me at the airport—about an hour from the centre of the city—&
drove me to my hotel: right in Manhattan, among the unreal, shooting
skyscrapers, and my room was on the thirtieth floor. Then we drove
around the city, me gawping, like the country cousin I am, at this titanic
dream world, soaring Babylon, everything monstrously rich and strange.
That evening, I went to a party, given in my honour by the Professor of
English at Columbia University: pack full of American dons, critics,
writers, poets, all of the older & more respectable kind.[1] Then home to
the 30th floor, to hear, all night, the roaring of heavy lorries, the hooting
of ships from the East River—I could see the Queen Mary, or Elizabeth,
from my window—& the banshee-screaming of police and ambulance
sirens, just as on the films. There seems, at first sight, to be no reality at
all in the life here: it is all an enormous façade of speed & efficiency &
power behind which millions of little individuals are wrestling, in vain,
with their own anxieties. The next day, Brinnin took me touring over half
of this mad city: Broadway, Harlem, the Wall Street area, the East Side
(where the Dead End Kids come from). I drank huge icy milkshakes in the
drugstores, and iced lager beer in the Third Avenue saloons almost every
one of which is kept by an Irishman; I ate fried shrimps, fried chickens, a
T-bone steak the size of a month's ration for an English family. I went to
the top of the Empire State Building, the tallest skyscraper in the world,
had one look at the nightmare city, & came down quickly. That night I
went to a party given to me by some of the younger writers. The next day
Brinnin & I did little but prepare my itinerary, which seems to take me to
every state in the U.S.A., & that evening I made my first public
appearance before an audience of 800 people. The reading seemed to go
very well. After that, a reception, so-called, in the flat of a young man
whose name I didn't catch: flats are called apartments here, but this one
had 20 rooms. The next day all over the city again, meeting many people,
mostly, again, writers, painters, or actors. And yesterday, Saturday, my
second appearance in the same hall as the first: 800 again, the full seating
capacity. Today, Sunday, I go to the country, with Brinnin, until Tuesday
when I make my way to Yale University & from there to Harvard, Boston.
After that, I've got about 10 readings in 20 days. Don't you worry about
me, now. I'm feeling tiptop. By the way, the first people to come along to
the stage-door after my first reading were three people from Llanelly,
utter strangers, now living in N. York. I'll write again next week. Tell me
everything. *And Get Stronger.* My forwarding address is c/o John Brinnin,
Valley Road, Westport, Connecticut. All my love to you both. I think of
you. Give my regards to Billy & Mrs. Thomas.

D.

SL

MS: Thomas Trustees

---

[1] This sedate party is not mentioned in Brinnin's *Dylan Thomas in America.*

CAITLIN THOMAS
[about March 11 1950][1]   [headed paper: 1669 THIRTY-FIRST STREET
WASHINGTON]

Kiss Colum again. Put	I shall write lots & lots
your hand on your heart	& lots to you from now, on
for me	the endless trains.

Caitlin my own own own dearest love whom God and *my* love and *your* love for me protect, my sweet wife, my dear one, my Irish heart, my wonderful wonderful girl who is with me invisibly every second of these dreadful days, awake or sleepless, who is forever and forever with me and is my own true beloved amen—I love you, I need you, I want, want you, we have never been apart as long as this, never, never, and we will never be again. I am writing to you now, lying in bed, in the Roman Princess's sister's[2] rich social house, in a posh room that is hell on earth. Oh why, why, *didn't* we arrange it *somehow* that we came out together to this devastating, insane, demonaically loud, roaring continent. We *could* somehow have arranged it. Why oh why did I think I could live, I could bear to live, I could think of living, for all these torturing, unending, echoing months without you, Cat, my life, my wife, my wife on earth and in God's eyes, my reason for my blood, breath, and bone. Here, in this vast, mad horror, that doesn't know its size, or its strength, or its weakness, or its barbaric speed, stupidity, din, selfrighteousness, this cancerous Babylon, here we could cling together, sane, safe, & warm & face, together, everything. I LOVE YOU. I have been driven for what seem like, and probably are, thousands of miles, along neoned, jerrybuilt, motel-ed, turbined, ice-cream-salooned, gigantically hoared roads of the lower region of the damned, from town to town, college to college, university to university, hotel to hotel, & all I want, before Christ, before you, is to hold you in my arms in our house in Laugharne, Carmarthenshire. And the worst, by a thousand miles—no, thousands & thousands & thousands of miles—is to come. I have touched only the nearest-together of my eternally foreign dates. Tomorrow, I go back from Washington, hundreds of miles, to New York. There I talk to Columbia University. The very next day I start on my pilgrimage, my *real* pilgrimage, of the damned. I go to Iowa, Idaho, Indiana, Salt Lake City, & then a titanic distance to Chicago. All alone. Friend Brinnin leaves me at New York. And from Chicago I fly to San Francisco, & from there I lurch, blinded with smoke and noise, to Los Angeles. The distance from New York—where I shall be tomorrow—to Los Angeles is further than the

---

[1] Thomas read in Washington DC on March 9, then in New York on March 13.

[2] Katherine Biddle (1890–1977), one of Marguerite Caetani's two sisters (in fact, half-sisters), to whom Thomas carried letters of introduction. Her husband, Francis Biddle, belonged to a prominent Philadelphia family and was U.S. Attorney-General, 1941–5. Katherine Biddle gave money to cultural causes and herself wrote poetry. Thomas retaliated by stealing some of Biddle's shirts when his hosts had left for Bermuda.

distance from London to New York. Oh, Cat, my beautiful, my love, what am I doing here? I am no globe-trotter, no cosmopolitan, I have no desire to hurl across the American nightmare like one of their damned motorcars. I want to live quietly, with you & Colum, & noisily with Aeronwy, & I want to see Llewelyn, & I want to sit in my hut and write, & I want to eat your stews, and I want to touch your breasts and cunt, and I want every night to lie, in love & peace, close, close, close, close, close to you, closer than the marrow of your soul. I LOVE YOU.

Everything is not terrible here. I have met many kind, intelligent, humorous people, & a few, a very few, who hate the American scene, the driving lust for success, the adulation of power, as much as I do. There is more food than I dreamt of. And I want to tell you again, my Cat, that I still drink nothing but ice-cold beer. I don't touch spirits at all, though that is all that anyone else seems to drink—-& in enormous quantity. But if I touched anything else but beer I just *couldn't* manage to get along. I couldn't face this world if I were ill. I have to remain, outwardly, as strong as possible. It is only in my heart and head that the woes and the terrors burn. I miss you a million million times more than if my arms, legs, head, & trunk were all cut off. You *are* my body, & I am yours. Holily & sacredly, & lovingly & lustfully, spiritually, & to the very deeps of the unconscious sea, I love you, Caitlin my wild wise wonderful woman, my girl, the mother of our Colum cauliflower. Your letter I read ten times a day, in cars, trains, pubs, in the street, in bed. I think I know it by heart. Of *course* I know it by heart. Your heart, alive, leaping, & loving, is in every word. Thank you, my dear, for your lovely letter. Please write as often as you can. And I will write too. I have not written since my first letter because never for a second, except for falling, trembling & exhausted thinking, thinking, thinking, of you, have I stopped travelling or reading aloud on stages and platforms. This is the first day on which I have had no work to do. I waited until I was in bed until I wrote to you. I can cry on the pillow then, and say your name across the miles that sever you from me. I LOVE YOU. Please, love & remember me & WAIT FOR ME. Keep the stew waiting on the fire for me. Kiss Calico Colum for me, & arrant Aeron.

I hope you got the stockings I sent you. I sent a pair to Ivy too. Today I had sent from a big shop in Washington lots of chocolates, sweets, & candies, for you, for Aeron, for my mother. Darling darling, I am sorry I could do nothing for dear Aeron's birthday. Dates & time were a maze of speed & noise as I drove like a sweating, streamlined, fat, redfaced comet along the *incredible* roads. But tell her many sweets & things shd reach her in a few days. From N York tomorrow, I shall also send some foodstuffs.

About the Ungoed cheque: if my chequebook is in the bottom of my suitcase, I shall write him a cheque & put it into this letter when I post it tomorrow. If it is not in my suitcase, but in my other suitcase in Brinnin's house, I shall send it separately tomorrow. I cannot look in the case now.

It is downstairs. The house is dark. I shall lie here & love you. I DO Love You, Angel. Be good to me & ours.

What can I say to you that I have not said a thousand times before, dear dear Cat? It is: I love you.

P.S. Always write me c/o Brinnin.

MS: Thomas Trustees

CAITLIN THOMAS
[March 15 1950]   c/o Brinnin Valley Road Westport Conn

from your lost, loving Dylan.

Darling my dear my Cat,
    I love you.
    You're mine for always as for always I am yours. I love you. I have been away for just over 3 weeks, & there's never been a longer & sadder time since the Flood. Oh write soon, my love, my Irish, my Colum's mother, my beautiful golden dear. There isn't a moment of any insane day when I do not feel you loving and glowing, when I do not grieve for you, for me, for us both, my sweetheart, when I do not long to be with you as deep as the sea. Only three weeks! Oh God, oh God, how much longer. I wrote you last from be-Bibbled Washington. Then back I sweated to New York. Then I read in Columbia University, New York. Then I flew to Cornell University, read, caught a night-sleeper-train to Ohio, arriving this morning. This evening, in an hour's time, I do my little act at Kenyon University, then another night-train, this time to Chicago. I never seem to sleep in a bed any more, only on planes & trains. I'm hardly living; I'm just a voice on wheels. And the damndest thing is that quite likely I may arrive home with hardly any money at all, both the United States *and* Great Britain taxing my earnings—my earnings for us, Colum, Aeron, Llewelyn, for our house that makes me cry to think of, for the water, the heron, old sad empty Brown's. I am writing this in a room in Kenyon University, & can find no paper or sharp pencil & am too scared to go out and find somebody to ask. As soon as I raise the courage, I shall write Ungoed's cheque—it wasn't, of course, in my suitcase in Washington at all but in Brinnin's possession in N York—& address the envelope & have the letter air-mailed. I love you. Every *second* I think of and love you. Remember me. Write quickly. You are all I have on earth.
    Did you get nylons & candy?
    And please, when you write, tell me how the money's going at home, how you are making out.
    Kiss Colum & Aeron for me.
    Have you thought of having Mary Keene or Oxford Elizabeth down?

Tell me everything.
Love me, my dear love Cat.
Be good.
Write quickly. What can I send you?

I LOVE YOU   XXX

Found a razorblade to sharpen my pencil, but no more paper. Out on the grounds—they call it the campus—of this College the undergraduates, looking more like bad actors out of an American co-ed film, are strolling, running, baseballing, in every variety of fancy-dress. Someone in the building is playing jazz on an out-of-date piano: the saddest sound. In a few minutes now I go out for cocktails with the President. I do not want to have cocktails with any President. I want to be home. I want you. I want you with my heart and my body because I love you. Perhaps, perhaps, perhaps, the door may suddenly open & in you will come: like the sun. But I do not think it likely. I love you, my pet

MS: Maurice Neville

CAITLIN THOMAS
[March 16 1950]   [headed paper: The Quadrangle Club Chicago]

Cat: my cat: If only you would write to me: My love, oh Cat. This is not, as it seems from the address above, a dive, joint, saloon, etc, but the honourable & dignified headquarters of the dons of the University of Chicago. I love you. That is all I know. But all I know, too, is that I am writing into space: the kind of dreadful, unknown space I am just going to enter. I am going to Iowa, Illinois, Idaho, Indindiana, but these, though mis-spelt, *are* on the map. You are not. Have you forgotten me? I am the man you used to say you loved. I used to sleep in your arms—do you remember? But you never write. You are perhaps mindless of me. I am not of you. I love you. There isn't a moment of any hideous day when I do not say to myself, 'It will be alright. I shall go home. Caitlin loves me. I love Caitlin.' But perhaps you have forgotten. If you have forgotten, or lost your affection for me, please, my Cat, let me know. I Love You.

Dylan

The address is still Brinnin. He forwards all mail to my lost addresses. I love you.

MS: Maurice Neville

CAITLIN THOMAS
[about April 5 1950]   c/o Witt-Diamant[1] 1520 Willard St San Francisco

My love my Caitlin my love my love

thank you (I love you) for your beautiful beautiful beautiful letter and (my love) for the love you sent. Please forgive, Cat dear, the nasty little note I sent about your not-writing: it was only because I was so worried and so deeply in love with you. This is going to be the shortest letter because I am writing it on a rocking train that is taking me from San Francisco—the best city on earth—to Vancouver in Canada. And with this tiny, but profoundly loving, letter, I also send you a cheque to Magdalen College for £50 & a cheque for £15 to you: that £15 seems an odd amount, but God knows how much is in the Chelsea bank. I unfortunately can't find the Dathan Davies bill you sent, so can you pay it out of this. Please, my own sweetheart, send all the bills & troubles to me after this. And I hope the cheques are met. The train is going so fast through wonderful country along the Pacific coast that I can write no more. As soon as I get on stationary land I will write longly. I said San Francisco was the best city on earth. It is incredibly beautiful, all hills and bridges and blinding blue sky and boats and the Pacific ocean. I am trying—& there's every reason to believe it will succeed—to arrange that you & me & Colum (my Colum, your Colum,) come to San Francisco next spring when I will become, for six months, a professor in the English department of the University. You will love it here. I am madly unhappy but I love it here. I am desperate for you but I *know* that we can, together, come here. I love you. I love you. I love you. I am glad you are stiff & staid. I am rather overwrought but am so much in love with you that it does not matter. I spent last evening with Varda, the Greek painter, who remembers you when you were fifteen. I wish I did. A long letter tomorrow. O my heart, my golden heart, how I miss you. There's an intolerable emptiness in me, that can be made whole only by your soul & body. I will come back alive & as deep in love with you as a cormorant dives, as an anemone grows, as Neptune breathes, as the sea is deep. God bless & protect you & Llewelyn & Aeron & Colum, my, our, Colum. I love you.

Dylan

P.S. Write, air mail, to the above address. I return to S. Francisco in a week.

P.S.S. Darling, I realise fifteen pounds is inadequate, but let that big £50 get thro' the bank alright & then I can send more. I can send you a cheque

[1] Ruth Witt-Diamant (b. 1895) taught English at San Francisco State College. Thomas had a letter of introduction to her, which he showed to college students he met in a bar. When they telephoned her, she invited him to leave his hotel and stay at her house, which became his refuge on the West Coast. In 1954 she founded the San Francisco Poetry Center.

in dollars next week, which you can cash through the account of my poor old man or through Ivy.

I love you.

MS: Maurice Neville

CAITLIN THOMAS
7th April 1950

Caitlin. Just to write down your name like that. Caitlin. I don't have to say My dear, My darling, my sweetheart, though I do say those words, to you in myself, all day and night. Caitlin. And all the words are in that one word. Caitlin, Caitlin, and I can see your blue eyes and your golden hair and your slow smile and your faraway voice. Your faraway voice is saying, now, at my ear, the words you said in your last letter, and thank you, dear, for the love you said and sent. I love you. Never forget that, for one single moment of the long, slow, sad Laugharne day, never forget it in your mazed trances, in your womb & your bones, in our bed at night. I love you. Over this continent I take your love inside me, your love goes with me up in the aeroplaned air, into all the hotel bedrooms where momentarily I open my bag—half full, as ever, of dirty shirts—and lay down my head & do not sleep until dawn because I can hear your heart beat beside me, your voice saying my name and our love above the noise of the night-traffic, above the neon flashing, deep in my loneliness, my love.

Today is Good Friday. I am writing this in an hotel bedroom in Vancouver, British Columbia, Canada, where yesterday I gave two readings, one in the university, one in the ballroom of the Vancouver Hotel, and made one broadcast. Vancouver is on the sea, and gigantic mountains doom above it. Behind the mountains lie other mountains, lies an unknown place, 30,000 miles of mountainous wilderness, the lost land of Columbia where cougars live and black bears. But the city of Vancouver is a quite handsome hellhole. It is, of course, being Canadian, more British than Cheltenham. I spoke last night—or read, I never lecture, how could I?—in front of two huge union jacks. The pubs—they are called beer-parlours—serve only beer, are not allowed to have whiskey or wine or any spirits at all—and are open only for a few hours a day. There are, in this monstrous hotel, two bars, one for Men, one for Women. They do not mix. Today, Good Friday, nothing is open nor will be open all day long. Everybody is pious and patriotic, apart from a few people in the university & my old friend Malcolm Lowry—do you remember Under the Volcano —who lives in a hut in the mountains & who came down to see me last night.[1] Do you remember his wife Margery? We

---

[1] Malcolm Lowry (1909–57), British writer, had lived in British Columbia with his second wife, Margerie, since 1940.

met her with Bill & Helen in Richmond, and, later, I think, in Oxford. She, anyway, remembers you well and sends you her love.

This afternoon I pick up my bag of soiled clothes and take a plane to Seattle. And thank God to be out of British Canada & back in the terrible United States of America. I read poems to the University there tonight. And then I have one day's rest in Seattle, & then on Sunday I fly to Montana, where the cowboys are, thousands of them, tell Ebie, and then on Monday I fly—it takes about 8 hours—to Los Angeles & Hollywood: the nightmare zenith of my mad, lonely tour.

But oh, San Francisco! It is and has everything. Here in Canada, five hours away by plane, you wouldn't think that such a place as San Francisco could exist. The wonderful sunlight there, the hills, the great bridges, the Pacific at your shoes. Beautiful Chinatown. Every race in the world. The sardine fleets sailing out. The little cable-cars whizzing down the city hills. The lobsters, clams, & crabs. Oh, Cat, what food for you. Every kind of seafood there is. And all the people are open and friendly. And next year we both come to live there, you & me & Colum & maybe Aeron. This is sure. I am offered a job in two universities. When I return to San Francisco next week, after Los Angeles, for another two readings, I shall know definitely which of the jobs to take. The pay will be enough to keep us comfortably, though no more. Everyone connected with the Universities is hard-up. But that doesn't matter. Seafood is cheap. Chinese food is cheaper, & lovely. Californian wine is good. The iced bock beer is good. What more? And the city is built on hills; it dances in the sun for nine months of the year; & the Pacific Ocean never runs dry.

Last week I went to Big Sur, a mountainous region by the sea, and stayed the night with Henry Miller. Tell Ivy that; she who hid his books in the oven. He lives about 6,000 feet up in the hills, over the blinding blue Pacific, in a hut of his own making. He has married a pretty young Polish girl, & they have two small children. He is gentle and mellow and gay.

I love you, Caitlin.

You asked me about the shops. I only know that the shops in the big cities, in New York, Chicago, San Francisco, are full of everything you have ever heard of and also full of everything one has never heard of or seen. The foodshops knock you down. All the women are smart, as in magazines—I mean, the women in the main streets; behind, lie the eternal poor, beaten, robbed, humiliated, spat upon, done to death—and slick & groomed. But they are not as beautiful as you. And when you & me are in San Francisco, you will be smarter & slicker than them, and the sea & sun will make you jump over the roofs & the trees, & you will never be tired again. Oh, my lovely dear, how I love you. I love you for ever & ever. I see you every moment of the day & night. I see you in our little house, tending the pomegranate of your eye. I love you. Kiss Colum, kiss Aeron & Llewelyn. Is Elizabeth with you? Remember me to her. I love you. Write, write, write, write, my sweetheart Caitlin. Write to me still c/o Brinnin; though the letters come late that way, I am sure of them. Do not despair. Do not be too tired. Be always good to me. I shall one day be in your arms, my own, however shy we shall be. Be good to me, as I am always to you. I love you. Think of us together in the San Franciscan sun, which we shall be. I love you. I want you. Oh, darling, when I was with you all the time, how did I ever shout at you? I love you. Think of me.

Your
Dylan

I enclose a cheque for £15.
I will write from Hollywood in three days.
I will send some more money.
I love you.

MS: Maurice Neville

CAITLIN THOMAS
18 April [1950]   c/o Witt-Diamant 1520 Willard St San Francisco

P.S. Sorry darling. Just been to bank &
50 dollars is only £17.15 shillings
(seventeen pounds fifteen shillings).
Will send another fifty dollars in
two or three days. *All* you have to do
with this cheque is to take it to
Barclay's Bank, Carmarthen. I love you.

Be good to me as I am good,
forever, to you, my love. I love you
every second of the day.

Darling my own, my Cat, my dear,
    Just returned from Los Angeles to S. Francisco to find your beautiful letter, my true love, & your very good, but heartbreaking, poem. I know it must be a hell of a battle with the small amount of money I could leave; here is a cheque for 50 (fifty dollars) which you can take to any bank in Carmarthen & get cashed. It should be worth about £20 (twenty pounds) & will help a little. Perhaps it would be a good idea to see the man in the Laugharne little bank—he comes twice a week—& he may be able to cash this cheque himself. Anyway, he will tell you about it. I cannot send an English cheque as I have none left, so I have to give an American one & then have an American one written for me by my host or hostess. It's all very complicated. This is a tiny letter which says nothing of my great love for you, & has no news. I just want you to have this small amount of money straightaway. I shall write tomorrow with all news—some of it

good, none bad, except that I am without the one thing in life that matters to me, which happens to be a small unhappy blonde in Laugharne, Carmarthenshire. Went to Hollywood, dined with Charlie Chaplin, saw Ivan Moffat,[1] stayed with Christopher Isherwood, was ravingly miserable for you my true, my dear, my one, my precious love. I shall write to Llewelyn too tomorrow. Love to all our children. Regards to Elizabeth. I'm glad she is with you.

I LOVE YOU   XXX   D.

MS: Maurice Neville

CAITLIN THOMAS

May 7 1950   [headed paper: Hotel Earle Washington Square N W
New York 11, NY]

My Darling

Darling darling dear my dear Caitlin, oh God how I love you, oh God how far away you are, I love you night, day, every second, every oceanic deep second of time, of life, of sense, of love, of any meaning at all, that is spent away from you and in which I only think of coming back, coming back, to you, my heart, my sacred sweetheart, Caitlin my dear one.

It will not be so long now, in terms of days & weeks, before I come back to the true world; but, in terms of lonely, sleepless nights, of heartbreak & horror, it is an eternity. I do not yet know when I can get a boat to sail back on; I know I cannot travel any more by plane. I have three more engagements, one in New York, the other two quite near, & then I am free. I am free from the 15th of May. But boats are hard to get, because of American tourists travelling to Europe, especially to Italy & Holy Year. I have good chances of getting a boat a few days after May 15, but dare not bank on it. So I have reserved a passage, anyway, for June 1st. But, by praying, perhaps I can leave a whole ten days or more before that. But I am coming to you. I love you. I knew, always, I loved you more than any man has ever loved a woman since the earth began; but now I love you more than that. I love you, my dear golden Caitlin, profoundly & truly & forever. Pray God you have not forgotten me. I love you. Pray God you are always good to me, as I to you. Pray God you love me still. I need you. I want you. Oh *dear dear* Cat! Oh my angel. Sometimes I think I shall go mad, & this time properly, thinking of you all day & night as I fly over the continent from university to university, hotel to hotel, stuffed-shirt to stuffed-shirt, heat to heat. It is getting abominably hot. Since I last wrote I have been in Florida, Wisconsin, Indiana, hell getting hotter all the time; I have been in Detroit, the worst city, the home of motorcars; & in and

---

[1] Ivan Moffat, an American script writer, worked for Strand Films in London during the war.

out of New York. I have been so exhausted I was quite incapable of writing a word. After readings, I fell into bed, into sweaty half-awoken nightmares. I couldn't write but I *do* hope you got the £17 cheque from San Francisco & the one last week from Boston. And I hope they helped a little. I think of you, my lovely dear, with all the children screaming in far Laugharne, with Oxford Elizabeth bitching on you, with Cordy[1] running away, with Mary & Alice arriving, with too little money, waking up alone in our beautiful bedroom—please Christ, my love, it *is* always alone—waiting for me, for nothing, for something, listening to Ma Long, hearing the curlews, seeing the herons, wailed at by old ill Thomases. Wait for me a little longer, my own true love. It was, you remember, the end of May on which I was supposed to return. How did I know 3 months could be like the distance from the sun to the earth, only infinitely lonelier. I love you.

I have heard nothing yet from San Francisco about our very possible year's visit there, but will hear before I leave for you. I have also been offered a lovely house in an orange ranch in Florida, but would be paid no money there. Whatever happens, we will return here for a year, you & I & Colm—kiss him for me—to California or the South. Kiss Aeron, too. And later on tonight—it is Sunday midnight in this little hotel in Greenwich Village—I will write to Llewelyn. I am lonely as the grave. This pen will not write. I want you. I love you.

I will write tomorrow to the parents. I have a whole day off before I commit my last few readings. If only *you* were here, we could be happy. I want you in my arms. I want to kiss your breasts! I want to make love to you, to sleep with you, to wake with you, us two in our house, warm, quiet, dear, & holy to one another. I love you.

I am glad Charlie Chaplin wired to you. He said he wanted to send his greetings. He's a very fine man. I was only 2 days in Hollywood, staying with Christopher Isherwood who took me along to Chaplin's to dinner. Chaplin danced & clowned all the time. I met also Ivan Moffat. Ivan says I could get a script to write almost any time. Once we are in San Francisco, we will see: it is not far away.

Next week I will send money again. Sorry it is always for such a curious amount: it is the English equivalent of 50 dollars.

Who is in our house now?

Think of me, my sweet wife, as I think of you.

I Love You. It Won't Be Long Before I am with you, God willing. I'll write very soon. Write to me dear, at this hotel.

I love you, dear dear *dear* darling Cat. I kiss your heart.

Dylan

MS: Maurice Neville

[1] Cordelia Sewell.

D. J. AND FLORENCE THOMAS
[unposted][1]
May 22 1950   [headed paper: Hotel Earle etc]

My Dear Mother & Dad,

How are you both? How, especially, is Dad? I think a great deal of you both, and very often, though I know you would hardly think so from my not-writing for so very long. But indeed, you are constantly in my mind; I worry very much about Dad's health, or lack of it; and, though I hear about you quite often from Caitlin, I still do not really get a clear picture of how you are. Is Dad in bed all the time? Oh, I do hope not. And he doesn't still have to have injections, does he? And how is Mother walking now?

I am sailing for home on June the first, on the Queen Elizabeth. It will take four and half days. So, somewhere in the first week of June, I shall be seeing you. And I am looking forward to it terribly.

At last my tour is at an end. I have visited over forty universities, schools & colleges, from Vancouver, in British Columbia, to Southern Florida. I have travelled right through the Middle West, the North West, & on to the Western Coast of California. After a reading in Indianapolis, a man came up to me & said, in a strong Swansea accent, 'How's D.J. these days? He used to teach me English before the last war. I've been an American citizen now for 25 years.' And he sounded as if he'd just stepped out from Morriston. I didn't get his name, because just then I was captured by someone else. I've met Welsh people after every public reading I've given, several of them from Swansea, Carmarthen, & Pembrokeshire, and all of whom knew Laugharne—or, at least, Pendine. And was, in nearly every case, offered the hospitality of their homes: which I never had time to accept. It has been the time element in this tour that has been most tiring; and the reason, too, I have hardly written any letters at all. I have almost never had a moment to myself, except in bed and then I was too exhausted to do anything. And the varying kinds of climates and temperatures have lessened my energy, too. In Chicago, it was bitterly snowing; a few days later, in Florida, the temperature was ninety. And New York itself never has the same sort of weather 2 days running. So one of my greatest troubles has been to know what to wear; my second greatest trouble, as I flashed round the continent, was that of laundry & cleaners. Sometimes I have to buy a new shirt in each town.

I am writing this in bed, at about seven in the morning, in my hotel bedroom, which is right in Washington Square, a beautiful square, which is right in the middle of Greenwich Village, the artists' quarter of New York. Today I have lunch with my American literary agent, & supper with Anita Loos, who wrote a best-seller years ago called 'Gentlemen Prefer Blondes'. She is interested in a play in which I might appear, as an actor, sometime, though of course it is all very much up in the air.

---

[1] The letter was with Brinnin's papers. It has no alterations and doesn't appear to be a draft.

I am longing to come home.
How is Caitlin *really*? And Aeron & Colm?
Excuse this very bad pencil, & scrappy letter.

Love to you both,

Dylan

MS: Delaware

MARGARET TAYLOR
Sunday June 18 1950   Boat House

My dear Margaret,
   This is my first letter to you for a very long time. Too long. I should
have written, for I wanted to, out of America, but was dizzily dippy most
of my stay there that never stayed quiet. I was floored by my florid and
stertorous spouting of verses to thousands of young pieces whose minds,
at least, were virgin territory; I was giddy agog from the slurred bibble
babble, over cocktails bold enough to snap one's braces, of academic
alcoholics anything but anonymous; I was sick from the muted, boring
thunder of planes in the stratosphere, an unlikely place of little interest; I
was gassed and whimpering after the ministrations of all the sweet, kind
hosts and hostesses who desired their guests to die, in delirium of only
the very best Scotch. I managed to write a few times to Caitlin, mostly
about domestic, that is, financial, matters, and once to the Pelican.[1] To
Llewelyn I sent candy but, much to his disgust, no note. And nothing
more. To you I wanted to send all the whirligig news of a three months '-
and-longer hysterical, thumping chore-and-more, but couldn't get around
to it for blather, haranguing, and rye, for the hospitable hawk-pounce, the
gimlet questions, the dentist-drill telephone, the violent, tentacular in-
timacies of strangers who forget one's existence a moment later, and the
jailing islands of hotel bedrooms from which one must escape at once
even if it is into the hands and un-mercy of bewildered but energetic
poets who sit, downstairs in the lobby, sweating into their lyrics and all
nice as birds.
   I met quiet people and had quiet times without Buchman, but with
those and in those I wilted so gladly I hadn't the strength to lift a pen: all I
could do was dawdle in powerful cars at seventy miles an hour tearing
from Joe's Place to Mick's Steakery, from party to quiet party where
almost nobody got hurt and the first guests to leave left, always, before
dawn. I met contemplative people, brooding among the jukeboxes and
hammering out their lonely poems, on typewriters big as tanks, to the
accompaniment of television, traffic off its head, street fights & acci-

---

[1] The house in Laugharne where his parents now lived, owned by Ebie and Ivy
Williams.

dents, the deaths of dogs and babies, the iceman coming who cometh all the time, and the telephone insistent as a Jacques Tati hornet. But, for the most part, things were loud; louder than people; and, Christ, the music that the police sirens sang!

So I couldn't write, not at all. And even now I can't write the kind of fruity farrago I would like (and you wouldn't) because I must try to answer the questions you put me, in your last letter, about the position of Poets in Universities.

The majority, the big majority, of poets in America *are* attached to universities. Quickly, I can, at the moment, think of only two well-known poets over there who are not: Wallace Stevens, Vice President of an Insurance company, and E. E. Cummings, President, Treasurer, Secretary, & all the shareholders of E. E. Cummings Ltd, a company that exports large chunks of E. E. Cummings to a reluctant public. If the name of a poet is mentioned in passing, someone is sure to say: 'Where does he teach?' But most of these poets are engaged as English lecturers & professors in the ordinary academic run of things. And it is, of course, with the others that you are concerned.

You mentioned Frost in your letter. Robert Frost, the G.O.M. of American poetry, is an exception to all rules, and isn't really to be considered. He is attached, in an honorary capacity, to several universities, but does little more there than give an occasional, perhaps, in some cases, yearly lecture. The universities just use his name, add lustre to their own reputations by *his* reputation, and also, of course, find it a way of paying him honour for his accomplishment and age.

The poets you are most interested in would be, I imagine, far younger men. And a good example might be the young poet, Robert Lowell.

The Library of Congress, at Washington D.C., have, for some few years now, instituted a Chair of Poetry. This is held by a different poet each year, & those who have held it include Allen Tate, Louise Bogan, & Elizabeth Taylor. Lowell had this Chair last year. His job was to be a Poet in Residence, to be the temporary host of visiting writers to the capital, American & foreign, to introduce other writers to them, & to make recordings, many of them later to be issued in albums, commercially, of certain chosen poets.

This year, Lowell is running a Poetry Workshop in Iowa State University, there to 'discuss the demands of the craft, to criticise the individual works of student members of the workshop, and to foster enthusiasm for poetry & the sense of criticism among them.' He attends the workshop a few times a week. He is called a Poet in Residence. There is, in Iowa University, also a writer who runs a prose workshop—for fiction & imaginative writing only—along the same lines.

Lowell is paid the same salary as an Assistant Professor: in his case, between 5 & 6,000 a year. The disparity in incomes, & in spending power, between America & here is so great that this can, of course, give little or no indication of what money a similar post, if established here, would demand.

There are also, in many other universities, other Poetry Workshops. In some of these, the procedure is the same as in Iowa. In some of these, the Poet in Residence is engaged for one year only, to be followed by another poet. In other universities, the Poet is engaged for far longer periods, sometimes permanently. And in many cases, the Poet attends the university only for one, or for 2, terms a year. In other cases, he turns up only a few times a year, to give readings & lectures to all the students of English & to the English faculty.

I think that, for English universities, a plan might be arranged combining all of these different procedures. That is, perhaps the Poet would be in residence the whole of one term, on tap, as it were, to discuss the poetry of students & preside over the criticism of poetry by other students; & he would give occasional readings, lectures, etc, the other two terms. It should not be too difficult to arrange a scheme satisfactory to the poet & to the students alike.

Also, the Poet in Residence could arrange for other poets to come along occasionally as guests, & supervise the activities of the workshop (if it could be called that) for one session or more and/or to read or lecture.

And, also, students could be allowed, & invited, to send along their poems for criticism when the P. in R. is not present at the University.

The whole thing, I think, should be as informal & as give-and-take as possible.

There could, too—as there often is in the U.S.A.—[be] special provision for advanced students, certain periods being set aside when the P. in R. wd be available, for advice & discussion, either in the workshop or in his own rooms, to those who are most serious about being poets & who have produced some real stuff or, at least, the proper beginnings of it.

And I think the idea of a summer seminar for foreign, & U.S.A. students, should thoroughly be gone into.

Many universities, for example, run Writers' Conferences. I enclose the syllabus of one such Conference.

As you can see, I am vague, but extremely enthusiastic, about all this.

Yrs Ever,   Dylan

For your benefit:

1) I visited about 40 universities, including Yale, Harvard, Princeton, Cornell, Columbia, Vassar, Brynmawr, Holyoke, Kenyon, Amherst, Illinois, Notre Dame, Iowa, Los Angeles, Pomona, Santa Barbara, San Francisco, Mills, Brandeis, Seattle, Chicago, Washington, Vancouver, Salt Lake City, Hobart, Florida, Detroit, Indiana, Philadelphia; and recorded poems, later to be made into an album and issued commercially, for the Library of Congress. Also, I recorded for the Library of Harvard, and read in the Museum of Modern Art, New York.

2) I read only modern British poems, from Thomas Hardy to today. I read Hardy, Binyon, Edward Thomas, W. H. Davies, Wilfred Owen, Edwin

Muir, Robert Graves, Andrew Young, T. S. Eliot, W. H. Auden, David Gascoyne, George Barker, Alun Lewis, W. R. Rodgers, Vernon Watkins, W. B. Yeats, de la Mare, Louis MacNeice, Edith Sitwell, Alex Comfort, D. H. Lawrence, John Betjeman, James Stevens, all chosen carefully for what, I hoped, would be an immediate impact upon the audience. They were all, or should have been, clear at a first hearing: or, at least, *much* of their meaning would come immediately across. And it did. The audiences—in some cases, as many as a thousand—were all extraordinarily enthusiastic.

3) Before leaving for the States, I wrote out a large anthology in long-hand. (This helped, of course, to get me thoroughly acquainted with all the poems.) And I never read the *same* selection at more than one place. Thus, I hoped to keep away from any staleness. I used to have all the poems on my lectern, & select from them, as I went on, according to the 'feel' of the audience.

4) Very often, at the end of a reading, I would meet a group, sometimes small, sometimes large, of interested students often in their common room, & talk, & answer questions informally. Sometimes I was invited to a students' party. Sometimes to a very small group in someone's house. I always tried to talk to the students,—never from the platform, this put too much of a formal distance between us—because the readings were for them. And from these meetings I got to learn what, of the poems I had read, they most appreciate, so that I often selected the poems for the next readings as a direct result of what I had learnt.

5) I always prefaced each poem with some prose comments. These, at the beginning of my tour, I wrote out in full; but as I grew more experienced I dispensed with these notes & talked off the cuff, which was far more satisfactory all round.

6) I was invited by the University of California at Berkeley to join, for a year, their Department of Speech. I don't quite know what the function of this Department is, but my appointment wd be as Poet in Residence to discuss & criticise the poems of the students, to foster enthusiasm for poetry & for criticism. No date for my possible appointment was mentioned, but I gather that it is under discussion now.

7) And that's about all.

I hope this, & the preceding pages, will be of some little use.

I hope your & the Registrar's as-yet nebulous plans *will* come to something. And, God, I need some stability.

Stability. You wanted to know some of the details of my—sweet words —financial embarrassments, so that your ravens may help.

Altho' I left Cat £10 a week—not in one sum, but to be delivered by the Bank—& also sent her several cheques from the States, the extravagant woman managed to chalk up, at the Chemist's, a bill for £150.[1] Also, I

---

[1] The Laugharne chemist's was more than a pharmacy, and sold groceries and liquor.

owe Llewelyn's school fees for this term, & Stanier *must* be paid the £50. And I owe Ebie for *many* taxis & for the Pelican. Say another £50. Altogether, £250. And I can raise, immediately, only £50 which I cannot send Stanier as we must manage to live here. I am starting to write some U.S.A. articles for Vogue, etc, but this will take a little time. Oh, ravens, come quick, come quick. Is there any hope? And desperately soon?

Write, please, M, anyway.

And I shall write again, & not all about Poets-in-Bloody-Residence and Work-Bloody-Shops.

Love,
D.

I had a very sweet letter from Dick. He, too, wants me to come to London & look about and try to cash in with newspapers & films. I'll go to London next week.

MS: Texas

JOHN F. NIMS and MRS NIMS[1]
17th July 1950   The Boat House Laugharne Carmarthenshire

My dear Bonnie and John,

Remember me? Round, red, robustly raddled, a bulging Apple among poets, hard as nails made of cream cheese, gap-toothed, balding, noisome, a great collector of dust and a magnet for moths, mad for beer, frightened of priests, women, Chicago, writers, distance, time, children, geese, death, in love, frightened of love, liable to drip.

I never managed to come back, although I so much wanted to. I never answered your nice letters, nor acknowledged the hollyhocks. My only damp excuse is that animal-trainer Brinnin ('Bring 'em back half alive') whipped me all over the wilds after I reluctantly left you, from British Columbia to Florida; I hardly ever knew where I was; I lost the ability to form words on paper; I ranted through my one-night stands like a ruined, sonorous mule; I spent one liquid, libidinous fortnight in New York and was wheelbarrowed on to the Queen Elizabeth by some resident firemen, a psychoanalyst's insane wife, Oscar Williams and *his* wife, whip-cracking Brinnin, a hosier from the Bronx, an eminent playwright (if anonymous), three unidentified men who came either from the Museum of Modern Art or from McSorley's Saloon, a lifelong friend of half an hour, a glossy woman who had made some mistake, and hairy people. Lots of hairy people, all sighing with relief. I shared a cabin with an inventor of a new kind of concrete, called, so far as I could gather, Urine—the inventor,

[1] John Frederick Nims (b. 1913), poet and teacher, had been Thomas's host at the University of Notre Dame, Indiana.

not the concrete—and spent my days with salesmen at the bar. As a result, I have never felt physically better in my life, and go for long walks, healthy as a briar pipe, and sing in the bath (which does not exist), and have clear eyes and a new front tooth—which must have grown, for I have no memory of going to the dentist—and a spring in my step and a song in my gut and poems to write and no need to hurry to write them. I must ruin my health again: I feel so preposterously *well*.

But I do wish I had been able to return to Niles and Schmoo myself to sleep and meet your friends again. Not coming back was one of the things, in all my silly panting around, I most regret. But, if Caitlin and Colm and I come to the States next year—though how we shall achieve this, I don't know yet—may we stay for some days?

And if ever you manage to visit this country, beds, couches, cots, playpens, fish, cockles and mussels, flat warm Welsh bitter beer, affection, a dog as balanced and gifted as yours, sea and river, are all yours in this arsehole of the universe, this hymnal blob, this pretty, sick, fond, sad Wales.

Have you, John, a book of your poems to send me? I shall be giving some radio readings of American poetry, and want very much to read you and Lowell. In return I can send you an old bicycle or a new poem or a picture of Laugharne or any book you want.

Is there any news of the vague project you said you would work on for Caitlin and me and the hornless fiend who is playing at my feet with a scissors?

When you have time, will you write anyway & let me know how you are?

> Love,
> Dylan

Only source: SL

RUTH WITT-DIAMANT
[card, postmarked July 27 1950, London NW8] [written jointly with Stephen and Natasha Spender. Only the sentence beginning 'And this' is in Thomas's hand]

Dear Ruth, Dylan says he loves
you and is as grateful to you
as we are. We have been
meeting and singing your
praises. Stephen. And this is
to say how useless it is to say,
because you know it, that what
Stephen and Natasha say is true.
> Dylan

Elizabeth Matthew & I send lots
of love Natasha.

MS: Berg

JEAN LEROY
August Bank Holiday 1950   The Boat House Laugharne
                                                    Carmarthenshire

Dear Miss LeRoy,
    In answer to your note of August 1st: The fee of ten guineas, plus
£2.15.od expenses is okay for my part in the New Judgement on Edgar
Allan Poe programme broadcast on 23rd July, in the Home Service. My
fares in connection with this broadcast were: [*a blank space*]
    I'd be very much obliged if you would have the cheque sent to me at my
above home address, & *not* to my bank.
    In late reply to yours of 13th July, yes, please do let us close on the basis
that I am paid 50 guineas *on acceptance* of my script, *Letter to America*.[1]

                                                    Yours sincerely,
                                                    Dylan Thomas

MS: Texas

JEAN LEROY
21 Aug 1950 (Wants payments expedited. See Appendix 57.)

PRINCESS CAETANI
[?late summer 1950]   9 Drayton Court Drayton Gardens London S W 10

My dear Madame Caetani,
    A very hurried, & late, note to apologise, profoundly, for all my past
carelessness, & to thank you, from my heart, for the cheque you sent me.
The cheque I have just received. We can pay some bills, and eat. Thank
you, all my life.
    I hurriedly send you a poem, hoping you will like it. I have worked for a
long time on it.

---

[1] Thomas had proposed a 30-minute script about his U.S. trip for the Home Service. It was
   not written.

Also I enclose a Note, for your possible interest, of where this poem will, one day, I hope, find its place.[1]

All I want to do is to be able to write that long, intended poem.

I will write, tomorrow, a letter of all my disastrous news. But not until tomorrow, though I could write, now, a little War & Peace—without much peace—about it. Not until tomorrow, because now I must go out, buy provisions, send off to a Welsh tradesman a months-old howled-for money-order. Because I must tell Caitlin.

I will tell you, tomorrow, why the BBC job failed, why I came back from America without money but happy to have been.

Our domestic life is a pit & trough. On top of it all, poor Caitlin is pregnant again & wants so much to stop it.

When I write tomorrow, I will try to give you my news without too much grovel & self-pity.

In the meantime, do read the poem.

My *deepest* thanks, & apologies.

> Affectionately yours,
> Dylan

Do you think the poem could be typed before you read it properly? I think the difficulty of handwriting, and of my dreadful pen, hinder the reading a lot.

MS: Camillo Caetani Foundation

HELEN MCALPINE
Thursday 14 9 50   Boathouse

Helen,

A very special note, please, dear, to be destroyed straight after reading. I came back to find Caitlin terribly distressed, but managed to tell her that all that that grey fiend had pumped into her ear was lies and poison. And so it was. And Cat believed me. And now we are happy, as always, together again, and that other thing is over for ever.[2] So, please, Helen:

---

[1] The poem was 'In the white giant's thigh'. Thomas had been writing it since the previous year; a worksheet of the poem (at Indiana) has phrases from the letter of 24 November 1949 on the reverse. It was intended to be part of a longer poem (along with 'In country sleep' and 'Over Sir John's hill') to be called 'In Country Heaven'. 'In the white giant's thigh' was completed in time to be broadcast on the Third Programme, 25 September 1950. *Botteghe Oscure* VI (November 1950) published it with a 'Note' about the 'Country Heaven' concept.

[2] While in the U.S., Thomas had an affair with a woman in publishing. Early in September 1950 she visited London—Brinnin came over at about the same time—and she and Thomas saw much of each other over a period of days. According to Brinnin, Thomas said to him, 'I'm in love with [her] and I'm in love with my wife. I don't know what to do.' Margaret Taylor is thought to have told Caitlin. Despite Thomas's efforts to camouflage the episode, it soured their marriage for months to come.

remember; for Cat's sake if not for mine: all, all, all that grey scum said was LIES. When Cat asks you, as she will, you must, please, say: 'It is all LIES. I met the girl with Dylan, and that is all there was to it.' You *must*, Helen, please. Don't answer this, I trust you with everything: which is Cat's happiness. And she is happy with me, though terribly miserable in Wales. We are coming, for a week or two, to London about the 24th of this month. Cat's mother is taking Colm and Aeron for that time, and Llewelyn returns to school. We'd love it if you'd put us up for that short time, but, if you can't, we'll see lots of you anyway. Will you write to Cat about this: I mean, *only* the putting-up part.

Do destroy this. I trust you and my dear Bill implicitly, as you know. All was LIES. And, incidentally, it was. And incidentally, the girl has gone to France, not to return.

Ever,
Dylan

TS: J. M. Dent. The MS is not with other letters to the McAlpines at Buffalo.

RUBY GRAHAM[1]
15 September 1950   The Boat House Laugharne Carmarthenshire

My dear Ruby,
I should have written before—oh, how many letters start like that !—but I have been in London nearly all the time, trying to settle some of my grisly problems and sell myself to Metro-Korda-Odeon as a Celtic Noël Coward, a Welsh J B Priestley, a Swansea Rattigan, a Laugharne cockle. That is, I mean that my last filmscript contract has ended and I have been hunting another down the labyrinthine ways of the nasty studios. This takes a long time; each meeting leads to a conference, each conference to a dinner, each dinner to a hangover, and then in the morning nobody, including oneself, can remember anything and one has to start all over again. However, I have just landed a pretty good picture—good for me, though I never succeed beyond the B's—which begins quite soon.[2]

And now the object of all this hoo-ha? It's to say: Please, Ruby, can I have a little time, quite a short time, before I pay you for all those marvellous fripperies and furbelows Caitlin bought in your shop?

Normally, I'm fixed well enough, in my sordid way, but now, on top of the death of my last contract, the Income Tax Dracula has now got me into such a corner that I've had to agree, through an accountant and agents, to hand him over every single penny I earn until what he wants is

---

[1] Mrs Graham was director of a dress shop. She and her husband Malcolm, who acted with Thomas in the Swansea Little Theatre in the 1930s, were old acquaintances.
[2] This may be an optimistic reference to a documentary he was to write for the Anglo-Iranian Oil Co.

fully paid. So I live, temporarily, on nothing, while working hard for that fiend.

Can you wait a little? I'd be terribly grateful. We're all in such a money mess here, now, in our little howling home full of napkins and old poems.

I hope a lot to see you [. . .]—when I'm able once again to come to S'sea to show Caitlin the big world.

Sorry about all this, but I *do* hope you won't mind.

Love from both

Dylan

MS: Clive Graham

PRINCESS CAETANI

11 November 1950   27 Cranley Mews   Cranley Gardens London S W 7

My dear Madame Caetani,

First of all, and as too often in my miserably too few letters, apologies and apologies to you for this long delay in writing. I had wanted to write at once, to thank you forever, to say how deeply glad I was that you had liked the poem. But I have been ill for several weeks, in and out of sick-beds in several, and increasingly depressing, furnished London rooms and spiritual orphanages. I caught lots of chills, and they jaundiced me, and I lay snarling at the edge of pleurisy, and I couldn't write or read and I didn't want to think. Caitlin went to an illicit hellhole to have her pregnancy killed because she cannot and will not deal with another child in the topsy-turtle life we reluctantly lead, and now is sad and weak. And I just couldn't thank you for your great generosity, though it was upon that we built our breath those days. Please, in your goodness, accept, once again, my saying: Forgive me for the long, ill delay, and it was not caused by my lack of gratitude nor by my not thinking of you with sincere affection. London I find bad, though maybe only for me. So many of my friends here are friends only so long as I am hopeless, lost, merry, and noisy. I want to be quiet and found, unhappy at home or at anywhere but not here, not here—not in a borrowed room in a crabbed and feckless house, all lumped together in a soya bean mock-sausage, twanging on each other's nerves like Saint Vitus on a harp. It's really the squalid devil, all in one London room with napkins and food and spilt books and flung clothes and a baby rampant & all the radios of hell turned on full moron-tilt. And there's that small house in Wales, seemingly secure, snug, & all-to-be desired, from this distance, as a house in Trollope. But I can't return to it until I have finished some work here; then, with the money derived from the work, I'll be able to pay some, a few, of the bigger and fiercer Welsh debts; but here it's so hard to work. And Caitlin won't return alone, for the loneliness there is as dispiriting to her as the sardine-cluster here. My, my, what misery!

And all this is one of my old squeals. I shall fashion a morose bagpipe for it, and play all night in the rain.

I made money in America, but returned with very, very little. Firstly, the man who arranged my programme of lectures—I read & lectured only at Universities & Colleges, with three exceptions—arranged it, though kindlily, badly. I found I had enormous air-trips to make between engagements, and these, almost always, I had to pay myself. He'd omitted to make allowances for considerable travelling expenses. Secondly, I had, at the end of my engagements, over a month in New York. There I had to live, at my own expense, in an hotel. Thirdly, the American Income Tax took about 30 per cent of what remained. And, when I returned to England, I found that the broadcasting job I had been promised would not materialise after all.

Now, I am writing a long radio play, which will, I am sure, come to life on the printed page as well. I should like you to see this, when it is finished. With luck—I mean, if I can live till then—it will be finished early in the New Year. I am enjoying writing it enormously. It is not like anything else I have done, though much of it is poetry.

And I will have a new poem—part of the long poem—for you *by Christmas*.

Oh, & I forgot. Please do print the prose note about the long poem if you want to.

You'll try to forgive me, won't you, for not writing for so long & for not acknowledging the money which saved us from—I hear the squealing bagpipe of my woe again, so I'll say only that it saved us. Will you forgive me? I do feel still so beastly unwell.

Write when you can; and the Christmas poem is certain.

Thank you, very much.

Yours affectionately,
Dylan

MS: Camillo Caetani Foundation

DOUGLAS CLEVERDON
[?late 1950]   [headed paper: SAVAGE CLUB]

Douglas Cleverdon (b. 1903) was a bookseller and publisher who joined the BBC in 1939 and became a key producer of literary features for the Third Programme after the war. He used Thomas often as actor and reader, and hoped to produce his as yet unfinished radio play on the Third Programme. Its title was not yet *Under Milk Wood*. Cleverdon wrote to Thomas, 20 October 1950, to say that the Third Programme 'have agreed to take The Town that Was Mad (or whatever title you prefer)'. On November 3 he urged Thomas to press on with it. On December 12 he wrote again, this time calling it 'The Village that Was Mad'. Thomas's letter sending the 39 pages is in the BBC file at this point. It was another three years before the play was finished.

Many apologies for having forgotten
the books.   Tomorrow.

Dear Douglas,

Here are the first 39 pages of the provisionally titled 'The Town That Was Mad'. I hope it won't be too hard for whoever types it to follow. No notice should be taken of the rings round several of the words.

I've just read these pages over again & am very enthusiastic to finish the thing. And quickly.

The whole play will, I think, take more than an hour.

See you Friday.

Dylan

Quite a number of the short introductory bits will be extended.

MS: BBC

CAITLIN THOMAS
5.30 Sunday [?1950]   On the Train

I'll wire you to tell you
what train I catch

Leaving you, my love, without kissing you, or being kissed by you, hurt more than my legendary back, my ham of misery. And all the way, limping and squealing along the cliff, I hoped & hoped I was too late for the car. But go I would have to, whether then or Monday morning, so perhaps it wasn't too bad that I caught the train and now, in the buffet car, am writing to you to say: I love you for ever, day & night, all my life & death, I love you, Caitlin. Forgive my bellows when I'm hurt, my snarling recriminations which are really only against the weather, the world, God, bombs, penury, drink, myself, but *never* you. Never you, my dearest wife. The waiters in this buffet car are the same we met when you & Ivy and I went together to London on Sunday, nearly a year ago, and they all asked fondly after you. Everybody asks fondly about you, but I am the only one who loves you always; and you are mine.

The train is a horribly slow one, stops at every station. It won't be in Paddington until about 9.30, which will hardly give me time to have a drink with either John D. or Bob. I don't know yet whose house I grace: probably Bob, because he is nearer to the BBC & my Celtic huddle of poets. I'll tell Bob & [?Shelah][1] you are writing, and, myself, find out what they intend to do about Christmas. If they come, would they stay in the Pelican and eat with us? I love you. The waiters have just asked me to play cards, & so I will. One of them I told about my injured back, & he said, without interest, 'Too bad. Now *I've* got a little pimple just inside

---

[1] Bob Pocock and his wife.

my nose—look here! you can hardly see it—and it makes me feel all nose. It's burning all the time.' I gave a cry as my back hurt me, & he said, 'That's what I feel like doing about my nose too.' People are very selfish. I love you for ever, my darling, my beautiful dear Cattle-Anchor, & I want you too.

Dylan

MS: Maurice Neville

CAITLIN THOMAS
[1950?] [on a torn scrap of paper]

Please my own Caitlin my dear darling I love I you I love you my dear. And forgive my bad temper this morning: it was because I knew I had to leave you, in the vile cold. Caitlin my darling I love you forever.

Dylan

I might try to come back tonight. But certainly sometime tomorrow. I'll ring.

MS: Thomas Trustees

BENJAMIN ARBEID[1]
December 7 1950 [draft]   The Boat House Laugharne Carmarthenshire
Wales

Dear Mr. Arbeid,
   Will you forgive me, please, for not having answered your letter of months ago? It was extremely kind of you to write, and I must seem most ungrateful not to have answered at once. I've been away from this address for some time, and the local post office, while forwarding some letters, decided to slip others into the letter-box so that they might wait, un-opened, on the mat for, so far as they cared, ever. I have just found your own letter today.
   Thank you for reading my very briefly suggested treatment of 'The Shadowless Man'—though it is so long ago now that very likely you may have forgotten it. And thank you for saying such very encouraging things about it. [*the next sentence has been deleted*: I did, of course, realise at the time how impracticable a subject it was in the light of Wardour Street's reaction to it.] Your suggestion that I should try it out on Cocteau, I shall certainly do something about.
   [...] hope that the possibility of you and your associates, sometime in

---

[1] Ben Arbeid, later a film producer, was then a freelance production manager.

the future, contacting me with regard to a possible film-writing con-
signment; I do hope this hasn't vanished into thin air. I'm about to go to
Persia to write a filmscript for Anglo-Iranian Oil—some kind of technicolor documentary, though God knows what it will turn into—but I
shall be returning to London in February.[1] Could we perhaps meet then?
Or, anyway, I should be very glad if you could drop me a line.

Yours sincerely,
Dylan Thomas

MS: Texas

HAROLD NICOLSON

Dec 7 1950   The Boat House Laugharne Carmarthenshire

Dear Mr. Harold Nicolson,

  Will you please forgive me for not answering your letter at once? It was very
very kind of you to write to the Secretary of the Royal Literary Fund about me,
and I'm extremely glad you will put my name forward.[2] It must, I know, seem
very rude indeed of me not to thank you a long time before this: I've been ill,
too ill to do anything but moan about it and my difficulties, and there was a
lot of trouble about changes of addresses and losing of letters, and then my
wife brought me home to get well in the country, and then, at home, the
difficulties came piling on me more heavily than ever, and I think I lost heart.

  The Secretary of the Fund wrote to me, and sent me a form of
application for a grant. This, too, I was unable to answer in time, and now
I find that my application can't come up at the next meeting on December 13, as the Secretary has to have it, along with some letters
supporting my case, at least seven days before the meeting. I've written
him today, but my case must, I'm afraid, wait now until January 10. I do
hope a grant will be made me. It's very urgent.

  I hope you will forgive me for this long delay.

And thank you very much.
Yours sincerely,
Dylan Thomas

TS: Royal Literary Fund

---

[1] The film, directed by Ralph Keene, was to show what benefits Western technology was
bringing Iran.

[2] Once again Thomas turned to the Fund. The author Harold Nicolson (1886–1968) had
written to the secretary, now J. G. Broadbent, in November to recommend him. On
December 8 Nicolson wrote again: '. . . I should of course have to disclose to the Committee that he is a very heavy drinker . . . you may have encountered similar circumstances
in which the money is paid in such a way as not to be spent entirely on drink . . . I gather
that his wife is almost equally unreliable. On the other hand, he is one of our best poets,
and if the Literary Fund exists for anything, it exists to enable such people to write a few
more poems before they go completely to pieces.'

UNKNOWN ADDRESSEE[1]
[?1950] [fragment; probably a draft]   The Boat House Laugharne
                                                    Carmarthenshire

Dear Sirs,
   I am applying for a Grant because I most urgently need financial help so
that I can go on working and be able to make enough money to keep
myself and my family.
   I am extremely badly in debt; these debts are pressing, and daily and
horribly becoming more so; and it seems that I cannot think of anything
else at all.
   Surrounded by these debts, hurt and worried to despair in the very
middle of them, and seeing and hearing my home crumble because of
them, I cannot write, they come between me and everything else I do.
And, as I can't write, I can't make any money, and so new day-by-day
debts arise; and I can't see any good end to this, and I would be insane if I
could.
   Less and less do I seem able to concentrate on anything except these
worries and despairs—(the writing of this letter is a kind of torture, my
mind keeps jerking painfully away to the thoughts of writs and
tradesmen's bills)—and more and more important grow these beastly
little griefs to me

MS: Texas

A BANK MANAGER
8 December 1950 [draft]   The Boat House Laugharne
                                                    Carmarthenshire

Dear Sir,
   Please forgive me for not being able, as I very much wanted, to come
along & see you in London about my rather strained financial affairs. I
was caught up with very frenzied preparations for my Persian visit, & also
with domestic crises, including illness.
   I am sorry that, through no fault of my own except carelessness—probably, to one's Bank Manager, one of the worst faults of all—I wrote, while
in London, cheques for which there was [not] enough money in my
account to provide for. I had been informed that a cheque for a £100 was
on its way to your Bank, & accordingly, & foolishly, though not, I swear
dishonestly, took premature advantage of it. I shall have, now, to come
back to London early next week to see that that £100 is paid in at once.
   Also, I should tell you now, as I shd have told you in our interview that,
unfortunately, never took place, that I have seen Mr Anthony Hubbard

[1] The letter may have been connected with his Royal Literary Fund application.

about that cheque I made out to him, payable on June 1, & he has agreed that he & I shd deal with it privately.

And now, a most sincere plea: I have had to cash, locally, a cheque for £5, dated today, the 8th, & made payable to I. Williams. Will you *please* see that this is honoured. If it was dishonoured, I should be in a *very* painful situation here, & here is a very narrow & hidebound small Welsh town: my fellow countrymen are not, as you know, altogether anti-pathetical to money. Will you please do this for me? I *had* to cash the cheque. And I shall pay in a £100 this week.

MS: Texas

MARGARET TAYLOR
[?1950]   Laugharne

My dear Margaret,

I was so very sorry to have had to ask you, yet again, for money. I hate doing it; especially as I know how difficult it is now for you, with all your great kindness, to help me.

The coalmen would give us no more coal unless we paid their bill. This bill I had to pay by cheque. And there was, in my bank, no money to meet it. Therefore, the cheque would be returned. Therefore, the coalmen would be vile, & there would be no more coal. So, I had to have £20 to send in to the bank to say: 'Do what you must with other cheques, but *please* honour the cheque to Frank H. Brown'. If I get your cheque, by Saturday—I'll just save things. If I don't, we must, I suppose, leave Laugharne.

Thank you, *a great deal*, for trying to help; & I hope to God you can.

Sorry for my exhausted bloodiness the last day of my London visit.

I shall, I hope, if I can raise the fare, see you Monday.

Yours,
Dylan

MS: Texas

JEAN LEROY
15 Dec 1950 (Details BBC expenses due. See Appendix 58.)

JOHN DAVENPORT
19 12 50   The Savage Club   1 Carlton House Tce   London   SW1

Dear Brother Savage John Davenport,
    It is a time-honoured custom of the Club to which we both have the
honour to belong, to address one another fraternally thus. If this were not
so, the appellation I should, in all honesty, be compelled to attach to your
name would be one singularly lacking in cameraderie.
    Your cherished illusion is, I must suppose, that your fellow members
remain in a state of ignorance as to the real purpose for which you joined
the Club. May I point out to you that one member, at least, is under no
illusion as to that purpose, which is to purloin from the Smoking Room
the only copies of The Stage and The New Yorker?
    If, as is obvious, you have no respect for other members who might
wish to peruse those periodicals, have you none for Literature? This, as
you well know, is a Club which regularly wines & dines such notable
practitioners of that Art as Reginald Arkell, Alec Waugh, Tschiffeley,
Louis Golding, Dale Collins, and L. I. F. Brimble. Are you not letting
down their good name, and the good name of all your fellow-scribblers —
under which heading I humbly class myself—when you stoop so low as
utterly and wantonly to disregard the injunction, Not To Be Taken Away,
which is stamped upon every periodical in the Smoking Room?
                                        Yours sincerely,
                                        Dylan Thomas, F.R.S.L.

MS: Texas   *SL*

JOHN DAVENPORT
19th Dec 1950   The Boat House Laugharne Carmarthenshire

Dear John,
    Many thanks for writing. The messages of good will were indeed
welcome, and are reciprocated. I trust that the New Year will find us both
in better financial fettle.
                                        Yours,
                                        Dylan

MS: Texas

JOHN DAVENPORT
[?December 1950]   Boat House

My dear John,
   The Pococks are going back to London on the 27th. I am going to
London on the 2nd of January. Can you come down between those dates?
We would love to have you, & are looking forward immensely to it. *Do
try*.

                        Love to Margery & Hugo & Roger,
                                              Dylan

MS: Texas

J. G. BROADBENT (Royal Literary Fund)
January 1 1951   The Boat House Laugharne Carmarthenshire

Dear Mr Broadbent,
   Thank you very much for your letter, and please excuse my (once more)
very long delay in answering: I have been ill again, all over Christmas
unfortunately, & for some time before. I am afraid my recurrent illness
has set back a lot what hopes I had of being helped by the Royal Literary
Fund, but it was, quite obviously, unavoidable. I still do hope something
may come of my application when it is, as I so much trust it will be,
brought to the notice of the Committee on January 13.
   In your letter, you said you wanted to know the amounts of my various
debts. Well, here they are, & I am afraid they are enormous: written
down, they seem more frightening to me than ever.
   For my son's schooling, I am in debt £100. (He goes to Magdalen
College School.) For one year's rent of my own house—I mean, the house
in which I & my wife & children live—I owe another £100.
   And I owe yet another £100 for the rent of my parents' house.
   Tradesmen's bills in the town amount, approximately, to £60.
   And our clothing bills come to, approximately, £30.
   I know this amounts to quite a hideous sum, but there it is.[1]
   My present income is, as I think I tried to explain in my letter to the
Committee, frightfully erratic, coming only from my poems, occasional
stories, & some freelance work for the radio.
   My commitments for the near future—& I'm glad to be able to strike
one slightly happier note in all this woeful parade of debts—will be

---

[1] Thomas was given a grant of £300, but it was instantly swallowed up by debts, which the
Fund appears to have paid direct. Magdalen College School (where Llewelyn was a
boarder) received £147; a girls' school (Aeronwy was also a boarder), £18; Savage Club,
£15; Laugharne pharmacy and post office (with whisky and Guinness prominent on the
bill), £50 on account of £117 owing.

covered by a film-writing job I am just about to do. But that job—very possibly the only lucrative one I shall have this coming year—is meant to keep us while I do more work at home to get money. What I just *cannot* do, by myself, is pay the past, & increasingly pressing, debts.

Sorry if this letter is vague: I still feel pretty groggy.

Thank you again for your letter. I hope that, by this time, you've received two letters to support my application: I wrote to Augustus John & Lord David Cecil, both of whom agreed to speak, or, rather, write for me.

Yours very sincerely,
Dylan Thomas

MS: Royal Literary Fund

CAITLIN THOMAS
[Jan 1951]   c/o Information Dept Anglo-Iranian Oil Co Avenue Shah
(Naderi) Tehran Persia

Caitlin my darling, dear, dear Caitlin, oh my love so far away I love you. All these strange, lost days I love you, and I am lost indeed without you my dear wife. This is so much further than America, and letters will take so much longer to travel to you and yours to me if you will ever write to me again oh *darling* Cat. And if you do not write to me, and if you do not love me any more, I cannot go on, I cannot go on sleeplessly thinking, 'Caitlin my Cattleanchor, my dear, does not love me, o God let me die.'[1] I can't live without you; I can't go travelling with this long, wan Bunny[2] through this fearful, strange world unless I am sure that at the end we will be together as we are meant to be together, close & alone except for our cuckoo whom I miss very very very much, more than I could dream of. But you: I miss you more than I would miss my life although you *are* my life. I can see now, in this grand over-hot Oil-Company Guest House where we are staying, your smiling and your anger, your coldness with me, your once-love for me, your golden hair & blue eyes and our wedding ring from a cracker, I can see you coming to bed, I can feel your coldness turning, in my arms, to warmth and love, I can hear you so beautiful with Cuckoo Colm Colum Column, I can hear you saying, 'I love you', 'I hate you', 'Go away', 'Come close' to me all the blessed days of our life. Caitlin beloved, unless you write to say that we will be together again, I shall die. I love you I love you, day, night, waking, sinking into some kind of sleep. This letter may take a week to reach you, or it may take three days; however long or short a time, oh darling darling write to me. There

[1] Thomas had left on the documentary-film trip with the row over his American mistress (who was already an ex-mistress) ringing in his ears.
[2] Ralph Keene.

will be nothing but pains & nightmares & howlings in my head and endless endless nights & forsaken days until you say, 'I am waiting. I love you.'

Forgive me, darling, for this business of money. I went with John D., as you know, on Tuesday to London & left you ten pounds to last a week. Then, when I rang on Saturday, you said the money had gone & you must have more. I know, I know, it goes terribly quickly, but somehow ten pounds a week *must*, I'm sorry dear, see you through. You said, in your lovely letter that I picked up on Sunday from John, that the Princess had wired to say she was sending more money. But, until her cheque is in the Bank, I can't let you have a cheque for Dathan Davies. So: will you see which of the letters that has arrived for me bears Italian stamps, open it, and if it has the princess's cheque (probably for £50) in it, send it on to me at the c/o Information Dept address, and I will send a cheque for the whole amount to you *at once. Or*, you can sign the cheque on the back with *my name*, if you like, and put it through my father's account. *Or*, you can sign the cheque with my name, give it to Dathan Davies in payment of their account & then have the £10-odd change for yourself. Do one of these things *as quickly as possible*. And, please, forward my letters as quickly as possible too: there should be a cheque in one of them with which I can pay Llewelyn's school fees. Now, for the moment, all I can pathetically do is enclose a cheque to Eric Jones made out for £5. This sounds absurdly small an amount to send all the way from Persia, but it's all I dare do until I know there is some more money in the Bank: and the only way I can know that is to see the letters which have arrived since I left. You will be receiving, at the beginning of each week, ten pounds in notes from Bunny's firm, for five weeks—by which time I shall be back in England. By which time, if you will ever have me again, I shall be at home with you. I love you, darling darling, darling. I LOVE YOU. I know I should have written to you in the five days I was in London before I and that long drip flew away, but I knew I would phone at the end of the week. Oh, *please* forgive me. I love you so much, so very much I can think of nothing else. I love you. I love you Caitlin. Please write at once, please forward all letters. Please read carefully that bit about the Princess's cheque. The sun's shining, & I'm in darkness because I do not know if you will ever love me again. And I'll die if you do not. I mean that. I shall not kill myself: I shall die. Our life together is for ever & ever amen. I love you.

I have to go out to see the town of Tehran which, at a quick look, seems depressing and half-made. When I come back, I shall write you again today.

The plane trip took 24 hours &, on arriving, Bunny had a collapse.

I LOVE YOU, MY ONLY CAITLIN DARLING.

> Love to our children.
>
> Your husband in the darkness,
> Dylan

MS: Maurice Neville

CAITLIN THOMAS
[January 1951] c/o Information Department Anglo-Iranian Oil Company
Avenue Shah (Naderi) Tehran Persia

I will write to
Llewelyn & Aeron, &
my mother & father
from Abadan. My love
Cat. Write to me quickly.
I love you.

Dear Cat Catlin darling, I love you. There's no meaning to anything without you. There's no meaning without us being together. I love you all the day and night, and I am five thousand miles away. Until I hear from you, Cat, every minute of the day and night's insane. I have to dope myself into nightmare sleep with tablets from Bunny's enormous medicine-chest. I wake up before it is dawn, in this great undersea bedroom under snow-mountains, and turn the echoes of your voice over and over in the dark, and look into your blue beautiful undersea eyes five thousand miles away: they're all that is real, the deepnesses of your eyes [...] the shadows of your voice, East, [...] or anywhere in the world.[1] Write [...] Cat dear. Say that you want me still, [...] you will wait for me. I love you. [...] of you all day and night: you in [...] saken seahouse in God knows what [...] misery and rain and hate of me: [...], in the snow & the sun, understanding nothing of the savage town around, wanting to know nothing of ugly, dirty, dinning Tehran with mosques and sores and disease and Cadillacs. I think of you always. I love you, Caitlin my wife for ever though you throw away my life. Write to me, Cat. My dear.

The long Bunny is still in bed, groaning: he has a 'little chill', he says, has a huge fire in his room, two hotwaterbottles, an array all over his bedside table of syrups, pills, syringes, laxatives, chlorodyne, liniments and compresses; he uses a thermometer every hour. And I? I go with horrible oil-men to interview horrible government-men; I sit in the lounge of this posh Guest-House for horrible oil-men and listen to Scotch engineers running down the Persian wops; I go, with a pleasant Persian guide, through endless museums, palaces, libraries, cou[...] law, houses of parliament, till my [...] and my boredom bleed. What for, what [...] for? Only the bazaar was wonderful [...] Tehran bazaar, the largest in Persia [...] all the things one's read about [...] bazaars, all the bits of films of [...] one's ever seen, haggling and cursing and grinning and smelling everywhere round one: miles of covered bazaar, smelling of incense and carpets and food and poverty. And women with only their eyes showing through tattered, dirty, cobble-trailing thin black sack-wraps; or lifting their wraps high to miss the mud and showing men's ragged trousers or baggy

[1] A corner is missing from one sheet.

black bloomers; and lots of them with splayed and rotting high-heel shoes. Only the very poor—that is, the vast majority—of women wear these wrappings, not only of black but of grey, earth-brown, filthy white —and they wear them only to cover up their rags. They huddle their horrible poverty inside these chadurs as they slipslop through the foul main streets or the shouting, barging aisles of the bazaar. Often there are babies huddled in with the poverty. And beautiful dirty children in little chadurs slip-slop behind them. The poor in the streets & the bazaar wear every kind of clothing, so long as it's dirty and wretched. Men wear little green brimless bowlers, or caps like scavenging tram-conductors', and old army overcoats, British, German, American. Poor children all have cropped heads. Well-to-do children have their eyes darkened with kohl or mascara.

The only water for the poor in Tehran—the capital city of Persia—runs down the public gutters. I saw an old man pissing in the gutter, walking away a few yards, then cupping his hands & drinking from it. This running cesspool is the only drinking & washing water for the poor. I love you. I love you. I love you in this dirty city. I love you everywhere.

There is no nightlife at all in Tehran. Moslems are not supposed to drink, though some do. Only in one or two expensive hotels for Europeans can you buy a drink. There seems to be no fixed price for any drinks. I was charged six shillings for a bottle of beer, Bunny twelve shillings for a small whiskey. Only in welltodo houses—and in this Guest-house for oil-men—can one drink at all. In four days I have had eight pints of beer: all lager. I love you, I love you in this dry city. I love you everywhere.

Write to me quickly, darling. Tell me tell me. Shall I bring back Persian sweetmeats? (I cannot send them: they would evaporate or burst.) There are wonderful liqueur chocolates you would love. But not so much as I love you. I love you. I love you. I love you Cat.

D.

MS: Maurice Neville

CAITLIN THOMAS
16th January [1951]   [headed paper: Ahwaz Persian Gulf]

Caitlin dear,
    I do not know if this letter will reach you at all, or if my other two letters have reached you. I do not know if, whether any of these letters has reached you or will reach you, you will reply to them. I do not know anything, except that I love you. And I do not know if you love me. I love you enough for both of us, but I must know, still, if you are waiting for me, if you want me, if I may come home to you, if there is any cause for

me to live. I love you, Caitlin darling dear. Perhaps my letters take very long to travel the miles between us, and so that is why I do not hear from you. Perhaps you have said: 'He is dead to me'. And, if you say that, indeed I will be dead. I love you, love you, love you, always, always, beautiful Cat my love. What I am doing here, without word of you, I just don't know. Yesterday I left Tehran for Abadan, and am stopping here for the night, in an Arabian house, after a twenty-four [hour] train journey. By plane, the journey would have taken 2½ hours. And so the powerful, tireless Bunny with his immense pharmacopeia, decided to go by train. It, of course, nearly killed him; and it has done me no good either. But, if I heard from you, if I knew, for one second, that you are mine, as I am yours, that you might again love me as I love you forever, I'd travel a thousand hours on the roof of the train. I grope through the nights and days like a blind man; even English around me is an unknown language; I am writing to you, my love, my wife, my darling dear Cat, the one soul and body in the world, as though I didn't know words: stiltedly, awkwardly. I love you. I can at least write that.

Yesterday morning, in Tehran, I went to a large hospital. In the children's wards, I saw rows and rows of tiny little Persian children suffering from starvation: their eyes were enormous, seeing everything & nothing, their bellies bloated, their matchstick arms hung round with blue, wrinkled flesh. One of them was crying: only one. I asked the English sister why. 'Poor little thing', she said. 'His mother went out every day begging in the streets, & he was too weak from hunger to go with her & she was too weak to carry him. So she left him alone in her hovel. The hovel had a hole dug in the earth floor where a fire always was; or at least hot cinders, ready for cooking. The child fell down into the fire & lay there *all day* burning till the mother came home at dusk. He is getting better, but he's lost one arm & all his toes.'

After that, I had lunch with a man worth 30,000,000 pounds, from the rents of peasants all over Iran, & from a thousand crooked deals. A charming, and cultivated, man.

Now all the weather's changed. In Tehran, it was brisk, sunny spring. A wonderful climate. Here, 24 hours nearer the Gulf, I'm sitting dead still and panting & sweating. What it's like in the summer, Christ knows. In Tehran, they said: It will be cold down here. I brought a tweed suit & a duffle, & the temperature's nearly a 100. There are great palm trees in this garden, & buzzards overhead. At every station of this 24-hour journey—& the stations are very odd; they cater for no-one—children rushed up to the train from the mud-hut villages: three quarter naked, filthy, hungry, and, mostly, beautiful with smiles & great burning eyes & wild matted hair: begging for the smallest coins, pieces of bread, a sweet, anything. I gave the first lot my lunch, & woof! it went in a second. I love you. So write to me please, if you value me at all. Goodnight, my love.

Oh, it would be wonderful to be with you, to be in your lovely arms, my love. It's seven o'clock in the morning; I'm lying in bed; already it's awfully hot; together we could be happy, we could go out into the garden in the sun, into the striped streets, on to the river banks. Yesterday evening, just before dusk, I saw four men, in long Arabian dress, squatting in a circle on a tiny mudbank in the middle of the river. The mudbank was just large enough to hold them. The sun was going down quickly, the river was rising. The four men were playing cards. Together here, or anywhere, in any dusty sunfried place, we could be happy, my dear love. I love you. I feel you & smell you, & hear you everywhere all around me. I see you in our pink house, so far away, I could yell till I die. Remember me, sweetheart. If I didn't think that, at the end of this wandering rubbish, I'd be with you again—and we could together prepare to be somewhere else; I wrote, last week, to San Francisco—I'd melt away, saying your name, into the hot sea. I love you love you love you love you, & I am yours & you are mine. Tell me, when, & if ever, you write, how you dealt with the Princess's cheque. If you forward letters, I will see if there is any money in the Bank & then I can send you some. BUT WRITE. I'm lost without you. Tell me about Colm, Aeron, & Llewelyn. I'll send Llewelyn stamps of Iran. My dear!

Dylan

MS: Maurice Neville

A WOMAN FRIEND[1]
[about January 17 1951]   Abadan

[...]

I am writing this in a tasty, stifflipped, liverish, British Guest House in puking Abadan on, as you bloody well know, the foul blue boiling Persian buggering Gulf. And lost, God blast, I gasp between gassed vodkas, all crude and cruel fuel oil, all petroleum under frying heaven, benzola bitumen, bunkers and tankers, pipes and refineries, wells and derricks, gushers and super-fractionators and [?Shatt]-el-Arab and all. Today I was taken to see a great new black-towered hissing and coiling monster, just erected in the middle of the refinery. It cost eight million pounds. It is called a Cat-Cracker.

Abadan is inhibited almost entirely by British—or so it seems. There are thousands of young Britishers in the bachelor quarters, all quietly seething. Many snap in the heat of their ingrowing sex and the sun, and are sent back, baying, to Britain. Immediately, their places are taken by fresh recruits: young wellgroomed pups with fair moustaches and briar pipes, who, in the soaking summer, soon age, go bristled about, chainsmoke damp hanging fags, scream blue on arak, toss themselves

---

[1] Thomas's relationship with this woman, who is still alive and unwilling to be identified, dates back to his American visit the previous year.

trembly all sleepless night in the toss-trembling bachelors' quarters, answer the three-knock knock at the midnight door, see before them in the hot moonlight wetmouthed Persian girls from the bazaar who ask, by custom, for a glass of water, invite the girls in, blush, stammer, grope, are lost. These old-young men are shipped back also, packed full with shame and penicillin. And the more cautious stay on, boozed, shrill, hunted, remembering gay wonderful London so white-skinned and willing.

I visited oil-fields in the mountains last week. By night, the noise of frustrated geologists howled louder than the jackals outside my tent. Utterly damned, the dishonourable, craven, knowledgeable, self-pitying jackals screamed and wailed in the abysses of their guilt and the stinking garbage pails. 'Rosemary', 'Jennifer', 'Margery', cried the nearmale un-sleepers in their near-sleep. And the hyenas laughed like billyho deep down in their dark diseased throats. O evergreen, gardened, cypressed, cinema'd, oil-tanked, boulevarded, incense-and-armpit cradle of Persian culture, rock me soft before lorn hotel-bedtime. I have nostalgia and gout. [...] My toe pulses like a painful cucumber in the arraky bar. O city of Hafiz and Sad'i and Mrs. Wiltshire the Consul's wife, tickle me till my balloon toe dies [...] A lonely country. And so is stricken Persia, mosque and blindness, fountains and mudhuts, Cadillac and running sore, pomegranate and Cat-Cracker. Beer in an hotel bar costs ten shillings a bottle; whiskey, one pound a nip. There is no nightlife. Shiraz sleeps at nine. Then, through the dark, the low camel bells ring; jackals confess their unworthiness to live in an ignoble fury of siren howls and utter their base and gutter-breathed gratitude to the night that hides their abominable faces; insomniac dogs rumpus in the mountain villages; the Egyptian deputy-Minister of Education, who has the next hotel room, drunkenly gallumphs with a thin, hairy secretary; dervishes plead under my bed; there are wolves not far away. There is no night life here; the moon does what she does, vermin persist, camels sail, dogs defy, frogs gloat, snow-leopards drift, ibex do what they do, moufflon are peculiar, gazelles are lonely, donkeys are Christian, bears in the high hills hug [...]

                                                                    Dylan

TS: J. M. Dent   *SL*

CAITLIN THOMAS
[January 1951]   Isfahan Iran

Caitlin dear,
    Your letter, as it was meant to, made me want to die. I did not think that, after reading it so many times till I knew every pain by heart, I could go on with these days and nights, alone with my loneliness—now, as I know too well, for ever—and knowing that, a long way and a lifetime

away, you no longer loved or wanted me. (After your cold, disliking letter, you wrote: 'All my love, Caitlin.' You could have spared that irony.) But the bloody animal always *does* go on. Now I move through these days in a kind of dumb, blind despair, and slowly every day ends. It's the nights I fear most, when the despair breaks down, is dumb and blind no longer, and I am only myself in the dark. I am only alone in an unknown room in a strange town in a benighted country, without any pretences and crying like a fool. Last night I saw you smiling, glad, at me, as you did a thousand years ago; and I howled like the jackals outside. Then, in the morning, it was the same again: walking, in despair, frozen, over a desert. It was even a real desert, the camels aloof, the hyenas laughing. I'm writing this, perhaps last, letter, just before I go to bed in an hotel full of brutes. If only I didn't have to go to bed. Nobody here, in this writing room, the wireless shouting Persian, can see anything wrong with me. I'm only a little fat foreigner writing a letter: a loving, happy letter to his wife 'waiting at home'. Christ, if they knew. If they knew that the woman I am writing to no longer needs me, has shut her heart & her body against me, although she is my life. I cannot live without you—you, always—and I have no intention of doing so. I fly back, from Tehran to London, on, I am almost certain, the 14th of February. I shall cable you from Tehran the time of my arrival. You said, before we parted, that you would come up to London to meet me on my return. You will not, I suppose, be doing that now? If you are not, will you please—it is not a great deal to ask—leave a message at the McAlpines. I will not come back to Laugharne until I know that I [?am] wanted: not as an inefficient mispayer of bills, but as myself and for you. If you do not meet me in London, I shall ring the McAlpines. If there is no message there from you, I shall know that everything is over. It is very terrible writing this such a great distance from you. In a few minutes I shall go to my bedroom, climb into bed in my shirt, and think of you. The bedroom knows your name well, as do many bedrooms in this country. 'Caitlin, Caitlin', I will say, and you will come drifting to me, clear & beautiful, until my eyes blur and you are gone. I love you. Oh, darling Cat, I love you.

Dylan

MS: Maurice Neville

JOHN DAVENPORT
[?1951]   *You know where*

John my dear,

How's everybody who's nobody in, dear, dead Chelsea these excruciating days? How's little Mary, the twenty-seventh Mews? and her oh so tantalising spraygun Michael? Still sculpting away? What a bore for the bronze! And, yes, do tell me, in words of one *shocking* syllable—how I *wish* I could speak in asterisks!—the faring of the Langhams, those conjugal double djinns. Has he found a complexion yet to match his shirt? And *credulous* my Mrs [?Smith]? we really *must* send her on a holiday to Prague: she'd love to see so many dishonoured Czechs all together! And Bunny too? that long, failed stoat? How *unfair* of him to have had piles! What will Persia give the dear fellow, I dare wonder? Maybe the mosques will get him yet! or am I confusing my religions?

Oh, how far, far away I feel, here in my *horribly* cosy little nest, surrounded by my detestable books, wearing my odious, warm slippers, observing the gay, reptilian play of my abominable brood, basking in the vituperation of my golden, loathing wife! How distant the trilling ripple of delighted laughter from the naughty Fulham inns as ebullient Beulah trapezes on a phrase! How *exquisitely* far off the rapier play of Ross, the Caspar sally, the limpid grace of that little silver lady who, even now, is delicately dropping down the mouth of a white telephone her perfect, pearl-like turds of ingenious insanity![1]

How adorably dim sound the great bar bells of London town!

How near is Brown's! How carcass dull! How slow! How higgledy! How me-embracing! And there I wend my day.

Ever yours,
You know who

MS: Texas

CAITLIN THOMAS
Monday [?1951]   4 St James Tce[2]

Cat darling dear, I miss you I miss you more, it seems, than ever before. Cat sweetheart my love, I love you. I love you for ever. You are everything that exists to me. You're my life and my love and I love you. London is terrible without you, and I know that Laugharne is terrible too. Since you left in the sun, leaving me broken and hollow and very near to crying, it has been dark yellow in the streets, with a fine thin dark yellow rain all the time as well. The days have been thousands of years long; the nights in our grandish but now almost pigsty McAlpine bedroom have been sleepless & feverish & sick and screaming with worry; I have had no money, and none—so far—of my appointments have led to any definite job. Tomorrow I meet Arbeid, who's been ill; he's going to Paris to see Dick & Hilda Sims;[3] he wants them in a film of his; and he wants me to

---

[1] A few of the cryptic references can be decoded. The Langhams were a couple, vaguely remembered. 'Bunny' was Ralph Keene. Robert Beulah, a portrait painter. 'Caspar', probably Admiral Sir Caspar John, son of Augustus John, who had a flat near the Davenports.
[2] The McAlpines' address.
[3] Hilda Simms, American actress.

write the film. But it isn't immediate. Whatever happens, I'll return on Wednesday even if it means coming back to London a week later to see Arbeid on his return from Paris. Also, I fell halfway downstairs here & cut my head and blacked my eye. I look repellent. Oh, Cat my Cat my true Cat my dear poor darling, I love you beyond any words, beyond the stars. I think of you all night & day. Everywhere you are with me, and not with me. I'm terribly sorry, darling, I can't send any money in this letter: I've only a few shillings. Somehow I'll get some to bring back on Wednesday. I want to be with you. I am lost without you. The already damned dark world darkens again. Every sun goes in. I love you & want to be with you always, until the end of time. You are my Caitlin, & I love you. Kiss the cuckoo for me. Love to Aeron. To you, all I have, which is bloody little. I love you love you love you. If you came into this posh musical room at this moment, I would cry & die I need you so. It is drizzling, afternoon. Helen is sewing downstairs. I am waiting till six o clock when I meet Ted Kavanagh again.[1] He's hopeful of us working together, but nothing is immediate. And it *has* to be. But please, my love, do know that I am trying everything I know. I am not drinking—I can't, anyway, but I don't want to. I am quiet, very sad, & wanting you all night and day. Please, dear dear Cat, try to endure the—I love you—long sad Laugharne end-of-the-world days for a little longer.

> *Dear* Cattle anchor
>
>> Yours eternally affectionate,
>> black-eyed, profoundly
>> depressed
>>> Dylan

MS: Maurice Neville

TED KAVANAGH
[1951]   The Boat House Laugharne Carmarthenshire Wales
                                        Tel: *Laugharne 68*

Dear Ted,
    Thank you for the Quid's Inn outline.[2] 'Rudest comments appreciated', my black eye! I think it's a very very good idea indeed, lusty, twisty, thirsty, and with enormous, almost frighteningly so, possibilities. It's a whole new, old, rough and alive comic world you're thinking of conjuring and gingering up: all the rich, rooted, fruity past of the rural gallimaufry loud alongside with the world of to-now. (I'd like to see John Q. bring in

---

[1] Ted Kavanagh (1892–1958) was a radio scriptwriter whose wartime comedy show, the weekly *ITMA*, became a national event. He never repeated the success. In 1951 he hoped to collaborate with Thomas in a BBC comedy series, but it was not written.
[2] 'Quid's Inn' was the working title of the series.

the stocks and the ducking stool again.) The whole thing is, to me, a wonderful and exciting gamble—and, what's bettingly best about it, you can go wrong from the very beginning. But I don't think you will. Everybody'll want to go to Quid's Inn, in whatever village it is—Little Fiddle on the Grog or anywhere, though not, by God, that—and I want to go myself. I want to hear the village and the village singers—Al Rhubarb and his Glee, though not, by God, that—noising in the upstairs Music and Recreation Room; and the meetings of the local John O' London's, or Will O' Birmingham's, Literary Society, or the P.E.N. or N.I.B. (National Institute of Bards?) Club, and to hear, not sopping dance lyrics, but, affectionately guyed, such ballad-concert favourites as 'Drake's Drum' and 'King Charles'. And, oh, the societies of cranks!

I think, myself, by the way, that it would be wrong to use the Colonel again.[1] A drunk, certainly, if you like, but a truly rural one: the last of the red-faced squires, maybe, or the wicked, poaching Jack-of-all-trades, like Bob Pretty in the W. W. Jacobs Cauliflower Inn stories. (And I want to hear, very much, the medley of all English country accents, and the coming of the Australian, and the frightful visitations of the enemies from over the borders, the haggisy stone-snaffling Scotch and the hymnal, leeky Welsh.)

I want to go to Quid's Inn every week, and I'd like, if I could, to try to help to make it the best, funniest, truest, and most exhilarating pub and meeting place in the indestructible country. In fact, I really would like to have a bang with you at all this, and do feel that I could add something. I think it can be great stuff.

Will you drop me a line, or wire me, or phone me at Laugharne (pronounced Larne) 68, whenever you feel like it? I'd be up the next day, and perhaps we could have straightaway some drinks and/or lunch.

I've lots of ideas and suggestions and characters all floating about like kidneys.

Yours,
Dylan T

MS: Texas

PRINCESS CAETANI
March 20 1951   The Boat House Laugharne Carmarthenshire
                                                                    Wales

Dear Marguerite Caetani,
I have been ill, with almost everything from gastric influenza to ingrowing misery. And only now my wife Caitlin has given me a letter that Davenport had forwarded from you nearly six weeks ago: She didn't know

---

[1] 'Colonel Chinstrap', an alcoholic character in *ITMA*.

who the letter came from, and had half-mislaid and half-forgotten it in the general hell of sickness, children, excruciating worry, the eternal yellow-grey drizzle outside and her own slowly accumulated loathing for the place in which we live. I was distressed that the letter had remained unanswered for so long, and doubly distressed that you should have no letter from me after yours of December 14th. I wrote, at length and wildly, my thanks and affection and small mouse-on-a-treadmill news, at once to your Paris address. I suppose I put the wrong address. I am sorry that you should, through my apparent carelessness, have come to think of me as unmannerlessly grateful—as I am sure you must have come to think, for that long, hateful silence of mine, though unpremeditated, was the nastiest answer in the world to your great kindness to us and to the fond, nice way you are kind. I have a poem nearly finished, which will be about 50 or 60 lines long[1] and is coarse and violent: I will send it as *soon* as it is done—when I can, if I can, shake off this nervous hag that rides me, biting and scratching into insomnia, nightmare, and the long anxious daylight. But I won't mind a bit if you do not want to use it:—(of course, I shall mind a bit, but only in a hidden, unimportant way). I want to write poems so much—oh, the old pariah cry!—but I worry too much: I'm at my worries all day & night with a hundred crochet hooks. Will you forgive me for worrying you with my limp but edgy letters? And will you forgive me for the silence before this whimper? I did not mean it. Thank you again, and the poem will come: the crotchety poem not quite clean, but worked at, between the willies, very hard.

I wish I knew what to do. I wish I cd get a job. I wish I wish I wish. And I wish you a happy Easter, with all my heart. The sun came out this morning, took one look at wet Wales, and shot back.

Yours affectionately,
Dylan

MS: Camillo Caetani Foundation   *SL*

OSCAR WILLIAMS
25 March 1951   Boat House Laugharne Carmarthenshire Wales

My dear Gene and Oscar,[2]
Ten months, nearly, since I saw you last, and longer, much, since I wrote. I meant and I meant and I meant, but somehow I never did write, although there was so very much to thank you for, fondness, beer, cheques, poems, paintings, a tooth. And books as well. I never thanked you for the new Modern Poetry which I recently took for a ride to Persia and read lots of in Isfahan and Shiraz and all the oily places. The Anglo-

---

[1] 'Lament'.
[2] Oscar Williams was married to Gene Derwood, poet.

Iranian Oil Company sent me out to write a filmscript to show how beautiful Persia is and how little as a mouse and gentle is the influence there of that Company: my job was to help pour water on troubled oil. I got out just before martial law—a friend of marshall plan's—and perhaps, disguised, will be sent back to write a script to show, now, suddenly, how beastly Persia is and how grandly irreplaceable is that thundering Company.[1] Incidentally, the biggest thing in the Oil Refinery at Abadan is costing eight million pounds to put up, and is called a Cat-Cracker. I'd crack a lot of cats for that. Thank you, a *great* deal, for selling that piece of cheese for such a splendid sum.[2] I'm enclosing the 2 Exemption Certificates, & hope I've filled them in correctly. I have a couple of poems, but can't find them; when I do, I'll send them on. I saw John Malcolm in London last summer, for a few revolving days. When I send the poems on, I'll write a longer letter with what grey and drizzly news I have. It has been raining in Wales since last June. I hope to come, with Caitlin, to the States next year: if there are any and if there is one. How are you both? Before a long letter, goodbye for a bit. And love, always, to you both.

Dylan

MS: Harvard   *SL*

ALEC CRAIG
7th April 1951   The Boat House Laugharne Carmarthenshire Wales

Dear Alec,
    Thanks for the letter. Yes, May 7th—7 o'clock programme—would suit me very well, and thank you for the invitation.
    I'd like to read other people's poems as well as my own, so perhaps it would be best to call my little do just 'A Reading of Poems,' which allows me to bring in what I like—especially poems by little-known modern British & American. Okay?
    It was nice to see you again.

Yrs,
Dylan

MS: Thomas Trustees

[1] The country's nationalist movement had begun, and the Anglo-Iranian Oil Company was taken over in April.
[2] The 'piece of cheese' was 'How to Be a Poet', a tongue-in-cheek article written for a British magazine, *Circus*, the previous year. Williams sold it to *Atlantic* for $250.

ANEIRIN TALFAN DAVIES
7th April 1951   The Boat House Laugharne Carmarthenshire

My dear Aneirin,
   Thank you for writing. I'd be delighted to do a Festival talk for the
Welsh Service; and I think the Festival Exhibition on the South Bank—or
the Festival Gardens & Funfair (what *is* the official title?) in
Battersea—would be grand. Which do you favour? And have you a rough
date for the talk?[1]

                                             Yours,
                                             Dylan

MS: BBC

JOHN DAVENPORT
12 April 1951   Laugharne

Dear John,
   Sorry to have missed you my last London visit. What a word visit is for
my kind of occasional agitated bumbling in frowsy streets, unkind pubs,
deleterious afternoon boozers, snoring cinemas, wet beds! I stayed all the
time in the McAlpines', Bill frenziedly protecting his period furniture as
though I were going to lay an egg on it, Helen singing Irish ballads to West
Indians. And every day I was chasing money and jobs. I have found a job,[2]
and a very fishy one too I will tell you about when we meet over flat beer
in some chill emporium, but no money yet.
   And this job may make me stay in London for a long time, in which
case Caitlin will have to be with me too—and of course her cockalorum.
That is presumably what Mad Mags[3] meant when she told you about our
giving the Boat House up. She's wrong again, I've no intention of giving it
up. But we probably will want a flat or house in London, & M said she had
found half a house in Cheyne Walk by the chimneys which she was
enquiring about. Also, she *has* bought a cottage in Laugharne, in the
downtown square or Grist, for her & her horrors in the holidays. So has
Mary Keene bought a cottage there. We have reasons for leaving. It's like
seeing a new wing built, for obstreperous incurables, on to a quiet bin one
has got used to.
   I should be up next week, and will get in touch. And I'd love to meet
Canetti. I'll look out for Richard Jones's letter.

---

[1] The Festival of Britain, centred on the South Bank of the Thames, was a national occasion,
    aimed at inspiring the people as postwar 'austerity' faded. The talk was first broadcast on
    5 June 1951.
[2] Perhaps the script-writing with Kavanagh, of which Thomas had high hopes.
[3] Margaret Taylor.

A pile of poems from Douglas Phillips, the butcher's son—remember? —arrived a few days ago. I haven't read them properly yet, but think they've got a lot. All about masturbation, sin, violent death, decay, wet dreams, impermanent love, hatred of Carmarthen, and—looking, at random, at the words of one poem—festering seashores, wet vulva lips, gaseous virgins, putrid flame, lewd men, raving swordfish, sensual whips, tortured women rending wedding-gowns, charred mates, smiling cream over lips' soft brim, lascivious farmers, shaven thighs, childhood captured in rubber sheaths, love's limpets sucking oval stones, rubber wives ripping blubbered membrane veils, plasmal fruit, burst plackets, fishes' bladders, bloated pelvis, vulpine fur, etcetera. I can't understand why he doesn't show them to his father. A few memorable lines:

1) '... the pus of sin
   That feeds each female with male cheer.'
2) 'The tiles are wreathed in smiles when chimneys copulate.'
3) 'O sexual scholar in masturbatory cell,
   Your writhing brain fictitious children sperms.'
4) 'What can I do when bugle-bellied wives
   Reveal the bedpan secrets of their lives?
   Can I bend down and crouch beneath their skirts
   To ease my bullying blow-boy where it hurts?'[1]

You never can tell now, can you?
But every now & then there are good bursting bits.
Stop press: M comes down on the midnight train tonight to discuss 'the Cheyne Walk Project'. If it comes off, I shall have a town house & a country house, and I have just borrowed 5/- from Ivy Williams to run them both.

Love,
Dylan

MS: Texas   *SL(R)*

JOHN MALCOLM BRINNIN
12 April 1951   Boat House Laugharne Carmarthenshire Wales

Dear John,
    How nice, nice, nice! Oh, my conscience, I had feared that you left London[2] breathing—no, I can't possibly mean that—had left London saying: 'No more of that coarsened looby and his backstairs drizzling

---

[1] Douglas Phillips has pointed out that Thomas's summary of the poems, most of them part of a sonnet sequence, is not very accurate, although the quotations are. He also notes Thomas's generosity to a young writer—see Thomas's letters to him, pages 800 and 803. Two of the poems were later published, in *Dragons and Daffodils* (1960) and *Texas Quarterly* 1968.
[2] Following Brinnin's visit the previous September.

town. Foul enough in my America, feebly lascivious in his pigsty in the Earle, puking in Philadelphia, burgling the Biddles, blackmailing psychiatrists' mistakes for radiosets and trousers, fanging through the lesbians, hounding poor Oscar, but there! there in that English sink, intolerable, dribbly, lost. And, oh, his so called friends! toadying slaves of the licensing laws, rats on a drinking ship'—or didn't we meet any friends? I can't remember. I remember I liked, very much, our being together, though you were in that Royal (was it?) jail and I in my false bonhomous Club. I remember meeting you at the station, and that was fine. And the London frowsty Casino, a memento of which I enclose: who are those perhaps-men, one bluebottle-bloated, one villainously simpering, with floral and yachting ties, so untrustworthily neat and prosperous with their flat champagne? I remember the Thames and old Pearl—whom I saw something of later but who, I imagine, left London, as I imagined you had done, rasping to herself: 'No more of that beer-cheapened hoddy-noddy snoring, paunched, his corn, his sick, his fibs, I'm off to Taormina where you know where you are: oh, his sodden bounce, his mis-theatrical-demeanour, the boastful tuppence!' I haven't heard from her since she went away.

Now, for your letter. First: Next time I am in London I shall see what boys I know in the black rooms of the BBC and tell them that you are coming to London in July and that, if pressed in a vice, bribed heavily and dined, you might just possibly think of reading, on the Third Programme, your poems, the poems of America, or of assessing the contemporary literary situation in Massachusetts, Virginia, and the Whaler Bar. I'll do my very best. You couldn't, I suppose, persuade your publishers to send me the shiny anthology and the new book of poems? I'd like them, a lot, anyway. And I will talk to the Institute of Contemporary Arts. I am so glad, indeed, that you will be here in July; and I shall be less revolting than last time, whatever the sacrifice. And let us meet the tiny great for tea, and go to Oxford where I know a human being. Caitlin will be in London in July, which will not make things any quieter. We both will probably be living there for some time: I am about to take on a new job: co-writing, with the best gagman in England—he is an Irishman from New Zealand[1]—a new comic series for the radio. I have already thought of two jokes, both quite unusable. And may I come to Edith's party for you? Her parties are always brilliant opportunities for self-disgrace.

Give my love, if ever you see them or believe it, to Pearl, Lloyd & Loren, Marion & Cummings, Stanley Moss, Jean Garrigue, Gene Baroff, Jeanne Gordon, David Lougée, Howard, [*a word is crossed out*] the one I crossed out, Patrick Boland, and any ugly stranger in the street.[2] Have a thousand boilermakers for me, and send me your stomach: I'll put it under my pillow.

---

[1] Ted Kavanagh.
[2] The poet Lloyd Frankenberg and his wife, the painter Loren McIver; the poet E. E. Cummings and his wife Marion Morehouse. Patrick Boland was Thomas's host in Detroit, and a poet, as were Jean Garrigue, Stanley Moss and Gene Baroff.

I have written three new poems, one alright, which I will, if you like, send you when I can find them.

I have no news at all. I am broke and in debt. And that reminds me to thank you very much for sending to my, my, my! Chartered Accountants that quite legendary-looking account of my howl-for-my-supper earnings. The Accountants tell me I shall, probably, not have to pay any Income Tax on anything earned in the U.S.A. *except*:

(1) The amounts remitted by myself or by my Agent to this Country: i.e. remittances made to my wife, bank, or any other person.

(2) The amount brought in by me when I arrived back in this Country.

Can you help? I think, through you, I sent about three small sums to Caitlin. Can you remember? And I came home, I think, with about 200 dollars.

If you can remember what amounts of money I sent to Caitlin with your knowledge, would you be so kind as to write to Leslie Andrews & Co., 10 North Street, Horsham, Sussex, England, and let them know? And then that will really be the end of your agental duties *until next time*.

Now, next time: I would very much like (I'd adore it) to be imported to the States next year, 1952. The Poetry Center paying my passage and the first fee. I would bring Caitlin with me, if by that time I have made, as I intend to do, much money from my ha ha scripts. And would you, *could* you, act as Agent or Christ knows what for me again? I do not think I would wish to go through the Middle West, excepting Chicago, again, but anywhere, everywhere, else, unless I have quite ruined myself in all those places where you were not with me. Could you put out feelers, spin wheels, grow wings for me? I am so deadly sick of it here. I would bring great packages of new poems to read, and much more pre-written prose to pad them in. I would be much better than I was: I mean, sick less often. I mean, I would so much like to come. Could you write to any friends or acquaintances I might have made and see if they would help? Would you, now?

No, Persia wasn't all depressing. Beautiful Isfahan & Shiraz. Wicked, pompous, oily British. Nervous, cunning, corrupt and delightful Persian bloody bastards. Opium no good. Persian vodka, made of beetroot, like stimulating sockjuice, very enjoyable. Beer full of glycerine and pips. Women veiled, or unveiled ugly, or beautiful and entirely inaccessible, or hungry. The lovely camels who sit on their necks and smile. I shan't go there again.

No news. Still broke and in debt. I spent all the Persian money on beetroot vodka, glycerine beer, unveiled ugly women, and, as you conjectured, the camels, the camels, the camels are coming.

Yes, I *do* want to come to the States early next year. But I shall see you before then, & will do all I can do to make you a very little money on the BBC. But naturally don't count on that. You will be here during the Festival of Britain, though nobody here has any idea of what we have to be festive about. And mostly, I suppose, the BBC will be plugging homegrown poetry. However, I know some unpatriotic people on the Third Programme, and they owe me something for the pleasure they've got in my not being on the Third Programme recently.

I'm sick of Laugharne. It has rained here since last June.

Write soon.

Love to you,
Dylan

MS: Delaware   *SL*

ANEIRIN TALFAN DAVIES
1 May 1951 (About Festival of Britain visit. See Appendix 59.)

ANEIRIN TALFAN DAVIES
[May 1951] (Sends Festival script. See Appendix 60.)

PRINCESS CAETANI
17th May 1951   The Boat House Laugharne Carmarthenshire Wales

My dear Madame Caetani,

First of all: all, all my thanks for your last letter and the cheque out of the great blue that made our life here temporarily bearable and made me, once more, so deeply grateful to you I should never, however long I lived, be able to say how much. It's fine to think that you think of me here, there in your Rome, & I love your letters. I wish I could write more often, with all my news, but all my news is bad & nervous and I'm sick of my always hurdygurdying these little griefs out and me like a monkey on the top of it all with my beggar's cap. But one day I shall write calm & at length, though, God, not now.

No, I'm sorry I never received the last number. It must have gone to a dead address. And I'm sorry I don't speak French.

Here is a poem you mightn't like at all, but do read it, please. I hope you understand my painfully shaking writing. Though on the wagon now, I'm like a St. Vitus leaf. Tell me about the poem, anyway. It is, of course, yours if you want it. I have nearly finished two other poems, much slower & sadder than this, also yours, which I will send you as soon as I can.

I'm just beginning the beastly process of selling up my house here to pay debts etc, a very shaking thing to do because I am so fond of it. And we will have to try to get furnished rooms in London, if we can. But I'm going to keep my books anyway.

If you don't like *Lament*, please slam it back. And perhaps you'll like the ones-in-progress much better.

I'd like to have a copy, very much, one day, of the last Botteghe.

Now thank you, with all my heart, again.

> Yours affectionately,
>
> Dylan

MS: Camillo Caetani Foundation

UNKNOWN

27 May 1951 (About a writers' group. Draft only. See Appendix 61.)

OSCAR WILLIAMS

28 May 1951   Boat House Laugharne Carmarthenshire Wales

Dear Oscar,

I'm afraid I'm sending you only one poem—and that only the first section of a poem, though nobody need know that. I mentioned the title and idea of this poem over a year ago, in pretty New York, but scrapped all of it I had written on my return. I have only recently finished this version.[1] The other poems I found since last writing to you, I have sent to Botteghe Oscure. This means, I get paid by them *well*, first, & then can sell the poems (well again, I hope) in the States. If I publish the poems first in the States, Botteghe Oscure doesn't want them. So, when they're printed in Italy, I'll send them along. I've no spare copies now. And my newest poems aren't yet finished. Sorry I couldn't type this one out. A few words, on looking through it, seem hard to read. The first word on line 7 is PLEADING. The fourth word in the third line from the end of page one is LANES. On page 3, in the 3rd line, the word is ROISTER. In the 7th line of page 3, the word GAMBO means a farm-cart. In the last line but one from the end of page 3, it is THEY with the Simple Jacks. On page 4, line 7, RAIN and WRING are 2 separate words. I am sure this complicates matters. It's a conventionally romantic poem & perhaps you won't like it at all. But could you sell it for me for a LOT of money? I'm desperately in need of it. If you can get a cheque sent soon, will you see that it is made out on a *London* bank. Your last two lovely cheques took about 6 weeks to clear. I'm in such a state of debt & brokeness, I'm having to sell up my house as soon as I can & move to London which I hate.[2] The

---

[1] 'In the white giant's thigh'.

[2] The house, which in any case belonged to Margaret Taylor, was not being sold. But she found the cost of upkeep a burden. The latest plan was to find the family another, temporary house in London, where Thomas would be nearer the sources of work and income, and might not need to visit America again.

house—what I own of it—will all go towards debts—& then not all of them, by a hell of a long way. I hope to keep my books. Oh, oh, oh! Misery me. Do what you can about this lush poem. And please excuse rushed writing & no news.

Love,
Dylan

MS: Harvard

SL

T. S. ELIOT
28 May 1951   The Boat House Laugharne Carmarthenshire

Dear T. S. Eliot,
  Very many thanks indeed for your letter & your cheque. It was extremely kind of you, and the cheque helped to ease my difficulties here. I was, as you know, very nervous in writing to you at all to ask your help; and especially since your recent reputation for wealth. It was in spite of this, that I managed to write my begging letter. I was, anyway, writing to the best poet I know, and not to a supposedly monied man.
  Thank you, again, most sincerely.

Yours,
Dylan Thomas

MS: Texas

LAURENCE GILLIAM
28 May 51   The Boat House Laugharne Carmarthenshire

Dear Laurence,
  About the possible Festival Fantasia. I couldn't get in touch with you—my fault—on my last few London days.
  Any suggestions about the F.F.? Treatment? Length?
  And, *terribly* important to me, ADVANCE, IMMEDIATE?
  I returned to find my local debts even more stridently urgent. I owe every tradesman in town, and just can't think how I'm to pay them. I can't even get down to work here unless I can pay them a little bit peace-offering.[1]

---

[1] Gilliam replied (May 30) to say that 'Third are very interested in the idea of a Festival Fantasia, but on checking with Copyright department I find that they have a working agreement with your agent that payment for commissioned work is only made on delivery of script. I am sorry, but I cannot get round this ruling . . .' Thomas's failure to deliver either *The Plain Dealer* or *Peer Gynt* was to blame.

Can you do your best?
Or any other suggestions?

>Tremblingly, & very
>much in earnest,
>Dylan

MS: BBC

PRINCESS CAETANI
28 May 1951   The Boat House Laugharne Carmarthenshire Wales

My dear Madame Caetani,
  I hope you've had, by this time, my brief, troubled letter and my rough, untroubled poem.
  I have just finished the short poem I enclose.[1] If you like the other one, the 'Lament', well enough to print, I think this little one might very well be printed with it as a contrast.
  In spite of all the things that go with selling-up home, I am still trying to work. (Indeed, I am still trying to sell up home, which has to be, and quick.) And I hope to finish soon a longish play, as yet untitled, in verse and prose which I have been thinking of for a long time. I will send it to you soon. I *do* hope you will publish it—unless, of course, it is too long (or too bad)—as I am, at the moment of working on it, pleased & excited with it. It is gay & sad and sentimental and a bit barmy. So am I. I'm looking forward to hearing from you.

>Affectionately,
>Dylan

The only person I can't show the little enclosed poem to is, of course, my father, who doesn't know he's dying.

MS: Camillo Caetani Foundation   SL

DOUGLAS PHILLIPS[2]
June 24 1951   Boat House Laugharne Carmarthenshire

Dear Douglas Phillips,
  First of all, I want to say how very sorry I am not to have written to you a long time ago, when you sent me that packet of animal bombs by post:

---

[1] 'Do not go gentle into that good night'. Published, with 'Lament', in *Botteghe Oscure*, November 1951.
[2] See letter to John Davenport, page 793.

they burst all over the place, cocks and cunts and blood and stars and great green cabbages. I read the poems right through quickly, bits of them aloud and always with excitement, for it is exciting being in at the beginning of a new talent, however mixed-up it may be at the moment. Then I had to put the poems away and go to London. I should have written to you then, briefly, to say I'd had the poems and was enormously struck by them, and would write again about them. But I didn't, and I'm sorry.

Now I've read the poems again, and will read them again. This is only to say what I should have said in March: I feel privileged to be allowed to read your poems in manuscript; you really have got a lot of something there, and a rage and a fire and (over-churning) movement of your own, and a weltering violence; and I'd like, if I may, to write about some of the poems in detail as soon as there's a proper lull between my bread-and-butter jobs.

I hope you're writing now, and I'll be very glad to see anything new at any time.

Soon I'll write a better letter.

Congratulations!

If any of this sounds like an elder poet writing, throw it in the fire.

Yours sincerely,
Dylan Thomas

MS: National Library of Wales

OSCAR WILLIAMS
10th July 1951   Boat House Laugharne Carmarthenshire Wales

Dear Oscar,

Many many thanks for selling my poem so quickly & for so much.[1]

I'm typing—or, rather, having typed—a few other ones which I'll airmail next week.

I enclose the Exemption Certificates, signed. I don't know what else to fill in.

Thank you for getting the cheque sent to a London Bank. I hope you can manage to send the $45 cheque to a London Bank too.

You are very good to me. (Even to the stamped envelope.)

I hope to come to the States early next year again, with Caitlin. Poetry Center & Museum of Modern Art (for whom I will read King Lear) will be helping.

---

[1] 'In the white giant's thigh'. *Atlantic* magazine paid $150 for first U.S. and Canadian rights. A steady stream of dollars was reaching Thomas via Williams, bypassing David Higham.

I hope something will come of the possibility you mention: that of a group of midwestern colleges planning a good sum, or offer, for me.

I have to catch the post, but will write at length when I send on the new poems.

I read some of your poems aloud to a Welsh Society last week. Liked.

Love to you & Gene from C. & me.

Dylan

I think I'll be seeing J. M. Brinnin in London this month.
I'm going to live in London for the winter which I shall hate.

MS: Harvard

PRINCESS CAETANI
July 18 1951   The Boat House Laugharne Carmarthenshire Wales

Dear Madame Caetani,

Many, many apologies. Of *course* I should have written at once to say: Thank you for your letter, for Botteghe Oscure, for the cheque which came zooming out of the Roman blue in time to pay a summons. But day after day I put off writing, because, each day, I hoped to finish the longish (about 100 lines) birthday poem I was—and still am—writing. I wanted to send it to you with my letter of gratitude: it is a much, much better poem than the 'Lament' & the villanelle to my father: I like it better than anything I have done for a very long time (which does not say a great deal: I do not like reading my poems at all; only writing them). But I couldn't finish the poem quickly enough, & now I *must* write to you without it. Today is Wednesday: I hope very much to finish it by this coming weekend, & will send it, arrogance, obscurity, & all, straightaway to Switzerland.

The play—did I say it was a radio comedy about Wales, & not a stage play?—I've temporarily shelved to write the poem which I have been wanting to write for a long time, ever, in fact, since my last year's birthday, which is what the poem is, in its way, all about. I'll send on the play, of course, as soon as it's finished. But the poem you shall have much first: in time, perhaps, (& if you like it) for the coming number (and perhaps if there is room). (and if there is time.) it was your fond mention of Cummings in your last letter that topples my punctuation about like this. And, yes, what a very fine man he is. I hope to see him again next year in New York, if ever I get there. The Museum of Modern Art has, for some erratic reason of their own, asked me to read King Lear; and Columbia & the Poetry Center have invited me over too. But I shan't go unless I can take Caitlin (who still, I believe, thinks that America is either all Hollywood or Senator McCarthy). Did you, by the way, say that you would be in London this autumn for your daughter's wedding? (Will you give her my kindest regards?) If you do come, I very much hope we shall meet.

Thank you, deeply, again. And expect my new poem *very* soon. I trust, early next week.

Yours,
Dylan

PS I enclose the pale [?page] proofs, but there is nothing to correct. Only, please, make it a bigger dash than a hyphen after 'good bells jaw' at the end of the last-but-one line on the first proof page.[1]

MS: Camillo Caetani Foundation

GRAHAM ACKROYD
18 July 1951   Boat House Laugharne Carmarthenshire

Dear Graham Ackroyd,

Sorry not to have written much before this: I've been away, and didn't get any letters.

And I'm very sorry, too that my Miller letters are gone. Pinched. I'd kept them in a book of Miller's, and after a party I found that all the signed books were gone. And the letters.

About my visit to Miller at Big Sur: it was very short, nothing happened, and I remember v. little of what was said. But I could run out a very short, uneventful piece about it, if you *really* liked.[2]

Anyway, good luck with the book. And apologies again about this delay in writing. I can't apologise about the stolen letters: I can only think and curse.

Sincerely
Dylan Thomas

TS: Thomas Trustees

DOUGLAS PHILLIPS
Wednesday [July 1951][3]   Laugharne

Dear Douglas,

Thanks for the letter & the three poems. I like the first two poems very much, & think they contain some of the best lines, and brief passages,

---

[1] 'Lament': 'I lie down thin and hear the good bells jaw'.
[2] Ackroyd writes: 'I must have had some daft idea about starting a literary magazine.'
[3] Date supplied by recipient.

you have yet written. I am not sure, myself, of the third poem, but will read it very carefully again, as I also will the other two.

I'm writing to Botteghe Oscure this week, and will, with your permission, send the editor the first two of the new poems and tell her that I have many more to send her of yours if she likes these.

Don't worry about your behaviour here, it was alright. I'm a pretty silent person at home, too, & just go on dumbly & dully reading, but it doesn't mean anything. One should be able to be silent with one's friends, when one wants to.

Come down for a week-end when you can.

Yours,
Dylan

MS: National Library of Wales

DONALD TAYLOR
31st August 1951   Boat House Laugharne Carmarthenshire Wales

Dear Donald,
I had a foggy feeling, after our Lordly day[1] and the evening with the afflicted Americans, that you and I had fixed a date to meet, but, for the death of me, I couldn't remember if or no or, if, when and where. I hope I was mistaken, and that we hadn't arranged to meet, which sounds, maybe, discourteous, but you know what I mean. I tried to get in touch with Higham, but his nose was being scraped. If we did have a date, & I didn't (as was obvious) keep it, please forgive me. And, if we didn't, let's make another soon. I've such a lot to talk about, and that day (for me, at least) wasn't half long enough and was interrupted too much by bad cricket, indifferent drink, and mad women and fat men.

We come to London to live at the end of September, money willing and Caitlin's mumps gone—(she's moaning now, like a sad football). But, before I make that complicated move, I want to have, fixed as firmly as possible, if even only in the mind, a programme of work to keep me in creditless London. Have your plans moved any, and do they still, after a day in which I am sure I spoke very little sense, include me? (It was very good to see you, and I make no apologies for my senselessness: I was quite happy.) I must know as soon as possible—though I realise that nothing happens quickly, except disaster, in your and my world.

I told you about my American commitments. Today—one reason I am writing this—I heard from America the very final dates they have fixed for me. My first lecture is at Columbia on January 30th, & my last in the Museum of Modern Art in the last week of February. Therefore, my

---

[1] Watching cricket at Lord's.

whole trip would take, at the maximum, six weeks. I *must* reply, in the next few days, to my American sponsors & say, quite definitely, Yes or No. Suppose—and, Lord, I hope so—you and I are working, soon, fully together: could I, then, take six weeks off from January, say, 20th on? Could you let me know how you feel about this? You know that, above everything, I want to work with you, again, on films, and exclusively, if possible, on feature films this time. And you know, as I told you at probably incoherent length in the Insipid Writers' Club, that I must have a regular job this winter. If six American weeks interfere with these two things—and I do so hope that both things are the same: i.e., that the regular job is to write scripts for and with you—then I'll cancel the lectures. But I must say Yes or No to Columbia University etc. straightabloodyway.

A pity we can't meet again very soon. I *could* come up to London; but I wish you could come to Wales: our house is almost childless now, and the weather, for the moment, windily good.

Have you any stories in mind which, perhaps, I could read or think about?

Anyway, do please write quickly about these points.

I saw T.V. people a few days after seeing you. They're full of work to do, but offer lamentable pay. And, help us, we all do need so much these once-longed-for but execrable days.

I am writing a plotless radio play, first thought of as a film.

Two acquaintances of mine have committed suicide within the last fortnight; one of them was a painter, Ralph Banbury: do you remember him? A tall, languid man, friend & pupil of Cedric Morris, with a Chinese grandmother.

Love,
Dylan

MS: Buffalo   *SL*

DAVID HIGHAM
August 31 1951   The Boat House Laugharne Carmarthenshire Wales

Dear David,

Thank you very much for arranging, from your sinusoidal bed, for fifty quid to be advanced to me on future earnings. It was very kind of you, and I felt most callous to have had to ask you this when you were ill. I hope you're quite recovered now.

I hope, too, that the fifty quid can be paid back to you in a lump sum soon, and not taken, bit by bit, from small BBC cheques etcetera.

I wrote to Donald Taylor today, asking him if his film-plans were moving any, and telling him that I had just heard from America: the

Poetry Center of New York *must* know, straightaway, if I can keep my dates there: the first is, Columbia University 30 January 1952, the last in the Museum of Modern Art the last week of February. Taylor will probably write to me directly about this; but, if you *do* happen to be getting in touch with him in the immediate future, perhaps you could stress the urgency of my knowing how soon to expect a regular contract job from him. As I told you when we briefly met, I'm coming to London to live at the end of this month, and really must have a regular job then to keep me there: or, at least, the tangible prospect of one very soon. There could, I suppose, be no question of Taylor giving me, from the end of September, a retaining fee until he starts his firm properly?[1] But perhaps I had better wait to hear from Taylor before you, possibly, put out any feelers in this direction.

Thanks again for the advance, which covered me over a particularly bad spot.

Yours,
Dylan

MS: Texas

JOHN MALCOLM BRINNIN
August 31 1951   Boat House Laugharne Carmarthenshire Wales

Dear John,
A very brief note of apology and affection. Your letter, waiting for me in John Davenport's, I mislaid, and now don't know where you'll be or when, for a moment, you may come to London. (I've written to Reggie Smith, who's on holiday, but couldn't give him a date, except that I *thought* it to be early in September. I know he will fix a recording if he can: probably of verse.) But from your littler letter I see you will call at the American Express, Paris, around Sept 1–4. I *do* hope this will find you then. And I *am* so sorry I couldn't get up to London after you left Laugharne,[2] & that I lost your letter, & that I haven't written. I've been in a mess about money, and, in London, about trying to fix a film-job for the winter. Caitlin has mumps, badly, and oh! oh! oh! I'm vague & distressed about me and poems and Laugharne & London —and the States. But, of course, I'll be there for the Columbia date on January 30. I hope, very much, we can meet in London before you return: I want to ask you about these dates, about what sort of poetry you think I should read, what kind of prose I should write for the several occasions. Also, I should like very much to see you again, before next January.

I hope you didn't have too muddled a time down here. Regards to Bill.[3]

---

[1] Taylor's plans came to nothing as far as Thomas was concerned.
[2] Brinnin visited Europe again in July, and went to Laugharne for the first time.
[3] Brinnin's friend Bill Read, later the author of *The Days of Dylan Thomas*, who came with him to Europe.

Please write soon, if ever you get this, and I'll write back fully.
Try to make London.
Caitlin sends you her love. And I send mine.

Dylan

MS: Delaware   *SL*

PRINCESS CAETANI
31st August 1951   The Boat House Laugharne Carmarthenshire Wales

My dear Madame Caetani,

I owed you, before, a letter, a poem, and an apology. Now, Lord help us, I owe you a whole sackful of apologies; this letter must necessarily be sad and short; and there is no poem.

I took the new poem—it is the first of three poems linked together by the occasion of a birthday—up to London with me on my last, just-over visit, meaning to typewrite it there and send it straight to you. Nothing, however, went right with my plans—it was my hope to arrange a job for myself for the winter, when we must move from here to London—and I decided to go, with no hopes, home. But I hadn't the money to go home, couldn't arrive home with no money, and was forced to sell my poem to a London magazine for ten pounds.[1] I don't think I need—I know you now, so well, from letters—tell you how ashamed I am. The poem, good or bad, was for you; I wanted, more than anything, for it [to] appear in Botteghe Oscure, the only periodical. But I had to have a little money at once; I knew no-one; and I had nothing to sell but this laborious lyric.

I will, of course, if you still want them, send to you the next two poems that will make the whole poem. But I would not be surprised if, after the breaking of my sincere promise, you found that you did not want them.

I do assure you that only the most drastic need would make me sell my work in this way.

You say that you will be in London for three weeks from the 15th of next month. I do hope we can meet during that time.

I am very sad about the poem; but I hope that, (somehow,) I shall be able to write the next two & make them better than the first.

Yours,
Dylan

MS: Camillo Caetani Foundation

[1] Presumably *World Review*, where 'Poem on his birthday' appeared in October 1951. Thomas also sold the poem to the *Atlantic*. See letter to Oscar Williams, page 817.

DONALD TAYLOR
13 September 51   Boat House Laugharne Carmarthenshire

Dear Donald,
    Thank you for the letter. I'm delighted you are making progress, and
that we may be working together in a matter of a few weeks. I do hope so.
This is only to tell you telephone number: Laugharne (pronounced Larne)
68, when you want to ring. I have severe gout, and am quite laughable,
but not to me. Write or ring soon.

                                              Love,
                                              Dylan

MS: Buffalo

PRINCESS CAETANI
September 15 1951   The Boat House Laugharne Carmarthenshire
                                   Telephone number: Laugharne 68

My dear Madame Caetani,
    First of all: Thank you, very deeply, for your forgiving letter and for the
money which you should not have sent me, because I had broken my
word, but which I was so terribly glad you did, and surely that sentence is
askew. The money saved my life again, or, rather, paid a horned and
raging bill. Oh, how many times you've saved my lives now! I've as
many, I suppose, as a Hallowe'en of cats. And the lovely letter of forgiveness was so good to have, though it made me feel only more ashamed
that, in a moment of need, I had to sell my best poem for years to an aloof
stranger.
    Perhaps Davenport, who rang me this morning, will have told you how
this came about. Day after day, in London, I tried to get settled some jobs
which were (and still are, I hope) to support me this winter; and one of
them, I was led to imagine, was to begin at once. So it didn't matter, then,
in London, not having any money at all, nor not being able to send any
home, because soon, very soon, I said to myself, tomorrow perhaps, or the
rich day after, the job would just BE, like that, quick as a flick of the
fingers, and then everything would be allright and the bills would be paid
and the summonses silenced and we'd buy new clothes and the bells
would ring fit to bleed; it was nice thinking this. But, of course, and a
hundred of courses, the jobs, day after broke day, drifted further & further
away. 'Oh, yes, they *would* materialise', the suave men said, 'Eventually.
You must learn to take the long view. And, yes, yes, yes, we know you
must come, at once, to London to live, because you can live no longer in
your ivory Laugharne, but remember: home was not built in a day'. And
the daft bellringing billpaying dreams, full of new suits and gold boots
and flowers in the buttonholes and Something Coming In Every

Week—(the wonderful wish words that sing like thrushes at night, out of the down-at-heel darkness, to the dispossessed in their little black beds)—they all faded. And there I was, not a potential man of affairs any more, solid shrewd and distinguished as a whiskey advertisement, with a smile that would float a merger, but a lost, plump bum with a bucket of words wailing 'Woe and woe' and nowhere to go. Or, at least, I felt as outcast as that. Or I romanticised myself into that shabby posture, and looked at the greasy, inviting Thames with wild (but, thank God, craven) eyes.

Caitlin was ill, at crumbling home, with, of all things, mumps. I almost wish it had been a more imaginative, and dolorous, illness. I had wired her to say, 'Okay, all in hand', meaning the work and the money was mine. And she had wired back to say how good that was and would I please come home that day and bring some money which was so much needed for the carping shops. But nothing was okay, and all was out of hand, and I couldn't even buy a ticket for the journey. I thought, then, of sending that beastly poem—how over-important all this dreary business makes it! and it's no Paradise Lost!—straightaway to you and wiring you that it was on its way and could, would you, please, please wire me some money for it. But I couldn't. It was too damned abrupt. And it would take too long, however quick. I was quite sick with despair. So many days had come to this black blank. I had to get away. And so, having nothing else, I took the detested poem to a magazine and sold it there and then and bought a present, vainly to try to lessen the pennilessness of my arrival, and took the night-train back that said all the way: Welsh fool, Welsh fool.

I wrote to you a letter in a scrambling hurry. And then your letter came, and thank you again for it. I'm busy now piling up books and bits and pieces to take, when we can, to London, if there's anywhere there, and have lost your letter in this sad and grisly bustle, your letter that told me when, and for how long, you would be in England. Then, this morning, Davenport rang and said that you were leaving for France very early in the week of the 17th of September. I'd thought you were staying, oh, very much longer. And so now, I suppose I can't see you at all? There are several things I should like to talk to you about; and I do very much want to meet you. If there is any chance of your staying a day or so longer, could you wire me or ring me—my number is at the head of all this rigmarole—and then, perhaps, with luck and some scraping together I can come up to see you before you vanish again? I very much hope this can happen.

And thank you, once more. And I grieve that poem like hell.

Affect yours,
Dylan

MS: *Camillo Caetani Foundation*

FRANCIS BIDDLE[1]
15 September 1951 The Boat House Laugharne Carmarthenshire Wales

Dear Mr. Biddle,
   Only today I heard that you and Mrs. Biddle were in London, or, rather, that you had been in London, were on your way to Ireland, and would be returning to London in about a fortnight. I do hope this good news is true. I would so much like to meet you on your return. Would you, if we could meet, write to me and tell me when you'll be in London? I'm going up in about a week's time.
   I'm awfully sorry I never wrote to you after Washington, and have no excuse, except that I had a very frantic & flying—oh how I loathe that endless air—two months after leaving you and ranted hoarsely all over the place, in California, Florida, and Canada, and never seemed to have any time to write & thank you for being so kind to me. I'm afraid I was very dim & shy.
   My wife and I are going to the States in January, but I do hope I can meet you long before that, in London, and I'm looking forward a lot to seeing you both, if that is possible.

With all best wishes,
Dylan Thomas

TS: J. M. Dent

OSCAR WILLIAMS
31 Sep 51

Dear Oscar,
   In a frightful hurry for post.
   Permission slip signed & enclosed.
   'Immortal Poems'—my!
   Am sending you 3 new poems today.
   When do I get the 125 dollars? Am in trouble, serious.
   Will write with the poems.

Love,
Dylan

My 1st N. York date is January 30. I *shall* be free for a week in Feb.

MS: Harvard

[1] See note, page 751.

ROBERT POCOCK
[postcard] 2 October 1951   Boat House Laugharne Carmarthenshire

Can you, will you, send me that ms of 'Adventures In The Skin Trade', which I think you still have and which I want to work on and get money from, at once. I'd be v. grateful; in fact, I shall die if you don't.
We hope to be in our town residence in about a fortnight's time. There will be a small, and disastrous, warming up.
Love from us both to you both,

                                                    Dylan

MS: Texas

RUTH WITT-DIAMANT
10 October 1951   The Boat House Laugharne Carmarthenshire Wales

Darling Ruth,
  By this long time you will have, if not forgotten me—who *could* forget that lordly, austere grace and grave demeanour, the soberly matured wisdom, dedicate, reverend, chaste and aloof, that incorruptible ascetic, that Santayana of Wales?—at least have come most justly to loathe the very hiccup of my name. (Of Tram's opinion of me, I daren't think. I found, this week, a long, fond letter to him in a pile of socks and poems, unposted since last Christmas. I am writing to him on bent knees, wagging my bum like a spaniel, but expect no answer. Give him my love. I very often think of him and Bill, of Gavin,[1] and, of course, of you who made my ranting holiday ridiculously happy, who showed me the exhibitionist floodlit seals and the pansied Pacific baths and the starry city and Miller's mountain, and gave me polar beer and artichokes, and laughed with me and at me till I felt more at home than at home where it's only at, and made me want more than anything to lurch back to the beautiful West where men are sometimes men and the bars are always exultantly open and the wind and sea and people are right and raffish and tins of fruit juice breed in the ice box.)
  How could I not have written, when every week of the piggish year I mean to with all my heart, that poor bloody muscle? Oh, easy, easy. The son of a sloth and a turnip, either I hang by my whiskery toes, thinking of nothing and lust, or sit bigheaded in the wet earth, thinking of turnip poems; and time snails by; and San Francisco's six thousand lamenting miles away; and Wales is dead from the eisteddfodau up; and day after day I grow lazier and fatter and sadder and older and deafer and duller; grey

[1] Tram Combs, a bookseller; William Swan; Gavin = Chester Alan Arthur III, grandson of a U.S. President. All were friends of Mrs Ruth-Diamant. Information from notes by Tram Combs in the Berg Collection.

grizzles in my dry hairmat; gout snarls in my big toe; my children grow large and rude; I renounce my Art to make money and then make no money; I fall in love with undesirable, unloving, squat, taloned, moist unlovely women and out again like a trout; I quarrel with Caitlin and make it up in floods of salt self pity; I fall downstairs; I frighten myself in the night, my own plump banshee; I celebrate other people's birthdays with falsely bonhomous abandon; I daydream of Chile, a place I never want to visit; I write poems and hide them before I can read them; and next week I shall be thirty-seven horrors old.[1] Does that, in any way, explain, dear Ruth, why I haven't written? Of course it doesn't. I've no excuse, but *please* try to forgive me. And are you well? and would you like to see me again? At the end of January, Caitlin and I are going to New York, financed by the Poetry Center, Columbia, and the Museum of Modern Art in collaboration, and I should hate it if I didn't, somehow, manage to get to California and (if you could bear it) stay with you for a week. Do you think some Universities would pay me enough, for readings, for us to be able to travel there from New York? And, if I am only but a little bit forgiven for my long and wicked silence, could you begin to try to find this out for me? My New York readings—at the Museum of Modern Art I read, Christ help me, scenes from King Lear, and a fine King Lear I'll look in my little shiny suit—will be over by the end of February, and I needn't return to England until the end of March. Will you see if anything can be done?

We're leaving Wales for London in a few weeks' time, to a house an insane woman has bought us. I'll hate to leave this sea but I must earn a living and will be writing filmscripts, class very B.

How is your wonderful city? Is your son home? Will you write soon? And I'll write again, a letter full of woes and useless news and little dirty drawings in the margin.

I'll have a drink with you tonight in the forlorn pub where ragged, romantic, weatherbeaten fishermen talk about motorcars and the dollar crisis, and to your memory in, I'm afraid, tepid cat-sour beer. Have a drink with me, in your nice hill house, or in Gavin's tumbledown castle, or with Tram and his beard amen.

All my love to you,
Dylan

MS: Berg

---

[1] Thomas's birthday was not until October 27.

PRINCESS CAETANI
October 1951   The Boat House Laugharne Carmarthenshire Wales

My Dear Madame Caetani,

Thank you for your telegram from Paris. And I hope my letter, addressed to Brown's Hotel, was forwarded to you.

This is a difficult letter to write, because I am asking a great request of you.

But let me first explain. The enclosed manuscript is called, as you will see, 'Llareggub. A Piece for Radio Perhaps', though the title is most provisional.[1] And it is the first half of something I am delighting in doing and which I shall complete *very* shortly. Only very special circumstances—and I'll tell you of them in a moment, if I may—are preventing me from carrying on with it every minute of the working day.

I told you, as you may remember, that I was working on a play, mostly in verse.[2] This, I have reluctantly, and, I hope, only temporarily, abandoned: the language was altogether swamping the subject: the comedy, for that was what it was originally intended to be, was lost in the complicated violence of the words: I found I was labouring at each line as though I were making some savage, and devious, metaphysical lyric and not a play at all. So I set the hotchpotch aside, and am prepared to wait.

But out of my working, however vainly, on it, came the idea of 'Llareggub'. (Please ignore it as a final title.) Out of it came the idea that I write a piece, a play, an impression for voices, an entertainment out of the darkness, of the town I live in, and to write it simply and warmly & comically with lots of movement and varieties of moods, so that, at many levels, through sight and speech, description & dialogue, evocation and parody, you come to know the town as an inhabitant of it. That is an awkward & highfalutin way of speaking: I only wanted to make the town alive through a raw medium: and that, again, is wrong: I seem hardly able to write today, or, at least, to write *about* Llareggub: all I want to do is to write the damned thing itself.

Reading (as I hope you will) the first half of this piece as it stands, you'll see that I have established the town up to a certain moment of the morning. And the effect you will find, probably, rather jerky and confusing, with far too many characters and changes of pitch and temper. But the piece will develop from this, through all the activities of the morning town—seen from a number of eyes, heard from a number of voices — through the long lazy lyrical afternoon, through the multifariously busy little town evening of meals & drinks and loves & quarrels and dreams and wishes, into the night and the slowing-down lull again and the repetition of the first word: Silence. And by that time, I hope to make you utterly familiar with the places and the people; the pieces of the town will fit together; the reasons for all these behaviours (so far but hinted at)

---

[1] Thomas had resurrected the joke-name that he first used in the 1930s.
[2] If this is true, the work isn't known.

will be made apparent, & there the town will be laid alive before you. And only you will know it.

Let me particularise, & at random. As the piece goes on, two voices will be predominant: that of the preacher, who talks only in verse, and that of the anonymous exhibitor and chronicler called, simply, 1st Voice. And the 1st Voice is really a kind of conscience, a guardian angel. Through him you will learn about Mr. Edwards, the draper, and Miss Price, the sempstress, & their odd and, once it is made clear, most natural love. Every day of the week they write love letters to each other, he from the top, she from the bottom, of the town: all their lives they have known of each other's existence, and of their mutual love: they have seen each other a thousand times, & never spoken: easily they could have been together, married, had children: but that is not the life for them: their passionate love, at just this distance, is all they need. And Dai Bread the baker, who has two wives: one is loving & mothering, sacklike & jolly; the other is gypsy slatternly and, all in love, hating: all three enjoy it. And Mrs Ogmore-Pritchard who, although a boardinghouse keeper, will keep no boarders because they cannot live up to the scrupulous & godlike tidiness of her house and because death can be the only boarder good enough for her in the end. And Mr. Pugh, the schoolmaster, who is always nagged by his wife and who is always plotting her murder. This is wellknown to the town, & to Mrs. Pugh. She likes nagging; he likes plotting, in supposed secrecy, against her. He would always like plotting, whoever he lived with; she would always like nagging, whoever she lived with. How lucky they are to be married. And Polly Garter has many illegitimate babies because she loves babies but does not want only one man's. And Cherry Owen the soak, who likes getting drunk every night; & his wife who likes living with two men, one sober in the day, one drunk at night. And the cobbler who thinks the town is the wickedest place to live in in the world, but who can never leave it while there is a hope of reforming it; and, oh, the savour his cries of Gomorrah add to the pleasures of the little town wicked. And the old woman who every morning shouts her age to the heavens; she believes the town is the chosen land, & the little river Dewi the River of Jordan; she is not at all mad: she merely believes in heaven on earth. And so with all of them, all the eccentrics whose eccentricities, in these first pages, are but briefly & impressionistically noted: all, by their own rights, are ordinary & good; & the 1st Voice, & the poet preacher, never judge nor condemn but explain and make strangely simple & simply strange.

I daren't look back over what I have written: I wrote it v. quickly, & most probably it reads like nonsense. But I *terribly* want to finish the piece. And it *will* be good (of its own kind). And this is where my great request of you at last comes in.

Can you pay me—and, I am sorry, *at once*—for this half of 'Llareggub' just as though it were finished? For without being paid well and at once, I cannot finish it.

In the middle of next week, we finally leave Laugharne for London. I mean, we *have* to leave: the house is sold. But, still, I *cannot* leave without paying the whole of the debts I owe to this town. And they amount to about a £100. If I can pay this, we can leave for London, where I have borrowed a flat, and I can get on, at once, with the rest of 'Llareggub'. Oh, I want to so much. I can finish it in two weeks. But only if I can settle all up here.

I know the amount I am sending you of Llareggub (and, of course, quite possibly the quality: you may loathe the thing) is not worth a £100. But what I want is to be paid now for the *whole* piece in advance. Is that possible? I am pinning every bit of faith on to that.

Can you cable me your answer?

Wouldn't it be awful if you thought the whole thing bunk. My head is full of it, I *must* go on.

Please forgive this letter.

Ever,
Dylan

MS: Camillo Caetani Foundation   *SL*

MARGARET TAYLOR
Wednesday [?October 1951]   Laugharne

Yes, it *is* a long time since I wrote to you last. Before, perhaps, you housed us, so snug and beautiful, in Laugharne, in the imperishable Boat House down whose kitchen steps, some Saturday nights ago, I fell like a barrel?[1] I was in bed, then, for days, with a rumpled back, and gout came too, grinding gout, and went to bed in my toe, and a Summons arrived to pay a firm of plumbers for the work they did, last December, in extricating, from the W.C. pipes of a London flat we were living in, a bottle of Hammerton's Stout thrown down by Colm. And, when I could walk again, I quarrelled and fought with Caitlin over something now forgotten but which I remember in every detail, and huffed out of the house to Swansea where I stayed with a barrister who uses brandy like salt or sauce, pouring it over everything, meat, potatoes, porridge, and even boiled egg. And Caitlin & Lizzie Lutyens came & reclaimed me, and, though I am writing this in the upper room of the Pelican, (for my shed keys are lost once more, for I think the sixth time) I can hear Lizzie hissing and gushing and drooling & bubbling about Edward,[2] money, the BBC, twelve tones, Constant[3] & babies, men, men, men, all the way from

---

[1] If this was, in fact, the first letter Thomas had written Mrs Taylor since moving to Laugharne in 1949, it should come much earlier. But its references to the move to London date it to late 1951.

[2] Edward Clark, Lutyens's husband.

[3] Constant Lambert, composer and conductor.

her bed in the Boat House where she lies all day monologuing herself to death. Lizzie came into the Pelican yesterday afternoon, raving drunk, and gave my father a heart attack. Today, he is still shaking. Caitlin's black eye has just faded; a boy fell from a tree where he was picking conkers, quite near your Grist house, and his shoulderblade broke & pierced his lung, and at the postmortem in Carmarthen Infirmary they found he had been eating stamps; a white owl breathes on a branch right outside Phil the Cross's bedroom window, like a hundred people making love, and inflamed Phil so much he ran, for the first time in years, to his wife's bed and set about her so fiercely he nearly died of a fit of silicotic coughing and couldn't go to work next day; a printed form has just come that tells me I shall be prosecuted herewith unless I send in my National Insurance book fully stamped for 1950; Ivy's front teeth fell out one evening while she was playing skittles, and yesterday she told me she had been blind in one eye for twenty years; Colm's scalded chest is better, but he still has nightmares; there is little other news.

I do hope it will be possible for us to come up to London towards the end of next week. That is the date we had looked forward to, too. But, as you know, and as we said this morning on the telephone, It All Depends. I couldn't go into any details on the phone as weazel-eared Lizzie was lying in bed in the same room, reading a book on Erasmus Darwin upside down. After our conversation, I talked to Caitlin about the position, and she said—as, indeed, I do myself feel most sincerely—we shouldn't take any money from you who has already given us two houses and much, much more besides. I hope some other money will arrive before the end of next week, from America; some is due to come, but of course, it may take a month. Anyway, and in spite of my better feelings, and feeling every kind of calculating and ungrateful monster, I made out a careful and detailed list of my Laugharne & Carmarthen debts and found them far more dreadful than I had imagined. Ivy, I can stall, I think. I do not believe the Post Office will mind waiting. And my poor Mother, from whom I was obliged to borrow to avoid yet another prosecution, would wait until after the grave. But certain debts in the town are desperately urgent, and *must* be paid before I can leave; and I do not see how I am to pay them. *First*, there is that summons, Plumber v Colm, which I mentioned earlier: this amounts to £6.10.0. & must be paid in five days. *Second*, there is a bill of Sydney Heath, Carmarthen, for Llewelyn's new mackintosh & socks, & this must be paid at once as they do not know or trust us: £7. *Third*, there is a bill of Keene's, the Grocer, for £11. *Fourth*, there is a bill of Fred Phillips for £17, due since July. *Fifth*, there is a Turpin greengrocer bill of £10. *Sixth*, there is a personal debt to Phil of £4 which I am, in honour & friendship, bound to pay. These six items amount to £54.10.0., and, as I say, I cannot leave Laugharne for Delancey Street[1] without settling every single penny of it.

---

[1] Where Mrs Taylor had bought a house; it is in Camden Town.

I shall be getting, for a poem, a small cheque, amount as yet unknown, which will take us up to London; and, after that, myself & London will see what we can do. That side of our gigantic move, I don't need help. This, the seaward, is the side that counts. We will both be terribly disappointed if we cannot come up next week to your/our new house.

Donald's film job is quite certain, as he wrote to me a few days ago, & will begin in 'some weeks'.

But, here in Laugharne & now, that doesn't mean anything, not to our summonses, grocers, greengrocers, clothiers, & candlestick makers.

Thank you for everything, for the beautiful Boat House, & for Delancey Street, for the caravan, for the Manor House, for the Little House, for a lot.

I shall show you my new poems in London—if ever, O God, we get there.

I am now going to borrow five shillings from someone for Woodbines & a Felinfoel.

Love,
Dylan

MS: Texas

OSCAR WILLIAMS
[October or November 1951]   Boat House Laugharne Carmarthenshire
Wales

S. Howard Moss, of the New Yorker,[1] wrote to me asking for poems. This is no good for him, I suppose?

My dear Oscar,
   Herewith a long new poem.[2] It's wonderfully good of you to take my bits and sell them so quick and so very well. I've spent months writing this poem, and hope you can squeeze out a real huge cheque from some moneyed illerate—it's me that's illerate, I meant illiterate—bastard for it. Months and months, and I think it's the best I've done. As always, I need money in a *terrible* hurry. Particularly urgently now, as next week we move to London, to stay in lodgings at the beginning & then to move into a house. I have gout, strained back, bronchitis, fits, and a sense of disaster, otherwise very ill. My love, and Caitlin's, to you & Gene whom we'll be seeing a lot (I hope) of in February. Please, old crazy friend, get me a lot of dough bloody bloody *quick*. And thank you a great lot for the 50 dollars.

Dylan

MS: Harvard

---

[1] Howard Moss, poetry editor of the *New Yorker*.
[2] 'Poem on his birthday'. The editor of *Atlantic*, Edward Weeks, was 'captivated' by it. He paid $200, grumbling slightly, and published it the following March.

DAVID HIGHAM
3 12 51   54 Delancey St Camden Town London NW1

Dear David,
Thank you for arranging that advance. And for writing to Leslie Andrews. If he still takes 75 per cent,[1] & you take your advance also, in bits, off the bits I earn, God alone knows how I'm going to live, and with bloody Christmas coming too.

Enclosed, is the Poem I imagined, incorrectly, was entitled 'Shabby & Shorten'.[2] Can you let Bozman have it? I saw him after leaving you & discussed the Collected Poems. He said also he would like to publish 'The Doctor & The Devils' at the end of next year. But—is there no chance of selling this *as a script* to a film company still?

Yours,
Dylan

MS: Texas

JOHN MALCOLM BRINNIN
3 12 51   54 Delancey Street Camden Town London NW1

Dear John,
Your letter just forwarded from Laugharne to our new London house or horror on bus and nightlorry route and opposite railway bridge and shunting station. No herons here.

Your letter, just read, has scared the lights out of me. First date in N.Y. January 23rd? I'll have to look lively. I'll also have to look like hell for money (£100) to keep girl & family here while Caitlin and I are junketing abroad.

Questions & answers:
(1) How long do we plan to stay? Between two & three months.
(2) Do we want to confine our movements to east & middle west or do we also want to go to the west coast?
   We certainly want to go to California, after the other dates you have arranged. Ruth Witt-Diamant, of San Francisco, (address: 1520 Willard St, S.F.) has recently written asking us the same question, or roughly the same. She says she will, given due warning, be able to arrange some S. Francisco readings. I am sure that Hunter Lewis, of B.C. University, Vancouver, would also invite me again. He said so in a letter this year.
(3) I don't think Florida for a month. A Californian month (or less) for

---

[1] As provision against income tax.
[2] 'Once below a time'. ('The criers of Shabby and Shorten./The famous stitch droppers'.)

us after New York. And then New York at the end again. I would, incidentally, like to go to Washington. Would that club like me again? The shirtless Biddles have invited Caitlin & me to stay with them there.

(4) Yes, yes, yes. I *do* want you please to be my little guide & agent.

On to other things. Oscar Williams, in his last letter to me, said that a group of mid-Western universities were getting together to invite me for a jolly week with them at a figure like one thousand dollars. He did mention mid-February, but I see that that now conflicts with my pre-arranged New York commitments. I shall write to him today; but do you think you could, as little agent, also get in touch with him and find out if the date—if it is a real date—can be moved to end of February or first of March. Then we could go on to S. Francisco in March sometime. I could leave Caitlin there while I went anywhere else on Pacific Coast where I was invited.

The Socialist Party in New York City—address 303 Fourth Avenue, N. York 10, tel. Gramercy 5-6621—have written to me to ask me for a poetry reading. They say they're a small body (like me) & can't pay much at all, but I would like to do it for them if you can arrange it. Oh, the chairman of the Finance Cte of the S. Party is, if you didn't know, a Jane Browne.

Next things you want to know: (1) Visa. I haven't got one yet. My passport is left in Laugharne, & I will try to go down & get it at the end of this week. Before I get the visa, I am almost certain to need—as before — papers from you, as my agent, explaining the purpose of my visit to the States and instancing some of my more worthy-looking engagements. Perhaps, if easily & quickly obtained by you, a letter from Columbia to you about me, from the Center, and from anywhere important else, would considerably help. Anyway, let me have some official papers of confirmation to show the scared baiters in power here.

(2) I have made no ship reservations for Cat and me, not knowing when I was due in N. York. I'll try to do this this week early, following your instructions about getting the steamship line to have their N. York office contact you at once at Poetry Center for payment.

(3) Caitlin will be coming with me, but *not* the baby.

(4) It's okay to say to the New School I'll do them a second programme of dramatic readings.

Now to *my* questions. What sort of poetry would, d'you think, most of my sponsors like me to read? Modern? including modern American, or is that presumptuous? Blake, Keats, Donne, Hopkins, Owen? And what about 'dramatic excerpts'? Marlowe, Shakespeare, Webster, Tourneur, Beddoes? Do tell me what, from your previous experience of 'my audiences', they most would like from me. I don't want to read too much of my own, except for a few recent ones. Laughlin, by the way, is bringing out a pamphlet of new poems for my visit.

What news of [. . .]? I hope, God bless her, she's in Brazil. How are *you*?

How goes Sidney G.? He was moaning for weeks about his companions, Raine & Gascoyne.[1] 'Och, there'll be wee orgies with those two sparocks.'

I'll get this off straightaway, without any news or affection; and will see about steamer bookings & visas *very quickly*.

Please you write quickly, too; & do let me know your suggestions as to the contents of my programmes. And do do something about West Coast. That's what Caitlin wants most.

Love,
Dylan

PS. Mebbe, after all, a bit of Florida would be good, if possible. Miami? Gainesville first, & then Miami?

PSS. A very important point I forgot. If we're to spend one whole month in N. York, *in an hotel*, we'll be desperately broke. Is there anyone who would put us up for, say, a week while we look around for someone else to put us up for the next week, and so on? It really's important. The money I earn we want for The Sights, not for board. Can you delicately hint around?

PSSS. I'm writing today to Ruth Witt-Diamant, but perhaps you could write as well—her address is on page one—to see what, if anything, she has done?

D.

MS: Delaware   *SL*

ANEIRIN TALFAN DAVIES
3 December 1951 (Agrees to reprint of BBC talk. See Appendix 62.)

DAVID HIGHAM
Thursday [marked '14 Dec 1951 recd']   54 Delancey St Camden Town
London NW1

Dear David,

When I was talking to Leslie Andrews' man the day before yesterday, I mentioned the fact that I was having an advance on a new book very shortly & that I very much hoped I could have this sum intact & that no tax deduction be made from it. He agreed to this, saying that the monies you had for him would keep the Income Tax wolf well at bay & that this advance need not be touched. So will you *please* let me have the

---

[1] W. S. Graham, Kathleen Raine, David Gascoyne: all poets.

American Diary £100[1] without any tax deduction &—*very* much please again—without deducting from it anything towards the money I owe your firm. This £100 will pay immediate debts & see my family over beastly, expensive Christmas. Can you see to it that I get this sum whole —(minus, of course, your usual agent's fee). I am doing two broadcast jobs just after Christmas, & the 50 tax per cent can be taken from those, which will, now, I think, nearly clear the Tax debt. Also from these can be taken the rest of what I owe you. But please (once more) let me have the *whole* of that £100. *It is urgent.*

I am posting Laughlin's proofs direct to him tonight.[2] Is that okay? I would have posted them sooner, but am going to read most of them tonight at the Institute of Contemporary Art & have no other copy.

Yours,
Dylan

I'll ring you about this, very briefly, tomorrow.

MS: Texas

JOHN MALCOLM BRINNIN
6 January 1952   54 Delancey Street Camden Town London NW1

Dear John,

Thank you for your two letters, official & not.

Thos. Cook have just written me to say you've paid for Caitlin's & my passage on the Queen Mary on January 15. Thank you. I only hope to the Lord I can make it. The difficulty is over my visa. The American Consulate would not revalidate it until they had 'investigated' me. They're presumably in the process of doing that now. The snag seemed to be a visit I paid to Prague in 1949—the year *before* I came to the States last. I'm *hoping* to get the visa this week. Do you know anyone important your end who'd say a word to the Embassy, or Consulate, that I'm not a dangerous Red? I'll be seeing a British Foreign Office man myself tomorrow. But perhaps everything will work out okay. It's just that there's such very little time. If the worst comes to the worst, and my visa is withheld *after* the 15th, I'll cable. I'll cable you, anyway, if the Q. Mary sails with us. Will you meet us? Please?

Any hope of accommodation yet—or should we stay in a hotel for the first part of our visit?

Heard from Ruth Witt-Diamant about possible Californian readings?

I must read Lear again: haven't looked at it for years.

---

[1] Higham had negotiated a £400 contract with the London firm of Allan Wingate for an 'American Journal' of 60,000 words, to be delivered on 30 June 1952. The first £100 was paid on signing. The book was not written.

[2] Presumably *In Country Sleep and Other Poems*, published February 1952.

I enclose a letter from McGill University, Montreal. This letter seems, to me, to mean that McGill is prepared to transport me (I suppose at a good fee) all the way from Wales to Montreal. And (I suppose) back. They seem to know nothing about my coming to the States in January. *So*: as my transportation from N. York to Montreal will be so much less than from Wales to Montreal, the fee, surely, must be commensurately (or proportionately, I don't know the words) increased. I've written to Stors McCall, saying, 'Yes, delighted', & that I'd be in N.Y. the end of January. I told him that you, as my dear little agent, would be getting in touch with him as you, and you only, knew what my N. York commitments were, & when. Will you write to him, quickly? And as I don't particularly want to go to Montreal, soak McGill for twice (at least) as much as I get in the States—plus, of course, full expenses *by air*!

I'll be cabling you. Keep your fingers crossed for us.

I'm looking forward, a lot, to seeing you. And I hope I can.

Cat got her visa straightaway.

Love,
Dylan

MS: Delaware

JOHN MALCOLM BRINNIN

[Telegram, January 16 1952, from SS Queen Mary]
SEE YOU PIER 90 SUNDAY BRING CARPET LOVE DYLAN CAITLIN.

Original: Delaware

MARGARET TAYLOR

10th February 1952　　　　　　　　　　Hotel Chelsea　222 23rd St W
New York[1]

My Dear Margaret,

I've been meaning, & meaning, to write a letter, a proper letter, but this poor little scribble is so far the best I can do. (I've not even written to my parents, though Cat has.) It's the terrible speed & noise of this place, the parties piling, the faces blurring, the endless insistent killing kindness that's the reason I haven't, long before, said How are you? & how is dear Aeron? How is everything? I promise to write properly soon.

Dylan

MS: Texas

[1] A large, economical hotel, beloved of writers, near the Greenwich Village district. Thomas and his wife arrived in New York on January 20, but he had no engagements until January 30.

SOPHIE (?WILKINS)[1]
Thursday [February 21 1952]

Dear Sophie,
I'm terribly, *terribly* sorry—and so is Caitlin, who sends her regards —
that I can't come along tonight as I very much wanted to & looked
forward to. I've been sick as hell all day, really physically sick in the most
obvious & unpleasant way, & could only just get through a reading at the
NYU.[2] Now the reading is over, & I'm going back to bed, hotwater bottle,
& sleeping draught.
A great many apologies, & I hope, a lot, to see you soon. (We'll be in the
White Horse,[3] at about [?4] o'clock on Sunday, on Hudson & 11th Street,
& would like to see you & apologise in person—if you'll excuse the
phrase.)

Fondly,
Dylan Thomas

DAVID HIGHAM
26 Feb 1952   [headed paper: Hotel Chelsea, etc]

Dear David,
Caitlin & I are getting very anxious—to put it mildly. Today we heard
from Dolly Long, 49 Orchard Park Estate, Laugharne, Carmarthenshire,
the girl who is looking after our baby; she told us she had received no
money from you in spite of my cable & Caitlin's letter. Do you remember, we arranged together that you would pay Dolly Long £3 a week
for three months (or, if necessary, longer) out of the three monthly
cheques for £50 each delivered you by Charles Fry?[4] I realised that I owed
Pearn & Pollinger & Higham £50, so perhaps you have taken the February
Fry £50 for that debt. If this is so, WILL YOU VERY MUCH PLEASE send
to Dolly Long—I repeat the address, 49 Orchard Park Estate, Laugharne,
Carmarthenshire—the WHOLE of the March Fry £50? And can you,
please, *CABLE* me at the above address. If Dolly isn't paid—the main
reason I arranged to write a book for Fry, a book which is shaping well,
though roughly—then we shall have to return to England somehow
rightaway, breaking all my university lectures etc., as Dolly Long is poor
& cannot look after a child for nothing.
So, PLEASE: Send her the whole (minus, of course, ten per cent) of Fry's

---

[1] The Thomas Trustees have a photocopy of this letter; the addressee is said to have been
Sophie Wilkins.
[2] Thomas read at New York University on Thursday February 21.
[3] A Greenwich Village tavern that Thomas made his drinking headquarters.
[4] Charles Fry, of Allan Wingate, had commissioned the 'American Journal'; further
advances of £50 a month were due in January, February and March.

forthcoming *March* cheque. This is most urgent. Caitlin's breaking her heart about the baby. AND DO PLEASE CABLE TO RELIEVE OUR DEEP ANXIETY.

I've seen Helen Strauss, by the way, & Mike Watkins.[1] Mike wanted me to stay on with him, but, of course, I've followed your advice & instructions & told Helen Strauss that, along with your other writers, I have moved over to her. She is now in the process of settling some gramophone record contract for me.[2]

I'll write again when there is news. My lectures—readings, rather—are going extremely well. We start for the middle west in the middle of March.

But the main purpose of this very worried letter is:

Please Pay Dolly Long the whole March £50. AND *PLEASE* CABLE us you're doing so.

I'm sick with anxiety.

Yours,
Dylan

MS: Texas   *SL*

RUTH WITT-DIAMANT

March 9th 52   c/o J M Brinnin   100 Memorial Drive   Cambridge   Mass

Darling Professor

Every day, since we arrived in the States, nearly three ulcering months ago, I've been meaning to write & say: 'Darling Professor, How are you? We will be in San Francisco towards the end of March. Can we stay with you for a week or two?' But I haven't been able to write a *single* letter. John Brinnin has again fixed me up with a breathless & bloody pro-gramme—though in S.F. there is little for me to do, thank the sunny Lord, but sit & like & be with you & see the seals & Big Sur & the Pacific baths. What a pity Tram & Bill are gone. And Elaine. I saw Donald Weeks in Washington a few days ago: he says she's getting married, lucky nasty man.

We are leaving New York on March 16, making our way to San Francisco & you via Chicago & Arizona, where for a few days we stay with Max Ernst.[3] We will be in S.F. some time between the 22nd & the 24th of March. I'll wire you from the Ernsts the *exact* date of our arrival. I'm longing to see you. And Caitlin sends her love.

---

[1] Strauss and Watkins were with the Ann Watkins literary agency.
[2] Two young women, Barbara Holdridge and Marianne Mantell, had started the Caedmon record company. They recorded Thomas in New York, reading poetry and prose, in 1952 and 1953: a far-sighted investment.
[3] Max Ernst (1891–1976), painter.

John Brinnin, with whom we are staying for a few days while I rant at Harvard, says he will write to you tomorrow *in detail* about the Berkeley engagement etc. I think he needs a bit of assistance from you.

It's going to be grand.

Ever,
Dylan

MS: Berg

JOHN DAVENPORT
March 21 [1952] [postcard]

Am staying, very near here, for a few days with the Max Ernsts, though not in the villa in the foreground. A killer-diller of a journey so far. On our way, next week, to San Francisco. (By the way, Time Magazine will be approaching you in London about me. They're doing a piece, & wanted a London friend who Knew All.)

Love to you & Marjorie & the little others, from Caitlin & me.

Always
Dylan

MS: Texas

DANIEL JONES
[postcard] March 21 [1952]

Caitlin & I are buried in the Tuzigoot stone teepee
on the Other side of this card.
We were killed in action, Manhattan Island, Spring, 1952,
in a gallant battle against American generosity.
An American called Double Rye shot Caitlin to death.
I was scalped by a Bourbon.
Posthumous love to you & Irene & Dylan & Catherine[1] from
Caitlin & Dylan

MS: Texas   *SL*

---

[1] Mrs Jones and their two children.

OSCAR WILLIAMS
[postcard, with four signatures] [March 1952]

Wild & Western Love to Gene and Oscar from—
           Max Ernst
           Dorothea
           Dylan
     and   Caitlin   X

MS: Harvard

BILL MCALPINE
[card, postmarked March 28]

X marks where we are staying
I'm going to write you & Helen a long daft letter as soon as we arrive in
San Francisco after a (so far) tumultuously exhilarating & axe-splitting
tour. But for the moment, just this idea—though it's not, for a moment,
as sensational as the desert itself—of where we are on the 21st of March.
Love to you both.

                                        Always,
                                        Dylan
MS: Buffalo

JOHN MALCOLM BRINNIN
4th April [1952]   c/o Witt-Diamant 1520 Willard Street San Francisco
                                                                California

Dear John,
     Three letters lie—I don't, of course, mean that—before me: dated
March 20, March 26, & April 1st. Here's a brief, but none the less stupid,
reply to them all.
     I'm awfully sorry, re March 20, that you've been sick. And not of us? A
mysterious illness; probably test-tubing out from M.I.T.—to whose English students, & professor of English named maybe Fudge O'Dell, I owe a
forever unwritten apology for never turning up. But I'm very glad you're
better (April 1st) now, & on such a good day.
     Thank you for the damnably urgent & answerable letter from Higham.
I'm supposed, as perhaps you read, to write an introduction to the English
forthcoming edition of my Collected Poems, which, I suppose, entails my
reading them all. Daft I may be....
     Now, re March 26th. Those 'ridiculous mishaps' that caused you to
miss my wire from Sedona[1] proved agonising to us. Caitlin was frightfully

---

[1] At Max Ernst's home.

ill all the way from New York to Pennsylvania State College (where [. . .] was an old fool & more, but the audience gallant) and on the night-train to Chicago. During the Chicago journey, my bottled up bottle illness also grew severe; indeed, we were both so near to undignified death that, on reaching Chicago, we just *could* not go straight across the city to catch our next train to Arizona but *had* to lie down, dying, in an unrocking bed. (Incidentally, a roomette is only for *one* traveller, & Christ help him. We had to change to a bedroom. Dearer.) So we went to a cosy little hovel of an hotel (the [. . .]) & wept & sweated there until next day. The hotel was fabulously expensive; the Pullman reservation for Tuesday, the 18th, fell out of date; I had to buy a new one; & so we arrived at Flagstaff with less than a dollar. The Ernsts were lovely, charming, & hospitable, but had no ready money & none to lend. We stayed there, absolutely penniless, for 8 days, being unable to buy our own cigarettes, to post a letter, or stand with a beer at Sedona's cowboy bar, or even wire you again. We stayed there, saying 'Beastly John Brinnin', until help came from San Francisco. Arriving at San Francisco, we found your 2 letters, & 2 cheques, & also a letter from the headmaster of Llewelyn's school saying he would be thrown out unless a £100 were paid by April 5. I then wired you again. You sent a cheque for 200 dollars. And so I had 400 dollars altogether. 300 dollars I wired to Llewelyn's school. The other 100 I spent on a Vancouver ticket. So (again) *HELP*.

(On top of this, Caitlin had carefully arranged for some laundry to be sent on from New York to San Francisco. This cost 40 dollars.)

I can just manage to get to Vancouver, & I'll leave Caitlin the fee for my S.F. State College reading which is tonight & which will be only 50 dollars.

About other engagements: Is the date, on April 26, at the University of Chicago the *same* as that, on April 24, at the Northwestern University, Chicago? Or can't I read?

It's summer here, not spring. Over 80. At Easter we go to Carmel & on to see Miller at Big Sur. We are both well.

Please write very soon, [*the remaining words form a large circle*] with any news, some love & a *Bit of Money*. Caitlin sends her love. And, as always, so do I.

Yours, Dylan

MS: Delaware *SL*

HENRY MILLER
[April 1952]   1520 Willard [St] San Francisco

Dear Henry,
   I'm back here once more, staying with Ruth Witt-D for a week or so. This time my wife Caitlin is with me.

We're driving out your way next—Easter—weekend. Shall we call & see you? I'd love to. It would be on Easter Saturday or Sunday.

If it's no good to you, perhaps you wouldn't mind dropping a card to me?

But I hope it is all right.

Yours,
Dylan Thomas

TS: J. M. Dent

JEAN GARRIGUE[1]

April 5 1952   c/o 1520 Willard St San Francisco California

Dear Jean,

Your letter's just come from the Chelsea. I *did* miss seeing you in New York; though I knew, from Stanley Moss, that you were teaching at Bard:—I hoped you might visit the city some weekend, & that we could meet. But even hearing from you I like very much.

Look: To whom do I say what I'd like to say about your poems for the Guggenheim you *must* get? To you? or to the, to me, nameless & addressless Guggenheim people themselves? I can do either, or both.

As perhaps you know, should know, or don't know, I think your poems are beautiful; they are subtle & exciting; they're the work of a deeply serious poet with a fine ear and a lovely, dangerous, voice of her own.

Isn't that awful, when all I mean is that I like them a *lot*, that I re-read them, remember them, & was moved, & made full of wonder, by the new poems in Botteghe Oscure.

To whom shall I say something like that? or something, I hope, much better said?

Write, if you will, to the address above, which I leave on April 17. After that, my best address, as I'm moving quickly all over the place, is c/o John Brinnin, 100 Memorial Drive, Cambridge, Mass.

Caitlin & I get to New York on April 30, & leave for England on May 16. Any chance of meeting between those dates?

Always,
Dylan

MS: Berg

---

[1] Poet (b. 1914). She taught at Bard College, 1951–2.

KARL [*probably* SHAPIRO][1]
[May 1952]   [headed paper: Hotel Chelsea, etc]

Dear Karl,
Thank you for the Rhyming Dictionary. I'll write something so soon as I get back to England, doom, & duty.

Had the bad news, on arriving here, that my son had been thrown out of his school because past fees had not been paid. Also, that the rent on my parents' house was so overdue that they, too, (crippled, blind, etc) may be thrown out.

Will this melt a rich bitch heart? Can you try?

Caitlin (who sends her love to you both) seems to imagine that Mrs (Meat) Prince[2] would be sympathetic. Do you?

Anyway, can you try to do something for us? Otherwise, we'll arrive back with nothing but debts & gloom & nowhere to go & no time to write.

We leave on May 16th. You were both fine to us in Chicago.

Ever,
Dylan

[*printed at foot of page:* LARGE and SOUND-PROOF ROOMS]
[*written beside it:* Don't you believe it]

MS: Carbondale

GENE DERWOOD
[card, posted at sea, postmarked May 23 1952]

So sorry we didn't manage to say Goodbye to you—Terrible [*illegible*] and muddly as usual. Tell Oscar will send manuscript to him when I can get him something decent together.
Very rough & rocky in mid ocean.
                    XXX   Love Caitlin & Dylan
MS: Indiana

OSCAR WILLIAMS
[?May 1952] [postcard]

Can you see a X on postcard? That's us. Hope you'll see it closer, one day, soon.
MS: Harvard   Dylan

[1] Poet (b. 1913). He edited *Poetry* (Chicago).
[2] Perhaps Ellen Borden Stevenson (former wife of the politician Adlai Stevenson), patron of the arts.

P. H. NEWBY[1]
4 June 1952   The Boat House Laugharne Carmarthenshire Wales

Dear Mr. Newby,
   Thank you very much for your letter about 'Personal Anthology'. It
was waiting for me when I returned from the States to London last
week, but, in travelling home to Wales, I'm afraid I somehow mislaid it.
Would it be an awful nuisance for you to tell me once more the details
of time, length, date etc? I'd like, a lot, to do a 'Personal Anthology', &
can put it together very quickly. What about an Anthology of modern
American verse?
   Sorry about the delay, & my carelessness in losing your letter.
   Hoping to hear from you soon,
                                                Yours sincerely,
                                                Dylan Thomas

MS: BBC

DAVID HIGHAM
28 June 1952   The Boat House Laugharne Carmarthenshire

Dear David,
   Thousands of apologies. That's so easy to write, but I mean every one.
Though small, I must be one of your most infuriating thorns.
   When in London, I spent a lot of time in Lord's—(where lazy thorns go,
when they're not pricking their agents)—bareheaded and balding in the
sun. I developed what I thought to be sunstroke, and, by kind daft friends,
was put, moaning, into a sleeper and trained home. But it wasn't
sunstroke: I had pleurisy, and I'm only just recovered. Not *serious*
pleurisy, except to me whom the States have taught an obsessive, and
intriguing, hypochondria. But serious or not, I couldn't write. Now I'm
resuming what I imagine to be work.
   1) I saw Bozman, and got fresh proofs from him.[2] I promised him the
preface in a week, but illness supervened. And now I have to confess that
I can't write an ordinary prose-preface at all, having no interest whatsoever in it. What I *am* doing, and doing quickly, is writing a Prologue in
verse: not dense, elliptical verse, but (fairly) straightforward and colloquial, addressed to the (maybe) readers of the Collected Poems, & full (I

[1] Percy Howard Newby (b. 1918), novelist, who joined the BBC as a talks producer in 1949.
[2] Of *Collected Poems*.

hope) of references to my methods of work, my aims, & the kind of poetry I want to write. I hope it will be interesting; I know I'm interested in writing it. It will be about 160 to 200 short lines of verse, of which I have written about 80 so far.

2) I saw Donald Taylor. But far from *my* charming him out of his attitude, he, with his airy-fairy lackadaisical blarney charmed *me* into a kind of acquiescent and doped silence. 'Just leave everything to me. Everything will be all right. I'll see (or write to) Higham & Bozman. Just don't you worry. I'll do what's best for us both', is, I dreamily believe, what he told me.[1] Have you heard? Should I drop him a line? I can be much more definite with written words than I can in pleasant, lulling, and responsibility-procrastinating company.

The script work he has for me is still vague, though he is, of course, most optimistic.

3) I didn't see Fry. I rang him up to put off our lunch-date till the evening; &, by the evening, was, as I thought then, struck dumb & giddy by the sun. I'm writing to him this week-end, however, with explanation, and to give him an idea of how I intend to do the book.

4) A letter came to me from Kilmartin, so I didn't need to see him. He was keen on having articles on America for the Observer.[2] These articles, however, cannot now be chunks of the Wingate book, as that will be mostly of a fantastic nature & quite unsuitable for a newspaper. But I hope to be able to write, for Kilmartin, separate, straight pieces.

5) I've written to P. H. Newby about 'Personal Anthology', & will finish the anthology (of American modern poetry) as soon as a couple of books I am waiting for arrive from London. This is a quick job.

6) I couldn't of course take part in the MacNeice programme, which took place when I was ill.

I shall be in London for the Newby recording in the middle of July, & will ring you then. I have bought a panama hat for Lord's, to keep off the pleurisy.

Hope to hear soon about Laughlin.

And all my sincere apologies again. Don't despair of me.

Yours, Dylan

PS. By the way I forgot to give you my home phone number. It is: LAUGHARNE (pronounced Larne) 68.

MS: Texas   *SL*

---

[1] *The Doctor and the Devils* was still unpublished. Dent wanted Dylan Thomas to be shown as the sole author; Donald Taylor complained that it was he who 'initiated, constructed and partly wrote' the script. As published (1953), it is 'by' Thomas, 'from the story by' Taylor.

[2] Terence Kilmartin, literary editor of the *Observer*.

DAVID HIGHAM
21 July 1952   The Boat House Laugharne Carmarthenshire

Dear David,

I had a nice letter from Fry, and an enthusiastic one from Bozman about the verse prologue to the Collected Poems. I posted, today, a short note to Donald Taylor, telling him I'd be in London this week—for a recording of American poems—and want, very much, to see him about Hedgerley Films (whatever they might be) and, in view of Bozman's final refusal to print it unless it bears my name alone, about the ill-fated Doctor & the Devils.

Now the verse prologue should have been finished by this time, and *would* have been hadn't a London visit and two Welsh university lectures cropped up. The London visit was for various recordings for the 3rd Programme, and was interrupted by an urgent call to return to Carmarthen to meet the Income Tax Commissioners along with Leslie Andrews who was contesting their right to tax me, for my 1950 visit to the States, on £1,907. Andrews was defeated, & now it's up to me & him to plug in lots more expenses. Whatever happens, there's going to be a lot deducted from this coming winter's earnings. And the university lectures, in North Wales, an area harder to get to from S. Wales than Ireland would be, took up a lot of time; I had to do them, though, as they made a few necessary pounds. I have to come to London again this week, to continue the recordings that were interrupted by the Income Tax trolls; but, immediately on my return at the end of the week, will hurry up & finish the prologue for Dent.

Which leads me to a very urgent matter: Last week, right after the horror of the Tax tribunal, an inspector called here from the Ministry of National Insurance. I'd filled up only one of my insurance cards since the scheme began, and had put off and forgotten, in about equal parts, the whole thing until this Inspector came. And now I have to pay £50. 12. 6d at once—last day tomorrow, Tuesday, 22nd July,—or they will prosecute me & Make A Warning of me. So can you *please, please,* pay £50 into my bank—Lloyd's Bank Ltd., 164 Kings Road, Chelsea, S.W.3.—tomorrow, the 22nd? That is, can you, please, advance me £50 on the strength of the Dent Collected Poems & on the various BBC jobs I'm now doing? There is nowhere else to approach in such a terrible hurry as this, & you've always been wonderfully good to me (better than I deserve) in the past.

If you could ring me up here, at Laugharne 68, when you have received this letter, and say that you can do this for me & that the £50 is on its way to my Chelsea bank, then I can write a cheque for that amount and take it in to the National Insurance office that day. That very Tuesday, the 22—

or I am *done for*. The Inspector, otherwise, will prosecute *from that moment*. Please, David.

And once the verse prologue is finished, I can get down, fast & properly, to the American fantasia.

Yours,
Dylan

I'll wait in all morning for your *prayed-for* call.

MS: Texas   *SL*

R. D. SMITH[1]
22 July 1952   Boat House Laugharne Carmarthenshire
                                                          Laugharne 68

Dear Reggie,

Did you get that sketch of mine typed? If you did, thanks very much my boy & will you send it to me so that I can make it better? And if it isn't typed, don't bother a bit but do please [send] the ms on just as it is: it's not too good as it stands, but I *can* make something of it if I work more carefully at the end. It's hot & lovely here, and I'm sitting in my pink skin in a garage, writing this, and looking hellish.

Love,
Dylan

MS: Dr Cyril James

DOUGLAS CLEVERDON
19 August 1952   Boat House Laugharne Carmarthenshire

Dear Douglas,

At long last—and with many apologies—'Spoon River Anthology'.[2]

You will see that I have chosen too many poems, probably, but I think it worth duplicating too many in the script for you to work on with the readers. The order need not be kept in the way I have indicated, but can—and should—be changed about, according to voice, mood etc. I'm

---

[1] Reggie Smith, BBC producer.
[2] Thomas was compiling a radio programme from the book, *Spoon River Anthology*, a collection of short poems by the American writer Edgar Lee Masters, first published 1915.

sorry I couldn't arrange the poems better—that is, make a real programme of them, alternating grim & (fairly) gay, etc—but I had only that one afternoon in the library with the book. I didn't write much then, only got engrossed in the poems until 6 o'clock.

I hope the introduction isn't too long and/or tendentious.

Will you drop me a line about this?

And, if it *is* possible to get a little money soon, could it be got, somehow, straight to me, & not through my agents, d'you think? I'm in a hell of a money mess, sued on all sides; trying to finish several things, including 'Llarreggub' & a long poem, but worried to death; ill with it.

Ever,
Dylan

I remember, when we last talked of this programme, your suggestion that there shd be a few words by me between each poem. This, really, isn't any good. After the introduction, the poems, I think, *must* come one after the other, with only the pause when the Narrator says 'Joe Smith'.

MS: BBC

DOUGLAS CLEVERDON
23 Aug '52   The Boat House Laugharne Carmarthenshire

My dear Douglas,

Thank you very much for your letter. I enclose a formal note about (I hope) BBC payment for 'Spoon River'.[1] And, *please*, make it come, if at all, terribly quickly.

Delighted to think you might be coming here about the middle of September. There is, of course, a bed for you here.

I'm glad you and Laurence[2] & all want to get 'Llareggub' on the air. I want, myself, to finish it more than anything else. I'm longing to get to work on it again. I have only to finish one job, which I should do by the end of the week of the 25th, and then I can—BUT: I can't without money.

This is the position. I'll want a month or 6 weeks to complete it, working on it every day: I write very slowly when I'm very much enjoying it. And I can't work on anything for a month, without the money to keep us going during that time. I have to write little things & pack them off straight away for money by return; and this is obviously death to any project that needs a month or six weeks' full concentration. If the BBC could pay me a weekly sum, (not less than £10 a week, for the period of 6 weeks) I could shove all other small jobs aside & work on 'Llareggub'

---

[1] Thomas wanted to be paid direct, circumventing David Higham and the income-tax deductions.
[2] Laurence Gilliam.

only; and guarantee the script complete at the end of that time. That's really the only way it can be worked.[1]

Could you talk to Laurence about this?

I could devote my time, with the greatest enjoyment, to writing imaginative full-length things for the radio if I could be paid a weekly wage. Otherwise, it's bits & pieces for me all the time; this does not get me enough to live on; & is in every way unsatisfying.

Will you do what you can?

And, in the meantime, *please* do try to get me some 'Spoon River' money. I'm being sued by the National Insurance people, among other people.

Yours ever,
Dylan

MS: BBC

DOUGLAS CLEVERDON
[*enclosed with previous letter*]
23 August 1952   The Boat House Laugharne Carmarthenshire

Dear Mr. Cleverdon,

This is to authorise the B.B.C. to make their payment for 'Spoon River Anthology' direct to me at the above address.

Yours truly,
Dylan Thomas

MS: Texas

MARGED HOWARD-STEPNEY
Another Thomas benefactor, Marged Howard-Stepney (1913–53) came from a wealthy Anglo-Welsh family. She was an eccentric who dismayed her advisers by handing out presents to the needy, and spent much time drinking with Thomas. This letter-as-poem is taken from a heavily-altered worksheet, and probably was never sent.

[?1952] [draft]

My dear Marged, You told me, once, upon a time, to call on you when I

---

[1] Cleverdon, knowing that advance payment was impossible, proposed to his superiors that the BBC give Thomas five guineas (£5.25) for every thousand words of the script he delivered. Cleverdon even offered to have the money deducted from his own salary, should the BBC suffer any loss. 'It will be a tragedy for the Corporation, no less than for himself,' he wrote, 'if he cannot bring to fruition the works of creative imagination of which he is capable.' The plan was agreed, but had little effect. *Under Milk Wood* was completed hurriedly in 1953 for stage readings in the United States. It was not broadcast until after Thomas's death.

was beaten down, and you would try to pick me up. Maybe I should not have remembered

> You told me, once, to call on you
> When I was beaten down ...

Dear Marged,

> Once upon a time you told me,
> I remember in my bones,
> That when the bad world had rolled me
> Over on the scolding stones,
> Shameless, lost, as the day I came
> I should with my beggar's cup
> Howl down the wind and call your name
> And you, you would raise me up.
>
> The same very same time I told you,
> And swore by my heart & head,
> That I would forever hold you
> To the lovely words you said;
> I never thought so soon I'd lie
> Lonely in the whining dust;
> My one wish is to love and die,
> But life is all mustn't & must.
>
> I mustn't love, & I must die
> But only when I am told,
> And Fear sits in the mansioned sky
> And the winged Conventions scold,
> And Money is the dunghill King
> And his royal nark is the dun;
> And dunned to death I write this jingling thing
> Dunned to death in the dear sun.
> This jingling thing

MS: Texas

CAITLIN THOMAS
[?1952]

Two conjectures are involved in trying to place this despairing letter. 'That Marged gin woman' suggests it was written after Caitlin had found and read the previous piece of doggerel. And 'the Insurance thing summons' may place it near similar references in letters to David Higham of 21 July and Douglas Cleverdon of 23 August.

Caitlin,
  Please read this.
  That letter you saw was horrible, it was dirty and cadging and lying. You

know it was horrible, dirty, and cadging and lying. There was no truth in it. There was no truth meant to be in it. It was vile, a conscientious piece of contrived bamboozling dirt, which *nobody* was supposed to see—not you, or that Marged gin woman. I wrote it as I will tell you. The fact that you read it has made me so full of loathing & hatred for myself, and despair, that I haven't been able to speak to you. I haven't been able to speak to you about it. There was nothing I could say except, It isn't true, it's foul, sponging lies. And how could I say that when you'd *seen* it? How could I tell you it was all lies, that it was all made up for nothing, when you'd seen the dirty words? You'd say, If you didn't mean the dirty words, why did you write them? And all I could answer would be, Because I wanted to see what foul dripping stuff I could hurt myself to write in order to fawn for money. I'd as soon post that muck as I'd swim, I was going to tear it up in a million bloody bits. Marged told me, when she was drunk with that [. . .], to write to her about what I owed the Insurance things & others, or that's what I gathered—as much as anyone could gather. Or perhaps that's what I wanted to gather. Anyway, I put the Insurance thing summons in an envelope & explained, in a note, that I'd spent the other half of the money she'd given us for that, & that there were other real debts too. Then I went on writing something else—those endless rotten verses of mine, which I almost agree with you about—and then, when I came to a dead bit, to a real awful jam in the words, I saw—on the other broken table—when I'd written to Marged & started writing a proper sycophantic arselicking hell letter, putting in pretentious bits, introducing heart-throb lies, making, or trying to make, a foul beggar's lie-book of it. I only just avoided tuberculosis & orphans. There's no excuse for my writing this. I'd no idea it would go further than the floor of this shed. I was all wrong to drivel out this laboured chicanery. So wrong, & ashamed, I haven't been able to say a word to you about it. The misery I'm in can't make up for, or explain the misery I've made for you by my callous attempt at a mock-literature of the slimiest kind.

I love you.

Dylan

MS: Thomas Trustees

BBC
5th Sept 1952   The Boat House Laugharne Carmarthenshire Wales

Dear Mr Layton,[1]
    Thank you for yesterday's letter. I enclose the Talks Contract, signed.

---

[1] The addressee was Miss E. M. Layton, Copyright Department.

I do hope you can let me have your cheque for 20 guineas as soon as possible.[1] That, indeed, is the reason I asked, in this particular case, for you to negotiate directly with me instead of with Pearn, Pollinger, & Higham, in the usual way: I thought it would be a bit quicker, as I'm going through one of those times when all the bills are coming in together and I want whatever money's due to me with all the speed possible.

When, however, it comes to negotiations about the feature programme 'The Town That Was Mad', that I have been asked to write, I should like you, please, to deal with P.P. & H., my agents.

Thanks very much.

Yours sincerely,
Dylan Thomas

MS: BBC

E. F. BOZMAN
10 September 1952   Boat House Laugharne Carmarthenshire

Dear Bozman,
More apologies than there's paper, for this crippling delay.

I intended, as you know, to write a more-or-less straightforward & intimate prose preface, and then funked it. And then I began to write a prologue in verse, which has taken the *devil* of a time to finish. Here it is, only a hundred & two lines, and pathetically little, in size & quality, to warrant the two months, & more, I've taken over it. To begin with, I set myself, foolishly perhaps, a most difficult technical task: The Prologue is in two verses—in my manuscript, a verse to a page—of 51 lines each. And the second verse rhymes *backward* with the first. The first & last lines of the poem rhyme; the second and the last but one; & so on & so on. Why I acrosticked myself like this, don't ask me.

I hope the Prologue *does* read as a prologue, & not as just another poem. I think—though I am too near to it now to be any judge—that it *does* do what it sets out to do: addresses the readers, the 'strangers', with a flourish, and fanfare, and makes clear, or tries to make clear, the position of one writer in a world 'at poor peace'.

I will have a proof of this, won't I?

I'm writing to Higham, to say that the Prologue and the proofs are at last in your hands. And I'm begging him to have my contract with you settled *as quickly as possible*. Though the result does little to show it, I've spent 2 months at this poem, working hard at it every day and doing no other work-for-money at all. And consequently I've got very badly into debt, am faced with summonses, and cannot even now buy myself a beer

[1] For *Spoon River Anthology*.

and cigarettes. And daily it gets worse. So, please, do do all you can to let me have my advance royalties on the Collected Poems really quickly. It's very urgent. I'm in quite a desperate position, even to a few pounds, and day-to-day wants & needs.

You asked me, in a previous letter, about possible interviews with the press when the book comes out. Of course, I'd be pleased & will do whatever you can arrange.

All my apologies again.
Yours,
Dylan Thomas

PS. I shd, if possible, like a dedication: just

To Caitlin.

Proofreading the Collected Poems, I have the horrors of 'Paper & Sticks' on page 116. It's *awful*. I suppose it's *quite* impossible to cut it out? I shd so like it, somehow, to be omitted.[1]

D.T.

MS: J. M. Dent   *SL*

GILBERT PHELPS
3 October 1952 (Discusses BBC programme arrangements. See Appendix 63.)

E. F. BOZMAN
6 Oct 1952   Boat House Laugharne Carmarthenshire

Dear Bozman,
  Hope this is satisfactory, & that you can get it in in time. *Do* try, please. And apologies again for my terribleness.

Sincerely,
Dylan Thomas

MS: J. M. Dent

---

[1] 'Paper and Sticks' was first published in the magazine *Seven*, Autumn 1939. It was reprinted in *Deaths and Entrances*. The poem was deleted from the 1952 collection, and replaced by 'Do not go gentle into that good night', at proof-stage the last-but-two poem in the book.

GILBERT PHELPS
8 October 1952 [postcard]   Boat House Laugharne Carmarthenshire

Good. October 16th then. And yes let's have lunch. I'll meet you in the
Cock, Great Portland Street, at one? Okay? The Cock's to avoid wicked
friends in other pubs. Unless I hear from you, then.

Dylan

MS: BBC

OSCAR WILLIAMS
October 8 1952   Boat House Laugharne Carmarthenshire Wales

Dear Oscar,
   How are you and bless you you Little Treasure.[1] Our love from us,
looking over wet sand at nothing with some birds on it, to you eagled
there looking out at the Statue of—what's its name? I think it has
something to do with what Our Side gives to people after it has napalmed
them. If anyone in any uniform said to me, 'Now we're going to make you
free', I'd cut my throat with a blunt cunt. How are you, you label-less red
hot red potato you, I salute you from this bronchial heronry.
   Thank you, very, very very much, for the two letters and the two
cheques, they arrived in the old nick of time when every lane was
mantrapped for me and grocers were armed to their sandy fangs and I
couldn't even afford to go to the brewers' annual picnic which, everyone
assured me afterwards, was the best for years, chaos, blood, disaster,
singing, from beginning to end.
   Thank you, *very* much, for working so hard to get me some of that
money, damn and blast it with a great big kiss. And I'm terribly glad you
think you might be able to send along, from Miss Gardner[2] (whom God
wing!) the balance in full of a hundred and fifty dollars this month. I'm
very poor now. I've been working on a poem, and it takes so long, and I've
no time, then, to do any other jobs for our bread, marge, and gristle, so the
money'll be wonderfully welcome. I'm sorry not to have written long
before: I've had pneumonia etcetera and the etcetera was worse. But it's
not through not thinking of you, cock, and that's a cockney expression
and doesn't mean balls.
   I saw John Brinnin and Howard Moss off on their backbound train,
Howard being kissed goodbye by an adolescent boil with simper and
spindles attached. I see Gene Baroff in London, who is so Anglicized, who

[1] Among the anthologies Williams edited was *A Little Treasury of Modern Poetry*.
[2] Isabella Gardner, patron and poet, purchased many Thomas manuscripts. A receipt (at
Indiana) dated October 15 shows her paying Williams $250 for 143 worksheets of 'Poem
on his birthday', a holograph ms of the poem, and a letter.

corsets and straitjackets his vowels so cruelly, he faints. I'm giving a reading on the BBC 3rd Programme of Roethke this week, and of Robert Lowell next week. Half an hour each. I'm trying to arrange a Williams (not WC). Good news about Poetry. (I mean, of course, Poetry Chicago. What *could* good news about poetry be? Bishop Eliot defrocked?) Oh, yes, and I'm introducing & arranging a half hour of Spoon River, and also a Personal Anthology—the B.B.C. has been running a feature called this for about six months now—devoted to Masters, Lindsay, Robinson & Sandburg,[1] a fine old four for a programme and a boozeup. But going back to Karl[2] and Poetry Chicago: Thank you—this is thankyous today, and about bloody time—for suggesting and making possible that number you talked about. I'm sorry I can't send on my new poem, myself, for that number, but my agent here, David Higham, will be doing so, direct to Karl. You see, the poem is a 'Prologue' to my Collected Poems, due to be published any moment now, and, had, therefore, to go through Higham's hands. I told him that Poetry, Chicago, wanted a poem, so perhaps Higham has already sent it along.[3] (The Prologue, by the way, is a complete poem by itself, not just something written especially for a collected volume.) Any money coming from that Prologue will have to go through Higham, of course; but any other money from Karl—for the printing of the manuscript pages, for the possible prize you hinted at—can come, thank God, direct to me. And do I need it! And do I need it now! We are entirely without money, & want some more urgently, if that is possible, than ever before. Here, as you know, we are not as we are in the States, where we don't think or care about what we spend. Here, we have nothing to spend, and think and care about it all the time. So please, cock. (I've asked for a copy of Collected Poems to be sent to you.) I've another vast wodge of working-sheets for the Prologue Poem: want them, for sale? I'm enclosing a copy of that poem, too, for you yourself: on fine, thick paper it can take the place of a window pane, can be a very small tablecloth, or you can race cockroaches on it. How is Gene? Caitlin's & my love to her and to you, always.

Dylan

The copied-out poem is really in 2 verses. I forgot, & have drawn in a line. Unnecessarily, & with great trouble, I have, as you might notice, rhymed all the way back from line 51 to line 1.

MS: Indiana   *SL*

---

[1] Edgar Lee Masters and (probably) Vachel Lindsay, the 'jazz' poet; E. A. Robinson; Carl Sandburg.
[2] Karl Shapiro.
[3] 'Prologue' appeared in the *Atlantic*, January 1953. Nothing appeared in *Poetry* (Chicago).

DOUGLAS CLEVERDON
9 October 1952   Boat House Laugharne Carmarthenshire
                                                          Laugharne 68

My dear Douglas
   Oh, dear dear! I've been so looking forward to your coming down here,
and the very date you manage to get away I'll be in London. I'm going to
lecture in Oxford on Wednesday the 15th, & on Thursday the 16th I'm
recording a new poem of mine for John Lehmann's programme in London
with Gilbert Phelps. I want to return to Laugharne on the Thursday night
train, arriving there Friday (17th). Is it possible for us to do something
about this? (You must, of course, stay with us.) Could you ring me at
number above, or drop a card? Surely, we can fix something somehow. I
do hope so. (Going to start work on Llarregub today.)[1]

                                                              Ever,
                                                              Dylan

MS: the recipient

JOHN ALEXANDER ROLPH[2]
October 9th 1952   Boat House Laugharne Carmarthenshire

Dear Mr. Rolph,
   Thank you very much for your letter. Indeed, I remember your talking
to me about a bibliography of my writings—how could I forget? It seems
such a fantastic project—and I'm glad, & amazed, it's actually made
progress. Yes, of course, I'll help you all I can about dates & placings of
early poems etc, but I must warn you I won't remember much. I know I
did quite a lot for the New English Weekly—poems & stories—which I've
never gathered together or reprinted. But, anyway, I'll do all I can, & I'm
sure it can be done by correspondence.
   I'm very grateful to you for the trouble you are taking in such a peculiar
cause, & for your very nice letter.

                                                          Very sincerely,
                                                          Dylan Thomas

MS: Texas

---

[1] An engagements book that Thomas used in 1952 is at Texas. Cleverdon is shown as
visiting Laugharne on October 17 and 18. On October 19 Thomas wrote 'SOLID WEEK
ON LLAREGGUB TO FINISH IT'. Then he altered 'WEEK' to '16 DAYS'.
[2] J. A. Rolph, bookseller; author of *Dylan Thomas: A Bibliography.*

GUGGENHEIM FOUNDATION
October 17 1952 (Formal letter seeks award for Oscar Williams. See Appendix 64.)

GWYN JONES
October 28 1952   Boat House Laugharne Carmarthenshire

Dear Gwyn Jones,
   Thank you & your wife very much indeed for asking me to stay with you when I come up to read poems to the Arts Society on November 12th.[1] I'd love to. Looking forward to seeing you again after so many cruel, fattening, short, delicious, or abysmal, years.

Sincerely,
Dylan Thomas

MS: the recipient

E. F. BOZMAN
28 Oct 1952 (Sends copy of 'Prologue'. See Appendix 65.)

PRINCESS CAETANI
6 November 1952   The Boat House Laugharne Carmarthenshire
Wales

My dear Marguerite Caetani,
   It was beautiful to have your letter, and it made me a hundred times more ashamed, if that were possible, of my wretched, long, dark silence. Your letter was so warm, and good, as though I had never been barbarously bad to you at all, and as though, almost, I was forgiven for the breaking of promises, the filthy discourtesy incomprehensible to me also, even the whole dead year's dumb insult itself. It was beautiful to hear from you. I don't deserve one warm word but only bashing on the head and then forgetting cold as ice. I don't understand why I never wrote, why I never wrote if only to *explain*, to explain why I could not, at that time,

---

[1] Gwyn Jones was then Professor of English at University College, Aberystwyth.

in spite of my promises, finish the second half of my piece for you. Many times I began a letter, and then put it aside because the piece was not finished. And the drafts of letters piled up, and time lapped on and thickened, putting on skins of distance, and daily, and even more so nightly, I grew more ashamed of my silence and more angry with my procrastination until, at last, I couldn't write at all. I buried my head in the sands of America: flew over America like a damp, ranting bird; boomed and fiddled while home was burning; carried with me, all the time, my unfinished letters, my dying explanations and self-accusations, my lonely half of a loony maybe-play, in a heavy, hurtful bunch. These ostrich griefs were always with me, and whispered loudest in the late night when, indeed, I was all sand. 'Put it off, put it off', 'It's too late now', 'You can never be forgiven', 'The past is as dead as you'll be', 'Burn the daft drafts, unwind the half-play in your head so that nothing's left', 'Forget, you damned Welshcake, for doom'll nibble you down to the last loud crumb', 'Strangle your litter of wits in a sack, and splash!'—these agenbite-deadeners did their long-night worst, but the little voice in the dark, oh, throb, throb, throb it went across Kansas and in all the ovens of the hotel bedrooms. (These pages, I think, are wilting in the grey nearly permanent drizzle that sighs down on to this town and through the birdscratched matchboard roof into my wordsplashed hut. It isn't rain, it must be remorse. The whole fishy bay is soaked in guilt like the bad bits of poems-not-to-be oozing to the marrow on the matchsticked floor, and the half-letters curling and whining in the warped drawers. I'm writing this guilty noise in a cold pool, on a November afternoon, in mists of depression. Forgive me even for this, if you can. I find my pitiful wallow in the drizzle of regret an indulgence I can't pity. This weather gets me like poverty: it blurs and then blinds, creeps chalky and crippling into the bones, shrouds me in wet self, rains away the world.)

I can't explain why I didn't write to explain why I couldn't finish the piece. (No, I can't explain. When I try to explain my fear, the confused symbols grow leaden and a woolly rust creeps over the words. How can I say it? I can't. I can say: One instinct of fear is to try to make oneself as little, as unnoticeable, as possible, to cower, as one thinks, unseen and anonymous until the hunt is past. My fearful instinct is to bloat myself like a frog, to magnify my unimportance, to ring a bell for a name, so that, as I bluster and loom twice my size, the hunt, seeing me monstrous, bays by after different & humbler prey. But that is not what I mean: the symbols have wet-brain, the words have swallowed their tongues.)

All that I can't explain. But why I didn't finish the piece there and then, as I said I would, is another matter. I was, as you know, leaving home—though, am, miraculously, home again now in this tumbling house whose every broken pane and wind-whipped-off slate, childscrawled wall, rain-stain, mousehole, knobble and ricket, man-booby-and-rat-trap, I know in my sleep. I was leaving for ever, it seemed, had nowhere to go, nothing to go with, and, after you had wonderfully helped me to pay off some of my many debts here, I went to London, which, to me, is nowhere, and lived by odd reviews—and they were odd, too—odder broadcasts, pretending to women's clubs, putting off, putting off, all the nasty time, the one thing I wanted to do: finish my piece for you, and make my peace. But nothing could happen. Then I went to the States with my luggage of dismays and was loudly lost for months, peddling and bawling to adolescents the romantic agonies of the dead. I made money, and it went, and I returned with none; and once more, with the unfinished letters, poems, and play weighing much more heavily now on a mind nearly out of its mind with its little, mountainous anxieties and aches, reviewed, begged, lectured, broadcast, waited, with no hope, for the time when I could come back here and write truly again. I waited, and I put off, full of fear and wishes.

It is all a very inadequate explanation, and it cannot call itself an excuse, and indeed my fears are inexcusable though very real to me in their mean, mad way. And my talk, though terribly but weakly true, of 'putting off' all the time, is terribly putting off, I know.

These are the reasons, however—and expressed in depression and with little hope of them being believed or thought worthy—for my silence and my broken promises. About John Davenport and René [?Clair] I had heard nothing until your letter; and, even if I had heard, how could that, in any way in the world, affect you and me: your goodness to me, your faith in me, and my affection and gratitude kept, so it would appear, so obstinately secret?

I'm trying to work again now, and faithfully promise you the rest of the thing, and whatever other work I have, by, at the latest, the first of February. I won't fail you. Or have I joined forever the folds of the snarling and letting-down black once-friendly sheep? Oh, I do hope not.

It is so difficult for me to live and keep my family alive. There are many petty jobs which would make me just not enough money for tradesmen and rent, for clothes and school, for parents, shoes, and cigarettes, but these petty jobs, by their nature and by the time they claim, stop me writing as I would wish to write. But how, without these jobs, am I to live, to write, at all? These problems keep me treadmilling small nightmares all the waking nights.

About another visit to the States, I don't know. Though I can only play a poet there, and not make poetry, yet there I can, if only for a few months, live and send money home. I may have to go again. I cannot go on thinking all the time of butchers and bakers and grocers and cobblers and rates and rents until I bleed. After I have finished what I am now working on, I may have to give up writing altogether. (My need—as I imagine it—to write, may be all conceit. The bellows that fan the little flicker is nothing but wind, after all. And writing is certainly not one of the ancient secrets of the head-shrinking tribes. Ach, my endless bleating of private woes because I am not 'allowed' to write, as though the trees would grow inward, like toenails, if I renounced this passion for self-glorification. 'Peace, let me write. Gag the tradesmen, I must write. Alms, for the love of writing.' Perhaps I should be better off pulling teeth. But even this momentary disgust I blame upon the weather. And even this disgust is 'material for writing' just as trees, and toenails, and glorification, and teeth.) I think it's time to stop this. I wanted, at first, only to say that I am profoundly ashamed of my silence and of my broken promises, and that I will not fail you again, and that I do, with all the bloody muscle of my heart, ask for your forgiveness. But the letter got caught up with my despairs, though, always, I want, one day, to write you a happy letter. Because I am very often happy, and not always, here by the sea, without cause.

Please forgive me, and try to trust me again.

The old, cold pool of the day is a little warmer now.

Yours ever,
Dylan

MS: Camillo Caetani Foundation   *SL*

MIMI JOSEPHSON[1]
7 Nov 1952.   Boat House Laugharne Carmarthenshire
                                                    Laugharne 68

Dear Mimi Josephson,
    I was, honest to God, and in spite of my 'idiosyncracy' that I do not answer letters, about to write to you. You'll see, from the word in quotes, that Dent's have passed on your letter to me.
    And isn't it awful, but I'm afraid I *won't* be staying in London after Monday the 17th. I'm going up to London on the 14th, and will be about that night and on the night of the 15th. If you could be in town then, let's have a drink. Otherwise, what about coming down here—not really to be recommended—or to Swansea some time soon. Yes, Swansea best, as I love any excuse for going there. That sounds ungallant, but I don't mean it. The thing, anyway, would be to have a drink together, in Swansea or in London 14th or 15th (evenings). Do let me know which is best for you, and I'm sorry I didn't write before.

Sincerely,
Dylan Thomas

MS: the recipient

[1] Mimi Josephson was a freelance journalist in Cardiff, interested in poetry and poets.

MIMI JOSEPHSON
[telegram, November 15 1952, Laugharne]

FRIGHTFULLY SORRY IMPOSSIBLE LAST MOMENT MEET
SWANSEA TOMORROW WRITING. DYLAN THOMAS

Original: the recipient

MIMI JOSEPHSON
Fri 21 [November] 52   Boat House Laugharne

Quickly, and with much disappointment: I can't turn up this Saturday
in S'sea as I'm in bed with bronchitis I caught—if it is a thing you
catch—in London from which I've only just returned. Many apologies &
regrets. Thank you, a lot, for the poem and the terrifying things it says. As
soon as I'm audible again—I can't speak at all now, only croak,—& out &
about, I'll get in touch with you. And this will be quite soon, I hope.
Awfully sorry again.

Dylan Thomas

MS: the recipient

GWYN JONES
21 Nov 1952 [postcard]   Laugharne

Thank you both, a lot, I loved being there, you were awfully kind, I had a
fine audience at the reading, and the memories of Icelandic firewater
lasted well until Shrewsbury. I've just come back from a loud week in
London, with bronchitis and an overpowering sense of fear. I hope never
to move again from this wet lost spot—except, of course, to Aberystwyth
and Iceland. Hope to see you again soon,

Dylan

MS: the recipient

A. G. PRYS-JONES[1]
21 November 1952   Boat House Laugharne Carmarthenshire

Dear A. G. Prys-Jones,
    First of all, do please forgive me for not answering your dizzyingly kind letter long before this, and for not acknowledging the typescript of the review—a review I am quite dumb before. I've been away in London, no letters were forwarded from Laugharne, and in that ghastly city I caught so much cold I'm still croaking and snuffling about the house like an old, slippered crow.
    It was extremely good of you to send on the full copy of the review,—but in face of its staggering praise of my poems, what can I say? Cold 'thank you', even, could sound damnably immodest, as though perhaps I were thanking you for something which I expected, something I thought my due. Which is light years from the case. I was amazed at the praise; honoured by the constructive work and care which had gone into the appreciation of these often absurdly difficult poems; and, of course, delighted by the fact that you understood, so deeply, the underlying purpose and direction of the stuff itself—even though some of the poems, and many of the passages and lines, I had, I know, made impenetrable to others by my own tortuous ignorance of the particular dark in which I was trying to move.
    Yes, amazed, honoured, & delighted, that's all I can say. And thank you, too. (But I could have written so much more freely if you had damned the book to little wild bits.)
    I'm hoping to have a Collected Stories, including some new ones and many that have appeared only in small, forgotten magazines, at the end of next year. My next book will be pretty awful: a film-scenario I wrote some years ago, which no-one would film, and which Dents seem to think is worth printing, as a story in itself. I just don't know: it's a long time ago & all over to me. It will be called 'The Doctor & The Devils'. And I'm also hoping to bring out an extravagant play, as yet unfinished & maybe the radio will do it first, about a day's life in a small town in a never-never Wales. It sounds very ordinary, but it isn't that anyway, it's odd as anything, & I'm enjoying writing it. No title yet, only an unprintable one.
    Once again, but never finally, all my thanks and regards.

Very sincerely yours,
Dylan Thomas

MS: Texas   *SL*

---

[1] Arthur Glyn Prys-Jones (b. 1888), educationist and writer, reviewed Thomas's *Collected Poems*, published November 10, in the Cardiff *Western Mail*.

STEPHEN SPENDER
22 November 1952   Boat House Laugharne Carmarthenshire

Dear Stephen,

Were you at Edith's on Monday? I couldn't turn up, I was sick and wretched though I wanted very much to see you and Natasha again and to say goodbye to Edith, and now that I'm more or less home again I'm wretcheder than ever. I seem to be finally caught and tangled. I knew, when I was in London helping to raise Cain,[1] that I had left scores of unsettled debts behind me and that there were several summonses on the way. Then, on Monday morning, more dreadful letters were forwarded. I got back here to more bills, and to hear that the bailiffs will be moving in unless I pay what I can never pay because I have no money at all, even for bread or cigarettes but have to borrow the shillings for these. The bailiffs will be moving in because I can't pay enough, on account, of the income-tax I owe on money I earned, and spent, in America in 1950. And I have nothing to go on with day to day.

There's no need to write out a hideously long list of all I owe and all I must pay at once at once because I'm not asking you for anything but— *Do* you know anyone who could help me *now*? I don't know anybody. I can't write properly. I can't write anything anyway, I can't work or sleep because of this. From all I earn, anyway, the Income Tax, for that damned American trip, take 75 per cent & will now take everything. Of course I've no savings, and this house isn't mine to sell. Only immediate help can save me from I don't know and I can't say because I have never been so full of despair nor Caitlin neither. Do you know anyone you can ask? I can provide that anyone with a real long row of my debts so that he can see that it isn't for me to spend. I can't go on like this. I'm used to living up and down and mostly down, but this is over the edge and the end. I've been helped before, in the past, & that was wonderful. But I've never needed it as I need it now. I'm sorry that my first letter for so long to you should be like this, but I don't know who to turn to and perhaps you do know someone. *Surely* there is someone—though I'm sure I don't know why. It's nice, I suppose, to be overpraised, as I've been recently, but it makes this despair much worse, if that were possible and I suppose it always is, to know that those over-words were about somebody quite else, somebody I don't know at all, and not about who I am and what I am and the hating, unwanting where-I-am, and all the misery because I haven't a couple of hundred pounds or so and never bloody will. (Here they are, and I did want to keep them out, near-hysteria and rage and selfpity.) Please help if you can. And *surely*, *surely* there's someone somewhere, I'll keep on saying to myself till I hear from you.

                                        Love to you and Natasha,
                                              Dylan

---

[1] A reading of Edith Sitwell's 'The Shadow of Cain'.   [Cont.

I'm sending this to John Raymond at the New Statesman to send on to you.

MS: Harvard   *SL*

A. J. HOPPÉ
22 Nov 1952   Boat House Laugharne Carmarthenshire

Dear Mr. Hoppé,
   Many apologies for not returning, & commenting on, the rough design & blurb for 'The Doctor & The Devils' long before this. I've been away in London, unfortunately no letters were forwarded to me there, & since my return I've been in bed with bronchitis.
   I think the rough design is adequate, if not exciting. But the sub-title doesn't seem [what] we want at all. I've been trying to think of others — such as, A Film Without Pictures—but none was successful. But I don't think, anyway, the suggested subtitle should stand. What is a film scenario anyway but a story written for films, as the script of a play is a story for the stage. One might as well say, 'A Story In A Stage Play'. I may be wrong indeed, & scenario may mean something else. But the subtitle on this jacket does seem to me, at least, awkward & repetitive.
   Wouldn't it be possible to have the jacket without any subtitle *at all*? and let the blurb say in what form 'The Doctor & The Devils' is written?
   I know you want to sell this to general readers of fiction, & perhaps readers of thrillers, & that some suggestion, on the jacket, that [it] *is* fiction would be a help. But I think myself that if you're going to try to combine 'story' & 'scenario' on the jacket you're going to find it very difficult; & reviewers will have a fairly easy time picking whatever subtitle you choose to bits.
   Yes, really, for me, no subtitle on the jacket. The blurb straightaway *does* say, 'D & D' is written in such & such a form, & is 'a gripping' story about murder. So much for readers of general fiction & thrillers.
   I notice that in neither the blurb nor the brief note for the half-title is there any mention of Donald Taylor. I know that he & Dents have come to some arrangement as to the use of his name, but shouldn't it be referred to, even in passing, in the blurb? In the 3rd paragraph of the blurb, for instance, if you put after 'two things stand out … in this scenario', just the words, 'which is based on a story-line of Donald Taylor'— wouldn't that meet the case? I don't, of course, know what sentence Dent's & Taylor had arranged to cover his share in the thing: mine was merely a suggestion.
   What a pity, by the way, the *second* name for Robert Knox, the name thought of after the ms was in Dents hands, hadn't been used throughout. Thomas Rock is so much rockier, & nearer the original, than the wet,

lame William Salter. It *would* make an awful difference, I think, to the whole story if its principal figure had a dynamic kind of name you could believe in & credit him with.[1]

But this letter's already too long.

Sorry again for the long delay.

Yours sincerely,
Dylan Thomas

MS: J. M. Dent

ELLEN KAY[2]
[November 1952]

Dear Ellen,

Will this ever reach you? There's one of your names missing, too, and the typed poems I have of yours, with all your names, are somewhere else.

It was lovely to see you, if only for a moment, after I'd helped to raise Cain that Sunday. I had to go off with a lot of awful people because I'd promised.

I shall be in London, on this Friday evening, the 28th. Would you like to meet me? I wish you would. I shall be in a pub. Now which pub? Do you know the Salisbury, next door to the New Theatre in St. Martin's Lane? I'll wait there from six till seven.

Or, if you get this and can't come, will you ring Primrose 0529 some time on Friday. I won't be there but you can leave a message. And I'll ring up there as soon as I arrive in London from Cambridge, where I'm just going.

This sounds so complicated; and it would be so simple if you *could* come to the Salisbury, this Friday evening, between six and seven.

Yours,
Dylan

MS: Pierpont Morgan Library

---

[1] Dent deferred to all Thomas's suggestions.
[2] Ellen de Young Kay (b. 1930) was an aspiring poet, who met Thomas when he read at Mills College in Oakland, California, April 1950. She saw him a number of times over the next year or two, in America and London, and thinks she may be 'the only woman who went out with him in two continents but never went to bed with him'. She is now an Episcopalian nun of the Order of St Helena.

JOHN BELL[1]
2nd December 1952   Boat House Laugharne Carmarthenshire

Dear Mr. Bell,
    Thank you very much for your letter. I'm very interested indeed in your suggestion that I should write, for children, a book of the old stories of Wales; and though I've never written for children, or thought about it, I really would like to try: especially on such themes.
    My trouble is one of time. I've a prose-book to finish for a publisher—I've only very recently begun it—before I can touch anything else. The book's overdue, badly, already, and I must get down to that and nothing else. This will take me some months; I'm afraid I can't say exactly how many. After that, I'd be delighted to start on the Welsh legends: to start, anyway, reading the old collections of them, gathering & selecting. But all this may be far too vague for you.
    My agent, by the way, is David Higham, of Pearn, Pollinger, & Higham, 39–40 Bedford Street, Strand, W.C.2. And details—if you felt, after this unsatisfactory letter, that you could wait until I'd finished this commissioned book I'm working on now—would have to be gone into with him. But I *would* appreciate it if you would let me know, too, what you think. Could you? Thanks again.

                              Yours sincerely,
                              Dylan Thomas

MS: Oxford University Press

JAMES JONES[2]
2 December 1952   Boathouse Laugharne Carmarthenshire

My dear Jim,
    It was fine to hear from you after the centuries that have passed since Warmley, the impromptu chambermusic, complete with Woolworth whistles & saucepan lids, the great unknown composer Dr. Percy, your wonderful hot jazz, and the banging on the wall of the Careys (wasn't it?) next door. I don't often see Dan, though we're less than fifty miles apart: when I do get to Swansea, we drink champagne, go to horror films, and (sometimes) have a little nap on Constitution Hill on the way back to Rosehill Terrace. I wish we all could have met when you were down in Swansea last summer. Fred Janes I see even less often than Dan; and Tom Warner has disappeared, to me, altogether. I often see, in the Evening

---

[1] Of the Oxford University Press. The proposal was for a book of 'Welsh Fairy Tales', but it was never begun.
[2] Dan Jones's brother, a journalist.

Post, pictures of the Rev. [. . .], Vicar of St. Somewhere, who—remember?
—had a cleft palate and was an authority on tramcars.

I'll be listening to Dan's Symphony on the 17th.

Thanks a lot for writing. Your telephone exchange is, I notice, rather
reminiscent of Warmley.

Hope to be seeing you,

Ever,
Dylan

MS: Texas

MR EVANS[1]
3 December 1952   Boat House Laugharne Carmarthenshire

Dear Mr. Evans,

I can't tell you how very deeply disappointed I am not to be able to
make my visit, as President, on Friday; and I do wish it had been possible
for me to let you know this miserable news far sooner, so that any
preparations could have been postponed. As it is, I'm afraid I've left it to
the last moment. I could not be more sorry. My father, who lives in the
same village, has been blind and very ill for a long time; but, in the last
few days, his condition has grown desperate, and I cannot possibly leave
him, as my mother is a permanent invalid and cannot take care of him at
all. I *had* hoped that perhaps a slight improvement in his extremely
serious illness would allow me to make my visit to Bangor, and, with that
in mind, put off writing to you until this last moment. But he is weaker
than ever today, and delirious, and his doctor has just told me that I
should be on hand day & night. I know you will understand; and I do hope
you know, too, how much I was looking forward to the whole evening.

Is it possible for the Dinner & Address to be postponed, and not
cancelled? I could come up any time you suggest in the New Year.

My deep apologies again,

Yours sincerely,
Dylan Thomas

MS: National Library of Wales

---

[1] Thomas's host-to-be at an unidentified function in North Wales.

CAITLIN THOMAS

For Caitlin Thomas on Her Birthday[1]
8th December 1952, from her Husband.

Caitlin I love you
And I always will.
I love you in Brown's Hotel,
The Cross House, Sir John's Hill,
London, New York, bed.
In any place, at any time,
Now, then, live, dead—

This is all that I
Have to say
On your birthday,
My Caitlin:
As sure as death is sure,
So is my love for you everlasting

MS: Maurice Neville

ELLEN KAY
9 December 1952   Boat House Laugharne Carmarthenshire

My dear Ellen,
I hoped that that was what had happened. I don't mean I hoped my letter would be too late for you to come to meet me, but I mean that I hoped it was the lateness of the letter and not anything else, such as your just not wanting to come and meet me. I mean—but you know what I mean. I was very sorry to miss you, and moped, and snarled at every one I saw, and cursed America—and especially San Francisco—and drank limitless pints of liverish liquorice unlibidinous Guinness, and was melancholy, tragic, and a bit sick—like an old, round adolescent. But, even if my note had reached you, it would have given you very little time. As soon as I know I'm going to London next, I'll give you plenty of warning, and if you don't come I'll cut my throat on a rusty poem. I don't know if I can get to London before Christmas. I want to, very much, but am too poor now. By poor, I mean, simply, I have no money at all. If I had, I would come to London. What is maddening is, that usually I am in London, where I do not want to be, every couple of weeks; and now that I want to be there, I can't. (It makes me cross, too, to think that you have been in England so long, and that I never knew it. You said you wrote. Did you write to the Savage Club? I haven't been there this year. I am a fool. I

---

[1] Caitlin Thomas was thirty-nine.

should die.) Thank you for your sonnet. I really did like it a lot, and it was lovely to have it, and to know that it is mine. 'Esq.' looks wonderful, like a little silk hat. I liked the way the poem moves; and most of all, perhaps, the movement of the first six lines. I hope I can somehow see you very soon. If not, then in January.

Yours
Dylan

MS: Pierpont Morgan Library

STEPHEN SPENDER

9 December 1952   Boat House Laugharne Carmarthenshire

My dear Stephen,
  This isn't about the same miserable subject as my earlier letter —though the situation is, if that were possible, worse than it was then, and it certainly looks as though it's going to be worms and water for Christmas—but only to thank you, very much indeed, for your notice, of my Collected Poems, in the Spectator.[1] You were, as you know, the very first person ever to write to me about a poem of mine; and this is now the clearest, most considered and sympathetic, and, in my opinion, truest, review that I have ever seen of my writing. I mean, that your statement of understanding of my aim and method seems to me to be altogether true; and no critic has attempted, in writing about my most uneven and unsatisfactory work, to set out, plainly, the difference between the writing of poetry towards words and the writing of poetry from words — though that's, of course, oversimplification. No writer before you; and I do want, please, to thank you again very much.
  I do hope, by the way, that my first, almost despairing letter, wasn't a dreadful nuisance to you, and didn't seem an impertinence. I had, & have, no-one to turn to, and felt sure you would understand my present, beastly difficulties.
  Please thank Natasha for her telegram. I will write her separately, if or if not this wretchedness is somehow lifted or even eased.
  Oh, & I forgot. I'm not influenced by Welsh bardic poetry. I can't read Welsh.[2]

Yours,
Dylan

MS: Harvard   *SL*

---

[1] Spender called him 'a romantic revolting against a thin contemporary classical tendency . . . In [his] poetry the reader feels very close to what Keats yearned for—a "life of sensations" without opinions and thoughts'.
[2] Spender: 'His poetry is not so much influenced by, as soaked in, childhood experiences of the Bible, and doubtless, also, Welsh bardic poetry.'

JOHN ALEXANDER ROLPH
11 December 1952   Boat House Laugharne Carmarthenshire

Dear Alexander Rolph,

So very sorry not to have written long before. Thank you, a lot, for your letters, and your awfully kind offer to try to get hold of any difficult-to-get items for me should I need them: I won't forget that. You said you were moving to Weybridge in the new year. When? I don't think I'll be in London until about the 12th or 13th of January: about that date I'm helping to raise Cain again, or his Shadow rather, this time without Edith S. and at the Albert Hall. If you haven't moved by that time, do let's fix up to meet for some drinks one evening round then.

I'm afraid I'm going to be nearly no good at all to you in answer to these questions about when & where etc. My memory's bad, I keep no files or old numbers of periodicals.[1]

New English Weekly. Yes, perhaps I did contribute to it *after* 1935, though I'm not sure. I seem to remember 2 poems and another prose piece than 'After the Fair'. And a regular novel review in, about, 36, 37, or 38.

Of the periodicals you mention, all, I think, are finished. And 'Caravel' was the only one I believe to be not British. If you like, I could put you in touch with Ruthven Todd, in New York, whose knowledge of these fly-by-night magazines *used* to be enormous.

Do you know my American selection of poems & stories called 'The World I Breathe', brought out by New Directions in 1939. There are 4 stories in that that don't appear in 'Map of Love'. Of these, one, 'A Prospect of The Sea', was, I think, printed in a Penguin of Modern Welsh Stories. Again, I don't know if it was reprinted from a periodical: I rather think I sent, on request, the manuscript to the editor. 'The Burning Baby', also in 'The World I Breathe', was published in Roger Roughton's 'Contemporary Prose & Verse', just before the war.

A London magazine called 'Janus' published a story of mine called 'The Horse's Ha', which hasn't been in book form yet. And another little magazine, called 'Yellow Jacket', edited by Constantine FitzGibbon (who's brought out a couple of novels fairly recently) printed 2 stories, called, as far as I remember, 'The Vest' and 'The True Story'.

Robert Herring's 'Life & Letters ToDay' printed, I think, 2 or 3 stories, including one called 'The Lemon', which also has not yet been in a book.

The Booster was edited by Henry Miller in Paris before the war: I'm afraid I don't know when. (Miller's address is, I think, quite simply Big Sur, California.) There were certainly very few numbers of it brought out under Miller. It was, I think, originally a little 'organ' run by, or for, American business-men visiting Paris, full of rotarian-like gossip. Miller, as an American exile living in Paris, somehow got temporary hold of this bit of hail-fellowry, & immediately printed Alfred Perlès, Lawrence

---

[1] There are some mistakes in Thomas's account.

Durrell, very odd drawings, himself, & one contribution by me—all to the surprise of the subscribers.

The Map of Love. My memory's almost gone here. *Some* of the stories, I believe, *were* printed in periodicals. One of them, at least, I am sure appeared in 'New Stories', a brown magazine, & was later reprinted in one of E.J. O'Brien's Best Stories of The Year, or whatever he called it. 'The Orchards' was, I think, published in Elizabeth Bowen's 'Modern Short Stories', which was an early Penguin, though whether she reprinted it from the 'Map of Love' or from a magazine I can't remember.

And I feel pretty certain 'The Tree' was published somewhere. Maybe in the N.E. Weekly.

Any other things I can remember about poems & stories—especially about stories in The Map of Love—I'll send you.

Oh, I do remember. 'The Mouse & The Woman', in 'The Map of Love', was, I'm fairly sure, published in 'transition' just before the war.

Enough to go on with?

Let me know about the date of your going to Weybridge, & whether we can meet in London round about Jan. 13.

Yours,
Dylan Thomas

PS. Some prose was printed by Keidrych Rhys in his 'Wales', now also defunct. 'Prologue To An Adventure', printed in 'The World I Breathe' appeared in one of the New Directions yearly anthologies—& also somewhere, forgotten, else. 'The Holy Six' & 'The School For Witches', in the same 'W. I Breathe', haven't been published in periodicals.

MS: Texas   *SL*

MARY DAVIES[1]
16 December 1952

Dear Miss Davies,
    You will, I know, be very sorry to hear that my father died today. It was a very peaceful death.[2]
    You will excuse my mother not writing personally to you, at this moment. She is bearing up, however, wonderfully well, and sends her fondest love to you.

Yours
Dylan

MS: John Wilson

---

[1] A family friend in Carmarthen.
[2] D. J. Thomas was seventy-six.

VERNON WATKINS
29 December 1952   Boat House Laugharne Carmarthenshire

Dear Vernon,
    Thank you so much. I miss him a great deal.
    This is only a little—after, years?—to say Happy New Year to you &
Gwen & the children.
    I hope I'll see you soon. I am going to read 3 ballads of yours from
Swansea on the 14th of January. Can we meet for lunch that day?
    It will be wonderful to see you again.

                                            Ever,
                                              Dylan

MS: British Library   *VW*

E. F. BOZMAN
29 December 1952   Boat House Laugharne Carmarthenshire

Dear E. F. Bozman,
    You wrote me, on the 11th, about John Alexander Rolph, modern rare
bookseller, who's planning a bibliography of my writings and wants to
know if you would publish it. And you wrote back to him, you said, &
told him you'd prefer to wait a few years. I shd think so, too. Let's have
something to bibliographize first. But as to his wanting to 'establish a
priority on his own behalf' to be my bibliographer, I shd certainly say,
Yes. I've been in correspondence with him for quite a time, have met him
once or twice, and he seems excellent, to me, & very keen. He knows
more than almost anyone wd want to know about the scores of fly-by-
night little reviews of the thirties, in which such a lot of my stories etc.
appeared; & I think that when and if ever the time comes when a
bibliography of my at-present all too meagre writings could be considered
saleable, then Rolph is the very man.
    Thank you again for your Christmas greetings, for the Fables, and for
your kindness in allowing me to anticipate such a *very* welcome chunk of
my next spring's royalties.
    By the way: Have you thought again of having that insipid 'William
Salter' changed to rugged 'Thomas Rock' in the 'Doctor & The Devils'? I
know the expense wd be considerable; but the script wd, in my opinion,
gain *enormously* in strength & distinction just from that alteration. I do
think it important.·

                                    Yours sincerely,
                                      Dylan Thomas

PS. Donald Taylor sent a copy of 'Doctor & Devils' to James Bridie once, for his opinion, & because Bridie had dealt with *exactly* the same theme in that wellknown play of his whose name I've now forgotten. Bridie liked it, but the first thing he said, as far as I remember, was: *Do* change Knox's name to something good and strong. I shd, of course, have done it before the manuscript was submitted to you. But I'm mentioning this now only because of my great respect for Bridie's opinion on anything, big or small, of dramatic value.

D.T.

PSS The name of Bridie's play was, of course, 'The Anatomist'. I had not read it when I helped to write Doctor & Devils, but, reading it later, I found a *great* deal of resemblance in the treatment.

D.T.

MS: J. M. Dent

MR MORGAN[1]
30 December 1952   The Boat House Laugharne Carmarthenshire

Dear Mr. Morgan,
   My mother has asked me to write to you, to thank you, very deeply, for your kind and consoling letter on my dear father's death. I and my family wish to join her in thanking you. Your tribute to my father's teaching I very much appreciate and shall always remember. I was taught Shakespeare and Milton by him in the old Grammar School, and owe my first love of poetry to him. He had been suffering for a long time, and towards the end of his life was nearly blind.
   Uncle Arthur died in 1947, and my father's ashes were buried with his.
   It was good to hear from one who had known not only my father but my grandfather as well, whom I never knew.
   Thank you again for your letter, and your prayer that we may be blessed & sustained in our sorrow.

Yours very sincerely,
Dylan Thomas

MS: National Library of Wales

OSCAR WILLIAMS
Jan 5 1953   Boat House Laugharne Carmarthenshire

Dear Oscar,
   Love to you & Gene from Cat & me, always.
   This is only a little note, because Christmas here has been so confused

[1] A family friend.

that I'm still ½ daft with it. My father, in great pain, & blind, died a few days before Christmas, & I had a lot of sad business to attend to: I'm the only one left, if you exclude, as well you may, a sister in Bombay.[1] The children have been ill. Caitlin's pregnant again. The water pipes have burst & the house is flooded, etc. etc. And the etceteras are almost worse than the rest. So this, before a real letter, is only to say: Thank you, thank you, for the cheque for 150 dollars, previously unacknowledged, and for the last, December 8, cheque for 100 dollars. Oh, Mrs. Stephenson, would you were the first lady of the land, you old bag![2] *And, please*, I *would* like, *straightaway*, the balance due to me, on that piece of Chicagoanery, of 200 dollars. Without those cheques you've been whistling across the water, we couldn't have lived through these foul months.

New York I am supposed to come to end of April; alone, maybe, at first, to be joined by Cat in the early summer.

I return, signed, the Golden Treasury slip. You do me over-proud.

The 'Prologue' sheets I shall send this week, along with a short story.

Also, I received the Skin-Trade 198 dollars, praise be.[3]

(And am *longing* for the last Stephenson 200 dollars.)

No news now; just thank yous, please send, & all love.

Doctor & Devil is a bad book: an old commissioned filmscript. Let's all forget it.

What Guggenheim news?[4]

Again,
Yours,
Dylan

MS: Harvard   SL

ALFRED JANES
5 Jan [1953]   Boat House   Laugharne   Carmarthenshire

Dear Fred,
Thank you, very very much indeed, for writing on my father's death. Poor old boy, he was in awful pain at the end and nearly blind. The day before he died, he wanted to get out of bed & go into the kitchen where his mother was making onion soup for him. Then, a few hours afterwards, he suddenly remembered everything, & where he was, & he said, 'It's full circle now'.

---

[1] Nancy, aged forty-six, was seriously ill.
[2] Ellen Borden Stevenson, misspelt by Thomas.
[3] The previous year, New American Library had bought rights in *Adventures in the Skin Trade* for $397.50. This was precisely calculated, 15,900 words at 2½ cents a word. The $198 seems to have been the second-half payment.
[4] Oscar Williams had applied for a Guggenheim award.

My mother is very good & brave about it; and she wants to thank you very much, as well, & to wish you a good New Year.

I do hope to see you soon.

Ever,
Dylan

MS: Eric Barton   SL

REV J. OLIVER STEPHENS
5th January 1953   Boat House Laugharne Carmarthenshire

Dear Professor Stephens,

My mother wants to thank you and your sister very very much indeed for your sympathy on my father's death and for your warm, consoling letter; and may I and my family join her too in thanking you with all our hearts. My father was in great pain and distress at the end, and nearly blind; but though we wished him peace and rest, his death was a terrible loss to us all.

My mother knows you will forgive her for not, at this time, writing to you herself.

I do hope we shall meet again one day. I remember, with very much pleasure, our last all-too-brief meeting.

Thank you again, both of you, from all of us.

Yours sincerely,
Dylan

TS: Thomas Trustees

E. F. BOZMAN
6 January 1953   Boat House Laugharne Carmarthenshire

Dear E. F. Bozman,

Thank you for your last letter of the 2nd of January, in which you mentioned the possibility of an autobiography, especially in relation to my early years. Well, of course, I have produced a more-or-less auto-biography in my 'Portrait of The Artist As A Young Dog'. And I really haven't enough desire, or material, to try to write another. And the childhood broadcast you mentioned—I'm afraid I don't know which one it was—is one of only six similar broadcasts: not nearly enough for even the smallest book. These six were, incidentally: Two on *Memories of Christmas*,[1] one on *Memories of August Bank Holiday*, one called just

---

[1] Only one radio essay was about Christmas; the companion piece, 'Conversation about Christmas', was written for *Picture Post*

Memories of Childhood & the other *Early One Morning*, and the other, in dramatic radio form, called *Return to Swansea*.

I have also a recent short story, about the adolescent period, called *The Followers*.[1]

In an American book of mine, published by New Directions, called 'The World I Breathe'—a book of verse and prose—there are five stories which haven't appeared in an English book: 2 of them haven't appeared in any periodical. These five are:

> The Holy Six,
> A Prospect Of The Sea,
> The Burning Baby,
> Prologue To An Adventure
> The School for Witches

and are all very young & violent and romantic.

There are also, in periodicals, 4 stories of a similar kind:

> The Lemon,
> The Horse's Ha,
> The Vest,
> The True Story.

I think that the broadcast reminiscences, all fairly riotously innocent, *together* with the death-&-blood other group typified by the Burning Baby, would make an interesting volume: especially if somehow, through a longish introduction, through an introductory story, or through some as-yet-unthought-of prose-links, I could explain their origins & bring them closer together.[2]

If you would be interested in this, I could have the five stories from 'The World I Breathe' typed out, write to a friend on the B.B.C. to gather together the reminiscent broadcasts, of which, unfortunately, I have no copy, and ask John Alexander Rolph, my bibliographist-to-be, to find the four stories in the old, fled periodicals. Perhaps we could discuss this on the 20th or 21st.

Yours sincerely,
Dylan Thomas

This wd, I realize, be a hotchpotch of a book, but the separate items cd be introduced, in some way, so as to make them cohere into a kind of oblique autobiography: *a growing-up told (a) in stories written while growing up, and (b) in memories of childhood written when grown up.*

MS: J. M. Dent   *SL*

---

[1] Published in *World Review* October 1952. It is a not very successful attempt to repeat the *Portrait* formula.

[2] Bozman, like Church before him, still found some of the early stories unpalatable. See note, page 882.

GWYN JONES
6 January 1953   Boat House Laugharne Carmarthenshire

My dear Gwyn,

Thank you for the letter and Adelphis,[1] and I'm very sorry not to have written much sooner. My father died last month, and the children were whining sick, and there was black wet Christmas, and I've been terribly busy failing to write one word of a more or less play set in a Wales that I'm sad to say never was, and as for money I've been up and down up and down for weeks like a prick in a box.

I liked the three stories very much indeed: real stories in wonderful words. And I hope to be able to say so, in a review, when Shepherd's Hey[2] comes out—along with a few carps about characterisation. Thank you a lot for sending them. Caitlin loved them too.

I haven't anything yet to send Ifor Evans, but will *as soon* as I have. It's good of you of both of you to want me to (as Fowler puts it).

I'm reading some poems of Vernon-Watkins from S'sea on the 14th, if you ever listen in. And of course if you don't, I'll still be reading them. What do you think of his poetry? I forgot, sipping that Faxafloi water,[3] to ask you.

All good wishes to both,
Yours,
Dylan

MS: the recipient

A. G. PRYS-JONES
6 February 1953   Boat House Laugharne Carmarthenshire

Dear Prys,

Of course you can persuade me to come to the Cardiff Literary Society —but, oh, what a long time away! If living, then I'll boom, with pleasure, on December 10th, and thank you for asking me. Fee fine.

Yes, the Foyle prize was certainly better than a slap in the belly with a wet poet.[4]

Looking forward to meeting you again; though before the end of the year, I hope. If in Cardiff at any time, may I give you a ring?

And thank you a lot, for sending me the two books. I like your own verse, and the Bible isn't bad either.

[1] The magazine *Adelphi* was edited by a Welshman, Sir Ifor Evans (referred to later in the letter), who was seeking contributions.
[2] A collection of stories by Gwyn Jones.
[3] Faxafloi, Faxi's inlet, in Iceland. Gwyn Jones was serving schnapps.
[4] The Foyle's Poetry Prize, worth £250, was awarded to Thomas for *Collected Poems*.

Very sorry I couldn't write to you much sooner than this: I've been in London, and letters weren't forwarded. Perhaps you have left Porthcawl by this time, but I'll take a chance.

Yours,
Dylan

MS: Texas

JOHN ARLOTT
6 Feb 1953   Boat House Laugharne Carmarthenshire

John,
Very many apologies. I've been away, missed your letter until today, and now am ill with flu, bronchitis, etc. croaking and snuffling. Thank you very much for the letter, for thinking about me, for suggesting that piece, & for pushing up the price. I'm awfully sorry I can't do it: not because I don't want to, but because I *daren't* promise that I could turn it out by mid-February: I'm in a tangle of doubts & debts, as well as shoved to the eyebrows with frogs' catarrh, and am disastrously behind in two commissioned jobs. But thanks a *great* deal for the offer of the job, which I'd like to do, & the money, which, dear, I'd simply adore.

Did I ever thank you for that bit of practical help you sent along so kind & so quick? If not, I should have very much indeed; and if so, I do it again.

Dylan

MS: the recipient

DAVID HIGHAM
6 February 1953   Boat House Laugharne Carmarthenshire

Dear David,
From a sickbed of bronchitis and doubts, I croak my sincere apologies for not having answered letters. I feel awful. I've been away for some little time, trying to think straight, returned feeling more crooked than ever, tried to do 4 recordings from the S'sea BBC, failed entirely because of lack of voice, & coughed back to bed where I now am. I'll try to do the recordings (I suppose Jean Le Roy knows about them) again on Monday.

a) I'm writing, *really*, a *really* explanatory letter—& one which I hope will allow me grace—to Charles Fry this weekend; as soon as I get up.
b) Yes, please do go ahead with the O.U.P. agreement.[1] I want very much to do it.

[1] The 'Welsh Fairy Tales'.

c) My 'affairs in general' are in a hell of a mess, and thank you, very very very much, for being so willing to try to help me with them.[1] As soon as I possibly can—very soon; next week, I hope—I'll come up to London to see you. Could we meet outside the office, d'you think? For lunch somewhere? or a drink at the Savage?

Oh, splutter & bark, I'm full of toads & Friar's Balsam.

Apologies once more.
Dylan

MS: Texas

—A LETTER FROM CAITLIN THOMAS—

Burdened by debts and broken promises to publishers, but most of all desolated by what he feared was a decline of his creative powers, Thomas had entered the last and bleakest period of his life. Early in 1953 he was again looking to America as an escape from reality. His wife Caitlin, as incapable as he of breaking the spell, wrote to their American friends, Oscar Williams and his wife Gene Derwood, on 9 February, 1953. Williams was interested in poems and a diary she had written. It is the only letter in this book not by Thomas.

> I've been meaning to write to you both, believe it or not, ever since I came home [*from their U.S. visit a year earlier*]. But life in this spartan country is so rigid, rigorous, & righteous, that I find it very hard to imagine myself ever frolicking, though that is hardly the word, in your gardens of ease, and fruity succulence. Or meeting such mythological angels as you two, who actually work to make money for other people. That is surely unheard of, today or any other day. I must thank you, here & now, Oscar, and most profoundly, for saving our lives so many times. The trouble is our lives are permanently in need of being saved, and I doubt, very forcibly, that they are worth it. I can't tell you how many times your soothing cheques have arrived, at the most urgently opportune moment [...]
>
> I know you are haunted with this money bugbear too, which makes it all the better of you to bother with Dylan's vast complications and wangles. And since he has, as good as, given up writing, for the actor's ranting boom, and lisping mimicry, anything he sells is either a re-hashed bubble and squeak of adolescence, or a never to be fulfilled promise in the future. Which obviously, when the future comes, and it always does in the end, makes things very difficult. And the only way out is to run, which we are just about, on the verge, of doing again.
>
> And what is more, it looks ominously like, in your direction. So look out, and bolt the doors ... We are losing this humble house, which was supposed to be ours for ever, owing to the changing whims of our

---

[1] Higham had written on January 8: 'If there is a crisis in your affairs that you would like to talk over with me, I'd be more than ready to do so.'

[?failing] Patroness. What an unreliable breed they are, one minute up, the next down, and us as rustically dull, that is probably the trouble, and the same old mules, as ever. I would much rather have a patron, but they are much harder to find. And sugar daddies are not so acceptable, apparently.

Dylan has set his mind on returning to America to start the old racket in full swing again. But, bringing all the Welsh craft and acumen to bear, leaving *the wife* and family behind this time, until he should see fit to send for them. When, according to him, he has amassed the mythical dollars. I am a great fool, but not quite so great as to fall for that one. So it seems there may be some little dissension, to put it mildly. And talking of greatness, were we? Where is that great work I was going to send you?

Well I think it must have landed in my belly, that is the only place that got pregnant, and nothing, not a flicker of inspiration, came out of anywhere else. In fact I am feeling like death at this moment, after a horrible abortion, much too late, and as empty as the day I was born. It is partly this stinking, long, punishing winter, and all the domestic worries and abominations, that nip any poor wee buds of spontaneity at sight. Plenty of good excuses, see, but more likely I am quite simply barren. I am impatiently waiting for the Spring to start the blood circulating again, if it ever will [. . .]

I am terrified of being swallowed up again in your great, flattering, pampering Continent. We are not used to so many temptations and the result is disastrous. Good love. XXX. Caitlin.

MS: Harvard

GLYN JONES
15 February 1953   Boat House Laugharne Carmarthenshire

My dear Glyn,

Thanks very much for writing. So sorry not to have been able to answer at once: I've been away, in Swansea & in London. But I'm writing to Idris today. I've known him, off & on, and always, unfortunately, in little bits, for years & years; and I was terribly sorry to hear from Vernon, & from you, about his illness. I think he's a fine chap and a real poet, God bless him.[1]

I'm so glad you liked being in Vernon's company. So do I. I saw him in Swansea only a few days ago & he talked about you then: a real sign of affection: as you know, he usually talks about nothing but poetry and its synonym, Yeats. Keidrych is, I see from the correspondence column in the Western Mail, ranting in Llandilo now. I don't know what happened to him & our Dumb Friends. Do you think something similar happened to his little charges as did to Carlyle's dog? Carlyle used to talk to it for hours, week after week, year after year, and at last it could bear it no

---

[1] Idris Davis (1905–53), Welsh working-class poet, was dying of cancer.

longer & threw itself out of the window. Have you read anywhere recently of a mass animal suicide?

By the way, is the poetry society you mentioned in your letter anything to do with Prys-Jones? Because if it is, I've agreed to go & read poems in Cardiff—invitation from Prys—some time in October. So perhaps we *will* get our annual hour. But I hope it's sooner.

Ever
Dylan

MS: Carbondale

JOAN BOWLES[1]
15 Feb 1953   The Boat House Laugharne Carmarthenshire

Dear Miss Bowles,

Will you forgive me, please for not having answered your extremely kind and very welcome letter long before this? It's nearly a month since you sent it; but since then there have been all kinds of illnesses and little disasters happening here, and I really haven't been able to do anything much but grieve and sneeze. It was very good of you to write to me after I helped to raise Cain in the Albert Hall before such a tiring audience. And thank your friend for me, too, for encouraging you to write to me. I felt encouraged as well to think that you were so moved by the whole performance. Yes, the Radio Critics (whom I didn't hear, except at second hand, when they dug their little claws in me) are a mealy, genteel drawl and giggle of parasites. Glad you dislike them too.

Thanks again for all the nice things you said.

Yours sincerely,
Dylan Thomas

TS: Thomas Trustees

CHARLES ELLIOTT[2]
15 February 1953   The Boat House Laugharne Carmarthenshire

Dear Mr Elliott,

Thank you very much for your letters. And will you thank the committee of the College English Society for their kindness? It was good of them to forgive me for mislaying, somehow, the original letter, & very nice of them to say that an early meeting cd be arranged—even one in the afternoon. I think poetry aloud sounds better (& often louder, too) in the

---

[1] An admirer.
[2] Secretary of the English Society at University College, Cardiff, where he was on the staff of the English department.

evenings; and so could you tell the committee I'd be glad if they could arrange a meeting, at the *usual* time for meetings, in the evening, about the middle of March some time? About money: it's not that my time's precious, but that money is to me. Can you pay ten guineas, plus Laugharne return-fare? Thanks again for writing. Will just a return of poems do, by the way, with a few comments?

Sincerely,
Dylan Thomas

MS: Columbia University

CHARLES FRY[1]

16th February 1953   The Boat House Laugharne Carmarthenshire

Dear Charles,

First of all, a *tremendous* number of apologies, profound, very very nervous, terribly late, too late perhaps. These apologies, we both know, are childsplay to make and we're not children (though I feel, sometimes, even now, as useless as a fat child in a flood) and contracts and the writing of books aren't playing. And what perhaps kills trust between persons most, is silence: that dead, muffling, insistent, insolent silence of which I've been guilty for so very long. All I can say at the beginning of this inadequate, breathless, and honest-as-I-can-be letter is: my apologies come from my head and my heart. And the silence, which I hate, came from no intended insolent carelessness or any desire to dishonour a promise I was longing to keep, but from one tortuous cause alone, which I will try to explain: a cause that, aggravated by guilt and grief and illness, became daily more intolerable to me until now, at this most urgent moment, I can still hardly write at all.

Let me straightaway apologise, please, for never having had the courtesy to answer a letter, or the courage to write directly to you and to try to explain my one real problem which has, for a year now, nagged and savaged me and made me lose nearly every shivering ounce of faith in myself. The reasons I didn't answer, I couldn't answer, your kind and justifiably firm letter of December were, mostly, all circumstantial ones, though magnified and distorted, no doubt, by my small, deep hell of the last year. These 'circumstantial' reasons were: my father died that month, blind, of cancer, and everything that had to be done was done by me: this included the care of my mother, who is a permanent invalid, and her maintenance, for the pension she and my father existed on died with him. The children got sick, and I had no money. Early this year, my best friend in the world, a woman of my own age, died of drink and drugs.[2] And I've been ill too. So far, so very obviously bad, a mockRussian whine

---

[1] Of the publishers Allan Wingate.

[2] Marged Howard-Stepney, 'that Marged gin woman', died in London on January 22. The inquest was told that she suffocated after a dose of sleeping pills; the verdict was misadventure. It is said that she meant to take over the Boat House from Margaret Taylor and pay its expenses for the Thomas family.

or drab borrowed slice of Gissing. Perhaps these recent happenings *could* just about pardon my not writing letters. But they have, of course, nothing to do with your chief worry and mine: why the book I promised, and so very much want to write, is not yet written. These happenings can't pardon that, and my detailing of them is not intended to. The 'nagging, savaging, destroying' problem, the real reason why the book is as yet unwritten, *that* is what you want explained. And how can I write that reason down? *That* is the thing itself: for a whole year I have been able to write nothing, nothing, nothing at all but one tangled, sentimental poem as preface to a collection of poems written years ago.

Perhaps it doesn't seem and sound—that phrase, 'I have been able to write nothing'—the throttling bloody hell it's been to me for this whole waste of a twisted year. And this letter is sure to be silly and pretentious enough without my griping on about words being the light and reason of my life etcetera. I went to America, as you know, about this time last year, and kept a jungle of a diary[1] which I felt quite certain that I could, on my return to this wet idyllic tomb on the coast, shape and order into a book neither you nor I would be ashamed of; and I was excited, as I still am, at the thought of wheedling and hacking a proper work out of the chaos of places and people I'd scrawled in planes and trains and bedrooms-like-boilers. I went on all over the States, ranting poems to enthusiastic audiences that, the week before, had been equally enthusiastic about lectures on Railway Development or the Modern Turkish Essay; and gradually I began to feel nervous about the job in front of me, the job of writing, making things in words, by myself, again. The more I used words, the more frightened I became of using them in my own work once more. Endless booming of poems didn't sour or stale words for me, but made me more conscious of my obsessive interest in them and my horror that I would never again be innocent enough to touch and use them. I came home fearful and jangled. There was my hut on a cliff, full of pencil and paper, things to stare at, room to breathe and feel and think. But I couldn't write a word. I tried then to write a poem, dreading it beforehand, a few obscure lines every dumb day, and the printed result shook and battered me in any faith in myself and workman's pride left to me. I couldn't write a word after that. These are the most words I have written for a year.

And then, because I wouldn't write at all, I got broke—I'd brought little or no money back from the States—and kept the wolf just a hairy inch from my door and my sleep by croaking poems, and such, on the air: an appalling retrogression to an American habit that had gone bad on me. I didn't croak enough to keep me going, and lectured, then, to English women: less intimidating, maybe, but less profitable, too, than American. And all the time I couldn't, I really couldn't, do the one thing I had to do: write words, my own words, down on paper.

[1] If Thomas kept an American diary, it has never been seen.

Now I can understand what one ordinary, I suppose, reaction would be to this endless jumbled dull confession: Here's somebody who read aloud and lectured too much too often and too long in a too-hospitable place and who became sated with public words and with his own ex-hibitionism. On his return, he couldn't get down to work; he missed the willing audience, the easy, but killing, money; as time went on, he became frightened of his failure to meet his literary commitments and now, groaning as though all disinterested heaven were lurching on to his head, conjures up, to a squeal of Welsh bagpipes, some vague psycho-logical hoo ha to account for his timidity and sloth.

I know it goes deeper than that, I've lived with it a long time, or so it seems, and know it horridly well, and can't explain it. I haven't been able to write a word, of anything. Behind me, all the time, I heard, And you'll never be able to write a word again. I thought it would break me up into little self-pitying bits.

But an odd thing's happened, and only now. Or perhaps it isn't odd, and time alone has done it. Whatever the reason, since the disasters, big and midget, I mentioned some time ago, on page 93 of this letter, I've got unknotted. Now for God's sake I can't explain that; but there it is. And Higham is going to get lots of other difficulties straightened out, so that I can get down to those ogre words again without nightmares of doubt and debt, and my dear diabolic family shall be protected for a time. And I'll write that American book, or die.

I'm coming to London Monday next. Higham, I hope, has fixed up a time to meet you. (For me to meet you, I mean.)

I daren't read back over these pages, in case I scream with denial & embarrassment.

It *must* be time alone that's done its work.

Please try to forgive me for my mean, tortured silence; and for this letter.

> Yours ever,
> Dylan

MS: Texas   SL

E. F. BOZMAN
18 February 1953   Boat House Laugharne Carmarthenshire
                                                       Laugharne 68

Dear Bozman,

So very sorry to be so late with these proofs. I've been ill, & unable to do much; & when I got better I lightheartedly—or lightheadedly, rather —thought I could get through the Doctor & the Devils in half a day. It's proved gruelling, & I've just finished. It looks an awful mess, I'm afraid;

& do you think I shd have a quick look at a second proof? If you do, I guarantee to let you have it back the next day. Of course, changing Salter to Rock throughout has helped to botch the pages; & then the whole typographical form is difficult too.

I shd have most of the material for the next book in hand this month.

I'm coming up to London on Monday, & will give you a ring.

Yours,
Dylan Thomas

Yes, I *do* think I should have a look at a second proof, don't you? I certainly might have missed a few things in all that mess.

MS: J. M. Dent

GRAHAM ACKROYD
20 February 1953   Boat House Laugharne Carmarthenshire

Dear Graham Ackroyd,

Thank you very much for sending Philip Callow's 'In the Wonder', along to me: I was interested to read it, but don't by any means agree with what you say about it.[1] He's obviously a man of some deep feeling; but there is, to me, no sign, in these pieces, that he is a poet at all. He appears to believe that all he has to do is to scribble down, on separate lines, a few soulful sentimental stale-phrases in the lack-of-rhythm of weak back-broken prose, utter a few passionate bleats, throw in an ill-assorted handful of abstractions, sew on, most untidily, a few threadbare coloured ribbons from old bad half-remembered twilight verses, and wind up cosy and mysterious with God—and there, by God, is a poem. This is probably horribly, and cheaply, unfair to someone of sincerity and conviction; but he must know, sooner or later, that poems are made out of living words; and that his words are all dead. 'In The Wonder' is, in my nasty opinion, tepid and spineless gush. Don't, please, show this to your friend, who may be all you say: perhaps this is a blind day to me.

How are you these days? And when are we going to have a drink in London together? Sorry I've still lost the Miller letters. How is he? and how's the picaresque novel—I'd like to see it a lot.

Sorry I can't help with Philip Callow's stuff.

Yours,
Dylan Thomas

MS: Texas

[1] Philip Callow (b. 1924), better known as a novelist and biographer, also published some volumes of verse.

JEAN LEROY
20 Feb 1953 (Thanks her for BBC contract letter. See Appendix 66.)

OSCAR WILLIAMS
27 February 1953   Boat House Laugharne Carmarthenshire   Wales

Sending work-sheets
separately
                        D.

Dear Oscar,
   The New American Library cheque has just arrived. I cannot take my
sticky eyes from it, and I remember that great line: 'the heel's wide
spendthrift gaze towards paradise'. Thank you, so very much, for the
bother and speed & business of it. And forgive me, please, for the asthmatic brevity of this. I'm about to catch a bus to catch a train to catch a
film-man and, almost certainly, to miss the bus. I'm so fat now I can't
hurry; I have elephantiasis: a huge trunk and a teeny mind. It's full-moon
time, & the town is baying. And I'm awfully worried about my scheduled
visit to the States. I have to write a book by June, & haven't begun it.
We're being thrown out of this house—though only we would live in it,
over-run by rats: us *and* the house.[1] I hardly dare write to Brinnin to say it
is all too difficult, but must do so quickly or he will need a hundred new
kinds of pills all big as roc eggs. Perhaps if Caitlin were settled in some
new warren, I could fly over for a few dates: but we're moving to Christ
knows where by the sea. I want very much to meet the mogul you
mentioned & to find out about that 4000 a year each etc: it sounds
wonderful: we could go anywhere on that, except Laughlin's heart and
ski-run. But I don't know how I'm going to see you at all this year, with
the commissioned book yapping at me, the house being pinched, and all
my depression at the thought of ever moving again except into my long
and dirty home. I'll write you again when I hear from John Malcolm once
he has heard from me in a re-balding letter.
   I enclose the signed note for the Prologue poem; also the work-sheets. I
do hope you can sell them for an impossible sum. My agent here has said
he will help me with my debts but allow me no money: so I must have
some of the stuff on the side. You must take some money yourself from
whatever you can get for these messy sheets—poems won't change the
sheets for their guests—so that we can both celebrate. Please.

---

[1] Margaret Taylor found it increasingly difficult to finance the Boat House. But the
  Thomases continued to live there.

The trivial short story I can't find but will. It was published in World Review.[1]

Caitlin's no longer pregnant: it cost five broadcasts and a loan, and I wish I could have announced, on the air, the reason for these broadcasts.

The bus is getting up steam.

Love to you & Gene from us all, and thank you deeply.

I look forward to a letter.

Yours Ever,
Dylan

I'll be doing a broadcast of your poems some time this spring. Will let you know when. The BBC doesn't much like doing American copyright poems: they hate spending dollars. I *may* have to put some English poems in the same programme: if I have to, I'll choose very good ones.

MS: Indiana   *SL(R)*

KEITH KYLE[2]
27 February 1953   The Boat House Laugharne Carmarthenshire

Dear Mr. Kyle,

Thank you for your letter of February 19th, and I'm sorry not to have answered straightaway.

I read, with great interest, the four scripts, in the 'This I Believe' series, you enclosed. Thank you for asking me to contribute to the series: I'd very much like to, and will send you the 3½ minute script as soon as possible. Perhaps you could let me have a recording date—or even one or two to choose from?—when you have the script? Is it, by the way, possible to record from the Swansea studios?—only an hour or so away from me. Anyway, I'm in London often.

Yours sincerely,
Dylan Thomas

MS: BBC

CHARLES ELLIOTT
27th Feb 53   Boat House Laugharne Carmarthenshire

Dear Mr Elliott,

So sorry not to have answered your letter: I've just come back from

---

[1] 'The Followers'.

[2] A producer in the BBC's North American Service. He sent scripts by Viscount Kemsley, John Lehmann, Peter Ustinov and Aneurin Bevan. Thomas didn't contribute to the series.

London. Yes, March 10, Tuesday, 6.30's fine. I can't think of a title, as I'll probably be reading some modern poets & also a chunk of a kind-of-play of mine. 'Some Recent Writing' might do.

I'd like to spend the night in Cardiff. Anywhere. And I'll send you a wire to say time of my arrival.

Very many thanks for all the *great* amount of trouble you're taking; & your kindness in arranging things.

Sincerely,
Dylan Thomas

MS: Columbia University

DAVID HIGHAM
March 2 1953   Boat House Laugharne Carmarthenshire

Dear David,

Thank you very much for lunch & for the consoling talk about my wretched affairs. Sorry I was so out-of-sorts that day: I don't know: I'd only just arrived in London, the place that usually out-of-sorts me but takes some days to do so. I hope you'll have lunch with me soon, and that I'll be brighter. But, in spite of my dimness then, I do hope I managed to make you understand how grateful I am to you for the bother you're taking to more or less take care of me—so far as debts go &, of course, so long as I work like a beaver. You asked me to send you a list of my local debts: I enclose the largest: far larger, by the way, than I had, even at my gloomiest, expected. If more details of the bill are wanted, they can be provided: I think the house rent[1] comes to about 165 & the hiring of taxis, over a long period, makes up the rest. Ebie Williams is a friend of mine & will be satisfied, to begin with, with whatever you can send him from the kitty. I have two other bills here, for about £20 each. What shall I do with them? The rest are small bills I'd like to pay myself *if I had the money*. Could you put something in the bank for me straightaway, so that I can pay these. 25? I've a weekly girl to pay, as well, apart from my own day-to-day expenses. (Ebie Williams, of our local Brown's Hotel, is very pleased, by the way, that his bill is being sent to you, however slow the payment of it might be. He's my friend, as I said, & therefore he knows me.)

I went to see Charles Fry, & arranged to deliver manuscript by end of June.

Thank you for sending the old magazine material. I'm dealing with it. Bozman wants to bring the book out in October. No title yet.

I wrote to Michael Powell.[2]

---

[1] Of The Pelican, where his mother lived.
[2] A short film on a classical theme, to be written for the director Michael Powell, seems to have been mooted.

Thank you again, sorry for my dyspeptic vagueness at our lunch, & I hope you can put a sum in the bank right away & also let the owner of the Pelican House (where my mother lives) have something. Also, shall I send the two other £20 bills?

Yours,
Dylan

MS: Texas

OSCAR WILLIAMS
March 3 1953   Boat House Laugharne Carmarthenshire

Dear Oscar,
Work sheets of 'Prologue'. Perhaps a typed copy of the final poem, on top of the sheets, wd look well to a maybe buyer, I don't know. I've tried to keep the sheets in some sort of order, from the very first germ of the poem—it was going to be a piece of doggerel written to someone in the States on my return from there to Wales, but soon grew involved & eventually serious.
Hope you can sell this.
Hope you've had my letter.
I've got gout today. God, that reads like GOAT. I mean, the one in the toe.
Every time a bird flies by, I yell, thinking it might land on my toe. All I can think about is TOE.
Hope you're having a good toe.
Toe to you both.
I'll write soon properly long.

Ever,
D.

MS: Indiana

E. F. BOZMAN
16 March 1953   Boat House Laugharne Carmarthenshire

Dear E. F. Bozman,
Sorry to be late with the enclosed proofs: I've been away, broadcasting.
I'm afraid I don't know how to answer the proofreader's queries about Donald Taylor's account (page 135).[1] But I do suggest that the

---

[1] *The Doctor and the Devils* included a brief essay by Taylor, 'The Story of the Film'.

penultimate paragraph be deleted: it seems a little smug & apt to forget that this film is only a melodrama & much of it probably wildly inaccurate. I have also ventured to correct Taylor's grammar on page 136 & insert one or two commas. I was very sorry not to have been able to see you during my last London visit. I had to hurry home after only a day & a half. The gathering of material for the new book of stories is going on well: I am waiting, however, for some more stuff from Rolph the bookseller. And, as you suggested very kindly, it would be a great help if the material could be typed for me when it is ready so that I could go through it carefully in typescript rather than in proof.

I hope to see you when I am next in town.

Yours,
Dylan Thomas

MS: J. M. Dent

DAVID HIGHAM
17 March 1953   Boat House Laugharne Carmarthenshire

Dear David,

I do hope you got my last letter, written just after we met in London. I've been expecting an answer, and am worried about it. I hope you aren't ill; or that anything, in my letter or at our lunch, offended you: I'm awfully sorry if it did.

If you got that letter you'll remember I enclosed with it a bill from our local Brown's Hotel, mostly for the letting of a house, for £190. Now that—though it must, of course, be paid, eventually, however slowly—is not, at this moment, nearly so urgent as other quite small ones which have cropped up in the town and which I really *must* pay at once. (Friendly Brown's can wait. These tradesmen and rates-men can't.) And the most urgently pressing bill is one for £35 to Magdalen College School, Oxford. As soon as I won that Foyle's award, the very first cheque I wrote was to the School, for that amount; but they kept the cheque, without presenting it, for so long that when they *did* present it it was returned by the Bank, the Foyle's money being by that time finished. This is really distressingly important for me to pay *now*.

I don't know how my account stands with you, but you should have received, from the BBC over £100 for four Personal Anthologies I recorded in the Swansea studios several weeks ago and which have been broadcast, on the Welsh Region, week by week. Also, I recorded a Childhood Reminiscences sketch for the Welsh Region, from Swansea, last week, for £20 (twenty pounds) and this coming Friday am to record two more, at, I believe, the same fee.[1] So that there should be a £100 in the kitty, and £60

---

[1] These talks were some of the old reminiscences, being rebroadcast.

coming. The £100 should *certainly* be there by now. Can you, therefore, let me have the money for Magdalen College School, or arrange to pay it, at once? And can you, *please*, pay into my Bank all you possibly can, *at once* as well. I need £50 for various small bills here which simply *must* be paid this week. I have no money at all.

I'll ring you, at your office, in the morning, hoping that you will have read this by that time and that you will be able to let me have £50 directly in the Bank & enough to pay the School. The Income Tax *must*, this time, wait for its share.

And, also, when I ring I do hope I'll find that you aren't ill or offended.

Yours ever,
Dylan

MS: Texas   *SL*

JOHN ALEXANDER ROLPH
17 March 1953   Boat House Laugharne Carmarthenshire

Dear John,

Very many apologies for this delay. I shd have written weeks ago, to thank you for the letter & for all you're doing to try to get these scraps & stories of mine together. And to say, Sorry, too, that our evening in town—or our hour, rather—was such a mess. I do hope we'll have another evening soon without so many people & so much confusion. The thin, pale woman with us—Marged Howard-Stepney—who drank sherry very quickly, died the next evening of an overdose of sleeping drug.

Since seeing you, I've managed, myself, to get hold of *Janus* (May 1936) and *Yellowjacket* (May 1939), with my stories, 'The Horse's Ha', 'The True Story', & 'The Vest', in them. Also I've found two forgotten ones: 'Prologue To An Adventure' in *Wales*, Summer 1937; and 'Adventure From A Work in Progress' in *Seven*, Spring 1939.

What I *wd*, & urgently, like from you is: 'After the Fair', N.E.W. March 1934; & any other N.E.W. story. And 'Quite Early One Morning', the only copy of which I've lost. Is it possible for me to have them soon? Then I can let Bozman have at least 17 items towards that book, which he wants to bring out as soon as possible. Do let me know.

Yours,
Dylan

MS: Texas

CHARLES ELLIOTT
17 March 1953   The Boat House Laugharne Carmarthenshire
                                                        Laugharne 68

Dear Charles Elliott,
    Thank you for my evening at Cardiff, all the kindness & hospitality. It was a wonderful audience.
    I wonder if I can ask one more favour of you. Do you remember that I had with me a suitcase & a briefcase, & that I transferred, some time in the evening, some of the contents of the briefcase into the suitcase? Well, anyway, I left the briefcase somewhere. I *think* it must be in the Park Hotel. I've written to the manager; but could you possibly, when & if passing by, drop in & see if it is there? It's very urgent to me: the only copy in the world of that kind-of-a-play of mine, from which I read bits, is in that battered, strapless briefcase whose handle is tied together with string.[1]
    If the thing isn't there, do you think you *could* find out where the hell I left it? I didn't leave with it on Wednesday morning when I caught the train.

                                Thank you again, & sorry for all this.
                                Dylan Thomas

MS: Columbia University

JOHN MALCOLM BRINNIN
18 March 1953   Boat House Laugharne Carmarthenshire Wales

I shall be applying for a visa next
week: in Cardiff, this time. I do not
think they are quite so screening-
strict there as in London. URGENT,
& just remembered: Let me have, at
once, a formal and official Poetry
Center letter Dear Mr. Thomas-ing
me and saying what cultural &
important engagements you have
fixed up for me.

Dear John,
    After all sorts of upheavals, evasions, promises, procrastinations, I write, very fondly, and fawning slightly, a short inaccurate summary of those events which caused my never writing a word before this. In the

---

[1] This may have been the first time an audience heard parts of *Under Milk Wood*. In October Thomas lost the manuscript again. Douglas Cleverdon found it in a London pub.

beginning, as Treece said in one of his apocalapses, was the bird; and this came from Caitlin, who said, and repeated it only last night after our Boston-Laugharne babble, 'You want to go to the States again only for flattery, idleness, and infidelity'. This hurt me terribly. The right words were: appreciation, dramatic work, and friends. Therefore I didn't write until I knew for certain that I could come to the States for a visit and then return to a body and hearth not irremediably split from navel to firedog. Of course I'm far from certain now, but I'm coming. This unfair charge—flattery, idleness, etcetera—kept me seething quiet for quite a bit. Then my father died, and my mother relied on me to look after her and to stay, writing like fury, pen in paw, a literary mole, at home. Then a woman—you never met her—who promised me a real lot of money for oh so little in return died of an overdose of sleeping drug and left no will,[1] and her son, the heir, could hardly be expected to fulfil *that* kind of unwritten agreement. Then a publisher's firm, which had advanced me money for an American-Impressions book of which I never wrote a word, turned, justly, nasty, and said I had to do the book by June 1953 or they would set the law on me. Then Caitlin was going to have another baby and didn't want it. Then Margaret bloody Taylor said that she was going to sell the rickety house we wrestled in, over our heads and live bodies. So this was the position I was in, so far as my American visit was concerned:—Caitlin was completely against it, and was going to have a baby; my mother was against it, because I should be near her and working hard to keep the lot of us; and I was reluctantly against it, because I was without money, owing to an unexpected suicide, and I could not, naturally, leave a mother and pregnant wife and three children penniless at home while I leered and tubthumped in Liberty Land; and the publishers were legally against it, because I had to write a book for them quickly; and on top of all that, the final reason for my knowing I could not come out this spring was the prospect of the rapid unhousing of dame, dam, chick-to-be, and the well-loved rest. (I write like a cad. I should whip myself to death on the steps of my Club for all this.) Well anyway: I won a prize, for the book of the year, of £250 (pounds), which put paid to baby through the wicked good will and skill of a Pole like Conrad Veidt.[2] And a brother-in-law in Bombay said he would look, from a distance, after my mother's welfare. And Margaret bloodiest Taylor has, temporarily, relented. And I think I can give the demanding publishers the script of 'Under Milk Wood' (when finished) instead of, for instance, 'A Bard's-Eye View of the U.S.A.' And Caitlin's hatred of my projected visit can be calmed only by this: that after no more than 6 weeks' larricking around I return from New York with enough money to take Colm, her and me for three winter months to Portugal where all, I hear, is cheap and sunny. Or, alternatively, that I find, in a month, a house for us, in your country, and

---

[1] Marged Howard-Stepney.
[2] Conrad Veidt, German actor, first seen in the early horror film, *The Cabinet of Dr Caligari.*

can send for Caitlin to join me in the early summer and keep us going, through summer and autumn, by work which is not cross-continental reading and raving. Of the alternatives, she would far prefer the first. So do you think it possible? Do you think I can earn a lot in six weeks: enough, that is, for a Portuguese winter? I do not care, in those six weeks, how much I read, or how many times, or where. I think, for economy, it would be best for me to stay in a New York hotel—the Chelsea, I trust— for only a little time and then to move in, manias and all, on to friends. I am hoping that perhaps my old friend Len Lye, who lives in Greenwich Village, near Ruthven Todd, will put me up: I am only small, after all, and alone, though loud. I haven't his address, but will get in touch with him once in Chelsea'd New York. So, friend and agent, as much as I can do in six weeks please is perhaps best for us all.

I have put down, in more or less true detail, all the above little hells to show why I have been unable, till now, to write and say: 'It is fine. Go ahead.'

About 'Under Milk Wood'. I shall not have the complete manuscript ready until the week of my sailing. I have, anyway, some doubts as to the performance of it by by myself and a professional cast. Some kind of an approximation to a Welsh accent is required throughout, and I think I could make an hour's entertainment out of this myself. Shall we discuss it later? I shall have the m.s. with me, embarking from the liner, and if you still think, after reading it, it needs other and professional voices, then I don't believe it would need all that 'careful preparation' you mention. I should be *very* glad, by the way, to hear from you, as soon as possible, about any ideas you might have as to what I shd read aloud in my general verse-reading programmes. What poets, and of what centuries? I'd like a wide repertoire. Caitlin sends her love to your mother.

Yours always, dear John
Dylan

MS: Delaware   *SL(R)*

JEAN LEROY
30 March 1953   The Boat House Laugharne Carmarthenshire

Dear Jean Le Roy,
    You asked about a piece which has just appeared, in Paris, in the new literary magazine, Les Lettres Nouvelles: a piece called Le Bébé Ardent. This, I suppose, is a translation of a story of mine called 'The Burning Baby'. I've got an awful memory, but I *do* just seem to remember hearing from a new French magazine about this story; but I very much doubt if I

answered it; if it *did* ever come, I lost it immediately. Anyway, I've had no copy of the magazine. Sorry to be so useless.

Yours,
Dylan Thomas

MS: Texas

E. F. BOZMAN
30 March 1953   The Boat House Laugharne Carmarthenshire

Dear E. F. Bozman,
   Enclosed are some of the books & magazines in which appear 12 of the stories & sketches for the new book. I do hope it won't be too much of a nuisance to have these typed. And could I have the typescript as soon as possible? Also the books & magazines. I'm leaving for New York, for a month's lecturing, on April 16th, and would like to read through the typed 12 stories before then. Also before then I hope to get together the other 9 or so items to make the book complete. What of a title? As it is a book about, & mostly by, adolescence, perhaps the title of one of the sketches would do: 'Quite Early One Morning'. Otherwise, I suggest 'The Burning Baby'. What d'you think?
   I will be seeing you before I leave for N. York.

Yours,
Dylan Thomas

MS: J. M. Dent

E. F. BOZMAN
31 March 1953   Boat House Laugharne Carmarthenshire

Dear E. F. Bozman,
   I hope that by this time the first quite big chunk of material for the new book has reached you, & also the accompanying letter. I don't remember, however, if I indicated, in my letter, what material exactly was to be typed (& it was extremely kind of you to suggest that you might get it typed for me). In case I didn't, the list is:

> The Followers (World Review)
> Holiday Memories }
> Quite Early One Morning } (typescript)
> Adventure (Seven)
> The Vest }
> The True Story } (Yellowjacket)

The Horse's Ha (Janus)

The School For Witches
The Holy Six   (This World I
The Burning Baby   Breathe)
Prologue To An Adventure
A Prospect of The Sea

I've heard today from friends of mine who've helped me collect the above that I can expect to have nearly all the rest next week. This will include 'Return Journey', a long piece, 'Memories of Childhood', and 'Memories of Christmas', all originally broadcast: that is, written to be *spoken* aloud but also, very much, to be read. 'The Crumbs of One Man's Year', that was broadcast one New Year's Day & is, I hope, quite a good piece. A short story of the fantastic kind, called 'The Lemon'. Another Christmas piece. And a little very early story called 'After The Fair', which appeared in the New English Weekly many years ago. My bibliographer-to-be, John Rolph, has tracked this last down to the files of a public library but is not allowed to take the copy out and, having no shorthand, cannot easily copy it. I shall have to think how to get hold of this as—whatever its literary merits; I can't remember a thing about it now—I *should* like to include it: it's the earliest story of mine & will take its place next to some little piece describing the author just about that time of his life.[1]

I'll write again; & I do hope we can hurry a contract up. I'm going to the States, for 6 weeks lecturing, on April 16th, and *must* have some money to keep my family going while I am away and to settle some outstanding debts before I leave. I'm desperately broke.

Yours,
Dylan Thomas

MS: J. M. Dent   *SL*

---

[1] Many of the stories and radio talks listed by Thomas were collected in book form, in the UK, soon after his death: in *Quite Early One Morning* (1954) and *A Prospect of the Sea* (1955). But the more violent and sexual stories remained under a cloud as far as his British publishers were concerned: a reader's report dated January 1954 said 'The Burning Baby' was 'a horrible fantasy', 'Prologue to an Adventure' a 'welter of pornographic filth' and 'The Horse's Ha' 'disgustingly obscene'. It was 1971 before these and similar stories from Thomas's list appeared in a British book, in *Dylan Thomas: Early Prose Writings:* more than thirty years after they were written.

KEITH KYLE
31 March 1953   Boat House Laugharne Carmarthenshire

Dear Mr. Kyle,
    Thank you for your letter, & the enclosure from Cecil Day Lewis. Yes, certainly I'll write to David Higham, my agent, asking him to waive that ban in this particular case and to get in touch with you immediately. I didn't know the ban existed, myself.[1]
    I've written Day Lewis to the same effect.
    Sorry not to have sent my script 'This I Believe' much sooner. I've had bronchitis. I'll send it on in the next few days.

Sincerely,
Dylan Thomas

MS: BBC

DAVID HIGHAM
31 March 1953   Boat House Laugharne Carmarthenshire

Dear David,
    I enclose a letter from Keith Kyle of the BBC, and a note from Cecil Day Lewis. I think we should, if possible, waive that ban they refer to, in this particular case. (I didn't know the ban existed.) As Day Lewis says, if he can't get my permission he'll go no further with the project. And I think those talks *shd* be heard in the U.S.A. If you agree, could you let Kyle know?
    Writing soon at more length about other things.

Yours,
Dylan

P.S. Both letters in sad disrepair, I'm afraid.

MS: Texas

---

[1] C. Day-Lewis had included Thomas's poem 'A Refusal to Mourn' in a radio programme that was to be distributed in the U.S. by the BBC's Transcription Service. Thomas's agents didn't allow this use of his material.

THEODORE ROETHKE[1]
31 March 1953   Boat House Laugharne Carmarthenshire Wales

Dear Ted,

Sorry not to have written before to thank you for sending the Dancing Poems. I think they're wonderfully good. I kept putting off writing until I knew when I'd be in the States, so that I could say, See you, I hope, in the so-and-so. Now so-and-so is April 21st, and I'll be in and around New York until June 5. Any chance of seeing you for a few hours, evenings, days? A line to me c/o Brinnin, saying, Yes, or even, Yes, perhaps, would be fine to look forward to.

I asked the BBC, officially, about getting hold of a copy, for you, of the recording I made of the three poems of yours, but the BBC said, We never, we never, we never. Which is not true. Now I'm climbing into the BBC by the back door, and falling over the slimy accents, and hope to get a copy soon. I'm glad and proud you want one: I hope I haven't boomily buggered the poems up. The recording got several letters: 'terrific poems', 'gibberish', etc, and one or two simple serious & passionate ones from people I didn't know of that did show how disturbed they were by the strange things that had happened to them across the air. You still have a grotesquely small audience here, but very fierce.

Had your wedding card. Congratulations. Best wishes, & sympathy, to your wife. Hope you had a nice, loud, elbowy, dancing time and fell on some guests.

I haven't seen a copy of Poetry Chicago yet with your piece about my book.[2]

Are you writing poems? I want very very much to see them. And do try to meet; New York or Chicago. Or anywhere.

Yours,
Dylan

MS: Washington   *SL*

E. F. BOZMAN
April 6 1953   Boat House Laugharne Carmarthenshire

Dear E. F. Bozman,

I'm sorry our telephone conversation was obscured by the failure of my telephone apparatus to make my really great gratitude heard. Thank you very very much for saying that you would arrange for £250 to be paid to

---

[1] Thomas and the American poet Roethke (1908–63) became friends during the American visits.
[2] A review, in the December 1952 issue, of *In Country Sleep and Other Poems* (New Directions, 1952), under the pseudonym 'Winterset Rothberg'.

me, this Tuesday, tomorrow, on advance of our contract: things have been difficult for me lately, indeed stopping me writing at all because of nagging and bewildering financial worry; and this considerable kindness on your part will ease them all. I could not have left for the States without paying some of my outstanding debts in this tolerant village, nor without leaving my family enough money to live on in my absence. Thank you again. I am writing, after writing this, to David Higham, to ask him to send on immediately as much of that generous advance as he, and the Income Tax, allow.

Your letter, about the stories & sketches which I sent you, did not really surprise me; I realised, I think beforehand, that the early violent stories *were* very raw. I myself thought that their rawness would, in contrast to the maturer, remembering, sketches, be acceptable; but I do appreciate all you say. I *would* like, one day, to have those other stories printed in book form, but I shall leave them now, and I look forward to talking with you about them before, visa willing, I set out on my short, and maybe vain, in both senses, American tour.

I shall send along the rest of the acceptable material as quickly as possible.

Yours very sincerely,
Dylan Thomas

MS: J. M. Dent

DAVID HIGHAM
April 6 1953   Boat House Laugharne Carmarthenshire

Dear David,

I sent the first big chunk of the material towards the new proposed book of short stories for Dent's, to Bozman a few days ago. The later ones he liked, but the early ones he considered 'too raw for publication under the Dent imprint'. This was a disappointment to me, as I had considered that the juxtaposition of the early violent stories and the calmer prose-memories would make an interesting book. However. Bozman wants now to make a volume of the later sketches & stories, although these do not, as yet, number more than 8 altogether, including the 3 which Bozman is now having typed. And I am persuaded, by him, to leave those early stories alone at the present moment.

Two days ago, Bozman phoned me to say that—perhaps in view of the fact that he had to turn these raw stories down—he was prepared to advance me, on my contract, the sum of £250 immediately. This seems extremely generous, and I have written very thankfully to him. He will be in touch with you tomorrow (Tuesday), and promises to let you have a cheque, at once, for this amount. I do hope you will be able to let me have, for myself, the most substantial part of this cheque: indeed, all that is possible out of it. I am due to sail, visa willing, for New York on Thursday the 16th of this month, for a reading-tour, in the Eastern States, of about 5 or 6 weeks, probably six. And I can't leave without settling outstanding debts & arranging for my family to live in my absence. So that: please do let me have nearly all of that advance—sent to my bank. I'm in an awful mess, as usual, and in a frightful flap about leaving: visas, ticket, etc. I have a television show, from Cardiff,[1] & two recordings—one from London, for Cleverdon, & one from Swansea—before leaving; and a packet of small debts, etc., to see to; and a quick script to write.

I'll ring you in the morning. I have written to my bank telling them to expect a good deal of money by Wednesday, and am already drawing on this.

Yours,
Dylan

MS: Texas

DAVID HIGHAM
16 April 1953[2]   as from The Boat House Laugharne Carmarthenshire

Dear David,
   Thanks for everything you're doing. This is just to give you my American address: c/o J. M. Brinnin, 100 Memorial Drive, Cambridge, Mass. And to say: will you, for the next 5 weeks—i.e. until I come back from the States—send whatever monies come in to me (I mean, the 50% of them) direct to Caitlin, at Laugharne, and *not* to my bank? Please.

Yours ever,
Dylan

MS: Texas   *SL*

CAITLIN THOMAS
Monday 20 April 53   [headed paper: United States Lines]

Oh Caitlin Cat my love my love, I love you for ever & ever, I LOVE YOU CAT, if only I could jump over this rocking ship-side into the awful sea and swim to you now, I want to be with you all the time, there isn't one moment of the endless day or night on this hell-ship when I'm not

---

[1] 'Home Town—Swansea. A programme in which viewers meet some of the interesting people who live in this old Welsh town.' 9 April 1953. Alfred Janes, Dan Jones and Vernon Watkins took part with Thomas. Wynford Vaughan-Thomas introduced it.
[2] The letter was written just before Thomas left on his third trip to the U.S.

thinking about you, feeling through the dark and the rolling and the wind for you and talking to you. Don't be lost to me, darling; forgive me for all my nastiness, mad-dog tempers, of the last days & weeks: they were because I didn't want to go, I didn't want to leave you in old dull Laugharne with children and loneliness, I didn't want, I promise you before God, to move at all, except with you. I longed to be with you, terribly close as we very often are, as we nearly always are, sitting in the shed and writing, being with you, & in your arms at night. And here I am, on this huge hot gadget-mad hotel, being tossed and battered; the sea's been brutal all the time; I can hardly write this at all, in the tasteful, oven-ish, no-smoking library-room, for the rattle & lurch; everybody's been sick every day; for one whole day, full of dramamine, I groaned in a fever in the cabin which I do not share, alone in my horrible rocking hothouse where there's no time, no night or day; occasionally now I manage to rock, like a drunk, to the bar where a few pale racked men are trying the same experiment as me, and then, after an ice-cold couple, stagger back to my room, to pray that I was with you, as I always wish to be, and not on this eternal cocktail-shaker of a ship—or if I *have* to be on it, which God knows I don't have to be, then oh Cat oh my sweetheart, then why why aren't you with me too. I've spoken hardly a word to anyone but one stout barman; the people who share my table—when any of us is well enough to appear—are a thousand times worse than those dumpling (Dolly's kind of dumpling) Dutchmen: there's a middle-aged brother & sister, and a little sophisticated German woman; the little German woman's beastly, and told me, when the brother & sister weren't there, that she'd thought of asking the purser to move her to another table: 'I don't like', she said, 'having my meals in the company of a woman who reminds me of my cook'—which seems one of the oddest things I ever heard said. There is also a German count, or mock-count, with whom I have exchanged half a dozen words: he looks, speaks, & acts like Charles Fisher. Otherwise, not a word to anyone. Every one is very clean & well-dressed and moneyed; the only one possible thing I have in common with them is that we all feel ill. It is nine o'clock in the morning; tomorrow we dock at New York; breakfast has been & gone. I love you, Caitlin, oh my darling I love you. To think that *I* was angry because *you* did not want me to go away. I was angry, really, only with myself, because I did not want to go away and yet was going. But I shall bring money back & we will go [to] the sun very soon: that is sure. I'll write properly when I'm on land: this rocking is getting unsteadily worse. And I'll send some money in the letter, just as soon as I get any. Higham's number is TEMPLE BAR 8631 in case you feel like ringing him about the letter I wrote to him on the morning of my going away: I told him then to send any money coming to me *direct* to you. I love you. Please, my darling, try to love me, and wait for me. Wait for me, dear, I'll hurry like hell through this sad month-and-a-bit. I can see you now. You're more beautiful than ever, my own true love. Kiss the children and beat them to death. I hope the sun is out, and that you can buy the canoe. Be good to me: you are everything. Why did I snarl when you only wanted me to stay? I love you.

Now I am going to the bar for a cold beer, then back to the bloody cabin to lie on the unmade bed & to fall into a timeless dream of you and of all I love—which is only you—and of the sea rocking & the engines screaming and the wind howling and the despair that is in everything except in our love.

Oh, Cat,
I love you
Dylan

MS: Maurice Neville

CAITLIN THOMAS
April 22 [1953]   as from 100 Memorial Drive Cambridge Massachusetts

Darling,

Arrived in NewfilthyYork two days ago. Staying in Chelsea for 3 days, in small room exactly under our old one. Chelsea staff very disappointed you didn't come. If *they* are, what do you think I am? I love you my love for ever & for ever and wish to be with you always on earth & in heaven.

Oscar & I are together at this moment in a post-office, so this is very short. Here's a cheque for 100 dollars—about 37 pounds. I'll write a letter from John B's at Memorial Drive, where I go tomorrow.

I love you,
Dylan

MS: Thomas Trustees

CAITLIN THOMAS
[about May 23 1953]   [headed paper: The Poetry Center]
as from 100 Memorial Drive Cambridge Mass

> P.S. If you write again to [*an arrow points to Brinnin's address*], darling please put c/o J.M. Brinnin. Letters to me just at 100 Memorial Drive don't get delivered, it's such a huge building, and one letter from you, love, to me, has been sent back to England.   XX I kiss you.

Cat sweetheart,

Caitlin my love three thousand miles away darling Cat you are so near.

And your beautiful letter tore all the time and distance away and I was with you again, again in our bed with the beating seaweather, as I read the words of the letter over & over and as I saw your hand writing it and as I could see your face & hair and eyes my darling darling. You are with me always, Cat, as God is with the devout; other people around me are lousy with their personal interests, are unhappy & lost, but I am certain in my body & my heart & that makes all the miraculous difference. I'm certain that we are together; I am sure that I love you; I know that you are Caitlin; and I am smug about it. But always through the smugness comes the terrible fear: Caitlin may always be distant, perhaps she or I will die, my true incredibly-lovely Cat doesn't, can't, love me any more. I love you, Caitlin Macnamara, I love & love you. People here know that, although I would never say it. They can see the love for you around me; they can know I'm blessed. I'm damned if I'm blessed, but all the eyes of the strangers can see that I am in love with you. I love you. I'm writing this again in Brinnin's Memorial Drive; Brinnin is away; his mother is shopping, I suppose. And I love you.

This trip is nearly over. There is one foul thing, though. The aeroplane I was to have caught on May 26th has been removed from the passengers' list because of the Coronation: that is, so I understand, rich bitches have bought it out so that they can get to London to look at the Queen. And so I have to get the next poor-available plane, which is on June the first, arriving on June the second, the day of the Coronation. I'm sorry, my love, my own, Caitlin my Cat, but there is no other way. I shall telegram the exact hour of my arrival in London on June 2nd to Laugharne & to Helen's address in case you are there. Meet me, Cat: oh, what [am I] without you? I love you. It is only 4 days later.

June the 2nd, then in London. And may Laugharne stop raining. And then: can you—this is important—make plans well-beforehand to be away with me the whole of July. Alone, without Colm or Aeron. You & me. I know that at the end of July, Llewelyn comes out of school, but somehow it must be arranged. You and me must, at the beginning of July, go together to Hollywood. We can get a boat from London, direct but slow, to San Francisco, & then fly to Los Angeles in an hour or so. Outside Hollywood, in a huge easy house in the hills, we're to stay for the month with Stravinsky. I've seen him, just now, in Boston, and we've thought of an opera and it is—for me—so simple that the libretto can be written in the time we're there.[1] That's not just optimistic: it *can*, & will be. In advance, I'll be given 500 pounds & our passage, firstclass, & then another £500—& then royalties until we die. We'll go back from

---

[1] Boston University's Opera Workshop cabled Thomas on May 21, to ask if he would consider writing a libretto for Stravinsky. He met the composer briefly at an hotel in Boston. They discussed a story about a world reborn, perhaps colonised from outer space after a holocaust: a new Eden. But it was a tentative plan, not a commission. Boston still had to raise the money.

Hollywood to Laugharne, &, in the winter, we'll go to Majorca. There'll be plenty of money. This time it's working. Majorca seems to be the cheapest place in the sun there is: I've got lots of information about it. We can stay at a pension, & then get a house & two servants. It sounds mad but I think it's true & can be done. I love you.

Biddy rang me up & came along & gave me a rather moth-eaten camelhair coat for you. I'm going to send Ivy a lot of rich sweets; buy a shirt for Phil; something cowboy for Ebi; bring along a piece of finery for my mother. For you, Caitlin, only my eternal untouched love, my wonder at *your* love, my heart & my gout. I'm going to buy Welly a leather travelling-bag to go with his travelling rug. And whatever I can think of for darling Colm & dear Aeron. I am sick damp drivelling *and* strong with my love for you. Oh, Cat, this letter sounds so cheery & so silly. I'm desperate really to be with you. The pictures of you & me on John's walls here make me shout & cry and weep.

Is my sister dead?[1]

I'll try to write to my mother.

I've finished that infernally eternally unfinished 'Play' & have done it in New York with actors.[2]

I've seen Dave & Rose.[3]

But it's *I* who love you, even though Rose says she does.

I love you.

I love your oh I don't know just everything of you.

I'm going back to New York tomorrow to do the 'PLAY' again. Tomorrow I'll send some money. It will come in 4 or 5 days. About sixty pounds, for bills.

Why am I here? I want to be with you. We will never again be not together.

> I love you I love you I love you I love you

> > I love you
> > Oh Cat.

And please do, carefully, the preparations for Hollywood July.

> > I love you my Cattleanchor my dear
> > dear dear

MS: Maurice Neville

IRENE JONES (Mrs Daniel Jones)
[postmarked June 14 1953] (Sends her names of doctors. See Appendix 67.)

[1] Nancy had died on April 16.

[2] *Under Milk Wood* had its first performance at the Poetry Center on May 14.

[3] Rose Slivka, then married to the sculptor Dave Slivka, was Caitlin Thomas's closest friend in America.

ELIZABETH REITELL
June 16 1953   Boat House Laugharne Carmarthenshire Wales,
                                 but as from, privately, The Savage Club
                                     One Carlton Terrace London SW3

Elizabeth Reitell (b. 1920), was a wartime lieutenant in the U.S. Women's Army Corps, then an artist, and from 1951 to 1953 worked with J. M. Brinnin as assistant director of the Poetry Center. There she met Thomas in the spring of 1953, helped him prepare *Under Milk Wood* for production, and fell in love with him. She had been married twice.

Liz love,
    I miss you terribly much.
    The plane rode high and rocky, and over Newfoundland it swung into lightning and billiard-ball hail, and the old deaf woman next to me, on her way to Algiers via Manchester, got sick in a bag of biscuits, and the bar—a real, tiny bar—stayed open all the bourbon way. London was still glassy from Coronation Day, and for all the customs-men cared I could have packed my bags with cocaine and bits of chopped women. All my friends, including the Irish ones I stay with, were, early that morning, in the middle of Coronation parties that had already lasted a week, and did not seem to think that I had been away: my broken bone, of course they took for granted, and they showed me an assortment of cuts, black eyes, & little fractures to prove that they too had suffered for Royalty. I came back here, to the always sad West drizzle, the following week, the candies running in my bag, and have just been sitting around, getting accustomed. These are the first words I've written, and all they mean to say is: I miss you a great, great deal. We were together so much, sick, well, silly, happy, plagued, but with you I was happy all the time.
    No, don't send that stupid Prologue to Richman, but please to me. And also, if you can, any other reviews and also some of the poems among the papers.
    I saw my Welsh solicitor, and he did not appear to know why I had gone to see stuffy Maclean O.B.E. I told him he had written to me to ask me to go, but he said no. Who is right, if anybody, can you remember? Now he says that he intends to go on with the anti-Time case only in Europe whose libel-laws he understands, and to leave the American side altogether.[1] I told him about that New Directions digest of reviews, on yellow paper, that you were going to send Maclean. If you haven't already sent it to Maclean, would you send it to me to give to the Welsh solicitor. If Maclean has it, he, Welsh solicitor, will write Maclean for it. All this is

---

[1] *Time* magazine published an article about Thomas on 6 April 1953. Thomas objected to a passage that said he guzzled beer and smothered truth and fact in 'boozy invention'. The article continued: 'He borrows with no thought of returning what is lent, seldom shows up on time, is a trial to his friends, and a worry to his family.' His solicitor (and friend) in Swansea, Stuart Thomas, issued a writ on April 30. *Time* responded by putting a private detective on Dylan Thomas's tail when he made his next and final visit to the U.S.

disjointed & probably confusing. Hope you can disentangle it. And I'm sorry, Liz dear, that, all these miles away, I am still worrying you over such small things. I wish I was worrying you, very near.

Later today—this is the wet, gray morning, all seabirds & mist and children's far-off voices and regret everywhere in the wind & rain,—I'll write to Stravinsky, and then soon may know a bit more of where I shall be & what I shall do this fall. I've been asked to go to an International Literary Conference—oh God, oh Pittsburgh—in October, with Eliot, Thomas Mann, Forster, Elizabeth Bowen, Camus, Hemingway, Wilder, Faulkner, and my agent in London says I certainly should and I probably shall. With those boys' names, there *must* be money. Oh, and Arthur Miller will be there too, so he and I can be avant-garde together and write a play in which *everybody* takes his clothes off in a sewer. It's a shame our sweet little David couldn't have had that bunch all together in his party. Remember me to [...] if ever you see him. And to Ruthven, please? With thanks for housing my cases of rubbish. And to Mr. Campbell in the bucketing rain in F. Street, and to the so liberal party, and to Herb at the Crucible, and to Charlie Read chasing you—which is more than Herbert will do this year at Harvard.[1] And always to John, to whom I shall write this long, trembling week.

My arm is still in plaster: new Welsh plaster. I haven''t yet found a Doctor like Milton, nor will I ever. All my best wishes to him: he picked me out of the sick pit with his winking needle and his witty wild way.[2]

Oh, I miss you, Liz.

I've put 2 addresses at the top of this letter. The first is for Poetry Center. The second—deep as a grave full of comedians—for you and me should you write, one day, from you to me.

I'm sending this to Charles Street. Next month I'll write to you at Dundee.

What are you doing?

> Love, love, to you,
> Dylan

MS: Elizabeth Reitell Smith

---

[1] Herbert Hannum, an architect, was later Elizabeth Reitell's third husband.
[2] It was Dr Milton Feltenstein's 'winking needle' that injected Thomas with half a grain of morphine on 4 November 1953, and led directly to his death.

JOHN MALCOLM BRINNIN
16 June 1953   Laugharne

My dear John,

Just arrived back here, fractured and barmy, to torpor and rain and Ivy's dungeon, and I've nothing to tell you except a thousand thankyous and how much I miss you. In spite of Milk fever, bonebreak, some nausea, Carolina and Richman, old Captain Oscar Cohen,[1] I enjoyed myself an awful lot, especially in Cambridge & Boston. And thank your mother too for every kindness.

I haven't heard yet from Sarah Caldwell[2] about the opera, and wrote to Stravinsky only today, so I don't know yet any autumn plans. But there's an International Literary Spender-less Conference at Pittsburgh in October, to which I've been invited, and, though to hell with Conferences, I shall quite likely go there on the way (I hope) to California via (somehow) Memorial Drive; and with Caitlin, too.

I'm going to start work tomorrow and shall revise Milk Wood for publication and broadcasting here. I'll also be seeing David Higham soon, and will get Milk Wood copyrighted as a play for public performance. Could you, then, d'you think, do something, with Tom Brockway and with the woman of Wolfe & influence, whose name I've forgotten, about getting it done across the States? And then, after finishing 'In The Skin Trade', I want to begin on a new, and, in one sense, proper-er, play. About this I'll tell [you] in—is it?—August. Do write to me, however briefly, though please not shortly; and could you let me know Sarah Caldwell's address at Boston University?

The very best to Joe.

Ever,
Dylan

MS: Delaware   *SL*

IGOR STRAVINSKY
16th June 1953   The Boat House Laugharne Carmarthenshire Wales

Dear Mr. Stravinsky,

I was so very very glad to meet you even for a little time, in Boston; and you and Mrs. Stravinsky couldn't have been kinder to me. I hope you got well very soon.

I haven't heard anything yet from Sarah Caldwell, but I've been thinking a lot about the opera and have a number of ideas—good, bad, and

---

[1] 'Captain Cohen' is Oscar Williams. Richman is probably Robert Richman, who founded the Institute for Contemporary Arts in Washington DC.
[2] Of the Opera Workshop.

chaotic. As soon as I can get something down on paper, I should, if I may, love to send it to you. I broke my arm just before leaving New York the week before last, and can't write properly yet. It was only a little break, they tell me, but it cracked like a gun.

I should like very much—if you think you would still like me to work with you; and I'd be enormously honoured and excited to do that—to come to California in late September or early October. Would that be convenient? I do hope so. And by that time, I hope, too, to have some clearer ideas about a libretto.

Thank you again. And please give my regards to your wife and to Mr. Craft.

Yours sincerely,
Dylan Thomas

MS: Paul Sacher Foundation, Basle.   *SL*

THEODORE ROETHKE
19th June 1953   Boat House Laugharne Carmarthenshire Wales

Telephone: Laugharne (pronounced Larn) 68

Dear Ted,

I missed, very much, seeing you in America, heard you were with your wife, you normal old thing, in Wystan's in Ischia,[1] and hoped, a lot, I'd be back in time to see you hereabouts. I returned, on June the third, just missing the crowning horror, with a broken arm and rhubarb eyes and feeling like the Island of Bourbon—which, according to the Encyclopaedia Britannica of 1810, the only work of reference in Laugharne, has ſpiders of the ſize of a pigeon's egg, moſt enormous bats, and a burning mountain which throws out vaſt quantities of bitumen, ſulphur, and other combuſtible materials and makes all about uſeleſs. And I got somehow back to our very small house in the grey perpetual rain with a party of Liverpool-Irishmen who insisted on carrying my crippled and fear-dumb mother (who lives nearby), down the dangerous cliff-path, dropping her every now and then with cries of 'Watch out, Ma', and who all fell asleep on the floor and then, fully clothed, went riding the children's rubber animals and birds on the rough sea: none was drowned, but one very nearly, and the village's opinion of him was, 'He wasn't fit to be on a swan'.

I had a good bad enough time in Mew York and in Cambridge too where I met some old and fond friends of yours whose names I never caught, suffered in Syracuse and Carolina, made them suffer in Amherst, was called a Red in Washington but so was Mr. Taft, felt curiously thwarted

---

[1] W. H. (Wystan) Auden had a villa at Ischia.

in Bennington which talks of you with a reverent terror, Winterset, and signed an excellent paper-back book contract—copies in every drugstore, with a suggestive cover—for the story you read a bit of in New World Writing.[1] That story is what I'm about to work on now. I haven't tried to write poetry since last October. *Your* new poems—written in Europe? not, I suppose, that it matters where—I think are beautiful. I'd like to hear you read them, and to go through them very carefully with you. Perhaps we can learn a little from each other, and anyway it will be very enjoyable if we learn and know nothing and only blunder loud about. I'll find out what I can about publishers in England for the Waking Poems, and we'll see Louis MacNeice together, a very good chap, about a rant at the BBC. And so: when *can* we meet? I shall be in London, taking up the revised version of the kind-of-play to the publishers, at the very beginning of July, and then have to come back, on July 6, to Llangollen in North Wales to report, for the Welsh BBC, on an International Eisteddfod there, which lasts until the 11th. I have a suggestion for after that. You said you were going on to Ireland after London. Caitlin, who comes from County Clare, and I want to go to Ireland, too. So, if I can raise enough money, shall we all go together? Laugharne is only about 30 miles from Fishguard from where the boats cross to Rosslare. And from Rosslare we could go into County Cork by train, eat and drink a bit in the West, and wind up in Dublin. Perhaps you and your nameless wife—my very best to her — would spend a day or two here on the way from London to Fishguard, before all setting off. Can we talk about this in London—if you can be in London anytime from July 1 to 5 or 6? If you can't, do write please. Ireland together would be wonderful, I hope.

Here—for any news & nonsense I have can keep until London, Laugharne, or/and Ireland—are two songs, from the play, to fill up the page.

1st Song

Johnnie Crack and Flossie Snail
Kept their baby in a milking pail
Flossie Snail and Johnnie Crack
One would pull it out and one would put it back
O it's my turn now said Flossie Snail
To take the baby from the milking pail
And it's my turn now said Johnnie Crack
To smack it on the head and put it back

Johnnie Crack and Flossie Snail
Kept their baby in a milking pail
One would put it back and one would pull it out
And all it had to drink was ale and stout

---

[1] *Adventures in the Skin Trade.*

For Johnnie Crack and Flossie Snail
Always used to say that stout and ale
Was *good* for a baby in a milking pail.

2nd Song

I loved a man whose name was Tom
He was strong as a bear and two yards long
I loved a man whose name was Dick
He was big as a barrel and three feet thick

And I loved a man whose name was Harry
Six feet tall and sweet as a cherry
But the one I loved most awake or asleep
Was little Willie Wee and he's six feet deep

Oh Tom Dick & Harry were three fine men
And I'll never have such loving again
But little Willy Wee who took me on his knee
Little Willy Weazel was the man for me.

Now men from every parish round
Run after me and roll me on the ground
But whenever I love another man back
Johnnie from the hill or Sailing Jack
I always think as they do what they please
Of Tom Dick & Harry who were tall as trees
And most I think when I'm by their side
Of little Wille Wee who downed and died.

Oh, Tom Dick & Harry were three fine men
And I'll never have such loving again
But little Willy Wee who took me on his knee
Little Willy Weazel was the man for me.

Now when farmers' boys on the first fair day
Come down from the hills to drink and be gay
Before the sun sinks I'll lie there in their arms
But I always think as we tumble into bed
Of little Willy Wee who is dead dead dead.

Oh, Tom Dick & Harry were three fine men
And I'll never have such loving again
But little Willy Wee who took me on his knee
Little Willy Weazel was the man for me.

> From us both to you both,
> Dylan

MS: Washington   *SL*

JOHN ALEXANDER ROLPH
20 June 1953   Boat House Laugharne Carmarthenshire

Dear John,

Thank you for your last letter. Sorry I haven't written before: I've been back from America only a very short time, with a cracked arm and the quivers, and have only just come to. Come to what, I don't know yet. And thanks for trying to dig out more stories from old magazines: an awful job, I know, & I don't wonder it's failed. The copy of 'Wales', by the way, was very useful.

The paragraph John Davenport referred to in his Observer review of my bad 'Doctor & Devils'[1] came, as you guessed, from an 'Horizon' questionnaire. The questionnaire is, I believe, quoted in full in Connolly's new 'Ideas & Places'.[2] I can't remember a word of my own contribution to it.

How is the new business coming on? Hope to see you in London one day.

Yours,
Dylan

MS: Texas

DAVID HIGHAM
June 20 1953   Boat House Laugharne Carmarthenshire

Dear David,

Sorry not to have got in touch with you as soon as I came back. I broke my arm just before catching a New York plane for London, and it's rather hindered me. 'Under Milk Wood' is finished; it was performed, twice, in the Poetry Center, New York, with a cast of six, as a 'play for voices', to two audiences of a thousand each—mostly theatrical audiences, including lots of producers & playwrights—& went down extremely well. And I also gave a shortened reading of it, by myself, at Harvard. I've got three good notices of it, from the New York Times, the Saturday Review, & the leading Boston daily, which I lent to some woman who's doing an article on me for John O'London's weekly. I've written to her, today, to send the notices directly on to you so that you, if you will, may send them along to Charles Fry. He might like to see that, anyway, it *has* been well thought of. I'm busy now revising the play, but will have it ready by the end of this month. It definitely does need revising for publication; many phrases & whole passages I had to alter for dramatic performance, & will now have to change them back. Also, the two performances have

---

[1] *The Doctor and the Devils* had been published, at last, on May 14.
[2] *Ideas and Places* (1953) reprinted Connolly's essays from *Horizon*.

shown me several weaknesses in the writing which I am now going (I hope) to better. I'll be up on the 30th of June myself, and will ring you at once. Either then, or on the 1st of July. And either I shall bring the ms. with me or send it on to you beforehand. I'm afraid there will only be one copy, & that not perfectly typed by any means: it will be the copy I used on the stage, with alterations & many new passages in writing (but clear writing).

Thank you very much indeed for looking after Caitlin, & all the other things, so wonderfully well when I was away.

Looking forward to seeing you.

Dylan

I saw the S'sea solicitor.

MS: Texas

CYRILLY ABELS[1]

June 20 1953 [draft][2]   Boat House Laugharne Carmarthenshire Wales

Dear Miss Abels,

Thank you very much for writing to me. I did enjoy meeting you, and Miss Bolster, and the very pleasant cameraman, for that very short time in the hotel; and I only wish I cd have been more helpful to your guest-editor. I felt like an old pudding with feet. Perhaps I shall be able to meet you again in New York. We might be doing 'Under Milk Wood' once more at the P.C. in October of this year: a revised and, I hope, a much better script. I'm working on it now.

And thank you for photographs; it was nice of you to let me have a set for myself. My wife said one of the pictures looked a bit blurred, but I said it was me; and indeed it was. The pictures were awfully good.

I got the little interview, and there was of course nothing wrong. I'll look forward to seeing the feature.

Thank you again.

Yours

[on *reverse, draft lines from* Under Milk Wood: Captain Cat, at his window thrown wide to the sun and the clippered seas he sailed long ago when his long-ago eyes were blue & bright, slumbers & voyages;]

MS: Texas

[1] Cyrilly Abels was managing editor of *Mademoiselle*. She had sent Thomas text and photographs of an article in their August feature, 'We Hitch Our Wagons'.

[2] When *SL* was in preparation, Abels supplied a photocopy of the letter as received by her. This is lost, Abels is dead, and all that remains is Thomas's draft.

JOHN DAVENPORT
20 June 1953   Boat House Laugharne Carmarthenshire

Dear Brother Sly Boots,
   I shall listen in, twice, tomorrow, Sunday, to hear the midday rats at
my cheese, and, later, Miss Powell. Thank you. I saw a review by
Bonhomie Dobbin in the Spectator.[1] I wish I'd seen yours in the Observer.
   It was lovely to see so many of you in London and in Bach's-a-poor-
man's guineapig-catty flat. I'll be up again on July 1st about, to deliver a
ms, and will ring the BBC for you.
   Ted Roethke will probably be in London at the same time. He's been
staying in Wystan's nest in Ischia. He wants to know if he can have a
pitch on the BBC all for himself to read some of his own poems. He reads
awfully well. Can you do anything?[2]
   So Bill & Helen are going to Tokyo in October. Helen comes back with
an Irish accent after a week in Kerry. I can't phrase or illustrate the
gesture needed to describe the effect upon her of four Japanese years.
                                                        Love
                                                        Dylan

MS: Texas

MIMI JOSEPHSON
June 20 53   Boat House Laugharne Carmarthenshire

Dear Mimi Josephson,
   It was very pleasant to see you in Laugharne, even for such a short time,
and I do hope we'll meet again when I'm in Cardiff: I'll be there sometime
in August to do a television story, and, if you'll give me your number, I'll
ring you up, if I may.
   I realise that you felt you couldn't, with Fitzgerald & the cameraman
there, ask me as many, or the sort of, questions you wanted to; and I find
I'm no good talking to on the telephone: I know I give the impression of
being terse and in a hurry, when indeed I'm anything but. So, if there's
anything you want me to say, do write me a line and I'll answer by return.
   Two things: one, will you let me see the article?[3] and, two: will you,
please, send on the 3 cuttings about 'Milk Wood', from the American
papers, which I lent you, to my agent, David Higham, of Pearn, Pollinger,
& Higham, Ltd., 39–40 Bedford St., Strand, W.C.2. Can you do that

---

[1] Dilys Powell was reviewing *The Doctor and the Devils* for the BBC. Bonamy Dobrée had
   reviewed it in the *Spectator*.
[2] Davenport was working for the BBC.
[3] Mimi Josephson was preparing an article about Thomas for *John O'London's Weekly*. It
   appeared on August 7, 'Poet in the Boat House'.

straightaway? Sorry to be a nuisance, but he wants them at once to show to the publisher (Allan Wingate) who'll be printing the play this year. You've probably picked out what lines, if any, you want to use from those notices by this time. Can you let Higham have them as soon as you receive this? Thanks a lot.

And don't forget to write if there's anything I can do. I look forward to seeing you again.

Yours,
Dylan Thomas

P.S. Caitlin told me you just rang up. The photograph of the man with the striped tie, on the fire-escape of his New York apartment: W. H. Auden. Other photographs in my hut are of D. H. Lawrence & Thomas Hardy, there's a big photograph of Walt Whitman over my table, just under the roof, and a portrait of Blake. There are also, pinned about, pictures of monkeys & naked women.

MS: the recipient

OSCAR WILLIAMS
June 22 1953   Boat House Laugharne Carmarthenshire Wales

Dear Oscar, Little dear Honourable Treasurer of mine, how are you? Did you discover Columbus well? and give my best to Long Don Drummond the Potent Man? I missed you a lot my last days, and was Lizzed away to the plane alone. I almost liked the plane-ride, though; it was stormy and dangerous, and only my iron will kept the big bird up; lightning looked wonderful through the little eyeholes in its underbelly; the bar was open all the way from Newfoundland; and the woman next to me was stone-deaf so I spoke to her all the way, more wildly and more wildly as the plane lurched on through dark and lion-thunder and the fire-water yelled through my blood like Sioux, and she unheard all my delirium with a smile; and then the Red Indians scalped me; and then it was London, and my iron will brought the bird down safely, with only one spine-cracking jar. And, queasy, purple, maggoty, scalped, I weak-wormed through festoons, bunting, flags, great roses, sad spangles, paste and tinsel, the million cardboard simpers and ogrish plaster statuettes of the nincompoop queen, I crawled as early as sin in the chilly weeping morning through the city's hushed hangover and all those miles of cock-deep orange-peel, nibbled sandwiches, broken bottles, discarded vests, vomit and condoms, lollipops, senile fish, blood lips, old towels, teeth, turds, soiled blowing newspapers by the unread mountain, all the spatter and bloody gravy and giant mousemess that go to show how a loyal and phlegmatic people—'London can break it!'—enjoyed themselves like hell the day before. And, my God, wouldn't I have enjoyed it too! In the house where I stay in London, a party was still going on, at half-past seven in the wet, beige morning, that had started two nights before. Full of my news, of the latest American gossip from the intellectual underworld, of tall goings-on, of tiny victories and disasters, aching to gabble I found myself in a company of amiable, wrestling, maudlin, beetleskulled men, semi-men, and many kinds of women, who did not know or care I had been so far and wildly away but seemed to think I had been in the party all the whooping time. Sober, airsick, pancaked flat, I saw these intelligent old friends as a warrenfull of blockish stinkers, and sulked all morning over my warm beer as they clamoured and hiccupped, rolled rodgering down, fell gaily through windows, sang and splintered. And in the afternoon, I stood—I was the only one who could—alone and disillusioned among the snorers and the dead. They grunted all around me, or went soughing and green to their Maker. As the little murdered moles in the Scotch poem, like sma' Assyrians they lay. I was close to crying there, in the chaotic middle of anticlimax. It was all too sordid. Oh how I hated these recumbent Bohemians! Slowly, I went upstairs to bath. There was a man asleep in the bath. And tears ran down my cheeks. Two creatures stretched dead in my bed. And, now, rain was boo-hooing too all over London.

P.S. I am sorry to add to this that by the end of the day I was happy as a pig in shit myself, and conducted the singing of hymns with my broken arm, and chased people and was caught, and wound up snug as a bugger in Rugby. Oh, my immortal soul, and oh, my tissues!

I returned to Laugharne ten days later; and now, in my left mind again, I shall begin to go on with the Adventures In The Skin-Trade. It is still raining here, just as when I left, but the sun hops in and out between the drizzles and fish skip in the sea and the old people are dying off like moths and our murderer goes around with an axe hanging by a string from his belt and white owls wheeze in the castle and there was a fight in the churchyard last night and I can hear now the cries of the village idiot being tortured by children in the Square and Aeron my daughter rides the waves proud on a rubber swan and Colm on a red duck and Ted Roethke is coming down in three weeks and we're going to Ireland together and Caitlin's brown as a berry from the bits of the sun through the West rain and I've revised 'Under Milk Wood' for an English publisher, adding many pages, and here comes the sun again and things, all said and done, all dead and gone, are just about liveable, praise bloody be!

I could find no silver belt, but, before leaving, commissioned someone to search for and buy one and I know she will; so any day now, Gene will have it, with my love. I hope she is well again.

Thank you very much for the photographs of you, Cecil Scott, and me: we all look like vampires full of breakfast.

Did I see you before I recorded for the Hairies?[1] I took your advice, and

[1] Thomas's nickname for the founders of Caedmon, Barbara Holdridge and Marianne Mantell.

read only my poems on both sides of the disc. The Yeats I had no time to do—my own recording lasted all night long—but I will record when I return. I may be returning—though my Californian plans are still cloudy—in October. Another performance of Milk Wood has tentatively been dated for October 6 or 7, and I've been invited to an International Literary Conference at Pittsburgh a few days later. So I may see you quite soon, with Caitlin too, and see more of you, and clearer, than this last muddled time.

I am giving some radio readings of American poets in August, but cannot find the copy you gave me of your book of American Poetry. Could the publishers send me one, do you think? I do hope so: it is a fine book, and I should like it very much, and it will be useful.

And I would, a lot, appreciate Mrs. beautiful Adlai's last hundred dollars (minus expenses) as there are hundreds of debts to settle here. Could you, *quickly*?

The murder of the Rosenbergs should make all men sick and mad.[1]

Yours always,
Dylan

Thank you for everything you did for me, Oscar, during my stay, before & after, for the Mentor contract[2] & countless kindnesses, and for being in New York and for being at all. Caitlin sends her love.

MS: Harvard   *SL*

MEREDITH JONES
22 June 1953 [draft]   Boat House Laugharne Carmarthenshire

Dear Meredith Jones,

Thank you very much for your letter. I'm so glad I'm not too late to come & talk at the Summer School, & I'll look forward to Porthcawl on the 5th of August. And many thanks for your kind invitation to stay with you that night: I'd be very glad to.

As to a fee: I suggest 15 guineas, plus return railway fare from Laugharne. If this is considered *too* handsome, I'll not bite the hand that gives me ten. But naturally I prefer 15, & do consider it appropriate for an hour's fairly strenuous reading of poems with comments. If you want a title, would just that do: 'A Reading of Poems, With Comments'? I think of reading a collection of modern British & American poems, with passages of introduction, explanation, & criticism, etc. Wd that do?

I hope to hear from you again about further details.

And once more, I'm very pleased I'll be able to come along.

Yours

MS: Texas

[1] Julius and Ethel Rosenberg, convicted of spying against the United States for the Soviet Union, were executed on 19 June 1953, despite international appeals for clemency.
[2] The *Skin Trade* paperback contract.

LLEWELYN THOMAS
23 June 1953 [draft, incomplete]   Boat House Laugharne

Dear Llewelyn,
   I've been back here now about three weeks, as Mummy probably told
you, with a broken arm. I managed this just before catching the homeward plane in New York. When we all came back from Italy, I did at least
wait till we had got to London before tripping over a wire. This time, it
was in an hotel bedroom in the dark: I woke up & couldn't find the light
and got out of bed & tripped over my suitcase—crack! I screamed and
screamed, but nobody came so I had to go back to bed.
   I may be returning to America this autumn for another month or two,
to write the libretto of an opera. But what I really want to do is to go with
you & Mummy to Majorca for a holiday. I don't know about the others.
Try to find out what

MS: Texas

LLEWELYN THOMAS
[?] [draft]

My dear Llewelyn,
   What are you doing, always catching colds? You are the coldest boy in
England! You should be an Eskimo

living in a

and fishing in a

DAVID HIGHAM[1]
[early July 1953] [incomplete]

[...] I enclose a copy [of *Under Milk Wood*] *unrevised*. This is the version which was performed—or, rather, spoken in performance—in New York. I am now *adding* quite a lot to this, and changing quite a bit which is more effective on the stage, I think, than it would be on the printed page. The greatest amount of *addition* will take place late in the script, after page 47. The play (for voices), as you know, is an evocative description of a Welsh town-that-never-was from, roughly, midnight to midnight. And in *this* version, it will be seen that *dusk* arrives too sharply and suddenly and that the whole of the day *up to* the dusk much overbalances, in emphasis and bulk, the day *after* dusk. This was all right on the stage: the thing ran an hour and twenty minutes, straight dramatic reading with no intervals, and it was about as much as, in my opinion, an audience could be expected to take. Now, however, I am paying as much attention to the evening as, say, to the morning; and I hope to improve MILK WOOD very much structurally by this.

It's extremely concentrated—in parts, anyway—and *has* to be short anyway. It can be made to *look* quite a nice book, I think. And I've got a lot of faith in it myself—perhaps because I enjoyed it so much, and am still enjoying the additions and alterations.

Please take no notice of the dim red lines on the enclosed script.

P.S. This, looking at it again, will be quite a *lot* altered in small detail.

TS: J. M. Dent

P. H. NEWBY
15 July 1953   Boat House Laugharne Carmarthenshire

Dear Mr. Newby,
I'd be delighted to read Sir Gawain and the Green Knight—(did J. R. R. Tolkien write a very good children's book, The Hobbit?)—and thank you very much for asking me.[2]

Yes, I *was* going to America this month, but have put it off now until October. More than likely I'll be back before Christmas—but, anyway, would it be possible to do the recordings any time before October?

I'm coming to London next week. Shall I give you a ring? Perhaps we could have a drink together. And could I get, then, a copy of the translation?

---

[1] Quoted in a letter from David Higham to E. F. Bozman at Dent, 8 July 1953. Thomas's letter has disappeared.
[2] Tolkien had made a new translation of the medieval poem. Newby wanted six 30-minute readings.

I must apologise to you—& to my friend, Gilbert Phelps—for never having done anything about that Personal Anthology. I'd still like to do a reading of modern American poets. Perhaps we can talk about that when—as I hope—we meet? Anyway, I'll ring you early next week. And thank you again.

Sincerely,
Dylan Thomas

MS: BBC

MR [?RIOEDAN]
15 July '53 (Gives permission to quote from poems. See Appendix 68.)

MR DAVIES[1]
July 16 1953 [draft]   Boat House Laugharne Carmarthenshire

Dear Mr Davies

I'm so sorry not to have answered your letter long before this: I've been away, and unfortunately no letters were sent on. And I'm sorry, too, I'm not the chap you thought I was. After such a charming letter, I feel I really should be, but I just *can't* change Swansea Grammar to Pencader Grammar School however hard I try. The time is right, about 25 years ago; it's the place that's the trouble. But it's strange that photograph that rang a bell in your belfry. My parents never told me of a twin brother banished to Pencader—I apologise for the word 'banished': that other boy's parents wd have considered Swansea the place of banishment—and I have, I'm *very* glad to say, never as yet seen any human being look quite like me. (Even *I* don't look like me half the time, which is some consolation.) So I'm afraid it's a mistake. But thank you indeed for being so very pleasant to me, & I'm delighted that you like my writing. I do hope you've thoroughly recovered from your operation now.

With all best wishes,

Yours sincerely,
Dylan Thomas

(of S'sea, I'm almost sure, not Pencader. You see that grain of doubt you've planted in my mind?)

MS: Texas

[1] An unidentified correspondent.

THEODORE ROETHKE
17 July 1953   Boat House Laugharne Carmarthenshire
                               Telephone Laugharne (pronounced Larn) 68

Dear Ted,

Thank you for your letter & enclosures. I liked the revision of the fine poem, and the other two poems, Squeeze & Dinky, are better, or nicer anyway, than Goethe.

I don't think damn it I'll be able to raise enough lovely to get to Ireland in the *very* near future—bills suddenly stormed in, and the Eisteddfod cost a tiny fortune and my health—but I'll try. I'll try all right.

I'm coming to London on Monday the 20th. I don't know where I'm staying yet, as where I stay isn't any more, but will you *please* leave a message at the Savage Club, 1, Carlton House Terrace, London, S.W.3.—the number's in the telephone book.

If you haven't found one yet, a pretty good hotel is the Royal Court, Sloane Square, Chelsea—but just a little stuffy.

The BBC Third Programme is *longing* for you—the word is the word of the old fat friend, John Davenport, I got hold of on the BBC—&we'll see him when we meet & fix up a torrential recording.

Hope this reaches you at the American Express.

I'm glad your wife was Beatrice O'Connell & is now Roethke. My wife was Caitlin Macnamara and is now unfortunate.

All the best to you both from both of us.

                                                        Dylan

MS: Washington   *SL*

THEODORE ROETHKE
[July 1953] (Note, with instructions for reaching Laugharne. See Appendix 69.)

JEAN LEROY
28 July 1953   Boat House Laugharne Carmarthenshire

Dear Daphne Richards,
I mean, Dear Jean LeRoy,

Sorry not to have written before: I've just got back here. And back to find I haven't a spare copy of 'Under Milk Wood' to do the Mademoiselle cuts on.[1] The copy I have I'm working on, slowly, in a quite different way:

[1] Extracts from the play appeared in *Mademoiselle* in February 1954.

I'm adding to it. The only other copy, Bozman of Dent's has. I think he'd part with it. If you let me have it then at once, I could send it back by return or, if you wished, airmail it direct to Cyrilly Abels. It's all a nuisance, I know, but it's not all my doing: the number of typescripts was, in the first case, very limited, most of these going to the cast that read it in New York; Cyrilly Abels returned her copy to Poetry Center, New York, where the thing was performed, asking them to let me have it to cut. This copy was sent to me, & I sent it to Higham who gave it to Bozman. I cut the end of the page as I'd added yet another complication which is best, at the moment, forgotten.

Can you do anything?

About Muggeridge & Punch.[1] I *haven't* written any satirical verses about America, but only a piece of satirical prose, which I used as an introduction to some poetry readings there and is (a) unsuitable, (b) incomplete as a piece. By 'unsuitable', I mean I don't think it's good enough for Punch. But I would very much like to write a piece, or pieces, *for* Punch as soon as I can.

And please thank Mr MM for asking me.

Yours,
Dylan Thomas

MS: Texas

OSCAR WILLIAMS
[28 July 1953]   Boat House Laugharne Carmarthenshire

Our Dear Oscar,

Very many thanks; which always begins every letter to you. For your own letter; for the Selected Williams—thank you for sending the *right* Williams; and for the American Anthology. This is very brief because I have just come back from London, rain, despair, Roethke, publishers, agents, wee brawls, schoolboards, snubs, snobs, ulcerous luncheons, and am depressed here & insolvent in Wales and rain. I'm enclosing, signed, the note of permission. 14 poems! Dear God, we'd better not become any better friends, even if we could. And it's wonderful of you to say you think you can manage to get the * 'round fee' for me straightaway. Oh, I *do* hope so. I'm down the drain again, and have arranged to send Aeron to a boardingschool next term, which is hideously expensive, and what with taxes and the immortal soul it's hardly worth keeping your head above the shit. (Surely, by the way, I did, didn't I, damn me, acknowledge the last lovely manuscript hundred you sent? If I didn't, I do now most gratefully. If I did, I do again.) And another by-the-way, though a furious one this time: the Caedmon Hairies, Marianne & Barbara, paid me only 200 dollars of the 500 dollars they were supposed to pay me—on signing of contract—for that last recording of my own poems. They promised to send me—personally, not to my agent—the other 300 by July 1st. I'm writing this, rot them, on July 28. I want their hairy money.

I read American poems, including, of course, yours, to the University of Wales a week or so ago. And will be broadcasting some soon again. I'll let you know details.

Caitlin sends her love to you & Gene and so do I.

I do hope (again) you can airmail that cabbage back (see asterisk on first page).

Ever,
Dylan

Just finishing final revision of 'Under Milk Wood'. It's quite a bit better. Would you like the ms? or, rather, bunches of the working sheets?

D.

Do you know—I mean, can you get for me—the Hairies' address? I'll send them the crabs of a letter.   D.

I'll write *fully* next time, v soon.

MS: Harvard

ELI MORTLAKE[1]

28 July 1953 [?draft]   Boat House Laugharne Carmarthenshire

Dear Eli Mortlake,

Yes, I had heard about Helen's death, and was very sad. I would have written you, but had no address.

Certainly I would like to write something—'anything', as you say —about Helen, but it is extremely difficult: I knew Helen very little indeed, though the little I knew made me most fond of her; and I hadn't seen her for years. Also, I'm awfully bad at remembering times and places. I know the first time I met her was in Glasgow, and the other times must have been in London —usually, I imagine, with Sydney Graham and Colquhoun & MacBryde.[2] But the details are irredeemably blurred, and all I remember really, from these occasions, was Helen's sweetness, strength, and humour. I wish there something of use that I *could* write.

I shall be in London very soon. Would you care to meet and have a drink? If you'll let me know, I could drop you a line to say just when I'd be there.

Thank you very much for the letter.

Yours,
Dylan Thomas

MS: Texas

[1] Unidentified correspondent.
[2] The painters Robert Colquhoun and Robert MacBryde.

RALPH WISHART[1]
July 28 1953   Boat House Laugharne Carmarthenshire

Dear Ralph,
I'm really terribly sorry about the misunderstanding and you've every right to think I'm a dirty dog. Well, I am, if you like, a middle-aged dog with a dirty mind, but of course I was coming to see you, and still am, and always will, and the reason for my not coming in on Monday or afterwards is very simple. I was driven up from Laugharne on the day of that broadcast, arriving in good time—good time, that is, for a quick one in the King's Head—about seven o'clock in the evening. You were, of course, shut. After the broadcast was, to the relief of thousands, over, I was driven straight back to Laugharne—if you can call it straight, stopping about thirty times—and I haven't been to Swansea since.
I didn't write to explain, as perhaps I should, because I knew I was coming up to Swansea any time to call on the B.B.C. and I would be meeting you then. Now I'm coming up, for the first time since I saw you after my Llangollen visit, tomorrow, Thursday, to see D.J.T.V. Thomas.[2] I'll drop in after lunch—with, I hope to God, a cheque.
How's Dan? I'll be seeing him too, I hope. Thanks for everything, & sorry again.

                                   All the best,
                                   Dylan

Only source: SL

FELIX GERSTMAN[3]
28 July 1953 [draft]   Boat House Laugharne Carmarthenshire Wales

Dear Mr Gerstman,
Very many thanks for your letter, which interested me considerably. I'm grateful to Mr Watson Pierce for introducing us.
I hope to be in New York for a short visit in October, and would very much like to get in touch with you then. There are a number of things I would like to discuss. I'll let you know well beforehand my New York dates so that—as I hope—we can arrange to meet. Thank you again.
                                   Sincerely yours
MS: Texas   Dylan Thomas

[1] Ralph Wishart (1911–75), 'Ralph the Books', a Swansea character, had been a second-hand bookseller in the town since the 1930s.
[2] David J. Thomas was the BBC producer in charge of 'A Story'. Thomas performed it on August 10 in a makeshift studio, a clergyman's library with a camera rigged up; it was his only solo appearance on television.
[3] An agent with whom Thomas hoped to arrange a more lucrative U.S. lecture tour.

DANIEL JONES
Monday August 24 1953   Laugharne

Dear Dan,
   Will you be in Swansea this week? John Ormond came down here,
warbling and nut-fed, a few days ago, and said you were in Cardiff. If you
aren't, and are home again, will you let me know quickly? I don't want to
come to adanabandoned Swansea.
   I owe you some money, and hope to give it to you when I see you. Did
you see [. . .], after his intentional and contemptuous failure to turn up? or
had he forgotten? I can only suppose he never meant a word of it, and
thought it fun. I still need fifty pounds *terribly*, which should make him
laugh his head off.
   I have to see T.V.D.J. Thomas in Swansea, *and* Aneirin, but will get
that over quickly and then—oh, to bask unasked in a Bass cask, etc!
   Isn't life awful? Last week I hit Caitlin with a plate of beetroot, and I'm
still bleeding. I can't finish a poem, or begin a story, I chew my nails down
to my shoulders, pick three-legged horses with beautiful names, take my
feet for grey walks, moulder in Brown's, go to bed as though to an office,
read with envy of old lonely women who swig disinfectant by the pint,
think about money, dismiss it as dirt, think about dirt.
   Do write a postcard, if you're at home, or telephone Laugharne 68.

                                                        Ever,
                                                        Dylan

MS: Texas   *SL*

MIMI JOSEPHSON
25th August 1953   Laugharne

Dear Mimi Josephson,
   Thank you so much for sending me John O'London. Naturally, I liked
your article a lot, and thought it awfully well done and full of fun and
sense. 'Naturally', because it made such a splendid rumbustious figure of
this melancholy bad-natured slob mouldering away in his mud-hole by
the wish washy water. But I think you did a really warm, and lively, and
imaginative job. The portrait was excellent, and depressing. Caitlin says,

by the way: we have *six* rooms and a kitchen; but that is another storey. Many thanks again.

Yours,
Dylan Thomas

TS: J. M. Dent

PETER DAVIES
25th August 1953 (Agrees to sign books. See Appendix 70.)

ALAN HODGE[1]
August 25 1953   Boat House Laugharne Carmarthenshire

Dear Alan,

So sorry not to have written long before this. I lost your letter almost as soon as I got it, and didn't know where to write you. I found the letter this morning.

I'm very glad you and Robert Graves are hoping to get a publisher to bring out a collected Norman. And of course I'd like to write down some of my memories of him. I was awfully young when I first knew Norman in the early 30's, and so bloody full of myself, or full of my bloody self, that that wonderful time is mostly vague and muddled now; I remember all the feel of it, but not many happenings or details. But I'll try, I'll try all right.

I'm coming to London next week. Would you meet and have a drink? Perhaps you'll make me remember some more. I'm even dim about Night Custard, though I was there at its first stirring. I remember better the Unpopular Man, that Old Normal and I made together.

Shall I give you a ring at History Today?

Yours ever,
Dylan

TS: Jane Aiken Hodge

[1] Alan Hodge (1915–79), author and historian. He had written to ask Thomas for his recollections of Norman Cameron, who died earlier in 1953. A draft of the letter is at Texas; a typescript copy was with Alan Hodge's papers.

STEPHEN SPENDER
August 25th 1953   Boat House Laugharne Carmarthenshire

Dear Stephen,
 Sorry not to have written much sooner about *Encounter*:[1] I mislaid your letter.
 I'm glad you want something of mine, and wish I had something to send straightaway. I'm working on a small poem now, and will let you have it when ready. As for that extract of a novel you saw in New World Writing: do you remember which extract it was? Two have been printed in New World Writing so far. The first extract, 'A Fine Beginning', has been printed in England. But the second—which appeared in the last number of N.W.W.—called 'Four Lost Souls' hasn't been printed anywhere except there & I'm sure you could get permission to use it. I hope you do.[2]

                                                   Yours,
                                                   Dylan

MS: Harvard

CYRIL CONNOLLY
5 9 '53   Boat House Laugharne Carmarthenshire

Dear Cyril,
 Here's *my* permission to include the three poems you wanted in The Golden Horizon.[3] The book-publishers of the three poems were, in England, J. M. Dent, &, in America, New Directions.

                                                   Yours ever,
                                                   Dylan

MS: Texas

E. F. BOZMAN
11th September 1953   Boat House Laugharne Carmarthenshire
                                                   Laugharne 68

Dear E. F. Bozman,
 I was sorry I wasn't able to see you when I came to London last: I'd a

---

[1] Spender was a founding editor (with Irving Kristol) of *Encounter*, first published October 1953.
[2] 'Four Lost Souls' didn't appear in *Encounter*.
[3] *The Golden Horizon* (1953), an anthology of extracts from the magazine.

very short time there—just for a little broadcast, and to see about my daughter's new school—and David Higham told me that, so far as he knew, there was nothing very urgent to discuss. I wanted to meet you anyway; and I do hope now we'll be able to lunch together before I go to the States early in October.

Well before I leave, I'll have finished the final corrections and amplifications of 'Under Milk Wood'. I think it's much better now—(it sounds as though it had been ill). One of the reasons I'm going to America is to take part in three public readings of it, with a professional cast, at the Poetry Center, New York. (The other, and main, reason is to go to California to begin work with Stravinsky on a new opera.) And, when I return some time in December, I hope that it can be given one or more reading-performances, most likely on a Sunday night, in London; with any luck, I'll be able to get firstrate Welsh actors to read it. Higham, in the meantime, and as soon as he has my complete version, will see to it that someone like Sherek[1] has a chance of reading it with this in mind. 'Under Milk Wood' will also be broadcast next year, in full, and it should be possible to arrange this broadcast to happen about the same time as publication. I myself have good hopes altogether of the success of Milk Wood; and I'm *very very* grateful to you for taking it over.

About the *Book of Stories*—I suggest, tentatively, the title of 'Early One Morning', the title of one of the stories:—I have reckoned out that there are now eleven of these, including a very recent one that will, I think, be appearing in next week's 'Listener'.[2] And I want to write two or three more, still on a childhood theme, to complete the book. In spite of what you very rightly say about the 'rawness' of the other, and earlier, stories I sent you some time ago, I still think that one, and one alone, of these 'A Prospect of The Sea' could well take its place in the volume. Perhaps, when you have the rest of the stories together, you would consider this again? (Though I may very well be completely wrong about it.) And, thinking back, *yes*, 'Early One Morning' does seem to me a good title.

Higham told me that you were prepared to consider again the short novel, 'Adventures In the Skin Trade'. I'm so glad. When I come back from America, I intend to settle down & finish it. And, after that, another 'Play for Voices', using the same form as in Milk Wood.

Now to a much more difficult part of this letter. Straightaway, I just *must* say that I'm in money trouble again, and this time quite seriously again. And I'm wondering, and hoping terribly much, that somehow you can help me. I really do need help at this very moment. As perhaps you know, David Higham has taken over what I suppose I must call my 'financial affairs' in a very expert way. As well as seeing to my eldest children's school-fees—my daughter will be beginning boarding-school next week—he also keeps money aside for income-tax and allows me a

[1] Henry Sherek (d. 1967), theatre producer.
[2] 'A Story', the television broadcast.

sum per month for personal expenses. But I'm afraid that that sum isn't enough to pay tradesmen's accounts etc. and now I'm being pressed to pay at once some most urgent debts I have simply had to incur over recent months. I cannot ask Higham to help me with these: he is doing all he possibly can with the money at his disposal. And I do not know what on earth to do. I'm trying to put this down as simply and flatly as I can; but, really, I'm *sick* with anxiety, and find it terribly hard to work. What's particularly infuriating is, that I'm about to make quite a lot of money in the States. The Stravinsky libretto is, in itself, an assurance of that. (I hope one day you'll publish the libretto.) And I'm going to give a short series of very well paid commercial lectures—(I mean by that, not to universities, as on my previous visits, but in town halls & to large unacademic paying audiences. The lectures, incidentally, won't be lectures, but readings of poetry). There money is, a lot of it, so near; and here I am in the most awful position, owing money to everywhere here and the debts mounting every day nightmarishly. I can't say 'Stravinsky' to tradesmen, insurance, etc. etc. Oh Lord, I am in a mess.

Can you help? I don't know how. And really, I need help without Higham's—no, I can't say 'knowledge', that sounds like working behind his back; perhaps I mean his friendly superintendence. He thinks me extravagant, as perhaps I am. But my debts are all for unextravagant country living, & they've mounted up horribly. Have you any suggestions? Could Dent advance me any good sum on 'Milk Wood', or on 'Early One Morning'. Or could I somehow borrow money & pay it back from my American earnings in October & November? It's so hard for me to think. We haven't, now, even enough to take Aeronwy & Llewelyn to their schools next week; & it seems so silly; but the silliness is frightening in this remote place. Or in any place, I suppose, except that here nearly everyone is very poor: certainly, all my friends. Now I am beginning to gabble.

Can you write me, or ring me?[1]

When I rang this afternoon, I felt too awkward to say anything. I couldn't even *ask* for your private address, which is what I had rung for. Forgive me. And for this letter.

I just realised: in one breath I talk of going to the States in a very few weeks, probably three weeks or less, & in the next breath say we cannot afford the trains to London. This sounds absurd. My American ticket is, of course, paid for by the Poetry Center New York. But before I go, I *have* to clear up everything here & leave it (almost) sweet & smiling.

Yours,

Dylan Thomas

---

[1] Bozman sent a stern but kindly reply, refusing to cheat Higham. 'You have every reason, Thomas,' he wrote, 'to look forward to a brilliant and successful future, not only in fame *but FINANCIALLY*!' On Bozman's letter Thomas drew a gargoyle with a squint, and wrote the name of a horse for the 4.30.

And I daren't look back over the last part of this letter in case I cross it all out in horrified embarrassment.

MS: J. M. Dent   *SL*

PRINCESS CAETANI
[?1953] [incomplete draft][1]

Dear Marguerite Caetani,
    What can I say?
    Why do I bind myself always into these imbecile grief-knots, blindfold my eyes with lies, wind my brass music around me, sew myself in a sack, weight it with guilt and pig-iron, then pitch me squealing to sea, so that time and time again I must wrestle out and unravel in a panic, like a seaslugged windy Houdini, and ooze and eel up wheezily, babbling and blowing black bubbles, from all the claws and bars and breasts of the mantrapping seabed?
    Deep dark down there, where I chuck the sad sack of myself, in the slimy squid-rows of the sea there's such a weed-drift and clamour of old plankton drinkers, such a mockturtle gabble of wrecked convivial hydrographers tangled with polyps and blind prawns, such a riffraff of seabums in the spongy dives, so many jellyfish soakers jolly & joking in the smoke-blue basements, so many salty sea-damaged daughters stuffing their wounds with fishes, so many lightning midnight makers in the luminous noon of the abysmal sea, and such fond despair there, always there, that time and time again I cry to myself as I kick clear of the cling of my stuntman's sacking, 'Oh, one time the last time will come and I'll never struggle, I'll sway down here forever handcuffed and blindfold, sliding my woundaround music, my sack trailed in the slime, with all the rest of the self-destroyed escapologists in their cages, drowned in the sorrows they drown and in my piercing own, alone and one with the coarse and cosy damned seahorsey dead, weeping my tons.'
    What can I tell you? Why did I bray my brassy nought to you from this boygreen briny dark? I see myself down and out on the sea's ape-blue bottom: a manacled rhetorician with a wet trombone, up to his blower in crabs.
    Why must I parable my senseless silence? my one long trick? my last dumb flourish? It is [not] enough that, by the wish I abominate, I savagely

---

[1] There is no version of this letter in the Caetani archive. It was probably drafted at Laugharne during Thomas's last summer there, and left unfinished to be found by one of the collectors who descended on the Boat House after his death. Texas has several sheets, covered with trial phrases: 'babbling and blowing bubbles, like a wheezy Houdini', 'don't I smell fishy as I ooze webfooted', 'arse over head', 'dandruff over corns', 'up to their sockets in snails', 'up to their skulls in crabs', 'spare me a copper for a cuppa for my supper'. And 'down at eel'.

contrive to sink lashed and bandaged in a blind bag to those lewd affectionate raucous stinking cellars: no, I must blare my engulfment in pomp and fog, spout a nuisance of fountains like a bedwetting [?whale] in a blanket, and harangue all land-walkers as though it were their shame that I sought the sucking sea and cast myself out of their sight to blast down to the dark. It is not enough to presume that once again I shall weave up pardoned, my wound din around me rusty, and waddle and gush along the land on my webbed sealegs as musical and wan and smug as an orpheus of the storm: no, I must first defeat any hope I might have of forgiveness by resubmerging the little arisen original monster in a porridge boiling of wrong words and make a song and dance and a mock-poem of all his fishy excuses.

The hell with him.

MS: Texas   *SL*

PETER DAVIES
15 Sept 1953   Boat House Laugharne

Dear Mr. Davies,
    Sorry not to have answered straightaway. Yes, do come down if you want to this week: any day except Thursday. I won't be at my house, as all the family's gone to London: but you can leave a message for me at Laugharne 13: the pub.

                                                        Sincerely,
TS: Thomas Trustees   Dylan Thomas

IGOR STRAVINSKY
September 22 1953 The Boat House Laugharne Carmarthenshire Wales

Dear Igor Stravinsky,
    Thank you very very much for your two extremely nice letters, and for showing me the letter you had written to Mr Choate of Boston University. I would have written again long before this, but I kept on waiting until I knew for certain when I would be able to come to the States; and the lecture-agent there in New York, who makes my coming across possible, has been terribly slow in arranging things. I heard from him only this week. Now it is certain that I shall be in New York on the 16th of October; and I'll have to stay there, giving some poetry-readings and taking part in a couple of performances of a small play of mine, until the end of October. I should like then, if I may, to come straight to California to be with you and to get down together to the first stage of our work. (I'm sure I needn't tell you how excited I am to be able to write down that word 'our'. It's wonderful to think of.)

One of my chief troubles is, of course, money. I haven't any of my own, and most of the little I make seems to go to schools for my children, who will persist in getting older all the time. The man who's arranged my readings in October, at a few Eastern universities and at the Poetry Center, New York, is paying my expenses to and from New York. But from there to California I will have to pay my own way on what I can make out of those readings. I do hope it will work out all right. Maybe I'll be able to give a few other readings, or rantings, in California to help pay expenses. (I'd relied on drawing my travelling expenses etc from the original Boston University commission.) I want to bring my wife Caitlin with me, and she thinks she can stay with a friend in San Francisco while I'm working with you in Hollywood. Anyway, I'll have to work these things out the best I can, and I mustn't bother you with them now. Money for California will come somehow. I'll pray for ravens to drop some in the desert. The *main* thing, I know, is for me to get to you as soon as possible, so that we can begin—well, so that we can *begin*, whatever it will turn out to be. I've been thinking an awful lot about it.

I was so sorry to hear you had been laid up for so long: I hope you're really well again by this time. My arm's fine now, and quite as weak as the other one.

If you don't write to me at Wales before I leave, about October 7th, then my American address will be: c/o J. M. BRINNIN, POETRY CENTER, YM-YWHA, 1395 Lexington Avenue, New York 28. But anyway I'll write again as soon as I reach there.

I'm looking forward enormously to meeting you again, and to working with you. And I *promise* not to tell anyone about it—(though it's very hard not to).

Most sincerely,
Dylan Thomas

MS: Paul Sacher Foundation, Basle

CLIFFORD ROBERTS
9th October 1953 [?draft]   The Boat House Laugharne Carmarthenshire

Dear Mr. Roberts,
Thank you very much indeed for your kind invitation to me to attend the Port-Reeve's Annual Breakfast this coming Sunday. Unfortunately, I am going to London today, & from there to America, and will have to miss the pleasure of the Breakfast. I am indeed sorry, but wish you a very successful Sunday morning & the best of wishes over the coming year.

Yours sincerely,
Dylan Thomas

MS: Thomas Trustees

JOHN MALCOLM BRINNIN
[telegram, October 17 1953, from London]

TICKET ARRIVED COUPLE DAYS TOO LATE NOW CATCHING
PLANE 7.30 PM MONDAY 19TH DESPERATELY SORRY. DYLAN.

Original: Delaware

ELLEN STEVENSON
[telegram, October 25 1953, 9.51 pm, New York]

DEAR ELLEN OSCAR WILLIAMS HAS TOLD ME THAT YOU WOULD
LIKE ME TO PRESENT MY PLAY ENTITLED 'UNDER MILKWOOD'
IN CHICAGO I SHALL BE DELIGHTED TO DO SO WITH OR WITH-
OUT CAST BUT NOT WITHOUT CASH SOME TIME BETWEEN
NOVEMBER 12TH AND NOVEMBER 15TH ON MY WAY TO HOLLY-
WOOD WOULD YOU KINDLY GET IN TOUCH WITH MY MANA-
GER JOHN BRINNIN 100 MEMORIAL DRIVE FOR FULL DETAILS
THANK YOU VERY MUCH LOOK FORWARD TO SEEING YOU
WITH WARM REGARDS DYLAN THOMAS

Original: Texas   *SL*

Dylan Thomas's last public engagement was a lunchtime reading at the City
College of New York on Thursday 29 October 1953. He spent much of the next
few days with Elizabeth Reitell. He seemed exhausted and unwell, and drank
heavily. The detective hired by *Time* magazine padded along behind him and his
friends. On the night of Saturday October 31, Thomas, in a bar on 7th Avenue,
was heard to say that all women were only substitutes for Caitlin. He was also
seen to be taking benzedrine. On the night of Wednesday November 4 the
assiduous detective noted a 'get-together' at the Chelsea. The friends left;
Elizabeth Reitell remained. In fact, the doctor with the 'winking needle', Milton
Feltenstein, had injected Thomas with half a grain of morphine to relieve the
symptoms caused by alcohol. This amounted to an overdose. About 1 am on
November 5, Thomas collapsed in a coma. He died in hospital without recovering
consciousness, four days later, at lunchtime on Monday 9 November 1953.

APPENDIX A
Incidental Letters

The letters here—chosen by rule-of-thumb as being of no great importance—have been separated from the main text, where the place of each is marked.

1 PAMELA HANSFORD JOHNSON

[Editor's note:]
The play, 'Spajma and Salnady' (the names are anagrams), is in *Early Prose Writings*, which omits two lines that follow the play: 'And in the distance, Pamela, I think I can hear the baying of the 147 Jews. Forgive much. Write soon. Dylan.' She noted its receipt in her diary, January 17.

MS: Buffalo

2 GLYN JONES
[Christmas 1934]   5 Cwmdonkin Drive Uplands Swansea

Dear Glyn,
  This, at the moment, is how the position stands: I wrote you a letter on Wednesday night, addressed, probably, to a legendary street in Cardiff, I having lost your last letter, and in that letter of mine I explained that I was home for Christmas & would be unable to see you before Saturday. Now, I am afraid, the date is Monday, as my sister can't travel before Sunday afternoon. I asked you—in the letter that you probably won't ever receive—to call at 5 Redcliffe Street, S.W.10, where my partner, Janes, would be expecting you; my bedroom is empty & welcome to you, & comrade Janes will see to your home comforts etc. Every-thing's in a devil of a mess, isn't it? If this letter gets you before Monday, *do* follow my instructions & sleep in Redcliffe St. Directions to reach my habitation: Take the 14 bus from Piccadilly, up Brompton Road & Fulham Road to the Redcliffe Arms at the corner of Redcliffe Gardens. Walk straight up Redcliffe Gardens, & my street is about the fourth or fifth on the right.
  Now, if this letter gets you *on* Monday, please do 'phone me immediately: This is my phone number: FLAXMAN 1644. We can then meet, arrange sleeping & accom-modation details, & see everyone we can see together. But don't forget: unless I see you before, *do* go to Redcliffe St & let Janes put you up. He's a very nice chap. Anyway, above is my number. Don't forget it. Monday, then, if not before.

[Cont]

Talk to you about everything then.

The usual apologies
for slackness

Dylan

MS: Carbondale

3   DENYS KILHAM ROBERTS
[?winter 1935/6]   5 Cwmdonkin Drive Uplands Swansea

Dear Mr. Roberts,
    Herewith is the proof of my poem—all correct except for the one singular instead of plural in line [*number missing*] of the verse, which I have corrected.

Dylan Thomas

I suppose I will be notified when the anthology is to appear.

MS: Texas

4   JOHN JOHNSON
[late June 1936]   5 Cwmdonkin Drive Uplands Swansea

That's fine: Saturday 27th; Vianis, 1.15. You'll recognise me easily. I'm short with lots of hair. Sincerely,

Dylan Thomas

TS: Thomas Trustees

5   DENYS KILHAM ROBERTS
[?summer 1936]

   Here are lots of poems for you to see.
   The one beginning, 'A Grief Ago' was printed in 'Oxford Programme'.
   The one beginning, 'Hold hard, these ancient minutes' in 'Caravel', Majorca.
   The one beginning 'Foster The Light' in 'Contemporary Prose & Poetry'.
   The one beginning, 'Do you Not Father Me?' in the 'Scottish Bookman' (now dead, I think).
   The one beginning, 'Ears In The Turrets Hear' in John O'London's Weekly. (Don't I get around?)
   The one beginning, 'Today, this insect', & the one beginning, 'Then Was The Neophyte' are to be printed in 'Purpose'.
   The first seven poems (each *quite* complete by itself) from 'Poems For a Poem', were, as you see, printed in 'Life & Letters To-Day'. The last three have been, or will be, printed in 'Contemporary Prose & Poetry'.
   I've had several fairly recently in New Verse, but I expect you've got all the New Verses: I haven't any copies.
   I do hope you'll be able to use one or some of these.

I hope, really, you'll like one or two of the 'Poems For A Poem'; though they are linked together by a certain obscure narrative, they're entirely self-contained.

Yours sincerely,
Dylan Thomas

MS: Texas

6 JOHN HADFIELD (Publicity Dept, J. M. Dent)
1st September 1936   5 Cwmdonkin Drive Uplands Swansea

Dear Sir,
I'm enclosing a fairly recent photograph of myself as you asked me to. Would you, I wonder, send it back to the address behind the photograph—when you've finished with it.

Yours faithfully
Dylan Thomas

MS: J. M. Dent

7 HERMANN PESCHMANN
January 3 1938   Blashford Ringwood Hants

Dear Mr. Peschmann,
I'm sincerely sorry not to have answered your letter before this. I've been in town recently, & all my papers have been left here, so I couldn't get your address as there was no-one to forward anything. And even now—I do hope you'll excuse my vagueness and carelessness—I can't find the particular letter of yours in which you suggested a reading date for January. I seem to remember it was the 27th(?). Would you be so kind—in spite of this rude delay of mine—as to tell me on what date you had invited me to read, & whether the invitation is still open. I'll be in town from the end of next week on.

Apologies again,
Yours sincerely,
Dylan Thomas

MS: Texas

8   DAVID HIGHAM
January 19 1938   Blashford Ringwood Hants

Dear Higham,
    Thank you very much for managing to get hold of the O.U.P. money so soon; it
was very kind of Charles Williams.
    I'm enclosing the gramophone 'agreements'.
    Hope you can get the short stories along to me soon.
                                        Yours,
                                            Dylan Thomas

MS: Texas

9   JULIAN SYMONS
20 January 1938 Saturday   Blashford Ringwood Hants

Dear Julian Symons,
    I'll be able to let you have a poem by the end of next week. Is that too late?
Poem of abt 40 lines.
                                        Sincerely,
                                            Dylan Thomas

MS: Texas

10   JULIAN SYMONS
[?January 1938]   Blashford Ringwood Hants

Dear Symons,
    Your urgent note has just been forwarded here. I can't think what became of the
poem I sent. Anyway, here is another copy, which I do hope isn't too late; perhaps
the original copy has arrived by this time.
                                        Happy New Year,
                                            Dylan Thomas

MS: Texas

11   DENYS KILHAM ROBERTS
26 February 1938   Blashford Ringwood Hants

Dear Mr Kilham Roberts,
    Of course you have my permission to include *Where once the Waters* and *The
Force that through the Green Fuse* in the Penguin anthology. You needn't write to
ask them, but acknowledgement to the Parton Press—who published my *18
Poems* in which these two poems appeared—should also be made.
                                        Yours sincerely,
                                            Dylan Thomas

MS: Texas

2 JAMES LAUGHLIN
June 1 1938   Gosport Street Laugharne Carmarthenshire S Wales

Dear Laughlin,
Delighted to hear you're in England. Yes, do please come down for the weekend—& for as long as you care to stay. We've a poky cottage, but there's room for you, & extremely welcome.

You take a train from Paddington to Carmarthen and then take a 'bus from Carmarthen to Laugharne. (The 'buses run every hour.) Or else you take a train from Paddington to St. Clears (just beyond Carmarthen) & taxi from there. But I advise the first: to Carmarthen & then 'bus. When you get to Laugharne, go into Brown's Hotel—anybody will tell you where that is—& enquire our whereabouts. It's very easy.

It's about 5 hours, I think, altogether from London to Carmarthen, & then about ½ hour from Carmarthen to Laugharne.

Looking forward very much to seeing you. We expect you Saturday. Start in the morning, early as possible.

> Yours,
> Dylan T.

MS: the recipient

3 BBC
15 October 1938   Sea View Laugharne Carmarthenshire S Wales

Dear Sir,
In reference to your last letter, of October 13: I authorise the broadcast of my poem, 'This Bread I break was once the Oat', as proposed, & agree to the fee of one guinea. Is the day for its performance October 22?

I should very much appreciate being paid as soon as possible the copyright fees for both these poems, as I need badly everything I can get.

> Yours faithfully,
> Dylan Thomas

MS: Texas

4 DAVID HIGHAM
14 May 1939   Sea View Laugharne Carmarthenshire

Dear Higham,
Since posting my letter to you this morning, I've finished my proofs and sent them to Dent's. I'm letting you know this immediately, as you wanted me to.

> Yours,
> Dylan Thomas

MS: Texas

15 J. M. DENT
May 15 1939   Sea View Laughharne Carmarthenshire S Wales

Dear Sir,
   Returning your information sheet. Long delay because I couldn't find a photograph or get one taken. Sorry my answers are so unhelpful. I just live in this small
town on the coast & write as much as I can.
   I enclose two photographs; you can use either, they're privately taken.
                                        Yours truly,
                                        Dylan Thomas

MS: J. M. Dent

16 DAVID HIGHAM
May 16 1939   Sea View Laugharne Carmarthenshire

Dear Higham,
   Thank you a lot. The cheque was tremendously helpful and has the tradesmen
smiling.
   I'll be sending the proofs back this week, & will let you know exactly when.
                                        Yours,
                                        Dylan Thomas

MS: Texas

17 J. M. DENT
August 22 1939   Sea View Laugharne Carmarthenshire

Dear Sir,
   I wish to have 3 more copies—3 copies, that is, over my author's allowance of 6,
which I've received—of my book 'The Map of Love', due out on the 24th of the
month. And could the price of these—at 25% less than the published price, as my
contract says—be deducted from future royalties on the book? I hope you will let
me know if this system of buying extra books is permissible?
                                        Yours truly,
                                        Dylan Thomas

MS: J. M. Dent

18 DAVID HIGHAM
12 Sept 1939   Sea View Laugharne Carmarthenshire

Dear Higham,
   Here are the filled-up forms. I hope, very much indeed, something will come of it.
                                        Yours sincerely,
                                        Dylan Thomas

MS: Texas

9   VERNON WATKINS
30 Nov 1939   Sea View Laugharne

Dear Vernon,
   Would you mind forwarding this letter to Taig? I've been asked to do a one-act play here for something or other, & can't think of a play—I want Taig's advice. Lost his address.
   We'll be seeing you v. soon now, I hope.

                                        Love,
                                          Dylan

MS: British Library

0   LAURENCE POLLINGER
Jan 3 1940   Blashford Ringwood Hants

Dear Pollinger,
   Just to let you know that I am staying at the above address for a few weeks.
   When my monthly Dent cheque comes to you, will you send it on here?
                                        Sincerely,
                                          Dylan Thomas

MS: Texas

I   LAURENCE POLLINGER
March 13 1940   Blashford Ringwood Hants

Dear Laurence Pollinger,
   Thank you for making an exception, and not deducting from my March cheque the money I borrowed from you in advance.
   I haven't been able to return to Wales yet, as I've been waiting to hear from London whether there was the possibility of me getting a war job. I've just heard there is a possibility, and I have to come to town to see about it. Can I be a nuisance again? Will you make another exception? I've had £3, which leaves £4.4.0 (that includes your agency deductions) to come to me next month. Can you advance me that 4 guineas straight away, and take the whole of Dent's next cheque? I may have a little money next month, of my own, but I haven't any this & I've got to get to town. I apologise for making our small transactions so complicated, but I do hope you will let me have, in advance, that remaining 4 guineas. Then everything will be quite clear: Dent's April cheque goes straight to you. I'll be terribly grateful. This job, if I get it, will probably mean a lot to me.
                                        Yours sincerely,
                                          Dylan Thomas

MS: Texas

22   LAURENCE POLLINGER
4th April 1940   Sea View Laugharne Carmarthenshire S Wales

Dear Laurence Pollinger,
    Just to let you know I'm back in Wales, so that any news etc you might have
[for] me can be sent direct. Anything from America? I'm relying on magazines
there (heard from Ann Watkins?) or on Laughlin, New Directions, for some
money soon.

Yours,
Dylan Thomas

MS: Texas

23   MISS M. CRANSTON (Secretary to Laurence Pollinger)
Aug 6 1940   at The Malting House Marshfield nr Chippenham Wilts

Dear Miss Cranston,
    Thank you for your letters. Yes, of course quote Methuen a fee & give them
permission to include my three poems in Day Lewis's & Strong's anthology. Do
you think you could see if I could get the fees for the poems paid *before*
publication? Preferably straight away? I need money urgently.
    If you haven't yet written to your New York people asking for a report on
Laughlin, please don't bother. I have heard from him, he has sent me the $50
dollar cheque &, because of my present position, I will have to accept it. But I
should like to hear about the short story situation: if Ann Watkins can't sell
them, I should like them returned to me.

Yours sincerely,
Dylan Thomas

MS: Texas

24   LAURENCE POLLINGER
[summer 1940]   Malting House Marshfield nr Chippenham Wilts

Dear Pollinger,
    Here is the contract, signed.
    As to clause 15: Laughlin says 'on terms to be arranged', & if, over my next
books, his terms are awful—can I refuse them? Because my next prose book might
sell well.

Sincerely,
Dylan Thomas

Hope you can get the Methuen fee. And that I can hear about Ann Watkins &
those stories.

MS: Texas

5   BBC
28 x 40   At The Malting House Marshfield Chippenham

Dear Sir,
    I thank you for your cheque for twelve guineas (12.12.0.); but feel you must have overlooked the payment for 'COLUMBUS', which was written for Mr. Morley's production about three weeks ago. The fee agreed upon was fifteen guineas (15.15.0).

                                        Yours truly,
                                        Dylan Thomas

MS: BBC

6   H. J. C. MARSHALL
17 Jan 1941   Marston Bishopston Swansea nr Glamorgan

Dear Mr. Marshall,
    Enclosed, two of my last three published books, as requested.

                                        Yours sincerely,
                                        Dylan Thomas

MS: Royal Literary Fund

7   M. J. TAMBIMUTTU
19 February 1941   Marston Bishopston Glamorganshire

Dear Tambimuttu,
    Here are some poems by a friend of mine. Will you read them, please, carefully, and consider them for publication in 'Poetry'? I like them a lot.
    Will you return the ones you don't want to
                        Veronica St. Clear Maclean,
                        Monmouth House
                        24 Lawrence St
                        S.W.3.

                                        Best wishes,
                                        Dylan Thomas

P.S. I haven't finished my own thing for the next number. Will it do for the number after next? Sorry.

MS: Texas

28   M. J. TAMBIMUTTU
May 21 1941   at: Laugharne Castle Laugharne Carmarthenshire

Dear Tambimuttu,
   I haven't heard a word from you yet about the poem I sent you at the end of last month. You did agree that you would pay me at once. I don't wish to be a nuisance, but I must ask you again. *Could you pay me by return?*
   Hope you've come through all the bombing all right.
                                        Yours,
                                           Dylan Thomas

MS: Carbondale

29   BBC
[?1941]   Mars Hotel Frith St Soho

Dear Sirs,
   I apologise for the delay in returning the contract sheet signed. It was not forwarded to me here immediately, by some mistake.
                                        Yours faithfully,
                                           Dylan Thomas

MS: BBC

30   PETER LUNN LTD
25 Sept 44   Majoda New Quay Cardiganshire

Dear Sir,
   Thank you for your note.
   I shall call at your office on Friday, Sept. 29, at 3 p.m., as suggested.
                                        Yours faithfully,
                                           Dylan Thomas

MS: National Library of Wales

31   BBC
16 Feb '45   Majoda New Quay Cardiganshire

Dear Sir,
   I enclose the Reply Sheet, signed.
   The bus fare from New Quay to Carmarthen—return—is five shillings.
                                        Yours faithfully,
                                           Dylan Thomas

MS: BBC

2   LAURENCE POLLINGER
24 March 45   Majoda New Quay Cards

Dear Laurence Pollinger,
   Just a note to say that I've lost Dent's address & am writing to R. Church care of
you. I do hope you'll get the letter to him straight away. Sorry for the bother.
                                                Sincerely,
                                                Dylan Thomas

MS: Texas

3   BBC
November 30th 1945   39 Markham Square Chelsea London SW3

Dear Mr. Alexander,
   Thank you for your letter saying that, in spite of my failure, through illness, to
turn in the script on Augustus John for the Hindustani Service, the fee of seven
guineas, rather than six, which you kindly arranged for me to receive for a 1,200
word script in English on 'Nationalism in Poetry' for the Belgian Service, still
stands.
   I return, signed, the corrected contract, and corrected from 6 to 7 guineas, as
you suggested.
                                                Yours sincerely,
                                                Dylan Thomas

TS: BBC

4   BBC
Nov 30 '45   39 Markham Square Chelsea London SW3

Dear Sir,
   I apologise for not having replied before to your letter of Nov 19 '45 in which
you said that you had enclosed two contracts in another letter to 37 (not my
address) Markham Square. You enclosed, in yours of the 19th, two duplicate
contracts which I now sign and return.
   I take notice of the fact that the contract for my selection & presentation of an
half hour programme of Welsh Poetry to be recorded on 2nd January '46 has been
sent to me on condition that you receive my script on or before the 15th of
December '45.
                                                Yours faithfully,
                                                Dylan Thomas

MS: BBC

5   MARGARET TAYLOR
(omitted from main text, p.579.)

First Poem:
   I find all such descriptive pieces, such nostalgic time-and-place evocations

relying on the impressionist expression of remembered detail, always rather baffling to read unless the actual objects—trees, river, wings etc—are *re-created* for me in a new light. I mean, unless the writer remembers that he is not re-creating *for himself alone* those objects he remembers in such a place and at such a time. He has been there before; I haven't. And therefore he must depict his recollected landscape (or whatever it may be) at several levels: he must see it, as it was, through his own eyes, and also make *me* see it as he saw it *then*; and, either afterwards or simultaneously, he must make us *both* see it freshly and anew.

And so, in this poem, though the words make me begin to *feel* what you felt when you saw that emerald river and those feathered trees, yet I cannot *see* them clearly. And the reason for that is because of the word 'impressionist'. I think it always unsatisfactory to put down the general word rather than the particular: in this instance, the river you describe as being 'spread impressionist' should be *defined* impressionistically. It may become, as it has become in the writing of many poets, a lazy mannerism to describe an object by a kind of group-word: 'cubist fields', 'symphonic rivers', 'architectural mountain': in those tiny examples, all of which have probably been used, there is no clarity of vision at all. To bring it down to complete absurdity: If a certain hill that you wish to describe seems to you architecturally composed and reminiscent of a certain style, it's laziness to say 'the Wren hill'. You should describe that hill in terms of pillar, dome, spire-like trees etc. I don't want to go on plugging this, and it may appear relatively trivial: all I want to do is to emphasise the need, in natural descriptive verse, of a fresh *conceiving* of each object. Emerson said to readers, 'You must read proudly.' I think he meant that readers should not be expected to do the writer's work. And when you use the word 'impressionist', you're asking the reader to project *his own images* into that word and to derive [from] them, what satisfaction he can. 'Here's a suggestion', the poet says, 'of what I mean. Now you work on it.' 'No,' the reader should say, 'take it back and give it again when *you've* put all you know and feel into it. I'll do the rest.'

In two other words of the first verse of poem one, I find rather a discordant ambiguity: the words are '*scorpion*' swans and '*crop*'. It's difficult, I think, leaving a queer, however good, adjective like 'scorpion' all alone in the air. And the verb 'crop', coming almost immediately after, does nothing to add to this word, to strengthen or illuminate it; indeed the verb contradicts and denies the adjective. And so both words lose their meaning.

The second verse has lovely movement, the floating and drifting of the mists implicit in the long-drawn rhythms. But, again, the word 'counterpoint', like the word 'impressionist', halts and hinders me. As a 'proud reader', I have to decline to accept a word upon which I myself have to work unduly. I'm prepared to accept, and to work upon, a difficulty, of meaning, syntax, image, symbol, but, not an evasion of a difficulty. Don't merely tell me there *is* a counterpoint: show it to me in words.

Will you take for granted my same criticism of each undefined generalisation, each group-word, each indefinition, each take-it-or-leave-it vagueness, each arbitrary abstraction, as it occurs in the rest of the poems? I wouldn't have laboured the point so, didn't I think it important and didn't I feel how a really lovely verse (verse two) could be marred by one inexactly realised word.

I like the last verse, though there are memories in it, for me, of passages in Eliot: particularly of passages in 'Burnt Norton' where he writes of 'at the still point of the turning world'. The resemblance, mostly of mood, was probably fortuitous, and matters very little anyway.

Poem Two. Here again, the question of texture is all-important (says Doctor Sneezer, failed B.A., Swansea). The deliberate movement and the careful grouping of words in the first four lines dwindle away as they reach the last, long 'impenetrable'. I should infinitely prefer here an *image* of impenetrability. A vague, unspecific word at the end of a verse in which all the other words are distinguishable objects moving harmoniously, can easily obfuscate, and nullify, them. It's impossible, of course, for me to suggest in what way you could objectify, make real, the 'impenetrable'. And the only general advice I can, misgivingly though sincerely, give is that you try to Think in Things.

In the second verse, I must merely repeat that the 'inner vision' should be particularised. What is it? If it is too vague to define, set down what *things* come nearest to being part of that vision. Sooner one solid glimpse of the inner world, [than] an amorphous statement of its existence.

The third verse is beautiful. (Mind, by the way, the spelling of 'bare'. What is this verse: a menagerie?) You can see in this how you have kept everything concrete to the very end. Here are no 'impenetrable visions' but honey, lion, and rose: all acquaintances, and given a new kind of life and meaning here. I do think, I do really think, you should work more, and very hard, on this poem, so that the third verse does not shine right out of it, as it does now, but is part of the whole radiance.

In verse four, a thousand times no! to 'ethereal as a dream'—phrases like that are written forever in the Oliver Sandys of time.

Poem Three:

I think that if you use this regular tumpty-tum beat (and, Lord knows, no disrespect to it, it can do wonderful things), you inevitably lead the ear to expect rhymes or assonances. And when, in lines three and four of each verse, and especially in line four, you give no rhyme or assonance, the ear, disappointed, rejects what it has already heard. The fourth line, in a verse using this metre, should tauten the whole verse, not leave it loosely unresolved. 'With every cloud that rides the skies,' though an absurdly banal line and only thrown out as a tentative first-thing-that-came-into-my-head suggestion, is the kind of line, only because of its ultimate rhyme, that shapes the verse as a whole. I like all the substance of the poem a great deal; it is only my ear, that red-lobed carper, that finds it unsatisfactory. I think the poem could be reshaped and rhymed to beautiful effect.

Poem Four:

From here, to Thirteen, it is, of course, quite a different kettle of poems. And I have far less to say about these poems in any detail.

I think that if you go on writing poetry, as I hope exceedingly you will, and indeed as I am sure you feel you must, you will find yourself writing in a kind of way which combines the full-imaged natural world of the first descriptive poems with the frail (but never weak) inner world of those very feminine (but *never* poetess-y) extracts of experience.

In this second group of poems, there is very little for me to criticise. More than the others, more than any kind of poem, these rely upon the immediate transference of an isolated emotion—though 'transference' is probably the wrong word. These poems must be *felt at once;* there is no time for them to creep in at a side-door, or seep down the chimney: they've got to come *right* in, without a waste syllable, expression, or gesture. Once they arouse in one any desire to analyse them, they fade. They're not written in invisible ink, but neither are they written in everybody's. There's a thin ice over the ink; and if one unbalanced word breaks that ice, down you go, poem and all, into a big blank blot. In this poem, beginning 'Dear Love, if you should cease to be', the word 'frightfulness' almost tips the whole thing into tenuous oblivion; but not quite. My objection to that word is the same as to the rest of the undefined generalisations etc of the earlier (in the folder, not by date) descriptive poems. I'm sure the one rule that can properly help, is: *Never* put down a word such as 'frightfulness'. Put down, instead, a frightful thing, symbol, image, or the precise words for a frightful feeling.

Poem Five Only two tiny points. Qualify, define, particularise—yes: but don't do these things to something that needs none of it. There is no need to say of a vacuum that it is 'where nothing is'. The Mediterranean is also tideless, and parallel lines, except to some scientists, do not meet.

And again I find the memory coming up of Eliot's 'at the still point of the turning world'. But I'm sure it's my memory, not yours. The words are common words.

Oh, and a third carp. *What* 'mysterious world'? You must say more. Neither does 'infinite space', 'celestial light', etc. mean anything to me.

Poem Six. 'The music in the hall' is, I think, almost exactly what you wish it to be, because it *is* exact.

Poem Seven, 'A Dedication'. I believe you could clarify the first verse, but the second is perfect: particular, minute, 'justly' observed, and not for a second's second is it petty.

(Incidentally, the 'pealing' of potatoes is most strange vegetable campanology.)

Poem Eight needs more concentrated working-upon. The words seems to me thinly spaced, and to have relationship to each other only through superficial *meaning*, not through texture: the sound, shape, weight, colour, density of language. Too often (in what one might call poems of emotional immediacy and what appears to be, but rarely is, spontaneous growth), unmarried words limp together towards the consummation of the last line, only to find it entirely unsatisfying, unrewarding of the intensity that has forced them towards the end.

I hope, in commenting so heavily, almost so blunderbussily, on a short and simple poem, that I'm not giving the idea that I would wish you to burden it with any intricate technical apparatus. All I mean is that a poet must endeavour to feel & weigh the shape, sound, content etc. of each word in relation to the words surrounding it—and that of however simple a nature the poem he is working upon. It isn't only the *meaning* of the words that must develop harmonically, that must weave in and out of each other, each syllable adding to the single existence of the next, but it is that which also informs the words with their own particular life: the noise that they make in the ear and the air, the contours in which they lie on the page and the mind.

Poem Nine, 'So quiet and still', is quiet and still as the breath itself; and beautiful, & not to be touched.

Poem Ten Only the same, now nearly threadbare criticism: 'Hardship's fierce frustration' has no place in any poem because it *escapes* the work of defining, poetically, the hardship and the frustration.

In *Poem Eleven*, 'The Sunday Street', there is something wrong, grammatically, with the first verse. This wouldn't matter if it did not hold one up.

I find the phrase 'with pleasurable surprise' a little too ingenuous, and would be inclined to write here a phrase reflective, in some slight, subtle way, of the character—as you see it in the poem—of the 'you'. But the end is lovely, & does so need lovely language—as simple as possble—to flow up to it.

Poem Twelve, 'Who Can Hear The Stars Sing', seems out of keeping with the rest of this very moving group; to have slid in from another world of experience; and from *another* need to write. Also, I think it too obviously reminiscent of Donne's 'Go and catch a falling star'.

Of the last poem, I have nothing to say except that I like it very very much. I told you, at the beginning of this letter, that I could never speak commonsensibly about what moves me & what seems to me inevitable. So I shan't *try* to speak about this. Maybe 'agitated breath' for a moment disturbs my appreciation: two words set together as one: a cliché, rather tired. But, maybe again, I am wrong. It *is* a good poem.

6 BBC
15 April '46   Holywell Ford Oxford

Dear Sir,

This is only to corroborate the letters you have already received from my agents, Pearn, Pollinger & Higham Ltd., of 39–40 Bedford Street, Strand, W.C.2., that contracts & payments for my future Talks & Reading engagements should be sent to them.

I had written to corroborate this some days ago, as Miss Pearn told you, I believe, when she spoke to you on the phone, but the letter was somehow mislaid.

Yours truly,
Dylan Thomas

MS: BBC

37 GODFREY THURSTON-HOPKINS[1]
April 27th 1946   Holywell Ford Oxford

Dear Sir,

Please do forgive me for not having answered your letter of March 15. I've been changing my address too often for the BBC to keep up with me, & your letter arrived only a day or two ago.

The 'Memories of Christmas' was printed in the Listener of December 20 1945. The recording you heard was called, I think, 'Second Hearing.' I haven't a copy myself, but the BBC is sure to have a back number.

I am very glad you enjoyed the talk, and I am really grateful to you for writing & wanting to see it in print.

Yours truly,
Dylan Thomas

MS: the recipient

[1] An admirer.

38   DAVID HIGHAM
July 19 1947

Dear David,
My address until August 10, when I travel home, is: *Albergo Elba, Rio di Marina, Isola d'Elba, Livorno, Italy*—just in case anything urgent crops up.
Will drop you a line as soon as I return.

Yours,
Dylan

MS: Texas

39   JEAN LEROY
19th September 1947   Manor House South Leigh Witney Oxon

Dear Miss LeRoy,
Your letter of yesterday. Please do accept on my behalf the fee of twelve guineas, plus one night expenses allowance of £1.7.6. for my part in the reading from Cervantes' THE DOG'S COLLOQUY on the 9th of October. But my return fare should now be from South Leigh, not from Oxford, as my permanent address is now the above. Will you see to that in future? Thanks very much.

Yours sincerely,
Dylan Thomas

MS: Texas

40   JEAN LEROY
12th November 1947   Manor House South Leigh Witney Oxon

Dear Miss LeRoy,
Many apologies for not having answered several letters much sooner. I have been in London, and no letters were forwarded.
Perhaps I [?shd], straightaway, give you a London telephone number where I can always be reached before 10 a.m., and in the evenings, and where any messages can be left for me—in case anything urgent arises. It's a nuisance not being on the phone here. The number is RICHMOND 5582.
Going back to your first unanswered letter of 31st October. I am very glad indeed that you managed to get the BBC to pay twenty five guineas for my poem, *In Country Sleep*, broadcast in 'New Poems' on 28th October. And I presume that you have accepted. I note, too, that they won't be paying the same fee for repeat broadcasts.
About your letter of 5th November. I see that the BBC now agrees to pay my return fare of 19/11d, as well as 2.15.0 expenses, for each programme in the 'Paradise Lost' series; and that they will be letting you have their cheque for £7.9.0 covering expenses due for 'P. Lost' of October 19th and 26th. Good.
About *Book* 4 of 'P. Lost', mentioned also in your letter of the 5th. The rehearsals were on Friday (7th) Saturday (8th) & Sunday (9th); and this does

definitely mean that I should receive *three* nights' expenses instead of two: our station here is on a very tiny, & inconvenient, branch-line.

Your letter of November 11th: *'P. Lost' Book 5*, to be recorded on 15th November. Rehearsals for this, I see, are on Friday, Saturday, & Sunday. Therefore in this case also, I should receive *three* nights' expenses instead of two.

'P. Lost' Book 6 Rehearsals Friday (21st) & Sunday (23rd). I should come back to Witney after the Friday rehearsal, and return to London *Saturday* evening, as there is no train from Witney on Sunday morning that would get me to the studio by 10 a.m. Therefore, I should receive *two* nights' expenses, and *two* railway fares.

Hope I'm clear.

Yours sincerely,
Dylan Thomas

MS: Texas

41   MR TURNER[1]
Dec 30th 1947   Manor House South Leigh Witney Oxon

Dear Mr. Turner,

Please forgive me for not having answered your letter long before this. It got mislaid.

I'm afraid my broadcast 'Return Journey' hasn't yet been published, and unfortunately I have no copy myself to send you. I am very glad indeed that you liked it so much. It will be coming out in a book of my sketches & stories either this coming autumn or spring 1948.

You wanted to know about any other prose of mine. Apart from the stories which make up the second half of my book 'The Map of Love' (J. M. Dent), I have published only one book of stories, 'Portrait of the Artist As A Young Dog' (also J. M. Dent).

Thank you again for your letter. And, again, apologies for this long, rude delay.

Yours sincerely,
Dylan Thomas

MS: Texas

42   KATHLEEN GURNER
April 27 1948   Manor House South Leigh Witney Oxon

Dear Miss Gurner,

I'm so sorry there's been this bother about copyright permission for my poem 'October' to be used in your Anthology for Schools. You certainly have my own permission, & I suggest you write to my agent, David Higham, Pearn, Pollinger, & Higham Ltd, 39–40 Bedford Street, London W.C.2., saying that you have my permission & asking them to obtain Dent's as quickly as possible. This they will do. What a nuisance it is!

Yours sincerely,
Dylan Thomas

MS: Texas

[1] An admirer.

43   MRS F. I. WEBLEY
June 25 1948   Manor House South Leigh Witney Oxon

Dear Madam,
Please forgive me for not answering, before this, your letter of June 14.
I thank you very much indeed for your kind invitation to me to lecture to the Newport & Mon. Literary Club, but am afraid that, reluctantly, I must decline. I am going abroad in the early spring of next year.
Thank you again for the invitation.
                                        Yours faithfully,
                                        Dylan Thomas

MS: John Wilson

44   JEAN LEROY
20 August 1948   Manor House South Leigh Witney Oxon

Dear Miss LeRoy,
Yes, please, do accept the BBC engagement for the reading of *Edith Sitwell's* poems on 28th September, in the 3rd Programme.
                                        Yours sincerely,
                                        Dylan Thomas

MS: Texas

45   JEAN LEROY
Nov 16 1948   Manor House South Leigh Witney Oxon

Dear Miss LeRoy,
I really don't feel that the fee and expenses offered by the BBC for my participation in the programme 'Trimalchio's Dinner', to be recorded on December 2, is at all adequate & I'm very glad you're questioning it.
To begin with: £1.7.6. expenses for 2 days and *nights* seems to me absurd. I *do* have to pay for my bed on each of my London visits, & two hotel bills for bed alone come to more than £1.7.6.
Also I think the fee itself, fifteen guineas, to be extremely poor.
I hope you will go ahead fiercely & try to obtain a much better offer.
                                        Sincerely,
                                        Dylan Thomas

MS: Texas

46   JEAN LEROY
25 Nov '48   Manor House South Leigh Witney Oxon

Dear Miss LeRoy,
   I've just today received, from your offices, the BBC cheque for my 'Extraordinary Little Cough'.
      For One British Broadcast Use—   20.10.0.
      "   One British Broadcast Performance—
      Reading   8. 8.0.
                                                                        28.18.0.

   I'm sorry, but I've mislaid your letter in which you detailed to me the fees of the
contract for that story, but I *definitely* remember that the Performance, Reading
fee was EIGHTEEN not EIGHT guineas. If it *had* been eight, I would have
protested at once.
   Do see, please, where the mistake has been made.
   And thank you *very* much indeed for saying how much you liked the story.
                                    Sincerely,
                                    Dylan Thomas

MS: Texas

47   JEAN LEROY
Dec 6th 1948   Manor House South Leigh Witney Oxon

Dear Miss LeRoy,
   Answering, late I'm afraid, your letter of Dec. 1st.
   Sorry about the typographical error. But thank you *very* much for getting the
BBC to pay me 12 guineas for the reading. And *of course* it's acceptable.
                                    Sincerely,
                                    Dylan Thomas

MS: Texas

48   JEAN LEROY
17 Feb 49   Manor House South Leigh Witney Oxon

Dear Miss LeRoy,
   Thank you for your letter about the BBC's offer of £75 for my adaptation of
Wycherley's Plain Dealer. Perhaps we should close for that. And let's try to get all
of all we can for my actual speaking part in the broadcast, please.
                                    Yours sincerely,
                                    Dylan Thomas

MS: Texas

49 ELWYN EVANS
14 March 1949   Manor House South Leigh Witney Oxon

Dear Mr Evans,
    Thank you very much for your letter, and please forgive me for not answering before: I've been abroad.
    And thank you for wanting me to give a talk on Hopkins in your new literary magazine; I only wish I could. But I've just got a new filmscript to write and a play-adaptation for the Third, and mustn't take on any other job, even a 15 minute one. But I would like, in the future, if I may, to talk in the magazine. And thank you very much for asking me.

                                        Yours sincerely,
                                        Dylan Thomas

MS: BBC

50 JEAN LEROY
March 14 49

                                        Manor House South Leigh Witney Oxon

Dear Miss LeRoy,
    Thank you very much for your letter of the 11th. I think the new figure, £100, for my adaptation of the Plain Dealer & my performance in it is very good & please do accept it. I'll get in touch with the producer myself. Thanks.

                                        Yours sincerely,
                                        Dylan Thomas

MS: Texas

51 DAVID HIGHAM
May 16 1949   The Boat House Laugharne Carmarthenshire

Dear David,
    I enclose the 3 Columbia contracts, signed by me, for you to send to Ann Watkins to see to &—eventually—to collect from. This shd go by air-mail, shouldn't it? It's been rather a long time (not all my fault).
    See you next month about things.

                                        Yours,
                                        Dylan

MS: Texas

52   ELWYN EVANS
July 3 1949   Boat House Laugharne Carmarthenshire

Dear Mr. Evans,
   Sorry not to have answered sooner. I've been away.
   I'll send along copyright details tomorrow.

                                        Yours sincerely,
                                        Dylan Thomas

MS: BBC

53   ELWYN EVANS
13 July 1949   The Boat House Laugharne Carms

Dear Elwyn Evans,
   Enclosed the brief E. Thomas script & also the Collected Poems. I've given page
numbers in Script. Hope you will keep the book for me. What time do you need
me on the night?

                                        Yours sincerely,
                                        Dylan Thomas

MS: BBC

54   JEAN LEROY
15 July 1949   The Boat House Laugharne Carmarthenshire

Dear Miss LeRoy,
   About the reading of Edward Thomas's poems for the BBC, from Cardiff on July
29th. Fee fine. The fare, return, from Laugharne to Cardiff will be £2.13.0. To get
the most convenient train I have to go from Laugharne to St. Clears (the nearest
station) by cab.

                                        Yours sincerely,
                                        Dylan Thomas

MS: Texas

55   G. V. ROBERTS
5 August 1949   The Boat House Laugharne Carmarthenshire

Dear Sir,
   Thank you for the invitation, from the Tenby & District Arts Club, to come
along & read or talk sometime during your autumn–winter session.
   As you see, I live near to Tenby, and am very glad to accept your invitation.
   If you could give me a choice of a few dates?

Thank you very much for what you said about my reading from Edward Thomas last week.

> Yours very truly,
> Dylan Thomas

MS: National Library of Wales

---

56   JEAN LEROY
16 October 1949   The Boat House Laugharne Carmarthenshire

Dear Miss LeRoy,
   Yours of the 14th. About the programme called 'Swansea & the Arts'. Twelve guineas seems alright, plus 2 return fares Laugharne–S'sea, & one night's allowance. The return fare Laugharne–S'sea is: 17/6. Two return fares make, according to me, £1.15.0.

> Yours sincerely,
> Dylan Thomas

MS: Texas

---

57   JEAN LEROY
21 Aug 1950   Boat House Laugharne Carmarthenshire

   Sorry not to have included fare detail in my note about E. A. Poe programme. Return fare, Laugharne–Paddington, for this broadcast was £3.5.0.
   I made a special journey to London for the John Donne broadcast of Aug. 14, & the fare was the same as above. Also there were the usual expenses for the day & accommodation overnight.
   I hope you can get these cheques through quickly, & will you please send them to me at the above address & *not* to my bank.

> Sincerely,
> Dylan Thomas

MS: Texas

---

58   JEAN LEROY
15 Dec 1950   The Boat House Laugharne Carmarthenshire

Dear Miss LeRoy,
   You asked me whether, in the programme 'Poetic Licence', recorded on the 11th December & broadcast on the 15th, I had any special expenses on top of my fee. Yes, I had returned to Wales a week before the recording, & had to travel to London for the recording. The fare is the usual return one, Laugharne to London.

> Yours sincerely,
> Dylan Thomas

P.S. Oh, & about that long-ago programme, 'Poems & A Commentary'. My expenses were: return fare Laugharne to London, plus one night's stay in London. Sorry not to have answered this before. Hope you can get the payments through before Christmas.

DT

MS: Texas

59 ANEIRIN TALFAN DAVIES
1 May 1951   Boat House Laugharne Carmarthenshire

My dear Aneirin,
    Sorry not to have answered long before.
    Okay, make it a fixed date for June 5th. I am going to London next week & will see the Exhibition then, & will let you have the script as soon after as I can. 15 minutes?

Yours,
Dylan

MS: BBC

60 ANEIRIN TALFAN DAVIES
[May 1951]   Boat House Laugharne Carmarthenshire

Dear Aneirin,
    Many apologies for this long delay in sending South Bank script. I've been ill.
    I'll ring you up Monday morning, to find out Tuesday rehearsal & recording times.
    Hope there's time to type the enclosed, & that you like it well enough.

Yrs,
Dylan

MS: BBC

61 UNKNOWN
27 May 1951 [draft]   Boat House Laugharne Carmarthenshire Wales

Dear Sir,
    I'm sorry I haven't been able to answer, before this, your letter wanting to know about the Writers Groups of the S.C.R. & my interest in it.
    I, too, belong to no political party. I am a Socialist, and, so far as I know, there is no Socialist party.

MS: Indiana

62   ANEIRIN TALFAN DAVIES
3 December 1951 [postcard]   54 Delancey St London N W 1

Yes, of course 'Dock Leaves' can print my talk on the South Bank Exhibition. But please don't send them the typescript you have, as there [are] many misprints in it and I should also like to alter a few lines & words for publication.

I have a copy somewhere, which I will correct this week. Shall I send it on to you, or will you drop me a line to tell me Dock Leaves address?

> Yours,
> Dylan T

MS: Texas

63   GILBERT PHELPS
3 October 1952   Boat House Laugharne Carmarthenshire

Dear Gilbert,
First I heard that I was taking part in 'New Soundings' was in your letter yesterday. But I do remember that my agent was sending my new poem, Prologue, to Lehmann, so I suppose that's it. I've just come back from London, & can't come up again until October 16. I'll be travelling down to London from Oxford the morning of the 16th. Is that day possible? I don't quite know how long the poem takes—ten minutes or more. Do let me know. I want, if possible, to catch the night train back to Wales on the 16th.
Want to see you about Personal Anthology too.

> Yours,
> Dylan

MS: BBC

64   GUGGENHEIM FOUNDATION
October 17 1952   Boat House Laugharne Carmarthenshire Wales

Gentlemen:
I write in behalf of Mr. Oscar Williams who has applied for a Guggenheim this year. He is without doubt a very real and important American poet and the help and encouragement a foundation like yours can give should do a great deal to keep his creative powers alive. His powerful imagery and unique personal idiom will add a permanent page to American poetry, I feel sure. I don't know of any poet in America, who has not yet received a Guggenheim, who deserves it more than Mr. Williams. I fervently pray that you will see your way clear to awarding him a fellowship so that he can write his new book of poems.

> Sincerely yours,
> Dylan Thomas

MS: Indiana [typescript, signed by Thomas]

65   E. F. BOZMAN
28 Oct 1952   Boat House Laugharne Carmarthenshire

Dear Bozman,
   You wanted me to send back this written copy of the Prologue: for an Exhibition of Books. Sorry I haven't anything else but stacks of worksheets.
                                        Sincerely,
                                        Dylan Thomas

MS: J. M. Dent

66   JEAN LEROY
20 Feb 1953   The Boat House Laugharne Carmarthenshire

Thanks for letter about BBC Welsh Home Service contract for my four Anthology programmes. You wanted to know the cost of two railway journeys Laugharne – Swansea. It is £1.6.6.
                                        Sincerely,
                                        Dylan Thomas

MS: Texas

67   IRENE JONES
[postmarked June 14 1953]
                                        Boat House Laugharne
                                        Laugharne 68

Dear Irene,
   Here are the addresses & names of 3 of the best bone-boys in the country.

Sir H. A. Thomas Fairbank
6M Hyde Park Mansions
Marylebone Rd.
H. Osmond-Clarke
80 Harley St.
Sir Reginald Watson-Jones
82 Portland Place.

The last is the best but all are top.

                                        Yours, with love,
                                        bottom.

MS: Texas

68   MR [?RIOEDAN]
15 July '53   Boat House Laugharne Carmarthenshire

Dear Mr. Rioedan,
   Please forgive me for not having answered your letter much sooner: I've been
away and no letters were forwarded.
   Yes, most certainly you have my permission to use those extracts from poems
of mine as chapter-headings for your novel: I'm glad they come in useful.
                                                    Yours sincerely,
                                                    Dylan Thomas

MS: Texas

69   THEODORE ROETHKE
[July 1953]   Laugharne 68

                    Dylan,
                    Boathouse,
                    Laugharne,
                    Carmarthenshire,

                    Book
                    From Paddington
                    Station
                    To
                    Fishguard
                    ——————
                    (I think |
                    you get
                    tickets all the
                    way through to
                    Dublin at
                    Paddington)
                    ——————
                    Stop at St. Clears
                    Station in Wales, where
                    [*illegible*] will meet you for Laugharne.

MS: Washington

70   PETER DAVIES
25th August 1953   Boat House Laugharne Carmarthenshire

Dear Peter Davies,
   Thank you for your letter. I'm sorry I couldn't answer it before this: I've been
away from Laugharne. Of course I'll be very pleased to sign any books, and to
meet you if you come down here. I'll be away all the week of the 31st of August,
but before then and after will be at home nearly all the time.
                                                    Yours sincerely,
                                                    Dylan Thomas

TS: Thomas Trustees

APPENDIX B
MISCELLANEOUS

A number of letters are known to exist, or to have existed, which are not included in this collection, or are present only in mutilated form.

To his sister Nancy, undated. Sold at Sotheby's, 1981. (See page 5.)

To Stephen Spender, 4 June 1940. (See page 453.)

To Elizabeth Lutyens, undated, but about August 1948. She quoted the following extracts in an article for the magazine *Adam*, no. 236, page 3, 1953, following Thomas's death:

'. . . it is pauper week in the Old Manor, and the bills are wailing. Next week, who knows? I may have gold boots. I haven't been in London much, am trying to write a poem about Heaven . . . I am supposed to be writing the script of a musical called 'Me and the bike,' but haven't got down to it yet. Our dog is horribly well . . . I'm going to Edinburgh next week to read poems at the Festival. My own poem is grand, purple, sonorous, odd.'

The following nine items were sold by Sotheby's between 1969 and 1982, but have not been traced:
To:
[Denys] Kilham Roberts, dated April 5 [1946].
Miss Field, 15 April 1946.
Ronald [Bottrall], 27 May 1951.
Society of Authors, 26 March 1946.
Mr Waits, 27 October 1946.
Unnamed woman recipient, 21 May 1945 (part of this letter, in a version taken from a bookseller's catalogue, is in the main text at the appropriate date).
Robert Byron, 3 letters between 20 September 1937 and 9 December 1937.
John Williams Hughes, 22 June 1953.
Miss M. E. Barber, (postmarked) 5 March 1946.

A letter to E. and J. Munro, 10 October 1936, mentioned in a Robert K. Black catalogue, asks to be forgiven for his failure to meet: he got fuddled in a pub. (A trivial note to the same E. and J. Munro appears in the main text, page 240, inserted there on the chance that the Munros would turn out to be interesting. They remain unidentified.)

A letter to Robert Herring, ascribed to November 1935, mentioned in a catalogue of 1958, is included on page 204 in the bookseller's version.

*

Other material:

The J. M. Brinnin papers at Delaware include a dozen telegrams from Thomas. Two of them are in the main text. The rest are not included. All are about arrangements.

Written on the back of an envelope addressed to Vernon Watkins, probable date 1944 or 1945 (MS: British Library):

P.S. If you can't manage to come down, I shall of course be able to meet you in Carmarthen—New Quay's two hours away from Carmarthen. But I will have to be alone. Write anyway. D.

An undated note to David Higham (MS: Texas):

Dear Higham,
    So sorry, I thought I'd sent these things before. Hope to hear from you soon.

Yours,
Dylan Thomas

An undated note to Stanley Moss, probably written in New York (MS: Texas):

Very sorry indeed, Stanley, but I was called a few minutes after you rang and hauled out of bed, and summoned to an agent-and-publisher party.
    Have to go.
    Do call me tomorrow.

Yours,
Dylan

An undated note to (probably) Sheila and Bob Pocock (MS: Texas):

Sex marks the window where I sleep.
Follow the arrow thro' the wall & that's
where, I hope, you'll sleep together
one day soon.

A note to an editor (MS: Texas):

Here are two poems for you to consider for the Poems Of The Year. The long one was printed in 20th Century Verse, the short one in Poetry, Chicago. They're all I have at the moment, as I'm working on a series of poems which I want, eventually, to be published at one time together.

Dylan

APPENDIX C
Letters made available since the original edition

[at page 350]

KEIDRYCH RHYS
7 January 1939   Blashford Ringwood Hants

Dear Keidrych,

Thank you for writing at last.

If you want me to write to Niall Montgomery – though why he can't write to me himself, I don't know – will you give me the *right* address. And when I write, what do I say? I've never read a line of his.

Augustus John said, only a few days ago, that he wrote you a letter about that portrait but that you never answered it. This must be due to the constant muddle of your addresses. I've had letters to you returned 'Unknown.' John *told* Sevier that you wanted the portrait to be reproduced, and Sevier said that he would 'see about it.' I don't suppose for a moment he's done anything. Also, Nicholson who runs the gallery in which Sevier had the exhibition has been warned by John that he must allow the portrait to be reproduced whenever you wish it. But the best thing is to write again to John, Fryern Court, Fordingbridge, Hants, & tell him your worries.

You know, half the trouble is not other people's. You're such a bloody mystery man. You begin something, get some support, then keep those supporters, suddenly, in the dark for months. Surely you said your object was to get 'Wales' out for Christmas: getting a good start on the Welsh Review.[1] And here you're hanging on into February. Incidentally, in your contents-list of the new 'Wales' – which looks as though it could be very good – you have an article on *Mary Butts*.[2] Now *why*, for God's sake? What has an old, dead Paris-Bloomsbury-Cornwall precious female pasticheur to do with a young, progressive Welsh magazine? She's a legend for middle-aged pansies (Cedric, Lett, Herring etc) to present with graceful, rather catty tributes in camp-quarterlies. All her work was a weak, drugged lie. Why not an article on Firbank, too? Are you Time-&-Tiding us?

Nobody, to my knowledge, has 'created dissension,' has tried to spoil your idea of making an influential group of writers in Wales. You yourself have been so evasive; you have dragged into your magazine all the little waste names – Potts, Heseltine, Todd, Symons, Agee – that belong to London rags & not, in thought or action or feeling, to anything connected with Wales. At a time when all your energies were needed – at the time of the conception of the Welsh Review – to

---

[1] February 1939 saw the first issue of Gwyn Jones's *Welsh Review*, 'A monthly journal about Wales, its people, and their activities.'

[2] Mary Butts (1892-1937), novelist, is best known for *Death of Felicity Taverner* (1932). She liked grand themes – among her subjects for novels were Alexander the Great and Cleopatra – and studied mysticism and religions.

keep your contributors, to build up a new interest in 'Wales,' to keep people like John & Hughes permanently on *our* side, you vanished. The contributors, thinking 'Wales' dead, agreed to support the Welsh Review; few, I think, ratted. Now your writers are dispersed, the policy of 'Wales' seems vague enough to include any backstairs London literary clique, & nobody outside a small circle knows whether 'Wales' will ever appear again.[1] I know you've had difficulties, & I'm not a good or happy lecturer. But really you have lacked drive & firmness, you've let the possibility of a possibly *great* magazine almost slip away. It mustn't slip away altogether. Whatever I can do, let me know. I'm no organiser, either. But between us we should manage a little solidity of concentration on making the *basis* of 'Wales' permanent & seeing that its integrity does not degenerate into fashionable, periodical literature such as any sap or crook like [. . .] or Grigson can produce so deftly & uselessly.

I don't quite know what Treece wants. Some sort of critical, though personal, appreciation from a Welsh point of view I should think. His address now is: The Grammar School, Caistor Rd., Barton on Humber, Lincs. Perhaps you could write & ask, or tell, him.

We'll be back in Laugharne at the end of February. Will you still be near? You must come then. There must be lots of work for us. Write soon.

Love,
Dylan

Are you doing a 'bibliography' of me? I can let you have a lot of material.

MS: Gabriel Pustel

[at or near page 460]

ROBERT HERRING
[? Summer 1940]   c/o Malting House

Dear Robert Herring,
Would you like to use this poem?[2] If you would, I could use a guinea.
Yours
Dylan Thomas

The poem may look very sprawly, but it's really properly formed.

MS: whereabouts unknown[3]

[1] The issue was published in March 1939 as 'Nos. 6/7.' No. 5 had appeared in summer 1938.
[2] Probably 'Into her lying-down head,' which Herring published in *Life and Letters Today*, November 1940.
[3] A transcript of the letter was made some years ago by Ralph Maud.

[at page 776]

AUGUSTUS JOHN
8 December 1950   The Boat House Laugharne Carmarthenshire

Dear Augustus,

Will you do something for me, please? It only means writing a letter, but it means writing a letter to:

The Secretary, The Royal Literary Fund, Stationers' Hall, London, E.C.4.

Would you, in the briefest of letters, support my claim, which I have already made in an official application, that I am a person known to you to be in financial distress, and also that, in your opinion, I am a person whose financial distress should rightly be alleviated by a grant from the Royal Literary Fund?

When I came back from London, I found that all my Laugharne cheques had bounced. You know what this means in a Welsh township not notoriously anti-pathetical to money. It is very painful here indeed.

Today I had a letter from the bank saying that all my London cheques had also been dishonoured. The English, too, are only nonchalant about money when you have it, and I expect London to be a painful place when I return.

I had thought there was money in the bank. There was; but none of mine.

This week, I have received a letter from Llewelyn's school at Oxford, saying that unless the last two terms' fees are paid he can no longer remain at that school.

And I owe, for the Pelican, Laugharne, which I rented for my father & mother, one year's rent. There is danger of their being evicted.

This little list of griefs does not include my long debts to every tradesman.

If I am not in 'financial distress,' then I am dangerously near it.

I have lots of work to do next year, but can do nothing while these debts are dogging.

So *would* you write that letter, please? The Royal Literary Fund is a last hope.

See you on the Cross,

                                   Dylan

MS: Whereabouts unknown[1]

[at page 776]

DOUGLAS CLEVERDON
Dec 8   50   Laugharne

My Dear Douglas,

See you, then, in your office at 3.15 on Monday, the 11th. Have you a copy of 'Spoon River Anthology'[2] in case I have mislaid mine?

Mislaid is, I'm afraid, the word for the Faber Book of Comic Verse. I'm dreadfully sorry, and will attempt to right it.

I'll tell you about the Mad Town[3] when we meet.

                                   · Ever,
                                     Dylan

MS: Rosenbach Museum and Library, Philadelphia

[1] The letter was sold at Sotheby's, London, in 1979.
[2] See footnote, page 833.
[3] This reference suggests the letter may be earlier than the undated letter to Cleverdon on page 773.

[at page 792]

MICHAEL FORTY[1]
7 April 1951   The Boat House Laugharne Carmarthenshire

Dear Michael Forty,
Thank you very much for your letter of December, 1950 – which has just been given to me by Russell Williams.[2] He suggests a good date for me to come to Swansea to bellow would be Wednesday, April 25th. The time, sometime in the afternoon. The 25th suits me, though I would really rather an evening date. Poems flag in the afternoon. But Russell says that it's difficult to get a crowd of people together in the evening, as they've gone, lots of them, or want to go, home to districts outside S'sea. If this is so, then let it be the afternoon.[3] R. also suggests I read to a lot of people, not to a small group. I don't mind either way. What I'd do would be to read modern poems, with a few silly comments. You could just call it 'Modern Poetry,' which is vague enough. Anyway, will you let me know what you think? Fix anything, any time of day you like, for the 25th. By the way, I'll be in London & will have come down specially, so that my expenses will be return fare Paddington – S'sea. Is that all right?

Yours sincerely
Dylan Thomas

MS: Michael Forty

---

[1] Chairman of the English Society at University College, Swansea, where he was a student.
[2] A fellow student at the university college. He lived in the Laugharne area.
[3] In the event, the meeting was held in the evening. Forty and another student met Thomas, who 'looked like a seedy commercial traveller in a shiny suit, carrying a little case,' at the station earlier in the day. Before and after the meeting, held in a basement room of the Students' Union building in Sketty Road, Thomas drank at the Uplands Hotel, once his neighbourhood pub, with students and staff from the university college. This was the evening sardonically described by Kingsley Amis, then a young English lecturer at Swansea, in the *Spectator*, 29 November 1957.

Index of Recipients

General Index

There is a separate Index of Recipients,
and recipients are not listed as such in the General Index.
Individual works by Thomas have their own entries.
'(P)' indicates a poem, '(S)' a story.